Germany
943 BIE

34267001036842

C0-DMC-767

Benbrook Public Library

European Nations

Germany
A Reference Guide from the Renaissance to the Present

Joseph A. Biesinger

An imprint of Infobase Publishing

Germany: A Reference Guide from the Renaissance to the Present

Copyright © 2006 by Joseph A. Biesinger

All rights reserved. No part of this book may be reproduced or utilized in any form or by any means, electronic or mechanical, including photocopying, recording, or by any information storage or retrieval systems, without permission in writing from the publisher. For information contact:

Facts On File, Inc.
An imprint of Infobase Publishing
132 West 31st Street
New York NY 10001

Library of Congress Cataloging-in-Publication Data

Biesinger, Joseph A.
  Germany : a reference guide from the Renaissance to the present / Joseph A. Biesinger.— 1st ed.
    p. cm. — (European nations)
  Includes bibliographical references.
  ISBN 0-8160-4521-6 (hc : alk. paper)
  1. Germany—History—Handbooks, manuals, etc. 2. Germany—History—Chronology. 3. Germany—Civilization—Handbooks, manuals, etc. 4. Germany—Encyclopedias. I. Title. II. Series.
  DD17.B54 2006
  943—dc222005023373

Facts On File books are available at special discounts when purchased in bulk quantities for businesses, associations, institutions, or sales promotions. Please call our Special Sales Department in New York at (212) 967-8800 or (800) 322-8755.

You can find Facts On File on the World Wide Web at http://www.factsonfile.com

Text design by David Strelecky
Cover design by Semadar Megged
Illustrations by Pat Meschino

Printed in the United States of America

VB Hermitage 10 9 8 7 6 5 4 3 2 1

This book is printed on acid-free paper.

CONTENTS

Foreword v

Introduction vii

History of Modern Germany 1

Tribal Origins and the Middle Ages 3
The Renaissance 13
Protestant Reformation 19
Counter-Reformation and Thirty Years' War 27
Age of the Baroque 32
Absolutism in the Habsburg Austrian Empire 39
Rise of Brandenburg-Prussia 50
Society and Culture in the Eighteenth Century 55
The Era of the French Revolution and Napoleon, 1789–1815 64
Restoration, Romanticism, and Revolution 68
Otto von Bismarck and German Unification 74
Industrial Revolution 82
Nineteenth-Century Culture and Society 88
The Second German Empire, 1871–1918 95
The First World War 102
November Revolution, 1918–1919 107
Versailles Treaty and Weimar Constitution 114
Weimar Republic, 1919–1933 120
The Nazi Dictatorship 135
World War II and Holocaust 144
Allied Occupation, Democratic Rebirth, Cold War 153

THE FEDERAL REPUBLIC, 1949–1990 160
THE GERMAN DEMOCRATIC REPUBLIC 178
REVOLUTION AND REUNIFICATION 185
POST-REUNIFICATION TO THE PRESENT 191

Historical Dictionary A–Z 201

Chronology 761

Appendixes 781
RULERS AND STATESMEN 783
MAPS 785

Bibliography 801

Index 827

FOREWORD

This series was inspired by the need of high school and college students to have a concise and readily available history series focusing on the evolution of the major European powers and other influential European states in the modern age—from the Renaissance to the present. Written in accessible language, the projected volumes include all of the major European countries: France, Germany, Great Britain, Italy, and Russia, as well as other states such as Spain, Portugal, Austria, and Hungary that have made important intellectual, political, cultural, and religious contributions to Europe and the world. The format has been designed to facilitate usage and includes a short introduction by the author of each volume, a specialist in its history, providing an overview of the importance of the particular country in the modern period. This is followed by a narrative history of each nation from the time of the Renaissance to the present. The core of the volume consists of an A–Z dictionary of people, events, and places, providing coverage of intellectual, political, diplomatic, cultural, social, religious, and economic developments. Next, a chronology details key events in each nation's development over the past several centuries. Finally, the end matter includes a selected bibliography of readily available works, maps, and an index to the material within the volume.

—Frank J. Coppa, General Editor
St. John's University

INTRODUCTION

The study of history as a liberal art is one of the educational means by which a person can develop a critical mind and other important intellectual skills. This reference volume of modern German history proposes to introduce the reader to the historical method of analyzing events through cause and effect and focusing on the roles of significant personalities, movements, political and economic systems, social structures, military power, and the expressions of religion and culture. Although it is organized as a reference book, this overview of Germany from the Renaissance to the present also has the qualities that make it an excellent textbook. Not only does it contain a lengthy survey to the present, but it also has more than 600 articles that focus on important personalities and other topics of political, economic, social, diplomatic, religious, and cultural significance. In addition it contains an extensive chronology of important events and, also, an excellent bibliography for further reference.

In order to understand the world during the last century, the study of German history is imperative. To live without this knowledge is to walk as a blind person in the midst of a storm and certainly not to understand modern world history. The world has truly experienced a storm of revolutions, world wars, and colossal change. Not that the German people are responsible for all of them, but there are some causes that lurk in the depths of German and European history that can only be learned by the study of German history. Some years ago Sebastian Haffner wrote:

> Whether we like it or not, today's world is the work of Hitler. Without Hitler, no divided Germany and Europe; without Hitler, no Americans and Russians in Berlin; without Hitler, no Israel; without Hitler, no de-colonization, at least not so fast, no Asiatic, Arab and Black-African emancipation, and no downgrading of Europe.

Without the phenomenon of Hitler there would not have been World War II and no Holocaust and no nightmares of those events and no innumerable millions of deaths. Hitler personified the German problem for Europe and the world, and for more than a century the German question has had a decisive impact on the history of the world.

The study of the history of the German people, however, has importance for other reasons as well. Some of the greatest philosophers, theologians, poets, writers, and artists and architects were born of German parentage and nourished by its culture. They have made substantive contributions to Western civilization, including the United States. The German people also have experienced a variety of political institutions—rule by emperors, kings, and princes, representative institutions and republics. In studying German history one can benefit from understanding the relationship between geography and the growth of military institutions. Germany has often been contrasted to Britain, which has been protected by the water, while Germany has lacked frontiers and required a strong military to defend it from potential enemies on all sides. Germany also was internally weak, even though it encompassed the Holy Roman Empire, which began with the Saxon, Otto I, who was crowned king in 962. By the end of the Middle Ages there were, however, some 300 states—duchies, counties, ecclesiastical territories, free cities, and other territories. There was no clear boundary to the west, where the German states were threatened by the French king, or to the east, where Slavic tribes predominated. During this period the Germans themselves colonized the east in one of the greatest movements of peoples before the American West was settled. Here the Germans settled in areas associated with the names of Mecklenburg, Pomerania, and Brandenburg, and they pushed into Silesia. This eastward expansion indicated a new direction of German influence, with which the Hohenzollern family, which created Prussia, was associated.

Many cleavages have divided German society throughout history. Ethnically, the Germans were not homogeneous. The religious conflicts between Protestants and Catholics during the Reformation created other serious divisions. Some historians even claim that Germany was never thoroughly Christianized, and its pagan tradition erupted again during the Nazi regime. Other divisions existed in the political and cultural realm and among the social classes. Political disunity, however, was the most obvious division. The Germans oscillated between universal empire and localism. When nationalism belatedly developed, attempting to bridge these differences, it ended up becoming a most violent kind. The 18th century saw the rise of the state of Prussia and the violent threat of the French Revolution and Napoleonic Wars, which revealed the weaknesses of Germany but led to a widespread growth of national feeling. Unfortunately, the Congress of Vienna militated against the growth of unity. The rivalry between Prussia and Austria prevented the growth of a true federation that might have led to a unified state. The revolutions of 1848 were a turning point for Germany, during which the Germans failed to turn toward democratic government and create a successful unified state based on a liberal constitution. In the end it was the authoritarian Prussian Junker, Otto von Bismarck, who set himself the task of destroying liberalism in order to strengthen conservative Prussia and maintain its position as a great power. Prussia and Prussianism eventually triumphed over the rest of Germany, which was more passive, liberal, and good-natured. Bismarck and Prussia impressed on the Germans a spirit of militarism and the Machiavellian doctrine of the reason of state, which justified every infringement of written and unwritten law. These were qualities that found even greater expression in the leadership of Adolf Hitler. The cleavages continued after World War II, as West and East Germany were divided between a democratic Federal Republic and a communist German Democratic Republic. Today the Germans are still trying to bridge those differences since they were reunified in 1990.

HISTORY OF MODERN GERMANY

Tribal Origins and the Middle Ages

German history recounts the experiences of the German tribes and their evolution into modern societies. Their origin has been traced as far back as the second millennium B.C. to Scandinavia. During the early part of the first millennium, even before the beginning of the Roman Republic, some tribes had moved southward. A western Teutonic branch of the tribes moved up the Elbe and Rhine Rivers, reaching the Main River about 200 B.C. This branch settled in what is now Germany, which distinguishes some of its regional and linguistic differences. The Alemanni ("all men") and the Suevi (Swabians) settled on the upper Rhine; the Franks ("free men") on the lower and middle Rhine; the Saxons ("swordsmen") between the Weser and the Elbe Rivers and the Harz Mountains, and the Thuringians south of the Saxons. The territory occupied by the Saxon tribe is about the same as Lower Saxony today. A mixture of Germanic and Slavic tribes settled the territory farther east in Upper Saxony, which later would include the Kingdom of Saxony.

The eastern branch of the Germanic tribes, the Goths, crossed the Baltic Sea between 600 and 300 B.C., migrated up the Vistula to the Carpathian Mountains and then toward the Black Sea. The Vandals settled in Silesia, and the Markommani in Bohemia. After reaching the Black Sea, the Goths divided into the Visigoths (West) and Ostrogoths (East), who mingled with local populations and established kingdoms in southern Russia. The Ostrogothic kingdom that had been established in the fourth century A.D. reached from the Black Sea to the Baltic. Later migrations of Germanic peoples included those of the Norsemen. To the east these migrating tribes subjugated the Finnish and Slavic peoples and established themselves around Kiev. In the west they invaded England, the area of Normandy, and even Sicily.

ROMAN GERMANY

German history also had its beginning in the interplay between the German tribes and the Roman Empire. For some time there had been interaction between the two peoples, and some Germanic tribes had even become allies of the Romans. In 12 B.C., however, the Romans, who already controlled Gaul, decided to conquer Germania between the Rhine and the Elbe Rivers and, along with the Danube, establish a new northern and eastern boundary for the Empire. The Romans were victorious against the Germans, under Drusus, the adopted son of Augustus (r. 27 B.C.–A.D. 14). The Romans completed the pacification of what was to be a new province. Tiberius, who had been leading the campaign, however, was diverted to quell an uprising in Austria and left the incompetent Varus in command. In A.D. 9 one of the most famous battles in Roman history occurred in the Teutoburg Forest of modern Westphalia. Varus let his legions be ambushed by the Germanic prince Arminius, whose warriors annihilated some 20,000 Romans. Only later under the reign of Tiberius (r. A.D. 14–37) was the honor of Roman arms vindicated. The costs of the campaigns convinced Tiberius to settle for a Rhine-Danube frontier instead of an Elbe-Danube frontier. West of the Rhine two border provinces of Upper (Superior) and Lower (Inferior) Germany were established. From late in the first century until the barbarian invasions of the third, these areas were extended to include a district bounded by the Rhine, the Danube, and 300 miles of fortifications between them called the limes. Had the Romans been able to conquer and colonize the area of Germania east to the Elbe, the course of German history would have been different. The pattern of division between Roman and barbarian Germany perhaps would not have occurred. During the Middle Ages the Romanized areas of south and west were culturally different from the more recently converted and colonized areas to the east. Later, during the Reformation, these northeastern non-Romanized areas became the centers of Protestantism and, during the last century, of racist nationalism.

GERMANIC MIGRATIONS AND CULTURE

The German tribes naturally expanded through mergers and population growth. The basic social unit of the clan usually grew into a tribe, migrated, and fought for new territory in which to settle. As the tribes expanded they threatened the fortified Roman borders. Although the Alemanni and Swabians threatened the borders along the Rhine, the most serious threats to the Roman Empire came from the great migrations. The formerly peaceful coexistence between the Romans and the German tribes ended when the Visigoths, who were fierce warriors, were pushed by the even fiercer Huns from northern China westward, where they met with the Burgundians, Vandals, and Langobards. The Goths were divided into two tribal groups, the Visigoths (western) and the Ostrogoths (eastern). Initially, the Visigoths were supposed to be allies (*foederati*) and defend the eastern frontier. Treated badly by the Romans the Visigoths soon rebelled, defeating the Roman legions under Valens at the great Battle of Adrianople in 378. After Adrianople the Romans permitted more settlements of barbarians within the Western Empire. The Vandals crossed the Rhine in 406, and within three decades gained control of Northwest Africa. The Burgundians ended up settling in Provence in Gaul. The Angles and Saxons settled in England. The most important tribes were the Franks, who settled in northern and central Gaul, the Salian Franks along the seacoast, and the Ripuarian Franks along the Rhine, Seine, and Loire Rivers. The Visigoths sacked Rome under the leadership of Alaric and his brother-in-law, Ataulf, and eventually settled in southern Gaul and Spain. Later, the Ostrogoths established a kingdom in Italy under Theodoric the Great (454–526). An interesting aspect of all these battles and victories is that more often than not, as in Theodoric's case, the Germanic leaders respected Roman greatness and tried to imitate it.

Even the ruthless Vandals under Geiseric sacked but did not destroy Rome. By the end of the fifth century the barbarians had completely overrun the Western Empire.

The German peoples lived in a tribal culture in contrast to the civilization of the Romans. The civilizations that had existed around the Mediterranean were based on urban life and a territorial state. The Germans had lived in northern and central Europe in heavily forested areas with swamps and steppes. Their basic social unit was the clan; the population was divided into two classes, freemen and slaves. The most prominent freemen were noblemen (*athelings*), whose lifestyle was migratory. They built no temples, cities, or states. The only structures of some importance were their walled fortifications. They hunted and did some stock farming for food but had no economic system. The land was communally owned, and each year the work was divided among families. Their cultural life was centered on feuds and plunder, massacring their enemies, and even offering up human sacrifices. Victory in battle was the most important value for men. They believed in the magic of blood, and so the descendants of great warriors were elevated above those of the ordinary freeman. Customs and tradition were important in the decisions of the assembly of freemen called the Ding, which also acted as a court of justice. The assembly also elected the king or duke (*Herzog*). There was no written criminal or civil law in the modern sense. Finally, in Germanic religion the gods were conceived as personal beings, beyond good and evil. The individual tribal member's relation to his gods was much like his relationship to his chiefs, involving mutual service, trust, and loyalty. Good and evil existed in the same god. Among the well-known gods was Wodan-Odin, who represented the mysterious and demonic elements in Germanic religion as well as the majestic god of wisdom, death, storm, and the battlefield. Wodan was extremely irrational and unreliable. Another was Thor, who was the guardian of pasture and protector of married life, but also, in contrast, the god of war.

It took centuries to make the transition from their tribal migratory customs to those of a settled agricultural civilization. Roman cities had declined to practical nonexistence and survived only as small administrative or ecclesiastical centers. Trade was practically nonexistent until its revival in the 11th and 12th centuries. The assimilation by Germanic peoples of Roman customs and state traditions was a process that lasted certainly until the High Middle Ages. As far as the German language was concerned the word *deutsch* was first used to identify the language spoken in the eastern territories, while Romance dialects also were incorporated into Charlemagne's empire. Later, the word used to identify the German language was applied to the territory they inhabited, hence *Deutschland*.

Some German terms became significant later. The supreme commander was called the *Herzog* or *Fürst* and was elected from those families ennobled by blood, and the whole family was elevated with the leader. Although the Romans called a "first" man a king (*rex*), a more accurate Roman term for such an official would have been *praetor* or *princeps*. The German term *König* meant "descendant of a noble family" and was used by the Romans as an equivalent for the Latin word *rex*. There was a hereditary aspect to Germanic leadership as they were elected from families supposedly endowed with supranatural gifts. This paradoxical combination of election and heredity helps explain why medieval German kings found it difficult to establish lasting dynasties. Another paradox related to this was the German desire for independence, which, however, was combined with a strong need to submit to sanctified authority. Another combination of cultural traits gave rise to medieval feudalism. It was found in the Germanic institution of Gefolgschaft, by which followers would promise personal fidelity to the leader. Personal loyalty (Treue) took precedence over bonds of kinship and the tribe. This strong Germanic custom merged with the Roman practice of dependency in the late Empire. Later the Germanic feudal empire had at its core a whole hierarchy of bonds and relationships, with mutual obligations and loyalties that created the relationship between feudal lords and vassals.

FRANKISH KINGDOM

The story of Germany during the Middle Ages begins with the fall of the Roman Empire in the West. The German tribes that took over the territories of the Empire were numerous and included the Goths, Vandals, Burgundians, the Franks, the Alemanni, and the Thuringians, from whom emerged the specifically German peoples. They primarily inhabited the river basins of the Rhine, the Meuse, the Elbe, and the Danube. Under the Frankish Merovingian king, Clovis, the Alemanni were conquered, which began the union of tribes that would compose the German peoples. Later rulers conquered the Thuringians and the Bavarians. While Charles Martel, the first Carolingian ruler of the Franks, subdued the Frisians, Charlemagne conquered the Saxons. In about 800 the Carolingian Empire established a common ruler and a primitive administration that was the foundation for the political history of medieval Germany. That ruler was Charlemagne or Karl der Grosse as Germans named him.

CAROLINGIAN EMPIRE

The Germans have long been fascinated with the heroic and commanding personality of Charles the Great. Not only were his achievements unprecedented, but his personality as recounted by his biographer, Einhard, was the stuff of which legends are made. Gigantic in stature, dynamic in vitality, sensual, cruel, courageous, and a victorious warrior, he provided what was to be a too short-lived period of peace and justice. It was during his reign that one of the most significant features of German medieval history began, the eastward migration of the German people. It was from the fortified border territories called marches and ruled by margraves that he defended his empire against attacks of the Slavic and Avar tribes. Charlemagne made the church a bulwark of royal authority, forging an alliance with the papacy, appointing bishops and employing them as counsellors and administrators. This culminated in the coronation of Charlemagne by the pope on Christmas Day in 800 as "Emperor ever august of the Romans." During what has been named the Carolingian Renaissance, he also facilitated the reform of education and the church, and produced the readable Carolingian script. The very limited administrative centralization that Charlemagne achieved was probably due to his strong personal authority. In accordance with Frankish custom, however, Charlemagne designated that the empire should be divided among his three sons. A settlement was finally reached in the Treaty of Verdun of 1843, which gave the western part to Charles the Bald and the eastern to Louis the German, while Lothair received a narrow corridor between them between the North Sea and Italy. Not only did Lothair receive the least viable territory, but also the imperial title without imperial authority over his brothers. The Carolingian empire was reunited only briefly during the reign of Charlemagne's grandson, Louis the German.

SAXON AND SALIAN DYNASTIES, 919–1125

The transition from the East Franconian kingdom to the German Empire (*Reich*) occurred when the first German king, the Franconian duke Conrad I, was elected in 911. The high nobility (magnates) elected the monarch, but he had to be a blood relative of his predecessor. There was no capital city. It was a mobile monarchy with the king moving from place to place administering justice and making laws. Imperial estates were the source of the royal income. Sometimes, powerful tribal dukes challenged his authority. Conrad's successor, the powerful duke of Saxony, Henry the Fowler (known for his falconry), was elected king Henry I (919–936), ruler of the kingdom of the Germans (Regnum Teutonicorum). This first distinctly German dynasty was called the Saxon or Ottonian, so named on account of his successor, Otto I (936–973). The Saxon dynasty ruled with the support of a powerful military aristocracy and the church, over which Henry had asserted his authority. Otto used his power over the church as a counterweight against the powerful dukes. While Henry had succeeded in defending the kingdom against the invading Magyars, both he and Otto were successful in forging alliances and exercising their authority. With Otto's coronation in Rome in 962, the German kings could claim the unique title of "Emperor" unifying the German monarchy and the Roman Empire.

From the coronation of Otto I in 962 to the death of Henry III in 1056 the papacy was dominated by the German rulers. Emperors such as Otto III (r. 983–1002) and Henry III (r. 1039–56) supported reform within the church, which helped lay the foundation for the later papal resurgence. The dynamic reform pope, Leo IX (r. 1049–54), became pope with the support of Henry III, promoting regional synods opposed to the selling of church offices and clerical marriage. The control of the church was, however, lost by his successor Henry IV (1056–1106). The reform pope Nicholas II in the Lateran decree of 1059 established the College of Cardinals, which henceforth instead of the emperor was to select the pope. Henry's conflict with Pope Gregory VII (r. 1073–85) occurred over the pope's prohibition of the appointment of bishops and other church officials by lay officials. The separation of church and state was opposed by the emperor and resulted in his excommunication, penance at Canossa (1077), and surrender of his authority over the church. The outcome of the "Investiture Controversy" was the Concordat of Worms (1122), which allowed Henry V to influence the selection of only the German but not Italian higher clergy. The church was the winner in this struggle, because the German prelates were able to exercise their independence.

HOHENSTAUFEN DYNASTY, 1138–1250

During this same period some of the great dynasties that were to become famous in German history emerged. First there were the Welfs of Saxony, then the Wittelsbachs of Bavaria and thirdly the Hohenstaufens, otherwise known as the Staufer dynasty. In 1138 the House of Hohenstaufen came to the throne and lasted until 1250. The political turmoil of the period was successfully dealt with by the emperor, Frederick I (Barbarossa, the "Red Beard") who had been duke of Swabia and whose strength, wisdom, and longevity were second only to

Frederick I (Barbarossa, the "Red Beard") *(Library of Congress)*

Charlemagne's. During his reign the term *Holy Roman Empire* first came into regular usage. With the help of the princes and the Roman Law, Frederick restructured Germany as a feudal, rather than the centralized, monarchy it had been. Frederick had presided over the constitutional transformation of the monarchy.

Although the prestige of the Empire and the decline of central authority along with territorial fragmentation began during the reign of the Hohenstaufen emperor, Frederick I Barbarossa (1152–90), the period was considered a golden age. Under his successors, Henry VI (1190–97) and Frederick II (1212–50), the princes, both ecclesiastical and secular, became semi-sovereign. Frederick II, sometimes called "The Wonder of the World," did establish a modern state in Sicily but sacrificed Germany for his Italian policies. He conceded control over the German Church to the papacy, granting free elections of bishops and abbots. Frederick also made irrevocable concessions regarding administrative and legal jurisdiction, taxes and coinage to the nobility. Both ecclesiastical and secular princes were made practically independent, even allowing the princes to establish their own systems of justice. Frederick II's eager compliance with the demands of the German princes amounted to a kind of Magna Carta, which made the princes little kings in their territories and ensured six centuries of division in Germany. The emperor's theoretical rule in the West now came to an end with the death of Frederick II's son Conrad in 1254. Perhaps more significant was that Germany was proceeding in the opposite political direction from France and England, which were laying foundations for their nation states. Frederick can be credited with assuring the fragmentation of Germany, which lasted until modern times. In 1257 shortly after Frederick's death (1250) the princes established their own electoral college of the emperor, which was officially recognized in the Golden Bull (1356).

HABSBURG DYNASTY

In 1273 the Habsburg family became the rulers in Austria and soon held the imperial title. The emperors Rudolf (1273–91) and his son Albert I (1298–1308) tried to centralize imperial power again, but that failed. Under Charles IV (1346–78) the anarchy of the princes was legalized in 1356 through the Golden Bull. The bull designated that the election of the emperor was to be restricted to an electoral college composed of seven great princes (the king of Bohemia, the duke of Saxony, the count Palatine, the margrave of Brandenburg, and the archbishops of Mainz, Cologne, and Trier). This legalization, of course, furthered the disintegration of Germany. Yet Charles was intelligent enough to realize that he could not reverse the trends that were strengthening princely territorial powers and consequently sought to rule through the princes and personal influence. With the Golden Bull he laid the constitutional foundations for the Holy Roman Empire until its dissolution in 1806. By the end of the 15th century, therefore, two levels of institutions existed: the Diets or Imperial assemblies (Reichstage) attended by the emperor, nobility, knights, and representatives of the towns; and second the diets of the local territories (*Landtag*) in which the princes met with the privileged groups to gain their support and raise taxes.

With the economically powerful towns the electors increased their power at the expense of counts, lords, and knights. From 1438 the office of emperor was for all practical purposes a hereditary monarchy in the hands of the Habsburg family. Even with the attempted reforms by emperor Maximilian I (1493–1519) the fragmentation continued. The emperor was pitted against the interests of the electors, princes, and towns. Their rights and privileges were always expanded at the expense of the imperial power. The Reich, the Holy Roman Empire of the German Nation, continued to protect the smaller states from foreign threats, and the imperial idea lived on until Napoleon's dissolution in 1806.

CITIES AND CRAFT GUILDS

In Germany cities originated and grew as isolated enclaves. They had no roots in German culture. In the west and along the Roman frontier, some cities had roots in Roman history, as for instance Cologne or Regensburg. While the English and French kings established permanent residences for their courts in London and Paris, the German emperors refused to settle in the cities of Gaul and continued to migrate from one of the Palatinates to another. During Merovingian times these were wooden structures with earthen ramparts. In Charlemagne's time stone architecture imitating monasteries and bishops' residences was begun. Feudal lords began to fortify their permanent residences, perhaps moving them to hilltops, out of which the castles (*Burgen*) evolved. Gradually towns formed around the castles, as is indicated by the names of such cities as Augsburg, Regensburg, Würzburg, and Magdeburg. But it must be emphasized that there were no direct connections between the German cities beyond the Rhine and the Danube and the Roman or German tribal past, except, that is, for the ecclesiastical officials, the bishops. They had to locate their sees at the sites of Roman towns, but when the apostle to the Germans, St. Boniface (680–754), founded new bishoprics in Bavaria and Hesse, he established them in rural areas.

In Germany the cities were by-products of the feudal empire and assumed importance only in the second half of the 13th century. The cities developed along purely economic lines. The German word for *city* is *Stadt* and has no connection with the Roman word *civitas*. *Stadt* simply meant a marketplace, a location where some activity takes place. The towns of the ninth and 10th centuries grew up around trade fairs associated with church settlements. In order to evolve into modern cities, they had to be emancipated from the control of the lord or bishop and to develop city councils. Second, a mercantile leadership had to take over the patriciate of the knightly traders and the Ministeriales. In the inland cities handicrafts, industry, and banking became important, which set the stage of the third step in the transformation of cities, at which time the craft guilds took over the city councils during the 14th century. This created the petty bourgeois character of urban life that craftsmen had won at this time and then continued to exercise. Only in the Hanseatic cities were the craftsmen not able to take over this leadership role. Through the predominance of the guilds whole cities were transformed into work collectives and generally became models of order and discipline. In contrast to the feudal interests of the lords, the cities became the first expression of the communal public interest that was served in administration, finances, defense, health, welfare, and education. These were not controlled by a ruling elite. It was the guilds that created the models for good government later imitated by the territorial states.

ORIGINS OF CAPITALISM

The social and psychological atmosphere of the inland cities reflected the ambivalence of the German character toward man and nature found in the rift between the city and the country. The organized character of the city was in opposition to the chaotic world outside its walls and nature. The social and psychological atmosphere that permeated the inland cities encouraged materialistic values and also the rise of capitalism. European banking on a large scale was developed in Renaissance Italy, but in Germany, where a middle class sought to make money and increase production as ends in themselves, this capitalism was more modern in its values, not as the Renaissance princes engaged in it to attain political power or fame.

As the Hanseatic towns declined and the focus of economic activity changed, Germany experienced considerable economic expansion, especially in the areas of mining and banking. Before the Spanish began to import silver from the New World, the Germans had become producers of silver, which was the medium of exchange. Such families as the Welsers and especially the Fuggers of Augsburg had become preeminent financiers, and even came to dominate the metal industry in Hungary. Unlike the kings of England and France, the German emperor was completely dependent on the princes for financial support and often had to rely on bankers. It is difficult to understand how the emperors were so poor and almost powerless to raise funds. We are told that Frederick III (1440–93), who was the last German emperor to receive his crown in Rome, became a fugitive in his own empire, seeking refuge in friendly monasteries and cities because of the resistance of rich merchants to his efforts to levy a special tax. Another humiliating example occurred when the emperor Maximilian I was prevented from leaving Augsburg because he could not pay his bills to the butchers and bakers. Intricately involved in imperial politics, the Fuggers, as the most powerful bankers in Europe, lent great sums of money to bribe the princes to ensure the election of King Charles of Spain as Emperor Charles V. Not only in Germany had banking acquired the power to influence political events, but the money traders also functioned according to purely economic motives. As the economic power of the middle class rose, so did their cultural and political influence. Yet it must be remembered that although social mobility existed, this was still a premodern society of estates based on ranking according to clergy, nobility, and commoners. As far as the majority of the population were concerned, the tide of population growth and inflation undermined any possible economic improvement.

LATE MEDIEVAL CULTURE

It is also in the late Middle Ages that the movements that flowered in the Renaissance and Reformation emerged. Mysticism in the spiritual and philosophical realms and humanism in literature, education, intellectual focus, and the arts established important precedents and foundations. Johannes Tauler and the disciples of Meister Eckhart preached the necessity of a personal relation between the soul and God, while Geiler of Kaisersberg inveighed against the ecclesiastical abuses of the time. In contrast to Italian humanism the origins of German humanism were associated with the establishment of universities. However, in Germany, where the princes were hostile to intellectual life, this establishment came later, and when the princes established universities, they did so in imitation of other European rulers. Some examples were first the University of Prague founded in 1348, followed by the universities of Vienna, Erfurt, Heidelberg (1386), Cologne, and Leipzig (1410). The humanist movement in Germany was also stimulated by Charles IV (elected emperor in 1346), who was influenced by Italian humanism and who patronized learning. In general, however, intellectual life was the province of the middle class, but middle-class people were unconcerned with the broader issues of politics and society. What resulted was a narrow-minded parochialism or an interest in utopian and abstract issues, which left its mark on German culture well into the modern age.

During the late Middle Ages and as the modern world was dawning, two major crises occurred that had far-reaching consequences. One was the population crash of the early 14th century due to overpopulation and the devastating effect of the bubonic plague (1348–50), when hardly a village in Germany was spared. The devastating epidemic was carried by fleas from rats, and it was spread by the sneezing of infected people. It reduced the European population by about two-fifths. It inspired an obsession with death and dying and encouraged a deep pessimism. It added to sinister forebodings of the end of the world. The dreaded figure of Death and the "Dance of Death" became familiar themes in preaching, theology, literature, and the arts. The second and perhaps more important development was an institutional and leadership crisis in the Catholic Church, which was of the greatest significance for the future of Christian unity. It had three aspects: the Babylonian Captivity of the church (1309–76), the Great Schism (1378–1415), and the Conciliar Movement. The Babylonian Captivity was a period of predominating French influence in papal elections and papal policies. The Great Schism created a disastrous division in the church when three claimants contended for the papal throne. The papacy was brought back to Rome and steadfastly opposed the conciliar theory that church councils should take precedence over papal decrees. The papacy denounced any future appeal to a general council. All of these conflicts led to the unfortunate postponement of needed church reforms that would eventually lead to the Reformation.

The Renaissance

The Renaissance marks the beginning of the modern world, its new learning, exploration, and the emergence of national monarchies. Except in the area of humanism, Germany did not share in those contemporary trends. The Renaissance in Italy, of course, was the movement that inspired all of Europe. In Italy humanism meant returning to the sources of Western culture in ancient Greece and Rome. In many ways it was a backward-looking movement, yet the goals of the humanists were to create a new view of man and the world. The Turkish conquest of Constantinople in 1453 brought Greek scholars who stimulated the study of ancient Greek culture. What made it possible for humanists in Italy and throughout Europe to reach a truly international public was the new technology of the printing press, which had been invented by Johannes Gutenberg (ca. 1400–68) in Mainz. In fact the spread of printing was one of the indications of a close literary relationship between Germany and Italy. There were linkages through the influence of the imperial court, the newly founded German universities, and the cultural interests of the urban populations of southern Germany. Yet the German humanists wrote in Greek and Latin, which confined their influence to a comparatively small intellectual class and never had much of an audience among the masses. German humanism also differed from that of other countries to the north by stimulating religious discontent and hostility toward Rome, rather than pressuring the local church to reform itself. On the other hand, the German humanists were too tolerant and too compromising to be rebels. In the end, however, they were swept away by Luther's religious revolution. At best their rationality contributed to the enlightenment of their German public and contributed to the reform of the universities, which up until 1500 had been dominated by Scholasticism. Under the leadership of the Alsatian scholar, Jacob Wimpheling (1450–1528), new humanist curricula were introduced.

Perhaps the earliest influences of Italian humanism were manifested at the University of Prague through the humanist chancellor, Johann von Neumarkt. The most famous work of early German humanism was the *Plowman from Bohemia*, written by Johannes von Saas in 1400. In this dialogue between the Plowman and Death, the dignity of man is emphasized and Death challenged. Other early cultural influences from Italy went back to the Council of Constance (1415). This phase died out with the riots that occurred as a result of the persecution of the religious reformer, Jan Hus (1372–1415), a precursor of Martin Luther. Contemporaneous to the rise of German humanism was the literature that reflected the culture and interests of the German townsmen (*Burgers*).

The best example of this literature was written by Hans Sachs (1494–1576), a shoemaker from Nürnberg. He wrote thousands of poems and many legends, farces, and Shrovetide plays (Fastnachtsspiele) and was German to the core. An enthusiastic follower of Martin Luther, he also was inspired to write the religious play *The Nightingale of Wittenberg.*

RUDOLF AGRICOLA AND CONRAD CELTIS

It was, however, in the latter 15th century that Rudolf Agricola (1444–85) fathered German humanism. His early education was in the Netherlands with the Brethren of the Common Life, and he prodigiously expanded his knowledge of the arts, philosophy, and theology at the Universities of Erfurt, Louvain, and Cologne. Like all the other German humanists he also was educated in Italy, where he spent 10 years. There he was inspired by Petrarch, but also studied the classics and the law. Returning to Germany he sought to spread Renaissance learning. A leading disciple of Agricola was Conrad Celtis (1459–1508), who became the foremost poet of the German renaissance, an outspoken champion of classical scholarship, an advocate of religious renewal, and a staunch patriot and admirer of medieval German literature. Celtis began as an itinerant poet and eventually became a professor in Vienna. In his verses he imitated the Roman writers Horace and Ovid. In his quest for new rules for life and education, Celtis believed in the power of the printed word and expected that the thought of the ancients would reveal the knowledge of the universe. He expressed a love for medieval German culture and a strong German patriotism, lectured on the Roman historian Tacitus, and published his *Germania* in addition to the plays of Roswitha of Gandersheim (latter 10th century), who was the first dramatist and poetess in German literature. Celtis and the other German humanists, like the Swabian, Heinrich Bebel, made their greatest scholarly contribution in the field of historical study. The study of the Roman past had made them curious about their German past. Celtis and Bebel made *Germania* by the Roman writer Tacitus the key book of German humanism.

A member of the clergy who was also a humanist was Jacob Wimpheling. His writings criticized the lax morals of some of the clergy, and he hoped to reform the Catholic Church from within. Another German humanist of the period was Willibald Pirkheimer (1470–1528), who was a patrician from the imperial city of Nürnberg. A dedicated intellectual, educated in Italy, he was a very competent Latin and Greek scholar. Mutianus Rufus (1471–1526) was an advocate of Christian humanism based on the moral teachings of St. Paul. At the University of Erfurt Rufus became a leader of the humanists and influenced many students there to practice a more devotional and ethical Christianity. As with other humanists there was a greater emphasis on moral living rather than theology.

JOHANNES REUCHLIN

Johannes Reuchlin (1455–1522) was the most respected and admired of the German humanists who mastered many areas of knowledge. He studied at many universities: jurisprudence at Orléans, philosophy at Paris, Greek at Basel and Tübingen—where he also taught Greek and served as a civil magistrate—law at Rome, and Plato at Florence. He was an eloquent Latin stylist and the first fully competent Greek scholar in Germany. The real passion of his life, however, was Hebrew, which was the key to unlocking the mysteries of the ancient Jewish Cabala. Before the turn of the century he mastered the cabalistic literature and published a study on it. In 1506 he went on to produce a Christian-Hebrew grammar, and in 1518 another treatise on Hebrew studies. Reuchlin became engaged in some controversies with the orthodox Thomistic professors at the University of Cologne who thought that his studies were heretical. It was the converted Jew, Johannes Pfefferkorn, however, who became his most vociferous enemy. Pfefferkorn intended to exterminate Judaism in Germany and demanded that all Jewish literature be destroyed, while Reuchlin defended their existence as sources of religious and cultural truths. A spectacular controversy ensued. The Dominican priests even opened inquisitorial proceedings against him. Reuchlin responded by publishing a collection of letters, *Letters of Famous Men,* from those who supported his ideas. Also coming to his defense were the humanists Ulrich von Hutten and Crotus Rubeanus, who wrote an anonymous and satirical collection lampooning Reuchlin's opponents entitled *Letters of Obscure Men.* The goal of Reuchlin's Hebrew scholarship was to purify the church so that it could provide a more meaningful spiritual experience. In his philosophical-theological works, *On the Wonder-Working Word* (1494) and *On the Cabalistic Art* (1517), he sought to integrate both ancient and modern philosophy to demonstrate divine truth.

ULRICH VON HUTTEN

Ulrich von Hutten was the chief nationalist among the German humanists and possessed a bitter hatred of the papacy, which he thought was the principal financial exploiter of the Germans. He was the scion of an impoverished Franconian noble family and received his early education in a monastery. Then he attended four universities, and in 1512 served in the imperial army. What made him famous was his sharp Latin diatribes against Duke Ulrich of Württemberg, who was responsible for the death of Hutten's cousin. His diatribes have been compared to the *Philippics* of Demosthenes. Nonetheless, in 1517 he was crowned poet laureate by Emperor Maximilian I for his Latin poems, and that same year defended Reuchlin against the Dominican priests from Cologne. In Hutten's view the emperor was the representative of the German people, who were the heirs of the ancient Romans, and the pope was the enemy. Hutten was disappointed that the emperor was a Spaniard, a foreigner, and a Catholic. Hutten's dialogues included *The Book of Dialogues* (*Gesprächbüchlein,* 1521), in which he condemns the papacy for immorality and greed. When he wrote the bitter dialogues, *Vadiscus* (1520), also directed against the papacy, he lost the patronage and protection of Archbishop-Elector Albrecht. Hutten later was estranged from Reuchlin when the latter publicly condemned the teachings of Martin Luther. Hutten was only one of two humanists who supported Luther, doing so for political reasons; the other was Philip Melanchthon (1497–1560), who did so for religious reasons. It was in *The Arouser of the German Nation* (1520) that Hutten announced his support for Luther as a fellow fighter for German freedom from the yoke of papal exploitation. He has gone down in history as one of the most outstanding controversialists in German literature.

PHILIP MELANCHTHON

Melanchthon was a humanist scholar and professor of Greek at the University of Wittenberg, which had become a Lutheran stronghold. The brother of his grandmother was the famous jurist and Hebrew scholar Johannes Reuchlin. Melanchthon lectured in Latin and Greek literature at the University of Tübingen. Early on he became involved in the controversies surrounding Reuchlin's ideas, helping edit his *Letters of Obscure Men*. At the age of 21 he became professor of Greek at Wittenberg and became close friends with Luther. Melanchthon became the chief systematic theologian of the Reformation, writing his *Loci communes*, a systematic exposition of the teachings of St. Paul. It was Melanchthon who formulated the statement of Protestant doctrine that was presented to the emperor Charles V in 1530, the statement known as the Augsburg Confession. In the true spirit of humanism he tried to reconcile the differences between Protestants and Catholics. He later mediated Luther's disputes with another reformer, Huldreich Zwingli, in the *Marburg Colloquy* of 1527 and with Martin Bucer in the *Wittenberg Concord* in 1536. Because of his excellent textbooks and educational reforms, the title *praeceptor Germaniae* is attached to his name.

ERASMUS OF ROTTERDAM

The leading spokesman of the Christian humanists and the greatest literary figure of his age was Desiderius Erasmus (ca. 1466–1536) from the Netherlands. Erasmus was cosmopolitan in his thinking and was overly optimistic in his hopes to reform universal Christian society. After living in Louvain and then in Basel, Erasmus had already become famous before taking up residence in Freiburg in Briesgau, which was under Habsburg rule. His edition of the New Testament was the capstone of a program of Christian reform in a number of books: *The Handbook of the Christian Soldier, The Adages,* and *Praise of Folly.*

In his early formation Erasmus came under the influence of the Brethren of the Common Life and their mystical piety. His monastic education, ordination to the priesthood, and the influence in England of the Oxford reformers in the circle of John Colet all had a great deal of influence. Erasmus was more of a moralist and was not a systematic philosopher. He presented his ideas in choice Latin prose with wit and irony. He spoke of the "philosophy of Christ" as though it could be learned. Once they were understood, Erasmus believed that the Christian virtues would reform the individual and the world, which could be improved by the morality of good people leading a Christlike life. Not surprisingly, Erasmus considered the church to be the greatest educational institution of mankind. Martin Luther utilized Erasmus's New Testament in his teachings on the Epistle to the Romans, but Erasmus's theology was too rationalistic and was rejected by Luther. Erasmus's theology, however, became a part of the thinking of Melanchthon and through him penetrated Lutheranism.

Zwingli, or Swiss "reformed" Protestantism was also strongly influenced by Erasmian thought.

PRINTING AND MEDICINE

As the beginning of modernity the Renaissance was reflected in the lives and accomplishments of a number of famous Germans. The technical invention of the printing press by Johannes Gutenberg (ca. 1400–68) made possible many of the revolutionary changes that are common in the modern world. The printing press facilitated the rapid dissemination of knowledge and ideas, undermined the restrictions placed on new knowledge by the Catholic Church, and served as an instrument for educating the general public. By the year 1500 there were some 9 million copies of about 30,000 titles available to readers. Without it the Lutheran Reformation would have been impossible. The widespread availability of the Scriptures made it possible for believers to read and interpret Scriptures for themselves. The printing press also made possible the scientific revolution and the dissemination of scientific knowledge.

One of the leading scientific figures of this transitional age from the medieval to the modern world was Paracelsus (1493–1541). The new optimistic attitude toward man's capacity for knowledge and power reflected in the Renaissance is present in Paracelsus. He learned from his father the art of healing and gained a great deal of knowledge of mineralogy and metallurgy. He studied the properties of herbs, plants, and minerals and the peculiarities of human illness. Basically, his approach to knowledge was experiential, which made him dispute the humanists and their reliance on ancient texts and, of course, the medical authority of his time, the Muslim Avicenna. Paracelsus was appointed city physician and professor at the University of Basel, preferring to lecture in German rather than in the traditional Latin. He believed that the physician was an intermediary between man, nature, and God. Paracelsus bridged the spiritual world of Christianity and the modern world of science. He believed that sickness was a disturbance of divine harmony but that the individual and the physician were able to study the book of nature and discover the appropriate treatment. His was a mystical nature philosophy, a sort of magical view of the universe that was common during the Renaissance, in which nature is a creative process. The influence of his thought reached into the 19th century, especially in the thought of Goethe and the romantics.

RENAISSANCE ART

The new currents of the age were to be manifested in the life and works of Albrecht Dürer (1471–1528). In the life of this great artist can be found the conflicts of his age in the striving for limitless knowledge versus the contemplative life of the Christian monk. The new artistic expression of the Renaissance made painting and sculpture independent of architecture. The artist now painted on an easel and for the commission earned from wealthy townsmen. Technical expression became independent of subject matter, and art became independent of religion, which was one of the most important features of the transition to modern culture. Dürer combined a minute rendering of detail with the Renaissance concern for anatomy and perspective. And more reflective of the currents of his age this great artist combined the spirit of the Renaissance in his scientific naturalism with that of the Reformation in his subjective individualism. His religiosity is reflected in his many portrayals of the passion of Christ, while his study of man and nature is evident in his engraving of St. Jerome, who is presented at work in his study.

Two other painters who were influenced by the art of the Italian Renaissance and were uniquely German in their themes and rendition of their art were Matthias Grünewald (1480–1530) and Albrecht Altdorfer (1480–1538). Grünewald was the most original of the German painters, and in his religious paintings his style is soft and colorful, emotional and realistic. Space is suggested through the use of light and shade. His most original work is the *Isenheim Altarpiece,* completed in 1515 and painted with oil on wood. Especially in the crucifixion panel Grünewald displays his mastery of gesture to express feeling. Albrecht Altdorfer was distinctly different, painting landscapes in the Danube style of Bavaria and Austria in which the atmosphere is very natural. In his religious themes, as in the *Birth of Christ* and *The Holy Family at a Fountain,* an intimacy with the subjects is evoked. His most important work is his depiction of Alexander the Great's victory over the emperor Darius. Another landscape painter was Lucas Cranach the Elder (1472–1553), who was stylistically related to the Danube school. He was particularly good at uniting figures with their backgrounds. He was the court painter to Frederick the Wise of Saxony and friend of Martin Luther. An example of his innovative style is represented in his *Portrait of a Saxon Lady.* The realism of his portraits and his technical skill were abundantly evident. A synthesizer of the German, Italian, and Flemish traditions was Hans Holbein the Younger (1497–1543), who became one of Germany's greatest Renaissance painters. He came from Augsburg but spent much of his life in England. His most impressive paintings were in portraiture, one of his most famous being that of Erasmus. He also completed drawings and portraits of members of the court of Henry VIII. The colors he employed were rich, and he left no visible brush marks. In the woodcut *Dance of Death,* satire and misery are expressed. His greatest portrait is that of Joseph Hubert Morett.

PROTESTANT REFORMATION

The reform of the Catholic Church initiated by Martin Luther was inspired by the Christian's quest for salvation. Even though the primary impulse was Luther's attempt to solve his personal need to be assured of salvation, it precipitated a backward-looking revolution that involved a humanist return to the sources, in this case the Scriptures. Luther's protest against the abuses in the church, his revival of Pauline and Augustinian theology on the role of faith in salvation, his denial of free will, and his challenge to the authority of the pope and councils set Luther on a course that would irreversibly destroy not only the unity of the church but also Christendom. Luther challenged the institutional authority of the Catholic Church and emphasized the personal interpretation of the Bible. The Protestant revolt divided Germany into two almost evenly divided denominations whose conflicts would irreversibly scar society, creating one of the many cleavages that divided it.

NEED FOR CHURCH REFORM

As we have already seen, the anarchical condition of the Holy Roman Empire in which the princes predominated made it difficult to produce church reform and certainly was an important factor in bringing about the Reformation. Another major cause of the Reformation was the moral decline of the church in general and the papacy in particular. Papal encroachments on local authority alienated the national churches, which prompted them to break with Rome and reorganize on a national basis. The English church broke entirely with Rome under Henry VIII, and the French church had gained autonomy under its "Gallicanism." What had occurred nationally in England and France occurred only locally within German cities and territories.

On the other hand, the Reformation also was the culmination of popular mystical movements and heresies that had been developing for centuries. From the Albigensians, Waldensians, Beguines, and Beghards of the 13th century to the Lollards and Hussites of the 15th, these lay religious movements shared the common goal of religious simplicity in imitation of Jesus. A century before Luther, Jan Hus (1372–1415) had preached the need for reform and been repressed. Ever since the Great Schism of the 14th century, the church councils had failed to bring about urgently needed reforms. While saints had prayed for reform, humanists tried to reform the church and society by intellectually raising individuals to higher standards of moral behavior. Their reform program for the church and society was founded on education, a knowledge of the classics, new translations of the Bible, and the writings of the church fathers. The approach of the humanists, however, was overly optimistic about human nature, something that Martin Luther's was not.

The problems in the church were enormous. Lax morality and corruption were rife. Ignorance and immorality, pluralism, simony (the buying and selling of church offices), and a preoccupation with worldliness were widespread among the higher and lower clergy. Papal taxes drained money from Germany, and the church came to be seen as oppressing the poor, as was the aristocracy. Many Christians who sincerely wanted to feel assured of salvation became disillusioned with the clergy who would not live up to their expectations. The horrors and catastrophic death rate due to the Black Plague created a fear of death that continued to be strong in Germany. It motivated many Christians to seek meaningful religious experience and a certainty of salvation. Besides the pious experiences associated with the Modern Devotion inspired by the mystical *Imitation of Christ* by Thomas à Kempis, there were other devotions associated with pilgrimages and veneration of relics. Perhaps the most controversial was what many considered the sale of indulgences. Based on the church's spiritual treasury of merits gained by Christ and the saints, a Christian could gain the remission of the temporary penalties of sin that he would have to suffer in purgatory. Conditions in the Papal Court in Rome under the Borgia and the Medici families were scandalously worldly and at times immoral. When Martin Luther visited Rome in 1511, these streams of criticism merged, linking the abuses in Germany with the authority of the church. And when Martin Luther in 1517 indicted the corruption involved in the sale of indulgences by the Dominican monk Tetzel, he unintentionally sparked the Protestant Reformation.

What had prepared Luther for the formulation of his Ninety-five Theses in 1517 was a new understanding of Scripture dating back to 1512 on the relationship between grace, the Scriptures, and salvation. Catholic doctrine had long held that both faith and good works were necessary for salvation. Disagreeing with Erasmus and other humanists that humans could do good works, Luther came to the conclusion that human nature was so depraved that a Christian could never produce the good works that were required for salvation. Luther wrote that he came to despise the phrase "righteousness of God," for it seemed to demand of him a perfection that neither he nor other human beings could achieve. Through long meditation on the Scriptures, particularly on St. Paul's letter to the Romans (1:17) that "the just shall live by faith," Luther came to the conclusion that salvation did not come from religious works and ceremonies; rather salvation was given to the believer standing before God who trusted in Christ and was therefore clothed in Christ's righteousness. Salvation came through faith in the promises of God earned by Christ's crucifixion.

At first neither the archbishop of Mainz, Albrecht von Brandenburg (1514–45) nor Pope Leo X (1513–21), took Luther's theses seriously, believing that the controversy would soon blow over. Yet, after they were translated from Latin into German and were printed, they rapidly stirred up great discontent in Germany. In December 1517 Archbishop Albrecht condemned Luther as a heretic. In October 1518 Luther was called to defend himself at the Diet of Augsburg, where the heretical and revolutionary nature of his doctrines became more apparent. There was a pause in the prosecution for two years due to political issues concerning the election of a new emperor. In 1520 Luther published three pamphlets that openly challenged fundamental Catholic doctrines and challenged the authority of the pope. The first was the *Address to the Nobility of the German Nation*, which was a plea to the princes to establish a reformed church in Germany. In the *Babylonian Captivity of the Church* he attacked the sacramental system administered by the clergy and demanded that clergy have the right to marry. Finally, *On the Freedom of the Christian Man* Luther elaborated on his doctrine of salvation through faith, though he did not deny the obligation of Christians to perform good works.

The seriousness of Luther's disbelief in traditional Catholic teachings finally brought a papal declaration of excommunication. In defiance Luther burned it. Then he was summoned by the new emperor, Charles V (1519–56), to defend himself at the imperial Diet of Worms (1521). Unwilling to recant, Luther said that neither could he violate his conscience nor change his position. The emperor Charles responded with the Edict of Worms (1521) demanding that Luther be captured and his teachings suppressed. Fortunately for Luther, he had the support of Frederick III, "the Wise," the elector of Saxony (1486–1525), and was protected in the fortress called the Wartburg. Luther's vigorous defense of his beliefs at Worms gained him the support of many Germans who also hoped for religious and social reform. A large number of princes proceeded to establish state-dominated churches in their territories. Luther also replaced the Catholic mass with a new liturgy based on the reading of the Scriptures, preaching, and the singing of hymns.

At the Wartburg Luther began his translation of the Bible. His teachings were now spread far and wide among the German people by his followers in the Augustinian religious order, the lower clergy, and various humanists. A propaganda war now also ensued between Catholics and Protestants. Not only oral but especially printed propaganda became a potent weapon. The printing press was a crucial medium that placed the dissemination of Lutheran ideas beyond the usual control of the church. Luther translated the New Testament in 1522 and the rest of the Bible by 1534. It is undoubtedly true that the religious revolution associated with the Protestant Reformation was due in large part to the availability of hundreds of thousands of copies of the Scriptures.

LUTHER AND MELANCHTHON

Philip Melanchthon (1497–1560) became Luther's close friend and collaborator. Melanchthon was a classical philologist who formulated the statement of belief of the Lutherans, the Augsburg Confession, which was presented at the Diet of Augsburg in 1530. The document was intended to facilitate compromise. Diplomatically, Melanchthon had left out some key positions of Luther, such as the priesthood of all believers, the rejection of papal primacy, and the denial of free will and belief in predestination. Luther, however, only reluctantly approved of the Confession. What Melanchthon had hoped would lead to a possible reunion of Lutherans and Catholics was opposed by the Catholics with the backing of Charles V. For his part Luther opposed all attempts to compromise, even challenging the churchmen at Augsburg with such statements as that he would be a "pestilence" to them and not leave them in peace until they mended their ways. Certainly Luther's personality was not given to compromise. Although Melanchthon failed here, it was his role in Lutheranism to provide Lutheran theology with a philosophical basis.

LUTHER AND ZWINGLI

Huldreich (Ulrich) Zwingli (1484–1531), who was an ordained priest, was influenced by Luther's ideas of reform. Zwingli had accepted the position as minister at the Great Cathedral (Münster) in Zurich, Switzerland, and proceeded to reform that church, but in a more radical direction than Luther. Zwingli prohibited the celebration of Mass and ordered the removal or destruction of statues and images. One of the most serious differences with Luther occurred over the meaning of the Lord's Supper. Whereas Luther had retained the literal and "real" interpretation of Christ's presence on the altar, Zwingli taught that Christ was present only symbolically. Luther refused to compromise

A lithograph showing a crowd gathered to watch Martin Luther posting his Ninety-five Theses to the door of a church in Wittenberg *(Library of Congress)*

been realized. As a result of the rebellion the princes became reactionary and opposed to any meaningful reforms.

REFORMATION AND THE TOWNS

The Reformation probably was more successful in the towns. The townsmen (*Burgers*) were more educated and more influenced by Luther's writings. Lutheran pastors propagated their beliefs wherever they could receive a hearing, much more so in the towns, which were small enough for there to be a real sense of community. Only Cologne and Augsburg had populations greater than 40,000. While the town councils had not been able to control the independence of the Catholic Church, a Protestant Church with its lay elders more easily controlled church finances and charitable services. Also, the married Protestant clergy were a more visible model for Christian family living than were the biblical examples of Joseph and Mary. Many towns were also centers of civic virtue where the townsmen had to perform various communal responsibilities. Membership in committees contributed to a sense of participation, and townsmen could gain entry into the ranks of the oligarchy. While the leaders of some towns were benevolent, others, of course, were interested in pursuing their own interests. The towns also tried to protect themselves against the tyranny of the princes, and some towns used Protestantism to revolt against their Catholic princes.

ANABAPTISM AND MÜNTZER

In the town of Müntzer one of the more radical millenarian phases of the Reformation took place. By 1532 the town had become Protestant. Two years later Johann Matthys, a baker by trade, came to Müntzer, announcing the imminent second coming of Christ. An Anabaptist by belief, he insisted on the rebaptism of believers and insisted that unbelievers be killed. It had already been prophesied by Merchior Hoffman that Müntzer was to be the site of the end of the world, which inspired more than 1,500 townsmen to be baptized and await Christ's second coming in what Matthys called the New Jerusalem. When this failed to occur, an Anabaptist council ordered the destruction of statues and other so-called works of the devil. Then the town was besieged by the bishop, making it even more radical. Matthys was killed by the bishop's army. Then a new council of elders crowned a Johan Bockelson, a tailor's apprentice, as King Johan the Just, a type of New Testament king. It all ended with the town being stormed and the Anabaptist leaders killed.

CALVINISM IN GERMANY

The belief in the omnipotence of God led John Calvin (1509–64) to different conclusions than it had led Martin Luther. In Lutheranism religious justification led the believer to accept the world and to fulfill the duties of his calling. For Calvin faith was only one part of Christianity, and action the other. In Calvinism the Christian was called to action to change the world. Ethics had with Zwingli's interpretation. This issue was debated at a theological conference in Marburg in 1529, since then known as the Marburg Colloquy. Interestingly, there had been agreement on 14 out of 15 articles, but not on that of the Lord's Supper. The contrast between Luther's emphasis on the Scriptures versus Zwingli's rationalism was very evident.

KNIGHTS REVOLT AND GREAT PEASANTS' WAR

The consequences of the Reformation went far beyond the religious sphere. Social, economic, and political unrest coalesced with religious protest, sparking the first revolutionary movement in German history. The imperial knights were the first to organize. In August 1522 the imperial knight Franz von Sickingen presided over a meeting of 600 knights at Landau on Lake Constance. They formed an association to defend their rights and the Lutheran faith. Their role in warfare had changed. Gunpowder had practically made their former role obsolete, so many became mercenary officers in new armies and others became robber barons or served the interests of princes. Most of the imperial knights lived in run-down castles. The knights revolted, and the upheaval ended when Franz von Sickingen was killed, many castles destroyed, and their lands confiscated. Later, the emperor enlisted the knights in his service against the princes who had been victorious in the struggle and had profited the most from the Reformation.

In June 1524 a rebellion of peasants (The Peasants' War) occurred after they had taken Luther too seriously on the issue of social reform. It was not the poorest of the peasants but the middle and upper peasantry who demanded the right to elect their own pastor and desired that their tithes remain in the village. As important were their economic demands. They had been losing in the struggle against the powerful who were impoverishing them. They wanted to reverse their loss of access to communal lands and forest, and desired that their relationships with their lords not be based on monetary interests but on Christian principles. They hoped that Luther would support their rebellion against their secular rulers. On the other hand, Luther thought that their rebellion was inspired by Satan and condemned it in his pamphlet *Against the Thieving and Murderous Hordes of Peasants,* in which he encouraged the princes to kill some 75,000. He truly believed as did Catholics that God had ordained rulers to keep law, order, and peace. His condemnation of the rebellious peasants reflected his own personal struggles, on the one hand to rebel and on the other the need to submit to authority. After defying the spiritual authority of the church, he also emphasized the need of all Germans to submit to temporal authority. The peasants established the "Christian Association." Most of the fighting took place in Swabia, but it also spread to Franconia and Thuringia. At one point the former mayor of Würzburg and famous sculptor Tilman Riemenschneider (1460–1561) supported their efforts. The princes brutally suppressed the rebellion, and the peasants slipped back into their despair. A consequence of the revolt was that Lutheranism became increasingly dependent for its success and protection on the princes. In reality the desire of the peasants for fundamental social reform was too utopian and could not have to apply specifically to the individual and the community, and the organization of the church was so ordered for the sanctification of the individual and the community. Calvinist church offices included ministers, teachers, deacons, and elders, which indicated the broad range of ministries. For Calvin faith was beyond human understanding, and the doctrine of predestination was the key doctrine that expressed the supremacy of God's will. Calvin wrote the greatest work of systematic theology in Protestantism, his *Institutes of the Christian Religion*, first published in 1536.

Germany generally did not accept Calvinism, except in the areas of Westphalia and northwestern Rhineland, where Calvinist refugees from the Netherlands had settled. Elsewhere the first prince of the Empire to accept Calvinism was Elector Frederick III of the Palatinate (1559–76), whose University of Heidelberg became the foremost center of Calvinism. The Calvinist churches came to be known as "the reformed" church in Germany. The Heidelberg Catechism of 1563 became the chief creed of the Reformed churches. Other locations where Calvinism took root were in Nassau, Bremen, and Anhalt. But German Calvinist churches were different from that in Geneva, did not accept its constitution or discipline, and neither did the Heidelberg Catechism mention predestination. Like their Lutheran brethren the Calvinist churches were authoritarian territorial units and did not follow the corporate or presbyterian form of government.

CHARLES V AND THE REFORMATION

At his first imperial diet Charles V declared Luther to be under the ban of the Empire in the Edict of Worms (1521). The attempts by the emperor to enforce the Edict of Worms, however, were generally unsuccessful. His efforts provoked the Protest of 1529, signed by a large number of princes and towns. This was followed by the Confession of Augsburg (1530), a vigorous exposition of the leading beliefs of the reformers. Between 1521 and 1524 Charles was distracted by a series of wars with the powerful French king Francis I (1515–47). As if this was not enough, Pope Clement VII (1523–34) decided to ally himself with the French king. The Ottoman Turks also were threatening Habsburg territory from the East. Finally, the internal divisions in the Holy Roman Empire were an insurmountable obstacle to Charles's goal of preserving religious unity. The independence of the hundreds of states ruled by princes, ecclesiastics, and imperial cities had since the Middle Ages resisted imperial domination. If the pope had called a general council to reform the Catholic Church, the efforts of Charles to stem the rising tide of Protestantism might have been more successful. In 1540 Charles sought to reach a settlement by agreement at the Conference of Regensburg. In spite of his goodwill and moderation, the conference broke down and the dividing line between the two doctrines became firm. As a result Charles resorted to warfare challenging the Schmalkaldic League formed in 1531 by the Protestant princes. Charles was at first successful, but then lost because the Leaguers had received support from France and the powerful Maurice of Savoy. By this time some four-fifths of Germany had become Protestant. Finally, Charles was compelled to agree to the Peace of Augsburg

(1555). This was a turning point in the Reformation because it acknowledged the equality between Lutheranism and Catholicism. The ideal of Christian unity was gone forever. The fundamental principle of the peace was that each prince was accorded the right to decide the religion of his own state. That did not mean religious toleration, which was a battle that had yet to be fought.

The Renaissance and Reformation ushered in sweeping and permanent changes in Europe, which developed into the modern period. The Reformation in Germany contributed to the beginning of a national consciousness and a specifically German culture and character. It meant that the dominance of the Catholic Church as the sole spiritual authority in Europe had come to an end. The Catholic Church had become one creed and religious institution among many others. Science and the arts now began to function independently of the church. The Renaissance and Reformation helped lay the foundations for a secular Europe. The Reformation under Luther's leadership, however, had other far-reaching consequences in German history. Luther's emphasis that every profession or trade was a true "calling" ordained by God had the consequence of inhibiting ambition to improve one's status in society, contributing to the stability or stagnancy of German society. Also when Luther equated divine with secular authority and denied the mediating role of the church between the government and the people, a great incentive was created for the modern German ruler to exercise unlimited authority. The obverse of this development was that unlimited obedience could be demanded of the modern German citizen. We will see both of these tendencies emphasized in the development of the Prussian state.

Counter-Reformation and Thirty Years' War

During the years between the Peace of Augsburg and the Thirty Years' War, forces for a fresh struggle were taking shape. A turning point in the Reformation took place during the pontificate of Pope Paul III (1534–39), who appointed a reform commission that clearly identified the causes of corruption in the Catholic Church. In 1545 he initiated the Council of Trent, which met in three sessions, concluding in 1563. In 1555 Pope Paul IV initiated a vigorous policy of Catholic reform that was continued by his successors. The papal court was purged of its worst evils. The Tridentine Decrees were the outcome of the third and most successful session of the Council of Trent. These final decrees were uncompromising and disappointed moderate Catholics who had hoped for concessions to Protestants. Papal authority was vindicated, the Catholic doctrine of faith and tradition restated, the seven sacraments and transubstantiation upheld, and an unmarried clergy was to be maintained. The machinery of church government was thoroughly reorganized. The Counter-Reformation went to war against heresy with the militant and learned Society of Jesus, the reformed monastic orders, and the great saints and mystics. Pope Paul III had already instituted in 1547 the Roman Inquisition and the Index of Forbidden Books as two of its weapons.

From the beginning Germany became the center of the Counter-Reformation where circumstances made rapid success most likely. The imperial authority could be counted on to support the Catholic cause. Ferdinand I, Charles V's successor in the Habsburg lands and the Empire, pursued a moderate policy, both from conviction and necessity. His successors, Maximilian II, Rudolf II, and Matthias, however, were Catholic zealots who worked steadily and with increasing fervor to eradicate Protestantism in their ancestral lands, and who threw all their influence on the side of Catholicism in the Empire. In addition to these challenges Protestantism was suffering from the lassitude that follows the successful emergence from a great struggle. Various factions divided it. Its lack of a center of authority and foundation on individual interpretation of Scripture encouraged variations in interpreting the Gospel message, and church organization became a source of division. There were extremists like the Anabaptists at Müntzer who had created a bad reputation for Protestantism through their lawlessness and defiance of authority. Competition from Calvinism, which had spread rapidly from Switzerland, had attracted many Lutherans because of its clear doctrine and cohesive organization. Calvinist states were mingled with Lutheran ones, and their rulers were more concerned with organizing leagues to advance their form of Christianity than to unite against the Catholics. Finally, the Peace of Augsburg contained within itself the roots of further conflict. Only those who had signed the Confession of Augsburg were considered Protestants and free to practice their faith, while Lutherans in Catholic states were not allowed freedom of religion. Also, no settlement had been made of the territories that had been under the rule of a bishop and were now Protestant. Between 1555 and 1618 many Protestants returned to Catholicism, which finally encouraged the Protestant princes to put aside their differences and resume the militancy they had known earlier. Now war appeared to be inevitable. Meanwhile France had overcome the problems of its religious divisions under King Henry IV and became interested in expanding its power in Germany, which continued to be divided. On the other hand, the French had to deal with the power of the Habsburgs in both Spain and Austria. With its plans to dominate the Baltic Sea, Sweden also was pleased that the power of the German states was too weak to resist its expansion.

THE THIRTY YEARS' WAR

What occasioned the outbreak of the Thirty Years' War, the Bohemian succession, was certainly not the war's main cause. Often called "the last of the religious wars," the sources were certainly religious, between a militant Catholicism and a militant Calvinism. On the other hand, secular dynastic interests were also at work: the interests of the German princes to resist the power of the emperor and the expansionist dynastic interests of other European monarchs. Since these were so powerful, involving the states of Denmark, Sweden, France, and Spain, perhaps the Thirty Years' War might be considered the first European civil war fought principally on German territory.

The Peace of Augsburg had been a compromise on the religious issue but did not satisfy the participants and broke down. Under the weak emperor Rudolf II (1576–1612), who had been brought up under Spanish and Jesuit influences, the Counter-Reformation began, which incited the renewed struggle between the confessions and the rulers who supported them. In 1608 the Protestant princes, under the leadership of the young Calvinist prince-elector of the Palatinate, Frederick IV, concluded an alliance known as the Union, while the Catholic princes promptly responded with the League, at the head of which was Duke Maximilian of Bavaria. While the main strength of Protestantism lay in the north and center of Germany, Bavaria became the center of the Counter-Reformation. Indicative of the temper of the leaders of the Counter-Reformation was one of the bitterest enemies of the Protestants, Archduke Ferdinand of Styria, who later became Emperor Ferdinand II (1619–37). He reportedly stated that he would rather rule over a land that was a desert than over one populated by heretics. No sooner did this prince come to the ducal throne than he annulled the religious liberty of his Protestant subjects, expelled their clergy and teachers, and forced both the nobles and the people to return to Catholicism.

A decade of tensions and crises preceded the immediate cause of the Thirty Years' War, just as later happened before World War I. When Ferdinand became king of Bohemia in 1617, the event mainly furnished the cause of the Thirty Years' War. As the result of a collision between the two confessions in Prague, the Protestants, who formed the majority of the population both there and in the rural districts, set up a government of their own. When Ferdinand II (1619–37) succeeded the emperor Matthias, the Czechs rebelled. Protestant princes met in a diet in the spring of 1618 and threw two of the Habsburg governors out the window of Hradcin Castle, which has been memorialized as the "defenestration of Prague." Then the Protestants chose the young elector of the Palatinate, Frederick V, the son-in-law of James I of England, as a rival king. Ferdinand responded to the challenge by sending a strong imperial army into Bohemia and crushed the rebellion at the Battle of White Mountain that November. With a fierce vengeance the insurgents were punished. Twenty-seven prominent leaders were beheaded in the marketplace of Prague; thousands of families were exiled and dispossessed of their houses and chattels; and Protestant churches and schools were appropriated by Catholic priests and Jesuit teachers. In the end Frederick, known as "the Winter King," lost both the Palatinate and the Bohemian throne.

The Protestant princes of Germany did not appear to be overly concerned for their coreligionists and stood by at the defeat and massacre of the Bohemians. Then Spanish troops under General Johann Tserklaes, count of Tilly, commander of the armies, ravaged the Palatinate. Not until the emperor outlawed the ruler of that territory and proposed to install the Catholic Bavarian duke Maximilian in his place, did the Protestant princes become alarmed. That would have increased the number of the Catholic electors of the emperor at the expense of the Protestant. Of the two German princes who should have taken the lead in resisting the challenge to their faith and their independence, John George of electoral Saxony became an ally of the emperor, while George William, elector of Brandenburg, did not get involved. In the end the emperor made Maximilian an elector by presenting him with the Upper Palatinate.

While Catholics were determined to eliminate heresy, Protestants wanted to expand their influence throughout Germany. Many princes also had material gain at heart, attempting to expand their power and territories. One example was Maximilian of Bavaria of the Wittelsbach family, who even desired to rival the power of the Habsburgs. Other princes had designs on their neighbors. The margrave of Baden desired Württemberg, while the city of Würzburg was desired by the landgrave of Hesse. Above all the emperor wanted to consolidate Habsburg territories and extend his rule over Germany. Foreign rulers were no less altruistic, whether they were Gustavus Adolphus, Christian of Denmark, Maurice of Nassau, or Cardinal Richelieu, who ruled in France during the infancy of King Louis XIII. For instance, Richelieu financially supported the invasion of Germany by Denmark, and after 1631 French money was the principal financier of the Swedish forces. What further complicated the dynamics of the war was that soldiers of fortune were selling their services to the highest bidders and contributed to the brutality of the campaigns through wanton destruction and unnecessary killing.

In the long struggle that began in this fashion, Austria and Spain, with Bavaria, supported the emperor and Catholicism, while Denmark, Sweden, Holland, France, and England supported the Protestant cause. The confessional questions over which contention first raged were soon overshadowed by those of purely political goals. There were actually four wars, fought for the most part in different fields: the Bohemian phase and Palatinate war (1618–23); the Lower Saxon and Danish war (1624–29); the Swedish war (1630–35); and the Franco-Swedish war (1635–48). King Christian of Denmark, duke of Holstein, entered the struggle at an early stage, bent on acquiring Bremen and other North German districts. France, which subsidized all the emperor's enemies in turn and attacked his armies in Spain, was primarily interested in weakening its southern neighbor. In 1630 Gustavus Adolphus, the warrior king of Sweden, invaded Pomerania with a well-equipped army of 15,000, said to be the only national army in the war. Over a year later at the battle of Breitenfeld north of Leipzig Gustavus brilliantly defeated the imperial army. This Swedish army moved westward toward the Rhine, then marched against the city of Nuremberg and then south into Bavaria. Although Gustavus was killed at the Battle of Lützen two years later, Sweden continued to fight throughout the phases. The involvement of England was mainly with money and naval assistance.

The war lasted until 1648, then was concluded by a series of agreements collectively known as the Peace of Westphalia (October 27), which partitioned a large part of Germany. Other agreements among the major European powers during the next two decades, as for instance between Russia and Poland in 1667, marked a major turning point in European history. The states that benefited the most from this 17th-century world war were France, Sweden, and the Netherlands, which won what Austria lost. While France emerged as the dominant power in Europe, Sweden gained supremacy in the Baltic. France obtained Metz, Toul, and Verdun, reaching the Upper Rhine, which had been her ambition for a century. Spain, Denmark, and Poland were also on the losing side. Bavaria lost the Rhenish and kept the Upper Palatinate. The Holy Roman Empire was irreparably weakened through the recognition of the independence and the sovereignty of the states. Both the United Netherlands and Switzerland became independent states. The religious provisions of the Peace of Augsburg were reaffirmed, and all religious groups, rulers, and subjects, including Calvinists, were given an equal status. Neither the Catholic nor the Protestant side achieved their goals, and Germany was still very much divided as before. The ruinous economic and social impact of the war has often been exaggerated, especially by German historians. The areas most affected by the destructiveness of the war were the militarily strategic ones along the Rhine, the Black Forest, the Leipzig plain, and the roads to the city of Regensburg and the Danube valley. Agriculture was hurt the most by the ravaging armies, but the disappearance of villages had begun already in the previous century due to the development of large estates. Economic breakdown in the commercial cities had already begun due to imperial bankruptcies, the inflation of the 1620s, and the changes in trade routes due to the Atlantic trade. It has traditionally been thought that there was a disastrous population decline of from 5 million to 8 million people. Undoubtedly, the movements of often undisciplined armies and population migration contributed to the spread of typhus, one of the greatest killers of the 17th century, plague, and even syphilis. Scientific demography was unknown by earlier historians, and it is now known that urban mortality in Germany was probably no greater than elsewhere. The apparent catastrophic decline in population was probably due to disease and migration and perhaps there even was a modest increase. The economic consequences of the war that had supposedly turned back German development for 100 years has now been reinterpreted as a period in German history in which income, productivity, and standards of living actually improved.

Age of the Baroque

Originally a word of Portuguese origin indicating irregularly shaped pearls, the term *baroque* came to identify the international architectural and artistic style that dominated principally Catholic Europe from the end of the 16th century until the middle of the 18th. Baroque artists tried to harmonize the classical styles of Renaissance art with the intense spirituality manifested during the Reformation. Not only was the architecture, sculpture, and painting of this period dramatically realistic, but it served as a stage setting for religious, political, and social ceremonials. It also was intended to represent the order of society and the universe, reflecting the new view of the universe emerging from the Scientific Revolution.

The baroque style was enthusiastically embraced by the Catholic Counter-Reformation. It was especially popular in the Habsburg courts of Vienna, Prague, Madrid, and Brussels, and eventually spread to Latin America. The Catholic Church commissioned many new monumental churches, providing for the faithful an earthly demonstration of the truth and power of the Catholic faith. It had its origin in Italy during the 16th century in Il Gesu (1568–84), the mother church of the Jesuits in Rome, which became the model for later baroque churches and palaces. The baroque spread to France in the second half of the 17th century, but its final and distinctive phase occurred in Germany. A great building era began in the 1680s and reached its peak in the first half of the 18th century. This building boom reflected the dynamism that spread from Vienna, which was flush from the victory over the Turks and the French, giving rise to a new consciousness of greatness, of imperial destiny, and a sense of unity involving the Habsburg dynasty, the Catholic Church, and the aristocracy.

ARCHITECTURE, ART, AND SCULPTURE

Baroque architecture aimed at dramatic effect, and baroque sculpture portrayed emotional intensity or imitated the realities of nature. The baroque was able to fuse elements inherited from past architectural styles. From the Gothic, baroque art took over a striving to express the supernatural and an interest in closely observed detail in nature, and from the Renaissance the baroque continued the use of classic forms in architecture. Contours were irregular, and the total effect of a building was indented rather than displaying the compact and solid nature of the classical style. Architecture also reflected the search for grandeur and power that was widespread in the 17th century. Magnificently ornamented facades, twisted and bloated columns, decoration that emphasized deep colors and iridescent gilding, framed in heavy draperies, achieved an overall splendor. All the parts of the baroque palace were subordinated to the grandeur of the total form and conveyed an impression of limitless space. The palaces usually included a sweeping grand stairway intended to impress visiting princes, great halls, expanses of mirrors, and long rows of windows that looked out over carefully clipped hedges and geometrically patterned walkways.

Numerous absolute rulers of the German principalities during the period from 1690 to 1770 aspired to reside in palaces that imitated the Versailles of Louis XIV. Examples were the Zwinger Palace in Dresden, designed by Mätthias Pöppelmann (1662–1736), and the episcopal palace of the prince-bishop of Würzburg by Balthasar Neumann (1687–1753). To this can be added the Heidelberg Castle and the Charlottenburg Palace in Berlin. In Austria the chief architects were Fischer von Erlach (1716–39) and Johann Lukas von Hildebrandt (1668–1745). Fischer von Erlach designed one of the finest churches of the high baroque period, the St. Charles's Church built by Emperor Charles VI. It was built on an oval plan with a mighty dome. Hildebrandt's masterpiece was the Belvedere Palace built in Vienna between 1700 and 1723 as the summer palace for Prince Eugene of Savoy. Its elegance and monumental scale made it one of the supreme achievements of the Viennese baroque.

The great monastic church of Melk was built by Jacob Prandtauer (1655–1727) and Josef Munggenast between 1702 and 1738 and dominates the landscape from a cliff above the Danube. Its festive interior of gray marble with gilt ornamentation replaced the largely white background of Italian naves. Balconies in baroque churches were placed between massive Corinthian pilasters and gilded and suggested a box at an opera. Grandeur in the use of domes was softened by delicacy of detail in sculpture and carving. An example was the facade of the Church of the Fourteen Saints by Balthasar Neumann. Sculptured figures of gods and saints came to dominate architecture, and they became indistinguishable from pictorial backgrounds. Perhaps the best-known example of a freestanding sculpture and classical influence are found in the bronze equestrian statue of the Great Elector by Andreas Schlüter (1664–1715) in the grand courtyard of the Charlottenburg Palace in Berlin. Other baroque ornamentation can be found in the church altars of Bavaria and Austria with their charming painted wood sculptures. The figures of the Virgin Mary, Mary Magdalene, the saints, angels, and representations of the Christ Child are so attractive that one would think the artist had searched for the most beautiful models. Their expressive features register grief, tearful sorrow, or radiant joy. The spread of a hand, the gesture of an arm, and the posture of the figures are lively and graceful. Franz Ignaz Günther (1725–75), court sculptor, had a large shop in Munich. His *Pietà* and *Annunciation* (1764) at Weyarn in Upper Bavaria represents the Bavarian rococo at its very best. Located in the Bürgersaal Church in Munich, the group of the *Guardian Angel* shows the Archangel Raphael leading young Tobias by the hand. The contrast of the haughty angel and the overawed but trusting youngster is unique in sculpture.

The pictorial nature of the art of this period emphasizes softened contours in light and shade, as in a Rembrandt painting. Baroque painting stressed space-enlargement, creating the illusion of vanishing walls and ceilings. Light and color were used to dissolve form as in paintings of Peter Paul Rubens. But art also strove to reflect the supernatural and also to glorify monarchs and princes, and inspire in the beholder feelings of grandeur or devotion. In defining the character of the baroque style Heinrich Wölfflin described it as "painterly" or pictorial in contrast to the sculptural character of the Renaissance. Portraiture now came to express the individuality of the subject. Whereas in the Renaissance landscapes were used as backdrops for religious topics, now landscapes came into their own as subjects of beauty. The art of the period now came increasingly to serve the interests of kings and princes, and the interest of religion only in baroque churches.

LITERATURE

Literature in Germany around 1600 produced nothing that was equal to that of the countries surrounding it. In Germany religious movements had dominated the first half of the 16th century, and thereafter a new beginning had to be made. During the 17th century Germany was dependent on foreign models, and its most original contributions to the baroque style occurred only after 1700. Yet at the beginning of the 17th century the reform of the German language was taking place. Luther's translation of the Bible, as great as it was, did not uproot the many German dialects, as the Bible and sermons were adjusted to the local vernacular. Only between 1590 and 1650 did High German become the standard language in the sermons and schools of North Germany. Yet throughout the century and well into the 18th century the German language still was an uncertain medium for literary expression. The literature of the 17th century is not memorable and certainly lacked the universality that makes literature endure. German literature was enslaved to foreign and especially French fashion.

Leadership for a new beginning, however, was provided by Martin Opitz, whose great desire was to create a German literature equal to that of France and the Netherlands with his book *On German Poetry* (1624), followed by a book of his poems. His rules were followed by generations of German writers, and he was proclaimed the "father of modern German poetry." Through his efforts the secular forces of German literature were freed from religious dogmatism. On the other hand, Paul Fleming (1609–49) did express a creative imagination in his lyric poetry, especially concerning his deep religious faith. Among Catholics, the Jesuit Friedrich von Spee introduced a mystical love of Christ into the religious literature. The mystical poems of Count Nicolaus von Zinzendorf (1700–60) influenced the Protestant circles of Pietism. And for the world of pantheistic mysticism, Johannes Scheffler (1624–77) provided insights through his poetry, but he also was an example of conversion from Protestantism to Catholicism and even was ordained a priest. The religious poet Paul Gerhardt (1607–76) was outstanding, and as an orthodox Lutheran minister followed only Martin Luther as the most creative songwriter of Lutheranism. Gerhardt's hymns expressed the faith of the individual believer in objective Christian truths and his poems emphasized the presence of God in the beauty of nature. The greatest talent of the period was the Silesian Andreas Gryphius (1616–64), who was both a poet and tragic dramatist. He wrote in a dramatic rhetorical style. One of the creators of a satirical baroque prose, and a dynamic, moralistic preacher, was the Catholic Abraham a Santa Clara (1644–1709), who impressed Viennese congregations with his imaginative language. Dramas of political and religious violence were common, and the theme of pending disaster is not so surprising in a century that witnessed the Thirty Years' War, plagues, and many other misfortunes.

The greatest work of German literature of the 17th century was the novel *The Adventurous Simplicissimus* (1669) by Jacob Christtoffel von Grimmelhausen (1625–76). It is largely autobiographical and is a great epic. Like Parzival in Wolfram von Eschenbach's epic, Simplicissimus experiences a life process leading from an original harmony in his youth through the failures and sins of life, finally realizing a vision of God. The author places his protagonist in the end of a historic epoch, but with hope for a regeneration of mankind.

MUSIC

The baroque witnessed the introduction of new musical forms such as the oratorio and opera. The oratorio flourished both in the Catholic south and the Protestant north, and found its way to England. The baroque is primarily associated with the names of Johann Sebastian Bach (1685–1750) and George Frideric Handel (1685–1759). Bach, whose life was profoundly influenced by his devotion to the Lutheran faith, concentrated on vocal and instrumental music for church liturgies, especially in the form of sacred cantatas, and for instrumental and organ music. While Bach's career started in Weimar, it was in Cöthen where the Calvinist prince Leopold did not require religious music that he composed his six famous Brandenburg concertos. Later in Leipzig he composed around 250 cantatas for church choruses. It was here that he also produced sacred works on the theme of Christ's passion, the *St. John Passion* (1723) and *St. Matthew Passion* (1729). These and his monumental Mass in B Minor elevated the German musical tradition to new heights.

Although Handel was born in the same year as Bach and came from the same general area of central Germany, Handel's career was quite different. Unlike the religious musical tradition in which Bach was nurtured, Handel went on to compose numerous operas for cosmopolitan audiences in Italy and London. In Hamburg he found a flourishing center of opera and Germany's first commercial opera house in which to develop his interest in opera, which would dominate his life. From there Handel went to Florence, where he staged his first opera, *Rodrigo*. From Florence he went to Rome, where he produced his first oratorio on the theme of the Resurrection performed on Easter Sunday. Eventually he returned to Hanover in northern Germany. After some visits to England during the reign of Queen Anne, he became the favorite composer of King George I (1714–27), who had been his employer earlier in Hanover. For George I he composed his famous *Water Music* (1717) and for the Royal Academy of Music he produced an amazing 14 Italian operas in eight years. During the reign of George II (1727–60), Handel developed a new genre, the English oratorio, the most famous of which was *Messiah* (1742), which was followed by 15 more. His last commission became one of his most popular, the *Music for the Royal Fireworks* (1749). In moving "sentimental language" Handel gave expression to the "passions of the human heart," which his epitaph expressed so very well.

SCIENTIFIC REVOLUTION

Most of the advances of the Scientific Revolution took place outside of Germany. That is not to say that Germans were not interested in the problems of nature. Germans had continued to study nature through observation in the manner that had been stimulated by the Italian Renaissance. But a method based only on sensory observation and imaginative description proved to be inadequate. A new and complex descriptive tool was needed to provide the key to unlock an exact understanding, and that tool was mathematics.

In the history of the Scientific Revolution Johannes Kepler (1571–1630) was the great astronomer who gave the Copernican system its mathematical basis and worked out the laws of planetary motion. He was the astronomer at the Imperial court, but lived in a European and not a German intellectual world. Although religion was the driving force behind his thinking, and he maintained his connection to the Lutheran Church, he sought to understand God as the creator through mathematics. He believed that reason was the only authority, and his scientific research led him to formulate the three laws of the movement of the planets. Kepler was guided by the popular Renaissance philosophy of Neoplatonism, which maintained that the world was harmoniously structured according to a geometric design. Kepler worked out the planetary orbits, concluding that they were elliptical in shape and the Sun lay at one end of the ellipse. Mathematical equations were used to prove that the planets did not revolve around the Sun in circular orbits but rather in an elliptical pattern. Kepler's laws were published in the *New Astronomy* (1609) and in the *Harmonies of the World* (1619). Through his planetary laws Kepler substantiated the Copernican theory, which postulated that the Sun rather than the Earth was the center of the universe, adding that the planets revolve around the Sun in an elliptical orbit rather than a circular one as Copernicus had maintained.

GOTTFRIED WILHELM VON LEIBNIZ

Gottfried Wilhelm von Leibniz (1646–1716) was one of the most universal minds in German culture, and among German thinkers only Johann Wolfgang von Goethe (1749–1832) can be compared to his genius and his range of interests. He was the son of a Leipzig professor and became an academic prodigy. He had international connections with kings, statesmen, and philosophers, traveled widely, was interested in numerous subjects, and was even elected a member of the English Royal Society. He became Germany's response to the new scientific method and philosophies being pioneered by Galileo, Newton, Descartes, Hobbes, and Spinoza. Leibniz had great ambitions, one of them being to reform the religious and political world. He proposed a plan for the reconciliation of Lutheran and Reformed churches and hoped for a reunion of the

Christian churches. Perhaps his most successful project was the foundation of academies of sciences. In Berlin the Society of Sciences was founded with the help of the first Prussian queen, Sophie Charlotte; another was founded in Dresden, and the one planned for Vienna with the support of Prince Eugene was not realized because of the lack of money in the Austrian treasury.

The central theme and goal of the philosophers of the age was epistemology, the relationship of the mind to nature. Leibniz denied the sharp distinction that Descartes had drawn between philosophical and mathematical truth on the one hand and theological truth on the other. All subject matter, Leibniz believed, could be understood through reason. However, he rejected a mechanistic interpretation of the world and preferred a teleological one that could be achieved through a new conception of "substance." To him the universe consisted of an infinite number of substances called "monads" and thus his system was called Monadology. Religion for Leibniz was different than it was for Luther. Man was not the object of God's creation and was not as Luther thought utterly depraved. For Leibniz God was not an angry creator but the architect and guarantor of the universe. In political life, unlike the English thinker Thomas Hobbes, Leibniz thought that the purpose of the state was a moral one and emphasized that the absolutist state was limited by the individual's right to education. He tried to improve the cultural foundations of German political life, and as a patriot he endeavored to improve the welfare and security of Germany. His place in German intellectual life is as the father of the German Enlightenment and the transmitter of Western European thought to Germany.

In philosophy and mathematics Leibniz expressed his genius. He expanded the mathematical and mechanistic worldview through his calculus, which he invented independently of Newton. Leibniz deserves the credit in the history of German scientific thought for the distinctive view of science in Germany. In contrast to France and England, where the concept of science applied exclusively to nature, in Germany all forms of scholarship including the liberal arts could be considered science (*Wissenschaft*) as long as they followed the methodology of their subject matter.

PIETISM

Pietism was a private form of Protestantism, which expressed a personalized attitude toward Christianity and was somewhat similar to Jansenism in France, or Puritanism and Methodism in England. Pietism began with the organization of special meetings for biblical study (*pietatis*) organized by Philip Spener (1635–1705), who wrote the movement's first treatise, *Pia Desideria* (1675). Pietism cared principally about the spiritual awakening of the individual, but also created an enthusiasm for social work and the establishment of workhouses along the English model. The movement spread rapidly, and the political and social conditions of Germany explain why it was more confined to the upper classes and was a revolt against authoritarian and institutionalized religion. The Pietists, unlike the Lutherans, stressed that the state was unfit to direct the religious life of its Christian members. Pietists believed that a true Christian moral life could be realized only in a community. It might be asked why the Pietists, unlike the English Puritans, did not simply separate themselves from the state. They could not because Imperial law forbade it. Socially, Pietism started among the upper burgher class and the nobility. It spread widely in the 17th century in the area around Frankfurt among the Imperial nobility. The nobility of Saxony and Prussia also favored it, while only in Württemberg was there widespread popular support among the lower classes. The source of supreme authority was the Bible, and its daily study the only means to salvation. Worship centered in the family, and personal religious experience was emphasized instead of regular church attendance.

ROCOCO

The rococo was the elegant concluding phase of the baroque. The middle of the 18th century saw the kings and aristocracy begin to prefer smaller residences where more intimate meetings of the salon could comfortably take place. Although rococo art no longer reflected the grandeur and flamboyance of absolutism and the design of an ordered society, it nonetheless achieved a certain elegance and grace. Two of the chief examples of rococo architecture actually were completed in the early part of the century, the Zwinger in Dresden (1711–22), already mentioned in reference to the baroque, and Frederick the Great's palace in Potsdam, Sans-Souci (1745–47). In Sans-Souci the decor is light and elegant in contrast to the grandiosity of the baroque. Residences generally were not very high, and their design enclosed gardens of the nongeometric English fashion, where trees and shrubs grew naturally. More than exterior design the rococo focused on interior design to accommodate social functions. For instance, chairs received backs, and bedrooms were separated from reception rooms. Windows bathed the interior with light, and the preferred colors were pastels. Music also reflected the new interests, as did dress. The powdered wig became a symbol of the age and the minuet the preferred form of dance. But it was in the Catholic south that Germany's great musical geniuses flowered. It was a golden age of German music that reflected a universality of meaning instead of a particular faith or region. The trinity of great composers were Joseph Haydn (1732–1809), Wolfgang Amadeus Mozart (1756–91), and Ludwig van Beethoven (1770–1827). Perhaps it was Mozart's chamber music that best expressed the elegance and grace of the rococo.

Absolutism in the Habsburg Austrian Empire

The Habsburg dynasty was first established in the archduchy of Austria after 1282. The family grew in importance so that between 1440 and 1806 a Habsburg wore the imperial crown of the Holy Roman Empire continuously with only one exception, the short reign of Charles VII (1742–45) from Bavaria. The Holy Roman Emperors were weak and lacked a strong central government. No emperor had established a system of common law nor a representative institution like the British Parliament. On the other hand, the Habsburg dynasty developed its strength as rulers in their own domains The Habsburgs commanded the allegiance of a dozen different nationalities, and their authority extended itself over a bewildering variety of societies and cultures, which included the archduchy of Austria, the duchies of Styria, Carinthia, and Carniola, the counties of Tirol, Istria, Vorarlberg, and Gorizia-Gradisca, the city of Trieste, the crown lands of Bohemia and Hungary, which included Moravia, Croatia, and Transylvania, and a miscellany of territories in the Austrian Netherlands, Lombardy, Mantua, Galicia, and even some fragments of Poland. It truly was a heterogeneous state, but not impossible to rule in an age before strong sentiments of national pride dominated politics. The Habsburgs were never a German dynasty, but they did play a significant role in German history.

During the 16th and 17th centuries the Habsburgs tried to master their realm through family ties and support for Roman Catholicism. They hoped that the dynasty and the church would provide the institutions that would provide enough cohesiveness for the diverse peoples under their rule. Austria supported the Counter-Reformation and achieved the highest degree of religious unity, dispensing with the rights given to Protestants in Catholic lands by the Peace of Westphalia. For two centuries between the division of family territories in 1519 to the end of the War of Spanish Succession (1701–14) the Habsburgs expended the resources of their lands in pursuit of dynastic goals throughout Europe, but failed to develop a stable political order. The Catholic Church encouraged the ambitions of the Habsburgs to be the defenders of Christian faith against the Turkish infidels. The defense of Vienna in 1683 led to a new crusade against the Turks, which was extremely costly and extended Habsburg borders ever farther to the east.

FRENCH ABSOLUTISM AND IMPERIALISM

The monarchical absolutism that was so fashionable in the 17th and 18th centuries gave the ruler almost unlimited power, an efficient administrative bureaucracy, and a fiscal policy that provided the means of taxation to build a strong army and state. State control of the economy called mercantilism also promoted economic growth, which made possible the buildup of military strength and the beautification of capital cities. It was the French monarchy that provided a splendid example of absolute monarchy for Austria, as well as Prussia and many of the other German princes of Bavaria, Saxony, and Hanover. The Treaty of Westphalia (1648) had given the German princes full sovereignty to control their states and conclude foreign alliances, as well as the independence to resist the authority and power of the Holy Roman Emperor. They could imitate Louis XIV, who followed the theory of princely absolutism to the letter and disregarded the traditional prerogatives of the Estates and the provincial diets so well expressed in his motto "I am the State." It should be remembered that princely absolutism did not begin in 17th-century France, for its code was already formulated during the Renaissance by the Italian Niccolò Machiavelli (1469–1527) and in France by the jurist Jean Bodin (1530–96).

Besides pursuing the ideals of absolutism, Louis XIV established the largest standing army that Europe had ever seen, and he was determined to protect France against Habsburg encirclement, and to extend France's frontiers into the territories of the Holy Roman Empire. Besides the independence given to the German princes by the Treaty of Westphalia, the treaty also provided France with the opportunity to influence German affairs. Louis XIV assumed the role of protector of the prerogatives of the German princes. The first such intrusion occurred at the death of the emperor Ferdinand in 1657, whereupon Louis tried to secure the election of the elector of Bavaria. The election of Leopold I (1658–1705), the Habsburg archduke of Austria, was immediately opposed by the "Rhenish League" of German princes in alliance with France. Louis's program of national aggrandizement included expanding France's frontiers to include most of the territories on the left bank of the Rhine. The Rhine River was to become France's natural eastern boundary. Unbelievably, most German princes supported him along with Sweden. In 1667 Louis invaded the Spanish Netherlands and managed to keep 11 cities in Flanders according to the Peace Treaty of Aachen (1668). After Louis ended the Dutch War with the Peace of Nijmegen (1678), he attacked the Holy Roman Empire and occupied Alsace and Lorraine and the Imperial city of Strasbourg. With the exception of Brandenburg, which was allied to the French, many German princes decided to join the emperor and the kings of Spain and Sweden in the League of Augsburg (1686), which led to the French attack on the Palatinate. Now the coalition against Louis was joined by England. The indignation of the German Protestant princes was aroused by the deprivation of religious freedom of the French Huguenots. Some 200,000 emigrated from France to Holland, England, and Prussia. In 1688–89 the cities of the Palatinate, including Worms, Speyer, Mannheim, and Heidelberg, were senselessly devastated, including their historic monuments and art treasures. The remains of the castle of Heidelberg still stands as testimony to the rapaciousness of the French. Louis lost the war in the Palatinate. By the Peace of Ryswik (1697) Louis lost most of his conquests with the exception of Strasbourg and the occupied areas of Alsace, which he was able to keep because the emperor was preoccupied with the renewed threat of a Turkish invasion.

TURKISH WARS

The siege of Vienna by the Turks in July 1683 was the culmination of a Turkish offensive against the West that had begun in 1645. The Turks had conquered Crete in 1669, had defeated the Poles in the Ukraine and Podolia in 1672, and had attacked and were defeated at Kiev, but Hungary was in rebellion and the way to Vienna now lay open to them. The terrible siege of Vienna lasted for two months, and Austria was slow to receive any help from Christian Europe. Soldiers finally arrived from Saxony, Bavaria, Franconia, and the Upper Rhine, but the army that played the most decisive role came from Poland and was under the leadership of John Sobieski. Charles of Lorraine was the chief field commander, and their combined forces defeated the Turks at the Battle of Kahlenberg (1683). Charles of Lorraine defeated the Turks again at Gran in 1685 and also captured Buda, the ancient capital of Hungary. In 1687 Charles was victorious over the Turks at the second Battle of Mohács, where Sulieman the Magnificent had been victorious in 1526, which had secured Turkish dominance of Hungary. In 1687 the Diet of Pressburg conferred the male line of succession in Hungary on an Austrian male heir. The first to be so crowned was the emperor Leopold's son Joseph on December 9, 1687. All of Hungary and Transylvania was given up by the Turks in the Treaty of Karlowitz (1699). The surrender of these areas by the Turks had great historic significance, marking the beginning of the Danubian empire of the Habsburgs, which was to last until 1918. With the fall of Budapest the emperor was able to impose a constitution, which made Austrian absolutism supreme in Magyar lands. An extensive protective belt now surrounded the Austrian homeland, and new resources were made available. The emperor now considered himself more Austrian than Roman. In 1713 the Habsburg family became the hereditary monarchs of the three thrones of Austria, Hungary, and Bohemia, which annulled the traditional rights of the Bohemian and Hungarian Estates to elect their kings.

Although the Habsburg monarchy emerged from the Turkish Wars considerably stronger and its reputation enhanced, its advisers had come to the conclusion that centralized institutions and a standing army were required to enforce the imperial will. They wanted to make the Chancellery (Hofkammer), and the Military Council (Hofkriegsrat) into instruments for increasing centralized administrative, fiscal, and military control. One of the strongest advocates for this centralizing policy was Prince Eugene of Savoy, a renowned hero and one of the greatest military strategists of his age. He had fought for the Habsburg dynasty not out of selfish interest and the pursuit of glory but for the Austrian state, which he thought could become a unifier of a Christian Europe. His political sagacity was probably equal to his military genius. In June 1703 Prince Eugene became the president of the Austrian war council appointed by the emperor, Leopold I, who was facing the successful armies of Louis XIV and a spreading revolution in Hungary. Earlier, in May 1701, Prince Eugene commanded the Austrian troops in Italy in the first campaign of the War of the Spanish Succession (1701–14), in which he conducted a brilliant campaign against French forces. It was here that the poverty of Austrian finances demonstrated itself when the treasury could not provide the necessary soldiers and equipment to support his campaign. The Grand Alliance of the emperor, England, and the Netherlands was the solution at this time. With Austria in great danger the Anglo-Dutch army in the Netherlands under the command of the great military commander John Churchill, duke of Marlborough, was permitted to enter Germany. Through cooperation with Prince Eugene the Grand Alliance prevailed at the Battle of Blenheim (August 13, 1704). At the Danube River one of the most murderous battles of the century occurred. The duke of Marlborough's tactical genius, however, made victory possible with the skillful support of Prince Eugene. Great losses occurred on both sides. It was the first great military defeat of the armies of Louis XIV. Germany was liberated, and Bavaria, an ally of Louis XIV, was occupied and almost annexed. Bavaria was saved as the emperor Leopold died on May 5, 1705, and was succeeded by Joseph I (1705–11). To his credit the young emperor aspired to reassert the role of the emperor within the Holy Roman Empire. Yet he did not live long enough to have any effect. His younger brother, Charles, then succeeded him as emperor Charles VI, the last in the male line of Habsburg succession. The empire of the Austrian Habsburgs had become the largest of the German states and the principal rival to Brandenburg-Prussia.

WARS OF AUSTRIAN SUCCESSION

The succession to the Austrian throne was an issue of top priority even at the beginning of the reign of Charles VI. After his firstborn male heir died in 1716 and the birth of three daughters followed by 1724, it was hard to suppress fears of challenges to a female successor. In 1718 the Austrian government publicly announced the Pragmatic Sanction (1713), by which Maria Theresa was to succeed her father, Charles VI (1685–1740), to the Habsburg throne. The Pragmatic Sanction was first approved by all the estates of the Austrian Empire by 1732, signifying the importance given to the indivisibility of the Habsburg empire, which was to be further demonstrated during the crisis years of the 1740s. The assent of foreign states and the Holy Roman Empire was obtained in the 1730s. Yet, no sooner did Charles die in 1740 than a number of sovereigns withdrew their assent to the Pragmatic Sanction. Maria Theresa's enemies who contested her succession were the elector of Bavaria, Charles Albert Wittelsbach (1697–1745), Philip V of Spain (1683–1746), Augustus III of Poland and Saxony (1696–1763), and Frederick II Hohenzollern, who in 1740 had just become king of Prussia. During the Wars of Austrian Succession that followed, the archduchess, Maria Theresa (1740–80), was challenged and humiliated most of all by Frederick the Great of Prussia. Maria had inherited her father's aged ministers, who favored compromise instead of resistance. No one would have been surprised if the monarchy had collapsed and Vienna no longer been the capital of a great power.

Frederick II was determined to take advantage of the situation by laying claim to Lower Silesia. Under the pretext that Austria was no longer strong enough to protect the Silesians, Frederick occupied the province in a surprise coup. Then, in order to obtain recognition to his claim, Frederick offered Maria Theresa an alliance and promised in compensation to support her husband, Francis of Lorraine (1708–65) as a candidate for Holy Roman Emperor. After his offer was rejected, Bavaria and France soon joined in an attack on Silesia. A Franco-Bavarian army captured Prague on November 26, 1741, and the Bavarian elector Charles became emperor Charles VII. Maria had to flee Vienna but succeeded in rallying the Habsburg cause, enlisting the support of the Hungarians and Great

Statue of Frederick the Great, Berlin *(Library of Congress)*

Britain. A Hungarian army occupied Munich. Great Britain now actively supported Austria with an army led by George II, who was also the elector of Hanover. Great Britain, the Netherlands, and Austria concluded, the Treaty of Warsaw, which recognized the Pragmatic Sanction. In September 1745 Maria Theresa's husband, Francis of Lorraine, was elected Emperor Francis I. Still hoping to recover Silesia, the Austro-Saxon army was defeated by the Prussian cavalry, for which Frederick came to be known as "the Great." The second Silesian war ended with the Treaty of Dresden (December 25, 1745), in which Frederick II recognized Francis I as emperor. More fighting continued. Peace was finally concluded in the Treaty of Aachen (1748). The succession of Maria Theresa was confirmed, but disappointingly, Prussia's retention of Silesia, one of Austria's richest provinces, was recognized as well. Austria also lost Italian districts of Parma, Piacenza, and Gustalla to France. The years between the Peace of Aachen and the beginning of the Seven Years' War (1756–63) were filled with intrigue and diplomacy, which produced a reversal of alliances known as the Diplomatic Revolution.

STATE REFORMS

Maria Theresa was an extraordinary and courageous German princess. She may have inherited her lively personality from her Guelph mother but was a true Habsburg in her strong belief in her dignity. She had a happy marriage but did not let her husband, who was unsuited to politics, affect her judgment. She had pride in her dynastic inheritance, strongly believed in her moral principles, and was able to create enthusiasm for her monarchy. Her government was not based on rational principles, but on strong convictions and a simple faith; she was free from bigotry but was religiously intolerant. She had an "insatiable" desire to have children, giving birth to 16 (five boys and 11 girls) and thought of her subjects in a maternal manner. Yet, after her experiences during the War of Austrian Succession, she became aware that changing ministers was not the answer to Austria's problems, but that a radical reform of state institutions was necessary.

Without prior training the 23-year-old empress surprised everyone, and with a strength of character, her feminine genius, courage, and determination, she rallied her ministers and mobilized the resources of her territories. She also realized that new policies were needed, in effect a revolution in government, and she relied on her husband, Francis Stephen of Lorraine, her cabinet secretary Ignaz Koch, and Johann Christoph Bartenstein, who was her foreign secretary. She discovered how the Provincial Estates could frustrate the policies of the central government. The estates controlled taxation, military recruitment, and supplies and used these to advance the interests of the provinces and the popularity of individual ministers. She felt that Providence had sent her Friedrich Wilhelm, Count Haugwitz, from Silesia, who was ideally suited to assist her in beginning her revolution in government. The actual work of reform was turned over to him. He established royal "Representation and Chamber" in every province with the exception of Hungary to take over the functions of the Estates. These chambers were made responsible to the central government in the Directorium under Haugwitz's control and which replaced the Austrian and Bohemian chanceries as well as the treasury. By 1749 this reorganization was completed, and the court became the administrative nerve center of the monarchy.

Centralization was the means through which reform was to be accomplished. Combined administrative departments of internal affairs, justice, commerce, war, and foreign affairs replaced the separate chancelleries of Austria and Bohemia. The Provincial Estates were deprived of their authority. In Hungary, however, the nobles maintained their independence by the recognition of their historic privileges, and traditional laws were upheld. The historic role of local diets was restricted, and new provinces were subdivided into districts, which furthered royal centralized administration at least in Austria and Bohemia, if not in Hungary, Italy, or the Netherlands. Executive and judicial branches were separated. The chief state offices of defense, foreign affairs, justice, interior, and commerce were made responsible to the monarch. The authority of the Estates in Austria and Bohemia was restricted by abolishing their right to collect taxes, which were now collected by royal officials. This department also paid troops and nominated officials. Industry was encouraged, which more than doubled the monies available for the military. But Maria Theresa restricted expenses rather than raised taxes. She made major tax reforms by requiring the church and nobility to pay their share of the taxes. A general tariff wall was also erected around Austria and Hungary.

After the conclusion of the Seven Years' War the revolution in government was broadened to include the common welfare and general prosperity, which meant raising the cultural and educational standards of the population. Recognizing the necessity of education, Maria Theresa started a system of elementary schools partly accomplished by reducing the independence of the Catholic Church. She appreciated the need to improve the social conditions of the peasantry. Maria Theresa was also responsible for major legal reforms. In 1768 a new penal code was instituted and in 1776 judicial torture was abolished. The penal code standardized judicial proceedings and punishments, making equal justice more likely. In religion she was intolerant, stressing religious unity through Roman Catholicism, and was especially intolerant toward Jews. She defended the rights of the state in relation to the church, not allowing communications from the papacy or pastoral letters to circulate without her permission. Religious holidays were reduced, and so were the number of religious orders. The Jesuits were banned from the Empire. Finally, she was aware of the peculiarities of different nationalities and their traditions, which was important in the peaceful governance of a multiethnic Empire. It was in response to conservative Catholicism and not the ideals of the Enlightenment that she sought to reform the government.

FOREIGN POLICY AND KAUNITZ

Although France had been Austria's principal antagonist to this point, Maria Theresa now had to focus on the dangers posed by Austria's new principal enemy, Prussia and Frederick II. Along with the revolution in governmental organization, Maria Theresa now adopted new foreign policy objectives.

Although Silesia had been reluctantly ceded to Prussia, the recovery of the lost province became the principal long-term objective of Austrian policy. She discovered the appropriate diplomat among her ambassadors, Wenzel Anton, Count Kaunitz (1711–94), who possessed great political vision and was influenced by the mechanistic rationalism of the Enlightenment. He had acted as her plenipotentiary at the Congress of Aix-la-Chappelle. In 1749 he was appointed the youngest member of the supreme advisory council, the Conference, then as ambassador to France, and finally in 1753 as head of foreign affairs as chancellor of state. With patience, daring, and rational calculation Kaunitz abandoned Austria's alliance with Great Britain and achieved an alliance with France. As the architect of this diplomatic revolution, Kaunitz became Maria Theresa's most influential adviser.

The so-called Diplomatic Revolution of 1756 came about in response to the danger that Prussia posed to Austria's goal of recovering Silesia. The alliance with France enabled Kaunitz to also bring Russia into a war with Prussia. In 1756 Austria was at the center of a strong alliance in which she could set her strong army against Prussia. At the Battle of Leuthen (December 5, 1757) Frederick defeated an Austrian army twice as strong as his, and the Battle of Rossbach (1757) stimulated a great deal of admiration for Prussia in Germany. While Austria's alliance with France was extremely unpopular in Germany, the military skill of Prussia was admired, which enabled Frederick to replenish his army with German troops. On February 16, 1763, the treaty of Hubertusberg was signed by a victorious Prussia, which retained Silesia after stopping one of the most powerful coalitions ever assembled in Europe.

After the Seven Years' War (1756–63) Austria abandoned the idea of regaining Silesia and adopted a peaceful foreign policy. Maria Theresa reluctantly took part in the first partition of Poland (1772) and the War of Bavarian Succession (1778–79). She was opposed to the further expansion of Prussia and Russia. In the 1772 partition Austria received Galicia. Prussia agreed to a compromise peace ending the Potato War, in which Bavaria ceded the Inn Quarter to Austria.

JOSEPH II AND REFORM

At the death of her husband, Francis I, in 1765, her son Joseph was appointed coregent, which lasted until 1780. He already had been crowned Holy Roman Emperor in 1764. Joseph was unlike his father and insisted on sharing in the governance of the Empire. The empress was opposed to giving her son this responsibility, but after many arguments she relented, allowing him to be in charge of army reform and sharing with Kaunitz the conduct of foreign policy. He was lacking in talent for either of these two areas. The struggle between mother and son lasted for 15 years.

Of her 16 children it was her son Joseph, her beloved "Phoenix," who succeeded her as Joseph II in 1780, although he had already become emperor in 1765. Of the kings of the 18th century Joseph was the most revolutionary reformer. He lacked the warmth of Maria Theresa, and because of his puritanical personality the atmosphere of his court was bleak and lacked the elegance of his mother's. Not only did he pursue further centralization, but he also tried to level class differences and secularize government. Unlike his mother, Joseph enthusiastically admired the French philosophes and their reforms for government and society based on reason. He dreamed of the Austrian Empire being transformed by the muse of philosophy. His program, however, was too radical and, like those of other visionaries, soon overturned. What did he try to change? First, he abolished the personal servitude of peasants. Serfdom no longer existed in Austria, but the peasant could not leave the land, and his lord still controlled his right to marriage. The peasant was freed from subjection to his landlord according to the edict of November 1, 1781, and now was a subject of the state. Furthermore, Joseph gave the peasants hereditary rights to land. The nobility saw these measures as revolutionary acts that alienated them. Neither the nobility nor the peasants could comprehend the drastic changes that he decreed. Most of the agrarian reforms were not retained after Joseph II's death, and the social and economic emancipation of the peasants in Austria was not achieved until the revolution of 1848–49. He ended the restrictions of the guilds and tariff barriers. Equality before the law, elimination of the death penalty, and religious toleration were also decreed.

Joseph's attacks on the institution of the Catholic Church and its monasteries aroused alarm in Rome and certainly were unwise. First, he desired to become the only sovereign over the church. Traditional ties with the archbishoprics of Salzburg and Passau were cut as were the connections with the papacy. Monastic orders were placed under the control of local bishops, and those monasteries not operating educational institutions or providing nursing care were dissolved, closing some 800 throughout the Empire. The education of priests was to be supervised by the state. Civil marriage was introduced and divorce made possible. The Edict of Toleration (1781) ended the identification of the state with the Roman Catholic Church, which had begun during the Reformation "Ferdinandean period." Non-Catholics were given full rights as citizens and allowed the private exercise of religion. This may have been the beginning of religious toleration, but full religious equality did not occur until 1861. For the first time the legal position of the Jews was addressed. Their status was understandably complex. While the Jews had been expelled from Vienna in 1670, it was belatedly discovered that rich Jews were needed to administer state finances. Samuel Oppenheimer was one such important Jewish financier during the reign of Leopold I. In any event Joseph II decreed that the Jewish religion must be tolerated and broadened Jewish social rights as to their occupations and place of residence.

With already too many enemies, Joseph II made even more when he humiliated other ethnic nationalities by making German the official language of government. In his drive to create a single unified Empire he created a central office for Austrian internal administration, the United Court Chancellery, which was divided into 13 departments. Indicative of his fanatic reforming zeal were the 6,000 edicts he issued in 10 years. Because he feared that they would not be executed, Joseph even organized an extensive police system throughout the provinces, responsible to the chiefs of provincial administration, who sent secret reports to the central government. Realizing the failure of his efforts, Joseph, writing the epitaph for his grave said, "Here lies Joseph II, who was unfortunate in everything that he undertook." His successors, Leopold II (1790–92) and Francis II (1792–1835) administered the suppression of his reforms out of the need for aristocratic support and fear of the French Revolution.

Yet the reforms initiated by Joseph II looked forward to the principles of liberalism. Joseph had conceived the state to be built on an egalitarian society and inspired by secular ideals that informed the French Revolution and the liberalism of the 19th century. Joseph remained a hero among the peasantry. His initiatives also contributed to the stability of the Habsburg monarchy as it withstood the challenges of the French Revolution and the Napoleonic wars. His successor, Leopold II (1790–92), also an enlightened despot, agreed with many of Joseph's goals but had more respect for constitutional forms. He reintroduced the Provincial Estates and the constitutions of Hungary and the Netherlands, although by and large government administration was still carried on in a centralistic manner. Joseph's concentration on the Habsburg Empire and preoccupation with Austrian problems came at the expense of his involvement in German affairs. Ironically, he was more interested in Germany than was Frederick the Great, but the king of Prussia had continually frustrated Joseph's German policies. In short, Austria's ties with the rest of Germany were loosened, and the creation of an imperial crown for Austria in 1804 would have been impossible without the unifying policies of Maria Theresa and Joseph II. The Holy Roman Empire was dissolved by Napoleon in 1806.

VIENNA AND ARCHITECTURE

Vienna was to the Habsburgs what Paris was to the Bourbon monarchy. Many splendid palaces and churches in the baroque style of southern Catholic Europe were built to display the glory of the monarchy. Prince Paul Anton (Pál Antal) Esterhazy rebuilt his castle at Eisenstadt where the great composer Haydn would conduct. Vienna became the music capital of Europe. The famous architect Johann Lucas von Hildebrandt designed the Belvedere Palace for Eugene of Savoy. But it was Austria's greatest architect, Fischer von Erlach, who drafted the plans for the Royal Library and the Imperial Palace of Schönbrun. In 1715 he began work on the St. Charles Church (Karlskirche) in Vienna, one of the finest churches of the high baroque, built on an oval plan with a high dome. It was built by the emperor Charles VI in fulfillment of a vow made during a plague and dedicated to St. Charles Borromeo.

On the banks of the Danube to the west of Vienna, Jakob Prandtauer built the most impressive baroque monastery in all of the Austrian lands, the Benedictine abbey of Melk. Salzburg was not to be left out of the competition for architectural beauty either. Under Archbishop Johan Ernst Thun (1687–1709) the famous Mirabell Gardens of Salzburg were constructed with beautiful sculptures by Fischer von Erlach adorning them. He was also responsible for 12 of the impressive structures in Salzburg, the Kollegienkirche being one of the most outstanding achievements of baroque architecture. Hildebrandt was responsible for the rebuilding of the Residenz and Schloss Mirabell.

During the reign of Maria Theresa court architecture moved from solemnity and the symbolization of power to an informality of joyous gracefulness, which was expressed in the restoration of her palaces. The architect in charge of producing this "Theresian" style was Nikolaus Pacassi. Schönbrun was rebuilt in the 1740s, and the palace in Innsbruck in the 1750s and 1760s. The main ceiling frescoes of Schönbrun and Innsbruck reflect the changing styles and values of the old and the new. The frescoes synthesized in their allegories the military prowess of the Habsburgs with the Enlightenment's neoclassical themes emphasizing nature's bounty and economic productivity. The uneasy juxtaposition of baroque and neoclassical style reflected the character of Maria Theresa's reign, harnessing new policies to traditional objectives. Neoclassicism triumphed between 1772 and 1778 as Maria Theresa had the park of Schönbrun Palace beautified. Chosen by Kaunitz as the chief architect, Ferdinand Hetzendorf von Hohenberg emphasized classical antiquity and the Enlightenment's challenge to traditional society. He even had Pacassi's rococo staircase rebuilt along classical lines. The gardens of Schönbrun reflected a nostalgia for classical antiquity. The sculptor, Johann Wilhelm Beyer, produced 30 life-size statues lining the avenue to the fountain of Neptune with figures from Greece and Rome. Here an important difference of emphasis is seen in contrast with the parks of Versailles and Trianon. At Versailles the emphasis was on the personalities of imperial Roman history, whereas in Vienna the heroes immortalized were those of Plutarch's republican Rome, representing the qualities of character that made it great.

Rise of Brandenburg-Prussia

Of the more than 300 sovereign states in the Holy Roman Empire after the Peace of Westphalia, only two were to emerge as great European powers. Austria was the major one, but Brandenburg-Prussia was to emerge in the 17th and 18th centuries as a significant second. The rise of Brandenburg and its expansion into modern Prussia was the work of the Hohenzollern family, which included the Great Elector, Frederick William (1640–88), Frederick III, who became Frederick I, the first king of Prussia (1688–1713), and the renowned Frederick the Great (1712–86).

THE GREAT ELECTOR

It was during the reign of Frederick William, the Great Elector, that Brandenburg was recognized as a leader among the German states. Brandenburg was a small, open territory that was impoverished and misgoverned when Frederick William began his reign. The misery and suffering of the Thirty Years' War had affected the peasants and townsmen the most, while the Junker aristocracy had become more powerful. Going back to the Reformation the Junkers had seized the common lands and forced the peasants to work on their estates in an increasingly commercialized agricultural economy. In order to get the financial and military support of the aristocracy the Great Elector granted the aristocracy almost complete control over their estates and the peasantry, including police, legal, and economic power. These powers were not lessened until the reform initiated by Baron von Stein during the Napoleonic Wars. Frederick William also inherited a disorganized and undependable force of about 3,000 mercenary soldiers, and in its place he began to organize a disciplined paid professional army. Initially he had difficulties recruiting from native manpower and the peasantry, having to rely on vagabonds and servants. Gradually the officers came from the landed aristocracy attracted by the financial benefits that could be had. By the last decade of his reign Frederick William had built up his army to the fourth-largest in Europe with 45,000 men, which had defeated the Swedes and established Brandenburg as a military power. The army was financed and was placed under the jurisdiction of a new agency called the General War Commissariat. Gradually the Commissariat became a bureaucracy and the basis for a civil administration.

The Great Elector laid the foundations for economic progress. He reformed the system of land tenure and introduced improved methods of cultivation, which helped make agriculture profitable for peasants. Encouraging trade and industry, he built roads and canals, introduced a postal service, and established schools. State-financed factories were established, often run by foreigners. After the repeal of religious toleration in the French Edict of Nantes, thousands of skilled Huguenots immigrated to Prussia and contributed to its industrial development. Frederick William even promoted trade with the Indies and established the first German colony on the west coast of Africa. A man of vision, the Great Elector can be said to have laid the foundation for the patriarchal state in Prussia, enabling it to unify Germany in the 19th century.

The religious mixture of Lutherans and Calvinists was undoubtedly a leading factor in making Prussia one of the most tolerant of the German states, although in the tradition of absolutism, decreed by the ruler. It is thought that when in the early 17th century the elector at that time, Johann Sigismund, converted to Calvinism, he found himself obliged to respect the rights of the Lutheran Church. The country was divided between a Lutheran aristocracy and a minority Calvinist urban middle class. Later in 1685 the Great Elector issued the Edict of Potsdam (1685), welcoming to Prussia the French Calvinist Huguenots who were expelled from France when the Edict of Nantes was revoked. These French Calvinists went on to make outstanding economic and educational contributions. In education, for example, they established the College Royal, which for generations educated many of Prussia's elite. The Academy of Sciences in Berlin also claimed a sizable minority of French Calvinists as its members.

FREDERICK III

The succeeding elector of Brandenburg was Frederick III (1657–1713), who was less of a statesman and soldier and more artistically and aesthetically gifted. Perhaps his most significant contribution was his assumption in 1701 at Königsberg of the title of Frederick I, king of Prussia (1688–1713), which, however, was outside of the Holy Roman Empire. It was only from Brandenburg that he derived his electoral title. Perhaps he was inspired by the fact that the elector Frederick August of Saxony had recently been crowned king of Poland. Even earlier in 1688 military assistance from Brandenburg had helped secure the English throne for William of Orange from Holland.

FREDERICK WILLIAM I, THE "SOLDIER KING"

Under his son, Frederick William I (1713–40), Prussian development proceeded in a more austere direction. Known as the "Soldier King," he devoted great financial resources to the development of the army. Taxes were levied on the aristocracy, and aristocrats were expected to serve as officers and their sons to be educated in military academies. By 1739 all of the generals were aristocrats and only about 5 percent of the 211 officers were not from the nobility. The Junker nobility came to be imbued with a sense of duty, obedience, and sacrifice, which made them great soldiers. The exaltation of these military virtues has historically been associated with Prussian militarism. All peasant males were required to serve in the army, while the urban bourgeoisie and property owners were exempted. The king took great pleasure in finding the best physical types for his regiments, sending recruiting agents throughout the country. By the end of his reign the army had grown to some 80,000 men and was still the fourth-largest in Europe. Next to his love for the army was the king's devotion to the administration of government. A highly efficient bureaucracy was developed in which the Junker aristocracy was again dominant. The General Directory, which was first organized to supervise the military, was used to direct other departments of government, including the police and the economy. Yet Frederick William also subjected his people to a hard discipline and expected them to be thrifty and to serve the king with their bodies, property, and consciences. He promoted commerce and agriculture and protected Prussian industries from foreign competition. Undoubtedly he personified what later came to be known as Prussian virtues, such as discipline, orderliness, and frugality, and vices such as extreme self-assertiveness, bellicosity, and thinking that only his own point of view was true.

This policy of the Prussian kings to favor the Junker aristocracy in order to create a strong army, however, held the danger of placing the peasantry at the mercy of the aristocracy, and in the case of the independent peasantry of threatening their extinction. The Prussian kings needed to maintain a strong class of peasantry because they served in the army, supported the army with their taxes, and worked for and provided supplies for the army. Consequently, in a series of edicts (1709, 1714, and 1739) the Bauernschutz was established, which attempted to protect an economically secure peasantry. Nonetheless, the taxes and services that the peasantry provided for the army were enormous. During the 1750s, for instance, a peasant in Lower Pomerania contributed an unreasonable 18 out of 22 thalers of his yearly income to the support of the army. Worse yet, all grown men in Prussia were subject to military law and were restricted in their travel; villages had to watch out for deserters; and soldiers were required to wear their uniforms during their months at home.

FREDERICK THE GREAT

Frederick William II of Prussia (1740–86), later known as the "Great," was reared by a father who was a stern and threatening taskmaster, Frederick William (1688–1740). According to the laws of modern psychology Frederick should have become a nervous wreck, certainly a hypochondriac and later in life gone mad. Yet Frederick became one of the best educated and cultured monarchs in Europe and the most brilliant soldier and statesman of his age, so much so that even to his contemporaries he was known as "Frederick the Great." It was his intention to be a well-rounded and enlightened man. A student of the Enlightenment he invited the French philosopher, Voltaire, and other enlightened authors to join him in stimulating discussions in the palace of Sans-Souci between 1745 and 1756. Claiming to be the first servant of the state, he implemented during the last 25 years of his reign reforms encouraged by the philosophers. He presided over the reform of the Prussian legal system, providing a common code of laws considered to be superior to a variety of local codes. Religious toleration was extended to all, and limited freedom of speech and press were allowed. With some exceptions, torture was abolished. Demonstrating that he was not a pure idealist, Frederick could not bring himself to outlaw serfdom even in the face of Enlightenment criticism. In his *Political Testament* of 1752 Frederick indicated his intention not to undermine but actually to strengthen the aristocracy. In this regard Frederick followed a reactionary policy that effectively closed the upper ranks of the civil service to all but the aristocracy. On the other hand, Frederick can undoubtedly be called an enlightened despot, having modernized the Prussian state and providing it with an efficient government by a capable bureaucracy and a good economy. The army was the model for the state, which was authoritarian and paternalistic. Prussian society was generally stable, but it also lacked those institutions and values that would encourage its members to emancipate themselves into a democratic form of government. The conditions among the middle class of the towns allowed them to pursue their economic interests and advance themselves in the bureaucracy. On the other hand, the option of entering the aristocracy was impossible in the 18th century, when the bridge of upward social mobility was closed off and the aristocracy made more exclusive.

SEVEN YEARS' WAR

Foreign affairs dominated the first part of Frederick's reign, and his achievements were dramatic. For more than 20 years he was engaged in an almost unbroken succession of wars that made great strides in consolidating the disjointed territories that made up the Prussian state. Altogether there were three Silesian wars: Frederick first seized Silesia, then held it, and finally was confirmed in its acquisition during the third, also called the Seven Years' War (1756–63). The occasion of the first Silesian war was associated with the war of succession to the imperial title. With the death of Emperor Charles VI in 1740 his daughter Maria Theresa was to assume the title based on the Pragmatic Sanction of 1713, which had secured the Habsburg possessions for her. Her title was challenged, however, by two very powerful rulers who had married daughters of Emperor Joseph I, the elector Charles Albert of Bavaria and the elector Frederick Augustus II of Saxony. Frederick thought it was a good time to advance the Hohenzollern claim to lands in Silesia, so without any warning he invaded Lower Silesia in December. How did he justify this occupation? He told the inhabitants that he had the legal right to do so and needed to occupy the territory to protect other Prussian lands. This, of course, was not to the liking of Maria Theresa, and therefore the first Silesian war and the War of the Austrian Succession were fought concurrently. Frederick's allies were France, Spain, Bavaria, and Saxony, while Maria Theresa had Russia, Holland, and England as allies. Through the Treaty of Breslau (July 1742) Frederick secured both Upper and Lower Silesia. This was followed by a second Silesian war in 1744, which essentially confirmed Frederick's possession of Silesia in the Treaty of Dresden (December 1745). As so often happened in the game of monarchical alliances, the allies were shuffled. In the meantime it was necessary to elect another emperor, and on this occasion Maria Theresa's husband won the title as Francis I (1745–65). But now complications and a further reshuffling of allies took place. England and France were already involved in war in North America. When George II of Hanover feared for the safety of his electorate because of the threat from France, he allied himself with Prussia, which now was opposed by Austria, Russia, and France. With this the Seven Years' War (1756–63) began. Although Frederick had some German allies, his armies had to fight against the allies of Maria Theresa, but also troops from Sweden, Bavaria, Württemberg, and Saxony. An unbelievable struggle ensued for six years. With the death of the Russian empress Elizabeth (January 1762) and the accession to the throne of Peter III, who admired Frederick, Russia, then Sweden, then France withdrew from the conflict. The Treaty of Hubertusburg (February 1763) ended the war, which essentially confirmed Prussia's claim to Silesia. Prussia also received the town of Gratz. The Seven Years' War took a great toll on all the participants, killing more than 1 million men and making large areas of Germany and Bohemia desolate.

Society and Culture in the Eighteenth Century

SERFDOM, POPULATION EXPANSION, AND DISEASE

In the 18th century Germany continued to be a predominantly agricultural society. Of the approximately 20 million people living in the Holy Roman Empire, more than a majority (80 percent) were still peasants living at a subsistence level. By the end of the century when the population had reached 24 million, 1 percent of the population, comprising 50,000 families, belonged to the nobility. The agricultural workers in the western portions of the Empire were freer and economically more independent and better off than their counterparts in the Prussian lands to the east. There peasants were under the bondage of serfdom in an almost slavelike condition. As far back as the Thirty Years' War agricultural estates in the east had grown larger through enclosures, which had led to an increase in peasant oppression. Frederick II had some success in reforming landholding in his estates through the reduction of the days of obligatory service to the lord and the establishment of some 50,000 privately owned farms. Generally, the Prussian aristocracy opposed any reforms, failed to modernize their estates, and were deeply in debt. Not until the defeat of Prussia at the hands of Napoleon did the aristocracy wake up to the necessity of reform. In the other German states to the west such as Baden and Bavaria the old feudal obligations were reduced but not eliminated and few peasants were able to purchase their lands.

Population expansion in the 18th century contributed to pressures on the land and to increasing poverty. Around the middle of the century the Habsburg subjects totaled about 6 million, which increased to more than 9 million at the turn of the century. Migration and immigration contributed to this growth as Germans from the south and west colonized Hungarian lands, which had been depopulated. Prussia, which in 1740 had an estimated population of 3.5 million, also tried to stimulate population growth through the immigration of almost 300,000 colonists. Other population movements occurred, and the most important one was the 100,000 or so settlers who immigrated to the United States. Like other German rulers, Frederick III of Hesse-Kassel, engaging in the trade of mercenary soldiers, sold more than half of his 29,000 German soldiers to Great Britain to suppress the American revolutionaries. Life expectancy in Germany was less than the 29 years of Frenchmen. If one wonders why the population was so small throughout much of the century, one need only look at the impact of epidemic diseases. Even though plague waned at the beginning of the century, it nonetheless killed off about one-third of the population of Prussia. Smallpox was the second-greatest check on population growth as one in 10 average deaths was attributable to it. Inadequate nutrition was also a contributing factor, and primitive medical practices ensured a low survival rate from other illnesses like pneumonia. Not until after 1800 did the potato improve the diets of the poor and bring an end to famines.

ECONOMY

Handicraft production, or the manufacture of products from some raw material, had for centuries been principally carried out in artisan workshops and closely supervised by the guilds. With the rise of a wage-based capitalism, the putting-out system expanded production by including home-based workers. The only large units of production consisted of pre-industrial enterprises called "manufactories." Hundreds of workers might be concentrated in one building for the more efficient utilization of their labor. These manufactories were owned by governments or capitalists and numbered about 1,000 in 1800. Although the Industrial Revolution occurred later in Germany in the mid-19th century, some early experiments had occurred, such as the construction in 1784 of the first cotton mill in Düsseldorf.

POLITICAL DECENTRALIZATION AND COURTLY LIFE

The political decentralization of Germany gave rise to many vibrant urban centers with an industrious middle class and royal courts. Munich and Dresden were court cities, while Mainz was important because of its cathedral; Nuremberg was an old imperial city, Hamburg a commercial center, and Göttingen a university town. The Holy Roman Emperor did not have a capital city as the French king had in Paris, where imperial coronations could take place or the emperor's residence was located and organs of government functioned. Regensburg was the city in which the imperial Diet had met since 1663, but the emperor generally lived in Vienna. In general the princes of Germany built their own versions of Louis XIV's palace of Versailles and enjoyed an extravagant court life, fleecing their peasants to pay their expenses. At Mannheim, for instance, the elector Karl Theodor of the Palatinate maintained a large orchestra, a ballet, and an opera company. In Pfalz-Zweibrücken the duke constructed an extravagant residence at an enormous cost. The landgrave of Hesse-Kassel found ingenious ways to finance his palace and art collection at Wilhelmshöhe, by selling his male subjects to Britain for use as soldiers against the American colonists. Each palace stimulated the local economy by relying heavily on numerous craftsmen to produce the gold and silver luxuries and other miscellaneous items thought to be appropriate to a princely lifestyle. The extravagance of one estate in Saxony illustrated well how a court provided hundreds of positions of employment not only for nobles but also for musicians, ballet dancers, actors, cooks, and other staff. In Würzburg and in Salzburg the prince-bishops lived in beautiful baroque palaces and entertained lavishly.

SOCIAL STRUCTURE

As elsewhere in Europe the social structure of German society was very hierarchical. The social position of most Germans was not one of choice but was determined by birth into a particular social estate. Like so many other things the occupations open to a person, educational opportunities, religion, clothing, and food were likewise prescribed. When social advancement did occur it was often the result of marriage, education, or service to a prince. Not yet organized into a modern class structure, society was still divided into four estates: clergy (*Klerus*), nobility (*Adel*), middle class (*Bürgertum, Burghers*) and peasantry (*Bauern*). Three-fourths of the German population, or 18 million, were farmers (40 percent were propertyless) and existed under the manorial system that defined legal and social relationships. The Protestant clergy were mostly of middle-class origin, while the higher clergy, the bishops and archbishops and prince-bishops, came from the nobility. The lower Catholic clergy came from middle-class and artisan families. As usual in premodern societies the tax burden was unevenly divided as can be seen in the status of the Catholic Church in Bavaria, which was exempt even while it owned approximately one-third of the land. Consequently, the Bavarian Wittelsbach monarchs sought to curtail inheritance donations of taxable lands to the church.

The nobility were the ruling elite and in the wealthier states of Germany attempted to live lives of luxury and splendor, while in eastern Prussia it was said that some aristocrats lived lives indistinguishable from their subjects'. Education was of little interest, and where the nobility could afford luxurious living one grand tour of famous places would suffice. The composition of the noble estate was not static, and wealthy members of the middle class could often purchase various titles of nobility. The middle class were positioned socially between the nobility and peasantry, living predominantly in towns and cities and approximating some 25 percent of the population. Their employment would range from wealthy merchants, lawyers, doctors, and civil servants in the upper middle class to domestic servants and day laborers in the lower. Politically, it was only the masters of the guilds who controlled town government. There were variations in legal status with approximately only 10 percent who could claim full status as free citizens (*Bürgerrecht*). While the richest might build fine residences, the general standard of living afforded wooden furniture and thatched roofs. More than half of the middle class belonged to the lower ranks who were very poor. The very poor often engaged in begging, which during the eighties in Berlin amounted to 5 percent of its 145,000 inhabitants. Finally, the peasantry amounted to 75 percent of the population. In the west and south land ownership was more prevalent, while in Holstein and Prussia an oppressive serfdom still prevailed. Except for the most well off, a meager subsistence was the rule, even extreme poverty and hardship similar to the animals they raised. On the backs of the illiterate peasantry the agricultural economy and grand lifestyle of the nobility rested.

In society and the family males were dominant. In Prussia women were subject to their fathers or husbands in careers, finances, and children. The purpose of marriage was not romantic love but to have children. Grounds for divorce in Protestant Prussia were codified in law. In Catholic areas divorce was not allowed.

CULTURE

One of the primary expressions of the refined culture of the aristocracy and the beautification of church ceremony was music. In the middle of the century Mannheim became a great musical center, where the model and rules for modern orchestras were established and what form the classical symphony should take. The "Berlin School" under Frederick the Great, who was an accomplished musician, composed music to the taste of the king. C. P. E. Bach was temporarily employed there as a harpsichordist, later moving to Hamburg for a more lucrative position. The career of George Frideric Handel (1685–1759) as a composer started in northern Germany but then took him to England, where he composed his great oratorio, *Messiah.* Vienna, however, was the music capital of Germany. It was the home of Johann Sebastian Bach (1685–1750), Joseph Haydn (1732–1809), Wolfgang Amadeus Mozart (1756–91), and Ludwig van Beethoven (1770–1827). Bach sought to give a musical expression to fundamental Christian truths in his *Passions,* while the secular *Brandenburg* Concertos honored the Hohenzollern monarchy. Franz Joseph Haydn composed primarily for the Hungarian aristocracy, developing the integration of stringed instruments in the orchestra. Out of his Enlightenment Pietist religious inspiration he composed *The Creation* in 1798. The Enlightenment also influenced Wolfgang Amadeus Mozart, who grew up in Salzburg and was employed in the court of the prince-bishop. This tragic genius composed operas in German, such as *The Magic Flute,* in which the characters were developed with a realism akin to Shakespeare. His *Requiem Mass* expressed his religious sentiments and beliefs that humans were capable of moral progress. The appeal of the Viennese composers to a European-wide audience attested to the universal quality of their music. The final composer in this group was Ludwig van Beethoven. He hailed the advent of Napoleon Bonaparte with his Third Symphony, and the stirring chorale of his Ninth Symphony joyously expressed the sentiments of Friedrich Schiller's *Ode to Joy.*

THE ENLIGHTENMENT

Germany was also influenced by the French Enlightenment. Called the Aufklärung in German history, it influenced a small part of the learned upper and middle classes. As in France, its goal was to liberate the individual from the conventions of society, and through the use of reason to challenge accepted traditions, ignorance, prejudices, and religious superstition.

The Enlightenment attempted to make reason completely autonomous and sought to derive all other authorities from it. The church no longer kept its dominating position, and even ideas of God, freedom, and immortality were derived through logical thinking. Not only did reason free itself from the restrictions placed on it by the churches, but it also became less concerned about religious dogma. The beliefs of the individual became less important than his thoughts and actions. Tolerance became an ideal and the quarrels between the denominations that had been so pervasive during the 17th century became less violent. The realm of the supernatural now ceased to dominate philosophical thinking and practical ethics formulated moral rules of behavior. Gottfried Wilhelm von Leibniz (1646–1716) went so far as to assert that the world we live in was "the best of all possible worlds," in which everything had a reasonable purpose and was the instrument of a benevolent divine will. It was an optimistic attitude in contrast to the pessimistic resignation to the will of God emphasized by the Reformation. Now the ideal man no longer sought to remove himself from the world, but was one who led a reasonable life and sought to abolish injustice in the world. Among the reforms that emanated from this application was the elimination of trials for witchcraft. It pleaded for dignified living conditions for the Jews and other minorities. It fostered the education of women and started the emancipation of the colored races.

Although the German Enlightenment challenged the religious traditions of the Catholic Church, it did not challenge princely power. Rather it sought to rationalize the use of state power and to secularize it. Leibniz, for instance, opposed revolution against rulers because he thought that the consequences would be worse than the abuses of authoritarian princes. German Enlightenment thinkers also did not challenge the hierarchical order of society. The most important theorists were Samuel von Pufendorf (1632–94), Christian Thomasius (1655–1728), and Christian von Wolf (1679–1754). None of these opposed the theory of absolute monarchy and did not support the idea of constitutional limitations. Instead, they concentrated their thought on the duties of the rulers, emphasizing their responsibility to guide the economy and provide education and social welfare.

Because the German Enlightenment took place later than that in France and England, it was strongly influenced by the English philosophers John Locke (1632–1704) and David Hume (1711–76). Both based reason on experience and therefore were called empiricists. Instead of starting with general principles, as did the French philosopher René Descartes (1596–1650), they began with the observation of detailed objects and only inductively derived their ultimate principles. Another important English influence in German literature was the thought of Lord Shaftesbury (1621–83), who applied empirical methods to the fine arts. The most important German representative of the empirical method was Gotthold Ephraim Lessing (1729–81). Another empiricist was the younger contemporary, Gottfried Herder (1744–1803), although he also considered unique historical conditions and human emotions. Immanuel Kant (1724–1804), the Königsberg philosopher, represented the culmination of empiricism, but also like Herder he opened a new chapter in German intellectual history.

Both rationalism and empiricism were ways of understanding the world as a meaningful system that followed its own laws. That does not mean that the existence of God was denied. Like the Deists in France it was thought that after God created the world it was left to function according to the perfect laws that he had established. Miracles and other interferences with daily processes were no longer believed to occur. The universe was autonomous and functioned according to God's laws. Man's actions were no longer directed nor his destiny fulfilled by God's involvement.

Both of the greatest philosophers of the Enlightenment, the Dutch Jew Baruch Spinoza (1632–77), and Leibniz thought that the existence of God could be arrived at only through faith but not proven through reason. They avoided the absolute rationalism of Descartes and the philosopher Christian von Wolff (1679–1754), who was the most popular of the disciples of Leibniz. The followers of Wolff employed the deductive method and tried to discover the reasons for all the processes and facts of life, creating great dictionaries for their definitions.

LITERATURE AND DRAMA

Modern German literature also took form in the life and work of Gotthold Ephraim Lessing (1729–81), Friedrich von Schiller (1759–1805), and Johann Wolfgang von Goethe (1749–1852). While the inspiration for the Enlightenment thinkers came from France, English literature was the predominant inspiration for the creation of modern German literature and came through William Shakespeare, John Locke, and writers of the 18th century such as Joseph Addison and Richard Steele. The first German poet of this modern period was Friedrich Gottlieb Klopstock (1724–1803). Sometimes called the German Milton, he liberated lyrical poetry from the dominance of French neoclassicism. His work was soon overshadowed by Lessing's, in particular *Minna von Barnhelm* (1767), which satirically depicted the sorrowful state of Prussian army veterans after the Seven Years' War. In *Nathan der Weise* (1779) Lessing pleaded for religious toleration and the Enlightenment ideal of humanity. Both plays laid a solid foundation for the modern German drama.

The storm and stress (Sturm und Drang) movement was one of youthful protest against stuffy elders and emphasized naturalism and individual liberties. One of its founders and philosophical leaders was the theologian Johann Gottfried Herder (1744–1803). His influence was that of a literary critic and philosopher of history. Herder glorified Shakespeare as the greatest dramatist since the Greek classical age. Poetry, he thought, should not imitate foreign standards, but emanate from the innermost soul of a people. Perhaps most significant was his *Ideas on the Philosophy of the History of Mankind (Ideen zur philosophie der Geschichte der Menschheit)*. In this classic on the philosophy of history Herder emphasized an "organic" interpretation of history in which the history of culture progresses through cycles of birth, maturity, and death. He saw each stage as a step toward the perfection of humanity.

During his studies at the University of Strassburg the youthful Goethe was influenced by Herder. Becoming the chief representative of the storm and stress movement, Goethe emerged as its leading poet, and author of its first important drama and novel. As the friend and adviser of the duke of Saxsen-Weimar, Goethe wrote some of his greatest love poetry. The rebelliousness of his young generation is expressed in his hymn *Prometheus* (1773). In the dramatic tragedy *Götz von Berlichingen* (1773), in which a rebel loses in a heroic struggle against corrupt civilization, Goethe reveals his anticlassical sentiments

Goethe's Monument, Frankfurt am Main
(Library of Congress)

and his belief that nature and simple folk are the source of strength. A novel of unhappy love and suicide, *The Sorrows of Young Werther (Die Leiden des jungen Werthers)* (1774) is filled with passion and sentimentality and protests against the French etiquette of love. This novel made Goethe famous throughout Europe. It was, however, Goethe's *Faust* trilogy (1773, 1806, and 1832) that was the most influential in German literature and its greatest masterpiece. In this dialectic between a variety of opposites like good and evil, reality and myth, and guilt and forgiveness, Dr. Faust, a magician, makes a compact with the devil to gain superhuman power. In the end Faust triumphs over evil because of his striving for a higher type of mankind, making this tragedy an archetype of German tragedy and "divine comedy" in the 18th-century classical humanist tradition. The essential aspect of Goethe's *Wilhelm Meister* is this pursuit of the ideal personality and of striving self-development, which Goethe thought should be the chief goal of society. Goethe was a true cosmopolitan and loved all of humanity.

A good friend of Goethe and the second-greatest figure of Germany's classical literature was Friedrich Schiller. A professor of history and philosophy at the Jena University, he set his dramas in historical and national settings and sought to communicate moral lessons. In *The Robbers* (*Die Raubers,* 1781) the theme of fraternal hatred and injustice brings the leader of the robbers in the end to atone for his rebelliousness. Other historical dramas included *Don Carlos* (1787), *Maria Stuart* (1800), and *Wilhelm Tell* (1804). In general, Schiller was a strong advocate of freedom of speech and was a critic of a corrupt aristocracy.

The romantic school of writers also had its origins in the 18th century and continued until about 1830. Even though they were influenced by the storm and stress writers, they were not youthful rebels. They included writers such as Jean Paul (1763–1825), Friedrich Hölderin (1770–1843), Heinrich von Kleist (1777–1811), and Friedrich von Hardenburg (1772–1801), known as Novalis. Others were Achim von Arnim (1781–1831), Clemens Brentano (1778–1842), Joseph von Eichendorf (1788–1857), and Ludwig Tieck (1773–1853). They idealized individual freedom, sensuousness, nature, and a poetic aesthetic sense. These writers emphasized the German people as a cultural group and humanity, but not political nationalism. They surprisingly idealized the medieval past and a Christian Europe presided over by the Catholic Church. They criticized the Reformation and the Age of Reason as having destroyed a united Christendom and for making God superfluous. They were cosmopolitans, many of whom converted to Catholicism.

PHILOSOPHY

It was, however, the philosopher Immanuel Kant (1724–1804) who was responsible for undermining the theological underpinnings of the traditional world outlook, liberating science from the dominance of metaphysics. In his *Critique of Pure Reason* Kant denied any respect for tradition, emphasizing that every idea had to justify itself. It was a Magna Carta for German scientific thinking. It also had political ramifications because as the old order collapsed so did the beliefs that provided its foundations. As Kant stated, "A free man is one who is autonomous. Man exists only as an end in himself. The highest maxim of morality and freedom is: Act so that you utilize the humanity in your own person as well as in the person of every other individual at all times as an end and never as a means." The concept of humanity and the goal of world peace through a world order were the themes of Kant's *Essay on Perpetual Peace*. World citizenship and the brotherhood of man were deeply held ideals in the humanist tradition and were given expression in Schiller's *Ode to Joy*. More important was the long-term influence of these ideals, which were foundational for German liberalism. Serious weaknesses, however, existed in this foundation, especially in the dichotomy between morality and legality, which in the end paralyzed the liberal and democratic movements in Germany.

SECRET SOCIETIES

During the last two decades before the French Revolution broke out in 1789, a number of secret societies were established that enlisted members from the middle class to the nobility. The Freemasons were perhaps the most numerous, and they were spread throughout the German states. They were egalitarian, humanitarian, and cosmopolitan and sought to transform society through influencing governmental ministers and rules. Their greatest enemy was the Catholic Church and its influence. Their cult of secrecy created fears of their power and influence. The Illuminati, a secret society founded by Adam Weishaupt, emphasized the importance of reason and education in order to raise the moral level of daily and political life. Its strength was primarily in Bavaria, where it had more than 600 members. Nonetheless, members of the lesser nobility joined as well as writers such as Goethe and Herder. Another society was the Rosicrucians, who sought to influence personal lives, politics, and culture, and had chapters in Prussia, Bavaria, and Austria. Spiritualistic seances were an important part of their meetings, which gave them a bad reputation. With the French Revolution both the Freemasons and Illuminati were suspected of supporting the radical Jacobins and were gradually suppressed.

The Era of the French Revolution and Napoleon

1789–1815

When the French Estates General convened in 1789 and began the process of change that is known as the French Revolution, one of history's most cataclysmic eras began. The Third Estate declared itself to be the National Assembly and began a reform of government and society that would change the nature of French and European history. The feudal social order that had existed since the Middle Ages was swept away. The nobility was abolished, feudal dues eliminated, guilds banned, a land tax instituted, and education secularized. A constitutional monarchy was established, and the Declaration of the Rights of Man assured liberty and equality for all. The Catholic Church was alienated by the Civil Constitution of the Clergy and the nationalization of church property. Fearing that the king was collaborating with foreign enemies, the revolutionaries had him executed. A republic was declared, and a radicalization of the revolution occurred, which led to a Reign of Terror during which thousands were executed.

The French Revolution was injected into the life of the German people more than any other nation in Europe. Initially, the most important intellectual and cultural leaders were very enthusiastic about the revolution. The young poet Hölderin wrote his enthusiastic "Hymn to Humanity" and "Hymn to Liberty." The educated middle class who were civil servants, judges, lawyers, professors, and doctors also embraced the egalitarian ideals of the French Revolution. Although the revolution was hailed by these groups, the idea of imitating the French and changing society by revolution was not. Neither the revolutionary implications of the doctrine of natural law nor of the social contract, which had been propagated by John Locke and Jean-Jacques Rousseau, found an echo in the thinking of German intellectuals of the Enlightenment. Some regional disturbances did occur, but at no time was there a revolutionary movement. The regions that were most sympathetic to the revolution were the state of Brunswick, the city of Hamburg, and the area of the Rhineland. Most of the other German states, such as Prussia, Austria, and the south German states were hostile to the revolution. The euphoria of the cultural leaders and the middle class, however, ended when the French Revolution turned violent with the beheading of the king and the Republic's Reign of Terror. The nationalist aggression of French armies against German territory purged German intellectuals of their cosmopolitanism and prepared the way for the rise of the spirit of German nationalism.

Among German rulers the image of the revolution was generally negative. Convinced that the success of the revolutionary doctrines would mean the overthrow of the established monarchical and aristocratic elites of Germany and the rest of Europe, the rulers of Austria and Prussia concluded a defensive alliance against the French in February 1792. In late summer 1792 small Austrian and Prussian forces marched through Luxembourg into Champagne with no very definite military plan, and in humiliating skirmishes were forced to retreat back over the Rhine as far as Frankfurt. With the execution of Louis XVI and the republicans challenging the princes and monarchs of Europe with death and destruction, the First Coalition was formed, which included Prussia and Austria, Great Britain, Holland, Spain, Sardinia, and Naples. After two years of fighting, little was accomplished, the alliance was dissolved, and the king of Prussia even made a separate peace with France in April 1795. From the beginning of 1796 Napoleon Bonaparte became commander in chief of the republican forces, and the French proved to be victorious against the Second and Third Coalitions. French armies defeated the Austrians at Marengo and Hohenlinden (1800), which was followed by the Peace of Lunéville (February 1801), in which Germany lost more than 3 million people and considerable territory. This partition of Germany begun by Napoleon was continued by the German princes, who compensated themselves for their losses. At the Diet of Ratisbon in February 1803 the ecclesiastical territories were secularized, and some 4 million subjects changed rulers. The medium-size states profited the most. In May 1804 Napoleon was crowned emperor of the French. Perhaps seeing the writing on the wall, the Holy Roman Emperor, Francis II of Austria, decided to constitute his Austrian territories as a hereditary empire. In 1805 Napoleon was victorious against the Third Coalition at the battle of the Three Emperors, also known as Austerlitz. In the Treaty of Pressburg (December 1805), which followed Austria's defeat, it ceded to France Italian territories and recognized Napoleon as king of Italy. More important, the rulers of Bavaria, Württemberg, and Baden were rewarded with German territory, and the first two were made kings. In 1806 Napoleon formed the Confederation of the Rhine, which consisted of 16 German princes. That same year the Holy Roman Empire was ignominiously dissolved and Francis II made it official with his formal abdication.

One of the most profound results of the Prussian defeat at the hands of Napoleon was the reform of the Prussian state, laying the foundations not only for its successful participation in Napoleon's defeat, but also for its future role in the unification of Germany. From 1807 to 1813 Prussia endured its humiliation. At the same time the reforms of farseeing statesmen like Baron vom Stein (1757–1831), Baron von Hardenberg (1750–1852), and Wilhelm von Humboldt (1767–1835), along with those of generals like Gerhardt von Scharnhorst (1756–1813), Neithardt von Gneisenau (1760–1831), and Gebhard Leberecht Blücher (1742–1819) were initiated. The chief architect of reform was Baron vom Stein from Nassau, who was an ardent opponent of the French Revolution, but who wanted to abandon the old systems of absolutism and centralization and mobilize the physical, intellectual, and moral energies of the people to serve their fatherland. The civic reformers believed that political and civic freedom would provide for the unity and security of the state. Their reforms were social, economic, administrative, educational, and military. The bold laws of Stein and Hardenberg abolished the legal aspects of serfdom and permitted peasants to assume mortgages and to freely marry and select occupations. Medieval economic corporations and regulations were eliminated, and freedom of occupation and contract were established. The reforms conferred on the towns extensive powers of self-government, thereby converting dependent subjects who had been divided into estates (*Stände*) into free citizens and modern social classes. Under the influence of Humboldt the educational system was reformed and extended. The unified school replaced the socially separate schools, and the University of Berlin was founded. A modern bureaucracy was organized in Prussia, which became a model of efficiency. Nothing materialized out of plans for a legislative assembly, which was not established until 1848. Patriotism was stimulated by the eloquent Addresses to the German Nation by Johann Gottlieb Fichte (1762–1814), and inspiring songs from poets like Ernst Moritz Arndt (1769–1860), Theodor Körner (1791–1813), and Friedrich Rüchert (1788–1866). Simultaneously the army was reformed, and many of the defects and abuses eliminated. For instance, the system of flogging was abolished as were the hereditary rights of the officer class. A system of universal service and a reserve militia (*Landwehr*) were instituted—the reserve pool of trained soldiers to secretly overcome the limitations imposed by Napoleon— which served to quickly expand the army during the War of Liberation and which provided a model for the German general staff after World War I.

The beginning of the end for Napoleon's domination of Europe was the catastrophic failure of his invasion of Russia in 1812. By 1813 Prussia and Austria were joined by Russia, Sweden and also Great Britain in what has been known in Prussian history as the "War of Liberation." The engagements culminated in the great three-day Battle of Leipzig (October 16–18), which was fought in Saxony and which ended in complete victory for the allies. By the end of March 1814 the victorious allies marched into Paris. Although the first Peace of Paris (May 30, 1814) restored the Bourbon family to the throne in the person of Louis XVIII, France was treated rather magnanimously and required only to withdraw her boundaries to the frontiers of 1792. The details were worked out at the Congress of Vienna, which met at the end of October 1814, but was interrupted by Napoleon's return from banishment on the island of Elba. On June 18, 1815, Napoleon and his armies were finally defeated at the Battle of Waterloo. The Second Peace of Paris was concluded on November 29, 1815. The allies forced France to withdraw its boundaries to those of 1790 and to pay for reparations and for a five-year occupation by allied forces.

As was to be expected, the Congress of Vienna, also called the dancing congress because of its numerous festivities, made some major alterations in the map of Germany. After the long French domination and the end of the Holy Roman Empire the boundaries of many states had been changed and many abolished. Even though there was widespread sentiment for the restoration of the old Empire, Prince Clemens von Metternich, the foreign minister of Austria, opposed it. In the end the negotiations at the Congress of Vienna and the resulting compromises were not completely satisfying or disappointing. Metternich was an exponent of the principle of legitimacy, which favored the restoration of former monarchies where possible. This was done in France and Spain and in some Italian states. On the other hand, the principle of compensation operated when it was in the interest of the allies. On the whole Prussia did quite well and was compensated for its loss of Polish lands with two-fifths of Saxony, though it desired to annex all of it. It also received part of Westphalia and the left/western territory along the Rhine. On the other hand, Prussia ceded some territories to Hanover. The new kingdom of Bavaria received Ansbach and Bayreuth from Prussia and Würzburg and Aschaffenburg from Austria. In turn Bavaria ceded the Tyrol and the famous city of Salzburg to Austria. Austria was compensated with the Italian provinces of Lombardy and Venetia for its loss of the Austrian Netherlands.

RESTORATION, ROMANTICISM, AND REVOLUTION

THE GERMAN CONFEDERATION

In place of the old Empire the Congress of Vienna devised a new and looser federal union called the German Confederation (*Deutscher Bund*). Its form, functions, and powers were expressed in the Federal Statute of June 8, 1815. The federation comprised 35 principalities and free cities of the old Empire, and not surprisingly, the hereditary presidency was given to Austria. As one statesman remarked, Germany was not much more than "a geographic expression," yet the territory it encompassed was larger than today and included all of the present states of Austria, Luxembourg, Limburg, and sections of Denmark, Poland, Italy, and Czechoslovakia. The powers and duties of the confederation were vested in its sole organ, the federal diet (*Bundestag*), a legislative council consisting of the plenipotentiaries of the member states. It met in Frankfurt am Main. Both Austria and Prussia had to agree before the Diet could act, and only three other states, Baden, Württemberg, and Bavaria could substantially influence its decisions. Since there was no popular representation, it generally attempted to keep the status quo of the restoration. Its main accomplishment was to suppress any efforts aimed at greater freedom and national unity. The press and publishing were kept under strict censorship, universities were closely supervised, and liberal political activity was suppressed. The most infamous legislation of this type was the Carlsbad Decrees (1819), which suppressed any expression of democratic ideas or advocacy of national unity. The latter was treated as a form of sedition and punished accordingly. The most zealous in executing the decrees was Austria, and Prussia under Metternich's influence was not far behind. When a liberal revolution broke out in Paris in 1830, liberal hopes were raised, but the power of reactionary rulers was too strong. In 1837, when Hanover became detached from the British Crown, its ruler demonstrated his opposition to the post-Napoleonic reforms by repealing the moderate constitution of 1819.

Metternich, a nobleman from the Rhineland, whose faith in the rationalism of the Enlightenment was crushed by the extremes of the French Revolution, believed that only the oligarchy of the landed nobility and state administrators could be relied on to govern. So Metternich followed an intransigent and reactionary policy for Austria, as did most of the other kings who had promised to their people direct participation in government. Certainly the Confederation was not the reward politically conscious Germans had expected for the fighting, support, and suffering during the War of Liberation. In a few states, however, like Baden, Bavaria, Hanover, Nassau, Weimar, and Württemberg, more enlightened princes did introduce constitutions (monarchical constitutions).

These constitutions did not provide for popularly elected assemblies but a very restricted suffrage with representatives who had to be civil servants of the state. Their concerns were limited to municipal government, taxation, and the elimination of old restrictions in the mercantile and farming community. Jewish emancipation also was a prominent issue.

The tremendous enthusiasm engendered in Germany during the War of Liberation against Napoleon subsided considerably during the years immediately following the settlement of 1815. The hopes of nationalists and reactionaries for glorious and final solutions to the problems of central Europe were left unrealized. A cultural style that developed during the restoration as people desired a more peaceful and traditional way of life came to be known as "Biedermeier." It was a social and political style that was typified by provincialism, middle-class social propriety, rococo furniture, the music of Schubert, the writings of Goethe's golden years, and a generally apolitical attitude. The German educational ideal of Bildung, which emphasized rationality and improvement, now focused more on the individual rather than on society. The period also manifested a reaction against the secular and anticlerical tendencies of the previous age and saw a strong revival of interest in religion.

THE ROMANTIC MOVEMENT

Even though the restoration period appeared to have settled the conflict between the old and the new, in reality it continued in the world of ideas. Ideological conflicts continued from 1815 to 1848. Culturally, this was a period when the heirs of the Enlightenment and rationalism fought a losing battle against the swelling tide of the new movement of romanticism, which had begun during the years after 1770 as a protest of youth against the standards of their elders. In literature and the arts it was a continuation of the storm and stress movement and a revolt against classicism. The romantic rebels believed that classicism stifled all that was creative and spontaneous in artistic expression. It was like a barbaric discharge of ardent and gay-colored things from an unrestrained and chaotic soul. It was a movement of art that stressed exaggeration, excitement, opposition to anything regulated, antipathy to the monotonous, the simple, and the logical. In general it was a reaction against the rationalism and systematic thinking of the 18th century. Whereas the rationalists of the Enlightenment had emphasized order, relevance, and utilitarianism, the romantics stressed traditionalism, and were fascinated by nature, the spiritual world, incoherence, contradictions, and complexities.

Romanticism was a movement of youth and of protest. The romantics expressed a rebellious desire to lead unfettered lives resulting in emotionalism, excess, and immorality. The romantics disagreed with Goethe and Kant that there were rules and limitations in one's moral life and literature. Preferring instinct over reason as a better guide to the basic truths of life, they also lacked the discipline of a Goethe to complete long works like novels. They refused to recognize that society had legitimate claims on the individual, and believing in a cult of individuality they claimed the right of superior individuals, or geniuses, to realize their potential at the expense of society. No single book had a greater influence upon the first romantic generation than Goethe's *Wilhelm Meister's Wanderjahre (Wilhelm Meister's Travels)* (1829). It is the story of an egocentric young man who left a comfortable life and promising career and whose life is transformed through work, renunciation, and travels. Other authors imitated this example of self-fulfillment and self-discovery through experiences and travel, assuming an almost mystical or quasi-religious significance. The romantics venerated the past and were fascinated by the study of history and such keys to understanding it as folk songs and fairy tales. Not only did they see in the Middle Ages Germany's imperial greatness and cultural oneness, but also the spiritual unity and doctrinal security of the Catholic Church. Many converted to Catholicism.

The culture of the romantic period was one of the richest in German history and perhaps modern European culture. This age was stimulated by the work of Friedrich Gottlieb Klopstock (d. 1803), Johann Gottfried Herder (d. 1803), Immanuel Kant (d. 1804), Friedrich Schiller (d. 1805), Christoph Martin Wieland (d. 1813), and Johann Wolfgang von Goethe (d. 1832). The writers of this new romantic age were Friedrich Hölderin (1770–1843), Jean Paul (1763–1825), August Wilhelm (1767–1845), and his brother, Friedrich Schlegel (1772–1829), Friedrich von Hardenberg (1772–1801) known as Novalis, Ludwig Tieck (1773–1853), Heinrich von Kleist (1777–1811), Ernst Moritz Arndt (1769–1860), Theodor Körner (1769–1860), Friedrich Rückert (1788–1866), Joseph Görres (1776–1848), Achim von Arnim (1781–1831), Clemens Brentano (1778–1842), Jakob (1785–1863) and Wilhelm (1786–1859) Grimm, Ludwig Uhland (1787–1862), Joseph von Eichendorff (1788–1857), Heinrich Heine (1797–1856), Ernst Theodor Amadeus Hoffmann (1776–1822), and Franz Grillparzer (1791–1872). Thinkers who made significant contributions to modern European thought were Johann Gottlieb Fichte (1762–1814), Georg Wilhelm Friedrich Hegel (1770–1831), Friedrich Schleiermacher (1768–1834), Friedric Wilhelm Joseph von Schelling (1775–1854), and Arthur Schopenhauer (1788–1860). In the realm of music the symphonies and other works of Ludwig van Beethoven (1770–1827) enthralled audiences. Other renowned composers of the period were Karl Maria von Weber (1786–1826) and Franz Peter Schubert (1797–1828). The most significant painters were Caspar David Friedrich (1774–1840) and Moritz van Schwind (1804–1871).

NATIONALISM AND LIBERALISM

German nationalism was a child of romanticism. Under its influence nationalism postulated that the collective past experience of an ethnic population was a guide to its future. That meant that each nation had a historic destiny that could be recognized through the study of its history. Fascinated with the Middle Ages, they interpreted the past Holy Roman Empire as a glorious symbol of Germany's future, and that a national state would occupy most of the territory of the old Empire. With dissatisfaction growing toward the repressive restoration policies and with the recognition that economic expansion was fostered by a common market, support for a nation state grew among the educated, urban middle class. By contrast, nationalism found little support among the rural peasantry and aristocratic elites.

Liberals presented themselves as a party of progressive change and the future. They were opposed to the forces of order, reaction, and the past represented in the practice of monarchical absolutism of the restoration period, aristocratic privileges, mercantilist economies, state-sponsored churches, and everything else that preserved the past. It is not that German liberals had idealized the French Revolution. On the contrary, they had little sympathy for its violence and democratic agitation. While liberals condemned state despotism and interference in private affairs, on the other hand they acknowledged that the bureaucratic state had often been an instrument of progress. Consequently, this proved to be one of the ambivalences that plagued the liberal movement, for liberals also hoped to use the state to achieve some of their own interests. While the greatest agreement among liberals was what they were against, they found it difficult to define and agree on their goals. Without question they favored greater political, economic, and social freedom, but they were deeply divided about the scope of freedom, its character and implications. One example concerned the nature of representative government and which people should be able to vote. Most assuredly, when liberals spoke of the people, they meant the middle class (*Mittelstand*) which was limited to only men of property and education. Disagreements existed over how democratic the suffrage should be, some wishing to include wage earners and farmers, but opposed to the enfranchisement of women, servants, and children. It was this question of who would have the right to vote that became the single most important constitutional question that liberals would have to face.

EARLY INDUSTRIAL REVOLUTION

Undermining the prevalent economic and social structures were the economic changes brought about by the early stages of the Industrial Revolution and by the Customs Union (Zollverein, 1834). Sponsored by Prussia and joined by most of the German states except the Austrian territories, it eliminated internal tariffs and stimulated economic growth. The proceeds of the taxes at ports of entry were redistributed to member states according to population. The period marked the beginnings of the transition from preindustrial to industrial capitalism, and the pace of change leaped forward with increasing speed. The length of the first train track that was built in Bavaria in 1836 between Nuremberg and Fürth was only six miles, but by 1840 that had expanded to more than 500. The Borsig locomotive works were established in Berlin. The building of the railroads was the decisive stimulus for the Industrial Revolution and had a major impact on the economy and society. Profits on railway investment ranged from 10 to 20 percent. Railways demanded tremendous amounts of iron, which stimulated mining and coal production. Eventually, transportation costs were reduced by 80 percent. The use of steam engines expanded throughout the economy with more than 400 steam engines operating in 1837, and nearly tripling (1,139) during the next decade. Monetary policy also helped stimulate business, as the stable Prussian thaler came to dominate. Tax policy also provided a stimulus for investment. No longer were there any restrictions on engaging in business. Most industrial goods were still imported from Great

Britain, yet German industrialization had begun. A new class of factory workers did also. With rapid population growth there soon was a labor surplus. Since there were no social welfare provisions, most workers endured a miserable existence. On the whole the decade of the forties was a difficult one, and in 1844 tensions exploded in Silesia when an uprising of displaced hand weavers occurred. It was suppressed by the Prussian army. Out of these experiences a workers' movement began. On the whole the German states were poised for a takeoff into a full-fledged industrial revolution in the fifties and sixties.

REVOLUTIONS OF 1848

In contrast to the negligible response in Germany to the French Revolution of 1789, the response to the revolution in France during February 1848 was an epidemic of uprisings in March throughout all the German states. Economic problems and disease in the countryside, urban unemployment and misery caused by industrialization, and increased political repression by governments trying to stifle criticism combined to create an atmosphere ripe for revolution. Protests by farmers in the countryside against taxation then spread to protests and uprisings in towns and cities, first in the west and south and then north and east, including Munich, Vienna, and Berlin. Some were armed clashes, while others consisted of peaceful demonstrations numbering some 30 separate revolts. During this first phase of the revolution the street fighting that took place in Berlin's Alexanderplatz killed some 230 people before Frederick William IV ordered his troops to leave the city and granted liberal reforms. In Vienna the revolutionary turmoil forced Metternich to hurriedly flee to England and the emperor to retire to Innsbruck. The three major goals of the revolutionary leaders were the common goal of establishing a nation-state; the liberal demands for basic civil rights and constitutional government with some measure of popular sovereignty; and social and economic reforms such as the complete elimination of serfdom, improved working conditions for urban workers, and economic freedom for business. There was an ultraradical group that preached a socioeconomic egalitarianism, but it must be emphasized that the revolutions were not caused by problems and class conflict emerging out of this early stage of the Industrial Revolution.

The revolts proceeded through four stages. During the first phase moderate liberal goals were achieved and political power was temporarily shared with the old ruler. In Berlin the king even toured the city blanketed with the new black, red, and gold flag. In May the German National Assembly, known as the Frankfurt Parliament, met in St. Paul's Church in Frankfurt am Main. During the second phase, lasting from June 1848 to April 1849, the old rulers attempted to regain the power they had lost. The Austrian army attacked the revolutionaries in Prague and Italy, proving that the army could still be counted on as a bulwark of monarchical conservatism. Encouraged by these victories, reactionaries began to reassert themselves in the other German states, which ended in the defeat of most of the liberal agenda. This period ended when the Prussian king, Frederick William, refused to accept the imperial crown of a united Germany in April 1848, which was offered to him by the Frankfurt Parliament. The third phase was a brief new wave of revolution that swept over most of the states between April and August 1849. Liberals and nationalists hoped to salvage at least a portion of their initial gains. In Saxony, the Palatinate, and Baden the lower classes and democratic forces rebelled when they realized that all of their sacrifices on the barricades had brought them no social or economic benefits. The repression of this third wave of revolutions occurred during the fourth phase, when the National Assembly also was disbanded. In the aftermath trials were held, thousands emigrated, and repression was instituted by the conservative governments of the 1850s.

One of the greatest debates by the National Assembly in Frankfurt was between those who favored a "greater Germany" versus a "smaller Germany," that is, which states and ethnic populations would be included in a German nation-state. Austria insisted on bringing into the Reich all of its ethnic populations, encompassing more than a dozen different nationalities. The "smaller Germany" solution, which excluded non-German ethnic populations, won the day. This was one example of the confusion and conflict among the three liberal revolutionary aims (national, liberal, and social). Middle-class liberals were forced to choose between unification and constitutionalism. The representatives at Frankfurt chose unification, which doomed both. The middle class also feared the egalitarian aims of the lower classes on whom they depended for their popular revolutionary support, which in the end made the middle class place their reliance on the conservative forces of order and stability.

It has often been said that Germany and Europe failed to make a decisive turn toward constitutional government during the revolutions of 1848. Although that was true, there were, however, lasting achievements. Major German states kept written constitutions with some degree of popularly elected parliaments. The freedom of peasants from manorial taxes and other burdens was not eliminated in Prussia, but artisans and journeymen in guilds were protected by the Prussian Commercial code of 1849. Neither was trial by jury eliminated nor the legal emancipation of Jews reversed. Economic liberalism was not retarded as the states continued to encourage economic modernization. And finally, as legal equality for the middle class was not reversed, its political and economic self-consciousness continued to grow.

Otto von Bismarck and German Unification

The suppression of the revolutions of 1848 continued to make Germany and Europe uncomfortable. Nothing had been solved in 1848, and the nationalistic desire for the unification of Germany and the liberal goal of more representative government remained. What was not accomplished by revolution in the streets, however, would soon be achieved by political leaders in cabinet rooms and through warfare. By 1859 Italian unification had taken place under the leadership of one such statesman, Count Camillo Cavour.

ARMY REFORM AND PARLIAMENTARY CONFLICT

The decade of the 1850s was years of industrial growth. Although Prussian productivity still lagged far behind that of Britain, it was growing faster. Heavy industry and mechanical engineering led the economy. Prussia with its Zollverein had become the predominant economic power, which strengthened the political self-confidence of the liberal middle class. The German Progressive Party (Fortschrittspartei) was formed in 1861 and quickly became the strongest in the Prussian parliament (Diet). It was this party that formed the basic opposition to the policy of the new Prussian king, William, and his minister of war, Albrecht Roon (1803–79), to reorganize and strengthen the Prussian army. Roon, the professional soldier, wanted to set the army apart from civil society and make it the bulwark of the monarchy. These goals were different from those of the liberal reformers who wanted the army through a strong National Guard to reflect the national spirit. It is not that the liberals did not want a strong Prussian army, but not one that would be a sort of praetorian guard for the monarchy. A struggle over army reform ensued, resulting in the budget crisis of 1862. The king then appointed Otto von Bismarck as Prussian prime minister. The new minister succeeded in conducting the government and collecting taxes without a constitutional budget. The Prussian people were ruled through administrative fiat, and the army was expanded and modernized. The Progressive Party passed votes of no confidence, but they did not turn to revolution to achieve their goals. The middle-class liberals had learned the lessons of 1848 well and feared that another revolution would again unleash the power and violence of the lower classes.

BISMARCK'S STATECRAFT

Otto von Bismarck (1815–98) was the great architect of German unification. It is often assumed that since he successfully guided Prussia's course of action, he had a carefully worked-out plan that achieved unification. Bismarck had a clear conception of his goals but was flexible in the means he took to achieve them. He did not plan wars but waged them only when diplomatic alternatives were exhausted. The so-called Iron Chancellor was a conservative statesman who believed that the state was the major agent of history and that all of history was directed by God. Bismarck took the raison d'état as the guiding star of his diplomacy, which has been called Realpolitik. As a statesman he was no opportunist but was flexible in the conduct of policy while holding strong ultimate goals. Pertinent here was his absolute aim to preserve the dominant position of the monarchy. That did not mean that he favored an autocratic king who suppressed his nobility and people. He believed that the nobility were the strongest possible supporters for the monarchy. He actually favored popular participation in the affairs of state and even criticism, but it was the king's prerogative to control the army and direct foreign policy. He was opposed to German nationalism as it was advocated by liberals and parliamentarians, and deeply resented the efforts of the National Assembly in 1848 to achieve German unification by democratic means. The only reform of the German Confederation that Bismarck would accept was that which would not change the character of the Prussian monarchy. As far as war was concerned he was not a warmonger and did not consider war lightheartedly. Rather it was a natural part of life and acceptable in accomplishing his political goals. He was opposed

Napoleon III and Bismarck, after a painting by Camphausen *(Library of Congress)*

to preventive war and wars for prestige but considered wars for the honor of the state to be acceptable.

Bismarck's political conservatism found its ultimate sanction in the Christian faith. He was opposed to whatever the French Revolution had birthed, as his mentor Leopold von Gerlach had held. For Bismarck patriotism meant subordination of all principles and sentiments to the interests of the state. Bismarck was willing to accept the German Confederation as insurance against revolution, but he was opposed to Prussian cooperation with Austria. Finally, it probably was in Bismarck's dealings with Napoleon III of France that he announced a modification of his position on foreign policy to a belief that principles could be changed. His firm adherence, however, to the principle of legitimacy gave Prussian policy continuity.

THE DANISH WAR, 1864

In the early 1860s the Schleswig-Holstein Question stirred up national passions in both Denmark and Germany. In 1863 a nationalistic and liberal Danish parliament approved a new constitution but also, contrary to international treaty, decided to annex Schleswig and Holstein, both of which had large German populations. German nationalists were outraged, but the Danes refused to cancel the annexation. The Great Powers discussed the problem but could not resolve it, and finally the German-Danish War (1864) broke out. Not willing to lose the duchies to the Danes, the German governments aimed primarily to prevent Schleswig and Holstein from becoming strongholds of liberalism. It was not the German Confederation but the conservative powers of Prussia and Austria that went to war and won, forcing Denmark to cede the duchies, which were to be jointly administered.

The important consequences of the Danish War for Prussia were fourfold. The Prussian army received some necessary combat experience, especially in the campaign in Jutland. The architect of the Danish victories, the chief of the general staff Helmut von Moltke (1800–91), proved himself to the king. Also the Prussian armies made a remarkable assault on the Danish stronghold of Düppel, which aroused a great degree of patriotic pride and weakened the liberals. Diplomacy also had proven itself inadequate in solving the international question of Schleswig-Holstein and unable to stop the warring parties.

The improved relations between Austria and Prussia that had resulted from the Danish War soon broke down. Austria wanted the make the duchies an independent state, while Prussia wanted extensive advantages for itself, including military and commercial rights. Desiring to absorb both duchies, Bismarck ably deceived the world concerning his real intentions. When Austria and Prussia failed to come to an agreement over the duchies, Austria broke the partition agreement and appealed to the German Confederation to solve the issue. The reform of the confederation and the creation of greater unity was also part of the conflict. Bismarck's desire to outdo Austria even led him to propose the establishment of a German parliament in Frankfurt based on universal manhood suffrage. He believed that he could manipulate and exploit national sentiment for his own purposes. His goals and means were certainly not conservative as he pursued national unity. He concluded a secret alliance against Austria with the Kingdom of Italy. The duration of the alliance was only for three months beginning in April 1866, Italy promising to go to war against Austria if war with Prussia broke out by that time. Italy was promised Venetia to complete her unification. Then Bismarck collaborated with the French emperor, Napoleon III, who agreed to remain neutral with the hope of compensation after the war with territory in the Rhineland. International diplomacy thus helped make war possible and winnable.

AUSTRO-PRUSSIAN WAR, 1866

Prussian armies invaded Bohemia in 1866 without a declaration of war, starting the Austro-Prussian War. Using its modernized army, benefitting from the combat experience in the Danish War, and relying on the efficiency of its railroads for rapid movement of armies, Prussia defeated Austria at Königgrätz (Sadowa) on July 3, 1866, after 10 days of fighting.

Why were the Prussians so overwhelmingly victorious over Austria in a campaign that lasted only seven weeks? First, the Prussian army had been modernized and had a superior general staff. Second, the Austrians had weak generalship. The emperor had switched the commanding generals, placing the former commander of the Italian area in the field to the north. Imperial favoritism had played a role in this decision, but commanders in the Austrian army had insufficient control over their subordinates. Furthermore, technology and tactics were also significant factors. The Prussian infantry was equipped with the Dreyse "needle gun," a breech-loading rifle, whereas the Austrian soldiers still fought with muzzle-loading rifles. Superior modern tactics were employed by the Prussians against the outmoded tactics of the Austrians. Another factor of great importance was the division of the Austrian armed forces between two fronts, fighting the Prussians to the north and the Italians, who had entered the war as planned, to the south. While the Austrians defeated the Italians at Custozza, they were not able to move their forces north because of the lack of railroad facilities, which makes the last reason for Austria's defeat. While the Prussians had had ample rail connections to mass their armies at the proper time, there only was one rail line between Vienna and the Bohemian plain, where the main theater of war was. Besides his general unfamiliarity with the site, General Benedek was also deprived of the necessary reinforcements that might have turned the battle in his favor.

In the Peace of Prague that July, Austria was excluded from a future role in a united Germany. It was forced to pay a small indemnity and cede Venetia to Italy. Prussia then formed the North German Confederation (Norddeutscher Bund) with the states north of the Main River and Bismarck as prime minister. This was to be the basis for the small German solution (Kleindeutsch) to the problem of unification. Bismarck had finally achieved his goal of making Prussia the dominant power in northern Germany and a great power in European affairs. The North German Confederation was a symbol of the success of Prussian counterrevolutionary conservatism. The liberals lost politically but gained economically. They had gained a democratically elected parliament but lost because it was powerless. They did gain, however, in the economic sphere, where the new commercial code removed the last legal and institutional barriers to Germany's rapid industrialization.

THE FRANCO-PRUSSIAN WAR, 1870–71

Since the 17th century French leaders had tried to prevent the rise of a united German empire across the Rhine. With Bismarck's diplomatic victories and Prussia's military successes in 1864 and 1866 there was increasing apprehension in France over the prospects of having a united and powerful German neighbor. The French emperor, Napoleon III, had remained neutral during the Danish and the Austro-Prussian wars. In 1866 he had expected the conflict to be prolonged and exhausting and end in a stalemate, thus weakening both Prussia and Austria. Based on a secret meeting with Bismarck at Biarritz in October 1865, where Bismarck made vague hints that Napoleon would be compensated along the Rhine if the French would not interfere in a conflict with Austria, Napoleon reasonably expected to be rewarded with territorial compensations. When in the summer of 1866 Napoleon demanded the left bank of the Rhine, including the city of Mainz, Bismarck categorically refused. Napoleon's demands aided Bismarck in the formation of an alliance with the southern German states against France. Napoleon also failed in his attempt to purchase Luxembourg in 1867 and the Belgium railroad system, which Bismarck and the governments of England and Russia opposed. Because of increasing internal opposition to the Second Empire, the monarchists believed that a humiliation of Prussia would restore the support of the French people for Napoleon. With his armies newly equipped Napoleon believed that the French army was superior and could successfully intimidate Prussia. Napoleon attempted but failed to successfully negotiate alliances with Austria and Italy and mistakenly hoped that the south German states would support France.

For his part Bismarck considered a war with France to be unavoidable. He also was convinced that the southern German states would support Prussia and that the European powers would remain neutral. He foresaw that such a war would irresistibly draw together all the provinces and people of Germany and that the anticipated victory would be crowned by the achievement of national unity. Not only had Bismarck gained for Prussia diplomatic protection, but Prussia's armed forces were well prepared. The Prussian general staff had worked out a detailed strategic plan and the armed forces and the trained reserves could be brought to full war strength at short notice.

Napoleon soon got the opportunity to administer the wished-for diplomatic humiliation of Prussia. As a result of a revolution in 1869 the Spanish throne had become vacant, and the Spaniards had offered the crown to Prince Leopold of Hohenzollern-Sigmaringen, a member of the Catholic branch of the Hohenzollerns and a distant relative of the king of Prussia. The French government immediately protested that this would resurrect the old threat of the Austrian-Spanish Habsburgs surrounding France. Aware that the candidacy of Prince Leopold was disagreeable to France, Bismarck secretly tried to secure the acceptance of the candidacy while Prussian king William, anxious to preserve the peace, tried to persuade the prince to decline the Spanish offer.

Even though Prince Leopold finally announced that he would not be a candidate for the Spanish throne, Napoleon listened, however, to the advice of the imperialist extremists in the French cabinet, and committed the greatest mistake of his political career. In July 1870, while King William was vacationing at Bad Ems, the French ambassador demanded of the king a formal pledge never again to give his consent to another candidacy of a Hohenzollern to the Spanish throne. The king of Prussia was angered and asked that Bismarck be informed by telegram of the French demands and of William's negative answer. The message was sent from Bad Ems to Bismarck, who then proceeded to condense and omit passages in his "Ems Dispatch." He made it appear that the Prussian king had been grossly insulted and that the French ambassador had been intentionally slighted. The Ems Dispatch was published in the press, and with inflammatory comments the demand for war became so great in France that Napoleon responded with a declaration of war (July 19). Unlike some historians who have claimed that Bismarck was trying to create a war, it is fairly certain that Bismarck did not plan a war, but the crisis that he encouraged and the maladroitness of the French government and popular passion conveniently provided a war of opportunity.

The German princes immediately rallied to the support of Prussia, placing their armies under the command of the Prussian general staff. The nominal commander in chief of the German armies was the king of Prussia, but all military movements and operations were directed by General Helmuth von Moltke, whose strategic genius had helped win the war against Austria. He divided his forces into three large sectors: a central army under the command of Prince Frederick Charles, a northern right wing under General von Steinmetz, and a southern left wing, consisting of contingents from Baden and Bavaria, under the crown prince of Prussia. Almost 1,830,000 soldiers were quickly mobilized within 18 days, unlike the slow mobilization of the French. About 462,000 were transported to the front. The Germans had the advantage with their railroads, supply system, high command, and general staff. This war also became a new kind of people's war and not the traditional type of 1866. New weaponry also made the battles more deadly as both infantry and cavalry were slaughtered with the French repeating rifle, the Dreyse needle gun of the Prussians, and the firepower of the breech-loading cannons of Krupp. As the widely dispersed French reserves struggled to join their armies, the Prussian armies broke through the Lorraine gap, winning the battles of Vionville-Mars-la-Tour, Saint-Privat, and Gravelotte, which placed them between Paris and the main French armies of Marshall, Bazaine, and MacMahon. Marshall was cornered into the fortress of Metz. When the armies of MacMahon and the emperor tried to aid Bazaine, some of the forces were destroyed while others were surrounded at Sedan and bombarded until they surrendered. Six weeks after the war began Napoleon and his army of 100,000 troops surrendered.

COLLAPSE OF THE SECOND FRENCH EMPIRE

Two days later the Second Empire of France collapsed and a republican provisional government of National Defense, headed by the French lawyer

Gambetta, was proclaimed in Paris. The army of almost 200,000 men under the command of Marshal Bazaine was besieged at Metz and surrendered on October 27. In the meantime the German armies had marched into the heart of France and had encircled the French capital. Paris offered heroic resistance, but after four months the beleaguered city was finally forced to surrender on January 28, 1871. A newly elected French National Assembly, convening at Bordeaux, chose Adolphe Thiers, a veteran French statesman and twice prime minister under Louis Philippe, as executive head of the French Republic (1871–73). He crushed an attempt of the radical Commune to establish a socialist regime in France and conducted the negotiations that led to the preliminary peace agreements of February 26. Thirty thousand German troops had staged a symbolic occupation of part of the French capital but were withdrawn after the French National Assembly had accepted the preliminary peace terms.

The final peace treaty was signed at Frankfurt on May 10, 1871. If Bismarck's counsel had prevailed in the peace settlement with France as it had in 1866 in the peace treaty with Austria, the terms would have inflicted no incurable wounds to French pride and self-esteem. On the other hand, had General von Moltke's goals prevailed, France's power would have been utterly destroyed and peace indefinitely postponed. Bismarck, however, was placed in charge of armistice talks, and was satisfied with a substantial indemnity of 5 billion francs and the cession of Alsace, the majority of whose population was German in language and cultural tradition. Without consulting the wishes of their populations, the provinces of Alsace and part of Lorraine were annexed by Germany and incorporated into the Prussian system of administration. Administrative autonomy was withheld from both provinces until 1918, and during all these years the Prussian government by a series of psychological mistakes kept alive popular resentment and tried to whip the provinces into line. In addition to these territorial losses, France agreed to the German occupation of her key fortresses until the payment of the war indemnity was completed

SECOND GERMAN EMPIRE AND NEW EUROPEAN ERA

At Versailles near Paris, King William I of Prussia was proclaimed German emperor on January 18, 1871, with most of the German princes in attendance. All over Germany victory and unity celebrations took place in a spirit of militaristic nationalism and religious fervor. Most Germans were elated over unification and believed that their victory was a manifestation of the favor of divine Providence.

The Franco-Prussian War ushered in a new era. It broke the long peace among the major powers that had lasted since the Congress of Vienna. It created a new and very strong German nation, the Second Empire. It also emphasized the value of large, well-trained, and well-equipped armies. It left a heritage of bitterness between France and Germany and aroused a fiercer nationalism throughout all of Europe. Instead of bringing peace among nations as the romantic nationalists had hoped, German and Italian unification was not accomplished by the people but from above by governments and armies. The seeds of discord and violations of international treaties contributed in the long run to the causes of both the First and Second World Wars.

Industrial Revolution

The Industrial Revolution was a great dynamic processor that transformed all the conditions and institutions under which people—in any nation—lived. In Germany it strengthened the paternalistic state, powerful economic interest groups, and militarism but weakened the liberalism of the middle class and created an atmosphere hostile to urban life. Industrialization had already begun in England some hundred years earlier and France thereafter, but was to occur in Germany during the latter half of the 19th century, much later, more quickly and thoroughly. Germany's economic transformation from a predominantly agrarian nation to a modern, highly efficient industrial and technological state occurred mostly during three decades. In England that process had taken more than 100 years and produced different results, strengthening the middle class and parliamentary government. Germany, on the other hand, had to borrow technical inventions, capital, and examples of business and industrial organization from abroad. Once adopted, however, the Germans systematically exploited and improved on these and by 1913 had become the leading competitor of Britain and the United States in steel production, world trade, banking, insurance, and shipping. The period of proto-industrialization before 1850 was not very promising in Germany. It cannot be said that the German people between 1815 and 1848 had become better off economically. Economic growth had hardly kept ahead of rapid population growth. Nonetheless, important social and economic changes were taking place. During the restoration period some rulers as in Prussia had liberated individuals from the corporate restrictions of the guilds, making possible a new system of production based on factories. In agriculture capitalistic enterprise was limited, and the emancipation of the peasants did not substantially improve their conditions. Migration to cities increased these markets and the availability of a mobile labor force. Textile factories were built. In capital-poor Germany between 1818 and 1849 only 18 limited companies were formed, but that was a start. An example of an early industrialist was Friedrich Harkort (1793–1880), who established a factory in the Rhineland that produced iron and machines, with the help of English engineers. Later, he also became involved in railroads and shipping. He strongly believed in economic nationalism and propagated the idea of individual initiative and self-reliance. Friedrich List (1789–1846), on the other hand, was more of a visionary who dreamt of a protectionist middle European customs union that could challenge England's industrial supremacy. Economic liberalism, however, was the predominant economic philosophy of the time. The real industrial revolution began in the 1850s and was linked with a general improvement in the world economy. The economic progress of the 1850s and '60s laid the foundation for the progress that was to follow with political unification in 1871. Political unity created an environment conducive to economic growth, including a unified market, unified economic legislation, a common system of weights and measures, a new unified currency based on the gold standard, and the establishment of a central Reichsbank in 1875.

The first major growth industries were the railroads and heavy industry such as machine tools. The coal and iron and steel industries were also fundamental. But the major development in railway construction and the building of a network began with small lines. By 1848 the existing German railroads radiated from a number of regional centers such as Berlin, Leipzig, Hanover, Hamburg, Cologne, Frankfurt, and Munich. The expansion of the 1840s, however, placed Germany ahead of France in railroad building. The railroads actually created a common market out of the Prussian Customs Union established in 1834. Although only 3,280 kilometers of track existed around 1845, this jumped by 1860 to 11,633 and to 18,560 in 1870, increasing to 41,818 in 1890, 49,878 in 1900, and to 59,031 in 1910. The railroads were highly profitable and paid out dividends of up to 20 percent in the 1860s. Private capitalization predominated in the early period, but as governments later became involved, Prussia brought its railroads under state control between 1879 and 1884. Ownership by the state of all German railroads took place after 1918.

As the railroads expanded, heavy industry in the production of steam engines and machine tools for other purposes expanded significantly. The accelerated exchange of goods and the widespread availability of coal now made the Customs Union into an engine of growth. Most of the big machine factories originated in this period, such as the Borsig Locomotive Works in Berlin. Using a model from the United States, August Borsig (1804–54) in four years produced the first railroad engine and within a decade was able to supply the requirements of the whole Prussian railroad system. Josef Anton Maffei (1790–1870) founded his machine factory in Munich, as did other industrialists in Karlsruhe, Esslingen, and in Kassel. The most significant growth, however, took place in the coal and iron industries. The principal coal fields were in the Ruhr in Westphalia, the Saar basin in Upper and Lower Silesia, and Zwickau in Saxony. One of the most powerful coal syndicates in Europe was organized in the Ruhr. The marriage of coal and iron produced the most powerful iron and steel industry in Europe. For instance, just in the period from 1871 to 1874 a tremendous number of iron industries and engineering firms were established in Prussia. To the Borsig factory in Berlin were added the Krupp industry founded by Alfred Krupp (1812–87), the Thyssen steel works in the Ruhr established by August Thyssen (1842–1926), and the iron and steel empire established by Karl Freiherr von Stumm-Halberg (1836–1901). In Silesia Prince Guido Henckel von Donnersmarck (1830–1926) expanded his coal and iron industry to become the second-richest man in Germany next to Alfred Krupp.

By the eve of World War I Germany had been able to forge ahead of England and was second only to the United States in iron and steel production. An earlier limitation of highly phosphoric iron ore deposits was overcome by the invention and importation of the Thomas-Gilchrist open-hearth method of smelting ore. This enabled Germany to exploit the iron ores found in Lorraine, which Germany had annexed after the Franco-Prussian War, and linked these with the rich coal deposits in the Ruhr. The annexation of Alsace-Lorraine also brought a mature textile industry and potash deposits for fertilizer, providing Germany with a near monopoly in Europe. The increased production of steel was used in machine tools, cutlery, and precision instruments, but predominantly to build up the railroads, to develop a great merchant and naval fleet, the armaments industry, and much later the automobile industry. The shipbuilding industry experienced a remarkable growth after 1880, transforming the merchant fleet to steam-powered steel ships. The major shipbuilding cities were Hamburg, Bremen, Stettin, Elbing, and Kiel. Only Great Britain led Germany in total tonnage. German shipyards produced for the mercantile fleet but also for the massive naval building program advocated by Admiral Tirpitz (1849–1930). The two largest shipping companies were the Hamburg-Amerika Linie (HAPAG) founded by Albert Ballin (1857–1918), a Hamburg Jew, and the North German Lloyd of Bremen founded in 1857 by Heinrich Herman Meier (1809–1898).

The chemical and electrical industries experienced their massive growth after 1880. Germany had more than adequate resources in salt, potassium, and the derivatives of coal and lignite, which were transformed by the talents of highly

The SS *Bremen* of the North German Lloyd Company, 1905 (*Library of Congress*)

trained chemists. These industries produced chemicals for industrial uses as well as pharmaceuticals. The most spectacular developments came in the field of synthetic dyes, synthetic substitutes for rubber, oil, nitrates, photographic supplies, anesthetics, and pharmaceuticals. Important corporations were Agfa, Badische Analin, Bayer, Höchst, and IG Farben.

Electrical engineering had its beginning with the introduction of the telegraph in the 1840s, but it was the telephone industry that stimulated the production of telecommunications equipment after 1877. One of the founders of this industry was Werner von Siemens (1816–92) who invented the first dynamo, which made it possible to generate electricity anywhere. Siemens also introduced the electric railways. Another pioneer of the industry was Emil Rathenau (1838–1915), who founded the German Edison Company (AEG) in 1883. In the 1890s the process of electrification of cities was undertaken as was the building of an electrical trolley system of transportation. The problems of long-distance electrical transmission were overcome as well as those of hydroelectric power. By the eve of World War I Germany was producing some 50 percent of the world's electrical equipment.

At the beginning of the Industrial Revolution in Germany the availability of capital for investment was very limited. The demand for capital was satisfied by the expansion of joint-stock investment companies and the development of large commercial banks. While in the 1840s only 18 investment companies existed, by 1859 another 251 had been added. While the number of industrial corporations grew by 295 between 1851 and 1870 a phenomenal increase of 857 occurred between 1870 and 1874. Political unification in 1871 and the influx from France of thousands of millions of marks as the result of the huge indemnity imposed by the victorious Prussians led to an unprecedented economic boom. The establishment of hundreds of companies led to unwise investments. In 1873 the stock exchanges in Vienna and then Berlin collapsed. As was the case in boom times industrial production exceeded demand and many companies went bankrupt. Some companies that had been formed without a solid basis, but with an expectation of future profits, did not survive this crisis. The German response to this phenomenon was to organize cartels or trusts by which companies controlled the market and fixed prices. This provided economic security in times of recession, but also limited competition. The crash of 1873 also shattered the self-confidence of the middle class and created a pessimistic outlook that dominated during the following years. A depression lasted until 1877, followed by a decade of slow recovery, then another depression occurred lasting to 1895. The new electrical industry sparked a boom between 1895 and 1900, followed by another recession until 1907. During the years prior to the First World War there was general economic expansion and prosperity.

The nature and growth of the German banking system was what facilitated the rapid growth of commerce and industry. German banks played a different role in the economy than did those of England or the United States. By comparison the German banks provided credit to companies to promote production and not credit for consumers. German banks were a combination of commercial bank, investment bank, and investment trust. They participated in the establishment of enterprises and participated directly in their management.

Exports were financed by them as were large-scale industries abroad, including railroads, telegraph, and many others. German banks helped finance the Northern Pacific Railroad in the United States and the famous Berlin to Baghdad Railroad.

The solution to the problem of finding adequate capital for financing Germany's industrial development was found in the example of the French joint-stock institution, the Crédit Mobilier. The first banks to follow this example were the Schaaffhausensche Bankverein founded by Gustav Mevissen and the Diskonto Gesellschaft founded by David Hansemann in 1851, followed by the Darmstädter Bank cofounded by Abraham Oppenheimer of Mannheim. The Berliner Handelsgesellschaft was founded in the 1850s, but expanded under Carl Fürstenberg, who had been trained by Bismarck's Jewish banker, Gerson Bleichröder. Although there were many banks that facilitated German industrialization, the greatest was the Deutsche Bank founded in 1870 by Georg von Siemens (1839–1901), a cousin of Werner von Siemens (1816–92), who was a famous leader in the electrical industry. Another was the Dresdner Bank established in 1872.

The building of the railroads and the expansion of heavy industry required an unprecedented growth in a nonagricultural workforce. As was the case elsewhere in Europe, population was growing rapidly during the 18th and 19th centuries. At the opening of the 19th century the total population of what became Imperial Germany was just a little over 24 million, which increased to 41 million in 1870, and by 1914 that number had multiplied to just under 68 million. Although the birth rate had climbed throughout the century, between 1900 and 1905 the absolute highest birth rate in German history occurred. The population in 1871 living in urban areas was only 36 percent, while in 1910 the percentages were almost reversed (60 percent), which meant that the movement of people into cities occurred very rapidly. Psychologically, however, Germans expressed negative feelings toward urban life. Emancipation of the rural population had proceeded apace (in Prussia serfdom was ended in 1810), which meant that internal migration could occur. Emigration to foreign lands, especially to the United States, had been high in the middle of the century, but as industrialization advanced fewer Germans took that route to a better life. A wave of internal migration created a human reservoir that the industrialists could tap. Between 1850 and 1870 the earlier agricultural and artisan proletariat was now being transformed into an industrial proletariat. Even artisans who previously had maintained their independence now sought work in the factories. The migration of a huge numbers of former agricultural workers from east of the Elbe River now became the workers in the factories of Rhineland-Westphalia. Working and living conditions in most instances were wretched. On the outskirts of Berlin and other industrial cities shanty towns grew up. Tenement houses were also built where on average six to seven people lived in one room. Workers often labored for 18 hours a day, and wages were so low that they often had to rely on bread lines. Child labor was common.

Workers' educational associations were formed, and many workers joined these self-help organizations. Numerous new types of organizations were established. The great Prussian architect and conservator of ancient monuments,

Karl Friedrich Schinkel (1781–1841), suggested vocational schools as did the Hamburg-born architect Gottfried Semper (1803–79), famous for his buildings in Dresden and Vienna. The industrialist Raiffeisen founded rural credit cooperatives, and Franz Hermann Schulze-Delitzsch (1808–83) started credit associations for small businesses. Consumer cooperatives and trade unions were formed. The Catholic and Protestant Churches also advocated reforms to improve conditions, as in the case of Bishop Wilhelm von Kettler (1811–77), and the operation of charitable and vocational associations for tradesmen and workers, as in the case of Adolf Kolping (1813–65). Both of these were the founders of the German Social-Catholic movement. These and others sought to reform the existing capitalist and industrial system.

The most prominent of those who opposed mere reform and demanded fundamental change in economic relations were Karl Marx (1818–83) and Friedrich Engels (1820–95). They insisted that the capitalist system had to be destroyed. During the 1848 revolution they had written *The Manifesto of the Communist Party*. It was written for Belgian workers, but it did not have any impact on that revolutionary year. Karl Marx was exiled and took up residence in London, while Friedrich Engels had set up factories in England. Marx began to research the forces and trends of the capitalist system in order to prove that a proletarian revolution was inevitable. In 1867 Marx published the first volume of *Das Kapital*. Workers themselves had set up the first workers' associations in the wake of the 1848 revolution. These were repressed, but the establishment of trade unions continued. In 1863 Ferdinand Lassalle (1825–64) founded the General German Workers' Association, which demanded equal and universal suffrage and state-supported companies. In 1869 a Marxist oriented Workers' Party was formed in Eisenach by August Bebel (1840–1913) and Wilhelm Liebknecht (1826–1900). Eventually, the party of Lassalle and that in Eisenach merged in 1875 in Gotha to form a united workers' party. In the Gotha program the Social Democratic Workers' Party advocated a mix of Marxist and Lassallean ideas.

Nineteenth-Century Culture and Society

The cultural trends of the latter half of the 19th century included realism, naturalism, materialism, impressionism, and expressionism, as well as the rise of modern anti-Semitism. Some of the intellectuals involved would praise the accomplishments of Bismarck and German society, while others reflected or severely criticized the materialism and militarization of German society. The romantic movement came to an end as the modern world tore apart its veil of fantasy and colorful illusions. The spread of the logic of Hegel's idealistic philosophy, the political struggles of liberalism against the old authoritarian monarchical order, the failure of the revolutions of 1848, the rising nationalistic spirit, the progress of natural science, the onslaught of the early Industrial Revolution and its factories and industrial working class—all were creating a world that needed to be described in new terms. Realism provided that new objectivity. The best literary works of realism were in the novels of such writers as Wilhelm Raabe (1831–1910), Theodor Storm (1817–88), and Theodor Fontane (1819–98). Fontane was the greatest of these novelists, while the age also brought forth one of the most outstanding lyric poets in the history of German literature, Annette von Droste-Hülshoff. She was deeply religious and combined realistic observation and deep psychological insight. One of her novels, *The Jew's Beech Tree* (1842), was the finest tragic narrative of the middle of the century.

On the other hand, there were those like the historian Heinrich von Treitschke, who praised the creation of the Second Reich and the use of military power to accomplish national goals. He influenced many of Imperial Germany's future leaders. Just as his writings reflected the militarization of the bourgeoisie, his interpretation of the problems of German industrial society was to blame the Jews as Germany's "national misfortune." His work reflected and contributed to the growth of anti-Semitism, a trend already seen in Gustav Freytag (1815–95), who in *Debit and Credit* (1855) sought to mirror the German problems of his time. He wrote one of the great realistic historical novels of the earlier 19th century in which he praises the enterprising spirit of German merchants. Another of the foremost realist novelists was Wilhelm Raabe, often called the German Charles Dickens. His pessimism about the materialism and nationalism of his age is apparent in his distinguished novel *Der Hungerpastor* (1864), which depicts the struggles of average people trying to achieve success and love in overcoming life's challenges. In other novels he dealt with greedy people and their morals and how some could be destroyed by the lies and the meanness of modern life. Both Freytag and Raabe, however, were influenced in their anti-Semitism by the thinking of the infamous anti-Semitic Frenchman

Count Gobineau. Although prejudice against the Jews had a long history, in 1873 Wilhelm Marr used the term *anti-Semitism* for the first time and alleged that Germany's problems were the result of a "Jewish conspiracy."

Out of realism emerged the more extreme literary form of naturalism. It had its forerunner in the socialistic novels of Friedrich Spielhagen (1829–1911) and the social perspectives of Theodor Fontane (1819–98). More important were the foreign influences of Leo Tolstoi, Henrik Ibsen, Émile Zola, Charles Darwin, and the scientific positivism and empiricism of the late 19th century. Before he turned against naturalism and socialism, Friedrich Nietzsche was also influential. The naturalist authors emphasized the misery of the slums, capitalistic exploitation, and social inequality. The middle class also was a target of the naturalists, and class struggle was emphasized. The vulgar language and the dialects of the common people were used effectively. Life was explained on a scientific basis, and sexual questions were freely discussed. The principal naturalist authors were Arno Holz (1863–1929), Gerhart Hauptmann (1862–1946), Hermann Sudermann (1857–1928), and Frank Wedekind (1864–1918). Influenced by the Swedish dramatist and novelist August Strindberg (1849–1956), Widekind started in the naturalist tradition but tended toward symbolism, employing grotesque and tempestuous messages in order to justify the power of man's sexual instincts, and he preached a gospel of amorality. In Widekind's attack on the rulers and middle class of Wilhelmine society he warned that dangerous forces of destruction were adrift. Considered by some to be a "genius of smut," his powerful dramas undermined the contemporary naturalist theater, paving the way for the expressionist dramas of the future. One of the writers of the realistic and naturalist schools whose writings were a clear reflection of problems connected with industrial, urban, and social change was Heinrich Mann. He wrote satirical novels criticizing bigotry, hypocrisy, and chauvinistic patriotism. Mann's *In the Land of Cockaigne* (1900) described the shallow humor and cheap intellectual ambitiousness of the newly rich in Berlin, where the population had more than doubled from 1870 to 1914 to around 2 million residents. His philosophy was one of "radicalized realism," which emphasized a psychological, social, and material determinism. In *Professor Unrath* (1905) he examined the power of sexual attraction and the ruination of a professor by a cheap nightclub entertainer. Mann also wrote a powerful condemnation of Imperial Germany in the trilogy *The Empire,* where he denounced government officials, middle-class servility, and the general German lack of "civic virtue." His best novel, *The Patrioteer* (*Der Untertan*), was the first in this series. Thomas Mann should also be mentioned in any discussion of naturalism, for early in his career he wrote *Buddenbrooks* (1901), which expressed with great refinement the decay of a proud patrician merchant family and its old middle-class values overcome by the challenges of industrialism and materialism.

Theodor Fontane (1819–98) wrote fascinating novels in the genre of social realism dealing with the conflict between a formerly dominant aristocracy and the newly rich bourgeoisie. He began his career as a journalist, then distinguished himself as a ballad writer, and only later did he become a novelist. He wrote one of Europe's greatest realistic psychological novels, *Effi Briest* (1895), the story of a German Madame Bovary married to a stern Prussian official and who is unfaithful in a short affair with a young major. There is a sense of being trapped as the young woman after an indiscretion is crushed by the lack of compassion of society. Infidelity was an unforgivable crime for the wife, but the double standard existed for the husband. Another novel on a different theme is the humorous satire of the rich and pretentious bourgeoisie in *Jenny Treibel* (1892). The city was the focus of Fontane's social realism as it also was for the contemporary writers, Friedrich Spielhagen (1829–1911) and Herman Sudermann (1857–1928). Spielhagen, like Freytag, sought to mirror the social problems of his time, especially the dangers of materialism and nihilism and the reactionary feudalism of Bismarck.

While Spielhagen belonged to the realist movement, Hermann Sudermann was a naturalist author and one of the most popular playwrights of his time. His dramas concerned such themes as the double standards in wealthy families as well as the conflicts between Prussian fathers and their daughters. The naturalist authors took up the battle for humankind's emancipation where the earlier generation of the storm and stress poets and the young Germans had left off. The naturalists, however, were much more radical and depressing in their descriptions of German life. They emphasized the raw and uncouth elements in life where the aesthetic elements of realism gave way to the propagandistic descriptions of the misery of the slums, as well as social hypocrisy and economic exploitation.

In Berlin a new era of theater also began. Die Freie Bühne founded in 1889 was dedicated to the modern drama. It presented the plays of Ibsen and Strindberg. Such German playwrights as Gerhart Hauptmann and Frank Wedekind, a forerunner of expressionism, had their works performed here. One of Germany's greatest playwrights was Gerhart Hauptmann, whose naturalist dramas vibrantly elicited compassion for the poor and man's powerlessness in a world of hostile forces. Hauptmann's naturalist drama *Before Dawn* (*Vor Sonnenaufgang*) (1889) is the story of an alcohol-infected family afflicted by despair and suicide. Hauptmann's greatest work was *The Weavers* (*Die Weber*) (1892), a socialist drama depicting the suffering and despair of Silesian weavers and their futile rebellion in 1844. Abandoning naturalism in the 1890s, Hauptmann turned to symbolism.

Two geniuses of this period whose influence had a far-reaching impact on German history and particularly National Socialism were Friedrich Nietzsche (1844–1900) and Richard Wagner (1813–83). Friedrich Nietzsche sarcastically criticized the materialism and philistinism of his generation. In the *Twilight of the Idols* (1888) Nietzsche lambasted his countrymen as being "stupid," resulting from German's power and prosperity. Trained as a classical philologist, Nietzsche led a radical revolt against the values and traditions of Western civilization. His famous themes included the "god is dead" gospel, "the superman" and "the will to power." Nietzsche's ideas anticipated Sigmund Freud's concept of the unconscious and the existentialist search for the meaning of life.

Richard Wagner was also a prominent critic of German society, a leading propagandist of Nordic racialism, and a brilliant composer of melodramatic operas based on medieval German legends. Along with Nietzsche he believed that Western civilization was in decline. He concluded that the German people could only be regenerated by returning to their ancient racial myths. He condemned

Jewish influence in German cultural life in his essay *Judaism and Music,* blaming the Jews for Germany's cultural decline. Wagner also opposed the liberalism, materialism, and intellectual progress of the middle class.

German music continued its excellence throughout the 19th century. Just as Mozart and Beethoven had dominated the musical scene in the late 18th and early 19th centuries, Felix Mendelssohn (1809–47) and Robert Schumann (1810–56) were the most important composers until mid-century. Both Mendelssohn and Schumann exemplified the romantic tradition, the former in his experiments and recycling of thematic material, and the latter in his moody nature and receptiveness to literary stimuli, and his demise through insanity. Schumann set to music poems by Heine, Körner, Eichendorff, Rückert, and Chamisso. Carl Maria von Weber (1786–1826) should also be remembered as a leading contributor to the romantic and nationalist movement and especially for his opera *The Free Shooter* (*Die Freischütz*). Franz Liszt (1811–86), who was half Hungarian and half German, does not fall neatly into the German symphonic tradition, yet his contributions were enormous. Not only was he an outstanding pianist, he also was the equivalent of the renowned Paganini. Liszt's decadelong career in Weimar produced the Faust symphony and many symphonic poems.

Two musical giants who dominated the second half of the 19th century were Johannes Brahms (1883–97) and Richard Wagner, although closely followed by Richard Strauss (1864–1949) and the Austrian composers Anton Bruckner (1824–96) and Gustav Mahler (1860–1911). Brahms was one of the greatest symphonic composers of the century; his *German Requiem* (*Deutsches Requiem*) (1868) and his Violin Concerto were among his greatest accomplishments.

On the other hand, Richard Wagner believed that he was creating the music of the future, which inspired him to compose his music dramas, *Der Ring des Nibelungen, Tristan und Isolde, Die Meistersinger von Nürnberg,* and *Parsifal.* It was his goal to achieve an organic union of music and drama in which each remained independent, the music reflecting the mood and passion while the drama carried the action. His heavy and pessimistic music was dazzlingly different from previous composers. Wagner experienced both marital and financial difficulties and was befriended by King Ludwig II of Bavaria who paid off his debts. It was therefore not until June 10, 1865, in Munich that *Tristan und Isolde* was first performed. Wagner also marks the transition from the more moderately liberal and nationalistic earlier 19th century to the more cynical and materialistic late 19th and 20th century.

On the more popular side are the operettas of Jacques Offenbach (1819–80) and the immortal Viennese waltzes by Johann Strauss the Elder (1804–49) and the Younger (1825–99). Offenbach was of German-Jewish origin but performed most of his burlesque operas in France. He is remembered mostly for his *Tales of Hoffman.* It was Offenbach who encouraged the younger Johann Strauss to write operettas, his most successful being *Die Fledermaus.* Just as Gilbert and Sullivan personified Victorian England and Offenbach the Second Empire in France, it was Johann Strauss and his son who dominated the musical life of Vienna. They composed waltzes, polkas, marches, and quadrilles, and the younger became known as the Waltz King, two of his most popular being "The Blue Danube" and "Tales from the Vienna Woods."

ART AND ARCHITECTURE

There was no productive relationship between politics and the arts in Imperial Germany. The arts were not of great interest to Bismarck, and the government lacked a policy to advance cultural activity. In fact cultural creativity was not respected as was the production of material goods. Materialistic values dominated the thinking of the middle class and were severely criticized by Nietzsche and other writers. Writers and artists were alienated by these realities, but their alienation was also caused by their conviction that their involvement in public affairs was contrary to their calling. In the German cultural tradition it was the inner life and not the external world that should be their focus. The culture of the Imperial establishment was oriented to the aristocracy and middle class, a static system in which militarism, narcissism, sentimentality, and literary hero-worship predominated. Art and literature reflected the contradictions of the age. Official art styles approved by the academies and the nation's elites were statues of military heroes and philistine paintings of the neo-idealist school. The neo-idealist school reflected Hellenism and romanticism; it was a patriotic art emphasizing imaginative, mythical, and intellectual qualities. It reflected the anti-French attitude so prevalent in German culture. It was a style opposed to the scientific emphasis of French naturalism and impressionism, which German audiences associated with unpatriotic and subversive radicalism, socialism, and polluting cultural degeneracy. Arnold Böcklin and Max Klinger were the leaders of neo-idealism, and their art took on patriotic significance in the 1890s. Their art was an antimodernist campaign for a return to a simpler preurban and preindustrialized world.

A younger generation of artists soon decided to secede from these officially approved styles. A group of artists united under the name the Artists Group Bridge, known as the Brücke, organized to promote the aesthetic of expressionism. Early members included such great artists of the movement as Ludwig Kirchner, Karl Schmidt-Rottluff, Emil Nolde, and Max Pechstein. The Brücke collapsed in 1913 and was followed by the Blue Rider group organized in Munich and named after Wassily Kandinsky's painting by the same title. Before 1914 the work of these artists was characterized by the use of bright colors and simplified forms. In its first exhibition in 1906 the Brücke announced its program to be a call to creativity and a break with hidebound German institutions and to shock the middle class. Nudity was a central motif for these artists, who worked communally.

These trends in art were similar to a new social movement of youth. The youth revolted against the rigidity of school curriculums, patriarchal dominance in the family, the prevailing repression of sexuality and bodily freedom, and the materialism of society. In 1906 the Free Youth Movement was founded, emphasizing a return to nature, nudity, and a life of physical fitness. This was an outgrowth of the organization in 1901 of the Wandervögel, an anti-hierarchical hiking group dedicated to group interaction and equality, physical activity, and natural foods. The Free Youth Movement spread throughout Germany and became both nationalistic and anti-Semitic. The ideas of the youth revolt and other interest groups spread rapidly through various mass media of the press, magazines, and photojournalism. During this age political satire and muckraking journalism were widespread and popular.

During the post-1871 founding era and into the Wilhelmian period, public architecture was pompous and the facades of buildings had extravagant ornamentation. The styles were unimaginative imitations of historical styles including neo-Gothic, neo-Renaissance and neo-baroque. Against this approved imperial style emerged a new style of art deco called Jugendstil, which favored designs that were lean and graceful.

SOCIAL STRUCTURE AND WOMEN

Nineteenth-century Germany was still a male-dominated society. Women were generally restricted to being wives and mothers, focusing on the three K's of children, kitchen, and the church (*Kinder, Küche, Kirche*). Women worked primarily in the home, and the largest number of women were employed on farms rather than in commerce and factories. Ownership of farms and control of female income was still in the hands of the husband. Of the 1.9 million female laborers in the Prussian workforce in 1861, most were agricultural laborers and half a million were servants. Only one in 10 employed women worked in factories. As the century progressed, married women increasingly were employed in factories, an increase that rose to 27 percent of the female workforce in 1907. During that same year at least 50 percent of the agrarian laborers were women, and servant girls accounted for another 16 percent of female workers. Certainly the majority of women workers did not enjoy the benefits that reforms in industrial employment had acquired for women, such as the 10-hour day, no work on Sundays and evenings, and eight weeks of maternity leave.

Women did not have the right to vote during the 19th century. In Prussia they also were barred from political participation in organizations and trade unions, while in more liberal states such as Bavaria and Württemberg women were allowed to join political movements. As women's organizations were founded to lobby for improved conditions—access to education, equal pay, equal property rights—it is no surprise that the Civil Code of 1900 established women as "legal persons." The Civil Code also made divorce easier, ending the requirement of the husband's consent. In 1908 women finally were allowed to join political clubs and after the turn of the century could attend universities. The female historian Ricarda Huch became the first woman to receive a doctorate.

The movement for women's rights first began with middle-class associations like the Federation of German Women's Associations (BDF), strictly middle-class in orientation and founded by Auguste Schmidt in 1894. It advocated for many reforms such as access to higher learning and the right to vote, but also for equal pay in factories and opportunities for professional women. In 1902 the German Union of Women's Suffrage (DVF) was organized by the radical feminist Anita Augspurg. Working-class women also began to organize and the Law of Association in 1908 allowed women to join the SPD with equal rights. One of the early advocates of working women's issues was Clara Zetkin of the SPD, who had founded the paper *Equality,* advocating feminine economic self-sufficiency. Other women authors who exposed the conditions of laboring women were novelists Clara Viebig, Anna Croissant-Rust, and Gabriele Reuter. At the beginning of the 20th century it is perhaps not surprising that there occurred a conservative backlash to the expansion of women's rights. A Social Darwinist orientation influenced the creation of the League for the Protection of Motherhood, which emphasized "racial health." Gertrud Baumer, a disciple of Adolf Stöcker and Friedrich Naumann, took over the BDF and advocated the protection of marriage and motherhood and was opposed to abortion on demand. Other leaders of the BDF sought to protect marriage for reasons of racial hygiene. The male reaction culminated in the League for the Struggle Against the Emancipation of Women, whose members included military leaders and other conservatives and cultural pessimists. Not surprisingly, some even linked the feminist movement to the myth of a Jewish conspiracy.

EDUCATION

German society was highly stratified, and the educational system helped keep it so. It tended to freeze the existing social system and was used by the government to reinforce loyalty to the existing order and obedience to authority. Through the elementary system most Germans learned to read and write, which helps explain why in the 19th century German workers were the best educated in Europe. Yet the educational system did not promote upward social mobility. Most of the school population were discouraged from entering secondary schools and obtaining their Abitur, which permitted the graduate to enter a university. Secondary education and university degrees were essential for government and professional employment. For the masses of students traditional values, discouragement by teachers, the expense and the heavy emphasis on learning all contributed to educational inequality in Germany well into the latter 20th century. The universities maintained their tradition of humanistic studies, but also after 1871 promoted the social and behavioral and natural sciences.

THE SECOND GERMAN EMPIRE

1871–1918

As Germany became unified in 1871, it was a nation undergoing a profound and complex process of change. It possessed an economy and society that was experiencing rapid industrialization and urbanization, a social transformation from a predominantly rural and agricultural society to one in which population was increasingly moving to cities and working in industries. Education was expanding; technological and scientific advancements were taking place; railroads networked the nation; and banks and capital markets were expanding. On the other hand, Germany was a nation that lagged behind politically. The new Empire had been created by leaders of the Prussian counterrevolution, who were opposed to effective parliamentary government with ministerial responsibility and real democracy. The new emperor, Kaiser William I, Bismarck, and the Junkers firmly believed that the absolute power of the Kaiser and the independence of his army were keys to the stability of society. Another characteristic of German history, its particularist tradition of federalism, also persisted into the new Empire, which divided sovereignty and complicated the development of a unified nation-state. Bismarck was willing to grant Bavaria and Württemberg certain constitutional privileges, including the continuation of their monarchies, the separate administration of their armies in time of peace, and an independent railway, postal, and telegraph system. Another symbol of its patchwork character was that all the German states were permitted to appoint ambassadors to foreign states. Special attention was given to Bavarian pride as King Louis II had been chosen to ask the Prussian king at Versailles to accept the hereditary imperial title and later in the constitution a Bavarian was always to chair the Committee on Foreign Affairs. Finally, Bismarck had to persuade the Prussian king to accept the title "German Emperor" instead of the title that William preferred, "Emperor of Germany," so that the sensibilities of the German princes would not be offended.

BISMARCKIAN "PSEUDO-CONSTITUTIONAL ABSOLUTISM"

The constitution of 1871 has been called the Bismarckian compromise and the government one of "pseudo-constitutional absolutism." It mixed conservative politics and economic liberalism. Written mostly by Bismarck, it intended to enhance the role and power of Prussia, and was not a foundational document for future constitutional development. It was illogical and filled with contradictions. For instance, the imperial government was not provided with administrative agencies that could execute policy and enforce laws. It also was supposed to be a federal state, but the states were unequal and dominated by Prussia. It had a parliament, the Reichstag, which was democratically elected by males over the age of 25, yet ministerial responsibility was lacking and legislation could not be initiated. So the new constitution was basically flawed, and critics have said that it was intended to ensure Bismarck's personal power. On the other hand, there was some accountability of the Reich chancellor (prime minister) to the emperor but not to parliament, and he did have to try to get majorities for his policies in the Reichstag. Although Germans called the Reichstag a talk-shop, it nonetheless had the potential of growing into an effective governing body. The Reichstag was a body of nationally elected representatives, a platform for the debate of policy; it did review laws and could veto the budget. Bismarck certainly valued the Reichstag as a counterweight to particularism, and in foreign affairs it was a good platform for discussion. The suffrage in the individual states varied; in 11 it was still based on the amount of taxes paid, while in four the voters were divided according to estates. At the turn of the century the south German states reformed their electoral laws in accordance with the Reich, while Prussia retained its undemocratic three-class voting system until 1918, which was a continued obstacle to reform.

The founding of the Reich created a unified economic and customs area that fostered rapid economic growth. Progress was gradually made in unifying important institutions such as transportation, the postal system, currency, banking, weights and measures, and the achievement of a uniform legal system. In 1872 a uniform penal code was introduced and in 1900 a code of civil law.

Nationality problems were bound to exist after unification. Instead of incorporating various ethnic groups such as the Poles, the German state attempted to integrate them through bureaucratic means. In 1872–73 the German language was made the only language used in schools in the Polish-speaking areas, and after 1876 also in business. Even the Germans in the imperial territory of Alsace-Lorraine, who had been favorably treated by the French constitution, resented being treated as second-class Germans.

POLITICAL PARTIES

The political parties in the Reichstag were the same that had functioned before in the individual states and in the North German Confederation. The conservatives were recruited chiefly from state officials and from owners of landed property. The liberals comprising the National Liberals who were monarchists, and the Progressives who were democrats were both advocates of laissez-faire (unlimited competition in economics) and of secularism (freedom from church influence) in politics, culture, and education. The Center Party, which received its name based on the central location of its seats in the chamber between the Conservatives and Liberals, was originally founded in Prussia in 1852 and reorganized on the national level in 1871 by Ludwig Windhorst. Though not officially associated with the Roman Catholic Church, the Center Party represented primarily German Catholics, and it sought to defend Christian principles in politics, society, and education. The seats on the extreme left of the Reichstag were occupied by the Social Democrats, the followers of the doctrine of socialism propounded by Ferdinand Lasalle, Karl Marx, and Friedrich Engels. Their anticapitalist, pacifist, and internationalist creed as well as their adherence to materialism and atheism placed them in opposition to all the other parties of the parliament. Their gospel of social compassion and their program for the redemption of the masses from poverty and social degradation, together with the ability of some of their leaders, gained so many members despite repression and persecution that it became the largest party in the Reichstag by 1912.

THE KULTURKAMPF, SOCIALISM, AND SOCIAL LEGISLATION

Bitterly and vainly Bismarck fought against "the enemies of the Reich," the Center Party and the Social Democrats. Typical of conflicts between church and state the first of these internal wars called a "Battle for Civilization" (Kulturkampf) was against the Catholic Church over state inspection of schools and the requirement for civil marriages. The radical and anticlerical minister of education in Prussia, Adalbert Falk, sponsored the May Laws (1873), which forbade the clergy to meddle in state matters, banned the Jesuit order, and placed the church and clergy under state supervision. Catholics rallied to the church, and by 1878 this campaign proved to be a failure. This struggle like that with the socialists proved that the new German nation would not peacefully work out its problems. While Catholics remained distrustful of the Reich, the Social Democrats were more hostile and determined opponents. Bismarck began his battle against social democracy in spring 1878 out of fear of a social and political revolution, blaming Social Democrats for two attempts that had been made on the Kaiser's life. The Reichstag was dissolved, and the Anti-Socialist Laws of October 1878 decreed that socialist organizations that "threaten to overthrow the existing state and social structure" were banned. In the next election this ensured a comfortable parliamentary majority for the government. The workers stood by their political leaders, but by 1890 it was clear that the repressive legislation had failed. The more positive counterpart to the repressive Anti-Socialist Law was the social insurance scheme by which it was hoped the workers would support the state. Bismarck's goal was not inspired by a humanitarian motive to protect workers from the uncertainties of the industrial economy but to win over the "great mass of propertyless people" to the conservative way of thinking. Yet, the "state socialism" of Bismarck's social legislation, covering sickness, disability, and old-age schemes, was without question an important step in social progress.

FOREIGN POLICY AND ALLIANCE SYSTEMS

The goal of Bismarck's foreign policy was to preserve the authoritarian system within the Second Reich. He claimed that his foreign policy was based on the unchanging principles that Germany was a saturated nation and no longer had territorial ambitions. The victory over France in 1871 gave Germany hegemony in central Europe. In order to stabilize the balance of power achieved in 1871, Bismarck believed that monarchical states were the most stable and best candidates for Germany's alliances. He had to isolate France and frustrate any attempt by her to form an alliance with Austria, Russia, or England. To do so, he built a system of defensive alliances with Austria and Russia and eventually Italy. In 1872 both Francis Joseph I of Austria and Alexander II of Russia visited Berlin, and Bismarck succeeded in forming the Three Emperors League, a friendly accord among the three monarchs. Bismarck's choice of allies, however, contained fundamental flaws inasmuch as Russia and Austria were countries in domestic turmoil and ones that pursued risky foreign policies, especially in the Balkans. Bismarck was fortunate in having Great Britain as another ally, at least until Germany began to acquire colonies in 1884, becoming one of England's rivals in colonial affairs. There also were strains in relations with Russia over its intervention in behalf of oppressed Christian minorities under Turkish rule. To check the expansion of Russian power, England had sent a fleet to the Black Sea and Austria fielded an army to block Russian expansion in the Balkans. Bismarck was permitted to arbitrate this dispute, which he did as an "honest broker" at the Congress of Berlin in 1878. Because of the resentment of Czar Alexander II over the partition of Bulgaria at the congress and the domestic demand in Germany to establish tariff restrictions on Russian grain imports, relations with Russia became strained. Bismarck then turned to Vienna and concluded with the Austro-Hungarian foreign minister Andrassy the Austro-German Dual Alliance (1879), providing for mutual assistance in case of Russian aggression and for the benevolent neutrality of either party if one of the two nations should be attacked by France. In 1882 Bismarck included Italy in his defensive plans in the Triple Alliance in order to encourage the Italians to clash with the French in North Africa rather than pursue expansion in southeastern Europe, where it would clash with Austria. Italy was the weakest link in this defensive alliance system, which proved to be the case when it failed to support its allies in 1914. The alliances had to be continually adjusted as when Bismarck in 1887 negotiated the Reinsurance Treaty with Russia because of fears of crises in the Balkans and France. Bismarck had obtained promises of Russian neutrality in case of French attack. Inasmuch as the treaty was not renewed in 1890, the system of alliances was at a crossroads. The contradictions inherent in simultaneous alliances with Russia and Austria, both having conflicting interests in the Balkans, proved unworkable. When William II became emperor, he refused to renew the treaty, and by 1894 France and Russia had concluded the Franco-Russian Entente and a future two-front war became almost inevitable for Germany.

BISMARCK'S DISMISSAL

In the 1880s Bismarck's popularity faded. It was not that his genius and accomplishments were not recognized, but as the Berlin novelist and perceptive critic Theodor Fontane reported, people questioned his character and concluded that he was "a small man." Bismarck had increasing difficulty constructing parliamentary majorities as the left liberals, the Center Party, and the Socialists voted against him. Alluding to the possibility of war with France, Bismarck used scare tactics to pass the budget in 1878. Because the Reichstag was becoming more difficult to control, the chancellor even contemplated abolishing the egalitarian right to vote. Then in 1888 Kaiser William I was succeeded by his liberal son, Frederick III, who tragically died of cancer within the year. His son, William, ascended the throne as William II (1859–1941) and ruled until the end of the Empire in 1918. Impetuous and desirous of popularity, William disliked Bismarck's complicated alliances, disagreed with the persecution of socialism, and was upset that Bismarck had even considered a constitutional coup. William forced Bismarck's resignation on March 18, 1890. Yet Bismarck had achieved German unification and afterward preserved European peace. His negative influences were many, including his fixation on monarchism and his persecution of opponents as subversives. The long-range impact of his methods harmed Germany's political modernization: his use of parliamentary tactics that damaged the future of liberalism, his alienation of many Germans from the government, the premium he placed on political conformity in the bureaucracy, the damage he caused to the independence of the upper middle class, and his abandonment of the lower middle class to a resentful political existence influenced by demagogues.

WILHELMINE GERMANY

The major domestic political issues of the era of William II (r. 1888–1918) were the fight against the rapidly growing Social Democratic Party, the tough policy pursued against national minorities, the restrictions on suffrage of the Prussian three-class voting system, and the failure to extend ministerial responsibility of the government to the Reichstag. The dynamic growth of Germany into the greatest European industrial state prevented the eruption of the many smoldering tensions. Public life was bureaucratized and militarized, while an imperialist foreign policy stirred people's emotions and bound them through nationalism and militarism with the monarchist authoritarian state.

William II was a man of interesting contrasts much like the times in which he lived. He was born with a physical disability that left him without the use of his left arm. He was ill-educated, impulsive, tactless, and lacking in culture; he liked rowdy parties and luxurious yachts, cultivated military bearing, boasted about Germany's power, and sought to assert himself in every aspect of Germany's policies. With all of these negative characteristics, the Kaiser also desired to be a modern monarch who was responsive to the needs of the people. Therefore he became preoccupied with public opinion in the press and concentrated on his public image.

William's advisers were mostly aristocratic and a politically and socially homogenous group who were reactionary and mediocre and numbered about 20. Until his death in 1909 the sinister Baron Fritz von Holstein had a perniciously strong influence on the Kaiser, discrediting the Kaiser at home and abroad. The Kaiser's other chancellors and their years in office were Count Leo von Caprivi (1890–94), Prince Chlodwig zu Hohenlohe-Schilingsfurst (1894–1900), Bernard von Bülow (1900–08), and finally Theobald von Bethmann-Hollweg (1909–17). They were all weak and provided no effective check on the emperor as Bismarck had been able to do with Emperor William I. The failure to check the Kaiser was also due to fragmentation and confusion in policy making. For instance, the military services were able to reverse or frustrate the decisions of the chancellor and the Foreign Office. Of critical importance in this regard was the naval staffs' consistent opposition to Chancellor Bethmann-Hollweg's attempts to reach a naval accommodation with the British, which might have avoided the naval arms race. Equally pernicious was the development of the Schlieffen Plan by the army's general staff to cope with a war with France. It required the violation of Belgian neutrality, of which the chancellor was not informed. Similarly in 1909 the general staff changed the defensive character of the Dual Alliance by a commitment to back Austria under any conditions. The Kaiser also had various advisers who were sometimes the heads of military cabinets and other times just traveling companions who plotted to change courses of action agreed upon with his chancellors. William II unfortunately chose mediocre chiefs of staff for the Prussian army, replacing in 1890 the famous General Helmuth von Moltke (the great) with General von Waldersee, then General Hans von Schlieffen, and then General Helmuth von Moltke (the younger), whose mediocre talent failed to bring Germany a quick victory in 1914. Finally, the Reichstag itself was responsible for not taking initiatives to change the balance of power in the government. A few of the causes of the failure of the Reichstag were due to the strong interest groups of agriculture and heavy industry, especially steel, which promoted tariff protectionism, imperialism, and militarism. Two incidents that provided opportunities for the Reichstag to challenge the Kaiser were the London *Daily Telegraph* Affair in 1908 and the Zabern Affair in 1913.

After some 20 years of economic recession, 1895 heralded the start of a new period of economic prosperity and rapid technical development for German industry. The expansion of the chemical and electronics industries in particular led to a second wave of industrialization. Powerful companies such as Krupp and Siemens were two that dominated the market. The shipping industry was also rapidly expanding under the leadership of the Hamburg-America Line and North German Lloyd. In order to promote their interests, employers formed large and influential organizations such as the Central Association of German Industrialists, which favored tariffs against imports of grain and steel, while the more export-driven chemical and electrical industries representing the more liberal of the middle class and National Liberal Party opposed them. A Federation of Farmers was organized to fight against the reduction in grain tariffs, which sought to gain support through anti-Semitic agitation. Trade unions already had been established in the 1860s, representing the interests of workers. They were unable, however, to develop large organizations until the Anti-Socialist Laws had been repealed by Kaiser William II. The Free Socialist Unions were organized into industrial federations and had 2.5 million members by 1913. The liberal Hirsh-Dunker labor association and the various Christian unions were of lesser significance.

The repeal of the Anti-Socialist Laws and the passing of social legislation in 1890 were aimed at reconciling the Social-Democratic Party to the state, although it was resisted by its leader, August Bebel. The Kaiser was very disappointed and resentfully described the workers as "treacherous comrades." Unable to reimpose the suppression policy, it was proposed by Chancellor Hohenlohe-Schillingfürst that political laws be tightened up (Subversion Law, 1894) and strikers be imprisoned (prison proposal, 1899), which was rejected by the Reichstag. The socialists started to question their adherence to the ideology of revolution and discussed the possibility of bringing about change gradually through reforms. Full employment and rising real incomes cast doubt on Karl Marx's theory of the impoverishment of workers. It was Georg von Vollmar and Eduard Bernstein who were the leading spokesmen of the reformists, and who were primarily supported by the trade unions. The opponents were led by the Marxist Karl Kautsky.

THE FIRST WORLD WAR

ALLIANCES, IMPERIALISM, AND THE ROAD TO WAR

After the dismissal of Bismarck by Kaiser William, a diplomatic revolution occurred resulting from the Kaiser's decision to steer a "new course" in world affairs. The young emperor repudiated Bismarck's policy toward Russia by not renewing in 1890 the Reinsurance Treaty of 1887, after which Russia turned to France for an ally. The Kaiser also proceeded to alienate England by building a large naval fleet and pursuing an imperialist foreign policy. The building of a "deterrent fleet," which was to be two-thirds of the size of England's, was a matter of prestige for him and his advisers, especially Admiral Alfred von Tirpitz (1849–1930). Although England and Germany could have been natural allies had Germany not pursued its naval and colonial policies, these placed Germany and England on a collision course. A naval arms race ensued in addition to the military arms race already taking place.

In the imperialist race to divide the world among the European nations, William II demanded a "place in the sun" for a German colonial empire. German navalism and imperialism went hand in hand with theories of Social Darwinism, which linked the struggle among nations and individuals to policies that would make Germany the strongest nation and the most fit in the struggle among nations to survive. German imperialism did not have any great success: Between 1897 and 1899 only Tsingsau, the Caroline-Marianne-Palau islands, and parts of the Samoan islands were colonized. The Kaiser's aggressive speeches and the brutality shown by colonial troops in suppressing colonial uprisings damaged Germany's reputation in the world.

Furthermore, the Kaiser interfered in the imperialist interests of Britain in South Africa, dispatching the famous Krüger Telegram congratulating the Boer Free State in repulsing the Jameson raid and also warning that Germany would not allow any attack on that Transvaal state.

Moreover, the Reich did not take advantage of the opportunity for a rapprochement with Great Britain when Anglo-French rivalry reached a peak over the Sudan in the Fashoda conflict in 1898. In addition to the building of a battle fleet, the Berlin to Baghdad railway project challenged British interests in the Middle East and India. In 1904 Britain and France finally settled their differences over colonial policy and signed the Entente Cordiale. German attempts to take control of Morocco failed over the joint opposition of Britain and France. The defeat of Russia in the Russo-Japanese War (1904–05) encouraged Russia to join with Britain and France in 1907 to form the Triple Entente, with the result that Germany began to feel encircled.

A World War I recruiting poster featuring a German soldier, which says "Everything for the Fatherland, everything for freedom" *(Library of Congress)*

The competition between Austria and Russia in the Balkans created further crises, especially when Russia and its ally Serbia backed down in 1908 over the annexation by Austria-Hungary of Bosnia-Herzegovina. The attempt made by the Balkan people to become united into nation-states during the Balkan Wars of 1912–13 by dividing up the European territories of Turkey further heated up the "powder barrel of Europe" in the Balkans. On June 28, 1914, the Austrian heir to the throne, Archduke Francis Ferdinand, and his wife were assassinated in Sarajevo by a young Serbian, Gavrilo Princip, working for the secret nationalist society the Black Hand. The Austrians decided to solve the problem of Serbian nationalism by resisting the Serbian government's practically complete acceptance of its ultimatum. The Austrian government was emboldened by the secret support it received from the German military. While German diplomacy was geared toward avoiding war, the army was not. Great Britain wanted to negotiate. On the other hand, France was bound to support the Russians in any Balkan conflict resulting from the agreement made in 1912 and thereby rejecting all Austrian annexation plans. When the Russians ordered a general mobilization on July 31, 1914, after negotiations between the Kaiser and the Russian czar failed to halt the march to war, Berlin decided in favor of a military solution, ordering mobilization. The organization of the European powers into two opposing alliance systems and the mobilization plans of their armies destroyed any hope of solving the conflict through negotiation. Although reluctant, Great Britain finally decided for war with Germany when the Germans violated Belgian neutrality.

THE QUESTION OF RESPONSIBILITY

The question of responsibility for the First World War has long been acrimoniously debated. All nations bore some responsibility. The major burden of responsibility, however, for causing the world war lay with Germany. Imperial Germany had encouraged Austria's local war with its so-called Blank Check against Serbia, and it did little to prevent a continental war that it was confident of winning. Germany certainly did not desire a world war, because it hoped to keep Britain neutral. It did, however, take the risk of expanding the war with its invasion of Belgium. The German general staff saw the assassination of the archduke as an opportunity for a preventive war. According to the papers of von Jagow, the German secretary of state for foreign affairs, the chief of staff, von Moltke, in June 1914 asked the government to start a preventive war, which was denied, though the government was confident of success in case war broke out. The generals had advised that war was inevitable anyway in about two years, and Chancellor Bethmann-Hollweg believed their assessment.

CONDUCT OF THE WAR

Enthusiastic crowds throughout Germany greeted the declaration of war on France and Russia in August 1914. Most people believed that the war would be short and the enemy quickly vanquished. When it was time to vote for the funds to fight the war, even the so-called enemies of the state, the Social Democrats, supported the government's request. The war did not turn out as expected. The first great strategy of the war was the Schlieffen Plan, which, however, failed to quickly defeat the French. The German advance was halted at the Battle of the Marne. The war of mobility quickly slowed, and before long, trench warfare ruled. No one had anticipated the results of industrial warfare with machine guns, poison gas, barbed wire, massive artillery bombardment, and airplanes. The new heavily destructive weapons made it difficult for either side to gain much territory as an unheroic war of attrition ensued. The second great strategy, the Verdun offensive, also failed to defeat the French. At home the Kaiser declared a truce between the political parties, declaring that all were "only Germans." Yet, martial law was declared, and effective civilian government and civil rights were curtailed. As the war progressed, the weak Reich chancellors had to submit more and more to the will of the army supreme command. The nominal head was Field Marshal Paul von Hindenburg, who had been recalled from retirement, but the real power was Quartermaster General Erich Ludendorff. Hindenburg had become famous by stopping the "Russian steamroller" in the east at the Battles of Tannenburg and the Masaurian Lakes. The naval strategy also failed as the High Seas Fleet remained at base in Kiel and Wilhelmshaven, fearing defeat by the superior Royal Navy.

The chief of the admiralty staff, Admiral Henning von Holtzendorff (1915–18), now argued in favor of a third great strategy: unrestricted submarine warfare, which would defeat the Royal Navy. Bethmann Hollweg and some other leaders of the German government were aware of the dangers, especially that it would bring the United States and other neutrals into the war. Hindenburg and Ludendorff along with the admiralty finally convinced the Kaiser that Germany could gain its imperialist objectives through submarine warfare, ignoring the political problems resulting from the entry of the United States into the war, which occurred after the sinking of the *Lusitania*. After the Bolshevik Revolution in October 1917, Russia under the leadership of Vladimir Lenin and Leon Trotsky left the war and accepted the Peace of Brest-Litovsk, by which Russia lost her western provinces and Ukraine was granted independence. Meanwhile, in 1916 the Germans became determined to win at all costs. The moderate Chancellor Bethmann Hollweg was dismissed, and Georg Michaelis was completely under the military dictatorship of Hindenburg and Ludendorff.

PEACE RESOLUTION, REFORM, AND THE ARMISTICE

In July 1917 the moderates in the Reichstag proposed a Peace Resolution emphasizing a negotiated peace, but were opposed by the annexationists of the Fatherland Party. Popular unrest began to manifest itself by strikes, demonstrations, criticism in the press, and a radicalization in the ranks of the socialists. The left wing of the Social Democratic Party formed the Independent Social Democratic Party (USPD), and a minority of radical socialists formed the Spartacus League under Karl Liebknecht and Rosa Luxemburg, later to become the German Communist Party (KPD). There also was pressure to reform the government, which only succeeded when the great spring offensive of 1918 failed. The October Reforms by the new chancellor, Prince Max von Baden, represented the first real step toward a parliamentary system of government. With the military situation at the brink of collapse, Ludendorff pressed the government to request an armistice. Ludendorff wanted to shift the burden of responsibility for the war and its loss on the civilian leaders, those who would be elected and have to sign the armistice and the peace treaty. This was the basis of the "Legend of the Stab in the Back," which would absolve the military and blame the leftist political parties for the humiliation of defeat. The political leaders accepted the opportunity to bring about political reform and hoped that the Allied peace terms would be lenient according to President Wilson's Fourteen Points.

NOVEMBER REVOLUTION

1918–1919

AN UNPLANNED REVOLUTION

The November Revolution came as an unwanted child in the midst of confusion that resulted from the armistice, which surprised most Germans. Some historians prefer to describe it as a collapse rather than a revolution. The last revolution in German history, which occurred during 1848–49, like the French Revolution of 1789 and the Russian Revolution of 1917, had been preceded by periods of preparation during which discontent was aroused by intellectual and political ferment. Preparation for these revolutions had also clarified political goals and identified some potential revolutionary leaders. No such tradition preceded the revolution in Germany in 1918. While the official program of the Social Democrats spoke of "revolutionary principles," the whole notion of causing a revolution was absent from the minds of Socialist leaders and party members. The events of November 1918 surprised most Germans. The Social Democrats essentially adopted the revolution after it had started, and their actions during the revolution went opposite to their traditions. They suppressed the radical Spartacists, and they preserved a middle-class instead of creating a working-class society and out of necessity recreated the army. The great tragedy for Germany was that the revolution produced few leaders who enthusiastically and passionately believed in republican and democratic ideals and institutions.

The notes of President Woodrow Wilson of October 14 and 23 emphasized the need for Germany to destroy those forces in Germany that had threatened the peace of the world. This included the surrenders of military leaders and the Kaiser. By October 31 external pressure for the abdication of the Kaiser had become so intense that the cabinet was forced to discuss the matter seriously. President Wilson's demand that the Kaiser abdicate was a powerful factor in turning the country against William, particularly after the four years of war and privation that had led Germany to a humiliating defeat. The popular mood and also that of Social Democratic leaders was not necessarily against the institution of the monarchy but was directed exclusively against the Kaiser and the crown prince. The Kaiser delayed his decision to abdicate, and the interaction between the desire for peace and the notion that the emperor was obstructing peace negotiations led to the agitation that resulted in the proclamation of a republic on November 9.

MUTINY IN THE NAVY

At this juncture discipline in the armed forces began to break down. The trouble started among naval units in Kiel and Wilhelmshaven. Since the Battle of Jutland in 1916 the German High Seas Fleet had been virtually confined to the North Sea ports as a defensive screen for U-boat warfare. On October 28, however, the fleet was ordered to sea for a major operation in the English Channel. Here was an example of the pride and egotism of the German naval staff, which was determined to end the war with an impressive battle. They also were trying to assure that the navy would outlive the war. The sailors had resented the harsh discipline imposed on them in port and mutinous outbreaks and refusal to obey orders had already taken place. Now they demonstrated, and soldiers were called out to restore order. Then both the soldiers and sailors joined together and hoisted red flags; the German revolution had begun. The Kiel mutiny was the first of a chain of revolts that spread across Germany in the next few days and that finally disrupted the German Empire.

POLITICAL PARTIES UNPREPARED

The left-wing political parties were unprepared when the revolution came. The Majority Socialists certainly did not want a violent upheaval even though they had peace and democratic reform as their goals. Surprisingly, they would have been happy with a monarchy that had real constitutional limitations. The Independent Socialists who had split off from the Majority Socialists had actually exploited unrest in their campaign for an immediate end to the war. Most of their prominent leaders—for example, Hugo Haase and Karl Kautsky—were more interested in peace than in revolution. Some of them had worked together with radical factory workers in large cities to further agitation for revolution. They did not, however, understand that the German state was vulnerable to revolution. The really revolutionary pressure group was called the Sparticists, who were politically radical and to the left of the Independent Socialists. What made political change possible was the sudden demoralization created within Germany by the news of impending defeat, which paralyzed the repressive forces of the regime. It was the soldiers in the rear areas who played a key role in overthrowing the German Empire. They alone could have suppressed the revolutionary movement, but they did not. Although they were affected by antiwar feeling, they had little inclination to revolt. Yet, they found themselves unable to shoot their countrymen just to continue a war that had been lost.

A REVOLUTIONARY PATTERN

A pattern of revolutionary activity made itself apparent. Mass meetings in favor of peace and political reform were held, followed by marches and demonstrations. Soldiers and sailors usually made up the most radical elements in these groups as well as in the leadership that emerged. The police and military found that they could not ban demonstrations and enforce restrictions. When officials retreated, this encouraged the demonstrators to take more dramatic actions. Majority Socialists sometimes were able to take over leadership of the crowds, but more often agitators would lead the crowds to barracks, prisons, and government offices. Soldiers were disarmed and persuaded to join the revolution. Political prisoners were released. Municipal and, in some cases, government authority was taken over by the rebels. Revolutionary power was then exercised by the so-called Workers' and Soldiers' Councils, otherwise known, as in Russia, as Soviets.

WORKERS' AND SOLDIERS' COUNCILS

The councils owed their conception to the Russian Revolution, but that is not to say that Russian agents had brought about the German revolution. Most Germans did not have a precise idea of the form and function of the Soviets, and few had a clear idea about what was happening in Russia. Much confusion existed in both socialist parties about the purpose of the councils. Most Majority Socialists considered it their task to prevent a chaotic civil war and starvation, and so the councils were seen as devices to maintain law and order. The Independent Socialists saw the councils as institutions of working-class expression and thought that they might inspire workers to be more politically active. Also, the councils were seen as a means to create more democratic institutions in Germany and to take some initial steps toward socializing the economy. Finally, an insignificant number of socialists thought the councils ought to be instruments of proletarian dictatorship, which would replace parliaments altogether.

KURT EISNER AND REVOLUTION IN BAVARIA

During the first few days after the disturbances at Kiel, political power had changed in only a few northwestern cities. On November 7, however, a more serious and significant disturbance took place in Munich, the capital of Bavaria. The Independent Social Democrat and journalist Kurt Eisner turned an election campaign into agitation for a German republic. Faced with a complete breakdown of police and military authority, the last of the Wittelsbach kings, the aged Ludwig III, left his palace in the middle of the night and never returned. On November 8 Eisner announced that Bavaria was a republic and he was its new premier. The significance of this event is that it sealed the fate of the German Empire. The Majority Socialists could not afford to let the Independents take the lead in winning power as they had in Bavaria. They had to act quickly if their party was to control events in the future.

A REPUBLIC PROCLAIMED

Meanwhile, in Berlin the situation had been deteriorating. A group of factory shop stewards in Berlin's heavy industrial plants were preparing for a revolution to take place on November 11. Workers' and Soldiers' Councils were being set up, despite the express prohibition of the Army High Command. Until then, the Majority Social Democrats (SPD) had managed to prevent any serious outburst among Berlin's factory workers. An ultimatum was presented on November 7 to the cabinet that if the Kaiser and the Crown Prince did not abdicate within two days the SPD would leave the coalition government that had been established. On November 9 Prince Max of Baden announced the Kaiser's abdication and handed over his office as Reich chancellor to the socialist leader, Friedrich Ebert, who offered seats in the cabinet to the Independent Social Democrats. It appeared too late to save the institution of the monarchy. Crowds of soldiers and workers were marching on the government buildings. Now the danger existed that the radical Sparticists and their leader, Karl Liebknecht, would take over the leadership of the revolution and declare Germany a republic. Faced with this situation, Philip Scheidemann went to a window of the Reichstag building and announced to cheering spectators that Germany had become a republic. The Social Democrats had not wanted a republic but now had declared one.

A SEVERE ARMISTICE

On the morning of November 10 the Imperial cabinet met for the last time. Friedrich Ebert took the chair as chancellor. A German armistice commission under Erzberger had already gone to negotiate with the western Allies and had relayed the conditions to be imposed upon the German armed forces The armistice terms were severe, but Ebert knew that nonacceptance meant that an Allied invasion would occur. So Germany's representatives signed the armistice on November 11 and hostilities ceased. But Ebert was haunted by the fear that a collapse of military discipline or public order in Germany might also bring Entente troops across the Rhine. Reports from German embassies in neutral countries suggested that if any sign of Bolshevism appeared in Germany an invasion might follow.

ESTABLISHMENT OF A REVOLUTIONARY GOVERNMENT

The next goal was to establish a revolutionary government. Real power in Berlin rested at that moment with the Workers' and Soldiers' Councils. The SPD campaigned vigorously to make sure that delegates who were sympathetic to them were elected to the councils. The speakers of the SPD were more experienced and better known. Ebert also persuaded the leadership of the Independents (USPD) to cooperate with him in forming a government. On November 10 the leaders met and formed a ruling cabinet called the Council of People's Delegates, composed of a total of six Majority Social Democrats and three Independents with Ebert as chairman.

The new revolutionary government was an uneasy but not impossible coalition. Its Social Democratic members were eager to reestablish order in Germany and to organize the election of a National Assembly. Once these objectives were gained it would be possible to negotiate a peace treaty with the Entente powers and begin the process of economic reconstruction. They believed that the sort of Germany they wanted could be created through the National Assembly with the aid of existing bureaucratic institutions. Ebert kept the civil service of the deposed Kaiser's Reich in office, expecting that they would be necessary to keep order and feed the population. The government under the Majority Socialists did manage to prevent a civil war and protect the republic against radical revolutionary groups. What they failed to realize was that the authoritarian forces from the old bureaucracy—the judiciary, the army, and industrialists—were strengthened. Instead of the nationalization of industry, an important decision on future worker-management relations in Germany was taken by the Stinnes-Legien Agreement of November 15, 1918, in which industry recognized trade unions as partners in negotiations on wages and working conditions, and in return the unions dropped their demands for nationalization of various industries. In reality this social partnership only meant a formal equality of status.

However, many problems made cooperation between the Majority Socialists and the Independents very difficult. Personal animosities created by the split in the German labor movement during the war were not easily forgotten. The SPD leadership had supported the war effort and had finally been included in the government. The USPD had been ostracized as subversives or even traitors. Some of them had suffered imprisonment, as did Kurt Eisner, who had led the revolution in Bavaria. They, in turn, regarded the collaborationist attitude of the SPD leaders as a betrayal of socialist principles. Ebert wanted to end disorders as soon as possible and call elections to a National Assembly, while the Independents considered the revolution as a victory and heroic achievement. Furthermore, they thought that German society ought to be fundamentally altered with immediate steps toward socializing large-scale industry. They believed that unless radical change was carried out as part of the revolution, it might never happen. The Majority Socialists thought that the National Assembly that would represent the nation should make that decision.

In the struggle between the Workers' and Soldiers' Councils and the state bureaucracy the authority of German officialdom proved too great for the councils. They were unable to exercise any real control over internal administration. A National Congress of German Councils met in Berlin on December 16 and voted for rapid elections for a National Constituent Assembly. Attempts by the congress to bring about socialization and army reform were evaded. A Central Committee was set up and dominated by Social Democrats.

EBERT MAKES A DEAL WITH THE ARMY

Despite the failures of the executive committee, Ebert's government was still faced with the problem of organizing an effective armed force for protection. Although the Soldiers' Councils had power among the troops in Berlin, they could not become the foundation of a republican army. Units were breaking up, and by the middle of December it appeared that the army was dissolving. Some soldiers remained in their barracks, but that was largely to obtain food and shelter. Indeed, some of them, like Adolf Hitler, who was in the barracks in Munich, were disgusted with the collapse of the imperial government and blamed the revolution and the Marxists for their humiliation. Since Ebert wanted to maintain order, he and General Groener of the army made an agreement known as the Ebert-Groener pact. On the night of November 9 General Groener had telephoned Ebert and offered him a deal. Having replaced General Ludendorff in the Supreme Command, Groener offered to cooperate with the Republican government if it was prepared to maintain discipline in the armed forces to prevent revolutionary disaffection from spreading to soldiers on the front. Once in Germany it was hoped that the Front Army would provide a reliable force with which to stabilize the situation within Germany. But Groener also wanted the officer corps to be free of civilian parliamentary interference and wanted to limit the activities of the Soldiers' Councils. Without consulting his colleagues, Ebert agreed. A private phone linked the High Command to the Reich Chancellery, and consultations between the two men were conducted without difficulty. Although the short-term practical needs of the republic for security were met in this way, Ebert's decision, unfortunately, left the military foundations of the Prussian-German authoritarian state intact and independent; the army remained "a state within a state." The Independents urged that an officer known to approve of the revolution be appointed as the head of the Prussian War Ministry, which administered military affairs. Ebert, unfortunately, disregarded their suggestion and chose Colonel Reinhardt, who was a monarchist but promised never to use his troops to attack the government. So the Independents and their supporters in the councils took the view that Ebert was giving way to counter-revolutionary pressure.

THE SPARTACISTS

When a conflict occurred between the majority Socialist leaders and a mutinous unit of sailors quartered in Berlin, the Independent Socialists decided to resign on December 29 from the government. Carrying on alone, Ebert and his colleagues faced a tense situation, which was made worse by Germany's difficult economic situation, in turn made more difficult by the continuation of the Allied blockade. The Spartacists and radical Independents did their best to mobilize support among the numerous unemployed workers and were now totally opposed to Ebert's government. The most consistent radical voices on the left belonged to the Spartacist Union, whose leaders, Rosa Luxemburg and Karl Liebknecht, argued that the November Revolution was a sham and that the proletariat must be mobilized to take over the government. On December 31 the Spartacists held a congress at which it was decided to break away from the Independents and form a separate German Communist Party. Under the leadership of Rosa Luxemburg the party seemed likely to follow an independent course from the Russian Communists, even though Karl Radek, a Bolshevik agent of Lenin, had been present at the foundation of the congress.

The German Communists in their meetings and their newspaper, *The Red Flag (Die Rote Fahne)*, were encouraging a new stage of revolution, an immediate insurrection. However, Rosa Luxemburg and Karl Liebknecht had no desire to initiate a coup, instead thinking that the German people had to be educated first on the conservative nature of the Ebert government, and then aroused to revolutionary action. Most of the rank and file were willing to risk a conflict, while Berlin was still in an atmosphere of turmoil. Successful large-scale demonstrations took place, and a revolutionary committee declared that Ebert's government was deposed. This Spartacist rising was virtually unplanned and chaotic. Once the fighting had started, however, Rosa Luxemburg believed that as a leader she ought not to desert the rebels or to encourage them to surrender. The rebels were crushed after some bitter fighting. The new defense minister in Ebert's government, Gustav Noske, made use of volunteers (Free Corps), raised and led by the old army commanders, most of whom were opposed to the revolution. The officers in one of these units murdered Rosa Luxemburg and Karl Liebknecht on January 15. Noske was then regarded on the left as the butcher of the working class. A hastily formed Soviet Republic was also violently repressed in Munich at the beginning of May 1919, when perhaps as many as 1,000 people were killed as the Free Corps entered the city. Noske's forces freed Berlin and Munich from the fear of communist insurrection, but working-class unity was destroyed and never repaired.

On January 19, when the elections for the National Assembly took place, the Social Democrats lost their monopoly over political life. The votes for socialist parties were in the minority, and the opportunity for fundamental social and economic change had passed. Now the middle-class parties of the majority favored a constitutional republic. The tide of revolution had turned.

INTERPRETATION OF THE REVOLUTION

Was the revolution a failure as some historians have claimed? It was neither an unequivocal success nor a failure. It was a failure in the sense that it did not bring socialism to Germany. Yet it may be doubted whether most Germans were prepared to accept large-scale social experiments as the revolutionary idealists desired. Certainly those who urged radical measures were probably inspired by the example in Russia, but there was a lack of agreement on goals and methods. The organs of working-class self-expression, the Workers' and Soldiers' Councils, could not assert themselves against the experienced labor leaders and civil servants, nor against the popularity of a representative parliament. On the other hand, the revolution had succeeded in overthrowing the old Imperial regime, even though the bureaucracy and army remained. It was clear that the new political institutions would be genuinely democratic in a way that they had never been before. Even though Germany had not been totally transformed, the limited goals of the Social Democrats and the compromises that were necessary promised to make the Weimar Republic freer and more egalitarian than Imperial Germany had ever been. In many ways the November Revolution succeeded in achieving the liberal goals of 1848.

VERSAILLES TREATY AND WEIMAR CONSTITUTION

A VENGEFUL PEACE

Even as revolutionary violence swirled around them, the leaders of Germany attempted to solve the serious problems that faced the defeated nation. They had to negotiate a peace treaty with the Allies and then draft a new constitution for the republic. They were more successful in writing a new democratic constitution than they were in obtaining a peace treaty that would ensure peace and stability in Europe. The victors and especially the French premier, Georges Clemenceau, turned out to be vengeful. They rejected President Woodrow Wilson's lenient Fourteen Points and sought to inflict a severe peace on Germany. During the Paris Peace Conference Clemenceau complained that it was far easier to make war than peace, which is far from true. It takes wise men to make a lasting peace. The victors could have learned from what had been done at the Congress of Vienna after the Napoleonic Wars. The diplomat and historian George Kennan would call the peace "vindictive madness" and *The Economist* stated that the treaty was the war's "final crime." The ill-conceived Treaty of Versailles would poison relations between Germany and the rest of the world. Even more unfortunate was that the republican politicians in Germany who were not responsible for the war would be blamed by most Germans as having signed a humiliating peace treaty. The Weimar Republic would never be able to escape from under the shadow of Versailles. In the end the treaty and the reparations that followed would be major reasons for the fall of the Weimar Republic and the birth of the Nazi dictatorship.

THE NATIONAL ASSEMBLY

After months of waiting, more than 80 percent of the German electorate went to the polls on January 19, 1919, to elect 435 members to the National Assembly, each member representing 150,000 people. In this election the German people rejected the radical programs of the revolution, casting 76.2 percent of their votes for the moderate parties, 37.9 percent for the Social Democrats (SPD), 19.7 percent for the Center Party, and 18.6 percent for the Democrats (DDP). Together these parties, which had supported the Peace Resolution of 1917, formed what was called the Weimar Coalition. They would dominate the National Assembly and write the new constitution. The radical left-wing Independent Socialists (USPD) won only 7.6 percent of the vote, and the right gained only 14.7 percent of which 4.4 percent was for the German People's Party (DVP) and 10.3 percent was for the Nationalists (DNVP). The Communists (KPD) boycotted the elections in protest of the failure of the revolution to create a communist state.

On February 6, 1919, Friedrich Ebert, the head of the provisional government, opened the National Assembly, not in Berlin but in the peaceful city of Weimar, the home of Goethe. Ebert's speech praised the accomplishments of the provisional government and proclaimed a new era of freedom and prosperity for the Germany people, who were finally free of their despotic kings. Ebert also asked for the loyal support of the people, calling upon them to unite behind the republic. The head of the provisional government sharply condemned any attempt by the Allies meeting in Paris to impose a repressive peace on the republic.

THE GOALS OF THE PEACEMAKERS

While the delegates to the National Assembly occupied themselves with writing the constitution, the representatives of the Allies met in Paris to discuss the terms of the peace treaty. Unlike the Congress of Vienna, which rebuilt Europe after the Napoleonic Wars, the Paris Peace Conference refused to allow the defeated states to participate in its deliberations. Although the 27 victorious nations sent 70 men to discuss the future shape of Europe, the real power and decision making rested in the hands of the Big Four, Georges Clemenceau of France, David Lloyd George of England, Vittorio Orlando of Italy, and Woodrow Wilson of the United States. Clemenceau's goals were to weaken Germany so that it would never again be a threat to France and to seek French annexation of the left bank of the Rhine and former German colonies. Lloyd George had promised British voters that he would make the Germans pay for the war, place the former Kaiser on trial for war crimes, and weaken Germany so that she could never again menace the stability of the world. By comparison the goals of Vittorio Orlando were to annex the Italian-speaking areas of South Tyrol, Trieste, and Fiume. Woodrow Wilson idealistically condemned the old diplomacy and spoke of foreign policy being under the control of the people. Wilson spoke loudly of self-determination for all nations and the creation of an international organization that would use democratic procedures and make war obsolete. Unfortunately, Wilson abandoned most of his principles under pressure from the other statesmen in order that the international organization, the League of Nations, could be established. Wilson made no effort to fulfill his promise of peace terms based on his Fourteen Points. The Big Four met behind closed doors and prevented the Germans and their allies from even discussing the peace terms. Instead, the victors demanded acceptance of the peace terms under the threat of renewed fighting. The failure of Wilson to carry out his promise of open negotiations gave the Germans still another reason to feel betrayed.

When the sessions opened, Clemenceau immediately demanded a vengeful peace that would tear the left bank of the Rhine from Germany and give France the Saar valley with its rich coal deposits. The French premier further demanded the occupation of the Rhineland by Allied troops for 30 years. Striving to fulfill at least part of his promises, Wilson insisted that the period of occupation be cut in half and that the Saar valley be placed under the League of Nations for the same time. Attempting to placate the French, Wilson proposed to grant the French title to the coal mines in the Saar as compensation for the French mines destroyed in the war. The French also demanded that the new Polish state be awarded the city of Danzig and the surrounding areas as an outlet to the Baltic Sea. This was resisted by Lloyd George, who insisted that the city be placed under the mandate of the League of Nations and that Poland, which would not be awarded the city, would get an outlet to the sea through the Vistula valley. It was also decided that the mixed German-Polish population of Upper Silesia could decide their future through a plebiscite.

TERMS OF THE TREATY

On May 7, 1919, the Germans were shocked to receive the terms of the peace treaty. The Reich would lose large areas, including Alsace-Lorraine, a few towns in Belgium, most of Posen and West Prussia, and all former colonial possessions. Both the Saarland and Upper Silesia would be detached from Germany and their futures determined by plebiscites to be held under the supervision of the League of Nations. While some of these territorial losses, for example, Alsace-Lorraine, could be justified, others were questionable because many Germans living in the lost areas failed to be granted the right of self-determination as promised by Wilson. The Germans were especially angry over the creation of the Polish Corridor in former German areas, separating East Prussia from the rest of the Reich. The territorial arrangements would substantially contribute to shattering the peace and stability of Europe.

The treaty also called for the destruction of the German military. In the future the German army could consist of no more than 100,000 men. It was forbidden to possess large guns and was allowed only a limited number of smaller ones. For the navy submarines were expressly forbidden, and only six warships and smaller craft were allowed. The prohibition of conscription had unintended consequences, for it ensured that the German army would remain an elite corps of professionals, loyal only to their commanders and their interpretation of nationalism. This served to further strengthen the power of the officer corps and prevented any attempt to replace the professional force with a more democratic army, as German liberals had hoped for more than 100 years.

WAR GUILT AND REPARATIONS

Perhaps the most severe aspects of the peace treaty were the provisions designed to fulfill Wilson's demand for compensation for the destruction of the war. The victors required the Germans to accept the entire guilt for the outbreak of the war in Article 231 of the treaty and to pay for all civilian damages and cost of the armies of occupation. The Allies forced the Germans to turn over to them all German merchant ships of more than 1,600 tons, half of those between 800 and 1,600 tons, and a quarter of the fishing fleet. The winners of the war also demanded that the Germans build 200,000 tons of shipping annually to be given to the Allies without payment. Not only did the losers have to deplete their shipping fleet, but they also had to deliver large quantities of coal to France, Belgium, and Italy during the next 10 years. All German property in the Allied countries was to be sold, with the proceeds going to the victors. Finally, the Germans had to internationalize all their rivers and to allow Allied warships to pass through the Kiel Canal. By March 1 the Germans had to agree to deliver 20 billion gold marks worth of goods, which was the beginning of reparations with a total bill coming at a later date. The economic aspects of the treaty proved to be its most severe section. The Germans ended the First World War with a national debt of 144 billion gold marks. The burden of reparations in material and money harmed the already weak Germany economy, helping to cause serious inflation and leaving thousands of workers without jobs. The War Guilt Clause was clearly based on a total misrepresentation of the facts and unjustly made the Germans accept the blame for causing the war. The Germans were certainly to blame for bloodshed, but so were the Serbs, the Russians, and the French.

DENUNCIATION AND RELUCTANT ACCEPTANCE

The publication of the terms of the peace treaty shocked the German people. When Germany surrendered, it was believed that the peace would be based on Wilson's Fourteen Points, which were in spirit rejected. The National Assembly met in special session in Berlin on May 12 to discuss the document. One by one the political leaders of all the parties rose to strongly denounce the treaty and demand its revision. After the stormy session ended the angry delegates stood to sing the German national anthem, "Deutschland über Alles." Ebert, who had been elected president of the republic on February 11, asked the Allies to reconsider, only to be told that Germany had to sign by June 23 or face severe consequences. A major political crisis resulted, and the entire ministry resigned in protest as no politician wanted to bear the blame for accepting the harsh terms of the treaty. Ebert even asked General Groener if the army could protect the country should the Allies invade. In no way was the army capable, Groener replied, and told Ebert that he had no choice but to sign with the hope of a revision in the future. A new coalition government headed by Gustav Bauer recommended that the National Assembly approve the treaty, which it did on June 23 by a vote of 237 to 138. Some delegates abstained, and some refused to participate in the national humiliation. The treaty was signed by two obscure German politicians in the Hall of Mirrors at Versailles, where almost a half century before the German princes had proclaimed William I their emperor. When the full impact of the treaty and the reparations were felt by the German nation, disillusionment with Wilson's broken word and the harsh terms of the Treaty of Versailles grew. Many vowed to revenge the disgrace and overthrow the leaders and the republic that had accepted its humiliating terms. Had the Allied leaders realized how much responsibility the treaty would have for the failure of Germany's democratic republic and rise of Nazi tyranny, they might have done otherwise.

THE WEIMAR CONSTITUTION

In the meantime the National Assembly completed its work on the constitution and overwhelmingly approved it on July 31, 1919, by a vote of 262 to 75. The Weimar Constitution went into effect on August 14, 1919. Konrad Haussmann said of the Weimar Constitution that it was "born in suffering" and that it represented "the law of a people oppressed by the enemy." Although it reflected the condition of the German people in their hour of defeat, it also reflected their desire for government to strengthen the Reich, based on freedom and justice and to serve the cause of peace and progress. It was a democratic document emanating from the sovereignty of the people with guarantees for civil rights. The legislative branch of the government was to consist of two houses of parliament. The lower house or Reichstag represented the people and was to be elected by universal, equal, direct, and secret ballot every four years. The upper house, the Reichsrat, represented the states. The representatives to the Reichstag were not elected by majority vote as in the United States, but rather by a complicated system called "proportional representation," which was designed to give political parties the same percentage in the lower house as they received at the polls. Although democratic and protective of small parties, this proved to be one of the constitution's major flaws because it made possible a multitude of political parties. It made it very difficult to form ministries with the support of the majority of the Reichstag and caused considerable instability. The states, which had been reduced from 25 to 18, retained their old rights and chose the representatives to the Reichsrat. The constitution established a centralized state in which the central government retained all executive, judicial, legislative, and financial power over matters of national concern. Thus, the National Assembly rejected Hugo Preuss's proposal in favor of a stronger federalism, which like the royal governments it replaced jealously guarded their rights.

The president would be elected in direct popular election for a term of seven years and serve as head of state to the new Germany. In some respects his powers were greater than those wielded by the German emperor. Thus, he could dissolve the Reichstag even without the consent of the upper house, the Reichsrat, which the Imperial Constitution had required. In an effort to prevent the president from becoming a republican kaiser, the constitution required that his actions be countersigned by the chancellor or cabinet officer concerned. The constitution also gave the Reichstag the right to remove the president by a two-thirds vote, subject to approval by a national referendum. The president's chief duty was to appoint the chancellor and the ministry, with the requirement that the cabinet enjoy the support of the majority of the Reichstag. The president also was commander in chief of the armed forces, which the Kaiser had been only in time of war. Despite the limitations placed on the power of the president by the constitution, he was granted extraordinary emergency powers under Article 48 of the constitution. In case "public safety and order were seriously disturbed," the president could rule by decree and even suspend fundamental rights such as habeas corpus, secrecy of the mails, freedom of expression, inviolability of the home and of private property, and could use the army to enforce his decrees. Although this power was theoretical unless approved by the Reichstag, he could suspend the parliament and rule without it for 60 days. It must be emphasized that Article 48, which appeared necessary because of threats against the Weimar Republic, became a dangerous provision for it allowed the president to make himself a dictator and rule by decree. During the Weimar Republic the two presidents used it more than 200 times, thereby paving the way for Hitler's dictatorial rule. Had the National Assembly not made the fatal mistake of placing Article 48 in the constitution, Hitler's seizure of power would not have been so easy.

WEIMAR REPUBLIC

1919–1933

Why did the German people's first bid for democracy during the Weimar Republic fail? In some respects the obvious problems of military defeat, revolution, and a dictated peace made it remarkable that it ever survived the circumstances of its birth. The idea of republican government was never less welcome. There were too few people who really desired to make democracy work. And unfortunately, the Kaiser and the other men who started World War I were relieved of the onerous burden of concluding and taking responsibility for the peace. The Social Democrats who dominated in the provisional government were held responsible for the lost war by the "stab-in-the-back" legend. Accordingly, the complementary myth was spread that Germany had not been defeated by the Allies but by its own traitors. Another indictment against the republic was that the democratic form of government was alien and unsuited to the German political way of thinking and had been forced on Germans by Woodrow Wilson and the Allies. Lastly, the Weimar Republic soon became identified with the acceptance and execution of the crushing burdens of the Versailles Treaty imposed upon Germany by her enemies. Consequently, the republic rapidly became unwanted and unacclaimed, despised and denigrated, and the target of attack by extremists from the left and the right. What the republic needed was friends, time, and a period free of crisis, none of which it received.

The four years that followed the promulgation of the Weimar constitution were years of continual crisis. Besides the dangers caused by international pressures, there were always fewer devoted friends of the republic than there were opponents, and many Germans simply remained neutral. The extremists on the right and the left tried everything to destroy the republican experiment. The Nationalists on the right were monarchists, landowners, and industrialists who regarded the Majority Socialists as dangerous as Communists. Even further on the right were the extremist anti-Semitic, anti-communist, and generally anti-democratic groups that would form the Nazi Party. On the left were the Communists and some Independent Socialists who believed that the Majority Socialists had betrayed the revolution. In the center of the political spectrum was the Catholic Center Party, which though part of the Weimar Coalition also had conservative members who were neutral toward the republic. Many members of the German People's Party of Gustav Stresemann could not be counted on as republican supporters.

Among public officials upon whom the republic depended for carrying out its policies, most officials in the universities, schools, the courts, the police, and the army had not been replaced by republicans and could also not be counted on to serve the new government. Examples could be found among teachers who glorified the imperial past to police who treated terrorists and assassins on the political right differently from those on the left. Light sentences were given by judges to men charged with the desecration of the symbols of the republican regime and even the murder of leading statesmen, such as Matthias Erzberger and Walter Rathenau. The army was also unreliable and mostly staffed with royalist officers and former members of the Free Corps (Freikorps). The army continued to be a state within the state and claimed to be the best judges of what was in the best interest of the nation. For example, the chief of the army, General Hans von Seeckt, between 1920 and 1926 defied the Versailles Treaty by making secret agreements with the Soviet Army. Until Seeckt was relieved of command, he carried on a subterranean campaign of opposition to Stresemann's Locarno Policy.

The efforts of the republic's leaders to carry out the terms of the Versailles Treaty led to the Kapp Putsch of March 1920, the first serious attempt by the right to overthrow the republic. This coup was a result of the Allied demand that the army be reduced to 100,000 officers and men. Units of the Freikorps had just returned from the Baltic and were ordered to demobilize. The commandant of Berlin, General Walther Lüttwitz, ordered the Ehrhardt brigade to take over Berlin. General Ludendorff was also involved, but the head of the new government was to be a politician, Dr. Wolfgang Kapp. The regular army under General Seeckt refused to use force against the rebels, and the government had to flee the city. What ended the Kapp Putsch was a general strike called by the Socialist Party and the trade unions, which paralyzed Kapp's government and the city, besides the passive resistance of bureaucrats who refused to provide the cash with which Kapp wanted to pay his soldiers.

Instead of punishing the army that had failed the republic, Ebert had to call on it to suppress a Communist uprising in Berlin, Münster and the Ruhr. It was estimated that a 50,000-man "Red Army" had captured several industrial towns and the area around Düsseldorf. For almost a year the force remained in the field before the Freikorps defeated them at the cost of some 3,000 dead and 1 billion marks in damages. As a result of this conflict Gustav Noske, the defense minister, was disgraced and was replaced by Otto Gessler, the mayor of Nuremberg.

The SPD also came to regret its failure to purge the German judiciary in 1918. Statistical analysis perhaps best reveals the nature of class justice under the republic. For the period 1918–22, 22 members of the left were tried for murder, in contrast to the right where 354 were tried for murder, but only one was convicted and none executed. Also time in jail was radically different; for political crimes by the left 15 years was average, whereas on the right only four months. Germans also undertook political murder without restraint. The killings of Rosa Luxemburg, Karl Liebknecht, and Kurt Eisner in 1919 were followed by the murders of the Communist editor Leo Jogiches, the pacifist Hans Paasche, and the Bavarian Independent Socialist deputy Karl Gareis in 1921. In August 1921 the nationally known Center Party politician Matthias

Erzberger was murdered, and in June 1922 Foreign Minister Rathenau was assassinated on his way to his office. Most of the assassins came from the Freikorp units such as the Oberland and Ehrhardt Brigades as well as the latter's successor, Organisation Consul.

The first election in the republic after that for the National Assembly was held in June 1920, and it proved disastrous for the republic's founders. The Social Democratic vote fell by 17 percent, that of the Democratic Party by 10 percent, while the Center Party's support held at 18 percent. What this meant was that support for the Weimar parties fell from 76 to 47 percent, depriving the three parties of a parliamentary majority. Conversely, the extreme left (USPD and KPD) tripled its share of the vote to 20 percent. The right (DNVP and DVP) managed to double its share to 28 percent, which gave the parties opposed to the republic 48 percent of the votes cast.

INFLATION, REPARATIONS, AND RUHR INVASION

The Weimar Republic inherited a considerable degree of inflation as a result of the war and the way it was financed. Whereas the British increased taxation to pay for the war, the German government floated war bonds and German investors expected to draw interest even after the war. Some of the economic problems facing the republic included a decrease in industrial capacity, the depletion of raw materials, a loss of tax revenue from the Rhineland, the loss of its merchant fleet and overseas markets, the staggering costs of demobilization, and unemployment relief. By 1918 the German mark had already lost two-thirds of its value against the dollar. Government expenditures were not financed through taxes to which the voters would have reacted by voting the Weimar Coalition out of office. So the government decided to print money to pay its bills. The faster money was printed the faster it depreciated. Although Matthias Erzberger, who was finance minister in 1919, imposed new taxes, he did not stop the printing presses. Even the president of the central bank (Reichsbank), who should have known better, justified the printing of even more paper money in order to cover its international trade deficit.

A major problem facing the chancellor from the Center Party, Konstantin Fehrenbach, was the reparations problem. In July 1920 Fehrenbach went to Spa in Belgium and three months later to Brussels to attend reparations conferences, trying to obtain accurate information as to exactly what amount of money and goods Germany was expected to pay. The demands were finally specified and handed to the German delegation at the London Conference of March 1, 1921. It stated that Germany was required to pay 132 billion gold marks within a period of 30 years. At first these demands were rejected, but later accepted by the new government headed by the Center Party deputy, Joseph Wirth, who announced that Germany would fulfill its obligations. This was followed until the beginning of 1923. It was in this context that the German government continued to borrow and print new money. A severe inflationary spiral started. Foreigners lost confidence in the currency, and it depreciated rapidly, having immediate repercussions. People began to try to turn their money into goods, while owners of goods were reluctant to exchange them for currency. Prices began to rise faster and faster. Then the French occupied the Ruhr in January 1923, which turned the decline into an avalanche. The German government not too wisely answered the French action with a policy of passive resistance that was enormously expensive and had to be financed by more printed money. By the end of 1923, 1,783 printing presses printed so much paper money that the mark stood at 25 billion to the dollar. Some Germans profited from the inflation, such as industrialists and other wealthy persons who were able to pay off their debts in inflated money. Hugo Stinnes built up his business empire by buying up weaker companies, which concentrated an enormous amount of economic power in his hands. The main victims of the inflation were people who subsisted on interest from savings and who saw their assets disappear. White collar workers like civil servants were also adversely affected. Workers, on the other hand, had to work longer hours and experienced a decline in income that brought hunger and sickness to their families. There was also a nationalist motive behind this inflationary monetary policy. Some people believed that the complete collapse of the currency would persuade the Allies to terminate reparations payments. Reparations were by no means the only cause of this inflationary catastrophe. The psychological effect was shattering and explains why so many people turned to demagogues to save them from these problems.

The economic conditions threatened to undermine the republic. The extremists of the right blamed all the problems on the Versailles Treaty and the policy of fulfillment of Germany's reparations obligations. In August 1921 fanatics assassinated Matthias Erzberger, the outstanding leader of the Center Party and one of the signatories of the armistice. In June 1922 a band of young men shot and killed Walther Rathenau because he was seen as the embodiment of the policy of fulfillment. Rathenau had planned Germany's wartime mobilization and as foreign minister during the republic had negotiated the Treaty of Rapallo. Other republican leaders were targets of attacks and murder attempts. The government appeared powerless to check the breakdown of law and order.

Greater threats against the republic occurred in 1923. One of the effects of the French invasion of the Ruhr was to stimulate attempts by groups of separatists to set up an independent Republic of the Rhineland. When it became known that the French had encouraged this attempt, it was discredited. More serious problems occurred in Saxony and Thuringia, where Communists and left Socialists took over the state government in October. The Berlin government intervened, deposing the state government and establishing martial law. The situation was more dangerous in Bavaria. There the state government had been dominated since 1920 by Gustav von Kahr, who had made himself the head of an antirepublican conspiracy that included Bavarian separatists, supporters of the Hohenzollern and Wittelsbach dynasties, anti-Semites, and those who wanted to imitate Mussolini. Kahr had attracted General Ludendorff and won the confidence of General von Lossow, the commander of the Reichswehr units stationed in Bavaria. He even tried to get the support of Adolf Hitler. Kahr's objectives were not entirely clear, but he apparently planned to strike against the government of the republic. General von Lossow, the commander of the Bavarian army group, was an ally of Kahr, and General von Seekt of the army command refused to have his soldiers shoot at other army (Reichswehr) troops.

On this occasion Hitler carried out the so-called Beer Hall Putsch. On the evening of November 8, 1923, Hitler broke into a meeting of Kahr and his supporters and declared that the National Revolution had begun. Then he made Kahr and Lossow pledge their support for his government. Later that night they changed their minds and decided to defend the constitutional order against Hitler's coup. Then, on the morning of November 9, Hitler and Ludendorff and the storm troopers (SA) marched into the city to the Odeonsplatz. There police and army troops fired on the column; Ludendorff was captured; Hitler was apprehended two days later. This eliminated the last serious threat to the republican government and made possible plans for recovery.

THE STRESEMANN ERA, 1923–1929

In the midst of the crisis, starting in August 1923, the tide began to turn. One reason was that the leading statesmen on the European stage changed. In France Edouard Herriot replaced vengeful Raymond Poincaré; Ramsay MacDonald became Britain's first prime minister from the Labour Party; and most important, Gustav Stresemann became the German chancellor and foreign minister. At the same time it became abundantly clear that the catastrophic chaos in the Ruhr had to end, along with the German policy of passive resistance. To Stresemann's credit he took the first step to break the deadlock. Gustav Stresemann had developed from an ardent nationalist and monarchist into an equally determined advocate of international understanding and a republican by rational decision. Convinced that the prolongation of the Ruhr struggle could only lead to national ruin, Stresemann ended passive resistance on September 26, 1923, and began negotiations with France. Voluntary German reparations deliveries were resumed, and conditions in the Ruhr District gradually returned to normal. Stresemann's next step was to stabilize the currency, which he accomplished by the establishment of the Rentenbank, which issued a loan to the Reichsbank which in turn issued a new Rentenmark in November 1923. This currency was backed not by gold but by a mortgage on the entire agricultural and industrial assets of Germany. In spring 1924 a permanent reichsmark, was issued. To demonstrate their serious intentions, the Germans balanced their budgets, making drastic budget cuts for 1924 in local, state, and federal governments. The new president of the Reichsbank, Hjalmar Schacht, restricted credit and raised interests rates. The budget balancing needed to stabilize the currency had negative social consequences, as it was done at the expense of layoffs and pay cuts of government employees.

While Stresemann was chancellor, he also had to deal with the triple threat of civil war. A monarchist-nationalist revolt of the Fridericus Rex movements in Pomerania was crushed by the army as were the communist uprisings in Saxony and Hamburg mentioned earlier. Additionally, the most formidable attempt at counterrevolution was successfully opposed in Bavaria, where Hitler and Ludendorff aimed at abolishing parliamentary institutions, suppressing civil liberties, expropriating Jews, and liquidating political opponents.

Not that Stresemann's efforts were appreciated by all groups. His policy of liquidating passive resistance in the Ruhr was criticized by the nationalists on the right and by the Social Democrats for having been too lenient with the enemies of the republic. The Social Democrats consequently withdrew from the coalition government and formed a new one composed of Stresemann's German People's Party, the Center and Bavarian People's Party, and the Democrats. The new cabinet was headed by Wilhelm Marx of the Center Party. Fortunately, for the republic Stresemann was given the post of foreign minister, an office to which he was returned again and again in a series of coalitions.

The period during which Stresemann directed Germany's foreign policy was generally characterized by international cooperation, transforming the harsh and punitive so-called spirit of Versailles into a more hopeful "spirit of Locarno." The Allies were increasingly willing to aid in Germany's recovery and to restore her to full equality in the family of nations. At the request of the German government the Reparations Commission appointed two committees of financial and economic experts to deal with the problems of currency stabilization and economic rehabilitation. In summer 1924 these experts met under the leadership of Charles Dawes, the president of the First Bank of Chicago and later to become vice president in the administration of Calvin Coolidge. The resulting Dawes Plan was the first attempt to settle the problem of reparations on a purely economic basis divorced from political considerations. The plan did not alter the total amount of reparations of 132 billion marks, but set up a schedule of payment. Adopted on August 16, 1924, by the Conference of London, the plan stipulated that Germany was to pay 2.5 billion marks every year for an unspecified number of years. The annual payments were to be raised by mortgages on German railroads and industries, by contributions of the German government, and by foreign loans and credits. After five years the annual payments were to be readjusted based on Germany's ability to pay. The Allies also arranged for a loan to Germany of $200 million by a consortium of American banks in order to provide hard currency. The Reich's reparation payments were established at 2.5 billion Reichsmarks. A reparations agent, the American banker Parker Gilbert, established an office in Berlin to oversee the transfer of funds. The Dawes Plan furthermore called for the reorganization of the German Reichsbank, making it independent of the state and placing it under a new directorate, half of whom were non-German.

Elections reflected the political mood of the country at the end of 1924. In the Reichstag elections of December 1924 the antirepublican German National People's Party (DNVP) became the second-largest party, which returned the conservatives to prominence. Further reflecting the move to the right was the election of Field Marshal Hindenburg as president during spring 1925. At the end of February Friedrich Ebert died. The electoral law provided for two ballots if one of the candidates did not receive a majority on the first ballot. The conservatives had nominated Karl Jarres, the mayor of Duisburg, who failed to win on the first ballot. Some of the other parties could not agree on a common candidate so the votes of the Weimar Coalition were fragmented. In the runoff election the SPD,

DDP, and Center Party agreed on the current chancellor, Wilhelm Marx, from the Center Party. Then the conservative nationalists changed their candidate to Field Marshal Paul von Hindenburg. It was the sister party of the Center, the conservative anti-socialist, Catholic-oriented Bavarian People's Party that broke ranks and secured the nomination of Hindenburg for the right. At the time Hindenburg was already 76 years old and did little campaigning, but with his reputation he won the election, although narrowly. Only a plurality of votes sufficed on the second ballot. Although an avowed monarchist, Hindenburg disappointed all those who had voted for him to restore the monarchy. He kept his oath of office loyally and gave strong moral support to the policies inaugurated by Gustav Stresemann. Only after Stresemann's premature death in 1929 did the soldier-president gradually succumb to the influence of rightist and reactionary politicians.

STABILIZATION AND LOCARNO, 1925–1929

The crowning achievement of Stresemann's tireless efforts in behalf of the pacification of Europe and international cooperation was the negotiation of the Locarno Pact. Germany and the Allies signed this treaty on October 16, 1925. In it Germany guaranteed the inviolability of the borders between France and Germany established by the Treaty of Versailles. The only flaw in this international agreement was that it left the question of Germany's eastern frontier unsettled. The reason for this omission was Germany's unwillingness to recognize as permanent the situation created by the Polish Corridor and the separation of Danzig from the rest of the Reich. German refusal to follow up French desires for the signing of a Locarno Pact for the eastern borders prompted the French government to enter into new military alliances with Poland and Czechoslovakia. Yet the Locarno Pact was a great achievement. Stresemann had first discussed the possibilities of the plan with Lord d'Abernon, British ambassador in Berlin, who then convinced Sir Neville Chamberlain, the British prime minister. On November 27, 1925, the Locarno Pact was endorsed by the Reichstag. The parties that opposed it were the German National People's Party, the National Socialists, and the Communists. The fruit of the "spirit of Locarno" was the withdrawal of French and Belgian troops from the Ruhr in 1925, the evacuation of the Allied occupation from the zone of Cologne in the Rhineland in 1926, and the withdrawal of the Inter-Allied Military Control Commission. An invitation to Germany to join the League of Nations was accepted.

On August 27, 1928, Stresemann scored another triumph of his policy of international reconciliation. Most of the larger nations of the world, including Germany, signed the Kellogg-Briand Pact (1928) in Paris, outlawing aggressive war and pledging the solution of all international conflicts by peaceful means. The chief shortcomings of the pact were its failure to define aggressive war and to provide for adequate sanctions against aggressors. Meanwhile, with the acceptance of the Dawes Plan, there occurred a remarkable recovery of the German economy, stimulated by some $16 billion in foreign capital in German industry, public utilities, housing enterprises, and public works. By 1929 both the German national income and industrial production were nearly twice what they had been before inflation. New industrial cartels came into existence, savings increased, and employment figures in 1927 were the highest since the end of the war. However, prosperity was illusory inasmuch as it was an artificially stimulated expansion depending on the flow of foreign credit. It was bound to collapse when prices declined and the stock market crash of October 1929 forced the withdrawal of foreign capital. The condition of the Reich budget and the general economic life was far from healthy. Dangerous tendencies in government finances alarmed the agent-general for reparations, Parker Gilbert. Besides the already mentioned overexpansion, the central, state, and municipal governments had increased their expenditures and borrowing. Gilbert advised that the reparations problem should be reviewed in order to reach a final settlement. A committee was organized under the chairmanship of Owen D. Young, and by June 7, 1929, presented its report in what has been called the Young Plan. It set the total of German reparations at 34.9 billion gold marks and fixed the payment schedule to last until 1988. In return the Allies agreed to end their control over the German railway system and the Reichsbank.

In 1928 the German political situation again experienced important changes. The success of Stresemann's foreign policy was reflected in the Reichstag elections of May 1928, in which the Social Democrats gained more than 2 million votes and the right-wing parties were weakened. The Nazi Party won only 18 seats in the election. The new party alignments made it possible for the Social Democrats to be included with a chancellor, Hermann Müller, of the SPD. The parties of the right felt that their arguments against the fulfillment policy were losing ground, as the Versailles Treaty was being successfully weakened. The parties of the right now collaborated more closely in an intense campaign against the Young Plan. The right lashed out against the enslavement of future generations. The German Nationalists (DNVP) made Alfred Hugenberg their chairman, a powerful businessman who owned a large chain of newspapers, magazines, motion pictures, and other media.

At the Hague Conference in August 1929 convened to consider the Young Plan, Gustav Stresemann fought the final battle of his life trying to achieve the evacuation of the Rhineland. He was dying, and in order to achieve his heart's desire he agreed to additional burdens on the economy. He was assured that part of the evacuation would begin during September and be completed after the ratification of the Young Plan. He did not live to see the evacuation and died on October 3, 1929. The Stresemann era ended when the Young Plan was approved on May 17, 1930.

CULTURE AND SOCIETY

Weimar culture gave birth to many modern cultural movements. The new ideas, styles, and movements included expressionism in drama, art, and literature; the Bauhaus school of architecture associated with the architect Walter Gropius; atonalism in music associated with composers Arthur Schönberg and Paul Hindemith; the physics of relativity formulated by Albert Einstein; the theory and practice of psychoanalysis of Sigmund Freud; and the sociology of knowledge formulated by Max Weber and Ferdinand Tonnies. Those who created Weimar culture believed they were living in a new age. The war and revolution had smashed the institutions, traditions, and values of Imperial Germany. For many there was a sense that all things could be created anew, or at least could be different. There was an eagerness to experiment, creating new art forms, styles, and values in order to improve the quality of life.

Although expressionism in art and literature began during the latter phase of Imperial Germany, the world war, revolution, and the republic gave the expressionists with their utopianism and highly charged emotion a wider audience. The artists and writers had almost complete freedom, which they had lacked during the Empire. The shared experiences of war, revolution, suffering, hope-

A poster for the Bauhus movement, featuring a photograph of Walter Gropius *(Library of Congress)*

lessness, and alienation were relived in their art, literature, and in film. They were concerned with society's problems, but they also were elitist and sometimes religious. One of the leaders of the expressionist movement was Max Pechstein, whose paintings communicated religious rather than political messages. Pechstein and Ernst Kirchner had been members of the prewar artist group known as the Bridge. Kirchner's themes differed from those of Pechstein, who painted depressing and horrifying themes of the war and Berlin life. Max Ernst was early associated with the Dadaists but soon painted in the surrealist style. Otto Dix also had been associated with the Dadaists but, as an expressionist artist, memorialized the horrors of war in his painting *War Cripples*. Most held high expectations of the improvements in life that the revolution should have made possible. Some of the artists and many of the writers rejected the republic and its lack of idealism and longed for a restoration of the monarchy or some idealized future Reich. As a mass culture emerged, the culture of the intellectuals, however, was not what most Germans preferred or consumed. Most readers still favored the more commonplace entertainment of the adventure stories of Karl May, who wrote about the American West, or popular stories of the sea and patriotic themes. Thomas Mann, Erich Kästner, and Erich Maria Remarque did, however, make the list of best-selling authors. Intellectuals were faced by the challenge of mass culture, technological innovation, and mass consumption. The radio and film, for instance, were growing mediums of mass entertainment, and increased leisure time became available as wages rose.

A revolution in manners and morals occurred during the 1920s. Churches experienced a weakening of their influence, partly due to general secularization and because of their excessively patriotic attitudes during the war. The challenge to parental authority by young people was commonplace. Youth were no longer deferential to parents or obedient to traditional codes of behavior and morality. The authority of teachers was less respected. Women experienced a liberation from traditional expectations of their roles as mothers and homemakers. More of them had entered the labor force during the war, and some 11 million worked full time during the republic. The constitution gave them the right to vote, and educational opportunities opened up. Female bodies no longer were expected to be corseted, and short new hair styles like the *Bubikopf* became fashionable. Taboos against the use of tobacco, liquor, and premarital relationships weakened. Yet most women probably were still guided by traditional conventions and morality, and there was considerable ambivalence even among liberated women. Even though some women were pleased with the weakening of the old moral conventions, most voted for political parties that opposed their freedom. One widely read writer, Ina Seidel, emphasized the traditional values of motherhood, family, home, and soil.

Three identifiable phases of cultural expression emerged during Weimar. The time from November 1918 to 1924 was a time of experimentation, reflecting the revolution, civil war, foreign occupation, political murder, and fantastic inflation. Expressionism dominated in both art and theater. Between 1924 and 1929, when Germany enjoyed fiscal and political stabilization, prosperity, and renewed international prestige, the arts entered into the phase called New Objectivity (Neue Sachlichkeit) or matter-of-factness. The New Objectivity called for realism, simplicity, clarity, and accurate reportage. Cynicism and resignation were the negative side of the New Objectivity. In the final phase, between 1929 and 1933—during the Depression and government by decree, decay of middle-class parties, and the resumption of violence—culture mirrored events rather than critiqued them.

An important feature of Weimar cultural life was the hostility of its leading writers toward the government and parliament of the republic. In the ranks of this opposition were a good many journalists, writers, artists, professional men, and academics. Their political views were often too idealistic, naive, and muddled. Many of the expressionist writers and artists had entertained unrealistic expectations of the November Revolution's ability to change society. Having no real understanding of social forces, they were repelled by the compromises that helped solve the problems of the early republic. The left-winger Ernst Toller, for instance, expressed his personal feelings of outrage at the failure to destroy the old authoritarian bureaucracy, the old military caste, the prewar social system, and bourgeois ethical and moral standards. None of these alienated writers ever became convinced supporters of the republic. Some moved to extremes, such as Bertolt Brecht, who turned to communism. In his *Threepenny Opera* (1928) Brecht expressed cynical social satire. Hermann Hesse assaulted the middle class and its hypocrisy in *Steppenwolf* (1930). Both Hermann Hesse and Thomas Mann were fascinated by what they thought was the general decline of Western society and the corrupting influence of its materialism. Mann wrote of the conflict between anarchy and authoritarianism in an age of crisis in his novel *The Magic Mountain* (1924), which cast doubt on the ability of reason to sustain society. Hesse shared his doubts when he stated in *Klingsors Last Summer* (1920) that rationality had become madness and that all that was good and unique had died. More deliberate in their attacks upon the republic and its values and institutions were the writers who were associated with the New Objectivity movement. They exposed the weaknesses, injustices, and hypocrisies of their time and were pessimistic about possible improvement. In Alfred Döblin's greatest novel, *Berlin Alexanderplatz* (1929), the main character is determined to reform himself, but is overwhelmed by forces beyond his control. Erich Kästner's view of German society is even gloomier, and his opinion of the capital, Berlin, even worse. The best example of a merciless critic on the political left was the satirist Kurt Tucholsky. He fought against antidemocratic forces and was a merciless critic of the lack of civic virtue of the middle class. He was as intemperate as any critic from the right, condemning the Social Democratic leadership for defeating the revolution in 1918. Tucholsky's attitude was a common one among left-wing intellectuals

Right-wing ideologues joined in the criticism of the republic, but they also repudiated the Empire and presented an apocalyptic vision of a new revolution and a new Reich. They rejected rational political action and idealized violence; most were patriots, but they were also nihilists and certainly irrational. They foreshadowed the coming of the revolution from the right, that of Adolf Hitler and National Socialism. Among those on the radical right were Arthur Moeller van den Bruck and Oswald Spengler. Moeller's epic *The Third Reich* denounced the republic and called for a neoconservative revolution. Oswald Spengler in his *Decline of the West* predicted the end of European-American culture, the decay of democracy, and the replacement of technology by brainless brutal dictators. Both neoconservatives were cultural pessimists in the tradition of Friedrich Nietzsche, Paul de Lagarde, and Julius Langbehn. Both were opposed to modern capitalism and modern science, which they believed stifled freedom and individuality. Moeller, it should be noted, was the first and most influential preacher of the "stab-in-the back" theory.

ROAD TO DICTATORSHIP, 1930–1933

Four general factors contributed to the accelerated growth and success of the Nazi Party after 1928. First, the onset of the world economic crisis in 1929 destroyed the foundations that had been laid for the further stabilization of the Weimar Republic. As a direct consequence, economic, social, and political conflicts arose, increasingly small and large businesses collapsed, unemployment rose rapidly, and a great panic filled the middle class and peasantry. The panic increased attacks on the Versailles Treaty and reparations. Among the lower middle class there was a fear of being reduced to working-class status. Ideologically, it surfaced as a fear of communism. The radical parties on the left and right that rejected the parliamentary system increasingly blocked the formation of democratic majorities. The middle-class democratic parties became fragmented and multiplied but continually lost support to the radical right. National Socialist propaganda with its anti-Versailles revisionism, anticapitalist, anti-Marxist, and anti-Communist propaganda seemed to offer the simplest and most persuasive alternative. For many the best way out of the crisis appeared to be an authoritarian government that would be above individual and party interests. The economic factors of the Depression offered the partially submerged destructive forces of antidemocratic radicalism a major opportunity.

The takeover of the republic by the Nazis was not inevitable. What made it possible was, first, the crisis of the Depression, which was interpreted by many Germans as a crisis of the democratic parliamentary system of the Weimar Republic. Second, the German National People's Party (DNVP) was taken over by Alfred Hugenberg, and Hitler's association with him gave Hitler social respectability, political influence, and access to necessary financial resources. Third, after Stresemann's death governmental crises smoothed the road toward an extraparliamentary quasi-dictatorship. Between 1929 and 1933 the influence of the democratic parties was weakened in favor of the power of the president, the army command, and the bureaucracy. The crises of these years prepared public opinion for dictatorial solutions. Democratic responsibility diminished after the change of governments in 1930, and more particularly in 1932. Political life was reduced to government by the emergency law Article 48; faith in democratic methods disappeared. A power vacuum occurred with wide opportunities for radical groups, especially the Nazis. Fourth, the National Socialists, who in the 1920s had patterned their method of seizing power after that of Mussolini, shifted their tactics after 1928 to winning elections, a kind of pseudo-legal electoral politics using mass communication, force and persuasion, terror and propaganda, deception and violence. In the process the Nazis became the largest of the political parties. Hitler decided to hold out for his appointment to the top position as chancellor.

In March 1930 the Socialist chancellor, Hermann Müller (1876–1931), resigned when the German People Party (DVP) refused to remain in his coalition government. In order to cope with the economic pressures of growing unemployment, Müller had proposed to raise additional funds for unemployment compensation. Unfortunately, both business and labor opposed the necessary contributions required from them. Then, when he requested permission from President Hindenburg to use the emergency powers of Article 48 to deal with the economic crisis and the growing disorders in the streets, the conservative Hindenburg refused. The president would not entrust the emergency powers to a Socialist. So, in Müller's place Hindenburg selected Heinrich Brüning (1885–1970), who was a fiscal expert, a conservative centrist, and at heart a monarchist. He proceeded to form a cabinet that excluded the SPD, making it clear that he would not be dependent on any coalition of parties. Consequently, he constantly resorted to Article 48 to achieve what he could not achieve through ordinary legislative processes. This cabinet marked the end of the parliamentary system and the beginning of a quasi-dictatorial presidential cabinet system without the consultation of the political parties. The political parties lost their sense of responsibility for constructive cooperation. Brüning, who would come to be known as the "hunger chancellor," bears responsibility for hastily dissolving the Reichstag in July 1930 because it had understandably rejected his radical austerity program. It was his false hope to gain a wider support-base from the new elections. The economic situation was getting worse and worse, and street battles between opposing paramilitary factions became common. Unfortunately, the elections produced a landslide for the radical parties of the right and the left. Universal shock and amazement occurred when the Nazi delegates to the Reichstag increased from 12 to 107. There continued to be an upward surge to the radical parties when in the next Reichstag election of July 1932 the Nazis won 230 seats. That did not mean that Hitler was appointed chancellor through a parliamentary majority. The electoral success of the Nazi Party throughout 1932 only set the stage of the drama, but the plot of the drama focused on the political activities of an influential group of critics and opponents of the Republic. Beginning with Brüning, a procession of ambitious and misguided men sought to reconstruct the republic in a more conservative direction. The others included President Hindenburg, Franz von Papen, Kurt von Schleicher, Hindenburg's son, and the state secretary Meissner. Instead of Hitler's dictatorship being inevitable, these men manipulated events to make it possible.

Despite his difficulties, Heinrich Brüning's government lasted for more than two years. He used Article 48 and placated enough factions to remain in power. He was a conservative centrist, a nationalist, and his goal was to rebuild Germany, renounce the Versailles Treaty, and end the payment of reparations. Also, he favored a union (*Anschluss*) with Austria, and at the Geneva Disarmament Conference in 1932 insisted on "equal rights and equal security for all peoples."

He favored the army and attempted to alleviate economic distress by classical conservative measures of budget-cutting and retrenchment of social services.

Hindenburg, although initially a president loyal to the constitution, was filled with a profound distaste for civilian republican politics. This field marshal whose reputation was made at the Battle of Tannenberg was ill-qualified to head the republic. With the onset of the Depression crisis, he permitted his advisers to push him further along the road of authoritarian, extra-parliamentary experiments. Instead of using far-reaching emergency powers of Article 48 to protect the republic as the first president, Friedrich Ebert, had done, he allowed their use to undermine it. In Hindenburg's hands the Reichstag was suspended, authoritarian experiments by Franz von Papen and Kurt von Schleicher were supported, and the state government of Prussia was taken over and its democratic government abolished. Ultimately Hindenburg permitted a terrorist power grab by a minority government under Hitler after January 30, 1933.

Although the expansion of the Nazi Party appeared to be unstoppable, it might have been countered in two ways. By permitting a carefully contained National Socialist participation in a parliamentary government, their chances of opposition might have been limited. Or, legal and political action against their antidemocratic activities might have been attempted. In fact, however, nothing was done, even though the Nazi camouflage of legalism for their radicalism was clear. The antidemocratic antiparliamentarian nature of the Nazi movement was readily apparent. One of the most notorious examples of the failure of the judicial authorities to take action against the Nazis occurred during autumn 1931. At that time a secret plot was uncovered, detailed in the "Boxheim documents," which were the plans for a terrorist regime after a Nazi seizure of power. The documents revealed plans for shooting enemies, the suppression of public life, and a dictatorship by the Nazi Party. Central and regional governments now had unmistakable evidence of Nazi plans, but used only feeble countermeasures.

In the midst of these political and economic problems Hindenburg's presidential term expired. It was symptomatic of the shift to the right that Hindenburg, who in 1925 had been a candidate of the conservatives, in 1932 became a candidate of the moderates and even the Socialists in 1932. Despite the senility of the 84-year-old general, the Socialists had no better candidate to compete with Hitler and defend the republic. Actually, Hindenburg felt uncomfortable being the candidate of the left, but did so anyway. There had to be two ballots, and Hindenburg was reelected by 19.3 million votes against Hitler's 13.4 million. Nevertheless, Hitler staged a remarkable and dramatic campaign using the airplane and other technology to drum up 13.4 million votes. "Hitler over Germany" was the slogan that represented Hitler's impressive campaign.

Another example of the government's failure to stop the Nazis involved the Storm Troops (SA) in spring 1932. When the acting minister of the interior, General Wilhelm Groener, finally outlawed the SA, President Hindenburg objected and dismissed Groener. It was, however, a financial scandal that ended Brüning's career as chancellor. Even though he had tried to help the East Elbian landholder friends of Hindenburg with financial aid (*Osthilfe*), Brüning was resented and finally dismissed by Hindenburg when he resisted the inclusion of Nazis in his cabinet. Hindenburg now betrayed the forces that reelected him president, and he followed a right-wing authoritarian solution by selecting Franz von Papen (1879–1969) as chancellor.

On the advice of General Kurt von Schleicher (1882–1934) and the Harzburg Front, Hindenburg on June 1, 1932, appointed von Papen, who had friends among the nobility and who was a confident master of intrigue who believed he could keep Hitler out of power with a coalition of conservative aristocrats, industrialists, and army men, in short, a cabinet of barons and army officers. Von Papen made concessions to Hitler to get Nazi support and opened the path to dictatorship. One of the concessions was the dissolution of the Reichstag in June 1932, resulting in the July Reichstag elections in which the Nazis polled their highest vote (230 seats) ever. Von Papen also made the mistake of eliminating the ban on the SA, which brought him into conflict with the state governments that wanted to continue the ban. Pitched battles occurred in the streets of Berlin between Nazis and Communists, which led von Papen to take dictatorial measures deposing the socialist prime minister of Prussia in a coup d'état on July 20 because he supposedly was unable to maintain peace in his state. Von Papen violated the constitution when he placed Prussia under martial law in order to please the ultraconservatives. Not only did von Papen get control of the Prussian police, but he also established a precedent for the Nazi policy of coordination (*Gleichschaltung*), which they implemented seven months later. Von Papen even attempted to make a bargain with Hitler to join the government, but Hitler demanded the full powers of chancellor. Von Papen also proposed the long term-suspension of parliament as an opportunity to institute authoritarian constitutional reforms that would give the president wide dictatorial powers. After von Papen dissolved the Reichstag, he proposed a coup d'état of the Reich government and a ban on all political parties, which would permit the chancellor to govern without the Reichstag. Hindenburg rejected this proposal as unconstitutional. Finally, von Papen resigned and a new cabinet was formed by General Schleicher.

Schleicher's government lasted only two months. He had persuaded Hindenburg that he was capable of solving the crisis without forcing the president to break his constitutional oath. He had become fearful that Hitler's personal army was a threat to the army, and now was determined to stop the Nazi steamroller. Schleicher was unable to split the Nazi Party as he had hoped, and he was unable to deal with the economic crisis. There was endless intrigue, and in the end von Papen succeeded in convincing Hindenburg to dismiss Schleicher. In the meantime Hitler had abandoned his demands for exclusive power and was willing to join a coalition government, however with himself as chancellor. As a result Hindenburg agreed to appoint Hitler as chancellor on January 30, 1933. When Hitler moved into the chancellery in Berlin, he is supposed to have remarked to Goebbels: "No one will ever get me out of here alive!"

THE NAZI DICTATORSHIP

As we have seen, Hitler became chancellor legally. That does not mean that he was the choice of the majority of the German people. At most the Nazis received 37 percent of the vote. In fact, at the very time that he was appointed, the strength of the Nazi Party was already declining. Why then was he chosen chancellor? Hitler was accepted at the last minute by conservative elites who were frightened by General Schleicher's attempt to obtain mass support for his policies from the left. They feared a Communist takeover. All of these conservatives, however, underestimated Hitler's political skills, and they assumed that he could be controlled by them. They were not expecting him to make himself a dictator nor to create a totalitarian state. Hitler outsmarted them all and created the foundations for the "Führer state" within a short two months. Using Article 48, which enabled him to be appointed chancellor, Hitler used it to abolish civil liberties. In the cabinet of ministers of which he was the prime minister, only three members were Nazis, and Hindenburg always had the power to dismiss him. In fact, many observers did not think that he would last very long. The Nazis, however, had a critical advantage in having control of the police in Prussia. Hermann Göring had taken control of the police in the largest state of Germany, and Wilhelm Frick, as Reich minister of the interior, had control over the remaining forces. Furthermore, the minister of defense, General Werner von Blomberg, favored the Nazis and would not have used the army against them.

ESTABLISHMENT OF THE DICTATORSHIP

In his first cabinet meeting, January 31, Hitler along with the naive von Papen announced that the next election would be the last and mark the end of the parliamentary system. On February 1 Hitler dismissed the Reichstag and called for new elections on March 5. Hitler truly expected the Nazis to be so successful at the polls that they would receive a majority and be able to "legally" vote to end the parliamentary system. The goal of the national government was a "national revolution," creating a unity above the divided parties. Using the fear of communism, Hitler convinced Hindenburg to issue an emergency decree restricting freedom of the press and public meetings. In the electoral campaign the Nazis effectively used the state public radio. Communists were considered enemies of the state and could be legally attacked. The SA (Sturmabteilung) and SS (Schutzstaffel) were made auxiliary police in Prussia, and terror was unleashed on the streets. The Socialists were unwilling to use force to protect

Poster featuring Adolf Hitler (right) and Paul von Hindenburg, which says "The Reich will never be destroyed when you stay united and loyal" *(Library of Congress)*

themselves. On February 27 the Reichstag building caught fire, and the incident was blamed on a communist "red threat." The next day Hindenburg issued a decree that provided the "legal" foundation for the future police state. It was called the Decree for the Protection of the People and the State. Communists were arrested, and the meetings of other political parties were harassed. Anyone could be imprisoned without trial. Even with all of the pressure of terror on their side, the Nazis still received only 43.9 percent of the vote. Since the German Nationalists (DNVP) won 52 seats, together with the Nazis they had a narrow majority of 51.7 percent. Then they took over the state governments. Attacks on the Communists and Socialists gained the support of Hitler's nationalist allies. On March 21 a magnificent national celebration was staged at Potsdam to bolster the image of a "bloodless" revolution. On March 23 the Enabling Act was passed, which gave the government the right to enact laws without the consent of the Reichstag. It was the legal sanction for the establishment of Hitler's dictatorship. Most of the delegates in the Reichstag voted for it, only 94 Socialists against. The 74 favorable votes of the Center Party gave Hitler the required votes to pass the law. When Nazism was on trial after the war, the Center Party was judged to have been unwise in its decision but not guilty. Hitler had stayed within the limits of the constitution and the "legality" of the passage of the Enabling Act gave judges and civil servants justification for supporting the regime. By a law of July 14 the National Socialist German Worker's Party was made the sole legal party in Germany, and any attempt to organize new political groups was made a crime. As the propaganda minister, Joseph Goebbels stated that National Socialism could allow no opposition and required that it control all power.

CONSOLIDATION OF POWER

Internal consolidation of power occurred between spring and summer 1933. The next stage after the seizure of power was that of coordination (*Gleichschaltung*). It meant that the social and political institutions of Germany, its political parties, state governments, bureaucracies, professional organizations, and trade unions were brought under Nazi control. To transform Germany from a federal into a unitary state, governors were appointed to supervise the administration. The Nazis also divided all Germany into districts called *Gaue*, each of which was under the authority of a *Gauleiter* (district leader). This provided two channels of authority and control, one through the official government and the other through the Nazi Party. At the same time, the cabinet was made impotent. Ministers no longer were allowed to vote on decisions, which gave Hitler absolute power over decisions. A law for the "Rehabilitation of the Civil Service" also gave Hitler power to purge unwanted government employees, especially to dismiss all Jews. Strikes were forbidden in May, after which all labor unions were abolished, eventually to be replaced by the German Labor Front, which included both management and labor, supervised by the Nazis. Meanwhile, Goebbels began to infiltrate education, art, theater, newspapers, and literature in order to eliminate from German culture all politically unreliable elements and to use them to spread Nazi ideals. To provide the country and foreigners with some show of popular support for Nazi policies, meaningless mock elections were still held, as in November 1933. The Nazi Party was the only party on the ballot and received an amazing 92.2 percent of the vote, yet 3.4 million voters still voted against the regime. The one-party state had been achieved, and even Hitler was amazed that the republican system had collapsed so easily.

By the end of summer 1933 the coordination process had been completed. However, there were still some sources of opposition possible. One was President Hindenburg, who could dismiss Hitler, but there was no danger of that, for on the whole the president was pleased. The army could stop the Nazis, but the minister of defense and many officers were pro-Nazi. The only threat came from Hitler's own SA. Once the Nazis had seized power, the rivalry between Roehm's SA and Himmler's SS, the black-shirted elite guard, had become more pronounced. The brown-shirted SA, which had some 2.5 million members, desired a more thorough social revolution. They also wanted more of the rewards of victory and wanted their units incorporated into the regular army (Reichswehr). Hitler was strongly opposed to the SA's demand to be the core of a new German army. President Hindenburg and the army leadership made it clear that they were opposed to any replacement of the army by the SA. Hitler then decided to crush the independent power of the SA. On the weekend of June 30 a massacre occurred, the Night of the Long Knives, as the purge came to be known. Hitler personally supervised the arrest of Roehm and other SA leaders, all taken to prison and shot. Göring executed the SA leaders in Berlin. The SS was used by Heinrich Himmler and Reinhard Heydrich to shoot accused traitors or homosexuals in their homes throughout Germany. Also included in the purge were other enemies of the regime, such as General von Schleicher, Gregor Strasser, prominent Catholics, and some monarchists. After the event Hitler promulgated a law retroactively legalizing the killings as emergency measures.

The final step that made Hitler the "Führer of the German People and the Reich" came on August 2, 1934, when President von Hindenburg died. A law was promulgated that combined the offices of president and chancellor, which made Hitler the commander in chief of the armed forces. Barely hours after Hindenburg's death the army (Reichswehr) was required to taken an oath of allegiance to Hitler as its new commander, promising unquestioning obedience. To stress the break with the past, Hitler changed the name of the German army from Reichswehr to Wehrmacht. A plebiscite approved the union of the offices of president and chancellor.

Hitler was convinced that it was his destiny to achieve a total revolution, to transform Germany in all aspects. Although he wanted to make Germany a world power again, at the core of Nazi ideology was the goal to create an Aryan racial state. The massive support for the Nazi Party in the early 1930s had actually come from its being a party of protest against the Depression and the Weimar system. Nazi propaganda had downplayed anti-Semitism in favor of nationalism, anticommunism, and economic issues such as not charging interest on loans and closing department stores. Some anti-Semitic steps were taken during the early years, but until about 1938 Hitler felt that he needed to cooperate with the forces that had made Nazi successes possible, which included the conservatives in the army, big business, the civil service, and the landed aristocracy. So conservative economic policies still predominated, interest was charged on loans, and department stores remained open. Price and wage controls remained. Yet there was a gradual shift. Hitler insisted on government-sponsored public works and a dramatic buildup in military spending. A dramatic link between public works and defense spending came about in the construction of the strategic superhighways, the *Autobahnen.* Nazi popularity soared; they were the leaders who could "get things done." By the end of 1933 unemployment fell by a third from 6 million to 4 million. A policy of deficit financing of public works projects occurred. The fiscal conservative head of the Reichsbank, Hans Luther, resigned and Hjalmar Schacht, the financial wizard of German recovery, took his place. The government also followed policies that were intended to achieve self-sufficiency (autarchy) in raw materials and food. Bilateral agreements were negotiated that bypassed the need for hard currency. This worked to some degree, but Germany lost traditional markets in North America and western Europe. It also hampered the rearmament program. Some believe that the Nazis cured the Depression, which was not the case, but they did enable Germany to come out of its depths more quickly than did other industrialized nations.

THE NAZI "TOTAL" STATE

The meaning of the Hitler state was that public political power emanated from the personal power of Adolf Hitler. "What benefits the state is right" became a favored motto. The individual German was left only with duties to the state. The state, on the other hand, had no duties to its citizens or to humanity at large, but only rights relative to other states. It was as if the state had a life of its own and followed its own laws based on blood community. Individualistic thinking had to be eliminated. According to Hitler the state had no moral scruples and lived by the instinct of survival, through brutal struggle. Control of the state by Hitler came through the Nazi Party. A phenomenal increase of 1.6 million in party membership occurred during the first three months after January 30, 1933, constituting 65 percent of the membership. So enrollments were closed until 1937. Most vocational groups joined in the expansion of the party, while the sociological composition of the party changed only slightly. As before, the working class was underrepresented; the lower middle class increased its support; lower-level civil servants and teachers expanded their representation, while the upper middle class and aristocracy were overrepresented in comparison to their percentage of the population. The organization of the party included leaders in all regions of the state, and local block leaders kept their surveillance of groups of families. The leaders of the party shared Hitler's vision of Nazism as a crusade that would save Germany and create a new national community. In addition, there were other organizations such as the SS, the National Socialist Motorized Corps, the police called the Gestapo, the German Labor Front, the German Labor Service Battalions, the League of German Women, the Hitler Youth, the Union of German Girls, and dozens of others that were hierarchically organized, thoroughly disciplined, and subject ultimately to the Führer.

The Nazis also turned Germany into a unitary state more susceptible to totalitarian control. In 1934 they abolished the remaining sovereign rights of the states as well as those of the Reichsrat, the upper house of parliament. Totalitarian control also required new concepts of law and legality. Law became politicized in all its aspects and was deprived of its traditional principles and moral basis. Hans Frank, the Nazi Reich commissioner for justice did his best to abolish the old idea that punishment could occur if a law was violated. People's actions, according to Frank, were to be judged on the basis of the National Socialist worldview (weltanschauung). The legal system was supposed to serve the Nazi movement. According to Herman Göring the protection of the law was to be extended only to true National Socialist–minded citizens. Those who disobeyed Hitler committed crimes against the German people and did not deserve the protection of the law. A special People's Court (Volksgerichtshof) was set up in 1934 to judge cases of treason, which could mean almost any political offense and from which there were no legal means of appeal. In this way a constitutionally based state was transformed into one based on the sentiment of the nation as interpreted through Nazi ideology.

Much of the law, however, was administered through the Gestapo. A system of surveillance and terror, including the Gestapo and the SS along with other secret agents, was established. Those arrested were interrogated and sent to a concentration camp for a few months or years, intended to be a warning to others discontented with the regime. In February 1933 the first of the concentration camps was set up for political internees (Communists, Socialists, Jews, priests and ministers, defeatists, speculators, and intellectuals) ultimately reaching some 300 camps. The SS (Schutzstaffel) became Hitler's bodyguard and a "state within a state." Members considered themselves part of a new ruling elite. They swore total obedience to Hitler and pledged themselves to fight even when all appeared hopeless. By 1939 the SS together with the Gestapo was occupied with persecuting opponents of the regime. During the war the SS was expanded to include military units called "Waffen-SS," which were assigned special duties in the occupied territories, such as exterminating the Warsaw Ghetto in 1943 and operating the death camps.

PERSECUTION OF THE JEWS

The origins of anti-Semitism can be traced back to the 19th century, and for Hitler it was the central belief of his philosophy. With the aid of the party philosopher, Alfred Rosenberg, and the application of pseudoscientific ideas, the Nazis developed racial theories that became a creed in their movement. Rosenberg asserted that race was the primordial force in society, the basis of language and cultural traditions, of art, beauty, progress, and achievement. Among the races, the Nordic Aryans were not only considered to be the best but were destined to rule the so-called lower races—Latins, Slavs, Semites, and Negroes. Superior racial stock, however, was not based on race alone but also on the soil that produced the people's soul (*Volksseele*), and it was blasphemous to allow German soil to be contaminated by an alien (Jewish) race. The extermination of the Jews became a goal of Nazi ideology. The Nazis were obsessed with racial impurity that resulted from racial mixing. As early as July 1933 the Nazis passed their first Eugenics Laws, designed to supervise the breeding of future generations. Strict medical exams were required before marriage. A Hereditary Health Court was established with the powers to issue sterilization decrees for the mentally or physically diseased. Healthy Aryans were encouraged to propagate. State subsidies were provided for large families. To justify demands for more living space (Lebensraum) the Nazis actively encouraged Germans or their descendants living abroad to return.

Racial fanaticism, ingrained anti-Semitism and the need for a scapegoat stimulated the Nazis' persecution of the Jews. Hitler even called them "the eternal parasites." Nazi propaganda drummed into audiences the idea that Jews lurked behind all enemies and were the cause of Germany's problems. No Jew could be a fellow German. The consequent persecution of Jews initially lacked any formal policy. In April 1933 an unofficial boycott of all Jewish businesses and professional services was inaugurated. Some Jews were beaten up and imprisoned, and the emigration of Jews began. The dismissal of Jewish judges and civil servants heralded the systematic elimination of Jews from all elements of society. Increasing use was made of the legal basis for this action, the "Aryan paragraph" (bylaws of organizations intended to exclude Jews) against doctors, dentists, chemists, lawyers, solicitors, artists, and journalists. Universities and state-run schools were now open to an increasingly smaller number of Jews. They were also barred from tax and social benefits, from military service, and from all clubs and associations. Jews were prevented from entering bars, sitting on park benches, and using public baths. By 1935 discrimination and persecution became systematized. Through the Nuremberg Laws and the Nationality Acts of September 1935 Jews were legally defined as anyone with a single Jewish grandparent. They were deprived of their citizenship and designated as "members but not citizens of the state," which automatically barred them from the civil service, the legal profession, the Labor Front, and all official organizations. Mixed marriages between Jews and non-Jewish Germans or sexual relations between them were prohibited by law.

In fall 1938 anti-Jewish legislation and harassment increased. Using as a pretext the murder of a secretary of the German embassy in Paris by a young Jew, the Nazis unleashed ruthless attacks on the German Jews. In what came to be known as the "Night of Broken Glass" (Reichskristallnacht), about 1,000 synagogues throughout Germany were burned; Jewish homes, apartments, and shops were destroyed. Wealthy Jews were arrested and sent to concentration camps. A collective fine of 1 billion marks was imposed upon the Jewish community. Thereafter, more anti-Jewish legislation was issued almost weekly. Jews were barred from attending theaters, concerts, movies, or other public performances. They were forced to sell their real estate and businesses at ridiculously low prices. Nor could they walk on certain streets. They had to assume biblical names such as Israel and Sarah on their identity papers that clearly marked them as Jews. Finally, they were forced to wear large yellow stars. Even before the outbreak of World War II some Jews were being restricted to ghettos.

RELIGION AND THE CHURCHES

Hitler's use of such religious terminology as soul and spirit were not Christian concepts, but rather mystical forms of nationalism. When he invoked the name of God, it was not the Christian God but a Germanic god who could best be served by devotion to the German people. According to Hitler's way of thinking, a person was either a German or a Christian, the Old and New Testaments were Jewish swindles, and although he tolerated the churches he promised to eradicate Christianity after the war. Yet for tactical reasons, in 1933 he promised not to meddle in religious affairs and sought to give the impression that he was a protector of Christianity. He gave his consent to the attempt to create a Protestant Reich Church, which was to be coordinated with the state. In July 1933 Hitler concluded a concordat with the Catholic Church. The pope hoped to obtain the protection of the church's traditional rights in the new Reich. In return for their assurance not to get involved in politics, Hitler granted Catholics freedom of religious activities. His main aim, of course, was to undermine the remaining strength of the Center Party and of the Catholic labor unions, and to get valuable international recognition for the new government. In the end Catholics were disappointed that the concordat did not protect them as expected, and persecution of the church occurred. In 1937 Pope Pius XI in an encyclical denounced the Nazi regime's violations of the concordat and the deification of race. On the other hand, the Protestant churches were disunited in their attitude toward the Nazi regime. On the one extreme there were the "German Christians," who supported the regime and thought that God's law was being fulfilled by the National Socialist state. At the opposite pole were those led by Pastor Martin Niemöller, who opposed the Nazis' attempt to convert their church into a political arm of the state. He and like-minded ministers formed the Emergency League of Pastors in 1933, which became the German Confessional Church. They objected to the oath of allegiance required of the state-controlled Reich church. Rebellious pastors, like the Catholic priests, were arrested and disappeared into concentration camps. The failure to develop a state church that would be obedient to the regime led Hitler to develop a savior myth that he was the second Messiah. Faith in Hitler was given truly religious significance, and party rallies and pageants were turned into gigantic acts of devotion.

FOREIGN POLICY

National Socialist foreign policy went beyond the revision of the Treaty of Versailles. It entailed the acquisition of new living space (Lebensraum) and the establishment of a "Great German Reich of the German Nation." In the first years of the regime Hitler pursued only a revisionist policy. As he continued to be successful, he finally embarked upon an imperialist expansionist policy when he occupied the rest of Czechoslovakia in spring 1939. In 1933 the foreign office still remained unaffected by the seizure of power, and a revisionist policy of the Weimar period continued. After the concordat with the Vatican in July 1933, Hitler signed a nonaggression pact with Poland in January 1934, easing tensions in German-Polish relations. The increase in Hitler's international standing weakened internal opposition to him. The reoccupation of the Saar in January 1935 was seen as further success in Nazi foreign policy. So far Hitler had not violated the Treaty of Versailles. By contrast, however, the reintroduction of conscription in March 1935 and the reconstruction of the air force

(Luftwaffe) were violations of the treaty. Germany left the League of Nations in 1933, which brought condemnation of Germany's violations, but the European powers failed to form a united front against Hitler. Instead of imposing sanctions, the foreign powers effectively approved such violations of the treaty. The Anglo-German Naval Agreement of June 1935 averted the threat of German isolation and encouraged Hitler to violate the treaty yet again by ordering German troops into the demilitarized Rhineland in March 1936. When the Spanish civil war broke out in July 1936, the German "Condor Legion" was sent to support the anti-republican Falangists of General Franco. The weapons, which had been developed as a result of the German policy of rearmament, were tested for the first time in Spain. Nevertheless, Hitler saw Mussolini rather than Franco as a potential ally of his own military plans, and the two reached an agreement on the demarcation of their respective policies of expansionism in October 1936 in the formation of the Rome-Berlin Axis, which was a prelude to the future wartime alliance. The agreement also paved the way for the annexation of Austria to the German Reich. In March 1938 German troops marched into Austria and were met by jubilant crowds, and the country was annexed as "Ostmark." Thus the Greater German Reich was established by a policy of surprises and blackmail. The Gestapo accompanied the German troops into Austria, and by December 1938 had taken more than 20,000 people into custody. The Anschluss with Austria was another violation of the Treaty of Versailles. England and France continued to follow their policy of appeasement. In September 1938 they agreed to cede the Sudetenland in Czechoslovakia because they did not yet feel ready for a military conflict with Germany. Hitler, of course, was not satisfied; his next aim was the takeover of the remaining areas of Czechoslovakia. The alleged persecution of the German minority by the Czechs served as a pretext. The press were given orders to dramatize their reports of horror, murder, and mistreatment in order to demonstrate the barbaric nature of the Czechs. Hitler also used the conflict between the Czechs and the Slovaks as an excuse for ordering German troops to the area that became known as "the protectorate of Böhmen and Mähren," through which Slovakia became an autonomous state under the protection of the German Reich. As a reaction to his open aggression Great Britain and France issued a joint declaration guaranteeing protection for Poland. The Anglo-German Naval Agreement was revoked by Hitler in April 1939. The "Pact of Steel" firmly committed Italy to Germany's expansionist policy. Then, to the astonishment of all of Europe, Hitler and Stalin signed a Nazi-Soviet nonaggression pact in August 1939, which protected Germany from the prospect of a two-front war. Hitler's decision to invade Poland on September 1, 1939, in blitzkrieg fashion (a "lightning war" through the use of mechanized armies and overwhelming air power) started World War II as Great Britain and France declared war in fulfillment of their treaty obligations to Poland.

World War II and Holocaust

There is no doubt that World War II was Hitler's war. It was rooted in the ideology of National Socialism and the quest for living space (Lebensraum) and began with the invasion of Poland. Hitler intended to reverse the Treaty of Versailles, which had made the German city of Danzig a free city and provided Poland with a corridor to the sea, an area composed of former German territory that also had cut off eastern Germany from the rest of the Reich. Now he demanded the return of Danzig and a territorial path through the corridor. Secretly instructing his generals to prepare a military campaign to solve the Polish problem, Hitler also diplomatically prepared the path for war by abrogating Germany's nonaggression pact with Poland. Then, on August 23 a nonaggression pact was signed with Russia, which protected the German armies from being attacked by the Soviet Union. Hitler's orders to his generals indicated the character of the coming war. They were to act brutally, without pity, and completely annihilate Poland.

The German invasion of Poland truly was a lightning war (blitzkrieg). Having learned from the slaughter of trench warfare in World War I, the German army wisely created a plan of invasion that used speed and efficiency, employing mechanized columns of panzer divisions (300 tanks) supported by massive air power in order to penetrate enemy lines and encircle and destroy entire armies. Needless to say, the Polish army was outnumbered and poorly equipped and was quickly defeated. To make matters worse, Russia attacked Poland from the east. Even though Hitler had desired to avoid a European-wide war, Britain and France disappointed him when within two days they declared war on Germany. However, that did not matter as French armies never attacked in the west, even though German defenses were weak. Within four weeks all Polish resistance ended. On September 28, 1939, Poland was divided by Germany and Russia. A stalemate resulted when the Western democracies took up defensive positions and did not attack Germany's vulnerable western border. Lasting the winter, the stalemate was called "the phony war."

WAR IN THE WEST

Resuming the offensive, Germany attacked Denmark and Norway on April 9, 1940. Those areas were of strategic importance as Great Britain had already set mines to stop the supply of Swedish iron ore from Norwegian ports, one that was essential for German steel production. Denmark surrendered immediately, but the Norwegians after a strong resistance with the assistance of 50,000 British troops capitulated on June 9. The Norwegians did some harm to the German navy by sinking the cruiser *Blücher* and damaging the battleship

Deutschland and the cruiser *Emden*. Nevertheless, the Germans seized the capital and established their own puppet government under Vidkun Quisling, whose name became synonymous with *traitor* during the war. A positive result for the democracies, however, was the fall of British prime minister Neville Chamberlain, whose policy of appeasement had failed to prevent war. As an advocate of taking a hard line toward Hitler, Winston Churchill now became England's new prime minister on May 10, 1940. He had been an early and forceful critic of Hitler and the British policy of appeasement.

On May 10 the Germans launched their attack on the Netherlands, Belgium, and France. Instead of repeating their World War I strategy and being unable to directly assault the Maginot defensive line through Belgium, the Germans planned to attack through Luxembourg and the Ardennes forest. The success of this strategy made its author, General Erich von Manstein, famous. The panzer divisions raced across northern France and split the Allies, trapping the British army at Dunkirk. From there the British accomplished what was a heroic and remarkable rescue of some 330,000 troops. On June 5 the Germans invaded southern France and were joined by Italian forces after Mussolini declared war on France. The French were never able to mount a counteroffensive and surrendered on June 22. At the end of the campaign the German armies occupied about three-fifths of France while the Vichy regime headed by Marshal Henri Pétain controlled the rest. The Vichy regime was a puppet state, and the French government took up residence in England. Hitler was overjoyed that he had revenged the German defeat of World War I. He also proved to himself that he had been correct in pursuing the risky policies that had brought Germany a resounding victory and that the generals and diplomats who had opposed this strategy were wrong. The dictator was now convinced that he was a military genius, and the German people hailed him as a conquering hero.

THE BATTLE OF BRITAIN

The problem of Britain remained, however, and Hitler was unsure of how to deal with it. He undoubtedly admired the British for their skill and racial superiority in building the world's largest empire. He was even prepared to allow Britain to retain its empire in return for allowing Germany a free hand on the Continent. His main goal was to invade Russia, defeat communism, and acquire living space. Winston Churchill, a descendant of the duke of Marlborough, who had fought to prevent Louis XIV from dominating the Continent, rejected Hitler's offer to make peace. In response Hitler decided to launch an invasion, issuing the directive Operation Sea Lion, even though he considered it very difficult. Because he believed that Britain would surrender once Russia had been eliminated, in July he ordered the army to prepare for an invasion of the Soviet Union, which he unrealistically set for September 15. Nevertheless, plans continued for the invasion of Britain and control of the air was a priority. The first strikes by the German air force (Luftwaffe) were against airfields in southeastern Britain. Despite a spirited defense by the Royal Air Force (RAF), the Germans might eventually have gotten the upper hand. When the British retaliated with air raids on Berlin and other cities, Hitler sought revenge by directing the

Luftwaffe to bomb London. Nightly bombing destroyed a considerable portion of London, and some 15,000 people died. However, the idea of victory through air power proved false. Although the British were outnumbered, they were able to concentrate their Spitfires and Hurricanes and destroy twice as many German planes as the Royal Air Force lost. Furthermore, the British had developed a radar system that warned them of an approaching attack, and the Ultra system provided them with intelligence as to where and when German planes would strike. Hermann Göring, commander of the Luftwaffe, and Hitler made serious mistakes that saved the British air bases and eventually cost the Nazis the Battle of Britain. The invasion plan had to be abandoned.

An alternative to the invasion of England was to capture Gibraltar and close the Mediterranean to the British navy. Admiral Raeder urged Hitler to capture Gibraltar and the Suez Canal and then advance through Palestine and Syria to Turkey. Hitler was disappointed that Spain's General Franco would not enter the war and gave up on the capture of Gibraltar. The Italians, who were supposed to defeat the British in North Africa, were pushed back into Libya by January 1941 after initial successes. Hitler also was forced to divert his attention from the Russian invasion to the Balkans to help the Italians in Greece. He also decided on a large-scale intervention of armored forces under the command of General Erwin Rommel, who came to be known as the Desert Fox. By May 1941 Rommel had reached the Egyptian frontier but was forced to a halt due to lack of reinforcements. The price of all these diversions, however, was a significant delay of the start of the Russian campaign and perhaps the loss of the war.

INVASION OF RUSSIA

With no immediate hope of defeating England at the end of 1940, Hitler issued the directive Operation Barbarossa for the destruction of the Soviet state. The plan included an enormous encirclement of the Russian army. The main centers of Soviet industry and agriculture were to be captured and a defensive line established from Archangel in the north to the Caspian Sea in the south. After the delay because of the Balkans Operation, Barbarossa was launched against Russia on June 22, 1941. Despite their deep suspicion of Germany the Russians were taken by surprise. Stalin had not fortified the border or ordered his armies to withdraw when attacked. In the first two days some 2,000 Russian planes were destroyed on the ground. The primary objective was to destroy the Russian armies, and with their quickly moving armored divisions the Germans captured more than 2 million Russian soldiers. The invasion force was an enormous force of 180 divisions, which included 20 panzer divisions with 8,000 tanks. Although so many Russians were captured, the Germans miscalculated about the available Russian reserves, which were able to provide 300 new divisions. Nevertheless, the Russians lost 2.5 million men, most of their tanks and with the Germans at the gates of Moscow a German victory appeared imminent. However, as winter set in, the Germans could not deliver the final blow. In August they had delayed their advance while Hitler planned strategy. The generals had wanted to concentrate forces to take Moscow before winter, and had that been done the war might have been won. However, Hitler diverted forces to the south, and when they returned to the Moscow front it was too late.

Winter devastated the German army, which was not appropriately dressed or equipped. This was one of Hitler's biggest mistakes and prevented a German victory in 1941. Another of Hitler's mistakes was his refusal to allow his armies to withdraw and regroup for the following spring. Then, on December 19, Hitler made another error overestimating his ability to take over operational command of the army and punishing the generals who had recommended withdrawal or retreat. Neither did the Germans make a wise decision in their harsh occupation policies inspired by Hitler's racist attitudes toward Slavic peoples. This inspired anti-German sentiment and guerrilla warfare against the Germans. Finally, Hitler's decision in December 1941 to declare war on the United States was a fundamental mistake that made his defeat inevitable.

German tanks bogged down in the heavy snow outside Stalingrad (Library of Congress)

HITLER'S PLANS FOR EUROPE

Hitler often spoke of the "new order" that he intended to impose after he had established his Third Reich. He predicted that his own empire would last for a thousand years. If his organization of Germany before the war is a guide, he had no single plan of government but relied frequently on intuition and pragmatism. His organization of conquered Europe also had patchwork characteristics. Some conquered territory was annexed to Germany; some was not annexed but administered directly by German officials; other lands were nominally autonomous but were ruled by puppet governments. The use of terror was essential in providing living space (Lebensraum) for the German people in areas occupied by inferior races. In Poland the Germans forced Poles from their land and employed them as cheap labor. Hitler had similar plans on an even greater scale for Russia. The Russians would be driven eastward into central Asia, while Germans resettled the land and the Russians would be kept in check by frontier colonies of veteran soldiers. In areas racially akin to the Germans, germanization would take place. The people of Scandinavia, the Netherlands, and Switzerland would be absorbed. Even some 15,000 girls from Ukraine were resettled in Germany as servants and wives. Economically, Hitler regarded conquered lands as a source for plunder. In eastern Europe industries were removed, and land was confiscated in Poland and Russia. In the west the occupying army had to be supported by the country and was stripped often of necessities.

TURNING OF THE TIDE, 1942–1943

Throughout most of 1942 it appeared that the Germans might still win the war. In 1942 Hitler's armies advanced deeper into Russia and almost reached the Caspian Sea in their drive to control Russia's oil fields. In Africa, too, Axis fortunes were high. Rommel drove the British back into Egypt toward the Suez Canal until he was stopped at El Alamein, only 17 miles from Alexandria. German submarines still threatened British supply lines. In the North Atlantic German submarines continued to successfully attack Allied ships. By 1942 the number of German submarines had increased to 250, and in the first half of 1942 had sunk 4.5 million tons of shipping.

In November 1942 an Allied force landed in French North Africa under General Dwight D. Eisenhower and pushed eastward. After defeating Rommel at El Alamein, the British field marshal Bernard Montgomery pushed westward, defeating Rommel again in Tunisia. The Allies then controlled the Mediterranean and were in a position to attack southern Europe. In July and August the Allies took Sicily. Mussolini fell from power, and the Italian government declared war on Germany. The Germans, however, occupied Italy and doggedly resisted the Allied advance.

On the eastern front the turning point came at the Battle of Stalingrad. After the Germans had captured the Crimea, the generals had recommended the capture of the oil fields in the Caucasus. Hitler, however, decided that Stalingrad, a major industrial center, should be taken first. The battle for Stalingrad raged for months because Hitler again overruled his generals and would not allow a retreat. Catastrophically the entire German Sixth Army of 300,000 men was lost at Stalingrad. By February 1943 German forces in Russia were back to their positions of June 1942. By spring 1943 it became clear that the Germans would not defeat the Soviet Union. In summer 1943 Hitler's generals urged him to build an east wall based on river barriers to halt the Russians. Instead, Hitler gambled on taking the offensive by making use of newly developed heavy tanks. In one of the greatest tank battles of the war, the Battle of Kursk, which the Russians considered the decisive turning point of the German-Soviet war, the Russians defeated the Germans, who lost 18 panzer divisions. Afterward the Russians advanced relentlessly.

THE HOME FRONT

During the first two years of the war Hitler demanded few important sacrifices from the German people. Spending on domestic projects continued, and food was plentiful. At this time the economy was not on a full wartime footing. The failure to quickly defeat the Soviet Union changed everything. Food could no longer be imported from the east. Germany had to mobilize for total war. In 1942 Hitler ordered a great expansion of the army and armaments production. Now the government began to demand major sacrifices from the German people.

Albert Speer (1905–81), who had been Hitler's personal architect, was appointed minister for armaments and munitions and began to direct the economy to meet its military needs. The government sought the cooperation of major German businesses to increase war production. Between 1942 and 1943 Speer tripled war production despite intense Allied air raids. Speer pleaded for the total mobilization of resources for the war effort, but that did not occur until July 1944, when it was too late to affect the outcome of the war. Between 1942 and 1944 more men were drafted from industry into the army, resulting in a decline of military production. Shortages of consumer goods became serious. Prices and wages were controlled, but the standard of living of German workers fell. Burdensome food rationing began in April 1942, but to make up for food shortages the Nazis seized more food from occupied areas.

By 1943 serious labor shortages appeared. Foreign workers and even slave labor was used to enlarge the labor force. The Nazis required German teenagers and retired men to work the factories, and encouraged women to join them. Nazi resistance to female employment declined, and propaganda emphasized a woman's role as coworker in addition to the ideal of motherhood. It is interesting that women did not wholeheartedly heed the government's call to aid war production. There was only a slight increase in female employment between 1939 and 1944. Films portrayed ordinary women who became especially brave and patriotic during the war and remained faithful to their husbands fighting for the Fatherland. The wartime activities of women, whether as air raid wardens or factory workers, were pictured as the natural fulfillment of their maternal roles. Women as farmers were providing for their soldier sons and husbands, and as frugal housewives they also helped win the war. Finally, women were told that they were protecting racial purity through chastity.

The war years saw an intensification of political propaganda to encourage the civilian population in support of the war effort. Nazi propaganda blamed the outbreak of the war on the British and the Jews. It also stressed the power of Germany and the inferiority of its enemies. Propaganda Minister Josef Goebbels used both radio and film to boost morale and the Nazi cause. Movies of the collapse of Poland, Belgium, Holland, and France were shown to demonstrate German might. The Nazis also used the mass media to frighten the population of the conquered territories. As the Russian campaign turned from victory to defeat, propaganda aimed to stiffen German resolve and frighten Germans about the consequences of defeat and the Allied policy of unconditional surrender.

After May 1943, when the Allies began their major bombing offensive over Germany, the German people feared the dangers of the continual bombing and destruction of their cities. It is believed that German morale was not undermined, but in fact that resistance was stiffened. Yet, the war brought great changes and vast physical destruction, invasion, and occupation. Germany had become transformed, but not according to the ideals of National Socialism.

THE RESISTANCE

Germany had its resisters and groups that opposed the Nazi regime even before the war began. As the SS and SD increased their control over everyday life, resistance became more dangerous and ineffectual. One noteworthy wartime effort was the White Rose movement, which involved a small group of students and one professor at the University of Munich. They distributed pamphlets denouncing the regime as lawless, criminal, and godless. Its members were caught, arrested, and promptly executed. Likewise, Communist resistance groups were mostly crushed by the Gestapo. Only one plot against Hitler and the Nazi regime came close to succeeding. It was the work of a group of military officers and conservative politicians who were appalled at Hitler's conduct of the war and were sickened by the wartime atrocities committed by German forces. One member, Colonel Count Claus von Stauffenberg, believed that only the elimination of Hitler would bring the overthrow of the Nazi regime. On July 20, 1944, he planted a bomb in Hitler's East Prussian headquarters; the bomb exploded but failed to kill the dictator. The plot involved the security service that was to take over the government. Quickly uncovered and crushed, the plot involved thousands of people and some 5,000 were executed.

D-DAY TO DEFEAT NAZI GERMANY

On June 6, 1944, known as D-Day, American, British, and Canadian troops landed on the coast of Normandy. The long-awaited second front was finally opened. Although the German defenses were strong, the Allies were able to establish a beachhead because of the delayed German response to the invasion. The Germans thought that the real invasion might occur to the north. In mid-August the Allies landed in southern France to put more pressure on the enemy and by September France was liberated.

The Battle of the Bulge through the Ardennes forest in Belgium was the last major counterattack of the war. The Germans were able to push forward into the Allied line, which was called the Battle of the Bulge. The Allies soon recovered their momentum and moved eastward. They crossed the Rhine in March 1945, and German resistance rapidly crumbled. By March 1945 the Russians were near Berlin. Because the Allies insisted on unconditional surrender, the Germans fought until May. Hitler, Eva Braun, Goebbels, and his family all committed suicide in an underground bunker in Berlin on May 1, 1945.

THE HOLOCAUST

The most horrible aspect of Nazi rule arose from the inhumanity and brutality inherent in Hitler's racial doctrines. He considered the Slavic people to be subhuman creatures, who like beasts did not have to be treated as human beings. In parts of Poland the upper and professional classes were entirely jailed, deported, or killed. Schools and churches were closed; marriage was controlled by the Nazis to keep down the Polish birth rate; and harsh living conditions were imposed. In Russia things were even worse. The Russian campaign, according to Hitler, was a war of extermination. Heinrich Himmler planned to eliminate 30 million Slavs to make room for the Germans. The number of Russian prisoners of war and deported civilian workers who died under Nazi rule reached about 6 million.

The control of Poland provided Hitler with the territory outside of Germany in which to execute the Final Solution to the Jewish question. The responsibility for the systematic murder of the Jews called the Holocaust lay primarily in the hands of Adolf Hitler, Heinrich Himmler, Reinhard Heydrich, and Heydrich's successor, Ernst Kaltenbrunner, who had been head of the Austrian SS before the Anschluss. All of them were fanatic anti-Semites who firmly believed that the world war was a battle between Aryans and Jews for control of the world. The SS was given responsibility for what the Nazis called the Final Solution to the Jewish problem. Heydrich, head of the SS's Security Service, was given administrative responsibility for carrying out the annihilation. Systematic planning for the Holocaust began in February 1939, when Heydrich ordered Adolf Eichmann to forget about encouraging emigration and make plans for the ghettoization of Jews. During the invasion of Poland the roving killing squads, the Einsatzgruppen, simply executed thousands of Polish Jews. After the defeat of Poland Heydrich ordered the Einsatzgruppen to concentrate Polish Jews in ghettos established in some Polish cities. In June 1941 the Einsatzgruppen followed the regular army's advance into Russia and executed Jews in their villages and buried them in mass graves. An estimated 1 million Jews were killed by the Einsatzgruppen. This method of eliminating the Jews, however, was judged to be too inefficient.

Between July 1941 and January 1942 the machinery for the Holocaust was set in motion. Although there was no written order by Hitler, he was known to be responsible for authorizing Göring's order to Heydrich to begin drawing up plans for the Final Solution. In January 1942 Heydrich presided over the Wannsee Conference, which organized the methods and location where the extermination would occur. The plan involved the roundup of Jews who were to be transported in freight trains to Poland, where six extermination centers were to be constructed. Auschwitz-Birkenau was the most infamous. The use of Zyklon B (hydrogen cyanide) was to produce an efficient killing of many people in gas chambers, and then they were to be cremated. By spring 1942 the death camps were in operation. Jews were brought from all over Europe, even from Berlin as late as 1943. Despite the pressures of transporting military supplies, the movement of Jews took priority. Some argued that the Jews could be used for military production, but extermination took precedence. When Jews arrived at Auschwitz, about 30 percent went to the labor camp while the

This 1945 photo was taken at Buchenwald concentration camp by a member of the U.S. 80th Infantry. *(United States Army)*

remainder were executed. More than 6 million Jews were killed, more than 3 million in death camps. More than 90 percent of the Jewish population of Poland and some other countries were killed, which was the equivalent of 2 out of 3 European Jews. Only 1 million Jews remained alive and those in pitiable condition.

Allied Occupation, Democratic Rebirth, Cold War

Not since the Thirty Years' War had Germany been so devastated when the German armed forces surrendered unconditionally on May 8, 1945. As the German historian, Friedrich Meineke, stated, it was "a burned-out crater of power politics." Years of bombing had left German cities like endless rows of empty shells. People were hungry and miserable. Millions had war disabilities; millions were widowed and orphaned. Most suffered from malnutrition. Refugees and expellees moved endlessly here and there. The housing shortage was severe. Eighty percent of the houses in Cologne and 50 percent in Hamburg were destroyed. Only half of the 4.3 million prewar population of Berlin still lived there. The transportation system had broken down due to the destruction of thousands of locomotives and freight cars, 3,000 railroad bridges, including all the bridges on the Rhine and Weser Rivers, and two-thirds of those on the Danube. The Ruhr coal industry was producing only one-sixteenth of prewar production.

ZERO HOUR AND NEW BEGINNINGS

While after World War I the administrative apparatus of the state continued to function and provided stability and continuity, in 1945 the administration disintegrated and disappeared. German constitutional life had reached "point zero" as one commentator put it. The Allied powers were literally forced to assume authority over Germany. This second defeat signaled the end of the German nation state established by Bismarck. Prussia, the heartland of this empire, was divided and lost its eastern provinces, and national unity was lost.

One lesson learned from the peacemaking after World War I was that Germany should be occupied until such time as a peace treaty could be signed with a democratic government. At a series of wartime conferences in Teheran (1943), Moscow (1944), and Yalta (1945), the Allied powers decided to divide Germany into four zones of occupation. The British received the northwestern industrial area; the United States occupied the southwest area, including Bavaria, Hesse, and part of what is now Baden-Württemberg; the French received parts of the British and American zones, occupying an area bordering the Rhine; the Soviet Union received eastern Germany, which it already occupied. The capital, Berlin, was subjected to a special four-power administration, though it was located entirely in the Soviet zone. The Western powers had agreed in principle to some territorial compensation for Poland at Germany's expense. This had already been accomplished by the Russians, who as they advanced into Germany acted unilaterally, taking over large parts of eastern Germany and assigning them to

Poland in compensation for eastern Polish territory seized by Russia. The Soviets also seized the northern part of East Prussia, including the city of Königsberg, which had been a center of German commerce and culture since the Middle Ages. All in all the Soviets severed from Germany territory east of the Oder River and Neisse River. Although this was supposed to be only provisional, it turned out to be permanent. Germany lost one-quarter of its prewar territory and some 9.5 million of its population.

ALLIED PLANS AND CONFERENCES

The arrangements for the immediate future of Germany went through further refinements at the American-British-Soviet summit conference in Potsdam just outside Berlin during July 1945. France was not invited. It was decided that Germany should undergo a process of denazification, demilitarization, democratization, decentralization, and decartelization. For the time being no central German administration was to be formed, but responsibility for the government of the whole of Germany was to be in the hands of an Allied Control Council formed of the commanding officers of the four powers. Executive authority in each of the occupation zones was in the hands of the military commandants, who were responsible to their governments. It was intended that Germany was to be treated as a single economic unit during the period of occupation. The Potsdam agreements also provided that reparations in the form of industrial equipment and goods could be extracted instead of the financial payments that had been so troublesome after World War I. Since the western zones possessed major industrial areas, the Russians were to receive a portion of what was extracted there and in return foodstuffs and raw materials were to be shipped to the western zones. The conference placed the eastern German territories, which had been occupied by Poland and the Soviet Union, under their administration. The final borders were to be determined by a peace conference. The Potsdam Agreements also provided for the humane transfer of German populations living east of the Oder-Neisse line in addition to those in Czechoslovakia and Hungary. More than 14 million Germans were involved, and almost 2 million died in the process. Nearly 8 million people found a home in what would become West Germany or the Federal Republic, and more than 4 million were settled in eastern Germany, which became the German Democratic Republic.

DENAZIFICATION

The Allies decided as early as September 1943 that the punishment of the Nazi regime's major leaders would be their joint responsibility, while denazification of German society would be handled by each occupying government. Beginning in November 1945, 24 civilian and military officials of the Nazi regime, including Göring, Ribbentrop, Hess, Speer, Keitel, and Streicher were tried by the International Military Tribunal (IMT) in Nuremberg. Martin Bormann, the general secretary of the Nazi Party, though absent, was tried and convicted. Those on trial were indicted for crimes against peace, war crimes, unleashing aggressive war, and crimes against humanity. Eleven out of 22 were sentenced to death, some received prison sentences, and a few were acquitted, such as Franz von Papen and Hjalmar Schacht.

Each zonal commander then conducted his own denazification program. The Russian campaign was the swiftest and most radical and was concluded by 1948. Some 45,000 leading industrialists, landowners, military officers, civil servants and Nazi Party officials were punished, and many were sent to labor camps. The Russians were quick to brand as fascists those who opposed the creation of the Russian-styled "people's democracy." On the other hand, the American military courts conducted trials that were conscientious and time-consuming. Following a policy that attributed a person's guilt according to the governmental office that each had held by the end of 1945, the Americans jailed 100,000 former Nazis, more than any of the other Allies. In February 1946 the Americans required Germans to fill out a questionnaire as to their activities during the Nazi period. Some 3 million persons were identified as requiring a hearing. However, massive difficulties were encountered because the Americans had too few personnel and the German denazification tribunals were too lenient. By 1947 the political climate had changed, and denazification became less important; among other things there was a need for business people who might have been active Nazis to manage the revitalized economy. On the other hand, the British were wiser in sorting through lists of former officials, realizing that local officials and teachers might have joined only to keep their jobs. Reeducation was also a major part of the denazification process. Educational reform was difficult to accomplish because of destroyed schools, the influx of refugees, and the need for new textbooks. Each Allied zone tried to use its own educational system as a model for the Germans to follow. In the American zone the traditional three-tiered school system, including the Gymnasium, was kept, and the new texts were written from the point of view of Christian Catholic humanism, which had had a strong tradition in southern Germany.

POLITICAL PARTIES AND TRADE UNIONS

Initially, the occupying powers had prohibited all political activity. This changed, however, with the need to install mayors and state (*Länder*) councils in order to rebuild administration. The conditions for democratic life were created only gradually, starting with permission for German newspapers to be published and for new radio stations to broadcast, although the Allies strictly supervised their operations.

In June 1945 the Soviet Union became the first occupying power to give the green light to the establishment of political parties and trade unions, with the aim of influencing political developments throughout Germany. The Soviet administration (SMAD) forced the union of the Social Democratic (SPD) and Communist (KPD) parties to create the Socialist Unity Party (SED). The Americans and the British hesitatingly followed suit in the late summer, and the French fell into line toward the end of 1945. Following the failure of short-lived attempts to form coalitions on the left and the right, the establishment of four parties was permitted in each zone with few exceptions. Initially, the parties were constituted on a regional basis, but after August 1945 national parties were allowed. Already in April 1945 former Social Democrats led by Kurt Schumacher came together and reconstituted the Social Democratic Party. Schumacher's office in Hanover became the temporary headquarters of the party, which was able to build on a long democratic tradition. The task of reorganizing the Christian, Liberal, and Conservative Parties proved to be more difficult because of the many splinter parties that had been formed in the Weimar era. For Christians the divisions that kept them from forming one party had been lessened by their combined resistance to the immorality of Nazism, which gave them an incentive to cooperate in the postwar period. In December 1945 many local groups merged to form the Christian Democratic Union (CDU), which was known in Bavaria as the Christian Social Union (CSU). These parties intended to bridge denominational and social differences and made Christian ethics the guideline for their political activity. Not until December 1948 did the various Liberal Parties unite to form the Free Democratic Party under the chairmanship of Theodor Heuss. Many other parties, such as the German Party, the German Center Party, the German Communist Party (KPD), and the Bavarian Party, were formed but were short lived.

LOCAL STATE FORMATION

In all zones new state (*Länder*) boundaries were drawn in 1945/46, partly because Prussia was broken up. These states played a particularly prominent role in American policy. The military government transferred all functions that had previously been controlled by the central government (Reich) to the prime ministers (*Ministerpräsidenten*) of the states, who were elected by parliamentary assemblies, and to the state (*Länder*) councils that they formed. In addition, the Americans insisted on the speedy establishment of constitutional parliamentary democracy. So by the end of 1946 constitutions were written and functioning in Bavaria, Hesse, and Baden-Württemberg. They were written by the state assemblies and approved by the voters. This political process, which preceded the formation of federal institutions, influenced the important role of the states and their representatives in the political structure of the future Federal Republic.

PARLIAMENTARY COUNCIL AND THE BASIC LAW

In July 1948 the three Western military governors recommended to the prime ministers of the states that a Parliamentary Council be assembled. It should be composed of members from the state legislatures (*Lantag*) with the purpose of writing a constitution for the three Western zones, which after approval by the occupying powers would be ratified by the people. The prime ministers objected that the drafting of a constitution should be delayed until Germany was reunited, which would provide a sufficient degree of German sovereignty. It took further negotiations for the prime ministers to finally declare that they were ready to assist in the development of a parliamentary democracy. Yet, it had to be temporary until a free vote had been taken on a constitution by the whole

German nation. A committee of experts drew up a document that recommended alternative proposals as a guideline for the Parliamentary Council. There were debates over the question of financial administration and the representation of the states. Other differences with the military governors threatened the success of the Parliamentary Council's work, but a compromise agreement was achieved at the end of April. On May 8, 1949, the Parliamentary Council approved the Basic Law for the Federal Republic of Germany by a vote of 53 to 12. After the miliary governors had given their consent, the document was submitted for ratification to the state parliaments. Only the Bavarian legislature rejected the Basic Law because it was considered too centralist. Nevertheless, at a state ceremony in Bonn on May 23, 1949, the Basic Law was proclaimed.

The deputies to the Parliamentary Council still had vivid memories of the weaknesses of the Weimar Constitution and of the totalitarian rule of the National Socialists. They therefore sought to build effective safeguards around the new democracy to protect it against totalitarian influences from the left and right. A stable democracy was provided for in Article 20, based on the constitutional principle that all state actions have to be based on the rule of law, the democratic principle that people participate in approving of state actions, the social welfare principle that the state promotes equal opportunity and social justice, and the federalist principle that state powers are divided between the federal and state levels. The first article dealing with human rights had its roots in the liberal tradition of the Constitution of 1848. Some of the efforts made to correct the weaknesses of the Weimar Constitution included weakening the powers of the federal president to a ceremonious role and making the electoral law for the legislature (Bundestag) a dual system of proportional representation and single-member constituencies. The delegates who wrote the constitution also tried to reduce the likelihood of splinter parties; the state could also ban totalitarian parties that were a threat to the republican constitution. The legislature was made the most important organ in the decision-making process, reflecting the sovereignty of the people. To reduce the possibility of cabinet crises through a parliamentary vote of no confidence, the Basic Law stipulated a "constructive vote of no confidence," which required that the opposition parties must have a replacement cabinet ready. Civil liberties were guaranteed, but advocacy of anti-Semitism, racism, or the overthrow of the democratic form of government was prohibited as an abuse. While the proposal of the SPD to include "socioeconomic rights" was rejected, the state promised to support the family and the church. States' rights were represented in the second or upper chamber of the legislature, the Bundesrat, and the Federal Constitutional Court was clearly modeled after the Supreme Court of the United States.

ECONOMIC RECONSTRUCTION

The economic conditions of Germany were terrible, and in 1945 there was not much hope of improvement. Industrial production had sunk to one-third of prewar levels and food was in such short supply that during the severe winter of 1946–47 daily rations were about 1,000 calories. The economic policy of the occupation forces were primarily dominated by the aim of destroying Germany's war-waging potential and acquiring compensation or reparations for their wartime losses. U.S. economic planners had some contradictory goals. Their list of some 1,210 industrial plants to be dismantled would have reduced German industrial capacity to 75 percent of 1936 levels. Yet, if this would have been carried out, the other American goal of making their zone economically self-sufficient would not have been possible. The winter of 1946–47 proved that German production had to be increased or the western zones would become permanent financial liabilities for the United States and Great Britain, which itself depended on America for aid. Consequently, only a small number of plants were ever dismantled, contrary to the massive number removed from the Soviet sector. Simultaneously, the cold war was beginning, and a fundamental change in U.S. policy took place as announced by Secretary of State James F. Byrnes, who promised a continued military presence in Germany and economic aid. The United States and Britain then economically united their zones in January 1947 into the Bizone, which was gradually administered by the Economic Council, which met in Frankfurt am Main. This body made a momentous decision to establish a market economy and rejected the system proposed by the Social Democrats, which was based on

Ruins of a large building after Allied bombing in Berlin, 1945 *(Library of Congress)*

planning and socialization. One of the market economy's most determined advocates was Professor Ludwig Erhard, who later served for many years as minister of economics.

In June 1947 the Marshall Plan, or European Recovery Program, was announced, through which the United States would fund the economic reconstruction of Europe. The western zones received a large addition to the regular aid they received. The Marshall Plan helped direct economic planning away from nationalization, which was quite popular, toward a free market system, and it made the American dollar the dominant currency. It also speeded up, however, the division of Germany and Europe until the end of the cold war in 1989. What further aided economic recovery was the long-planned currency reform. On June 20, 1948, the almost worthless reichsmark was redeemed at the rate of 10 reichsmarks to one deutsche mark. Every resident was at first given 40 of the new deutsche marks (DM) and later another 20. On June 23 the Soviet Union announced a currency reform in its zone and in all of Berlin. The Western Powers declared this measure to be void in their sectors of Berlin and introduced the DM there as well. In addition, Ludwig Erhard eliminated all economic controls and forms of rationing. These decisions bolstered the industrial upturn, which had already begun. Amazingly, by the end of 1949 prewar levels had almost been reached. The population at first did not benefit as much as expected. Shop windows filled up, but prices rose steeply and wages were frozen, resulting in rising unemployment.

THE FEDERAL REPUBLIC

1949–1990

ADENAUER ERA

In 2003 Germans were asked to name the greatest person their country had ever produced. To the surprise of many Konrad Adenauer received more votes than other famous personalities such as Martin Luther, Otto von Bismarck, Ludwig van Beethoven, or Johann Wolfgang von Goethe. Their choice was a good one because his leadership made possible the resurrection of a German state after World War II, which not only became a parliamentary democracy but also a trusted Western ally against the Soviet Union. His leadership was the greatest asset of the fledgling Federal Republic. He already had been an important political figure during the Weimar era as mayor of Cologne before his dismissal by the Nazis in 1933. A conservative Catholic who detested totalitarianism but did not actively participate in the resistance, he nonetheless was arrested and managed to experience the pain of concentration camp life. He was again made mayor of Cologne in 1945 by the military government, but his proud independence and criticisms of the occupation led to his dismissal by the British, which nonetheless contributed to his popularity among the Germans. He was then free to organize the Christian Democratic Union (CDU) first in the British zone and then in the rest of West Germany. He became the leading figure in the CDU and in 1949 was chosen the Federal Republic's first chancellor. His patience and negotiating skill helped him gain concessions from the Western Allied powers. His dislike of Prussia and Berlin meant that he would have little hesitation to move the capital from Berlin to Bonn in his native Rhineland, "where Germany's windows are wide open to the West." His Catholicism also became an advantage as so many Protestants were located in East Germany behind the Iron Curtain. He was patriarchal and a "father figure" for millions of Germans in the difficult transition from Hitler's dictatorship to democratic self-government. It was also good for Germany's economic future that he favored free market principles and rejected the demand for the nationalization of basic industries that so many Germans preferred. He chose as his minister of economics Ludwig Erhard, who had dismantled price controls and rationing imposed under the Allied occupation. Criticized for allowing former Nazis to occupy political offices, he replied that only unrepentant Nazis should be kept from holding office. Besides bringing the Federal Republic into the Western fold as part of NATO (North Atlantic Treaty Organization), he made a priority of reconciling differences with France. He cultivated a friendship with Israel and recognized the need to pay restitution to Jews for Hitler's crimes. Finally, Adenauer's control over the cabinet and parliament was so firm that it was said he had invented a new political system known as "Chancellor-Democracy."

Yet, even with such an impressive figure in a position of leadership, the shadow of the failed Weimar Republic hung over the revival of German political life. People wondered if democracy could ever be revived or ever succeed. What then were the factors that made it possible for the Federal Republic to become a successful liberal democracy? There was no unpopular treaty to defend as Weimar had to do with the Versailles Treaty. The Potsdam Conference had set the geographic boundaries for the postwar German state, and the historic state of Prussia was dissolved, which eliminated the basis of power of the conservative elites (Junkers). There also was to be no "stab-in-the-back-legend" that civilians were to blame for Germany's defeat as was the case after 1918. The defeat of the military was quite clear, and no longer would there be a state within a state, as was the case with the army before and after World War I. A more homogeneous population emerged after 1945. Regional differences

U.S. Air Force C-54s are lined up awaiting takeoff from Rhein-Main Air Base in Frankfurt for Berlin during the airlift. *(United States Air Force)*

were diminished, and the war had brought about an unprecedented mingling of peoples from different classes and regions. The population of the Federal Republic was 20 percent larger than it was in 1938, while a considerable area of agricultural land was lost. Some 7 million refugees from eastern Europe were resettled in Germany, which considerably changed the population. For instance, the refugees from the Sudetenland of Czechoslovakia provided a stimulus for industrial development that had been missing, especially in Bavaria. Due to the excesses of the war, nationalism declined and the "reformed Germans" were accepted into the European community. Most Germans turned their backs on the recent past and did not resist the Allied occupation or parliamentary democracy, which was backed by the United States.

The emergence of the cold war as early as 1946 led to the Berlin Blockade of 1948. The Soviets had reacted to the currency reform in the western zones on June 24, 1948, by imposing a blockade on all land and water routes to West Berlin. The Western powers responded to this by instituting an air lift lasting for 11 months, which supplied the city of 2 million. It was finally lifted on May 12, 1949. The division of political life was complete. The Allied High Command and Soviet authorities split up on June 16, 1948. Meetings of city councils were transferred to the western sector, and by the end of the year separate administrations took up residence in different sectors of the city, ending the effort to integrate West Berlin into the Soviet zone. Two German states were then set up. On May 23, 1949, the Federal Republic of Germany was officially established following the publication of the Basic Law. The Soviet Union followed suit on October 7, 1949, by setting up the German Democratic Republic, which made the division of Germany complete.

BUNDESTAG ELECTION AND ADENAUER CABINET

At first the elections in the Federal Republic kept a traditional multiparty character. Thirteen parties were listed on the ballot. After a fierce election campaign voters went to the polls on August 14, 1949. One of the major issues debated during the campaign was the future economic policy of the Federal Republic. The CDU and CSU emerged as the strongest party group with 31 percent of the votes cast, closely followed by the Social Democrats with 29.2 percent. The liberal Free Democratic Party (FDP) established itself as a third force, and in addition eight other parties succeeded in winning parliamentary seats. Thus a clear majority of the electorate had voted in favor of the parties that supported Erhard's policy of a capitalist social market economy. Nevertheless it was not yet clear whether these parties would be able to agree upon the formation of a coalition government. Konrad Adenauer with great tactical skill helped form a middle-class coalition with the FDP and German Party (DP). As part of the negotiations the chairman, Theodor Heuss, was chosen as federal president on September 12, 1949. Three days later, Adenauer himself was elected as federal chancellor by only a one-vote majority. Yet by the end of the 1950s the two parties, the CDU/CSU and the SPD, appealed to a wide spectrum of voters across class and geographic divisions. The liberals of the FDP trailed behind and became a swing party, sometimes allied with the CDU/CSU and sometimes with the SPD.

It was largely due to the charisma and abilities of Konrad Adenauer that the CDU/CSU succeeded in transforming itself above class and religious divisions into a majority party, receiving more than 50 percent of the vote in 1957.

That is not to say that the transition to democratic government was not without its difficulties. In his search for experienced civil servants, Adenauer followed a policy of forgive and forget, sometimes appointing ex-Nazis who were repentant to high governmental posts. One of his high-profile choices was Hans Globke, an ex-Nazi, as minister of the interior to run his chancery. Globke had been one of the architects of the infamous anti-Jewish Nuremberg racial laws, which tainted the Federal Republic with accusations of pro-Nazi sympathies. Denazification became an obvious victim of the Adenauer government in which 60 percent of all government section chiefs were chosen from former Nazi Party members. As the British High Commissioner Sir Ivone Kirkpatrick remarked, he constantly ran into former Nazi administrators in industry and society. The reliance on former Nazi administrators was explained and justified by an interpretation of the Nazi dictatorship as an accidental aberration of German history outside of the German tradition.

Interpreting their role in the Nazi tyranny, both Protestant and Catholic churches had differing responses. At a meeting of the Protestant Church leaders in Stuttgart on October 19, 1945, a statement of admission and repentance was issued for the church's cooperation in the suffering that Germany had inflicted on so many peoples. Noticeably absent was any reference to the Jews or the Holocaust. Martin Niemöller, a concentration camp survivor, confessed to the Christian's sins of omission. At this time the Catholic Church was less repentant and did not admit to cooperation with the regime. It resisted the concept of collective guilt that all Germans were responsible for the crimes of the Nazi period. In the debates about and the writing of the Basic Law, the Church's Concordat of 1933 was confirmed as valid, still governing church-state relations.

Besides dealing with the denazification process, Adenauer's first government had to deal with the potential opposition by the Union of Expellees and Dispossessed (BHE), which lobbied for Germans who had lost their properties in the East. Organized in 1950, it made a strong showing in Schleswig-Holstein, and the 1953 Bundestag elections returned 27 deputies. Many of these voters gradually were coopted by the CDU, discontinued their opposition, and were convinced to join a mainstream party to achieve their goals. By 1957 the BHE could not meet the Basic Law's requirement that small parties must receive 5 percent of the vote in order to return deputies. Another example of the way the Federal Republic avoided Weimar's polarization of the electorate was the case of the Communist Party (KPD) and the neo-Nazi Socialist Reich Party (SRP), whose voter support was minimal. When it became clear that the SRP had fascist goals, the Federal Constitutional Court outlawed it.

REGAINING SOVEREIGNTY AND INTEGRATION WITH THE WEST

The rapid acquisition of sovereignty by West Germany was to a great degree due to the advent of the cold war. Adenauer's goal was to have the Federal

Republic rejoin the family of nations. Three issues were fundamental in his thinking. West Germany had to maintain a friendship with the United States and France. He decided to place West Germany firmly in the Western camp and not flirt with the Russian attempt to neutralize central Europe. In November 1949 Adenauer negotiated the "Petersburg Agreement," in which he promised to cooperate in economic and political matters with the Western Allies and give up the possibility of rearmament. The "chancellor of the allies," as he was labeled by his political opponent, Kurt Schumacher of the SPD, realized that if Germany took the part of the West in the cold war the Western Allies would gradually relinquish control. In 1951 Adenauer took another step toward his goal, agreeing to the establishment of the European Coal and Steel Authority, which placed Franco-German coal and steel production under one authority. This Schuman Plan began the integration of West Germany into Western Europe. The Korean War provided the next opportunity. Since the United States was interested in lightening its defense burden in Europe, Adenauer proposed the creation of a border patrol force and military units to form part of an all-European army. For their part the Allies agreed that the Federal Republic could establish a foreign office to conduct a foreign policy and the legislation of the German states would not have to be approved. Opposition to German rearmament came from France and within Germany from various groups. Yet Adenauer pushed it through the parliament (Bundestag). The rewards were many. On July 9, 1951, the end of the state of war was declared. In 1952 the General Treaty formally abolished major parts of the Occupation Statute of 1949 and promised to defend West Germany against a Soviet attack. Adenauer also agreed to the desire of the United States that Germany reestablish its armed forces. The rearmament was opposed by the Social Democrats. A temporary setback occurred in August 1954, when France rejected the European Defense Community. Nonetheless, Washington and London decided to include German forces in the North Atlantic Treaty Organization (NATO). In return, the Germans renounced the production of atomic, biological, or chemical weapons. On October 23 the Paris Accords were signed, which admitted the Federal Republic into NATO with the Germans agreeing to contribute 500,000 men. German sovereignty was restored when the Paris Treaty came into force in May 1955. The new German army was integrated into the democratic political structure of West Germany, and care was taken that the old army, independent of civilian control, would not be reestablished. In October 1955 after a plebiscite and without alienating France the industrialized Saarland was reunified to Germany. Finally, it must not be forgotten that Adenauer's early decision to make reparation payments to Israel contributed to the Federal Republic's acceptance into the family of nations.

RECONSTRUCTION AND THE "ECONOMIC MIRACLE"

After the war Germany was a landscape of destroyed cities, hunger, cold, and joblessness. Its industrial production in 1946 was one-third of a decade earlier.

Yet by 1953 the western half of Germany had exceeded the gross national product of 1936, with only 53 percent of the land area and 75 percent of its population. Although initially the results of this recovery were unevenly distributed, average wages reached prewar levels in 1950 and doubled by 1965. This extraordinary recovery and period of economic prosperity became the cornerstone of the political and social stability of the Adenauer era. The annual growth rate was 10 percent, and gross national product tripled between 1950 and 1960 with an inflation rate below 3 percent. The export-driven economy brought increasing gold and currency reserves into the central bank (Bundesbank). By 1961 full employment had been achieved. The West German economy grew into the third-strongest in the world and second only to the United States in world trade.

How was this so-called economic miracle made possible? There were many factors that contributed to this astounding recovery. The foundations were in the removal of price controls and monetary reform in 1948. The new currency remained stable and was controlled by a politically independent central bank (Bundesbank), which encouraged savings and investment. The Marshall Plan aid stimulated the economy further but supplied only 7 percent of Germany's capital. The demand created by the Korean War and the general worldwide economic upturn further stimulated growth. Efficient management, a large supply of skilled labor provided by refugees, and a docile labor force were important. Labor unions restrained their demands for wage increases, which kept the price of German goods competitive on the world market. The Federal Republic avoided the pitfalls of the labor-management problems of the 1920s by negotiating labor's success in gaining equal representation on the supervisory boards of the iron and steel industry. The replacement of old with new modern equipment was stimulated by the destruction of the war and the reparations for the dismantling of factories by the Allies after the war.

A great deal of the credit must also be attributed to the welfare-state capitalism that was fostered by the economics minister Ludwig Erhard. The model he chose was called a social market economy, based on a free market economy relying on private enterprise, allowing market forces to dominate and keeping state intervention to a minimum. The best solution for unemployment Erhard maintained was economic growth that would create jobs for all. The role of the state was focused on preventing economic concentrations that hampered competition and canceling the social inequalities that capitalism created. Those Germans who had hoped for at least the reduction of socioeconomic inequalities that had embittered German politics in the past were disappointed by Erhard's policies, which maintained the traditional relation between capital and labor. The economic boom of the 1950s made it possible for the Federal Republic to address some of its social problems. The main tasks were caring for war victims, solving the housing shortage, and integrating refugees and expellees into society. In addition to state-financed housing construction another key policy was the equalization of the tax burden, involving a redistribution of wealth that favored the war victims, refugees, and others hurt by the currency reform. Other social reforms followed, which allowed for a 40-hour workweek and pension reform that linked pensions to the rising cost and standard of living.

TRANSITIONAL YEARS AND ECONOMIC CRISIS UNDER LUDWIG ERHARD, 1963–1969

After the retirement of Konrad Adenauer, Ludwig Erhard was elected Federal chancellor by the Bundestag on October 16, 1963. His government, like its predecessors, was based on a coalition between the CDU/CSU and the FDP. Erhard was increasingly faced by new challenges, however, and some old problems. The cold war had entered into a new period of détente after the Cuban missile crisis and Nikita Khrushchev's dismissal, which threatened to make permanent the division of Germany. An economic crisis had become evident by 1964–65 especially in the energy industry, where the Ruhr coal industry could no longer compete with oil and imported coal. Fear of inflation led to inadequate countercyclical measures, which made unemployment rise rapidly, and recession aroused exaggerated fears and worries. The economic crisis gave rise to a neo-Nazi revival and electoral successes for the National Democratic Party (NPD), which had been founded in 1964. Simultaneously, there was a dramatic trial of former SS officers from the concentration camp at Auschwitz and a stormy public debate over the extension of the time during which former war criminals could be tried. The government's foreign policy also had its limitations. Although the Federal Republic negotiated nonaggression declarations for the first time, Erhard nonetheless continued to refuse to recognize the legitimacy of East Germany (GDR) and the status quo in Europe. Adding to this was a debate between "Atlanticists," who thought that close German-American relations provided better security for Germany, and "Gaullists," who wanted to forge special links to France. Gradually Erhard's position was undermined, and failing to solve a crisis in the coalition, a new Grand Coalition was formed.

THE GRAND COALITION AND YOUTH PROTEST

After the fall of the Erhard government, the CDU/CSU nominated Kurt Georg Kiesinger, the minister-president of Baden-Württemberg, as the third chancellor of the Federal Republic. The so-called Grand Coalition was formed, which included the CDU/CSU and the SPD, and it was agreed that the alliance would last for only a short time. The formation of the coalition was motivated by fears of the neo-Nazi (NPD) successes in the state elections of Hesse and Bavaria and the desire of the SPD to test its capacity to govern after 17 years in opposition. Led by the economics minister, Karl Schiller, neo-Keynesian measures were used to fight the recession. The budget was balanced and taxes raised, mostly on consumers, and before long in fall 1968 unemployment became minimal. During the Grand Coalition the Basic Law was amended quite often. Financial laws were adapted to modern economic management. These and other governmental reforms were adjustments to the requirements of an industrial society and were some of the most important achievements of the Grand Coalition.

As important were the political debates and public opposition to the Emergency Powers Acts that the Bundestag passed in May 1968. These acts amended the Basic Law and ended the veto powers of the Allies, creating specific policies for emergency situations, especially defense. There also was intense debate over

Willy Brandt *(Library of Congress)*

whether the Federal Republic should embrace a two-party instead of a multi-party system. The proposal was rejected because of opposition by the SPD and public protest. The small liberal party, the FDP, probably would have dissolved.

The 1960s also saw the rise of protest movements that were critical of West German materialism, affluence, and unwillingness to confront the past. Student protests and criticism were sparked by the out-of-date structures of the university system and inadequate educational facilities. When a student was shot by the police on June 2, 1967, during a demonstration against the state visit of the shah of Iran, the violence spread from West Berlin. Yet it was more than a protest against the academic system. The protest movement paralleled the U.S. student movement, which opposed American intervention in the Vietnam War and against dictatorial regimes around the world. In Germany the movement was also against the solidarity of the Grand Coalition, its passage of the Emergency Powers Act, and the lack of a meaningful political opposition. The younger generation was reacting against traditional authority and demanded changes and democratization in all spheres of life. The most serious level of violence occurred after an assassination attempt against the life of Rudi Dutschke, a student leader in Berlin. Violent street battles protested against Axel Springer, the famous publisher who was blamed for inciting the assassination plot. Although the movement gradually declined, criticism and dissent became institutionalized. The questioning of the traditional German way of life and behavior was a lasting consequence of the movement. Yet, in the confrontation with state authority violence unfortunately became a weapon of political conflict.

THE SOCIAL-LIBERAL COALITION

On October 21, 1969, Willy Brandt of the SPD was elected chancellor by a narrow majority, the first Social Democratic head of government in the Federal Republic. The FDP and SPD formed a Social-Liberal governing coalition, which became the first transfer of power to an opposition party in the Federal Republic and lasted from 1969 to 1982. Willy Brandt became the second of West Germany's great chancellors and in 1971 was the first German leader since Gustav Stresemann awarded the Nobel Peace Prize. As mayor of Berlin in 1961 he had witnessed the city's physical partition with the erection of the Berlin Wall. His new foreign policy personified a spirit of reconciliation between Germany and the peoples of Eastern Europe and the GDR.

The domestic policy of the new government was summed up in Chancellor Brandt's first speech, which announced that not only the government but all aspects of society would be democratized. That was too bold a claim as political realities limited the ability of the government to carry out such a plan. The government proposed to improve the educational system, modernize the legal system, extend the social security network, strengthen the rights of workers, and open their opportunities to participate in the management of companies. Besides the disputes over the Eastern treaties, there were other differences of opinion that hampered the democratization initiatives. One of the contentious reforms concerned the issue of worker participation in company management and that of the laws governing abortion. The initial bill on abortion was declared incompatible with the Basic Law by the Federal Constitutional Court, and was followed by a guideline regulation. One of the most significant changes concerning family law was the introduction of no-fault divorce. The debate over worker participation in workers' councils continued until 1976, when a law was passed for equal representation of workers on the councils in all large-scale companies, but the shareholder representatives remained dominant in conflict situations. Some reforms were made in education, and the university system was expanded, which provided for greater equality of opportunity. In social welfare the most significant measures included a flexible system for old-age pension eligibility, an improved system of sickness benefits, and a reform of family allowance and rent laws. The economic crisis of 1974–75 proved that the expansion of social programs had reached its limit.

OSTPOLITIK (FOREIGN POLICY WITH THE EAST)

The chancellorship of Willy Brandt coincided with the era of more peaceful relations (détente) between Russia and the United States. The superpowers desired more peaceful relations between West and East Germany, a desire that coincided with the goals of Brandt and Walter Scheel. These leaders were among a group of policy makers called the "new realists" who competed with such older points of view as the "Atlanticists" and the "Gaullists," who believed that European interests did not always coincide with those of the United States. What Brandt and Scheel wanted to accomplish was to improve East-West relations, create stability for West Berlin, and improve contacts between East and West Germans. In return the West Germans would agree to give up the Hallstein Doctrine and accept the post-1945 boundary changes in Eastern Europe. These policy changes had been prepared in some small way by attempts during the Erhard government to create a thaw in East-West relations. Then a behind-the-scenes adviser to Brandt, Egon Bahr (SPD), promoted the idea of friendlier relations, "change through rapprochement" between East and West. Out of this optimistic thinking emerged a new and realistic policy toward the East, rather than that based on the Hallstein Doctrine, which refused to recognize the regime of the GDR and attempted to isolate it internationally. The new Ostpolitik of Willy Brandt was both a process and a goal, which resulted in a series of bilateral agreements between West Germany and the Soviet Union, then the Communist regimes of Eastern Europe, and finally the GDR.

The Treaty of Moscow, signed on August 12, 1970, was the basis of the system of Eastern treaties devised by the SPD/FDP government. The nonaggression agreement and the recognition of existing borders, which the treaty contained, also formed the basis of later treaties with Poland, Czechoslovakia, and the GDR. Linked with the treaty was the four powers' agreement on Berlin, the Basic Treaty of 1972, which eased restrictions on traffic to West Berlin. It also made possible visits by West Berliners to the communist eastern part of the city. The problems that were confronted in crafting an agreement over Berlin were enormous. Since the Allies retained sovereign rights over the Western sectors of the city, talks between the four powers were necessary. After months of negotiation the Big Four powers finally concluded the 1972 agreement, which gave recognition to East Germany while the Russians and the GDR agreed to respect the ties of West Berlin to West Germany.

Since the foreign policy debates of the 1950s there had never been such bitter political struggles in the Federal Republic. Opposition to the treaties was led by Franz Josef Strauss, leader of the CSU, Helmut Kohl, deputy chairman of the CDU, and Erich Mende of the right wing of the FDP. The conservatives tried to oust Chancellor Brandt by a constructive vote of no confidence, which failed, though the debates did not subside until the parliamentary elections of

November 19, 1972. Brandt made sure that elections would occur through a no-confidence motion, which ensured the elections and confirmed the social-liberal coalition in office. The conservatives even rejected the treaties during the confirmation process. Nevertheless, that was all part of the growth of West German democracy. A different political approach was followed in the GDR, where the hard-liner, Walter Ulbricht, still ruled. Ulbricht disagreed with Brandt's proposals and was soon undemocratically replaced by Moscow with the more agreeable party leader Erich Honecker.

Against considerable opposition from the CDU/CSU, Brandt was able to push through a series of treaties and agreements that culminated in the Basic Treaty between East and West Germany in December 1972 and ratified in May 1973. The two Germanies accepted equality of status in relations with each other. In September 1973 both Germanies were accepted as independent states in the United Nations. Even though both Germanies recognized each other, that did not mean that they accepted the other as a foreign state, but in a special relationship exchanging "permanent representatives" and not ambassadors. Brandt's new eastern policy succeeded in easing tensions between the two Germanies and made West Germany a participant in détente.

Brandt's coalition soon faced troubled times. The Yom Kippur War of October 6, 1973, in which Egypt and Syria attacked Israel, led to the Arab oil embargo. An economic downturn resulted because the industries of West Germany were mostly dependent on Middle Eastern oil, which tripled in cost. Inflation had already damaged the economy, due to massive government spending on education, social welfare, and defense. As Brandt's popularity declined, international terrorism at the Olympic Games in Munich during 1972 also embarrassed the government when a helicopter sent to rescue the Jewish athletes exploded. Unfortunately and unknown to Brandt his close personal adviser, Günter Guillaume, was an East German spy, which after his exposure led to Brandt's resignation. Although Brandt continued as chair of the SPD and went on to become president of the Socialist International, his colleague, Walter Scheel, was elected federal president and Hans-Dietrich Genscher (FDP) became foreign minister.

CULTURE AND SOCIETY

The German experience with Nazism separated artists and writers from earlier traditions, leaving them rootless and confused. Nazi culture had so debauched many German words and ideas that it made it difficult for writers to use them again. Perhaps it can be said that literature reached its lowest point during the Nazi period. One of the major traditions in German culture had been philosophic humanism, which was highly personal and introspective in character. After the war some authors like Heinrich Böll rejected that tradition and attempted to describe the events of everyday life. Böll and the younger writers of the postwar period had belonged to the intellectual circle called Group 47. It had been organized in 1947 by the two left-wing authors and provided stimulation, criticism, and encouragement for the next two decades. Besides Böll, other members included Albrecht Goes, Ingeborg Bachmann, Wolfdietrich Schnurr, Hans Magnus Enzensberger, Günter Grass, and Uwe Johnson. In their practical political involvement they departed from the German intellectual tradition, wherein writers lived in their ivory towers and wrote about personal subjects. A large number of works of the postwar period deal with Nazism and war. All of the writers believed that they wanted to play a role in shaping the new German democracy. Some were politically active, such as Günter Grass, who actively campaigned for the SPD. Albrecht Goes was an especially relevant writer shortly after the war, writing two short works, *The Unquiet Night* (1949) and the *The Burnt Offering* (1954), the latter depicting the suffering of the Jews and the desire for atonement by some Germans, reflecting the author's religious and humanitarian attitude toward life.

Less religious and more objective and detached were the three major authors of the postwar period, Heinrich Böll, Günter Grass, and Uwe Johnson, each representing the eclecticism of the new literature. Heinrich Böll received the Nobel Prize in literature in 1972 for the novel *Billiards at Half Past Nine,* which critically commented on the society of the Adenauer era. Son of a cabinetmaker from Cologne and defender of the underdog, he had a sense of humor and social satire common to the Rhinelanders. Other novels of his included *Adam, Where Were You?* (1951), *The Clown* (1963), and *Group Portrait with Lady* (1971). *Adam, Where Were You?* is an excellent war book without a plot and depictions of fighting, which nevertheless depicts the war as cruel, absurd, and grotesque. Günter Grass came from the prewar city of Danzig and wrote of the Nazi period that he experienced as well as the horrors of war. The dominant theme in his Danzig trilogy, *The Tin Drum* (1959), *Cat and Mouse* (1961), and *Dog Years* (1963) is the failure of the German people to critically deal with their Nazi past. As a socialist he also campaigned for the SPD, and during the campaign for reunification in 1990 not surprisingly opposed it. The novelist Martin Walser also wrote satirically about the middle class and their competitive status consciousness. Hans Magnus Enzensberger was a scathing critic of the society created by the prosperity of the economic miracle. Playwright Rolf Hochhuth employed political themes in *The Deputy* (1963), in which he accused Pope Pius XII of silence and moral indifference about the Holocaust.

SOCIAL STRUCTURE

Although reflective of postwar German society, what the writers emphasized was only part of the story. The social structure had changed. The old upper classes of landed aristocracy, army officers, and government bureaucracy were no longer dominant. The prosperity of the economic miracle did create a so-called leveled-off, larger middle class consisting of businessmen, skilled workers, and technicians. Yet it was not a classless society as has often been presumed. Former elites like university professors, businessmen, and church leaders still persisted. Some upper-class families retained the *von* in their names and could be found in leading roles. Although less powerful than it used to be, a German upper class still existed and exercised both economic and political influence. Most of the wealthiest families in Germany had acquired their wealth during the period of industrialization, such as the Krupp, Bosch, and Siemens families.

Some others arose earlier, such as the Haniel family, which was granted the right to build a warehouse in Duisburg by Frederick the Great. Another wealthy family of historical interest is the Thurn and Taxis family, which founded the postal service of the Holy Roman Empire. The educational system remained traditional, largely reproducing the social status of the parents until the reforms of the Brandt era. Few areas adopted the comprehensive school, and most operated with the three-part selective system that favored the children of middle-class professional families. Working-class and rural children were not given the opportunities to achieve their potential. As the economy shifted from a predominantly industrial to a service economy, there developed a considerable amount of structural social mobility. It also must be emphasized that in West Germany all sectors of the workforce were well trained and qualified for their occupations.

WOMEN'S ROLES

Women were generally expected to choose between family and a career. After the heyday of the postwar "rubble women" women reverted to their traditional roles, which emphasized the bearing of children, cooking in the kitchen, and attending church. Educationally, women did not receive apprenticeship training that led to higher paying jobs and were underrepresented at the higher levels of the educational ladder. Those employed outside the home tended to be found in lower-status and lower-income employment and more often than men employed in smaller companies. Overall, women had lower occupational attainment than men and received less education than women in other industrialized nations. Despite government efforts and the feminist movement, women generally were expected to choose between raising a family and working in a career. Child care provisions were not conducive to a household with working parents. In general, Germany has had the greatest gender inequality of any of the advanced industrial countries. There was hope, however, that through the efforts of the Social Democrats and the Greens that significant changes in the field of gender equality would occur.

CULTURAL VALUES

Cultural life during the early decades of the Federal Republic was decidedly materialistic and reinforced traditional values. The medium of communication remained newspapers, magazines, and books in addition to radio and later television. Besides being more avid readers, Germans also frequented movies and appreciated concerts. Perhaps as much as any other group activity, Germans had always been active in social and athletic clubs. As prosperity took hold, they also loved to go on vacations, especially in warmer climates like the Mediterranean countries of Italy, Greece, Spain, and Turkey. Television in Germany was publicly financed and not commercial as in the United States. The films that Germans preferred showed happy family life, entertaining comedies and, of course, American imports. American popular music and jazz also had a large audience.

In the 1960s and '70s the younger generation came of age, and the population increased to slightly more than 60 million by 1980. Student revolts, rock-

and-roll music, and disdain for the values of their elders were reflected in the idealism of youth. The younger generation favored European integration, desired greater social mobility, and were ecologically minded. The realization of some of their dreams was made possible by the institution of the comprehensive 12-year school system, which in some areas replaced the three-tiered system. The expansion of the university system broke the control that tenured professors had over the universities, and the number of college age students enrolled rose from 2 percent in the 1950s to 20 percent in the 1980s, although nowhere near the almost 50 percent in American institutions of higher learning. Institutional growth in higher education also occurred, expanding the number from 26 to 49.

FOREIGN WORKERS

West Germany also possessed a large group of foreign guest workers, who became an under class. In the early years of the republic refugees had been abundant and provided a cheap labor force. When the Berlin Wall was built in 1961, this source dried up and workers came from Mediterranean countries and even Turkey. Before long, Turkish workers and their families became the single largest foreign group helping provide cheap nonunion labor for an expanding economy, paying taxes and performing jobs that Germans no longer were willing to do. The foreigners, however, did not qualify to become citizens. Germany's conservative political elites maintained that Germany was not an immigrant country like the United States. With the economic recession of the 1970s and 1980s and the rise of unemployment incentives, the Kohl government even offered foreign workers incentives to return home, not an easy task when these noncitizens composed one-10th of the West German population. Also these minorities resisted cultural assimilation and created social problems. Rising racial hostility was evident in the rise of right-wing political movements that opposed their presence.

SCHMIDT ERA: SOCIAL UNREST, TERRORISM, AND THE END OF DÉTENTE

Helmut Schmidt, who followed Willy Brandt as chancellor, was a Social Democrat from Hamburg. He had the reputation of a tough administrator, and had been a minister of the interior and leader of the SPD's Bundestag caucus. In the Brandt-Scheel cabinet he was an outstanding minister of defense. In 1974 when Brandt left office and Scheel became federal president, Schmidt became chancellor and Hans Dietrich Genscher (FDP) became Schmidt's coalition partner for the next eight years. The alliance between the two, however, did not work as well as did that of Brandt and Scheel. Genscher was too independent and his personality too secretive. During their tenure of office Germany faced serious problems of social unrest, economic disruption, political terrorism, and foreign policy challenges.

Schmidt did reap some of the benefits of Brandt's eastern policy. On July 10, 1974, Germany and Czechoslovakia established formal diplomatic relations and together abrogated the old Munich Agreement of 1938. The next year Schmidt joined the Conference on European Security and Cooperation at Helsinki. With Erich Honecker of the GDR, Schmidt agreed to safeguard human rights. Schmidt also aimed at achieving progress in the field of European unity and harmonizing the economic policies of industrialized nations. However, from 1974 to 1977 the terrorist Red Army Faction (RAF) tried to destabilize the Federal Republic through murder, kidnappings, and bombings. The West German government responded with arrests and loyalty oaths. Schmidt was also criticized by the growing environmental movement. Fear of a nuclear accident, acid rain and water pollution, and the placement of nuclear weapons on German soil also led to the formation of the Green Party, which later entered the Bundestag in 1983. Nevertheless, the Schmidt/Genscher government won a clear majority in the parliamentary elections of October 1980. The SPD, however, became divided over the placement of American intermediate missiles to counter the threat of Soviet SS 20 missiles. Major economic policy differences between Schmidt and Genscher and welfare spending cuts led to another vote of no confidence, which ended Schmidt's career on September 17, 1982.

Helmut Schmidt's chancellorship was not marked by outstanding success in domestic affairs. Schmidt's image was that of a perceptive, cultured, and well-spoken leader, but also a vigorous, resolute, and conscientious realist who thought that Germany's problems could best be handled with careful, clear-eyed management. Schmidt, however, failed to adequately consider the philosophical as well as the purely political aspects of the problems he faced. Schmidt's firm, centralist style of leadership had some successes. But his inability to produce a convincing political rationale to underpin and connect his policy decisions and his failure to win political support for those decisions contributed to the unraveling of his chancellorship.

THE KOHL ERA, 1982–1998

Chronic economic problems and the end of détente had undermined support for the Social-Liberal coalition that had been in power since 1969. After the FDP agreed on a program with the CDU/CSU, Helmut Kohl on October 1, 1982, was elected the next chancellor following a constructive vote of no confidence against Schmidt. The new government decided to call early elections for March 6, 1983. The CDU/CSU increased its share of the vote to 48.8 percent, and the Green Party passed the 5 percent hurdle and became the fourth party in the Parliament for the first time since the 1950s. Structural problems in the economy proved that the "economic miracle" was over and that the two oil shocks of the 1970s had disrupted world trade. So the voters protested against the inaction of the Schmidt-Genscher government, which had failed to effectively deal with the problems.

When Helmut Kohl became chancellor, little did he realize that he would become the longest-serving official in that capacity in the history of the Federal Republic. Kohl had begun his political career when he was elected to the state legislature of the Rhineland-Palatinate in 1959, where he then served as minister-president from 1969 to 1976. In the 1970s he directed the reorganization of the CDU's organization and was selected leader of the party in 1973.

Running unsuccessfully for chancellor in 1976 and deferring to Franz Josef Strauss's candidacy in 1980, Kohl in 1982 became the youngest chancellor in the Republic's history.

Kohl was committed to two ideals, that of states' rights against the centralizing tendencies of the SPD, and binding the Federal Republic to the Common Market. Based on the program of the CDU, which was adopted in 1978 at the Ludwigshafen convention, Kohl defended the free market economy and insisted on reducing the welfare budget. In doing so his conservative government tried to reduce the size of government but did not pursue radical economic restructuring and privatization. In order to stimulate the economy and increase investment, tax cuts and other incentives were introduced. Although a difficult challenge, the government tried to change the expectations that Germans had about social welfare. In other areas the government also implemented environmental reforms. Low-emission car engines and unleaded gasoline were among the measures that were introduced. Underlying structural problems in the economy nevertheless persisted, especially in the labor market, where job losses increased in the traditional sectors of shipping, coal, and steel, negatively affecting areas in the north and west. Strikes actually increased, and laws were proposed to limit them. The unemployment rate did not go down even though new jobs were created in high-tech industries. Most of these problems were due to changes in the world economy. In regard to the European Community, in December 1985 Kohl and other heads of government approved the revisions for the Treaty of Rome, which provided for the completion for an internal market, the development of monetary union, and expanded power for European institutions.

In foreign policy Kohl refused to accept the division of Germany, demanding self-determination for the people of the GDR, and he proclaimed that there was only "one German nation." In the area of foreign policy Kohl was weak, and his foreign minister, Genscher, was responsible for seeing the positive potential in the reforms of Gorbachev. Yet, no sooner had Kohl taken office than he was faced with a crisis concerning the great missile debate—whether or not the Americans could place missiles on German soil. A mass of 400,000 people demonstrated against the American policy, but Kohl successfully pushed the missile bill through the Bundestag in November 1983. Under Kohl the military alliance with the United States was strengthened, and he committed Germany more closely to the European Union. On the other hand, NATO's force modernization program placed a strain on relations with the Soviet Union and the GDR.

Kohl also tried to create a more positive national identity for the German people, rejecting the concept of collective guilt for the Nazi crimes of the past. A wave of Nazi revivalism, including the publication of the forged diaries of Adolf Hitler, embarrassed his administration. Anguish over the Nazi past was also manifested in Kohl's attempt during his visit to Israel to avoid responsibility for the crimes of the Nazi regime. Kohl also attempted reconciliation with France at the 1916 battlefield of Verdun, and in 1985 with the United States at the military cemetery at Bitburg, where he shook hands with President Ronald Reagan on the 40th anniversary of the end of World War II. For this effort Kohl was misunderstood, and he was criticized as insensitive to the Nazi past. Debates by leading historians over German responsibility for the Holocaust occurred between 1985 and 1988 in what came to be known as the Historikerstreit. Scholars such as Ernst Nolte, Andreas Hillgruber, Klaus Hildebrand, Hagen Schulze, and Michael Stürmer all questioned whether all Germans could be held responsible for Nazi crimes and whether Nazi crimes were unique. The philosopher Jürgen Habermas, who initiated the debate with these conservative historians, accused them of moral relativization and neonationalism. Even the respected president of the Republic, Ernst von Weizsäcker, felt he had to publicly remind his countrymen of the tyranny and brutality of the Nazi regime. Scandals and corruption also plagued Kohl's administration. In 1988

German chancellor Helmut Kohl stands behind U.S. president Ronald Reagan during Reagan's visit to Bonn. *(Reuters/Landov)*

the ministry of defense permitted plans for submarines to be delivered to South Africa. Other serious embarrassments concerned Iraq, to which Germany had sold weapons and contributed to its poison gas arsenal while German companies had even built Saddam Hussein's bunkers.

Kohl's greatest achievement was his leading role in the reunification of Germany, an achievement that favorably compares to those of Konrad Adenauer. Although Kohl's popularity was waning and the CDU suffered electoral setbacks in 1987, the changes propose by the Soviet leader, Gorbachev, were inevitably leading to the end of the cold war. As a good politician Kohl sensed the inevitability of reunification and proposed his Ten Point program, in which he envisaged a confederation of the two Germanies. As the crisis of population loss and economic instability continued in the GDR during 1989–90, the emphasis on unity became predominant. As demonstrations were taking place in the GDR during fall 1989, the crowds at first chanted "We are the people," but by the end of November they declared "We are one people," expressing sentiments for unification. At Christmas 1989 Helmut Kohl was given a tremendous welcome in Dresden, and he seized the initiative for unity, with American backing. In the campaign for the March 1990 elections to the People's Chamber (Volkskammer) Kohl promised East Germans quick unification and rapid economic integration as well as currency parity. The CDU backed the East German Alliance for Germany, which was victorious. The Two-Plus-Four talks began in May between the two Germanies and the four great powers, the United States, the Soviet Union, France, and Great Britain. Kohl and Genscher ably handled the talks; they agreed to guarantee the German frontier with Poland. During the summer, on July 14, Kohl and Genscher met with Mikhail Gorbachev, who did not object to a united Germany within NATO. Then the Caucasus Agreements allowed for unification in return for economic and military concessions. Shortly thereafter, on September 12, Germany was recognized as a sovereign state. The Treaty of Unification was signed on August 31. In the first all-German elections on December 2, 1990, Kohl was elected the first chancellor of a united Germany. A reunified Germany now had to face the problems of creating a common democracy, economic reconstruction of the bankrupt East, and the reestablishment of social relations between societies that had many differences.

The German Democratic Republic

As Germany lay in ruins in 1945, no one was certain what the future would hold. Although the emergence of the cold war made the division of Germany inevitable, that was not the intention of the Western Allies nor Stalin. The disagreements about the future of Germany were already evident during the conferences that the Allies held in Teheran (1943) and Yalta (February 1945). While there was agreement on dividing Germany into zones of occupation, differences arose over the issues of reparations and the western boundaries of a reconstituted Poland. At the Potsdam Conference from July to August 1945, it was, however, agreed that Germany would be denazified, demilitarized, and democratized. This did not mean that a uniform policy would be applied in the four zones of occupation. The agreements of the Potsdam Conference were applied in each zone as the occupying power saw fit. No peace treaty could be signed since no German government existed.

In the Russian zone, however, the most radical changes were implemented. Under the instruction of the Russians the German Communist leaders began to take some control. Many of these leaders, such as Walter Ulbricht (1893–1973), had been imprisoned in Nazi concentration camps or they had spent their years of exile in Moscow. Walter Ulbricht became the German Communist Party's effective leader in 1945 and remained its first secretary until 1953. With the backing of the Russians the German Communist leaders punished the former Nazis and their accomplices. Full-scale communization was to take place later. Initially, some multiparty pluralism was permitted with the Christian Democrats and the Liberal Party competing in the early elections. Walter Ulbricht believed that a one-party system could not be imposed as under Nazism, but as he said in May 1945: "It must look democratic, but the power must be in our hands." As early as April 1946, however, the Communists forced the Socialists to merge with them and created the Socialist Unity Party (SED), which became the ruling party in the GDR. On May 24, 1949, when the Federal Republic was formally set up in Bonn and the Basic Law went into force, the Russians reacted swiftly and established a state of their own. Consequently, the German Democratic Republic was set up on October 7, 1949, proclaimed by the East German People's Council (Volkskammer) after so-called elections with one list of candidates. The Socialist Unity Party (SED) consolidated its power, setting up a National Front organization to supervise society at the local level. It also purged thousands of pro-Westerners from public positions. In 1951 Soviet-style collectives were introduced in the factories, and a year later the collectivization of agriculture was intensified. All of these measures involved the use of terror against whole social groups. Since the borders were still open, this provoked a growing exodus to the West of middle-class and professional people as well as farmers and others.

East Germany had a "people's democracy" according to the first constitution of October 1949. The country was organized as a federal state divided into five regions (*Länder*), which had been states in the Weimar Republic: Brandenburg, Mecklenburg, Saxony, Saxony-Anhalt, and Thuringia. These were abolished in 1952 and replaced by smaller districts, which were more easily controlled by the central government. In 1958 the chamber representing the original five regions was abolished. The constitution described the political system as a political democracy with civil liberties, which sounded very democratic but was only a facade for the political practice of "democratic centralism" as was determined by the ideology of Marxism-Leninism. While elements of the middle class remained, it was the proletarian working class that was to provide the leadership for the transformation into socialism. In structure and ideology the SED followed the example of the Soviet Union. Although there were elections, a Party Congress, and a Central Committee, these did not provide the opportunity for debate or free decision making. The members of the Central Committee appointed the officials who headed government and the party. An example of the increasing alignment of the SED with the Communist Party in the Soviet Union was the result of the 1950 Party Congress, which led to the purge of some 150,000 party members who supposedly sympathized with Marshall Tito of Yugoslavia.

The recovery of the economy in the GDR was slow, struggling as it did with the reparations that the Soviet Union extracted. Machinery and even whole factories were shipped to the Soviet Union, and when that proved inefficient, industries were taken over and their profits expropriated. The inefficiencies caused by the massive nationalization of industry and collectivization of farms also placed a severe strain on the economy still struggling to recover from the war. The reaction of the government was to demand higher goals and workloads from workers while their living standards hardly improved. Problems resulting from these hard-line policies multiplied in 1952 and 1953. Food shortages, the reduction of demand for consumer goods, and a wave of secret police arrests produced a rapid increase in the flight of East Germans to the West, an increase from 72,000 to 110,000 from the first to the last half of 1952. By the end of 1952 some 15,000 farmers had left for the West, leaving 13 percent of the arable farmland unproductive. A crisis situation had developed.

UPRISING OF JUNE 17, 1953

Discontent over the new work quotas caused workers on June 16 to lay down their tools and march in protest on union headquarters and the Council of Ministers building. Then the construction workers in East Berlin revolted by stopping work and calling for a general strike on June 17, 1953. Their strike quickly spread to other branches of industry, to more than 200 other locations and especially some other large cities such as Leipzig and Magdeburg. At first the government responded cautiously, but when some of the demonstrators began to make political demands for free elections and the restoration of unions, Walter Ulbricht called for Russian help, and tanks from the army garrison rolled into action. The revolt was quickly suppressed. It was the first revolt of its kind in postwar Communist eastern Europe. In the eyes of many anti-Communists it was an example of Soviet brutality, while an assessment more favorable to the regime was that Russian firepower was used sparingly, resulting in the deaths of only 21 people. Before the revolt a thaw of Stalin's harsh policies was going on in Russia after his death in March 1953. Under consideration in Moscow was the replacement of Walter Ulbricht. Yet, the result of the uprising ironically strengthened his position. Besides being a genuine protest after eight years of socialism and repression, the uprising also was a product of disillusionment expressed by others, such as playwright Bertolt Brecht, who had been sympathetic to the new regime. He regretted the government's explanation that the people had betrayed the government's trust. Brecht responded, "Would it not have been simpler if the government had dissolved the people and elected another?"

Coming after the death of Stalin and the opening of a new era of liberalization in Russia, a modest degree of moderation also ensued in the GDR. The so-called Russian revisionists were allowed to criticize aspects of the regime and to propose changes. But shortly afterward the uprising in Hungary in November 1956 again changed things for the worse. After the Russians suppressed the Hungarian Revolution, gloom again descended on those who had hoped for a less rigid form of socialism in the GDR. The exodus to the West again increased. It had averaged about 230,000 per year between 1949 and 1960, rising to 30,000 a month during the first part of 1961. Half of all those who left were under age 25, while the older ones included many thousands of engineers, doctors, and other specialists important to the economic life of the GDR. It was this drain of intellectual and professional leadership that in August 1961 led Walter Ulbricht to stop this hemorrhage by building the Berlin Wall. It was a confession of failure and defeat in the propaganda battle over the value of the GDR, but necessary to block this easy escape route from East to West Berlin. It did provide a new lease on life for the GDR. At first East Germans reacted with despair at being imprisoned, but soon they acquiesced and made the best of it. Ulbricht was able to promote economic reforms and tried to inculcate some sense of national identity and pride in the citizens of this artificial state.

ECONOMIC SYSTEM

The economy of the GDR followed the model imposed on all the Soviet bloc countries in eastern Europe. Eastern Germany had few mineral resources and was the least industrialized part of Germany prior to the war. The economy was less damaged by the war than in the West, but huge reparations were extracted by the Russians, totaling almost 25 percent of production between 1945 and 1953, plus the removal of whole factories and even household plumbing fixtures. The Russians reduced the East German industrial capacity by about 40 percent. The new Communist leaders also had to gradually nationalize and collectivize the economy and then learn how to run it efficiently. The growth of the economy in the GDR, however, was impressive. By the 1980s the GDR had become the strongest economy in the Soviet Bloc and the world's 10th-leading industrial power. As compared with the living standards in Russia, East Germans had a higher standard by 50 percent.

After Stalin's death and the establishment of COMECON, the Soviet Bloc's newly created planning system, the GDR like the other members was required to specialize. The GDR was supposed to concentrate on precision instruments, machine tools and other complex machinery, and some chemicals. Moscow set the prices and often penalized the Germans, while imports of oil and natural gas from the Soviet Union were inflated over those of the world market. The centralized planning was inefficient. While some small private businesses were allowed to exist, mostly in craft and service sectors, some 10,000 firms were nationalized. The principal large industries were regrouped into combines that operated under fixed production quotas, prices, and distribution outlets that were fixed by five- and seven-year plans. In 1963 some changes occurred with more autonomy and emphasis on managerial skills. Retrenchment occurred in 1968 partly as a reaction to the liberal ideas of the Dubcek government in Prague, Czechoslovakia, which had been repressed by the Soviets during that year. In the agricultural area collectivization proved to be a disaster. By the 1980s some 95 percent of the land was farmed by cooperatives, but productivity was 15 percent less than on West German farms. The government also tried to balance public and private ownership by allowing farmers use of some livestock and 1.2 acres for personal needs.

East Germany developed a socialistic welfare state, certainly different from that of West Germany. Although East Germans' lives were restricted and supervised, a generous welfare state emerged. Major inequalities of class and income differences were ironed out, while a reasonable standard of living was provided. In the constitution every citizen had the right and duty to work. The system guaranteed employment, and the fixed numbers of students at the universities and technical schools were assured jobs after graduation. As compared with businesses and factories in the West, overstaffing by 30–40 percent was the rule, which contributed to the huge unemployment problems after reunification. Massive subsidies of basic necessities like housing and fuel were provided; for example, rents accounted for only 5 percent of average income and fuel only 2 percent. Food, transportation, and entertainment were also subsidized. Wage differentials were small; for instance, factory managers and senior professionals received approximately twice the income of the average workers. From a national perspective 40 percent of the state budget went to subsidize 80 percent of consumer goods. Obviously, the system distorted economic realities and impeded modernization.

SOCIETY, EDUCATION, AND CULTURE

In contrast to the Federal Republic, women and mothers were encouraged toward independence, and 87 percent did work outside the home. A second income was often necessary. Although women constituted 50 percent of the teachers and judges, it was rare to see women in senior political positions. The government gave young couples incentives to get married and have children and provided generous family allowances and paid maternity leave. Abortion and the pill also were readily available, and the divorce rate was twice that of the West German figure. Health services were adequate and efficient.

All education and cultural efforts were guided by the philosophy of Marxism-Leninism. Education was foundational to the GDR's cultural politics, essential to the upward mobility of the working class and crucial for economic and political stability. A larger share of GNP was devoted to education in the GDR than in West Germany. Children attended school from age six to 16 and were trained early in life in collective living, social obligations, and patriotism. An indication of what was to be a new guide to morality was the "Ten Commandments of

A weary woman from the East Berlin sector clutches a bottle of milk she purchased on the West Berlin border at a relief station, 1953. *(Library of Congress)*

Socialist Morality," which stressed the interests of the working class rather than the Bible. Math and science were emphasized as was history, literature, and Russian language. But all education was partially vocational, focusing on biweekly visits to factories and farms, and at age 16 students entered an apprenticeship system. Generally, the system emphasized the development of conformity and social responsibility. Most students belonged to the Free German Youth Movement (FDJ), which provided them with opportunities for idealism and social service. Participation in sports and Olympic competition were used to boost domestic morals and patriotism and to win international recognition.

In 1951 the SED inaugurated a cultural policy based on Marxism-Leninism, which was called Socialist Realism. This was copied from Russia and used by the SED to provide guidance for writers and artists. Writers were directed to present a "positive" image of what society and the individual could become and what the "self-realized man" of the socialist world was. The new policy was directed against traditional German culture, and it considered the Western styles of art and literature to be degenerate, including expressionism, naturalism, and abstractionism. As far as what East Germany produced, the cultural world of the 1950s that conformed to Socialist Realism was a wasteland of production-oriented art and literature. Those writers who had been in exile and had returned to the GDR, such as Bertolt Brecht, Arnold Zweig, and Anna Seghers either wrote on historical subjects or wrote poetry. Although there was some freedom after the 1953 uprising, the Hungarian Revolution in 1956 again brought about a reaction back to a form of Socialist Realism called the Bitterfield Movement, which started in 1959 and encouraged writers to work on collective farms or in factories to experience the actual life of workers. The associated attempt to make writers out of industrial workers failed to discover much talent. Efforts at cultural isolation also failed.

After the erection of the Berlin Wall, there was a temporary relaxation of controls over artists, architects, and writers during the 1960s. The Stalinist style of architecture gave way to a style similar to the Western "international style." Abstract art and experimental theater was acceptable. The theme of alienation was popular with many of the authors of the 1960s as they attacked the SED or socialist society. In 1963 the novel *Divided Heaven* by Christa Wolf depicted some of the shortcomings of the GDR and the difficulties that East Germans faced. After 1965 a cultural freeze was again imposed. On the other hand, Christa Wolf was allowed to publish in the West *Thoughts About Christa T.* (1968), in which she wrote about a woman who committed suicide because she could not maintain her individuality. It was criticized by the regime for its failure to praise socialism. Erwin Strittmatter's *Old Beehead* was the most popular novel of the 1960s, relating the story of a small farmer whose efforts were undermined by party functionaries.

Despite some liberalization during the Honecker regime the distrust between the leaders and the people continued. In 1975 Stefan Heym's *Day X*, about the 1953 uprising, had to be published in the West. But the brief period of openness was characterized by such controversial works as Volker Braun's *Unfinished Story* (1975) and Christa Wolf's *Patterns of Childhood* (1976). The liberalization was largely negated by the practice of *Aüsburgerung*, whereby writers were deprived of their rights as citizens. A most notorious example of this concerned Wolf Biermann. His poetry had criticized party functionaries, so he was not allowed to return to the GDR after a 1976 concert tour in the West. Practically every well-known author signed a statement of protest against this measure of the government, which resulted in 30 of them being expelled from the Writers' Union, which practically silenced them. Christa Wolf and Stefan Heym were two of these writers. Nevertheless, during this period East German culture was constantly influenced by Western values through radio and television, even though the clothes, the mannerisms, the rowdyism, and the music all were condemned.

RELATIONS WITH THE FEDERAL REPUBLIC

Until Willy Brandt became chancellor of West Germany, relations between the two German states were icy. The earlier period was dominated by the Hallstein Doctrine initiated in the late 1950s by Walter Hallstein, which was a policy intended to boycott and undermine the GDR. According to that doctrine the Federal Republic threatened to cut off aid and break diplomatic ties with any state recognizing the GDR. In 1969, when Brandt and the SPD came to power in Bonn, relations began to improve. This was the period of détente between Russia and the United States. Walter Ulbricht was a rigid and hostile Communist who resisted this thaw in East-West relations. So in 1971 Ulbricht was eased out of power and replaced by Erich Honecker (1912–94), who had been his heir apparent. Honecker was more flexible and less involved in the Stalinist years, had served as chairman of the East German Youth Organization (FDJ) from 1946 to 1955, and was elected to full membership in the Politburo in 1958. Honecker was a pragmatic party official who was mainly concerned with the preservation of the SED's power in the GDR. He rejected the inclusion of Ulbricht's concept of "a socialist state of the German nation" in the constitution of 1974 and talked of the real socialism that existed instead of Ulbricht's ideological-sounding "developed socialism."

Brandt's eastern policy (Ostpolitik) considerably improved relations with Honecker and the GDR. They exchanged permanent ambassadors. Trade was substantially increased, and West Germans were allowed to visit the GDR. The foundation of right of access by the Allied powers to and from West Berlin was guaranteed. Honecker allowed mainly elderly East Germans to travel to the West. West German television was permitted, which opened East Germans to the freedom and living standards in the West. Censorship in literature and the arts was relaxed, and some independence was permitted for the Protestant Church.

Revolution and Reunification

The revolution of 1989 in the GDR was successful in reuniting the two Germanies but did not, as revolutions should, bring about a reform of the state. The GDR had been an artificial state defined geographically by the Soviet occupation zone and politically by the Communist Party as a socialist alternative to the Federal Republic. The GDR had survived and created its own political identity by the 1980s, except that the political environment created and maintained by the Soviet Union in Eastern Europe began to disintegrate. In autumn 1989 hundreds of thousands of East German citizens took to the streets of major cities, demanding the political and social changes that others who had fled to third countries had given up hope of ever experiencing. The pressures created by fleeing Germans and the internal protests brought about change in the Socialist Unity Party (SED) and state leadership, as well as the opening of the GDR's borders. The very nature of the state now was questioned by democratic elections. Finally, the process of unification with West Germany was set in motion with all of its political, economic, and social ramifications.

In the later 1980s the Soviet Union began to weaken its grip on Eastern Europe. Under the reforming leadership of Mikhail Gorbachev a process of political democratization and economic restructuring was initiated. While freedom of expression was the watchword in Moscow, the process of political democratization was extended to Poland, where a non-Communist government took control, and in Hungary, where non-Communist political parties were allowed to organize. The GDR under Honecker resisted these changes, prohibiting the organization of independent political groups. This caused considerable dissatisfaction among the East Germans, which a strong government might still have managed to suppress. But Honecker had fallen ill that spring with gallbladder surgery and liver cancer. With his absence for a long period, the stage was set for revolutionary developments.

Throughout 1989 there had been an increase in officially approved requests for emigration to the West. The East German government regularly delayed approval of applicants, and by January a huge backlog had developed. The first incident in which applicants for emigration lost their patience occurred when some 20 occupied the West German mission in East Berlin. These eventually were able to emigrate after assurances by the East German authorities that their papers would be quickly processed. In August that happened again, although this time it was 100 East Germans encamping at the mission, and this time they were sent home without their emigration being assured. In the meantime during that February, border guards had killed a young man trying to climb the

Berlin Wall. In Hungary that summer a reformist government decided to dismantle its fortified boundary with Austria. This presented the 220,000 East Germans vacationing there with the opportunity to flee to freedom. Some 20,000 decided to take that path. They were jubilantly received into refugee camps in Austria with offers of jobs. Now the process expanded to include others who decided to flee for Hungary via Czechoslovakia, while others invaded the West German embassies in Prague and Warsaw. While the West German government began to worry how it would handle these thousands of émigrés, the government of the GDR realized that it was in a state of crisis.

Besides the drama surrounding the émigrés, other sources of protest for internal reform began to be heard. One such source was in the Protestant Churches, where discussions and prayer vigils were being held. In the Nicholas Church in Leipzig Monday evening services were followed by demonstration marches demanding political reforms. Security forces tried to control these demonstrations, but soon the hundreds of marchers turned into hundreds of thousands. There was fear that the marchers would be suppressed by the army as was the case in China. On October 9, 1989, an event of great significance occurred; the East German authorities renounced the use of force against their own people. It was a major turning point and indicated that a peaceful revolution might be possible. Earlier, on September 25, the GDR had celebrated its 40th anniversary. With Gorbachev in attendance, what Honecker believed would crown his career turned out to be the beginning of his demise. Gorbachev insisted that changes be made in the leadership. In order to forestall a revolution by the people from below, the Politburo on October 18 replaced Honecker, as general secretary of the SED, with Egon Krenz, who was a hard-liner and had been Honecker's handpicked successor. Demonstrations now continued in cities and towns throughout the GDR with an estimated 500,000 people participating in Berlin. Meanwhile, in September and October a number of new political parties were established, the most important being New Forum. Krenz was unable to convince the populace that real changes were possible. On November 7 the government headed by Willi Stoph resigned and a new government headed by Hans Modrow, a reformist party secretary from Dresden, was elected by the parliament (Volkskammer) on November 13.

On November 9 a dramatic turn of events occurred. Egon Krenz had drafted a new travel regulation that enabled East Germans to cross over into West Berlin with visas granted upon short-notice applications. When this was announced at a press meeting on the evening of the 9th, it was incorrectly interpreted as beginning right away instead of the next day. The border crossing was overwhelmed with people as East and West Berliners rushed to the Wall. The border guards opened the gates letting everyone through. A party atmosphere ensued as revelers danced on top of the Wall. The next day the press announced that the Berlin Wall was gone! During the following days East Berliners shopped the streets of West Berlin, taking back home all sorts of consumer items. During the ensuing weeks the crisis deepened. The demonstrations continued. The debate over reforms by the new government was broadened when Chancellor Helmut Kohl of the Federal Republic announced his Ten-Point plan for the two Germanies, but it envisaged a federation and not complete unity. Now the debate was internationalized as the solution to the German question involved the Allied powers, NATO, and the Warsaw Pact.

As the revolutionary events unfolded, domestic political change occurred peacefully and rapidly. Egon Krenz was replaced by the young Gregor Gysi. The SED adopted a new image, calling itself the "Party of Democratic Socialism" (PDS). It became apparent how artificial the large membership of the SED had been when in January 1990 a shocking 50 percent of the membership resigned. The former parties subservient to the SED now were also reorganizing with new programs, joined by New Forum, Democracy Now, and Democratic Awakening, as well as the SPD. Then a group called the Round Table under sponsorship of the church was organized with the goal of democratizing the GDR. As the Modrow cabinet tried to cope with a rapidly declining economy, it also had to deal with a medical crisis that was due to the huge exodus of workers and medical personnel. During all of 1989 some 344,000 had left the GDR, but by mid-March another nearly 150,000 had disappeared westward. Now sentiment was increasing for unification and not reform. Whereas in the early days of the revolution the marchers chanted "We are the people!" by the end of November the chant had changed to "We are one people!" expressing sentiments for unification. In December 1989 Kohl and Modrow met and agreed on a "treaty community," which had been part of the Kohl proposals for a gradual process aiming at unification, but one that would realistically have taken years. Yet events were to outrun their plans. In the middle of January Stasi headquarters was stormed and under pressure from the Round Table, which represented reform groups and demanded that the Stasi be disbanded. Discussions between the government and opposition groups grew more strained. Elections were then scheduled for March 18. While these events were taking place, the economy was collapsing, with West German money and goods flooding the country, which was further complicated by an illegal currency market and smuggling. By February 1990 even Modrow admitted that the economic situation in the GDR was so desperate that he had changed his mind in favor of economic and monetary union.

As the power of the SED-PDS declined and New Forum failed to seize the initiative to replace the once dominant Communist Party, the West German political parties entered into the election campaign with their strong organizations and well-financed campaigns. The CDU, SPD, and FDP found new partners in the GDR. The CDU formed the Alliance for Germany with the old CDU, the German Social Union (DSU), and the Democratic Awakening. The FDP united liberals in a League of Free Democrats. What had been New Forum became Alliance 90, teaming up with other smaller groups such as Democracy Now and Peace and Human Rights Initiative. Helmut Kohl's Alliance for Germany campaigned on a platform of unification and rapid economic integration. The Alliance did not win an absolute majority, but did win 192 out of 400 seats and was able to form a cabinet with the SPD (88 seats) and the League of Free Democrats (21 seats). Lothar de Maizière, leader of the CDU, led the new government. The election spelled the end of the GDR as the other political groups won only a small number of seats.

The idea of German unification received the support of the United States, but was resisted by Mikhail Gorbachev and Margaret Thatcher of Great Britain. Kohl realized that he had a narrow window of opportunity to realize political unification and seized it. That February it had been agreed that Two-Plus-Four talks would take place between the two Germanies and the former allied powers. The strength of the German mark made unification appealing. On April 23 it was agreed that the exchange rate would be 1:1 on wages and private savings. The next day Kohl and Maizière agreed on a monetary union, which was to take place on July 1, 1990. The border was opened at midnight on June 30, the currency shared, and shops opened for business. In the meantime Kohl was busy obtaining the agreement of the Soviet Union to unification. He understood Russian objections to a united Germany within NATO. When he visited Gorbachev in mid-July, he was surprised when the Soviet leader gave his approval to Germany's NATO membership. The Two-Plus-Four talks were concluded in Moscow on September 12, followed by the signing of a German-Soviet cooperation treaty concerning Soviet troop withdrawal and German economic assistance. The treaty of German unification was signed on August 31, and on October 2–3, 1990, Germany was reunified and Berlin made its capital again. The former GDR was divided into the states of Brandenburg, Mecklenburg-Western Pomerania, Saxony, Saxony-Anhalt, and Thuringia. In the federal elections of December 2, 1990, the CDU/CSU won 43.8 percent of the vote, which gave Helmut Kohl a strong majority in the first parliament of the united Germany.

CONSEQUENCES AND PROBLEMS OF UNIFICATION

It cannot be denied that unification took place too quickly, but an open window of diplomatic possibilities in international affairs necessitated swift action. It was difficult to predict how long the Soviet reformer, Gorbachev, would remain as premier. Using currency unification between the GDR and the Federal Republic as a bridge to unification made a rapid transition to a market economy in the new states necessary but also made economic collapse inevitable. Few could have foreseen the challenges in transforming the GDR's planned economy into a largely free market economy as there were no precedents. Living standards unfortunately improved too slowly, and it was understandable that Easterners would grow impatient with the difficulties involved. People should have known that prices for basic essentials and services would have to rise because so much had been heavily subsidized in the GDR. It did surprise Westerners how unmotivated East German workers had become, how inexperienced they were with competitive market conditions, and how untrained they were to handle modern technology. Inflationary pressures also resulted from the demand for wage increases because Easterners grew impatient with pay scales that were half that of Westerners. It also should not have come as a great shock when unemployment rose rapidly as a result of the closing of state-run companies. Everyone knew that the state-owned enterprises were hopelessly overstaffed and that workers had not been dismissed even when unneeded. Unemployment reached 15 percent in some areas but more than 30 percent in others. By some estimates there were 50 percent fewer jobs in the eastern industrial sector than before unification, which naturally led to increased social tensions.

The West German government had underestimated the economic and social changes that were necessary in the GDR. The whole economy had to be restructured along capitalist lines. Although some German firms may have profited by purchasing the former public properties offered by the Trust Agency, the federal government had to absorb the costs of modernization and environmental cleanup and vast infrastructure improvements. There also was a great need for an efficient public administration to replace the old bureaucracy that had operated under the SED. West German experts were required to help with public administration and the judicial system, but few wanted to live in the East. Civil servants and judges were not used to making independent decisions without being directed by the Communist Party. Legal claims on property, houses, and businesses necessitated extensive legal proceedings, long delays in business development, and fears about the loss of homes.

Another negative result of reunification was a currency crisis and a large increase in the national debt and inflation. In 1990 the Federal Bank had warned that the German government's policy of supporting high wages without the equivalent productivity would be inflationary. Then the German unions demanded wage increases to cover the rise in the cost of living. The bank responded by raising interest rates by three percentage points as an antiinflationary measure at the time that American rates had hit an all-time low. With a surge in foreign investment in German bank deposits, the value of the mark rose and other European countries raised their interest rates in order to maintain a fixed exchange rate required in existing agreements. As a consequence the British and Italians pulled their currencies out of the fixed rate system.

With a faltering economy, the rising cost of German unification, second thoughts about European unity, spreading disillusionment with political parties, and growing resentment against foreigners, there was a resurgence of right-wing parties. The rise of neo-Nazism was associated with violence against foreigners. The neo-Nazis took over the skinhead groups that had always been opposed to the establishment. Economic discontent in the eastern states helped make this possible, but most of the incidents were located in the former West Germany. In the former GDR the worst spasm of nativist violence since the days of Adolf Hitler was prompted by the victory of skinheads over the local authorities in the Saxon town of Hoyerswerda at the end of September 1991. While foreign mining workers had left after unification, several hundred asylum seekers arrived from 23 different countries. The "skins" first attacked Germans but then turned to the Vietnamese. Related to this extremism was the need to revise Germany's very liberal asylum laws. In article 16 of the Basic Law all victims of political persecution are able to apply for asylum and are supported by the German government for up to three years. In 1991, for instance, there were some 260,000 seeking asylum.

Finally, a crisis of identity grew among former East Germans. While they had rejected communism, West Germans had not considered them as equals but as backward country cousins. In establishing a new identity, there not only was a need to deal with their Communist but also their Nazi past, which had never been admitted by East Germans. Even though East Germans had been in favor of unification, they soon developed the attitude that they were being taken over and colonized by the West Germans.

Post-Reunification to the Present

ECONOMIC UNIFICATION, STAGNATION, UNEMPLOYMENT, AND EURO CHALLENGES

After reunification the German economy was challenged as never before since the immediate postwar era. The task of merging the two economies did not work out as smoothly as had been thought by West German leaders. The predictions of rapid rebuilding, economic integration, and a rosy prosperity did not come true. Everyone had been confident that private and public investment along with job retraining would successfully modernize the economy in the former East German states. The program for this enterprise was optimistically called "Cooperative Enterprise for the Upswing in the East." The privatization process was carried out by a Trusteeship Agency (Treuhandanstalt). Both German and foreign investors were invited to purchase plants and properties. Unfortunately, they were overvalued at above 1 trillion German marks (DM), and in the end instead of making money it cost the German government 250 billion marks. Not surprisingly, the Trusteeship Agency had difficulty selling most of the properties, and before a buyer would conclude a deal, the government had to pay for such things as modernizing the plants and environmental cleanup. Furthermore, the former markets in Eastern Europe for the inferior East German products now had disappeared. The federal deficit for 1994 alone reached 71 billion marks and the national debt skyrocketed. Then interest rates rose. Unemployment in the former East German states averaged around 15 percent, but some areas reported more than 40 percent. It must not be forgotten that the infrastructure, whether trains, roads, or communications, were substandard, which required the federal government to finance a vast modernization project. In order to pay for all this and not ruin the economy, an agreement was reached in 1992 called the "Solidarity Pact," which was to raise some 100 billion marks by extra taxes and spending cuts.

A national debate erupted over how to solve the economic problems facing a unified Germany in the European and global market. In the past Germany had been praised as "Model Deutschland," a cooperative model of how an industrial society ought to be organized. Numerous solutions were suggested. The main alternatives, however, consisted of two: (1) to allow the capitalistic forces of the marketplace to bring about the necessary adjustments, or (2) for the government to craft an industrial policy that would provide goals and direction, and to promote change with tax and investment laws. The conservatives focused on the obvious need to lower the normally high wages of German workers who had negotiated higher than usual labor contracts since 1989. The euphoric predictions of a prosperous future resulting from reunification led to an astronomical 58 percent wage increase, which was also due to the German system of industry-wide collective bargaining of contracts. Not to be forgotten were the exceedingly generous social benefits to which Germans had become accustomed, which even the newly elected chancellor, Gerhard Schroeder of the SPD, admitted in 1998 had to be reduced. Chancellor Kohl (CDU) also wanted to reduce the environmental restrictions that increased business costs and restricted new construction. Another constraint on the economy was the huge amounts of money the federal government was obligated to spend to modernize and integrate the former Communist states. Increasing government deficits and mushrooming national debt all contributed to a low growth rate and unemployment, which by 1997 had reached an average postwar high of 11.3 percent, partly due to the high rates of unemployment in the East, where so many plants were closed down.

Short-term solutions to the economic problems were attempted. The Kohl government announced an austerity program that included reduced sick pay and fewer job guarantees. The government also began to divest the state of its investment in publicly owned enterprises, such as Lufthansa, the national airline, the railroads, which had been state owned since the 19th century, the postal service, and the telephone system. Shares were sold to private investors, but the government had to take over the debt of these corporations, which further pushed up the national debt. Although these measures removed the government's responsibilities, it did not solve the fundamental economic problems. Although Kohl had negotiated reunification, he undoubtedly had failed to modernize the German social-market economy during his administration. By the time he left office, Germany's ranking among industrial nations in economic competitiveness had fallen to 24th.

The tax reforms that the Schroeder government finally initiated in 2001 reduced one of the great obstacles to economic reform. Income and corporate taxes had been linked to the generous social services to which Germans had become accustomed. The Christian Democrats (CDU) and Liberal Democrats (FDP) favored a reduction in direct taxation in order to spur new investment, while the SPD wanted tax reform to be linked to policies that provided incentives, for example, on energy use and job creation. Tax reform, however, was slow to happen because compromise between the major political parties and federal versus state conflicts was so difficult, as had been proven with the failure of an earlier reform bill in 1997.

In May 2001 the pension reform plan proposed by Chancellor Schroeder was approved by the upper house of the parliament (Bundesrat). The plan decreased the benefits paid directly by the government. Employees in private industry were encouraged to invest their retirement savings in government-supported private investments. This was later expanded to public employees. It was the beginning of a shift from large-scale social programs supported by high taxes. The old system was no longer affordable because the ratio of workers paying into the system to retirees being paid would not hold in the future.

By 2003 the laws affecting everything from hiring and firing workers to environmental restrictions, to health care and pension laws were still too rigid and frustrated efforts to revive economic growth and provide new jobs. Some changes in the laws affecting layoffs and pensions had taken place, but they only highlighted the urgent need for broader structural changes.

The German economy was further challenged by the introduction of the euro currency on January 1, 2002, which replaced the German mark (DM) with the new European currency. Although the euro initially declined in value in reference to the dollar, by the beginning of 2004 it rose some 40 percent and pushed prices higher throughout Europe. Consumers and companies became more cautious, which inhibited growth and the creation of new jobs. Furthermore, Germans saved more than their American counterparts, which also hampered economic growth. In fact, the slow growth of the economy prompted Germany and France to abandon the continent-wide commitment to keep the government's deficit to no higher than 3 percent, allowing it to rise to 4 percent of GDP.

German companies needed more flexibility in setting their own management policies, rather than being tied to region-wide or sector-wide agreements that governed hiring, firing, and wage policies. In the past the German economic model had emphasized cooperation instead of conflict as has been the case in the United States. The establishment of wages had traditionally been settled by forging agreements between employers, unions, and the government concerning wages, benefits, and working conditions. The issues usually were resolved in an evenhanded fashion by taking into account the concerns of all sides. So, it is not at all surprising that Germans have had a great deal of difficulty in making even minor reforms. Take for instance Chancellor Gerhard Schroeder's success in 2003 in changing some labor rules, which was laudable as far as it went, but did not make the necessary fundamental reforms. Companies have decided to make the best of the situation as has the automaker Audi AG. It has experimented with a new pay structure that eliminates the fixed hourly rate and replacing it with pay scales based on worker productivity. Germans also were not happy with Schroeder's attempt to trim the welfare state. Some 100,000 protested in Berlin against the cuts. Critics claimed that taxes fell unfairly on the elderly and the unemployed. As an alternative to the benefit cuts, some lawmakers demanded a rise in the inheritance tax, which would hit the wealthy the hardest.

Mergers and acquisitions have been ways in which German companies have adjusted to the world market. A prime example of the mergers that swept across the world in the late 1990s was that between Deutsche Bank AG, Germany's largest bank, and Dresdner Bank AG, the third-largest along with Allianz AG, an insurance firm. The German banking industry was overcrowded and required consolidation to enable it to compete with worldwide conglomerates. The merger began the unraveling of Germany's elaborate system of cross-holding of the limited 10 percent market share of each bank. Not only did the merger bring the German banking system into line with that of other European nations, but also made the merged bank the second in size in the world.

UNIFICATION POLITICS AND ITS NEW CHALLENGES

The reunification of Germany was Chancellor Kohl's greatest achievement. It is easy to see why he was reelected in 1990 and again in the 1994 parliamentary elections. The official interpretation of unification was that it was the work of both West and East Germans, and although opposed by some of Germany's neighbors was aided especially by the Americans and Russians. As true as this was, there was another reality that lurked behind these noble words, and that was that the GDR imploded and then was for all practical purposes annexed by West Germany. Even the Treaty of Union between the ex-GDR and the Federal Republic, which had provided for a special commission to reexamine the Basic Law and recommend changes, turned out to be like window dressing. In July 1994 the commission concluded that no changes were necessary. The first all-German election since the end of World War II took place on December 2, 1990, when some 17 million voters went to the polls. The CDU remained the largest party, receiving with its coalition partners, the CSU and FDP, 54.8 percent of the vote. Surprisingly, the CDU did remarkably better than the SPD in the East German states, due to the latter's ambivalent stand on unification. The Free Democrats (FDP), due to the popularity of Hans-Dietrich Genscher, actually received a 1 percent higher vote in the East (12 percent) than in the West. The extreme right-wing party, the Republikaner, fell short of the 5 percent of the vote necessary for a party to be represented in the Bundestag. The successor to the SED, the Party of Democratic Socialism (PDS), received only 2.4 percent of the vote nationwide. Because of their opposition to rapid reunification, the Greens received only 3.9 percent of the vote but remained in the Bundestag due to an alliance with the East German Alliance '90. Voter participation decreased only slightly from a high of 84.3 percent in 1987 to 77.8 percent in 1990.

Kohl soon had to face the realities of governing a newly united nation. After promising no new taxes, Kohl in fact had to raise taxes. Political corruption scandals also tarnished his coalition. Because of economic difficulties he was increasingly reluctant to tolerate criticism. Then Kohl attempted to force the CDU to accept his choice of a successor to Richard von Weizäcker, the federal president, which created considerable problems in the governing coalition. Roman Herzog, the chief judge of the Federal Constitutional Court, was finally chosen in 1994. In the five new states many difficulties arose in dealing with their Communist past. As trials were held, often lower-ranked officials were punished while leaders were not.

Other problems plaguing the country concerned the rise of extreme right-wing groups, which were opposed to the large number of asylum seekers flooding into Germany due to the extremely liberal asylum law. Virtually any foreigner could ask for and receive asylum and then benefit from the social service benefits. A wave of neo-Nazi violence targeted foreigners and left 30 dead and hundreds injured between 1990 and 1995. All of this created resentment against foreigners, which expanded even to long-term resident Turks, often in the form of violence. One violent example occurred on November 23, 1992, in the town of Moelin, where extremists killed three Turkish immigrants through fire bombing. After this the government announced a program to crack down on right-wing neo-Nazis.

In the Bundestag elections of 1994 the CDU/CSU coalition won with 41.5 percent of the vote. The party strategists featured Kohl as the "chancellor of unity" whose down-home personality and increasingly heavy weight appealed to the electorate. The CDU convention also chose a new party platform that emphasized an "ecological" social market economy and favored the European Union. A campaign stressing "security, stability, and the future" and an improving economy helped reelect Kohl's coalition. By 1998, however, Kohl's star was fading. Too many struggles and too many unfulfilled promises about Germany's future had disillusioned many voters. He had failed to solve the country's economic problems, which resulted from reunification and from the global recession of the early 1990s. To counter this, Kohl tried to make his experience as chancellor for 16 years a campaign issue. CDU posters claimed that he was a "world class" politician for Germany, had orchestrated Germany's reunification, and played a major role in the establishment of a unified European currency. While Kohl represented stability, the SPD candidate, Gerhard Schroeder, represented change, which is what many voters wanted. In his appearance and thinking Kohl was showing his age, 67. His usual campaign speech focused on Germany's past and not on a vision for its future. Kohl understandably refused to face the telegenic Gerhard Schroeder in a televised debate. A widely publicized debate before the Bundestag did occur in which Kohl warned that change was dangerous, while Schroeder accused Kohl of being in office too long and out of touch with the voters. In a version of "it's the economy, stupid" Schroeder accused Kohl of failing to reduce the country's high unemployment and widening the gap between rich and poor. Embarrassingly, Helmut Kohl became the first chancellor to be ousted from office in an election. With the passing of the "unity chancellor" who had bridged preunification and unification Germany, a new postwar generation had arrived to lead Germany into the future and to give new form and meaning to German identity.

During the election Gerhard Schroeder managed to project a much more youthful and dynamic image. He was a surprising choice because his ideas reflected a centrist position and not the traditional socialist position of the party leader, Oskar Lafontaine, who became the powerful finance minister in the new government. Not only had Schroeder earlier gained notoriety in addressing the Bundestag without wearing a necktie, it was also well known that after a night of drinking he walked in front of the chancellor's residence and shouted, "I want in there!" As head of state government in Lower Saxony he had courted businessmen, which alienated some leftist party members. Schroeder said he represented the New Middle and borrowed from the campaigns of Tony Blair in England and Bill Clinton in the United States. For perhaps the most media-savvy politician that postwar Germany produced, now the politics of personality took center stage. Without specifics Schroeder offered himself as the symbol of change, a man of action and a manager who had everything under control. Schroeder's admiration for his predecessor, Helmut Schmidt, inspired him to project the image and style of Schmidt. He claimed to be a modernizer of government, reformer of social welfare, and the creator of a public-private alliance necessary for success in the global economy. An energetic campaign promised a brighter future and was enhanced with rock music, videos, the photogenic images of Schroeder and his wife, and imaginative political commercials. The public clearly preferred Schroeder as their new chancellor. The issue of unemployment, of course, was an important campaign issue. More than 80 percent of the public thought that unemployment was the most important problem facing the nation. A mood of discontent also contributed to Kohl's defeat, a mood of frustration with expectations and realities concerning unification. The public wanted a change of leadership that could reform the tax laws and social welfare programs.

The SPD increased its share of the vote by 4.5 percent over 1994, making modest gains in both western states among the new middle class and in the east among blue collar workers. The mixed partial proportional electoral system worked to the advantage of the SPD, giving it 13 extra seats in the Bundestag. The CDU/CSU came second, followed in third place by the Green Party. The SPD and Greens then formed the Red-Green coalition, giving it a 345 to 324 majority. The other parties, such as the reformed Communist Party, the Party of Democratic Socialism, won 36 seats with 6.2 percent of the vote, managing to surmount the 5 percent threshold. The two right-wing parties, Republikaner and German People's Party, received only a combined vote of 3 percent. The governing coalition of the SPD and Greens then agreed on a program to attack the problems that had led to Kohl's defeat. Yet there were divisions within and between these coalition partners, which made a consistent policy difficult. Besides the conflict of ideologies between Schroeder and Lafontaine, the Greens were also divided by the Fundi and Realo factions, which further complicated the alliance's attempts to forge a New Middle. One such conflict between the Greens and the SPD concerned the closure of Germany's nuclear power plants, with the Greens favoring an immediate closure versus the SPD's more practical support for gradual closure. Other divisions concerned the question of Germany's role in its military alliances and changes in its citizenship laws. Even more fundamental were the difficulties in arriving at a consensus on how to deal with unemployment, tax reform, and reduction of social services.

When Schroeder took office he was confronted by economic uncertainty, mass unemployment, and a general apprehension about the implications of globalization. Many Germans questioned the ability of the government to deal with these problems. In order to meet these challenges, Schroeder projected an image of a man of action who had everything under control. Yet his management skills were far from outstanding, and he failed to demonstrate any creativity in solving Germany's problems or formulating solutions. Just as bad he failed to martial the political support needed to pass his reforms. Unfortunately, the inexperience of his administration led to inadequate preparation and frenetic action, much as in the early administration of President Clinton.

After one year in office Schroeder's coalition proposed a structural reform plan for the social welfare programs. It was soon scrapped, however, when voters were so opposed to the reform program that many even abandoned the party in several state elections. Later, in 2001, a pension reform plan was passed by the Bundestag. The plan cut the amount of benefits directly paid by the government and encouraged individuals to invest their retirement savings in government-supported private investments. Workers and management in the metal and electrical industries also agreed to allow employees to invest a small portion of their pretax wages into retirement investments. The Bundestag also approved a plan to shut down all of the nuclear power plants before 2021.

In November 2001 Gerhard Schroeder was overwhelmingly reelected as the head of the Social Democratic Party. In the parliamentary elections in September 2002 he was reelected with a five-seat majority with 306 seats in a 603-seat Bundestag, although the vote for the SPD declined slightly to 38.5 percent from 40.9 percent in 1998. The Greens with the help of the popular Joschka Fischer in the foreign ministry polled 8.6 percent of the vote, up from 6.7 percent. The opposition center-right coalition of the Christian Democratic Union and the Christian Social Union also won 38.5 percent of the vote, up from 35.1 percent in 1998. Yet, why was Schroeder reelected after failing to reduce Germany's unemployment as he had promised? One reason was his excellent handling of flood relief during the devastating floods in eastern Germany. Analysts also attributed it to his very popular opposition to the proposed U.S.-led military intervention in Iraq. However, following the election, Schroeder proposed tax increases that again were resisted by SPD members. Also reflecting voter dissatisfaction in February 2003 was the CDU defeat of the governing SPD in two state elections.

A turning point in postwar German history came when Chancellor Schroeder on March 14, 2003, announced Agenda 2010. It proposed structural reforms in social welfare programs by reducing entitlements and making labor market reforms that had been recommended by economists and business leaders. The agenda's provisions were expressions of Schroeder's New Middle philosophy between that of Keynesian economics and neoliberalism. Some of the provisions included allowing small companies to lay off workers, the reduction of unemployment benefits, and drastically reducing the eligibility period for benefits. In health services employees were made responsible for the burden of payments; co-payments by employers were eliminated to reduce business costs. Perhaps 50 percent or more of SPD members opposed the cuts proposed by the agenda, but with Schroeder's threat to resign as chancellor the delegates at a party conference reluctantly supported the agenda. Should the reforms in Agenda 2010 be enacted, it was expected that the SPD would be defeated in the next parliamentary election and that the future cohesion of the party could be threatened.

By February 2004 opposition from the liberal core of the Social Democratic Party to Agenda 2010 had become so strong that Schroeder decided to step down as leader of the SPD, although he continued in the office of chancellor. The political marriage between Schroeder and the Social Democrats had begun to fall apart during summer 2003, when critics accused him of catering to corporations and the wealthy. Opinion polls showed that Schroeder's reforms and his failure to lower unemployment had reduced the party's popularity among voters to 26 percent. The most recent complaints concerned Schroeder's proposed reductions in worker compensation programs and a plan to require patients to pay the equivalent of $12.50 for their initial visit to a doctor, hardly an economic burden when compared to the costs faced by the average American.

FOREIGN POLICY

The ratification of the Unification Treaty and the Two-Plus-Four Treaty terminated the rights and responsibilities of the World War II Allied powers in both Berlin and Germany as a whole. Germany had therefore regained sovereignty over both its internal and external affairs. Responsibility for its foreign policy now assumed primary importance. Germany had to allay the fears of the nations surrounding it that it would not repeat its past history of aggression. In order to accomplish this goal, Germany had to settle all remaining boundary disputes. Also, it had to solidify its relationship with France, which Chancellor Kohl had seriously nurtured. Certainly the French were concerned that a united Germany not return to its old ways of again threatening France or follow an independent foreign policy. Chancellor Kohl was also determined to integrate Germany into a strengthened European Union. Kohl realized that Germany's internal unity as well as Germany's European and global responsibilities were all interrelated.

In order to further European unity it was essential to strengthen the relationship with France. In December 1991 the Maastricht Treaty was signed, which was intended to bring about economic and eventually political union. The treaty provided for the creation of a common currency, the elimination of tariff barriers between members of the European Community (EC), common recognition of diplomas, and European citizenship. Maastricht was negotiated too quickly, and opposition developed in various countries concerning its goals. For instance, resistance against the common currency delayed the introduction of the euro until 2001. Not until 1993 did the Federal Constitutional Court decide that the Maastricht Treaty was compatible with the Basic Law. Also lacking was a formula for the political and military role of Germany in Europe.

The relationship with the newly liberated countries of eastern Europe and especially Russia was a particularly difficult challenge. Germany worked cooperatively within the European Union, signing a Partnership and Cooperation Agreement with Russia on June 24, 1994. Extensive foreign aid of more than 90 billion DM was also given to Russia to aid in the process of democratic transformation there. That did not include private donations between 1990 and 1992, totaling 650 million DM. In addition, the federal government had to support the withdrawal of Soviet troops from eastern Germany to the tune of 14.6 billion DM. The Federal Republic also provided massive amounts of aid to the successor states in eastern Europe to aid in the transformation to market economies. Resentments against Germany were still harbored in Poland and the Czech Republic. Economic and cultural agreements, however, improved relations with Poland, while the more complex relationship with the Czech Republic was improved by the admission of mutual wrongs. The Kohl government also sponsored Poland, the Czech Republic, and Hungary for membership in NATO, which occurred later in the decade. As important a demonstration of its being a good European citizen was the Federal Republic's support for the European Commission's 1997 agreement to extend EU membership to the states of eastern Europe, including Estonia and Slovenia, but also to the Mediterranean island of Cyprus.

On a global scale Germany continued its financial aid to developing countries and was especially concerned that the recipient countries respect human rights. Support for the United Nations also remained strong, Germany being the third-largest contributor to the UN budget and providing almost one-quarter of the budget of NATO. For the first time a unit of the Bundeswehr participated in the UN operation in Somalia. After a good deal of controversy the Federal Constitutional Court decided that the military could participate in operations within the framework of NATO or in implementation of decisions of the UN Security Council. In 1993–94 German participation in UN operations was limited to peaceful operations, providing medical and humanitarian aid in Cambodia and Bosnia. During the post-unification period Germany also was permitted to occupy one of the rotating seats on the Security Council.

When Gerhard Schroeder became chancellor in 1998, President Bill Clinton of the United States, who had cultivated an extremely close relations with the pro-American Helmut Kohl, was optimistic about working with Schroeder. Conservative President Chirac of France also congratulated Schroeder, while Labour Party leader Tony Blair of Great Britain was perhaps the most pleased to see a center-left government in Germany. Schroeder quickly reassured French political leaders that the German government would continue its close diplomatic ties, a promise that was later to be realized in their common front against American policy in Iraq. Yet before that opposition took place, Schroeder did commit 3,900 German troops to the U.S.-led military campaign in Afghanistan, which according to the constitution required the Bundestag's approval for troop deployments outside of NATO countries. Schroeder's decision was at first opposed by the radical and pacificist rank and file in his coalition partner, the Green Party. That position, however, changed at a Green Party conference that produced enough votes accepting the deployment of German troops against the terrorists. Later, on December 16, Schroeder cautioned the United States against expanding the war on terrorism to include Iraq without better evidence linking Saddam Hussein to terrorism. Frosty relations with the United States were made colder during the September parliamentary elections. Besides Schroeder's antiwar statements, one minister equated President George W. Bush's foreign policy methods with those of Hitler and another compared Bush to the Roman emperor Augustus, who had subdued the German tribes. Schroeder's conciliatory gestures of removing the offending ministers were ignored by the United States. In the meantime Germany was designated to become the president of the UN Security Council on January 1, 2003. In the Security Council Germany along with other U.S. allies continued to refuse to support an invasion of Iraq without UN authorization.

GOVERNMENT AND ELECTIONS, 2002–2004

Throughout the years of Schroeder's term of office as chancellor, Germany's economic woes continued to plague the nation. In 2003 he finally decided to outline a major program of reforms, which he called Agenda 2010, that combined tax cuts and cuts in the social welfare system, which included health insurance, unemployment payments, and pensions. The continuing high unemployment rate (joblessness exceeded 4 million) became one of the most conspicuous failures of his chancellorship, which was aggravated by the national recession driven by a global downturn. All of these were very unpopular with many SPD voters. In May of 2005, the SPD lost the state election and control of the government in its traditional stronghold of North Rhine-Westphalia. The result prompted Schroeder to call for a vote of no confidence in the Bundestag, which made early national elections inevitable. Actually, Schroeder was facing a rebellion in his own party over his economic reform program. Schroeder miscalculated in his expectations that he and the SPD could defeat the CDU and its leader, Dr. Angela Merkel, in the elections that were held on September 18, 2005. Schroeder was still the more effective campaigner, while Dr. Merkel was a lackluster candidate. The election ended almost in a tie, with both Schroeder and Merkel claiming victory. The Christian Democrats actually finished first, with 35.2 percent of the vote, even though their lead in opinion polls had dropped 20 points in the two months prior to the election, while Schroeder's SPD received 34.3 percent. Merkel did unbelievably poorly in the former East German states, where the CDU's share of the vote dropped to 25.3 percent. The division of seats in the Bundestag was 225 for the CDU and 222 for the SPD. Under Germany's election law, Dr. Merkel was given the first chance to form a new government, which she succeeded in doing. A coalition was formed with the SPD, which was to receive eight ministries, while Merkel became chancellor and the CDU was given six ministries.

HISTORICAL DICTIONARY
A–Z

A

Aachen

The old imperial city of Aachen is situated on the border between Germany, Belgium, and the Netherlands. It was the favorite residence and coronation site of the emperor Charlemagne (742–814). Charlemagne, king of the Franks, and ultimately emperor of the HOLY ROMAN EMPIRE, is considered the founder of the Christian West and the political progenitor of Europe. The prominent position of the Carolingian empire in the world soon became manifest in its extensive network of foreign relations, which included the Byzantine imperial family and with Harun al-Rashid, the caliph of Baghdad. Charlemagne settled in Aachen, where he erected a magnificent imperial residence inspired by Roman and Byzantine models. Charlemagne made Aachen the second city of his empire, the center of culture and learning in what has come to be known as the Carolingian Revival. German kings were crowned in Aachen well into the 16th century, which event was moved to FRANKFURT AM MAIN in 1562. The city was fortified in the late 12th century and became a free imperial city in 1250. One of the most famous landmarks from this early period is the tomb of Charlemagne, over which hangs a bronze chandelier presented by Emperor Frederick I Barbarossa in 1168. The Palace Chapel of Charlemagne, built between 790–805, houses his throne and other medieval crafts.

At the end of the 17th century Aachen was the scene of several peace conferences at the end of the War of Devolution in 1668. In 1748 Aachen was the location of the peace conference at the end of the WAR OF AUSTRIAN SUCCESSION. After occupation by France in 1794 Aachen was annexed by France in 1801. It was then given to Prussia in 1814–15 by the CONGRESS OF VIENNA. After WORLD WAR I, Belgium occupied the city. During WORLD WAR II it was seriously damaged and became the first German city to fall to the Allies on October 20, 1944.

Aachen has served as a railway hub and as an industrial and commercial center of the coal mining region. Almost every branch of the iron and steel industry functions in the vicinity of Aachen. Textiles, furniture, glass, and machinery are also produced there.

absolutism

Centralized political power in the hands of princes and kings emerged in the 17th and 18th centuries. While in the HOLY ROMAN EMPIRE the estates expanded their power, the territorial princes emerged as rulers with unlimited power in their own states in respect to state administration, the fiscal system, and the army whether they abolished or merely tolerated the cooperation of the estates. The will of the prince was supreme. The most typical representatives of this absolutism were August I of SAXONY (1553–86), who was the leader of the Lutherans, and MAXIMILIAN I of BAVARIA (1595–1651), the leader of the Catholics. In Bavaria the estates had already been deprived of their political power by 1618. The principle of religious uniformity was the lever that accomplished this. In AUSTRIA, on the other hand, large groups of nobility and the towns formed powerful associations to protect their political rights. But the bloody conflicts that occurred in Austria ended with the Battle of White Mountain (1620) in complete victory for the royal power.

The power of August I and Maximilian I grew through the expansion of bureaucratic organization, mercantilistic economic practices, and military power. Government by princely ordinance increasingly assumed priority over customary arrangements and the decisions of the diets. Now officials were recruited from the universities and the middle class, whose servility and subservience became increasingly evident. The power of the prince was, however, mitigated, especially in Lutheran states from 1550 to 1650 because rulers and their subjects shared a strong bond of duty and obligation. There was a sense of calling and a personal sense of duty that permeated the social and political order. It was not until the century after the PEACE OF WESTPHALIA (1648) that bureaucratic functionalism and courtly ceremony created a wide chasm between the ruling classes and their subjects.

Many of these absolute princes made their residences the center of cultural life. They invited theater groups and orchestras to the court, and they were very partial to Italian opera. Many established collections of works of art, and others founded libraries. The most famous architects, sculptors, and painters were employed to build and decorate their magnificent palaces, which were located in the city center, as in BERLIN, DRESDEN, and Würzburg. Some followed the example of Versailles, which lay outside of Paris, as in Numphenburg near MUNICH and Ludwigsburg near Stuttgart. The age of absolutism reflected BAROQUE CULTURE at its height. Some rulers also were exponents of "enlightened absolutism," encouraging science and philosophy and establishing various academies and universities.

Through complete control of commerce and trade the absolutist states were able to increase their economic power. Thus, states such as Bavaria, BRANDENBURG (later Prussia), Saxony, and HANOVER were able to develop into independent centers of power. Austria, now the residence of the Habsburg emperors, repelled the Turks and acquired Hungary as well as parts of the former Turkish Balkan countries, enabling it to become a major power. It was challenged by PRUSSIA, which, under FREDERICK THE GREAT, became a leading military power.

The success of the Bavarian and Austrian rulers in depriving the estates of political power was complete. No diets were called in Bavaria after 1667, and religious uniformity was strictly enforced when, in the Upper Palatinate, which Bavaria acquired after the THIRTY YEARS' WAR, Protestantism was purged from the province. In the late 17th century the model of princely absolutism was provided by the great French king Louis XIV. In the 18th century it was the enlightened absolutism of Frederick the Great and his Austrian disciple, Emperor JOSEPH II, who provided the example of the rational organization of the state.

Abwehr
(Amt Auslandsnachrichten und Abwehr)

The Abwehr was the office of intelligence of the High Command of the German Armed Forces (OKW: Oberkommando der Wehrmacht). The intelligence office was the largest office in the OKW and was under the command of Admiral Wilhelm Canaris. It controlled the collection and dissemination to the armed services of all clandestine military intelligence and conducted military sabotage and counterintelligence efforts.

The activities of the Abwehr were well organized under Canaris but soon received interference from the Security Service of the SS (SD: Sicherheitsdienst) under Reinhard HEYDRICH, which was supposed to ferret out all the enemies of the state. The overlapping functions of the two groups caused an intense rivalry until Heydrich became the dominant figure on September 27, 1939, when he was placed in charge of the RSHA (Reich Security Main Office), the organization coordinating the police and security operations of the Reich and Nazi Party under the supervision of Heinrich HIMMLER.

Adenauer, Konrad (1876–1967)
first chancellor of the Federal Republic of Germany

One of Germany's greatest post–WORLD WAR II leaders, Konrad Adenauer helped establish the CHRISTIAN DEMOCRATIC UNION (CDU) and became the first chancellor of the FEDERAL REPUBLIC OF GERMANY (FRG) from 1949 to 1963, presiding over its remarkable economic recovery and leading it into the anti-Communist NATO alliance.

Born in the Rhineland city of Cologne in 1876 into the family of a Prussian Catholic minor civil servant, thrifty and hard-working, he studied law and political science, earning a law degree, and joined the Catholic German Center Party, becoming assistant to the mayor of Cologne in 1906 and in 1917 the lord mayor. He remained Cologne's mayor during the WEIMAR REPUBLIC and also was chairman of the upper house of the Prussian state legislature from 1920 to 1933. Opposed to the Nazis, Adenauer was forced out of office in 1933. During the Nazi dictatorship he avoided politics and refused to participate in resistance to the regime, yet was sporadically persecuted by the GESTAPO and imprisoned twice.

Although restored by the U.S. military authorities as mayor of Cologne, he was dismissed by the British occupation authorities in October 1945 due to conflicts with them. It was at this point that he joined the already established CDU, a new political party based on Christian principles, including members of both Catholic and Protestant denominations. Adenauer rapidly rose from being a local leader to chairman of the party for all of West Germany in 1949. In 1947 the Americans and British created the Bizone, which gave Adenauer the opportunity to form a coalition of parties against the SOCIAL DEMOCRATIC PARTY (SPD), which he considered similar to the Communists. In 1948 he became president of the Parliamentary Council and was instrumental in writing the BASIC LAW, a provisional constitution for a new government. In the first parliamentary elections for the BUNDESTAG (Federal Parliament), the Christian Democrats and their ally the CHRISTIAN SOCIAL UNION (CSU) won enough votes to form a coalition government and Adenauer's selection as the first postwar chancellor, to be reelected in 1953, 1957, and 1961. The great electoral victory of 1957 was the only absolute majority ever won by a party in the history of the FRG.

Adenauer had a conservative philosophy favoring a society that protected the individual citizen through the law. He was opposed to socialist and egalitarian ideas, yet compromised with the majority, which favored strong social insurance programs. Economic policy was left in the hands of Ludwig ERHARD, who directed a remarkable economic recovery. In foreign affairs Adenauer was absolutely opposed to the expansion of Communism, seeing it as a threat to Western humanistic individualism and Christian values. His goal as a statesman was to integrate West Germany into Western Europe. This resulted in a Franco-German rapprochement, membership in the Council of Europe, contributions to the European Defense Community, sovereignty for the Federal Republic, and in

Konrad Adenauer *(Library of Congress)*

1955 membership in NATO. With the cold war heating up as a result of the Korean War, Adenauer sought to rearm Germany, which was resisted by the Allies until West Germany's entry into NATO. In 1957–58 Adenauer made the Federal Republic a founding member of the European Economic Community (EEC).

Refusing to negotiate with the Soviet Union over German reunification, Adenauer believed that a rearmed Germany in a strong Western alliance was the best policy to get the Russians to compromise. One example of his hard-line approach was his rejection of Khrushchev's ultimatum in 1958 that Berlin become a "free city." Adenauer's ambition to create a nuclear capability for the West German army and subsequent demand for influence on NATO's nuclear strategy was resisted by the Kennedy administration. Always unsure about the American commitment to defend West Germany, the chancellor feared German interests would be sacrificed in negotiations between Washington and the Soviet Union. During his visit to Moscow in 1955 he did, however, establish diplomatic relations in order to gain the release of German prisoners of war.

Called Der Alte (the Old Man), Adenauer, the father figure, brought strong leadership and stability to German democracy, sometimes being criticized for being too authoritarian. Yet he was able to keep the radical forces of the right in check but also was instrumental in the pardoning of war criminals. Along with Ludwig Erhard he presided over the German "Economic Miracle" but also favored a strong system of social security. Close ties with Israel were established and reparations begun. Yet as a more liberal generation came of age in the 1960s he lost touch. His political career ended when he was forced to retire in October 1963, due in part to the scandal uncovered by the SPIEGEL AFFAIR.

Afrika Korps

The term *Afrika Korps* (Africa Corps, Deutsches Afrika Korps, DAK) was popularly used to designate all Axis forces in Africa, but technically it only meant the 5th Light Infantry Division, including its armored regiment, and the 15th Panzer Divisions, which were commanded by Lieutenant General Erwin ROMMEL. The first German troops arrived in Tripoli on February 11, 1941, in order to reinforce the rapidly retreating Italian army in Libya in its battle with the British. In two months the British had captured 114,000 prisoners. In August 1941 Rommel's command was raised to the status of a panzer group. Later it was renamed the 21st Panzer Division. In addition, Rommel had the support of the German 90th Infantry Division and six Italian divisions.

After Rommel the command of the Afrika Korps was placed under Lt. General Ludwig Cruewell. After he was shot down in May 1942, he was replaced by Major General Walther Nehring, who was wounded at Alam Halfa. His replacement was Lt. General Ritter von Thoma, who also was unfortunate enough to be captured at EL ALAMEIN. Other generals involved in command were Field Marshal Albert KESSELRING, Col. Fritz Beyerlein, General Gustav Fehn, General Hans Cramer, and Lt. Gen. Heinz Ziegler.

The African campaign began with a counterattack by Rommel on March 30, and by the end of May the Egyptian frontier had been reached. Unfortunately for the Axis, Adolf HITLER never adequately supplied the Afrika Korps with men and material. British control of the Mediterranean Sea obstructed the resupply. Nevertheless, Rommel launched another offensive against Egypt in May 1942, but was halted at El Alamein some 60 miles west of Alexandria. Although Rommel remained optimistic, the British launched their offensive on October 23, 1942, and by the end of May 1943 all active resistance was crushed. Part of the significance of the loss of North Africa was the loss of the opportunity to capture Gibraltar or the Suez Canal.

Agadir Incident (1911)

Agadir was a small port on the Atlantic coast of Morocco and became the center of the international crisis known as the Second Moroccan Crisis. Tension over French troop movement in Morocco, which represented a possible threat to German interests there, led the German government to make a demonstration of force by sending the gunboat SMS *Panther* there. The German foreign secretary, Kiderlen-Waechter, believed that French intrigues had broken the agreement reached five years earlier at ALGECIRAS and that a display of strength would gain compensation for Germany. Britain, on the other hand, was alarmed that Germany wanted to establish a naval base there, close to Gibraltar and Britain's vital trade routes. Lloyd George, the British leader, gave a stern warning to the Germans, which was interpreted by them as a threat of war, and the Germans denied that they had any intention of annexing Moroccan territory. The crisis was peacefully resolved by slight French concessions in the French Congo in return for German recognition of French rights in Morocco. Unfortunately for Germany, the crisis gave the impetus for a closer Anglo-French understanding.

Agrarian League
(Bund der Landwirte)

The Agrarian League was a powerful pressure group and prototype of extra-parliamentary mass mobilization efforts. It was one of a number of mass organizations that sought to influence the government outside of the Reichstag.

The Agrarian League was founded in 1893 by the JUNKERS (East Elbian large landowners). It grew quickly into a formidable organization with some 300,000 members by the eve of WORLD WAR I. Most of its members were farmers from all over Germany, but the leaders were the Prussian Junker aristocracy. The principal goal of the organization was to protect German agriculture through tariff protection against lower cost imports. It was the liberal tariff policies of the Caprivi government (1890–94), especially the commercial treaties with Russia, that were the catalyst for the organization of the Agrarian League.

Neither Caprivi nor German farmers foresaw the collapse of the international grain market in 1893. The newly formed Agrarian League clamored for the renegotiation of the Caprivi treaties to protect them from cheap agricultural imports from Russia and America. At that time the Agrarian League failed to raise the Reich's tariffs, because of opposition from Germany's rapidly growing export industries, which preferred lower food costs. Germany's wealth was increasingly based on manufacturing exports such as chemicals and electrical products, which were the lifeblood of the economy. Although Caprivi lost his job over the tariff disputes, his successor, von BÜLOW, worked out a compromise solution by giving agricultural interests increased export subsidies and cheaper credit.

Its public relations campaign lobbied for higher tariffs and against political reforms. Although officially nonpartisan, the Agrarian League kept close ties with the leaders of the conservative parties, helped place friends into government positions, favored a policy of imperialism, and sought to affect public opinion against constitutional reform. The agenda of the league came to dominate the political outlook of the GERMAN CONSERVATIVE PARTY (Deutschkonservativ Partei). In an attempt to strengthen its influence, it formed alliances with other economic interest groups such as the Central Association of German Industrialists (Centralverband Deutscher Industrieller (CdI).

After the war the Agrarian League merged with other groups into the Reichslandbund, which supported the GERMAN NATIONAL PEOPLE'S PARTY (DNVP). In 1929 with the Union of German Farmers it formed the Green Front to advocate even higher protective tariffs and after 1930 increasingly supported the NAZI PARTY (NSDAP). Under the Nazis it was coordinated into the Reich Food Estate.

Agricola, Rudolf (1444–1485)
German humanist

Roelof Huysman, who adopted the Latin name Rudolf Agricola, was born near Groningen in Frisia in 1444. Because he was so intelligent he was able to attend the University of Erfurt when he was 12. After Erfurt he went on to study at the Universities of Cologne and Louvain. Between 1469 and 1479 he studied and wrote, learning Greek and writing a biography of Petrarch, a founder of the Italian Renaissance. Returning to Germany in 1479, he carried with him the humanist intellectual life of Italy, becoming the founding father of German humanism. He had an attractive personality, had many friends, including Desiderius ERASMUS and Stephen MELANCTHON, and was sought after by many. In 1482 he served in the court of the Emperor MAXIMILIAN for six months. Then the elector of the Palatinate was able to bring Agricola to the University of HEIDELBERG. While there he educated some younger humanists. Agricola's works were written in Latin, the most important of which was an introductory manual entitled *On Dialectical Invention.*

Air Force
(Luftwaffe)

The German air force originated before 1914 and grew rapidly during WORLD WAR I. It was generally employed for reconnaissance, air combat, and some long-range bombing missions over London. After the war it was disbanded and forbidden by the TREATY OF VERSAILLES. In 1922 Germany again was allowed to build civil aircraft, and Lufthansa airlines became the most advanced airline in the world. German civil aviation was largely controlled by the military (Reichswehr) under the leadership of General Hans von Seeckt. During the 1920s a highly efficient aircraft industry developed, which included such aircraft manufacturers as Focke Wulf at BREMEN, Dornier at Friedrichshafen, Heinkel at Warnemünde, Junkers at Dessau, and MESSERSCHMITT at AUGSBURG. Not only had German designers developed all metal planes, but also variable pitched propellers and retractable landing gears.

As soon as Adolf HITLER assumed power, he set about funding a new air force (Luftwaffe) and by 1935 it was officially established. Hermann GÖRING was placed in charge as Reichskommisar for Air, and State Secretary Eduard Milch and under him General Walther Wever were made responsible for its development. Secretly, they built factories for aircraft production, constructed airfields, and established training schools. Within two years Hitler announced to the world that he had an air force of 20,000 officers and men and had more than 1,800 planes. In 1936 General Albert Kesselring succeeded Wever as commander of the Luftwaffe.

German bomber, HE 111, during flight *(Library of Congress)*

The basic tactical unit of the Luftwaffe was the group, which was composed of three wings. Each wing was composed of three squadrons of 12 to 16 aircraft. A wing included 40 planes and a group about 120. Some of the nomenclature included the Fighter group (JG), Bomber group (KG), Night fighter group (NJG), Fast bomber group (SKG), Dive bomber group (StG), and Transport group (TG).

The Spanish civil war marked the beginning of its use in war. In August 1936 the Germans became involved in Spain, and their approximately 200 aircraft became known as the CONDOR LEGION. Its transports ferried thousands of General Francisco Franco's troops from Morocco to Spain, and other aircraft assisted the Fascist cause in the civil war, providing the Germans with invaluable experience. The air force was not used in the ANSCHLUSS nor in the crisis over Czechoslovakia in 1938. The invasion of Poland, however, involved some 1,600 aircraft. Hitler's infamous BLITZKRIEG relied on speedy fighter planes and Stuka dive bombers, which bombed Polish airfields and provided support for panzers and ground troops. Later, continued successes occurred during the invasion of Denmark, Norway, the Netherlands, and Belgium. The story changed somewhat in France. The Luftwaffe was unable to stop the evacuation at Dunkirk and turned to supporting the tanks racing toward Paris. In France they met an air force with equal competence and equipment.

The BATTLE OF BRITAIN was a real turning point for the Luftwaffe in the battle for the skies. Before the Germans could invade Britain by sea, they had to defeat the Royal Air Force (RAF). The Germans started out with an armada of some 2,600 aircraft. The attack began on August 13, 1940, and by the end of September it became evident that the air war would not succeed in subduing Britain. The British Hurricanes and the Spitfires began to turn the tide of battle, and it became evident that preparing Britain for an invasion would take more than the light bombers. The change in German tactics from concentration on airfields to cities greatly benefited the RAF and its ability to repel the Luftwaffe. The British also possessed the new invention of radar, which helped in the defense of Britain.

The German strategy of air-army cooperation in offensive operations worked well on the Russian front until 1942, but left the Luftwaffe inadequately prepared for other tasks. For instance, too few fighters were available to defend the homeland when the massive Allied bombing raids began. When fighters were taken from the Russian front to help in home defense, the division of aircraft was inadequate for both fronts. Aircraft production had also languished between 1939 and 1942, new planes failed to materialize, and the renewed effort to produce more planes was too late. No wonder that the Allied landing on D-DAY was successful when one considers that 12,000 Allied planes faced only 500 German aircraft. In 1944 it is also astonishing that German factories produced 39,000 aircraft, which were shortly destroyed on the ground or in brief combat operations. In February 1945, when the Luftwaffe was essentially beaten, some 3,000 aircraft remained grounded without fuel. Also, between 1939 and 1945 the Luftwaffe had lost too many pilots and crews, killed, wounded, or captured. The hopes that Hitler had placed in new weaponry to win the war were illusory. The V-2 rockets had a minimal impact and the invention of jet aircraft in the Messerschmitt Me 262 also failed to save the Third Reich.

Albert (Albrecht) of Brandenburg (1490–1545)
elector and archbishop of Mainz

Albert of Brandenburg was born on June 28, 1490, the younger son of John Cicero, elector of Brandenburg. His older brother became elector Joachim I of Brandenburg. Albert studied at the University of Frankfort on the Oder, then entered the ecclesiastical profession, and in 1513 he became archbishop of Magdeburg and the administrator of the bishopric of Halberstadt. At the young age of 24 he became archbishop of the electorate of Mainz in 1514, which was important in the selection of the emperor. It might appear that Albert's acquisitions of multiple religious offices was exceptional, but it was a common practice among aristocratic German families. It was, however, a costly affair because the pope demanded 30,000 ducats for the privilege. On the other hand, the new archbishop had to raise the necessary funds by obtaining a loan from the AUGSBURG banking house of the FUGGERS. At the same time Pope Leo X granted him permission to issue indulgences to finance his transactions. He was allowed to keep half of the proceeds in order to repay the Fuggers and the other half was to go to the Holy See. Albert's financial needs and his association with his employment of the Dominican friar John Tetzel were not conducive to conveying the impression of religious respectability. John Tetzel's dramatic and exaggerated preaching of the indulgences left a scandalous impression, but so did Albert's luxury loving and sensual life as he traveled about with his mistresses piquantly clad in male costume. Martin LUTHER objected to Tetzel's scandalous promotion of indulgences, posting his Ninety-five Theses and sending a letter to archbishop Albert. Luther's communication about the indulgences was not answered, but referred to the Holy See, and it was reported by Albert that Luther was spreading new doctrines. Whether or not Albert could have handled the situation locally is difficult to determine, but needless to say he was not a competent theologian and was irritated by any interference with his financial dealings.

In 1518 Albert was created a cardinal as a reward for his services to the church. The next year his vote became important in the election for emperor, which was being contended by Francis I, king of France, and Charles who was elected CHARLES V with the help of Albert's vote. Albert received a considerable sum of money from Charles for his support. Albert also was one of the most significant patrons of the arts in Germany. He was friends with the humanists Desiderius ERASMUS and Ulrich von HUTTEN. Among his accomplishments in architecture was the sumptuously adorned Stiftskirche at Halle and the cathedral in Mainz.

After Luther's ideas began to spread, the reformers hoped that Albert would be won over to Lutheranism. During the PEASANTS' WAR of 1525, however, he decided to side with the Catholic princes in the defense of Dessau in July 1525. As Albert opposed the spread of Lutheranism in his own diocese, it did not deter many from accepting the reformers' doctrines. During his latter years Albert was less tolerant of Protestant teaching and invited the JESUITS to teach in his dominions. In 1541 Albert found it necessary to grant his subjects their religious liberty, but exacted from them 500,000 florins to pay off his debts. Yet, Albert was not so hostile to Protestants as was his brother, Joachim. Albert was involved in peace efforts, but also was a member of the League of Nuremberg, which was formed in 1538 against the protestant SCHMALKALDIC LEAGUE. As the REFORMATION progressed, Albert became instrumental in fostering the COUNTER-REFORMATION, although he soon died on September 24, 1545, in Aschaffenburg.

Albert V (1528–1579)
duke of Bavaria and Renaissance prince
Albert was duke of Bavaria from 1550 to 1579 and one of the most influential German princes of the COUNTER-REFORMATION. He was significant as one of the founders of the Bavarian quasi-absolutist state in the 16th and 17th centuries. His education was strongly influenced by his training in the Jesuit college at Ingolstadt, where he acquired a strong sense of Catholicism along with a deep appreciation for Renaissance humanism. He spent extravagantly on Renaissance art, sculpture, music, and architecture, which almost bankrupted the state.

Albert's father, William IV, hoped that Albert's marriage to the eldest daughter of Emperor Ferdinand I would bring BAVARIA an electoral title, which did not occur. On the other hand, the prince's authority was enhanced when for the first time the Bavarian decree on primogeniture was enacted, which declared that the territory of Bavaria was indivisible. It was promulgated not by his father, but by Duke

Albert IV on July 8, 1506, which increased centralized political control.

Beginning with Albert V the politics, religion, and family interests of the WITTELSBACHS became increasingly intertwined with that of the Catholic Church. Earlier in his rule Albert had tried to compromise with the Protestants in the Bavarian diet, whose financial support he needed to help pay for his extravagance. Albert made concessions to them and also convinced the pope to allow communion in both bread and wine. However, Albert's dogmatic Catholicism won out in the struggle. As the Protestant nobles resisted his centralizing efforts, Albert moved to crush the Protestants and reduced the power of the Bavarian assembly. Even Catholic nobles who tried to free themselves from his authority lost their independence. To suppress the Protestants he employed what was known as the Spiritual Council controlled by his secular advisers. Churches were inspected annually, strict censorship was imposed, and the JESUITS were given control of schools and universities.

Albert also sought to extend his family's interests outside of Bavaria by attempting to acquire bishoprics for family members. He acquired that of Freising outside of MUNICH, and after the death of his father and the succession of William V, Ernest came into possession of the bishoprics of Hildesheim, Münster, Halberstadt, Lüttich, and Cologne.

Algeciras, Conference of (1906)

The international conference of the Great Powers at Algeciras in southern Spain was intended to settle the conflict between France and Germany over imperialist influence in Morocco. In 1905 the French government began to extend its control over Morocco, which the German government decided to challenge. In March 1905 the German emperor interrupted a Mediterranean cruise to make a theatrical landing in Tangier, where he visited the sultan, promising him German support to protect Morocco's independence. Behind the emperor's visit were advisers (Friedrich Holstein and Prince Bernhard von BÜLOW, chancellor, 1900–09) who were hoping to humiliate France and weaken the new alliance, the Entente, between France and England.

The conference was held between January and April 1906. The Germans had insisted on the conference in the hope of inflicting a diplomatic humiliation on France and destroying the growing friendship between Britain and France. Largely through the skill of the British delegate, Sir Arthur Nicolson, the Germans were isolated and outvoted, and reluctantly had to accept the "Act of Algeciras," which authorized France and Spain to police Morocco under a Swiss inspector general and respected the sultan of Morocco's authority. The close collaboration of the French and British representatives is of greater historical importance than the terms of the actual settlement; by their cooperation they strengthened the Anglo-French Entente and showed Russia the advantages to be gained from a similar understanding with Britain.

Allied Control Council

The Allied Control Council was established at BERLIN in June 1945. It was an organization agreed upon by President Franklin Roosevelt, Prime Minister Winston Churchill, and Marshal Joseph Stalin in accordance with agreements made at the YALTA and POTSDAM CONFERENCES for the administration of the whole of occupied Germany. The council was located in Berlin and was made up of the supreme commanders of the four occupation powers. It was a complex organization of 12 directorates and 170 subsections. Acting under the general guidance of the council, each of the four Allies was responsible to administer its own zone, and each military governor retained virtually complete autonomy to make decisions in their zones that they deemed necessary.

The four representatives to the council were General Eisenhower (U.S.), General Montgomery (Britain), General Zhukov (USSR), and De Lattre de Tassigny (France). The first formal meeting took place on June 5, 1945, when proclamations establishing the council and its responsibilities were signed. A month later on July 10 the first business meeting was held. In 1948 the Soviet representative left the council, which brought an end to its meetings.

Alsace-Lorraine

These provinces on the eastern border of France were linked in name only after annexation by BISMARCK in 1871. The area is divided into three regions: Lorraine, Lower Alsace, and Upper Alsace. The provinces were continually fought over by France and Germany. Most of Alsace was first occupied by the French in 1648 (PEACE OF WESTPHALIA), 10 "free cities" being annexed in 1681. Lorraine was formally added to the French Kingdom in 1766. After the Franco-Prussian War and the Treaty of Frankfurt (1871) both provinces except for part of Lorraine around Belfort were ceded to Germany. On June 3, 1871, they were declared "Imperial Territory" (Reichsland). Until Bismarck's fall in 1890, Alsace and Lorraine were administered with severity, but thereafter tension relaxed and the Germans made an effort to assimilate the territory, even granting it a degree of autonomy in 1911. At the same time the industrial yield of the iron-ore deposits of Alsace and Lorraine was considerably increased by the perfection of the Gilchrist-Thomas process of steel making in 1878. A number of incidents showed Alsatian dissatisfaction with German administration; the most famous of these occurred in November 1913 at Zabern, where riots broke out following insults heaped on Alsatian recruits by a German lieutenant. In France there was continuous resentment against Germany for having annexed Alsace-Lorraine; in Paris the statue representing the city of Strasbourg was permanently veiled from 1871 to 1918. The territories were restored to France by the TREATY OF VERSAILLES, 1919. Between the wars conflicts over religious policy led to occupational demands of autonomy. In 1940 Alsace-Lorraine was made an integral part of Hitler's Germany, but was liberated once more in 1945.

Altdorfer, Albrecht (1480–1538)
Renaissance painter, draftsman, printmaker, and architect

One of the leading landscape painters of the Danube school of BAVARIA and AUSTRIA, a lifelong resident of REGENSBURG, Bavaria, Altdorfer became a member of the city council and was appointed city architect. The city council in 1533 adopted Lutheranism, which he presumably supported. In 1538 he died and was buried in the Augustine cloister. His earliest drawings demonstrate the influence of Italian RENAISSANCE painting. He displayed a poetic feeling for the smallest details and light of the landscape. In *St. George in a Wood* color and detail are almost indistinct from the figures. In *Holy Night* the moonlight has a mysterious quality. In his religious paintings such as The *Birth of Christ*, The *Holy Family at a Fountain*, and the *Birth of the Virgin* there is a romantic intimacy. After 1510 his paintings became more monumental with bold spatial effects and vivid coloring. It was during this period around 1521 that he produced *The Danube Landscape* near Regensburg. During the last period of his life starting about 1526 he became more influenced by the Renaissance, interested in color and architectural construction, as in the *Emperor's Bath* in Regensburg. His use of Italian figures had a decidedly German quality. His engravings share the qualities of the Nuremberg school, whose graphic art was determined by Albrecht DÜRER. Altdorfer's most important work, *The Battle of Alexander* (1529) was executed in Munich and commissioned by Duke Wilhelm IV of Bavaria. The armies of Alexander and Darius are locked in a monumental battle scene. The organization of the miniature size of armies numbering in the thousands makes Alexander and Darius's fate seem inconsequential.

Amiens, Battle of (August 1918)

The Battle of Amiens between August 8 and 11, 1918, was decisive in bringing WORLD WAR I to an end.

The final German offensive of World War I, the Michael Offensive, was launched in March 1918, which was the last gamble for enough military gains so that the Allies would agree to peace on Germany's terms. That offensive ground to a halt, and it was the Battle of Amiens, August 8–11, that turned the momentum in favor of the Allies. Sir Henry Rawlinson's Fourth British Army supported by French units struck with suddenness east of Amiens.

The British Fourth Army was speedily organized and moved into forward positions with extraordinary stealth. Fourteen divisions of infantry, three cavalry divisions, 2,000 guns and 450 tanks were secretly moved into position along a 10-mile front. The guns were moved by railway at night and camouflaged by morning. The rumble of the tanks getting into position was smothered by a noise barrage of the Royal Air Force. To increase the smash surprise, no practice maneuvers were held. Air cover was provided with 800 aircraft with the British forces and 1,104 with the French First Army. Added power for the offensive was provided with the French Third Army and 90 tanks. In summary, Generals Foch and Haig proposed to retake the old Somme battlefield.

When the battle began, the Germans were completely surprised. Two thousand guns roared across the plateau, the infantry moved rapidly across no-man's-land. Units leapfrogged one another as they moved quickly ahead. At one time the British took more than 16,000 prisoners in less than two hours. By August 11 German resistance hardened, and it was time to stop. A great battle had been fought and won, and the German front line pushed substantially back.

The significance of the battle was that as a result of the "Black Day" the German leadership came to the conclusion that the war could not be won. Ludendorff's equilibrium was shaken. On August 11 the emperor summoned a meeting of the High Command and decided that the war had to be ended. Ludendorff decided that German offensives were unable to force the enemy to sue for peace, which now had to be secured through diplomacy. By September 29 Hindenburg and Ludendorff advised the emperor to negotiate an armistice.

Anabaptists

Anabaptists were those Protestants who emphasized adult baptism as a free act of the acceptance of Christianity, and not the traditional Catholic sacrament removing original sin. They first appeared as a distinct group in Zurich, Switzerland, being forced to leave by Ulrich ZWINGLI, moving northward along the RHINE and eastward to Moravia. They had much in common with the Zwickau radicals such as Thomas MÜNTZER. One also had to be saved and regenerated to become a member of the community by baptism. They emphasized the communal ownership of goods. They subscribed to the belief in the internal light of prophecy as a balance to the Scriptures and sacraments. A true Christian had to live according to the personal piety and ethics taught by Christ in the Sermon on the Mount. Most Anabaptists believed that the church was visibly composed of true believers. All service to the state was forbidden as an expression of idolatry. A chiliastic belief predicted that the Day of Judgment was imminent when the children of God would rise up to slay all nonbelievers, preparing the way for the return of Christ. Secular authorities reacted with alarm to such teachings that all service to the state was idolatry and a revolutionary restructuring of society should take place. This resulted in secular authorities arresting, imprisoning, and executing thousands of Anabaptists. The policy was confirmed by the imperial diets of Speyer (1529) and AUGSBURG (1530) when the ancient Roman Justinian Code was reiterated condemning rebaptism as punishable by death.

Although some Anabaptists were inclined to withdraw from the world, others felt called to destroy the ungodly. Leaders who believed this, such as Jan Mathys and John of Leyden, took over in Münster, where they established communal sharing of goods and the introduction of polygamy. It was an Anabaptist dictatorship noted for its brutality and extremism. It was here that a coalition of both Catholic and Lutheran princes laid siege to the city and executed its leaders. Following the revolution in Münster another leader, the Dutch reformer Menno Simons (1496–1561) established a peaceful and pious movement whose followers became known as Mennonites, becoming the largest of the Anabaptist sects. The Mennonites eventually migrated to North America and had considerable influence on Quakers and Baptists.

Anglo-German Naval Treaty (1935)

On June 18, 1935, Germany and Great Britain negotiated a bilateral agreement on naval armaments that permitted the Nazis to substantially exceed the naval limits set down in the VERSAILLES TREATY.

The Anglo-German naval treaty established a "permanent relationship" between the German and British navies. The treaty set the total tonnage of the German fleet at no more than 35 percent of the aggregate tonnage of naval forces of the British Commonwealth. It also permitted Germany to build a submarine fleet equal to the total submarine tonnage of the Commonwealth. The agreement unilaterally modified the naval terms of the Versailles Treaty and particularly disturbed France, which was less convinced than Britain that Adolf HITLER would honor his commitments. Hitler proved the French to be right when he denounced the treaty on April 28, 1939.

This naval accord was a diplomatic victory for Hitler and was significant in that the British recognized Germany's right to rearm and indirectly to break the Treaty of Versailles. It also initiated the policy of appeasement based on the belief that satisfying the demands of the powers dissatisfied with the treaty would ensure European stability. From the British point of view they had gotten the Germans to agree to specific armaments restrictions. Diplomatically, the naval accord weakened the Allied front toward Germany because the French were not consulted and became suspicious of British actions.

Anschluss

Anschluss is a German term for the union of post–WORLD WAR I AUSTRIA with Nazi Germany in 1938. It was a political, diplomatic, and economic triumph for Adolf HITLER, through which he created a Greater German Reich, which not even Otto von BISMARCK had accomplished.

After World War I and the disintegration of the multinational Austro-Hungarian Empire the remaining German part of the Empire forming the Austrian Republic voted overwhelmingly to be united with the new WEIMAR REPUBLIC. This was forbidden by the Allies in the TREATY OF VERSAILLES and the Treaty of St Germain. Agitation in favor of Anschluss continued throughout the 1920s, especially in the Tyrol and Salzburg. In 1931 a projected Customs Union between Germany and Austria had to be abandoned because France and the Little Entente complained that this would have been a first step to a political union of the two countries. Demands for union increased in 1933 after Hitler became German chancellor. A Nazi coup in Vienna in July 1934 failed, although the Austrian chancellor, Engelbert Dollfuss, was murdered. Internal discord in France and the reconciliation of Fascist Italy and Nazi Germany in 1936 left the Austrian government isolated in the face of Hitler's demands. In February 1938 Hitler asked the new chancellor, Kurt von Schuschnigg, to meet him at Berchtesgaden and demanded concessions for the Austrian Nazis, including participation in the government. Hoping to forestall Hitler by a public relations coup in favor of Austrian independence, Schuschnigg planned a plebiscite on the question. Hitler was furious and countered by submitting an ultimatum on March 11, 1938, demanding the resignation of Schuschnigg. He was forced to resign in favor of the Austrian Nazi Arthur Seyss-Inquart, who invited the German Army to occupy Austria on March 12 to maintain "law and order," which was met by near universal acclaim. On the next day Seyss-Inquart proclaimed union with Germany. That same day Hitler arrived, making a triumphal tour of the country, which culminated in front of the old imperial castle in Vienna to an audience of 100,000 cheering admirers.

In 1938 France and England limited their protests to the Anschluss with diplomatic notes. This was partly the result of the APPEASEMENT POLICY adopted by the governments of England and France, through which they hoped to contain Hitler's revisionist foreign policy. It failed because in some months they would be faced with Hitler's threat to the independence of Czechoslovakia.

Anti-Comintern Pact (1936)

This pact between Nazi Germany and Japan was important primarily for its propaganda value demonstrating that Nazi Germany was opposed to communism. On the surface this political treaty was directed against the communist international organization, the Comintern, but was secretly an agreement against the Soviet Union.

The German foreign minister, Joachim von RIBBENTROP, came up with the idea of establishing a special relationship with Japan. Through conversations with the Japanese military attaché in Berlin Ribbentrop proposed a treaty against the Soviet Union that would be disguised as simply an anti-communist front. Adolf HITLER encouraged the conversations and approved the final agreement, which was concluded in November 1936, the same month that Mussolini proclaimed the formation of the AXIS. Hitler had wanted a stronger anti-Soviet commitment, but Japan had little desire to be drawn into a European war. The agreement became more serious after war began between China and Japan (China incident) of July 1937, when Japan requested a cessation of aid that the Germans had been providing to China.

Japan decided to enter the agreement after the Soviet Union had signed a mutual assistance treaty with Outer Mongolia, which Japan interpreted as a direct threat to its interests. There was a secret protocol attached to the Anti-Comintern Pact, by which each party committed itself to neutrality if the other was at war with the Soviet Union. When Italy joined the pact in November 1937, the protocol did not apply to it. The pact was expanded to Hungary, Spain, and Manchukuo in 1939 and in 1941 Bulgaria, Croatia, Denmark, Finland, Romania, Slovakia, and the Chinese government in Nanking.

anti-Semitism/Jew hatred
(1500–1848)

Before the advent of modern concepts of race, anti-Semitism should more accurately be described as prejudice or hatred toward the Jews because of their religion, cultural separateness, or economic power. During the late Middle Ages the image of the Jew became fixed as a symbol of hidden menaces and was stripped of normal human characteristics that would control civilized conduct toward them. Outbreaks of violence occurred frequently in northern Europe, and although the popes tried to protect Jews, Christian teaching continued to define them as religious antagonists. Sporadic popular outbursts by rioters found it easier to identify their victims when they were forced, as in Bamberg, to wear yellow patches or horned caps. Sometimes Christian merchants were jealous of Jewish peddlers, while others may have wanted to free themselves from debts to Jewish moneylenders. Then, between 1290 and 1421, secular rulers expelled Jews from their lands, and specifically in the HOLY ROMAN EMPIRE, from Prague in 1400 and Vienna in 1421. Compulsory segregation into ghettos began in Venice in 1516, and by 1600 the physical and economic segregation of Jews throughout Europe was mostly complete.

The Lutheran Reformation in Germany held out prospects of some relief. LUTHER at first hoped that Jews would convert to his brand of Christianity, but disappointed by their continued resistance, Luther published *Concerning the Jews and Their Lies* (1543). Fortunately, Luther's admonition of harsh punishment for the Jews was not adopted. Conditions improved in Protestant Europe because of the rejection of the Catholic doctrine of transubstantiation, which reduced accusations of ritual murder against Jews and the generally better treatment of Jews in Calvinist areas. The Catholic COUNTER-REFORMATION reemphasized hostility toward the Jews. During and after the THIRTY YEARS' WAR the conditions somewhat improved as the various German states sought the aid of Jewish lenders to rebuild their lands. Many territorial princes even invited Jewish settlement and Court Jews (Hofjuden) played an important role in financial administration. Brandenburg-Prussia probably demonstrated the greatest degree of toleration. Being a Court Jew, however, did not always protect one, as was the case for Joseph Süss Oppenheimer, who, even though he had been the banker of Duke Karl Alexander of Württemberg, was tried and executed after the duke's death. More generally, Jews were regularly expelled from cities and states and were segregated, impoverished, and treated with contempt. When the Jews were expelled from Vienna in 1670, some 50 families were invited to Prussia, where they played a significant economic role helping the country recover from the lengthy and devastating SEVEN YEARS' WAR. During the latter 18th century it appeared possible that an integration of rich Jewish families in BERLIN and the enlightened aristocracy and middle class might have been possible. The philosopher Moses MENDELSSOHN and his daughter, Dorothea Mendelssohn Veit, conducted a reading and discussion society in Berlin, which played a significant role in demonstrating that the differences between Jews and Germans could be bridged. Contrary to expectation, the rationalism of the ENLIGHTENMENT did not free Judaism from the criticism that thinkers like Immanuel KANT leveled against all religions. Judaism according to his viewpoint was primitive and intellectually stagnant. There were those, like Christian Wilhelm Dohm, who advocated toleration and emancipation and believed that Jews were equal human beings, with which much of the population probably disagreed.

During the French Revolution French Jews were given full civil rights in France. In Prussia Wilhelm von HUMBOLDT argued for emancipation, but a condition was added that they assimilate into German society. Only under pressure of the French conquerors did Jews receive the rights of citizenship through the introduction of the Napoleonic Code in the Rhineland, in most German states between 1806 and 1808, but not in Prussia until 1812. When the French left Germany and a severe economic depression occurred, there was a revival of Jew hatred and a revisionist mood that sought to abolish their citizenship or limit its practice. While the issue of Jewish rights was being debated at the CONGRESS OF VIENNA, local governments in Frankfurt, Bremen, Lübeck, and Hamburg already had withdrawn the rights granted Jews during the French occupation. In fact, in Lübeck and Bremen Jewish families were expelled and sporadic attacks by mobs occurred. A notable instance of Germans coming to their defense occurred at the University of Heidelberg, where students were inspired by the famous jurist Anton Thibaut, an advocate of legal reform.

A considerable amount of anti-Semitic literature was published after the Napoleonic period, undoubtedly influenced by romantic nationalism. This form of nationalism admired everything rooted in German culture and history, emphasized a feeling of exclusivity deepened by suffering and struggle, and demanded the purification of the German people (*Volk*) of alien elements. At this point the motivation was not racial but religious. The Christian faith was considered an essential part of German identity, and Jews had to convert in order to become members of the German nation. Even when Jews tried to assimilate and become "good" Germans, they were often criticized for their arrogance and judged as "un-German" as was the case of Heinrich HEINE.

The REVOLUTION OF 1848 spread anti-Semitism throughout Europe. Jewish emancipation was an objective of the liberals and radicals, and some of the revolutionary leaders were Jews, which reinforced the negative connection with the threat of subversion. Nationalism also became a source of conflict between Jews and Gentiles, and the so-called Jewish question was dominated by such fundamental issues as Jewish radicalism, economic domination, media control, and whether the gulf between Jew and Gentile could be bridged.

anti-Semitism (1871–1945)

The term *anti-Semitism* appeared in Germany in 1879, first being used by the journalist Wilhelm MARR, indicating a new attitude toward Jews and Gentiles in a secularized Europe. Modern political identity, he thought, was based on race and nationality, and the differences between Jews and non-Jews were irreconcilable because they were racial. Anti-Semitism implies more than a distaste for Jews or intense emotional hatred; it advocates a goal of committed action against the Jews. It was no longer just a personal hatred nor an issue of religious conversion, nor mob action. What was new and menacingly different about anti-Semitism was its institutionalization, that is, its embodiment in permanent political parties, associations, and published journals. Not even racism was the distinguishing characteristic between anti-Semitism and the Jew hatred of the past. Racism had existed before 1879 and was not universally part of the new outlook, especially in eastern Europe, where, for instance, the most significant anti-Semitic book of the 20th century was *The Protocols of the Elders of Zion*, which did not conceive the Jewish question to be racial.

It was the abolition of discriminatory laws through emancipation that empowered the Jews and reversed the relation between Jews and non-Jews. To their enemies emancipation had been an invalid bestowal of rights, which Jews would use to control the nation. Anti-Semites were usually powerless "little people" who thought that anti-Semitism offered them a way of achieving power and of acting out their hateful feelings toward Jews, although conservative groups and parties could also use anti-Semitism to get votes and protect their interests.

The anti-Semitic movement of the 1870s arose in response to Jewish migration to cities, attendance at universities, entrance into the professions, and participation in public and cultural life. Their upward mobility became highly visible. Also significant was the economic depression of the 1870s, which worsened the already difficult situation and created resentment in the lower middle class and peasantry, who were having a difficult time adjusting to a capitalistic market economy. In modern history anti-Semitic resentment usually appeared much stronger during economic crises, such as that of the 1870s, and then later in the aftermath of WORLD WAR I and during the GREAT DEPRESSION of the 1930s. Anti-Semitism first took organized political form in Germany, where it became a fundamental platform of the CHRISTIAN SOCIAL PARTY, launched in 1879 by the court preacher Adolf Stöcker, who depicted Jews as agents of social decay, revolutionary discontent, and subversive to German hierarchical patriarchal society. It also appeared in Austria-Hungary as an artisan defense movement and was politically successful when Karl Lueger was elected mayor of Vienna. Germany's most famous nationalist historian, Heinrich von TREITSCHKE, warned against the Jewish threat to the national unity of Otto von BISMARCK's new German state, coining the infamous phrase, "the Jews are our misfortune." Most of the anti-Semitic politicians, however, came out of the ranks of failed academics, journalists, and would-be intellectuals who blamed Jews for most of the economic, cultural, and moral evils of the time. The new anti-Semites believed in a Jewish world conspiracy, had a theory of history, and were committed to fighting against the Jewish danger. They institutionalized anti-Semitism in journals, newspapers, reform clubs, and political parties.

None of these groups and political parties developed into strong mass movements nor became powerful enough before World War I to pass laws in the REICHSTAG to restrict Jewish rights. This, however, opened the way for those anti-Semites who rejected conventional parliaments as a manifestation of the evil Jewish influence. The Russian Revolution of 1917 and German defeat in 1918 had proven the worst fears of these anti-Semites. Postwar resentments fueled the proliferation of radical right organizations, especially in BAVARIA with large numbers of ex-servicemen who were anti-republican and anti-Semitic and willing to use violence and political assassination. For instance, Walter RATHENAU, the famous Jewish foreign minister, was assassinated in 1922. The Republic lacked legitimacy in the eyes of anti-Semites; in fact, it was difficult for the republican government to fight against anti-Semitism. German economic and educational elites were willing to use anti-Semitism to fight for their interests and finance anti-Semitic publications. The NAZI PARTY espoused extreme anti-Semitism in order to mobilize a mass following. After Hitler became chancellor, the persecution of Jews became commonplace and their rights were eliminated. Jews were excluded from public life and government service; then deprived of citizenship through the NUREMBERG LAWS of 1935; and finally expelled from professions and commercial life by 1938. The Nazi state made the solution to the Jewish question one of its chief tasks.

The culmination of modern anti-Semitism came after the outbreak of WORLD WAR II. Jews were deported to ghettos in eastern Europe and then to extermination camps like Auschwitz. Nazi leaders were responsible for the decision of the FINAL SOLUTION, but collaborators in the occupied areas made the genocide possible. All the participants were motivated in this mass genocide by the anti-Semitic prejudices, racism, conspiracy theories, and demonic images that had dehumanized the Jews and made it acceptable to deprive them of their human rights.

Anti-Socialist Law (1878)

The Anti-Socialist Law of October 19, 1878, gave the German government the authority to suppress all independent labor organizations, all of their political and economic associations, newspapers, periodicals, and printing presses. The government was given power to declare a state of siege wherever necessary in order to take action against them.

The German chancellor Otto von BISMARCK had become alarmed at the rapid growth of the socialist vote during the 1870s. As far as he was concerned the SOCIAL DEMOCRATIC PARTY was not just another political party like the NATIONAL LIBERAL PARTY or the CENTER PARTY, but the Socialists were enemies of the state and also of the German way of life. He already had taken administrative action trying to prevent socialist influence in the army and the civil service. In 1877 he began to consider how to ban the Social Democratic Party altogether. Since a bill to do that had to be introduced on the federal level in the Reichstag, the National Liberals and the Center Party had the opportunity to vote against such political repression. A struggle over constitutional liberties was in the making as the government and the parties stood at odds.

Events then played into Bismarck's hands. At first one and then two attempts were made to assassinate the emperor, which then Bismark used to scare the population into suppressing the Socialists. On May 8, 1878, a half-witted tinkerer from LEIPZIG named Hödel attempted to kill the emperor but failed. In response Bismarck introduced a bill into the Reichstag embodying anti-socialist measures, which were again successfully opposed by the Liberals and the Center. Not even a month later, on June 2, another attempt on the emperor's life was made, this time wounding him seriously. The assassin was a Dr. Nobling, not associated with the Socialists but who it was claimed acted on their behalf. Besides unleashing a violent campaign against the Socialists, Bismarck also dissolved the Reichstag and with new elections hoped to capitalize on the public outrage against the Socialists. The National Liberals remained the largest party, with the other parties gaining or losing only a few seats. This time, however, the proposed anti-Socialist legislation passed (229 to 149) because of Liberal support along with the Conservatives and the Reich party. The Anti-Socialist Law of October 19, 1878, forbade all associations and publications that sought to subvert the existing social order or showed "socialist tendencies," so that professional socialist agitators could be banned in certain affected communities. It gave the police such large powers of interrogation, arrest, and expulsion that suspected Socialists lost the customary protection of the law. Freedom of assembly and freedom of expression could be restricted in "imperiled areas." Their party was forced to become a clandestine organization. It also struck a blow at the Independent Trade Unions, which were closely associated with the Social Democratic Party. For the remainder of Bismarck's years the Socialists were subject to arrest by local police.

Initially passed for the duration of three years, it was periodically renewed until 1890. The Anti-Socialist Law was a public admission by Bismarck that he believed royal authority had to be maintained by restricting freedom of political choice. As serious as the persecution was, it was milder than the terror enacted by the French government after the Paris Commune in 1871. The Anti-Socialist Law completely destroyed the existing institutions of the SPD. During the 12 years that the law was in force, 900 persons were expelled from their homes and 1,500 were imprisoned. The party's leaders were forced to leave the country and others were arrested. The party press had to be printed outside the country. Socialist leaders who were in the Reichstag and enjoyed immunity could not speak or campaign in public. The congresses of the party had to be held in Holland or Switzerland. But the voters continued to support the party in the Reichstag elections. By 1884 through shrewd underground organizations the workers cast more ballots for the Socialists than in 1878, and by 1890 the vote had tripled.

appeasement policy

The appeasement policy was the invention of Prime Minister Neville Chamberlain of Great Britain. The term *appeasement* became synonymous with the international negotiations between Britain and France and Italy and Adolf Hitler's Germany, which resulted in the Munich Agreement of September 29, 1938. Germany was allowed to take over a portion of Czechoslovakia called the Sudetenland, which contained one-third of the population of Czechoslovakia. In exchange all four states guaranteed the rump of Czechoslovakia against unprovoked aggression.

Neville Chamberlain who became prime minister in 1937 had distinguished himself in domestic ministries, but was notoriously ignorant of foreign affairs. His brother, Austen, once corrected him in a conversation on foreign affairs, "Neville, you must remember you don't know anything about foreign affairs." Strong-willed and self-confident, he intended to be his own foreign minister and sought to solve the problems facing him. He considered the premises of British and French policy toward the totalitarian states of Italy and Germany to be mistaken. Hitler had succeeded in altering the balance of power in Europe. He had repudiated the arms clauses of the TREATY OF VERSAILLES and had remilitarized the Rhineland. In addition Ethiopia had been invaded by Mussolini, and both dictators had assisted General Franco in defeating the republican forces in Spain. Based on these harsh realities, the businesslike Chamberlain thought that the Versailles system could no longer be maintained. Instead, through realism and accommodation bargains should be made with the dictators, satisfying their wants and thus achieving a peaceful détente. Chamberlain's assumption that Hitler was a rational politician and valued peace as did Chamberlain turned out to be the principal fallacy of the appeasement policy. Actually, appeasing the dictators helped to bring on the war by encouraging the dictators and convincing them of the weaknesses of the democracies.

The adoption of the policy of appeasement by the British government, however, had the approval of the majority of the British people. Many Britons in the 1920s had come to think that Germany had been badly treated at Versailles, which feelings Hitler exploited in the 1930s. Many Britons had come to think that

WORLD WAR I had been caused by an excessive emphasis on ideas of national prestige. Therefore, many thought that it was better to attempt to resolve every plausible national grievance that might lead to war. Hitler had argued that German grievances—in the Rhineland, in Austria, in the Sudetenland—were, after all, based on an old liberal doctrine of national self-determination.

It should be emphasized that contrary to appearances neither Stanley Baldwin nor Neville Chamberlain was a pacifist. They actually were rearming Britain while they were appeasing Hitler, and their policy had the support of the public. Although it was callous to allow Nazi Germany to take over the Czechs, it should be remembered that the British had suffered 2.5 million casualties just a short time earlier and viewed a major new war as a greater evil. Czechoslovakia was, after all, a faraway country to fight for and the prime ministers of the Commonwealth countries were urging caution.

Before 1939 many appeasers understood Nazi Germany as just another European state maneuvering in the international balance of power in a diplomatically rational manner. Hitler, it should be remembered, had maintained that illusion in official documents and in his repeated assurances of his desire for peace and his personal assurances to British visitors. Thus, the appeasers placed too much faith in treaties, were unaware of Hitler's secret plans, underestimated the speed of German rearmament, and were too optimistic about their ability to defend themselves. In addition it should not be forgotten that they also took comfort in Hitler's strong anticommunism and the expectation that Germany would be a bulwark against the Soviet Union. This illusion was also shattered by the NAZI-SOVIET (Hitler-Stalin) PACT of August 1939. Hitler's desire for war and the failure of appeasement made it clear when war came that there was no alternative to military resistance.

Ardennes, Battle of the (December 1944)

The Battle of the Ardennes forest or Battle of the Bulge was the last attempt by the Germans to break through the Allied front in the West. Their goal was to capture Antwerp and cut off Allied troops in northern Belgium and the Netherlands who were preparing to invade Germany. Because the Americans were holding the Ardennes with a minimum of troops, Adolf HITLER decided on a counterattack through this difficult terrain of forests and a minimum of roads. The weather was harsh with fog, wind, and snow. In the past German armies had successfully invaded through the Ardennes in 1914 and 1940.

The offensive was a total strategic and tactical surprise launched in poor weather. In order for the breakthrough to be successful, Hitler created the Sixth SS Panzer Army with four SS panzer divisions and placed his favorite, Sepp Dietrich, in command. While he was to attack to the north, at the same time another new panzer army under General Manteufel would attack in the center. To the south Lt. General Erich Brandenberger's Seventh Army would attack. An amazing total of 30 divisions were amassed along with 1,000 aircraft in utmost secrecy. The commander in chief of the West, General von Rundstedt, had been kept in the dark and was appalled when he learned of the campaign. Rundstedt thought the campaign lacked all the right conditions for success.

General Eisenhower appointed Field Marshal Montgomery to temporary command of the front, even though the heaviest fighting involved American troops. American forces resisted the German onslaught as well as possible, but Manteufel's panzers broke through and headed for St. Vith and Bastogne. At Bastogne the 101st Airborne Division and part of the 10th Armored were rushed to establish a perimeter defense around Bastogne. Eisenhower was informed by ULTRA intelligence that the Germans were heading toward the Meuse, and ordered General Patton to attack northward. Part of Patton's 7th Corps was used to blunt Manteufel's 2nd Panzer Division. Resistance was so stiff at Bastogne that nine panzer divisions had to get involved in the battle. Runstedt requested Hitler to let his forces withdraw, but was refused. At the same time the skies cleared and Allied planes by the thousands bombarded the Germans on December 23–24. The Allies launched their counteroffensive on January 3, 1945, and forced the Germans to retreat by mid-January, losing some 100,000 out of the half million men they had committed to the battle. Nearly all the tanks and aircraft were lost. Churchill called the battle the greatest of the war. The American army in four days doubled its infantry and tripled its armor. The German losses were so severe that subsequently they were not able to hold the defenses of the Rhine, and the failure of the offensive dissipated Germany's reserves and hastened the final defeat of the Reich.

Arendt, Hannah (1906–1975)
German-Jewish philosopher

Hannah Arendt was a philosopher and political scientist who focused her research on the totalitarian regimes of the 20th century. Born in Hanover, she was the only child of middle-class Jews of Russian descent. A brilliant student, she studied with such great scholars as Rudolf Bultmann in the New Testament, Martin HEIDEGGER in philosophy at Marburg, with the phenomenologist, Edmund HUSSERL at Freiburg, and the existentialist Karl JASPERS at Heidelberg.

When the Nazis came to power, Arendt moved to Paris, engaging in social work for a French organization responsible for finding homes in Palestine for Jewish orphans. She immigrated to New York, where she helped Jews flee from Nazi-occupied Europe. She embarked on a career in journalism, writing on such topics as racism, imperialism, and nationalism. In 1949 Arendt became the executive secretary for the Jewish Cultural Reconstruction Incorporated, which collected writings the Nazis had banned.

In 1951 she published the work that made her famous, *The Origins of Totalitarianism.* It explored the historical conditions that gave rise to the oppressive movements of fascism and Soviet communism. She explained how modern European states were influenced by ANTI-SEMITISM, racism, and imperialism. She explained how people could come to be totally controlled by their political systems. The tools of power the dictators used were their ideologies (political belief systems), terror, concentration camps, and the permanent abolition of civil liberties.

Her second major work was *The Human Condition,* in which she examines the human predicament in a world faced with radically new problems. After this book's publication she was appointed the first woman professor at Princeton University. In 1961 she was an observer at the trial in Jerusalem of Adolf EICHMANN, who was a Nazi bureaucrat responsible for sending an untold number of Jews to the gas chambers. Her observations were published in *Eichmann in Jerusalem* (1964), in which she concluded that Eichman was a bureaucrat whose participation in the evil of genocide was more banal than radically evil. Her public reputation suffered from these eccentric judgments. She also taught at the University of Chicago and the New School for Social Research, where she stimulated many students. Other books included *The Great Philosophers* (1962), *Men in Dark Times* (1968), and *The Life of the Mind* (1979).

aristocracy

The German aristocracy constituted the landowning rulers of the HOLY ROMAN EMPIRE. They did not constitute a modern social class, but the first estate in the premodern political system. German society of the early modern period breaks down into three main groups with substrata in each group: the nobility, the bourgeoisie, and the peasantry. There were also a variety of minorities and outsiders who were not an integral part of it. The clergy was divided among the three groups.

By 1800 it is estimated that some 50,000 noble families with 250,000 members existed. The most important division was between the imperial nobility, who were directly responsible to the emperor, and the territorial nobility, who were responsible to a regional or local territorial lord. The former included the secular and ecclesiastical territorial princes, and the imperial counts and knights. In order to restrict employment in the church, around 1700 a distinction was made between "old" and "new" nobility, the old predating 1400 and given preference. There was another category of nobility including some patricians in the cities. Sometimes even commoners could be ennobled, but that was rare.

Within the nobility there were different rights of lordship (*Herrschaftsrechte*), which was the most distinctive qualifier of status from the highest of the territorial princes and imperial nobility to the lowest local lord. Nevertheless, all nobles enjoyed certain privileges not possessed by the rest of society. These were special judicial treatment, freedom from direct taxation, special hunting rights, and freedom from state interference in their lives. Between 1500 and 1800 the aristocracy increasingly lived a variety of lifestyles, had different amounts and sources of income, worked at an assortment of occupations, had greater education and were more cultured, and no longer resided only in rural areas. Territorial princes included the emperor, whose courts, armies, and governments employed many thousands of nobles who no longer could support themselves from agriculture. Consequently, nobles were increasingly employed in civil administration or military command. By the 18th century an increasingly large number of nobles derived much or all of their income from service to the state. Perhaps not typical, but nonetheless indicative, was the fact that by 1718 four-fifths of the adult Prussian nobility were employed in the civil or military service. Employment in state service also changed the way the nobility thought about education. Since state service required juristic or other specialized knowledge, university training became necessary. As the nobility increasingly worked and resided in cities, they also mixed more frequently with the upper bourgeoisie as the leaders of city administration, the cultural elite, and professional people. In the 17th and 18th centuries they also increasingly participated in literary and cultural societies that had mixed memberships of nobles and bourgeoisie. They also mixed with the upper bourgeoisie in the hundreds of lodges of the Freemasons and other patriotic and literary societies. The German nobility made an important contribution to society, was not parasitic but dutifully employed, and the territorial princes, by providing employment in their courts, government, and armies, contributed to their reputation of a true service class. This new lease on life that they acquired in this period of transition helps explain how they survived the upheavals of the period of the French Revolution and why the institutions of nobility and monarchy were so accepted in Germany.

It was, however, the Prussian nobility who were preeminently dedicated to state service. In return for service King FREDERICK WILLIAM I decreed that the nobility of the sword would be the "first estate of the realm." The king had established the CANTON SYSTEM, which divided the kingdom into military districts and the districts into cantons. Each canton had to provide a regiment, and officers and men had to live in their home districts. There no longer was a distinction between private and military life. The JUNKER was both lord and officer, while the peasant was both serf and soldier.

Nobles continued to maintain their prestige, identities, and political influence throughout the 19th century. Neither the REVOLUTION OF 1848 nor unification and the establishment of the Second Empire eliminated them. In fact, they dominated the government of the empire and were predominant among the officers. They continued to be distinguished by their region, religion, wealth, and type of land ownership. They, of course, were faced by numerous challenges due to commercial development and the INDUSTRIAL REVOLUTION. Besides rivaling the nobility in wealth, the middle class also purchased their landed estates with increased frequency. Nonetheless, the nobility were able to adapt to the political and economic consequences of industrialization. Nobles with estates modernized them and used their political power to raise tariffs against grain imports. Others were employed in bureaucracies as well as in the military. Through patronage they even maintained influence in the Protestant and Catholic Churches. They also played prominent roles in the conservative AGRARIAN LEAGUES (Bund der Landwirte) and in two of the imperial political parties, the Protestant CONSERVATIVE PARTY and the Catholic CENTER PARTY.

During the WEIMAR REPUBLIC the influence of the nobility declined, but manifested itself in monarchist and nationalist groups and especially in the GERMAN NATIONAL PEOPLE'S PARTY. Some nobles, such as the President Paul von HINDENBURG and the Catholic Franz von PAPEN contributed to the fall of the republic. Many younger nobles supported the NAZI PARTY and believed that its authoritarianism was preferable to the democracy of the republic. Once in power, the Nazis did not break up the large estates on which aristocratic wealth depended. Aristocratic enthusiasm for the Nazis dampened with the Nazi persecution of the Christian churches, Hitler's assumption of the command of the military, and the belief that his wars were going to destroy Germany. Some joined the anti-Nazi RESISTANCE. Not until the end of the Third Reich were the aristocracy permanently undermined. The Prussian Junkers were eliminated by the GERMAN DEMOCRATIC REPUBLIC and the loss of eastern territories to Poland. In the FEDERAL REPUBLIC aristocratic titles remained, but their social status and influence depended on how well they adapted to the capitalist democracy.

Armed Forces (Wehrmacht)
(1939–1945)

Besides being limited to armed forces of no more than 100,000 men, both the General Staff and the General Staff Corps were prohibited by the TREATY OF VERSAILLES. Yet, as in other areas, the Reichswehr had circumvented these limitations by using different designations until 1935. In that year the chief of the general staff also became the chief of the general staff corps. In 1935 the German armed forces received their new name, the Wehrmacht. Ultimate authority was placed in Adolf HITLER's hands, and below him stood a war minister who exercised authority over the various services. Hitler undermined the independence of the armed forces when he dismissed Generals BLOMBERG and FRITSCH. Accomplishing this, he created a Wehrmacht High Command (OKH) under the spineless General Wilhelm KEITEL. Yet Hitler did rely on the OKH to plan the campaigns against Poland, France, and Russia. When the German armies failed to take Moscow in December 1941, Hitler assumed supreme command of the army.

For the invasion of Poland, the German Army had about 60 divisions available, which included six panzer divisions and eight mechanized divisions, involving close to 1.5 million men. In May 1940 the army mobilized a total of about 5 million men. Of these some 2.5 million were deployed in the west in 135 divisions, which included 10 armored divisions and between six and nine motorized divisions. The panzer units included about 2,500 tanks. When the invasion of Russia took place in 1941, the army had assembled about 3 million men, including several hundred thousand from satellite countries. These were organized in 160 divisions, including 19 panzer and 14 motorized. About 3,000 to 4,000 tanks were available. In order to defend against the expected Allied invasion, the Germans also deployed 58 divisions in the west, of which 10 were panzer divisions. Overall during the war, the Wehrmacht mobilized about 12.5 million men; about 3 million were killed, and more than 7 million were wounded. Another estimate, including losses of the navy and Luftwaffe, amounted to losses of more than 8,300,000 men.

The Wehrmacht became increasingly dominated by the Nazis and Nazi ideology. Because of this the army was responsible for collaborating in the genocidal war against the nations of Europe. This was especially true in the eastern European theater, where the war became barbarized in its treatment of prisoners of war, civilians, the Jews, and other ethnic minorities. The role of will power and courage could not make up for the mistakes of Hitler, the Nazi leadership, and the early failure to fully mobilize the economy for war in order to provide enough equipment for a protracted fight. Yet, it has been noted that "seldom have armed forces fought better in a worse cause than did Hitler's Wehrmacht." Finally, the leadership of the armed forces was defective in their lack of long-range planning beyond the immediate needs of the battlefield.

Armed Forces (Bundeswehr): Federal Republic

The armed forces of the Federal Republic, the Bundeswehr, were formed at the beginning of the cold war and were integrated into NATO.

At the end of WORLD WAR II and the defeat of Nazi Germany, no one would ever have expected that Germany would have been rearmed within the decade. With the advent of the cold war, the Berlin Crisis and airlift of 1948, and the Korean conflict, a number of steps led in that direction. The negotiation of the GERMANY TREATY, the failure of the EDC, the inclusion of West Germany and West Berlin into a Western defense perimeter, the U.S. need for extra military support in Europe as the Korean War involved it in Asia, and Konrad ADENAUER's desire to make the newly constituted Federal Republic a military contributor to Western defense, led to the establishment of the Bundeswehr. The issue was hotly debated in Germany and especially opposed by the SPD. The Paris Treaties of 1955 made rearmament possible and allowed the Federal Republic to join NATO.

The Bundeswehr has been a conscript-based military force, under thorough parliamentary control for the first time in German history, and has no identification with any political party or interest group. All men have been liable to the draft since 1957, but since 1996 the period of compulsory service has been reduced to 10 months. With the failure of the EUROPEAN DEFENSE COMMUNITY, West German troops became part of NATO in 1955. By the early 1960s Germany's contingent of 500,000 men was organized in 12 divisions and turned over to NATO command. That strength continued until reunification, with 340,000 in the army, 106,000 in the air force, and 36,000 in the navy, and with 11,000 employed in an inter-service role.

The Bundeswehr is allowed by the BASIC LAW, which forbids aggressive war but allows participation in collective security. The Bundeswehr's only role has been the defense of the Federal Republic along with NATO. It could not be employed outside of the NATO area, although since reunification that has changed. It also has not been allowed chemical or nuclear weapons. There is today a reluctance of German men to serve in the army, with more conscientious objectors than those conscripted. The imbalance is even greater when those with medical exclusions are included. There is also an unwillingness of the German government to commit troops to anything other than humanitarian causes, which has stirred a national debate on the future of the German army. There are current plans to reduce the number of draftees from 70,000 to 30,000 a year.

Changes have recently occurred in the employment of German troops in peacekeeping missions in places such as Afghanistan, Bosnia-Herzegovina, Kosovo, Djibouti, and other trouble spots. As was widely reported, Chancellor Gerhard Schroeder declined participation of German forces in the war in Iraq nor to be involved in peacekeeping there.

Army (Prussian to 1860)

It was FREDERICK WILLIAM, the Great Elector, who was the founder of absolutist government in Brandenburg-Prussia, and who also established it as a military power. In 1657 Frederick William received the sovereignty over PRUSSIA and was convinced that the estates should support a standing army. The army, however, came directly under the elector's control, and he used it to overwhelm internal opposition. The army became the center of the new Brandenburg-Prussian state and grew in size from about 2,000 men in 1656 to 12,000 in 1672 and to 45,000 during the period of war with the Swedes, when in 1678 he defeated them at Fehrbellin, establishing BRANDENBURG as a military power. The army became a state enterprise, and private military entrepreneurs were eliminated. Beginning with the Great Elector, the social composition of the officer corps slowly became dominated by the JUNKER nobility.

The Great Elector's son in 1701 became king of Prussia as FREDERICK I. He used the army he inherited largely as the bulwark of his authority. His son, FREDERICK WILLIAM I (1713–40), who thought that the international position of a prince was based on the size of his army, increased it to 64,000 men in 1725 and 89,000 men in 1740. Nicknamed "the sergeant king" he enforced severe discipline. Because of the enormous number of desertions, he turned to making military service legally binding upon all his subjects. Frederick William abolished the militia organizations and decreed that emigrants who intended to escape military service would be treated as deserters. More significant, in 1732–33 the Prussian CANTON SYSTEM was established. Every regiment in the army was assigned a specific recruiting district, and all young males were enrolled on the regimental recruiting list. If voluntary enlistments did not make the necessary quotas, then the difference would be made up from the rolls. Although the universal obligation to serve became part of customary law, in practice because of economic considerations liberal exemptions were allowed to those in trade and industry, so the obligation fell on agricultural workers and poor peasantry. The impressment of foreigners was continued. In 1740 there still was a 2 to 1 predominance of foreigners in the army. During the wars of FREDERICK THE GREAT the ratio was 1 to 1, dropping to 1 to 3 during the SEVEN YEARS' WAR (1756–63).

Standardization, new tactics, and centralization also improved the army. Military uniforms and weapons were standardized; in 1714 the king wrote the first comprehensive military regulations to be issued to the army. Tactical exercises and endless drilling produced an infantry that had flexibility and precision as well as rapidity and accuracy of fire, which were to make Prussian armies famous. In 1723 Frederick William I established the GENERAL DIRECTORY, which centralized military, economic, and political authority. It shaped economic growth to the needs of the military. Out of war commissariats of the Great Elector grew the formidable administrative apparatus of Frederick the Great's Prussia. But this centralization stopped at the gates of the nobility.

During the reign of Frederick William I a fully hierarchical officer corps was developed. The army became increasingly attractive to the Junkers as the revenues from their estates declined in the early 18th century and the king gave them the opportunity in the army to enjoy a monopoly in the higher ranks and be able to preserve their privileged position. By 1724 there was scarcely a noble family in the Hohenzollern domains that did not have a son in the officer corps. The officer corps became a new caste rooted in social privilege and dominance in the most important profession in the state. It became the chief defender of the existing political order. Even under the enlightened Frederick the Great the nobility had an almost absolute monopoly on commissions and a right to the highest posts in the civil service. Through the cantonal system, the mobilization of the nobility for the officer corps, and an economy that was geared to the maintenance of a large army, an antiquated social order and an authoritarian and increasingly militarized society was held together.

The army declined during the latter years of the reign of Frederick the Great and his successor, FREDERICK WILLIAM II (1786–97). The turning point came with the military defeats at JENA (1806) and AUERSTADT (1806) and the dismemberment of Prussia.

Within six years after the defeat of the Russians and the Treaty of Tilsit, however, Prussia was able to provide the leadership to defeat Napoleon. Then arose a group of leaders, among whom were Freiherr vom Stein, Gerhard Scharnhorst, August von GNEISENAU, Hermann von Boyen, and others who were able to reform both the military and the state. In July 1807 King Frederick William III appointed a Military Reorganization Commission headed by Scharnhorst to recommend reforms. The commission might only have accomplished minor reforms were it not for the leadership of Scharnhorst and his disciples. Scharnhorst's goal was to create a national army in which every citizen was called to miliary service and was to be founded on the virtues of courage, gallantry, and honor. Voluntary enlistments and the brutal penal code were eliminated. Primary importance was placed on limiting service in future armies to Prussian citizens. The reform plan of 1807 called for a standing army and a national militia. A new patriotism was to be linked to the old Prussian military virtues, which involved a complete program of education. The result of these ideas was the creation of an army of the line side by side with a militia (*Landwehr*) and levy of the people (*Landsturm*). The militia was to consist of some 150,000 reservists between the ages of 20 and 35; the *Landsturm* was the general mobilization of the whole male population over 35. The latter were to serve only within the country, wear no uniforms, and employ no weapon. It was in French terms a *levée en masse*. As important was the reform of the officer corps. Scharnhorst ruthlessly purged from the corps all those commanders who owed their positions to social prestige rather than to personal qualifications. The middle class were allowed into the officer corps, but after the War of Liberation the nobility reasserted their dominance.

Training also changed. Old drill techniques were eliminated, and smaller army units composed of all branches of arms were organized. The cooperation of infantry, cavalry, and artillery in such units adapted the army to fighting in broken terrain and to attacking in deep columns. Rigid single battle lines were abandoned, and new tactics placed greater responsibility on subordinate officers and required more personal self-reliance in the lower ranks. The excellent staff work was one of the most important features of the new army and provided the roots for the Prussian general staff system. Different reformers like Gneisenau, Grolman, Boyen, and Carl von CLAUSEWITZ served as chiefs of staff with the individual corps commanders. At the decisive BATTLE OF LEIPZIG the Prussian forces fought heroically and made a significant contribution to the Allied victory.

During the Restoration conservatives demanded an end to universal military service and the renewal of the cantonal system, eliminating the *Landwehr*. Nevertheless, as the reaction set in after the CARLSBAD DECREES were issued in 1819, the social and educational reforms effected in the officer corps by Scharnhorst were weakened. Deliberate evasions of the educational requirements for a commission maintained aristocratic preponderance in the officer corps. The *Landwehr* was reorganized and placed under the close supervision of the regular army. Professionalism and the concept that the army was a special calling and the old antipathy between the army and civilian society reasserted itself. This time an organized liberal movement inspired by desires for constitutional reform became increasingly critical of the government and the army. Between 1819 and 1840 the efforts of Scharnhorst and the reformers to reconcile the military with civilian society were shattered. The army was again considered an obstacle to social progress.

The Prussian army played a decisive role in the REVOLUTION OF 1848 and widened the gulf between the military and civilian society. It was the conduct of the troops in Berlin and the attitude of its leaders that precipitated the uprising of March 18; it was the withdrawal of troops that placed the constitutional reformers temporarily in control of events. Of course, the reformers realized their insecurity as long as they did not have control of the military. When the NATIONAL ASSEMBLY convened in April 1848, it drafted military reforms to restrict the power of the king over the army and to make it responsible for defending the constitution. The memory of the March days by army leaders made them fearful of revolutionary agitation in the future and convinced them for the next decade that the army should be primarily used as a domestic police force. The Revolution of 1848 demonstrated to Prussian leaders that the survival of the monarchical order depended on the exclusive royal control of the army.

After 1848 the main concern was not over the threat of foreign armies but domestic civil disturbance. The law governing the state of siege gave the army wide powers in the event of civil unrest. The *Landwehr* was purged of liberal elements and placed under the control of the army. After the economic crisis of 1857 plans for army reform were designed to make the army a reliable defender of royal absolutism. These reforms precipitated a constitutional crisis. The Liberals demanded constitutional concessions in return for support for the military reforms. General Manteuffel wanted a showdown, but the calmer von Roon was prepared to accept some kind of compromise with the *Landtag*. In September 1862 the situation reached a complete deadlock when the *Landtag* refused to vote any further funds for army reform. In desperation Otto von BISMARCK was appointed minister president of Prussia with the task of solving the crisis.

Army (Second Empire, 1871–1918)

The Prussian army was the most obvious instrument of power and influence in the Second Empire. Technically, a "German" army did not exist, but the Prussian army by law was extended to the entire Reich, and the army became one unified army under the immediate control of PRUSSIA. All of the states except three, BAVARIA, SAXONY, and Württemberg, transferred their military powers to Prussia. Only the three retained independent military contingents, which in time of war came under Prussian control. The king of Prussia, as emperor, was commander in chief and was in complete control of the army. Allegiance was sworn to the emperor and not the constitution. The hopes of the liberals that the army would be under parliamentary control were not realized. The military, not subject to constitutional requirements, was thus removed completely from the constraints of the constitution. The army was the core of the Prussian state, "the state within the state."

The Prussian soldier-state was recognized by most Germans as having been responsible for the unification of Germany. Political thought as well as political action throughout Germany, therefore, was deeply influenced by the Prussian crown, the Prussian general staff, and the Prussian army. It was a truism that the primary means used in creating the new German Reich was the forces of the Prussian military, and that continued to preserve it. As the eminent historian Friedrich Meinecke wrote "It was the Prussian military state with all that goes with it—its royalist and aristocratic traditions and its favoring of those social classes that made up the core of the officer corps—that has remained the most firm pivot of internal policy and at the same time the citadel of the entire fortress."

The army did, however, play an essential role in bringing about national integration after 1871. It absorbed generations of conscripts into the one institution that symbolized the Empire. Although the army had preferred to recruit its officers from the nobility, the expanded army had to reach into the upper middle class to fulfill its requirements. It became an honor for the middle classes to obtain officer's commissions, and its impact on their social consciousness has been called the "feudalization of the middle class." The middle-class officer candidates had to be Christian in religion, politically conservative, and as feudal-minded as the JUNKERS themselves.

In order to escape from the possible constraints of revolution and the liberal parliament, the political generals decided to withdraw most of the vital military matters from the war minister and place them in the hands of constitutionally irresponsible agencies like the General Staff and the Military Cabinet. Second, they decided to make the officer corps a bulwark of royal absolutism by withholding officer commissions from candidates with unorthodox social and political ideas. The officer corps thus became a sort of praetorian guard.

With the Franco-Russian alliance of 1894 the general staff was convinced that Germany had to be prepared to fight and win a two-front war and that it should be fought on enemy territory. The development of the SCHLIEFFEN PLAN was a strategy that made that possible. General Schlieffen's strategy was predicated on a quick defeat of

France while holding Russians in the East. It also planned on the violation of Belgian neutrality, logistical difficulties, and little leeway for the problems characterizing modern warfare. Military leaders in Germany and Austria-Hungary increasingly felt that a war was inevitable and the sooner the better if they were to win. Although the REICHSTAG resisted increasing military budgets, the budget for the navy was increased to the point that peace with Britain was threatened. By 1914 the army had a peacetime strength of 800,000 men with a war footing of almost 4 million. As Germany stood on the brink of war, there were weaknesses manifested in its reserve system, where half of the men conscripted during a year saw no military service.

Between 1890 and 1914 military leaders appealed for funds to increase the size of the army comparable to its enemies. General Schlieffen believed that all men capable of service had to be trained, but they could not without new budget increases and reforms, which meant more appeals to the Reichstag for funds. The difficulties of getting the Reichstag to vote for these increases were made more difficult by the constant criticism of the emperor and his military clique over making any concessions to the parliamentarians. There was also the problem of internal competition within the army, and the war of opinions was one of the army's greatest weaknesses at the beginning of WORLD WAR I. Equally evident was the growth of military absolutism as the army claimed immunity to the law and a significant part of the officer corps looked down upon society with contempt and hostility. A classic illustration of this problem was the ZABERN AFFAIR of 1913, in which a young officer insulted the people of Alsace and his commanding officer declared a state of siege and made wholesale arrests of those who mocked his troops. The privileged position of the army as a state within a state was not changed until after World War I.

During World War I a number of failures in the German war effort led to its eventual defeat. The High Seas Fleet that Admiral TIRPITZ had built up at great expense not only had turned the British to the side of the Allies but was completely ineffective in defeating England on the sea. Then the Schlieffen Plan was fatally altered and the stiff Belgian resistance slowed the German advance to the advantage of the French. The British forces arrived earlier than the German leaders had expected and stopped the Germans at the Marne. Another radical change in the Schlieffen Plan moved the left wing into an offensive against Nancy. On the eastern front the Russians launched an offensive earlier than expected, but General HINDENBURG defeated them at the BATTLE OF TANNENBERG and Battle of the Masurian Lakes. The Austrians, on the other hand, in the battles of Galicia and Serbia lost the best of their junior and noncommissioned officers. Worst of all, the Central powers had begun the war without a coordinated plan and knowledge of one another's capabilities. The war began with three major campaigns: one into France, a second into Serbia, and a third into Galicia. All failed. Later, in January 1917, the Germans again tried a go-for-broke strategy with unrestricted submarine warfare. This only managed to bring the United States into the war. Unable to force a decision in the west, they turned to defeating Russia. The Russian Revolution had occurred, and Lenin decided to make peace, which resulted in the TREATY OF BREST-LITOVSK, through which Germany and Austria gained control of eastern and southeastern Europe. In the meantime, Hindenburg and LUDENDORFF had become military dictators and in 1918 planned a spring offensive, again gambling unrealistically that the gains would force the Allies to agree to peace on German terms. To obtain this goal, the generals had precalculated a casualty figure of 600,000 men. The offensive failed, and an armistice was negotiated on November 11, 1918.

Army (Reichswehr, Weimar Republic)

The German armed forces during the WEIMAR REPUBLIC were called the Reichswehr (1919–35).

At the end of WORLD WAR I the German High Command was anxious to disassociate itself from the war, which it had promoted and lost. It therefore fabricated the "Stab in the Back" legend blaming the war protesters, Social Democrats, and revolutionaries for Germany's defeat. They also followed a political plan to burden the civilian government with the responsibility for the armistice negotiations and also the TREATY OF VERSAILLES.

Initial efforts to create a new army along republican lines were made difficult by the turmoil of the REVOLUTION OF 1918–1919 and a fear of communism. As a consequence of these problems the Reichswehr had to rely on the former members of the army and navy, who were governed by the agreement arrived at in the EBERT-GROENER PACT, by which the officer corps would be free from parliamentary interference in return for maintaining orderly demobilization and internal security. The leadership of the Reichswehr was generally opposed to the concept of a parliamentary republic but decided to uphold the state. They also distrusted the radical-right paramilitary groups called the Free Corps (Freikorps). The KAPP PUTSCH of March 1920 became a turning point in relations between the Reichswehr and the civilian government. Even though the defeat of the Kapp Putsch was a great victory for republican forces, it failed to lead to the needed reform in the Reichswehr of eliminating monarchist and antirepublican officers.

The Reichswehr was composed of the army and navy, although it mainly refers to the army alone. The strength of the army was fixed by the Treaty of Versailles at 100,000 men and the treaty also specified what proportions should go to the various services. Universal conscription was abolished, the General Staff was forbidden, and therefore the army became a highly trained group of professionals. According to the treaty it was not to possess tanks, aircraft, or heavy artillery. The navy was reduced to a few cruisers with its personnel set at 15,000, and all submarines were forbidden.

The generals leading the Reichswehr were unenthusiastic supporters of the Weimar Republic. General Hans von Seeckt (1866–1936), who had distinguished himself in the war, gave up the Versailles-prohibited title of chief of the general staff and assumed his new title of Chef des Truppenamtes on November 24, 1919. Under his leadership the Reichswehr developed into a state within a state, serving successive civil governments loyally but without enthusiasm. Seeckt was adamant that members of the Reichswehr remained totally independent of politics considering the parliament (REICHSTAG) "the cancer of our time." Seeckt's goals were to preserve as much of the prewar army as possible. Rather than resisting the Versailles Treaty, Seeckt thought it more important to keep the army in being and preserve the possibility of a military resurrection. Under the Treaty of Versailles Seeckt could not create a "shadow army," as had been done by the great Scharnhorst and GNEISENAU during the Napoleonic period, because of the treaty's requirement of 12-year enlistments. With patience and determination, however, Seeckt conducted his covert campaign against the restrictions of the treaty by establishing the Reichswehr as a true military elite, an army of leaders. Every member was trained so that he was capable of filling the next highest position. Seeckt even figured out how to circumvent the closing of the War Academy for the training of staff officers. Essentially, the training was distributed to the military districts under control of the Truppenamt. Although the treaty forbade the Great General Staff, it did not forbid the Operational General Staff, which Seeckt hoped to use to carry on its traditions. In order to circumvent the prohibition on military aviation, Seeckt set up a "secret flying group" within the Reichswehr Ministry. Within the government office of air transport civilian aviation was guided in accordance with military needs. As a reservoir of military manpower Seeckt used the civilian police, where combat-hardened officers who could not be taken into the Reichswehr joined the state and border police. Even the prohibition on submarine design and construction was circumvented as KRUPP set up a dummy Dutch company that built and sold submarines to foreign governments out of Germania shipyards at Kiel. Other circumventions also occurred.

In 1921 during maneuvers in the Harz Mountains motorized infantry were loaded onto trucks in place of the mounted forces allowed by the Allies. Other elaborate schemes in 1921 included the unofficial training of transport troops as artillerymen.

In foreign affairs Seeckt was anti-Polish and pro-Russian. The new state of Poland had just won a decisive battle against the Russians at the gates of Warsaw, and Vilna was seized. Germany's problem with the new Poland resulted in an alliance between Germany and the Soviet Union, which came into being as a result of the Treaty of Rapallo in April 1922. For Seeckt friendship with Russia was integral to his whole political outlook. Its communist philosophy meant little to him, and more important it had not signed the Treaty of Versailles and was also shut out of the LEAGUE OF NATIONS. Seeckt also thought that a Russian alliance would help in the struggle against Poland in Upper Silesia and that Communist-inspired social unrest in Germany might be reduced. So the Polish question became the godmother of the alliance between the Reichswehr and the Red Army. There was also an economic connection because the Communists needed to industrialize and Seeckt wanted a place where prohibited German industries could be shipped. Within Germany the restrictions of the treaty were also circumvented, and clandestine rearmament begun. So-called black production centers for war materials were created and hidden from the Control Commission. For instance, within the firm of Rhein-Metal, which constructed railway carriages, artillery construction was located. That many types of weapons were forbidden did not hinder their development. In 1922 the Reichswehr signed a contract with the firm of Krupp for the development of German artillery, which firm also contributed to the development of tanks.

The minister of defense was a civilian to whom the Reichswehr was theoretically responsible. The first was Gustav Noske (1868–1946), whose short term lasted from 1919 to 1920, followed by the conservative Otto Gessler (1875–1955) from 1920 to 1928, and finally General Wilhelm Groener from 1928 to 1932. A common commitment to revising the Treaty of Versailles brought about cooperation with the foreign office. After Paul von HINDENBURG, an unreconstructed reactionary and trustee of the traditions of the officers' corps, was elected president of the Republic in 1925 the Reichswehr hoped for a reorganization of the state along authoritarian lines, which actually began with the presidential cabinet in 1930. The crowning achievement of the Reichswehr's political influence was the appointment of General Kurt von SCHLEICHER as chancellor in 1932.

Schleicher's attempt to establish an authoritarian state with a mass base of support failed. The leaders of the armed forces looked down on Adolf HITLER and National Socialism, but later approved of the possibilities for the revival of German power. A Nazi government appeared to offer the best opportunity to build up the Reichswehr and rearm the nation. The soldiers offered no opposition to Hitler's appointment as chancellor and the violence used to establish a dictatorship; they cooperated in the blood purge of the radical SA in 1934. Under the Nazi regime after the death of President Hindenburg, General von Blomberg as Reichswehrminister introduced the oath of personal fealty in 1934, placing the armed forces under Hitler's direct control. In 1935 the name of the armed forces was changed from Reichswehr to Wehrmacht, with the divisions Heer, Marine, and Luftwaffe. In 1938, during the Blomberg-Fritsch crisis, Hitler even took personal command of the military.

Asylum Law

The BASIC LAW includes the Asylum Law (article 16 and 16a), which provides the right of asylum for politically persecuted foreigners. The law is the most liberal in the world. Virtually any foreigner has been able to ask for political asylum in Germany, and once the application has been submitted the individual is free to stay and benefit from the German social service system until their case is decided. Nonetheless, every person whose application for asylum has been rejected may still appeal to the Federal Constitutional Court. The German right of asylum has existed since 1949 and has no equal in the world.

The number of asylum seekers increased dramatically in the late 1970s, from its previous level of between 5,000 and 10,000 annually to 33,000 in 1978 and 108,000 in 1980. Between 1980 and 1992 many Eastern Europeans who could travel abroad applied for asylum, their number increasing from 108,000 to 430,000 per year. Most (68.3 percent) have come from eastern and southeastern Europe, but others are from Asian and African countries. After 1990 the number even skyrocketed more. In 1992, for instance, Germany alone took in nearly 80 percent of all people seeking asylum in the European Community. At the same time the proportion of those who could be recognized as genuine victims of political persecution fell to less than 5 percent. In 1993 up to the end of August, some 322,600 asylum seekers entered Germany.

Many of these were not fleeing political persecution anymore but were seeking to enter Germany, where they could achieve a higher standard of living. Affluent West Germany, with its generous social services, became a prime European destination for asylum seekers. Meanwhile, the state and local authorities (i.e., cities, towns, and villages) were required to provide the asylum seekers with housing, medical services, and an allowance to cover living expenses, which may create resentments with local populations.

As the number of applicants rose astronomically, there were pressures to amend the asylum law. In force since 1993 "the asylum compromise" has sought to bring the right of asylum back to its original purpose to protect those actually suffering persecution. Applicants from democracies could now be returned without a judicial hearing, but what makes it more controversial is that the countries of eastern Europe have been declared democratic. Foreigners who enter Germany from a safe third country may no longer invoke this basic right. Germany also has reserved the right to identify countries where according to public information no one is subject to persecution and no one has grounds for seeking asylum. When the new legislation on the right of asylum became effective in July 1993, the number of applicants fell significantly; in 1994 only 127,210 people sought asylum with a similar number of 127,937 in 1995.

Atlantic, Battle of the (1939–1945)

The Battle of the Atlantic was not a battle as such, but a long naval struggle between 1939 to 1945 to keep open the sea routes between the United States and Great Britain. It primarily was a war between German submarines and Allied antisubmarine forces.

The German navy was woefully unprepared for a major naval war, while the British held naval superiority. The war began with unlimited submarine warfare. During the early stages of the war the goal of the German navy was to stop Allied shipping, an effort conducted by surface ships. The surface fleet made major contributions to the Norwegian campaign but suffered great losses. The battle began after the fall of France in June 1940. The main strategy was to defeat Great Britain by severing her maritime links to war materials. Norwegian bases also permitted German U-boats to escape the Allied blockade. Yet during the winter of 1940–41 the German navy was unable to successfully restrict imports to Britain. Large surface raiders were rendered inactive, and large ships like the *Bismarck* ended the use of heavy ships in the Atlantic. It was left to the submarine fleet to do the job, but Admiral DÖNITZ had only 27 submarines operational. Even though submarine production rapidly increased, after the spring of 1941 the window of opportunity for success had passed.

In order to defend themselves against individual surface nighttime attacks, the British developed a centralized system of convoy routing, dispersed ships widely, and strengthened escorts, all of which made it more difficult for U-boats to find and attack convoys. The Germans then countered with the "wolfpack" system, which made their attacks more successful. As U-boats extended their range farther into the Atlantic, convoys had to be escorted across the

German submarine being launched *(Library of Congress)*

entire ocean. After the Japanese attacked Pearl Harbor and war was declared against Germany, the U.S. Navy became officially involved but had to learn by experience. The U-boats even extended their range into the coastal waters of the United States and the Caribbean and scored a high level of kills during summer 1942. Shipping losses continued to be heavy during winter 1942–43, especially in the North Atlantic.

Help, however, was on the way. Two technical developments aided the Allies; radar and airborne depth bombs. Radar could detect surfaced U-boats at some distance. Increased shipbuilding and especially the smaller escort aircraft carriers (CVEs) provided patrol planes for convoys and were part of convoy escort forces, which patrolled submarine operating areas. The year 1943 was a turning point. U-boat warfare became primarily defensive, many were sunk in encounters, and others did not go out to sea. Winter 1944–45 was better for the U-boats, but again new technology, especially more sensitive radars, tipped the scales in favor of the Allies. In the end it was the improvement of convoy operations that proved a greater success than the conduct of patrols. The balance of sinkings was 2,753 Allied ships against 733 German and 79 Italian submarines.

Auerstadt, Battle of (1806)

Fought at the same time as the BATTLE OF JENA, Napoleon's forces defeated the Prussians at the Battle of Auerstadt just as they did at Jena.

While Napoleon won the Battle of Jena almost before it began and faced the smaller of the two Prussian forces, he sent Marshal Davout to Auerstadt, where he was surprised by the main Prussian army under the duke of Brunswick. He deployed his three divisions in a defensive line and fought off multiple attacks by the Prussian infantry and cavalry. The Prussian army lost its leaders; the duke of Brunswick was wounded and then died, and General Mollendorf was then captured by the French. Into the confusion stepped King Frederick William III, who tried to coordinate the efforts of the army and save the day. He launched a series of poorly planned assaults on Davoust's troops, which were easily repulsed. During the battle his son, Prince Louis, was killed. Frederick William launched a counterattack but was unable to stop the French. Although the Prussian troops fought bravely, they broke into a rout under French pressure. The Battle of Jena-Auerstadt was a decisive French victory.

Augsburg

Augsburg was established as a military colony by the Romans about A.D. 15–16 and derives its name from the Emperor Augustus. It became an administrative center during the Carolingian Empire. During his long episcopacy Saint Ulrich (923–973), who strengthened his power as the secular lord of Augsburg, also contributed to stopping the Magyar invasion of Germany. Established as a center for commerce and crafts during the 11th century, its citizens gained the right of self-government by 1276, and its status as a free imperial city was affirmed by a charter in 1316.

During the 15th century Augsburg reached the peak of its prosperity as the center of trade between southern Germany, Italy, and the East. It also had a community of humanists whose famous leader was the patrician Conrad Peutinger (1465–1547). Augsburg also was the home of the artist Hans Holbein the Elder (1470–1524), whose paintings hang in the cathedral. Two of Augsburg's most famous families—the Fuggers and the Welsers—rose to prominence as international merchants and bankers. Jacob Fugger (1459–1525) spent some of his considerable wealth for charitable purposes, endowing the Fuggerei, a unique experiment in social welfare for poor older citizens.

Augsburg was the location of important imperial parliaments (diets) during the Reformation. In 1518 Luther's meeting with Cardinal Cajetan took place, while the classic expression of Lutheran doctrine, the Augsburg Confession, was submitted to the emperor Charles V at the imperial diet of 1530. Many Augsburgers converted to Lutheranism, although some like the Fuggers remained loyal to Catholicism. To punish Augsburg for participating in the Schmalkaldic War, Charles V in 1548 abolished the guilds and abrogated the constitution of 1368, which restricted to the patricians three-fourths of the seats on the town council. Catholics were sufficiently numerous so that under the Peace of Augsburg of 1555, both Protestant and Catholic worship coexisted, which did not often occur during the Reformation. The Fuggers withdrew from financial life and became landed aristocrats, while the Welsers went bankrupt in 1614. Among the civic buildings erected during this period was the magnificent town hall built between 1615 and 1620 in Renaissance style by the municipal architect Elias Holl, who transformed Augsburg into the "Pompeii of the German Renaissance." The prosperity came to an end during the Thirty Years' War.

Augsburg became part of the kingdom of Bavaria in 1806, and in 1817 it became the administrative center of the region of Bavarian Swabia. Yet even before the end of the Holy Roman Empire Augsburg's economy was reviving as a center of cotton weaving and banking. The factory of the "German cotton king," Johann Heinrich von Schüle, was built in 1770–72, beginning Augsburg's history as a textile manufacturing center. This began a new age of prosperity. Engineering firms also were established, which still exist today. During World War II about half of the city was destroyed. The city was rebuilt and enlarged in 1972, when land from neighboring communities was incorporated. A vibrant cultural life is enjoyed by its citizens and a new university was opened in 1970.

Among the famous Germans born in Augsburg were Rudolf Diesel (1858–1913), who invented the revolutionary internal combustion engine. The controversial dramatist Bertolt Brecht (1898–1956) also was born there. The aircraft designer Wilhelm Messerschmidt (1898–1978) established an aircraft factory and designed one of the superior fighter planes of World War II, the ME 109. One of his planes was the first to break the sound barrier in 1943.

Augsburg, Diet of (1530)

This was the first meeting of the imperial estates after the DIET OF WORMS in 1521. Emperor CHARLES V had called the meeting after having been crowned emperor by the pope. Determined to settle the religious turmoil in the Empire, Charles needed aid from the estates to defend the Empire against the advances of the Turks. Although the diet passed economic legislation restricting price cartels, speculative trading, and activities of the Jews, its principal goal was to settle the issue of religious diversity and achieve some degree of reconciliation between Protestants and Catholics.

The moderates among the Protestants and Catholics appeared to be in a position to achieve a compromise. An important influence in the attempt to effect a reconciliation of the diverse Protestant groups was Ulrich ZWINGLI (1484–1531), whose goal was like that of Desiderius ERASMUS (1465–1536), to achieve moral reform. He and Martin LUTHER (1483–1546), however, disagreed about the nature of the Lord's Supper, Luther being very reluctant to accept any basic changes in religious forms or the political and social order. On the other hand, Philip MELANCTHON (1497–1560), who was also strongly influenced by Erasmian humanism, was inclined to effect a reconciliation. The Protestant estates drew up their articles of faith and submitted them to the diet. Most important was the statement by the Lutherans, the Lutheran Confession, which subsequently came to be known as the AUGSBURG CONFESSION. Mainly composed by Melancthon but approved by Luther, after extensive debate and argument by theologians the diet rejected the Augsburg Confession. The Confession, however, remained a doctrinal statement of Lutheran belief.

Catholics scholars and theologians like the papal legate, Cardinal Compeggio, had come to the meeting to mediate the religious crisis. Also attending were ardent opponents of Luther's teachings, such as the theologian Dr. Johann Eck (1486–1543) of Ingolstadt, who claimed that he had found some 400 errors in Protestant teachings. Compeggio was attempting to bring about a peaceful reconciliation, bringing the Protestants back into the fold, but most likely he thought, it would take force. These and other Catholic leaders produced a refutation of the Augsburg Confession called the *Confutatio*.

Most Protestants left Augsburg after efforts at mediation failed. It was the Catholic estates that were left which made the decision, the recess dated September 22, that all deviations from Catholicism were forbidden. The document reaffirmed the EDICT OF WORMS (1521) and aimed at the suppression of Lutheranism, Zwinglianism, and Anabaptism. The recess legislated against Protestant practices and the means employed to spread the Protestant Reformation. The Protestants were threatened with prosecution by the Imperial Cameral Court if they did not accept these provisions by April 15, 1531. In their defense the Protestant estates formed the SCHMALKALDIC LEAGUE later that same year.

Augsburg, Religious Peace of (1555)

The DIET OF AUGSBURG met from February to September 1555. The diet decided that both Lutheranism and Catholicism were to be officially recognized religions in the Empire. Only those Lutherans, however, who accepted the statement of faith in the AUGSBURG CONFESSION of 1530 were permitted the legal right to exercise their religion, although it was not a modern policy of religious toleration. Neither Calvinists nor Zwinglians called "Sacramentarians," nor Anabaptists called "Sectarians," were given the legal right to practice their faith. Freedom of conscience for individual Germans to pursue their own religious convictions was not recognized, while the princes and territorial knights were granted the right to decide on which religion could be practiced in their territories. Individual subjects and their families were allowed to emigrate, but this was not easy in an agrarian economy. They had to sell their properties and pay a tax to be released from feudal services to which they still might be obligated. Nonetheless, this probably saved many of strong religious convictions from the Inquisition in Catholic areas and Protestant jails in Lutheran territories. The prince could also change the religion of his territory and had the right to administer its religious affairs. Yet the rights and privileges of the prince was limited to his territory; neither was he allowed to protect his coreligionists elsewhere nor engage in missionary activity. These rights and obligations were later to be defined as "He who owns the land determines its religion" (*Cuius regio, eius religio*).

The peace was a political solution to the intractable religious divisions caused by the Reformation. Ferdinand, the brother of CHARLES V, had become king of Hungary and Bohemia, and archduke of the Habsburg possessions. Ferdinand had been given authority to "act and settle" as Charles already in 1554 had begun to divest himself of his dignities as emperor. Many princes did not attend, and most sent diplomatic representatives to the diet. Nevertheless, the rights granted to the princes were extended to the imperial nobility, while free cities had to observe certain provisions. For instance, where Catholic churches and monasteries had been reopened in a number of cities that were predominantly Protestant, the imperial cities were obligated to allow and protect the rights of the Catholic minority to worship there.

Catholics were especially insistent that the ecclesiastical principalities not be secularized. Protestants already controlled the secular college of electors, while the college of princes had a Catholic majority. It is true that many of the bishops and abbots had proven themselves incompetent in the fight against the spread of PROTESTANTISM. The emperor willingly suspended the jurisdiction of the bishops over Protestant territories, but not in Catholic lands. The bishops had stood out as the symbols of the union of imperial and hierarchical authority in the HOLY ROMAN EMPIRE. In order to prevent the further secularization of Catholic Church properties, the Ecclesiastical Reservation was formulated, which stated that Catholic archbishops, bishops, and abbots could not force their subjects to convert to Protestantism as a secular prince could, but had to vacate their offices and lose their benefices, rights, and privileges. An orthodox successor could be chosen by those responsible. Lutherans, of course, opposed the Ecclesiastical Reservation, but the emperor insisted, and it was promulgated on imperial authority and not included in the Augsburg Treaty. The reservation saved many Catholic properties and was partly responsible for the survival of Catholicism. Protestants, however, continued to secularize bishoprics and abbeys, especially in northern Germany. In order to get the acquiescence of Protestants to the Ecclesiastical Reservation, Ferdinand in a secret document did declare that the ecclesiastical estates that had already introduced Protestantism should be maintained. More than any other decision at the diet the ecclesiastical reservation saved the ecclesiastical principalities for another 250 years and contributed substantially to the survival of German Catholicism.

The Religious Peace of Augsburg failed to restore the unity of Christendom. Protesters and heretics now for the first time obtained equal status with the established church. The emperors had failed to regain the monarchical power they lost in the 13th century and neither the Protestant nor Catholic princes were brought under imperial control, and the divisions between the princes deepened. The Peace of Augsburg also furthered the process whereby the religious issues and struggles of the Reformation became political. Little attention was paid to the sincere practice of religion, while sweeping authority was given to secular princes to determine religious faith in their territories. The Reformation's ideal of freedom of conscience was now violated by the authoritarian state. The political consequence for the Empire was its disintegration into territorial units, each with its absolute ruler.

Augsburg, War of the League of (1688–1697)

Although there were minor causes of the war, the major one was the desire of Louis XIV to expand French power. One ground for the war was the dispute over the election of the archbishop of Cologne. The pope, Innocent XI, had given his support to the emperor and BAVARIA in the choice of Prince Joseph Clement of Bavaria, while Louis was resolved to secure it for von Fürstenberg, bishop of Strasbourg. In 1681 French forces had conquered the free city of Strasbourg, which prompted new defensive coalitions to form against Louis. One of these was the League of Augsburg, created in 1686 to resist French expansion into Germany, which included the Austrian emperor, LEOPOLD, the kings of Sweden and Spain, the electors of Bavaria, of SAXONY, and the Palatinate. Meanwhile, the French revocation of the Edict of Nantes produced more unfavorable feeling in Protestant Europe toward France for its persecution of PROTESTANTISM. When William of Orange from the Netherlands took over the throne of England in 1688, both England and the United Provinces joined the alliance against Louis.

The strained French economy was not capable of fighting a prolonged war, which, however, did last for nine years. At first Louis hoped that a show of force would convince the Germans to recognize French conquests and predominance. Finally, when the French invaded, they found little resistance on the left bank of the RHINE. From the outset the French were determined to spread terror. The French minister of war, Louvois (1641–91), expressed the harsh sentiment that the Germans would respect only guns and fortresses. The French were mistaken that this might be an easy victory. The emperor Leopold decided to actively resist and had the support of the German princes. He even decided to fight on two fronts because the Turks were attacking from the east. In 1688–89 the French devastated the cities of the Palatinate, including Worms, Speyer, MANNHEIM, and HEIDELBERG, including their historic monuments and art treasures. The remains of the castle of Heidelberg still stand as testimony to the rapaciousness of the French. Louis XIV lost the war in the Palatinate with the League of Augsburg. Stalemate and exhaustion made both sides agree to a compromise settlement in the PEACE OF RYSWICK in 1697. By the Peace of Ryswick Louis lost most of his conquests with the exception of Strasbourg and the occupied areas of Alsace, which he was able to keep because the emperor was preoccupied with the renewed threat of a Turkish invasion. The treaty did thwart Louis's expansion into Germany and secured Holland's borders.

Augsburg Confession
(Confessio Augustana)

The Confession of Augsburg was drawn up on the emperor's request to be presented at the DIET OF AUGSBURG (1530). It was drawn up by Philip MELANCTHON (1497–1560) a close friend and collaborator of Martin LUTHER. It was a carefully and shrewdly worded document that left the door open for a compromise with the Catholics. It summarized some of the agreements on doctrine concluded between various evangelical groups. The document was emphatic on principal Lutheran beliefs of justification, of its concept of the church, and of its understanding of the importance of preaching. On the other hand, it was compromising and omitted such controversial topics as the papacy, the ministry of all believers, indulgences, purgatory and the Lutheran challenge to the seven sacraments. The sacrament of the Lord's Supper, however, was close enough to the Catholic position, while on the other hand the Zwinglian or other sectarian positions were excluded. The *Augustana* or Augsburg Confession thus included 21 articles of faith and seven on rites.

Luther was not happy with its conciliatory tone, but he could not personally attend the diet and remained in the Coburg Castle. Melanchton was labeled as compromising too easily, but he was fearful of civil war in Germany and the decline in public morals and education that he witnessed. He saw compromise as the only way to preserve the unity in the church. The Augsburg Confession was signed by the princes who had made the protestation at Speyer and the two cities of Nürnberg and Reutlingen. It was read in both Latin and German to the emperor CHARLES V, who attended. While the Catholic princes refused to make a similar statement of faith, which they said was widely known, the Catholic theologians critiqued the Confession.

Augspurg, Anita (1857–1943)
radical feminist

Anita Augspurg, a teacher, lawyer, and journalist, was one of the radical leaders of the middle-class women's movement. She was a member of the General German Association of Women Teachers along with Helene Lange, Gertrud BÄUMER, Auguste Schmidt, Hedwig Doh, and Minna Cauer. Most of these leaders had not married and were explicitly forbidden to do so if they worked in state schools. They considered the "woman question" first and foremost as one of education and employment.

The women's movement after 1900 increased its struggle for the right to vote. Anita Augspurg and other radical feminists in 1902 created the German Union of Women's Suffrage (DVF), which grew to a membership of 10,000 by the beginning of WORLD WAR I. It formed the radical wing of the middle-class women's movement as the Federation of German Women's Associations (BDF) became more conservative on women's issues and in 1914 supported the annexationist war aims. The suffragists following Augspurg broke from the BDF and became active in the peace movement and sought an end to the war without annexations or indemnities. The stresses of the war divided the women's movement as much of the rest of German society.

After women received the right to vote in the WEIMAR REPUBLIC, Anita Augspurg and other radical feminists became pacifists and formed the Women's League for Peace and Freedom and edited journals such as *Woman in the State*, fighting for women's absolute equality. It may seem strange, but Augspurg's feminist message proved too strong for socialist women. Middle-class women were alienated by their demand for social justice. Support for Augspurg's feminist message declined, so she turned to the International Women's League for Peace and Freedom for support. That also was no solution, because sociologically many younger women had become apathetic about women's rights issues and did not join the organizations. They saw Augspurg and other leaders as "shrill and douty," believed that women's rights had been won, and were optimistic about their opportunities to have a career and be married. Newer organizations became successful with a new focus on sexual reform and motherhood. Augspurg's movement with its emphasis on pacificism and feminist reform therefore declined. Augspurg's organization and Helene Stöcker's League for the Protection of Motherhood with its emphasis on sexual pleasure both were banned by the Nazis. While vacationing in Italy during winter 1933, Augspurg and her associate, Lida Gustave Heymann, decided not to return to Germany until HITLER was defeated. She died before 1945.

Auschwitz-Birkenau

The principal Nazi camp for the extermination of the Jews, Poles, and Slavs was Auschwitz, located some 33 miles west of Cracow, Poland. A former military barracks acted as the initial headquarters. In 1941 Rudolf HÖSS was directed to enlarge Auschwitz as a major annihilation camp for the FINAL SOLUTION because of its ready railroad connections and its isolation from populated areas. By 1943 the camp had been expanded to house 30,000 slave-labor prisoners confined in rows of barracks. With the additional extension of the camp to Birkenau, the capacity of the camps was expanded for 200,000. Rudolf Höss testified at the NUREMBERG TRIALS that he held some 140,000 prisoners there, many of whom worked at special war plants operated by I. G. Farben and other armaments industries.

Höss described what faced the arrivals at the camp in the following words: "We had two SS doctors on duty at Auschwitz to examine the incoming transports of prisoners. The prisoners would be marched by one of the doctors who would make spot decisions as they walked by. Those who were fit for work were sent into the camp. Others were sent immediately to the extermination plants. Children of tender years were invariably exterminated since by reason of their youth they were unable to work." After undressing and being told that they were to be deloused, they were gassed with Zyklon B (hydrogen cyanide), which was very efficient for killing large numbers of people. The process took three to 15 minutes. After the bodies were stripped of valuables, they were burned in large crematories that could burn some 9,000 bodies in 24 hours. It is estimated that some 2 million people were annihilated at Auschwitz-Birkenau between 1942 and 1944. As the Russian army approached the camp, about 58,000 prisoners began a forced march to camps in Germany. The camp was liberated by Soviet soldiers on January 27, 1944; they found some 5,200 prisoners alive.

The following details create a more comprehensive picture. On April 27, 1940, Heinrich HIMMLER ordered the construction of Auschwitz. May 20 saw the first 30 prisoners arrive, German criminals whose job it would be to control the future inmates. The first 728 Polish political prisoners arrived on June 14. In September 1941 the first test of gassing with Zyklon B killed 850 Poles and Russian POWs. That October Birkenau was set up as the first of 40 subsidiary labor camps. In January 1942 the killing of Jews began at Birkenau, initially in two gas cambers located in converted houses. By spring 1943 four new gas chambers went into operation at Birkenau with the killing capacity of 8,000 corpses in 24 hours. In May 1943 Josef MENGELE arrived to become the camp doctor, beginning his horrible medical experiments. In spring 1944 about 800,000 prisoners were killed. By the end of summer (August) the Nazis began the dismantling of the camp, evacuating prisoners to Germany. On October 7, 1944, Jewish prisoners managed to blow up Crematoria IV and revolted, 450 of them being killed. The total number of prisoners sent to Auschwitz was more than 1.3 million, out of which some 200,000 survived. About 90 percent of Auschwitz's dead were Jews, including 46,000 from Czechoslovakia, 69,000 from France, 55,000 from Greece, 438,000 from Hungary, 60,000 from the Netherlands, and 300,000 from Poland. The remaining non-Jewish victims included 75,000 Poles, more than 20,000 Gypsies, 15,000 Soviet POWs, and 25,000 people from other nationalities.

Austerlitz, Battle of (1805)

Austerlitz was the decisive battle of the War of the Third Coalition fought in Moravia on December 2, 1805, between Napoleon and combined Austro-Russian forces. Six weeks earlier Napoleon had forced the surrender of another Austrian army at Ulm on October 20 and had entered Vienna on November 13. The remnants of the army of Emperor FRANCIS II (Francis I of Austria) were joined by fresh Russian troops and gave the allies an advantage of 86,000 men to the approximately 67,000 French. Napoleon realized that he was not strong enough to attack the Austro-Russian forces so he feigned weakness and retreated, trying to make the allies attack him.

Czar Alexander and Emperor Francis had their armies advance to the village of Austerlitz. Napoleon tricked the allies into thinking that a retreat was in progress by commotion in the French camp that night. Napoleon called up reinforcements of Bernadotte's I Corps from Brno and Davout's III Corps from Vienna to increase his army to 67,400 men. While the two emperors were on the Pratzen heights, watching the allied advance, Napoleon anticipated the attack and made his main thrust against the center with Soult's IV Corps and Bernadotte's I, breaking the allied army in half. Part of the allied force was driven south over the frozen lakes and marshes of the Litava. Cutting off their retreat, Napoleon with cannon positioned on the heights smashed the ice under them and destroyed them. When the battle was over that night, the allies counted 27,000 casualties, 12,000 of them prisoners, while the French lost about 9,000.

The significance of the battle was that within 24 hours Emperor Francis sued for peace, which resulted in the TREATY OF PRESSBURG (Bratislava) signed on December 26, 1805. The defeat at Austerlitz had devastating consequences. It shattered the Third Coalition, forced the Russians out of central Europe, and isolated the Prussians to be defeated the following year.

Austria

Austria originated in the geographic area of the narrow funnel-shaped Danube corridor where it opens onto the Vienna basin, which continues onto the Pannonian and Carpathian plain. Austria was established as a defensive Eastern March against the aggressive Hungarians. It was first referred to in 996 as "Ostarrichi." Austria was originally a margravate with its capital in VIENNA and ruled by the Babenberg family. It became a duchy in 1156. This family then acquired Styria in 1192 and what today is upper Austria. During the 13th century Ottokar II of Bohemia came into control of Austria. To these territories were added Carinthia and Carniola in 1335, Fuino in 1335, and Trieste in 1382. After Ottokar's defeat by the German king Rudolf I in 1278, it passed to the Habsburgs, who ruled it until the collapse of the Austrian Empire at the end of WORLD WAR I (1918). With hereditary domains in Switzerland and southwest Germany and controlling the important Alpine passes and the Vienna basin, the Habsburgs were able to build a great empire primarily through marriage and inheritance. The Habsburg dukes became Holy Roman emperors from 1273 to 1308 and from 1438 to 1806. During the REFORMATION Austria was threatened by a significant spread of PROTESTANTISM, but during the COUNTER-REFORMATION that was reversed through a strong pro-Catholic policy. During the THIRTY YEARS' WAR Austria was the strongest German state. By this time it also had become a multiracial state, including Germans, Czechs, Hungarians, and Croats.

In the 18th century Austria engaged in a power struggle with Prussia for dominance in the HOLY ROMAN EMPIRE. The empress MARIA THERESA and King FREDERICK II of Prussia fought each other for control of SAXONY. Then the NAPOLEONIC WARS demonstrated Austria's weaknesses, and in 1806 the Holy Roman Empire was dissolved by Napoleon. In 1804 Emperor FRANCIS II, who had perceived the coming end of the Holy Roman Empire, had himself proclaimed Francis I, emperor of Austria. Under Prince Clemens METTERNICH it led the coalition of allies, which defeated Napoleon and convened the conference in Vienna, known as the CONGRESS OF VIENNA. At the congress the territories that would compose the modern Austrian Empire were Austria, Hungary, Bohemia, Moravia, Galicia, Silesia, Slovakia, Transylvania, the Bukovina, Croatia-Slavonia, Carniola, Gorizia, Istria, Dalmatia, Lombardy, and Venetia. This included 11 nationalities, and with an absence of geographical and economic unity the empire was hampered from establishing an effective central government. From 1815 to 1848 Austria was the principal power in Europe, upholding the conservative order along with czarist Russia. The REVOLUTION OF 1848 almost overthrew the monarchy, but it was suppressed by the army. Between 1848 and 1866 Otto von BISMARCK of Prussia outmaneuvered the Austrians. In the Austro-Prussian War (Seven Weeks' War) Bismarck secured the exclusion of Austria from the GERMAN CONFEDERATION. In response to the Hungarian demands for additional rights, a compromise was reached called the Ausgleich and subsequently, between 1867 and 1918, the empire was known as Austria-Hungary.

Since Austria-Hungary was allied with Imperial Germany and lost the war, it was inevitable that the empire would disintegrate. The various nationalities demanded their independence. The Treaties of St. Germain and Trianon (1919–20) formally recognized the empire's end. After the fall of the Habsburgs in 1918 only German Austria remained along with Salzburg and parts of Tyrol. The non-German nationalities were formed into the successor states of Czechoslovakia, Hungary, Poland, Yugoslavia, and Romania. A republic was established in Austria in November 1918, a constituent assembly met in March 1919, and Karl Renner was elected chancellor. Although the Austrians wanted to be united to Germany, that was forbidden by the treaty of St. Germain-en-Laye. What remained was called the Federal Republic of Austria and was organized as a federation according to a Swiss model. There was little positive feeling of support for the republic, and the Viennese especially suffered economic privations. While the Viennese voted primarily for socialist parties, the provinces supported church-related (clericalist) political parties. Under the new chancellor, Engelbert Dollfuss (1892–1934), a virtual fascist constitution was adopted. Then an abortive Nazi putsch in July 1934 killed Dollfuss. His successor was Kurt von Schuschnigg (1897–1977), whose authority was weakened by Nazi pressures. In March 1938 the Nazis conducted an ANSCHLUSS, an annexation, by which Nazi Germany occupied Austria, giving it the name Ostmark. From 1938 to 1945 Austria formed a province of "Greater Germany."

The Soviets occupied Vienna in April 1945 and divided the country into four zones of occupation. Under Allied occupation a Federal Republic was established, and Karl Renner became its first president. By the Austrian State Treaty of 1955 the Allies recognized Austria's independence and neutrality and their troops were withdrawn. The federal republic is based on parliamentary and democratic principles. There are nine provinces with each electing its own provincial assembly (*Landtag*) and head of government (*Landeshauptmann*). Vienna is the capital and itself a province. It has a municipal council, which is also a provincial assembly. The mayor (*Bürgermeister*) is chairman of the Municipal Senate (*Stadtsenat*). The parliament of the republic is the Federal Assembly (*Bundesversammlung*) and consists of two houses. The head of state is the federal president (*Bundespräsident*), who appoints the federal government presided over by the federal chancellor (*Bundeskanzler*).

Austrian Succession, War of
(1740–1748)
In accordance with the terms of the PRAGMATIC SANCTION (1713), MARIA THERESA (1717–80) succeeded her father, CHARLES VI (1685–1740), to the Habsburg throne. No sooner did he die than a number of sovereigns as might have been expected withdrew their assent to the Pragmatic Sanction. Those who contested Maria Theresa's succession were the elector of Bavaria, Charles Albert Wittelsbach (1697–1745), Philip V Bourbon of Spain (1683–1746), and August III Wettin of Poland and Saxony (1696–1763). It was FREDERICK II Hohenzollern of Prussia who had just become king of Prussia (1740) and was determined to take advantage of the situation by laying claim to Lower Silesia. After taking over Silesia in December 1740 Frederick offered to compensate Austria with an indemnity. Frederick even promised to support the candidacy for the imperial throne of Maria Theresa's husband, Francis of Lorraine (1708–65), as compensation. After his offer was rejected, BAVARIA and France soon joined in the attack on Silesia. A Franco-Bavarian army captured Prague on November 26, 1741, and the Bavarian elector Charles became Emperor Charles VII. Maria Theresa fled from Vienna but succeeded in rallying the Habsburg cause, enlisting the support of the Hungarians and the English. A Hungarian army succeeded in occupying Munich. England now actively supported Austria with an army led by King George II, who was also the elector of Hanover. Then Great Britain, the Netherlands, and AUSTRIA concluded the Treaty of Warsaw, recognizing the Pragmatic Sanction.

In September 1745 Maria Theresa's husband, Francis of Lorraine, was elected emperor Francis I (1745–65). Maria Theresa still hoped to recover Silesia, but the Austro-Saxon army was defeated by the Prussian cavalry, for which Frederick came to be known as "the Great." The Second Silesian war ended with the Treaty of Dresden (December 25, 1745) in which Frederick recognized Francis I as emperor. More fighting continued. Peace was finally concluded in the Treaty of Aachen (1748). The succession of Maria Theresa was confirmed, but Prussia retained Silesia, one of Austria's richest provinces. Austria also lost the Italian districts of Parma, Piacenza, and Gustalla to France. But France was unhappy with the requirement that she withdraw from the Austrian Netherlands. In reality it was a truce rather than a real peace since none of the signatories was really satisfied. The years between the Treaty of Aachen and the beginning of the SEVEN YEARS' WAR (1756–63) were spent in active diplomacy, which ended in the reversal of alliances and came to be known as the DIPLOMATIC REVOLUTION.

autarchy

Autarchy was the economic policy that Nazi Germany followed starting in the 1930s. It was intended to produce German economic self-sufficiency, especially for the purposes of gaining independence in foodstuffs and raw materials. It reflected a critique of liberal capitalism and the free-market system. Hitler, like many Germans, believed that the Allied blockade of WORLD WAR I led to revolution and defeat in the war. German farmers favored controlled markets and stable prices. It was hoped this would lead to increased food production and self-sufficiency. Heavy industry also favored autarchy. But problems were quickly evident because German economic growth had been fueled by exporting finished goods and importing raw materials and foodstuffs. With the drop in exports there was a corresponding drop in currency income needed to pay for raw material imports necessary for rearmament. By 1936 a severe currency crisis existed. Hjalmar SCHACHT, who was president of the Reichsbank from 1933 to 1939, tried to solve the problem by regulating imports. One solution was bilateral trading agreements, which worked in eastern and southeastern Europe and South America, but did not in North America and western Europe, where Germany lost markets.

Hitler and those who favored autarchy now pushed for self-sufficiency through a FOUR YEAR PLAN, which was supposed to prepare the economy for war in four years. With the exception of coal Germany lacked any significant amounts of mineral resources. This was an area in which Hitler especially desired to gain independence. The manufacture of synthetic substitutes for rubber and gasoline from coal became a priority. The project was terribly expensive and inflationary. In the end the Four Year Plan was a failure.

autobahns

A system of superhighways known as autobahns had already been planned during the WEIMAR REPUBLIC. It was during the DEPRESSION, however, and the early Nazi regime that road building projects became priority public works programs. The Nazi program of road building begun in 1933–34 was part of a broader effort to encourage the expansion of automobile transportation. But the Nazis had other motives, that is to create a system of strategic superhighways as part of rearmament. The building of the autobahns came under the direction of Fritz Todt, and he created a gigantic state building concern. The autobahns were highly visible and popular. It offered jobs for construction workers and engineers as well as being a stimulus of the automobile industry.

Many roads had to be rebuilt after the war. The Brandt-Scheel government in coping with the recession of the late 1960s funded the extensive improvement of infrastructure, including an extensive expansion of the autobahns.

The Autobahn with service station and a view of the countryside *(Library of Congress)*

Axis, The

The term *Axis* was originally applied to the alliance between Fascist Italy and Nazi Germany (Rome-Berlin Axis) between 1936 and 1945. The metaphor Axis was invented by Mussolini in a speech at Milan on November 1, 1936: "This Berlin-Rome line is . . . an axis" around which states with a common interest might collaborate. The speech followed a visit by Ciano, the Italian foreign minister, to Hitler, resulting in an Italo-German statement of common interests (October 21, 1936) known as the October Protocols. This was expanded on May 22, 1939, into a formal military alliance known as the Pact of Steel. The Axis was expanded when Japan, which had previously signed the ANTI-COMINTERN PACT, adhered to an agreement for a 10-year military alliance with Germany and Italy (September 27, 1940). Smaller countries, including Hungary, Romania, Slovakia, Bulgaria, and Croatia subsequently joined the Axis. Because she had fought the Soviet Union, Finland was a participant in the war on the Axis side, and Spain, although a nonbelligerent, supplied some troops (the Blue Division) for the Eastern Front.

B

Baader, Franz von (1765–1841)
Catholic philosopher

Franz von Baader, the son of a Munich physician, became a mining engineer and was appointed in 1826 to the chair of speculative theology at the University of Munich during the reign of Ludwig I. Baader called attention to the growing seriousness of the social problems that resulted from the early Industrial Revolution and urged the Catholic Church to take the lead in their solution. Baader had lived in England for four years, observed the social problems there, and was influenced by the ideas of the Frenchman Félicité Robert de Lamennais (1782–1854), who already saw the dangers that threatened from the division of society into a propertied and a proletarian class. Baader noted that the industrial machines had a depersonalizing effect on workers and that the law of declining wages would impoverish them. He demanded limitations on free competition. He also thought that the church and the state should act as a "Christian deaconry" and jointly carry out a social policy on their behalf.

Back in Bavaria Baader was employed in the department of mines, operated a glass factory, and retired in 1820. In his speculative thinking he was eclectic and wrote on philosophical and theological subjects. Like his fellow romantic thinkers he was concerned with the process through which human beings learn about the external world. His solution was a blend of natural science and religious mysticism. He thought that he would find the answer in a "world soul," which he believed bound all things together. His thinking was a mixture of science and alchemy, theosophy and logic. His search for an ordering intelligence never had the success that the philosopher Georg Wilhelm Friedrich Hegel (1770–1831) achieved in his system of philosophy. Baader believed in the religious primacy of the individual, was critical of but ignored by the hierarchy of the church, and believed in the possible union of the Christian denominations. His idea of a holy alliance was used by Metternich for his reactionary policies during the restoration.

Baader-Meinhof Group (BMG)/Red Army Faction

Between 1970 and 1974 the secret Red Army Faction became a Communist urban guerrilla band attempting to destabilize the Federal Republic. The media created the popular designation of the terrorist organization as the Baader-Meinhof Group, which West German police labeled an organization of violent anarchists. They committed robbery and arson and murdered 30 people. They kidnapped numerous others and bombed U.S. and German government installations.

Despite its sinister reputation the Baader-Meinhof Group had a hard core of only four militants. Ulrike Meinhof (1934–76) and Gudrun Ensslin were women students who were deeply influenced by a morally rigid and radical Protestantism. Of the two men, Andreas Baader was magnetic and brutal, while Jan-Carl Raspe was rootless, and both were less intellectual and more impulsive than the women. They never developed a coherent political ideology but believed that the only way to change the established political system was to employ violence. Gudrun Ensslin, a Lutheran pastor's daughter, was once quoted as saying "Violence is the only way to answer violence" and oppose the cold war. They were a heartless part of the alienated postwar "Auschwitz generation." Following the 1972 bombing campaign the core members of the BMG were arrested and tried. Members of the original "gang of four" were tried for five murders and 54 attempted murders. Meinhof and Ensslin hanged themselves in prison while Baader shot himself.

The goals of the terror campaign grew out of the 1960s student movement and its demand for free speech and of the Socialist Student Organization (SDS), which was a leading organization of the extraparliamentary movement (APO) of the late 1960s. Its roots, however went even further back to the 1950s and the German protest movement against NATO membership, rearmament, nuclear weapons, and the revulsion felt against the West German government for allowing former Nazis to hold high positions. Leftist intellectuals initially had sympathy with the BMG's goals, although not its methods of violence. Two famous supporters were the novelist Heinrich BÖLL, and Peter Brandt, the son of Willy BRANDT. Ulrike Meinhof had taken part in the 1958 antiatom death campaign and edited a leading radical student monthly in HAMBURG, *Konkret*. She was antiauthoritarian, opposed to the consumer society of West Germany, and advocated an "armed struggle." It was she who wrote the first manifesto of the group, which introduced the concept of the "urban guerrilla," and who tried to provoke the repressive potential of the West German state. Along with Meinhof, Baader had lost patience with debates and protests and believed that only a resort to violent political action could change political structures. In 1967 the movement decided that physical force was a necessary means of resistance against what they considered a fascist state. In 1968 Baader, Ensslin, and two others decided to fire-bomb two department stores in FRANKFURT AM MAIN. Although convicted for the arson, both fled the country, returned, were rearrested, and freed in a jailbreak.

After the deaths of the initial leadership, the Red Army Faction's (RAF) second generation, continued its reign of terror. These included bank robberies, bombings, kidnaps, and murders. The RAF succeeded in the assassinations of prominent West German politicians and businessmen. Government officials also were kidnapped. Throughout their campaign the BMG-RAF committed 28 assassinations, injured 93, and attempted to take hostages 15 times. Even after unification in 1990 the RAF murdered the chief executive of Deutsche Bank and the director of the Trust Agency (Treuhandanstalt). The wave of terrorism climaxed in the autumn of 1977 when attempts were made to free Baader and other prisoners. In 1977 Baader shot himself in prison, and Ensslin committed suicide. As a result of this campaign of terror the Federal Government restricted the civil liberties of younger leftists and the defense lawyers in what was called the Contact Ban Law of 1977.

Bach, Johann Sebastian (1685–1750)
greatest composer of the baroque period

Johann Sebastian Bach is undisputedly considered the greatest composer of the BAROQUE period. He was born in Eisenach, Thuringia, the most famous member of a family that produced six generations of musicians. The family was Lutheran and remained loyal throughout the THIRTY YEARS' WAR. His father instructed him in the violin, and he sang in the choir at St. George's Church. He became orphaned at an early age, was taught keyboard lessons by his brother, then joined a choir in Lüneburg. Later, he became the organist at the New Church in Arnstadt in the Thuringian Forest. Not long thereafter, he became court organist at Weimar, was encouraged by Duke William Ernest, but failed to be appointed musical director in Weimar. Near the ELBE RIVER in Saxony-Anhalt lies the city of Köthen, where Bach served for six years as musical director to the court of the prince of Anhalt-Köthen, where his musical talents reached their greatest expression, especially in chamber and orchestral music. In 1721 he became director of church music in LEIPZIG and then city music director (court composer for the elector of Saxony) in 1723, a post he occupied until his death. An especially noteworthy experience was the opportunity in 1747 to play for FREDERICK THE GREAT at Potsdam. All of Bach's four sons led musical careers.

Bach's works encompass more than 1,000 works and cover all the musical genres of the baroque period. Bach's sacred works include cantatas, passions, the Christmas Oratorio, and many organ works. These have been considered by many to have been the epitome of church music. Many of his choral and organ works were composed during his lengthy tenure as musical director of the Church of St. Thomas in Leipzig. He also composed vocal works, including more than 200 cantatas. His great choral masterpieces were the B Minor Mass, the Christmas and Easter Oratorios and the *St. Matthew* and *St. John Passions.* Bach also created secular works of unparalleled beauty. These included the six Brandenburg Concertos, but also violin and keyboard concertos, some called *The Well-Tempered Clavier.*

Baden-Württemberg

The pre–WORLD WAR II states of Baden and Württemberg were combined into this federal state in southwest Germany. Its capital is Stuttgart. Its first minister president was Reinhold Maier (1889–1971) of the Free Democratic Party.

The state of Baden has had a long, distinguished history. In the 18th century Baden had been a margravate ruled by the enlightened Carl Friedrich of Baden-Durlach, who came to the throne in 1738. Karlsruhe had became the capital in 1715 under his predecessor, Carl Wilhelm of Baden-Durlach. By the time of Carl Friedrich's death in 1811 Baden had become the third-largest state in southern Germany. His paternal, cultured, and enlightened rule laid the foundation for Baden to become a kingdom during the Napoleonic era. The peasants were among the freest in Europe, but their primitive farming techniques kept them at a subsistence level. In the 19th century Baden possessed a strong liberal movement and favored the REVOLUTION OF 1848. In the 1860s it experienced a struggle between liberals and Catholics over a new school law. The conflicts became complicated as crosscurrents of animosities fueled it. Catholic leaders mobilized opposition to the government, while liberals organized to fight clericalism. Baden favored Austria during the Austro-Prussian War, but joined with Prussia in establishing the Second Empire. Baden was a state both in the Empire and the WEIMAR REPUBLIC.

In the 18th century Württemberg was ruled by the despotic Duke Carl Eugene, who reigned from 1737 to 1793. Educated at the court of Prussia, he came with a love of soldiers but also

Johann Sebastian Bach *(Library of Congress)*

of extravagance, living like a sultan, spending money on palaces, mistresses, hunting, and festivities at court. His excesses led to near financial ruin, but fortunately they were stopped by his wife. In the 18th century Württemberg did not follow the path of bureaucratic absolutism characteristic of other German states. A complex compromise existed by which the estates retained considerable power. Frederick II, who became duke in 1797, instead of being forced by the French to reform his government in favor of the estates, was aided in creating administrative centralization. By cooperating with Napoleon in 1805 the elector was made a king. After the historic estates were dissolved, the king himself controlled the government in tyrannical fashion. In 1819 a constitution was adopted much like that in Baden and BAVARIA. There was support for unification in the fifties and sixties but not under the leadership of Prussia or AUSTRIA.

After World War II Baden and Württemberg were formed into one state, which became a stronghold of the Christian Democratic Union (CDU). When the coalition government of Reinhold Maier (CDU) fell, the CDU monopolized politics with Kurt Georg KIESINGER (1904–88), Hans Filbinger, and Lothar Späth becoming minister-presidents. Baden-Württemberg is one of the wealthiest of the states in the FEDERAL REPUBLIC, with both a diverse economy and varied geography. Agriculture is still a vital part of the economy. The state has a primarily industrial economy with a diversity of companies. The three leading industrial products are precision tools, automobiles and auto parts, and electronics and computers. Bosch and Daimler-Benz are the preeminent companies, and IBM and Hewlett-Packard have their headquarters there. There also are handicraft products. Tourism adds to the diversity of the economy with the attractions of the Black Forest.

Important cities include the capital Stuttgart, and the cities of MANNHEIM, Karlsruhe, Freiburg im Breisgau, HEIDELBERG, and Ulm. Stuttgart is the home to Daimler-Benz-Porsche. Other industries include precision engineering, optics, textiles, and a wine-producing center. Stuttgart has two universities and an Academy of Fine Arts. Mannheim is a beautiful city of squares as the city was laid out by Palatine Elector Frederick IV in 1607. Mannheim was an important center for music in the 18th century but is an industrial center today. Karlsruhe was the former baroque grand-ducal capital and lies at the northwestern foothills of the Black Forest. Going back to 1715, the city was laid out in a fan shape from the palace. It had been the home of the FEDERAL CONSTITUTIONAL COURT. Freiburg im Briesgau is a commercial and administrative center, has a university dating back to 1457, a Gothic cathedral, and lies on the southern slope of the Black Forest. Heidelberg is a university town and features a late Gothic church, the Old Bridge with the Neckar Gate, and the ruins of its famous castle.

Baden-Württemberg is rich in cultural opportunities. There are nearly 1,000 museums and state and city theaters. Religiously Roman Catholicism predominated in Baden, while PROTESTANTISM, especially PIETISM, predominated in Württemberg. It also has a strong intellectual tradition with both romanticism and rationalism having strong roots in the area. Famous Germans born here were Friedrich SCHILLER (1759–1805), Friedrich HÖLDERIN (1770–1843), Georg Wilhelm Friedrich HEGEL (1770–1831), Friedrich Wilhelm SCHELLING (1775–1854), and Martin HEIDEGGER (1889–1976). The Stuttgart Ballet and the Bach Academy are internationally famous.

Ballin, Albert (1857–1918)
shipping magnate

Albert Ballin was the chairman of the world's largest steamship company, the Hamburg-American Line, for 30 years. Of Jewish ancestry, he nonetheless became one of Imperial Germany's foremost businessmen and special friend of Kaiser WILLIAM II.

He was born poor, but through his keen intelligence and flair for business was able to work his way up the ladder and become chairman of the steamship company. The Hamburg-American Line offered competitive prices and efficient service both in passenger travel and freight and soon took over the lead that British steamship companies had monopolized for decades. Although Ballin believed that Germany's destiny was to be a world economic leader, he attempted to work out conflicts that arose between Great Britain and Germany over commercial interests and especially the growing naval rivalry that Admiral TIRPITZ and the Kaiser were promoting. Since Ballin knew the Kaiser, and William was his frequent guest, Ballin counseled that Anglo-German competitiveness be kept within bounds so as to preserve peace. Obviously, the Kaiser disregarded his advice. Ballin died on November 9, 1918.

Barbarossa, Operation

Barbarossa was the German code name for the invasion of the Soviet Union during WORLD WAR II. It was based on Adolf HITLER's Directive No. 21, issued on December 18, 1940. Operation Barbarossa was named after the medieval emperor Frederick Barbarossa (Red Beard), who legend had it did not die, but was only sleeping in a cave until he returned to lead Germany to power. The goal was to destroy the Russian army by "deeply penetrating armored spearheads," and blocking its retreat eastward. Another goal was to push the Soviet Union's borders to the east so that its planes could not bomb Germany.

Hitler appropriately set the starting date for spring on May 15, 1941. Due to Hitler's misconceptions about the Russians, he believed that it would only be a short campaign of perhaps five months. Unknown at the time was the future German involvement in the war in the Balkans, which was to delay the invasion until June 22, 1941. The campaign began on the plains of Poland, which Hitler and Stalin had conquered and divided in the fall of 1939. There the Germans smashed through, turned north to encircle Leningrad, turned south to seize the immense natural resources of Ukraine, and finally drove ahead to within 20 miles of Moscow, where the German army was finally stopped for the winter. The war went on with renewed successes in 1942, the defeat at Stalingrad, the great tank battle at Kursk, and then the fall of BERLIN.

Barbie, Klaus (1913–1991)

Nazi SS leader

Klaus Barbie was the SS captain known as "the butcher of Lyons," who headed the anti-Resistance operations in France during the Nazi occupation. After graduation in 1934 he joined the HITLER YOUTH and when he was 22, the SS in 1935. A short time later he joined the security service, the SD (Sicherheitsdienst) headed by Reinhold HEYDRICH. After Germany invaded France, Barbie became head of anti-Resistance efforts there. As head of the GESTAPO in Lyon he was responsible for actions against French Jews, and in one raid of a Jewish orphanage some 50 boys and girls were sent to AUSCHWITZ. Barbie was ruthless and fanatical and regularly used torture in his interrogation of prisoners.

When the war was over, Barbie hid until he was recruited by the American Counterintelligence Corps as a spy. Within the next four years he ran a spy network in East and West Germany and France. When French war crimes investigators became aware of him, American intelligence aided his escape to South America in 1951, first to Buenos Aires and then to Bolivia, under the name of Altmann. Soon he became an adviser to the Bolivian secret police. The Bolivian military regime protected him, but after a civilian government assumed power he was extradited to France in 1983. He was convicted of at least four murders and 15,000 deportations to death camps and was the last ranking German war criminal to be tried. He was sentenced to life imprisonment, but in 1991 died of cancer in prison.

Barmen Declaration (1934)

The Barmen Declaration was a statement of belief of the CONFESSING CHURCH. It expressed its opposition to the official national church and the new ideology of the GERMAN CHRISTIANS, rejecting the totalitarian claims of the Nazi state on the church.

The purpose of the Barmen Declaration was to give the traditionally divided German Protestant churches a basis for cooperation and a defense against the onslaught of the "Faith Movement of the German Christians" from within their own churches, and against the increasing encroachment of the Nazi state and party on church institutions and activities. Such a uniting creedal document was drafted and accepted, and further elaboration of the document within the different denominations was planned but never materialized.

Most of the pastors delegated to the Barmen Synod of May 1934 had been members of the Emergency League since 1933, and as members of this league each one had to sign that the application of racial laws (i.e., the "Aryan paragraph") to the church community was a violation of the Christian creed. Some of the leading members that drafted the declaration hoped, after winning unity among the heterogeneous groups of different Protestant denominations, that a theologically revived and unified church would oppose the nonbiblical racism of the Nazi movement—a belief that turned out to be naive at best. The Barmen Declaration meant different things to different people; it has been called a bridge, rather than a new foundation for the various churches that agreed to it, and it was certainly realistic that any explicit political agenda would have had no chance of being adopted. Nevertheless, the Confessing Church did appear, at home and abroad, as "the last refuge of freedom and independence in a land locked into gear and oppressed."

The Barmen confessional corresponded significantly with the teaching of the theologian Karl BARTH. According to Barth, "The church is that community which derives its being from the decisiveness of God's presence among men in Jesus Christ and lives by acknowledging and confessing that fact before men." Barth interjected his own brand of aggressive theology by urging participation of Christians within the community of men. He knew that serious differences existed between the Nazis and the church. Barth attempted to redress the polarization of church and state so that these differences could be contested. For him it was more than just a matter of jurisdiction. It was not enough to merely accept the existing role of the church; the church was also responsible for the state in times of political misconduct. Although Barth was interested in redressing state policies, most Confessing Church members tried to achieve a modus vivendi with the Reich government and supported Nazi policies so long as they did not intrude upon the autonomy and prestige of the Protestant Church. The church was attempting to regain its hegemony within the realm of religious affairs.

baroque culture, German

The term *baroque* applies to the style in the arts of painting, architecture, and sculpture that expressed dynamic energy, flux and swaying movement, and dramatic contrast. It was a significant part of the culture of the 17th century but lasted in some cases into the 18th. Baroque artists tried to harmonize the classical styles of Renaissance art with the intense religious feelings manifested in the REFORMATION. The pictorial nature of the art of that period emphasizes softened contours in light and shade, as in a Rembrandt painting. Baroque painting, sculpture, and architecture stressed space and used light and color to dissolve form. Contours were irregular, and the total effect of a building was indented rather than the compact and solid nature of the classical style. Baroque architecture aimed at dramatic effects, and baroque sculpture portrayed emotional intensity or imitated the realities of nature. The baroque was able to fuse elements inherited from the past. From the Gothic, baroque art took over a striving to express the supernatural and an interest in closely observed detail in nature, while from the Renaissance the baroque continued the use of classic forms in architecture.

The baroque style began in Italy in the last quarter of the 16th century and then moved into Germany and AUSTRIA. Architecture reflected the search for grandeur and power that was widespread in the 17th century. Overall splendor with magnificently ornamented facades and sweeping staircases were meant to impress princes and awe a ruler's subjects. The numerous absolute rulers of the German principalities during the period from 1690 to 1770 aspired to reside in palaces that imitated Versailles of Louis XIV. Two examples were the Zwinger Palace at Dresden designed by Mätthias Pöppelmann and the Würzburg and Bruchsal Palaces by Balthasar NEUMANN (1687–1753). In Austria the chief architects were Johann Bernard FISCHER VON ERLACH (1656–1723) and Johann Lucas von HILDEBRANDT (1668–1745).

The baroque style was enthusiastically embraced by the Catholic COUNTER-REFORMATION. It was especially popular in the Habsburg courts of Vienna, Prague, Madrid, and Brussels. Eventually it spread to Latin America. The Catholic Church commissioned many new monumental churches, providing for the faithful an earthly demonstration of the truth and power of the Catholic faith. Grandeur in the use of domes was softened by delicacy of detail in sculpture and carving. An effective exterior is the facade of the Church of the Fourteen Saints by Balthasar Neumann. Classical motifs such as pilasters and pediments were used in an original attempt to reproduce the verticality of the Gothic. Andreas Schlüter created perhaps the best-known baroque bronze in the equestrian statue of the *Great Elector* in Berlin. It incorporated various influences, especially the Marcus Aurelius statue of ancient Rome. The painted wood sculptures of Bavaria and Austria in church altars are so realistic and charming that one can imagine oneself in their presence. The figures of the Virgin Mary, Mary Magdalene, the saints and angels, and representations of the Christ Child appear to be representations of beautiful models, while their features and gestures are expressive of grief, tearful sorrow, or radiant joy. At Weyarn in Upper Bavaria Franz Ignaz Günther (1725–75) sculpted his *Pietà* and *Annunciation* (1764) representing Bavarian rococo at its very best. In MUNICH's Bürgersaal Church there stands the unique statue of the *Guardian Angel*, which shows the Archangel Raphael leading the young, overawed, and trusting Tobias by the hand.

In the 17th century German literature was still enslaved to foreign and especially French models. Yet, leadership for a new beginning was provided by Martin Opitz, who was the father of modern German poetry and provided rules for generations of German writers. Paul Fleming expressed his creative imagination in his lyric poetry, while Friedrich von Spee introduced a mystical love of Christ into religious literature. The most conspicuous writer, however, was Andreas Gryphius (1616–64), who was both a poet and tragic dramatist. He wrote in a dramatic rhetorical style. One of the creators of a satirical baroque prose was Abraham a Santa Clara. Dramas of political and religious violence were common, and the theme of pending disaster is not so surprising in a century that witnessed the THIRTY YEARS' WAR, plagues, and many other misfortunes. The greatest work of German literature during the 17th century was by H. J. C. von Grimmelshausen (1625–76) in his *Adventurous Simplicissimus,* which followed the pattern of the Spanish novel and breathed the reality of German life into his story of a poor boy during the horrors of the Thirty Years' War. The great intellectual and father of the German ENLIGHTENMENT and progenitor of German IDEALISM, Gottfried Wilhelm von LEIBNIZ (1646–1716) has also been grouped with writers of the baroque. While Leibniz thought of Samuel PUFENDORF (1632–94) as a "mere jurist," he nonetheless along with Christian THOMASIUS (1655–1728) and Christian von WOLFF (1679–1754) followed the English philosopher Thomas Hobbes; they, however, disagreed with his idea of a chaotic and antisocial beginning of human history and instead believed in a two-fold social contract within the community and between the community and the ruler. Finally, Nikolaus Ludwig von Zinzendorf (1700–60) should be added to the list of baroque writers. He gave PIETISM a new direction and organizational form. He wrote more than 2,000 religious poems that gave expression to the mysticism in Protestant Pietism.

The baroque witnessed the introduction of new musical forms, such as the oratorio and opera. The oratorio flourished both in the Catholic south and the Protestant north. Yet, the baroque is primarily associated with the names of Johann Sebastian BACH (1685–1750) and George Frideric HANDEL (1685–1759). Bach concentrated on vocal and instrumental music for church ceremonies, especially in the form of cantatas, and music for the organ. Bach's *Passions* and his monumental Mass in B Minor took the German musical tradition to new heights. Handel, on the other hand, composed some 35 operas for much more cosmopolitan audiences in Italy and London. He also composed works for the organ and great oratorios, such as *Messiah*.

Barth, Karl (1886–1968)
theologian

Karl Barth was a famous Swiss (Reformed) theologian who was opposed to liberal theology and became a proponent of so-called dialectical theology. He was famous for his opposition to the Nazi regime. He played a significant role in the formulation of the BARMEN DECLARATION of the CONFESSING CHURCH.

Karl Barth was born in Basel, Switzerland, on May 10, 1886. He was ordained a pastor in the Reformed Church in 1911. During WORLD WAR I he developed pacifist views. Receiving his first professorship in 1921 at the UNIVERSITY OF GÖTTINGEN, he later moved to Münster and BONN. Barth's teachings emphasized the absolute difference between man and God, man's inability to solve his own problems, and his complete dependence on revelation. He was opposed to liberal theology and developed a so-called dialectical theology, which became a center of theological debate. Seeking to end the subservience of theology to the interests of the state, he focused on the theme of the revelation of God as the "Wholly Other." It was a theology focused on God's work and critical of human endeavor. It was not, however, a distant Calvinist God, but under the influence of Martin LUTHER, a more human concept of God. His *Epistle to the Romans* of 1919 was the first work in this theological existentialism. The dialectical school was one of a number of schools of thought that wanted to restore the absoluteness of the Christian religion.

Karl Barth was the leading theologian behind the Barmen Declaration of 1934. To Karl Barth the beliefs of the GERMAN CHRISTIANS were heretical. They had made race an expression of sacred truth, part of God's revelation, and thus opened up German Christianity to a flood of non-Christian and anti-Christian beliefs, attitudes, and activities. Barth like other theologians, however, failed to see that the racism of the German Christians was rooted in anti-Jewishness. On the other hand, he wrote: "Protest against the German Christian heresy cannot simply begin with the Aryan Paragraph, nor with their rejection of the Old Testament, the Arianism of their Christology, the naturalism and pelagianism (a heresy in the early church) of their teachings of justification and sanctification, nor the idolization of the state that characterizes German Christian ethics." Rather, the error of German Christians was to place the Germanic race (*Volkstum*) as a revelation equal to that of Holy Scripture.

Because Barth refused to take an oath of allegiance to HITLER, he was removed from his professorship at Bonn. He was commanded to begin his lectures on God each day by raising his arm in salute and saying "Heil Hitler!" which he denounced as blasphemy.

After being expelled from Germany, he spent the rest of his career at the University of Basel and was also well known in the United States after the war. He died on December 10, 1968.

Basic Law, The

The Basic Law for the FEDERAL REPUBLIC OF GERMANY was adopted in 1949. Its authors intended it as a "temporary" framework for a new democratic system, not as a definitive constitution. The Basic Law called upon the people "to achieve in free self-determination the unity and freedom of Germany." A parliamentary council, whose 65 members had been designated by the state parliaments, drafted the Basic Law as the constitutional foundation for the future West German state. The Parliamentary Council adopted the Basic Law with a large majority on May 8, 1949. After having been approved by the military governors, the constitutional instrument was endorsed by the parliaments of all the states except BAVARIA. Konrad ADENAUER, the president of the Parliamentary Council, promulgated the Basic Law on May 23, 1949, after which it became effective. At first the Allied occupying powers retained substantial sovereign rights, but these were gradually transferred to the Federal Republic of Germany (FRG) and the GERMAN DEMOCRATIC REPUBLIC (GDR). The Allies retained responsibility for Germany as a whole, however, until October 3, 1990, when the German Democratic Republic acceded to the Federal Republic of Germany, thus uniting the two German states.

The Basic Law provided the foundation for a stable democracy and thus prevented the kind of situation that during the end of the WEIMAR REPUBLIC made it possible to establish the Nazi dictatorship. One of the first requirements was to limit the powers of the state so as to protect the rights of the individual citizens. The Basic Law also created a system of values within which protection of individual freedom and human dignity is the highest principle of law. The citizen, however, is not viewed as an individual separate from the rest of society but as a part of the community.

According to Article 20, four fundamental principles determined the political and social structure of the Federal Republic, and Article 79 expressly states that these four central principles may not be amended. The Basic Law affirmed that the state is based on democracy, the rule of law, social justice, and that it is not a unitary but a federal state. Under the democratic principle all authority (sovereignty) comes from the people, and state authority is effected through an elected representative democracy. The Basic Law provided for direct decisions by the people through referendum, but only where federal territory is to be reorganized. The rule of law principle meant that the actions of the state are to be governed by the law and justice. The functions of the state were intended to be exercised by independent legislative, executive, and judicial authorities. All government measures may be reviewed by independent judges to determine whether they are in accord with the law.

The basic rights enumerated in Articles 1 to 20 reflected the liberal tradition expressed at the constitutional meetings in FRANKFURT during the REVOLUTION OF 1848. Citizen rights have been protected by the law against arbitrary actions of the state. The parliament (BUNDESTAG) is also bound by the constitution, and its laws must be consistent with it. The social-state principle recognized the responsibility of the state to ensure that members of the community are free from want, can live in dignified humane circumstances, and share in the nation's prosperity. This requirement was intended to balance social discrepancies and to assure social security and social justice. The federal system was chosen because of Germany's deep-rooted federalist tradition, which also left scope for the expression of different cultural and political traditions. At the same time a separation of powers was established with the division of legislative, executive, and judicial powers, which strengthens constitutionalism. It was intended to prevent excessive concentrations of power and the abuses that can result. A FEDERAL CONSTITUTIONAL COURT was also established to ensure that all laws conform to the constitution.

Basic Treaty (1972)

The Basic Treaty was a part of the OSTPOLITIK of the administration of chancellor Willy BRANDT, which fundamentally changed the way both Germanies related. It was an agreement that ended their refusal to recognize each other's existence. In the treaty both German states renounced the use of force and agreed to accept and not violate the existing frontier between them, and agreed to respect each other's authority and independence. For its part the FEDERAL

REPUBLIC abandoned its long-standing claim to be the sole legitimate expression of the German nation. For their part the East Germans agreed to respect the human rights as stated in the United Nations charter and agreed to permit brief visits by its citizens to the West in cases of family need. Full diplomatic recognition was not accorded to East Germany; instead of permanent embassies, "permanent missions" were established in BONN and East Berlin. The Federal Republic did not recognize the GDR as a foreign country but as a sovereign state within the German nation. The treaty did not solve the "national question" of how Germany would be reunited. For West Germany the decision to create practical cooperation with the East Germans was a gamble. It was feared that the official relations and legal autonomy might give sanction to the East German regime and help its development as a separate identity. In fact, the opposite occurred as the travel and communication resulting from the Basic Treaty actually reinforced the attractiveness of West Germany.

Bauernschutz
(Protection of the Peasantry)

The Bauernschutz was a series of 18th-century Prussian edicts that attempted to protect the economic and social security of the peasantry. The Prussian kings FREDERICK I and FREDERICK WILLIAM I realized that the Prussian army depended on the stability of the peasantry on the land for several reasons, the most important of which is that they paid most of the taxes that supported the army. Their well-being was also important because they provided the supplies and were called upon to work for the army, in addition to supplying the majority of the soldiers.

The Prussian peasantry were threatened by two major factors. One was the JUNKER nobility, which the kings also needed to provide officers for the army and whose increasing power threatened the peasants; second were the forces of modernization based on scientific agriculture and capitalism, which sought to establish free-market and wage labor conditions. Consequently, in a series of edicts of 1709, 1714, and 1739, attempts were made to secure the status of the peasantry. Even FREDERICK II realized the dangers and added other edicts to protect their status. Inasmuch as peasants were treated as army deserters who abandoned their lands, now also the nobility who evicted peasants from their lands were punished as deserters.

Even though such efforts were made to maintain a strong class of peasantry, the conditions that inevitably resulted when peasants were away performing military service resulted in the seizure of their farms by the Junkers. No state action could stop this process. As a result even before the emancipation of the peasantry took place during the Napoleonic age, an increasingly large rural wage-earning class was coming into existence.

Bauhaus (1919–1933)

The Bauhaus was a school of experimental design in art, architecture, and design located in Thuringia during the WEIMAR REPUBLIC. It opened in 1919 under the direction of the 36-year-old architect Walter GROPIUS, who declared that its purpose was break down barriers between artists and craftsmen, integrate art and technology, and create new architectural designs. As would be expected, local conservatives and reactionaries accused the school of being a center of Communist Jews. Not that it was, but at first it did attract a student body of bohemians who had countercultural lifestyles as vegetarians and believers in eastern religions, communal living, pacifism, and even the occult.

The students first took a course in design by the Swiss artist Johannes Itten, who encouraged them to forget what they had learned about art and rely on spontaneous impulses in order to develop their sense of color and space. They also studied design and production under such distinguished artists as Lyonel Feininger, Paul KLEE, Wassily Kandinsky, and Josef Albers (painting) and László Moholy-Nagy (photography), Herbert Bayer (graphics), Annie Albers (weaving), Oskar Schlemmer (stage design), Gerhard Marcks (sculpture), and Marcel Breuer and Mies van der Rohe (architecture and furniture design).

Early in the 1920s Gropius had lost his patience with the mysticism and backward-looking philosophy of Itten and replaced him with the more forward-looking László Moholy-Nagy, who was devoted to the art and technology movement. Although not original, the characteristic Bauhaus style was a union of art and technology that emphasized simple lines and the use of steel, glass, and concrete. The style had been influenced by the aesthetics and designs of Le Corbusier and van Doesburg. The Bauhaus held its famous exhibition of 1923 under the banner "Art and Technology—a New Unity," which attracted some 15,000 visitors. There was ballet, new concepts of stage design, and a musical program by Stravinsky and Hindemith. Mies van der Rohe exhibited a model of a glass skyscraper, and Marcel Breuer exhibited some chairs of modern design.

Reactionary right-wing groups continued to criticize the school, believing that there were dangerous goings-on and the artists were daring to flout tradition. When the socialist government was replaced in 1925 by a more conservative one, the school was closed. Gropius moved the school to Dessau, where it was well received. There art and technology triumphed over the other arts. A number of the teachers resigned, such as Kandinsky and Klee, whose notions of art were more imaginative than technical, and Gropius resigned in 1928 to design cars. Near the end of its existence the school concentrated on design rather than art. In 1932 the town council closed the Bauhaus, and Mies van der Rohe, the director since 1930, moved it to Berlin. After HITLER came to power, Mies dissolved the movement and, like Gropius and other artists, immigrated to the United States. The accomplishments of the school during its 14 years had "revolutionized industrial design and helped invent a new architecture."

Baumer, Gertrud (1873–1954)
leader of middle-class women's movement
A child of a Protestant pastor, trained as a teacher, Gertrud Baumer possessed a strong sense of Christian duty. She was moderate in her politics, a nationalist, and advocated the expansion of career opportunities for women in education and social services. A writer and politician, she became president of the Federation of German Women's Associations (BDF) from 1910 to 1919. During the war she encouraged women to support the war effort and furthered their cooperation by organizing the National Women's Service.

Although opposed to the TREATY OF VERSAILLES, she served on the LEAGUE OF NATIONS commission for social and humanitarian questions. During the WEIMAR REPUBLIC she served in the National Assembly and then in the REICHSTAG from 1920 to 1932 as a representative for the liberal GERMAN DEMOCRATIC PARTY (DDP). That does not mean that she thought democracy was the best form of government, being critical of its pursuit of self-interest. She supported protective legislation for women workers, opposed the legalization of abortion, and was especially concerned with issues confronting youth.

When the Nazis came to power, Baumer was supportive. When the Nazis dissolved the BDF, Baumer, however, did not receive a position in the Nazi bureaucracy. Nevertheless, she was allowed to continue publishing the magazine *The Woman* (*Die Frau*) until 1944. After the war she was declared rehabilitated by U.S. occupation authorities, and she expressed the judgment that Hitler's dictatorship was demonic. Now she encouraged women to help rebuild German society in a new book, *The New Path of the German Woman*. As a Christian conservative she helped found the CHRISTIAN SOCIAL UNION (CSU) and was active in the CHRISTIAN DEMOCRATIC UNION (CDU).

Bavaria

As one of the tributary duchies in the Carolingian Empire, Bavaria was ruled by the Agilofinger dynasty. Until 1255 its capital was REGENSBURG. Later the WITTELSBACH family ruled from 1180 to 1918. The duke of Bavaria became an elector (*Kurfürst*) in 1623, succeeding the elector of the Palatinate, Friedrich V, who was deprived of his electoral privilege after being defeated in the THIRTY YEARS' WAR. The new elector also received the Palatinate, which continued as part of Bavaria until 1945. During the COUNTER-REFORMATION Bavaria became a principal supporter of Roman Catholicism. In the 18th century Bavaria sought unsuccessfully to rival AUSTRIA as the leading state in Germany.

The French Revolution and Napoleonic periods significantly influenced Bavaria. In 1805 under Napoleon Bonaparte Bavaria became a monarchy when the elector received the title of King Maximilian I Joseph (1806–25). Bavaria was also geographically enlarged with predominantly Protestant areas in Franconia and Swabia being added to an almost exclusively Catholic state. While Bavaria was Napoleon's ally, it made a significant contribution to Napoleon's invasion of Russia but turned against him during the WARS OF LIBERATION, which allowed Bavaria to retain most of its territorial gains at the CONGRESS OF VIENNA.

Under the succeeding king, LUDWIG I, Bavaria became a center of the arts, especially in MUNICH. The REVOLUTION OF 1848 forced him to abdicate, and he was succeeded by MAXIMILIAN II. On the national question Bavaria favored the greater German solution, the inclusion of Austria in a united Germany. In 1866 Bavaria supported Austria against Prussia in the Seven Weeks' War but was invaded, defeated, and forced to pay reparations. Having been forced by Otto von BISMARCK to sign a defensive alliance with Prussia, Bavaria was drawn into the Franco-Prussian War and was included in the new Second German Empire on January 18, 1871. As part of the bargain of accepting membership in the new German empire, certain rights were reserved for Bavaria, reflecting its attempt to preserve its identity. Bismarck allowed Bavaria to maintain a separate army and command structure in peacetime, separate diplomatic representation abroad, and a separate rail and postal system. Bavaria retained permanent seats on the Imperial committees of defense and foreign affairs. In addition it retained its taxes on alcoholic beverages, independent control of citizenship, residency, colonization, and emigration. King LUDWIG II also received a secret fund from Bismarck, despite the lack of enthusiasm demonstrated by his absence at the coronation ceremony of the emperor at Versailles.

Bavaria was a predominantly Catholic state, but was administered by a liberal government and bureaucracy. It soon was at odds with Bismarck over the KULTURKAMPF. The Bavarian Patriots' Party founded in 1869 represented the interests of the Catholic majority as would the Bavarian wing of the Catholic CENTER PARTY. The late 19th century was also a period of social and economic change in this still predominantly agricultural region. Industrialism and urbanization first affected AUGSBURG and NUREMBERG and later MUNICH. The capital also flowered as a center for literature, theater, art, and architecture. After the strange death of Ludwig II in 1886, his successor, Otto, was mentally incapable of ruling. From 1886 to 1912 Prince Regent Luitpold remained nominally king until 1913, when Ludwig III succeeded him.

During WORLD WAR I Bavaria contributed some 900,000 soldiers to the war effort with some 200,000 killed. As elsewhere the population suffered, but Bavarians became especially resentful toward BERLIN's centralization of power. With the end of the war the revolutionary turmoil of 1918 first toppled the Wittelsbach dynasty, which was swept away by Kurt EISNER, who established a socialist republic. Munich was one of the few German cities to experience a Soviet-type republic during spring 1919 and its brutal suppression. Although Bavarians initially supported the WEIMAR CONSTITUTION and the WEIMAR REPUBLIC, the political trend was to the right and proto-Nazi paramilitary groups called Free Corps were tolerated. Bavaria's native conservatism was represented by the BAVARIAN PEOPLE'S PARTY (BVP), which also significantly contributed to the election of Paul von HINDENBURG as president of the Reich in 1925. In November 1923 the Nazis under the leadership of Adolf HITLER failed in their attempt to take over the government. Hitler was tried and convicted, and spent a short period in Landsberg prison. During the period when the Nazi Party dramatically expanded between 1930 and 1933, the Bavarian People's Party steadfastly opposed it. After the "seizure of power" in 1933 Bavaria like the other German states became a party district (*partygaue*) and succumbed to Nazi control. The first concentration camp of the Third Reich was established by Heinrich HIMMLER in DACHAU. The war severely affected Bavaria, and it experienced the same catastrophic destruction as the rest of Germany.

With the division of Germany into occupation zones, the principal southern part of Bavaria came under the American occupation authorities, while the Bavarian Palatinate was lost to the French zone. DENAZIFICATION, as well as political and economic reconstruction occurred under Allied tutelage. Bavarian political leaders in keeping with their historical traditions favored a decentralized federal government as a protection against another dictatorship. Between 1946 and 1948 the successor party to the Bavarian People's Party was formed, now constituted as the CHRISTIAN SOCIAL UNION (CSU), which supported the inauguration of the FEDERAL REPUBLIC of Germany in BONN in May 1949. The CSU continued to be the most outspoken champion of federalism and states' rights in the new era.

Developments over the decades leading up to reunification in 1990 witnessed many changes. As an interdenominational party the CSU was popular enough to control every Bavarian government except one. By 1970 Bavaria also was rapidly becoming an industrial state. Economic modernization was achieved especially in the fields of automotives, machine tools, electronics, aerospace, and tourism. The influx of some 2 million Sudeten German refugees added significantly to this economic transformation. Bavarians liked to call their economic transformation the "Isar Valley" in imitation of California's Silicon Valley. Agriculture, however, remained an important part of the economy and provided a conservative base of support for the CSU. In national politics the CSU was allied with the CHRISTIAN DEMOCRATIC UNION (CDU), which gave the Bavarians influence in the highest government circles, symbolized by the career and influence of Franz Josef STRAUSS (1915–88).

Bavarian People's Party (BVP) (1918–1933)

During the WEIMAR REPUBLIC the Bavarian People's Party (Bayerische Volkspartei) was a regional party centered in BAVARIA. The party was opposed to the centralistic character of the WEIMAR CONSTITUTION and strongly opposed to Prussian hegemony. Until 1923 it was antirepublican and then turned more moderate. The BVP was instrumental in the election of Paul von HINDENBURG as president in 1925 and later strongly opposed the rise of the NAZI PARTY.

The initiative for the establishment of the Bavarian People's Party came on November 12, 1918, from the REGENSBURG faction of the Bavarian Center Party, where the Bavarian Peasants' Association and its leader, Dr. Georg Heim, was influential. Dr. Heim and others opposed the national Center Party's leftward orientation under Matthias ERZBERGER. Their platform for a new German state was that it follow the Christian-democratic ideal, appeal to all social classes and faiths, advocate federalism, and call for a Christian moral and cultural renewal. It supported the protection of the family, private property, the right of inheritance, and agrarian reform. A republic for Germany was accepted with some reservations, but it was proposed that the permanent form of the Bavarian state had to be decided by the voters. The party espoused a federalistic character, was determined to end the hegemony of Prussia, and was opposed to the unitary policies of the Socialists. Its slogan was "Bavaria for the Bavarians."

Throughout 1919 the BVP followed a policy of cooperation and compromise with the Republic, but in 1920 the Weimar Constitution was increasingly criticized as a product of the Revolution, and constitutional revisionism became the chief driving force within the BVP. The BVP's collaboration with the KAPP PUTSCH made it clear that it was willing to employ unconstitutional methods to achieve its ends. Even though the rightist policies

Poster from the Bavarian People's Party that reads: "The Bolshevik is coming! Throw him out on Election Day!" *(Library of Congress)*

of Gustav von Kahr were discredited in 1921, no reorientation of the party to the left took place. In the intraparty struggles to gain the upper hand, the right wing of the BVP outmaneuvered the moderates. On a national level the BVP still promoted a federal reform program through a series of attempts at placing its proposals before the REICHSTAG, then also at the time of the Reichstag elections in 1924 and the presidential elections in 1925. Locally, the BVP failed to prevent the emergence of Adolf HITLER and the Nazi Party. The Nazis even were allies of the BVP against the federal government and the Socialists.

After Hitler's BEER-HALL PUTSCH the leadership of the party came increasingly into the hands of right-wing figures such as Dr. Heim, Anton Pfeiffer, Franz Xavier Lang, Karl Schwend, Martin Loibl, and Fritz Schaeffer. They were nationalistic and militaristic, promoted the "stab in the back legend," condemned the Revolution, were loyal monarchists, and waxed enthusiastic over the military virtues. Their influence was critical in the BVP's decision in 1925 to support the conservative candidacy of Paul von Hindenburg for president of the Republic, a decision that was decisive in his election victory against the candidate of the Center Party, Wilhelm Marx. Otherwise, a more moderate position was taken by Heinrich Held (1868–1938), the minister-president from 1924 to 1933. The BVP participated in several national cabinets from 1924 to 1928 and supported the anti-depression policies of Heinrich BRÜNING. While the Nazi Party attacked the BVP during the period from 1930 to 1933, the BVP also strongly opposed the increasing strength of the Nazi Party, as did other Catholic leaders. In the presidential elections of 1932 the BVP was a supporter of Hindenburg's reelection. After the Nazi seizure of power in Bavaria on March 9, 1933, many party officials were removed from office. In May–June thousands of party leaders were arrested and imprisoned, and the party was finally dissolved by the regime.

Bavarian Succession, War of the
(1778–1779)

The War of the Bavarian Succession was precipitated by the extinction of the direct WITTELSBACH line of Bavarian electors in 1777. Maximilian III Joseph, who had been the elector since 1745, died childless, and so the succession passed to a collateral Wittelsbach, the elderly Karl Theodore (1724–99), elector of the Palatine (1733). This increase in the power of the Wittelsbachs upset the emperor, JOSEPH II (1741–90) of Austria and his mother, MARIA THERESA (1717–80). Austrian troops were sent into Bavaria to annex certain areas, but with the agreement of Karl Theodore, who was conniving to make his children princes of the Empire. Karl Theodore agreed to cede Lower Bavaria to Austria in 1778. Now FREDERICK THE GREAT of Prussia (1712–86) and Saxon troops of Elector Frederick Augustus III (1750–1827) intervened to prevent this extension of Austrian territory and power.

The armies of both sides marched around, avoiding a general engagement, although some Prussian detachments were defeated in three engagements. Troops spent most of their time foraging and being concerned with supply lines, so the war has been nicknamed the Potato War. The czarina Catherine II (1729–96) of Russia mediated the quarrel, and a peace was signed at Teschen on May 13, 1779. For Frederick the Great the loss of 40,000 troops was disastrous, losses mainly due to sickness and desertion. The Austrians had to give up their designs on Bavaria, except for a small area including the town of Braunau. The Prussian monarchy secured recognition of its hereditary rights in Ansbach and Bayreuth. Karl Theodore died in 1799 and Maximilian IV Joseph (1756–1825) succeeded him, becoming king of Bavaria, and Maximilian I Joseph after 1806.

Bayer AG

Bayer AG became one of the world's leading chemical and pharmaceutical companies. It began with the manufacture of synthetic dyes and expanded into pharmaceuticals such as aspirin, as well as health care, photography, polymers, and agrochemicals.

Friedrich Bayer (1825–80), a merchant, and dyer Johann Friedrich Weskott (1821–80) established on August 1, 1863, the company Friedrich Bayer and Co., a general partnership in Wuppertal-Barmen to manufacture synthetic dyes. Its success led to the establishment of new factories and research laboratories, so that on June 1, 1881, it went public, a joint-stock company called Farbenfabriken. In the new scientific laboratory, which it soon set up, such pharmaceuticals as aspirin were developed, as well as chemical dyes. In 1888 a pharmaceutical department was established. With the expansion of the use of photography in 1904 the company developed chemicals for developing film. Carl DUISBERG became the managing director starting in 1912, established a second production site in Leverkusen, near Cologne, and moved its headquarters to this new site. From 1881 to the eve of WORLD WAR I the company's workforce increased from 300 to 10,000. Not long after the company was founded it expanded abroad to the United States and to Russia. Before long new factories were set up worldwide.

The war and its aftermath seriously affected the company's business and profits. As it was integrated into the war economy, it was required to produce war supplies such as explosives and chemical weapons. During and after the war the company's foreign assets were confiscated, and it was excluded from foreign markets. Because of many difficulties in remaining competitive, the German chemical companies merged and formed I. G. Farben conglomerate (I. G. Farbenindustrie AG, which ended Bayer's separate existence). Nonetheless, for pharmaceuticals the Bayer name continued to be used. The new areas of research in which I. G. Farben was involved were in synthetic rubber, polyurethanes, and therapeutics for infectious diseases. During WORLD WAR II, I. G. Farben produced for the war effort, employed forced labor, and was involved in production at concentration camps such as AUSCHWITZ.

After the war was over, I. G. Farben was broken up by the Allies. Successor companies were set up during the ECONOMIC MIRACLE and Farbenfabriken Bayer AG became involved in the production of plastics, fibers, agrochemicals, and pharmaceuticals. Evidence of dynamic revival and expansion are such vital statistics as employing 78,000 workers and marketing 8,500 different products. The corporate health of Bayer was also demonstrated when it acquired two American laboratories in 1974 and 1978. By the end of the 1980s Bayer was employing 153,000 people worldwide in 150 countries.

Bayreuth

In 915 Germany's oldest castle, Burg Lauenstein, was built. Bayreuth's history, however, mainly goes back to the 12th century, when it was an important early trade route. At the time the House of Merano built a fortified castle on the banks of the River Main. From 1604 to 1768 Bayreuth became the residence of the margrave of Brandenburg-Kulmbach and until 1791 of the margrave of Ansbach. Under these margraves BAROQUE and ROCOCO palaces were built. Under the margrave Frederick (1753–63) and his wife, Wilhelmina, who was the favorite sister of FREDERICK THE GREAT, the great Margraves' Opera House was constructed, which today is the oldest theater in Germany.

Bayreuth's modern fame rests with the career of Richard WAGNER and his wife, Cosima, who settled in Haus Wahnfried. He designed and built the Wagner Festival House (Festspielhaus) from 1872 to 1876 in the north of the city and began to perform his operas there. The first to be featured was the *The Ring Cycle*.

Bayreuth has also had a bad reputation because of the close association between Adolf HITLER and Wagner. Both Wagner's operas and his anti-Semitic views had a considerable impact on Hitler.

Bebel, August (1840–1913)

founder of the Social Democratic Party (SPD)

August Bebel in association with Wilhelm LIEBKNECHT (1819–1900) founded the GERMAN SOCIAL DEMOCRATIC PARTY in 1869 and was its uncontested leader from the founding of the German Empire until the eve of WORLD WAR I. He influenced the development of the labor movement in the 1860s and learned about socialism from another leader of the movement, Ferdinand LASALLE (1825–64). Bebel only had an elementary school background, and his occupational training was that of a woodturner. But his mental and personal characteristics provided him with abilities to distinguish himself as a leader. He had personal charisma and was a forcefully effective public speaker, great at organizational tasks, and was a very capable parliamentary politician. He served as a representative to the REICHSTAG of the NORTH GERMAN CONFEDERATION in 1867 and then in the imperial Reichstag until his death in 1913. Bebel also associated the party with the First International, led by the exile Karl MARX (1819–83).

Bebel was persecuted and imprisoned for six years along with other socialist leaders under BISMARCK'S ANTI-SOCIALIST LAW. The laws were finally repealed in 1890, but in the meantime the party had acquired new voter support, growing most rapidly to become the largest party in the Reichstag. It did not help that Bebel had opposed German unification during the Franco-Prussian War, which created conflict between the party and the new Imperial government. Bebel increasingly came under the influence of Marxism. Although he was the practical leader of the party, it was Karl KAUTSKY (1854–1938) who was the academic theoretician. Kautsky was responsible for the formulation of the ERFURT PROGRAM adopted in 1891, which was based on the philosophy of class struggle. It paved the way for the future development of the party. Although he was an advocate of moderate policies, he opposed the reforms proposed by Eduard BERNSTEIN (1850–1932), but managed an acceptable compromise. Nevertheless, Bebel at the party conference of 1903 in Dresden declared himself to be the unalterable "deadly enemy" of middle-class capitalist society in order to undermine and eliminate it. Besides providing an authoritarian type of leadership and creating a disciplined party, Bebel also wrote what was the most popular book of the movement, *Woman and Socialism*.

Beck, Ludwig August Theodor (1880–1934)

German general

As chief of the General Staff from 1933 to 1938 Ludwig Beck was responsible for rebuilding the German army. He opposed HITLER's invasion of Czechoslovakia. In retirement he and Carl Goerdeler became leaders of the conservative resistance against Hitler.

Ludwig Beck was born on June 29, 1880, in Biebrich on the Rhine, the son of a wealthy industrialist. In 1898 Ludwig joined the army, distinguished himself on military theory, and was invited to join the General Staff as a captain in 1913, continuing to hold staff positions during WORLD WAR I. The bloody battles of the war and the humiliation of retreat left a deep and lasting impression on him. He also would not believe that the German army had lost the war, and like so many others believed "the stab in the back" legend. As would be expected, he opposed the Revolution and the WEIMAR REPUBLIC. In the Reichswehr, the German army under the Republic, he held staff and command positions. Beck was impressed with Nazi electoral successes after 1930 and then welcomed Hitler's appointment as chancellor.

Beck was promoted to lieutenant general and given command of a cavalry division as a result of writing a handbook on tactics. After October 1933, as chief of the General Staff, Beck pushed for speedy rearmament and expansion of the army. He also was behind Germany's withdrawal from the Disarmament Conference and the LEAGUE OF NATIONS and favored the reoccupation of the Rhineland in violation of the TREATY OF VERSAILLES. He also thought that only the army should be able to use force, so he favored the assassination of Ernst RÖHM and other SA leaders while also opposing the SS under HIMMLER. His favorable attitude toward the Nazis began to change with their attacks against Christianity and the false charges against General FRITSCH for homosexuality. Beck also became wary of Hitler's aggressive foreign policy. As early as 1935 an operational plan for war against Czechoslovakia prompted Beck to threaten to resign should Hitler proceed with the plan. Beck wrote warnings before the occupation of the Rhineland and before the annexation (ANSCHLUSS) of Austria.

In 1938 Beck again insisted that a German attack on Czechoslovakia was bound to involve France and England and start a European war that Germany could not win. He did not share Hitler's belief that the army could quickly penetrate the Czech defenses; a delay would provide France time to invade Germany because the German West Wall was not completed. He also thought that Germany did not have the resources to fight a long war and would meet with a disastrous defeat. At a meeting of the commanding generals under General Brauchitsch's chairmanship, Beck's analysis of the military situation was approved. Beck also proposed to Brauchitsch that the generals should go on strike, resisting any orders for war. When Brauchitsch met with Hitler, he failed to communicate to the Führer the opposition of the generals to war. Unable to convince others in the army leadership to join him, Beck resigned in August 1938, but it was kept a secret until after the Czech crisis was over. Beck had come to the realization that true patriotism demanded opposition to Hitler. He said, "The soldiers' obedience has a limit where their knowledge, their conscience, and their responsibility forbid the execution of an order." He believed that soldiers had a responsibility to "the whole people" and not just to carrying out military orders.

After his retirement he joined forces with the conservative politician and mayor of LEIPZIG, Karl Goerdeler, as leaders in the conservative opposition to Hitler. Most of the war years were spent in planning resistance and making plans for a post-Nazi government with himself as its head. He also realized that only a military defeat would create the climate for a successful coup against Hitler. Then, as a result of his involvement in the abortive coup of July 20, 1944, he was executed.

Beckmann, Max (1884–1950)
artist

One of Germany's most famous postimpressionist artists, Max Beckmann displayed characteristics of expressionism and the NEW OBJECTIVITY movement. His art evoked spiritual and mythic expressions of the individual person in the modern world.

Instead of studying architecture first as some artists such as Ernst KIRCHNER had done, Max Beckmann studied art from the beginning (1900–03). Quickly becoming successful, he moved his studio to BERLIN in 1904. He joined the Berlin Secession movement, and in the years between 1906 and the outbreak of WORLD WAR I his reputation spread widely throughout Germany as he exhibited his paintings in Magdeburg, Weimar, and Berlin. During the war he served as a medical orderly, and the horrors of war and mutilated bodies led to his nervous breakdown. In 1925 he was appointed masterteacher at the Stadelschule in Frankfurt, and in 1926 his first retrospective was held at the museum in Mannheim. He also was honored with a special room in the National Gallery in Berlin to display his art. After the Nazis came to power, he was persecuted with the closure of this room, the removal of 530 paintings from various museums, and the incorporation of 21 of his paintings in the DEGENERATE ART exhibition. Moving to Amsterdam for the duration of the war, he immigrated to the United States in 1947 and remained there until his death.

Beckmann's motifs explored the spiritual and psychological themes in "complex allegories and containing a highly personal and autobiographical imagery." Grotesque forms reflect the psychoanalytical expression of complexes and reflexes. Like Ernst Kirchner, his wartime art responded to its horrors with expressionistic distortions of reality. Sometimes human beings were depicted as robots performing mechanical automatic functions. Although Beckmann never identified with only one school of art, he was determined to use his art in the social struggles of the postwar period. He also joined the New Objectivity (Neue Sachlichkeit) movement in protest against the extremes of abstract art. Some of his social commentaries were found in *Königinen II* (1922) depicting the newly rich of the Weimar era dancing with abandonment, *Man with Fish* (1934) with almost Picasso-like imagery, and *Circus Caravan* (1940) showing distorted circus performers and their loneliness. Americans are lucky to have readily available to them in the Museum of Modern Art in New York Beckmann's famous large-scale triptych, the *Departure* (1932–35), which depicts in mythic form the problematic place of the individual in the modern world.

Beer-Hall Putsch of 1923
(Hitler-Ludendorff Putsch)

The Beer-Hall Putsch (coup) of November 8–9, 1923, was the attempt by Adolf HITLER and the NAZI PARTY along with the moral encouragement of General Erich LUDENDORFF to take over the Bavarian government and march on BERLIN. The other conspirators, including Gustav Ritter von Kahr, backed down from overthrowing the government, and Hitler and the Nazis marched into MUNICH, where they were stopped by the army. Hitler was captured, tried, and imprisoned.

The Beer-Hall Putsch was a response of ultranationalists in BAVARIA to the Ruhr crisis of fall 1923. A new Reich government under Gustav STRESEMANN had ended the German passive resistance against the French occupation. As a result, the Berlin and Bavarian governments came into conflict, the latter declaring a state of emergency on September 26, giving Kahr dictatorial authority. The Berlin government now tried to restrict the Nazis in Bavaria by closing their newspaper, the *Völkischer Beobachter,* which the commander of the Bavarian military district, General Otto von Lossow, refused to obey. In the meantime Hitler had become the leader of a right-wing paramilitary group, the Combat League (Kampfbund), which sympathized with Kahr and hoped to march on Berlin (as Mussolini had marched on Rome in October 1922) to overthrow the republican government. Kahr and his fellow conspirators began to grow cautious, especially when General Hans von Seeckt (chief of the Army Command, 1920–26), became fearful that an abortive coup would harm the army. So the stage was set when on November 6 Kahr cautioned Hitler against hasty action, but Hitler decided instead to force the Bavarian leaders to join the Combat League in a march on Berlin.

On the evening of November 8 Kahr held a meeting of some 3,000 of his supporters at the Bürgerbräu Keller, a large beer hall in Munich. On the platform were local dignitaries, including General von Lossow, commander of the army in Bavaria, and Col. Hans von Seisser, chief of the

Bavarian State Police. Hitler and the storm troopers surrounded the hall, led a detachment down the aisle, fired a shot at the ceiling, and shouted that the "National Revolution" has broken out and the Reich and Bavarian governments were deposed. After jumping on the podium, Hitler forced the dignitaries into a side room and made them pledge their support to his new government. After recovering their wits, the three leaders of the Bavarian regime began to berate Hitler, challenging his plans. This so infuriated the Führer that he went back into the hall and proclaimed to the crowd: "Tomorrow will find a national government in Germany, or it will find us dead!" It all appeared to be a comic opera. Ludendorff entered the hall and denounced Hitler for starting a revolution without his approval. Hitler ignored him, saying that he would be victorious. Behind the scenes Kahr, Lossow, and Seisser escaped and reneged on their promises. In Berlin General Seeckt ordered the rebellion crushed. After planning his strategy all night, Hitler by morning then felt his plans had misfired, but Ludendorff insisted that there be no retreat.

At 11 A.M. the assembled Nazis with their swastika banners and flags began their march into the center of Munich to the Marienplatz, then on the narrow Residenz strasse to the Odeonsplatz. They were led by Hitler, Hermann Göring, Ludendorff, and Julius Streicher. When the marchers reached the Odeonsplatz, they were met by a force of army troops and police. Hitler called on the police to surrender; they responded with a volley of bullets. Hitler hit the pavement and in the confusion escaped by car while Ludendorff walked straight through the ranks of police who showed him the respect of a war hero. Fourteen storm troopers were killed, becoming the first Nazi martyrs.

Hitler's abortive putsch put an end to the Kahr conspiracy and eliminated the threat to the Republic. Hitler's abysmal failure, however, inadvertently turned into a brilliant achievement. Previously he had been just a regional rabble-rouser and political nobody, and afterward a national figure. At his trial he made a fool of the Republic. Besides, Hitler learned an important lesson: that violent takeovers by political minorities were not the best way to achieve power. Instead, after his release from Landsberg prison, he decided to follow a legal path of gaining electoral victories in order to control the government.

Beethoven, Ludwig van (1770–1827)
composer

Born in Bonn in 1770, Ludwig Beethoven was the son of a Flemish family of musicians who had immigrated to the Rhineland and established themselves as musicians to serve the Rhenish electors. At age 11 he had to leave school due to his father's alcoholism. By age 12 he was already an accomplished keyboard virtuoso and talented pupil of composition. His teacher helped him obtain a position as assistant organist at the court of the elector of Cologne, Maximilian Francis, the brother of Emperor Joseph II. The elector thought so highly of the young organist that he sent him to Vienna, the music capital of Europe, to study with Mozart. After two months, however, he had to return to Bonn due to his mother's death. In 1792 he again went to Vienna to further his training and career. There he studied with Haydn and entered the musical circles of the Viennese upper classes. Beethoven's boorish and unpleasant personal habits combined with crude social behavior made it surprising that he had friends and that women fell in love with him. From 1792 until his death at age 57 Beethoven lived amid a circle of friends, never married, rarely traveled, and did not depend for income on an official position. His tours as a concert pianist and composer were successful until progressive deafness, which he had begun to experience before 30 years of age, caused his playing to degenerate. Beethoven tried to hide his defect, which made communication difficult and caused him to be suspicious of others. He also was afflicted by periods of depression.

In the three major phases of his life he composed nine symphonies, seven concerti, 32 piano sonatas, and more than 67 songs (lieder). His First and Second Symphonies and his first two piano concerti were composed during the first period of his life. During the second period the Third through the Eighth Symphonies and the opera *Fidelio* were completed. His Third Symphony (1804) was dedicated to Napoleon, but then revoked when Beethoven, a convinced republican, learned that Napoleon had been crowned emperor. During the third period of his life he composed the *Missa Solemnis* (1823) and the Ninth Symphony (1824). In the final chorus of that great symphonic work, Beethoven set to music the hymnic verses of Schiller's *Ode to Joy*. Whereas before Beethoven instrumental music was considered inferior to vocal music, he raised it to the highest artistic level and was the heir of Haydn.

During the last 10 years of his life Beethoven's music reached new heights, which included his last five piano sonatas and the Ninth Symphony. He died in Vienna in great agony on March 26, 1827, of cirrhosis of the liver.

Benjamin, Walter (1892–1940)
cultural critic

Born in 1892 to affluent Jewish parents in BERLIN, Walter Benjamin became one of the most significant cultural critics during the WEIMAR REPUBLIC. Unsuccessful in pursuing an academic career, he became a Marxist and supported the writings of Bertolt BRECHT. Benjamin abandoned the German tradition of Hegelian idealism and set out to interpret poetic works on their own terms. He discovered the relevance of German romantic philosophy to theories of modernity. Few cultural critics have acquired a greater importance since WORLD WAR II. In *On the Concept of History* (1940) Benjamin strove to reconcile the messianic anticipation of salvation in Jewish mysticism with the Marxist materialistic philosophy of history. Although Benjamin's thinking was influenced by philosophers such as Immanuel KANT, Edmund HUSSERL, and Sigmund Freud, Benjamin's thinking cannot be easily categorized.

After the Nazis came to power in 1933, Benjamin fled to Paris, where he continued to contribute to the work of the Frankfurt Institute for Social Research under the eminent leadership of such philosophers as Max Horkheimer and T. W. Adorno The institute later developed into what became known as the Frankfurt school, a circle of specialists from various fields whose common theme was social theory. In his writings at this time Benjamin focused on the archaeology of early consumer capitalism and on theories of remembrance. Like so many others, Benjamin became a victim of Nazism. At first he left Paris when the German army occupied the French capital, fleeing south to Vichy France, but was lucky enough to obtain a visa to enter the United States through the intervention of his friend Max Horkheimer. At the Franco-Spanish border he and friends were stopped for lack of exit visas. Fearing the prospect of being turned over to the GESTAPO, Benjamin committed suicide.

Benn, Gottfried (1886–1956)
expressionist poet

Born the son of a Lutheran minister in Mansfield, Prussia, Gottfried Benn became a leading expressionist writer. Educated in theology and philology and then receiving a medical degree in military medicine, Benn became a specialist in skin and venereal diseases and conducted a medical practice among the poor in BERLIN. After the war he continued to pursue both his medical and literary careers. His brief support for Nazism was inspired by the hope of creating a new German society based on the philosophy of Friedrich NIETZSCHE. Benn was quickly alienated by the regime. During WORLD WAR II he served as a medical officer. Afterward his work was banned by the Allies, but later his poems and essays were published and he received recognition as a major poet.

Benn's writing depicted scenes of horror and dying. In his first published collection, *Morgue*, one of the poems, "Beautiful Childhood," dwelled on decaying flesh, and the collection observed how nature was indifferent to human desires. Reflecting his repugnance of life, his expressionist poems in *Flesh* (1917), and after the war *Rubble* (1924), depicted hideously morose and despairing scenes. A universal nihilism permeated his work, indicating that all of human experience and suffering were meaningless. Modern science, he thought, had destroyed an anthropomorphic interpretation of the universe, which also made history meaningless. Although he published collections of his poetry during the WEIMAR REPUBLIC, his more positive though misguided prose works, *Nihilism* (1932) and *The New State and the Intellectual* (1933), optimistically believed in the renewing possibilities of Nazi political theories. He soon realized, however, that the Nazis meant to politicize art, which he opposed along with their idealization and use of violence. His work was criticized by the regime, and he was forbidden to publish in 1938. After the war he became one of Germany's leading poets, publishing *Static Poems* (1948) and *Intoxicated Tide* (1949). His nihilism continued to permeate his work though he admitted that some happiness could be experienced through the art of the "absolute" poem written only for itself.

Bennigsen, Rudolf von (1824–1902)
National-Liberal politician

Throughout the first decade of the NATIONAL UNION (Nationalverein) and the first three decades of the NATIONAL LIBERAL PARTY, Rudolf von Bennigsen was its moderate liberal leader.

Rudolf von Bennigsen was born at Lüneberg on July 10, 1824, into an old aristocratic family of HANOVER. He studied law at GÖTTINGEN and then became a judge. He was inspired by the liberalism and nationalism of the REVOLUTION OF 1848 and during the 1850s became opposed to the reactionary government in Hanover. In 1856 he was elected to the legislature and in 1859 became a founder of the National Union. That August in the city of Eisenach there was a meeting of liberals from various German states. All the groups wanted to reform the constitution of the Confederation and advocated Prussian leadership to unify Germany. Emerging out of these discussions the National Union was formed in September 1859. Bennigsen was among its active leaders and was selected to be its head. During the next decade the National Liberals stirred up liberals and the middle class to support unification under Prussian leadership.

Beginning in 1867, Bennigsen began a decade of cooperation with BISMARCK and helped create the institutions of the new German Empire. Bennigsen was a calm parliamentarian and was influenced by English political ideas. He was an effective speaker, was able to mediate disputes, but was indecisive and lacked the dynamism to hold the party together. Under his leadership, however, the National Liberals supported Bismarck on broad issues and opposed him only on minor ones. Strongly anticlerical, the party was Bismarck's main ally in the KULTURKAMPF. By 1877 the Liberal agenda was nearly complete except for the issue of getting Bismarck to share some of his power. After a long discussion with Bennigsen, Bismarck offered him the post of the Prussian minister of the interior, trying to split the party. Bennigsen had also asked Bismarck to take two more liberals into the ministry in order to wield some influence in policy matters, which Bismarck had no interest in doing. The affair marked the end of the relationship between the liberals and the chancellor. Bismarck turned from Bennigsen and the liberals to look for new allies among the CONSERVATIVE and CENTER PARTIES.

During the next several years the left wing oppositional faction in the party seceded. For two more years Bennigsen headed the rump party and then resigned, withdrawing from Parliament and returning to Hanover. In 1887 he returned to the REICHSTAG but had little influence. Retiring in 1898, he died not long after at his estate on August 7, 1902.

Benz, Carl Friedrich (1844–1929)
automobile pioneer

Carl Friedrich Benz was born on November 25, 1844, in Karlsruhe, Germany. His major contribution to history is his invention of the modern automobile along with Gottlieb DAIMLER (1834–1900). As a boy he developed skills in technical matters. When he entered the secondary schools, his interest and competence in technical matters grew, qualifying him to become an assistant to his physics instructor. He attended Karlsruhe Polytechnic, where he obtained experience in the manufacture of engines. By 1872 he was able to open his first shop to produce engines. A decade later he was able to find investors and founded Benz and Company in October 1883, which produced stationary gas engines.

From the plans he had developed, Benz produced his first motorized tricycle, which was publicly tested in fall 1885. His patent was #37435. Perhaps his most important contribution was the invention of a four-stroke engine far superior to the ordinary two-stroke of the day. Adding a carburetor gave the engine greater fuel efficiency, while an ignition system was developed whereby a battery provided spark to a plug to start the engine. His motorized tricycle also had rear springs, rack-and-pinion steering, and water cooling. In 1890 a fourth wheel was added, which assured its economic success. The first mass-produced car in the world was the small Benz Velo (1894). By 1900 the Benz company with 400 workers was the largest car company in the world. In 1903 he withdrew from management. The company concentrated on luxury cars and marine and aircraft engines. A distinctive contribution to fuel efficiency was the invention of the diesel engine. Shortly before the GREAT DEPRESSION the Benz Company in 1926 merged with its competitor, the Daimler-Motoren-Gesellschaft, becoming Daimler-Benz AG. The father of the motor car died in 1929.

Bergen-Belsen

Bergen-Belsen was a CONCENTRATION CAMP built on the Lüneberg heath near Celle in northwest Germany. It was opened in 1941 to house up to 8,000 ailing prisoners of war, and thousands of Soviet prisoners of war died there between 1941 and 1942. In 1943 it came under the control of Heinrich HIMMLER, who converted it into a camp for Jews and incapacitated prisoners from other camps such as BUCHENWALD, DACHAU, Flossenburg, and Natzweiler. It was overcrowded with some 42,000 prisoners in transit by March 1944. Lack of hygiene and a typhus epidemic killed many prisoners as effectively as gas chambers elsewhere. Some 35,000 to 40,000 prisoners died of starvation, disease, and hard labor. Josef Kramer, the "Beast of Belsen," took over command of the camp at the end of 1944 and was responsible for many deaths and executions. Anne FRANK died in Bergen-Belsen in March 1945. The camp was the first liberated by the British on April 15, when it still contained some 60,000 inmates with about 500 dying each day. The Bergen-Belsen staff was tried in a British military court in October 1945.

Berghof

The Berghof was Adolf HITLER's private mountain retreat, the so-called Eagle's Nest. Literally it was a "mountain court" on the mountain named Obersalzberg in southeastern Bavaria. Originally the Berghof was a small country house called Haus Wachenfeld, and it was enlarged by Hitler according to his own design in 1935. It was at that time that it became known as the Berghof. Because the old house was preserved within the new one and the two living rooms were connected, it was not well designed to receive official visitors. Nevertheless, it had a most impressive view from an enormous picture window, which looked out over the villages of Berchtesgaden and Salzburg to the surrounding mountains. Many famous people were guests, including Neville Chamberlain in 1938. Hitler also liked to visit here with his friends. His female companion, Eva BRAUN, lived there until she joined Hitler in his Berlin bunker in 1945.

Berlin

The origins of the city of Berlin are to be found in the settlements of Berlin and Cölln, which were settled by itinerant merchants in the valley of the Spree River during the 12th century. When the HOHENZOLLERNS arrived in BRANDENBURG, the city became the urban center and fortress of the March Brandenburg. Berlin's designation as residence of the elector of Brandenburg in the mid-15th century enhanced the city's political, administrative, economic, and cultural importance. Schools were established, and culture was stimulated. Printers set up shop, and the first plays were performed in the city. In 1617 Berlin's first weekly newspaper began publication. Architecturally, the city was being constructed in the Renaissance style. Another factor that had a strong impact on Berlin's overall development was the influx of Huguenot refugees from France, who were offered refuge by FREDERICK WILLIAM (1620–1688) who was the elector of Brandenburg from 1640–1688.

The THIRTY YEARS' WAR had a disastrous impact on the city, with the population dropping by half (12,000 to 6,000). The city lost its wealth to war, was pillaged, homes were burned, and many people committed suicide. After the wars were over, the city was reconstructed. The mercantilist policies of the 17th century sought to develop the city's economic base and supported manufacturing industries. A decisive trigger for the city's economic development was the construction of a canal that linked the Oder and Spree Rivers, providing a waterway from BRESLAU through Berlin to HAMBURG.

The Great Elector had a positive effect on economic and cultural growth. He allowed the French Huguenots (Calvinists) and Jews to take refugee in Berlin. About 5,000 French Protestants came, creating new businesses such as paper, glass, and silk industries. In 1688 Frederick III (son of the "Great Elector") became the elector of Brandenburg. He commissioned baroque architects to construct new buildings. His wife, Queen Sophie, encouraged art, science, and philosophy. In 1696 the Academy of Art was founded. Consequently, Berlin came to be known as Athens on the Spree. In 1701 Brandenburg and the duchy of Prussia were joined to form the Kingdom of Prussia, and Frederick was crowned "King in Prussia" in 1701. Then FREDERICK WILLIAM I, king of Prussia from 1713–40, known as the "soldier king," laid out massive parade grounds in Berlin such as the Pariser Platz, Mehringplatz, and Tempelhofer Feld (later to become Tempelhof Airport, which became famous during the Berlin airlift (1948). In 1735 a wall was built around Berlin for the purpose of collecting tolls. When FREDERICK II known as "the Great" ruled from 1740 to 1788, he expanded the arts building, the State Opera House (Staatsoper). The ENLIGHTENMENT was in full swing, and Berlin residents such as Gotthold Ephraim LESSING and Moses MENDELSSOHN made their contributions.

During the NAPOLEONIC WARS Prussian national pride suffered due to the defeats at the BATTLES OF JENA and AUERSTADT in 1806. Napoleon even marched his victorious army through the Brandenburg Gate. After the WAR OF LIBERATION Berlin was at peace again. The railroads made their appearance with the first line constructed between Berlin and POTSDAM. The Berlin Zoo was founded in 1844. The population of 400,000 had grown too large, as at least half were impoverished and about 40 percent of the city budget was earmarked for charity. This was one of the reasons why the REVOLUTION OF 1848 spread to Berlin. Two hundred people were killed as citizens took to the streets. The revolution collapsed. In 1862 Otto von BISMARCK was appointed minister-president of Prussia and in eight years brought about the unification of Germany. In 1871 Berlin was designated the capital of the German Empire and seat of the newly established Reich administration. The population expanded to 3.7 million by 1910. A municipal water system was built as well as elevated railways and electric street lighting. Berlin also became an industrial city as the home of a large working-class population. Class struggles developed and there was a huge increase in support for the SOCIAL DEMOCRATIC PARTY. WORLD WAR I created unrest and eventually led to massive strikes against the war. During the revolutionary events of November 1918 Germany was declared a republic.

During the WEIMAR REPUBLIC Berlin continued to be the capital but also became an international center of intellectual and cultural life. It had a vibrant social life as all classes participated in Berlin's so-called decadent nightlife. Babelsburg on the outskirts of the city was the home of Europe's largest film industry. Movies such as *Metropolis* and *The Cabinet of Dr. Caligari* were produced there, while Greta Garbo and Marlene Dietrich went from Berlin to Hollywood. Berlin also became an important publishing center, printing some 150 daily and weekly newspapers. When the DEPRESSION hit, the unemployment of some 600,000 people rocked the city while Nazis and Communists had open battles in the streets. HITLER became chancellor in January 1933, imposing a reign of terror that repressed dissent. The REICHSTAG BUILDING was burned. The Jewish population was persecuted, and most left the city for foreign countries or concentration camps. Concentration camps were set up in the Columbiahaus in Tempelhof and in Oranienburg outside of Berlin. The war had a horrific impact on Berlin as Allied bombing and the Russian army destroyed or damaged 39 percent of its housing and 35 percent of its industrial plant.

At the end of WORLD WAR II the Allies assumed supreme power in Berlin. In 1948 the BERLIN BLOCKADE by the Russians attempted to starve the Western sector, and the BERLIN WALL was built in 1961 to keep the East Germans from escaping to the West. West Berlin had special status in the FEDERAL REPUBLIC. It no longer was the German capital, which had been moved to BONN, the new capital of the Federal Republic. East Berlin, however, remained the capital of the GERMAN DEMOCRATIC REPUBLIC. On June 17, 1953, workers in East Berlin and other parts of the GDR went on strike and started a near revolution, which was crushed with the help of the Russian army. In West Berlin many foreign workers, especially Turkish guest workers, took up residence in Kreuzberg. The reunification of Germany in 1990 presented the city with the task of harmonizing the different structures and social conditions that had developed during the 40 years of division. The unified German government decided to move its capital from Bonn back to Berlin, which has been undergoing great changes due to the massive construction projects. The Kurfurstendamm is no longer separated, and one can walk through the Brandenburg Gate unhindered.

Berlin, Battle for (Fall of) (1945)

There never had been any doubt that the Russians would be victorious in the Battle for Berlin. The Soviet army had massed 4 million men in Poland for the final assault, with 2.7 million along a front stretching south to the Adriatic Sea. The German armed forces facing them were only a shadow of the great fighting machine that had invaded Russia. The Luftwaffe had been blasted out of the skies and no longer represented an effective air force that could provide cover for German troops. German troops were predominantly older men and younger boys from the VOLKSTURM. Although the Germans still had thousands of tanks, they were running short of fuel. BERLIN had been bombarded by air raids, and the city's 3 million residents were desperate for food, fuel, and medical supplies, and extremely fearful of what awaited them from the Russians.

The general offensive on Berlin was to last some 45 days by as rapid an advance as possible. In January 1945 the Russians held a line along the border of East Prussia, down the Narew River to Warsaw, then along the Vistula River. They possessed a clear military superiority. The Soviet offensive began with a tremendous bombardment one week earlier than planned because of the stunning German counterattack in the BATTLE OF THE ARDENNES on the western front.

The Russians renewed their offensive on Berlin after a two-month lull on April 16, and by May 8 it was all over. The Russians massed some 2.5 million men and more than 6,000 tanks against about 1 million Germans with 1,500 tanks. The Soviets were massed in three army groups: the first Belorussian Front under Marshall Zhukov, the First Ukrainian Front under

Konev, and the Second Belorussian Front under Rokossovsky. Zhukov was to attack Berlin directly out of the Küstrin bridgehead, while Konev was to attack in three directions—toward Berlin, toward Czechoslovakia, and toward the ELBE RIVER to meet the Americans. Rokossovsky was to attack in the north. After bitter fighting the Russians were able to cut through the German lines, bypassing Berlin, and on April 24 the armies linked up and Berlin was cut off. Some 200,000 German troops were isolated in the city, and another 200,000 were surrounded in a pocket west of Berlin. On April 25 American and Soviet troops met at Torgau on the Elbe. The suburbs of Berlin had already been invaded on April 21, and on April 30 the REICHSTAG was stormed.

Meanwhile, Adolf HITLER and his associates were in their underground bunker, issuing orders, hoping beyond hope for a split among the Allies and miracle victories from secret weapons. On April 30 Hitler and Eva BRAUN committed suicide, and Joseph GOEBBELS and his family soon followed. The battle aboveground ended on May 2 when the commander of Berlin defenses, General Helmuth Weidling, surrendered. The Germans fought tenaciously for Berlin, fearing the worst from the Bolshevik hordes from Russia. Barbarous acts were in fact committed, as an estimated 2 million German women were raped by Soviet soldiers. German soldiers were marched off to camps in Siberia.

Joseph Stalin had an obsessive fear that the American and British armies would reach Berlin first. Stalin knew the psychological importance of conquering the German capital, but he also knew that the Americans had invented an atomic bomb. He hoped to strip Berlin's atomic research labs of their equipment, scientists, and uranium. Consequently, Stalin goaded his military commanders into competition to reach Berlin first. Americans, however, did not understand the strategic importance of controlling Berlin and Germany and wanted to quickly end the war, save American lives, and concentrate on defeating Japan. The American willingness to leave Berlin to the Soviets led to a rift in the alliance with Britain.

Berlin, Congress of (1878)

The congress convened by Otto von BISMARCK was intended to revise the Treaty of San Stefano of March 1878, which had expanded Russian power from the Straits to the Adriatic, more to the liking of the Great Powers. The Near Eastern Crisis and Russo-Turkish War had led to the utter defeat of the Turks by the Russians. The decline of the Ottoman Empire had now opened sources of conflict between czarist Russia and Austria-Hungary, Bismarck's allies in the Three Emperor's League (1873). Bismarck had refused to give the Russians a guarantee of support should a war occur with Austria-Hungary over the Balkans. So the forced settlement of San Stefano after the Turkish defeat had led to the creation of a pro-Russian Bulgarian state in the Balkans. As late as 1877 the Russians and Austrians thought they were in agreement about common interests in the Balkans and that the Russians had no intentions of building up a larger Slavic state, which would create unrest among the Slavic peoples in the Austro-Hungarian Empire. Consequently, the Austrians felt betrayed. The British also objected to the expansion of Russian power through San Stefano and demanded a review of the peace treaty. British imperial interests could not tolerate the Russian control of the Balkans, which involved control of Turkish affairs. In this tense situation, which could have escalated into a war, Bismarck stepped in as an "honest broker" and sponsored the 1878 Berlin Congress.

The congress was the most distinguished diplomatic meeting between the CONGRESS OF VIENNA and the Paris Peace Conference. Bismarck did not have a direct interest, except if war broke out between Austria and Russia, making Germany choose sides or remain neutral. Actually, it was concerning this affair that Bismarck made the famous remark that the Balkans were not worth the bones of a Pomeranian grenadier.

The settlements confirmed in the Treaty of Berlin made few happy, and Russia was especially troubled at what she had to give up. Even though the British foreign secretary, Lord Salisbury, felt that Bismarck had favored the Russians more than the British, the Russians blamed their losses on Bismarck, which soured relations between St. Petersburg and Berlin. The negotiations resulted in the following: Bulgaria was made an autonomous principality free from any further Turkish interference, which nevertheless was galling to the Russians because Bulgaria had lost Eastern Rumelia and its access to the Aegean Sea; the independence of Serbia and Montenegro was confirmed; the independence of Rumania was also confirmed, (a process that had begun in 1856) and she obtained northern Dobruja in return for ceding Bessarabia to Russia; Russia was confirmed in its occupation of the Caucasus; and without any effort Austria-Hungary received the right to occupy Bosnia-Herzegovina and Novibazar, while Britain received the right to occupy the island of Cyprus. The other territories in the Balkans, which were taken from the Ottoman Empire, were returned.

Berlin-Baghdad Railway

While Otto von BISMARCK would not allow any economic enterprise in Turkey to interfere with his foreign policies, when WILLIAM II came to the throne, imperial policy changed. William saw in Turkey a potential ally and an opportunity for German economic expansion. The emperor, who regularly spoke publicly in undiplomatic terms, in 1898 on a trip to Palestine claimed to be the protector of 300 million Muslims. Against whom? The following year a German company, Deutsche Bank, received the concession to construct the port of Haidar Pasha and then a railroad from Baghdad to Basra on the Persian Gulf. The bank had hoped to involve other countries in the project, especially the British, but the German government urged the company to go it alone. Already in 1888 the Deutsche Bank had received from the Turkish government the concession to build a railroad from Constantinople to Ankara. This so-called Anatolian Railroad was supposedly the first part of a projected railroad to run from Constantinople to the Persian Gulf.

As German financial interests already dominated the railroads of central Europe and the Balkans and had already been active for six years in Turkey, the project received the title Berlin-Baghdad Railway. It was resented by the Russians, who believed it would strengthen the Turkish empire, but who also incidentally had plans to build a Persian railroad. The project met with divided reception from the British, some thinking it would create antagonisms between Germany and Russia and others considering this land route to the Persian Gulf a competitor to the Suez Canal and sea route to India. As the Entente alliance took shape (France, Russia, and England) British opinion hardened against the railway project. Russo-German differences were settled by an agreement in 1911, and agreements in 1911 and 1914 satisfied British and French objections. However, by the beginning of WORLD WAR I only a small part of the railway line had been built.

Berlin Blockade (1948)

The Berlin Blockade was the outgrowth of the division of Germany and the inability of the Allies to agree on its future. The split between the Allies became clear at the London Conference of Big Four foreign ministers in December 1947, at which neither side was willing to compromise on Germany. As a result, the Russians solidified their control of eastern Germany and Europe. On the western side the Allies decided to integrate their zones into one economic unit. The Soviets reacted to the currency reform in the western zones by closing all the approaches to Berlin by rail, land, and water on June 24, 1948. Only the air corridors to Berlin were left open. It was made clear by the Soviets that their efforts at blockading Berlin were meant to halt the emergence of a West German state and not to expel the Western powers from Berlin. The Soviets did not want to lose their influence in the Western zones.

Although General Lucius Clay proposed to break through the blockade with an armed convoy, neither Washington nor Moscow wanted a direct confrontation. Almost all the supplies of food and fuel for all the sectors of Berlin came from the Soviet zone. About 2.5 million people lived in the Western sectors, and the prospect of supplying them appeared overwhelming. Nonetheless, the air corridors were open, and it was decided to attempt an airlift. For 11 months the city was supplied exclusively from the air. Planes landed nonstop in West Berlin's Tempelhof Airport, bringing some 4,500 tons of supplies per day, which increased to 8,000 by the end, demonstrating that Berlin could be supplied indefinitely. Yet, the coal allotments were so small that only a mild winter saved the population while industrial production in Berlin was reduced 50 percent and unemployment skyrocketed.

While the airlift was in progress, the political split was also sealed. The Soviet representatives had already left the Allied Kommandantura on June 16, 1948. The city legislature also transferred itself to the Western zones in September because of Communist demonstrators. At the end of 1948 separate municipal administrations were in place in the Western and Eastern sections of the city. The confrontation over Berlin froze the divisions into two separate administrations. The BERLIN WALL of 1961 had not been built yet, but the city now had two separate municipal governments. One was freely elected, while the other, under Russian control, had its government installed by SMAD (Soviet Military Administration for Germany). The introduction of the deutsche mark, the new currency in West Berlin, meant that the economy would be integrated with that of the Federal Republic and Western Europe.

Berlin Conference (1884–1885)

In winter 1884–85, 15 nations, including the Great Powers, met in Berlin at the invitation of Otto von BISMARCK to ease tensions among the European powers over the partition of Central Africa and to reach agreements over trade, navigation, and boundaries. The immediate cause of tension was British and Portuguese distrust of Belgian and French ambitions in the Congo and of German expansion in East Africa and the Cameroons. Even though Otto von Bismarck had no great personal interest in Africa, Germany had entered the colonial race exclusively for domestic reasons in order to support mercantile interests. Only as recently as 1884 had Germany entered the race for colonies, and in a short 12 months had proclaimed protectorates over Southwest Africa, Togoland, and the Cameroons, and the territories in East Africa. Germans like the Bremen merchant Adolf Lüderwitz, the Hamburg merchant Adolf Woermann, and Carl Peters, who organized the "society for German colonization," pressed for government involvement.

Bismarck's continental diplomacy enabled him to win colonies overseas. The state of foreign affairs between 1883 and 1885 made it possible for Bismarck to ignore England's opposition to German colonial expansion. Tensions between England and France in Egypt and revolts in the Sudan neutralized England. France, on the other hand, was involved in Tunisia and Indochina and had decided to cooperate with Germany in the colonial field. The noteworthy cooperation with France climaxed in the Berlin Conference of 1884–85 over the Congo, where France and Germany placed limits on England's colonial predominance.

The first thing the conference needed to judge was the conflicting claims in the Congo Basin, where the explorer Stanley had made claims that conflicted with the Portuguese and the British. The conference concluded by recognizing the Congo State and gave it access to the sea. Even though the title to the Congo Basin was given to the International Association, Leopold II of Belgium still controlled it and regarded it as his personal possession. Methods to suppress slavery and the slave trade were decided. Freedom of navigation on the Congo and Niger Rivers was also guaranteed. The conference made decisions concerning spheres of influence for the European powers so as to prevent a scramble for colonies that would lead to a major war.

The Berlin Conference stirred European activity in Africa by facilitating trade on the Congo and Niger Rivers. The way international law was conveniently applied to Africa was that any state could acquire territory by occupying it and notifying the other powers. As a result of the publicity the conference gave to Africa, the European powers completed the division of the continent during the next 10 years.

Berlin Wall (1961–1989)

The Berlin Wall was conceived as a means of stopping the increasing exodus of population leaving the GDR for the West. By 1961 more than 2.5 million East Germans had fled. Beginning in late 1959, the regime initiated a drive to collectivize the remaining private farmland. About 15,000 then abandoned their farms and fled to the West instead of submitting to collectivization. Skilled labor was also departing. Food shortages developed, while the Russian leader, Nikita Khrushchev, made threats concerning West Berlin. Within the first eight months of 1961 some 155,000 East Germans had registered as refugees. If one counts all those who fled Communist rule since the end of the war, it added up to 3 million.

In the early morning hours of August 13, 1961, the regime began to seal off East from West Berlin. Barbed wire was used to block street crossings. The construction of the wall had begun. Guards stopped all Germans who lacked permission to cross. Then a multilayered wall of concrete and barbed wire was built all around West Berlin, reaching 100 miles in length. No attempt was made to remove the wall, which, though an embarrassing symbol of East Germany's prisonlike status, served its purpose. The number of refugees was reduced to a trickle. Windows and doors of apartment houses first were blocked with barbed wire and then bricked up to prevent their use to flee. In succeeding years the annual outflow would amount to 6,000 but decline to a few hundred by the 1980s.

The consequences of the Berlin Wall were many. It diffused the Berlin crisis. The Kennedy administration actually was relieved, and it is believed gave tacit approval for the wall. Yet the Soviet Union had challenged the Four Power Occupation Agreement and agreements at the YALTA and POTSDAM CONFERENCES; not challenging their actions was embarrassing for America. Another consequence affected both German states. For the East German regime their problem was temporarily solved, and it allowed the GDR to develop its economy and identity. For West Germany the question of German reunification had to be reconsidered, which led to the new OSTPOLITIK of Willy BRANDT. The suffering of the families separated by the wall is difficult to assess, but undoubtedly tragic. The significance of the wall for the survival of the GDR for

A demonstrator pounds away at the Berlin Wall as East Berlin border guards look on from above the Brandenburg Gate, November 11, 1989. *(Reuters/Landov)*

three decades is made clear when one realizes that the end of the regime began on the night of November 9, 1989, when the wall came tumbling down.

Bernstein, Eduard (1850–1932)
Revisionist socialist

Eduard Bernstein was born in BERLIN in 1850, the son of a poor Jewish locomotive engineer. Not finishing high school and not attending the university, he nevertheless was very intelligent and capable. He joined the SPD, helping to organize the Gotha Congress of 1875, and after leaving Germany due to the antisocialist laws he became the Zurich editor of the *Social Democrat (Der Sozialdemokrat)*, the party's main newspaper. Thereafter, he was deported to London, where he became a correspondent for the Berlin socialist party newspaper, *Vorwaerts*. He was closely associated with Friedrich ENGELS, the Fabian socialists in England, and Karl KAUTSKY.

Until 1878 he was a bank clerk for the Rothschild brothers in Berlin, where he learned about capitalism. While an exile in London, he had numerous occasions to learn about socialism from Friedrich Engels. Bernstein explained his revisionist position in his book *Evolutionary Socialism* (1899). With statistics Bernstein critiqued the premises of Karl MARX's prediction that capitalism was on the verge of imminent collapse and that there would be an inevitable transition to socialism. Instead of workers becoming poorer and poorer, he demonstrated that they actually were improving their standard of living. He searched for a workable solution to the tremendous social problems resulting from progressive industrialization. He did not seek to change middle-class society through revolution but to reform it very much like the Fabians in England. Revisionism was condemned by the SPD in 1903. The split in the party between the revolutionary and evolutionary wings lasted until after 1945, when many of Bernstein's arguments were incorporated into the party's program.

Bertram, Adolf (1859–1945)
bishop and cardinal

Adolf Bertram is primarily remembered as the leader of the German Bishops' Conference under the Nazi regime and for his policy of "petition politics" (*Eingabenpolitik*), which involved private protests instead of public resistance against the Nazi regime's persecution of the Catholic Church and treatment of the Jews.

Born in Hildesheim into a shopkeeper's family in 1859, Adolf Bertram was educated early in life for the priesthood. Growing up during the persecution of Catholics in Prussia at the time of the KULTURKAMPF, he had to attend the University of Würzburg in BAVARIA. He was ordained in 1881, received a doctorate in theology in 1883, and the next year a doctorate in canon law at Rome. He was assigned to administrative duties as a cathedral canon in 1894, vicar general in 1905, bishop of Hildesheim in 1906, and in 1914 an archbishop of the large Catholic community in BRESLAU. After the war he was named a cardinal in 1919.

Starting in 1920, this obedient and good administrator was appointed president of the German Bishops' Conference, which first only included the Fulda organization of bishops and in 1933 was enlarged by the addition of the Bavarian Bishops Conference. His efficient and moderate but not aggressive or prophetic leadership was acceptable during the peaceful years of the WEIMAR REPUBLIC, but under the Nazi dictatorship and the church-state treaty (1933) of the CONCORDAT these characteristics led to an unsuccessful resistance against Nazi persecution and the perpetration of the HOLOCAUST. It is assumed that the lessons Bertram learned during the Kulturkampf included the belief that massive resistance to the government would result in greater persecution and the deprivation of the ministry of the clergy for Catholics. For Bertram and the other bishops fear of persecution was reinforced by their moral obligation to obey lawful authority as long as it did not violate divine law. The obligation of obedience was reinforced by the loyalty to the state, which the Concordat required. This is not to say that all the bishops unanimously or enthusiastically supported Bertram's policy of "petition politics."

The reputation of the Catholic Church for its lack of protest against the treatment of deported Jews was permanently damaged. Cardinal Bertram was not convinced by the pleas of Cardinal Konrad Preysing for an outspoken protest. The mantle of authority in the Catholic hierarchical system rested, however, on the shoulders of this autocratic and mistrustful old prelate (age 79 in 1937), whose diplomatic style failed to protect not only Catholics of Jewish descent but even the church. Certainly the obligations of the Concordat reinforced Bertram's natural obedience and loyalty to authority. It can reasonably be argued that expressions of loyalty to a head of state were justified, as were Bertram's greetings on the occasion of Hitler's 50th birthday (April 20, 1939) used to remind him of complaints that Catholics had with the government. Nevertheless, what is less understandable occurred after Hitler's death, when the aged Bertram continued to express his loyalty and requested priests to offer solemn requiem masses in Hitler's memory.

Bertram was too old (83) in 1942 to continue his duties as conference president, so he resigned the position but had to continue bearing its responsibility when no replacement was found. Surviving the war, he died on July 6, 1945.

Bethmann Hollweg, Theobald von
(1856–1921)
statesman

As chancellor Theobald von Bethmann Hollweg was an important leader who led Germany into WORLD WAR I and helped conduct the war during its first three years. He was partially responsible for the development of the crisis that led to World War I and failed to prevent the establishment of a dictatorship by HINDENBURG and LUDENDORFF in 1916, which led to unlimited submarine warfare and Germany's defeat.

Theobald von Bethmann Hollweg was born on November 29, 1856, into a family of bankers and landowners in Hohenfinow, BRANDENBURG. Belonging to an aristocracy of officials, he was well educated in the humanities and then studied law at Strasbourg, LEIPZIG, and BERLIN. Moderately conservative, he served in a variety of civil service posts as senior president in Potsdam (1896), president of administration in Bromberg (1899), Prussian minister of the interior (1905), and state secretary in the Ministry of the Interior in 1907. After the fall of Bernard von BÜLOW in 1909, he was appointed Imperial chancellor. While in the Interior Ministry during 1911 he accomplished a comprehensive social insurance law and alienated conservatives with a liberal constitution for ALSACE-LORRAINE. He was not able, however, to change the minds of Prussia's upper class, which benefited from the unequal PRUSSIAN THREE CLASS VOTING SYSTEM.

At the time that Bethmann Hollweg became chancellor, Germany was beset by difficulties posed by Serbian nationalism in the Balkans, which affected its alliance with Austria-Hungary. Germany also was diplomatically isolated and worried about the growing strength of Russia. Worst of all, he could not stop Germany's naval arms race with Great Britain. The AGADIR crisis in 1911 convinced him that some accommodation with Great Britain was imperative. He could not, however, overcome the strident nationalism of the PAN-GERMAN LEAGUE and the NAVY LEAGUE. When the British war secretary, Richard Haldane, came to Germany in 1912, Bethmann Hollweg's attempt to be conciliatory was undermined by the insistence of Admiral Alfred von TIRPITZ on a new naval bill.

During the July crisis of 1914 that arose after the assassination of the archduke Francis Ferdinand by a Serbian terrorist, the emperor of Austria informed Kaiser WILLIAM II that Austria intended to demand satisfaction from the Serbian government. The Balkan situation had already hung heavily over the decisions of German policy makers in 1913 as has been recorded in the gloomy reflections of Bethmann. In July 1913 Count Berchtold had clearly emphasized that Austria required better support from its German ally against Serbian expansionism, which had Russian support. On July 6, 1914, the morning after the Austrian emperor's memorandum was discussed, Bethmann Hollweg issued the "blank check" to Austria with the assurance that Germany would support its ally whatever that would be. Bethmann hoped that if Germany acted vigorously in support of Austria, perhaps the Russians would hesitate to support the Serbs, and then the French and the British would also stop from entering the war. Things did not work out to fulfill the hopes of Bethmann's strategy. Actually, Bethmann was pessimistic about a successful outcome and called it a "leap in the dark." Perhaps it was his hope that a daring action would have a remedial effect on Germany's ills. But realities of human and institutional behavior got in the way. First the Austrians procrastinated with their ultimatum to the Serbs. Then the German military became nervous about mobilization timetables, which led to the German military's urging the Austrians into full mobilization against Russia. The Russians responded with their own full mobilization, which brought German mobilization and declarations of war against Russia and France. When Germany attacked France by way of neutral Belgium and Bethmann remarked that the guarantee of neutrality was just a "scrap of paper," Britain declared war against Germany.

It is true that once war broke out Bethmann followed a policy of moderation. He opposed the annexationists who advocated adding large territories to Germany. He rather preferred that areas such as Poland and Belgium be quietly dominated by Germany but not annexed. The chancellor also opposed the policy of unlimited submarine warfare, which he thought was bound to bring the United States into the war. As a rationalist he was, however, not so perceptive about personalities. The failure of General Erich von FALKENHAYN, the army chief of staff, to win a decisive victory at Verdun prompted him to promote the candidacy of the heroes of the eastern front, Paul von HINDENBURG and Erich LUDENDORFF, to take over the high command. They proceeded in establishing a military dictatorship, thwarted efforts by the Americans to effect a compromise peace in 1916, and insisted on unrestricted submarine warfare, which brought the United States into the war. Under pressure of these generals Bethmann Hollweg had to resign from office.

Bethmann Hollweg was a tragic figure in German politics; his policies were thwarted by people and events he could not control. The remainder of his life was spent at Hohenfinow, writing his memoirs. He died there on January 1, 1921.

Biedermeier (1815–1848)

The term *Biedermeier* was condescendingly applied to a cultural style that emphasized the parochial lives, and the complacent middle-class family culture and unpolitical attitudes in the states of the GERMAN CONFEDERATION during the Restoration between 1815 and 1848. The term *Biedermeier* was derived from the name of a fictitious comic poet, Gottlieb Biedermaier, who was satirized in the Munich humorous weekly *Fliegende Blätter*.

To begin with, Biedermeier was applied to the prevailing fashion of interior decoration and modes of dress. It reflected the homely frugality and limited possibilities of middle-class life during the restrictions of the Napoleonic period. The economic depression that followed the WARS OF LIBERATION also played its restrictive role as did other measures of the period of the Restoration. Soberness and simple comfort encouraged solid craftsmanship and harmonious design in home furnishings.

On a cultural level Biedermeier reflected a sentimentalism in literature, music, and art. Its most characteristic expression occurred in Vienna. Austrian culture had managed to incorporate baroque, romantic, and classical elements. The conservative romantics also had found a home in the culture of southern Germany. Classicism associated with Goethe moved away from the grandeur of the Weimar period into a middle-class soberness. The baroque also persisted in the theater and in the literature of Franz Grillparzer, who followed the models of Spanish dramatists of the Golden Age. Music also was part of the

Biedermeier style, moving into the middle-class home, which involved family participation. Its popularization was reflected in the works of Franz SCHUBERT, Johann STRAUSS, and Felix MENDELSSOHN. Landscape art was also popular, especially that of the great Otto Runge (1777–1810). Also Caspar David FRIEDRICH endowed romantic scenes with distant horizons and an unearthly glow. Finally, Ludwig Richter (1803–44) and Moritz von Schwind (1804–71) provided the chief illustrations of German domestic life, fairy tales, and legends.

Biermann, Wolf (1936–)
singer and songwriter

Wolf Biermann was an original lyric poet and songwriter in the GDR, who became a political dissident and celebrated case. The "Biermann affair," demonstrated how the Communist regime dealt with writers and artists who criticized it.

Born in 1936 in HAMBURG to a family that was persecuted by the Nazis and whose father was a Communist dockyard worker and resistance fighter killed at AUSCHWITZ, Wolf grew up in West Germany and at age 20 immigrated to East Germany in 1956. He studied at the Humboldt University, and between 1957 and 1959 participated in the theater group Berliner Ensemble. Later, he started his own Berliner Arbeitr- und Studententheater, which met with government disapproval and began his long negative relationship with the Communist regime. In 1962, because of a performance at the Academy of Arts, he was forbidden to perform publicly and his application for membership in the SED (Socialist Unity Party) was rejected. There was a temporary ban on his work until 1963, which was followed by a permanent ban in 1965. In 1964–65 he was allowed to perform in West Germany and had a collection of his songs and poems, *The Wire Harp*, published, which, however, led to a ban that lasted until 1976.

In 1976 the government allowed him to leave the GDR and perform in concert in West Germany. While there, his citizenship was canceled to prevent his return. This "Biermann affair" led to protests and an exodus of East German writers, which included artists such as Stefan HEYM and Christa WOLF. Biermann then settled in Hamburg, where his popularity declined. In the 1980s he supported the West German peace movement.

As a writer he was influenced by BRECHT and HEINE. His subject matter varies from political and social criticism to love poetry. In his music he employs a variety of instruments as a means of varying textual perspectives. His publications include *The Wire Harp* (1965), *With the Tongues of Marx and Engels* (1968), *Germany, A Winter Tale* (1972), and *Prussian Icarus* (1978).

Bismarck, Otto Eduard Leopold von (1815–1898)
statesman

One of Germany's most famous statesman, Otto von Bismarck was responsible for the unification of Germany by the creation of the Second German Empire in 1871. During his tenure as chancellor of the Reich he waged a cultural war (KULTURKAMPF) against Catholicism, opposed the rise of socialism, instituted state-sponsored social insurance, and protected Germany diplomatically through the Triple Alliance.

Otto von Bismarck was born on April 1, 1815, to Ferdinand Bismarck, a typical estate owner in Pomerania, and Wilhelmine Mencken, whose lineage included bureaucrats and professors. His mother was educated in the thinking of the English Utilitarians, French Positivists, and German LIBERALISM. On her insistence, the family moved to BERLIN, where he attended a gymnasium. He studied law at the University of GÖTTINGEN, Germany's seat of liberalism, and subsequently at Berlin. Not accepted for a position in the foreign ministry, he began a civil service career in the judiciary. His lifestyle was characterized by laziness, drinking, and atheism, his body afflicted by a number of diseases, and his personality probably neurotic. Developing a contemptuous attitude toward the bureaucracy, he left to manage the family estates from 1838 to 1847. In the process of reforming his life, by 1847 he had abandoned his skepticism, adopting Christian PIETISM, which stressed subjective religious experience, acquired a sense of mission, married Johanna von Puttkamer, and entered politics.

His opportunity to enter politics came when the king, FREDERICK WILLIAM IV, called for a meeting of the Prussian Diet to consider new taxes. Here he gained a reputation for himself as a staunch defender of conservatism against the liberal majority. During the REVOLUTION OF 1848 he helped plan its defeat. In 1851 he was rewarded with an appointment to the prestigious position of Prussian representative to the Diet of the GERMAN CONFEDERATION, where he obstructed AUSTRIA. Subsequently, he was appointed to a series of diplomatic posts at Vienna in 1854, at St. Petersburg in 1859, and briefly at Paris in 1861.

In 1862 the new king, WILLIAM I, faced a constitutional crisis over budgetary increases to pay for the expansion of the army and the increase of the length of compulsory service from two to three years. Since the Prussian parliament refused to support this policy, the king needed a strong minister-president who would stand up to the opposition. Believing that he was the right man for the job, Bismarck wrote to the minister of war, Albrecht von Roon, who invited him to come to Berlin and meet with the king. Received in audience with the despairing king, Bismarck offered to lead the fight against Parliament. According to Bismarck, the king appointed him "not as a constitutional minister in the usual sense of the word but as the servant of Your Majesty." Yet, the king was unenthusiastic about his choice of this wild, witty, and notoriously reactionary JUNKER, but felt that he had no alternative than "mad Bismarck" to teach the democratic opposition not to challenge the king's desires concerning his army. The new minister-president continued to run the government, collected taxes, and expanded the army against the will of Parliament, which continued to refuse to pass a budget. One of the most enduring images of Bismarck as the "blood and iron" minister who favored war over parliamentary speeches was created in 1863, not from a speech given in the Parliament, but from remarks made in a small budget committee.

Otto von Bismarck *(Library of Congress)*

Bismarck's character as a diplomat and his achievements are not easy to explain. He was impatient, arrogant, and inclined to bluff. Later in life, through his memoirs, speeches, and conversations he explained that he had foreseen and planned his successes. In reality he was a master at seizing opportunities as they came. In German affairs his goal was to gain parity for PRUSSIA with the Austrian Empire. Bismarck sought to isolate Austria by gaining the diplomatic support of Russia and France. The Crimean War (1854–56) had embittered relations between Austria and Russia, while Prussian neutrality ensured that Russia would not intervene in a German conflict. At the same time economic expansion had created increasing demand for national unity throughout the German states. Being a very astute diplomat, Bismarck liked to keep his options open and, during these years, followed a policy that favored unification within the GERMAN CONFEDERATION. Bismarck's opportunity to demonstrate his skills came with the complicated problems concerning Schleswig and Holstein. These German provinces were part of the Danish kingdom but had been promised in 1852 that they would be separate from the Danish state. In 1864, however, much like 1848, the Danish king absorbed Schleswig into Denmark. In response to an aroused German national feeling, the German Confederation decided to take action against Denmark. Although Bismarck secretly desired to incorporate the duchies into Prussia, by dealing with the problem as a violation of the Treaty of London (1852), he kept France and England out of the coming conflict. Austrian and Prussian troops attacked Schleswig, quickly defeated the Danes, and the Austrians and Prussians agreed to administer the duchies in the Bad Gastein Convention (August 1865).

There is little doubt that Bismarck intended to provoke a war with Austria. While criticizing Austria's administration of Holstein, Bismarck appealed to German liberal national sentiment, demanding that a parliament be elected for all of Germany by universal manhood suffrage in order to deal with this problem. In response, Austria mobilized the military forces of the Confederation against Prussia. Bismarck already had protected his flank through a secret treaty with Italy and had obtained a promise of neutrality from Napoleon III, suggesting territorial rewards along the RHINE. When the prewar crisis came to a head, the other German states in the Confederation sided with Austria. Bismarck responded that the Confederation was dissolved, and without a declaration of war invaded Bohemia, instigating the Austro-Prussian War (1866). What was expected to be a long-drawn-out conflict with an Austrian victory ended up being decided in only seven weeks with a crushing defeat of Austria at the BATTLE OF KÖNIGGRÄTZ (Sadowa). Bismarck convinced the Prussian king not to further humiliate the Austrians with a march to Vienna and to offer a lenient peace in the Treaty of Prague. Prussia now annexed Schleswig-Holstein, HANOVER, Hesse-Kassel, and the city of FRANKFURT. In the new NORTH GERMAN CONFEDERATION, Austria was excluded, an assembly was popularly elected, with the king of Prussia as its executive. A defensive alliance was also negotiated with BAVARIA, Württemberg, and Baden. Back in Berlin Bismarck's prestige soared and the liberals in Parliament actually retroactively approved his four years of unconstitutional government, which proved to be disastrous for the future of German liberalism. The Iron Chancellor also was granted funds to buy an estate in Pomerania.

Bismarck's diplomatic genius was again evident during the events leading up to the Franco-Prussian War (1870). Napoleon III became resentful when he failed to receive Belgium as a reward for his neutrality in 1866. The French were further antagonized over Bismarck's support of Leopold von Hohenzollern-Sigmaringen's claim of succession to the Spanish throne. The French ambassador was sent to discuss the problem with the Prussian king, who was on holiday at the resort of Bad Ems. The French demanded assurances that Leopold's candidacy would be permanently withdrawn, while the king declined to make such a commitment. Receiving a telegraph concerning what had occurred, Bismarck then attempted to embarrass the French by editing the famous EMS TELEGRAM. All the conciliatory phrases were left out before it was released to the press, which fomented volcanic eruptions of nationalism and prowar sentiment in both Paris and Berlin. According to Bismarck, he pushed both countries to the brink of war because it was an "unavoidable necessity," when he realized that France would never peacefully allow Germany to unite. It was, however, the French who first declared war on July 19, 1870. Six weeks later, they were quickly defeated when Napoleon III and his army surrendered at the Battle of Sedan on September 2,

1870. In Paris, however, a republic was declared, and the new government continued to resist the Germans. The Prussian victory led to the formation of a unified German Empire, including the South German states. ALSACE and LORRAINE were annexed, ensuring that the French would seek revenge in the future. In the Hall of Versailles the king of Prussia was proclaimed William I, German emperor. As a reward for this triumph Bismarck was granted the title of prince.

Bismarck remained chancellor of the German empire and prime minister in Prussia until 1890. The constitution, largely written by Bismarck, maximized his personal power on the federal level and weakened the possibility for the REICHSTAG and the political parties to challenge his authority. It combined conservative authoritarian political ideas with liberal economic precepts. The hereditary leadership of the Empire was vested in the Prussian king with the title of German emperor, who appointed the imperial officials, including the chancellor, directed foreign affairs, commanded the army, made war and peace, and initiated domestic legislation. Not only had Bismarck succeeded in creating an authoritarian emperor, but he had dangerously done so in what was to become the most powerful nation in Europe. Of crucial importance was the lack of ministerial responsibility over the army and foreign affairs. In the area of economic modernization Bismarck worked with the NATIONAL LIBERAL PARTY to transform Germany, despite the crash of 1873 and periods of depression and deflation through the next two decades. But Bismarck's other major internal policies were never so successful. His attempt to stop the Catholic CENTER PARTY and his struggle during the Kulturkampf with the Catholic Church was a failure. After 1878 his policies to suppress socialism were also unsuccessful, as the GERMAN SOCIAL DEMOCRATIC PARTY continued to increase its support among voters. To combat the threat of socialism, Bismarck sponsored the first comprehensive program of social insurance covering health, old age, and unemployment benefits.

Bismarck's diplomatic efforts after unification were directed at consolidating and protecting the German Empire, especially against French revenge. In 1872 he established the Three Emperors' League (1872–1878, 1881–1887). In 1879 he negotiated the Austro-German Dual Alliance and in 1882 the Triple Alliance with Austria and Italy. In 1887 the Russo-German Reinsurance was signed. In 1878 he presided over the CONGRESS OF BERLIN, which dealt with the issues of imperialism. In general his diplomatic skills helped Europe avoid a general war until 1914.

Bismarck continued in office after the death of WILLIAM I, through the unfortunately short reign of FREDERICK III (died June 15, 1888), and for almost two years for his son, WILLIAM II. Disagreeing with Bismarck's control of ministers and his Russian policy, William accepted the chancellor's resignation. Bismarck retired to his family estates, criticized his successors, and wrote his memoirs. He disavowed the policies of the emperor until his death on July 30, 1898.

blank check

The blank check was a promise of support by Emperor WILLIAM II for whatever the Austrians determined was necessary to punish Serbia for her involvement in the assassination of the archduke Francis-Ferdinand on June 28, 1914. When the Austrian delegation met with the Kaiser, no specific action was indicated, but military methods were not ruled out. Reflecting the unrestricted power of the Kaiser was the fact that he did not consult with either the military chief of staff or the chancellor, Theobald von BETHMANN HOLLWEG, who was only subsequently informed. Impulsively, William made a hasty decision, priding himself in his ability to reach quick and correct decisions. Balance-of-power considerations were also made as Austria was Germany's only remaining ally. Furthermore, both states were interested in curtailing Russian influence in the Balkans through her ally Serbia. Domestic politics also were involved in that William thought that winning a limited war would unite the German nation and deflect the demands for political modernization at home. He certainly did not contemplate starting a world war. William's blank check strengthened those in Austria who favored a preventive war against Serbia. At first a secret, the Austrians kept the information about issuing an ultimatum to Serbia until July 23. With the ultimatum the assassination at Sarajevo became an international crisis. Within two weeks Europe would be at war. The ultimatum placed 10 demands on Serbia, all of which were agreed to except one. The Austrians were determined to teach the Serbs a lesson and on July 28 Austria-Hungary declared war on Serbia.

Bleichröder, Gerson von (1822–1893)
banker

Gerson von Bleichröder, the head of a private bank, was one of the most successful of the German-Jewish bankers during the latter 19th century. At 49 he was Berlin's most renowned private banker. Not only was he Otto von Bismarck's private banker, he also advised the German government on government policy and diplomatic matters. His bank had interests all over the world. He had been present at the creation of the Empire in Versailles in 1871 and had gained the respect of other bankers and his fellow Jews.

Gerson was born to Jewish parents in BERLIN in 1822. Full emancipation had not yet taken place and would not until under Bismarck's government. Gerson was born into an oppressed social group popularly thought to be depraved. As a youth his life was circumscribed by his Jewish faith, filial piety, and hard work. The first Bleichröder to appear in the records was in the 18th century, a Gerson Jacob, born in the 1740s, who was allowed to reside in Berlin as a gravedigger for the Jewish community. He married the daughter of a protected Jew who performed services for the state. One of Gerson Jacob's sons, Samuel, was Gerson Bleichröder's father, who opened a money exchange office, and by the time Gerson was born became a merchant banker and late in the 1820s had established connections with the Rothschilds, who institutionalized international banking, and who raised Samuel and his son Gerson above most other Berlin bankers. Gerson entered the father's business in 1839, in 1847 he became a partner, and in 1855 head of the firm when his father died. He made a lot of money in the economic expansion of the 1850s, and by 1861 Bleichröder had purchased an impressive mansion in the heart of Berlin. His Jewishness, however, made him vulnerable as he moved in the world of German high society. He lacked many of the qualities that were valued in the gentile world around him.

Diplomacy was Bismarck's passion. With diplomacy and war Bismarck had built the Second Empire, but it took Bleichröder's advice and money. He helped finance the wars of unification, money that was needed because the Prussian Parliament had refused funding during the constitutional conflict over the reform of the army. He continued to provide funds for domestic and foreign policy initiatives. When asked about what size of indemnity should be imposed on the French in 1871, he actually suggested a figure below the 5 billion francs that was imposed and which was paid off too quickly As a Jewish banker Bleichröder was accused by the conservatives of controlling German policy. Influential but not controlling, Bleichröder's financial power supported Bismarck's antisocialist legislation, railway nationalization, protectionism, the campaign against the Liberals, and imperialism.

As with Bismarck, foreign affairs was Bleichröder's world, too, as he had interests in almost every country in the world. Foreign bankers needed his support, and he needed their business. His economic interests were connected with the political interests of Germany. As a banker Bleichröder was a man of peace, which he believed brought prosperity while war bred economic uncertainty. Information that he gained from his relationship with Bismarck and his connections with other bankers, especially the Rothschilds in Paris, provided Bleichröder with profits and honors. He was ambassador extraordinary in charge of relations with France. He had a major role in loans to Russia, was the "czar's banker" and interceded for Russian Jews who were being seriously persecuted. His position in high political circles in Germany made him disliked, while anti-Semites slandered him.

Blenheim, Battle of (1704)

The Battle of Blenheim is known in German history as the Second Battle of Hochstädt, which occurred in August 1704. The commander of the imperial forces was EUGENE, PRINCE OF SAVOY (1663–1736), who was assisted by English forces under the command of John Churchill, duke of Marlborough. The combined forces defeated the Franco-Bavarian army near Hochstädt, BAVARIA, and forced the Bavarian elector, Max Emanuel (1679–1726), to withdraw from the war. Germany was liberated from the French.

During the first battle of Hochstädt in 1703 Max Emanuel had defeated the imperial armies of AUSTRIA and was able to occupy the whole Danube line as far as REGENSBURG and Passau. Louis XIV then sent his main forces to Bavaria, which Prince Eugene had attempted to stop from crossing the Black Forest and joining up with the Franco-Bavarian army under Max Emanuel. The HOLY ROMAN EMPIRE now was threatened by the Franco-Bavarian army as also was Vienna. Emperor LEOPOLD I (1658–1705) then requested the aid of his allies, England and the United Provinces. The war in Germany was popular neither in England nor the United Provinces, but the duke of Marlborough received permission to march his troops to the Danube and met up with the imperial armies under the command of Prince Eugene of Savoy and the Prince of Baden. The cooperation that ensued between Marlborough and Prince Eugene was rare. Marlborough and Prince Louis defeated the Bavarian army at Donäuworth. Then, with 55,000 men Marlborough and Prince Eugene defeated the Franco-Bavarian army at Hochstädt. It was primarily a victory for Marlborough as he routed the French forces of Marshal Tallard while the rest of the Franco-Bavarian forces retreated. The French were pushed beyond the Rhine. The battle produced the greatest number of casualties of the war, killing or wounding about 12,000 on either side. It was the first in a series of military reverses for Louis XIV. Other consequences were that it liberated all of Germany, lifting the morale of the German princes. The Habsburgs were able to continue the war, while Bavaria was forced out. The Austrians now came to administer Bavaria and treated it like a conquered state.

blitzkrieg

This strategy of warfare was first formulated by General Hans von Seeckt (1886–1936), commander of the Reichswehr during the WEIMAR REPUBLIC. Its basic premise was that rapidly advancing armored forces operating on their own could swiftly envelop the enemy and bring about a quick victory. Seeckt foresaw that this use of armored forces would create mass armies. When the German armies overran Poland and then France, the Netherlands, and Norway, the term came to mean the use of air power, armored forces, subversive warfare, and sometimes the use of airborne troops to quickly overwhelm the enemy. This worked in France but not in Russia, where logistics were unable to keep up with the armies.

Blomberg, Werner von (1878–1946)
minister of defense

Werner von Blomberg served at the request of President Paul von HINDENBURG as minister of defense and supreme commander of the armed forces from 1933 to 1938. He ardently supported HITLER's rearmament program. His presence was imposing, and he was the epitome of the Prussian officer, "a Siegfried with a monocle."

Blomberg was born in Stargard, Pomerania, on September 2, 1878. His military career began in 1897, and by the time WORLD WAR I occurred he had risen to become an officer on the General Staff. After the war he entered the republican army, the Reichswehr, and from 1927 to 1929 he was adjutant general of the Reichswehr. He visited Russia and was favorably impressed by the Soviet army. In 1930 he was placed in command of Defense District I at Königsberg, where on a visit he met and was impressed by Hitler and hoped that he would eventually make the Reichswehr a popular army. Although not a convinced Nazi he was loyal to Hitler and shouldered responsibility for the military buildup in the Third Reich. At first he was named minister of defense on January 1, 1933; then he called on the army to take a personal oath to Hitler after the death of Hindenburg; and in May 1935 he was named supreme commander of the new army, the Wehrmacht. He was one of the most important officers present at an important conference of senior officers on November 5, 1937, during which Hitler announced his plans for another war to achieve living space (LEBENSRAUM) by force. Minutes of the meeting were recorded by General Friedrich Hossbach which came to be known as the HOSSBACH MEMORANDUM. Both Blomberg and Col. General Baron von Fritsch, who was commander in chief of the army, opposed Hitler's plans. This made their futures highly questionable as events were soon to prove.

Now the needs of Blomberg's personal life intersected with the intrigues of the Nazi regime and destroyed his career. He had been a widower, and at the end of 1937 decided to marry his secretary, a Fräulein Eva Gruhn, who had a past as a prostitute. He should have known better, because such a marriage was not socially respectable for the commanding general of the officer corps. To make matters worse, Hitler and GÖRING were witnesses at the wedding. Meanwhile the chief of the Berlin police had been collecting a dossier on Eva, went to Göring, who went to Hitler, who became angered and dismissed Blomberg. Fritsch was also forced to retire when unproven allegations arose that he had committed homosexual acts. Although exonerated, he was forced to resign. The end result of the scandals was that Hitler used them to make himself the supreme commander of the armed forces. Blomberg's humiliation, however, did not dampen his admiration for the Führer as it should have. He supported Hitler to the end of the regime. After the war he was arrested and testified before the Nuremberg Military Tribunal (*see* NUREMBURG TRIALS) and died from illness in prison on March 22, 1946.

Blücher, Gebhard Leberecht von (1742–1819)
military leader

A Prussian field marshal, Gebhard von Blücher commanded the Prussian armies against the French during the latter Napoleonic wars. He was born in Rostock in the northern state of Mecklenburg on December 16, 1742, the son of a captain in the cavalry. He became an officer in the Swedish Cavalry during the SEVEN YEARS' WAR, but then entered the Prussian service and became a captain in a hussar regiment. In 1770 he incurred the displeasure of FREDERICK THE GREAT and was brutally dismissed. In 1787 he returned to the army under FREDERICK WILLIAM II and distinguished himself during the French Revolutionary Wars in 1793–94. He rose rapidly to a general's rank.

When Napoleon defeated Prussia in 1806, Blücher continued to resist even after the fall of BERLIN. His anti-French views led to his removal from command in 1811. He played a prominent part in the 1813 campaign, gaining a decisive victory on the Katzbach in Silesia and in the fighting at LEIPZIG. During this campaign he was made a marshal. In 1814 he led the Prussian troops in France and entered Paris. Recalled upon Napoleon's return from Elba, Blücher was given command of the Army of the Lower Rhine. He was wounded at Ligny, but two days later arrived with reinforcements in time to outflank the right of the French position at Waterloo at a decisive point in the battle.

Böll, Heinrich (1917–1985)
novelist and Nobel Prize winner

Heinrich Böll was one of West Germany's most popular and prolific authors. His short stories, novels, and lectures criticized German society from the Nazi period through the ECONOMIC MIRACLE and into the 1980s. He was a member of Group 47 along with others, such as GÜNTER GRASS. Böll's novels have a strong ethical perspective stemming from his personal philosophy of Christian Humanism and sympathy for the downtrodden. His central themes are the complicated responses of the German people to the Nazis and the war, the role of Catholicism in society, and the corrupting influence of the prosperity and consumerism of the postwar economy. He did not shun controversy. His criticisms of the Catholic Church included the papal encyclical *Humanae Vitae*. In politics he opposed the decision of the SOCIAL DEMOCRATIC PARTY to join the CHRISTIAN DEMOCRATS in the Grand Coalition in 1965. He denounced the materialistic attitudes of the German people and nuclear armament. His militant political activism irritated his contemporaries, but he was also an ally to dissidents in Eastern Europe, enabling the Russian novelist Alexander Solzhenitsyn to emigrate from the Soviet Union. In 1972 Böll was awarded the Nobel Prize in Literature.

Born in Cologne to a father who was a humble joiner, Böll was apprenticed to a bookseller and completed only one semester at Cologne University. His parents were devout Catholics but liberal, which perhaps influenced his embrace of humanistic ideals early in life. He refused to join the HITLER YOUTH, but was drafted into the army in 1939, was wounded four times, and returned to Cologne after the war.

Böll's early works focus on the impact of Nazi rule on ordinary people. His first novel, *The Train Was on Time* (1949), emphasized the stupidity of the war on the Russian front. In *Adam, Where Wert Thou?* (1951) he reacted to the horror of war with anger and condemnation in a story about the retreating German army. In the 1950s he wrote about the miseries of the postwar period in *Acquainted with the Night* (1953), *The Unguarded House* (1954), and *The Bread of Early Years* (1955). In *The Valley of the Thundering Hoofs* (1957) several young people find the enjoyment of the prosperity of their parents distasteful. One of his most famous novels, which climaxed his work in the 1950s, was *Billiards at Half-Past Nine* (1959), which provoked criticism from the church, the CDU, and others. It is a complicated novel, spanning three generations and the two world wars. It focuses on one family and probes the guilt of the Nazi past through reflections and flashbacks.

His disillusionment with postwar Germany and disapproval of the postwar German state and the church again appears in *Views of a Clown* (1963) through the story of a frustrated performer who exposes the hypocrisy of his own family and of society. *Group Portrait with Lady* (1971), Böll's longest novel, is more complex and is structured like a biography based on accounts of the friends of the protagonist. *The Lost Honor of Katharina Blum* (1974) is an indictment of journalistic and judicial malpractice and escalating violence in society. Böll attacked the journalism of the Bildzeitung of the Axel Springer press empire and its coverage of the urban terrorism of the BAADER-MEINHOF GROUP.

Compared to Ernest Hemingway, literary critics have described Böll's prose as concise, direct, and in a simple way unlike formal classical German literature, able to communicate both feeling and ideas. His extensive writings are often sentimental and idealistic, often polemical, but also are a critical commentary of West Germany since the war. The political content of his novels has been more often the subject of criticism, however, than his literary merits.

Bonhoeffer, Dietrich (1906–1945)
Protestant theologian

Dietrich Bonhoeffer was the most famous Protestant theologian executed by the Nazis because of his association in the German resistance to HITLER. His theology of Christ in community has influenced postwar Christian theology.

He was born in BRESLAU into a family of intellectuals, his father a psychiatrist. Dietrich studied theology under Karl Barth and taught at the University of Berlin. He was influenced by his stay in the period 1930–31 in the United States at the Union Theological Seminary, where he became interested in the example of Gandhi. Bonhoeffer sought support from international Christian leaders for the German Christians who were opposed to the Nazi control of the Protestant churches. Recognizing the evil in Nazism, Bonhoeffer organized the Pastor's Emergency League, which became the nucleus of the CONFESSING CHURCH. In 1935 he founded a clandestine seminary to train pastors for the illegal anti-Nazi church. Out of his experiences at the seminary in Finkenwalde he wrote *The Cost of Discipleship* (1937) based on Christ's Sermon on the Mount and *Life Together* (1939) on the nature of Christian community.

Bonhoeffer sought support for the anti-Nazi opposition from Bishop Bell of Sweden. He also joined the resistance movement and worked for Germany's defeat, becoming convinced that Germany deserved to suffer a harsh peace in order to atone for the crimes of Hitler's aggression and racial oppression. As a result of his activities he was arrested in 1943 by the GESTAPO, and after the assassination and coup attempt of July 20, 1944, failed, he was executed by hanging on April 9, 1945, in the Flossenburg concentration camp. While in prison he had smuggled out letters and papers that later were published as *Letters and Papers from Prison* (1972). The papers included reflections on the role of the church in politics. Bonhoeffer believed that Christians should not be narrowly religious but should be involved as disciples in the secular world.

Bonn

In 1949 Bonn became the provisional capital of the new FEDERAL REPUBLIC, which continued until it was decided in 1991 to reestablish Germany's permanent capital in BERLIN.

Bonn was first founded as one of the earliest Roman fortresses along the RHINE and then one of the first German cities. During the High Middle Ages it became the seat of the archbishop of Cologne from 1238 to 1794. One of the finest Romanesque churches in the Rhineland, Saints Cassius and Florentinus was built there during the Middle Ages. In the 18th century Ludwig van BEETHOVEN was born there in 1770. Under the youngest son of MARIA THERESA, Maximilian Francis, the elector-archbishop in 1784, the academy in Bonn was changed into a university, where members of the clergy were required to study. After the CONGRESS OF VIENNA when Bonn became part of PRUSSIA the university was refounded in 1818. Part of the university was housed in a baroque residence and in the Poppelsdorfer Palace. The city hall was built in the ROCOCO style and was residence for the electors from Cologne.

After the end of WORLD WAR II the American military established its regional headquarters on one of the hills (the Petersberg) outside of Bonn, which was one of the reasons that the West German capital was located there. Besides, it also was near the home of Chancellor Konrad ADENAUER. Also, the city was located in the more liberal and westward area of Germany, symbolizing the new Federal Republic's liberal orientation. The city grew from some 30,000 inhabitants in 1948 to 300,000 in 1990. Although initially the city had inadequate facilities to accommodate the growing state administration, improvements were made in the 1960s and 1970s. More than 100 foreign embassies were built, political parties got new headquarters, the Bundestag and Chancellery received new buildings, and Bonn took on the appearance of a permanent capital. After reunification occurred, the location of Germany's capital was seriously debated in 1991, and Berlin became the choice for a new reunified nation.

Bormann, Martin (1900–1945)

secretary to Hitler and director of the Nazi Party Chancellery

Martin Bormann was born in Halberstadt, worked on a farm, served in the artillery during WORLD WAR I and after the war joined the FREE CORPS. In 1923 Bormann was arrested for a political murder, and after release from prison joined the Nazi Party in 1927. He held posts of Nazi press officer in Thuringia in 1926, was made deputy leader of the Storm Troops (SA) and director of the party's insurance plan. In 1933 he was appointed as chief of staff to Rudolf Höss and became a member of the REICHSTAG. Both Höss and Bormann worked behind the scenes, formulating the laws and decrees promulgated by the regime. Bormann was an obsessive power seeker and brought himself to HITLER's attention by administering the construction of Adolf Hitler's BERGHOF retreat in Berchtesgaden. Also a good manager of finances, he was placed in charge of the income Hitler received from the sale of his publications, especially *Mein Kampf.*

After Rudolf Höss (deputy leader of the Nazi Party) flew to Great Britain in 1941, Bormann succeeded him at the post of director of the Party Chancellery. This gave him authority over the regional party leaders (Gauleiters) and senior party officials, and he related to them brusquely and harshly. As Hitler's personal aide and confidant he was able to control access to Hitler, which other party leaders strongly resented. Bormann had a great influence on decision making during the later years of the Third Reich. Bormann was one of the more radical Nazis and pressed for greater action against the churches, advocated extreme measures against the Jews, and had a role in looting artistic and cultural properties in eastern Europe and expanding the German slave labor program. After Hitler's suicide on April 30, 1945, Bormann fled the Berlin bunker. Bormann was indicted and later found guilty of war crimes and was sentenced to death by the International Military Tribunal at the NUREMBERG TRIALS on October 1, 1946.

Born, Max (1882–1970)
physicist

Max Born made a great contribution to modern physics concerning the basic laws of quantum mechanics. He gave a basic foundation to the work of Wolfgang Pauli, Werner HEISENBERG, and Erwin Schrödinger, showing the probabilistic nature of quantum mechanics allowing a statistical interpretation on the atomic level.

Born in BRESLAU in 1882, Born pursued his university studies at a time marked by radical changes in the fields of physics and mathematics. In 1912 he visited the United States, giving a lecture on relativity at the University of Chicago. Born was friends with Albert EINSTEIN and at one time took over the teaching responsibilities at the University of BERLIN. At the University of GÖTTINGEN, Born worked with a group of associates, which included Heisenberg, Enrico Fermi, Pascual Jordan, and Robert Oppenheimer, who would ultimately become the most prominent physicists of the 20th century. In the area of quantum mechanics, which seeks to understand the behavior of particles inside atoms, the theories of classical physics were inapplicable. Following his appointment at the University of Göttingen, Born developed a theory for understanding these elementary properties of matter.

In lectures and books Born elaborated his ideas. Perhaps the first book on quantum mechanics was a collection of his lectures, *Problems of Atomic Dynamics.* Two books that became classics were *The Atomic Theory* (1935) and *The Restless Universe* (1936). He also published a textbook on optics and a book on philosophy, *Natural Philosophy of Cause and Chance.*

Like so many other scientists Born left Germany when the National Socialists came to power. He immigrated to England, while Fermi and Oppenheimer went to the United States. Born returned to Germany after the war. In 1954 he belatedly was awarded the Nobel Prize for his scientific achievements. He was concerned with the role of science in human culture and was not very optimistic about the future. He died in Göttingen in 1970.

Borsig, August (1804–1854)
industrialist

August Borsig was one of Germany's leading innovators, along with Friedrich Harkort in the machine industry. He started the first German locomotive factory and along with other manufacturers succeeded in eliminating English competition in locomotives in the expanding German railway system.

Born into a lower-class artisan family, August Borsig learned to be a master mechanic. He had attended the Gewerbe Institut, through which the Prussian government was attempting to stimulate industrial development. Borsig received subsidies from the Prussian government and in 1837 was able to establish his business as a machine maker in BERLIN, employing 50 men, which during the next decade expanded to around 1,200. At first he supplied steam engines for sugar beet refineries. Within four years after opening his factory he produced his first locomotive, based on an American model. He began to compete with English manufacturers of locomotives, and by 1848 he was almost able to supply the whole demand of the Prussian railroads. By 1854 his company had produced 500 locomotives.

To place Borsig's accomplishment in some perspective it is helpful to look at other factories opened during this period. About this time Josef Anton Maffei opened his machine works in MUNICH and began producing locomotives as did Emil Kessler in Karlsruhe and Esslingen. In Kassel the Henschel works produced their first engine, the Dragon, in 1848. By the middle of the next decade German manufacturers began to export their locomotives. In Ruhrort in the Rhineland the firm of Haniel, Huyssen and Jacobi operated a big engineering works that operated according to model English methods. Among other things, they built river steamboats. The firm also controlled large ironworks at Sterkerade and Oberhausen. At Oberhausen the firm employed more than 1,000 workers (many of whom were peasant, landowning wage-earners) and used Nasmyth's steam hammer imported from England. Another important example occurred in Essen, where KRUPP and Co. produced such high-quality steel that it could be sold as English. Werner Siemens also laid the foundation for his industrial enterprise during the 1840s. He was an enthusiastic innovator who on borrowed money started a firm to manufacture telegraph apparatus.

Bosch, Robert (1861–1942)
industrialist

Robert Bosch was the founder of the Robert Bosch GmbH Corporation, which became a leading producer of automotive technology and a variety of other products. He contributed substantially to the expansion of the automobile industry.

Born on September 23, 1861, near Ulm in Württemberg, Robert Bosch received his education at the Technical University at Stuttgart. He also was trained in mechanics as an apprentice in Ulm and as a journeyman in Great Britain and the United States. At age 25 he opened his own company, Workshop for Precision Mechanics and Electrical Engineering. In 1887 his first invention was a magneto for gas engines, which appeared in an automobile engine a decade later. Among other inventions that improved the operation of automobiles was his spark plug. His ambition and talent as an industrialist motivated him to expand, adding new products and thousands of workers by the eve of the world war. His company made a great deal of profits from the war, but because he abhorred profiteering from war, he donated 10 million marks back to the German people. Like other companies after the war Bosch industries were hurt through the constriction of the economy. In 1927, however, he diversified and expanded again into the production of power tools, and other products such as cameras, radios, refrigerators, and television sets.

Bosch was concerned for the welfare of his workers and for the improvement of society. Even before the eight-hour day was widespread during the WEIMAR REPUBLIC, he already had introduced it in his company in 1906. Between the wars he made efforts to bring understanding between the German and French people. Bosch opposed the Nazi regime, supported the RESISTANCE, and aided Jews and other persecuted people. In 1964 the Robert Bosch Foundation was established.

Bosnia-Herzegovina

Bosnia-Herzegovina is the Balkan region where Archduke Francis Ferdinand was assassinated, which precipitated the Bosnian crisis and led to WORLD WAR I.

Bosnia-Herzegovina was occupied by the Turks in the 15th century. In the 1870s nationalistic agitation created enthusiasm for union with their fellow Serbians, and in 1875 there was an uprising that the Turks cruelly suppressed. At the CONGRESS OF BERLIN of 1878 Austria-Hungary was given the right to administer the provinces, although they remained part of the Turkish Empire. The Austrians, however, developed Bosnia and treated the provinces as colonies. The emergence of the Young Turk movement around the turn of the 20th century threatened Austrian rule, which led them to annex the provinces in October 1908. The annexation and the increase in Austrian power in the Balkans precipitated the Bosnian crisis. Although the Russian foreign minister, Izvolsky, had approved the annexation in advance with the understanding that the Russians would win free access to the Straits of the Dardanelles, the deal was cancelled by Izvolsky, who was now under pressures from his ministerial colleagues and the Pan-Slav movement. To make matters worse, he demanded that the Austrians be taken before an international conference for their violation of the Treaty of Berlin. In the settlement of the conflict Austria's ally, Germany, took a menacing attitude, which forced Russia resentfully to accept the annexation (March 1909). As a result, a considerable animosity was created, which inspired the Russians to support the Serbians against Austria. The Serbians living in Bosnia began a terrorist agitation against Austrian rule, which culminated in the 1914 assassination of Archduke Francis Ferdinand and his wife on a state visit in Sarajevo, which led to the world war.

Brahms, Johannes (1833–1897)
pianist and composer

Johannes Brahms joined Ludwig van BEETHOVEN (1770–1827) as one of the greatest symphonic composers of the 19th century. His position is midway between the classic tradition, which imitated Felix MENDELSSOHN (1809–47) and the futurists, Franz LISZT (1811–86) and Richard WAGNER (1813–83). Seeing himself as belonging to the mainstream of the German symphonic tradition and infusing it with romantic melodies, he expanded Beethoven's method of composing by motifs. The music he created marks one of the high points of the romantic period.

Brahms was born in HAMBURG on May 7, 1833, the son of an innkeeper who also had musical talent and was the first teacher of his son. He began his study of the piano at seven, learned theory and composition, and in order to help with family finances, played at lower-class dance halls and sailor's haunts, which proved to be harmful to his health at age 14. At this young age he also performed some concerts.

His acquaintance with the Hungarian violinist Eduard Reményi introduced him to the gypsy music that influenced many of his mature compositions. He visited with Franz Liszt in WEIMAR. A turning point in Brahms's life came in 1853, when he was introduced to Robert and Clara SCHUMANN in DÜSSELDORF, both of whom became his enthusiastic supporters and closest friends. Robert Schumann arranged for the first publication of one of Brahms's works, and in 1854 Brahms honored Schumann with his composition *Variations on a Theme of Schumann.* Sadly, Schumann died later that year, and Brahms looked after his widow but fell in love with her, an unrequited love that, however, ended in a friendship. During the latter fifties he completed his First Piano Concerto, which he had begun at the time he met the Schumanns. When his mother fell ill and died in 1865, he composed the famous *German Requiem* in her memory, which was published in 1869, the year after he moved to Vienna. During the later 1860s he published *Variations on a Theme of Paganini* Then he responded patriotically to the German victory in the Franco-Prussian War by composing the "Song of Triumph" (*"Triumphlied"*) in 1871.

The phase of his life during which he composed his symphonies occurred in the 1870s. Brahms finally completed the First Symphony at the encouragement of Clara Schumann, which he had worked on for 20 years. The Second Symphony and the brilliantly melodic Violin Concerto were completed during summers spent in the Austrian countryside in Carinthia. The University of Breslau conferred on Brahms an honorary doctorate, for which in appreciation he composed the Academic Festival Overture. In 1881 he completed the Second Piano Concerto in B-flat, which expressed great power and vitality. That same year Hans von Bülow, the conductor of the Meiningen Court Orchestra, gave Brahms the opportunity to try out his new works, the Third and Fourth Symphonies. Before his death on April 3, 1897, due to liver cancer, Brahms also composed many songs, as well as piano and chamber music.

Brandenburg

Brandenburg was an electorate of the HOLY ROMAN EMPIRE and was the territorial base of the HOHENZOLLERNS. It was merged with PRUSSIA in 1701. After WORLD WAR II it was a state of the GDR, but was dissolved in 1952, and since reunification is one of the new federal states.

Beginning in 1157 Albert I the Bear called himself the margrave of Brandenburg. In 1237 the city of BERLIN was founded. In 1415 Frederick VI Hohenzollern was given the hereditary possession of the Mark Brandenburg. FREDERICK WILLIAM, the Great Elector, margrave of Brandenburg, after having freed East Prussia from Polish overlordship in the course of the THIRTY YEARS' WAR acquired eastern Pomerania and some other territories in the Treaty of Westphalia (1648). By inheritance in

The Brandenburg Gate, Berlin, 1946 *(Library of Congress)*

1614 the three small duchies of Cleves, Mark, and Ravensberg on the lower RHINE had also become part of Brandenburg Prussia. In 1688 his son Frederick (1657–1713) succeeded the Great Elector to the electorate (1688) as Frederick III. In 1701 Frederick III was crowned Frederick I, king of Prussia, merging Brandenburg with Prussia. It was a province of Prussia from 1815 until 1945. After World War II Brandenburg lost the region east of the Oder.

During IMPERIAL GERMANY Brandenburg industrialized, mainly in the Berlin area. In the administrative district of Potsdam the population tripled. Politically, the SOCIAL DEMOCRATIC PARTY obtained 54 percent of the vote in 1912, and during the WEIMAR REPUBLIC the representation of workers' parties remained above average. Under the Nazis Brandenburg became one of the centers of arms production. After the war in the GDR steel and rolling mills, machine and vehicle construction and chemical plants were built. With reunification the entire industrial base of Brandenburg went into crisis, creating about 15 percent unemployment.

With reunification Brandenburg became one of the new federal states and possessed a small population of 2.65 million. The state surrounds Berlin and is subdivided into administrative districts. In June 1995 the Berlin House of Representatives and Brandenburg State Parliament approved the state treaty on the merger of the two states around the turn of the millennium. In the referendum held on May 5, 1996, however, the voters of Brandenburg turned down the merger. With its economic difficulties the successor to the SED, the PARTY OF DEMOCRATIC SOCIALISM, increased its vote from 13.4 percent of the vote to 18.7 percent in 1994, when its support equaled that of the CHRISTIAN DEMOCRATIC UNION. The elections of 1999 saw a sharp increase in support for the radical right and the election of five members for the German People's Union (Volksunion).

Brandt, Willy (1913–1992)
first Socialist chancellor of the Federal Republic
Willy Brandt, a Social Democratic chancellor, was one of the eminent statesmen who shaped Germany's postwar history. He was born with the name Herbert Frahm in the North Sea port of Lübeck on December 18, 1913, the illegitimate son of working-class parents. Only later when the Nazis came to power in 1933 did he change his name to Willy Brandt. Early on he found fellowship in the youth organizations of the SOCIAL DEMOCRATIC PARTY (SPD). He graduated from the Lübeck *Gymnasium* in 1932. Fortunately, he escaped capture by the secret police and confinement in a concentration camp, which happened to so many other socialists, by fleeing first to Norway and then in 1940 to neutral Sweden. Throughout his exile he worked as a journalist and finally returned to Germany at the end of the war to cover the NUREMBERG TRIALS. In 1949 he succeeded in being elected SPD representative from Berlin in the new West German BUNDESTAG. In 1957 he became the mayor of West Berlin. He became internationally famous in resisting Soviet and East German pressures on the city. During the Berlin crisis of 1961 he was forced to witness the city's partition when the BERLIN WALL was erected in 1961.

Meanwhile the Social Democratic Party was seeking ways it could attract more moderate voters and enhance its chances to become the majority party. Although the SPD had long ceased to favor revolutionary change, it decided to change its official Marxist program in 1959 at the Bad Godesburg Convention. A new program was approved, which abandoned Marxist determinism and affirmed the religious and philosophical roots of democratic socialism and the parliamentary system. The program also supported the idea of free competition and modified its demand for nationalization of the economy. Brandt now became an attractive and youthful candidate for the leadership of the party and became the party's candidate for chancellor in 1961, 1965, and 1969. In 1966 the SPD entered the "grand coalition" with the CHRISTIAN DEMOCRATIC UNION (CDU), and Brandt became foreign minister. In the 1969 elections Brandt won the chancellorship. Domestically, he initiated many reforms in education and the economy. Not abandoning Germany's commitment to Western European economic integration that Konrad ADENAUER had begun, Brandt initiated a policy of improved relations with East Germany, East European Communist countries, and the Soviet Union, called OSTPOLITIK. Treaties on the renunciation of force were concluded with Moscow and Warsaw, and the Quadripartite Agreement on Berlin was signed. Brandt relaxed tensions between the two Germanys, so that both were able to enter the United Nations and Germans able to cross borders. It also led to his reception of the Nobel Peace Prize in 1971 for his efforts to promote international understanding. A scandal concerning an East German spy, Günter Guillaume, led to his resignation.

Besides chairing the SPD until 1987, Brandt also became president of the Socialist International, which was a general organization of all Social Democratic Parties. He also chaired the Brandt Commission, which advocated the more equitable distribution of the world's wealth. Brandt prepared the way for the reunification of Germany in 1989, an event that occurred much sooner than he had anticipated.

Brauchitsch, Walther von (1881–1948)
commander in chief of the Wehrmacht

From 1938 to 1941 Walther von Brauchitsch was the commander in chief of the Wehrmacht. He was the commander during the campaigns against Poland, France, Yugoslavia, Greece, and the Soviet Union.

Brauchitsch was born in BERLIN on October 4, 1881. He joined the army, was commissioned a lieutenant in 1900, and had his first command as an artillery officer and later a staff officer during WORLD WAR I. Afterward he served as a training officer and also as an inspector of the artillery. Under HITLER he was named commander of a miliary district in East Prussia and in 1937 he took over the 4th Army Group at LEIPZIG. After General von Fritsch was forced to resign due to allegations of homosexuality, Hitler appointed Brauchitsch commander in chief of the army.

Brauchitsch was a compliant follower of Hitler. His position was complicated as he found himself bound by his oath to Hitler and his belief in the rule of law. General Ludwig BECK of the RESISTANCE appealed to him a number of times to join in stopping Hitler, but he hesitated for personal reasons. His second wife, who was a fanatic Hitler admirer, urged him to support the Führer. On the other hand, if Brauchitsch had supported Beck and his fellow conspirators in 1938, Czechoslovakia might have been saved and the road to WORLD WAR II avoided. Brauchitsch was overwhelmed by Hitler's fits of rage and continued to resist Beck's pleas. As a consequence, Beck resigned.

The campaigns against Poland and France were well planned, and Brauchitsch became more subservient to Hitler and less willing to support any conspiracy. On July 19, 1940, he was promoted to field marshal. He executed the initial phases of the campaign in Russia until December 1941, when German forces failed to capture Moscow. Brauchitsch recommended to Hitler that the army withdraw to a defensive line. It was at this point that Hitler relieved him of his command. The excuse for his retirement was that he was gravely ill. Hitler, in fact, held his army commander in chief responsible for the military failure in Russia. That Hitler also sacked the commanders of two army groups and four armies and then assumed command of the army himself makes it highly unlikely that illness was the cause of Brauchitsch's retirement. Although he remained on active duty, he was not assigned any duties for the duration of the war. Suffering from cardiac disease at the end of the war, he was arrested by the British and died in a military hospital on October 18, 1948, before his trial for war crimes.

Braun, Eva (1912–1945)
Hitler's mistress

Eva Braun, a photographer's assistant, became Adolf HITLER's mistress after 1931 and his wife on April 29, 1945, one day before their suicide.

Born in MUNICH into a middle-class teacher's family, Eva Braun became a photographer's assistant in the studio of Heinrich Hoffman. Hoffman happened to be Hitler's photographer and introduced the young woman to him. She was pretty in appearance, tall and slim with a good figure probably due to her interest in swimming, skiing, gymnastics, and mountain climbing. She also had professionally studied dancing. She fit into what Hitler expected from women—besides being attractive, she was shy and not opinionated about politics, she read novels and watched motion pictures, and she was especially attentive to and not interfering with his work. Hitler loved to be around beautiful women, but feared being controlled by petticoat politics. Not that beauty and intelligence could not coexist in the same woman, but Hitler was quoted as saying that intelligent men ought to have women who were primitive and stupid. Interestingly, he rejected striking blondes with Nordic features. Hitler was protective of Eva and solicitous of her well-being and health. Incidentally, he also made her a wealthy woman.

Eva Braun fit in well with Hitler's associates. At first she lived in his apartment in Munich and later moved to the BERGHOF, Hitler's estate and chalet on the Obersalzberg above Berchtesgaden. Outside of socializing with his associates, she kept pretty much in the background. He had limited time to give her, especially during the war when he was away at his military headquarters. Suffering from neglect, she brooded but did not complain. The servants were forbidden to talk to her, and when Hitler entertained important guests she had to remain in her rooms. To occupy herself, she read, exercised, and wrote letters and diaries. Yet that did not relieve her melancholy, so she attempted suicide several times. Near the end of the war Hitler sent her to live in Munich, but she insisted on staying with him in the bunker in Berlin. Eva longed to be married to Hitler, and he finally agreed. The brief wedding ceremony took place in the bunker; guests were greeted, a wedding breakfast was eaten, and Hitler went off to dictate his last will and testament. Eva proudly told a servant that she could now be called Mrs. Hitler. In the afternoon on April 30, 1945, she took poison and died at Hitler's side.

Braun, Karl Ferdinand (1850–1918)
physicist

On June 6, 1850, Karl Ferdinand Braun was born in Fulda, Germany, the son of Konrad and Franziska Braun. He attended the gymnasium in Fulda, studied at the University of Marburg, and completed his doctorate at the University of BERLIN in 1872. Braun was an itinerant professor whose career started at the University of Würzburg, then moved to a gymnasium in LEIPZIG and then the University of Marburg. For three years he was professor of physics at the Technical High School in Karlsruhe and then stayed for 10 years at the University of Tübingen.

He became famous for two technological achievements: (1) the coupled transmitter and receiver for improved wireless performance, and (2) the cathode-ray oscilloscope. The study of wireless transmission fascinated him, and he found an answer to the troubling question of why the range of transmission was no longer than 15 kilometers. He found that the answer lay in a sparkless antenna circuit. In 1909 he received the Nobel Prize along with Guglielmo Marconi for achievements in radio telegraphy, including transmission of electromagnetic waves, crystal detectors, and the use of radio transmissions for navigation. Braun also introduced the oscilloscope, which used alternating voltage.

In 1915 Braun traveled to the United States to testify in a case concerning radio telecasting for the Telefunken Co. He was unable to return to Germany because of the war and died unhappily on April 20, 1918.

Braun, Otto (1872–1955)
Prussian prime minister

Otto Braun was the Social Democratic prime minister of the state of PRUSSIA between 1920 and 1932. Over the years he tried to transform the aristocratic-dominated Prussian state into a democratic republic. In July 1932 the chancellor of the Reich, Franz von PAPEN (1879–1969), removed him from office in a coup d'état.

The son of a shoemaker, Braun learned the printing trade, becoming head of the SOCIAL DEMOCRATIC PARTY organization in Königsberg and editor of the local party paper. A good organizer and administrator, he was elected to the party's central committee. Between 1913 and 1918 he served as a representative of the party in the Prussian Parliament. In 1919 he became a member of the Weimar NATIONAL ASSEMBLY and then served in the REICHSTAG between 1918 and 1920. Braun was a highly patriotic and moderate politician. He voted with the Social Democrats, who approved of the war credits to finance the war; he lost his only son to the war in 1915; and fought against the left-wing antiwar faction in the SPD. During the NOVEMBER REVOLUTION of 1918–19 he participated in the Berlin workers' council, but was against the Spartacists and in favor of the constitutional assembly. Serving in the Prussian agricultural ministry, he tried to remove reactionary bureaucrats and proposed rural settlement programs for war veterans. As Prussian prime minister he favored a coalition government of moderate parties (SPD, DDP, CENTER, and DVP), and as Prussian prime minister between 1921 and 1932 made Prussia the democratic bulwark against the rising tide of Nazism. In the 1925 presidential elections he was the candidate of the SPD on the first ballot; on the second ballot, however, the Centrist candidate Wilhelm MARX (1863–1946) represented the Weimar Coalition and lost to General Paul von HINDENBURG (1847–1934). During the political turmoil of 1932 the Prussian cabinet tried to get Braun out of office by declaring that the head of state had to be elected by the state legislature. Braun remained in office, but while on vacation he was replaced by von Papen. Refusing to endorse the use of a general strike, Braun fought the coup through the courts, though failing in health. When HITLER came to power, Braun immigrated to Switzerland, where he lived until his death.

Braun, Wernher von (Wernher Magnus Maximilian, Freiherr [Baron] von Braun) (1912–1977)
rocket engineer

Wernher von Braun was the rocket expert who developed one of HITLER's secret weapons, the V-2 rocket.

Born in Wirsitz, PRUSSIA (now Poland), on March 23, 1912, Wernher von Braun was the son of the minister of agriculture. He studied mechanical engineering at the Technical University in BERLIN (1930–32) and there joined the Association for Space Travel and experimented with rocket engines at the testing site in Reinickendorf. After graduation in 1932 he became a civilian employee at the Army Ordnance Office, where he continued experimenting with rockets. Writing his dissertation on liquid-fueled rocket engines, he received his doctorate from the Humboldt University in 1934. In 1937 von Braun became technical director at the new rocket weapons center at Peenemünde, where he worked on the construction of the A-4 rocket, which developed into the V-2 rocket used against England in 1944–45. Surprisingly, he was imprisoned briefly by the GESTAPO for saying that he hoped to use the rocket to reach the Moon. (It appears that his principal interest in rocket research from the time he was a boy was for space travel.)

In 1945 at the end of the war von Braun and his team of experts left Peenemünde to escape the Russians and fled to BAVARIA, making contact with the U.S. Army. After being interrogated in London, he was soon in the United States in a secret operation that brought German scientists to the United States in violation of American laws. After some time he was brought to Huntsville, Alabama, where he worked on the army's missile program at the Redstone Arsenal. It later became NASA's George C. Marshall Space Flight Center, where they developed the Jupiter-

C rocket, which in 1958 launched the *Explorer I* satellite into orbit. In 1960 he became the director of the center and played an important role in the development of the Saturn rockets. The Saturn V rocket was used in the Apollo lunar landing program. In 1970 von Braun became deputy associate minister for planning at NASA. Then, between 1972 and 1975 he went to work for the Fairchild Corporation. On June 16, 1977, he died in Alexandria, Virginia.

Brecht, Bertolt (1898–1956)
playwright
Born on February 10, 1898, in AUGSBURG, Bertolt Brecht was the son of a Catholic businessman and Protestant mother. He studied medicine and philosophy at the University of MUNICH. During the war he served in a military hospital, which made him vehemently opposed to war and sympathetic to the Socialist revolution of 1919. After the war he wrote plays and as a resident of the Munich Kammerspiele had some of his plays staged. Before moving to BERLIN in 1924, Brecht gradually freed himself from the idealistic expressionist conventions of the avant-garde. In Berlin he was associated with Max Reinhardt's theater. His style turned more terse and intellectual and from Erwin Piscator he learned the techniques of experimental theater, such as the use of film and slides. During this period he also began his study of Marxism.

The first play to make Brecht famous was *The Threepenny Opera*. It was based on a translation of the 18th-century *Beggar's Opera*, which he transformed through the use of his own special language containing street-colloquial, Marxist, and biblical diction. He borrowed heavily from others such as Rudyard Kipling. He wrote several more plays with music in collaboration with Kurt Weill and Paul HINDEMITH. Brecht's term for his theatrical innovations was *epic theater*, through which he hoped to awaken the minds of spectators and speak truth to them. He opposed the hypnotization of the audience. Brecht also tried to create alienation in his audience through the elimination of most conventional stage props and the involvement of the audience. Brecht was highly critical of the politics of Germany, and he used his plays as a medium of criticism of social and political issues.

The day after the REICHSTAG fire on February 28, 1933, Brecht left Germany until 1948. It was his exile that established him as a prominent playwright in Great Britain and the United States. Before coming to the United States in 1941, he resided for a while in Scandinavia and then in the Soviet Union. In 1933 his books were publicly burned by the Nazis, while he directly attacked Hitler's regime in *Fear and Misery of the Third Reich* and the *Private Life of the Master Race*. His greatest plays, however, opened with *The Life of Galileo* and *The Good Person of Szechuan*. In *Mother Courage*, which takes place during the THIRTY YEARS' WAR, he demonstrated the folly of collaborating with the social system, which destroys the main character.

During WORLD WAR II when Brecht was in Hollywood, he worked as a screenwriter but was largely ignored. Because he was an outspoken anti-Nazi, his plays were not staged in Germany, but some were staged in Switzerland. In summer 1947 *The Life of Galileo* was finally staged in California. Returning to Berlin in 1948, he and his wife founded the Berliner Ensemble, a group that became the most famous theater group in East Germany. With the exception of *The Days of the Commune* he wrote no new plays.

Bremen/Bremerhaven
Bremen is the second-largest port and maritime trading city in Germany. It is the capital of the smallest federal state, encompassing the city and the port of Bremerhaven.

The city has medieval roots and became the see of a bishop in 787 during the reign of Charlemagne and an archbishopric in 845. In the 11th century under Archbishop Adalbert, Bremen became prosperous. As a trading city and secular state it became a member of the Hanseatic League (Hanse) in 1358. During the REFORMATION it became Protestant. In 1646 it became a free imperial city. In 1827 it developed its outrigger port of Bremerhaven. It became one of the largest ports, where emigrants sailed to North America by way of the major shipping firm, North-German Lloyd (Norddeutscher Lloyd). During the 19th century it became Europe's largest transshipper of cotton and coffee.

Bremen was Prussia's second-largest city during the latter part of the 19th century with its population increasing from 83,000 in 1871 to 247,000 in 1910 and peaking at the end of the 20th century at 672,000. It had become part of the GERMAN CONFEDERATION in 1866 and joined IMPERIAL GERMANY in 1871. Its strong labor movement led to strong opposition to WORLD WAR I, and it became a base for the INDEPENDENT SOCIAL DEMOCRATIC PARTY (USPD) and Communists (KPD). A socialist republic was established after WORLD WAR I but quickly was overthrown by military intervention.

The city government is dominated by a city council, which is largely SPD. The GREEN PARTY grew steadily after 1979 with a voter support of 5 percent rising in 1995 to 13.1 percent. Much of the population is employed in commerce and shipbuilding-related trades. Its problems are those of other cities with a large number of unintegrated foreign workers, racist incidents, and high unemployment of youth.

Brentano, Elizabeth "Bettina"
(1785–1859)
author and salon hostess

Elizabeth Brentano was one of the 20 children born to an Italian businessman, Maximiliane Brentano, in FRANKFURT AM MAIN. Her brother was Clemens Brentano. Her mother died in 1793 and her father in 1797. From 1793 to 1798 she was educated in a convent and then went to live with her grandmother. From her childhood she lived in the circle of the best-known literary figures, which included J. W. GOETHE, who was a good friend of her aunt, and Ludwig van BEETHOVEN. She met Goethe in 1807, but in 1811 he severed all contact with her because of the way she treated his wife. Bettina's first book was an imaginative presentation of her correspondence with Goethe, which was followed by other works of correspondence rich in charm and feeling.

Bettina married the poet and novelist Achim von Arnim (1781–1831) in 1811, whom she first met in 1808. She conducted a lavish correspondence with many writers, musicians, and artists, which became the sources for some controversial books. Her reputation in German romanticism is the greatest as a hostess for all the poets, musicians, professors, artists, philosophers, theologians, and scientists who visited her salon in BERLIN after her husband died in 1831. Among those who visited her home were Friedrich Heinrich Jacobi (1743–1819), L. TIECK (1773–1853), Friedrich SCHLEIERMACHER (1753–1854), Jakob (1785–1863) and Wilhelm (1786–1859) GRIMM, and Alexander (1769–1859) and Wilhelm (1767–1835) von HUMBOLDT. She was a delightful, witty, and knowledgeable conversationalist.

In her famous correspondence with Goethe, *Goethe's Correspondence with a Child* (1835), she related her sublime meeting with Beethoven on a showery afternoon when he sang and played for her. In the true manner of a genius in the romantic age Beethoven declared himself to be more than a mere technician but an interpreter of divine inspiration, a holy vessel whose creations attempt to interpret the overwhelming forces and revelations that possessed him. To Bettina Beethoven manifested himself as a romantic giant whom God had called.

She was more than a delightful conversationalist, but once a widow took an active interest in politics and social questions. She was active as a social reformer of the many ills afflicting Berlin. She investigated the causes of poverty, violence, and disease in the Berlin slums. She wrote polemical treatises for such liberal causes as the rights of workers and women. She hoped to move the Prussian king and public into action, but was unsuccessful in her efforts. Besides taking a positive view on socialism, she was also progressive in her views on the emancipation of women. Her most famous political work was a declaration of her principles in *This Book Belongs to the King*. She died on January 20, 1859.

Breslau

Originally and presently Breslau is the Polish city of Wroclaw in Silesia. It originated as a trading and cathedral town in the Middle Ages and attracted German immigration in the 13th century. In 1335 it became part of Bohemia. During the WAR OF AUSTRIAN SUCCESSION in the 18th century it became part of PRUSSIA. With the expansion of industry it became Prussia's second-largest city between the REVOLUTIONS OF 1848 and 1871. Otto von BISMARCK followed a policy that made the population largely German by WORLD WAR I. After the war it remained in the WEIMAR REPUBLIC along with Lower Silesia. It also was an important episcopal seat for the Catholic Church over which Cardinal Bertram presided. What remained of the German population at the end of WORLD WAR II was expelled when Silesia was added to the state of Poland after the war.

Brest-Litovsk, Treaty of (March 1917)

During WORLD WAR I a peace conference was held at Brest-Litovsk on December 3, 1917, between the revolutionary Russian bolsheviks (Communists) and the Central Powers headed by IMPERIAL GERMANY. Russia was undergoing a revolution, which started in October 1917, and the Germans had facilitated Lenin's return to Russia, hoping that he could fulfill his promise of removing Russia from the war. The Germans hoped to end their two-front war to enable them to concentrate on the western front.

Leon Trotsky headed the Russian delegation, and in three months of brilliant debating tactics wrangled with the Germans over the peace terms. Trotsky hoped that during the delay the revolution would spread to Germany and AUSTRIA. Irritated by this delay the Germans on February 18 resumed their military advance into Russia, which prompted Lenin on the 28th to order the acceptance of the German terms and the signing of the treaty three days later. The very severe terms imposed on Russia included the surrender of all of Poland, the Baltic states, Finland, large parts of Belorussia, Ukraine, and part of Transcaucasia. This amounted to the loss of 62 million people and 1.3 million square miles. Fortunately for Russia the treaty was invalidated by the armistice terms (November 1918) and abrogated by the TREATY OF VERSAILLES in June 1919.

The Bridge
(Die Brücke)

The group of artists known as The Bridge was formed in DRESDEN on June 7, 1905. Ernst Ludwig KIRCHNER, a student of architecture in Dresden and MUNICH took the initiative in its formation. Being more interested in the graphic arts, his enthusiasm for painting influenced three of his fellow architectural students, Fritz Bleyl, Erich Heckel, and Karl Schmidt-Rottluff, to join him. Other artists who soon associated with the group were Emil Nolde and Max Pechstein in 1906, Kees van Dongen in 1907, and Otto Mueller in 1910. Some artists only temporarily associated and exhibited with the group, artists such as Nolde, who left in two years, and van Dongen even in less time. Non-German artists such as the Swiss painter Cuno Amiet and Axel Gallén-Kallela also were participants for a short time. The main members of The Bridge were Kirchner, Heckel, Schmidt-Rottluff, and Pechstein, who lived and worked together, shared materials, models and money, and jointly produced the group's bulletins, catalogues, posters, woodcuts, and lithographs.

The name, "The Bridge," was taken from a passage in *Thus Spake Zarathustra* by Friedrich NIETZSCHE where he reflects that man is "a bridge and not a goal." In their founding manifesto the four members of The Bridge viewed themselves as an elite whose purpose it was to free themselves from the old established order and carve out space in the art world for their work. In their motto the group appealed to progressive artists everywhere to create a revolutionary artistic existence. Their appeal had some international response from Amiet, Kallela, and Edvard Munch, who participated in their group exhibitions between 1905 and 1913.

As the group lived and worked together, they used the same models but changed perspectives.

They worked rapidly, drew automatically, and practiced a summary painting style looking for simplified forms. They spent some summers together vacationing and painting in the beautiful Moritzburg Lakes outside of Dresden. In the world of nature they saw themselves in harmony. For a while they painted similarly, and together were fascinated by the people of the South Pacific and sub-Saharan Africa, which they studied at the Dresden Museum of Ethnology. This was the inspiration for their use of "black contours, angular figure types, masklike faces and vital poses of figures." Another example of foreign influences existed in the work of Kirchner, who was inspired by ancient Indian paintings. In 1910 a Gauguin exhibit in Dresden inspired the group in the depiction of non-European cultures. When the artists moved to BERLIN in 1911 they came into contact with literary expressionism through the revolutionary journal *Der Sturm,* one of whose editors was the figurative expressionist Oskar KOKOSCHKA and the radical antibourgeois circle that published *Die Aktion.* These influences moved the artists to emphasize content much more and to become involved in other fields of creative work.

With the move to Berlin divergences occurred in their responses to the cosmopolitan life of the capital city. It undermined their collective mentality and work, and their different orientations became evident as each member now preferred his own idyllic place to which he could escape. The final breakup occurred on May 27, 1913.

Britain, Battle of (1940)

The Battle of Britain was a massive air battle fought during 1940 in the British skies between German and British aircraft to determine air superiority over Britain before a German invasion could be launched.

The conflict between the Royal Air Force (RAF) and the German Air Force (Luftwaffe) occurred over Britain between July 10 and October 31, 1940. In mid-July the Germans began probing attacks on coastal towns and shipping but then began their serious attack on August 13, 1940. The Germans called their air assault Adlerangriff. Reichsmarshal GÖRING had collected some 2,500 planes in three air fleets. The first was under Field Marshal Albert Kesselring, the second was under Field Marshal Hugo Sperrle, and the third was under General Hans-Jürgen Stumpff. The Germans had an initial force of more than 1,300 bombers and 1,200 fighters. The German plan had as its priority the destruction of RAF planes and the airfields. They counted on surprise, but this was denied them by the British development of radar and the ULTRA intelligence system, which helped the British effectively concentrate their planes. The RAF was under the command of British Air Marshal Sir Hugh Dowding, who had only 660 operational fighters in 52 squadrons. The British were at a decided disadvantage, being outnumbered by a ratio of 3 to 1.

On August 13, 1940, the Luftwaffe made 1,000 fighter sorties and 485 bomber runs, losing 45 aircraft to the British 13. Two days later, it made 1,266 fighter sorties and 520 bomber runs, losing 75 planes. As the Germans continued to meet fierce resistance, they switched to heavy attacks on air bases between August 24 and September 5. Large bomber formations escorted by 100 fighters forced their way through, damaging air fields, communications, and control centers. In this phase the Luftwaffe almost broke the RAF by destroying about 450 planes, killing 103 pilots, and wounding another 128. The planes and pilots could not be rapidly replaced so a serious crisis faced the RAF.

What saved Britain was Hitler's decision to seek revenge for the British bombing of BERLIN. Interestingly, the Germans had bombed London by mistake and the British responded by an attack on Berlin. The Germans then decided to concentrate on bombing London, which was called the Blitz. While this was going on, the British repaired their airfields and regrouped. The climax of the battle fell on September 15, when 56 German planes were destroyed. The German plans for an invasion were postponed, and the Germans resorted to indiscriminate bombing of larger cities, especially London. German daylight attacks declined, with the last one occurring on September 30. During the 12-week battle 1,389 German aircraft were destroyed, while the British lost 792 aircraft.

Churchill immortalized the Battle of Britain with his "finest hour" speech. Churchill honored the pilots of Fighter Command when he said, "Never in the field of human conflict was so much owed by so many to so few."

Brüning, Heinrich (1885–1970)

Heinrich Brüning was born in Münster on November 26, 1885. After joining the Christian Trade Union Movement, he became its general secretary from 1920 to 1930. He also was a REICHSTAG deputy from the Catholic CENTER PARTY between 1924 and 1932. His most important political role was as Reich chancellor from 1930 to 1932, being dismissed by the ungrateful President Paul von HINDENBURG that May. That same month he took over leadership of the Center Party, and conservatism took the party in a rightist direction. Brüning was forced to dissolve the Center Party in July, 1933, as the Vatican was negotiating the CONCORDAT with the German government.

His financial expertise was used during the GREAT DEPRESSION to balance the government's budget by raising taxes and cutting expenditures. He utilized classic remedies and did not expand credit to strengthen buying power and create more jobs. He rather tried to lower wages and prices, increasing the deflationary spiral of the economy. Brüning's government functioned by presidential decree under Article 48 of the WEIMAR CONSTITUTION without a parliamentary majority, which paved the way for HITLER's dictatorship. His general plan had a foreign policy focus to revise the TREATY OF VERSAILLES and reduce reparations.

Brüning avoided imminent arrest by the Nazis by immigrating to the United States, where he was appointed a professor at Harvard. After his return to Germany in 1952, he was appointed professor in Cologne. He died in Norwich, Vermont, on March 30, 1970.

Buchenwald

Buchenwald was a major Nazi CONCENTRATION CAMP established four miles north of WEIMAR for political prisoners in 1937. On July 19 the Nazis with 149 prisoners from Sachsenburg concentration camp began building one of the regime's most notorious concentration camps, which became synonymous with Nazi barbarity. It was built on forested land on the Ettersberg Mountain high above the city of Weimar. It was intended to be one of three camps forming the initial nucleus of the concentration camp system. The other two were DACHAU in the south, Sachsenhausen in the north, with Buchenwald at the center. The railroad station from which the prisoners had to march at double time was at the base of the slope. In 1937 some of the pastors of the CONFESSING CHURCH, including Pastor Paul Schneider and even Martin NIEMÖLLER, were sent there.

The camp commandants were Karl Otto Koch (1937–41) and Hermann Pister (1942–45). Both Koch and his wife were sadistic, hoarded food and wine, and embezzled funds. He was tried and found guilty by an SS court and executed shortly before Americans liberated the camp. Hermann Pister, on the other hand, received his punishment from an American military court, which sentenced him to death in 1947. Other SS guards escaped punishment in the future FEDERAL REPUBLIC. Torturous treatment began when prisoners first arrived and were forced to march along the "the street of blood" in a tilted position as SS guards beat them and quite often killed them before they had even entered the camp. Initially, Buchenwald held mostly German communists, socialists, Jehovah's Witnesses, pacificists, homosexuals, and others the regime classified as "antisocial." The first shipment of Jews came in June 1938, and within two months 150 of them were dead. Later in September about 2,000 Jewish political prisoners were shipped from Dachau and another 450 Austrians, including former officials, professors, and military officers. In November 1938, when the pogroms against Jews started, many were interned in Buchenwald, some were killed, but most responded to this pressure and emigrated from Germany. Later,

Cremation ovens at Buchenwald, 1945 *(Library of Congress)*

when Jews were again shipped to the camp, they were more often in transit to AUSCHWITZ for annihilation. The total camp population that year had reached 7,000 to 8,000 men.

Myths about camp life that have been proven false were that persecution drew all the prisoners together in solidarity, whereas people were actually transformed into wolves. Prisoners stole from one another to survive. Another myth concerned Ilse Koch, the commandant's wife, which asserted that she used human skin from inmates to make lamp shades, which was believed by the prisoners and later American liberators. Later tests showed that the lamp shades were made from pigskin. An SS doctor actually collected tattooed skin from inmates and often had inmates killed to add to his collection. A Nazi device, not a myth, was called "an exchange of victims," which placed prison leaders in life-and-death dilemmas, choosing people for work details that meant certain death, choosing prisoners for execution when an example had to be set for the rest, and for medical experiments.

At its peak about 85,000 people were incarcerated in Buchenwald. Within less than eight years close to one quarter of a million prisoners were interned, tortured, and tormented. It is estimated that between 55,000 and 70,000 prisoners died there of malnutrition, disease, exhaustion, beatings, tortures and overcrowded sleeping conditions, and medical experiments. Pseudo-experiments were conducted by injecting prisoners with deadly vaccines and infectious diseases.

At one stage the Nazis allowed the common criminals to manage the camp's day-to-day affairs. Later, when inmates were needed for slave labor and a more efficient administration was required, they turned this task over to the political prisoners, led by German Communists. After the BATTLE OF STALINGRAD many qualified craftsmen were put to work in armaments production. They managed to alter blueprints, sabotage or delay production, produce carbines out of the wrong material, or use materials for personal products. Resistance cells began operating in 1938, aided by political prisoners who handled most of the camp administration. Just before liberation, the fleeing SS troops rounded up 27,000 prisoners, mostly Jews, and sent them on a death march through freezing weather to the Flossenburg camp. After the SS had fled, the prisoners seized control from the remaining guards. On April 10, 1945, Buchenwald was liberated by the U.S. 80th Division, which found 21,000 prisoners still there.

Bülow, Bernhard von (1849–1929)
Imperial chancellor

Prince Bernhard von Bülow was a statesman who became the fourth chancellor of IMPERIAL GERMANY, serving the Kaiser the longest of any of his chancellors. He was the son of Ernst von Bülow (1815–79). The younger Bülow entered the German diplomatic service in 1874 and eventually became ambassador in Rome (1894) and in 1897 foreign minister. He was at first especially favored by Kaiser WILLIAM II, who appointed him chancellor in 1900, hoping that he would become a second Otto von BISMARCK. Although he was an able diplomat, he was essentially a weak man who had few strong ideas on domestic or foreign policy and was dominated by others such as Baron Holstein, who was the counsellor of the Foreign Office, and Admiral TIRPITZ. Yet after 1897 Bülow promoted Germany's aggressive world policy (*weltpolitik*) to gain a "place in the sun" and until shortly before his resignation favored Tirpitz's naval program to which he subordinated German foreign policy. During the crises over Morocco and Bosnia he alienated the other European powers, leading to Germany's encirclement in the Triple Entente (1907). In domestic policy he failed to halt the growth of the SOCIAL DEMOCRATIC PARTY, rallied nonsocialist forces around the monarchy, and continued to shun any fundamental reforms.

When the Kaiser failed to consult his ministers before granting an interview in the *Daily Telegraph* in October 1908, the deterioration in relations between Bülow and the Kaiser culminated with Bülow's resignation in July 1909. In December 1914 Bülow returned to Rome as ambassador, trying to prevent Italy from leaving its alliance with Germany.

Bundesrat

The Bundesrat is also known as the Federal Council (or Council of Constituent States) and is the representative body of the states (*Länder*) of the FEDERAL REPUBLIC. Unlike the U.S. Senate, where senators are elected by the people, the members of the Bundesrat are appointed by the state governments. Through the Bundesrat the states participate in the legislation and administration at the federal level. Depending on the size of a state, it has between three and six votes, which may be cast only as a block vote on behalf of the state government concerned. Like the members of the federal government, the members of the Bundesrat may take part in all meetings of the BUNDESTAG and its committees. They may at any time intervene in a debate outside the agreed sequence of speakers.

More than half of all legislation requires the formal approval of the Bundesrat. This means that the bills cannot pass into law against its will. This applies especially to bills that concern the vital interests of the states, which include their financial affairs or their administrative powers. No proposed amendments to the constitution (BASIC LAW) can be adopted without the Bundesrat's consent by a two-thirds majority. In all other cases the Bundesrat only has a right of objection, but this can be overruled by the Bundestag. If the two houses of Parliament cannot reach agreement, a mediation committee composed of members of both chambers must be convened, which in most cases is able to work out a compromise. Federalism is very much active as the voting in the Bundesrat often reflects state and not party interests.

The Bundesrat elects its president from among the minister presidents (like U.S. governors) of the federal states for a 12-month term according to a fixed rotation schedule. The president of the Bundesrat exercises the powers of the federal president if the latter is not available.

Bundestag

The German Bundestag is the supreme legislative authority of the FEDERAL REPUBLIC OF GERMANY (FRG). It is the German equivalent of the U.S. House of Representatives. Its members are elected by the voting public (citizens age 18 and over) in general, direct, free, equal, and secret elections for a four-year term. The electoral system in which the representatives are chosen is a combination of proportional representation and direct election of candidates. Half of the members are elected directly, the other half via the state lists of candidates nominated by their respective parties.

The responsibilities and rights of the Bundestag include: the adoption of federal laws; determining the federal budget by legislation; ratification of all international treaties; parliamentary control over the federal armed forces; the right to request information from the federal government; the election of half the judges of the FEDERAL CONSTITUTIONAL COURT, while the other half are elected by the BUNDESRAT; participation in the appointment of the judges of the supreme federal courts. The Bundestag also elects the president of the Bundestag and the vice presidents. The chancellor is elected by the Bundestag upon nomination by the federal president. In order that the government always has a chancellor in office, which was a problem during the crisis years of the WEIMAR REPUBLIC, the Bundestag can remove a chancellor from office only by electing a new one. The Bundestag also participates in the election of the federal president. In case of an attack by a foreign power, the Bundestag determines the state of defense.

The members of the Bundestag are called upon to serve the whole people and not only their party. Pursuant to Article 38 of the BASIC LAW they are "not bound by orders and instructions, and shall be subject only to their conscience." Two privileges help them preserve their independence: indemnity and immunity.

Burschenschaft

Burschenschaft is a term originally applied to the student body at a university. In 1815 there was disappointment among the younger generation of Germans at the failure of the CONGRESS OF VIENNA to create a united Germany, so the name was applied to the student movement that grew out of the WARS OF LIBERATION. At JENA some 500–600 students formed a society pledged to combine personal virtues of sobriety and chastity with the patriotic purpose of achieving national unity. Similar societies were formed at 15 other universities. The festival at the WARTBURG on October 18, 1817, was the symbol for the union of all these societies in one national body. The Burschenschaft was hostile to the reactionary policies followed by most German rulers and desired the national unity of Germany. The murder of playwright August von Kotzebue in 1819 resulted in a ban on the society through the CARLSBAD DECREES.

The local Burschenschaft continued to meet clandestinely in many places, and the trend was for it to become more radical. After the HAMBACH FESTIVAL in May 1832 the students attacked a police headquarters in Frankfurt, which led to a wave of arrests. The students continued to be politically active, and many politicians in the FRANKFURT PARLIAMENT of 1848 had been associated with the organization. In the latter half of the century the Burschenschaft officially united as the Deutsche Burschenschaft in 1881 and developed into a union of social clubs of nationalistic and anti-Semitic character. A rival and somewhat more liberal organization, the Allgemeiner Deutsche Burschenbund by 1924 also demanded proof of Aryan descent. Under the Nazis the two groups were coordinated in 1934 and dissolved in 1935.

C

Calvin, John (1509–1564)
Protestant reformer

John Calvin was a French Protestant reformer who emphasized predestination in salvation and espoused a theocratic view of the state. His influence on PROTESTANTISM in the HOLY ROMAN EMPIRE was located primarily in Switzerland and the Rhineland.

John Calvin was born at Noyon, France, on July 10, 1509, into the bourgeois family of Gerard Cauvin, a lawyer and administrator. At first headed for an ecclesiastical career, Calvin later turned to the law. In 1523 he went to the University of Paris, where he studied Latin under the great teacher Mathurin Cordier, and like Martin LUTHER began his philosophical and theological studies under Nominalist influences. At Orleans and Bourges he studied law and Greek, graduating with a bachelor of laws degree in 1531. Calvin was more broadly educated than Luther, schooled in classical languages, philosophy, and theology, and then the law, but not least in the Bible. During this time Calvin fell under the influence of Lutheran teachers, particularly Jacques Lefèvre, a father of French Protestantism. Earlier at Bourges Calvin had met the German professor of Greek, Melchior Wolmar, a Lutheran who also is believed to have had a decisive influence on his life. After his father's death in 1531 Calvin felt free to give up the law and returned to Paris and to renew his linguistic, classical, and biblical studies. In 1532 he wrote his first book, a commentary on *De Clementia* by Seneca, whose stoic moral philosophy influenced him as it did the reformer Ulrich ZWINGLI.

Sometime in 1533 he was converted to Protestantism under the influence of his many instructors and his resentment of the condemnation of his father for embezzlement and his excommunication. Nevertheless, Calvin explained his conversion as an act of God by which his heart was subdued. Calvin also experienced the mental pain and dread caused by the thought of sin and divine judgment and was provided some consolation by Luther's theology of justification. There was a great and terrible distance between God and the individual believer that could be mediated only by Christ. Calvin emphasized the power of God over sinful and corrupt humanity; his God thundered and demanded obedience. In 1534 Calvin wrote an inaugural address for his friend and rector of the university, Nicholas Cop, a speech that contained some ideas of Martin Luther on salvation and good works. Pressure to flee came from the French church, which in 1534 supported by royal decree, declared Protestants to be heretics and subjected them to arrest and execution. Some months later, he ended up in Basel, Switzerland.

In 1536 Calvin published his *Institutes of the Christian Religion,* a primer and catechism in six chapters and expanded threefold in the second edition of 1539. The majesty of God is its basic theme, and that the main duty and purpose of man was to glorify God. An extremely logical and terrifying book, it stresses that between God and humans there is an unbridgeable gulf that makes it impossible for a person to gain salvation through his or her own efforts. In his omnipotence and omniscience God has foreordained all things that will ever happen. This truth led to

John Calvin *(Library of Congress)*

Calvin's principle of divine predestination whereby people are destined to either heaven or hell and cannot do anything to alter the intention of God. To those whom God has chosen to be saved, he has granted the gift of faith, which is undeserved. No one is worthy of salvation, and most are damned because of God's justice. It is only through God's mercy that the elect enter heaven. This doctrine of predestination did not originate with Calvin, but no one had ever expressed it so uncompromisingly.

Calvin's ideas differed from Catholicism and Lutheranism. He believed that the Creator's decision on who shall be damned is immutable. Therefore, unlike Catholicism he rejected the doctrine of purgatory, where people's sins were supposed to be cleansed so that they could enter heaven. Prayer, Calvin taught, did not change God's will and humans must worship God even though they be damned. The Catholic Mass, Calvin said, was sacrilegious because priests claimed that the bread and wine were changed into Christ's body and blood. On the other hand, Calvin believed that Christ is present only in spirit whenever believers gather together prayerfully. As far as the sacraments were concerned, none were necessary for salvation, but two were retained: Baptism, which was to be a seal and sign of grace; and the Lord's Supper, which was the spiritual flesh and blood of Christ. In regard to the Lord's Supper Calvin refused Catholicism's doctrine of transubstantiation, the Lutheran doctrine of consubstantiation, and Zwinglian symbolism. Calvin also believed in the existence of two churches, the visible comprising all believers and the invisible, which was composed of the predestined. He did, however, reject Luther's separation between the church and state, a worldly and ecclesiastical sphere, and insisted on a theocracy. Calvin rejected all other so-called sacraments as not founded in Scripture.

Calvin established an unofficial theocracy and a "Protestant Rome" in Geneva, Switzerland—a society in which Calvinist elders regulated the personal and social lives of the citizens and did so through church courts. Calvin acted as virtual dictator from 1541 until his death. The older and more pious members were the elders of the community who governed the city. A consistory of five pastors and 12 lay elders examined and regulated the conduct of all citizens. They imposed strict discipline in dress, sexual mores, church attendance, and business affairs and severely punished sinful behavior. Prosperous merchants and shopkeepers saw in the rigid social discipline Calvin imposed on the people a justification of the discipline they already imposed on themselves. Calvin saw nothing sinful in commercial activities and approved of charging interest on loans.

During his last years Calvin elaborated Geneva's laws, wrote against his enemies, and labored on the theology in his study, the *Institutes*. Geneva became a model church with discipline and order, and it became the center of international Protestantism. Calvin trained a new generation of reformers of many nationalities who carried his message back to their homelands. Besides its influence in Switzerland, the Netherlands, Scotland, France, and in Hungary, in Germany it made considerable inroads in the south, was centered between Worms and Strasbourg in the Rhineland, around Wittenberg, and later all the areas in Germany to which the French Huguenots emigrated during the reign of the Great Elector. It is also thought that Calvinism with its emphasis on austerity and hard work contributed to the development of modern capitalism. In America it was influential among the Puritans.

On May 27, 1564, Calvin died after a long illness.

Canisius, Peter (1521–1597)
Jesuit educator

Peter Canisius was the first German member of the Society of Jesus, the JESUITS. Besides being an influential preacher he played an important role in the COUNTER-REFORMATION in Germany, where he won over Catholic princes. He also made important contributions to raising the educational standards of Catholic youth. He was so popular and influential that Germans called him a "Second Apostle of Germany."

Peter de Hondt, later known as Peter Canisius, was born in Nymwegen, Holland, in 1521. In his education he was influenced by a study of the *devotio moderna* as cultivated by the Brethern of the Common Life and by reading about the mystical contemplatives of the later Middle Ages. He was accepted by the Jesuits in Cologne in 1543. After a long period of education in Cologne he was ordained a priest in 1546, and in 1548 he received a doctorate at the age of 27. He attended sessions at the Council of Trent as the "procurator" of Cardinal Otto Truchsess von Waldburg. Soon afterward he was called to Rome by Ignatius Loyola himself.

His missionary activities in Germany began in BAVARIA, AUSTRIA and Bohemia, where Catholicism was still strong. Through these activities he saw that what was required was a well-trained and devout priesthood. He devoted himself, therefore, to founding Jesuit colleges at Ingolstadt, Prague, MUNICH and Innsbruck, and Fribourg (Switzerland) and encouraged those already in existence in Cologne, AUGSBURG and Würzburg. Another major task of Canisius was to raise educational standards among Catholic youth so as to match the excellence of Protestant schools, which had improved under the influence of Philip MELANCHTHON. Canisius engaged in educational reforms in Vienna, Ingolstadt, and Fribourg.

Canisius also served as an adviser to numerous princes and bishops, urging them to take a determined stand against Protestants in imperial diets and church councils. At the request of the emperor Ferdinand, Canisius composed a catechism that became the standard book of religious instruction for youth. All these activities extended over half a century.

canton system

The canton system was a Prussian method of military recruitment that applied chiefly to peasants. In 1733 during the reign of FREDERICK WILLIAM I the recruitment of Prussian subjects was formalized by royal edicts. Frederick William divided the kingdom into military districts and allocated so many districts to each army regiment. Each district was subdivided into cantons, which were assigned to individual infantry, cavalry, or garrison companies for replacement purposes. Each canton was made of just so many fireplaces, 5,000 for infantry regiments and 1,500 for cavalry. This meant that military units could draw their recruits only from the cantons in their area. Eligible male children had to be enrolled on regimental lists at the age of 10 and had to take a military oath after they had been confirmed in the church and received the Lord's Supper.

The obligation rested mostly on peasants and journeymen in the crafts, which was due to the many exemptions that were allowed. It was not a system of universal military service. Whole social groups were exempted, namely all middle-class people, educated people, and also the workers in specialized manufacturing. Some regions of the country were also exempted, which was expanded under FREDERICK II, because of manufacturing in BERLIN, Potsdam, and BRANDENBURG. Foreigners were still hired and also impressed. In 1740 the army had two foreigners to one Prussian, and during Frederick's wars the ratio was as high as 1 to 1. Economic policy dictated that too many Prussians should not be taken from employment. Because army service was for 20 years, soldiers were allowed leaves to return to their villages; in the case of the JUNKERS they were able to keep most of their laborers. So generally, the Prussian army was composed of Prussian peasants and craftsmen and foreign hirelings. For the Prussians they were called up as needed.

For an army of 42,000 the cantonal system supplied enough troops. In 1808 the Military Reorganization Commission recommended introducing universal service and creating a reserve militia. However, in order to create a system of universal military service, all that was needed was to remove the exemptions from local and social groups. But Frederick William III did not approve of it because he was frightened of such a revolutionary move. But after 1806–07 reform-minded military leaders came to the forefront in 1813. The idea of an obligation to military service was resented by the nobility and the middle class, and the middle class especially complained that this was their only special privilege. The only way of evading the terms of the Paris Convention of 1808 and Napoleon's restrictions was to call up additional men for brief periods of training, made possible by sending home each regiment's older soldiers.

Carlsbad Decrees (1819)

The Carlsbad Decrees were a series of repressive measures enacted by representatives of eight German states meeting under the presidency of Prince Clemens von METTERNICH, ratified by the Frankfurt Diet, and applied to the GERMAN CONFEDERATION in September 1819. The measures prohibited political meetings, provided for the dissolution of the BURSCHENSCHAFTEN, and introduced a general surveillance of the educational system in all German states and strict censorship of the press. Moreover, a commission was established to study the discontent in Germany and begin proceedings against subversive individuals and organizations.

The event that occasioned the decrees was the stabbing to death of a playwright named August von Kotzebue (1761–1819) (who wrote reports on German conditions for the czar and was reputed to be a Russian spy) by an impressionable student, Karl Ludwig Sand. Actually, it is thought that Sand had come under the influence of the philosophy and doctrines of Karl Follen, a young University of Giessen lecturer who justified the murder of tyrants, a sort of German Robespierre. The assassination also was the culmination of a series of patriotic demonstrations in the universities by the Burschenschaften societies, whose aim it was, unlike other fraternities, to work for the moral and political regeneration of Germany and the cause of national unity. These had been organized into a national federation with branches at 16 universities. In 1817, in celebration of the fourth anniversary of the BATTLE OF LEIPZIG and also the 300th anniversary of Martin LUTHER's resistance to authority, the Burschenschaft at the University of Jena conducted a national assembly and meeting at the WARTBURG CASTLE. As might be expected, speeches were made about unity and freedom, and of course the students defamed the princes who had failed to grant constitutions to their people. They also built a bonfire into which they cast numerous hated symbols of Prussian autocracy. Two years of demonstrations like this led to Kotzebue's assassination and gave Metternich the excuse to promulgate the repressive measures. The Carlsbad Decrees were enforced by a harsh police system, which eventually led to the minor revolutions in 1830 and the more widespread and radical revolutions of 1848.

Celtis, Conrad (1459–1508)
humanist poet

Born into a Franconian peasant family in a village near Würzburg, after leaving home Conrad Celtis was educated at the Universities of Cologne, HEIDELBERG, Rostock, and LEIPZIG. Celtis was one of the first German humanists to visit Italy (1486–87). After 10 years of wandering he came to resent the Italian attitude of cultural superiority and was determined to rescue his fellow Germans from medieval barbarism. He sought to promote literary societies among the humanists as a means of combating the scholastics and of creating a truly German culture. After his time in Italy he studied mathematics and poetry at the University of Cracow. Then he became a professor of rhetoric at the University of Ingolstadt and in 1497 accepted an invitation from the emperor MAXIMILIAN to be a professor at the University of Vienna. There he established a College of Poets and Mathematicians, wrote poems and plays, and taught until his death in 1508.

Conrad Celtis earned a reputation as the finest lyric poet among the German humanists. His reputation as a poet resulted in Emperor Frederick III's crowning him as the first German poet laureate of the Empire. In his verses he imitated the Roman writers Horace and Ovid. His poetry described mountains and streams that are alive in the spirit of a nature pantheism that sought inspiration in the religion of forest and field and of the ancient Germans and in the teachings of the Druidic priestly fraternity.

Celtis was an outspoken champion of classical scholarship. Perhaps he had an exaggerated faith in the power of the printed word and expected that the thought of the ancients would reveal the knowledge of the universe. He expressed a love for medieval German culture and a strong German patriotism. Celtis along with Heinrich Bebel made Tacitus's *Germania* the key book of German HUMANISM, on which he published and lectured. His study of the Roman past made him curious about his own German past. He and his friends contributed to his *Germany Illustrated*. His epic poem, *Ligurinus*, praised Emperor Frederick Barbarossa, as his poem *Norimberga* praised Nürnberg.

Center Party

The Center Party (Zentrumspartei) represented Roman Catholics in the Prussian Diet and in the REICHSTAG after 1871. The name was derived from the location of its seats in the seating chart of the Reichstag. It was founded in Prussia shortly after the outbreak of war in 1870. Its roots went back to Catholic caucuses in the FRANKFURT PARLIAMENT of 1848, was revived in opposition to German unification under conservative Prussian PROTESTANTISM and anticlericalism of the NATIONAL LIBERALS. In the small-German (*Kleindeutsch*) solution to German unity, the Catholics became a permanent religious minority. The primary role of the party was to defend Catholic rights in areas of government financial support for Catholic education and other church institutions. Most of the voters of the Center were middle-class and rural voters and especially women in the Weimar era, while industrial workers often voted for radical parties. It must be emphasized that the Center was a lay organization and was not controlled by the Catholic hierarchy.

Ludwig Windhorst, who had been the last minister of justice in the Kingdom of Hanover before it was taken over by Prussia, became the leader of the party. Otto von BISMARCK hated him so much that he accused him of being an enemy of the state. Bismarck thought there was a link between the creation of the Center Party and the pope's declaration of papal infallibility, and that Catholics who supported the Center were hostile to Bismarck's solution to German unification. Bismarck considered them enemies of the Reich. A period of religious persecution, known as the "cultural struggle" (KULTURKAMPF) followed, with Catholic political resistance being led by the Center Party. In response to persecution Catholics rallied to the "Center Tower," which increased its seats in Prussia from 52 in 1873 to 90 and from 63 to 91 in the REICHSTAG. The conflict between church and state did not last that long and ended when a new pope, Leo XIII, sought a peaceful resolution and Bismarck found new allies in his struggle against socialism. The Center Party was in a position to block legislation in political and economic matters in return for government support of its religious and federal interests.

In the final decade of the century the Center had become the most important party and always was anxious to avoid being branded as unpatriotic. In response to Germany's quest to gain an imperial place in the sun, the Center was at first supportive, considering colonial expansion a means of providing security for Catholic missionaries, but also accepting of the common belief that Europe was spreading the benefits of civilization as long as moral principles were not violated. When Catholic missionaries endorsed the peaceful protests in German Togo after 1902 and were themselves imprisoned, the partnership between the government and the Center collapsed and the Reichstag dissolved in 1906.

During WORLD WAR I the Center supported the German war effort and in 1916 even went so far as to endorse unrestricted submarine warfare. By 1917, however, Matthias ERZBERGER, persuaded his party to support the Peace Resolution with the SOCIAL DEMOCRATIC PARTY (SPD). At the end of the war the Center helped write the WEIMAR CONSTITUTION. During the republican years the Center participated in many of the government coalitions and made great efforts to make the parliamentary system work. Although it supported its own candidate, Wilhelm Marx, for the presidency in 1925, its sister party, the BAVARIAN PEOPLE'S PARTY, made it possible for the conservative general Paul von HINDENBURG to become president. In 1928 the Center came under the control of the conservative prelate Monsignor Ludwig Kaas, who considered the SPD as its primary enemy while the Center's parliamentary caucus was led by Heinrich BRÜNING, who went on to be the unpopular chancellor during the GREAT DEPRESSION. Unfortunately, the Center voted for the ENABLING ACT in March 1933, which gave Hitler dictatorial powers. Very soon thereafter the party voluntarily dissolved after the Reich CONCORDAT was concluded.

Chamberlain, Houston Stewart (1855–1927)
author

Chamberlain was an Anglo-German author who became famous for *The Foundations of the Nineteenth Century* (1910), which glorified the Germanic race. The thesis of the book is that modern culture is the work of the Germanic race. The Jews embodied only negative traits and could not have produced a Christ, who, according to Chamberlain, was Nordic, blond, and blue-eyed. Chamberlain's thought influenced Nazi ideology.

Chamberlain was born on September 9, 1855, in Southsea, an English resort town, the son of an admiral. Educated in France and Germany, he studied the sciences in Geneva and philosophy in Dresden. He settled in BAYREUTH after marrying the daughter of Richard WAGNER (1813–83). He fell under Wagner's spell, first his music and then his thought. From 1882 on he participated in the Wagner cult along with other members of the family.

Along with the Frenchman Arthur de Gobineau, Houston Stewart Chamberlain popularized the idea of race as the crucial factor in human history. Through his *Foundations* Chamberlain had a special impact on Germany. He argued that the Aryans (Indo-Europeans), of which the Germans were the foremost element, were the true creators of culture, while the Jews were simply parasites who destroyed culture. The Aryan race, he thought, had to be prepared to fight for civilization itself. Because of such biological arguments, the Jews were now viewed in racial terms: All Jews supposedly had immutable characteristics harmful to the *Völkish* state that bore Aryan culture. Inasmuch as the Jews created a worldwide conspiracy against the Aryan race, the Jews would have to be eliminated from the life of the German nation.

HITLER's racial theories were strongly influenced by Chamberlain's *Foundations*. It is clear that even if Hitler had not read Chamberlain's work he had learned of his ideas secondhand and included them in *MEIN KAMPF*. Chamberlain's lack of vulgarity and his pseudo-scientific scholarly tone made racist thought available to all levels of readers.

Charles V (1500–1558)
Holy Roman Emperor

Charles V became the Holy Roman Emperor during the beginning of Martin LUTHER's efforts to reform the Roman Catholic Church. Charles inherited the thrones of the Habsburgs in Germany, in the Netherlands, and in Spain. Born in Ghent on February 24, 1500, Charles was the oldest son of Philip the Fair of Habsburg (of Burgundy) and a Spanish mother, Joanna the Mad of Aragon and Castile. Through the death of his maternal grandfather, Ferdinand, in 1516 he inherited in 1518 the throne of Spain, and when his paternal grandfather the emperor MAXIMILIAN I died in 1518, he succeeded to the Habsburg possessions and was crowned emperor in AACHEN in 1520. Not that his election was uncontested, because the French king, Francis I, had offered large bribes to the electors, which Charles was able to outbid with the loans he received from the FUGGER and Welser bankers of AUGSBURG.

The major task facing Charles in Germany was to solve the problems raised by Martin LUTHER and the REFORMATION. In his confrontation with Luther at the DIET OF WORMS in 1521 Charles firmly declared that he intended to crush the Lutheran Reformation. By the EDICT OF WORMS Luther was placed under the ban of the Empire. The publication of Lutheran literature was forbidden. Charles favored the settlement of the Lutheran controversy through a general council of the church. As Lutheranism spread, Charles changed his goals toward reforming the abuses and doctrines of the church, which had led to Luther's revolt. But Pope Clement VII not only feared the changes that a council would make, but also the extension of the emperor's power in Italy. After a struggle, the capture of the pope, and the sack of Rome in 1527, a reconciliation occurred that led to the coronation of Charles at Bologna in 1530, the last time an emperor was crowned by any pope. Charles finally gained papal cooperation from the next pope, Paul III, who convened the COUNCIL OF TRENT on December 13, 1545.

Two of the major distractions facing Charles that weakened his attempts to suppress Lutheranism were the French-Habsburg wars over control of Italy and the threat of the Turks. The emperor's victory over Francis I was at the expense of the deterioration of his position in Germany. Also, the Turks were advancing in Hungary and even laid siege to Vienna in 1529. The absence of Charles from Germany during the 1520s gave the German princes the opportunity to consolidate their opposition to the emperor. The princes used the religious issues to break with the emperor while Ferdinand, Charles's brother, left religion in the hands of the princes while he fought off the Turks. Although Charles was a moderate on the religious issue, he strengthened his orthodox position at the Diet of Speyer in 1529. At this meeting the Lutherans defied him, protesting his position, which resulted in the dissenters being labeled as Protestants. The DIET OF AUGSBURG took place in 1530, and again a hoped-for reconciliation did not take place. The 1530s did not improve Charles's position. He failed to enlist the German princes against the Turks, he lost the support of Henry VIII of England due to his divorce from

Charles V, Holy Roman Emperor *(Library of Congress)*

Charles's aunt Catherine, and the Protestant princes led by Philip of Hesse entered an alliance with France against the emperor. Even his brother, Ferdinand, was alienated when as emperor-designate Charles tried to change the imperial succession to his son, Philip.

In the end all the efforts of Charles to guarantee the unity of his empire and a universal imperial authority failed. In 1547 Charles succeeded in defeating the Protestant SCHMALKALDIC LEAGUE, but this proved of little consequence. An anti-Habsburg alliance soon again emerged, including the new French king Henry II, the defection of Pope Paul III, and the move of the Council of Trent to Bologna for fear of the emperor's influence; both Protestant and Catholic German princes opposed his proposals for constitutional reform in the HOLY ROMAN EMPIRE. A rebellion occurred against Charles in the 1550s, forcing Charles to sign the Treaty of Passau in 1552, which was finalized in the TREATY OF AUGSBURG (1555), which gave Lutheranism equality with Catholicism and placed religion under the control of each of the German princes. This made the princes the ultimate victors in their struggle with the emperor. It was Ferdinand who negotiated with the princes while Charles retired to the Netherlands. Charles abdicated his many crowns in 1555–56. Austria and the Holy Roman Empire he bequeathed to Ferdinand, and the Netherlands and Spain to his son, Philip. Charles died in Spain on September 21, 1558. His goal of uniting a Catholic Europe under his imperial rule never was realized.

Charles VI (1685–1740)

Holy Roman Emperor

Charles was the second son of Emperor LEOPOLD I. In 1703 he became king of Spain, and on the death of Emperor JOSEPH I in 1711 he was elected to the imperial title and the Habsburg dominions. In appearance he was short and ugly, with a typical Habsburg lip and brown hair. He possessed a reticent personality. So without the characteristics of a great emperor and, like his father, not fond of governing, the prospects for his reign did not appear to be promising. On the other hand, his education and interests oriented him toward music, and he became a talented musician and a patron of the opera.

At the death of King Carlos II of Spain, Leopold I went to war with Louis XIV of France to press the Habsburg claim to the Spanish Empire. The Habsburg campaign in Spain was unsuccessful, however, in that on the death of Emperor Joseph in 1711, Austria's allies refused to support Charles VI's claims and opposed a personal union of Spain and the Habsburg lands. Every member of the Grand Alliance except the Habsburgs concluded the Treaty of Utrecht in 1713. The treaty recognized the monarchy's conquests on the Italian peninsula plus Sardinia, and it confirmed Philip V's hold on Spain and its overseas empire. Although opposed to the Treaty of Utrecht, Charles realized it was hopeless to continue the struggle without the Netherlands and Great Britain. Charles acquired Milan, Naples, and the Netherlands. There was a renewal of efforts to change this settlement, and in the end Charles exchanged Sardinia for Sicily.

The issuance of the PRAGMATIC SANCTION was one of the consequences of the impossibility of regaining Spain. Charles wanted to ensure that Habsburg territories would pass intact to his heirs. The Pragmatic Sanction declared that all of the Habsburg possessions were indivisible and could be inherited in both male and female lines. The problem concerned his eldest daughter, MARIA THERESA, whose succession Charles wished to secure through the consent of the great powers. Securing the Pragmatic Sanction dominated foreign policy for the next two decades. Concessions were required. For England's consent Charles abandoned the Ostend Company. In the Treaty of Berlin (1728) Prussia accepted the female succession. For the consent of Frederick Augustus of SAXONY Charles had to support his candidacy to the Polish throne. Neither the War of the Polish Succession (1733–38) nor the second Turkish war worked to Charles's advantage. In the peace (1738) AUSTRIA lost Naples and Sicily to Spain and in return received Parma and Piacenza. Francis Stephen of Lorraine, the husband of Maria

Theresa, lost Lorraine in exchange for Tuscany. Perhaps it would have been wiser to follow the advice of Prince EUGENE OF SAVOY and guarantee the succession with a strong army and full treasury.

In contrast to the disasters of the Polish War, Charles did fairly well during the first Turkish war. Charles had formed an alliance with Venice against the Turks, who were trying to reverse the settlement at Karlowitz (1699). Charles, realizing that the Turkish victories against Venice would endanger Hungary, sent Prince Eugene of Savoy against the Turks; he won the battle of Peterwardein (1716). In the Peace of Passarowitz (1718) the Turks kept Morea, while the gains that Charles made in Serbia, Wallachia, and Bosnia were lost in the second of his Turkish Wars (1737–39). He retained the banat of Temesvár.

Austrian finances were in a state of near bankruptcy in the 1730s, even though Charles had made some efforts to improve trade and transportation. In 1740 Charles VI unexpectedly died, and the WAR OF THE AUSTRIAN SUCCESSION began in an attempt to divide up the Habsburg lands.

Charles VII (1697–1745)
Holy Roman Emperor

Charles Albert was the son of MAXIMILIAN EMMANUEL, the elector of Bavaria and his second wife, Theresa, the daughter of the king of Poland, John Sobieski. During Charles's youth the Austrians occupied BAVARIA in punishment for having sided with the French king, Louis XIV, against Emperor LEOPOLD I in the War of the Spanish Succession (1701–14). With the conclusion of peace Maximilian was restored to his electorate and Charles and his brother returned from Vienna to MUNICH. For a while Charles was loyal to the Habsburgs, serving courageously in the struggle against the Turks under EUGENE, PRINCE OF SAVOY. Charles then married the younger daughter, Maria Amalia, of the deceased emperor JOSEPH I. Even though she had renounced her rights to the Habsburg succession, it was these claims that Charles used to press his claim for the imperial title. The young prince had agreed to recognize the PRAGMATIC SANCTION in 1732, but with reservations. Earlier, in 1714, Maximilian had signed a treaty with France, which promised support for the WITTELSBACHS in their claim to the Bohemian crown lands.

The significance of Charles Albert is that he initiated the WAR OF THE AUSTRIAN SUCCESSION (1740–48) when CHARLES VI died. The elector refused to recognize the validity of the Pragmatic Sanction and the succession of the emperor's eldest daughter, MARIA THERESA. In 1742 the Bavarian elector was elected Holy Roman Emperor with French support, the first time that a Habsburg was not chosen since 1438, Bavaria then suffered Austrian occupation. His declaration as king of Bohemia was short-lived. The king of Prussia, FREDERICK II, helped him return to Munich, but the elector was defeated and impoverished. He died in 1743, and his replacement on the imperial throne was Maria Theresa's husband, Francis of Lorraine. In 1745 his son, Maximilian Joseph, signed the peace Treaty of Füssen with Austria.

Charlottenburg, Palace of (Berlin)

The palace of Charlottenburg, which lies in the old town of Charlottenburg in BERLIN was built by a succession of architects of the BAROQUE and ROCOCO styles. It was planned and constructed as a royal seat. It includes a long row of 1,830-foot frontage of 17th- and 18th-century buildings. In 1695 the countess and later queen of Prussia (1658–1705), Sophie Charlotte, had a summer residence built for her some five miles outside the gates of Berlin by the master builder Arnold Nehring. During the 18th century this was extended into a royal residence with a memorial courtyard and French-style gardens. The court architect Esoander von Göthe added the 470-foot Orangerie on the west side. Göthe also added the picturesque dome in the center of the palace. Under FREDERICK II (The Great) court architect von Knobelsdorff added the New Wing (Neuer Flügel) to the east. Completing the palace precinct was the court theater designed by C. G. Langhans in 1790 where the Museum of Pre- and Early History and a small Orangerie is located today.

Although originally located at the Lange Brücke, an equestrian statue of FREDERICK WILLIAM, the Great Elector, designed by Andreas Schlüter, stands (after being stored for safekeeping in Potsdam during WORLD WAR II) in the courtyard. The historical apartments are in the central area of the buildings. In the Knobbellsdorff wing are further historical apartments and the Museum of Applied Art, which contains the Guelph Treasure on the ground floor, also including the rooms occupied by Frederick the Great. The Golden Gallery is on the upper floor. In the Schlosspark is the simple mausoleum of Queen Louise and her husband, King Frederick William III, and of Emperor William I and his wife, the Empress Augusta (d. 1890). The noble marble sculpture is by C. Rauch and E. Encke. In the Belvedere is a collection of Berlin porcelain made in the Royal Porcelain factory.

Christian Democratic Union
(CDU, *Christlich Demokratische Union*)

The Christian Democratic Union is the political heir of the prewar Catholic CENTER PARTY. Although all Catholics did not support the Center Party, it had considerable support from Catholics, especially women after 1919, and had some clerical leadership. Protestants had not had a single party representing their denominational interests. The physical devastation and corruption of Christian moral values that HITLER had brought on Germany led many German Christians to look to their religion as the only social force that had not been perverted by Nazism and that could provide guiding principles for political life in postwar Germany. During and after the war Christian Democracy became a popular political creed in many countries of devastated Europe. So parties formed locally in the Western zones of occupation, based on Christian ideals but without denominational distinction. The main centers were in the RHINELAND, BAVARIA, and BERLIN.

CDU officials established a Christian party designed to appeal to all social classes and regions. The CDU was eager to bridge the Catholic and Protestant denominations. The Catholic Church gave its blessing and believed that an interdenominational party could also be of help in its Christian mission. The party followed a pragmatic program, which appealed to conservative secular voters, and the CDU benefitted from the loss of Germany's eastern territories, which were predominantly Protestant and would have been less sympathetic to an interdenominational party with strong Catholic influence. The significance of the word *Union* in the party's name signaled a determination to create a loosely federated structure that would be sympathetic to regional interests and not be controlled by bureaucrats from a central party headquarters. So the CDU was structured like a federation, leaving considerable autonomy to state party organizations.

As early as December 1945 with Allied and especially U.S. blessings, the Christian Democratic groups met in Bad Godesberg to form a new political organization. The CDU leaders knew that Allied approval of their nominations to party offices would depend on their nominees having anti-Nazi records. The logical choice to head the CDU was Konrad ADENAUER, a former mayor of Cologne from 1917 to 1933. At the end of the war U.S. officials reinstated him as mayor, but later he was dismissed by the British who accused him of noncooperation with them. That did not last long, and by February 1946 Adenauer was head of the CDU in the Rhineland. The main contest for the leadership post was from Jakob Kaiser, one of the founders of the CDU in Berlin. Adenauer prevailed with his emphasis on local controls over Kaiser's centralized organization. By 1948 the Soviets were forbidding the Berlin and eastern zone CDU representatives to attend Western meetings.

In 1947 the CDU drafted a basic program that emphasized the party's commitment to Christian ethics rather than materialism. They wanted the power of the state to be limited and the rights of individuals protected. Economically, the program opted for a middle-of-the-road course between private enterprise favored by conservatives and state socialism favored by the SPD. Adenauer and other conservatives recognized that many voters were attracted by progressive Christian values, but not socialist ones, so backed a mixed economy with some nationalization, for instance, of the coal industry and reorganization of steel and chemical industries. In practice, the Ahlen program was disregarded, and the CDU supported the capitalist system, backing the ideas of Ludwig ERHARD, who was director of economics in the Bizonal Administration of the Americans and the British. What ended up being put into practice was a "social market economy" a mixture of free enterprise system and social protection for the underprivileged. The conservative direction of the CDU provided its ideological orientation for the future. Adenauer expressed his support for a strong procapitalist, pro-Western, and anticommunist views.

From 1946 to 1949 the strength of the CDU was already evident in five of the 11 states that had elected CDU-led governments and in the Parliamentary Council, which was to draft a constitution. In the first federal elections in 1949 the CDU/CSU alliance won a majority of the seats in the BUNDESTAG. The CHRISTIAN SOCIAL UNION (CSU) was the more conservative sister party of the two and based largely in Bavaria with its electoral support from Catholics and conservatives. Adenauer became chancellor of the fledgling FEDERAL REPUBLIC. They called him *Der Alte* (The Old One), an affectionate term. In 1950 at the first West German convention of the CDU he eliminated his rivals. Without a central party organization the CDU had managed to govern in BONN. In the first two decades the local organizations were satisfied to be a purely electoral organization led by Adenauer and his successors, Ludwig Erhard and Kurt Georg KIESINGER operating out of the chancellor's office. The party won the elections in 1953, 1957, 1961, and 1965. The SPD did not win enough votes until 1969 after the CDU had been in office for 20 years and then another 16 years under Helmut KOHL, starting in 1982.

Christian Social Union
(CSU)

The Christian Social Union (CSU) is the successor to the BAVARIAN PEOPLE'S PARTY (BVP) of the WEIMAR REPUBLIC. The CSU is the sister-party of the CHRISTIAN DEMOCRATIC UNION (CDU). While the CDU is organized throughout the rest of Germany, the CSU competes for votes only in BAVARIA. The CSU was founded by Adam STEGERWALD (1874–1945), a trade union leader during the Weimar Republic, and Josef Müller, who had been active in the resistance against the Nazis.

While the prewar BVP had appealed mainly though not exclusively to Catholic voters, the CSU like the CDU attempted to create a popular party based on Christian principles able to attract a wider spectrum of voters from other Christian denominations. Denying that it represented only traditional Bavarian interests, the program of the CSU attempted to appeal to all social and occupational groups in society and be a true party of the people (*Volkspartei*), which the BVP was not. The CSU also hoped to bridge the political differences that had splintered the political opposition to the radicalism of the NAZI PARTY.

Between 1945 and 1949 there were two groups that competed for power within the party. The more liberal group, led by Stegerwald and Müller, wanted to steer the new party away from the very conservative orientation of the former BVP. Their influence enabled the CSU to attract voters among Protestants and industrial workers. The second group formed around the conservative leaders of the former BVP, Anton Pfeifer and Fritz Schaeffer, who represented the interests of Roman Catholicism and southern Bavarian traditionalism. These conservatives won out in the struggle for leadership of the party, when in 1949 Josef Müller was forced out as chairman of the party, which reduced the influence of the liberal wing of the party. The most famous of the leaders of the CSU was Franz Josef STRAUSS, who became the CDU/CSU candidate for chancellor in 1980.

The reform of postwar Germany in a federalist direction was one of the party's principal goals. Its leaders believed that only a federal system could prevent another dictatorship like that of the Nazis, or a new Communist one, while also protecting Bavaria's cultural heritage. The CSU also took a firmly conservative position on almost every political issue. During the years after the war it contributed to the success of democracy in the West German FEDERAL REPUBLIC. In the debate over the organization of the federal government the CSU favored the existence of a separate upper chamber of the federal government, the Federal Council (BUNDESRAT), which was to be selected by the state governments. Interestingly, the CSU initially voted against the adoption of the BASIC LAW because it considered it insufficiently protective of states' rights, although it eventually agreed to adopt it. Between 1945 and 2003 the CSU established itself as the dominant power in the Bavarian government. It promoted a modern entrepreneurial capitalist agenda, and since the 1960s Bavaria's predominantly rural economy has become industrialized.

Civil Code, German (Revised 1900)

The old Prussian Civil Code of 1794 had given the man a privileged position in the family. Married women had a restricted legal status. The husband had the right to make all the decisions affecting the family. He made the decisions concerning education; he was the child's legal guardian; he controlled the wife's wealth, which she brought into the marriage or inherited. The new revised German Civil Code of 1900 (Bürgerliches Gesetzbuch), which remained the law even past 1945, for the first time made women "legal persons," that is, married women were granted full legal capacity and competence. Husbands lost legal guardianship of their spouses, and the money a woman earned was now rightfully hers. Women were allowed to engage in legal contracts. Women also could enter universities, which some did in 1901 at Freiburg and HEIDELBERG. The first German woman to earn a Ph.D. was the historian Ricarda HUCH.

In the special case of divorce law the German Civil Code was even more backward than the Prussian Code of 1794. It reduced the number of legitimate reasons for ending marriage, which hurt women more than men because they were the more likely to initiate divorce proceedings in unsatisfactory marriages.

After WORLD WAR II the BASIC LAW decreed that male-female equality was binding in all aspects of the law. Nevertheless, there still was certain legislation that explicitly discriminated against women. For example, the 1950 provisional Federal Personnel Law included a clause on celibacy for female public officials. The family law that was part of the 1900 Civil Code was still valid in 1953 and was not replaced until 1958 with the Law on Equality. But married women actually had to wait until 1977 before genuine improvement in their status took place. In the First Law on the Reform of Marriage and Family Law, a new image of marriage was finally presented as a partnership of equal and shared responsibilities.

Clausewitz, Carl von (1780–1831)
Prussian general and theorist

The standard work on the theory and conduct of war, Carl von Clausewitz's *On War*, has become a classic and can be found in the library of every military academy. It is a work that defines war in political terms, that it "is simply a continuation of politics by other means." Clausewitz was one of a group of Prussian reformers that included Baron Karl vom und zum STEIN, Gerhard von Scharnhorst, and Neithardt von GNEISENAU. The phrases most often used to describe Clausewitz are the "philosopher of war," "a capable Prussian general," and "soldier and thinker."

Clausewitz was born in Burg near Magdeburg (the capital of the state of Saxony-Anhalt) on June 1, 1780, the son of a retired Prussian officer. He joined the army at the age of 12, experienced active service in the French campaigns of 1792–93, and was commissioned at 15. He was captured at JENA. He entered the War Academy in BERLIN at age 21 and had the good fortune to be influenced by the great military reformer Scharnhorst. In despair over the Prussian king's policies toward France, he immigrated to Russia and served in the War of 1812 and the WARS OF LIBERATION. After 1815 he held various appointments. In retirement he wrote extensively, especially *On War*, and died of cholera at BRESLAU in 1831.

Besides *On War*, Clausewitz wrote other works on military history. In 1807, for instance, he wrote three articles on the French victories at Jena and AUERSTADT, and on the subsequent collapse of the Prussian armies. During the Wars of Liberation he wrote an account of the spring campaign of 1813. From then on until his death he wrote voluminously but did not publish. In 1832 the publication of his collected military works began. Out of a total of 10 volumes (*Hinterlassene Werke*), the first three contain his unfinished manuscript *On War*. In the remaining volumes he wrote seven campaign histories from the 16th century to the BATTLE OF WATERLOO. Besides studies on political and cultural subjects there is a biographical essay on Scharnhorst, the leader of the Prussian reform movement. Through philosophical reasoning and astute judgment of human nature, Clausewitz probed deeply into the essence of war. He saw war as a continuation of politics. He advocated the idea of national war that should be ruthlessly and swiftly conducted so as to achieve decisive results in a minimum of time.

concentration camps

Concentration camps were enclosures for political dissidents and racially persecuted peoples of the Nazi state, intended for their correction, punishment, and eventually execution. The camps were officially known as State Camps for Rehabilitation and Labor. As the Prussian minister of the interior, Hermann GÖRING, in charge of the police and the GESTAPO as well as the secret security police, quickly placed Nazi enemies in "protective custody" in camps hastily established by the SA and SS in the state of PRUSSIA. On February 28, 1933, Chancellor Adolf HITLER obtained from President Paul von HINDENBURG an emergency decree that abrogated the constitutional rights of German citizens, and after Hitler was given dictatorial power, political opponents were incarcerated. In BAVARIA, where Heinrich HIMMLER was police president, he directed on March 21, 1933, the construction of the "model" concentration camp (*Konzentrationslager*, or KL) in DACHAU, which was placed under the command of Theodor Eicke. Dachau became infamous as the training center for SS guards and administrators for other camps. Rudolf HÖSS, who later became commandant at AUSCHWITZ, and Adolf EICHMANN, a chief administrator of the FINAL SOLUTION, were trained there. Other camps that followed were Ravensbrück (est. 1934) in Mecklenburg; Sachsenhausen (est. September 1936) near Berlin-Oranienburg; BUCHENWALD (est. July 1937) near WEIMAR; Flossenburg (est. May 1938) in the Upper Palatinate; and Mauthausen (est. 1938) near Linz in AUSTRIA. In 1934 Himmler and the SS took over the operation of the camps and established procedures for admission and supervision. Along with political reeducation for dissidents, flogging and torture also were used as means of coercion.

The number of camps increased from more than 30 principal camps to a total of 1,000 lesser camps supplying labor for war industries. Their purposes changed as new economic objectives were established. Between 1936 and 1941 up to 75,000 prisoners worked in quarries and the building of camps. Beginning around November 1938, with Kristallnacht (*see* NIGHT OF BROKEN GLASS) and the invasion of Poland, Jews and Poles were increasingly brought into the camps and used as forced labor. Industries even built factories near some camps to avail themselves of the labor. New camps opened up as the war progressed. Some of the prominent ones were Theresienstadt in Bohemia; Auschwitz, Maidanek, and Stutthof in Poland; Natzweiler-Struthof in Alsace; Kaunas and Riga in the Baltic states; and BERGEN-BELSEN and others in Germany.

In summer 1941 Hitler decided to initiate the Final Solution under cover of a war in which he assumed Nazi Germany would be victorious. The principal purpose of the Final Solution was the annihilation of the remaining Jewish population of Nazi-occupied Europe. The technical challenges in achieving this goal were enormous. Rudolf Höss was directed to enlarge Auschwitz because of its ready railroad connections and isolation from populated areas. Four million Jews and others were killed at Auschwitz and another million at Maidanek. Other major annihilation camps were built in the so-called General Government area of Poland; intended principally for the annihilation of Jews were Chelmno (340,000), Belzec, Sobibor, and Treblinka each with a daily killing capacity of 15,000–25,000. There were many other camps at which both Jews and non-Jews were forced to labor and were tortured, starved, and murdered.

It is complex to explain exactly why the camps operated as they did. Beginning in 1936 the SS camp guards were called the Death's Heads Corps (Totenkopfverbande). Internal discipline was the responsibility of camp commandants, block chiefs, and Kapos. Some of the officers were German criminals, while other prisoners in the camps were inmates who had decided to collaborate to avoid death and were rewarded with privileges for good service, which rewarded unnecessary brutality. Divide and conquer was the method that contributed to efficient rule. Inmates were color-coded with symbols on the bodies. Starvation, torture, beatings, and medical experiments were part of the camp life. The camp doctor at Auschwitz, Josef MENGELE, became notorious for his extreme experimental surgery. The social interactions in the camps have been studied elaborately. While some of the operational characteristics of the camps were derived from Nazi culture and the regime's goals, other aspects of the terror of camp life resulted from the specific training of the guards and the "antagonisms and dependencies" in the camps. When prisoners were gassed their goods and their bodies were used for economic purposes: clothes, money, valuables, gold fillings, female hair. Even body ashes were used for fertilizer. Out of the 6 million Jews who were killed by the Nazi regime, about 3 million died in the death camps.

The camp system disintegrated with the advance of Russian and Allied forces. Auschwitz was closed down in January 1945. As the camps were closed, those who could move were forced on "death marches" to camps within Germany, where some 100 camps housed nearly 500,000 "Aryans" and 200,000 Jews. In the West when the British liberated Bergen-Belsen on April 13, 1945, they found some 10,000 corpses, and only about one-third of the remaining 38,500 still living survived. Although exact figures are difficult, it is estimated that between 7 million and 11 million individuals perished in the camps.

Concordat of 1933

Concordats are treaties between the papacy and a national church intended to protect the rights of the Catholic Church. The Concordat of 1933 was one of those treaties, this time between the papacy and Nazi Germany.

Pope Pius XI preferred to rely on concordats with dictatorships to protect the interests of the church against the uncertain policies of postwar governments and the threat of atheistic communism. During the WEIMAR REPUBLIC, although several attempts were made to conclude a concordat with the Reich government, one was never successfully negotiated. When HITLER came to power, his interest in a concordat arose out of his acknowledgment that the church and especially the political activities of the clergy were a fundamental obstacle to his establishment of a dictatorship. During his early months as chancellor Hitler pursued a sham conciliatory policy toward the church, promising to protect and strengthen Germany's Christian traditions and institutions. The German bishops, on the other hand, responded to Hitler's promises, threats, and pressures by reversing their earlier condemnation of National Socialism. During that same month in March the Catholic CENTER PARTY voted for the ENABLING ACT, which gave Hitler dictatorial powers. In April the Reich government initiated the negotiations for the Concordat, which took place between Papal Secretary of State Eugenio Pacelli, the former papal nuncio in BERLIN and future pope PIUS XII, and conservative Catholic vice-chancellor Franz von

PAPEN. Negotiations continued while hostile actions were aimed against the church by Nazi officials. The papacy hoped to erect a legal wall to defend the freedom and institutions of the church, especially denominational schools.

After the Catholic political parties (the Center and BAVARIAN PEOPLE'S PARTY [BVP]) had disbanded, the negotiations were concluded with a solemn agreement and ceremony. The Concordat was signed on July 20, 1933, and the ceremonial exchange of documents took place in the Apostolic Palace of the Vatican on September 10, 1933. The treaty established a permanent basis for the regulation of relations between the Catholic Church and the German state. Of the 33 articles, 21 pertained to the rights of the church. The Concordat guaranteed the church the right to teach and publicly defend Catholic principles. The right to operate Catholic schools was clearly recognized. The freedom of church organizations, especially Catholic Youth associations, was safeguarded, but they could not be politically oriented. Article 31 concerning religious, cultural, and educational associations was left purposely vague and subject to future negotiations. Explicit pledges safeguarded communications with Rome—canonical regulations governing religious orders and ecclesiastical property. Bishops were to have the right to approve instructors of religion in the state schools. Actually, privileges that had existed only in predominantly Catholic regions now were extended throughout the Reich, that is, the right to assure that religious education was in accordance with Catholic principles. Catholic parents could even demand the creation of confessional schools, whereas the WEIMAR CONSTITUTION (article 174) had prohibited them. The freedom to make ecclesiastical appointments was also included, though limited in some cases by German citizenship or a period of education in Germany. The state did not have the right to veto ecclesiastical appointments, but consultation was necessary. A secret military annex was included, which obligated seminarians to perform military service during a general mobilization. Article 16 required bishops to take a loyalty oath to the German government. The clergy were to be German citizens and have a German education. Religious education was intended to inspire patriotism and loyalty to the state. Article 21 provided that Catholic pupils would continue to have religious instruction in state schools. Article 32 fulfilled Hitler's goals of disbarring the clergy from politics, membership in political parties, or even the promotion of one.

The Reich Concordat followed the pattern established by the Lateran Treaty between Mussolini and the papacy and not the concordats concluded with individual German states. The state treaties had been negotiated through a process that involved the bishops, clergy, and laity, providing advice and influencing the final form of the concordat. The Lateran and Reich Concordats followed "an authoritarian model." Hitler had thereby fulfilled a goal he had already envisioned in 1929, when the Lateran Treaties were concluded by which he achieved the removal of the clergy from politics. Because of the Enabling Act, the provisions of the Concordat came into force without approval of the Reichstag. World opinion regarded the Concordat of 1933 as a diplomatic victory for Hitler.

Condor Legion

During the Spanish civil war a unit of the German AIR FORCE (Luftwaffe) known as the Condor Legion, was assigned to support General Francisco Franco's nationalist attempt to overthrow the Spanish republic. In addition to the aircraft about 5,200 troops were committed to the civil war.

The Condor Legion was composed of several squadrons of Junker-52 bombers and Heinkel-51 fighters. Carrying 18 men plus the crew, the Junker-52 was used to transport Franco's troops from North Africa but was principally used as a bomber to attack Spanish towns behind Loyalist lines. (Later the Junker-52 was made famous in the invasion of Norway when it transported 30,000 men and supplies). Field Marshal Hugo Sperrle (1885–1953), who had helped shape the doctrine and organization of the Luftwaffe in the interwar period, was appointed commander of the 100 German planes by Hermann GÖRING, who was head of the Luftwaffe and minister of aviation. Sperrle advised Franco's high command in their use of forces. One of the notorious bombing raids carried out by the legion occurred on April 27, 1937, against Guernica, which caused a great loss of human life. The raid was immortalized by Pablo Picasso in his painting by the same name, one of his most famous. In 1938 Sperrle's Condor Legion made bombing raids on the great city of Barcelona, which foreshadowed the bombing of urban centers during WORLD WAR II. As commander, Sperrle was succeeded by Maj. Gen. Helmuth Volkmann in November 1937 and by Brig. Gen. Wolfram Baron von Richthofen in November 1938.

Confederation of the Rhine

The Confederation of the Rhine was a Napoleonic creation set up by the Treaty of Paris of July 7, 1806. It resulted from Napoleon's successful Ulm-Austerlitz campaign, and its purpose was to consolidate the French hold on western Germany and to neutralize the influence of AUSTRIA and PRUSSIA. Napoleon made himself Protector of the Confederation.

The original 16 states that joined the confederation included BAVARIA, BADEN-WÜRTTEMBERG and Hesse-Darmstadt, whose princes became grand dukes, the principality of Berg (created from Bavarian and Prussian territory ruled by Napoleon's Marshal Murat) and the duchy of Nassau. Ten small "nonmediatized" counts or princes were included under the chairmanship of K. Th. von Dalberg, the prince-primate, who himself received his own principality composed of the Grand Duchy of FRANKFURT. The confederation grew to include 36 German states. With the end of the HOLY ROMAN EMPIRE the other states that joined were the cities of NUREMBERG and AUGSBURG, the new Grand Duchy of Würzburg and in 1807 the newly formed Kingdom of Westphalia. With the defeat of Prussia in October 1806, the kingdom of SAXONY also joined, as did Mecklenburg.

The confederated states were obligated to maintain armies of 63,000 men, which were commanded by French officers; the confederation also entered into a military alliance with France. The confederation received the advantages of the Napoleonic Codes and a formal constitution on the French model. There were about 8 million Germans who had now become subjects of the French Empire. The states of Bavaria and Württemberg jealously guarded their newly won sovereignty and resisted the development of a governing council for the confederation. Napoleon himself interfered little in the affairs of the confederation, except to recruit auxiliary troops and general support for his foreign policy. With the Prussian war and the chain of wars that occurred between 1806 and 1812, Napoleon neglected to strengthen the confederation's federal authority. On August 1, 1806, the Rhenish Confederation seceded from the Holy Roman Empire and on August 6 Emperor FRANCIS laid down his crown to the old German Empire. The confederation lasted until Napoleon's defeat in 1813 at the BATTLE OF LEIPZIG. When the French departed, the confederation disintegrated.

Confessing Church

The Confessing Church was a movement within the Protestant churches in Nazi Germany opposed to the corrupting influences of Hitler's German faith movement. The name was adopted in 1934 for those opposed to the attempts by the rival GERMAN CHRISTIANS to impose pro-Nazi ideas and practices on church life.

Shortly after coming to power, Adolf HITLER made it clear that he wanted a Reich church that supported his ideas on race and leadership. The group called the German Christians enthusiastically supported his ideas and with the help of Nazi agencies they gained control of Protestant church offices. On July 14, 1933, a new constitution for the Reich church was formally accepted by the REICHSTAG. Then there was a struggle over the election of the new Reich bishop, Ludwig Müller, who was supported by Hitler and who was elected on July 23. The German Christians called for the removal of all anti-Nazi elements from the church and the eradication of Jewish influences on Christianity.

In opposition to these moves, Martin NIEMÖLLER, a former U-boat commander and pastor of a fashionable church in BERLIN who was initially a supporter of National Socialism, came to the defense of the traditional church. He founded the Pastors Emergency League to fight for the independence of the church along traditional lines and especially opposed Nazi racial doctrines. Other clergymen followed, such as Karl BARTH and Dietrich BONHOEFFER, and by the beginning of 1934 some 4,000 pastors joined the league. Some pastors were reprimanded and some arrested. It was these pressures that led to the organization of the Confessing Church led by a Reich Council of Brethren under the theologian Karl Barth. The Confessing Church held a synod in Barmen in May 1934 and produced a statement of members' beliefs, the BARMEN DECLARATION, which expressed their opposition to the heresies of the German Christians and the totalitarian claims of the state on the church. The Barmen Declaration was not a statement of political protest, and the pastors remained loyal to Hitler, maintaining the traditional Lutheran respect for rulers. In 1936 the Confessing Church challenged Nazi racial doctrines and accused the party of trying to substitute a religion based on the glorification of race. This letter was read by three-fourths of the pastors in PRUSSIA. Between 1934 and 1937 the Confessing Church waged a valiant theological battle against the Nazis. The Nazis, however, understood this as resistance and increased their persecution and even arrested some Lutheran bishops. Niemoller himself was sent to a concentration camp in 1937. Demonstrations in cities resulted, and Hitler modified church policy by replacing German Christians with conservative orthodox bishops and officials. Nevertheless, church seminaries were closed and persecution continued. Leaders were defamed as unpatriotic, which caused confusion and division within the church. Many pastors were called into military service during the war but still were unpopular due to accusations that they were disloyal. In general, clerical opposition to the regime was mainly passive.

Congress of Vienna (September 1814–June 1815)

The international congress held during 1814–15 in Vienna, the capital of AUSTRIA, was assembled to work out a territorial settlement after the NAPOLEONIC WARS. The settlement reached at Vienna was based on the principles of compensation for the victors, the reestablishment of legitimate monarchs wherever possible, and the balance of power.

The Congress of Vienna was not a deliberative assembly, and most of its decisions were made by the Great Powers, the four Allied Powers of Austria, PRUSSIA, Russia, and England. Although there were many others, the chief delegates to the meeting were; Clemens METTERNICH (Austrian Empire); Karl August von HARDENBERG, who was assisted by Wilhelm von HUMBOLDT (Prussia); Emperor Alexander I, Neselrode, and the Prussian reformer Baron Karl vom und zum STEIN (Russia); Viscount Robert Castlereagh and the duke of Wellington (Britain); Talleyrand (France); and Cardinal Consalvi (the papacy). The secretary-general of the congress was Friedrich von GENTZ, a Prussian who had been in the Austrian diplomatic service since 1802 and had been Metternich's political adviser. Gentz supported Metternich's position at the congress and favored German unification. The representative from defeated France, Talleyrand, was representing the restored king of France, Louis XVIII. In comparing his presence at the peace conference in 1814–15 with the absence of German representatives at the peace conference after WORLD WAR I at Versailles, a moderate settlement was achieved in 1815 versus a very punitive one in 1919. Talleyrand was able to play off one rival group against the other, and his vote was important.

The territorial settlement was embodied in the Final Act of June 9, 1815, which generally was known as the Treaty of Vienna. First, three new states were created, one of which was a united Kingdom of the Netherlands (Belgium, Holland, and Luxembourg). The second and most important for Germany was the creation of a GERMAN CONFEDERATION (Deutscher Bund), which consisted of 35 monarchical states and four city republics loosely linked with no central administration, except a Federal Diet at FRANKFURT, which was to be the chief organ of the defensive confederation. Although the settlement flouted the principle of nationalism in Germany, its member states pledged mutual aid in defense of the confederation. The congress in a forward-looking decision stipulated that each member of the confederation should establish assemblies of estates. Third, a free city of Cracow was created. Two subject "kingdoms" were created: Lombardy-Venetia, whose king was the Austrian emperor; and Poland, which was to be ruled by the czar of Russia. The legitimate dynasties were restored in Spain, Naples, Piedmont, Tuscany, and Modena. Austria received not only Lombardy-Venetia, but Dalmatia, Carniola, Galicia, and Salzburg. The reestablishment of the the Swiss Confederation and the guarantee of its neutrality and independence was a very enlightened decision. What to do with the kingdom of SAXONY was one of the major disagreements at the congress. Saxony, which had been an ally of Napoleon, was a suitable compensation for Prussia to relinquish its Polish territories to Russia. The king of Saxony was allowed to remain on his throne and kept possession of the important cities of DRESDEN and LEIPZIG. Prussia also obtained Posen, DANZIG, considerable gains in Westphalia, and the former Swedish territories in Pomerania. The Norwegians were united to Sweden. Britain retained Malta, Heligoland, Cape of Good Hope, Ceylon, Tobago, Santa Lucia, and Mauritius and was also given a protectorate over the Ionian Islands.

The congress made several significant pronouncements. It established the principle of free navigation of the RHINE and the Meuse. It also formally condemned the slave trade. It also recommended an extension of the rights granted to the Jews, especially in Germany. The congress also established a system of ambassadorial precedence, which influenced international diplomacy throughout the 19th century.

conservatism (1815–1945)

Conservatism is an ideology (a set of moral, material, and political beliefs) that came into being in response to the revolutionary changes brought on by liberalism and democracy, which were spawned by the ENLIGHTENMENT and the French Revolution. As a modern political philosophy, European conservatism originated in 1790 with the English thinker Edmund Burke and his *Reflections on the Revolution in France*. Burke enunciated a philosophy of evolutionary conservatism and believed that society was a contract between the living, the dead, and future generations. He was opposed to revolutionary change. Burke was popularized in Germany and Austria by Friedrich von GENTZ. Their ideas were reinforced by the influence of French writers such as De Maistre, Bonald, and Chateaubriand and given form in Germany by romantic pamphleteers such as Adam Müller, August and Friedrich SCHLEGEL, and Franz von BAADER, all of whom gave expression to the conservative philosophy of the German Restoration.

Prince Clemens von METTERNICH was the best-known exponent of conservatism in the German states; he believed in the principle of legitimacy and sought to restore the old order of government and society wherever possible. The most important conservative German thinker in the years immediately after 1815 was Carl Ludwig von Haller (1768–1854), who opposed the secular abstractions of Enlightenment political theories. His influence rested on his six-volume study *The Restoration* (1816–22), in which he gave conservative political thought an intellectual foundation, replacing the social contract theory of the revolutionaries. He believed that a ruler's power was natural, that the state was not a sacred community different from other social institutions, and that the rights and powers of the state were based on the same principles as families and communities. The conservatives in general insisted that they were not opposed to liberty but mainly the emancipation promised by the Enlightenment. Rather, conservatives believed in a liberty that was rooted, defined, and protected by custom.

The philosopher of German conservatism, however, was Friedrich Julius Stahl (1802–61), a Jew who converted to Christianity. His rabbinical training left a deep imprint on him, causing him to stress the role of religion and ritual in society. Like Haller, he was opposed to the natural law doctrines of the French Revolution. He believed that kings were the agents of God on earth and the divine character of the state gave it its legitimacy and its right to exercise power over its members. The law of reason and impersonal laws were to be replaced by personalistic theism. The true state, he thought, was a Christian state, paternalistic and absolute. Constitutions were worthless scraps of paper. These were the doctrines in which the Prussian ruling class believed in its fight against the growing strength of constitutionalism, liberalism, and revolutionary nationalism.

Although conservatives had their differences, most of them favored obedience to legitimate political authority, believed that organized religion was a fundamental foundation to the social order; they hated revolutions, opposed liberal demands for civil liberties, representative government, and the goals of national unity. The community took precedence over individual rights, and tradition rather than reason was the appropriate guide for the social order. The groups that supported conservatism after 1815 were the hereditary monarchs, government bureaucracies, land-owning aristocracies, and the Protestant and Catholic Churches. Their dominance was almost overthrown in the REVOLUTION OF 1848, but they recovered in the counterrevolution with the help of the military. During the 1850s conservatives turned increasingly to political repression to prevent the revival of liberalism. Reform projects ranging from eliminating the last vestiges of feudal obligations in the countryside to increasing rights of self-government in the municipalities where liberal political influence was the greatest were stopped. With the ascension to the throne of King William I in PRUSSIA; a conflict between the new king and Parliament over army reform began in 1859 and lasted until 1866. The Conservatives had insisted that political authoritarianism was based on the union of throne, altar, and the army, and should prevail over popular elections and parliamentary government. Traditionally, the conservatives had also preferred Prussian particularism over German nationalism, agriculture over industry, and traditional responsibilities over individual freedom.

After Otto von BISMARCK brought about German unification, conservatives did not agree with all of the changes that occurred. Besides national unity, Bismarck also appealed to the liberals with a popularly elected REICHSTAG. But conservatives were also facing the changes brought about with the Industrial Revolution and the breakdown of traditional class structure. Conservatives became more divided over time, splitting into two groups: the GERMAN CONSERVATIVES and the Free Conservatives. They were united in defending the Prussian system of government established in 1851, but they differed over the new Empire. The German Conservatives, who were dominated by estate-owning JUNKERS in the Prussian east, were opposed to modernization and wanted to preserve traditional society and government. The Free Conservatives, on the other hand, supported unification and industrialization as a means of strengthening Prussian conservatism. The latter were known as the Imperial Party and had become insignificant by 1914. The NATIONAL LIBERAL PARTY also had conservative tendencies after 1890 as many of its backers were iron and steel industrialists. With military defeat and the abdication of the Kaiser, conservatism lost its influence. Its intransigence in opposing the reform of the PRUSSIAN THREE CLASS VOTING SYSTEM during peacetime blocked moderate constitutional reform and contributed to the November Revolution.

With the establishment of the WEIMAR REPUBLIC conservatives went into opposition. They hated the republic and its socialist and liberal leaders. Political conservatism established the monarchist GERMAN NATIONAL PEOPLE'S PARTY (DNVP) in November 1918. It supported the restoration of the monarchy or the creation of an authoritarian state. Conservatives appeared to gain in strength with the election of retired Field Marshal Paul von

HINDENBURG as president in 1925. By the end of the 1920s conservatives were fragmenting into many smaller parties. The DNVP became more radical under the leadership of Alfred HUGENBERG. Between 1930 and 1932 the crisis of Weimar conservatism was evident in the attempts of Heinrich BRÜNING with Hindenburg's support to reform the WEIMAR CONSTITUTION in a more authoritarian direction. Variants of the conservative ideology also arose that talked about revolutionary conservatism. Conservatism had become so fragmented that it could no longer present a common approach to the collapse of Weimar parliamentarianism. Some conservatives, however, supported the Nazis, while others remained suspicious of Nazi violence. It should be remembered, however, that it was conservatives like Hugenberg and Franz von PAPEN who paved the way for Hitler to be appointed chancellor by another conservative, President Hindenburg. Conservative organizations such as the Steel Helmets (Stahlhelm) and others were dissolved or co-opted. Conservatives did not respond as a group to Nazi programs or the war, some favoring the expansion of the military, and others, like General Ludwig BECK, opposing Hitler's march to war. Other conservatives participated in the RESISTANCE, objecting to the war, the persecution of the Christian churches and the destruction of the Jews. The conservative Count Helmuth James von MOLTKE played the major role in the abortive attempt on Hitler's life on July 20, 1944.

constitutional traditions

The old HOLY ROMAN EMPIRE, which ceased to exist in 1806, had no formal constitution. Although the Act of 1815 establishing the GERMAN CONFEDERATION declared that all member states should have a constitution, only the south German governments, including Nassau in 1814, BAVARIA and BADEN in 1818, complied with this requirement. In contrast to the constitutions of the United States and France, which had been fought for by its citizens, these constitutions had come about more or less reluctantly as concessions by German ruling monarchs.

It was not until the German REVOLUTION OF 1848 that the movement for a democratic constitution achieved its first breakthrough. The constitution that was drafted by the National Assembly met in Saint Paul's Church, FRANKFURT AM MAIN, adopting "the fundamental rights of the German people" on March 28, 1849. The document was the first in German history to lay down the individual's civil liberties. An important point of debate for the National Assembly was the question of which form of new government should be established in the Reich. The constitution followed the principle of the separation of powers, but final authority was to lie with the "Emperor of the Germans," to which office King FREDERICK WILLIAM IV of PRUSSIA was elected. The REICHSTAG was to form the legislative branch of government. Twenty-eight of the states in the German Confederation recognized the constitution, but the Prussian king refused to accept the imperial crown. The state constitutions that followed, as for instance the Prussian of 1848, were forced on the people by their monarchs. After the Austro-Prussian War even the purely organizational constitution of the NORTH GERMAN CONFEDERATION OF 1867, which later was expanded into the constitution of Bismarck's Second Reich in 1871, was not the product of democratic constitutional reform.

The principles and traditions enshrined in the 1849 draft were not revived until 1919, when the National Assembly, which met in WEIMAR, adopted the famous and very democratic WEIMAR CONSTITUTION. The inclusion of fundamental rights became a basic element of the Weimar Constitution. However, it proved unable to withstand the strain of Germany's political instability and the economic troubles of inflation and depression. Consequently, the constitution failed to protect the German people, and Adolf HITLER was appointed chancellor and the Nazis established a dictatorship.

Council of Trent (1545–1563)

From the beginning of the 16th century there was sentiment for calling a council of the church in order to correct scandalous abuses. A council could not be called over the head of the pope, but Paul III under pressure from the emperor and the growth of PROTESTANTISM finally overcame his fears that he would lose his primacy to a council. Although long delayed, the council met in the imperial city of Trent in northern Italy. There were three sessions spread over 18 years and the reigns of four different popes due to problems such as war, plague, and imperial and papal politics. Unlike the general councils of the 15th century, this council was under the control of the pope, and most of the ecclesiastics in attendance were Italians. Voting also was controlled, with only high churchmen able to vote, with theologians, clergy, and laity excluded. The purpose of the council was not to reach an accommodation with the Protestants as some had hoped, but to bring about internal reform and reaffirm Catholic doctrine. One of the most important reforms consisted of the condemnation of simony (buying and selling of church offices) and the requirement that bishops reside and preach in their dioceses. The council also gave the bishops additional authority to discipline popular religious practices. In order to improve the position of parish priests, the council insisted that priests be better educated, establishing seminaries in every diocese, and also be celibate and cleanly dressed. The Council of Trent reaffirmed the following: the scholastic education of the clergy; the authority of tradition; the importance of good works in salvation; the seven sacraments; transubstantiation of the Eucharist; clerical celibacy; the existence of purgatory; the veneration of saints and sacred images; and last but not least, the granting of letters of indulgence. An Index of Prohibited Books was created for protection against heresy. By 1564 censorship became a centralized institution in the church. Gradually, though over some resistance, the new legislation was effective and parish life was renewed.

The Council of Trent refused to abolish celibacy as the emperor requested. The clergy were required, however, to be better educated. At the time of the council few clergy in Germany had more schooling than the elementary city schools provided, and only a small number attended universities. Now seminaries were to be established where prospective priests were to be educated in the arts, theology, and the practice of the priesthood. But for a long time in Germany these standards were not met by the clergy, and by the 18th century few seminaries existed. The clergy were, however, to be provided with a new breviary, missal, and catechism.

The council achieved two other very important results. In philosophy the theology of St. Thomas Aquinas was given authority in the church as against the medieval philosophy of St. Augustine. There had been a revival of Thomist theology in the last years of the 15th century with the commentaries by Cardinal Cajetan. The advantages of Thomism to the 16th-century church are that it supported a monarchical conception of government as the church had under the pope, and it gave intellectual justification to the ordered and systematic administration of religion. This adoption of Thomism did not mean that the church was to follow an inflexible scholasticism, because numerous schools of interpretation grew up, from the literalness of the Dominicans to the flexibility of the JESUITS. What Thomism did reject was humanist education and criticism in favor of a scholastic commentary that affected generations of priests. The other lasting result was the confirmation of papal primacy with the popes emerging from the last session of the council in absolute control of the church. This monarchical outcome paralleled the monarchical trend then current in most of Europe.

Counter-Reformation
(Catholic Reform)

The Catholic Counter-Reformation was the response of the Catholic Church to the Protestant REFORMATION. Although it had roots in a renewed Catholic faith and piety, especially in Spain, it was mainly accomplished through the establishment of new religious orders such as the JESUITS and the meetings and reforms of the COUNCIL OF TRENT.

The need for church reform was evident to many Catholics during the century prior to the protests of Martin LUTHER. Above all, in the countries that were untouched by the waves of Protestant reform (Italy, Portugal, Spain, Poland, Ireland, and especially in Spain), ecclesiastical reform had first been initiated. The leader of the Spanish reform movement was Ximenes de Cisneros (1436–1517), the archbishop of Toledo (1495–1517), who became a cardinal in 1507. Through his connections with Ferdinand and Isabella he was able to reform the Catholic Church in Spain. Like many humanists he believed that the reform should be accomplished through the established church, which inspired the Catholic reform movements in other countries.

Especially important in the process of reform was the creation of new religious orders. Devout individuals desired to create brotherhoods and sisterhoods to revive Christian piety among the masses. The first was the Theatines founded in 1524, which aimed at influencing those in the church hierarchy. One of its founders was Bishop Carafa, the future Pope Paul IV. Another new religious order was the Capuchins, which sought to carry out the ascetic and charitable ideals of St. Francis. Another order, the Barnabites, was intended to help people in the war-torn areas of Italy. For women there was the new order of the Ursulines founded in 1535, whose purpose it was to educate girls from all social classes. The Oratorians were founded as an elite order of clergy to promote church music and religious literature. Mystics such as Saint Theresa of Avila and Saint John of the Cross also appeared and inspired the revival of mystical piety. Most of all, there were the Jesuits, a religious order that next to the Council of Trent was the most instrumental in the success of the Counter-Reformation. It was founded by Ignatius of Loyola (1491–1556), who had undergone a profound religious conversion. He and his companions offered their services to the pope and promised their obedience as "soldiers of Christ." In June 1539 the Society of Jesus was formally instituted. By the time Ignatius died, his foundation comprised 58 colleges and numerous seminaries. The first companions of Ignatius had received a humanistic education during their years of study in Paris, and they retained their high respect for the principles of liberal education, which was handed down to their successors. During the lifetime of Ignatius houses of study were established in most of the larger cities of Europe and in all the centers of academic learning.

coup of July 20, 1944

After repeated assassination attempts, Colonel Claus von STAUFFENBERG in what was named "Operation Valkyrie," succeeded in smuggling a bomb into Adolf HITLER's East Prussian headquarters, the Wolf's Lair. The bomb exploded but failed to kill Hitler, and the conspiracy collapsed.

After 1941 the military opposition to Hitler was joined by younger officers, including Colonel Stauffenberg, a relative of Count Peter Yorck von Wartenburg of the resistance group known as the KREISAU CIRCLE. Stauffenberg had been slower than others to liberate himself from his fascination for National Socialism but finally opposed Hitler and his policies; he believed that the primary goal of the resistance should be the assassination of Hitler and the overthrow of the Nazi regime. Stauffenberg created an extensive circle of younger officers who supported him, and some generals such as Friedrich Olbricht, chief of the Army Office in BERLIN, and General Henning von Tresckow. Since 1938 Olbricht had been a leader in the military opposition to Hitler. The conspirators planned to place pro-coup officers in army commands in Germany so that leaders of the NAZI PARTY and the SS in the major German cities could be seized the day Hitler was assassinated. Since no frontline commanders supported the coup, the main support had to be the conspirators in Berlin. Even before the BATTLE OF STALINGRAD Stauffenberg obtained the cooperation of Field Marshal Witzleben to head the military operation after the assassination. But by the beginning of 1944 the plotters grew anxious because the GESTAPO was breaking up the opposition, especially the Kreisau Circle led by Count Moltke. In addition, the important intelligence division, the ABWEHR, was discounted as Admiral Canaris was dismissed in February 1944.

With the invasion of Normandy in June 1944, the conspirators realized they had to act. Field Marshal ROMMEL and General von Stülpnagel, the army commander in France, were added to the conspiracy. It was lucky that Stauffenberg had been promoted, which gave him access to Hitler's military conferences. On July 11 and 15 Stauffenberg had failed in two attempts to kill Hitler. On July 20 Stauffenberg finally was successful in smuggling a bomb into Hitler's headquarters in Rastenburg. Stauffenberg had only part of one hand to arm the bombs; the other he had lost plus an eye when an allied plane had wounded him in April 1943. Stauffenberg was interrupted in the arming process, so only one bomb was ready. Nonetheless, he proceeded to the meeting and placed the bomb close to Hitler. Stauffenberg excused himself to make a telephone call. While four others died, Hitler, although injured, escaped because the force of the bomb was deflected by a large oak table, and the wooden walls of the building weakened the effects of the blast. If the meeting had been held in Hitler's bunker, the blast surely would have killed him. Stauffenberg flew off to Berlin to carry out the coup, not knowing that Hitler had not been killed. At the War Ministry in Berlin General Witzleben, the new supreme commander of the army, ordered that Nazi officials were to be arrested and SS offices seized. Conspirators in Paris, Vienna, and Prague started their coup plans. Even after hearing that Hitler had survived, Stauffenberg desperately tried to bring higher-ranking officers over to the side of the coup. Only when Hitler's voice was heard on the radio did "Operation Valkyrie" collapse. That very night Colonel Stauffenberg, Albrecht Mertz von Quirnheim, and Werner von Haeften were shot. General Ludwig BECK was forced to commit suicide, and Field Marshal Rommel, because of his popularity, was allowed to commit suicide and given an official funeral. In the following hours and days the Gestapo made some 7,000 arrests and tortured prisoners to gain information. The People's Court under Roland Freisler conducted mock trials. About 5,000 were executed, and overall some 10,000 members of the resistance became martyrs to the Nazi regime.

Cranach, Lucas, the Elder (1472–1553)
artist

A famous Renaissance painter, engraver, and designer of woodcuts, Lucas Cranach became court painter to FREDERICK THE WISE OF SAXONY. He was friends with Martin LUTHER and Philip MELANCHTHON and supported the Reformation by illustrating and publishing religious writings.

Born in Kronach, Franconia, Lucas learned the art of engraving from his father. He resided in Vienna between 1500 and 1504, painting expressive figures and dramatic landscapes. He married in 1504 and had five children, two of whom became painters. In 1505 he moved to Wittenberg, where he became court painter to three successive electors of Saxony, the most famous having been Frederick the Wise, followed by John the Constant and John Frederick Magnanimous. He held the civic offices of councilor and burgomaster, was prosperous and respected. In 1550 Cranach moved to AUGSBURG and then to WEIMAR, following the elector John Frederick into exile, where the artist died in 1553.

Cranach's earliest paintings were completed during his stay in Vienna. His style is expressive and lively in *St. Jerome in Penitence* (1502), *Dr. Johannes Cuspinian and His Wife Anna,* (1502–03). Departing from the popular iconographic style in the *Crucifixion* (1503), Cranach used a bolder style. His first signed painting was the *Flight into Egypt* (1504). Reflecting greater spiritual inspiration, the *Martyrdom of St. Catherine* (1506) depicted tongues of fire symbolizing the Holy Spirit. In 1509 he engraved his most famous, the *Penance of St. John Chrysostom.* Increasingly he stressed linear detail and clean contours, which can be observed in *Madonna and Child* (ca. 1510). He painted *Cardinal Albrecht of Brandenburg as St. Jerome in His Study,* which he modeled after the St. Jerome of Albrecht DÜRER. Cranach executed paintings on numerous themes, including portraits, hunting scenes, and classical motifs with nudes as in the *Judgment of Paris* (1530) and *Venus* (1532). His paintings in support of the Reformation were *The Fall from Salvation* (1529) and *Christ Blessing the Little Children* (1538). His most famous Reformation portrait was the frequently printed study of the head of Martin Luther's father.

cultured elites
(*Bildungsbürgertun*)

The idea of a cultured individual in the 19th century who had been educated in the classics was an educational ideal and ethic of the German elites, the upper and middle *Bürgertum*. Its closest parallel in the English-speaking world was the tradition of a liberal humanistic education of a gentleman. This education and formation was to begin in the Gymnasium and continue through the university. After graduation it would continue in a shared cultured way of life of attendance in theater, music, and museums.

The general concept of cultivation in which the a person's faculties were to be developed so that he would be an independent thinking and self-governing individual found its source in the thinking and writing of the great reformer, Wilhelm von HUMBOLDT. This Prussian reformer dreamed of overcoming social divisions of his premodern society where estates rather than social classes predominated. Humboldt had been inspired by Friedrich SCHILLER and the other intellectuals at WEIMAR to develop an educational ideal that would encourage rational thinking and self-directed study. It was part of Humboldt's struggle for spiritual reform when he spoke of private life. In PRUSSIA he was able to influence the development of the classical curriculum in the Greek spirit in the Gymnasium. He quickly discovered how difficult it was to separate the survival of the Prussian state from his cultural ideal. The reality was that for the educated elites holding an office in the state was the main avenue of status and power in a society that did not have too many job opportunities for the educated. Office for the elite *Bürghers* was the equivalent of property for the

Adam and Eve in Paradise, woodcut by Lucas Cranach the Elder, 1509 *(Library of Congress)*

aristocracy. The graduates of Gymnasiums (*Abiturienten*) and holders of university degrees (*Akademiker*) hoped to replace the aristocracy's hold on state positions by their superior performance on examinations. In society they enjoyed positions that were not merited on the basis of wealth or property through their cultural sophistication and even reserve officer's standing.

During the earlier 19th century the educated and cultured elites generally led social progress and had a liberalizing influence favoring constitutional government and nationalism. After the nation was unified, industrialized and technologically and scientifically advanced, the educational system became more specialized, and in society, more complex mass education developed. As a consequence educated elites were represented in a variety of political and social orientations. They might become more conservative, antiliberal, antimodernist, and perhaps even ANTI-SEMITIC. Many were nationalistic and proimperialist. Most probably supported WORLD WAR I. As was evident in the postwar writings of cultural leaders, they were very critical and opposed the government of the WEIMAR REPUBLIC as too socialistic and liberal. Some even supported National Socialism and its emphasis on authoritarian government. After WORLD WAR II many supported the reestablishment of its institutions and values in the FEDERAL REPUBLIC, while radical idealists favored the Communist government in the GDR.

D

Dachau

A CONCENTRATION CAMP was established by Heinrich HIMMLER at Dachau, located 12 miles northwest of MUNICH, BAVARIA. The first major concentration camp and a model for later ones, Dachau was one of three camps set up in 1933 to form the nucleus of the Nazi concentration camp system. It is said that the presence of the empty halls of the old ammunition factory was one of the reasons that Himmler chose to erect the first camp here in March 1933 to hold the great overflow of political prisoners that filled the jails and prisons of Bavaria. The police personnel protested against the lack of due process afforded all these prisoners, so they were displaced by SS personnel. On April 1, 1933, Himmler was granted authority over the camp by the Bavarian interior minister Adolf Wagner, who had placed Himmler in charge of the Bavarian Political Police and all concentration camps. From April to May the first commandant at Dachau, Hilmar Waecherle, allowed the execution of some 1,100 internees. All were Jews or Communist (KPD) officials. After protests from the minister of justice, Hans Frank, Himmler chose Theodor EICKE, who brought the camp under control and formed the SS camp guards, called the Death's Head Formations. The development of an independent political police (GESTAPO) and SS-controlled concentration camps directly under Himmler was an essentially revolutionary development.

Between March 22, 1933, and April 29, 1945, some 200,000 prisoners passed through the Dachau camp and its branches. More than 32,000 died through torture, execution, hunger, and especially the typhus epidemic that raged there in 1945. In 1941–42 about 500 operations were performed in the process of medical experimentation. Some experiments involved malaria. Captured American airmen also died in the camp.

Courageous citizens of the town of Dachau tried to smuggle food into the camp. When the end of the reign of terror was near as American forces approached, a group of citizens and escaped prisoners attempted to take over the camp. The uprising was bloodily suppressed. On April 29, 1945, American troops liberated the camp. One-third of the remaining inmates were Jews.

Daily Telegraph affair (1908)

Kaiser WILLIAM II was a misfortune for the German people. He was jealous of England's empire and desired that Germany develop its empire and have a place in the sun. The *Daily Telegraph* affair was an occasion when his impetuosity, enthusiasm, and small regard for constitutional practice was certainly evident. William's comments in the interview by Colonel Stuart Wortley were published in the London *Daily Telegraph* on October 28, 1908. In the interview the emperor made imprudent and offensive statements about the British and claimed credit for preventing the Russians from attacking Britain during the Boer War and devising the successful British war plan. Ignorant of basic political facts both in Germany and abroad, William made other statements that were politically indiscreet in an inept attempt to improve relations between Germany and England.

William's interview created a public uproar and a constitutional crisis.

In both England and Germany there was a storm of protest. It was another example of the emperor's irresponsibility at a time when public respect for him was already in question because of revelations of sexual deviance among some of his close associates. In the REICHSTAG there was a storm of protest and agreement by all parties demanding some restraint on the emperor's prerogatives in foreign affairs. One Berlin newspaper declared that to have the operations of government dependent upon the will of a single individual was "unbearable for a self-conscious nation."

Actually, William had acted constitutionally, because he had submitted the interview to Chancellor Bernhard von BÜLOW for review, who unfortunately had neglected to read it, leaving it to a lower official. Bülow neglected to admit this to the Reichstag, intimated his disapproval of the Kaiser's statements, and suggested that the emperor meant well. What the chancellor did extract from the emperor was a promise to observe proper constitutional forms for the best interests of the state. This was a personal instead of a constitutional guarantee against a repetition of the events.

The *Daily Telegraph* affair was a lost opportunity for constitutional change as had happened before in Germany's constitutional history. The debate in the Reichstag lacked discipline and organization, expressed indignation, but tended toward the usual oratorical exaggeration. The political parties temporarily united in a demand to reduce royal prerogatives and make the chancellor more responsible to the Reichstag as was the case of the prime minister in the English parliamentary system. Actually, the Reichstag lost its opportunity to control the emperor and reform the Bismarckian constitution. Apparently, few of the Reichstag members thought of exploiting the emperor's indiscretions to expand ministerial responsibility. Besides making the emperor so depressed that he contemplated abdication, the main political consequence was that Bülow lost the emperor's confidence and his job.

Daimler, Gottlieb (1834–1900)
inventor of the gasoline engine and automobile

A pioneer in the development of an internal combustion engine, Gottlieb Daimler was born on March 17, 1834, near Stuttgart. Attending technical school in Stuttgart and gaining experience at the Strassburg steam engine factory, he finally completed his training as a mechanical engineer at the Polytechnic school in Stuttgart. For a decade after 1859 he worked in heavy engineering working for Bruderhaus Maschinen-Fabrik in Reutlingen as a manager. Daimler then went to a mechanical engineering company in Karlsruhe as a director in 1869. In 1872 as chief engineer at Deutz Gasmotoren-Fabrik, he cooperated in the development of a four-stroke engine developed by Nikolaus August, which was highly profitable.

After Daimler met Wilhelm Maybach in the 1860s, they developed a lifetime collaboration. In 1882 they set up a factory in Stuttgart to develop internal combustion gasoline engines for use in vehicles. By 1883 Daimler had overcome problems in ignition, patenting a self-firing system. By 1885 Maybach and Daimler had fitted an improved version of their engine to a motorcycle, and a water-cooled engine was applied to a carriage. It was modified to drive locomotives, fire pumps, and streetcars. In 1888 it even powered a dirigible airship, marking the beginning of German airship history. They later developed a two-cylinder engine to power a motorcar, which was exhibited at the Paris Exhibition of 1889. Ironically, it gained the attention of French investors who began the manufacture of automobiles in 1891. For Daimler and Maybach they organized the Daimler-Motoren-Gesellschaft mbH in 1890. By 1895 Daimler came into full control of his company. During this period they continued experimentation, developing the two-cylinder V engine, the first four-cylinder in-line engine, the first gearbox, a water-cooling system,

A Mercedes-Benz four-passenger car, 1940 *(Library of Congress)*

and air mist carburetor. They participated in races and demonstrated the usefulness of the automobile. Daimler died in Stuttgart on March 6, 1900.

Danish War (1864–1866)

The German-Danish war of 1864–66 was the first of the three wars of German unification. The victory of the Prussian army proved the importance of the military reforms of 1862 and significantly weakened the ability of liberals to oppose the absolutism of the Prussian government.

Like most of history, events are much more complex than historians can briefly explain. Such is the case with the relation between the Danish kingdom and the two duchies of Schleswig and Holstein, over which the German-Danish War of 1864 was fought. The problem originated when a duke of the two provinces became king of Denmark and the provinces remained his personal possession but not part of the Danish kingdom. Prior to the age of nationalism this may not have mattered, but it now became a significant problem that the whole population of Holstein was German and a member of the GERMAN CONFEDERATION, while Schleswig was not a member although its population was two-thirds German and wished to join the confederation. This was opposed by the Danish minority, which wanted Schleswig to be absorbed by Denmark; this was about to happen with the promulgation of a new Danish constitution in 1863. Yet international agreements were also relevant to the crisis that was at the point of boiling into a war. In 1852 the European powers had signed the London Protocol, recognizing the Danish heir to the throne as the future monarch of the two duchies, and Denmark had promised to keep the German provinces separate from the main state. The promulgation of a new constitution in November 1863 violated this agreement by absorbing Schleswig. The new Danish king made the mistake of disregarding the London Protocol and repeated the annexation of Schleswig as had been done once before during the REVOLUTION OF 1848. Not surprisingly, German national feeling exploded. The liberals in the National Association (Nationalverein) demanded that Schleswig and Holstein be taken from the Danes, and the states of the German Confederation decided to take federal action. What was the attitude of the Prussian chancellor, Otto von BISMARCK? On the surface he declared his intention to maintain the London Protocol and the law of Europe. He was less than sincere, however, because his main intent was to prevent an independent German state from becoming a stronghold of liberalism. In addition, Schleswig and Holstein were of strategic importance to Prussia, and consequently Bismarck wanted the duchies to be annexed by PRUSSIA.

There was much oratory and discussion among the Great Powers. Bismarck urged the Austrian government to join Prussia in upholding international law, and the Viennese government reluctantly agreed. The two major German powers sent an ultimatum to the Danes to revoke the constitution and declared war when the Danes refused. This so-called Second Schleswig War commenced on February 1, 1864, and fighting ceased on July 20. It was a strange and uneven conflict. The Danes lacked the military strength to win against the Germans. The Danish army faced superior numbers and a modernized artillery that had more efficient breech-loading cannons with rifled bores, which improved accuracy. The Danish navy, however, proved its ability by blockading Prussian harbors and on May 9 defeating the Austrian fleet in the battle of Heligoland. With the invasion of 57,000 Prussian and Austrian troops under the command of General Wrangel, Danish commanders gradually withdrew the bulk of their 44,000 men to the fortress of Düppel and the island of Alsen, while the remainder of the Danish army retired to Jutland. While General Wrangel advanced into Jutland, the attack on Düppel began on April 2 and ended in the middle of the month. It was the major operation of the war, beginning with heavy artillery bombardment followed by a successful assault by Prussian and Austrian soldiers. Prussian troops fought gallantly and created a new pride in Prussian military prowess.

News of the victory created an electrifying wave of pride and patriotism in Prussia, which undermined liberal resistance to Bismarck's absolutist policies. An armistice brought a lull to the war during a conference in London, but fighting resumed in June with the German occupation of Alsen. The German fleets now occupied the islands off the west coast of Schleswig-Holstein, and the army moved to Friedrichshaven on the Danish border. A new armistice was declared on July 20, and on July 25 a peace conference convened in Vienna. Although the Danes had still hoped for the old partition, no concessions were forthcoming from the Germans. In the Treaty of Vienna the king of Denmark handed over Schleswig, Holstein, and Lauenburg to the king of Prussia and emperor of Austria. They became the personal properties of the monarchs, who agreed on the joint administration of the provinces: Prussia would administer the northern province of Schleswig, while Austria would administer Holstein.

Danzig
(Gdansk)

Danzig was the former German name of the present Polish city of Gdansk. It is located at the mouth of the Vistula River on the Baltic coast. It was first mentioned as a Polish city around the year 1000. In 1148 it was recognized as a Polish diocese and was granted municipal autonomy in 1260 as a trade center. The Polish king Casimir IV in 1466 captured the city and gave it autonomy due to its opposition to the Teutonic Knights. During the Renaissance it became the most prosperous port on the Baltic. Although populated largely by Germans, Danzig served as Poland's one seaport from the 15th century until 1793, when it was annexed to Prussia. Between 1813 and 1814 the city appealed for unification with Poland, but when the CONGRESS OF VIENNA partitioned Poland among Russia, Austria, and Prussia, Danzig went to Prussia, remaining German until 1919.

After WORLD WAR I the TREATY OF VERSAILLES, in order to give the reconstituted state of Poland an outlet to the sea, made Danzig a free city.

With about 400,000 inhabitants it had an elected senate but was administered by a LEAGUE OF NATIONS commissioner. Despite the predominantly Germanic population, Poland was given charge of foreign policy, commerce, and customs. Danzig became a symbol of German resentment against the Treaty of Versailles. A Polish corridor also separated the main territory of Germany from East Prussia, which contributed to irredentist claims to both Danzig and the corridor. From 1933 to 1939 the Senate of Danzig was Nazi-controlled. Polish-German relations over Danzig deteriorated in March 1939. On September 1 the local Nazi leader, Forster, proclaimed the union of Danzig and Germany, thereby unleashing WORLD WAR II. In March 1945 the Russians captured the city and in May handed it over to the Poles, who expelled the German population. As part of Poland it was named Gdansk.

Dawes Plan (April 9, 1924)

The Dawes Plan was a report issued on the German reparations problem by a committee appointed by the Allied Reparations Commission. The committee was headed by the American banker Charles G. Dawes (1865–1951) and was to report on the means of balancing Germany's budget, stabilizing the currency (the mark), and devising a realistic schedule for reparations payments. Germany had fallen into default on its payments, which had been imposed due to the War Guilt Clause #231 of the VERSAILLES TREATY, which held Germany and its allies responsible for all the loss and damage of WORLD WAR I.

The committee developed a plan whereby Germany would make reparations payments based on the stability of the German currency. The report was accepted by a conference of governments in August. It ended the French exploitation of the Ruhr and determined that sanctions could be applied in the future only if an arbitration board declared a flagrant default. It devised a more realistic schedule of reparation payments. To help pay its reparations debts, the railways and industrial plants were mortgaged. The schedule of payments was scaled back in favor of the Germans: a sliding scale ranging from 1 billion reichsmarks (RM), or $250 million, to 2.5 billion RM ($625 million) by 1929. The recommendations included a reorganization of the state bank and foreign loans, especially from the United States, which were to stabilize the currency. The Dawes Plan did not fix the total amount of reparations, but did determine that only one-half of the payments would come from the German budget and the rest from interest on the bonds issued for railways and industries. The plan also established a reparations agent in BERLIN, who would oversee the transfer issue. Although the occupation of the Ruhr did not end immediately, the Dawes Plan did solve the problem of inflation. A framework was, however, established for working out a permanent solution. Nevertheless, the German budget never was balanced before 1929 and the formulation of the YOUNG PLAN.

To most Germans the acceptance of any obligation to pay reparations seemed to be unpatriotic. Germans were irritated that their finances were under foreign control. Perhaps most aggravating was the fact that no final amount was established toward which the large reparations payments would be credited. The Dawes Plan certainly gave political ammunition to HITLER and the Nazis, who were opposed to the "dictatorship" of the Versailles Treaty. In his speeches Hitler emphasized that Germany still was under the control of foreign governments, and LUDENDORFF shouted that it was a disgrace for Germany and a "Jewish Tannenberg!" Even the REICHSTAG debate was a stormy one in which both right- and left-wing extremist parties assaulted the "policy of enslavement." Yet, the foreign loans helped stabilize the economy and provided a period of prosperity until the GREAT DEPRESSION.

D-Banks

The economic crisis and depression that began in 1873 inaugurated the process of centralization in Germany's banking system. The crash of the

Viennese stock market created problems for a number of German banks. An even greater impact came from the collapse of the Jay Cooke Bank in New York, which had obligations to the German institutions. In the next few years smaller private German banks were forced out of business, and the four large D-Banks emerged as dominant forces in the German banking and investment community.

Even before this, a German banking system had developed that actively aided in the development of the pre-imperial economy. Some of these early banks were the A. Schaafhausensche Bankverein (est. 1848), the Diskonto Gesellschaft (est. 1851), the Darmstädter Bank (est., 1853), the Berliner Handelsgesellschaft (est. 1856), and the Schlesische Bankverein (est. 1856).

The D-Banks included the Deutsche Bank (est. 1870), the Dresdner Bank (est. 1872), the Darmstädter Bank (est. 1853), and the Deutsche Industrie-und Handelsbank (est. 1856). The Darmstädter Bank was one of Germany's oldest banks and was founded two years after the French Crédit Mobilier in 1851. Interestingly, Abraham Oppenheimer of Mannheim, one of the founders of the Mobilier, was also one of the founders of the Darmstädter Bank. The Deutsche Bank and the Industrie-und Handelsbank both were headquartered in BERLIN, which had become a financial center since unification. The Deutsche Bank expanded rapidly and by 1876 had taken over two other banks, the Deutsche Union Bank and the Berliner Bank-Verein, becoming Germany's largest bill of exchange and investment bank. Deutsche Bank had only recently been chartered in 1870 and was founded as a joint-stock bank for the purposes of financing German trade. Until 1900 the management of the bank was in the hands of Georg von Siemens, the cousin of the electrical wizard, Werner von SIEMENS (who was aided by the Jewish banker, Max Steinthal), and Hermann Wallich.

The modern German bank, like the Deutsche Bank and the Berliner Handelsgesellschaft, played a very important role in Germany's industrial growth, as a combination of commercial and investment bank. It financed such enterprises as the Mannesmann Company, the electrical firms of General Electric Co. (AEG) and Siemens, and the construction company of Philipp Holzmann. The Deutsche Bank also merged with major regional banks. During the Weimar period it was active in financing such new industries as automobiles (Daimler-Benz), motion pictures (Ufa), and air transport (Lufthansa). Deutsche Bank also expanded into international investments in Asia and South America, as well as in North America, where it invested in the Northern Pacific Railroad.

D-Day (June 6, 1944)

D-Day was the name for the invasion of Normandy originally planned for June 5 but which took place on June 6, 1944, under Supreme Allied Commander General Dwight D. Eisenhower. On its outcome hung the fate of Europe. The invasion was history's greatest amphibious operation, which involved 5,000 ships, and approximately 11,000 air sorties. American planes alone numbered almost 13,000 aircraft, which included more than 4,500 big bombers. There were approximately 154,000 American, British, and Canadian soldiers. Of these, 23,000 were arriving by parachute and glider. In preparation there was a long-range plan of deception to obscure where the Allied landings were to take place. It also involved tens of thousands of resistance fighters in Nazi-occupied Europe.

While the Germans anticipated an invasion at the Pas de Calais, nobody informed the Seventh Army in Normandy. The German commanders, Gerd von Rundstedt and Erwin ROMMEL did not believe that an invasion was coming because gale-strength winds were churning the English Channel. While Rommel was visiting his wife and Hitler was sleeping, the first Allied soldiers came to Normandy in three airborne divisions. A panzer division was ordered to counterattack but was destroyed by Allied aircraft. The burden of defending the Atlantic Wall then fell primarily on those German soldiers in place.

At first Allied tactical bombers began to bomb the entire northwestern coast of France followed by a naval bombardment. At 6:30 A.M. the amphibious landings began at Omaha and Utah Beaches near the mouth of the River Vire. The most difficult landing was 10 miles away at Omaha Beach, where high cliffs aided the German defenders. The Americans there nonetheless succeeded in securing a beachhead during the first day, getting 34,000 troops ashore. The assault proved easier for the British and Canadian troops, and before the end of the day they had made contact with the airborne troops beyond the Orne River.

It was at 4 P.M. on D-Day that Hitler finally approved Rundstedt's use of two divisions from the large German panzer reserve. Because of false intelligence, Hitler later retracted the order and still awaited the imagined invasion at the Pas de Calais.

defenestration of Prague (May 23, 1618)

Two governors and a secretary representing the Catholic Habsburg Crown were thrown out of a window of the royal castle, Hradschin, the seat of Habsburg government in Prague, by a group of Protestant noblemen. The incident constituted a coup against the Habsburgs, which triggered the Bohemian revolt and led to the THIRTY YEARS' WAR.

Relations between Bohemia's Protestant nobility and the country's Habsburg rulers had been deteriorating due to the attempts by the Austrian government to strengthen the position of the Catholic Church and to counteract the Protestant movement. The Protestants had won great liberties with Emperor RUDOLF II's Letter of Majesty of 1609, which granted all Bohemians protection against the forceful imposition of religion. Particularly in the royal and ecclesiastical lands, both the Crown and church had the support of a strong group of the Bohemian nobility as well as the cities of Pilsen and Budweis. After FERDINAND II ascended to the throne, strong attempts were made to strengthen Catholic institutions, which greatly incensed the Protestant opposition among the nobility. Tensions reached a feverish pitch after Ferdinand, a zealous Catholic who had stamped out heresy in his domain, clashed almost immediately with the nobility. Early in 1618 he sought to stop the Protestants from building churches at the towns of Klostergrab and Braunau.

On May 23, 1618, about 100 Protestant noblemen appeared at the Hradschin castle to protest to the royal governors, who were fanatical Catholics. The stormy meeting led to a fight, during which the two governors and the secretary were thrown out of a window of the royal castle. This was an apparent imitation of the defenestration that had started the Hussite rebellion two centuries earlier. That none of the three were killed was surprising, but the incident was symbolic and made any compromise solution impossible. It constituted a coup against the Habsburgs.

The radical group of Protestant noblemen was now in control and organized a provisional government headed by Wenzel von Ruppa to organize the defense of the rights of the country. They voted to raise an army of 16,000 men under the command of Count Matthias Thurn. They tried to make distinctions, claiming that it was not a revolt against King Ferdinand, but against his governors and the JESUITS. They also hoped to receive support from other Protestant estates of other Habsburg lands, but except for Silesia, that did not occur. The revolt soon ended with a defeat of the Protestants at the Battle of White Mountain on November 8, 1620. This revolt triggered the international conflict of the Thirty Years' War and greatly altered the balance of power in Europe.

Degenerate Art

Adolf HITLER was opposed to all modern art forms from impressionism and EXPRESSIONISM to cubism, which he considered degenerate art (*entartete Kunst*). He preferred the realistic style. The Nazis persecuted modern artists, outlawing their works. The BAUHAUS was shut down. Artists were even forbidden to paint and were harassed with searches of their homes and studios. Many of the works seized were shown in the "Degenerate Art" show, which Hitler staged in 1937 in MUNICH. After this it was shown on a yearly basis to malign the art and the artists. Afterward, the art pieces were destroyed.

In 1935 Hitler had gone to DRESDEN to an art show called "Images of Decadence in Art." This exhibit gave Hitler the idea of presenting his own Degenerate Art exhibit, which opened on March 31, 1937. It included not only all the art of the Dresden exhibition but also some of the 12,980 works of decadent art that had been confiscated by Professor Adolf Ziegler, president of the Reich Chamber of Visual Arts, from more than 100 museums and 112 artists. Some of the artists with the greatest number of confiscations were Emil Nolde (1,000), Max BECKMANN (500), Oskar Kokoschka (400), and George Grosz (200). Also included were paintings by the non-German painters Cézanne, Chirico, Dufy, Gauguin, Matisse, Picasso, and van Gogh. Paintings were displayed in such a propagandistic fashion in order to demean their value. Some paintings were unframed, some hung upside down, and some with captions: "Thus did sick minds view Nature!" The exhibit also went on tour, drawing an estimated 2 million visitors. Later, in March 1939 some 4,800 paintings were burned in Berlin.

A concurrent art exhibit was sponsored by the Nazis to show paintings approved by the Nazi state. The exhibit had the title of the Greater Germany Art Exhibition and was held in Paul Ludwig Troost's new classically designed building called the House of German Art (Haus der Deutschen Kunst), still standing in Munich. The exhibit was to emphasize Hitler's ideal image of the Aryan race, glorifying the family, the honor of war, and the strength of the German soldier. Certainly, none of the cynical, pessimistic and antiwar scenes of modern art were presented, not any nudes or cubist women. It was the first of eight annual exhibitions of art approved by the Nazis.

denazification
The Allies decided as early as September 1943 that the punishment of the Nazi regime's major leaders would be their joint responsibility, while denazification of German society would be handled by each occupying government. Beginning in November 1945, 24 civilian and military officials of the Nazi regime, including Hermann GÖRING, Joachim von RIBBENTROP, Rudolf HESS, Albert SPEER, General Wilhelm Keitel, and Julius STREICHER were tried by the International Military Tribunal (IMT) in NUREMBERG. Martin BORMANN, the general secretary of the NAZI PARTY, though absent, was tried and convicted. Those on trial were indicted for crimes against peace, war crimes, unleashing aggressive war, and crimes against humanity. Eleven out of 22 were sentenced to death, some received prison sentences, and a few were acquitted, such as Franz von PAPEN, and Hjalmar SCHACHT.

Each zonal commander then conducted his own denazification program. The Russian campaign was the swiftest and most radical, and was concluded by 1948. Some 45,000 leading industrialists, landowners, military officers, civil servants, and Nazi Party officials were punished, and many were sent to labor camps. The Russians were quick to brand as fascists those who opposed the creation of the Russian-styled "People's democracy." On the other hand, the American military courts conducted trials that were conscientious and time-consuming. Following a policy that attributed a person's guilt according to the governmental office that each had held by the end of 1945, the Americans jailed 100,000 former Nazis, more than any of the other Allies. In February 1946 the Americans required Germans to fill out a questionnaire as to their activities during the Nazi period. Some 3 million persons were identified as requiring a hearing. There were, however, massive difficulties encountered because the Americans had too few personnel while the German denazification tribunals were too lenient. By 1947 the political climate had changed, and denazification became less important; among other things there was a need for businesspeople who might have been active Nazis to manage the revitalized economy. On the other hand, the British were wiser in sorting through lists of former officials, realizing that local officials and teachers might have joined only to keep their jobs. Reeducation was also a major part of the denazification process. Educational reform was difficult to accomplish because of destroyed schools, the influx of refugees, and the need for new textbooks. Each Allied zone tried to use its own educational system as a model for the Germans to follow. In the American zone the traditional three-tiered school system, including the Gymnasium, was kept, and the new texts were written from the point of view of Christian Catholic humanism, which had a strong tradition in southern Germany.

Denck, Hans (1495–1527)
pope of Anabaptists

Hans Denck was born in Habach, Upper Bavaria, educated as a humanist, and graduated from the University of Ingolstadt in 1519. He was proficient in Latin, Greek, and Hebrew, and taught in Regensburg and was headmaster in NUREMBERG. His linguistic proficiency enabled him with the cooperation of Ludwig Hetzer to make the first translation into German from the Hebrew of the prophetical books of the Old Testament.

Denck's religious formation was influenced by the tradition of German Catholic mysticism and especially that of St. Theresa and the Protestant Reformation. Seeing the dangers of legalism and the institutionalism of Lutheranism, he developed a more spiritual interpretation of the church. He believed in a concept of continuing revelation through the inner word, without which he believed the Scriptures were useless. He believed that a person had to have direct revelation from God about himself; it was not just Christians that knew God, because God spoke to all men in their hearts. Denck developed a concept of continuing revelation through the inner word. The sacraments were not necessary for salvation; his interpretation of Baptism and Holy Communion was decidedly spiritual. To Denck the only thing that mattered was rebirth itself and not the act of being rebaptized. Rebirth makes a person a member of the church, and baptism was nothing more than a recognition of that fact. In fact, Denck was rebaptized in AUGSBURG by the Swiss leader Balthasar Hubmaier. As far as his conception of the church was concerned, it was spiritual and invisible. Denck can be regarded as a philosophical exponent of the ideas that underlay all of Anabaptism.

His attempts to unify the ANABAPTISTS failed, which disillusioned him about the movement. In Basel he wrote a statement of his faith, *The Recantation of Hans Denck,* in which he abandoned his Anabaptist position. His influence continued through his written works. He died of the plague in 1527.

Depression, The Great (1929–1933)

The Great Depression was Germany's most serious economic crisis in the modern age. Although it was an international crisis, it affected Germany most seriously. Eventually, it was one of the major factors that led to the growth of National Socialism and the collapse of the WEIMAR REPUBLIC.

The German economy had never recovered from WORLD WAR I because Germany had fought the war on credit and had liquidated most of its foreign assets. The postwar depression and the inflation crisis of the early 1920s, along with the reparations burden, created further economic problems. The industrial economy also was undergoing a structural change, which created high unemployment. In 1928 and early 1929 the German economy had already been experiencing difficulties, and consumer industries were in recession. In mid-1929 heavy industry also began a serious decline. During the year and a quarter before September 1929 the stock market in Germany had dropped 14 percent and then another 15 percent by December 1929.

Capital for investment came primarily from the United States. According to tradition German banks borrowed money from private lenders on a short-term basis. American capital exports had already slowed as the stock market boom in the United States crested in 1928–29. So there already was a credit squeeze when the American stock market crashed on Black Friday, October 24, 1929. Enormous financial losses and massive failures of banks and businesses occurred. The Americans called in their short-term loans from Germany. The collapse of the stock and commodities markets produced an unprecedented economic disaster in Germany.

In 1928 unemployment had already reached considerably more than 1 million. By winter 1928–29 it had reached 2 million, and by May 1930 this number had risen to 3 million. At the end of 1932 it had reached a record high of more than 6 million. One in three workers was unemployed, and this was only those owed benefits and not the long-term unemployed who had exhausted their benefit rights. Unemployment hit those in the age group from 18 to 30 the most, and if they were still living with family, they were disqualified from receiving benefits. Every other German family was hit by the Depression whether they were middle-class or manual workers. The long-term unemployed suffered poverty, loss of status, and self-respect. They lost the opportunity to do meaningful work. The government's inability to provide adequate unemployment compensation led to great hardship, bitterness, and resentment against parliamentary democracy.

Hunger and despair were everywhere. Old people who once were well off now became street beggars. Tenants withheld rents because they had no money. Suicides were a daily occurrence. Comparatively speaking, in Germany out of 1 million people in 1932 there were 260 suicides, while in France there occurred 155, in the United States 133, and in England 85. Agricultural output in 1932 was only 65 percent of what it had been in 1928, while farms and estates were frequently auctioned off. The Ministry of Welfare in Prussia in 1931 wrote regarding the impact on children that parental unemployment resulted in lack of nourishment of children, and the neglect of hygiene caused disease to rise while there was no money for doctors or medicine.

Depressions (1873–1914)

Although Germany had already entered the modern age of capitalism and industrialism between 1850 and 1870, after unification its first great speculative boom occurred between 1871 and 1873 and was stimulated by the victory over France. Starting with the depression of 1873, Germany went through periods of recovery and renewed depression a number of times. Throughout this period industrial expansion occurred, and urbanization and social change accelerated, but it was generally a period of deflation and business concentration.

The phase in Germany's industrialization that began with a hyper-boom was stimulated by the infusion of capital into the economy from reparations at the end of the Franco-Prussian War. Because the French paid this indemnity in two years, the huge influx of capital produced a speculative fever stimulated by a 50 percent increase in the money supply, which touched every sector of the economy. Increased liquidity was not the only cause. Heavy industry especially related to railroads was swamped with orders. The war had used up railways and the annexation of ALSACE-LORRAINE required new lines. Grandiose business schemes were created to lure investors to build railroads all over eastern Europe. Laws also had been liberalized to allow joint stock companies, and every brewery or other establishment now became incorporated. In a two-year period more than 700 companies were founded. Many construction firms were established in BERLIN, where whole new neighborhoods were planned in the suburbs. If more money was needed, it could always be borrowed from the numerous new banks that sprang up, which also played a role in the stock market boom. This business frenzy came to an abrupt end as a result of a speech by Eduard LASKER, a liberal politician, which exposed the legal and business irregularities that were intended to swindle investors. The boom dissolved in collapse as public confidence evaporated.

The savings of small investors were swept away, but some important things remained as part of the new capitalistic economy. Banks played an increasing role in the economy and so did size as industry became concentrated. Four big banks (the D-BANKS) were to dominate the economy, as did giant companies in the metal trades and construction industry. Many who lost money, however, blamed Lasker and the liberals for their losses, and ANTI-SEMITIC feelings came to the surface as popular literature in such novels as *Soll und Haben* by Gustav FREYTAG and *Der Hungerpastor* by Wilhelm RAABE, which stereotyped the Jew as rapacious. Unfortunately, the Jew was identified with the stock market and capitalism, and many people began to believe in a Jewish conspiracy.

The cyclical nature of booms and busts in the industrial capitalist system had not yet become apparent. The bust and depression that began in 1873 lasted longer than expected until another upswing in the economy occurred in 1879. After a three-year period of prosperity ending in 1882, another depression occurred until 1886, and then another recovery until 1890. This was followed by a recessionary period until 1895, when an upswing in the economy occurred based on an expansion in the electrical industry lasting until 1900. Another recession occurred until 1907, after which there was prosperity up to WORLD WAR I. In this process the agricultural sector declined absolutely, as did old industries such as railroads, but iron and steel production soared as did the expansion of the electrical industry. A key problem was overproduction in boom times, which inevitably led to an oversupply of goods and decline in prices and the concentration of industry into cartels to control prices and markets.

détente

During the period of the 1960s and 1970s the United States and the Soviet Union entered a phase of their cold-war relation in which they agreed to reduce international tensions. Despite some lessening of tensions after the Cuban missile crisis in 1962, both the Soviet Union and the United States continued to build up their nuclear arsenals with intercontinental ballistic missiles (ICBMs) and MIRVs. These more complicated missile systems were then countered by antiballistic missiles (ABMs), whose purpose was to hit and destroy incoming missiles. In the 1972 ABM Treaty both nations agreed to limit these ABM systems. As far as Germany and Europe were concerned, the centerpiece of détente was the Helsinki Agreements signed in 1975, which also reduced tensions between the superpowers. The agreements recognized all borders in Central and Eastern Europe that had been established since the end of WORLD WAR II, which acknowledged the Soviet sphere of influence in Eastern Europe. The Helsinki Agreements also committed the signatories to recognize and protect the human rights of their citizens.

As far as the Germans were concerned, they benefited from the relaxation of tensions by having more open borders and increased trade with Eastern Europe. This period also witnessed the German policy of OSTPOLITIK. This policy of opening to the East, especially the GDR, began during the GRAND COALITION (1966–69) and flourished during the chancellorship of Willy BRANDT from 1969 to 1972. It reversed the cold-war policy of the HALLSTEIN DOCTRINE, which sought to undermine the GDR and isolate it in the international community. The key agreements marking détente in Germany were the Eastern Treaties signed with Moscow, Warsaw, and Prague, which recognized Germany's eastern frontiers. It also involved the BASIC TREATY with the GDR, which recognized its existence and improved relations with it. Because of his opposition to détente Walter ULBRICHT was deposed as leader of the GDR and was replaced by the more agreeable Erich HONNECKER. The latter, however, had his own reservations, insisting on Abgrenzung, that the two German states had distinctively different characters.

With the Soviet invasion of Afghanistan in 1979, the events in Poland, and the Soviet Union's arms buildup, détente ground to a halt. Germans debated to what extent they should fall in line with the U.S. response to these events. There were passionate debates centered on NATO's dual-track decision of December 1979, which provided for the deployment of American intermediate-range nuclear missiles in Europe should the Soviet Union not agree to dismantle its new SS-20 missiles.

"Deutschland, Deutschland über alles"

The "Deutschlandslied," also known as "Deutschland über alles," meaning "Germany is above everything" is a poem filled with national enthusiasm written in 1841 by the popular poet Hoffmann von Fallersleben to celebrate Germany. It was set to the rousing music that Franz Josef HAYDN had composed in 1791 and was entitled *"Deutschland, Deutschland über alles."* At first it was used as an Austrian patriotic anthem. In 1922 during the WEIMAR REPUBLIC it became the German national anthem to the words of the first verse referring to Germany's greater borders. After WORLD WAR II the second verse was used, which emphasized unity, right, and freedom.

Diesel, Rudolf (1858–1913)
inventor of the diesel engine

Born on March 18, 1858, in Paris of German parentage, Rudolf Diesel left France for England with his family during the Franco-Prussian War. From there he went to AUGSBURG, where an uncle saw to it that he received a good scientific education. In 1875 he attended the Munich Polytechnical School. He studied thermodynamics under Carl von Linde and designed an engine with a thermodynamic cycle. In 1880 he moved to Paris to work in refrigeration engineering constructing a plant for the Linde company. During the 1880s he married and had three children. In 1890 he moved to BERLIN, where he continued to work for Linde.

Rudolf Diesel invented the high-pressure oil combustion engine. In 1892 Diesel patented his design of an engine using highly compressed air and fuel, which would turn into a hot gas and combust. It was patented and described in "The Theory and Design of a Rational Heat Engine" in 1893. Diesel continued to work on the engine at Augsburg with the financial support of Maschinenfabrik, Augsburg, and Friedrich KRUPP of Essen. It was perfected by 1897, using a fuel oil that was heavier than highly combustible gasoline and had much better fuel economy. In its tests in Augsburg it attained an unprecedented efficiency for thermal engines. It was licensed all over the world, and various versions were designed for automobiles, ships, and trains. He never lived to see his most efficient engine employed in cars or trains. In 1913 he died, mysteriously falling from the steamship *Dresden*.

Dietrich, Josef "Sepp" (1892–1966)
general of the Waffen SS

Notoriously brutal, Sepp Dietrich, an early member of the NAZI PARTY, rose to the position of commander of HITLER's bodyguard regiment. He took a leading part in the Blood Purge of the SA in 1934. He commanded a tank corps in the attack on Paris, commanded an SS army on the Russian front and the Sixth Panzer Army in the ARDENNES offensive. During that offensive he was responsible for the murder of 71 American prisoners at Malmedy.

Josef Dietrich was born in Hawangen, near Memmingen, on May 28, 1892, the illegitimate son of a servant girl. A butcher by trade and with little education, he worked at various jobs until in 1911 he joined the Imperial Army. During WORLD WAR I he was promoted to the rank of sergeant and decorated for bravery. After the war he had a series of jobs from laborer to policeman. He was an early member of the NAZI PARTY and the Brown Shirts of Ernst Röhm. In 1928 he was made commander of Hitler's bodyguard and assisted in the formation of the Black Shirts (SS). In the REICHSTAG elections of 1930 he was elected from the district of Lower Bavaria. In 1931 he was promoted in the SS to lieutenant general (SS-Gruppenfuehrer). After Hitler was appointed chancellor, Dietrich selected Hitler's bodyguard regiment, which would become Leibstandarte SS Adolf Hitler. One of his notorious roles occurred in the NIGHT OF THE LONG KNIVES, also called the Röhm purge, against the SA in 1934. He carried out Hitler's orders and killed some of his closest associates. In 1938 the Leibstandarte unit became a motorized infantry unit under his command.

During WORLD WAR II Leibstandarte SS became a panzer division and remained under Dietrich's command until 1944. In 1940 he commanded a tank corps in the attack on Paris. Later, on the Russian front, he commanded an SS army. In 1943 Dietrich was given the responsibility to return Mussolini's mistress to him. In winter 1944 he commanded the Sixth Panzer Army in the Ardennes Battle of the Bulge offensive. When he did not succeed in achieving his objectives, the offensive failed. It was at this time that some of his troops massacred 71 captured American prisoners. In 1946 he was arrested and tried for his responsibility in this massacre and sentenced to 25 years imprisonment, of which he served 10. Later he was tried and sentenced in 1957 by a German court for his role in the Blood Purge. On April 21, 1966, he died in Ludwigsburg.

Diplomatic Revolution of 1756

After the conclusion of the WAR OF AUSTRIAN SUCCESSION (1740–48), Empress MARIA THERESA appointed Wenzel Anton, Count Kaunitz (1711–94), to the supreme advisory council. Kaunitz approached the problem of constructing a new foreign policy. He demonstrated the inadequacy of AUSTRIA's traditional alliances with the Maritime Powers and tried to show how they might be replaced by an alliance with France on the basis of making the dismemberment of PRUSSIA an objective of Bourbon foreign policy. After Kaunitz demonstrated on paper how this system might be brought about, Maria Theresa appointed him ambassador to France and in 1753 head of foreign affairs with the title of chancellor of state. At first France appeared uninterested. Then Austria allowed the alliance with the Maritime Powers to lapse to improve the chances of an alliance with France.

When in 1755 clashes between British and French colonists made an Anglo-French war appear imminent, Kaunitz told the French ambassador that the Habsburg monarchy would remain neutral even if the French occupied the Netherlands. Then, as if to sweeten the deal to win French support for Prussia's dismemberment, Kaunitz offered the French a part of the Austrian Netherlands. In order to replace Austria after its defection from the British alliance, Britain concluded the Convention of Westminster in 1756, which was a defensive alliance with Prussia's king, FREDERICK II (1712–86), who feared invasion by both France and Russia, to prevent the entry of foreign troops into the Germanies. The unthinkable now happened. Louis XV of France responded positively to Kaunitz's proposal of an alliance against France's archenemy Great Britain. Austria's goal of recovering Silesia now seemed assured. Kaunitz had succeeded in completely reversing the direction that French foreign policy had followed since the 16th century. Instead of fighting to constrain Habsburg power, France would now fight to restore Austrian supremacy in central Europe.

Dix, Otto (1891–1969)
artist

A prominent painter and graphic artist during the WEIMAR REPUBLIC, Otto Dix was a leading exponent of the NEW OBJECTIVITY movement. His bitter social, political, and antiwar criticism caused his condemnation by the Nazis as "degenerate."

Born on December 2, 1891, to working-class parents in Untermhaus, Thuringia, Otto Dix soon manifested inclinations for the practical arts. At school his talent became obvious so he was apprenticed to a painter in Gera. From 1909 to 1914 he studied at the School of Decorative Art in DRESDEN. His early artistic formation was influenced by Renaissance artists Albrecht DÜRER and Lucas CRANACH, but subsequently by modern impressionism and postimpressionism, and finally by expressionism, which became the style of his maturity. Like so many other young men, Dix enthusiastically volunteered for military service. It was the mass destruction of the war that inspired some of his famous war drawings. After the war he worked in Dresden from 1919 to 1922. Associated with the dadists in Berlin, he gained notoriety by having his work exhibited at the International Dada fair in 1920. He also was associated with the November Group, which tried to win support for the Weimar Republic. From 1922 to 1925 he went to the Düsseldorf Academy, where he later taught as a professor from 1927 to 1933. He enjoyed his first retrospective exhibition at the Galerie Nierendorf in 1926. After the Nazis came to power, he was forbidden to exhibit his works; some were included in the DEGENERATE ART exhibition in MUNICH during 1937, and some 260 of his works were sold or destroyed. He did not leave Germany during the war, was arrested by the GESTAPO in 1939, and even served in the defense of Dresden. After the war he continued practicing his art and enjoyed a number of exhibitions. During this early postwar period of his life he concentrated much more on lithography, and the motifs of his art were more religiously inspired. He died of a stroke at age 77.

Otto Dix is one of the typical representatives of expressionism along with George GROSZ and Max BECKMANN, who sought to use their abilities in the service of social struggle. They associated themselves with the New Objectivity movement, which emphasized representational art instead of abstractionism. During the war Dix had drawn his comrades in battle, *Two Gunners* (1917), showing frontline soldiers firing at the enemy from behind a mound of corpses, which conveyed the pitched intensity of combat. After 1921 Dix distanced himself from abstract expressionism and in 1924 commemorating the mobilization of 1914 published a series entitled *The War*, in which he depicted the grotesque face of a wounded veteran, including *The Transplant*, recalling the thousands of photographs of wounded veterans in medical journals. The two drawings were different in that *Two Gunners* bore witness to the horrors of the war through abstraction, while *The Transplant* did so in a more graphic representational manner. Other examples of Dix's new representational style were the graphite drawing, *Pimp and Whore* (1921), and the color lithograph *The Madam* (1923). Like Grosz, Dix was captivated by the Old Masters, especially the Renaissance painters Hans Baldung Grien and Matthias Grünewald. Dix used their old German glazing and the oil-on-tempera techniques and borrowed from the late Gothic painters compositional devices, expressions, and gestures.

Döblin, Alfred (1878–1957)
expressionist novelist

Born Jewish in Stettin, Alfred grew up in BERLIN. Educated in neurology and psychiatry, he conducted a practice in Berlin and during the war was a medical officer in the army. At the same time he wrote short stories for *Der Sturm*, an expressionist (*see* EXPRESSIONISM) journal he cofounded in 1910. Experimenting with narrative perspective, he gained recognition with his Chinese novel, *The Three Leaps of Wang Lun* (1915). A long historical novel, *Wallenstein*, was published in 1920. A more common expressionist topic was man's struggle against the mechanization of modern life, which he developed in *Wadzek's Battle with the Steam Turbine* (1918).

Döblin's most famous novel was *Berlin Alexander Square* (1929). It is written in a style similar to that of James Joyce's stream-of-consciousness writing, free association and jumbled realistic situations that are a radical departure from realism. He experiments with shifts in perspective. A participant in the NEW OBJECTIVITY movement, Döblin exposes the injustices of his time. The story is a pessimistic and very depressing one. A former convict, Franz Biberkopf, hopelessly struggles to regain his place in society, but the collective forces against him are overwhelming and crush his forlorn ego. The action takes place in Berlin, no longer the pride of Imperial Germany but after the war a "Sodom on the eve of its destruction."

Being Jewish, he had to flee Germany for France in 1933 and became involved in the Zionist movement. In 1934 he published *Babylonian Migration* (1934), which is about the cult of heroes. Other novels followed: *Men without Mercy* (1935), *Journey to the Land without Death* (1937), and *The Blue Tiger* (1938) were written in France. In 1940 he evaded the Nazis and got to the United States. He lived in Hollywood, converted to Roman Catholicism, and returned to Germany as an education officer after the war. In 1948 his novel *The New Jungle* dealt with the brutality of colonialism, foreshadowing the problems of the modern world. He returned to France in 1953, fell ill in 1956, and died near Freiburg.

Dönitz, Karl (1891–1980)
supreme commander of the navy

Karl Dönitz was appointed grand admiral and chief of the submarine fleet in 1936 and promoted to commander in chief of the navy in 1943. He was named HITLER's successor and head of a new Reich government on May 1, 1945, surrendering to the Allies on May 7–8, 1945.

Born in Berlin-Grüneau on September 16, 1891, he attended a semi-classical high school, and he joined the Imperial German Navy in 1910. During WORLD WAR I he served aboard the cruiser *Breslau* and then was assigned to submarine duty in 1916. He assumed command of two submarines and was captured by the British. After the war he joined the Reichsmarine of the WEIMAR REPUBLIC, his service culminating as a staff officer in the Admiralty's office in Wilhelmshaven. In 1935 he was placed in command of Germany's reconstituted submarine fleet. He developed the famous "wolf pack" tactics for submarine attack. The best time for Ger-

Admiral Karl Dönitz congratulating German U-boat sailors after returning from a successful mission, 1942 *(Library of Congress)*

man submarines was at the beginning of America's involvement in the war when two or three ships were being sunk daily. Soon, however, the Allies had developed the convoy system, long-range radar, and escort planes, which very quickly turned the tables in favor of the Allies. By 1943 the Allies had won the BATTLE OF THE ATLANTIC, and Dönitz had to withdraw his submarines because of Allied material and technological superiority. This infuriated Hitler. In the meantime, in 1942 he had been promoted to admiral and on January 30, 1943, he replaced Admiral Erich Raeder as supreme commander of the navy.

Efforts to develop new all-electric submarines were hopelessly late, as the first of the 107 Mark XXI boats were not operational until March 1945. In 1944, as the Germans were retreating on the eastern front, the navy supplied ground formations against the Russians. Also, the navy had the responsibility of evacuating more than 2 million Germans and transporting supplies. Just before Hitler committed suicide, he named Dönitz as his successor. Setting up a temporary government in Schleswig-Holstein, Dönitz hoped to provide enough time for as many German troops to surrender to the British and Americans. He was captured by the British on May 23, 1945, and was indicted as a war criminal by the International Military Tribunal on October 20, 1945. He was sentenced to 10 years, which he served at Spandau Prison.

Dresden

Dresden is the capital city of SAXONY and once was called the "Florence on the Elbe." Some of the architectural achievements that provided this reputation were the 18th-century Zwinger Palace with its noted museums, the Dresden State Opera House, which was once associated with Richard WAGNER, Carl Maria von WEBER, and Richard Strauss, the rococo Hofkirche (1739–51), and the Kreuzkirche dating from the 15th century.

Dresden was first mentioned in the historical record in the 13th century. Between 1485 and 1918 the city gained prominence as the capital of the powerful dukes (later electors and kings) of Saxony. The city emerged as a leading cultural center in the 17th century, most notably during the reign of Frederick Augustus I, elector of Saxony, and later King Augustus II of Poland. During this period the alchemist John Friedrich Bottger invented the Meissen porcelain technique, making possible European production of the porcelain previously imported from Asia. After suffering heavy damage during the SEVEN YEARS' WAR (1756–1763), Dresden was rebuilt and became known as the Florence on the Elbe. Napoleon achieved his last major military success here in 1813. During the 19th century Dresden developed into an important industrial center.

The economy centers on port activities and the manufacture of high-technology products. Some of the products include specialized optical and medical equipment, business machines, computers, musical instruments, machinery, and tools. Dresden china, which was once made in the city, is now produced in Meissen. Dresden Technical University (1828), Carl Gustav Carus Medical Academy of Dresden (1954), Friedrich List University of Transportation of Dresden (1952) and a school of music (1856) are in the city.

The bombing and destruction of Dresden during WORLD WAR II occurred on February 13–14, 1945, during the closing months of the war. It was the most intense incendiary bombing of Nazi Germany during the war. Dresden had little heavy industry and up until early 1945 had been attacked only once by the U.S. Air Force. The Soviet leader, Joseph Stalin, demanded that Dresden be bombed in order to hamper the retreat of the German army and speed its final surrender. The bombing was part of a broader campaign named Thunderclap, which also included other cities, such as BERLIN, Chemnitz, and Magdeburg between February 3 and 9. After delays due to weather, the attack took place on the 13th by the Royal Air Force, with 805 bombers dropping 1,478 tons of high-explosive bombs and another 1,182 tons of incendiaries, a combination that started a firestorm. A total of 2,500 tons of bombs were dropped by British and American planes. The burning of multiple buildings generated great heat, causing a convection that sucked in air, which started more conflagrations. Hurricane-force winds came from every direction, and temperatures of 1,000 degrees resulted. On the 14th the British raid was followed by 311 U.S. B17 bombers. Estimates vary from 50,000 to 135,000 of the total number killed in Dresden, including refugees.

After the bombing the morality and necessity of this form of attack were questioned. Winston Churchill himself came to question its necessity.

Droste-Hülshoff, Annette von (1797–1848)
poetess

Annette von Droste-Hülshoff was the greatest lyric poetess in German literature. Her poetry is rooted in her Westphalian homeland, and she possessed great gifts of realistic observation and deep psychological insight. The theme of her nature poems is the unfathomable in human existence. Her devotional poems reflected her struggle with Catholicism.

Born in 1791 into a Westphalian aristocratic and Catholic family, she lived her early life in the castle that her ancestors had occupied for 400 years. She grew up socially isolated but had a good education through private tutors, common to upper-class women of the period. Her interest in poetry was stimulated by A. M. A. Sprickmann, and her love of English literature was especially strong for Lord Byron. During 1820 she wrote a cycle of devotional poems, *The Spiritual Year,* reflecting the ecclesiastical calendar and revealing her ardent Catholicism and her struggle with doubts about the faith. Between 1828 and 1838 she wrote three epic poems that were published in her first collection of poems in 1838. Changes in residence and falling in love also affected her work. When her father died in 1826, she and her mother had to move to more humble quarters, the Rüschhaus. In 1835–36 she visited Switzerland for a long stay in the home of her sister Jenny and her husband. Then, in 1837 she fell in love with Levin Schücking. In 1841 she visited the castle of Meersburg in an idyllic charming town of timbered houses overlooking Lake Constance. The castle had been purchased by her sister's husband, and while there she wrote many of her landscape and nature poems while she visited with Schücking. Until her death in 1848 she was continually drawn to Meersburg.

Her reputation as a writer of fiction rests on *The Jew's Beech Tree* (1842), which turned out to be one of the finest mid-century narratives. It was a tragic tale of ignorance, crime, and racial prejudice in which the sins of the fathers are visited on their sons. Its central figure is the day laborer Friedrich Mergel, who gets more and more deeply involved in criminal activity and murders a forester, Brandes, who is tracking him. Friedrich's guilt concerning a stolen watch finally moves him to murder Aaron, a Jewish pawnbroker. Inept political officials cannot lay hands on him, but retribution could not be avoided. Slowly and inexorably his guilt catches up with the murderer, until he hangs himself from the same beech tree under which he had killed the Jew. It was a story about morality in the mountainous parts of Westphalia.

Dual Alliance (1879)

The Dual Alliance was the secret Austro-German alliance of 1879, which was the keystone of Otto von BISMARCK's international system. The two states promised to support each other if attacked by Russia.

After German unification Bismarck had been quite willing to pursue policies without firm alliances and commitments to other nations. The position of Russia in international relations changed, however, with the the conclusion of the CONGRESS OF BERLIN in 1878 after the Russo-Turkish war. The Russians were sorely disappointed by the outcome of the congress and blamed Bismarck for the little they had to show. In the first months of 1879 the Russians had more reasons to be hostile toward Germany. New tariff duties had been placed against their grain, cattle, and timber, in addition to quarantine measures against plague that had broken out in Russia. Also there were Russian troop movements in Poland, and the strength of Pan-Slavism was growing. So Bismarck feared that the Russians might revive an alliance with France and threaten Germany. He then sought to secure an alliance in case of war and turned to AUSTRIA.

While the German emperor preferred friendly relations with Russia, the Austrians wanted to keep on good terms, with France. So Bismarck, instead of making the treaty a general one and not identifying a possible enemy, had to agree to name Russia. It was a sign of Bismarck's insecurity that he agreed to a treaty that called for "mutual assistance" if either power were attacked by Russia and for "benevolent neutrality" if attacked by another state. This treaty was concluded in peacetime and was permanent, at least until 1918 at the end of WORLD WAR I. The treaty was a landmark in European history because most treaties had been concluded on the eve of war and for limited duration or for specific purposes. It was the first of a series of secret treaties that prompted other nations to negotiate similar treaties in self-defense, which eventually resulted in two great alliance systems on the eve of WORLD WAR I.

Dürer, Albrecht (1471–1528)
artist

One of the greatest artists of the northern RENAISSANCE, Albrecht Dürer introduced the artistic innovations of the Italian Renaissance to German art. His new style was a fusion of the German realistic tradition with the Italian ideal of beauty.

Albrecht Dürer was born in NUREMBERG on May 21, 1471, the son of the goldsmith Albrecht the Elder. Demonstrating talent at an early age, he apprenticed under the master painter and woodcut designer Michael Wolgemut. After traveling to the Rhineland and the Netherlands, by early 1492 he had settled in Basel, where he worked as a woodcut designer. In the scenes of daily life that he produced he demonstrated the influence of the prominent German artist Martin Schongauer, a major representative of Rhenish graphic art. In 1493 he painted the famous self-portrait in which he appeared as a young romantic artist. After returning to Nuremberg in 1494, he married Agnes Frey, who unfortunately did not appreciate his expanding intellectual interests and friends. Leaving for Italy that same year, he visited Venice, Padua, and Mantua. In Padua he spent some time with his friend, the humanist Willibald PIRCKHEIMER. Dürer studied the Renaissance masters and soon learned how to paint his figures with "anatomical exactness, classical pathos, and harmony." An interest in art theory also developed, and his travels over the Alps inspired excellent landscape drawings.

Having assimilated the spirit of classical art, he returned to Nuremberg in 1495 and opened his own workshop. There he completed the famous *Apocalypse* cycle from the Book of Revelation, which with broad contrasts of black and white revealed the destructive forces of the ride of the Three Horsemen and an atmosphere of imminent doom. During this period Dürer also produced a number of portraits: *Oswolt Krell* (1499), *Dream of the Doctor* (after 1497), and one of his most popular, *Prodigal Son* (ca. 1496). In *Nemesis* (1501–02) he revealed his interest in perspective, human proportion, and complicated humanistic allegory.

On his next trip to Italy in 1505 he was profoundly influenced by the art of Venice, where he became acquainted with artists, humanists, and noblemen. His *Christ among the Doctors*, however, was probably executed in Rome. Back in Nuremberg he carved a number of large altarpieces, including the *Heller Altarpiece* (1507–09), the *Adoration of the Trinity* (1511), and the *Martyrdom of the Ten Thousand* (1508). From 1513 to 1520 his humanistic interests and his knowledge of classical philosophy, especially Neoplatonism, were manifested in some of his most famous master engravings: *Knight's Death and the Devil* (1513), *St. Jerome in His Study* (1514), and *Melancholia* (or originally, *Melencolia*, 1514). These engravings were allegories of virtues of the three principal spheres of human activity, the soldier, the contemplative, and the intellectual, reflecting the widening horizons of the age in respect to the study of man and nature. Depicted in his study, St. Jerome, who provided the official Latin Vulgate translation of the Bible from the Greek into Latin, was a symbol for humanists of the combination of ancient cultural values and divine inspiration. Depicted with the tools of science and the crafts, *Melancholia,* a female figure overcome with depression, is brooding over man's failure to fathom the secrets of nature. Dürer also published books on nature, the study of perspective, and proportion of the human body.

One of Martin LUTHER's humanist supporters, Dürer became involved in the conflicts of the Reformation. In 1525 the city of Nuremberg decided to officially adopt Lutheranism, and the PEASANT'S WAR ended with the defeat of the rebellion. In celebration of these events Dürer painted the *Four Apostles,* Sts. John and Peter, Mark and Paul and presented it to the Town Council. Not surprisingly, these apostles appeared to be residents of the city, another of them being Philip MELANCHTHON, a colleague of Luther's. In the panels Dürer included quotations from these saints containing criticisms of "false prophets" who were springing up to challenge the new faith.

The diversity of Dürer's achievements make him a typical Renaissance man. In addition to his paintings and engravings, he published books manifesting his interest in the study of nature and the study of perspective and proportion of the human body. Creating modern tools for contemporary German artists, his art translated the Italian Renaissance into what northerners could understand and apply. His influence was perhaps the greatest of any of the northern artists.

Düsseldorf

The city had its origins as a fishing village in the 12th century along the lower RHINE RIVER. In 1288 it was granted a charter by Count Adolf von Berg to become a city. It gained significance in 1386, when Duke Wilhelm II established his capital there. In 1609 its territory was called the Bergishes Land and was absorbed by Palatinate-Neuberg. Its first castle was built in the ROCOCO style around 1662 in the area of Benrath. During the latter 17th century the elector Johann Wilhelm (1679–1716) made Düsseldorf his capital, attracting artists to his court. His successor, Karl Philipp, moved the capital to HEIDELBERG in 1716 and shortly thereafter to MANNHEIM in 1720. Nevertheless, Düsseldorf became an artistic center with the establishment in 1777 of an Academy of Art.

Its history was disturbed by the impact of the French Revolution. The French took control of the city in 1795 and again in 1806 under Napoleon Bonaparte. It was finally liberated in 1813. In 1797 Heinrich HEINE, later to become a great poet, was born in Düsseldorf to Jewish parents. Under Prussian control in the 19th century, the city became an important industrial center, and by 1900 the population had expanded to 200,000. Both world wars took their toll, but WORLD WAR II especially left the city in rubble. The city was located in the British-occupied territory after the war, and they made it the capital of the new state of North Rhine Westphalia. The city was rebuilt and the population expanded to some 600,000.

Düsseldorf is a fashion design center, an art center, and home to a university. The city has become a major site for art exhibits and fashion shows. The Opera House and Theater are among the best in the FEDERAL REPUBLIC, and the ballet company has an international reputation. Its symphony orchestra is widely respected. Musical giants such as MENDELSSOHN, SCHUMANN, and BRAHMS had conducted there. The city's reputation as an art center goes back to the establishment of the Academy of Art in the 18th century. During recent times it has been home to modern artists such as Ulrich Rückriem, Felix Droese, Gunther Uecker, Otto Piene, and Heinz Mack.

E

Ebert, Friedrich (1871–1925)
Social Democratic leader and first president of the Weimar Republic

Born in February 1871 the son of a Heidelberg tailor, Ebert learned the trade of leatherworking in school. He joined the saddler's union and the SOCIAL DEMOCRATIC PARTY before it became legal in 1890. A party organizer and agitator, he was an effective speaker and was often elected to union and party positions. He became editor of a Social Democratic newspaper in 1893, and secretary of the party executive in 1905. Elected to the Reichstag in 1912, he succeeded August BEBEL as elected party chairman in 1913.

When war broke out in August 1914, Ebert led the Social Democratic Party in its vote for credits to support the war. He was extremely patriotic and lost two sons in the war. Although he tried to maintain party unity, in 1916 he turned against the antiwar faction of his party. Ebert favored compromises and alliances with the middle-class parties in order to attain a nonannexationist peace. He worked for the peaceful settlement of the BERLIN munitions workers strike of January 1918. On November 9, 1918, he was named Reich chancellor by Prince Max von Baden.

During the REVOLUTION OF 1918–1919 he placed himself at the head of the revolutionary movement in order to control its direction. He made a secret and critical agreement with the military leadership to preserve its position and guaranteed the return of troops according to the armistice; they had to cooperate in restoring order. The Constituent Assembly elected him temporary president, and he was reelected by the Reichstag in 1922, a position he held until his death in 1925. Ebert often used the emergency powers available through Article 48 of the constitution to protect the republic from attacks by the right and the left. Because of political instability he had to re-create cabinets quite often. He was slandered by both the right and the left and had to undergo libel trials on charges of treason during the war. He was, however, a good president who represented the German people. A significant failure of his administration was his inability to control the military.

Ebert-Groener Pact (November 10, 1918)

The Ebert-Groener Pact was an agreement that established a tactical partnership between the provisional civilian government (the Council of People's Plenipotentiaries, CPP) and the Supreme Command of the Armed Forces (Oberste Heeresleitung, OHL). On November 10, 1918, Friedrich EBERT contacted General Groener, Erich LUDENDORFF's successor in the OHL at military headquarters at Spa, and offered to make an agreement beneficial to both. The provisional government would protect the officer corps from parliamentary interference and support efforts to restrict the activities of the soldiers' councils, which Paul von HINDENBURG and Ludendorff wished to see abolished. In return, the Supreme Command of the Armed Forces, the OHL, would assist the government in maintaining order within Germany and administer the demobilization of the troops at the front as demanded by the Allies. Fearful of a Communist takeover and civil war and lacking any reliable republican force, Ebert made the agreement without consulting his colleagues in the CPP.

Ebert's decision to allow the army and its Prusso-German authoritarianism to remain independent as a "state within the state" seemed unnecessary at a time when the army's prestige and confidence were at their lowest point in a century. The Social Democrats gave up their opportunity to create a republican army. The old-line generals retained their powers and functions within the army and control of the armed forces. The opportunity to rid Germany of its militarism was lost. Ebert, however, had immediate problems with which to deal, and the long-range implications of his agreement with the military were not uppermost in his mind. First, he had to evacuate 2 million German troops from France and Belgium within two weeks in an orderly fashion, which could not be accomplished without the help of the staff officers. The other challenge Ebert faced was an internal security problem, especially in BERLIN. There the Soldiers and Workers' Councils were the strongest, and there was no reliable force in the capital to protect the provisional national government. Ebert believed that an agreement with army leaders was the only way to save the country from Bolshevism and civil war.

Economic Miracle

After World War II Germany was a landscape of destroyed cities, hunger, cold, and joblessness. Its industrial production in 1946 was one-third of a decade earlier. Yet by 1953 the western half of Germany had exceeded the gross national product of 1936 with only 53 percent of the land area and 75 percent of its population. Although initially the results of this recovery were unevenly distributed, average wages had reached prewar levels in 1950 and doubled by 1965. This extraordinary recovery and period of economic prosperity became the cornerstone of the political and social stability of the Konrad ADENAUER era. The annual growth rate was 10 percent, and gross national product tripled between 1950 and 1960 with an inflation rate below 3 percent. The export-driven economy brought increasing gold and currency reserves into the central bank (Bundesbank). By 1961 full employment had been achieved. The West German economy grew into the third-strongest in the world, second only to the United States in world trade.

How was this so-called Economic Miracle made possible? There were many factors that contributed to this astounding recovery. The foundations were in the removal of price controls and monetary reform in 1948. The new currency remained stable and was controlled by a politically independent central bank (Bundesbank), which encouraged savings and investment. The Marshall Plan aid stimulated the economy further, but supplied only 7 percent of Germany's capital. The demand created by the Korean War and the general worldwide economic upturn further stimulated growth. Efficient management, a large supply of skilled labor provided by refugees, and a docile labor force were important. Labor unions restrained their demands for wage increases, which kept the price of German goods competitive on the world market. The FEDERAL REPUBLIC avoided the pitfalls of the labor-management problems of the 1920s by negotiating labor's success in gaining equal representation on the supervisory boards of the iron and steel industries. The replacement of old with new modern equipment was stimulated by the destruction of the war and the dismantling of factories by the Allies after the war.

A great deal of credit must also be attributed to the welfare-state capitalism that was fostered by economics minister Ludwig ERHARD. The model he chose was called a social market economy, based on a free market economy relying on private enterprise and allowing market forces to dominate with state intervention kept to a minimum. The best solution for unemployment, Erhard maintained, was economic growth, which would create jobs for all. The role of the state was focused on preventing economic concentrations that hampered competition and on canceling the social inequalities that capitalism created. Those Germans who had hoped for at least the reduction of socioeconomic inequalities, which had embittered German politics in the past, were disappointed by Erhard's policies, which maintained the traditional relation between capital and labor. The economic boom of the 1950s made it possible for the Federal Republic to address some of its social problems. The main tasks were caring for war victims, solving the housing shortage, and integrating refugees and expellees into society. In addition to state-financed housing construction, another key policy was the equalization of the tax burden, involving a redistribution of wealth that favored the war victims, refugees, and others hurt by the currency reform. Other social reforms followed, which allowed for a 40-hour workweek and pension reform that index-linked pensions to the rising cost and standard of living.

Edict of Toleration (1781)

The Edict of Toleration issued by JOSEPH II granted the private exercise of religion to Protestants in the lands under Habsburg rule. Full religious equality with Roman Catholics was not granted until 1861.

The Edict of Toleration was issued on October 13, 1781, by Joseph II, the Holy Roman Emperor (1765–90). It ended the "Ferdinandean period" of Austrian history, in which Catholicism and the monarchy were partners in attempting to restore the Catholic faith and restricting the religious practice of the Protestant minority. Under Joseph's edict all non-Catholics were granted full rights as citizens and the right to privately practice their religion. This obviously was not equality, but a step in that direction. Restrictions on public practice, such as not being able to build spires on their meeting halls, to ring bells, or to have entrances on main streets, connote a lack of equality. A symbol of Catholic superiority was that priests were still responsible to keep the public registers. But Joseph's edict was a compromise between his desire to have one church under state control and the new philosophy of the free exchange of ideas. It is not at all surprising that the loosening of control that the edict accomplished brought out the true allegiance of as many as 70,000 official Catholics, who during the first year of the edict converted to Protestantism. As far as the Jews were concerned the Edict extended toleration to their religion and considerably broadened their rights to choose their occupations and where they would live.

Ehrlich, Paul (1854–1915)
physician and chemist

Paul Ehrlich was a medical scientist who was a pioneer in hematology, immunology, and chemotherapy. With the assistance of Sāhachivo Hata, Paul Ehrlich discovered that Salvarsan was effective in killing the organism causing syphilis. He previously had won the Nobel Prize in 1908 for work in the field of chemotherapy.

Paul Ehrlich was born into a Jewish family in the Silesian town of Strehlen, PRUSSIA, on March 14, 1854. He attended the medical schools of BRESLAU, Strasbourg, Freiburg, and LEIPZIG. Early in his career he experimented with cellular staining, and from these experiments concluded that chemical agents could destroy infections, which discovery revolutionized the practice of medicine. After his appointment as head of the famous Charité Hospital in BERLIN, he developed techniques for the diagnosis of tuberculosis and typhoid, and discovered medications to control fever and methods to treat diseases of the eye. Ehrlich also founded the field of hematology by differentiating the types of blood cells. By 1885 he had already made some 37 different scientific contributions. After 1889 he joined Robert KOCH's Institute for Infectious Diseases and concentrated on the problem of the body's immune system. This led to the discovery of antibodies, which are produced by the immune system, a discovery used by Emil von Behring, who created an antitoxin against diphtheria. Ehrlich also performed pioneering work in serum research and developed a system to measure its effectiveness. In recognition for his contributions Ehrlich was made director of the Royal Institute for Experimental Therapy.

In an exhaustive series of experiments he discovered that Salvarsan—also called "healing arsenic"—could kill the causal organism of syphilis. The venereal disease of syphilis was one of the most devastating chronic diseases before the turn of the 20th century and often led to insanity. While its symptoms could be treated with moderate success, the pathogenic organisms lodged in the body were never killed. Paul Ehrlich achieved the decisive breakthrough in treatment. The essence of his new method of treatment was the use of chemical remedies.

Ehrlich had already been awarded the Nobel Prize in 1908 for his work in the field of modern chemotherapy, of which science he also is considered to be the founder. He died in Bad Homburg in 1915.

Eichendorff, Joseph von (1788–1857)
poet and writer

Joseph von Eichendorff is one of the finest poets in German literature. As the "last knight of ROMANTICISM" his poetry and prose was the best and the most beautiful expression of the literary tradition. He was one of the HEIDELBERG group of romantic writers. After his student years at Halle and Heidelberg Eichendorff served in the FREE CORPS in the war against Napoleon. After demobilization he became a government official, first in BRESLAU, then in DANZIG, then BERLIN, and finally Königsberg in 1824.

Two fundamental experiences influenced Eichendorff's work: his experience of the country (landscapes) and his Catholic religion, which actually strengthened as he grew older. The religious basis of his poetry is evident but is clearer in his narrative works, especially in his first novel, *Resentment and the Present* (*Ahnung und Gegenwart*, 1815) in which he expressed his romantic vision of nature and at the same time moral standards. The picture of the present storm-tossed time always seems to slip away to fears and intuitions of the future. It was God, nature folk, and fatherland that were the basic motivating forces in his life and work. Eichendorf shared with other romantics such as Arnim, BRENTANO, and GÖRRES a fondness for folk song and folk tradition, a love of the Middle Ages, and the ideals of chivalry.

The best known of his prose works is *From the Life of a Good-for-Nothing* (1826), which was a humorous tale that stresses the colorful description of detail and melodious moods. It was not a work of compact or systematic thought, but is certainly a gem of romantic fiction. The "good-for-nothing" is sent packing by his father and bounces around wherever life takes him. He has adventures and love affairs in a world that is always blissful, where it never rains and every night is full of moonlight. Themes of the romantic school included in the *Good-for-Nothing* are concerned with searching afar and then yearning for homecoming; the sweetness of human love and of striving as an expression of man's quest for his eternal home.

Eichendorff, like other romantic poets, expressed his own poetic feelings through the depictions of nature and society. Nature is a symbol and mirror of personal moods. For example, in *Twilight* the details of the forest are blurred, and as night approaches a landscape of fantasy emerges filled with foreboding. Eichendorff's poetry has a simplicity about it that hides the subtlety of rhythm and mood. Much of his poetry expresses a feeling of joy, confidence, and resolution in the battle with evil. Yet, he himself explained that the charm of his poetry is reflective of the happiness he experienced as a child in his ancestral castle of Lubowitz in Upper Silesia. Nevertheless, his poetry is his most original achievement. It even has singable qualities and has been set to music by Robert SCHUMANN.

In the latter part of his life Eichendorff lived in Moravia, DRESDEN, BERLIN, and finally Neisse from 1855 to 1857. During these years his publications were mainly concerned with the history of literature, which he approached from a religious perspective.

Eichmann, Adolf (1906–1962)
Nazi bureaucrat

Karl Adolf Eichmann was the SS expert on Jewish affairs, charged with the transport of millions of Jews to the death camps during WORLD WAR II. Eichmann was a bureaucratic mass murderer for whom obedience silenced questions of morality.

Adolf Eichmann was born in Solingen, Germany, near the RHINE on March 19, 1906, the son of an accountant for an electrical firm. He was not a very good student, and his dark complexion prompted students to harass him as "the little Jew." Early on, his mother died. His father moved the family to Linz, AUSTRIA, where Eichmann attended the same school that HITLER had attended years earlier. The nationalistic anti-Western and ANTI-SEMITIC propaganda so popular after the war affected him deeply. In the 1920s Eichmann studied electrical engineering but left school because of the inflation. Gradually, he transformed himself into an assertive, extrovert, hard-drinking young man, perhaps prompted by his career as a traveling salesman for an oil company. Ironically, he got the job through Jewish relatives of his stepmother.

Already a German nationalist in 1932, he joined the Austrian NAZI PARTY and the SS as a protegé of Ernst Kaltenbrunner, who later would become chief of the security services (RSHA) of the SS. Immigrating to Nazi Germany, Eichmann obtained a position in the SD. Heinrich HIMMLER, who believed that Eichmann could speak Hebrew, put him in charge of the Scientific Museum for Jewish Affairs. He was rapidly promoted from 2nd lieutenant to lieutenant colonel. Then he served in the RSHA (Reich Security Main Office) in charge of forced Jewish emigration between 1938 and 1941, then made chief of subsection IV, B-4 as an expert on Jewish affairs. In summer 1941 he was one of the first to learn about plans for the FINAL SOLUTION, and on January 20, 1942, attended the WANNSEE CONFERENCE. Eichmann's department was placed in charge of arresting and transporting European Jewry to the death camps. Jews were required to wear the yellow star of David for easy identification and assemblage for transport. The system sent children, mothers, and the elderly directly to the gas chambers, while the strongest 25 percent were spared for slave labor, many of whom soon died. Although records were not accurate, Eichmann reported to Himmler in 1944 that about 4 million Jews had been killed in the camps.

Eichmann was an intelligent bureaucrat who was convinced that he was making an important contribution. He was extremely inventive in camouflaging policies and actions so as to mislead Jewish victims and the non-Nazi world. He took an "uncommon joy" in performing his duties in catching and executing the enemies of the Third Reich. Eichmann silenced his conscience and shielded himself from the reality of what he was doing through psychological compartmentalization and bureaucratic language ("officialese"). At his trial in 1961 he revealed his bureaucratic mind-set, which considered Jews as objects and not human beings. In 1944 he also unsuccessfully sought to trade the lives of 1 million Jews for 10,000 trucks and food.

After the war Eichmann escaped detection in an American internment camp and through a secret SS organization, Odessa, escaped to Argentina in 1952. His new identity was Ricardo Klement, and he got a job at a Mercedes-Benz automobile factory in Buenos Aires, where his family soon joined him. His luck ran out on May

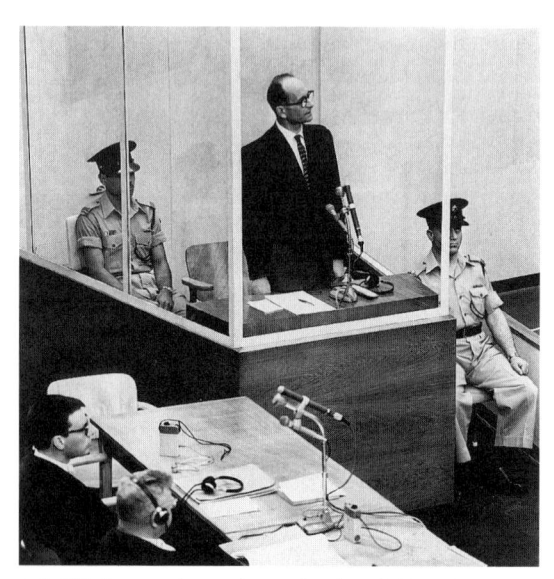

Adolf Eichmann during his trial in Israel, 1961 *(Library of Congress)*

13, 1960, when Israeli agents captured him and smuggled him to Jerusalem, where he stood trial, the first Israeli court to prosecute a perpetrator of the HOLOCAUST. Hannah ARENDT was an observer at Eichmann's trial and concluded in *Eichmann in Jerusalem* (1964) that his participation in the evil of genocide was more banal than radically evil. He was found guilty of crimes against the Jewish people and humanity, as well as war crimes. On May 31, 1962, he was hanged at Ramle.

Eicke, Theodor (1892–1943)
chief inspector of concentration camps

Theodor Eicke was born in Hampont, ALSACE-LORRAINE, in 1892, which at the time was part of the German Empire. After service in the army during WORLD WAR I he joined the police in Thuringia in 1919. He held a variety of positions, all of which he lost because of his hostility toward the WEIMAR REPUBLIC. In 1928 he joined the NAZI PARTY and its SA. Later, he transferred to the SS, where in 1931 he was made a lieutenant colonel (SS-Standartenfuehrer). He became involved in political terror bomb attacks for which he was imprisoned. Having escaped to Italy, he returned to Germany when HITLER became chancellor. In June 1933 Heinrich HIMMLER appointed Eicke to replace commandant Hilmar Waeckerle at the new DACHAU concentration camp, which gave him the opportunity to demonstrate his organizational abilities. He developed a company of well-disciplined SS camp guards called the Death's Heads Formations. In April 1934 Himmler appointed Eicke inspector of concentration camps and SS guard formations and promoted him to lieutenant general (SS-Gruppenfuehrer).

Next to Himmler, Eicke was undoubtedly the most influential in forming the organization and esprit of the SS camp guards. He issued precise regulations, which the guards were expected to follow to the letter on everything from beatings to solitary confinement. Guards had to be ruthless and without pity. A rigid person and narrow-minded in his thinking, Eicke was unable to consider future needs.

Examples of Eicke's short-range vision can be seen in the construction of camps at Flossenburg and Mauthhausen, which were built as work camps for quarrying stone, but which soon had to house many more prisoners as independent camps. The camps were built with too few barracks for their future use, which was largely Eicke's fault. Another example was the camp for women to be built at Ravensbrück, which Eicke insisted needed facilities for only 2,000 prisoners, while Oswald Pohl, who was a better planner, argued in favor of a larger capacity of 10,000. Eicke won out, but in the future Ravensbrück was to house 25,000 women in extremely overcrowded conditions.

For Eicke the concentration camps were a means to the end of expanding the number of guards in the Death's Heads units. He took great pains to provide for the comfort and furnishings of their quarters. Through his efforts the Waffen SS and the Concentration Camp SS were separated into different units after 1937. As he separated the more able soldiers into the Waffen SS, an increasing number of the remaining camp guards were mediocre or incompetent. Eicke overlooked the brutalities and bad conditions that existed within many camps and became more concerned with external matters. After the Waffen SS and the SS guards were separated, Eicke took greater interest in the Waffen SS.

Some Death's Heads units participated in the takeover of Czechoslovakia and were involved in the invasion of Poland. After the Polish campaign Hitler ordered Eicke to speed up the formation of a Death's Head division, and he was first promoted to lieutenant general and years later to general (SS-*Obergruppenfuehrer*) of the Waffen SS. Eicke replaced the units doing camp duty with reserves from the General SS. As the division was being assembled in 1940, Eicke was replaced as chief inspector of concentration camps by Richard Glücks. The Death's Head division participated in the French campaign and later in Russia. In February 1943 Eicke was killed on a reconnaissance flight near Kharkov in the Soviet Union, where his plane was shot down.

Einsatzgruppen
(SS mobile killing units)

The Einsatzgruppen were special mobile units assigned to kill the racial and ideological enemies of the Nazi regime. They were attached to RSHA (Reich Security Main Office) and operated under the personal direction of Reinhard HEYDRICH. The individual company-size unit was called an Einsatzkommando, the smallest unit was the Einsatztrupp, and the operations staff was an Einsatzstab. In general they were given the mission of supervising the FINAL SOLUTION. These units together with other security police killed up to 2 million Jews.

These units had been created during the annexation of AUSTRIA in March 1938 and the invasion of Czechoslovakia in March 1939 as strike forces for the political police and security intelligence services. At that time their task was to track down opponents of the Nazis. Six Einsatzgruppen were later sent into Poland, where they suppressed local resistance and eliminated hostile groups such as Poland's elite. Tens of thousands were executed, but the German military placed some limits on their ravages. They also were instructed to concentrate the Polish Jews living in the countryside into ghettos in the larger cities. All Jews were to be expelled from that part of Poland which was to be incorporated into Germany.

Although attached to the regular German army, their independence from military control was secured before the invasion of the Soviet Union. Four newly organized Einsatzgruppen totaling about 3,000 men followed the regular army into Russia and performed mass executions of Jews, Communist officials, and gypsies. Heydrich tried to inspire the fanaticism of the killers with HITLER's mixed-up racial beliefs that "Judaism in the East is the source of bolshevism." The leader of one of the groups, Otto Ohlendorf, later explained that the deception used by the Einsatzgruppen involved leading the Jewish victims to the killing field with an excavated tank ditch with promises of resettlement. They were then "shot, kneeling or standing, and the corpses thrown into the ditch." In the first six months some 700,000 were estimated to have been killed. A second sweep occurred in 1942 that brought the total to more than a million. German morale problems occurred with the barbarity and sadism of it all. Even Himmler was aware of the problems involved with the "repulsive duty" and claimed that he alone had responsibility before God and Hitler.

Einstein, Albert (1879–1955)
physicist

Albert Einstein, one of the greatest physicists of the 20th century, developed the special theory and general theory of relativity and the photon theory of light.

Albert Einstein was born in Ulm and studied mathematics and physics at the Polytechnic Institute in Zurich. While he worked in the Swiss Patent Office in Bern, his scientific research soon won him recognition, which brought him a professorship at the Technical University at Zurich between 1912 and 1914 and at the University of BERLIN in 1914.

In 1905 Einstein published two works that proved to be milestones in the history of physics: the photon theory of light, which was based on Max Planck's quantum theory and for which Einstein was awarded the Nobel Prize in physics in 1921; also the special theory of relativity, which constituted a new view of the world that superseded Newtonian thought. Several years later, Einstein developed the general theory of relativity announced in 1915, which enabled mankind to contemplate the structure of the universe from an entirely new perspective, a geometrical interpretation in a four-dimensional space-time continuum.

Before and after WORLD WAR I Einstein was an active pacifist and protested against German militarism. He also used his fame to support Zionism. The anti-Semites and Nazis attacked him and later burned his books. In 1933 Einstein was compelled to leave Germany due to his Jewish heritage. He accepted a new position in the United States at the Institute for Advanced Studies at Princeton University, where he continued his research. In 1939 he warned President Franklin Delano Roosevelt about the dangers of German research in nuclear fission. After the war, until his death, he campaigned against nuclear war.

Eisner, Kurt (1867–1919)
leader of Bavarian revolution and Republic

Kurt Eisner was a journalist and Independent Socialist who led the revolution in BAVARIA that overthrew the WITTELSBACH dynasty in November 1918 and proclaimed the Bavarian Republic.

Kurt Eisner was born on May 14, 1867, in BERLIN the son of a Jewish dealer in military decorations whose shop was located on the prestigious Unter den Linden. He attended a prestigious high school (Gymnasium) with the sons of officers and businessmen, graduating in 1886, after which he studied philosophy and German literature at the Friedrich Wilhelm University. Instead of completing his doctorate, he decided in 1889 to enter journalism in a job at a news agency, and in 1892 accepted a position at the night desk of the *Frankfurter Zeitung*. He entered journalism when Chancellor Otto von BISMARCK was dismissed from his job in March 1890. He married Elisabeth Hendrick, and they briefly resided in a Berlin suburb before leaving for FRANKFURT. At the paper he wrote approvingly of the recently rehabilitated SOCIAL DEMOCRATIC PARTY. He gained the respect of Wilhelm LIEBKNECHT, who was the patriarch of the SPD, and was accepted on the editorial board of *Vorwärts*, the SPD's leading newspaper. That did not last long, and he had to resign as his independent-mindedness brought him into disagreement with the coeditors. After a short time in NUREMBERG and a divorce he moved to MUNICH in 1910 and became the political editor of the socialist paper *Münchner Post*.

Eisner's writing reflected his critical and satirical thinking about the Empire, his optimism about the future of socialism, and an apology of his own life. He had published a critical study of Friedrich NIETZSCHE, considering his philosophy as oppressive and his influence perverse. More important was Eisner's recognition of the unreality of Nietzsche's "master morality." He rejected Nietzsche as socially unpragmatic and therefore did not give him his endorsement. The beginning of Eisner's thinking was that the triumph of socialism was inevitable. He rejected the evolutionary socialist revisionism of Eduard BERNSTEIN and his idea that there could be reconciliation between the ruling caste of Imperial Germany and the advocates of socialism.

What led to Eisner's leadership of the REVOLUTION OF 1918 started with his membership in the newly formed INDEPENDENT SOCIAL DEMOCRATIC PARTY (USPD) and leadership of the antiwar movement in Munich. After his release from prison on October 14 to run for Parliament as a candidate of the USPD, Eisner held some rallies in early November. On November 3 he addressed a large crowd on the Theresienwiese, where he criticized the government's plans for constitutional reform. He proposed that Bavarians proclaim peace along with the Germans in AUSTRIA who had already declared a republic. This desire for peace gave Eisner the moral high ground and prevented the government or rivals from restricting his activities. Then on November 7 Eisner took advantage of another rally dominated by the Majority Socialists who counseled for peaceful demonstrations, led a march on military garrisons and headquarters, and by nightfall had declared a Bavarian Republic. On the following day Eisner set up a cabinet of Independent and Majority Socialists, and he became both the prime and foreign ministers. The revolution in Bavaria made the fall of the Kaiser inevitable.

Eisner's attempt to govern the new republic faced numerous difficulties and ultimately failed. He was not satisfied with the Parliament, and he continued to rule with the support of the Soldiers', Workers', and Peasants' Councils that had become so powerful. Some of his initiatives were unpopular, such as the confession of German war guilt and his plan for socialization of the economy. The socialist leaders in Berlin mistrusted him, and the Majority Socialists tried to take over the government from him. Many people in

Munich considered the theatrics of his government a circus. With his government failing, he decided to resign. As Eisner turned the corner on the Promenadestrasse, a young right-wing fanatic, Count Arco Valley, who was a member of the racist Thule society, successfully assassinated him. Arco Valley was then shot by one of Eisner's guards. Within 60 minutes a member of the Revolutionary Worker's Council went to the Parliament and shot the Majority Socialist Erhard Auer. This was the dramatic end of the first revolution, and a second was soon to follow.

El Alamein, Battles of (July 1942, October/November 1942)

A desert railway halt about 60 miles west of Alexandria became the location of a major turning point in World War II, where the German army called the AFRIKA KORPS under the leadership of General Erwin ROMMEL (the Desert Fox) lost two battles to the British forces. The two battles at El Alamein were part of a German effort to save the Italian campaign against the British in North Africa, which had begun in September 1940, but by January 1941 the Italians were in retreat. Rommel and the Afrika Korps were sent by HITLER to Libya to lead the combined Italian-German forces. Rommel pushed the British to the Egyptian frontier by the end of May, but then because of insufficient troops and supplies he was stopped in July at El Alamein by British general Auchinleck. Stopping the Germans provided time for the Allies to reinforce their forces with thousands of new tanks, planes, and soldiers. Also to the British advantage was the appointment of new leadership under Generals Alexander and Montgomery. Rommel, on the other hand, was not adequately reinforced because of Hitler's preparations to invade the Soviet Union.

Extensively reorganizing and equipping his army, General Montgomery waited with his counteroffensive until October 23, 1942. Short of supplies and men, Rommel planned a defensive campaign, laying an extensive minefield. Unfortunately for the Germans, he returned to Germany for medical treatment. The British had overwhelming superiority of men and equipment and knowledge of German plans through the ULTRA intelligence system, and the second battle began with a horrific artillery barrage. The British eventually succeeded in penetrating the German defenses. Rommel quickly returned to Africa by plane and planned a counteroffensive, which failed. He began his withdrawal on November 2–3, 1942. Another significance of the battle was the beginning of Rommel's disillusionment with Hitler's refusal of his request to retreat in order to save his men. Hitler insisted on "victory or death." Less than a week after the reversal at El Alamein the Allies invaded North Africa. The loss of the Battle of El Alamein cost the AXIS some 50,000 men, about 30,000 captured, while the British lost about 13,500.

Elbe River

The Elbe is a major river crossing north central Germany beginning in Czechoslovakia and flowing in a north and northwest direction for 450 miles. It enters Germany from northern Czechoslovakia near DRESDEN, flowing northward past Torgau, Wittenberg, Magdeburg, in the direction of HAMBURG, flowing into the North Sea. During WORLD WAR II the Elbe and its tributary the Mulde were the meeting line for the Western Allies and the Russians. The British, however, were allowed to advance to Lubeck in the north, and an advance of American forces was allowed along the Danube into Czechoslovakia in the south. Based on prior agreements American forces were halted at the Elbe. The Russian and American armies met on April 15, 1945.

electoral system (Federal Republic)

In the national elections of the FEDERAL REPUBLIC each registered voter was allowed two votes. Voters used the first ballot to select the candidate of their choice from their constituency whom they wanted to represent them in the BUNDESTAG, the lower house of the Parliament. One candidate from each of Germany's 299 constituencies was therefore directly voted. The second vote was used to select which political party the elector preferred.

The percentage of party votes determined the number of seats each party would hold in the Bundestag, unless a particular party won more seats than what it received in the first vote. In those instances the party's representation in the Bundestag was instead determined by the first vote, and a number of seats—equal to the difference between the party's directly won seats and the lesser number of seats it would have been afforded by the second vote—were added to the Bundestag. These seats were called "overhangs."

Ems Telegram (July 13, 1870)

The Ems dispatch concerned the diplomatic conversations between the French ambassador and the Prussian king at the German resort at Ems. The subject was the candidacy of the HOHENZOLLERN prince, Leopold, to the Spanish throne. The Prussian king, William, had already forbidden Leopold from accepting the Spanish offer, but the French government decided that it wanted a diplomatic triumph. It consequently instructed its ambassador, Benedetti, to talk to King William again and get him to promise that a Hohenzollern would never again be considered for the throne. The king politely refused this request. A telegram was then sent by the king to Otto von BISMARCK in BERLIN describing the meeting. Bismarck decided to abbreviate the long description, making William's reply less polite and Benedetti's rebuff more insulting. The king also appeared to be insulted. When the telegram was released to the press and sensationalized it stirred up a great deal of national feeling in both Paris and Berlin. The news made compromise difficult. Paris mobs in the street demanded war, and the French Chamber was belligerent. The French government made the fatal mistake of declaring war on PRUSSIA on July 19, 1870.

Enabling Act (1933)

Officially called the Law for the Removal of the Distress of People and Reich, the Enabling Act was passed by the REICHSTAG on March 23, 1933. It gave the government the right to issue laws without the consent of the Reichstag, which indicated HITLER's hostility toward parliamentary government, suggesting that representative government was the cause of the people's suffering. Hitler had succeeded in destroying parliamentary government through parliamentary means, keeping with his strategy of legality after the failure of his attempt at force during the Munich Putsch. Hitler now received the right to make laws that deviated from the constitution. The power was to last only four years, and its purpose was to solve Germany's economic and social problems and create political stability. That meant no opposition to the NAZI PARTY and its goals to create a new Germany. The Enabling Act required a two-thirds vote of the Reichstag because it was a change in the WEIMAR CONSTITUTION. The Nazis and their Nationalist allies held 340 seats but not enough to pass the act. The Reichstag fire on February 27 had made it possible to pass an emergency decree, which the Nazis now used to jail and harass Communists and some Social Democrats, eliminating their opposition. Then the national celebration at Potsdam at the opening of the Reichstag presented a peaceful and patriotic image of the Nazis as being loyal to German traditions, President Hindenburg, and the army. Finally, the CENTER PARTY was intimidated by the Nazi threat to treat them like Communists or at least dismiss civil servants from their jobs, while if they cooperated the Nazis promised to respect the rights of Catholics. While the bill passed with 444 votes, only the courageous SOCIAL DEMOCRATS, under the leadership of Otto Wels, resisted with 94 votes against.

Engels, Friedrich (1820–1895)
social theorist of Marxism

Friedrich Engels cooperated with Karl MARX in the development of the theories of communism. They based their socialism and communism upon a materialist interpretation of the German philosopher Friedrich Wilhelm HEGEL.

Friedrich Engels was born on November 28, 1820, in Barmen, PRUSSIA, in the Wupper valley of the Rhineland, a son of a wealthy textile manufacturer. His father was an authoritarian religious fanatic who believed in PIETISM. From elementary school he went to one of the best Gymnasiums in Prussia. It was traditional in the Engels family that sons should study law and enter the Prussian civil service. So he studied law for a while, but in 1837 he left to follow his father's wishes to enter business. At the age of 20 he left the business world for a while and performed his compulsory military service. Opposed to organized religion, he embraced the radical ideas of the young Hegelians, particularly the materialist philosophy of Ludwig FEUERBACH. Engels's mind was brilliant and incisive and possessed of a great facility in learning many languages. Throughout his life he developed an understanding of the natural sciences and was a specialist on military affairs.

Working-class misery was one of the social forces that greatly concerned him. As a young boy he had witnessed "the victims of capitalism" being overworked in unhealthy and terrible working conditions. He again had the opportunity to view working conditions in England, which perhaps were worse than in Germany. In Manchester he went to work in a spinning factory in which his father was part owner. While there he studied classical economic writers such as Adam Smith and David Ricardo, and by the time he left Manchester in 1844 he had written his first important book, *The Condition of the Working Class in England in 1844*, published in German in 1845. It was a very accurate study for its time. Then in Paris he met Karl Marx for the second time, and because of their common beliefs they began a lifelong collaboration. Between 1845 and 1850 Engels lived in Germany, Belgium, and France, participating in revolutionary activities. In 1847–48 he and Marx collaborated in the publication of the *Manifesto of the Communist Party*. At the end of the REVOLUTION OF 1848 an uprising occurred in BADEN and the Palatinate, in which Engels participated. That failing, he escaped to England, where he returned to his father's business in Manchester. In the ensuing years of his friendship with Marx, Engels provided him with money to continue his research. Until 1863 his first Irish mistress was Mary Burns, and thereafter until 1878 he lived with her sister, Lizzy, as his common-law wife. In 1864 his father died, leaving him a partner in the firm, from which he retired in 1869. He finally was able to support himself as a middle-class gentleman and provide Marx with a yearly sum of £350. In 1870 he moved to London, where he closely collaborated with Marx.

In the 1870s he published a study of Germany's first revolution, *The Peasant War in Germany* (1870), and then his most important contribution to the study of socialist theory, *Herr Eugen Dühring's Revolution in Science* (1878), ranking equally with Marx's *Das Kapital*. Engels was a materialist who believed that all political and social institutions are conditioned by economic facts, and that ways of life change with changing methods of production and distribution. Engels and Marx predicted that this dialectical process would end up in the overthrow of capitalism and the establishment of a communist society. Perhaps the most important thing he did after Marx died in 1883 was to publish volumes 2 and 3 of *Das Kapital* from Marx's notes and manuscripts. Engels also clarified the concept of dialectical materialism, which had not been worked out by Marx. Other writings by Marx's lieutenant included *The Development of Socialism from Utopia to Science* (1882) and *The Origins of the Family, Private Property and the State* (1884), which provides a guide to the understanding of Marxist political theory. Finally, Engels interpreted the philosophy of Ludwig Feuerbach in *Ludwig Feuerbach and the End of Classical German Philosophy*, published in 1888. Afflicted by cancer, Engels died on August 5, 1895.

ENIGMA/ULTRA

ENIGMA was the code name of a ciphering machine invented by a Dutchman, H. Q. Koch, in 1919. A German, Arthur Scherbius, was marketing it in 1923, and the German army and navy bought it out in 1929, adapting it to military needs. The British and French obtained copies of it just before the invasion of Poland in 1939. The Germans considered their codes secure, more so because of daily changes in the codes. What the Germans did not realize, however, was that the Poles were reading ENIGMA messages in 1932, the French in 1938, and that the British had developed their own deciphering machine, which made them able to solve the code and its changes by 1940. Consequently, early in the war the British had the advantage of understanding all the radio transmissions between the German High Command and various field headquarters. ULTRA was the top security clearance given to the highly secret intelligence produced by the decryption of German radio messages. This intelligence coup was one of the Allies' critical advantages in the war, enabling their eventual victory.

Enlightenment

The Enlightenment was an intellectual movement patterned after that in France and England, which attempted to make reason completely autonomous and to derive all other authorities from it. The church no longer kept its dominating position, and even ideas of God, freedom, and immortality were derived through logical thinking. Not only did reason free itself from the restrictions placed on it by the churches, but it also became less concerned about religious dogma. The beliefs of the individual became less important than his thoughts and actions. Tolerance became an ideal, and the quarrels between the denominations that were so pervasive during the 17th century became less violent. The realm of the supernatural now ceased to dominate philosophical thinking. Practical ethics formulated moral rules of behavior. Life in this world as it was now became more important. The greatest of the philosophers, Gottfried Wilhelm von LEIBNIZ (1646–1716), went so far as to assert that the world we live in was the best of all possible worlds. Everything in this world was interpreted as having a reasonable purpose and was the instrument of a benevolent divine will. The Enlightenment fostered an optimistic attitude instead of the resignation to the will of God prevalent during the Reformation. Now the ideal humans no longer sought removal from the world but led a reasonable life and sought to abolish injustice in the world. They sought the practical application of Christian principles. Among the reforms that emanated from this application were the elimination of trials for witchcraft and the torture sometimes used. It pleaded for dignified living conditions for the Jews and other minorities. It fostered the education of women and started the emancipation of the colored races.

Because the German Enlightenment took place later than that in France and England, it was strongly influenced by the English philosophers John Locke (1632–1704) and David Hume (1711–76). Both based reason on experience and therefore were called empiricists. Instead of starting with general principles, like the French philosopher René Descartes (1596–1650), they began with the observation of detailed objects and only inductively derived their ultimate principles. Another important English influence in German literature was the thought of Lord Shaftesbury (1621–83), who applied empirical methods to the fine arts. The most important German representative of the empirical method was Gotthold Ephraim LESSING (1729–81). Another empiricist was the younger contemporary, Gottfried HERDER (1744–1803), although he also considered unique historical conditions and human emotions. Immanuel KANT (1724–1804), the Königsberg philosopher, represented the culmination of empiricism, but like Herder he opened a new chapter in intellectual history.

Both rationalism and empiricism were ways of understanding the world as a meaningful system that followed its own laws. That does not mean that the existence of God was denied. As with the Deists in France, it was thought that after God created the world it was left to function according to the perfect laws that he had established. Miracles and other interferences with daily processes were no longer believed to occur. The universe was autonomous and functioned according to God's laws. Man's actions were no longer directed nor his destiny fulfilled by God's involvement.

Both of the greatest philosophers of the Enlightenment, the Dutch Jew Baruch Spinoza (1632–77), and the German Leibniz, thought that the existence of God could be arrived at only through faith and not proven through reason. They avoided the absolute rationalism of Descartes and the German philosopher Christian von WOLFF (1679–1754), who was the most popular of the disciples of Leibniz. The followers of Wolff employed the deductive method and tried to discover the reasons for all the processes and facts of life, creating great dictionaries for their definitions.

While philosophical attitudes changed, so did religious ones. Subjective reasoning was accompanied by subjective feeling and faith. A personal attitude toward the Christian creed emerged in practically every nation of western Europe. Similar to the Jansenists in France, the Quakers and Methodists in England, Germany developed a parallel movement called PIETISM. The term was taken from a treatise by pastor Philipp Jacob Spener (1635–1705), which emphasized family worship and an active Christian approach to everyday life. Personal religious experience was emphasized instead of regular church attendance.

Erasmus, Desiderius (1466–1536)
leading northern humanist

The foremost exponent of European HUMANISM was Desiderius Erasmus of Rotterdam. He was the leading spokesman of the Christian humanists, a brilliant scholar and writer. In his satirically barbed writings, such as *Praise of Folly* and *Colloquia,* the Catholic theologian chastised both the ecclesiastical and secular dignitaries of his time. Notwithstanding his criticism of the institutions of the Catholic Church, Erasmus did not follow Martin LUTHER or John CALVIN, who started their own churches. Erasmus sought instead to reconcile the differences between Catholicism and the new theological movements of the REFORMATION.

Desiderius Erasmus *(Library of Congress)*

Erasmus was born illegitimately, the son of a priest and a daughter of a middle-class citizen of Gouda near Rotterdam. Educated at Deventer and later by the Brethren of the Common Life, he entered the Augustinian monastery at Steyn around 1486 and was ordained a priest in 1492. His monastic career produced a man who was meditative and scholarly but disliked the restrictions of the monastic life and who longed for the worldly intellectual life of ideas and letters. His employment as secretary with the bishop of Cambray opened the way out of the monastery when he was sent to Paris as a student of theology (1495–99). His most decisive intellectual experience came from a 1505 trip to England, where he was influenced by the humanists John Colet and Thomas More. They led him to the Gospels as a guide for the imitation of Christ, which gave him a spiritual focus, a return to the simplicity of the ancient faith in the teachings of Jesus as presented in the Gospels.

Returning to the Continent, he published a large number of works. The *Adages* were an insightfully annotated collection of classical proverbs; *Colloquies* were delightful dialogues and tales poking fun at the foibles of society; and *Enchiridion* was a penetrating handbook of Christian virtues and practice that summarized his faith and practical theology. He also published editions of Cicero's and St. Jerome's letters and a critical edition of Lorenzo Valla's *Annotations of the New Testament.* While living in the home of Thomas More in England, he wrote *The Praise of Folly,* which had a serious purpose and has remained the most enduring of all of Erasmus's works. In 1514 he was brought to Basel by Johann Froben, a printer, and he also began editing the works of St. Jerome, Seneca, Plutarch, and Cato, then published a critical Greek and Latin edition of the New Testament and wrote a handbook on the education of a Christian prince, which he dedicated to Prince Charles, who soon was to become Emperor Charles V.

As far as the Reformation was concerned, the popular saying has it that Erasmus laid the egg and Luther hatched it. Erasmus's Greek edition of the New Testament was the basis of Luther's Bible. Though Erasmus engaged in controversy with Luther on the question of free will, he was a pioneer of the Reformation. Later, however, he came to regard the Reformation as an enemy of learning. For him the church was the great educational institution of mankind, and he thought that as such it was deserving of a higher place than the states and political authorities that catered to the baser needs of man. The rationalistic theology and ethics of Erasmus were felt more indirectly. While Martin Luther rejected his theology entirely, they were potent elements in the thinking of Philip Melanchthon, who had a fundamental impact on Lutheranism. Ulrich Zwingli was from the beginning influenced by Erasmian thought, and the Swiss or "reformed" Protestantism was permeated with it. Even Catholic thought was influenced by his ideas. His widest support in Germany came during the years from 1515 to 1520, yet he also alienated many within the German church as it then existed.

Erfurt Program (1891)

In 1891 the reorganized Socialist Party held its first party congress in Erfurt after the lapse of the antisocialist legislation. Primarily formulated by Karl Kautsky, the new program differed from the old Gotha Program, which had derived its goals from law and philosophy in Marxist theory and explained a different path of socialist development. It also elaborated its social and political philosophy more precisely in an orthodox analysis based on the Marxian class struggle. It pictured the development of capitalist society and how the increase in monopolies was bringing about the decline of the middle class. A widening gulf was emerging between the exploiters and exploited, dividing German society into two hostile camps. The program analyzed the impact of economic crises (depressions) and pointed out that private property no longer adequately used the forces of production. Following this theoretical analysis was a list of practical demands, some of which repeated those of the Gotha program.

Erhard, Ludwig (1897–1977)
economics minister and chancellor

Ludwig Erhard was the father of the economic recovery of West Germany after World War II. His neo-liberal economic policies combined with social-welfare programs, the "Social Market Economy," led to the German Economic Miracle. He served as chancellor from 1963 to 1966.

Ludwig Erhard was born on April 2, 1897, in Fürth, Bavaria. He served as a sergeant in World War I and was severely wounded. After the war he studied economics and sociology at the University of Frankfurt, receiving his doctorate in 1924. After some years in business he went to work for the Institute for Economic Observation in Nuremberg, and in 1942 he became head of Nuremberg's Institute for Industrial Research. As a member of the "Freiburg School" under the inspiration of members of the

German RESISTANCE (Martin NIEMOELLER and the CONFESSING CHURCH) he had studied how to restructure the centralized economic planning of the Nazi state. After the war he was placed in charge of industrial reconstruction in the Nuremberg-Fürth area, appointed economics minister in Bavaria later in 1945, and named professor of economic policy at the University of MUNICH. In 1947 he became chairman of the bizonal committee for money and credit in Frankfurt. The following year he initiated the elimination of price controls, and on June 20, 1948, currency reform, which ended a controlled economy.

His economic philosophy was neo-liberal, and the system he advocated was called a "social market economy," which Americans can best understand as welfare-state capitalism. Erhard had to cooperate with the American demand for economic decentralization but also resist and convince the German political parties not to advocate a centrally planned economy. Although the SPD could not be convinced to alter its demand for state control of the economy, Erhard was able to convince Konrad ADENAUER of the CDU to create a free market economy with generous social programs. Erhard quickly became the main economic adviser to U.S. general Lucius D. Clay, the military governor of the U.S. zone, and advocated currency reform and the decontrol of prices. His philosophy of welfare state capitalism left capital and production in private hands, allowing market mechanisms to set price and wage levels. Profits, Erhard believed, provided the best incentive for productivity, and government intervention was advocated to assure an equitable distribution of wealth. In order to assure open and fair competition, the federal government attempted to combat cartels and other devices that restricted prices and production. By 1950 tax rates had generally been cut from 95 percent to 18 percent, and productivity quickly grew to prewar levels.

Shortly before the first parliamentary election in 1949, Erhard joined the CDU and became the economics minister in the new Adenauer government. He held that post until 1963, when he replaced the aged chancellor, "der Alte," in 1963. Unlike the more authoritarian and distant Adenauer, Erhard tried to be a "people's chancellor" with a more popular and direct contact with the people, which was not so successful as he hoped. His foreign minister, Gerhard SCHROEDER, pursued a foreign policy that promoted an easing of trade relations with Eastern bloc nations (1963–64). After his success in the elections of 1965 he sought to normalize relations with the Soviet zone countries of the WARSAW PACT. Erhard and Schroeder were termed *Atlanticists* for their support of strong ties with the United States and with NATO.

It is interesting that the German electorate could not trust Erhard to lift the country out of the recession caused by the German economy's transition from a production to a service economy. Since he could not overcome their fears of another depression crisis as in 1929, he had to resign his office on December 1, 1966. A year afterward he was named honorary chairman of the CDU. During his remaining years he enjoyed visiting professorships at Munich, BONN, and in the United States at Harvard and Columbia. He died at age 80 on May 5, 1977.

Ernst, Max (1891–1976)
artist in the dada and surrealist movements

Born on April 2, 1891, in Brühl, Germany, Max Ernst had early experiences that provided subjects for his later paintings. He studied philosophy and abnormal psychology at the University of BONN, started painting in 1912, but did not develop his own style until after WORLD WAR I. Illustrations from various magazines, used as bizarre images in his collages, were his main productions in the dada group in Cologne from 1919 to 1922. Dada was very irreverent toward conventional art, and the group staged the infamous 1920 exhibition in which the public had to walk through a public urinal. Moving to Paris in 1922, he painted in the surrealist dreamlike style irrational associations of images, desert landscapes, and an erotic atmosphere. One of his most famous paintings was *Two Children Are Threatened by a Nightingale.* In 1925 a new surrealist technique produced strange shapes by rubbing graphite on sheets of paper placed on floors, tiles, or bricks; called frottage, he later applied it to his paintings. He stopped using this style in 1930 and again turned to illusion and mythology.

As was the case with other surrealist painters, Max Ernst left Germany for the United States, where he lived until 1953. After marrying and divorcing Peggy Guggenheim, an art collector and dealer, he moved to Arizona, with the American painter Dorothea Tanning, his fourth wife, where he painted landscapes. He returned to Paris in 1953, and in 1954, at the Venice Biennale, Ernst received one of the greatest honors of the art world. After his death in 1976 major retrospectives exhibitions celebrated his achievements.

Erzberger, Matthias (1875–1921)
Catholic politician

Matthias Erzberger was best known for his sponsorship of the peace resolution that the REICHSTAG passed in 1917 during WORLD WAR I. He was a strong critic of submarine warfare and was a member of the German Armistice Commission in 1918. He also worked for the acceptance of the hated VERSAILLES TREATY. He was one of the many Germans assassinated by right-wing extremists in the early years of the WEIMAR REPUBLIC.

Born on September 20, 1875, in the town of Buttenhausen in the state of Württemberg, Matthias Erzberger prepared for a career as a teacher, but turned to journalism and politics. In 1896 he joined the Catholic CENTER PARTY and soon became editor of its publication, *Deutsches Volksblatt,* in Stuttgart. Entering the Reichstag in 1903, he soon became a leader of the Center's left wing. His mastery of finances inspired him to sponsor such major fiscal bills as the Finance Reform of 1909 and the military expansion bills of 1911–13. In 1905–06 he crusaded against abuses in colonial administration. Later, he crusaded for the rights of Polish Catholics in West Prussia. Before and during the war he represented the Kaiser's government to the Vatican. Erzberger's leadership influenced the Center to cooperate with parties on the left such as the Social Democrats. He favored constitutional reform. Although initially he had been a fervent annexationist, he came to realize that Germany had no chance of victory and advocated a peace of understanding. The horrible realities of WORLD WAR I motivated him to oppose unlimited submarine warfare and become a sponsor of the Reichstag Peace Resolution in July 1917.

In the midst of constitutional reform under the government of Prince Max of Baden, Erzberger became state secretary without portfolio. As an armistice commissioner he signed the armistice agreement for Germany at Compiègne on November 11, 1918, for which he was branded a "November Criminal." He became the most prominent spokesman for the ratification of the Versailles Treaty. In the first coalition government he tried to revise the tax structure in order to bring social justice. Political criticism intensified against him, and a subsequent libel suit forced him to resign. On August 26, 1921, he was murdered by two former military officers and members of an ultranationalist society.

Eugene, prince of Savoy (1663–1736)
Imperial field marshal and statesman

Prince Eugene of Savoy was a military genius and wise statesman. Dedicated, ascetic, and self-disciplined, he believed in the European mission of the Habsburg empire, its role in holding Christian Europe together. He was born in Paris in October 1663, the son of Prince Eugene Maurice of Savoy-Carignan, count of Soissons, who was in the service of France. His mother was an Italian-born niece of the powerful Cardinal Mazarin, although she was dissolute and eventually was banished from the court. The boy grew into a man physically weak and unprepossessing, not tall at all, but he transformed himself into a puritanical Spartan. Louis XIV thought that he would become a clergyman, but all the young man wanted was a military commission, the application for which Louis XIV personally rejected. So in 1683 Eugene went off to Vienna to serve LEOPOLD I, the Holy Roman Emperor. He was befriended by the Austrian chancellor, and his military career developed rapidly. He mastered the art of war in the school of Duke Charles V of Lorraine and eventually became the "first soldier of the empire."

Prince Eugene served in the Turkish Wars (1683–99) and the WAR OF THE LEAGUE OF AUGSBURG (1688–97). He participated in saving Vienna from the Turks in 1683, then in the capture of Budapest (1686) and the siege of Belgrade (1688). His military leadership was rewarded with an appointment to field marshal in the imperial army. In 1697 he proved himself as a commanding general after he succeeded Augustus II the Strong as commander in chief of the imperial army in Hungary, where at the Battle of Zenta, he defeated a Turkish army three times larger than his own, ending the Turkish war.

Although the Habsburg monarchy emerged from the Turkish Wars considerably stronger, Prince Eugene became one of the strongest advocates for centralized institutions and a standing army. He and other advisers wanted to make the Chancellery (Hofkammer) and the Military Council (Hofkriegsrat) into instruments for centralized administrative, fiscal, and military control. Eugene became president of the Council of War.

During the first campaign of the War of Spanish Succession (1701–14) Prince Eugene commanded the Austrian troops in Italy, where he conducted a brilliant campaign against the French army, but the lack of money prevented him from having the necessary soldiers and equipment to support his campaign against Marshal Vendôme. Leopold then called upon the "Grand Alliance" with England and the Netherlands to meet the threat from France. The Anglo-Dutch army under the command of John Churchill, duke of Marlborough, came to the assistance of Prince Eugene at the Danube, and they defeated the Franco-Bavarian forces at the BATTLE OF BLENHEIM (1704). In 1705–06 Eugene again defeated the French and drove them out of Italy. Eugene and Marlborough developed a strong friendship and continued to cooperate in battles against the French at Oudenarde and Lille (1708) and Malplaquet (1709). The allies abandoned the new emperor, CHARLES VI, concluding a separate peace at Utrecht (1713). Prince Eugene then counseled the emperor to end the war with France, which Eugene negotiated in the Peace of Rastatt and Baden (1714).

Eugene continued to serve the monarchy, and when war broke out again with the Turks the emperor Charles appointed him commander of the army in Hungary, where he defeated them at Peterwardein (1716), Temesvár (1716), and Belgrade (1717). The war was concluded with the Treaty of Passarowitz in 1718. By 1730 he was too old to successfully lead an army, but over his objections AUSTRIA became involved in the War of the Polish Succession (1733–35), and his command of the army on the RHINE defended Bavaria but little else.

The other area to which Eugene devoted considerable energy was the cultural life of the era. He became one of the largest collectors and most appreciative patrons of the arts. His extensive library, his art gallery, his magnificent palaces, his friendships, especially with the greatest intellectual of the period, Gottfried Wilhelm LEIBNIZ (1646–1716), manifest the same disposition to conquer the arts that he displayed in the arena of war. In 1736 Prince Eugene died and was buried in St. Stephen's Cathedral.

European Coal and Steel Community (ECSC)

The European Coal and Steel Community was an important step in the integration of the FEDERAL REPUBLIC into Western Europe. Based on the SCHUMAN PLAN, all French and German coal and steel production were brought under a common authority. The idea was to bind Germany economically and politically into the structure of Western Europe. It paved the way for the EUROPEAN ECONOMIC COMMUNITY, or Common Market.

On May 9, 1950, the French foreign minister, Robert Schuman, proposed a plan that had the goal of placing all Franco-German coal and steel production under a common authority. The French had been unable to dismantle the industrial capacity of the German industries in the

Ruhr, so the French politician, Jean Monnet, argued that it was best for France to bind the German industries of the Ruhr through both economic and political cooperation into Western Europe. Added to the French and German industries were those of Belgium, Holland, and Luxembourg. There was, however, resistance from German and French industry, which preferred self or regional regulation instead of submission to a central authority. Against this opposition, pressure from the United States, which desired to decentralize the Ruhr steel trusts, moved the Ruhr and Bonn governments to accept the treaty. In April 1951 the ECSC Treaty was signed and in August 1952 the Federal Republic with France, Italy, and the Benelux countries accepted permanent joint control of all national coal and steel industries. In order to gain support for the treaty from Germany's unions, Konrad Adenauer promised the unions that workers would have a major voice, called co-determination, in running private companies. In the ECSC coal and steel industries this resulted in workers' being allowed to elect 50 percent of the membership of the supervisory boards compared to the 33 percent of the seats in the rest of German industry.

It did not take much time for the High Authority of the ECSC to remove tariffs and quotas on the intra-Community trading of coal, steel, scrap, and iron ore. Subsidies were reduced, and discriminatory freight rates were abolished. Common guidelines were worked out regarding price and investment policies, and measures were taken to regulate competition and concentration and to influence production and productivity. Due to economic expansion there was such a high level of demand for the products of these industries that the High Authority did not have to interfere in production and employment. When the economy slowed in 1957–58, decisions on economic policy were left in the hands of the individual governments and not the High Authority.

The High Authority was one of four institutions that were the precursors of similar Common Market institutions: the High Authority, the Council of Ministers, the Common Assembly, and a Court of Justice. The High Authority corresponded to the EEC's commission. It was an executive body made up of nine members representing the member countries, with France and West Germany each having two. It could legislate binding decisions and issue recommendations, dismantle cartels, and levy taxes on the sale of coal and steel. The Council of Ministers was similar to the EEC's Council of Ministers and represented the national interests of member nations, which was to provide a balance to the High Authority. The Common Assembly corresponded to the EEC's European Parliament and possessed only consultative powers. The Court of Justice was similar to the EEC's Court of Justice and could make decisions on matters related to the ECSC treaty.

European Defense Community (EDC)

One of the primary goals of the government of Konrad Adenauer in the early 1950s was to integrate the Federal Republic into the Western Alliance. An important part of this effort was West Germany's willingness to supply military forces for the defense of Western Europe. This development aroused considerable controversy. As the Americans were involved in the Korean War, they readily endorsed a new German army.

In October 1950 there was widespread support for a West European army within the structure of the Council of Europe. The plans for the European Defense Community therefore would play a double role, the Germans providing their fair share of the defense of Western Europe and allaying French fears of a revived German military. A European Defense Community (EDC) provided for an integrated Western European army. It was negotiated at the same time as the General Treaty of 1952, under which the Allies agreed to abolish major parts of the Occupation Statute of 1949, without, however, making West Germany a sovereign nation. (Sovereignty was to be obtained by West Germany in the Germany Treaty of 1954). Through the EDC the six countries of Western Europe (West Germany, France, Italy, Belgium, Holland, and Luxembourg) were to place their armies under the control of an international command composed of officers from the six countries. Being placed under international control served to allay any fears that a West German army would threaten the other nations.

The EDC was controversial in both West Germany and France. In Germany the BUNDESTAG, however, was able to ratify the treaty and amend the BASIC LAW, removing constitutional prohibitions against a West German military. The French National Assembly voted against the treaty and put an end to the prospects of an integrated European military force. German troops ended up joining NATO forces in 1955, and two years later conscription was introduced again. In the 1960s German armed forces provided 12 divisions with 500,000 men.

European Economic Community
(EEC)

The European Economic Community was founded in 1958 by the Treaty of Rome for economic and political cooperation. It was originally composed of six members: Belgium, France, Italy, Luxembourg, the Netherlands, and West Germany (FRG). Others added later were the United Kingdom, Ireland, Denmark, Spain, Portugal, and Greece.

The initiative for the creation of the European Economic Community came from the French foreign minister Robert Schuman. He proposed to pool the iron and steel industries of France and Germany into a common market. It was thought that the revived industries of the Ruhr Valley would be better controlled through cooperation rather than the use of force. Out of this emerged the idea of an integrated market for French and German heavy industry, which resulted in the SCHUMAN PLAN. Through his leadership the original six members established the European Coal and Steel Community (ECSC). The ECSC abolished tariffs and created a common market for coal and steel products among the six countries. Even more important, control of trade and manufacturing levels of these products was turned over to an international High Authority, whose judgment superseded national decision-making bodies.

Efforts to create a more comprehensive economic union became a reality when the six countries agreed by the Treaty of Rome in 1957 to a number of cooperative agreements and to commit to a timetable for tariff reductions until all levies among the six countries were abolished. A Common Agricultural Policy (CAP) was established, which provided for massive subsidies to Europe's farmers. The administration of the Common Market was vested in a multinational European Commission, headquartered in Brussels, Belgium. Even though there were numerous compromises, the Treaty of Rome provided West Germany with equality, and she was finally accepted back into the European family of nations. Since West Germany (FRG) was the most advanced industrial country among the six partners, it benefited the most from the abolition of tariffs. The CAP, however, benefited France, the country that had the largest agricultural sector. On the other hand, West Germany (FRG) provided the largest amount of money for the EEC's farm subsidies, which also began a new era of improved relations between France and West Germany.

The EEC had gained momentum much more quickly than had been expected. As the economic decisions were made, a wide transfer of sovereignty rights occurred. The Rome Treaty had delegated the major decision making not to the EEC Commission in Brussels, the executive body representing Community interests, but to the Council of Ministers, who were the spokesmen for the interests of the individual nations. Since the treaty had merely outlined the objectives, the common rules and timetables for the envisioned economic integration, the formulation of policies had to be established in years of tough bargaining among the member nations by balancing their interests. As was mentioned earlier, French agricultural interests received increased benefits, while German industry was favored, and the smaller Benelux countries received advantages in commerce and the transit trade. The principal idea was to develop more than a trading bloc, to create a genuine economic community. Steps had to be taken to abolish barriers to the commodity trade and the free movement of labor and capital, to coordinate financial and general economic policies, and to adopt a common approach to agriculture, transportation, and foreign trade. The Rome Treaty had allowed 12 years to accomplish the gradual reduction of all tariffs among the six nations. Progress in this direction turned out to be much more rapid than originally planned due to Europe's prosperity and the favorable response of the business community. Business circles, which had had reservations or even opposed the Common Market, now rushed to meet the deadlines for competition at home and abroad. Changes in France also were beneficial. General Charles de Gaulle had become president of the Republic half a year after the creation of the Common Market, and due to increased prosperity, tariff reductions occurred more quickly. It has been said that prosperity created the Common Market, not the other way around.

European Union
(EU)

A cornerstone of postwar German foreign policy has been its cooperation with France, which culminated in December 1991 with the Treaty of Maastricht, which established the European Community. The treaty was signed at a solemn meeting of the government leaders of the member states of the Common Market in the Dutch city of Maastricht. The signatories were hopeful that the provisions in the 1,000-page agreement would be a major step forward to European cooperation and political unity. It provided timetables for the establishment of a European currency (the euro), the elimination of the last trade barriers among member countries, the establishment of a common European citizenship, and finally a name change from the European Community to the European Union (EU).

Although a step forward toward European union, the Maastricht Treaty did not fulfill the hopes of its backers. Helmut KOHL and François Mitterand neglected to prepare the groundwork for all the Europeanization measures that the treaty envisioned. For one thing opponents complained that the agreement did not provide for a strong European parliament, leaving unchecked the powers of the European Commission in Brussels. There were worries in Germany that the euro would weaken the mark. Small nations worried about being overwhelmed by the larger states. These reservations manifested themselves during the referendums for the treaty. At first Danish voters rejected the treaty, which subsequently they approved. French voters were only marginally in favor of the treaty. In Germany the treaty was approved in the BUNDESTAG but was challenged in the FEDERAL CONSTITUTIONAL COURT and in October 1993 was finally approved as not being in conflict with the BASIC LAW. Another weakness was the absence of any meaningful concept and institutions concerning the political and military role that the reunited Germany should play in Europe. Helmut Kohl had been enthusiastic about working for increasing powers for the European Parliament.

In 1992 Germans found themselves in a single European market and received a standardized European passport. It was the first hard evidence of steps toward greater union. It took a decade, but on January 1, 2002, the Europeans woke up to having a new money, the euro. In place of their marks Germans got euros, an important symbol of union. Monetary union was a prelude to further change. Former states from the Soviet bloc were soon to be admitted, including Poland, Hungary, Czechoslovakia, Romania, Estonia, and Slovenia. The islands of Malta and Cyprus also joined, and Turkey has applied for admission. Brussels' embrace will add 23 percent to the EU's landmass and bring in 75 million new citizens, making a Europe with 450 million people. The new members all hope for the prosperity Ireland and Spain achieved after entry into the European Community. Economic growth since 1995 reached 5 percent in the candidate countries of Eastern Europe. Trade with the EU accounted for more than 60 percent of the GDP of each future member.

euthanasia

Adolf HITLER's beliefs about racial purity and what was needed to improve the "national health" and "racial integrity of the German people" was promulgated early in his regime. On July 14, 1933, the Law for the Protection of Hereditary Health was made public. This was the beginning of a program of mercy killing of incurably insane and biologically defective German people and the mass killing and genocide of millions of people declared to be biologically inferior, such as Poles, Russians, Gypsies, and Jews. The program had three aspects: (1) euthanasia for incurables, (2) direct extermination, (3) mass sterilization.

Hitler believed that waiting until war would decrease the possibility of resistance to euthanasia on the part of the population and the churches. The churches had a long history of caring for the insane and crippled, and protests from several churchmen to reports of mercy killings began in summer 1940. Some took their protests to government officials. Protestant minister Friedrich von Bodelschwingh refused to hand over children from his asylum. The most famous protest was expressed by the Catholic bishop of Münster, Clemens von GALEN. He preached during summer 1941, condemning the euthanasia project. Copies of the sermons were distributed throughout Germany, and a strong public reaction occurred. Although Nazi leaders were outraged at the protest, Hitler wisely tried to soothe public opinion so as not to undermine the war effort. Hitler ordered a halt to the euthanasia program on August 28, 1941. The program had, however, provided some experience and training in the organized killing of people, which would quickly be applied in the extermination of Jews and other populations.

expressionism

Expressionism was a militant and aggressive artistic movement in art, literature, drama, and music. As a movement it had its beginning after the turn of the 20th century, rose to maturity during WORLD WAR I and declined in the 1920s.

In literature the origins of expressionism go back to the Swedish novelist and dramatist August Strindberg, in whose works men are driven by an omnipotent force that dominates them to perform good or evil. A new generation of writers rebelled against the values of the Empire and the depersonalization of modern industrial society.

Expressionist writers and artists also reacted against NATURALISM and neoromanticism. They attempted to show the truth by proclaiming man's mental phenomena, his aspirations, hopes, and fears. Expressionism was unique among the literary schools because its representatives did not try to imitate nature. They wanted to express their subjective, emotionally charged view of reality while it was fresh.

In the expressionist drama there also was a great deal of emotionalism. Drama was a more appropriate vehicle for their form of expression than was the novel, although some of Alfred DÖBLIN's novels were expressionist. In some respects expressionism was a type of social and political protest that was earlier seen in the storm and stress movement, of YOUNG GERMANY, and in naturalism. The tragedies of World War I and the Russian Revolution of 1917 gave a tremendous stimulus to the expressionist movement. Frank Wedekind (1864–1918) already in 1910 was an early representative of expressionism, manifested in his bizarre dramas' grotesque thoughts, tempestuous messages, and a mania for sex. The principal dramatists were antagonistic to material progress and the rise of an industrial and technological society. The expressionists were radicals whose interest was in a fundamental change in society and the regeneration of humankind. Other themes involved the conflict of generations and the battle of the sexes. The first play to be regarded as expressionist was *Mörder, Hoffnung der Frauen* (1910). Some of the principal expressionist dramatists were Ernst Barlach, Bertolt BRECHT in his earlier works, R. Goering, W. Hasenclever, H. Johst, and Georg KAISER (1878–1945). Kaiser was the leader in the field of abstract expressionism; he peopled his stage not with individual characters but general types of persons—the Mother, the

Engineer, the Millionaire, the Father. This form of drama was called Stationendrama. Among the great theater directors whose genius contributed to their development was Max Reinhardt (1873–1944).

Some of the greatest poets of the 20th century were expressionists, notably Rainer Maria RILKE (1875–1926), a poet who was a prophet, philosopher, and seer. He was unorthodox and mystical, trying to express the inexpressible. His visionary hymns of the *Duineser Elegien* can be counted among the works of the expressionists. Others are August Stramm, whose rhythmic poetry drives language to the extreme. Other important poets were Georg Heym (1887–1912), Johannes Becker (1891–1958), Gottfried BENN (1886–1956), Georg Trakl (1887–1914), and Franz Werfel (1890–1945). In their abandonment of poetic conventions their work reflected the distorted shapes and striking colors of expressionist painting.

Expressionism first became prominent in painting in the Blue Rider Group (Der blaue Reiter) and THE BRIDGE (Die Brücke). German expressionist artists included Ernst Ludwig KIRCHNER (1880–1938), Paula Modersohn Becker (1876–1907), Emil NOLDE (1867–1956), Max PECHSTEIN (1881–1955), K. Schmidt-Rottluff (1884–1976), and the most famous artist of The Bridge, Wassily Kandinsky (1866–1944). The movement lasted roughly from 1909 to 1921. The artists used abstraction and distorted images and bright colors to attack the conventions of art and society that the artists found to be dehumanizing and corrupting. After the war and the battles that were fought during the early republic, many of the artists became disillusioned and turned away from expressionism.

F

Falkenhayn, Erich von (1861–1922)
commander of German Army

Born on September 11, 1861, near Thorn, Erich von Falkenhayn was the son of an impoverished noble family. He became an officer in 1880, served on the General Staff, and commanded some of the European troops who suppressed the Boxer Rebellion in China in 1900. As a favorite of the Kaiser he was appointed to replace Helmuth von Moltke the Younger when he failed to fully implement the Schlieffen Plan in France and experienced an emotional breakdown. Many had doubts about Falkenhayn's own determination, but he was one of the military leaders who early on accepted that a quick victory was impossible. Falkenhayn realized that the war would be one of attrition following a strategy of "slowly wearing down" and "relentless bloodletting." He applied this strategy against Ypres and the ports along the English Channel and then the fortress at Verdun in 1916. These failed. He came to believe that the best Germany could achieve would be a negotiated settlement. Clashing with the generals who commanded the eastern front, he believed that the decisive front was in the West and not in Russia. The Kaiser was influenced by the eastern generals to dismiss Falkenhayn in August 1916 after a Russian advance during summer 1916 and the entry of Rumania into the war on the side of Britain and France. After his dismissal Falkenhayn proved himself to be an outstanding field commander in the successful invasion of Rumania. Subsequently, he served in the German support of the Turks in Palestine and took command of an army in Lithuania. He retired in 1919 to his family castle and died near Potsdam on April 8, 1922.

fascism

The term *fascism* was derived from the Latin *fasces*, which denoted a bundle of rods with a protruding ax head carried by the magistrates of ancient Rome. Though the original fasces symbolized justice, the alternative connotation of unity was more appropriate to the fascist movement intent on the reintegration of a society divided by social class and political strife. The term was used in Italy by both the left and the right. It had been used by a workers' association in Sicily in 1915, by Benito Mussolini's group, which favored intervention in World War I, and later it was applied to a parliamentary group for the prosecution of the war. Then it came to be applied to the "fasci di Combattimento" in 1919. In Italy many early fascists were left-wingers, and the question that often is raised is whether fascism is reactionary or progressive. Fascists claimed to represent the general interest against a restricted franchise dominated by a liberal oligarchy. Fascism promised to transcend this corrupt system. As fascism progressed through its phases from a movement to a political party and then to a regime, it was not static. While in 1919 most Italians did not know what it was, by 1921 it had organized into a political party. Mussolini himself had a leftist origin and as a socialist was pacificistic. When he converted toward military intervention in the war, he felt that war would unite the nation and would be a means toward a revolutionary end.

A Nazi official is shown leading a group of Hitler Youth and Italian children in a fascist salute. *(Library of Congress)*

Fascism was unique in its hostility to all the main established currents of the left, center, and the right. The Fascists actually cleared new ideological and political space in the political arena for themselves. Fascism was above all anti-Marxist, antiliberal, and anticonservative, but pro-collectivist. It emphasized the leadership principle (the Nazi *Führerprinzip*), used a party organized as an army, and pursued a totalitarian goal. Fascism sought to oppose international Marxism through fanatical nationalism, state centralism, and the elimination of the autonomy of individuals, groups, and institutions. In order to obtain power, fascist movements used legal and psuedodemocratic tactics. They possessed a similarity of style: elaborate liturgies in meetings, parades, decorations, and symbols; balcony speeches were common, wearing of colored shirts, shouts and salutes and large-scale party militias were used for political intimidation against parties and groups. The dictatorial party existed alongside the state and usurped many of its functions. The masses of the people were mobilized in order to demonstrate their apparent participation in the regime. It is clear that fascist state doctrine posited a new secular system, normally republican and authoritarian. The domination of the modern means of communications was also attempted. Fascists did have the common goal of a new economic structure and a functional relationship between social and economic systems. While Italian fascism emphasized corporatism,

Nazism explicitly rejected it because of its pluralism. Marxist writers have been wrong in their contention that the aim of fascist movements was to prevent economic changes in class relationships. Most fascist movements were imperialist, seeking a new order in foreign affairs through their alliances.

Fascist ideologies and ideas are often interpreted as opposed to the rationalism of the ENLIGHTENMENT because they scorned philosophical concepts and exalted action over theory. Yet, fascist ideas and goals were derived from the Promethean secular concepts of the 18th century. Fascism, however, diverged in its antimaterialism, its vitalism and idealism, and its metaphysics of the will. As a goal fascism, like communism, wanted to create a "new man." They hoped to recover a sense of the natural and enable the man of will and determination to go beyond himself and sacrifice for his ideals. In contrast to the structured and systematic thinking of Marxist-Leninism, fascism expounded a vague world view (weltanschauung). But even Italian fascism gave more evidence of a residual faith in human reason and perfectability of man than did Nazism. Hitler more than any other fascist leader was scornful of the masses of people, derided man's intelligence, substituting the "cult of primitive feeling," and made ANTI-SEMITISM into a fundamental doctrine.

Hitler's ideology was founded on race, while Italian fascism was based on political and cultural nationalism. Other fascists balked at official Nazi racial ideas. The Belgian Rexists and the Dutch National Socialists and the Italians up to 1937 did not mention the Jewish question in their manifestos. Both French and Italian fascism emphasized a joyous pragmatic activism, while Nazism believed in carrying out ideals programmatically with deeds. National Socialism tended toward revolutionary exclusivity, rejecting rival doctrines, while Italian fascism incorporated aspects of liberalism, conservatism, and socialism. As far as the goal of the development of a "new man" was concerned, Nazism formulated it in a new biological context, while the "fascist man" was to be developed through education. Finally, while the nationalism of the Italian fascism was based on Italian culture and national history, Nazi nationalism had a racial-environmental basis.

Fatherland Party

The Fatherland Party was a wartime nationalistic and xenophobic mass movement organized by the extreme right with the blessings of the German High Command (OHL) to oppose the Reichstag Peace resolution and lobby for the annexationist Hindenburg Peace.

A major vehicle for the propaganda effort of the High Command was the Fatherland Party, which was organized with its blessing on September 3, 1917. Paul von HINDENBURG and Erich LUDENDORFF wanted to mobilize public opinion in favor of the army's peace terms. The Fatherland Party attracted members from among conservatives and right-wing liberals of the late IMPERIAL GERMANY. Duke Johann Albrecht of Mecklenburg, a minor prince, and Admiral von TIRPITZ became its principal leaders. Tirpitz and Wolfgang Kapp were its actual founders. Kapp, a middle-class civil servant, and another leader, Heinrich Class, the chairman of the Pan-German League, were a new type of right-wing politician. The party's popularity can be assessed by the fact that it had almost a million members by September 1918 and had organized 2,536 local chapters. It achieved a long-standing desire of the political right for unity. Its sole purpose was to lobby for Hindenburg Peace, which was a vast annexationist program, including direct German control of Holland and Belgium, and German domination over Russia and Turkey. Its dominant ideological tone was set by the PAN GERMANS and radical nationalists. Although it had no parliamentary ambitions, it did favor the continuation of the Kaiser's authoritarianism at home. It also was another effort to bypass the regular constitutional channels of politics. The military propaganda machine of the OHL had already tried to create a cult of personality around Hindenburg with millions of posters and postcards asserting that the aged field marshal was the guarantor of victory.

After the Fatherland Party disbanded in December 1918 in the midst of the confusion of the REVOLUTION of 1918, its members drifted off into the parties of the far right during the WEIMAR REPUBLIC and eventually many supported the NAZI PARTY (NSDAP). Anton Drexler, the founder of the GERMAN WORKERS' PARTY (DAP), had been a functionary in the Fatherland Party and went on to become one of the original members of the NSDAP in MUNICH.

Federal Constitutional Court
(Bundesverfassungsgericht)

The Federal Constitutional Court is the supreme court of the FEDERAL REPUBLIC and has the competence to rule in disputes between the Federal Republic and the states. It has the power to declare unconstitutional the contents of a law or the actions of a political party. A most notable example of the latter was its ban on the Communist Party (KPD) in 1956.

In their desire to create checks and balances to governmental authority, the framers of the BASIC LAW were in general agreement on granting the courts the power of judicial review and on establishing a specific national-level court as the final arbiter in constitutional matters. The result was Articles 93 and 94 of the Basic Law, which established the constitutional court, assigned its competency and jurisdiction, and defined its composition. The court was a new addition to the postwar legal system and has become the most political of German courts. It is assigned the functions of judicial review, the adjudication of disputes between state and federal political institutions, the protection of individual civil rights as guaranteed in the constitution, and the responsibility for protecting the constitutional and democratic order against groups and individuals seeking to overthrow it. In this latter area the constitutional court has the right to ban such groups and their activities. Besides the ban on the Communist Party, the constitutional court has gained notoriety in adjudicating the reform of paragraph 218 of the constitution, the ASYLUM LAW, conscientious objections to military service, and the deployment of military forces.

Federal Republic of Germany
(FRG; Bundesrepublik Deutschland, BRD)

The Federal Republic was formed in 1949 out of the U.S., British, and French occupation zones, becoming a parliamentary democracy and prosperous capitalistic state. It comprised the western part of defeated Nazi Germany. In 1990 the Federal Republic absorbed the communist GERMAN DEMOCRATIC REPUBLIC to form a united German Republic.

The cold war led to the emergence of two separate states in Germany, the Federal Republic based on the occupation zones of the Western Allies, and the German Democratic Republic based on the Soviet zone. The process that created the Federal Republic was founded on the currency reform and the adoption of the deutsche mark. The BERLIN BLOCKADE contributed to the process, as did the convening of the Parliamentary Council on September 1, 1948, which wrote the provisional constitution called the BASIC LAW. The Basic Law was to be used until a new constitution for the whole of Germany could be adopted. The Basic Law called for a two-house legislature, the BUNDESTAG, which represented the population, and the BUNDESRAT, which represented the states. It was decided that the capital of the republic was to be in BONN.

The first period of the Federal Republic's history was presided over by the 73-year-old Konrad ADENAUER and the conservative coalition of the CDU/CSU from 1949 to 1963. When the Federal Republic came into existence, it was no sovereign state and was still governed under the Occupation Statute. Adenauer's most important foreign policy achievement was to integrate the FRG into a Western alliance by becoming a member of the NORTH ATLANTIC TREATY ORGANIZATION (NATO) and reestablishing German armed forces (Bundeswehr) by becoming a sovereign state in 1955, by joining the EUROPEAN COAL AND STEEL COMMUNITY (ECSC) and by signing the Treaty of Rome in 1957, creating the

European Economic Community (EEC). The economic foundation for the FRG's revival was the Economic Miracle. Under the stewardship of Ludwig Erhard and his neo-liberal economic policies, which included a social-market system, a tremendous economic boom was created. Rapidly increasing production, profits, income, and the standard of living contributed to the legitimization of the West German state system. Although Adenauer's star already was in decline by the end of the 1950s, it took until 1963 for him to resign over the Spiegel Affair.

A transition (second period) now followed from 1963 to 1969, during which Ludwig Erhard became chancellor, followed by the grand coalition of the CDU/CSU and the SPD under the chancellorship of Kurt Georg Kiesinger. Criticism of the government's economic policies was followed by a recession. The grand coalition overcame the economic problems with selective measures that stimulated economic growth. As this was happening, an extraparliamentary opposition was developing principally representing neo-Marxist views, which demanded radical change. As was happening in other countries, student protests were rampant. Finally, the grand coalition was torn apart by the election of the SPD candidate, Gustav Heinemann, as federal president.

The third period began with the SPD majority in the Bundestag elections of 1969. Willy Brandt became chancellor, and Walter Scheel (FDP) became foreign minister. The principal foreign policy initiative of Brandt's administration was his Ostpolitik, which opened up relations with the German Democratic Republic, Eastern Europe, and the Soviet Union. It was part of Détente between the superpowers. In domestic politics the SPD/FDP coalition extended the welfare state and liberalized society. An unfortunate spy scandal forced Willy Brandt to resign, and he was succeeded by Helmut Schmidt as chancellor and Hans Dietrich Genscher (FDP) as foreign minister between 1974 and 1982. The Social-Liberal coalition won the elections of 1976 and 1980. Among the domestic problems facing the government was the growth of terrorism of the Baader-Meinhof Gang. What became the main economic concern was the worldwide oil price explosion and the world economic recession, which hit the Federal Republic very hard. Gross national product stopped growing, unemployment and bankruptcies increased, the social security system was difficult to fund, and public debt was rising dramatically. It was difficult to find common policies to attack these problems, and the Social-Liberal coalition broke up and early elections were called for 1983.

The election was won by a center-right coalition led by the CDU's Helmut Kohl, initiating the fourth period of the republic's history. The 16 years of his administration began with the reassertion of national pride, a peace movement, protests against nuclear missiles, the rise of the pacificist and neutralist Green Party and its opposition to nuclear energy, and the rise of neo-nationalist parties and rightist fringe parties such as the Republicans. The deployment of nuclear missiles by NATO led to the 1987 U.S.-Soviet agreement on the elimination of land-based intermediate-range nuclear weapons in Europe. The growth of government borrowing was curbed, and a major tax reform program provided tax relief. Economic growth continued, and prices remained stable. Although there was an improvement in employment and new jobs were created, unemployment was still too high in 1989.

The collapse of the Soviet Bloc and the revolutionary events in the GDR during 1989 presented the opportunity for German reunification. As the East Germans reorganized their political parties and government, Kohl took the initiative and surprisingly won a victory in the all-German elections of 1990 by promising prosperity in a quickly reunited Germany. The union parties (CDU/CSU) won 43.8 percent of the vote against the Party of Democratic Socialism (the successor to the SED) which won only 11.1 percent of the vote. Reunification, of course, brought with it many new responsibilities and problems. Industries in the East collapsed and unemployment soared. There was no quick fix to the problems facing reunified

Germany. There was a resurgence of the extreme right. A high rate of unemployment continued. Kohl and the CDU won the election of 1994. Finally, the center-right coalition lost in 1998 to an SPD/FDP coalition headed by the new chancellor, Gerhard Schroeder.

Federation of German Industry
(Bundesverband der deutschen Industrie, BDI)

The Federation of German Industry (BDI) was founded in October 1949 by 32 industrial associations as an interest and lobbying group. It is the successor to the National Association of German Industry, which existed during the Weimar Republic and was disbanded in 1933. Thirty-four affiliated associations have composed the association, which represents some 80,000 industrial firms. The BDI represents the economic interests of German industry in relation to the German government and the European Community. Its headquarters is located in Cologne, while it also has offices in each of the federal states, and internationally in Brussels, London, Tokyo, and Washington. Policies are formulated by a wide range of individuals and groups, including the president of the BDI, the executive committee, specialized committees, and working groups. The policies are coordinated with other business organizations such as the Federation of German Employers' Associations, banking, insurance, and agricultural associations. The BDI is a member of the Council of European Industrial Associations.

The BDI has been very successful in promoting legislation that supports its interests. It does this by molding public opinion through the Institute for German Industry and the media. It maintains close contact and has successfully lobbied both Christian Democratic and Social Democratic governments. The association also has been successful in blocking legislation that it considers harmful to its members' interests. Most recently the BDI has recommended that the government promote an increase in private investment in eastern Germany, which, however, has not been implemented.

Federation of German Women's Associations
(Bund Deutscher Frauenvereine, BDF)

The Federation of German Women's Associations was founded in 1894. Auguste Schmidt, a trained teacher and member of the Association of Women's Teachers, became its first president. Its membership grew rapidly from 70,000 in 1901 to about 500,000 in 1914. The purpose of the BDF was to improve the lives of women by lobbying for equal secondary education, access to universities and all other institutions of higher learning, legal and economic protection for marriage and motherhood, equal pay for equal work in factories, greater opportunities for professional women, the right to qualify for jury duty, assured child support, equal parental guardianship laws, and finally the all-important right to vote. The federation even concerned itself with government for prostitutes. These goals indicate many of the areas in German society in which women possessed an inferior status to men and were without equal rights. Some of the goals were achieved in the revised Civil Code of 1900, which for the first time established women as "legal" persons and not subordinate to their husbands, who had been legal guardians.

There were a variety of associations for women throughout Germany, which makes clear that women were not only the cooks in the kitchen, worshipped at church, and cared for children (the KKKs) as the Kaiser William II would have liked. It is clear that women since the 18th century were part of the emergence of social associations that had an impact on the modernization of Imperial Germany.

feminism, 1815–1945

Those who labored for the emancipation of women had a number of characteristics in common. First, they believed in the validity of the female experience. Second, they considered the subordination of women not as a personal problem but an institutional one. Third, they sought to eliminate injustices by enhancing the power of women or limiting the coercive power of men and the state. The historical development of feminism accompanied the growth of democratization of nation-states, the spread of literacy, and the expansive growth of an urban and ultimately industrial capitalist market economy. The roots of the feminist movement were interrelated with the history of the ENLIGHTENMENT and the French Revolution, from which are derived some of its goals, such as liberty, equality, emancipation, liberation, justice, and sisterhood. The growth of feminism has to be understood in reference to the French Revolution, Napoleon's conquests, and the counterrevolutionary governments of the Restoration. After 1815 Prince METTERNICH and other German government figures sought to suppress the revolutionary influences from France and attempted to control public speech, associations, and debates over political liberties. Even in political theory relative to women's rights, Johann-Gottlieb FICHTE and Georg-Wilhelm Friedrich HEGEL stressed the importance for the state to have women and children subordinated to men in the family.

In the revolutionary climate of mid-19th-century Germany, the doors were opening to the critique of society by feminist activists. The central theme was "womanliness" and the contributions that women could make to the building of a new nation. This theme of "relational feminism" was espoused by Louise Otto, a well-educated woman of upper middle-class background. Otto also edited a revolutionary women's publication, the *Women's Newspaper.* Already in the mid-1840s she had campaigned for reforms in the education of women and improvements in working conditions in the new industrial cities. But Otto also thought that marriage was a degrading institution and that German women were lacking in character. German feminists at mid-century were also defensive against criticism of the way George Sand (a French woman writer) aped men by wearing men's clothing. The true German woman was idealized in Otto's eyes as one who was "virtuous, courageous, moralistic, patriotic and peaceable."

The early feminist associations generally worked for educational and professional advancement rather than for political rights. Their activities were hampered, however, by the Prussian Law of Association of 1850, which continued the reactionary policies of the post-Napoleonic period, prohibiting women from participation in political activities. Louise Otto was instrumental in the establishment of the first national feminist organization, the General Association of German Women (ADF), founded in 1865 and dedicated to the emancipation of women. Another association was the Lette Association, founded by Wilhelm Adolf Lette.

What was expected of women in Imperial Germany was, as Kaiser William II expressed it, that a woman's role ought to be confined to raising her children, cooking in the kitchen, and attending church. Among the feminist activists who thought otherwise were those who founded the Association for Women's Welfare in 1888, which advocated the right to vote. These were labeled radicals, while the more traditional feminists were called moderates. An umbrella organization, the FEDERATION OF GERMAN WOMEN'S ASSOCIATIONS (BDF), was established in 1893. In 1894 Auguste Schmidt became its president, and it lobbied for equal secondary education, access to universities, legal and economic protection in marriage, equal pay for equal work, equal property rights, and the right to vote. It was the more radical leaders who challenged the family law provisions of the new civil code of 1896 and the practice of state-regulated prostitution. The revised CIVIL CODE OF 1900 recognized women as "legal persons" for the first time. As a result, husbands no longer were considered legal guardians of their wives. On the other hand, more conservative groups formed, such as the German Protestant Women's League, which joined the BDF, adding to the strength of the moderates. In the 1890s a socialist women's organization also was formed under the leadership of Clara ZETKIN, but most of its efforts were directed toward achieving equality for women within the SOCIAL DEMOCRATIC PARTY. It was unfortunate that the middle class and the socialist feminists simply could not cooperate for the greater good of women.

Advances in the feminist agenda were increasingly apparent. In 1901 the gates to a university education were opened for the first time at HEIDELBERG and Freiburg, followed by the universities in PRUSSIA. On the eve of WORLD WAR I as many as 4,126 female students were enrolled. The Civil Code of 1900 also reversed the prohibition against divorce, allowing divorce by consent for childless couples. In 1902 the German Society for Women's Suffrage was founded by such radicals as Anita AUGSPURG and Lida Gustava Heymann. In 1908 restrictions against the participation of women in political activities were ended by the Reich Law of Association (1908). Women were now allowed to the join the SPD with equal rights. The Reich Law also helped women in their campaign for suffrage. Nevertheless, during the last decades of peace the women's movement like society in general became more conservative. One example of this was found in the leadership of Gertrud BÄUMER, who became the leader of the BDF in 1910. As a disciple of Adolf STÖCKER and Friedrich NAUMANN, she wanted to lead the organization in a more nationalist and traditionally conservative family direction. Women were told that marriage and motherhood were more important than careers, and she opposed abortion on demand.

Women did not get the right to vote, however, until after World War I in the WEIMAR CONSTITUTION. With the enfranchisement of women and the acceptance of legal equality in the Weimar Republic, the old goals had been achieved, which left the new female politicians promoting education, health care, and maternal and child welfare. Most observers were surprised to find that when women now voted they preferred candidates and parties with moderate to conservative views or in special cases the religious parties, the CENTER and BAVARIAN PEOPLE'S PARTY. The woman's movement became more conservative. Even the SPD took a more conservative position, which inspired socialist feminist leaders such as Louise Zietz and Clara Zetkin to switch to the INDEPENDENT SOCIAL DEMOCRATS (USPD). Middle-class feminists came to resemble their opponents, the anti-feminists directing women away from careers and back to housework. The main organization of middle-class feminists was the BDF, led by Baumer, which tripled in membership because other women's organizations joined, reflecting right-wing politics and even racism. The old-line feminists like Anita Augspurg and Lida Heymann decided to orient their interests internationally by playing leading roles in the International Women's League for Peace and Freedom. More left-wing reformers pushed for changes in the abortion law and making knowledge available about contraception.

The position of women in the workforce and the image of the "New Woman" were a subject of continuous debate during Weimar. The proportion of women in the workforce had not increased greatly from the Empire (1907) at 31.5 percent to 35.6 percent in 1925. It was in the internal makeup of the female workforce that the most changes took place and were so passionately debated. It was in the shift of gender-based employment that the greatest changes took place. New categories of women's jobs were created, such as shorthand typist, assembly worker, primary school teacher, and social worker. Female employment in these sectors became quite acceptable for single women, but a debate arose about when married women might be depriving a man of a job.

The Nazi male chauvinists never hid their hostility to the women's movement, stressing women's motherhood role, their subordinate position to men, and their responsibility for a separate sphere. Associated with the Nazi movement was the Nazi organization run by Gertrud SCHOLTZ-KLINK. All other feminist organizations were crushed, as were those dedicated to sex reform. Women were told they had separate spheres, and an unintended result was that many learned a variety of skills in the many leadership positions held open to them in Nazi women's associations.

feminism, 1945–2005

After WORLD WAR II had had such a destructive impact on the family, the smallest institution revived in the 1950s as the ideal form of security. For women that meant the housewife again was extolled. The numerous war widows and single working women who could not marry because of the shortage of males were seen as pitiable and marginal. Various forces combined to return women to the domestic sphere, actually reducing the number of women in the workforce. Some older feminists who had been active in the WEIMAR period were influential in the early FEDERAL REPUBLIC. For instance, through the efforts of Elisabeth Selbert the equal rights clause was included in the BASIC LAW of the Federal Republic. In the 1950s women in unions also were successful in fighting separate and lower wage classifications for women.

The notable women's rights movement, the "new feminism," emerged in the late 1960s. Rooted in the radical student movement of the late 1960s, it was first concerned with recognition of the equality of women's concerns in the student organizations. This new feminism mutated into a concern with the abortion issue when in 1971 hundreds of women publicized their abortions while protesting against West Germany's restrictive abortion laws. Abortion legislation was finally passed by the BUNDESTAG in 1975, which was, however, overturned by the FEDERAL CONSTITUTIONAL COURT. This setback was discouraging, and feminist goals were directed elsewhere. Systematic sexism became the enemy. Women now organized focus groups exploring their relation to the system. Feminist institutions also were organized such as bookstores, battered women's centers, and lesbian organizations. Some feminists turned to politics and influenced the organization of the GREEN PARTY, which fielded as many female as male candidates, unlike other political parties. In response, the SPD increased the number of its female candidates to 40 percent of its candidates in the 1998 elections.

Reunification brought on the third stage of postwar feminism. Laws regarding abortion had been more liberal in the GDR, and feminist pressure succeeded in stopping legislators from annulling that access, although the court again ruled against abortion. Other issues resulting from reunification were the difficulty of East German feminists in being able to get a place in the West's organizations. In society at large feminists were still concerned about the continued disadvantages that women face in their low representation in political life and low pay in their jobs. Yet even with these societal and political restrictions the success story of Dr. Angela Merkel is remarkable. She rose through the ranks of the male-dominated boardroom politics of the CDU to become Germany's first female chancellor at the end of 2005.

Ferdinand II (1578–1637)
Holy Roman Emperor

Ferdinand was the grandson of Ferdinand I and the eldest son of the ruler of Inner Austria, Archduke Charles (1540–90), and Maria of Bavaria. He was educated by the JESUITS at the University of Ingolstadt in BAVARIA. He was deeply influenced by Catholic teaching and intended to restore the Catholic faith in his domain. Consequently, in 1602 Protestant teachers and preachers were expelled from Styria, which he ruled under a regency, closing or destroying their churches and presenting his nonnoble subjects with the alternative of conversion or exile. Even the astronomer Johannes KEPLER (1571–1630) had to flee, placing himself under the patronage of RUDOLF II (1552–1612) in Prague. Since Rudolf and Emperor Matthias (1612–19) had no heirs, they renounced their rights of succession in favor of Ferdinand and engineered his coronation as king of Bohemia in 1617 and Hungary in 1618. In 1619 he was elected Holy Roman Emperor, succeeding Matthias. He was opposed by the Protestant electors, and in May 1618 the Bohemian nobility rose in revolt. The forces of the Catholic League under Count Tilly bloodily suppressed the Protestant rebels in Austria and Bohemia in 1620. It was Ferdinand's efforts to restore Catholicism that precipitated the THIRTY YEARS' WAR.

Pursuing his anti-Protestant policies, Ferdinand by 1627 banned all Protestant worship. This policy was combined with political repression when a new constitution eliminated the national liberties of the Bohemians. The Danish intervention between 1625 and 1629 was defeated by the coalition of the Catholic League under Generals Tilly and WALLENSTEIN, resulting in the Peace of Lübeck in 1629. Then Ferdinand issued the Edict of Restitution, which decreed that those lands that had been secularized since 1552 were to be restored to the church. Ferdinand was forced to dismiss General Wallenstein, which handicapped the imperial forces when the Empire soon was invaded by Gustavus II Adolphus of Sweden (1594–1632). Tilly was killed and his army defeated at Breitenfeld in SAXONY in 1631, forcing Ferdinand to reappoint Wallenstein. After some successes his army was defeated at the Battle of Lützen (1632), his army destroyed, and Gustavus Adolphus killed. As a result, Ferdinand had Wallenstein assassinated and the Edict of Restitution was modified, making 1627 the criterion for the ownership of church land. Ferdinand died at age 57 in 1637, before the Thirty Years' War was over. A devoted Catholic but not a wise political leader, he failed to suppress PROTESTANTISM in the Empire and widened the rift between imperial authority and the German princes. He did succeed in reuniting the principal Habsburg domains in central Europe.

Feuerbach, Ludwig Andreas (1804–1872)
materialist philosopher

Ludwig Feuerbach was a leading 19th-century philosopher of materialism, a critic of orthodox Christianity, and humanizer of God.

Ludwig Feuerbach was born in Landshut, BAVARIA, the son of a criminologist. For his education he at first studied theology, then switched to philosophy at HEIDELBERG and then under the renowned Friedrich HEGEL in BERLIN. He continued his studies and received his doctorate in 1828 at the University of Erlangen, where he was able to lecture for a while.

While Hegel's philosophy was suited for people who could be deeply convinced of the power of reason over reality and that progress toward freedom could occur in an authoritarian political order, orthodox theologians criticized Hegel for turning religion into mere logic. Some of his students took their teacher's ideas to their logical and radical conclusions. Leading to the radicalism of Feuerbach was that of David Friedrich Strauss, who alleged in *The Life of Jesus* (1935) that Hegel's divine spirit had created the New Testament as a myth. Feuerbach went on to call Hegel's universal spirit an abstraction and claimed the only reality was man and matter. Publishing his primary works, *The Essence of Christianity* (1841) and *The Essence of Religion* (1846), Feuerbach asserted that it was man who created God in his image and not the other way around. God became the purified essence of man and the unlimited ideal of his capabilities. His thesis that the supernatural was the creation of man's hopes and fears became an anthropology. Theology had now become a branch of anthropology and was rooted in matter. According to Feuerbach: "Man is what he eats."

Feuerbach's first publication, *Thoughts about Death and Immortality* (1830), wherein he denied the immortality of the soul, had already stirred up controversy. Other studies followed in *From Bacon to Spinoza* (1833), *Leibniz* (1836), and *Pierre Bayle* 1838). Since he was not allowed to teach because of his criticism of religion, he had plenty of time to write. He further clarified his position on God in *The Essence of Faith according to Luther* (1846) and *The Essence of Religion* already mentioned. He also proposed to reform philosophy in *Preparatory Theses on the Reform of Philosophy* (1842) and *The Philosophy of the Future* (1843), which had their bases not in the usual faculty of reason but in the materialism of the emotions and sensuality. In his latter life he studied and lived at Bruckberg and died in 1872 at Rechenberg near NUREMBERG on September 13.

Fichte, Johann Gottlieb (1762–1814)
philosopher

A philosopher responsible for contributing to the rise of a new aggressive German nationalism during the second half of the 19th century, Fichte thought that individual freedom could be attained only by identification with the nation. His belief in ethical idealism did not include a personal God, but the concept of an "infinite ego."

Johann Gottlieb Fichte was born the son of a Saxon weaver in Rammenau on May 19, 1762. Adoption by a nobleman provided him with educational opportunities otherwise denied to the poor. Initially attending school at Pforta, he later studied theology at the Universities of JENA, Wittenberg, and LEIPZIG. After his patron died, he obtained a tutorship in Zurich, where in 1794 he married Johanna Rahn. To gain the attention of KANT, he sent him the manuscript of his *Critique of All Revelation,* which gained Kant's praise. He published it, making Fichte's reputation. GOETHE's recommendation obtained him a professorship at the University of Jena, where he became a dynamic teacher and where he met Friedrich SCHILLER, the SCHLEGEL brothers, and Wilhelm von HUMBOLDT. During the next five years he expounded his ideas in a number of treatises. Because of his radical political ideas and unorthodox theological teaching that "there can be no doubt that the notion of God as a separate substance is impossible and contradictory," he was dismissed from Jena in 1799 on the grounds of atheism. After a few years in BERLIN he in quick succession taught one semester each at Erlangen University and then Königsberg. In 1810 he was appointed rector of the University of Berlin. Survived by his wife, he died of typhus on January 27, 1814, contracted during Napoleon's siege of Berlin.

The three foundations of his philosophy were the Pantheism of Spinoza, the concept of striving of LESSING, and the concept of duty of Kant. Contrary to the mechanistic explanations in Western science, earlier German thinking on the conception of the universe formulated by PARACELSUS, LEIBNIZ, HERDER, and Goethe held that it was a living organic process with which man must collaborate in order to realize its divine purpose. The dualism between nature and spirit had thus been overcome but was destroyed by a new dualism projected by Kant between the knowing mind and the unknowable thing-in-itself. Fichte took this dualistic philosophy a step further, arguing that the world outside the individual mind exists only to provide materials for the self-creative activity of the ego. The world can only be known, Fichte thought, to the extent that the knowing subject is continually involved in its creation. The youth of the romantic age saw in Fichte's creative ego, as presented in his *Science of Knowledge* (1794), not only a release from the bondage of the world but a call to action.

Fichte is among the disciples of Herder who began to change the character of German NATIONALISM after 1800. The differences between his concept of nationalism and that of Herder were in part due to his reaction to the French invasions of Germany and particularly to PRUSSIA's humiliation by Napoleon's armies. That occasion in 1806 prompted his famous series of lectures, *Addresses to the German Nation,* delivered in the winter of 1807–08, in which he called for a system of national education in Germany that would ultimately result in the moral regeneration of the German people. He thought that education should make Germans aware of their unique national character and teach them to love the Fatherland, enabling them to liberate themselves from the French. In describing the kind of spirit that should prevail in a time of national crisis, Fichte wrote, "[it is] not the spirit of the peaceful citizen's love for the constitution and the laws, but the devouring flame of higher patriotism, which embraces the nation . . . for which the noble-minded man joyfully sacrifices himself, and the ignoble man, who only exists for the sake of the other, must likewise sacrifice himself." Unlike Herder, however, Fichte attributed to the Germans an originality and a genius not possessed by other peoples. The Germans, he believed, were uncorrupted by civilization and therefore an original people. Whereas the Latin peoples had a civilization derived from a Roman heritage, the Germans both occupied an original homeland and used a language uncorrupted by importations. In the same vein he encouraged the Germans to throw off the political and cultural yoke of the French.

In his earlier works Fichte was concerned with the problem of individual freedom, and initially looked to the French Revolution to free mankind. Yet he became critical of the revolutionary emphasis on achieving individual liberty through the recognition of natural rights. He thought that recognition of natural rights limited the state's real sphere of action to give positive content to human freedom. Fichte, therefore, advocated a state socialism, not as a welfare institution, but to promote general education and communal work inspiring the highest ethical development of its citizens. The state also had to be restored as the lawgiver, not as the dictate of a ruler, but rather as an expression of the collective will of the German people.

Final Solution
(Endlösung)

The term *Final Solution* was applied to the Nazi plan to annihilate the Jews. It first appeared in the spring of 1940 in the context of a massive territorial resettlement program and apparently was not always a goal of Hitler and the NAZI PARTY. The year 1941 was a turning point in Jewish policy, which changed from forced emigration to genocide. The policy was to be carried out by systematic killing through the use of gas vans and the efficient use of gas chambers.

It is improbable that HITLER made the decision to annihilate the Jews as an inevitable result of his fervently held ANTI-SEMITISM. Persecution and forced emigration appear to have been the methods to cleanse Germany of the Jews. But military conquests had brought 3.5 million new Jews under direct German control, and the Russian war of destruction (*Vernichtungskrieg*) with its killing of Russian Jews broke the cycle of adding more Jews under German control. The term *Final Solution* appeared in dispatches in the middle of 1941 as emigration of such a large Jewish population was impossible. On July 31, 1941, six weeks after the invasion of the Soviet Union, Hermann GÖRING authorized Lieutenant General Reinhard HEYDRICH, chief of the Security Police and Security Service, to undertake "all necessary preparations with regard to organizational and financial matters for bringing about a total solution of the Jewish question in the German sphere of influence in Europe." It is clear that when the WANNSEE CONFERENCE occurred on January 20, 1942, the term *Final Solution* meant the genocide of the Jews. In the final analysis, this Final Solution or HOLOCAUST from the Jewish perspective, resulted from Hitler's fanatic hatred of the Jews, the competitiveness of the Nazi leaders who vied for Hitler's favor, the vulnerability of the European Jews, and opportunities of the war. Since no written document with Hitler's signature has been discovered, Hitler's exact role in the decision is the subject of historical controversy. Nevertheless, his oral authorization for the Final Solution was indicated by Heinrich HIMMLER.

Adolf Hitler had always associated Soviet communism with the Jews, so his war against the Soviet Union was a war against the Jews. Heinrich Himmler had shared Hitler's racial ideology of developing a pure Aryan race, so he and the SS were given responsibility for the execution of the Final Solution. The department placed in control was the Reich Security Main Office (RSHA) comprising the SD and the Security Police (SIPO), which consisted of the GESTAPO and the Kripo (criminal police) under the command of Heydrich. It was in Section B4 of the Gestapo that Adolf EICHMANN as an expert on the Jews came to control the Nazi machinery for the deportation of Jews from all over Europe to the death camps. Most of the annihilation took place in Poland. Jews had already been concentrated in a small number of ghettos in which many died and the remaining were later sent to the death camps. With the invasion of the Soviet Union four mobile killing units of up to 900 men (EINSATZGRUPPEN) were used as strike forces to search for and kill as many Jews as they could. A second sweep took place in 1942 and together some 1 million Jews were killed. The violent shooting methods of the Einsatzgruppen were horrifying and considered inadequate for other parts of Europe. Consequently, the death camps and their gas chambers were constructed as a more efficient method for the annihilation of the remaining millions of Jews.

The technical problems in the creation of physical facilities to kill so many people were almost overwhelming. SS officers experimented with gas vans and also with the improvement of gas chambers and ovens for cremation. In summer 1941 orders were given to Rudolf Höss to enlarge Auschwitz because of its railway access, and five other death camps became operative by 1942 at Chelmno, Belzec, Sobibor, Majdanek, and Treblinka. At Auschwitz up to 10,000 prisoners were sent to the gas chambers every day. Many other concentration camps existed in Germany such as Bergen-Belsen and Buchenwald, and in Austria, France, and Yugoslavia, where both Jews and non-Jews perished through forced labor, starvation, and murder. The campaign spread throughout Nazi-occupied Europe and continued even though resources were taken away from the war effort. During 1942 Jews were shipped from France, Belgium, Holland, and Norway. In 1943 Jews were deported from the cities of Berlin, Vienna, and Prague and the countries of Greece, Luxembourg, southern France, Italy, and Denmark. The survivors of the Jewish revolt in the Warsaw ghetto were sent to their deaths at Treblinka. Almost a half million Hungarian Jews were among the very last to be sent to Auschwitz after the Germans occupied Hungary in 1944. Most of the Jewish citizens of Poland, Greece, Czechoslovakia, and the Netherlands died in the gas chambers, while half the Jews of Romania and Hungary survived. After the fall of Mussolini, trains from Italy, Croatia, and Greece arrived at Auschwitz and Mauthausen. Most of the Jews of Denmark and Bulgaria survived, where the local populations actively aided them. Out of the 5 to 6 million Jews who were killed, about 3 million died in the death camps.

Although the Final Solution (the Holocaust) was one of the worst cases of genocide in modern history, it arose out of the prejudices and hatred that inspired a terribly misguided fanatical ideology aimed at one group of human beings. Although there had been pogroms and violence against Jews throughout their history, the enormity of the Holocaust and its stain on German culture have been unforgettable. Nevertheless, in his final testament dictated in his bunker beneath Berlin, Hitler repeated his anti-Semitic misconceptions and exhorted Germans to continue to follow his racial laws.

Fischer, Josef "Joschka" (1948–)

Josef Fischer was born the son of a butcher. Not lacking intelligence, he nevertheless did not perform well in school and dropped out. Educationally, he was self-taught. His early attempts at employment as a photojournalist and civil service employee were also failures. He married as a teenager and entered countercultural politics as a kind of "professional revolutionary." Involved in protests against the Vietnam War, he was consequently jailed. Afterward he held a series of jobs, factory worker, salesman, actor. For a period in the 1970s his youthful rebelliousness got him involved with the Sponti movement led by Daniel Cohn-Bendit in Frankfurt. He soon came to realize that extraparliamentary agitation and the pursuit of revolutionary ideals did not produce any meaningful results. He came to the conclusion that social and political reforms could be successful only if they were moderate and practical and occurred gradually. At the end of this road of maturation he finally entered the Green Party, where he found his calling as the party's parliamentary leader and was the first member of his party to become a minister in the ministry of environmental affairs.

In 1995 Fischer started to plan for a coalition government on the national level with the Social Democratic Party. Already in the late 1970s and early 1980s Fischer had decided to pursue practical political reform through parliamentary institutions, which brought him into conflict with other Greens such as Petra Kelly, who was among the "Fundis," and whose ideas were antiparty and extraparliamentary. Fischer was a member of the Realists or "Realo" faction, who believed that the party should seek office instead of pursuing direct democracy, pacificism, and the rejection of the postwar German socioeconomic order. He helped reorganize the party from a motley crew of antiestablishment protesters to candidates who could command the respect of voters.

After success in the parliamentary elections of 1998 the Social Democrats and the Greens formed a coalition government in which Gerhard SCHROEDER became chancellor and "Joschka" Fischer became foreign minister. Fischer's speech in June 1998 before the Germany Society for Foreign Affairs in BERLIN emphasized that Germany would continue to follow a policy of self-restraint and not one of national self-interest, which meant he would reject a policy of power politics. It was an antinationalist stance that was largely a reaction to postwar political management under the guidance of American leadership. So Germany was rehabilitated from its former national self-interested aggressiveness through its participation in the EUROPEAN COMMUNITY and its multilateral involvements.

Fischer von Erlach, John Bernard (1656–1723)

architect and sculptor

Fischer von Erlach was one of the most important architects of the age of the baroque. Along with Johann Lukas von Hildebrandt (1660–1750) he became a standard bearer of the new baroque style. Fischer received many commissions from the Austrian emperor.

Born in Graz, AUSTRIA, John Bernard was trained as a sculptor by his father. He received further training in Italy and perhaps was even influenced by Bernini. Returning to Austria in 1686, Fischer worked on small projects, medals, sculpturing, gardens, and vases. In 1689 he became the architectural instructor to Joseph I, king of Hungary. In 1691 following Joseph's coronation as Holy Roman Emperor he was appointed superintendent of imperial buildings and given the task of designing the triumphal arches for which he achieved public recognition. Fischer adorned the arches with a same sun motif utilized by Louis XIV of France and did so a second time in 1699, after Joseph's wedding to Wilhelmine Amalia of Brunswick-Lüneburg.

Fischer's grandiose plans for Joseph's palace at Schönbrun represented a direct response to Versailles. Although a design that would have made the Austrian palace grander than Versailles was first considered, the more modest alternative plan was adopted. The onset of construction of Schönbrun in 1694–95 inspired the ARISTOCRACY to build their own palaces with extravagant artificial gardens and many outbuildings. Besides Schönbrun Fischer designed the church of St. Charles Borromeo (Karlskirche), which, standing on grassy slopes outside of Vienna, became the most monumental baroque church in Vienna. It is a richly articulated building on an oval plan. After 1693 he worked for the archbishop of Salzburg and for other church and political dignitaries, such as Prince EUGENE of Savoy. After CHARLES VI became emperor, Fischer was reappointed as superintendent of imperial buildings after he presented to the emperor a series of monumental engravings. After John Bernard's death, his son, Josef Emmanuel, who was born in 1693 and also became an architect, completed the unfinished buildings of his father, including the imperial library and St. Charles Borromeo.

Fontane, Theodor (1819–1898)

realist novelist

Theodor Fontane was a novelist who depicted the BERLIN society of his time as it faced the process of change into an age of industrialization. He was critical of Prussian NATIONALISM and its chauvinism. Fontane believed that marriage and society represented principles of order, and unhappiness and tragedy followed those who violated them.

Among the many Huguenots who were forced to flee from France and who found refuge in BRANDENBURG was one of Theodor Fontane's ancestors, Jacques François Fontane. He settled in Eberswalde in 1694. Generations later Theodor was born in Neuruppin on December 30, 1819, the son of a pharmacist. Not inclined to pharmacy himself, Theodor decided to pursue a literary career. In his early twenties he demonstrated considerable talent by writing literary ballads that became popular and still appear in school readers. In 1852 he went to England as a newspaper correspondent, became an admirer of the work of Charles Dickens, and studied ballad origins. In 1855 he became editor of the Anglo-German news agency and an attaché to the Prussian embassy. Upon his return from England in 1859 he was employed on the editorial staff of the conservative *Kreuzzeitung* and reported on all three of the wars of unification. During the Franco-Prussian War he even experienced capture by the French who thought he was a spy. His travels were described during those years in *Travels through the Mark Brandenburg* (4 vols.), which served as a form of literary travel guide for visitors from other areas. For 20 years afterward he was a theater critic for the liberal Berlin *Vossische Zeitung*.

His most important contributions to literature and to an understanding of IMPERIAL GERMANY were his novels. *Before the Storm* (1878) was a historic patriotic story about the days before the downfall of Napoleon, uncharacteristic of his later works, which probed the problems of society. It was in his Berlin novels series that Fontane reached the height of his literary career. Of the three novels dealing with the painful consequences of adultery, *Adultery* (1882), *Trials and Tribulations* (1888), and *Effi Briest* (1895), *Effi Briest* is the best of the three and one of the great masterpieces of the European psychological novel. It is the story of a German Madame Bovary who marries a stern Prussian official twice her age. After the honeymoon she returns to a boring life in the provinces and has an affair with a handsome officer. There is a duel between the husband and the officer, who is killed. Because social custom dictates it, Effi is divorced by her husband and loses custody of her child. She must live the rest of her life isolated in Berlin. In the end Effi returns home, dying of tuberculosis and symbolically dying of a broken heart.

A gentle satire against the pretentiousness and shallowness of the rich MIDDLE CLASS of the new Empire is dramatized in *Lady Jenny Treibel* (1892). Fontane explores the social relationship between two Berlin families, the Treibels and the Schmidts. The novel is a witty, ironical comedy and recounts the short-lived betrothal of the wealthy and upwardly mobile Treibel son, Leopold, with Corinna, the intelligent daughter of Willibald Schmidt, an impecunious schoolmaster. Corinna is a modern woman, an "audacious breed" who wants to share in the rewards of material progress, even if she must do so through a marriage of convenience. In that context we see that Jenny, the mother, and her husband, an industrialist, are primarily motivated by money and social rank. Besides being a social climber, Jenny wants people to think that she favors art and culture, is for "poetry not prose," and in that, she confuses aesthetic aspiration with social superiority. All appears to end well with Corinna realizing her false sense of values and breaking off the relationship with Leopold and marrying someone of her own social class. Fontane expresses the hope that Germany can triumph over material greed and its better self can triumph.

In his late masterpiece, *Der Stecklin* (1899), Fontane mourned the passing away of the old aristocratic leaders. The story is about an aging widower, Dubslav von Stecklin, living in a dilapidated mansion. The novel does not have a plot, but Fontane expresses in masterly fashion the landscape around Berlin, and it is a fine study of unforgettable characters. Here Fontane is a sympathetic critic of William II's times. Sympathetic to the good old days and open to the ideas of the emerging age, he is nostalgic but outdated. Taken together, Fontane's novels are comparable to the best in the tradition of psychological realism.

Four Year Plan

HITLER's Four Year Plan was intended to alter the structure of German economic life, making it self-sufficient (AUTARCHY). He argued that it was necessary for Germany to fully rearm in order to protect itself against the Bolshevik threat, which in his racist conspiratorial view intended to bring the world under "Jewish domination."

The basic ideas of the Four Year Plan were recorded in a memorandum formulated at the BERGHOF. The main motive he claimed for the Four Year Plan was to speed up rearmament so that the German army would be prepared for war against the Soviet Union. At the annual party rally in NUREMBERG on September 9, 1936, Hitler announced his plan to make Germany independent of any foreign materials that could be made by German chemical, mining, or machine industries. In connection with the goals of the Four Year Plan Hitler sought to increase production of synthetic materials, which included fuel, rubber, fats, and light- and high-grade metals. The long-range solution, however, of Germany's resource needs was to be found in eastward expansion for living space (LEBENSRAUM).

Although Hitler threatened state control of the economy if private industry did not cooperate, he hesitated to impose totalitarian controls. The not so capable and overconfident Hermann GÖRING was placed in charge of the plan. His attempts to coordinate the many Reich ministries involved got him into conflicts with their directors, especially Hjalmar SCHACHT, the president of the Reichsbank and expert on rearmament. Schacht resigned in 1937 and was replaced by Walther Funk. Since the chief goal of the Four Year Plan was to spur the production of raw materials, a new Reich Agency of Economic Consolidation was created. General production of raw materials was downplayed in favor of strategic materials for rearmament. Between 1936 and 1942, 50 percent of total German industrial investment went into the Four Year Plan. Even with all these efforts the production of synthetic fuels accounted for only 20 percent of needs, and Germany still relied on foreign imports for one-third of natural resource requirements. The only areas in which the goals were reached were brown coal and explosives. The Four Year Plan was continued into the war years and employed forced labor. As a result of the plan industrial concentration increased in the German economy, and such giants as I. G. Farben became prominent in the field of synthetics.

Francis II (1768–1835)
Holy Roman Emperor

When the Holy Roman Emperor LEOPOLD II (1741–92) died in 1792, Francis, the oldest of his 16 children succeeded him. At age 24 the new emperor was immature, unimaginative, narrow-minded, and shy. There is no doubt that he was unsuited for the task of ruling the HOLY ROMAN EMPIRE and protecting the Habsburg lands, especially against the threats of the French Revolution and NAPOLEONIC WARS. It is said that he was devoted to the specifics of government and had no sense of the historical forces that manifested themselves during his reign. He followed the greatest monarchs of the 18th century such as MARIA THERESA and FREDERICK THE GREAT, and was representative of the monarchical mediocrity that was to follow. Considering himself too young and inexperienced to become emperor, he was faced with challenges that might have overwhelmed a greater man than he.

Scarcely a month after his accession France declared war on AUSTRIA. The DECLARATION OF PILLNITZ (August 27, 1791), which Leopold II had negotiated with PRUSSIA just before his death, made the war inevitable between France and the two German powers. This began a struggle that would last more than two decades, revealing the weaknesses of the Austrian monarchy. In the first phase the Austrians failed to decisively defeat France and in humiliating defeats lost all their Italian territories south of the Adige. After the Prussian defeat at Valmy on September 20, 1792, the Austrians lost their territories in the Netherlands. In 1793, when the revolutionaries executed the French monarchs, Louis XVI and Marie Antoinette, Austria joined the First Coalition against them. There was nothing but the humiliation of defeat for Austria, which came with the Treaty of Campo Formio (October 17–18, 1797). After Austria joined the Second Coalition military defeats at the battles of Marengo and Hohenlinden again followed, ending with the Peace of Luneville (February 2, 1801). Despite these military disasters Austrian NATIONALISM increased, as did the popularity of the emperor. To counter the French threat and the end of the Holy Roman Empire, Francis unified the Habsburg lands into the Austrian Empire and on August 10, 1804, proclaimed himself emperor. Under French pressure Francis agreed to the dissolution of the Holy Roman Empire, which was announced in Vienna on August 6, 1806. The medieval regalia and vestments were placed in the treasury of the Hofburg.

During the reign of Francis Austria lacked direction and resolve. Austrian diplomacy was weak, and military commanders and most officials were incompetent. The worse the situation became, the more Francis stuck to his old advisers, who resisted change. Fear of revolution within also made Francis more reactionary. The young emperor was further alienated from the progressive programs of his father and uncle because a revolutionary conspiracy was discovered and its leaders punished in 1794. Repression increased, and in 1801 censorship was placed in the hands of the police. Public discussion disappeared, the qualities of the ARISTOCRACY were defended as sources of stability and order, and the secular spirit of Josephinism was replaced by an emphasis on religious orthodoxy and piety.

In 1809 Austria again went to war with France. This time the general was the brother of Francis, the talented Archduke Charles, who won a small victory at Aspern-Essling, but was quickly defeated by Napoleon at the Battle of Wagram on July 5–6. Another positive change was the appointment of Klemens von METTERNICH (1773–1859) as the new foreign minister. Metternich arranged the marriage of the emperor's daughter, Marie Louise, to Napoleon. Metternich then maneuvered the defeat of Napoleon in the WAR OF LIBERATION 1813–15. At the end of war he organized the peace conference at the CONGRESS OF VIENNA (September 1814–June 1815), which redrew the map of Europe and restricted France's influence. Austria gave up western territories, but became a more compact empire and gained the presidency of the GERMAN CONFEDERATION.

During the restoration period Francis followed a reactionary conservative policy, which was executed by Prince Metternich. Along with Prussia, Austria adhered to the Holy Alliance of Czar Alexander I dedicated to suppressing any revolutionary activity. Internally, the age was called BIEDERMEIER, characterized by homely middle-class values and the creative music of Franz SCHUBERT and Johann STRAUSS. Those who espoused LIBERALISM were suppressed by a secret police symbolized by the fortress prison of the Spielberg. The policy of political reaction was formalized in the CARLSBAD DECREES of 1819, which were enacted after the assassination of August von Kotzebue. Austria also intervened in suppressing several revolutions. Censorship and the repression of the peasantry continued, and assertiveness by the nationalities in the Empire was suppressed. On the other hand, Francis retained some of the reforms of his father, especially state control of the church. Francis refused to exclude his retarded son from the succession to the throne. When Francis II died on March 2, 1835, it was Metternich who became one of the regents governing the Austrian Empire during the reign of Ferdinand.

Frank, Anne (1929–1945)
author

Anne Frank was a German-Dutch Jew who kept a diary of her life of hiding from the Nazis in Amsterdam. After she died from typhus in the concentration camp of BERGEN-BELSEN, her diary, which describes her life with other Jews in hiding between June 1942 and August 1944, was published by her father, Otto Frank, who survived AUSCHWITZ when the camp was liberated by the Russians in January, 1945.

Anne (Anneliese) Marie Frank was born in FRANKFURT AM MAIN on June 12, 1929, a daughter of Otto Heinrich Frank (1889–1980), a member of a banking family, and Edith Frank-

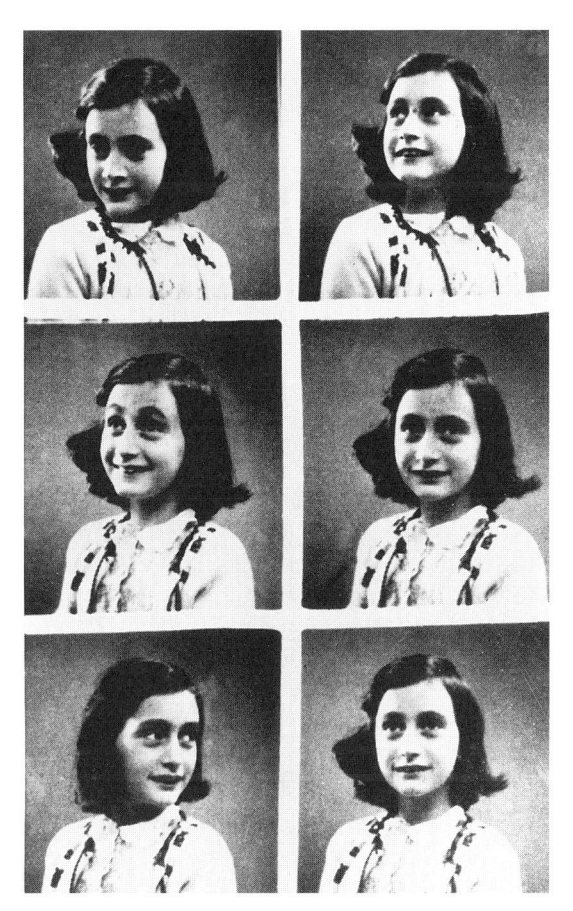

Anne Frank *(Library of Congress)*

Höllander (1890–1944), the daughter of a manufacturer in AACHEN. After the Nazis came to power, the family moved to Amsterdam, where her father established a business that produced pectin. The family lived a conventional life until the Germans invaded Holland. During the occupation the family and four friends (a total of eight) hid for two years in rooms behind a warehouse. Dutch friends helped them survive until the GESTAPO in 1944 discovered their refuge and sent them to Auschwitz-Birkenau. The group died in a variety of camps: Auschwitz, Mauthausen near Theresienstadt, and Bergen-Belsen, where Anne and her sister, Margot, died of typhus and starvation in March 1945, just weeks before the British liberated it and just short of Anne's 16th birthday.

Anne's diary is an amazing document for an adolescent girl. She described her life in hiding, her reactions, fears of discovery, quarrels, worries about friends, and stark accounts of the persecution of Jews in Amsterdam. In addition she recorded observations of her personal development. She even rewrote and edited her diary with the hope that some day it would be published. Anne's *Diary of a Young Girl* is a sensitive portrait of adolescence and a testament to courage and endurance.

Frank, Hans (1900–1946)
governor-general of Poland

Hans Frank was HITLER's lawyer and later was appointed the governor-general of occupied Poland. He was was born in Karlsruhe in BADEN on May 23, 1900. After serving in the war during 1918 he joined the FREE CORPS. Joining the German Workers Party he later became a Nazi when it became the NSDAP. Then he served in the Stormtroops SA. In the meantime he received legal training, which he completed in 1926, and because of his administrative abilities was promoted to head of the legal division of the NSDAP in 1929. As Hitler's lawyer he represented him in 150 lawsuits. When Hitler came into office in 1933, Frank was made minister of justice for BAVARIA, Reich commissioner of justice, and minister without portfolio. He founded and was first president of the Law Academy.

After the conquest of Poland, Frank was appointed chief civilian officer, or governor-general for occupied Poland on October 12, 1939. Frank described his policy in these words: "Poland shall be treated like a colony: the Poles will become the slaves of the Greater German Empire." From his headquarters in Wavel Castle, Cracow, he enslaved the Poles and exterminated the Jews. Already by December 1942 some 85 percent of Polish Jews had been transported to CONCENTRATION CAMPS. At the end of the war he was brought before the International Military Tribunal (IMT) (*see* NUREMBERG TRIALS) and placed on trial as a major war criminal. Frank had written 38 volumes of diaries, which were introduced as evidence on his behalf. He confessed his guilt, converted to Catholicism, and begged forgiveness of God. Now he also changed his view of HITLER and all the crimes he committed, accusing Hitler of betrayal of the trust of the German people. The court found Frank guilty of war crimes and crimes against humanity, hanging him on October 16, 1946.

Frankfurt am Main

Frankfurt is one of the most important cities in Germany. Its location makes it one of the most important commercial and economic centers in the FEDERAL REPUBLIC. It has long been a financial center and is the headquarters of the Federal Bank (Bundesbank). It is home to the leading German stock exchange and is the location of many trade fairs held throughout the year. Because of its location it also is an international junction for air, rail, and road traffic. Its Rhine-Main airport is one of the busiest in central Europe. Frankfurt also has been a cultural center, the University of Frankfurt being established in 1914.

Frankfurt's history goes back to the Roman Empire when it was a military settlement. In 876 it was described as the capital of the East Frankish kingdom. In the Golden Bull of 1356 it was designated as the traditional site of the election of the German kings and from 1562 the emperors were crowned at St. Bartholomew's Church. In 1372 Frankfurt was officially designated an imperial city, which status it maintained until the end of the Empire. The city's history as a commercial center also goes back to the Middle Ages, when the Draper's Hall was the site of a lively medieval cloth trade. Trade fairs emerged, and a stock exchange opened in 1585.

Its political history was stormy, like that of the rest of Germany. It had its share of civil unrest with the Fettmilch Insurrection between 1612 and 1616, when peasants rose against the ruling families. During the 18th century it was captured twice by the French. In 1806 Frankfurt became the seat of government for the CONFEDERATION OF THE RHINE, but was designated as one of the four free German cities by the CONGRESS OF VIENNA in 1815. From 1815 to 1866 it was the seat of the Federal Diet, and during the REVOLUTION OF 1848 the first German National Assembly was located in St. Paul's Church.

After unification in 1871 Frankfurt quickly became a busy and expanding city. Heavy industry developed, along with chemical and pharmaceutical industries such as I. G. Farben. The Rothschild banking dynasty also was located there. It became a major printing center. During both world wars it was important for the war effort. Because of its importance, it also was a major target of bombing raids during WORLD WAR II, when most of the city was destroyed. In 1945 the city was included in the American zone. Extensive rebuilding took place, and restorations were extensive.

Frankfurt is also known as the birthplace of Johann Wolfgang von GOETHE and the philosopher Arthur Schopenhauer. It also was the home of the Frankfurt Institute of Social Research, thanks to the philosopher Herbert Marcuse.

Frankfurt Parliament (1848)

The Constituent National Assembly that met in Frankfurt am Main during the REVOLUTION OF 1848 formulated the first German constitution for a united and parliamentary state.

The Frankfurt Parliament or National Assembly met on May 18, 1848, and lasted until March 1849. The mass protests throughout the German states for constitutional change in response to the February Revolutions in France resulted in the appointment of a committee of 17 by the Diet of the GERMAN CONFEDERATION to prepare a revision of its constitution. At the end of March 1848 a preliminary parliament (*Vorparlament*) was established under the leadership of Heinrich von GAGERN, a government official of Hesse-Darmstadt and a former member of the Burschenschaft. A committee of 50 representatives from the different German states discussed the ways and means of establishing both national unity and constitutional liberty for Germany. These liberal leaders then called for the election of a National Assembly. The Federal Diet (Bundestag) of the German Confederation then ceased to function.

The Frankfurt Parliament opened its sessions on May 18, 1848, in St. Paul's Church under the presidency of Heinrich von Gagern. The member states of the old confederation were represented, and independent male citizens over age 24 were eligible to vote. A minority of non-German members (Danes, Italians, Poles) were also present. Among the more than 600 members were Germany's most illustrious cultural leaders, most of them professors. They had the intelligence and enthusiasm to confront the issues that had divided Germans for such a long time: religious and cultural antagonisms, the rivalry between PRUSSIA and AUSTRIA, and the differences that divided those who favored a greater Germany that proposed to include Austria and those who favored a smaller Germany excluding Austria and under Prussian leadership.

While Heinrich von Gagern was a leading advocate of a united Germany under Prussian leadership, the parliament also elected the Austrian archduke, John, as imperial administrator and executive head of the new nation. The archduke also had liberal sympathies and had married a commoner. But the main obstacle was that any change in the constitution of the confederation had to be approved by both Prussia and Austria, which was very unlikely. From late autumn 1848 the parliament was divided between the greater and smaller German solutions to national unity. Complicating the debates was the rebellion that occurred in the duchies of Schleswig and Holstein. While Danish nationalists wanted to make the duchies part of Denmark, the German nationalists wanted them to be included in the German Confederation. A Danish victory occurred, but the duchies were to remain semiautonomous according to the Treaty of London (1852). The struggle, however, demonstrated that the Frankfurt Parliament was powerless in foreign affairs.

The constitution drawn up by the Frankfurt Parliament was a skillful compromise. The draft provided for a constitutional monarchy, a mixed form of government in which all the good features of monarchical, aristocratic, and democratic rule were present. The democratic feature was that the representatives were to be chosen by universal, equal, direct, and secret ballot. The German Liberals had drawn from the experiences of France, England, Switzerland, and especially from the United States. The federal structure of the constitution combined national unity and regionalism.

Two principal obstacles defeated this attempt at unification. The structure of the new state was to be a compromise, a larger federal state to include German Austria and a smaller federal state under Prussia. This did not satisfy the Austrians because Prince Swarzenberg, who was the head of the Austrian government, decided in March 1849 to include all of the Austrian Empire into the new German state. This resulted in a modified constitution that provided for a hereditary emperor, direct elections, a ministry responsible to Parliament, and an Imperial Diet (Reichstag) consisting of an upper and lower house. The king of Prussia, FREDERICK WILLIAM IV, was elected emperor by the assembly, but he rejected the crown, declaring that he could accept it only from the princes. Then Austria and Prussia withdrew their representatives, which was followed by other states. Mainly the republican left remained, and they were locked out. Moving to Stuttgart, fresh uprisings occurred in BADEN, the Palatinate, and SAXONY. The Prussian king then sent two army corps to suppress the rebellion. The German Confederation was restored.

Frederick I (1657–1713)
king of Prussia

The second and only surviving son of the Great Elector succeeded his father in 1688 as the elector Frederick III of BRANDENBURG. With the sanction of the Holy Roman Emperor, Frederick III literally crowned himself the "King in Prussia" on January 18, 1701, which was changed by his successors to "King of Prussia." Frederick's participation in the War of the Spanish Succession brought him the title of king. There were also other acquisitions, including the Spanish Gelderland, Neuchâtel, and Lingen as well as subsidies for his army. The duchy, which entitled him to the royal rank, was the duchy of Prussia, later East Prussia, although Brandenburg remained his electorate.

Frederick was a weak and indecisive king, inclined to fatalism, and one who interpreted events as the will of God. He avoided making difficult decisions and was exploited by members of his court. He was eclipsed by the superior talents of his father and his son whose energy, strength, and strong mind outshone him. Nevertheless, he hid his personal weakness through the pomp and magnificence with which he tried to endow his new kingship. He was dubbed the "ape of Louis XIV" because of the pomp and ceremony in imitation of Paris. He wanted to make BERLIN a city of culture and beauty. He enlarged the palace, built seven churches, and a massive arsenal, the Zeughaus. He became a patron of painters and musicians, and the architect and sculptor Andreas Schlütter, and established the University of Halle (1694), the Academy of Art (1696), the Berlin Royal Palace (1697), and the Academy of Sciences (1701).

Frederick II, "The Great" (1712–1786)
king of Prussia

Frederick II combined the qualities of a warrior king with those of an enlightened despot. As a prince he preferred books to the glories of war, but he was also an intrepid ruler and an eloquent conversationalist who attracted the most illustrious figures of the European intellectual and cultural scene. He was a patron of the arts and accomplished flautist, a hypochondriac plagued by doubts and loneliness, a genius at military strategy, and a charismatic statesman.

Born the eldest son of Frederick William of PRUSSIA and Princess Sophie Dorothea of Hanover on January 24, 1712, Frederick II at an early age rebelled against his soldier-king father, who wanted to mold him in his image. Frederick preferred French literature to German and the company of young pleasure-seekers to soldiers. When Frederick and his friend Lieutenant Katte planned an escape to England, they were arrested and condemned to death. After the execution of Katte, Frederick was imprisoned for six months, then was pardoned but had to learn how Prussian local administration worked. Having decided to obey his father, he learned how to be a good soldier and married the woman his father had chosen, although he never consummated the marriage. Between 1733 and 1740 Frederick also found time to study French literature and begin a correspondence with some of the most famous philosophes.

After his father died in 1740, Frederick became king and shortly became involved in the WAR OF AUSTRIAN SUCCESSION. He ignored the PRAGMATIC SANCTION to which Prussia had subscribed demanding the cession of the province of Silesia as the price of helping MARIA THERESA against France and BAVARIA. The demand was rejected, but after years of conflict Silesia was still in Prussian hands in 1748. The Austrians continued to be antagonistic over the loss of Silesia, and their new alliance with France in the DIPLOMATIC REVOLUTION led Frederick to promise Prussian neutrality (the Treaty of Westminster) in the war that had broken out in 1755 between England and France. With changes in the alliances Prussia faced an overwhelming continental alliance of AUSTRIA, Russia, France, and SAXONY. Frederick attacked Austria first and then fought the others individually. The superior discipline of the Prussian army allowed Frederick to march it to the theater of war in small detachments from various directions, uniting only shortly before the battle. In spite of superior tactics Prussia by 1762 was on the verge of bankruptcy, while Russian troops occupied BERLIN. The death of Empress Elizabeth of Russia and the succession of Peter III made Russia withdraw from the war. Frederick concluded the TREATY OF HUBERTUSBERG (1763) restoring the prewar status quo. Afterward, his policy was purely defensive. When

Austria and Russia were on the verge of partitioning the Ottoman Empire, Frederick managed to cajole Austria and Russia into a three-way partition of Poland. Two other ventures occurred. In 1778 Frederick reluctantly went to war against JOSEPH II of Austria to preserve the independence of Bavaria. In 1784 Frederick organized the League of German Princes to preserve the status quo in Germany.

Domestically, Frederick inherited a well-run state. Frederick worked hard at internal administration, ruling through ministers responsible to him and insisting that they work hard and be honest. The revenues of the state during his reign doubled, and the available reserves tripled through a system of indirect taxes and the establishment of state monopolies in salt, sugar, coffee, tobacco, and even porcelain. IMMIGRATION continued to be encouraged especially of peasants for underpopulated areas of the state. More than 300,000 colonists were settled in Prussia. To expand agriculture, marshlands were drained and turnips, beets, and potatoes encouraged. He refused to abolish serfdom, fearing that the landed nobility (JUNKERS) which produced both officers and officials, would be undermined. He followed the economic doctrines of mercantilism, which protected domestic industries. Frederick set up schools to train spinners and weavers and established cotton mills. Iron production was fostered in Westphalia and mining in Upper Silesia. He failed, however, to build a naval fleet, which made it impossible for Prussia to participate in the overseas trade of the 18th century.

During his reign little reform was accomplished. One exception was the area of judicial procedure where the efforts of his minister of justice, Cocceji, made progress in codification of the law, simplifying judicial procedure and replacing the jurisdiction of the nobility with a body of officials. The legal principle that the law should protect the poor and weak gained increased acceptance. Complete legal reform, however, was not achieved until 1781. Frederick had a reputation for being religiously tolerant. For Catholics he permitted them to build a church in Berlin and even invited the JESUITS to settle in Prussia. The same toleration was not extended to Jews.

Literature and music continued to be of interest to Frederick. At SANS-SOUCI he hosted the most famous salon in Europe. Voltaire was only the best known of the philosophes to take advantage of his hospitality. Frederick provided new subsidies for the Prussian Academy of Sciences, which subsidized figures of the French ENLIGHTENMENT. At the same time Frederick should be faulted for considering the German language a "barbaric" tongue. He had no respect for those who wrote in it. GOETHE and other German authors were thereby deprived of state support. Not content with being a patron of literature, Frederick also produced two books and a series of histories dealing with Prussia.

Frederick II died at his summer residence, Sans-Souci, near Potsdam on August 17, 1786. He has been blamed for being the inventor of

Frederick the Great, after a painting by Julius Antonio Schraber *(Library of Congress)*

German militarism, but that is a misunderstanding of his role in Prussian and German history. He never was a German nationalist, but rather a Prussian nationalist. He made war out of necessity or for political objectives. His interests especially in the latter part of his reign were generally nonmilitary and pacific.

Frederick III (1831–1888)
king of Prussia and emperor

In 1888, when Emperor William died on March 9, he was succeeded by his son, Crown Prince Frederick William, who took the title Frederick III. As crown prince he had endeared himself to his subjects by his military leadership in the wars of 1866 and 1870 and had been expected to open a new era of LIBERALISM. He had married the daughter of Queen Victoria, Princess Victoria, and was a believer in liberal and constitutional government. Perhaps that was one of the last hopes for liberalism in Germany, because BISMARCK had worked so hard to strengthen and entrench the conservative forces in Prussia. The new emperor, however, was already in the process of dying, as cancer of the throat had started the year before, and his sufferings practically incapacitated him. In the meantime, Bismarck remained in control of the government.

Born on October 18, 1831, Frederick was the only son of the king and emperor WILLIAM I. In his youth he shared the conservative political views so dominant at the Prussian court. At the encouragement of his wife, however, he developed relationships with prominent liberals. When Bismarck came into office and was the chief minister to his father, Frederick rejected his policies. Yet, although he favored constitutional monarchy, it has become clear that he did not favor the expansion of the powers of Parliament at the expense of the monarchy. His wife, Victoria, was disappointed to hear in 1870 that Frederick's hostility toward Bismarck softened when the chancellor assured him that German unification would be accomplished within a liberal-constitutional framework. For a while that appeared to be the case, but in 1879, when Bismarck changed his liberal alliances in favor of conservatives, Frederick fell into despair. He warned Bismarck not to subvert the constitution. Recent historians have proven that Frederick's reputation as a "progressive liberal" was a legend fostered by his wife in her correspondence after his death. He can be accurately described as a "constitutional liberal."

Frederick III, The Wise (1463–1525)
elector of Saxony

Frederick the Wise was one of the most influential princes in 16th-century Germany. Without the political protection of Frederick, Martin LUTHER and the REFORMATION would not have survived.

Frederick III, the elector of SAXONY, was the eldest son of Elector Ernest of Saxony, who succeeded to the electoral title as well as to the leadership of the Ernestine branch of the Wettin dynasty. His father died in 1486. Frederick received a good education and expressed an interest in scholarly and artistic matters throughout his life. He was interested in German history and had a deep respect for tradition.

Because of his political wisdom and personal reputation Frederick played an important role in national politics. He became involved with the attempt to reform the imperial constitution (1495). He held the title of imperial vicar and extended the authority of that office. In 1500 he was appointed president of the Imperial Council of Regency (Reichsregiment) by the emperor MAXIMILIAN I. Frederick declined to compete in the imperial election of 1519 against CHARLES V, recognizing the limitations of his own political power. He did, however, negotiate a deal with Charles, who pledged to repay the old Habsburg debts owed to Saxony. Frederick also played an important role with the seven electors in compelling Charles to sign an unprecedented election capitulation.

Frederick's enigmatic personality possessed a gift for silence. He was shy and reticent in personal contacts. Why he protected Luther is not entirely clear, but Frederick was a conscientious ruler who wanted to allow little intervention from Rome, particularly at his beloved University of Wittenberg, which he established in 1502. Frederick had decided at an early date that the reformer had to have a fair trial in Germany before being condemned. So he skillfully pursued a complicated series of negotiations that culminated in securing for Luther a safe public hearing at the DIET OF WORMS (1521). Even though Frederick could not stop the anti-Lutheran EDICT OF WORMS, he was able to secure the exemption of electoral Saxony from its enforcement.

During the PEASANT'S WAR Frederick was the only prince who entertained the hope of a peaceful compromise with the peasants, and he wondered if rulers had not given them a reason for their rebellion. Religiously, it is not known how far Frederick adopted Luther's teachings. Frederick owned a large collection of sacred relics that he treasured, devotion to which he slowly relinquished. Only on his deathbed did he accept the Lutheran practice of communion under both species. On May 5, 1525, Frederick died.

Frederick William (1620–1688)
"Great Elector" of Brandenburg

Frederick William, the only son of Elector George William and Elizabeth Charlotte of the Palatinate, was born on February 16, 1620. He succeeded as elector of Brandenburg in 1640. Raised as a Calvinist in the Reformed faith of the Hohenzollern court, he was religiously tolerant due to his experiences in the Netherlands at the University of Leiden. He inherited as widely scattered territories the duchies of PRUSSIA in the east and Cleve-Mark on the Dutch frontier. Having followed wise policies militarily and diplomatically, he acquired additional territories in the PEACE OF WESTPHALIA (1648). He added eastern Pomerania, which he received from Sweden, the bishoprics of Minden and Halberstadt, and the return of Magdeburg. Frederick continued to pursue an aggressive foreign policy, participating in the First Northern War between Sweden and Poland. By the Treaty of Oliva in 1660 his duchy of Prussia won its freedom from Polish sovereignty. His ambition to annex the Swedish Pomeranian area around the valuable seaport of Stettin, which he captured in 1677, failed. It was returned to Sweden due to the Treaty of Nijmegen and the opposition of Louis XIV. These additional territories made the possessions of the HOHENZOLLERNS second in size only to those of the imperial Habsburg family.

The Great Elector was the founder of both ABSOLUTISM and centralization in the Hohenzollern domains. During his reign the BERLIN government unified its administration and made the self-contained territories into the provinces of a greater state. The governments of the territories of BRANDENBURG, Prussia, Pomerania, Halberstadt, and Magdeburg lost their political and economic functions and were transformed into provincial courts of appeal. Frederick bargained with the diets for the right to collect taxes, appoint officials, quarter troops, and maintain appellate jurisdiction. He also took advantage of conflicts between the towns and the landed nobility to weaken his opposition. Each province sent agents to Berlin to attend the Privy Council, which was the central governing body over which the elector presided personally. But a new centralized administration superseded the administrative agencies of the estates and even the Privy Council. The elector was convinced that the estates, however, should provide enough money for the maintenance of a standing army. At the beginning of his reign the army was still largely a mercenary army, and only by the end of his reign was at least the officer corps composed of his subjects. To guarantee the support of the nobility (JUNKERS) to his reign and reforms, he granted them the exclusive right to own land, also having their seignorial jurisdiction over their estates reaffirmed. This even included the right to evict peasants and acquire their land. If that were not enough, the recess of 1653 allowed the Junkers to assume that every peasant was a serf unless he could prove his freedom, which opened the door for the expansion of serfdom. On the other hand, the right to appoint state officials became the exclusive right of the elector. More important, the army came under Frederick's exclusive control, which he used at times to overwhelm his opposition.

The elector followed mercantilist doctrines in his internal economic policies. A number of changes in taxation were attempted. Frederick attempted to replace direct taxes with excise taxes levied on the towns and on the officially tax-exempt Junkers, who collected their new share of the taxes from their peasants. The Junkers opposed the excise taxes on consumption, and so they were levied only on the towns and on trade. Within 15 years the excise tax was transformed from a municipal into a state tax, which provided a surplus to the government. Also important economically was the IMMIGRATION of 20,000 French Calvinist Huguenots who were forced out of France by the revocation of the Edict of Nantes; they brought important new business and manufacturing skills and cultural refinement. Also significant were the lessons that the elector derived from his observations of the prosperity of the Dutch, which was connected with their navy. Frederick attempted to build a navy and chartered Dutch ships to privateer on the Baltic Sea during a war with Sweden. In order to break into the overseas trade to Africa, he chartered two ships in 1680 to establish a colony on the Gold Coast and set up an African Trading Company, which traded in slaves with the West Indies.

A disciplined and hardworking ruler with a court that was simple and frugal, Frederick died in Potsdam on May 9, 1688.

Frederick William I (1688–1740)
king of Prussia

Frederick William I became the second king of PRUSSIA and one of its greatest administrators, not only of the army but also of internal state affairs. He came to the throne in 1713. Through rigid economies and improved administration he made Prussia financially independent, created a formidable army backed up by a full treasury, and established the Prussian civil service.

Born in BERLIN on August 15, 1688, Frederick William was the son of the elector Frederick III of BRANDENBURG and Sophie Charlotte of HANOVER. As a child he was headstrong and grew up with a great deal of physical energy, a violent temper, a robust personality, and a habit of strict discipline and hard work. Lacking trust in anyone, the king fired his father's ministers and required their successors to submit written reports while he made the final decisions. On the other hand, the king was boorish, lacked the cultural graces, besides being insensible to the feelings of fellow human beings. He became a formidable tyrant over his family, entourage, and the state.

Frederick's passion for the military was partly inspired by his acquaintance with John Churchill, duke of Marlborough, Prince Eugene of SAVOY, and Prince Leopold of Anhalt-Dessau. It was in the Great Northern War against Sweden that he realized the deficiencies of his army, so he increased its strength from 38,000 to 83,000 men. Unwilling to alienate the Prussian nobility, who insisted they could not spare their peasants for military service, he decided to hire troops abroad. Not until 1733 did he establish the CANTON SYSTEM, which allowed regiments to recruit soldiers from among the peasants and laborers in their home districts. By the end of his reign the size of the army had increased to such an extent that it was second only to the forces of the emperor. It should be kept in mind, however, that two-thirds of the Prussian army was composed of foreigners. Nonetheless, he instilled a new spirit, discipline, and efficiency, creating a professional army. He also mobilized the nobility into military service. The customary diversity of weapons, uniforms, and regulations ended. Yet, there were some distinctive curiosities about the king's army. He had a childish obsession with tall soldiers, which he liked to parade, and he thought of his soldiers as his children.

Frederick William established the foundations of the efficient Prussian civil service. He reorganized the government and unified the administration of the provinces. In 1722 he wrote the instructions for the GENERAL DIRECTORY of war, finance, and domains. He merged the separate administrations of the domains, the mint, the postal service, and customs into the general board of finance known as the Generalfinanzdirektorium, which approved all requests for money. Separate civil and military revenue administrations were combined under a supreme board and the provincial domains and commissariat administrations into collegial boards. Specific officials were made responsible for specific departments. A state-serving bureaucracy was thus formed. The king, however, instead of making decisions in the company of his state council, rather made decisions in private. His establishment of a centralized hierarchy of administrative offices represented the capstone in the structure of ABSOLUTISM.

Frederick William followed a policy of mercantilism in the colonization of East Prussia, the improvement of municipal administration, and the encouragement of the wool industry. He even converted his private estates into lands of the crown and converted hereditary leases of royal lands into short-term ones. The collection of revenues was achieved by replacing the feudal levy with a tax on the land of the nobles. He also placed excise taxes on luxury imports such as coffee, tea, sugar, and staple foods, which increased the state's yearly income some 250 percent.

His court was conducted on the basis of military principles that he also applied mistakenly to his family. The king's tyranny over his son, the future FREDERICK II, caused an unbridgeable rift between father and son. When the son attempted to flee in 1730, the king executed his best friend in his presence and then imprisoned his son in order to force his obedience. Frederick gradually was reconciled with his father, who died in 1740.

Frederick William II (1744–1797)
king of Prussia

Frederick William II was the nephew of FREDERICK II "The Great" and was crowned king of Prussia in 1786. During his reign the French Revolution broke out, but he failed to see the dangers it posed for monarchical power in PRUSSIA. He was overconfident in the quality of the army that he had inherited from his uncle, Frederick. In his eagerness to participate in the partition of the remaining territory of Poland in 1792, the Prussian campaign against France became ineffectual.

When Frederick became king, he was welcomed by the Prussian people. Most people were relieved when they heard the news of old Fritz's death. He had dominated the state with his will but had stifled individual initiative. His contempt for religion, his criticism of German, and enthusiasm for French culture, as well as excise taxes, generated popular resentment. So it was not surprising that there was a popular approval for the new king's appearance at church and his denunciation of French culture. He even eliminated the French character his predecessor had given to the Berlin Academy. The mercantilist policies of the past were liberalized, but it appears more with an eye to gaining popularity than a desire for permanent structural change. After a few years all liberal measures were abandoned, and taxes were increased on consumer goods because tax reform had diminished state revenues. In fact, the state treasury was in trouble due to numerous wars and political incompetence. Frederick's enormous war chest of some 50 million thaler was reduced in 10 years to a public debt of approximately the same amount.

Frederick William II was a friendly king with amiable gifts who unfortunately had no political talent and was manipulated by those who flattered him or who like his mistresses appealed to his sensuality. He had slight interest in military and political affairs, leaving the operation of state affairs in the hands of his ministers, the most important of which was J. R. Bischoffwerde, who was his foreign policy adviser. In military affairs his adviser was Johann Christoph Wöllner, who together with Bischoffwerde was among his Rosicrucian companions who staged unprecedented spiritualistic séances in the garden of CHARLOTTENBURG. Moral corruption from the court spread to BERLIN society, and criticism of conformity to traditional norms encouraged individuals to live according to their desires.

Both Prussia and AUSTRIA were initially little affected by the French Revolution, nor by the emigrant French nobles who were crowding many places in the Rhineland, particularly

Mainz and Coblenz. In August 1791 Leopold II of Austria and Frederick William II met in Pillnitz in SAXONY, where they rejected the demands of the youngest brother of Louis XVI, the count of Artois, to restore the political and social position of the crown and nobility. The German emperor and king of Prussia formulated the DECLARATION OF PILLNITZ, which promised to intervene to restore Louis XVI and introduce a moderate constitution. The condition which they set made it unlikely that any effort would be made. The Jacobin leaders in Paris, however, capitalized on the possible threat that Pillnitz posed, and before long Austria and Prussia found it necessary to conclude a defensive alliance in February 1792. With the declaration of war against Austria by the French legislature, Prussia mobilized the largest army, commanded by Duke Ferdinand of Brunswick. Due to an undiplomatic manifesto by the duke, he enabled the French revolutionaries to declare a war of national defense against tyranny. Although the Germans experienced successes and the way to Paris lay open, the duke hesitated for a variety of reasons and retreated to Germany. As the great German writer of the day, Johann Wolfgang von GOETHE predicted, on that day a new chapter in world history had begun.

With the formation of the first great coalition against the armies of the French Revolution, the German Empire finally declared war on France in March 1793, but the actual burden of fighting was carried by the Austrian and Prussian armies. After German victories in 1793 the tide of battle turned in favor of the French. Lazare Carnot, the Committee of Public Safety's "organizer of victory" enlisted new military leadership, including Napoleon Bonaparte, and created mass armies of as many as 800,000 men. The French armies gained superiority in 1794–95, while Prussian forces were weakened by disagreements with the Austrians and the need to suppress a revolt, which had emerged in Poland over the partition. The third Polish partition brought about the collapse of the Austro-Prussian alliance. With the exhaustion of Prussian finances, Frederick William II decided to sue for peace with France in the Peace of Basel on April 15, 1795. French troops were left in occupation of Prussian territories west of the RHINE. Resentment against Prussia was particularly strong in southern Germany, which was now exposed to French invasion. It was the beginning of an anti-Prussian attitude that was to last for decades. Prussia now became neutral for 10 years, leading to a situation in which Prussia had to fight Napoleon alone in 1806.

Two years after the third partition of Poland, Frederick William died. He was great neither as a man nor as a ruler. In intellectual and church affairs he was an obscurantist. In religion he insisted on narrow orthodoxy and rigid censorship; Protestant pastors could teach only what was in the official manuals. With the immorality of the court, society also experienced a decline of morals, while politics also degenerated. Even though Prussia had made some notable acquisitions, Prussia no longer merited the position to which it had been elevated by Frederick the Great. The campaigns of Frederick William brought no great victories, while the Treaty of Basel was disastrous for Prussia's future leadership among the German states.

Frederick William III (1770–1840)
king of Prussia

Frederick William III became king of Prussia in 1797, succeeding his unpopular father. Born in Potsdam on August 3, 1770, he had a timid and irresolute personality, but was strong enough to get rid of his father's ministers and mistresses and remove the restrictions on religion, abolishing censorship. The 27-year-old prince was honest, modest, with an aversion to luxury. His home life was Victorian with the middle-class values prevalent both in BERLIN and Potsdam. He displayed a respectable family life in his love match with Luise von Mecklenburg-Strelitz. The famous German historian Leopold von RANKE described Frederick William as a "simple" king, and to that we can add that he was one whose hesitancy to act was nearly pathological. But that was only half the story of the incompetence of this head of state. Frederick William even avoided consulting his appropriate ministers when making decisions, relying rather on so-called cabinet secretaries who were underlings and unstatesmanlike. This distressed the cabinet ministers and the bureaucracy, where considerable talent resided and whose pride had grown since the days of FREDERICK II. Frederick William was a very ordinary man who had the misfortune to be king during a time of revolutionary changes.

There were reformist energies present in Berlin at the turn of the 19th century, and the king must be given credit for seeing the need for fundamental social changes. He initiated the greatest agrarian reform ever made in Prussia, progressively freeing the peasantry on his royal domains between 1799 and 1805 and creating some 50,000 freehold farms. He was reluctant to declare the end of serfdom on the estates of the nobles but hoped his example would be followed. In the financial area the nobility held onto their vested interests, resisting the payment of a land tax, while the guilds resisted giving up their trade monopolies. When Baron Karl vom und zum STEIN became minister of taxation, he reformed the excise administration, which had separated the treatment of town and country. The king was also aware of weaknesses in the army in competing with the new type of citizen army fielded by the French. Strikingly, at least half of the Prussian army consisted of mercenaries and the rest of peasants and journeymen. The discipline of the nonmercenaries, however, had to be lightened. Also the army was too top heavy with old officers still around from the days of Frederick II. Half the generals were older than 60. The army had poor leadership and confused command structure, and the officers resisted reforms, all of which made the army the most obvious symbol of Prussia's weaknesses.

In foreign affairs Frederick William found it difficult to make decisions, preferring cautious policies and weak ministers. During the War of the Second Coalition against France in 1805 Frederick William clung to neutrality. As a result Austria was defeated at AUSTERLITZ in 1806. Then the king went to war against Napoleon at the least favorable moment, resulting in Prussia's military catastrophe at the BATTLE OF JENA. He was ignored in the negotiations at the Peace of Tilsit in 1807, and Prussia suffered the loss of its Polish and western territories, in addition to the disruption of its economy and financial ruin. The territorial losses amounted to roughly half of Prussia's territory. As a result of Jena in 1807, Frederick William made Karl von HARDENBURG his chief adviser, an outstanding official who in 1798 had been appointed to the GENERAL DIRECTORY and was placed in charge of foreign affairs. He counseled the king to resist Napoleon, who in response demanded that the king dismiss Hardenburg. This opened the door for the great Karl Freiherr von Stein, who wanted to replace the cabinet of the king's cronies with orderly and responsible ministerial government. In November 1808 Stein issued an edict establishing a centralized administration conducted by five ministers who had direct access to the king. With Stein's dismissal again in response to Napoleon, Hardenburg returned in 1810 to solve the fiscal crisis of the Prussian state. The reformers of the army, Gerhard Johann Scharnhorst and his idealistic fellow officers, had the goal of creating a citizen army led by an officer corps of talented professionals. As squeamish as ever, the king feared that this would endanger the state and refused to follow the call for national mobilization.

From the first defeats of Napoleon in 1813 until the CONGRESS OF VIENNA various statesmen proposed plans for the shape of a new Germany. Out of the complex negotiations and the unwillingness of most states to give up little, in the end the map of German Europe was redrawn. Prussia gained the most, receiving two-fifths of SAXONY, some Polish areas around DANZIG, what was lost at Tilsit, and territories in the Rhineland and Westphalia, which gave her a strong presence in western Germany. Although Frederick William in 1810 had promised a constitution with representative institutions, after the congress his willingness to grant a constitution declined. Napoleon's defeat and the settlement at Vienna decreased the need for change. The king's reactionary companions associated constitutions with foreigners and revolutionaries, while METTERNICH warned the king that a representative assembly would mean the end of Prussia. After the assassination of Kotzebue in 1819, the king's commitment to reaction was complete when he instructed Hardenburg to fully enforce the CARLSBAD DECREES. One year after the death of Hardenburg in 1822 the constitutional movement came to an end.

Two other changes during his reign included the merger of the Protestant churches and the establishment of the German Customs Union in 1834. A new order of worship was drafted by the king in the Agende of 1822 and through which he wished to make the AUGSBURG CONFESSION the official creed, which amounted to a declaration of royal opposition to the ideas of the ENLIGHTENMENT and modern German philosophy. In 1834 the German Customs Union was established to facilitate trade. It also facilitated the unification of Germany under Prussian leadership. Frederick William III died on June 7, 1840.

Frederick William IV (1795–1861)
king of Prussia

Frederick William IV was born on October 15, 1795, in BERLIN and became king of Prussia in 1840. He was very sensitive to criticism and self-conscious. On the other hand, he was sincerely a lover of peace, was broadly educated, and had good artistic tastes. As crown prince he was a student of the arts and had as close friends F. K. von Savigny, F. W. J. von Schelling, K. F. SCHINKEL, A. W. von SCHLEGEL, L. TIECK, Leopold von RANKE, Alexander von HUMBOLDT, and other leaders of the romantic movement. His national sentiment was stimulated by the WARS OF LIBERATION. On the other hand, he had developed a nostalgic admiration for the Middle Ages and thought it to be the apex of German history. The HOLY ROMAN EMPIRE represented the divine order on earth. He saw the GERMAN CONFEDERATION created by the CONGRESS OF VIENNA as the embodiment of the essential national traditions. He even wanted to create a unified German defense organization and nationally integrated economic policies. He was willing to let AUSTRIA renew the imperial Roman crown and to have PRUSSIA's kings be the hereditary marshals of the military forces. Frederick William was even more unyielding to liberal ideas than his father. Favoring a paternalistic monarchy based on divine right, he thought that constitutionalism, LIBERALISM, and democracy were products of irreligious rationalism. He was willing to have the king consult with a representative of the historical estates, but he would not be bound by parliamentary decisions. Popular humor around Berlin said of the king: "The Ghost of Frederick the Great is moving around the Palace of Sans-Souci, but without his head."

Frederick had a fervent desire to promote religion, but his choice of a minister of education and church affairs, J. A. F. Eichhorn, managed to alienate the universities and a large number of clergymen. Professors were again dismissed, one of which was Hoffman von Fallersleben, the author of the future German national hymn ("*Deutschland über alles . . .*"). More widespread was the reaction of church ministers against the pressure to conform to orthodoxy. Rationalistic ministers were forced to leave the church; they set up free churches and protested against the authoritarianism of church government. The movement of the Illuminati (*see* FREEMASONRY) was also strengthened and turned to promote common political ideals. A "German Catholic" movement also sprang up led by a suspended Silesian priest who protested against the hierarchical direction of the church and promised to free it from Roman bondage. He failed to have much of a following. Frederick also brought right-wing intellectuals to Berlin to uphold Christian dogma against what he considered the subversion of the philosophical ideas of Georg Wilhelm Friedrich HEGEL.

The central question was whether the king would move Prussia closer to a policy of liberal reform. Frederick William had drifted toward an authoritarian regime, but finally decided to implement the promise of his father to establish general estates. Instead of calling a popularly elected body, Frederick William called a united diet (*Landtag*) which was to be composed of the estates of the eight Prussian provinces. While the diet was asked to grant taxes and loans, it was not granted the right to meet regularly.

When the 1848 REVOLUTION broke out, Frederick was compelled to make an act of public mourning in the presence of the bodies of the revolutionaries whom his soldiers had shot. This was bitterly resented by conservatives as a humiliation of the monarchy. Two days later, Frederick William rode through the streets in a deliberate but unsuccessful attempt to appear as a popular leader and take over the Revolution. As far as German unity was concerned, he had no wish to exclude Austria from the new German state. The all-German FRANKFURT PARLIAMENT, on March 28, 1849, elected him emperor, and on April 3 a delegation offered him the imperial crown. The king declined the imperial title but declared his willingness to become the head of a federal state, though the princes had to give their approval. Many groups, including aristocrats, wanted him to accept the offer, but he rejected the popularly elected Frankfurt Parliament and its constitution. Frederick William IV had played the crucial role in wrecking the revolution and the hopes for German unity.

Afterward, an attempt by his adviser J. von Radowitz to create a union of German princes under Prussian leadership failed when combined pressure by Austria and Russia forced Frederick William to capitulate at OLMÜTZ in 1850. After that failure the king withdrew to his private artistic pursuits and left politics in the hands of his ministers. He suffered a stroke in October 1857 and mentally collapsed. His brother, William, ruled as regent until Frederick William's death in Potsdam on January 2, 1861.

Free Corps
(Freikorps)
The Free Corps were paramilitary units of veterans of WORLD WAR I who were unable to give up fighting and adjust to civilian life. They were recruited by the army and the government to circumvent the military restrictions in the TREATY OF VERSAILLES to repress leftist uprisings and to support right-wing causes after the war. The Free Corps were fighting not to save the WEIMAR REPUBLIC but to crush communism. One of the most notorious uses of the Free Corps was the suppression in April 1919 of the Soviet Republic in BAVARIA. Some members of the Free Corps became early members of the NAZI PARTY.

The name was taken from the first Free Corps (Freikorps), or voluntary units organized by a Major Lützow in 1813 as the basis of an army to free Germany from Napoleon. After 1919 the new Free Corps was composed of former officers, demobilized soldiers, military adventurers, and fanatical nationalists organized by Captain Kurt von Schleicher. Rightist in orientation and blaming the SOCIAL DEMOCRATS and Jews for Germany's defeat, they sprang up all over Germany. At first General Paul von HINDENBURG and other generals supported the Free Corps, but later military leaders found their behavior objectionable. Interestingly, the Allies approved of the Free Corps units fighting the Communists in Lithuania and Latvia in 1919.

Free Democratic Party
(FDP)
The liberal Free Democratic Party has played a pivotal role in West German politics since the founding of the FEDERAL REPUBLIC. The party often has been a member of governing coalitions both with the CDU and the SPD. Its leader, Hans-Dietrich GENSCHER, as foreign minister was very influential in the outcome of reunification in 1989–90.

In the postwar period there was an impetus to unite the various groups of liberals and their mildly different philosophies into one liberal party. It should be remembered that the liberals during the Second Empire and the WEIMAR REPUBLIC had been divided into at least two liberal parties which weakened their influence. In the late 1940s under the Western Allies the licensing policies permitted parties to form locally first and then at the state level. Out of these regional parties a loose union of the state parties was formed at a conference of delegates held in Heppenheim in December 1948. Theodor HEUSS, who became the first president of the Federal Republic, was the first leader of the party. The formation of the party did not mean that organizational unity equated with ideological unity. Going back to 1945 the liberals lacked homogeneity in the Western zones of occupation, much as they had during Weimar. There was a more liberal democratic wing centered in local parties in BADEN-WÜRTTEMBERG, HAMBURG, and BREMEN. There also was a right wing, which was more nationalist and free-market oriented and centered in Hesse and NORTH RHINE-WESTPHALIA.

In the early years of the Federal Republic the more conservative national-liberal wing was dominant until the death in 1961 of conservative Erich Mende. During that time the FDP participated in coalition governments with the conservative CDU/CSU (1949–66). The FDP had to compete for the nonsocialist vote. It was committed to free enterprise economics with a minimum of government interference in the economy and therefore favored the policies of Ludwig ERHARD, who was a former liberal though he joined the CDU. It also emphasized extensive civil rights, and recognized that the state has responsibilities for the poor. On the other hand, it advocated tax incentives for business and subsidies to farmers, both of which groups were part of its electorate. The FDP favored the separation of church and state, was anticlerical, and criticized the support of the CDU/CSU by the Catholic clergy and the reestablishment of Catholic schools in parts of the Federal Republic.

From 1966 until 1969 a reform and transition under the leadership of the liberal-democrats Walther Scheel and Hans-Dietrich Genscher occurred, which reoriented the FDP into an alliance with the SPD in the Social-Liberal Coalition in 1969. With the victory of the CDU in the elections of 1982, the FDP again changed alliances and entered a coalition with the CDU/CSU. During this alliance the free-market policies of the conservative liberals were emphasized in the policies of the 1980s, such as the reduction in the tax burden for companies. The party provided the foreign minister in all governments from 1969 until 1998 (Genscher serving from 1969 to 1992). Consequently, the FDP played a role in the formulation of OSTPOLITIK under Willy BRANDT and also promoted DÉTENTE in the governments of Helmut SCHMIDT (SPD) and Helmut KOHL (CDU), and in the complicated road to German reunification.

The party has always had to be concerned about getting enough votes to overcome the 5 percent level that parties must reach in order to gain representation in the BUNDESTAG. The FDP was able to overcome its minority status, getting between 6 and 12 percent of the vote. Its voter base comes from the self-employed and professionals but has no reliable voting bloc like the trade unions for the SPD and the churches for the CDU/CSU. The region in which the FDP was most successful has been in Baden-Württemberg. Between 1961 and 1983 it was the only third party in the Bundestag and the party whose support was needed to form a majority for a government. When in 1983 the GREEN PARTY entered the parliament, the FDP lost that exclusive position. In the elections of 1994 and 1998 the FDP tallied fourth among the parties behind the Greens. In all it served as an opposition party out of government only two times and participated in 13 out of 16 cabinets from 1969 until reunification.

Freemasonry/Illuminati

Freemasons formed secret societies to discuss and promote the principles of the ENLIGHTENMENT (Aufklarung). Freemasonry spread widely throughout Germany, and their program was also supported by the Bavarian Illuminati.

Modern Freemasonry began in England in 1717 with the establishment of the first Masonic "Grand Lodge." The purpose of the society was the construction of a so-called Grand Temple of Humanity, and the education of an enlightened humankind freed from superstition, from religious, political and social dogmas, and from various other restrictions. Individuals dedicated themselves to personal ennoblement, humanitarianism, and toleration. Deism was generally accepted, and Freemasons were dedicated to the creation of a natural religion. The Freemasonry of England and France cultivated a materialistic and atheistic outlook. Besides strict secrecy, it was a complex organization that developed an elaborate ritual derived from the medieval guilds.

Masonic lodges quickly spread throughout the German states and AUSTRIA. The first German Grand Lodge was established in HAMBURG in 1737, and a lodge in Mannheim during the same year. Some essential differences between German Freemasonry and that in England and France were the retention of the belief in God and immortality and the influence of the spirit of German classical literature and philosophy. The anticlerical character of Freemasonry was more pronounced in Catholic countries such as Spain, Italy, and France and in Catholic areas of Germany.

During the Enlightenment many of the political and intellectual leaders of Germany and Austria became members in a lodge. These included FREDERICK II (THE GREAT), KLOPSTOCK, WIELAND, HERDER, GOETHE, FICHTE, Josef von Sonnenfels, Mozart, and HAYDN. The husband of MARIA THERESA, Francis I of Lorraine, was a Mason, as were members of the HOHENZOLLERN dynasty in the 19th century, as well as most of the officials of the Prussian government. Gotthold Ephraim LESSING praised the ideals of Freemasonry in his *Discourses for Freemasons* as being in harmony with the spirit of the Enlightenment and true HUMANISM.

Some variations in the orientation of the lodges existed. Certain German lodges adopted the teachings of the Rosicrucians, who believed in an occult philosophy and were mainly conservative. On the other hand, other lodges associated with the Bavarian Illuminati adopted progressive and revolutionary goals. The "Order of Illuminati" (The enlightened ones) was founded in 1776 by Adam Weishaupt (1784–1830), who had formerly been a professor of canon law in the University of Ingolstadt in Bavaria. Although as in other lodges enlightened values were promoted, the antiauthoritarian and revolutionary attitude was stronger here than elsewhere. From Bavaria it spread northward under the leadership of Adolf von Knigge, but was suppressed in Bavaria in 1784 by the elector KARL THEODOR. It experienced a revival during the late 19th century.

French Revolutionary Wars

The wars of the French Revolution were triggered by the dangers of the revolution to other European states. They began in 1792 and lasted until the Peace of Amiens between England and France in 1802. These wars were followed by the NAPOLEONIC WARS, which ended at the Battle of Waterloo in 1815.

With the danger to Louis XVI and his family increasing and emigrant nobles fleeing to Germany and pleading for support against revolutionary France, the German powers faced difficult challenges. Wishing to avoid war with France, they issued the DECLARATION OF PILLNITZ, refusing to intervene on behalf of the émigrés. It actually increased the dangers of war and tempted the Girondins to use a war to divert attention from domestic problems and to spread revolutionary ideals. With the accession of Francis II in AUSTRIA, France declared war on Austria. A manifesto by Duke Karl Wilhelm Ferdinand of Brunswick on behalf of the émigrés provoked the storming of the Tuileries. When the Prussians crossed the RHINE to Verdun, the abolition of the monarchy was ensured. The Prussians were checked at Valmy, and before the end of 1792 the French armies occupied the Austrian Netherlands as well as Speyer, Worms, Mainz, and FRANKFURT.

By spring 1793 the Jacobins had executed Louis XVI and declared war on England and Spain. Out of this emerged in 1793 the First Coalition, which included the Netherlands, Sardinia, Spain, Naples, Prussia, Austria, and Portugal. Coalition forces invaded Alsace and threatened Paris. At this point the Jacobins reorganized national resistance under "Carnot the Organizer of Victory," who created a mass army of 800,000 men and adopted new methods of warfare. The French advanced, and as the first victories were won, the French gained superiority through sheer numbers and novel tactics. But Dumouriez's advance on the Netherlands was defeated at Neerwinden west of Liege by an Austrian army under Prince Josias of Saxe-Coburg-Saalfeld, and again at Louvain, whereupon Dumouriez concluded an armistice and defected to the Austrians. Prussian resistance slackened, then FREDERICK WILLIAM II deserted the coalition. In 1794 Prussia and Russia were preoccupied with their second partition of Poland and then the revolt of Thaddeus Koschiuszko in Warsaw. After negotiating a third partition of Poland in January, Austria concluded a treaty with England to subsidize the maintenance of 200,000 troops to drive the French from the Palatinate.

In the Peace of Basel (April 5, 1795) Prussia recognized the French Republic and was compensated for losses on the left bank of the Rhine. After others left the coalition, only Austria remained alone in the field against Napoleon. In the Peace of Campo Formio (October 1797) Austria recognized the Cisalpine Republic created by Napoleon in the name of the French Republic. Austria ceded the Netherlands to France and acknowledged the French acquisition of the left bank of the Rhine. The Austrians, on the other hand, acquired the Bavarian Inn district and the bishopric of Salzburg. The treaties of Basel and Campo Formio ended the wars of the First Coalition and resulted in the fulfillment of old French ambitions going back to the THIRTY YEARS' WAR.

The Second Coalition began in 1798. French conquests resumed, the Roman Republic proclaimed in the papal states, and the Helvetian Republic in Switzerland were the prelude to Napoleon's Egyptian campaign. Napoleon then returned to France and deposed the Directory and as First Consul in the Consulate took over the government of France. On June 14 Napoleon won the Battle of Marengo, to which General Jeane Moreau added the victory at Hohenlinden in Bavaria. Both of these battles decided the issue in favor of France. In the Treaty of Luneville Austria confirmed the conditions of Campo Formio and recognized the French possessions on the Rhine. France and Great Britain concluded the Peace of Amiens in the following year (1802).

Freytag, Gustav (1816–1895)
novelist

Gustav Freytag was a journalist, a cultural historian, and Germany's most popular novelist between 1850 and 1870. He wrote about the rising commercial MIDDLE CLASS, entertained an optimistic belief in progress, and thought that literature should not only entertain but be instructive. His dramas were vehicles for his views on modern problems.

Freytag was the son of the mayor of Kreuzberg, Silesia. He studied literature at BRESLAU and BERLIN, received his doctorate, and between 1839 and 1844 was a lecturer at Breslau. He gave up teaching for scholarship and writing. He published his first comedy in 1844 and was successful with his plays *Die Valentine* (1847) and *Graf Waldemar* (1850). With an interest in liberal politics he joined the journal *The Border Messengers* (*Die Grenzboten*), a LEIPZIG periodical espousing the liberal NATIONALISM of the National Association founded in 1859 and a predecessor of the NATIONAL LIBERAL PARTY founded in 1867. The National Association also was a forum for the discussion of literary REALISM. In 1854 he was very successful with *Die Journalisten* (1854), in which he portrays the representatives of the daily press and satirizes the methods of politicians and party bosses. In 1861 Freytag gave up journalism until 1867 and then resumed it during the years leading to German unification. As a liberal nationalist he supported German unification under Prussian leadership. In 1867 he was elected to the parliament (Diet) of the NORTH GERMAN CONFEDERATION. Then during the Franco-Prussian War at the personal request of the Prussian crown prince, Friedrich, he traveled with headquarters to France, where he conceived of the idea of the patriotic novel *Die*

Ahnen (1873–81), a fictional chronicle of German history. In 1851 he bought an estate in Siebleben near Gotha, where he spent his summers. In 1863 he wrote an essay on the technique of drama, *Die Technik des Dramas,* then a volume of reminiscences (*Errinnerungen aus mainem Leben,* 1887).

Freytag's novel *Debt and Credit* (*Soll und Haben,* 1855) was his most popular "realist" and significant chronicling of the life of the commercial middle class. The middle-class values Freytag emphasized were anticlericalism, antimaterialism, and anti-aristocratic pretentiousness. The goals that the middle class were supposed to strive for were work and nationalism. Freytag depicted the enterprising spirit of the middle class as the foundation for the new Germany. He skillfully portrayed a variety of characters and social types through the use of detail and humor.

In his multivolume *Scenes from the German Past* (*Bilder aus der deutschen Vergangenheit,* 1862) we have Freytag's first contribution to historical literature. It is a survey of Germany's historical past that combines historical research with a poetic style. Historical and literary landmarks were published with a running explanatory text. It still ranks high among works in German cultural history.

A realist writer of the mid-century and representative of a whole middle-class generation, he also has been criticized for his insensitiveness and ANTI-SEMITISM. In 1879 he retired to Wiesbaden, where he was honored until his death on April 30, 1895.

Friedrich, Caspar David (1774–1840)
artist

Caspar David Friedrich was the greatest artist of the romantic movement. He revived landscape painting in Germany, depicting an imaginary rendition of nature that expressed his melancholy moods, pantheistic beliefs, and nationalistic feelings.

On September 5, 1774, Caspar David Friedrich was born the son of a soap manufacturer in Greifswald. The traumatic deaths of his mother and brother produced a melancholy and a sense of guilt. His study of art began in 1788, and in 1794 he entered the art academy of Copenhagen. There he not only learned to draw scenes from nature but also was exposed to the theories of English romanticism. The NAPOLEONIC WARS aroused a strong hatred of France and love of Germany, and he became depressed at the news of Prussia's military defeat in 1806. In mountain scenes depicting lost French soldiers and monuments to German freedom fighters he chose to support the German WARS OF LIBERATION. During the following years his paintings became increasingly melancholic and gloomy. He protested against the reactionary restoration of the monarchy in Prussia in a painting of an ice-encrusted ship named *Hope* (1822). Earlier, Friedrich had come to feel that human beings were insignificant in the awesomeness of nature. In 1816 Friedrich became a member of the Dresden Academy, which provided him with a steady income that allowed him to marry in 1818. He was able to live a more fashionable life and wore the three-cornered hat symbolic of German nationalism. His fame inspired the Russian czarevitch to purchase several of his paintings in 1820. Because of his critical political attitudes and official criticisms of his art, his popularity declined. Enduring a depressed emotional state, he painted only watercolors between 1824 and 1826. As his mental and physical health declined, he experienced a stroke in 1835 and never again painted in oils. After 1837 he sketched only owls and gravestones, went insane, and died in DRESDEN during 1840. Except by a few friends, his subjective and emotional art was forgotten. It was rediscovered in the 20th century with the advent of EXPRESSIONISM.

At first imitative, Friedrich gradually developed his own style, rendering spacious landscapes populated by lonely figures and historic ruins. Friedrich thought that humans were part of nature like the trees in the scenes around them, so the motifs of his paintings usually showed individuals with their backs turned, set in dramatic but purely imaginative landscapes. Departing from the late 18th-century classical style of Carl Wilhelm Kolbe, Friedrich's *Woman* with *Spider's Web* presented a female figure in the midst of dense vegetation, intended to be a metaphor for confronting the divine. The woman's pose and gesture illustrated "the drama of the self facing the universe," a suspension between life and mortality. For Friedrich and his fellow romantics nature was, as the philosopher Friedrich Schelling believed, the spirit made visible and art was the means of making the finite infinite. Friedrich believed that all of nature and the human soul, in fact art, philosophy, literature, and science were unified and gave expression to the world spirit (*Weltgeist*). The romantic writers had convinced him that "art must have its source in man's inner being; yet, it must be dependent on a moral or religious value." Art, he thought, should be a mediator between man and the mystical sources in nature and should elevate spiritual awareness. Believing that present religions were passing away, he expected the future would bring a nondogmatic religious truth. In this light his painting *Cross in the Mountains* depicted a crucifix on a mountain illuminated by the setting sun, which represented man's continuing faith and hope in Jesus Christ despite the decline of institutional religion.

Fritsch, Werner von (1880–1939)
general

Colonel-General Werner von Fritsch was the commander in chief of the German army from 1934 to 1938. He was responsible for modernizing the German army and became a victim of HITLER's ambition to gain complete control of the armed forces.

Werner von Fritsch was born into an old Prussian military family on August 4, 1880. At 18 years of age he entered the army, and three years later his abilities were recognized with an appointment to the War College in 1901. In 1911 he was appointed to the General Staff, and during WORLD WAR I he experienced a variety of General Staff commands. During this period he became friends with the future leader of the army during the WEIMAR REPUBLIC, General von Seekt. During Weimar he served in the Reichswehr. Along with General Werner von BLOMBERG he supported the secret relation that the army had with the Soviet Union. He was prominent in General Staff circles and was promoted to lieutenant general in July 1932.

At first Fritsch hoped to be able to integrate Nazism into the nationalist perspective of the army. He was shocked, however, by Nazi lawlessness while attributing it to Nazi "youthful exuberance," but he remained silent. His military expertise made it possible for him to transform the small republican army into a large conscript one. As a leader he was a symbol of the non-Nazi officers. He feared that Hitler's anticommunism would lead Germany into a war with Russia, which turned out to be true. At the "Hossbach Conference" along with General Blomberg, both were horrified to hear of Hitler's war plans, which included the invasion of Russia. Fritsch was aware that the army was not ready, and he hoped that he could dissuade Hitler but was unsuccessful. Because of his opposition to Hitler's plans he got himself into trouble, and Fritsch's personal life then was to play a significant role in his fall from power.

Fritsch was reserved, had few female companions, and never married—being a bachelor who chiefly pursued his military career. This was used against him in the Blomberg affair (Blomberg, a widower, remarried a secretary who had been a prostitute) which scandal Hitler used to take control of the army. Fritsch was forced to resign on February 4, 1938, based on accusations of homosexuality which Hermann GÖRING and Heinrich HIMMLER had fabricated. Replacing Fritsch as commander in chief of the army was General Walther von BRAUCHITSCH. Fritsch was acquitted by a court of officers, was recalled to the army, but died in the invasion of Poland on September 22, 1939.

Fugger, Jacob "the Rich" (1459–1525)
early capitalist and banker

Jacob Fugger laid the foundation for the international banking house of the Fuggers. His banking house financed emperors, popes, mining, and long-distance trade.

Jacob was the second son of Johannes Fugger (d. 1409), a name that was first mentioned in the 14th century. Johannes had become a prosperous merchant and patrician in the imperial city of Augsburg. Originally intended for a career in the church, Jacob entered the family business after the death in 1473 of his eldest brother, Peter. Jacob was sent to Venice to learn bookkeeping and in 1485 was placed in charge of the Fugger business in Innsbruck. From there he got the bank involved in the mining industry in the Tyrol and by 1502 had extended the family's mining interests into Hungary and Silesia. Eventually he secured for himself a monopoly in the European copper market. In 1502 he became head of the family business interests and laid the foundations for the enormous fortune of the House of Fugger and its international prominence. He continued to expand his interests into other areas of commerce, including the spice trade to India, which generated a great deal of wealth.

The influence of the Fuggers was expanded as Jacob made generous loans to Archduke Sigismund of the Tyrol and Emperor Maximilian I. These and other loans were secured by the royal income from the salt mines. Other rewards for Jacob's services were the countships of Kirchberg and Weissenhorn, membership in the imperial nobility, and the title count of the Empire in 1514. In 1519 his loans were needed to secure the election of Charles, the grandson of Maximilian, as Holy Roman Emperor (Charles V) in 1519. Jacob lent more than half of the needed 850,000 gulden. He also got involved in church finance. Jacob loaned Albert of Brandenburg the necessary money to become archbishop of Mainz. This loan had unimaginable consequences, for it involved a sale of indulgences, which Luther protested and which led to the Reformation.

Jacob was the model of the early capitalist entrepreneur and banker. His motto was truly capitalist: "I shall gain while I am able." He had great business acumen and was a strategic thinker and diplomat. He was comparable to the princes of the Italian Renaissance even though he was a member of the upwardly mobile bourgeoisie. Jacob was also a philanthropist who endowed one of the earliest housing settlements for needy citizens in Augsburg, the "Fuggerei." Virtually, no other family wielded as much power or exerted as much influence on the politics and economy of their time as did the Fuggers of Augsburg.

Führerprinzip
(leadership principle)

Adolf Hitler believed in the leadership principle, a principle of rule whereby the dictator provided direction to the Nazi Party, the German people, and the state. As early as July 1921 Hitler insisted that the dictatorial leadership principle be the law of the Nazi Party. In *Mein Kampf* he denounced democracy as nonsense and made it clear that the future German Third Reich would be a dictatorship. Democratic parliamentarism with its many opinions could not possibly form the German people into a folkish (*völkish*) state resulting in a racial state (*Volkstaat*). Hitler conceived of himself as the supreme leader who embodied the will of the people. The leader would possess the right and power to command. After coming to power, Hitler put his leadership principle into action by establishing a dictatorship. Hitler's vision as an absolute ruler was expounded to the Hitler Youth on September 2, 1933, when he said that "one will must dominate us, we must form a single unity; one discipline must weld us together; one obedience, one subordination must fill us all, for above us stands the nation."

G

Gagern, Heinrich von (Wilhem Heinrich, Freiherr [Baron] von Gagern) (1799–1880)
liberal leader

Heinrich von Gagern became the leader of the liberal movement in HESSE-Darmstadt. He was elected the leader of the Frankfurt Parliament during the REVOLUTION OF 1848.

Heinrich von Gagern was born in Bayreuth in 1799, the second son of Reichsfreiherr Hans Christoph von Gagern, an aristocrat and descendent of a family of imperial knights who owed allegiance only to the HOLY ROMAN EMPIRE. Heinrich von Gagern studied at HEIDELBERG, Göttingen, and JENA. He was a veteran of the Battle of Waterloo. After the WARS OF LIBERATION he was influenced by the patriotic fervor of the student union (Burschenschaft) organization. In 1821 he entered the civil service and was elected to the state parliament (*Landtag*) of Hesse-Darmstadt between 1832 and 1836. During this period he was a successful Hessian landowner and chairman of the Rhine-Hesse Agricultural Association.

Gagern became a convinced constitutionalist and was one of a small group of aristocrats who were willing to cooperate with the liberal middle in the development of constitutional government. In Hesse-Darmstadt he became the leader of the liberal movement, which in the parliamentary (*Landtag*) elections of September 1847 won impressive victories. Chivalrous and idealistic, but not an original political thinker, he certainly was not a practical political tactician who was able to quickly grasp changing political situations. These undermined the possibility of his success in 1848. The qualities of his personality that were most admired by other liberals were that he was "passionate but restrained, idealistic but not doctrinaire, committed but dignified." For Gagern and other liberals belonging to a political party meant the formulation and discussion of ideas and secondarily the execution of policy. In 1848–49 these characteristics of the man would be sorely tested.

In March 1848 Gagern had become minister in Hesse-Darmstadt. Then he played a distinguished role in the pre-parliament (*Vorparlament*) for a national assembly. On May 19 the parliament elected Gagern as its president and under his leadership the parliament formulated rules and procedures that were to limit the long debates and speeches fashionable in 1848 so that decisions could be reached on major issues. Gagern was also mainly responsible for the establishment of a quasi-government, a central authority in the place of the hated Diet of the GERMAN CONFEDERATION. On June 29 the Parliament elected Archduke John, the youngest brother of Emperor Francis Joseph, "imperial regent." The archduke, who had the reputation of being a liberal sympathizer, organized a government of the Empire. When a deadlock occurred between the proponents of a larger and smaller German federation, Gagern proposed a compromise plan for a united Germany under Prussian leadership, which would be joined in a special relationship with the Austrian Empire. While the situation in AUSTRIA was moving in a counterrevolutionary direction, the Parliament finally passed a constitution that was ratified through Gagern's efforts. Then it elected the

Prussian king, FREDERICK WILLIAM IV, emperor, but the Prussian king declined to cooperate and rejected the imperial crown.

After the Constituent Assembly was dissolved on May 10, 1849, Gagern retired from politics. In 1850 he faithfully served in the war against Denmark. After 1862 he changed his 1848 position of favoring unification under Prussian leadership to support for the Austrian-oriented Greater German solution. Between 1864 and 1872 he served as Hessian representative in Vienna. He died on May 22, 1880.

Galen, Clemens August von
(1878–1946)

Catholic bishop of Münster and critic of Nazi regime

Clemens August von Galen was born into a family of Catholic aristocrats in Westphalia. After studying theology, he was ordained on May 28, 1904. He worked as a parish priest for some 30 years until he was appointed bishop of Münster on September 5, 1933. It is probable that his appointment was connected with the hopes connected in the CONCORDAT treaty of July 20 between the Vatican and the new government headed by Adolf HITLER. Galen was a dedicated German patriot who mistrusted the WEIMAR REPUBLIC and even the Catholic CENTER PARTY. His conservatism also led him to oppose Catholic renewal efforts such as the popular Catholic youth movement.

When the Nazis came to power, Galen pledged his loyalty to the new regime, hoping that the Nazis would retrieve the honor Germany lost through its defeat in 1918. Nazi policies and literature soon inspired him to oppose the regime. Anti-Catholic literature, especially that of the NAZI PARTY's chief ideologue, Alfred ROSENBERG, repulsed him. Galen launched a sharp attack against his racist views expressed in *The Myth of the Twentieth Century*. In 1939 Galen also deplored the procreation order of Heinrich HIMMLER for the SS, which encouraged women to bear children for the Reich whether they were married or not. What angered the regime the most was Galen's opposition to the T-4, the EUTHANASIA program that was intended to kill invalids, cripples, and incurables. He preached three now-famous sermons against it in July and August 1941. Galen believed that all life was sanctified by God and no one had the right to take a life. The Nazis debated what to do with him, but he was not incarcerated, although his brother was sent to Sachsenhausen camp in 1944. They did plan, however, to kill the so-called lion of Münster after the war. Galen has been criticized for not speaking out against the persecution of the Jews, but recent research indicates that Jewish leaders in Münster discouraged him from doing so for fear of Nazis reprisals.

After the war Galen's patriotism led him to criticize the occupation of his region by the British as shameful and inhumane. Pope Pius XII in 1946 bestowed on him the honor of a cardinalship. He died on March 22, 1946.

Gellert, Christian Fürchtegott
(1715–1769)

poet of pseudoclassicism

Christian Gellert was born of a poor preacher in the bleak Saxon Ore Mountains. He became one of the favorite authors of the period of pseudoclassicism between the BAROQUE and the age of storm and stress. Gellert embodied the sentimentalism and elegance of the baroque, but also the rationalism of the ENLIGHTENMENT, and was a kind man and prolific letter writer. Even FREDERICK II, who preferred French literature, thought Gellert was the only German author worthy of notice. Under French influence Gellert produced some of his best works, such as the poetic *Fables and Tales* (1746), which eulogized the noble savage theme and in which are found his moralism and introspection. Crystallized in his work were the forces attempting to overcome the dominance of the baroque.

Among the prose works produced by this professor at LEIPZIG were both didactic dramas and novels that expressed a lower middle-class moralizing and the usual sentimentality of the so-called Tearful Comedy. Among his dramas are

The Hypocrite, The Lottery Ticket, and *The Affectionate Sisters.* The best known of his prose works was the sentimental and moralizing *Life of the Swedish Countess G . . . ,*" (1746), inspired by the English novel *Pamela* by Richardson.

Another area of his best work was his inspiring church hymns, qualitatively far superior to his *Fables.* They continued in the hymnal tradition of the 17th century and were thought inspiring enough to be set to music by Ludwig van Beethoven, hymns such as "The heavens proclaim the honor of the Lord" and "God, Thy mercy extends as far as do the clouds." Gellert's hymns and writings were rationalistic and certainly not emotional like his successor Friedrich Gottlieb KLOPSTOCK, who wrote the cantos of his epic, *Messiah,* which had an ecstatic character and projected awe.

General Directory
(Generaldirektorium)

The General Directory was the central administrative organization founded by FREDERICK WILLIAM I in 1723 and completed by FREDERICK II. It combined the administration of the royal domains with the war commissariats. It made possible the organization of the resources of the state for national and military purposes. It provided the machinery for executing the policy that the king determined in his private cabinet.

The General Directory had four departments with one minister and a number of councillors. All decisions were made by a council of ministers. The four departments were divided territorially, but each had functional responsibilities. The ministers of the separate departments of the General Directory were invested with political and administrative responsibility. There also were intermediate boards established in the provinces, which were endowed with judicial powers in public law, and completely supplanted institutions of local government in the towns and in the western provinces. The first department was responsible for PRUSSIA, Pomerania, and Neumark, but also had responsibility for the provisioning of the army. After Frederick the Great became king, he added additional departments: commerce and trade (1740), military administration (1746), excise and duties (1766), mining (1768), and forests (1771).

The General Directory administered the royal domains, collected all taxes, and directed the operations of the mint, the postal system, and the royal monopolies. Besides directing the whole economic life of the state, it encouraged foreign IMMIGRATION, financed new industries, and generally shaped economic life to meet the needs of the military establishment.

Genscher, Hans-Dietrich (1927–)
foreign minister

Hans-Dietrich Genscher was the leader of the FREE DEMOCRATIC PARTY (FDP) from 1974 to 1985. He had been the longest-serving foreign minister in the history of West Germany from 1974 to 1992. He played an important role in the relaxation of the cold war with the Soviet Union in the 1980s and in German reunification.

Genscher was born on March 21, 1927, into a middle-class family in Reideburg in SAXONY. During the end of WORLD War II he was drawn into the war but ended in a prisoner-of-war camp. Afterward he studied law at the universities of Halle and LEIPZIG, receiving a law degree in 1949. He left the GERMAN DEMOCRATIC REPUBLIC (GDR) in 1952, settled in BREMEN, and started private legal practice. A lifelong liberal with an interest in politics, he joined the Free Democratic Party and focused on national politics. He soon became federal party manager and a protegé of the rising Liberal leader, Walther Scheel, who became party chairman in 1961. Genscher was elected to the BUNDESTAG in 1965 and became party whip. In 1968 Genscher became vice chairman of the party and chairman in 1969, when Scheel was elected president of the FEDERAL REPUBLIC.

In the elections of 1969 the SPD and FDP won a majority of seats in the Bundestag, and Scheel and Genscher agreed to form a Social-Liberal coalition government under Willy

BRANDT. Genscher was appointed interior minister, a position he would hold for the next five years. As interior minister during the terrorism of the BAADER-MEINHOF GROUP he successfully maintained individual rights and civil liberties. Five years later, when Helmut SCHMIDT succeeded Brandt, Genscher moved up to become vice chancellor and foreign minister until the mid-eighties. The elections of 1982 returned the CHRISTIAN DEMOCRATIC UNION as the majority party, and under the influence of the Liberal economics minister, Count Lambsdorff, Genscher led the FDP into a coalition with CDU under Helmut KOHL. The switching of coalition alliances opened the FDP to criticism of political betrayal, but Genscher became a symbol of continuity and moderation in foreign policy. In fact, when Genscher stepped down as party chairman in 1985 over a political finance scandal, it probably was a good thing as he was able to concentrate on foreign policy. During the next five years Gorbachev began reforming the Soviet Union and made possible German reunification.

Although Genscher did not originate OSTPOLITIK, he supported it and sought to improve West Germany's relations with the Communist nations of Eastern Europe. When he became foreign minister in the Kohl government, he maintained continuity, even though he had to endure criticism from some Christian Democrats who preferred a more confrontational policy. Genscher supported the evolutionary change that was occurring in Eastern Europe but was surprised when East Germans began to stream across the border and the Soviet Bloc began to crumble. As Chancellor Kohl supported rapid reunification, the pragmatic and steady hand of Genscher helped work out the necessary international agreements. Reunification made Genscher very happy, and his popularity in the former East Germany contributed to the electoral success of the Liberals in the first all-German Bundestag elections in December 1990.

Genscher surprised everyone when he resigned his position as foreign minister in 1992. He was replaced by Klaus Kinkel, the former justice minister, who pledged to continue Genscher's foreign policy. Genscher continued to play a role in world affairs and published his memoirs in 1995.

Gentz, Friedrich (1764–1832)
conservative publicist and adviser

Friedrich Gentz was initially a supporter of the French Revolution but later turned against it and translated Edmund Burke's *Reflections on the French Revolution.* Later, he entered the service of Prince Clemens METTERNICH and supported the settlements at the CONGRESS OF VIENNA. He became a proponent of German unification under Austrian leadership.

In 1764 Friedrich Gentz was born into a family of successful, upwardly mobile Prussian civil servants. He early drank deeply at the well of ENLIGHTENMENT thought. He was a student of Immanuel KANT and became a close friend of Wilhelm von HUMBOLDT after they met in 1790. As a young man Gentz was restlessly in search of a good cause and the early phase of the French Revolution and proclamation of freedom for humanity suited him. In 1791 he began to read the conservative Edmund Burke's *Reflections* on the revolution in France. Although at first he did not like it, as the revolution became violent and bloodied people's hands he realized the wisdom of Burke's commentary. In 1793 Gentz himself translated the *Reflections,* which established him as a antirevolutionary publicist. Burke's political vision made an important contribution to conservative criticism of the revolution and helped create an ideological justification for the old order.

Gentz became a successful polemicist, editor of conservative journals, and frequenter of the salons of BERLIN. His social talents were such that he could mix well in the society of the salons and be influential on the fringes of political power. Instability, however, was a hallmark of his life, with such experiences as divorce, bankruptcies, and scandal. These and disappointment motivated him to leave Berlin for Vienna, where he got a government job and was protected by Metternich. During the settlements at the CONGRESS OF VIENNA he supported its decisions. Afterward he abandoned liberal and nationalist views and became a strong advocate of national unification, but under Austrian leadership. In 1818 he founded the *Vienna Yearbook for Literature*, and in 1832 he died.

German Christians

In 1932 the Nazis encouraged the formation of a pro-Nazi organization within the German Evangelical Church called the German Christians. They were more significant when during the beginning of the Nazi regime they elected Ludwig Müller as Nazi Reich bishop.

The younger Protestant pastors were discontented with the existing Evangelical Church, which had strong nationalistic views and wanted a restoration of Germany's prestige. Under the leadership of such theologians as Paul Althaus and Emmanuel Hirsch they preferred a nationalistic interpretation of Christianity, which involved the elimination of Jewish and universalist traditions. They believed their anti-Jewish reforms would complete the REFORMATION of Martin LUTHER and restore Germany to its prominent place in the world. At first, the German Christians denied the canonicity of the Old Testament, but they soon rejected it on anti-Semitic grounds. The extremists, especially those from Thuringia, supported the elimination of the Old Testament entirely and the recognition of Adolf HITLER as the "redeemer" of Germany. The movement may have started out as an effort to create an Aryan church but ended up demanding the complete dejudaization of Christianity. They dejudaized the New Testament even faster than the Old and claimed that Jesus was not a Jew and the essence of the Gospels was hostility toward Jews.

German Christians considered themselves the "Stormtroopers of the Church" and supported the regime's racial doctrines. The German Christians wanted to establish the leadership principle (FÜHRERPRINZIP) in PROTESTANTISM by uniting all Protestant churches into a single Reich church under one bishop. In the church elections of July 1933 Hitler supported Ludwig Müller and Joachim Hossenfelder in their takeover of the church and also provincial church administrations. Ludwig Müller, a military chaplain from East Prussia, was ardent and became the Reich bishop.

Even though the German Christians initially succeeded in their attempts to gain control, it proved of short duration, because in September 1933 the Pastors' Emergency League was established by Martin NIEMÖLLER with the support of about 4,000 pastors. The Emergency League opposed nazification of church doctrine and the attempt to eliminate the Jewish heritage of Christianity. Besides issuing reprimands, Bishop Müller had pastors arrested. In April 1934 the CONFESSING CHURCH was established, which defended the church from Nazi influences. The Confessing Church was led by a Reich Council of Brethren under the leadership of the theologian Karl BARTH. When the Confessing Church had a national synod at Barmen in May 1934, it drafted the BARMEN DECLARATION, which denied the totalitarian claims of Nazism on the church. It was not a declaration of political protest as the theologians remained otherwise loyal to Hitler.

With the end of the war the German Christian movement came to an end, but its influence did not. Although most German Christians kept silent or repented, others were defiant. Besides resisting DENAZIFICATION, evidence exists that members denied the existence of the HOLOCAUST. With the apologies of others it was evident that many of their beliefs persisted.

German Communist Party (KPD)

The Spartacus League, which was the most formidable opponent of the chancellorship of Friedrich EBERT, became the Communist Party (KPD) in January 1919. It possessed two outstanding leaders, Karl LIEBKNECHT, who was the son of one of the founders of the SOCIAL DEMOCRATIC PARTY, and Rosa LUXEMBURG, a brilliant Polish revolutionary. On December 30, 1918, the founding convention of the German Communist Party (KPD) took place, and on January

1 the KPD was founded. This severed the ties that the Spartacus League had had with the USPD. Although Liebknecht and Luxemburg advised against it, the KPD boycotted the national elections. Then, under the leadership of the Revolutionary Shop Stewards, they staged the Spartacus revolt between January 5 and 12. It was a passionate revolt of large parts of the working population when they realized that the REVOLUTION OF 1918 had done little to change the class power relationships. Rudolf Hilferding called it "the Battle of the Marne of the German Revolution." During the uprising Liebknecht and Luxemburg were killed by members of the FREE CORPS. After the revolt was suppressed, the KPD boycotted the elections for the NATIONAL ASSEMBLY but did receive 2.1 percent of the vote in the Reichstag elections of 1920.

Before the deaths of Luxemburg and Liebknecht the party had considerable idealism, believing that the working class could march toward a common goal. Soon afterward factional conflicts developed between moderates and radicals. The factionalism, however, drove out of the party talented members such as Paul Levi and Ernst Reuter, and the party increasingly came under the control of Moscow. Instead of the espoused cooperation in the labor movement, the KPD increasingly competed with other groups. When the left wing of the INDEPENDENT SOCIAL DEMOCRATIC PARTY (USPD) split off from the party, it joined the KPD but soon regretted the move and returned to the SPD. Subsequently, the KPD also became adventurous and attempted an armed insurrection in Saxony, which had been urged upon them by the Hungarian revolutionary Béla Kun and the Russian Comintern. It ended as a tragic failure, and besides the dead there was a loss of about half of the KPD membership of 350,000. The KPD again involved itself in a fiasco during the Ruhr crisis in 1923.

By 1925 the party came completely under the control of Moscow through the leadership of Ernst Thälmann, who reorganized the party along Bolshevik lines. Moderates such as Heinrich Brandler and left-wingers opposed to Soviet domination such as Ruth Fischer were expelled from the party. By 1929 the KPD effectively had become the German branch of the Communist International. Throughout the Weimar period the KPD accused the SPD of being a traitor to the proletarian revolution, too tolerant of capitalism and sympathetic to the Western democracies. In the later 1920s it even labeled the Social Democrats, "Social Fascists." As the NAZI PARTY grew in strength, the KPD feared that the Nazis would attract many workers toward their program. As the depression deepened, the KPD sought to mobilize workers in their expanding network of factory-based revolutionary trade union cells. It hoped to create a revolutionary situation, but that failed to happen. The combat units of each party (the Communist Red Front and the Nazi Storm Troops) went into the streets and fought pitched battles. The KPD and the threat of Communist revolution became one of the chief battle cries of the Nazis. Unfortunately, the KPD failed to stop the Nazi march to power with Hitler's appointment as chancellor on January 31, 1933. The KPD became the Nazis' first target, as their leaders were imprisoned and organizations smashed; they represented the largest proportion of inmates in the CONCENTRATION CAMPS. Afterward the underground cells were discovered and suppressed by the GESTAPO. With the invasion of the Soviet Union underground, cells thrived in urban areas where the party had previously had support. After the end of the war and the establishment of the FEDERAL REPUBLIC the KPD did not do very well, eventually failing to receive adequate voter support above the 5 percent level.

German Confederation (1815–1866)

After the defeat of Napoleon the CONGRESS OF VIENNA (September 1814 to June 1815) redrew the map of Europe. The hopes of many Germans for a free, unitary nation-state were not fulfilled. The German Confederation replaced the old HOLY ROMAN EMPIRE (Reich) and was a loose federation of 35 monarchical states and four city republics. It was not a state but an association.

The Federal Act adopted by the German governments on June 8, 1815, declared as its objective "the preservation of the external and internal security of Germany and of the independence and inviolability of the individual German states." Its fundamental provisions were incorporated into the Vienna Treaty of June 9, 1815, and through Article 11 AUSTRIA, PRUSSIA, and all the other member states pledged mutual aid. The territories this left out were the Prussian provinces of East and West Prussia and Posen, as well as Austria's Polish, Hungarian, and Italian possessions. There were foreign princes of territories belonging to the confederation: the king of England as king of Hanover, the ruler of the Netherlands as duke of Luxembourg, and the Danish king as duke of Holstein and Lauenburg did not have to contribute to defense.

The sole organ of the confederation was the Federal Diet (Bundestag), which was located in FRANKFURT. It was not an elected but a delegated diet, able to act only if the two great powers, Prussia and Austria, agreed with each other. The Federal Diet was actually a permanent diplomatic conference. When it met as the Plenary Council, each of the members had at least one vote, while Austria and the five kingdoms had as many as four. The Plenary Council was to convene only for decisions regarding fundamental laws or organic institutions. It could reach decisions by a two-thirds majority, though on constitutional and religious matters unanimity was required. The Plenary Council rarely met between 1822 and 1847 and not at all thereafter. It was the Select Council that carried out regular business. Eleven of the larger states each had one vote as did each of the seven "curias" in which all the smaller states were bundled. The sovereignty of the member states was limited as they could not leave the confederation, nor could they conspire against one another to make a separate peace. The confederation formed a military organization in 1821–22 of some 300,000 men with Austria and Prussia contributing the largest contingents and the smaller states the rest. Who was to command this German army never was solved. As far as rights are concerned, those of individuals were the weakest.

The confederation saw as its main task the suppression of all aspirations to national unity and freedom. The press and publishers were subject to rigid censorship. The universities were under close supervision, and political activity was impossible. Although the confederation was not a national state, it did contribute to German national cohesion. Its diplomatic character allowed its member states to be the center of political life. It did provide a defensive organization so that the German states were better protected.

Meanwhile, the foundations of a capitalistic market system were emerging, which undermined these reactionary political systems. In 1834 the German Customs Union was founded, creating a small inland market. In 1835 the first German railway line went into operation. The foundations of industrialization were being established. A new class of workers emerged who worked in these establishments. A labor surplus occurred, and povemrty was widespread in the 1840s. Without a system of social welfare the mass of factory workers and displaced hand loom weavers lived in great misery. Tensions led to the uprising of the Silesian weavers, which was harshly repressed by the Prussian army. At the same time a liberal movement that favored freedom of the press, the elimination of restrictions on business, and constitutional government emerged to play a leading part in the REVOLUTION OF 1848.

German Conservative Party
(1876–1918)

The German Conservative Party represented the old feudal ideal of Prussian society and was known as the party of "throne and altar," meaning that it defended the ideals of divine-right Prussian monarchy, the organic theory of the state, and the protection of the Protestant Church.

The German Conservative Party was organized to represent the extreme right of Prussianism and to defend divine-right monarchy,

ARISTOCRACY, landed property, and the Protestant Church. The newspaper *Kreuzzeitung* was its principal organ. It had its main support in the electoral districts of the old Prussian provinces of East and West Prussia, Pomerania, Mecklenburg, and BRANDENBURG. They were the party of "authority rather than the majority," and of the Prussian land-owning class. Its political philosophy was in opposition to liberal and democratic theory. They emphasized that corporate entities rather than the citizens were the basis of the state. They believed in the organic theory of the state anchored in ROMANTICISM and emphasized the monarchical principle. They affirmed the virtues of inequality and the importance of the military, propagating the fiction that Germany was surrounded by enemies, a situation that required extensive armaments. Conservatives believed in social and political principles of Christianity, the divine-right theory of kingship, protection of the church, opposition to civil marriage, and education controlled by religious authorities. They also espoused ANTI-SEMITISM, declaring their opposition to the "destructive Jewish influences on our national life." They aimed to keep Jews out of universities, the bureaucracy, and the officer corps. Jewish influence was associated with capitalistic exploitation. In economics they were hostile to industrialism and emphasized the importance of agriculture. They thought BISMARCK was too liberal in allowing national suffrage and too nationalist in having submerged Prussia in the new Reich. In 1876, however, the party decided not to question Bismarck's constitution any longer.

The Conservative Party had influence far greater than its numbers, for it was closest to the government. As the party shifted its influence to economic objectives, it attracted more voters in the new Prussian provinces and outside of Prussia. In the elections of 1877 the Conservatives demonstrated that their power was weakening. In the REICHSTAG elections the party steadily lost ground. In 1890 the party had had some 73 delegates. By 1912 the Conservatives had been reduced to about 9.2 percent of the vote, which represented only 45 delegates.

In 1892 the Conservatives adopted a new manifesto, the Tivoli Program, in which they endorsed anti-Semitism and rejected parliamentarism and social democracy. It was an effort to stop the erosion of their popular support. They wanted to undercut the competition from the Christian Social Movement of Adolf STÖCKER and also that of the anti-Semitic parties. Surprisingly, the anti-Semitic parties all but disappeared, but the Tivoli Program made anti-Semitism respectable. From 1893 onward the Conservatives also received campaign support from the AGRARIAN LEAGUE. Even with these efforts to broaden the party's appeal its voter support declined.

During WORLD WAR I the younger leaders and members of the party advocated the annexationist demands of the PAN-GERMAN LEAGUE. The Conservatives also continued to demand no compromise on constitutional reform, in particular on the Prussian franchise and ministerial responsibility in the Reichstag. To this they added the "no surrender" position on the war. It was no surprise thereafter that Kuno von Westarp disbanded the party on November 11, 1918.

German Democratic Party
(DDP) (1918–1933)

The German Democratic Party was founded during the revolution of 1918 and was the party most closely associated with the founding of the WEIMAR REPUBLIC. It was a liberal party and had its roots in the PROGRESSIVE PARTY and the left wing of the NATIONAL LIBERAL PARTY of the Empire. It had won 18.5 percent of the vote for the NATIONAL ASSEMBLY and received 75 seats. Through Hugo PREUSS, a specialist on constitutions, the party had an important impact on the character of the WEIMAR CONSTITUTION. It was the largest nonsocialist and nondenominational party in the republic. Inspired by the ideas and leadership of Friedrich NAUMANN, the DDP sought to unite the more progressive members of the MIDDLE CLASS and nonsocialist working class into a pillar for parliamentary democracy.

The party was weakened from the beginning by disagreements over the TREATY OF VERSAILLES and lack of clear goals on social and economic policy. Within a year the party's strength was cut in half as the REICHSTAG elections of 1920 gave it a strength of only 39 seats. There also were difficulties within the leadership of the party, which was drawn from the prewar Progressive Party and from academic and professional groups that had little political experience. They may have been influenced by the IDEALISM and NATIONALISM of Friedrich Naumann and Max WEBER, but were not by nature democrats. They had hoped to achieve social reconciliation but found it difficult to relate to the electorate on terms that were meaningful, instead of on abstract principles. The INFLATION CRISIS of the early 1920s practically destroyed the national organization. So the German Democrats appeared as impractical intellectuals and based on newspaper press were considered by many to be the party of the Jews. In 1924 party representation fell to 25 seats, and it drifted to the illiberal political right. It failed to support the SPD in criticizing the army for meddling in foreign affairs, and it did support a bill that placed restrictions on freedom of the press in favor of protecting public morality.

While more liberal members such as Theodor Wolff, the editor of the *Berliner Tageblatt,* left the party, the new leader, Erich Koch Weser, and Gertrud BAUMER became critical of parliamentary democracy. Some democrats left the DDP for new special interest parties such as the Business Party of the German Middle Class. As Koch-Weser became worried about the future of the party, he worked out a merger and created the State Party, which was supposed to become a party of national consolidation. After a terrible showing in the September 1930 Reichstag elections, the DDP formally dissolved itself in November 1930.

German Democratic Republic
(GDR; Deutsche Demokratische Republik, DDR)

The German Democratic Republic was established in the Soviet Zone only after the ratification of the BASIC LAW and the formation of the FEDERAL REPUBLIC. The GDR was founded on October 7, 1949. A "Provisional People's Chamber" proclaimed the new state, which likewise formally declared that its aim was German unity. A constitution was written, and its first president, was Wilhelm Pieck, and Otto Grotewohl became the first minister-president. Now two states existed on German soil.

The constitution supposedly guaranteed civil liberties and established a parliamentary democracy and a multiparty political system. A bicameral legislature was established with the lower house, the People's Chamber (Volkskammer) being the most significant. There were four non-Communist parties to start with, but by the time the GDR was founded the Communist SOCIALIST UNITY PARTY (SED) dominated all political activity. The other parties were not allowed to run independent candidates. Throughout the history of the GDR all parliamentary bodies from town councils upward to the SED were elected on the basis of single lists. The SED's leading organ, the Politbureau, the real government of the GDR, had as early as 1950 only two former Social Democrats, in addition to seven Communist members. The party's general secretary was Walter ULBRICHT, who essentially was a dictator and dominated the GDR until his dismissal from power in 1970.

The development of socialism was seriously pursued starting in 1952, resulting in the transformation of the political and social system along Communist lines. The policy of socialization resulted in a catastrophic decline in living standards with emphasis placed on heavy industry to the neglect of consumer goods. With these political and economic pressures many East Germans left the GDR for the West. To prevent this "flight from the republic" extensive barriers began to be erected, which finally resulted in the uprising of June 17, 1953, which was suppressed by Soviet troops. With the death of the Russian dictator Joseph Stalin in 1953, there were some pressures to de-Stalinize, which Ulbricht resisted. People continued to flee, and year by year hundreds of thousands left, amounting to 3.5 million in 1961. Finally, the Communists built the BERLIN WALL to stop the flow of emigrants westward.

The result was a decade of stability and modernization of the system.

Walter Ulbricht was forced out of office in May 1971 because he opposed the new Soviet policy of DÉTENTE and was succeeded by Erich HONECKER, who led the GDR until the reform movement of 1989 led to reunification. Honecker was content to safeguard Communist control in the GDR; it was in the revised "Honecker's constitution" in 1974 that there was no mention of a German nation. Henceforth, the SED maintained that in both states two completely separate nations had arisen. The BASIC TREATY of 1972 was a step in normalization of relations between the two Germanies, but although West Germany recognized the existence of two German states it still was opposed to the recognition of the GDR under international law.

In domestic policy Honecker followed policies that tried to improve the economy. A new managerial elite emerged. Nationalization was further promoted, and centralization of economic decision making occurred. The planning priorities included an increase in consumer goods and efforts to improve the quality of important sectors of the economy such as precision instruments, chemicals, and electronics. Plans fell short of expectations as the price of raw materials rapidly rose during the 1970s, which made it difficult to earn the foreign currency to pay for food imports and improve the standard of living. The East German economy stagnated, and the external debt approached dangerous proportions, which helped the GDR live far above its means. With all of its economic shortcomings the GDR was in 10th place among the world's industrial nations and achieved the highest standard of living of the Soviet bloc nations.

State controls were eased, but surveillance of the population by the STASI (State Security Police) was widespread. People could watch television or listen to radio broadcasts from the Federal Republic. Artists and intellectuals received more freedom, but there still were serious restrictions on imports of books from the West. The regime did try to silence criticism by expelling prominent critics or depriving them of their East German citizenship. When Wolf Bierman, a poet critical of the regime, was expelled from the GDR, more than 100 leading artists and writers signed a statement of protest against the regime. Writers such as Stefan Heym and Christa Wolf were silenced. Inasmuch as consumerism was not as important as in the West, the East Germans were more interested in attending concerts and visiting museums. Popular discontent increased, however, during the 1980s, and the state allowed a limited number of applicants to resettle in the Federal Republic. Few East German citizens really believed that reunification was possible and did not see West German democracy as an alternative.

In 1989–90 the regime was overtaken by crisis, revolution, reform, and reunification. Honecker was deposed and replaced by Egon Krenz, followed by Hans Modrow. Free elections were promised for 1990 that became dominated by West German chancellor Helmut KOHL, who promised quick reunification based on the West German currency. With a conservative victory, the GDR came to an end.

German Labor Front
(Deutsche Arbeitsfront, DAF)
(1933–1945)

The German Labor Front was a monolithic organization established by the NAZI PARTY to coordinate unions and other labor associations in order to bring workers under its control. The organization had little to do in labor relations but was intended to support the regime's economic and rearmament goals.

The German Labor Front was led by Robert Ley (1890–1945) and was founded on May 10, 1933. Between May 1 and 10 some 169 trade union organizations were brought under Nazi control. The suppression of labor unions was part of the Nazi program against Marxism. The goals of the organization were varied and propagandistic and intended to create labor peace. It was not a labor relations mechanism, but was intended to control German workers, protect them from Marxist influences and make them patriotic and supportive of the regime's goals.

Before long the German Labor Front comprised the entire labor force of Nazi Germany and included about 20 million workers. Instead of striking for better wages, the Labor Front was intended to get workers to work together for the common good. Vocational training was provided not only to improve workers skills but also to integrate German workers into a racially based utopia. Incentives were used to get workers to become consumers of "people's products" like radios, refrigerators, bungalows, and cars like the Volkswagen, even though these products remained in short supply because of war production. The Labor Front distributed financial assistance, provided funds for workers' education and the construction of buildings, and stabilized wages. Other subsidiary organizations provided rest and relaxation. The "Strength through Joy" movement was designed to provide vacation trips, theater plans, music events, etc. to those who had a perfect party record. The "Beauty of Labor" organization had as its goal the improvement of conditions in factories, including canteens, sports facilities, and swimming pools. In 1938 some 7 million working took short trips, while only 130,000 were able to take advantage of cruises. The Labor Front reminded workers that Germany was creating a new national community in which class distinctions were disappearing.

Even though workers had gained benefits, they had lost their fundamental bargaining rights. The eight-hour day was stretched. Workers were given "work books" in 1935, which included their job qualifications. Agricultural workers were restricted from entering industrial labor, and Nazi control of labor, soon led to conscription of labor in order to build the defensive wall along the Franco-German border.

German National People's Party
(DNVP) (1918–1933)

Organized in the winter of 1918–19, the German National People's Party, DNVP, was the major conservative party during the WEIMAR REPUBLIC. It was the successor to and rallying point for the political forces of the Imperial parties of the right: it included the GERMAN CONSERVATIVE PARTY, the Free Conservatives, and the right wing of the NATIONAL LIBERAL PARTY, which did not heed the call of Gustav STRESEMANN to join the GERMAN PEOPLE'S PARTY, or DVP. Its heterogeneous membership was augmented by some arch-conservative leaders of heavy industry, some members of the ultra-nationalist FATHERLAND PARTY and the PAN-GERMAN LEAGUE. It also included the remnants of the old folkish groups and the Christian Social Party. The electoral basis of the party was no longer strictly East Elbian agrarian and Protestant, but now half of its voting strength came from western Germany. Its heterogeneity could also be seen in the makeup of its delegation in the REICHSTAG, which included the urban upper MIDDLE CLASS, industrial associations, associations of salaried employees, professional groups, the great landowners, and grain producers. The DNVP's share of the vote in federal elections was around 18–20 percent until it participated in the cabinet of Chancellor Wilhelm Marx (CENTER PARTY) in 1927–28, which resulted in a drop of its voter support to 14 percent. After that, Alfred HUGENBERG, a former director of KRUPP, an owner of a newspaper empire, and after 1927 Ufa, Germany's largest film company, took over the DNVP, moving it further to the right and helping Adolf HITLER to become chancellor.

The political position of the DNVP was dogmatic and ideological. It was monarchist, opposed to the TREATY OF VERSAILLES and the WEIMAR CONSTITUTION. With its radical rhetoric it invariably blamed the republic and the Allies for all of Germany's problems. In 1922 the DNVP did lose those folkish elements and those who favored the overthrow of the republic (putschists), which went on to form the German-Folkish Freedom Party (Deutsch-Völkische Freiheitspartei, DVFP). The experience of the inflation and the humiliation of the French occupation of the Ruhr hardened some, while it moderated others. The realists in the party favored the DAWES PLAN, while the ideologues were against it because it recognized the Versailles settlement. In 1925

Count Kuno von Westarp (1864–1945) along with Admiral von TIRPITZ prevailed upon the retired general Paul von HINDENBURG to be the conservative candidate for the presidency. With Hindenburg's election the conservative antirepublican forces in Germany made a good recovery.

From 1924 to 1928 the DNVP participated in a number of right-of-center cabinets. As Hugenberg gained control of the organization, he sought to mold it into an ideological bloc instead of a coalition of conservative groups. Like their attitude toward the Dawes Plan, the ideologues in the party opposed the LOCARNO TREATIES, which Gustav Stresemann had negotiated. In 1927 the German Nationalists made efforts to extend the influence of the churches in education. A school law was drafted under the direction of a German nationalist, which was to give the denominational school the same legal status as the interdenominational school. It was a direct attack on the Weimar Constitution in the area of education. Here the conservatives not only had the support of their Catholic counterparts in the BAVARIAN PEOPLE'S PARTY but also the moderate Center Party. The defeat of the bill temporarily weakened the DNVP but its anti-republicanism kept on growing. A plebiscite against the YOUNG PLAN failed. With the onset of the DEPRESSION right-wing voters increasingly turned to the NAZI PARTY. From 1930 to 1932 Hugenberg tried to influence Hitler by supporting a common candidate for the presidency in the Harzburg Front. That failing, when Hitler was appointed chancellor by Hindenburg, Hugenberg joined the cabinet of "National Opposition." The Nationalists won only 52 seats in the elections of March 1933 and voted with the Nazis to give them a majority in the Reichstag. Unable to influence Nazi policy, Hugenberg resigned from the cabinet. The party dissolved itself in June 1933.

German People's Party
(DVP) (1918–1933)

The German People's Party (Deutsche Volkspartei) was founded on November 23, 1918, by Gustav STRESEMANN. As a former parliamentary leader of the the NATIONAL LIBERAL PARTY he had wanted to join with other liberals in the GERMAN DEMOCRATIC PARTY (DDP). Because of his extreme annexationist position during WORLD WAR I, he was excluded from a leadership position and founded the DVP, which was one of the new parties like the German National People's Party (DNVP) formed during Weimar. It was opposed to the TREATY OF VERSAILLES and did not vote for the WEIMAR CONSTITUTION at the Weimar National Assembly.

The DVP was backed by powerful economic interests, especially in the Ruhr area. It was said to be the party of the wealthy industrialists and the highly educated. Although it served as the political voice for the academic community, they did not control of the party. Wealthy businessmen did, and some of the prominent ones who played leading roles in the party were Hugo Stinnes (1870–1924) and Albert Vögler (1877–1945), who had seats in the REICHSTAG. Also indicative of the influence of industrialists was the fact that in 1930 there were 10 Reichstag deputies who controlled 77 company directorships. Other socioeconomic groups supported the DVP, such as the independent MIDDLE CLASS, the professional civil service, and the white collar workers. A popular message of the party was: "What was good for business was good for the nation." The party also adopted an adamantly antisocialist stance with its slogan: "The DVP will set us free from Red chains;" it was strongly antirepublican in its program and revisionist in its foreign policy positions.

Support for the party increased as the electorate became more conservative. In the January elections for the Weimar Assembly the party polled only 4.4 percent of the vote, whereas as the mood of the electorate moved to the right, in the June 1920 Reichstag elections the DVP received 13.9 percent of the vote and 62 seats in the Reichstag. That high-water mark dropped in May 1924 to 9.2 percent, to 8.7 percent in 1928, and to 4.6 percent in 1930.

Stresemann became a supporter of the republic not out of inner conviction but because of changing conditions. With the economic situation steadily worsening and the resistance against Versailles and the Western Allies getting nowhere, Stresemann and the DVP leadership came to recognize that a mindless antirepublican obstructionism merely accelerated the plunge into total chaos. By 1923 some of the DVP leadership had become so worried about the consequences of German economic resistance in the Ruhr that Stressmann agreed to accept the chancellorship in September 1923. Runaway inflation, the French occupation, and antirepublican threats such as the HITLER'S BEER-HALL PUTSCH were solved through the suspension of parliamentary government. After this crisis Stresemann became foreign minister in a middle-class coalition, a position that he continuously held until his death in October 1929. Through the LOCARNO TREATIES Stresemann was able to "revise" the consequences of the Treaty of Versailles by accepting Germany's western boundaries in return for the removal of Allied occupation troops prior to 1935 and the readmission of Germany into the family of nations. He also supported rearmament and the army's (Reichswehr) clandestine cooperation with the Soviet Red Army.

Under the pressure of the DVP's industrial wing the party moved closer to the antiparliamentary right, refusing to continue its support of the cabinet of Heinrich BRÜNING in October 1931 while joining the "National Opposition." In the elections of March 1933, its vote fell to only 1 percent of the popular vote, and it dissolved itself along with the rest of the parties in July 1933.

German Progressive Party
(Fortschrittspartei) (1861–1918)

The Progressives consisted of the left-liberal segment of the MIDDLE CLASS. Among them were merchants and bankers of HAMBURG, BREMEN, and Lübeck, and of the central German cities. The party supported a British type of parliamentary democracy, capitalism, and a free trade policy.

The left-Liberals, Progressives, or the Party of Progress was the oldest of the REICHSTAG political parties. It originated in PRUSSIA in June 1861 and became the strongest party in the Prussian parliament (*Landtag*). Some of its leaders were Max von Forckenbeck, Freiherr von Hoverbeck, Hans Victor von Unruh, Hermann Schulze-Delitzsch, Theodor Mommsen, and Rudolf Virchow. The Progressive Party used this name until 1884, when it combined with the secessionist Liberal Union from the NATIONAL LIBERAL PARTY and called itself the German Free Thought Party (Freisinnige Partei), enlightened and anticlerical. It also was known as the Crown Prince's Party because he was the first to congratulate them. It included more than 100 deputies and had the potential of changing the imperial system with the future help of a liberal emperor like Crown Prince Frederick, which of course never happened.

The program of the Progressives reflected the ideals of the REVOLUTION OF 1848. They favored a full-fledged parliamentary state. In politics and economics they were laissez-faire. In general they were antimilitarist and were Otto von BISMARCK's main opponents on the Army Bill and the INDEMNITY BILL. They were also antistatist and opposed to socialism. Those who voted for the Progressives were the commercial middle class, artisans, small merchants, lower officials, and intellectuals. The forceful parliamentary leader of the Progressives was Eugen Richter (1838–1906). Richter always seemed to oppose whatever the government wanted and so irritated Bismarck that he left the chamber whenever Richter spoke. After Richter's death Friedrich NAUMANN emerged as the leader. He led the party away from dogmatic free market principles and preached the need to infuse social welfare into middle-class LIBERALISM.

When the liberal combination of the German Free Thought Party took place in 1881, the Progressives and Secessionists could claim 106 Reichstag seats. By 1884, however, the new party was able to hold onto only 67 of them, which was a defeat for political liberalism. In general, without a mass following the party received only between 12 and 17 percent of the vote cast in the Reichstag elections. Political liberalism stagnated. The Progressives and the National Liberals sent 118 delegates to the

Reichstag in 1890, which by 1912 had fallen to 87. The party splits of the Progressives clearly hurt them at the polls, and a united PROGRESSIVE PARTY did not emerge again until 1910. Some Progressives were willing to conclude electoral alliances even with the SPD. On the other hand, there were Progressives who supported imperial expansion and naval armament.

German Reich (Imperial) Party
(Free Conservative Party; Freikonservative Partei, RFKP)

The Reich (Imperial) Party (RFKP), the same as the Prussian Free Conservative Party, was an offshoot of the GERMAN CONSERVATIVE PARTY, which gave undeviating support to the policies of Otto von BISMARCK and supplied many ministers for his government.

On the national level the German Reich Party (Reichspartei) was founded in 1867 by those conservatives who considered themselves up-to-date and supported "Fatherland above Party." It split off from the German Conservative Party, which opposed Bismarck's policies. The German Reich Party represented the large landowners, industrialists, and capitalists from those areas outside the old provinces of Prussia, such as the Rhineland and Silesia. Well-connected, they also represented career diplomats and various state ministers. Unlike the Conservatives they approved of Bismarck's solution to national unification and his resort to LIBERALISM in his form of constitutional government. So the Reich Party along with the NATIONAL LIBERAL PARTY became the chief supporters of Bismarck in the early sessions of the REICHSTAG. Between 1867 and 1890 they also supported the KULTURKAMPF, Bismarck's policies against the socialists and protective tariffs. There was no question that they fundamentally supported monarchical rule. From their ranks also came many of its diplomats and senior civil servants.

It was said that the party was composed of notables who were like generals without troops and in their case without voters. Not that they lacked voters, but in the long run they did not adapt to the age of mass politics. In the Prussian legislature they were able to maintain between 50 and 65 deputies, but that probably was due to the restrictive PRUSSIAN THREE CLASS VOTING SYSTEM. In the Reichstag, where universal male suffrage prevailed, their electoral support dropped precipitously between 1878, when it received 14 percent of the popular vote (57 seats), and 1912, when it fell to 3 percent (12 seats).

After 1878 the Reich Party began to amalgamate again with the Old Conservatives and eventually merged with them. Their declining fortunes in the elections were due to a variety of reasons. The party was too heterogeneous and could not come to an agreement on a common platform. They disagreed over tariff policies and also Pan-Germanism. That does not mean they lacked influence in high places or even with Kaiser WILLIAM II, because the Saarland industrialists Carl Ferdinand von Stumm Hallberg (1836–1901) and Alfred KRUPP actually provided that. Another part of the party's problem was it never got down to building its organizational base, whether on the national, regional, or local level. Its failure to develop a mass electoral base doomed the party.

German Women's Bureau

The German Women's Bureau was established in 1933 in the process of GLEICHSCHALTUNG (coordination) of all women's organizations. It was a new national organization of women's cultural and social groups. The leader of the organization was Gertrud SCHOLTZ-KLINK.

All women's organizations were brought into line with Nazi ideology. HITLER regarded any kind of FEMINISM as forbidden activity, and he expected women to play a subordinate role in society, following the traditional ideals of children, church, and kitchen (*Kinder, Kirche und Küche*). Women's primary role was to bear children and raise the future leaders of the Nazi state.

Gertrud Scholtz-Klink, who also headed the National Socialist Women's Association, was made head of the new organization. She accepted the idea of the subservience of women to male leadership, but at the same time the women's organizations provided their own community independent of men in which she could be the strong leader of other women. Her blond hair and blue eyes plus the four children of an earlier marriage provided her with the correct Aryan image. As important as she was, Scholtz-Klink never once discussed Nazi policy with Hitler.

The Women's Bureau enrolled 1.6 million members by 1938 and did create some employment for women, but most of its activities were done on a volunteer basis. One of its major functions, the Reich Mother's Service, provided courses to help a woman run a home and raise her children. Welfare and Nazi ideology were also included in the 30,000 classes taught throughout Germany. Other activities were charity and volunteer work. The winter relief program for the poor was the biggest one.

German Workers' Party
(Deutsche Arbeiterpartei, DAP)

The German Workers' Party was an obscure radical right-wing group that was formed in MUNICH after WORLD WAR I. It was founded by a tool maker, Anton Drexler, and a journalist, Karl Harrer. It was one of several groups that emerged from the prewar FATHERLAND PARTY. At first it was just a political discussion group. Drexler decided, however, that this sort of activity had little potential influence, so he decided to create a political party alongside the discussion group in order to publicize the group's ideas. It was only in the summer that the party began to eclipse its parent organization, and by August was ready to schedule public rallies.

As a political indoctrination official for the army (Bavarian Reichswehr) HITLER was sent to spy on this group, and he decided to join it on September 19, 1919. The DAP had been prepared by Drexler with an organizational base and membership base that was ready for Hitler to build on. Soon Hitler became their best speaker and recruiter for an audience, and by the end of the year he became the chief of propaganda and a member of the executive committee. On February 24, 1920, Hitler made one of his most effective speeches and demanded that the party's Twenty-Five Points be adopted. In April 1920 the name of the party was changed to National Socialist German Worker's Party (NSDAP).

Germany Treaty
(Deutschlandvertrag) (1952, 1954)

The Germany Treaty of 1952, although not a peace treaty, ended the Allied occupation of West Germany and restored to the FEDERAL REPUBLIC its practical sovereignty. It was revised in 1954, when the Germans were included in NATO and the Federal Republic agreed not to develop nuclear or biological weapons.

In September 1951 the Western foreign ministers agreed to negotiate contractual agreements along with the participation of German forces in the EUROPEAN DEFENSE COMMUNITY (EDC). Among the most important were the convention on the rights and obligations of the Allied forces in the Federal Republic. Financial arrangements were also negotiated, and an arbitration tribunal was set up to negotiate between the Western powers and the FRG. A series of transitional provisions dealt with topics such as war criminals, decartelization, internal and external restitution, displaced persons and refugees, foreign interests in Germany, and civil aviation. Controversy arose over the Allied insistence on the right to declare a state of emergency and assume full authority. The final treaty specified the conditions under which such a state of emergency could be proclaimed and provided for full consultation with the German government.

The Germany Treaty was signed on May 26, 1952, after the EDC treaties were signed in Paris. When the French Assembly failed to approve German rearmament and defeated the EDC, the Americans agreed to a sweeping revision of the Germany Treaty. The Allies agreed to change the right to station forces in Germany from the category of a reserved right to that of an agreed treaty right under which the Allied troops would remain, but as allies. It also revised the state-of-emergency clause, practically eliminating it. Germany was also allowed to join NATO and the Western European Union. Germany became a sovereign nation able to conduct its own foreign policy. The Western Allies also recognized the Federal Republic as the sole and legitimate representative of the German people. The revised treaty was signed in September 1954 and came into effect on May 5, 1955. The Germany Treaty remained in effect until the Moscow Treaties of September 1990, which became the final peace settlement of WORLD WAR II.

Gestapo
(Geheime Staatspolizei)

The Gestapo was an acronym for the Nazi state secret police force that was dedicated to the task of maintaining the National Socialist regime. The political crimes against which the Gestapo defended the Nazi state included whatever was detrimental to the racial purity of the German people. The Gestapo became a symbol of the Nazi reign of terror.

The Gestapo consisted of professional police agents. It was known for its efficiency in dealing with opponents of the regime and did not feel bound by legal restrictions. Even accused individuals found innocent by a regular court could be arrested by the Gestapo after their release. Gestapo legality was rationalized by its lawyers on the basis that as long as the police carried out the will of the government they were acting legally, regardless of what they did.

The Gestapo had its origin in HITLER's personal bodyguard, the Headquarters Guard. During the late 1920s the SS came into being, and in

Gestapo officials record data on incoming prisoners at a German concentration camp. *(Library of Congress)*

1929 all units were united under Heinrich HIMMLER. In April 1933 Hermann GÖRING incorporated the political police of PRUSSIA into the Gestapo, as Office IV of the Central Security Office of the Third Reich (Reichsicherheitshauptamt). After a struggle between Göring and Himmler, the latter in April 1934 became head of the most important security force in the state. Command was given to Reinhard HEYDRICH, who also headed the SD. The Gestapo set up its own legal system and assumed control of citizens' lives. Not only did it use any method, it pursued all enemies of the Reich, whether Jews or Marxists. Even people who told jokes hostile to the Nazis were interrogated and imprisoned. Warnings might be given first, then suspects were placed in custody, ending with incarceration in CONCENTRATION CAMPS. Where legality was necessary, the accused were brought before the PEOPLE'S COURT (Volksgericht). Already by 1936 it was almost totally immune from external control.

The operations of the Gestapo were part of a totalitarian police state. The tentacles of its surveillance reached everywhere. For instance, auxiliary to Gestapo agents were block wardens who were supposed to keep close watch on the people living on their block. Block wardens visited every household at least once a week and made regular reports to the SD, who were intelligence agents. It also delivered "racial enemies" in occupied Europe to their designated concentration camps. Members of the Gestapo even commanded the EINSATZGRUPPEN.

In order to create an ideologically motivated police, Himmler integrated the SS with the Gestapo. By 1935 some 20 percent of the Gestapo were SS members, and after 1936 through the war more than 75 percent were SS. By 1945 the Gestapo had 32,000 members.

Gleichschaltung
(Coordination)

The policy of Gleichschaltung, or Coordination, was used by the Nazis to consolidate their power through the control of the institutions of German society. This was done by abolishing competing political parties and bringing all unions under control of one Nazi labor organization, or the control of state governments, bureaucracies, and professional and social organizations.

After the ENABLING ACT Hitler and the NAZI PARTY established their dictatorship through the control of the institutions and organizations of German society. The official name of the policy, through which all sectors of the state and society came under the control of the Nazi Party, was called Gleichschaltung. Three stages made up this process of Coordination. First, an increase of executive power and the elimination of all potential sources of opposition were achieved through intensifying the power inherent in presidential rule and by liquidating the constitutional pluralistic state and replacing it with a one-party regime. This was primarily made possible through the elimination of competing political parties and labor and social organizations, as well as the control of churches. The second stage brought the state bureaucracy and the federal structure as well as other organizations under central authority. This was accomplished by eliminating bureaucrats who were Social Democrats or Jews and other politically unreliable officials. Nazi leaders called Gauleiters were placed in charge of districts throughout Germany. The third phase neutralized the power of the SA and the army, the two remaining forces outside Hitler's control. The SA, for example, was brought under Hitler's control through the blood purge of the NIGHT OF THE LONG KNIVES, in which insubordinate SA leaders were killed. The army was brought under complete Nazi control through the BLOMBERG-FRITSCH crisis in 1938.

Gneisenau, Neithardt von
(August Wilhelm Anton Neithardt, Graf [Count] von Gneisenau) (1760–1831)
Prussian general and military reformer
Neithardt von Gneisenau was of Saxon origin (non-Prussian), the son of a middle-class family that had been recently ennobled. He had a noble mind, and the range of his emotions was broad

and deep. He had great political and military abilities, which his friends thought could have successfully competed with Napoleon's. He did successfully compete with Napoleon militarily as he strategized the defeat of Napoleon and completed Scharnhorst's work.

Gneisenau was first an officer in the army of Ansbach-Bayreuth when his services were sold to the English for use in the American colonies during 1782–83. Then he entered the Prussian army in 1786, serving as an infantry officer in the Polish campaigns of 1793–95. In the French war of 1806 he was present at Saalfeld and was a staff officer at the Battle of Jena. In 1807 he rallied the garrison and townspeople in defense of the fortress in the Baltic port of Kohlberg against the French. Along with Baron Heinrich Friedrich Karl vom und zum Stein and Gerhard Johann Scharnhorst he belonged to the circle of Prussian reformers. In 1809 Gneisenau visited London and St. Petersburg, and when he returned in 1811 to Berlin he became a strong advocate of resistance to Napoleon. He was disappointed when the Prussian king supported Napoleon's invasion of Russia, although without Napoleon's defeat in Russia, Prussia would not have had a chance to become liberated. In the Wars of Liberation from 1813 to 1815 Gneisenau was chief of staff of the Silesian army under General von Blücher and was the leading strategist of the Prussian army.

Gneisenau retired in 1816 and became governor of Berlin in 1818. In 1831 he was appointed to the command of troops sent to suppress the Polish uprising but died of cholera.

Goebbels, Joseph Paul (1897–1945)
Nazi propaganda chief

Joseph Goebbels was a close friend of Hitler and became the propaganda chief of the Third Reich. He created the Hitler myth.

Joseph Goebbels was born on October 29, 1897, in the Rhenish city of Reydt, the son of a bookkeeper in a small factory. He grew up in a strict Roman Catholic household. His Dutch mother continuously prayed that Joseph would be able to overcome his physical disabilities: infantile paralysis, a small body, and a club foot. These deformities exempted him from military duty in World War I, a stigma he resented. He attended the Gymnasium in Reydt and between 1917 and 1921 studied the German language, history, philosophy, and literature at a variety of German universities. At Heidelberg, where he received his doctorate, he studied under Friedrich Gundolf, the Jewish historian of German literature. Goebbels rejected his parents' hopes that he would become a priest and later even turned away from the Catholic faith. While at Heidelberg he had read Marx, Engels, and Lenin, and for a while he embraced communism and other leftist organizations. At first he was not anti-Semitic, but as his writings were rejected, anti-Semitism grew in response.

In 1922 Goebbels joined the Nazi Party. In June of that year he had heard Hitler speak at a political rally in the Cirkus Krone and was mesmerized like so many others deciding to follow Hitler. At first Goebbels was given a journalistic job with a racist paper in the Ruhr, then became business manager in a party district (*Gau*), and finally editor of *NS Briefe,* a publication of Gregor Strasser. Goebbels became embroiled in a controversy between the Strasser brothers and Hitler, with Goebbels siding with the Führer. In appreciation, Hitler in 1926 appointed Goebbels as the district leader (Gauleiter) in Berlin-Brandenburg in 1926. Starting with only 500 members, Goebbels through agitation and propaganda devoted himself to spreading the philosophy of National Socialism. From 1927 to 1935 he edited his own weekly newspaper, *The Assault* (*Der Angriff*), and used it to create the Hitler myth. Some of the themes he used described Hitler as the prophet, the fighter, a father-figure, or just a kind human being who loved children. Goebbels was also an effective speaker, second only to Hitler and able to fling insults at his opponents whether government officials, Communists, or Jews. In 1928 he was elected to the Reichstag from Berlin and so impressive was his work that in 1929 Hitler appointed him Reich Propaganda Leader. In 1932 he organized Hitler's campaign for the presidency and reorganized party campaigns for seats in the Reichstag.

After Hitler became chancellor, Goebbels was appointed on March 13, 1933, the Reich minister for enlightenment and culture. In this position Goebbels gained control of the press, art, film, radio, and popular culture of the Third Reich. Very few sectors of artistic expression evaded Goebbels in his position as Reich minister of propaganda. Always the master of propaganda, he kept Hitler as the main focal point in whatever ceremony was taking place. He staged every event to get a specific effect. An east-west avenue was built in Berlin on which army units would march past Hitler on his 50th birthday. Squares near the Reich Chancellery in Berlin and the Brown House in MUNICH were arranged for so-called spontaneous ovations of the people. Everything was choreographed. Film was a powerful tool that Goebbels used to manipulate the minds of the people. Goebbels also assumed power over the press and issued guidelines for editors. Through the Reich Chamber of Culture the art scene also was controlled. The German art world was purged of Jewish, Socialist, and Communist museum directors and art academy professors, purging the art world of undesirables. The Nazi "battle for art" was a campaign to discredit and eliminate modern DEGENERATE ART.

Goebbels often got into disagreements with others in the Nazi hierarchy, especially Hermann GÖRING and Joachim von RIBBENTROP. Goebbels married Magda Quant, who had divorced a Jewish businessman, and they had six children, all of whom were favorites in Hitler's circle. Goebbels had a number of affairs with film stars and even was beaten one time by an outraged husband. During WORLD WAR II he tried to keep up the morale of the German people, but as the war progressed that was more difficult to do. His most notorious speech, in August 1944, concerned his call for total war. In April 1945 he advised Hitler to remain in Berlin and end his life in a Wagnerian *Götterdämmerung* to maintain the Hitler legend. After Hitler and Eva Braun committed suicide, Goebbels and his family did likewise. In Hitler's political testament Goebbels was appointed his successor as Reich chancellor. After his wife poisoned the six children and killed herself, Goebbels took his own life.

Goerdeler, Karl Friedrich (1884–1945)
leader of the right-wing opposition to Hitler

Born in Schneidemühl to a Prussian district judge, Karl grew up to share many of his conservative viewpoints. His education focused on the study of law and public administration, which led to a career in government and economics. From 1920 to 1930 he served as a deputy mayor of Königsberg, and in 1930 he was elected lord mayor of the industrial city of LEIPZIG. During the DEPRESSION he tried to alleviate unemployment and in 1931 was appointed Reich commissioner for price supervision by Chancellor Heinrich BRÜNING. Later, under Adolf HITLER, his distinction as an administrator led to his appointment as an economic adviser and Reich price commissioner in 1934–35.

Goerdeler's political philosophy was conservative nationalist. Skeptical of the WEIMAR REPUBLIC, he joined the conservative antirepublican GERMAN NATIONAL PEOPLE'S PARTY. After the NAZI PARTY came to power, he became disillusioned with it, disagreeing with its lack of moral principles and its dictatorial political philosophy, in addition to its religious and racial policies. Despite his reelection as lord mayor of Leipzig, he resigned from the office after a trip abroad when the Nazis had removed the town's memorial to the Jewish composer Mendelssohn-Bartholdy.

In 1935 Goerdeler became involved with the resistance in Germany. He began corresponding with the chief of staff, General Ludwig BECK. Goerdeler was outspoken and courageous and brought a tireless energy to recruiting for the resistance. He felt that the West should be warned of Hitler's expansionist plans. He visited Britain and the United States, and in 1939 even met with Winston Churchill. After war broke out, he continued to encourage peace feelers through his contacts in Sweden and Switzerland. He and Beck became very active in planning for a government after Hitler's death.

Goerdeler was at first considered to be the perfect choice for the chancellor of this new government, but after several disagreements with his co-conspirators, they began to see him as more of a transitional figure in the new government. After several unsuccessful attempts to assassinate Hitler, the Resistance group planned another plot executed by Count Klaus von STAUFFENBERG on July 20, 1944. When the bomb exploded but failed to kill Hitler, retribution was swift and merciless. GESTAPO agents searched army headquarters, where in a safe they found documents that incriminated Goerdeler, who was designated to lead a new government. He was arrested on August 12 and executed by hanging on February 2, 1945, in Plotzensee Prison.

Goethe, Johann Wolfgang von
(1749–1842)
classicist and poet, novelist, playwright, natural scientist, statesman

Although a critic of the ENLIGHTENMENT, Goethe became one of the greatest expressions of its ideals. Ranking with Homer, Dante, and Shakespeare, Goethe was Germany's greatest literary genius. His accomplishments embraced many fields of endeavor. As a minister shaping the political, cultural, and economic fortunes of the grand duchy of Saxe-Weimar, his literary friendships, especially with Friedrich SCHILLER, set the standard of the "Weimar classical style." His literary accomplishments began with his novel *The Sorrows of Young Werther,* which made him famous early in life. On his travels to Italy he was decisively influenced by classical forms, which he then manifested in his masterpieces, such as *Iphigenie auf Tauris* and *Torquato Tasso*. Further examples of his rich literary work are poems such as the *Wanderer's Night Song* and *To the Moon,* his novels *Wilhelm Meister* and *Elective Affinities,* the cycle of poems *West-Eastern Divan,* and his autobiography, *Poetry and Truth (Dichtung und Warheit)*. *Faust* was the crowning achievement of his career.

Goethe was born on August 28, 1749, in FRANKFURT AM MAIN, the eldest son of a wealthy lawyer and imperial councillor, Johann Kaspar Goethe, and his wife, Katharina Elisabeth Textor Goethe. Of their children only Wolfgang and his older sister Cornelia survived. Both of them were educated at home by tutors who enkindled Goethe's intellect and imagination. Yet, some biographers attribute his personal qualities to his parents: his liveliness, impulsiveness, and imagination from his witty and storytelling mother; his stable character and reservedness from his father. He also had memorable experiences growing up in a large mansion. At 16 he went to study law at the University of LEIPZIG, where he remained for three years until an illness required him to go home. After two years he finally was healed, and he returned to legal studies, but this time in Strasbourg, the capital of Alsace, where his poetic genius was awakened. Here he met Gottfried von HERDER, who inspired him with the Gothic architecture of the cathedral, the Greek poets Homer, Pindar, and Ossian, and the plays of Shakespeare, all of which represented the spirit of their cultures and peoples. Goethe also took pride in Germany's cultural heritage.

Between 1772 and 1775 Goethe became the leader of the Storm and Stress (Sturm und

Drang) literary movement, which was a romantic reaction against the restrictiveness of classical and French influences on German literature. Its followers sought to break free of all authority, free of artificiality and contrivance, and return to "nature and reality" and to the intuitive and emotional side of man's nature. Goethe had been part of a "Knights of the round table" group at a local inn, calling himself "Götz von Berlichingen." In 1773 he finished his play of the same title, which brought Shakespearean drama to the German stage and started the storm and stress movement. Out of the agonies of a failed passionate love for Charlotte Buff, Goethe created his *Sorrows of Young Werther* (1774).

On the invitation of young Duke Karl August of Saxony-Weimar, Goethe left Frankfurt for a visit. They became fast friends, and instead of visiting for a few weeks, Goethe stayed in WEIMAR for the rest of his life (1775–1832). As an enlightened administrator he was placed in charge of finances and then interior affairs; soon becoming a privy councilor, he was granted a diploma of nobility, which allowed the use of *von* before his surname. Finally, he became prime minister. While in Weimar, Goethe pursued studies in mathematics, optics, geology, botany, and anatomy, which laid the foundations for scientific papers, in one of which he disagreed with Newton's theory of optics, and by his investigations into plant and animal life perceived the process of organic change, which he drew from the theory of Vitalism developed in the late Enlightenment.

Receiving time off to travel to Italy, he visited Rome, Venice, and Sicily from 1786 to 1788. The trip is said to have been the most important single event in his life. Escaping the burdens of governmental administrative work and the frustrating relationship with Frau von Stein, he found new inspiration in Rome viewing the monuments of ancient culture. The experiences caused him to affirm strictly classical ideals. He finished *Egmont* in Italy. Abandoning the romantic outpourings of his storm and stress period, he sought to give expression to the classical ideals of tranquility and harmony. He recast *Iphigenia in Tauris* in iambic classical form, then published *Roman Elegies* in superb elegaic couplets, which discussed his mistress, Christiane Vulpius, who eventually became his wife in 1806, but not until the French invaded Weimar and threatened her position. *Torquato Tasso*, produced in the classical style, was a dramatic but reflective story of an Italian poet of the late Renaissance; it describes the tragedy of being a supersensitive poet and the conflicting claims between practical life and the arts.

Returning to Weimar in 1791, he was appointed the director of the ducal theater, where he staged his own plays as well as those of his friend Friedrich Schiller. This second period of Goethe's life was extremely productive, and in cooperation with Schiller he created what scholars call German classicism. It attempted to use the classical past as an inspiration for a new German literary style whose goal was the elevation of humanity through classicism. Schiller and Goethe approached the goal differently. While Schiller emphasized the subjective nature of writing and the liberating aspects of intellectual and artistic freedom, Goethe was attracted to the objective side of knowledge and used natural science as a model for literature. Of the two, Goethe was the more intuitive thinker and natural poet. Goethe, however, owed to Schiller the encouragement to finish *Wilhelm Meister's Apprenticeship,* and the undertaking of studies that led to the epic *Hermann und Dorothea.* Schiller also urged Goethe to work on *Faust* again, of which he completed the first part. In 1797 Goethe completed *Hermann und Dorothea,* which ranks as one of his most perfect creations.

Between 1811 and 1814 Goethe published his autobiography, which ranks with other great biographies in Western literature. Entitled *Poetry and Truth* (*Dichtung und Wahrheit*), it charted Goethe's development through his youth. The work is beautifully constructed and modeled after his image of the spiral path of natural development and the interplay between poetic creation and subjective experience of personal development. It is not factually correct and is filled with an old man's recollections. As Goethe grew older, he was increasingly aloof from politics and literary movements. He disliked NATIONALISM, distrusted the masses, and had little in common with the young poets of the romantic age. He welcomed an escape from the turbulence of Europe with an interest in oriental culture, as if he were looking there for true humanity. Then Goethe met another sensuous young love, Marianne von Willemer, who seemed to step from the pages of a Persian manuscript. He wrote poems to her and she to him, which were combined in a collection, *West-Eastern Divan* (1819). It contains some of the happiest and most spiritualized love songs in the German language.

Between 1821 and 1829 Goethe published *Wilhelm Meister's Journeying Years,* which was to be a continuation of the earlier *Wilhelm Meister's Apprenticeship*. It was a series of loose episodes in novel form. He was no longer concerned with man as an individual, but with the problems of modern society as a whole. The Industrial Revolution had brought a whole set of new problems, and Goethe was one of the first to recognize them. Wilhelm and his coworkers direct uprooted craftsmen and farmers to Europe's open spaces and to emigrate to the New World. The year before his death Goethe completed his greatest work, *Faust* (1831), on which he had been working for more than 40 years. There are great differences between the first and second parts of this philosophical drama, reflecting both his youth and old age. The drama recounts the eternal saga of man's struggle for perfection. The first part is influenced by Marlowe's *Dr. Faustus,* describing Faust's pact with the Devil, who will claim his soul at the very moment when he gives him "something worth living for." Disenchanted in turn by knowledge, power, and sensual pleasure, Faust is truly happy when he becomes engaged in useful humanitarian labor. God then saves his soul at the moment that the Devil is about to claim it, which is a departure from the original legend. Faust's salvation occurs because of the action of both the feminine and masculine principles in his life, the feminine being the world's ordering force, while the masculine is the human striving for goals. The second part reflects Goethe's wisdom and philosophy of life, echoed in his famous phrase, "He who forever strives, he shall be saved."

At 83 Goethe died in Weimar on March 22, 1832. He was buried in the ducal crypt next to his patron, Duke Karl August, and his friend Friedrich Schiller.

Goethe was perhaps the last universal man and the most documented creative artist. He was one of Germany's most original and powerful lyric poets.

Göring, Hermann Wilhelm
(1893–1946)
Nazi leader second in command to Adolf Hitler

Born in Rosenheim, BAVARIA, on January 12, 1893, into a diplomatic family, Hermann Göring was educated in a military school and received an army commission by 1912. Serving with the highest distinction in the new German air force in WORLD WAR I, Göring was chosen to succeed the famous Manfred von Richthofen ("Red Baron") after his death. He was awarded the Pour le Merite and the Iron Cross (first class). After the war he was employed as a pilot in Sweden and Denmark. He met his first wife, the Baroness Karin von Fock-Kantzow, who divorced her husband to marry Göring in MUNICH. In 1922 he met Hitler, offered his services, and due to his background Hitler made him commander of the SA (Brownshirts). In 1923 he took part in the BEER-HALL PUTSCH, in which he was seriously wounded, escaping to AUSTRIA, where he became severely addicted to morphine. Returning to Germany in 1927 under a general amnesty, Göring rejoined the NAZI PARTY (NSDAP) and was elected as one of its first deputies to the REICHSTAG a year later. He was reelected in July 1932, when the Nazis won 230 seats, which placed Göring in a position to become president of that legislative body.

After Hitler became chancellor in January 1933, Göring became a member of the cabinet and minister of the interior in PRUSSIA, which enabled him to Nazify the Prussian police and to establish the GESTAPO. As creator of the new police state, Göring along with Heinrich HIMMLER and Reinhard HEYDRICH established the early CONCENTRATION CAMPS for the incarceration of political opponents. In 1936 Hitler made Göring commissioner for the FOUR YEAR PLAN for the war economy. He acquired considerable economic power, especially in the steel industry. Göring was appointed Reich Council chairman for national defense on August 20, 1939, and officially became Hitler's successor on September 1. He also directed the Luftwaffe's (AIR FORCE) campaigns against Poland and France, and in 1940 was promoted to Reich marshal.

Göring ordered extensive economic reprisals against Jews. In November 1938 he went further and warned of a "final reckoning with the Jews." On July 31, 1941, he instructed Heydrich to "carry out all preparations with regard to . . . a general solution of the Jewish question in those territories of Europe which are under German influence. . . ."

As director of the war economy and the Air Force Göring was involved in much political infighting, inefficiencies, and exaggerated promises of air strength, all of which had a negative effect on the war effort. He became increasingly despised by Hitler, who blamed him for Germany's defeats. Near the end of the war Göring made several attempts to negotiate with the Allies and suggested to Hitler that he step down and let Göring assume leadership, for which Hitler stripped him of his posts and expelled him from the party. He was captured by the Americans, tried, and sentenced to death at the NUREMBERG TRIALS, after which he committed suicide by poison on October 14, 1946.

Görres, Johann Joseph von
(1776–1848)
inspirer of Catholic political consciousness

Joseph von Görres was born in Koblenz during 1776, which marked the beginning of the American Revolution, and he died in 1848, just before liberal revolutions erupted all over the states of Germany. He started out as a true republican and went on to pioneer political journalism. He was the founder of political Catholicism in Germany. He also was a self-taught scholar who had an amazingly wide range of interests.

Görres was raised in Koblenz, which was the epicenter of the turmoil brought on by the French Revolution. He admired the philosopher Immanuel KANT (1724–1804) and the French romantic Jean-Jacques Rousseau. When the French invaded the RHINELAND, he considered them bearers of enlightenment and liberators of the Rhineland from clerical misrule and provincialism. Enamored by the revolution, he at first thought of France as his fatherland and dreamed of the union of the Rhenish provinces with France. In 1799 he visited Paris at the head of a delegation, but his experiences were disappointing, leaving him uneasy about the extent of the lawlessness. He also discovered that there were cultural differences between the French and Germans that could not be erased by common political ideals. In 1800, as a result of French rule in the Rhineland, he changed his views completely and became a fervent supporter of German NATIONALISM. Now his German national consciousness was no longer compatible with republicanism and the rationalistic ENLIGHTENMENT. He exchanged his journalistic career for secondary school teaching, and read romantic literature and idealist philosophy. Then he met Clemens Brentano (1778–1842) and Achim von Arnim (1781–1831) and joined them in their pursuit of German folk art, making a substantial contribution in his *Volksbücher* of 1807. As Napoleon's position became desperate in 1812–13, Görres thought an uprising of the German people against the French dictator was possible. He published a journal, *Der Rheinische Merkur*, which preached hatred for the French and cultural romanticism. After Napoleon was defeated, his journal urged the moral regeneration and political reform of Germany, which German rulers found threatening and stopped its publication, forcing him to flee across the border to Strasbourg.

Joseph von Görres was a political dissident. He found that PRUSSIA, like France, was unwilling to follow his solutions. For him both the Prussian state and LIBERALISM represented what he called "political protestantism," which he interpreted as the blind pursuit of self-interest unchecked by a duty to God. Both the REFORMATION and the French Revolution had emphasized a destructive individualism that atomized society. Both capitalism and ABSOLUTISM of the princes were an expression of egotism and undermined a moral culture. That is why in his Catholic old age he favored a return to a social and political structure that was based on the premodern estates. Voluntary associations and the church, he believed, were better vehicles for moral improvement than the state.

Returning to Catholicism during his stay in Alsace, he was offered a professorship in history at the new Ludwigs University in MUNICH. He became part of a circle of Catholic intellectuals who encouraged the Bavarian king, LUDWIG I (1825–48) in a more conservative direction. The main evil that Görres saw in German political culture was the selfishness of the German princes, placing their dynastic interests ahead of the common good. In 1838 Görres and others began publishing *Historisch-Politische Blätter für das katholische Deutschland*, in which they promoted Catholic political conservatism. At the end of his life, in addition to opposing Prussian absolutism and liberalism, he spoke out against radical class politics. He and the Munich political Catholics, the Prussian JUNKERS and Karl MARX were all hostile to capitalism and the marketplace. Greed and money, he predicted, would dissolve social relations and undermine family, church, and the larger community. Görres died on January 29, 1848, shortly before the upheavals of the REVOLUTIONS OF 1848.

Gotha Program (1875)

There had been two socialist parties in Germany, one under the leadership of Ferdinand LASALLE and the other under that of Wilhelm LIEBKNECHT and August BEBEL. Both merged in 1875 at a congress convened in Gotha on May 22, 1875. The Gotha Program was adopted by this new Socialist Labor Party of Germany. The Gotha Program combined elements from the Communist Manifesto of Karl MARX and the Eisenach Program followed by the Lasalleans. Two of these were Lasalle's stress on the role of the state and state-aid for producers' co-operatives. Some of the principles that the program proclaimed were that "labor is the source of all wealth and all culture"; the "means of production is in the hands of the capitalist class"; the misery of the working class is the result of their dependence. The only way that "labor may be emancipated," is that "the means of production must be transformed into the common property of society." The party advocated the use of "legal means at the establishment of a free commonwealth and a Socialist society" and recognized the international nature of the labor movement. Productive industrial and agricultural co-operatives "are to be on such a scale that the socialistic organization of the whole of labor" would be created. These theories then were followed by demands for the development of state political democracy and social reforms.

Göttingen, University of

Göttingen was founded in 1737 as a modern university for HANOVER by the elector Georg August of Lower Saxony, who was also King George II of England. It was the most modern university in the 18th-century HOLY ROMAN EMPIRE, and it provided major institutional support for the German ENLIGHTENMENT. It became the freest and most flourishing German university after 1750.

Göttingen had a new model of a university applied to its structure and curriculum, and it closely resembled modern research universities, a model that was subsequently perfected by Wilhelm von HUMBOLDT at the University of BERLIN. In the late 18th century in the United States Harvard University also remodeled its university after Göttingen. Based on the reforms begun some 40 years earlier at Halle, the traditional structure of the four teaching faculties (law, medicine, theology, and philosophy) acquired equal footing with theology, which also lost its power of censorship. Toleration was also adopted as official policy. This made it possible for Roman Catholics, Jews, and Calvinists to attend classes, although they had to worship privately. The students were usually from the MIDDLE CLASSES, but Göttingen also recruited young noblemen.

Seminars in philosophy and philology were established. Professors were supposed to teach and perform original research. Some faculty members established journals. The university also influenced the Enlightenment. Some of the strong disciplines at the university were mathematics, physiology, anatomy and medicine, political science, history, anthropology, and literary criticism. Some major intellectual figures were Albrecht von Haller, Georg C. Lichtenberg, Johann D. Michaelis, Georg Forster, and August Ludwig von Schlözer. The daughters of some of the professors also had a cultural role at the time. Especially noteworthy was Carolina Michaelis, who served as the companion and wife of both August Wilhelm SCHLEGEL and of Friedrich Wilhelm Joseph von SCHELLING. Some of its most famous students included Alexander von HUMBOLDT, the SCHLEGEL brothers, Prince Karl August von HARDENBURG, Friedrich von Gentz, and Baron Heinrich Friedrich Karl vom und zum STEIN. It was at Göttingen in the 1830s that the liberal commitment to constitutional government was dramatically expressed by the "Göttingen Seven" in their conflict with the Hanoverian government.

Gottsched, Johann Christoph
(1700–1766)

literary critic and theorist of aesthetics

Johann Christoph Gottsched was born in LEIPZIG, the son of a Protestant pastor. At Königsberg University he studied theology, literature, and philosophy, and by 1723 was qualified to lecture there. In order to avoid being drafted into King FREDERICK WILLIAM I's regiment of tall grenadiers, Gottsched moved to Leipzig in 1730 where he received an appointment at the university as professor of poetry. In 1734 he was appointed professor of logic and metaphysics.

In his efforts to reform German theater, he enlisted the support of Friederike Caroline Neuber, and together they founded a German-language theater, the Deutsche Gesellschaft, with a classical style. Until that time theatrical productions had consisted either of rather coarse popular amusements of burlesque horseplay or of court entertainment in the French language. Gottsched fought against the BAROQUE style, which expressed a transcendental view of life. In a dramatic ceremony, with the help of Frederike Neuber's troupe, he symbolically abolished the clown (Hanswurst or Punch), which had been introduced by English comedians a century earlier to the German stage. Inspired by the ideas of the ENLIGHTENMENT, Gottsched and Neuber wished to educate people to appreciate beauty, truth, and goodness, and foster the intellectual unity of Germany through a common high-standard language based on Saxon usage. Championing the cause of French literary classicism as formulated by Nicolas Boileau, he introduced the rules of this highly formal and rational literary mode into Germany. His enthusiasm for French tragedies inspired him to translate those masterpieces, but in stiff German alexandrine verses.

Gottsched also set about establishing a repertoire of modern German plays after the French classical model, publishing from 1740 to 1745 the six volumes of *The German Theater*. He also wrote a compendium of philosophy (1734) based on the teachings of Christian WOLFF. Through his various journals of literary criticism, Gottsched developed into a powerful critic hated by the younger generation of German writers.

His obstinate character involved him in sterile and sometimes ridiculous disputes. His dictatorial attitude provoked a growing opposition. Unfortunately, he had little critical insight into poetry. Almost every German writer of distinction was opposed to his domination over German taste in the 1730s. In his *Attempt at a Critical Art of Poetry* (1730) he explained in a didactic and boring manner how to write great classical literature. He fought energetically against the poetic imagination and those like influential

Miltonian-enthusiast Johann Jakob Bodmer, who criticized the application of reason and rule to literary production in the 1740s. By mid-century Gottsched's pedantic bigotry was eclipsed by a new aesthetic based on the creative power of intuition and imagination advocated by Gotthold Ephraim LESSING and Moses MENDELSSOHN. Lessing condemned the French classicists and their German imitators like Gottshed, whose productions had degenerated into endless monologues and analyses. Despite his limitations, however, Gottshed made some important contributions. Among them, he edited important collections of older German literature, paving the way for the scientific study of German literary history. In his advocacy of Enlightenment rationalism he fought ignorance and obscurantism and advocated better education for women. The professor died in Leipzig in 1766.

Grass, Günter (1927–)
novelist, playwright, poet

On September 30, 1999, the Swedish Academy awarded the Nobel Prize in literature to Günter Grass. He became the third German writer after Thomas MANN and Heinrich BÖLL to receive the prize. In his novels Grass explored the impact of Nazism on German identity from Hitler through the cold war to reunification, examined the "intertwined roots of good and evil," and fought against the amnesia and complacency of his countrymen. His first novel, *The Tin Drum*, published in 1959, helped revive German literature after decades of Nazi distortions. Grass did not hesitate to remind his countrymen of their history. He was bitterly critical of unification in 1990, describing it as another ANSCHLUSS, and expressed the belief that the HOLOCAUST had demonstrated that Germans were too dangerous to ever be united.

Born on October 27, 1927, in the city of DANZIG (now Gdansk, Poland), Grass grew up during the crisis years of the WEIMAR REPUBLIC and the Nazi dictatorship. He participated in the Nazi movement, believed in its ideals, served in the war, was wounded, and then was made a prisoner of war. He was angry about the sacrifice of his youth in the cause of German NATIONALISM. He pursued a nontraditional education, developed a distaste for theories, and preferred the school of experience in art and politics. At first he studied art, then wrote poetry published in the magazine of Group 47, a writers' workshop, then won a prize for chapters of his new novel, *The Tin Drum*, the first of the Danzig trilogy. In a surrealistic manner Grass satirizes the history of modern Germany through a narrator, a complex and self-willed dwarf named Oskar. The second novel of the trilogy is *Cat and Mouse* (1961), where Grass again uses Danzig as a setting. It involves a group of boys, one of whom has a deformed Adam's apple, and a cat that represents the human mob in unthinking pettiness, which pounces on the unusual boy's neck, assuming there is a mouse in it. In his third novel, *Dog Years* (1963), there are also symbolic projections of national guilt. The novel shows how the past determines the present. The dog years are not only bad years, but three generations of dogs play important roles in the action. In 1977 Grass published *The Flounder*, a bustling and mischievous story out of world history, which contrasts the destructiveness of men with the achievements and sanity of women. Grass always believed in "the literature of engagement" and was actively involved in politics, a supporter of Willy BRANDT and the SOCIAL DEMOCRATIC PARTY. In 1995 he angered his countrymen with the publication of *A Broad Field*, where he portrayed German business tycoons as ignorant and avaricious, having stolen the "people's property" of the former East Germany. Not unexpectedly the novel provoked harsh literary and political criticism.

Green Party
(The Greens)

Some of the young people who matured between the 1950s and the 1970s developed a different set of values than their elders. It was a generation that participated in the student movement, environmental protection, FEMINISM and women's rights, and the protection of individual rights and civil liberties. It also protested against nuclear power and nuclear weapons. The rise of the Greens can also be attributed to changing social structures and value priorities among West Germans. A new MIDDLE CLASS came to value postmaterialist quality-of-life issues. Some of this new generation joined communes, cooperatives, self-help groups, and the Greens. The impetus for environmental action and joining the Greens was the prediction of a worldwide ecological disaster unless citizens took measures to stop the process. Local activists had established citizens' initiative groups (*Bürgeriniativen*) to deal with the issues that the main political parties failed to address, even such issues as housing shortages and high rents. The leaders of these movements eventually formed environmental parties in the states and ran slates of candidates in local and regional elections. In 1972 an umbrella organization of these groups was formed as the Association of Citizen Initiatives for the Protection of the Environment (Bund Bürgerinitiativen Umweltschutz, BBU). By 1980 a national coalition of environmental parties founded the Greens to run candidates in municipal, state, and national elections.

Citizen's groups coordinated a campaign in 1979 for elections to the European Parliament and won 3.2 percent of the vote. This encouraged them to create a national organization in January 1980 at their founding conference in Karlsruhe, and two months later they formulated a party program in Saarbrüchen. The party entered the BUNDESTAG in 1983, when it received 5.6 percent of the vote and again in 1987 with 8.3 percent. In the 1990 elections after unification the vote for the party declined to less than 5 percent and therefore the Greens received no seats, which was due in part to its hesitancy over the quick pace toward reunification. (In hindsight their reservations were wise because of the economic problems of reunification, right-wing extremism, and the influx of asylum seekers.) The Greens did not expand their voter base with the additional voters from the former East, and consequently they were mainly a West German party. After 1991 the more radical left wing of the party, the so-called Fundis, left the party, which left the more pragmatic Realos in control. The foundation of their policies focused on environmental and ecological issues, gender equality, antimilitarism, internationalism, and participatory democracy, which made the party a good candidate in 1998 for a coalition partner with the SPD.

Looking back to the issues of the 1983 election, it was the Greens who opposed the stationing of American nuclear missiles on German soil and called for the dismantling of nuclear power plants, the outlawing of pesticide and herbicide use on agriculture products, the prohibition of the sale of war toys and advertisements featuring cigarettes, liquor, and candy, and the introduction of legislation banning discrimination against homosexuals. In addition to all these antiestablishment positions, the Greens called on Western and Eastern governments to begin nuclear disarmament. When they took their seats, the new deputies entered the Bundestag as a group, wearing jeans and sweaters, scattering flowers, and singing peace songs.

In 1997 the Greens had a membership of 49,000, with only 3,000 living in the new states. Only 35.5 percent of the membership were females. The Greens probably will never become a mass party like the SPD or CDU, and the leadership prefers a small party with direct links between leaders and members. Most of the members belong to the middle class, and three-quarters of Green Party supporters are under age 35. The party has received above average support from students and academic staff and from young professionals employed in education, health, and social services. Despite the Greens' many problems, from factionalism to organizational weaknesses, they have been on the cutting edge of politics. On the other hand they also have served as a safety valve in the political system. Not only have they made the German system more democratic, but as the largest environmental movement they have become the most influential antiestablishment party in Europe.

Grimm, Jakob (1785–1863), and Wilhelm Karl Grimm (1786–1859)
authors of fairy tales

The Brothers Grimm, Jakob and Wilhelm Karl, became famous as the authors of fairy tales. As scholars they also contributed to comparative linguistics. The Grimm brothers were the most important historians of medieval language and folklore.

A little over two centuries ago the Brothers Grimm were born in the small town of Hanau, Jakob on January 4, 1785, and Wilhelm on February 24, 1786. They grew up playing their games of make-believe together, and their lifelong close relationship made their accomplishments possible. The Grimm family lived nearby the magistrates' house between 1790 and 1796 while the father was employed by the prince of Hesse. The brothers attended school in Kassel, and both studied law at the University of Marburg. It was the inspiration of Friedrich von Savigny who awakened in them an interest in the past. In 1808 Jakob was named court librarian to the king of Westphalia, and in 1816 he became librarian in Kassel, where Wilhelm was also employed. They remained there until 1830, when they secured positions at the UNIVERSITY OF GÖTTINGEN.

The Grimm brothers published their first volume of fairy tales, *Tales of Children and the Home,* in 1812. They had received their stories from peasants and villagers. In their collaboration Jakob did more of the research, while Wilhelm, more fragile, put it into literary form and provided the childlike style. They were also interested in folklore and primitive literature. Between 1816 and 1818 they published two volumes of German legends and also a volume of early literary history.

In time the brothers became interested in older languages and their relation to German. Jakob began to specialize in the history and structure of the German language. The relationships between words became known as Grimm's Law. They gathered immense amounts of data. By 1830 the brothers moved to the University of Göttingen, where Jakob was named professor and head librarian. Wilhelm also became a professor in 1835. Both were dismissed that same year for protesting against the king's decision to abolish the Hanoverian constitution. Their last years were spent in writing a definitive dictionary of the German language, the first volume published in 1854, and it was carried on by future generations.

Wilhelm died in BERLIN on December 16, 1859, while Jakob continued work on the dictionary and related projects until his death in Berlin on September 20, 1863.

Groener, General Wilhelm (1867–1939)
general

General Wilhelm Groener was a senior military leader during WORLD WAR I who convinced the Kaiser to abdicate and accept the Allied peace terms. After the war Groener was responsible for establishing a provisional army, suppressing rebellions, and through the EBERT-GROENER PACT assuring the survival of the General Staff as the central institution of the army.

Wilhelm Groener was born in Württemberg in 1867, a son of a noncommissioned officer. He was extraordinarily capable and won the Kaiser's Prize for the top officer examination score. He was commissioned in the army in 1886, serving most of his career on the General Staff and in the railroad section. Between 1914 and 1917 he served in turn as chief of army railroads, Reich food office, and the General Staff's representative to the Bundesrat. In 1918 Groener took over Erich LUDENDORFF's position as first quartermaster general in October 1918. After the armistice Groener was responsible for bringing the army safely home, organizing a provisional army, and suppressing Communist rebellions in Germany. In return for supporting the civilian socialist government, Groener in the Ebert-Groener Pact assured the survival of the General Staff.

Before retiring in 1919, Groener helped to gain acceptance of the TREATY OF VERSAILLES. During the Weimar period he served as transport minister (1920–23) and defense minister (1928–32). As defense minister he supported military modernization and postwar rearmament. He made the mistake of sponsoring the rise of General Kurt von SCHLEICHER, who conspired against him with the Nazis when as Heinrich BRÜNING's interior minister he banned the brownshirted SA. Schleicher undermined Groener's standing with the army, while HITLER was promising to tolerate a new government if it lifted the ban on the brownshirts. On May 10, 1932, Groener, sick with diabetes, tried to defend the ban on the SA in the REICHSTAG, only to be violently attacked by the Nazi deputies. Groener was forced to resign on May 11, 1932. Brüning's position became increasingly vulnerable to his enemies in the entourage around the aging HINDENBURG, and he tendered his resignation on May 30, 1932. Groener died in Bornstedt, Potsdam, on May 3, 1939.

Gropius, Walter (1883–1969)
architect

Walter Gropius was one of the greatest architects of the 20th century and founder of the BAUHAUS.

Gropius was born in BERLIN on May 18, 1883, the great nephew of the 19th-century classical architect Martin Gropius. Walter studied in Berlin and MUNICH and practiced privately before serving in the army in WORLD WAR I. He was briefly married to the widow of Gustav Mahler from 1915 to 1919.

After 1908 Gropius started to search for an integrated approach to architecture, design, and town planning to create a new architectural form for industrial society. As for so many others, the war itself created a desire for ideas of utopian reform. Even earlier he was imagining ways to apply the latest technological discoveries to his structures. At several exhibitions he replaced the traditional ornamental facade with a transparent steel-and-glass curtain wall. From 1919 to 1928 he founded and was the director of the Bauhaus, a school of art and design that united art, industry, and daily life—a crafts-oriented reform institute. Together with artists such as Lyonel Feininger, Gerhard Marcks, Paul KLEE, Oskar Schlemmer, and Wassily Kandinsky, he worked first in Weimar and from 1925 onward in Dessau. In the process of design he emphasized that it had to begin with the search for the character of an object.

Walter Gropius *(Library of Congress)*

After the Nazis took over, he left Germany in 1934 and worked for two years in London, then in 1937 went to the United States, where he became professor of architecture at Harvard University. His main achievements were the pavilions at the Cologne Exhibition (1914), a factory at Alfeld (1914), a theater at JENA (1922), the Bauhaus at Dessau, and the Harvard Graduate Center (1950). He died in Boston on July 5, 1969.

Grosz, George (1893–1959)
artist

A famous artist during the Weimar Republic, George Grosz became notorious for his bitterly cynical social criticism of society in his drawings and paintings. Motivated by his Communist philosophy he visualized Weimar society as being dominated by militarists, capitalists, and middle-class oppressors of the working class.

Beginning his artistic studies in DRESDEN during 1909, he continued them in BERLIN and until 1913 in Paris. Like other young German artists he had to serve in the military, enduring two troubled tours. Yet, while out of the military, he was involved in antiwar activities and publications. With Germany's defeat and the outbreak of revolution in 1918, he became radicalized, and in 1919 joined the new Communist Party (KPD), contributing to a number of Communist-inspired satirical journals, one of them entitled *Everyone His Own Football* (1921). Grosz also became an aggressive member of the Dada movement in Berlin and had his first major exhibition in MUNICH during 1920. His anticapitalist and antimilitarist drawings appeared in a number of portfolios and cheap books, as, for example, his antimilitarist caricature "Kapp's Menagerie" of soldiers associated with the KAPP PUTSCH, published in *The Face of the Ruling Class*. He analyzed the role of contemporary artists in *Art Is in Danger*. On a trip to the Soviet Union in 1922 he met Lenin and Zinoviev. The middle class and their philistinism were the butts of Grosz's savage cartoons published in *The Philistine Mirror* in 1925 and the *New Face of the Ruling Class* in 1930. He also was known to publish in the famous liberal journal *Simplicissimus* between 1926 and 1932.

The Weimar Republic sought to protect itself by taking Grosz to court for his revolutionary and defamatory drawings of the army, public morality, and even blasphemy. Lucky for him he left Germany for the United States before the Nazis revoked his citizenship. Some 285 of his works were confiscated, and he was included in the DEGENERATE ART exhibition. In New York his drawings commented on the urban scene, but he also did a portfolio of drawings of HITLER's destruction of Europe.

A sample of his social satire can be seen in his painting *Metropolis 1917,* a view of wartime Berlin with its rich capitalist war profiteers and upper-class society of pleasure seekers. After the war he sketched himself drawing pornographic nudes, entitled *Self-Portrait for Charlie Chaplin* (1919). Reflecting his involvement in the Berlin Dada movement, the drawing *Dr. Huelsenbeck Near the End* (1920) pictures an elderly, well-dressed conservative-looking man stymied by the three other people representing various vices, such as a criminal and a prostitute. Grosz included this drawing in the moralistic-sounding portfolio *Ecce Homo* (*Behold the Man*), in which he critiqued the ruling classes for their greed, gluttony, and hedonism. This portfolio was condemned by the courts for obscenity, and most of the drawings were destroyed. Like so many of the Weimar artists, Grosz identified with the NEW OBJECTIVITY (Neue Sachlichkeit) movement, but like Max Beckman and Oskar Kokoschka, not all of its ideals. A prime example of Grosz's exploration of the New Objectivity style was his portrait of the writer Max Hermann-Neisse, in which he employed the Old Master techniques of painting in sharp contours, use of space, and a lack of central focus.

Guderian, Heinz (1888–1954)
expert on tank warfare

Colonel General Heinz Guderian has been called the "architect of the Panzer forces." He was a tank expert who along with the French general Charles de Gaulle and the British general J. F. C. Fuller designed modern mechanized warfare. Guderian along with General Erich von MANSTEIN can be credited with the development of BLITZKRIEG warfare. It was Guderian's training of German motorized forces that provided key elements in the early victories of the German army (Wehrmacht) in Poland, France, and the Soviet Union.

Guderian was born in Kulm, PRUSSIA, on June 7, 1888, into a family that traditionally served in the military. He attended military cadet school and in 1907 joined his father's elite unit. He gained experience in communications as a signals officer, which later was valuable in the development of radio control of large numbers of tanks. Otherwise, during the last year of WORLD WAR I he was assigned to the General Staff Corps and became familiar with the problems of supply in attack and defense. He remained in the army during the Weimar years. He was a liaison officer to a FREE CORPS division and became involved in nationalist politics. In 1922 he was recalled and began his career in modernizing and mechanizing the German army. He learned from theories and tests of armored warfare in England and France. While the French intended to use tanks as an infantry support weapon, Guderian proposed to use armored units that operated independently so as to pierce enemy lines, yet supported by mobile infantry, artillery, and engineers. Although Germany had been forbidden to build tanks by the VERSAILLES TREATY, secret work on tanks was occurring in Germany.

Guderian impressed HITLER with a demonstration of motorized troops in 1934. Then in 1935 he managed to win approval for the development of three panzer divisions, despite resistance from the traditionalists such as General Ludwig BECK. In 1937 Guderian published *Achtung! Panzer!*, which elaborated his lectures and discussions of tactics. In 1938 he was promoted to the rank of General der Panzertruppen, becoming the chief of mobile troops on the army General Staff. During the Blomberg-Fritsch crisis he was identified as pro-Nazi, which contributed to his rapid promotion. During the occupation of AUSTRIA his motorized units broke down. The invasion of Poland, however, proved that panzers were an essential part of blitzkrieg tactics and were an unqualified success. His panzer units destroyed thousands of cannons and several infantry divisions. With the invasion of France, Guderian supported General Erich von Manstein's plan to attack through the Ardennes forest. Guderian's units advanced so fast they were repeatedly ordered to halt by Hitler, who was worried that they might be cut off from the slower infantry. His push to the coast at Abbeville split the Allied armies in half.

Guderian protested against Hitler's plan to invade the Soviet Union, which would force Germany into an unfavorable war on two fronts. With his failure to convince Hitler, he dutifully prepared his units for the invasion. On June 22, 1941, the newly formed 2nd Panzer Army participated in the invasion and reached the outskirts of Moscow by December 1. In the autumn and winter conditions the panzer units broke down, and his troops froze in their summer clothing. Russian counterattacks occurred, and Guderian disobeyed orders, allowing tactical withdrawals. Hitler was so angry that he forced Guderian to resign and demoted him on Christmas Day. In 1943 he was recalled as inspector-general of armored troops, given the task of procurement and testing of equipment. The conspirators of the July 20, 1944, plot tried to recruit Guderian, but he remained loyal to Hitler. Guderian was appointed to the Court of Honor, which was to judge officers arrested in the conspiracy. The court expelled the officers from the army and transferred them for trial to the notorious PEOPLE'S COURT. After the assassination attempt he was promoted to chief of army staff, which he was to hold until March 1945, when Hitler forced him to take sick leave. Guderian surrendered to the Americans, was not found guilty of war crimes, and was released in 1947. His autobiography, *Panzer Leader*, was published in 1952. Shortly thereafter he died in Swangau bei Füssen, BAVARIA, on May 15, 1954.

Gutenberg, Johannes (1397–1468)
inventor

Johannes Gutenberg was not the inventor of printing but of uniform pieces of movable metal type, which for the first time made it possible to print books in large quantities. A revolution in printing made possible the rapid dissemination of knowledge and ideas, in effect creating a communications revolution. Without his invention the widespread impact of Martin LUTHER's

REFORMATION would have been inconceivable and the scientific revolution impossible.

Johannes Gutenberg was born with the name Henne Gensfleisch zur Laden about 1397, the son of a burgher in Mainz, Friele Gensfleisch. The name, Gutenberg, was derived from his father's residence in Mainz, the Haus zum Gutenberg. Nothing is known about his early life until in 1430 he was forced into exile in a dispute between the patrician leaders of the city and the guildsmen. He moved to Strasbourg, where he operated a goldsmith shop. In the process of his metallurgical experiments he discovered an alloy that could be poured into molds to form letters when cooled and which when assembled could form a page. This movable type, as it has been called, could be reassembled in an endless variation to print an entire book or many copies or many different books.

After returning to Mainz in 1448, Gutenberg borrowed money from a Johannes Fust in order to set up his press and print the Latin Bible. The sum of guilders was enormous, and Gutenberg was not able to pay it back. So Fust sued Gutenberg in 1455 and forced Gutenberg into bankruptcy and took over his press. Fust and his son-in-law, P. Schöffer, continued the business and actually were the printers of the first books. Gutenberg was not discouraged and began printing books again but on a smaller scale, in 1457 printing a Psalter and in 1460 a Latin dictionary. In 1462 the elector Adolf II of Nassau seized Mainz, and the burghers were driven out of the city. Gutenberg built another press in Eltville, and later was granted a pension in 1465 by the elector Adolf of Nassau. Gutenberg remained a bachelor and died still in debt on February 3, 1468.

Printing most probably was first invented in China, but for 150 years before Gutenberg's innovation texts had been printed in Europe from carved wooden plates. Gutenberg's movable metal type was made in a complex procedure and cast in a handheld instrument that Gutenberg himself invented. Gutenberg formulated his own ink, and his printing press was modeled after wine presses. His greatest accomplishment was the printing of 180 copies of the Latin Bible in double columns of 42 lines; it was 1,292 pages long. The printing of the Bible was made to look like a handwritten manuscript and took three years to complete.

H

Habermas, Jürgen (1929–)
philosopher and sociologist

Jürgen Habermas has been a challenging social scientist who built on the Frankfurt School in order to address the problems of political culture. During the 1970s he involved himself in political questions on the suspension of civil liberties. Between 1971 and 1983 he was the director of the Max Planck Institute for Social Research near MUNICH. In the 1980s he initiated the historical debate *Historikerstreit* with his criticisms of the neonationalism of conservative revisionist historians writing on Nazism and the world wars. He has affirmed human rationality and communication and elaborated a critical theory of modernity in his major work, *Theory of Communicative Action* (1981).

Jürgen Habermas was born in DÜSSELDORF on June 18, 1929, and spent his boyhood years in Gummersbach nearby. At the end of the war he reacted with horror to the revelations of the brutality of Nazi terror. In 1946 he began his university studies at BONN and read and speculated on the concepts of reason, freedom, and justice. He received his doctorate in 1954, writing his dissertation on the philosopher Friedrich von Schelling. Then he became an assistant to Professor Theodor Adorno, who was associated with the Frankfurt School. Later Habermas would become the successor to its tradition. His investigations gained him an international reputation as the first major German social and political theorist to make important contributions to the understanding of democratic societies.

The subjects on which he wrote ranged widely from analyses of postwar Germany to commentaries on MARX. Habermas's overall goal was to construct a social theory that could affect the emancipation of people from arbitrary social constraints. He pursued this goal in hundreds of articles and books. In *Theory and Practice* (1962) he analyzed how political ideals were realized in Western civilization. Then he compared the methods of the social sciences with those of the natural sciences and how scientific measurements could be applied to human beings in *The Logic of the Social Sciences* (1967). Then he followed with *Knowledge and Human Interests* (1981), in which he emphasized the importance of language in human evolution. In the early 1970s he examined the ideological roles that science and technology played in the modernization of society in *Toward a Rational Society* (1971), which was quickly followed by *The Legitimation Crisis* (1973), which analyzed legitimacy problems in modern societies. Many of these studies were published while he was director of the Max Planck Institute, where he had assembled scholars from different disciplines and tried to explain the basic conditions of modern society. Habermas's most important work was *The Theory of Communicative Action*, which built on his earlier work and developed a critical theory of modernity, which involved a concept of society that integrated what he called "the lifeworld paradigm" with its social context, or "system paradigm."

Although he had been a student of Marxism, he objected to Marx's reduction of history and culture to mere economic processes (economic determinism). In Habermas's *Theory of Social Action* (1981) and *Critique of Functionalist Reason* (1984) he provided a contemporary critique of older famous social thinkers such as Max WEBER, Emile Durkheim, Theodor Adorno, and Talcott Parsons in their methodology and conclusions.

Habermas continued to get involved in the political questions of the day. He has been critical of German politics, finding it deficient in democratic attitudes. During the student demonstrations of the 1960s he became an important spokesman for academic reform, but also blamed militant student behavior for interrupting democratic processes. When Germany was faced by the threat of terrorism, he opposed the suspension of civil liberties.

Habsburg dynasty

The Habsburg dynasty became the imperial family of Austria. The Habsburg family descended from the German Count Rudolf of Habsburg, who became Holy Roman Emperor from 1273 to 1279 and who bestowed the duchy of AUSTRIA on his son Albrecht. The male line died out in 1740, when Emperor CHARLES VI was succeeded by his only daughter, MARIA THERESA. She was married to the duke of Lorraine, and from 1745 the dynasty was known as the House of Habsburg-Lorraine. In 1804, with the proclamation of an Austrian Empire, the archdukes became emperors of Austria. In 1867 the Austrian Empire became the Austro-Hungarian Empire as a result of the *Ausgleich*. The Habsburgs acquired a new kind of constitutional significance in the personal union between Austria and Hungary. In 1918 the Empire came to an end, and German Austria was declared a republic. Until 1921 the Habsburgs technically remained the ruling dynasty of Hungary.

Apart from an interregnum (1740–42) and a second period when a WITTELSBACH (Charles VII of Bavaria) held the office of emperor, there was an almost continuous succession of Habsburg emperors from 1438 until 1806, when the HOLY ROMAN EMPIRE ended. Before 1438 other princes had held the imperial throne, but with the death of Emperor Sigismund (1410–37) during whose rule disorder in the Empire increased, the Imperial crown again reverted to the Habsburgs. A short reign by Albrecht II (1438–39) was followed by the election of FREDERICK III (1440–93), who devoted most of his efforts to the consolidation of Habsburg family possessions so that the power of the Habsburgs overshadowed the other principalities in the Empire. Frederick gave credence to the traditional saying "Let the others wage wars; you, happy Austria, may rely on marriage alliances." And so he did add Burgundy, a united Poland, and Bohemia when the male line of succession expired, Luxembourg and the Netherlands, and when Charles inherited the immense territorial possessions of his parents (Philip and Joanna) and at the death of his maternal grandfather, Ferdinand, in 1516, Charles also became the sovereign of Spain, Sardinia, Sicily, Naples, and the Spanish-Castilian possessions in the Americas. When Emperor MAXIMILIAN I died in 1519, the domains of his grandson Charles were further increased by the vast hereditary Habsburg territories in Germany. It was quite true that in the realm of CHARLES V the Sun never set.

Hallstein Doctrine (1955)

The Hallstein Doctrine was a foreign policy doctrine of the FEDERAL REPUBLIC (FRG) that sought to prevent international recognition of the GERMAN DEMOCRATIC REPUBLIC (GDR) by refusing to maintain diplomatic relations with countries that established relations with East Germany. The Hallstein Doctrine provided West Germany's basic foreign policy guideline from the mid-1950s to the OSTPOLITIK of Chancellor Willy BRANDT (1913–92).

Walter Hallstein (1901–82), a chief foreign policy adviser to and Foreign Office manager under Konrad ADENAUER, was a staunch advocate of Western integration and one of the authors of the Hallstein Doctrine. It was first enunciated in 1955 and threatened to terminate or not establish diplomatic relations with countries that recognized and established diplomatic relations with East Germany. The only exception to this rule was the Soviet Union, with which BONN established diplomatic relations and exchanged ambassadors in 1955.

The Hallstein Doctrine was based on the principle enunciated in the preamble to the BASIC LAW that the West German government in Bonn was the sole legal representative of Germany and spoke for all the German people until a government could be freely elected by the people in both East and West Germany. The Hallstein Doctrine effectively prevented Bonn from establishing formal diplomatic relations with the governments of Eastern Europe, which already maintained diplomatic relations with the Communist government in East Berlin. For example, when the government of Yugoslavia decided to diplomatically recognize the GDR in 1957, the Bonn government had to break its relations with Belgrade. In effect, the Hallstein Doctrine anchored the Federal Republic ever more securely to the West. It deprived the Federal Republic of having any diplomatic influence in Eastern Europe and eliminated any possibilities of trade with countries that had previously been active trading partners. This made the Hallstein Doctrine the subject of the criticism that it mainly served to consolidate the Communist regimes in Eastern Europe because they could justify their dictatorships by portraying the Federal Republic as a continuation of past aggressive German governments.

The Hallstein Doctrine worked to prevent Western nations from recognizing the German Democratic Republic; West German foreign aid programs also were used to influence underdeveloped countries in Africa and Asia not to recognize the GDR. There was, however, an unintended effect, which made the Bonn government susceptible to extortion when countries discovered that they could demand grants in exchange for not recognizing East Germany.

Hambach Festival (1832)

A high point in early German LIBERALISM was the great popular festival held at the old castle ruins near the town of Hambach in May 1832 in the Bavarian Palatinate. It was meant to be a German version of the revolutionary festivals held in France during the revolution. The Wartburg meeting of 1817 had been an earlier example, celebrating the *Volk* (German people), while in 1830 during the revolutions public political festivals again were held. The Hambach gathering was an extension of these earlier ones, but this time a festival celebrating constitutions, a Konstitutionsfest, with a variety of leaders and politically informed participants who were more socially diverse.

On May 27, 1832, almost 30,000 people gathered at Neustadt and marched with black-red-gold flags proclaiming Germany's rebirth. The festival was not intended to be a protest march or be violent, but rather an educational instrument attempting to teach about the reforms that were necessary. A diversity of speakers emphasized the common theme of a unified and free Germany, not with a conservative restrictive suffrage as in PRUSSIA, but popular sovereignty and economic freedom.

This presented the Austrian chancellor, METTERNICH, with another excuse to suppress liberalism. In 1830 the rebellions in Poland and Belgium had disturbed him, and he sent Austrian troops to Italy to restore order. In the weeks following the Hambach Festival, the chancellor tried to do what he had after the assassination of Kotzebue in 1817, that is to repress these expressions of liberalism. In early July the diet of the Confederation passed the Ten Articles, which emphasized the existing rules on censorship and dangerous political activity, promising military assistance to suppress political unrest. In June 1833 the Confederation decided to investigate troublemakers through a Central Bureau of Political Investigation. And in September of that year Metternich convened a meeting of the rulers of AUSTRIA, Prussia and Russia, where they pledged to firmly oppose revolutionary change. Since the Hambach Festival was held in Bavaria, King LUDWIG I appointed Prince Wrede as commissioner for the Palatinate, where he established martial law. Some speakers were tried and imprisoned, while others were deported or fled. The troops pacified the Palatinate, political organizations were dissolved, and the forces of reform crumbled. Reactionary governments in Hesse-Kassel, HANOVER, and SAXONY also followed Metternich's lead. Despite the victory of reactionary governments, their triumphs were short-lived, and political ferment continued throughout Germany.

Hamburg

Hamburg is Germany's second-largest city, its largest port and major center for shipping at the mouth of the ELBE RIVER, a federal state, and the largest city-state in Germany.

Founded in the early ninth century by Charlemagne, it soon became an archepiscopal see and a center for missionary activity. During the later Middle Ages it became an important port and regional city, becoming one of the founders of the Hanseatic League. In 1510 it became one of the IMPERIAL CITIES, and in the 1520s it was influenced by the REFORMATION. Hamburg became a Lutheran city and experienced a population growth with the influx of Protestant immigrants. This led to a tolerant attitude toward strangers, which gave way to an undisturbed development of trade. In the late 18th century the ENLIGHTENMENT restructured the political system of Hamburg. Reforms within the city included the promotion of the arts and crafts and under the sponsorship of the Patriotic Society, democratization, religious tolerance, vocational training, and social work. By the eve of the French Revolution Hamburg possessed a population of about 70,000 and was the third-largest city after Vienna and Cologne.

During the NAPOLEONIC WARS the French had a great impact on the city. In 1806 the French occupied Hamburg and forced some 20,000 citizens into exile. The hardships lasted until 1816, when the city reverted to the control of its city council. Hamburg became a member of the GERMAN CONFEDERATION as an autonomous state, which status it continued to enjoy after unification in IMPERIAL GERMANY (1871–1918). During the 19th century Hamburg emerged as a cosmopolitan city, and industrialization made it a center of the labor movement. Its trade also increased phenomenally, which made it one of the most prosperous areas in Germany. After WORLD WAR I the city was governed by a coalition government of the SPD and DDP, which lasted until 1933. With the Nazi regime the terror of the dictatorship affected Hamburg as elsewhere. Jews were persecuted, and during the Allied bombing raids of WORLD WAR II a great deal of destruction occurred, especially with the fire bombing of the city. Since the end of the war Hamburg has enjoyed more independence than ever before, while the SPD has dominated its politics, though the GREEN PARTY has challenged its dominance. Because of the loss of the city's hinterland to East Germany, its shipping declined. Other industries have taken its place, however, in the fields of banking, insurance, publishing, chemicals, and electronics. By the end of the 20th century the population grew to 1.7 million and the "guest workers," mainly Turks, make up more than 10 percent of the population.

Handel, George Frideric (1685–1759)
baroque composer

On February 23, 1685, George Frideric Handel was born in Halle, Germany. He was taught composition as well as the organ, violin, and oboe. Within 10 years he was composing for these and other instruments. Under the influence of Georg Philipp Telemann, Handel composed voluminously. In his early teens he was already a keyboard prodigy. His father died in 1697, and Handel kept a promise to him to complete his study of law at the university. In 1703 he decided to make a career of music and gained valuable experience in an opera orchestra. In 1706 he traveled to Italy, where he met the leading musicians and began his own operatic career.

Handel was a brilliant composer, interpreter, opera director, producer, impresario, and entrepreneur. During his four-year stay in Italy he composed the opera *Agrippina,* which met with sensational success and secured him a reputation throughout Europe. In 1712 Handel moved to London, where he spent the next 40 years and profoundly influenced English music. Outstanding among his numerous accomplishments are his organ works, the *Water Music* and the *Music for the Royal Fireworks*. His most inspired work comprised his biblically inspired oratorios, above all *Messiah*. Handel completed some 35 operas.

Hanover
(German: Hannover)

Hanover, also known as "the city of fairs" and "the garden city," is located in northwestern Germany on the Leine River and Mittelland Canal. It also is situated where the Harz Mountains meet the North German Plain. Hanover has a distinctive history, having been joined to the British throne, which was begun by Elector George Ludwig of Hanover, who became King George I of England and who joined England and Hanover in a personal union until 1837.

Hanover originated as a market town in the middle of the 12th century as *vicus Hanovere*. It received its municipal charter from Henry the Lion. With the division of the Welf (Guelf) possessions Hanover was ruled by the Calenberg family. In 1636 the duke of Calenberg moved his residence to Hanover. During the latter 17th century under the elector Ernst August (1679–98) the city enjoyed a cultural flowering, and LEIBNIZ stimulated the intellectual life with his presence. Duke Ernst August united the territory, and in 1692 Hanover became a principality. At this time the magnificent and famous Herrenhausen Gardens were designed in the BAROQUE style. In 1714 the elector George Ludwig of Hanover succeeded to the British throne as King George I, creating a personal union that lasted until 1837. The UNIVERSITY OF GÖTTINGEN also was located in the kingdom of Hanover, and it was here that the conflict of the Göttingen Seven professors with the new ruler, Ernst August, duke of Cumberland, occurred over his demand of an oath of

Osterstrasse, Hameln in Hanover, 1900 *(Library of Congress)*

allegiance. In the 19th century Hanover also enjoyed considerable prosperity and was the capital of the kingdom of Hanover from 1814 until 1866, when it lost its sovereignty by Prussian annexation after the Austro-Prussian War. This also gave rise to the German Hanoverian Party, which opposed the annexation and was the home state of Ludwig WINDTHORST of the newly formed Catholic CENTER PARTY. During WORLD WAR II approximately 60 percent of the city was destroyed, especially by the British. After the war that part of the city was totally rebuilt.

Known as a city of trade fairs, Hanover is also an industrial city and serves as one of the most important traffic junctions in northern Germany.

Hardenberg, Friedrich Leopold, Baron von (Friedrich Leopold Freiherr [Baron] von Hardenberg; Novalis) (1772–1801)

poet

Known as Novalis, Baron Friedrich Leopold von Hardenberg was the most important poet and imaginative writer of the early romantic movement. Both his prose and poetry express a mystical conviction in the symbolic meaning and unity of life.

Studying philosophy and law at the universities of JENA and LEIPZIG, he became friends with the philosopher Johann Gottlieb FICHTE, the poet Friedrich von SCHILLER, and with the romantic theoretician Friedrich von SCHLEGEL. After studying at the University of Wittenberg from 1794 to 1796 Novalis became a government official at Tennstädt. Engaged to Sophie von Kühn when she was only 13, he became distraught with sorrow when she died in 1797. Overwhelmed with her death, Novalis converted to a kind of Christian mysticism, which inspired him to become a poet. He did not remain single, however, and married Julie von Charpentier in 1798 while still continuing his "mystical union" with Sophie. His practical employment was in the area of mine inspector and later as supervisor.

His longings to be reunited with Sophie inspired him to his private lyrical agony in *Hymns to Night,* in which Novalis dreams of an infinity combining the world of light with the world of night and centering on the creative power of love, which he believed Christ has opened up. The *Hymns* are a Christian myth of redemption, which belong to the future, and the poet has to prepare the way for it by overcoming the visible world. Such thoughts as nature in the future changing into a world of spirits are found in Novalis's *Athenaeum* under the poetic title of "pollen." They were written under the influence of Fichte's *Wissenschaftslehre* and the identity philosophy of Schelling. The latter thought that nature was a gradual manifestation of the spirit.

Novalis thought that the natural world was composed of symbols and that poets could discover their meaning. He develops these in his unfinished novel, *Heinrich von Ofterdingen.* It relates the initiation of a young medieval poet into the mysteries of his calling. Going on a journey and as he receives his poetic instruction, he falls in love. The theme of the novel is the harmony and eternal significance of all life and nature and the union of reality and imagination. The poet's goal is to revive the Golden Age and overcome the domination of reason. The symbol of the "Blue Flower" is a sign that transforms all under it into one great whole. The "Blue Flower" later became the favorite symbol of the romantics for mystical aspiration.

Mysticism also found expression in his *Religious Songs* and an essay, *Christendom or Europe* (1799). Some of his writings were unfinished. But the mantle of mystical Christianity envelops the whole of Novalis's work. His own religious background was Protestant, but the trend of his personality and thought like many of his contemporary romantics was Roman Catholic. Here he found the power of the absolute and the importance of authority. Sick with tuberculosis, he died at age 29 on March 25, 1801, at Weissenfels.

Hardenberg, Prince Karl August von (1750–1822)

Prussian minister

Prince Karl von Hardenberg became PRUSSIA's leading minister of reform after its defeat by France in 1806.

Karl August von Hardenberg was born in Essenrode on May 31, 1750, and even as a young man demonstrated his abilities in the employ of Hanover, Braunschweig, and Ansbach-Bayreuth. In 1791 he became a servant of the Prussian state when Ansbach-Bayreuth was taken over that year. By 1804 his excellent service in diplomatic assignments led to his appointment as Prussian foreign minister. Hardenberg had great charm and knowledge of human nature. He also embraced ideas from both the French Revolution and the Napoleonic state administrative system. He continued the Prussian reform inaugurated by Baron Karl vom und zum Stein. His implementation of the emancipation of the peasantry and the emancipation of the Jews in 1812 reflected his ideas of civic equality.

In 1807 Hardenberg wrote his famous *Memoir*, in which he insisted on social and economic reorganization according to the principles of enlightened individualism combined with a strong centralized state bureaucracy. He advocated the reforms of the educational system according to the ideas of Johann Pestalozzi. Schools were to be separated from the state and the established church. Hardenberg supported the secularization of church property. The amount realized from the sale was to be applied to the national debt. In economics he abolished guild constitutions. With the new tax bills of 1811 he introduced a general ground tax, extending the consumer's tax and the duty on luxury articles over the entire country. Freedom of trade was proclaimed. Hardenberg agreed with Adam Smith that unlimited competition was "the best incentive and regulative principles of industry." The principles on which the new legislation was based were equality before the law, freedom of ownership, and freedom of contract. Understandably, opposition to this new legislation was strong among the nobility and large landowners. In agriculture he also applied the theories of Adam Smith, making the profit motive the basic principle of agriculture; the basis of the new system was the deathblow to the patriarchical economics of the landed nobility. It was through Hardenberg's power as chancellor of the state that he won over the forces of conservatism.

In foreign policy Hardenberg was the master statesman. He knew precisely when Prussia should reenter the war against Napoleon, and he upheld his reputation as an outstanding negotiator when he successfully represented Prussia in the territorial reorganization of Europe at the Congress of Vienna in 1814–15, at which Prussia was able to recover all the territory it had lost under the Tilsit Treaty in 1807. In the new Prussia enlarged at the congress he created an exemplary administrative system. He made continuous efforts to get Frederick William III to honor his promise to grant a constitution, but unfortunately the king and aristocracy were too wrapped up in the reactionary spirit of the times. Himself a liberal, Hardenberg was placed in an impossible position of representing Prussia at the postwar reactionary conferences whose goals it was to repress liberalism. On November 26, 1822, the great statesman died in Genoa.

Harzburg Front (1931)
conservative nationalists

The Harzburg Front was an alliance of right-wing nationalists meeting in 1931 in the town of Bad Harzburg in Brunswick (Braunschweig) to oppose the government of Heinrich Brüning and to establish a "national government." Represented were the Nationalists, the pan-Germans, the Stahlhelm, and the Junker Landbund. The list of prominent personalities included Adolf Hitler, Alfred Hugenberg, head of the German National People's Party, Fritz Thyssen, director of the United Steel Works, Franz Seldte, head of the Stahlhelm, and Hjalmar Schacht, banker and economics expert.

Hugenberg demanded that Germany be rescued from the Bolshevik peril and from bankruptcy, urged Brüning's resignation and new elections. He described Otto Braun and Carl Severing, the principal Social Democratic members of the Prussian cabinet, as "the German Kerenskys." He alleged that the Reich stood at a crossroads of choosing either the Russian or German way. In order to save the country from Bolshevism and economic bankruptcy, the national opposition was prepared to take over political control in PRUSSIA and in the Reich. Hitler also spoke and predicted that either Bolshevism or NATIONALISM would triumph in Germany.

At Harzburg a potentially mighty combination was being formed. It had the wealth, the prestige, and influence of a powerful political alliance. With Hitler's support it could have had the mass voter support also. Between the Harzburg Front and political power stood the president of the republic, Paul von HINDENBURG, who was able to keep a minority government of Heinrich Brüning in power through the use of Article 48. But Hugenberg's plan to create a shadow cabinet of national opposition and for uniting the right behind a single candidate for the upcoming presidential elections never materialized. Hitler had no intention of diminishing his own strength by combining with the Nationalists. Hitler wanted to stress the strength of the National Socialist movement. From the very outset of the rally he had tried to undermine the show of unity that Hugenberg had intended. And eight days later, a rally of 70,000 SA men descended on Brunswick to demonstrate the strength of the Nazi movement.

Hassel, Ulrich von (1881–1944)
diplomat

Ulrich von Hassel was a conservative critic of many aspects of the Nazi regime and was a leading diplomat in the RESISTANCE against HITLER. He was arrested and executed in connection with the July 20, 1944, plot to assassinate Hitler.

Born in Anklam, Pomerania, on November 12, 1881, he was raised in a deeply religious Christian and conservative patrician family. Educated in the law and languages, he entered the Foreign Office in 1909. In 1911 he married Ilse von Tirpitz, the daughter of the famous admiral and builder of Germany's naval fleet. During WORLD WAR I he served as a captain in the BATTLE OF THE MARNE and was wounded. An indication of his conservative beliefs in the imperial cause was his support for Germany's expansionist war aims and giving Generals Paul von HINDENBURG and Erich LUDENDORFF dictatorial powers in 1916. After the war he denounced the VERSAILLES TREATY and joined the ultra-right GERMAN NATIONAL PEOPLE'S PARTY (DNVP), which was hostile to the republic. Returning to the foreign service, he was stationed in Barcelona, Copenhagen, and Belgrade, and in 1932 in Rome.

At first Hassel approved the early achievements of the Nazi regime but then changed his opinion as the Nazis persecuted Christianity. He opposed the alliance with Italy (Rome-Berlin AXIS) and the Anti-Comintern Pact (the five-year anticommunist pact with Japan). Because of disagreements with Joachim von RIBBENTROP in the Foreign Office, he was dismissed by Hitler in 1937. Joining the Resistance, he associated with General Ludwig BECK and with the help of State Secretary WEIZSÄCKER and the English ambassador Henderson tried to prevent war just before the invasion of Poland. In 1940 he unsuccessfully sought a peaceful end to the war, but insisted that Germany retain some of its territorial acquisitions. Then he participated with other prominent resisters in the KREISAU CIRCLE on the nature of a postwar Germany. Perhaps his most significant contribution was the diaries he kept concerning the activities and problems of the Resistance. Their postwar publication as *The Von Hassel Diaries* (1948) have provided the best source on the Resistance. Hassel was arrested in connection with the July 20th plot to assassinate Hitler carried out by Claus Schenk von STAUFFENBERG. Tried before the PEOPLE'S COURT, Hassel was convicted and hanged at Plötzensee Prison on September 8, 1944.

Hauptmann, Gerhart Johann Robert (1862–1946)
dramatist and novelist

Gerhart Hauptmann was one of Germany's greatest playwrights and novelists. He was best known for naturalistic dramas. He was the leader of the literary school of naturalism coinciding with industrialization and material progress of the late 19th century. Reflected in his works are some of the dominant currents of scientific discovery, especially the effects of heredity and environment. His work also deals with the exploitation of workers, female subservience, the decline of morality, and the need of reform. Hauptmann progressed from NATURALISM to surrealism and reflected many of the prevailing trends in German literature. His mastery lay in the realistic development of his characters, his compassion for the poor and downtrodden, and man's helplessness in a world beyond his control.

Gerhart Hauptmann was born in Obersalzbrunn in Silesia on November 15, 1862, the son of a hotel owner. He was an art student at BRESLAU University, and after years of poverty married up socially to Marie Thieneman, which brought him financial security to pursue his studies at JENA, travel to Italy, and pursue his writing. After studying Charles Darwin, Karl MARX, and Henrik Ibsen, he first attracted the attention of his contemporaries with his naturalist drama *Before Dawn* (*Vor Sonnenaufgang*), which exposed the ugly conditions of the poor Silesian mining districts and advocated social reforms. It was performed in BERLIN during October 1889, supported by the society Freie Bühne. It used an analytical technique and emphasized the role of heredity. The degradation of a family hopelessly burdened by a variety of vices including alcoholism is not saved by a socialist reformer who breaks up with the woman, Helene, whom he fears will fall victim to hereditary alcoholism; she commits suicide in despair. Other plays followed exploring the role of heredity, but his greatest contribution was his play *The Weavers* (*Die Weber*) in 1892, which treated the historical revolt of the Silesian weavers in 1842. Here he portrayed the intolerable working conditions and the callous ignorance of employers, but also the lack of leadership among the workers; the revolt ends in failure. The scenes are vivid, dramatic, and emotional, and the dialogue is earthy. Because of strict censorship *The Weavers* provoked a court trial in 1892, after which other naturalist works were allowed to be publicly staged. Nonetheless, Kaiser WILLIAM II was so offended by *The Weavers* that he refused to attend any more plays and even refused Hauptmann the coveted Schiller Prize. Generally, Hauptmann was a critic of bureaucratic officials and imperial militarism. In 1912, however, he was awarded the Nobel Prize in literature.

In comedies such as *The Beaver Coat* (*Der Biberpelz,* 1894) Hauptmann proved himself a social satirist, applying the principles of naturalism to comedy and drawing an excellent sketch of a saucy and thieving washerwoman. Around the turn of the 20th century Hauptmann wrote two more impressive naturalistic plays, *Drayman Henschel* (*Fuhrmann Henschel,* 1899) and *Rose Bernd,* 1903. Both were tragedies and portray people's futile rebellion against the powers over them. Human loneliness and the inability to help one's fellows were presented in *Michael Kramer,* 1900.

Hauptmann soon broke away from naturalistic formula and experimented with symbolist works by applying the principles of naturalism to historical subjects, including dream figures. One of these experiments was *Hannele* (*Hanneles Himmelfahrt,* 1892), in which the poor daughter of a brutal mason, dying of cold, dreams in her last feverish moments of fairy-tale figures, or angels, and of the Lord Jesus. It is a dream play in a naturalistic setting. The principal theme is the daughter's visions, the compassion of angels, and Christ's help, and not the mistreated or dying child.

Hauptmann wrote 20 novels and narratives, developing psychological themes that he frequently combined with biography. The foremost among them was the apocalyptic novel *The Fool in Christ, Emanuel Quint* (*Der Narr in Christo Emanuel Quintl,* 1910), a tale of a humble Silesian carpenter and preacher who wants to emulate Christ. He is scorned and dies a miserable death. The moral of the story is that the modern individual would lock Christ up in an insane asylum rather than listen to him. Hauptmann's later novels included *Atlantis* (1912). It was a symbolic presentation of the entire bourgeois culture of prewar Germany, which was destroyed by WORLD WAR I.

As Hauptmann's fame grew, he was asked to write a play commemorating Napoleon's defeat at LEIPZIG, which became his only political work and was published as *Commemoration Masque* (1917), in which he embodied his convictions about Social Democracy. During World War I he wrote patriotic poems, and his responses to the war are contained in *Der weisse Heiland* and *Indipohdi*, both in 1920. The former play treats the story of Montezuma, and the latter places Prospero in a Renaissance Mexican setting facing the evil in the world. During the WEIMAR REPUBLIC he was the unofficial poet laureate and was even considered as a candidate for the presidency. After HITLER came to power, Hauptmann remained in Germany and gave up his last optimistic hopes for modern humankind. Too old to start over elsewhere, he did not oppose the Nazis and continued to write plays. He was criticized for being an opportunist and conformist. Although the Nazis dared not silence him, they treated him with suspicion. Suffering deeply from WORLD WAR II, he consummated his long career with *The Tetralogy of the Atrids* (1941–48), treating the same theme as Goethe had in *Iphigenie auf Tauris,* but in a new spirit. Hauptmann rejected Goethe's confidence in people's ability to master elemental forces in favor of the human struggle for goodness while enduring a series of defeats. Iphigenia commits crimes ordained by divine powers, and the struggle within her reflects a conflict among the gods. But what appears as nihilistic is cathartic, and although humankind does not understand what appears to be a futile effort, fate dictates a continuing struggle for goodness.

Hauptmann was extremely gifted, but did not have the intellectual abilities needed to develop these gifts to full advantage. Certainly his prose dramatic work was impressive in power and scope. He died on June 6, 1946, in his home in Agnetendorf and was buried on the Baltic island of Hiddensee, his favorite summer retreat.

Haushofer, Karl (1869–1946), and Albrecht Haushofer (1903–1945)
professors of political geography

Karl Haushofer was the founder of German geopolitics, a modern version of political geography. He thought that Germany needed more living space (LEBENSRAUM) and had to expand to the east. The theories of Karl Haushofer were used as rationalizations by the Nazis for national expansion. His son, Albrecht, also became a professor of political geography but joined the RESISTANCE against HITLER.

Karl Haushofer was born in MUNICH on August 27, 1869, was well educated, traveled widely, and served in WORLD WAR I as a brigadier general. In 1921 he became a professor of political geography at the University of Munich. He advocated the fusion of geography and politics, connecting political relationships and war to geography. He taught that Germany needed lebensraum and should add the agricultural Ukraine to the German industrial heartland. Haushofer influenced the thinking of the young student Rudolf HESS, who transmitted Haushofer's ideas to Hitler. When Hess flew to Scotland, he claimed that the idea came from Professor Karl Haushofer. Geopolitics became the fashion in Nazi Germany, and Haushofer won a reputation he did not want, as the "Man behind Hitler." Because of his son Albrecht's involvement in the July 1944 attempt on Hitler's life, he was arrested and after the war he committed suicide on March 13, 1946.

Albrecht Haushofer was Karl's son, born in Munich on January 7, 1903. He became a professor of political geography in 1940 at the University of BERLIN and during the same year went to work in the Foreign Office. More critical of Nazism than his father, he considered National Socialism a disaster and joined the Resistance. He was arrested in connection with the July Plot of 1944. He wrote the "Moabit Sonnets" in Moabit Prison in Berlin, which were preserved by accident and published later. The GESTAPO killed him on April 23, 1945, while he was being transferred to another prison just before the war ended.

Haydn, Joseph (1732–1809)
composer

Joseph Haydn practically invented the classical musical forms of symphony, concerto, string

Joseph Haydn *(Library of Congress)*

quartet, and sonata. It was his hard work and genius that laid the foundations for the great works of Mozart, Beethoven, and SCHUBERT.

Haydn was born in the village of Rohrau in Lower Austria near the border of Hungary. As he was one of 12 children, his father was unable to provide much education except what was available at the village school and church choir. It so happened that the Imperial choirmaster of St. Stephen's Cathedral in Vienna heard the superior soprano voice of the eight-year-old boy. For several years he was the leading boy soloist, but by age 17 he was out on the streets earning a living as a music teacher. His major breakthrough came when Prince Paul Anton Esterházy, one of the richest landowners of the Empire, heard one of his symphonies and offered him a job. Haydn was fortunate to have the use of a good orchestra and two theaters. In 1766 Haydn was given full control and became popular with the aristocratic visitors who came to the estate. Soon his name was widely known, publishers printed his works, and he was able to compose without financial anxiety. Even MARIA THERESA attended one of Haydn's symphonies in 1775. Haydn composed some 25 operas. A distinctive symphony, *The Farewell Symphony,* played with dramatic effects, was composed during the Storm and Stress period.

In the 1780s Haydn's reputation had spread rapidly, which allowed him to publish his works and to compose for other patrons. In 1785 he became a Freemason (*see* FREEMASONRY) and composed some works for a Parisian Masonic lodge, which resulted in the Paris symphonies (nos. 82–87). He was persuaded by the London impresario Johann Peter Salomon to visit England, where he was celebrated by the court and high society. In July 1791 Oxford University honored him with the degree of Doctor of Music, and the symphony played for the occasion was No. 92, known as the *Oxford Symphony.* His 12 well-received London symphonies (nos. 93–104) were commissioned by Salomon and were known as "Salomon" symphonies. In 1794 and 1795 he visited England again, but resisted King George's gracious invitation to stay permanently.

Haydn's perfection of the classical symphonic form has been described as one of the greatest achievements in the whole history of the arts. Yet he also composed great religious music. During his last years he returned to Vienna in the employ of a new Esterhazy prince who required sacred music for his court. Between 1796 and 1802 Haydn produced six Latin masses, including the *Mass in Time of War* and the *Nelson Mass,* which reflected the political turmoil of the NAPOLEONIC WARS. His last major creations were superb Handelian oratorios, *The Creation* (1798) and *The Seasons* (1801). He had the honor to compose the Austrian national anthem, "God Save the Emperor Francis."

On his 76th birthday he made his last public appearance at a performance of *The Creation* at Vienna University. In May 1809, during the Napoleonic occupation of Vienna, he died.

Hegel, Georg Wilhelm Friedrich
(1770–1831)
philosopher

The last romantic idealist philosopher, Georg Wilhelm Friedrich Hegel formulated a comprehensive philosophy stressing that the state was the highest expression of the development of universal reason. Some of his conclusions were incorporated into the German nationalist ideology. For Hegel the state was a manifestation of the "world spirit" operating in history. Antithetically, his view also led to the dialectical philosophies of Karl MARX and Ludwig FEUERBACH.

Born in Stuttgart on August 27, 1770, the son of a government official, Georg received a classical education and later with his Pietist father's encouragement entered the Lutheran seminary in Tübingen. He completed his theological education in 1793, although manifesting a greater interest in politics and the secular writings of Jean-Jacques Rousseau. At the seminary Hegel read German and Greek literature and enjoyed the friendships of the poet Friedrich HÖLDERIN and the idealist and romantic philosopher Friedrich Wilhelm Joseph von Schelling. All three sympathized with the French Revolution and its emphasis on freedom and reason. In 1797 Hegel was employed as a private tutor in FRANKFURT, where his employer had a fine library and where Hegel had time to write. After 1799 he began to prepare for an academic career, living with Schelling, then a professor at the University of JENA. Here he completed his first book on the differences between the philosophies of Johann Gottlieb FICHTE and that of Schelling, discovering that their philosophies were irreconcilable. Deciding to develop his own comprehensive system of philosophy, he wrote *The Phenomenology of Spirit*, completed in 1806, the very day that Napoleon's troops were occupying Jena. Over the next decade Hegel was editor of a newspaper, for eight years the headmaster of a secondary school (*Gymnasium*) in NUREMBERG, married in 1811, and appointed a professor of philosophy at the University of HEIDELBERG, where he published *The Encyclopedia of the Philosophical Sciences in Outline* in 1817, which furthered his philosophical thought, emphasizing that self-knowledge was the attainment of true freedom. That same year he was appointed a professor at the University of BERLIN and promoted to rector in 1830. Shortly thereafter, on November 14, 1831, he died during a cholera epidemic.

In *The Phenomenology of Spirit* Hegel discussed the manifestation in history of the Spirit possessed by all men. The Spirit is both general and particular to individuals, developing in stages. In his discussion Hegel proceeds from the simplest level of sense experience to abstract absolute knowledge. At the foundation of Hegel's philosophy of history is the progression of the Spirit according to the stages of a dialectical process through a succession of internal opposition and reconciliation. In the third stage of this process, the formation of culture (ethics and the administration of justice), there is also God's self-realization in man. Like the historian Leopold von RANKE, Hegel believed that there was an immanent divine providence in history.

Hegel also sought to demonstrate that reason expresses itself in the concrete events of history, not in the form of static concepts. Reason is embodied in the individual, concrete, historical states, empires, artistic styles, philosophies, and religions. The process by which reason manifests itself is through the union of opposites, which operates in historical development as it does in the logic of the individuals' reasoning. The reconciliation of opposites takes place in the dialectical fusion of thesis and antithesis to form a third higher level of synthesis. This process is continuous in history, leading to the unfolding of all the possibilities in the universal reason. According to his view of history, in the first, or oriental stage, the monarch alone had been free, but in the Greek and Roman stages an elite minority had achieved freedom. It was, however, in the last stage that the Germanic nations were destined to play a special role, bringing about the the advancement of universal reason and realization of freedom for all people. The highest expression of the development of the universal reason, however, was the state. Reacting to the ENLIGHTENMENT's emphasis on individualism, Hegel asserted that the state was much more than an institution for the satisfaction of individual needs, but had the historical mission to bring a nation to self-consciousness. The state was the essence of morality as a manifestation of the "world spirit" operating in history. The whole process, Hegel assumed, reached its consummation in the rational ideal order, the Prussian bureaucratic-military state.

Each age in history was regarded by Hegel as a stage in the onward march of the universal reason toward its consummation and the creation of an ideal society. The ambiguity of Hegel's famous phrase "what is real is rational and what is rational is real," has been used by both conservatives and radicals. Conservatives interested in justifying the status quo have emphasized that the present reality of existence is rational. Conversely, radicals such as Karl Marx have stressed the other half of the formula, that what is rational is the true reality and that the dialectical process of history would inevitably progress toward a rational proletarian society. So while conservatives found justification for the Prussian state, radicals also found a theory of historical development that envisioned progressive change, sometimes in revolutionary leaps forward.

The first complete edition of his works totaled 19 volumes published between 1832 and 1840, which contributed to Hegel's influence in Germany and the world throughout the latter 19th century and into the 20th. The influence of his thought was felt in Prussian and German cultural development and in secondary school development. It dominated German approaches to intellectual history and to the history of literature. His philosophy of religion has influenced German and well as English theology. But more significantly, Hegel also contributed to the peculiar development of German NATIONALISM. The belief in the special historical destiny of the Germanic peoples became an integral part of German nationalism. Although this is denied by some, Hegel gave his support to the Prussian state as an agent destined by history to bring the German people to self-consciousness, and contributed to the growing prestige of the Prussian monarchy throughout Germany. It is, however, undoubtedly true that Hegel provided the theoretical justification for the conservative nationalism of the late 19th century and the state worship of FASCISM in the 20th.

Heidegger, Martin (1889–1976)
philosopher

Martin Heidegger was born to Catholic parents in Messkirch, Baden. At first he studied to be a JESUIT priest, then served in WORLD WAR I and afterwards turned to the study of philosophy. He became privatdozent at the University of Freiburg, in 1923 a professor at Marburg, and in 1928 a professor at Freiburg. While a student at Freiburg, he had been trained in the phenomenological method of Edmund HUSSERL. Heidegger's first book, *Being and Time,* was dedicated to Husserl. In 1933 Heidegger became rector at Freiburg and reformed the university in line with his philosophy and with Nazism. In a public lecture titled "The Role of the University in the New Reich" he celebrated the advent of a new Germany. Soon he became disillusioned with Nazi leaders, resigning as rector of Freiburg, yet never disavowing his praises of the National Socialist movement.

Although he denied that he was an existentialist, he is widely considered the central figure in contemporary existentialist thought. Heidegger's greatest concern was for humans to understand the essence and meaning of being. In human existence "it is nature, the vocation of man, to ask the all important question, what is it, to be? And yet we fail to ask it, and it is our nature equally, or responsibility and our guilt, that we fail to do so." In his later work he focused on the essence of technology as a means of scientifically understanding humanity. Yet, his enduring concern for the nature of being led him to deny that realm to science but claim it for philosophy. Heidegger referred to Greek classical thought and the German poets, especially Friedrich HÖLDERIN. Holding to a mystical view of language, he subscribed zealously to the belief that philosophizing was possible only in German and Greek. In his later years he envisaged a post-technological era in which humanity might still be saved.

Heidelberg

Heidelberg is a university city located in the Palatinate in the present state of BADEN-WÜRTTEMBERG. It is 50 miles south of FRANKFURT AM MAIN. It occupies one of Germany's most picturesque sites along the Neckar River where it emerges from the Odenwald onto the Rhine plain. The location was of great strategic significance during the Middle Ages, since it guards the entrance to the Neckar Valley. In the 13th century the counts Palatine made their residence here, and it was the capital of the Palatinate until 1720. In 1386 Count Ruprecht I founded the famous university. He also began the construction of the castle. The city was ravaged during the THIRTY YEARS' WAR but was rebuilt afterward. Heidelberg Castle was made habitable, and the huge wine barrel was repaired. In the WAR OF THE LEAGUE OF AUGSBURG (1688–97) Heidelberg was devastated by the French armies, which destroyed the whole city and blew up the castle and other fortifications between 1689 and 1693. In 1720 the elector Karl Philipp moved his capital to MANNHEIM. In 1802 during the NAPOLEONIC WARS the Palatinate was taken from the WITTELSBACH dynasty and was given to the duke Karl of Baden.

The castle was one of the greatest examples of German Renaissance architecture. It was a magnificent residence of the electors built during the reigns of Otto Heinrich (1556–59), Friedrich IV (1583–1610), and Friedrich V (1610–20). After the French blew up the castle, it remained a picturesque ruin. The Friedrichsbau is an example of the mature German Renaissance, containing the statues of the rulers of the Palatinate.

The University of Heidelberg is the oldest in Germany. It was a center of Germanism in the 15th and 16th centuries and a center of Calvinism during the COUNTER-REFORMATION. It became famous during the 16th and 17th centuries. Duke Karl of Baden promoted learning, founded new colleges, and made it the state university of Baden. In the 19th century it became a center for the romantic movement.

During the 19th and 20th centuries sizable industries developed. Machinery, chemicals, precision instruments, and tools were the principal products. During WORLD WAR II it escaped damage, and during the U.S. occupation General Eisenhower made it army headquarters.

Heidelberg Confession/Catechism (1563)

HEIDELBERG became the foremost center of the Calvinist faith in Germany. The first prince who accepted it was Elector Frederick III of the Palatinate (1559–76), making Heidelberg into the leading German intellectual center. Consequently, the theologians at the University of Heidelberg composed the Heidelberg Catechism of 1563, which became the chief formulation of the Calvinist creed in Germany. Nowhere in Germany, however, was the constitution and discipline accepted. Interestingly, the Heidelberg Catechism did not mention CALVIN's doctrine of predestination.

A popular Calvinist movement only developed in the northwestern Rhineland and in Westphalia. The House of Orange in the Netherlands promoted Calvinism in Nassau, while the city of BREMEN also became Calvinist. Later, there were princely converts such as John Sigismund of Brandenburg, but outside these limited areas Calvinism achieved no deep social penetration. Its greatest German political philosopher was Johannes Althusius (1557–1638), who expressed some of the Calvinist democratic ideas. However, German Calvinism generally had to accept the close church-state patterns that were common within Lutheranism. Most of the German Calvinists followed the Lutheran pattern with a modified Lutheran or Philipist creed in which the doctrine of sacraments was the most divisive, although the two groups elaborated other differences in theology. Only a few German princes experienced the original Calvinism.

Heine, Heinrich (1791–1856)
poet

One of the greatest poets of late German ROMANTICISM, Heinrich Heine, was born in DÜSSELDORF on the RHINE, the son of a Jewish merchant. Unsuccessful in business, Heine studied law at the universities of BONN, GÖTTINGEN, and BERLIN, and converted to Christianity in order to pursue a legal career. At Bonn his literary talents attracted the attention of August Wilhelm SCHLEGEL, and his reputation grew as a lyricist. He was a member of YOUNG GERMANY, a group of writers who were nationalistic but not revolutionary. Nonetheless, Young Germany was considered subversive and was condemned by the BUNDESRAT of the GERMAN CONFEDERATION in 1835. In Berlin he had the opportunity to attend the lectures of the philosopher G. W. F. HEGEL. While there, he also frequented the salon of Rahel Varnhagen von Ense, which was attended by intellectuals such as Alexander von HUMBOLDT, Leopold von RANKE, A. Chamisso, and Bettina von Arnim. Heine published a collection of his poems. Besides prose travel books such as *Die Harzreise* in 1827, he published *Buch der Lieder* (1827), which laid the foundation of his reputation as a poet.

Unable to obtain a professorship in MUNICH and due to financial difficulties and problems with Prussian censors, Heine immigrated to Paris in 1831, inspired by the possibilities of a new world arising out of the July Revolution of 1830. He remained there until his death. The cynicism and bitterness of his thought some think was a reaction to injustice and persecution. In his younger years he loved to portray himself as a soldier in the movement to liberate humankind from its oppressors. The Germany of his time had not yet granted Jewish emancipation, and the privileges of the ARISTOCRACY were still entrenched. His personality was certainly complex, and he often contradicted himself, following no particular party or personal line. Yet, he passionately loved Germany. Although Heine's poetry treats of the themes of love and nature, his feelings and experiences are at the center of his art. A subtle lyricist and poetic virtuoso, he wrote songs and ballads, such as *The Book of Songs* in 1827 and *Romanzero* in 1851. Sometimes his poems were marred by sarcasm and witticisms. Some of his poems have been the source for many folk songs, such as "Die Lorelei" (*Loreley*), and non-Germans have been especially influenced in their perceptions of German romanticism. Important essays written in the 1830s, *The Romantic School* and *On Religion and Philosophy*, were intended to explain German culture to both the Germans and the French. Heine was critical of romanticism, interpreting it as a return to an outdated past and as a reactionary and irrational symptom of German backwardness. The German censors were also critical of his work, because in 1835 his works were officially branded as subversive in the German Confederation. He disliked the bourgeoisie but was also fearful of the French proletariat, hating the upheaval that took place in Paris during the REVOLUTION of 1848.

Heinemann, Gustav (1899–1976)
federal president

Gustav Heinemann served as president of the FEDERAL REPUBLIC (FRG) from 1969 to 1974. He was a politician who was committed to democracy and Christianity. A principled but pragmatic Protestant, he had been a member of the CONFESSING CHURCH, which opposed the Third Reich.

During the WEIMAR REPUBLIC he was politically active in a democratic student group. After receiving his doctorate of law, he worked as a legal adviser in industry, but during the Nazi regime he served on the board of directors of Rhineland Steel works in Essen, which was implicated in the armaments industry. A dedicated Protestant, he became a member of the Confessing Church, which influenced him deeply. In 1946 he became lord mayor of Essen.

Along with Konrad ADENAUER he became one of the founders of the CHRISTIAN DEMOCRATIC UNION (CDU), and as the most prominent Protestant in the party was appointed interior minister (1949–50) in the first Adenauer cabinet. Heinemann also played a prominent role in the postwar Protestant Church. From 1949 to 1955 he chaired the All-German Synod and signed the Stuttgart Declaration, by which the German Protestant Church accepted its guilt for involvement in Nazi Germany. Heinemann's principles led him to resign from Adenauer's cabinet, especially over issues on defense and rearmament. In 1952 he resigned from the CDU over Adenauer's policy of integration with the West, which he believed cemented the division of Germany. Then he cofounded the United German People's Party, which stood for a united and neutral Germany.

Heinemann's opposition to rearmament was related to his membership in the Confessing Church and the postwar Protestant Church. He felt that Christianity and the church had to remain independent of the state and avoid pitting the Christian West against anti-Christian communism. After the failure of his People's Party he joined the SPD in 1957, finding Christian values in the SPD, although he did not support the SPD's support for the nuclear armament of the army. From 1957 he was a member of the SPD's executive committee, was elected to the BUNDESTAG, was justice minister from 1966 to 1969, and elected federal president from 1969 to 1974. As a principled leader he contributed to the restoration of Germany's moral reputation.

Heisenberg, Werner Karl (1901–1976)
physicist

Werner Karl Heisenberg was the physicist who formulated the principle of indeterminacy and established the theoretical foundation for quantum mechanics, altering the view of the world. He worked on the development of an atomic bomb for Germany during WORLD WAR II. After the war he devoted his energies to building a free society in Germany.

Werner Karl Heisenberg was born in Würzburg on December 5, 1901, the son of August Heisenberg, a professor of Greek language and literature. He was affected by the lost war, the student youth movement, and the Bavarian Revolution in 1919. He soon attended university at GÖTTINGEN and MUNICH, studying theoretical physics, and took his doctorate in 1923. During the next two years he discovered the fields of quantum physics and atomic physics. With a Rockefeller grant he attended the Niels Bohr Institute in Copenhagen, where he studied with Niels Bohr the most recent speculations on atomic theory. In 1925 he published a paper calculating kinematic and mechanical relations in quantum mechanics through the use of matrix calculus. His recognition included an appointment as lecturer on theoretical physics at the University of Copenhagen. In 1927 he formulated the principle of indeterminacy or uncertainty. He was appointed professor of theoretical physics at LEIPZIG at age 25. In 1930 he published a classic in the field, *The Physical Principles of the Quantum Theory*. In 1932 along with Paul Schroedinger and Paul Dirac he won the Nobel Prize in physics. In 1941 he was called to BERLIN to hold the chair in theoretical physics at the University of Berlin and the directorship of the Kaiser Wilhelm Institute for Physics.

Heisenberg decided not to emigrate with the advent of the Nazi regime. He was concerned about the policies of HITLER's regime but did not join the resistance. On the other hand, he never was a member of the NAZI PARTY, and he continued to hold his prominent academic positions. When World War II began, Heisenberg was placed in charge of the project for the development of an atomic bomb. There is some controversy about the extent to which he was implicated in the Nazi efforts. After the war he claimed that he was trying to sabotage the German bomb efforts. On the other hand, it is believed that Heisenberg worked to develop the bomb, but failed because of lack of access to materials. It is possible that Heisenberg was trying to get out of a moral dilemma in his work on the bomb project by claiming he was trying to make the project fail.

After World War II Heisenberg reorganized the scientific research at the Max Planck Institute of Physics and of the Alexander Humboldt Foundation. One of his principal concerns during the 1950s was the formulation of a "unified theory of fundamental particles." In 1955–56 he presented the Gifford lectures at the University of St. Andrews, Scotland. His autobiography was entitled *Physics and Beyond* (1971). He retired in 1970, and later failing health brought serious illness; he died on February 1, 1976, in Munich.

Herder, Johann Gottfried von
(1744–1803)
philosopher

Philosopher, theologian, and literary critic who criticized the excessive dependence of the educated in Germany on French thought and manners, Herder was a theorist and leader of the storm and stress movement. His philosophy of history emphasized that each people possessed a unique spirit, culture, and history.

Johann Gottfried von Herder was born on August 25, 1744, the son of a schoolmaster in the town of Mohrongen in East Prussia. He mastered Latin and some Greek early, and in 1762 entered the university in Königsberg as a medical student. Turning to theology, he studied under Immanuel KANT and was also significantly influenced by the philosopher J. G. Hamann, who was intent on exposing the limitations of the rationalism of the ENLIGHTENMENT. Herder wrote his first important works on literary criticism in Riga, where he was employed as a teacher and minister between 1764 and 1769. Traveling widely, he met some of the philosophes in France and was privileged to have the friendship of GOETHE. Herder went to WEIMAR in 1776 as a superintendent of the Lutheran clergy. In the following decades he wrote extensively, publishing between 1784 and 1791 the four-volume *Idea for a Philosophy of History for Mankind* and his liberal *Letters for the Advancement of Mankind* between 1793 and 1797. In these works Herder incorporates elements of historicism. He thought that humans worked out their destinies interacting with institutions and environment. Rather than emphasize the progress of the individual, Herder believed that it is humanity that progresses through the providence of God.

Although Germans spoke a common language, they were divided into hundreds of petty states and lacked any conception of Germany as a distinct state. German intellectuals tended to share in the cosmopolitan outlook of the Enlightenment, and they generally admired the French philosophes. Herder objected to what he considered this excessive dependence and challenged his contemporaries to appreciate and develop their native German culture. He believed that bodies of persons sharing a common language possessed a unique spirit (*Geist*) or genius that had to be developed in its own particular way. For a culture to be authentic Herder thought it had to arise from the life of the common people (*Volk*) and be inspired by them. Herder was not concerned with politics and never argued that the political unification of Germany had to accompany its cultural renaissance. Herder's theory of national development was applicable to all peoples and did not imply that German culture was superior to others. Many literary figures of the German romantic school, such as the GRIMM brothers,

Johann Gottfried von Herder *(Library of Congress)*

took Herder's injunction seriously and in their writings explored Germany's cultural past through its folklore, law, and religion. Among some of Herder's disciples, such as FICHTE, German NATIONALISM began to change into the aggressive nationalism of the second half of the 19th century.

Herzog, Roman (1934–)
federal president

Roman Herzog was president of the Constitutional Court from 1987 and won election in 1994 as the CHRISTIAN DEMOCRATIC UNION's candidate for the presidency of a united Germany (1994–99).

Roman Herzog was born into a Lutheran family on April 5, 1934, in Lundshut, BAVARIA. His father was an archivist and director of a local museum. As a good student at the Gymnasium, he received a state scholarship to study law in MUNICH. In 1957 he passed the bar exam, and in 1958 he merited the degree of doctor of jurisprudence. In 1958 he married Christine, the self-confident and energetic daughter of a Lutheran pastor. This marriage produced two sons and a third who was adopted. From 1958 to 1964 he served as a legal assistant; from 1964 to 1966 he taught law at the University of Munich; in 1966 he received an appointment as professor of constitutional law and politics at the University of BERLIN. Moving to Speyer in 1969, he taught postgraduate courses to lawyers headed for public service, and then served as rector of the college in 1971–72.

His political career began in 1970 as he joined the Christian Democratic Union (CDU) and for five years served as state representative for the government of the Rhineland Palatinate under Helmut KOHL. Kohl had been impressed by Herzog's successful career and appointed him state secretary. In 1978 he was invited by Minister-President Hans Filbinger to become minister of education and of the interior in the state government of BADEN-WÜRTTEMBERG. In response to illegal student sit-down demonstrations, Herzog required them to pay fines to cover extra police costs and required that the police be better armed for the confrontations. He gave up this position in 1983 to become judge on the Federal Constitutional Court. At first he was elected vice president to the court and then court president in 1987. Surprisingly, on a case involving a state ban against demonstrations against a nuclear power plant, he voted to declare the ban unconstitutional, agreeing with the majority of the judges who had seen it as a violation of a citizen's right to free assembly.

When the famous and well-respected Richard von WEIZSÄCKER had completed his two terms as president in 1994, all the parties nominated their favorites. The first nominee of the CDU/CSU coalition was an ultra-conservative, Steffen Heitmann, who aroused widespread opposition within and without the party because of his volatile statements on social and political issues. Heitmann withdrew, and the CDU chose Herzog. The special assembly called to elect the president was composed of the members of the Bundestag and an equal number of representatives from the state parliaments. Herzog finally triumphed against the SPD candidate, Johannes Rau, on the third ballot when only a plurality of votes was needed (696 to 605).

Herzog decided to be more than just a figurehead president and made efforts to set the moral tone for the country as had Richard von Weizsäcker. He reminded Germans not to forget but not to be overwhelmed by the tragedies of their past in WORLD WAR II, and that racial and other prejudices should not be allowed to divide Germany. In 1992 he had already spoken out against the German radical right wing that was terrorizing Germany at the time. He continued to be a strong supporter of European integration and won the Charlemagne Prize for European unity in 1997. His term as president ended in 1999, when he was succeeded by Johannes Rau (SPD).

Herzog's duties did not restrict him from other services, for instance his chairmanship of the CDU/CSU Protestant Working Group. Besides being a prolific writer on legal issues, he found time to coedit a leading law commentary on the constitution and a Protestant encyclopedia, as well as teach courses at the universities of Speyer and Tübingen.

Hess, Rudolf (1894–1987)
deputy Reichsführer

Rudolf Hess was a young idealistic and introverted student at MUNICH University when he first met Adolf HITLER. Hess became intoxicated with his speeches and in 1920 once wrote an unsolicited letter eulogizing Hitler's political aims and skills. He wrote that Hitler was "an unusually decent, sincere character, full of kind-heartedness, religious, a good Catholic" and self-sacrificing, who had the welfare of Germany uppermost in his mind. Needless to say, Hess was naive, not a good judge of character, introverted, and a mediocrity whose main claim to fame was his relationship with Hitler.

Born in Cairo, Egypt, to German parents, Fritz H. Hess and Klara Münch, Rudolf received a German education in Alexandria and in Godesberg on the Rhine. In WORLD WAR I he served in the army, was wounded at Verdun, and later became a lieutenant in the AIR FORCE. In 1919 he attended Munich University, was influenced by and assisted the geopolitical professor Karl HAUSHOFER. During that same period he joined the anti-Semitic Thule Society. He joined the NAZI PARTY in 1920, participated in the 1923 Munich Putsch, and was tried and imprisoned in Landsberg, where he assisted Hitler in writing MEIN KAMPF (*My Struggle*). Most likely, the sections in *Mein Kampf* dealing with theories about living space and the British Empire were influenced by the ideas of Hess and Dr. Karl Haushofer. After the organization of the Nazi Party in 1925, Hess was made Hitler's personal secretary. In 1932 after Gregor STRASSER left the party, Hess was appointed the head of the Nazi Party's Central Political Commission. After Hitler became chancellor, he made Hess deputy Reichsführer. His responsibilities were to supervise the employment, promotion, and training of Nazis in all areas and later for the administration of the Nuremberg Laws on citizenship. Hess upheld Hitler's authoritarian and anti-Semitic principles. He may have saved some victims, but his administration established the categories of people intended for labor and extermination camps. In 1939 Hermann GÖRING was named Hitler's wartime "successor," and Hess became Göring's successor.

Perhaps the most notorious event in Hess's life was his flight to Scotland without Hitler's consent on May 10, 1941, landing by parachute on the duke of Hamilton's estate south of Glasgow. During the French campaign Hitler had discussed the possibility of a Anglo-German peace settlement in order to give Germany a free hand with Russia, giving a speech in July and making "peace feelers." Although never clearly explained, Hess hoped to reach some peace agreement with the Conservatives (Tories) who had favored the APPEASEMENT POLICY. Hess was treated comfortably in England, but all of his discussions were fruitless. He had no instructions or authority from Hitler to negotiate, and was denounced by the Führer as insane. After the war he was placed on trial before the International Military Tribunal (IMT) (*see* NUREMBERG TRIALS) claiming that he could not remember anything. He was judged guilty of crimes against peace (and on other counts) and was sentenced to life imprisonment. He remained in Spandau as the only prisoner remaining and committed suicide on August 17, 1987, at the age of 93.

Hesse

Hesse is one of the states of Germany. It was created through an ordinance of the U.S. Military government in 1945. It comprises the former Prussian province of Hesse-Nassau and the former state of Hesse on the right bank of the RHINE. Its largest city is FRANKFURT, and its capital is Wiesbaden, which is also the administrative center.

The state of Hesse emerged out of the Middle Ages as a group of temporal and spiritual principalities. By the 16th century it was a landgravate divided into a northern area, Hesse-Kassel, and a southern Hesse-Darmstadt. In addition to these was the free IMPERIAL CITY of Frankfurt. In 1866 Prussia annexed Nassau, Frankfurt, and the Landgravate of Hessen-Homburg, which were combined to form the Prussian state of Hessen-Nassau. The southern state, Hesse-Darmstadt, escaped the fate of Hesse-Kassel through its situation south of the Main River and so retained its identity as the Grand Duchy of Hesse. When its ruler abdicated in 1918, the grand duchy became a state in the WEIMAR REPUBLIC and then in the Nazi dictatorship until 1945. The fragments were united to form the state of Hesse.

The territory has also been the center of rapid population growth and rapid industrialization. Population has grown from 1.87 million in 1871 to more than 6 million in 2000. Frankfurt likewise grew from a population of 77,000 to about 600,000, Wiesbaden from 26,000 to 266,000, and Kassel from 39,000 to 185,000. The state is in the industrial heartland and has produced heavy machinery, railroads, electronic and chemical industries, plastics, and synthetics. Opel and Volkswagen both make automobiles here.

Politically, the state has been dominated by the SOCIAL DEMOCRATIC PARTY, especially between 1946 and 1974. All Hessian premiers (governors) were members of the SPD. Hesse was also the first state to experience a red/green coalition government, which lasted to 1987 and regained power after 1991. Joschka FISCHER was appointed environmental minister in the green/red coalition. From 1987 to 1991 and again after 1999 the CDU/FDP coalition ruled the state.

Hesse, Hermann (1877–1962)
novelist and poet

Hermann Hesse was an impressionist author and was strongly influenced by ROMANTICISM and Eastern philosophy. The heroes of his novels are often nonconformists who search for their identity outside of middle-class society. In his novels, especially *Steppenwolf,* youth discovered the spirit of revolt, but also the faith in reconciliation of the intellectual and the sensual, of science and art. He championed pacifism and international understanding.

Hermann Hesse was born on June 2, 1877, in Calw, in the Black Forest region of Württemberg. The son and grandson of missionaries, he grew up in a pious and educated household. In 1893 he attended the Protestant theological seminary in Maulbronn, but he soon rebelled against its disciplines. His parents could not understand his refusal to return and committed him to a nerve clinic, a humiliation Hesse never forgot. The experiences of rebellion and escape reappear in one form or another in almost all of his major works and stem from these experiences. He then worked in the book trade, read widely in German and foreign literature, and began to write lyric poetry and stories. He published his first works as *Romantic Songs* (1899) and *One Hour after Midnight* (1899), which were not serious and melancholic.

He achieved his first great success with the bildungsroman *Peter Camenzind* in 1904. In this story Peter, a young melancholic outsider, is cured by altruistic activity and a return to nature. The hero relinquishes his artistic calling and is cured amid the mountains of Switzerland. Besides other works that demonstrate his talent as a writer and his keen sense of psychology, the novel *Under the Wheel* (1905) stands out. It is an impressionist novel of the problems of puberty and a youth's tragic fight against the tyranny of a school system.

In 1912 he moved to Berne. As a result of a trip to India, he published *From India* in 1913. He opposed Germany's cause in WORLD WAR I, in some essays attacked German chauvinisim, and was in turn denounced as a pacifist traitor. Hesse's family life also broke down as his wife manifested mental disease and his third son became seriously ill.

His best-known books were published between the wars. *Demian* (1919) probes deeply into the problems of puberty and incest by portraying a delicate hero wavering between his demonic friend and his mother, an archetypical image of the eternal mother. He undergoes Jungian psychoanalysis and the emancipation of his personality from society's conventions. The act of self-liberation becomes even more violent in *Steppenwolf* (1927), in which the animal in man battles against the restrictions of civilization. *Steppenwolf* is Hesse's best-known novel. The key figure, Harry Haller, disappears after leaving behind a manuscript that tells how he has become a split personality that has been invaded by the spirit of a wolf from the steppes. He finds remission through friendship, dancing, and drugs. Other works of this period included *Klingsors Last Summer* (1920), *Siddhartha* (1922), and *Death and the Lover* (1930).

Hesse's last and most voluminous work is *The Glass Bead Game*, published as *Master Ludi* (1943), which he wrote late in life and which is a story taking place in a utopian life of harmony, an allegory whose story is told through high-level discussions. This work was especially mentioned by the Swedish Academy in awarding Hesse the Nobel Prize in 1946. He had earlier received the Gottfried Keller Prize in 1936 and another German award, the Peace Prize of the German Book Trade in 1955. He received an honorary doctorate from the University of Berne in 1947. In the 1960s Hermann Hesse became one of the favorite authors of rebellious German youths. He died in August 1962.

Heuss, Theodor (1884–1963)
president of Federal Republic

Theodor Heuss has the distinction of having been the first president of the FEDERAL REPUBLIC OF GERMANY. He used his office to reconcile the political differences among his fellow Germans, and internationally he was a convincing representative of the new democracy.

One of the founders of the FREE DEMOCRATIC PARTY (FDP) in 1946, he represented this party in the Parliamentary Council convened to draft the BASIC LAW, the constitution of democratic postwar Germany. Theodor Heuss was one of the few who had already worked to establish and defend democracy in Germany during the WEIMAR REPUBLIC. From his own experience he was well aware of the causes that had led to the Nazi dictatorship. Heuss was liberal politically as well as by conviction, serving several terms as a deputy in the Reichstag for the GERMAN DEMOCRATIC PARTY (1924–28) and its successor, the State Party, from 1930 to 1933. Critical of Adolf HITLER, he opposed the ENABLING ACT and tried unsuccessfully to get his party to vote against it, but in solidarity with his party voted for it.

Heuss was born in Brackenheim near Heilbronn, which lies deep in the Swabian countryside. He studied economics and completed his doctorate under the economist Lujo Brentano (1844–1931). Between 1905 and 1912 he was editor of *Die Hilfe*, a periodical founded by his mentor Friedrich NAUMANN, who influenced his thinking about social liberal reforms. After WORLD WAR I he became a leading executive in Naumann's Deutscher Werkbund. From 1920 to 1933 he lectured on politics at the Academy (Hochschule) for Politics in BERLIN. During the Nazi regime he worked on biographies, the best known on Friedrich Naumann. After the war he was appointed minister of education in the new state of BADEN-WÜRTTEMBERG and in 1946 was elected to that state's constituent assembly and parliament. In 1949 he was elected to the first BUNDESTAG and soon thereafter was elected federal president.

As the first president of the Federal Republic Theodor Heuss was an admirable choice for the growth of German democracy. His personality, dignity, and charm helped overcome some of the intense disagreements of the problems of the country and its division between West and East. His speeches contributed to the political education of his countrymen. He was reelected for a second term in 1954 and retired in 1959 to his home in Stuttgart.

Heydrich, Reinhard (1904–1942)
head of Nazi Reich Security Service and administrator of concentration camps

Reinhard Heydrich was born on March 7, 1904, in Halle, SAXONY, to a famous composer. He became an accomplished violinist. Too young to serve in the war, later in 1923 he joined the navy, but was dishonorably discharged in 1931 for an affair with a daughter of a senior officer. He joined the NAZI PARTY and then the SS (Schutzstaffel) in 1932. He impressed Heinrich HIMMLER and was promoted to a position second only to Himmler. Heydrich's appearance was the model of a blond athletic nordic type being popularized by Nazi ideologists. He had a leading role in the Blood Purge of 1934, which eliminated leaders of the SA and other opponents of the Nazis. He was made head of the Security Police and the SD and combined all offices and police agencies, such as the GESTAPO, under his direct command. By 1939 he was so powerful he could assume control of the RSHA, an enlarged terror organization, which included the SS and carried out Hitler's will. In 1940 he was elected head of the International Criminal Police Commission. Hitler appointed Heydrich acting Reich protector of Bohemia-Moravia in 1941 with the mission to suppress all Czech resistance.

Heydrich was the first to establish a ghetto for Jews and became the administrator of CONCENTRATION CAMPS. The most serious of his assignments concerned the FINAL SOLUTION. Hitler by way of Himmler and Herman GÖRING on July 31, 1941, authorized Heydrich to proceed with the plan on which he had been working. At the WANNSEE CONFERENCE on January 20, 1942, he was chosen to administer the genocide. He organized the special SS and police mobile killing units called EINSATZGRUPPEN that murdered more than 500,000 Russian Jews by spring 1942. Heydrich supervised the planning of the concentration camps where millions were gassed.

The Czech resistance succeeded in killing Heydrich. On May 27, 1942, two men waited for Heydrich's car at the edge of Prague and threw a bomb that wounded and eventually killed him. Hitler was enraged, considering the assassination as serious as a lost battle. Severe reprisals were ordered, almost a thousand were killed, and the village of Lidice was destroyed.

Heydrich has gone down in history as one of the great criminals of all time. His cold, cynical, brutal lack of compassion and respect for human life marked his character. He was never free of the torment and self-contempt arising from the fear that Jewish blood was in his family. Hitler and Himmler found him indispensible to their purposes, a man of great energy, obedient to orders, fanatical and zealous in carrying out plans.

Hildebrandt, Johann Lukas von (1668–1745)
architect

Johann Lukas von Hildebrandt, along with John Bernard Fischer von Erlach, was the greatest architect in AUSTRIA during the BAROQUE period. While Fischer von Erlach represented a more classical taste, his younger peer, Hildebrandt, designed his structures in a softer and more popular style. He began as a military engineer, being promoted to court engineer in 1701. Attracting the attention of Prince EUGENE of Savoy he designed a masterpiece of a palace, Belvedere, which was constructed between 1700 and 1723 as a summer residence for the famous prince. Its elegance and monumental scale made it one of the supreme achievements of the Viennese baroque. Prince Eugene already possessed a winter residence within the city walls, so Belvedere was built to overlook Vienna from the southeast. With its wonderful sense of proportion and scenic garden esplanade, Belvedere shone like a diamond among colored stones that represented the smaller, cramped palaces within the old city walls at a time when Vienna housed some 80,000 people. Belvedere was only one of some 240 aristocratic residences that sprang up in and around Vienna by 1730. To pay for their residences, the Austrian leadership was amply rewarded from the conquests in Hungary and elsewhere. For instance, Prince Eugene was rewarded with a bequest of 300,000 florins. This made it possible to employ perhaps hundreds if not thousands of artisans as well as free labor service (robot) of the peasantry.

Another great accomplishment of Hildebrandt was the monastery at Göttweg. It ranks with Jakob Prandtauer's beautiful Benedictine abbey at Melk and St. Florian, proud monuments of the baroque.

Himmler, Heinrich (1900–1945)
leader of the Gestapo and SS

Heinrich Himmler was born in MUNICH on October 7, 1900, into a middle-class Catholic family, the son of a former tutor of a Bavarian prince. After receiving a secondary education in Landshut, in 1917 Himmler joined the army as an officer cadet, but due to his frail health he never participated in military action. In 1922 he received a diploma in agriculture from a technical college in Munich. Later he worked briefly as a chicken farmer and a fertilizer salesman. He joined the growing NAZI PARTY and participated in the November 1923 BEER-HALL PUTSCH. Following HITLER's release from prison, Himmler rejoined him as the party's deputy propaganda chief. In 1929 he was appointed the commander (Reichsführer) of the blackshirted SS. Originally the SS had served as Hitler's bodyguard, but under Himmler's leadership the SS became a key element in the power structure of the Nazi state. By 1933 he had expanded its membership to more than 50,000. Himmler looked to aristocrats and other people of higher social status to fill the ranks of the SS and was able to secure their loyalty. Investigating potential leadership personnel, he would find out their weaknesses and vices in order to manipulate their loyalty.

By June 1936 Himmler had gained control of the entire German police forces, becoming head of the GESTAPO in addition to his leadership of the SS. He used these positions to create a reign of terror in Nazi Germany with the infamous KL (CONCENTRATION CAMP system). Dachau was the first camp created by Himmler in 1933. It was originally used to incarcerate and brutalize political dissenters and criminals. Homosexuals and Jews suffered there later on. The KL system was the perfect outlet for him to carry out his ideas concerning the virtues of German racial purity. From 1937 on the entire German population was screened for Aryan racial purity. In Eastern Europe Himmler's goal was to "Germanize" the occupied areas and to deport the native populations.

After the assassination attempt against Hitler in July 1944, Himmler became supreme commander of the home armies. Shortly before Hitler's death Himmler tried to negotiate a surrender, bartering Jewish prisoners for his own safety and proposing a German-Western alliance against the Soviet Union. When Hitler found out, he stripped Himmler of his offices. After being captured by the British, he committed suicide on May 23, 1945.

Hindemith, Paul (1895–1963)
composer, conductor, and violinist

Paul Hindemith was one of 20th-century Germany's most important composers in the neoclassical style. He is noted for his string quartets, symphonies, and operas.

Born on November 16, 1895, in Hanau am Main, he began violin lessons at an early age. In 1908 he was admitted into the Frankfurt Conservatory, later becoming the conductor of the Frankfurt Opera orchestra. In 1927 he accepted a professorship at the Berlin Hochschule für Musik. He also became a member of the Donaueschingen Festival, which was Germany's leading promoter of new music. The great poet Rainer Maria RILKE inspired the Rilke song cycle, *Scenes from the Life of Mary* (1922–23). More important was his later career as an outstanding violinist. He also played viola with the Amar Quartet formed in 1921, which performed contemporary works. He had the distinction in 1929 of being the first to play Walton's Viola Concerto. In a series of seven works Hindemith also developed an entirely different style of chamber music, drawing on BAROQUE forms and polyphony.

Why was Hindemith forced to leave Germany when he was not Jewish? Although he composed in the German neoclassical idiom, he also composed atonal music to which the Nazis objected. Furthermore, his wife was Jewish, and his association with Jewish musicians was objectionable. Considered a political radical, his music was placed on a proscribed list. The Nazis also banned his religiously inspired opera, *Mathis the Painter,* which dealt with the problems of the artist during troubled times and was based on the life of the 16th-century artist Matthias Grünewald. The opera was composed in 1935 and premiered in 1938 in Switzerland. That year he also composed one of his best-known works for the ballet, *Most Exalted Vision.*

After leaving Germany, Hindemith came to the United States in 1940 and taught at Yale University for 13 years. Some of his most popular works were performed during this period, such as *Symphonic Metamorphosis of Themes by Carl Maria von Weber* (1943) and *When Lilacs Last in the Dooryard Bloom'd* (1946). Leaving for Switzerland for the remainder of his life, he produced two major operatic works: *The Harmony of the World* (1957) and *The Long Christmas Dinner* (1960). On December 28, 1963, he died in FRANKFURT.

Hindenburg, Paul Ludwig Hans Anton von Beneckendorff und von (1847–1934)

field marshal and president of Weimar Republic

Paul von Hindenburg was born in Posen on October 2, 1847, the son of a Prussian army officer and JUNKER nobility. He was trained in the Prussian Cadet Corps. He distinguished himself in the last Prussian charge against the Austrians at Königgrätz in 1866 during the Franco-Prussian War, receiving a citation for bravery and the Iron Cross. He represented his regiment at the proclamation of the German Empire in the Hall of Mirrors at the palace at Versailles in 1871. In 1878 he began a 20-year service on the General Staff which alternated with field duty as a commander of the Fourth Army Corps at Magdeburg. He did not distinguish himself with strategic or tactical talent, but gained respect and promotions through hard work, loyalty, and noble bearing. In 1911 he voluntarily retired three years after the emperor criticized his conduct of maneuvers.

When WORLD WAR I broke out, Hindenburg was recalled to active duty and appointed commander of the 8th Army on the Eastern Front with Erich LUDENDORFF as his chief of staff. The new team was responsible for the decisive German victory over the Russians at the BATTLE OF TANNENBURG before invading Poland and winning the Battle of Lodz. In November Hindenburg was promoted to supreme commander of the Eastern Front with the rank of field marshal. In 1916 Hindenburg was made chief of the German General Staff with Ludendorff as chief of operations, the latter being the more influential. They pursued a policy of total war and all-out victory, which included submarine warfare; resistance to political reform at home made their power dictatorial. The unification of military command did not suffice to overcome the military superiority of the Allies. With the surrender in November 1918 and overthrow of the emperor WILLIAM II, Hindenburg's prestige did not diminish. He directed the withdrawal of German troops from France and Belgium before the deadline set by the Allies. After the Peace of Versailles was signed in June 1919, he retired again to HANOVER, where he occasionally expressed antirepublican views and cultivated his image as a national hero.

After the death of the first president of the republic, Friedrich EBERT, Hindenburg was nominated by the parties of the political right, including the BAVARIAN PEOPLE'S PARTY, the sister-party of the Catholic CENTER PARTY, and was elected president with a slight plurality. Although he desired a restoration of the monarchy, Hindenburg faithfully carried out his constitutional responsibilities. Hindenburg disappointed many people due to his support of various chancellors, including Wilhelm Marx, whom he defeated in the presidential election. He also supported the foreign policy of Gustav STRESEMANN, whose goal it was to bring about German reconciliation with France. Hindenburg also signed the YOUNG PLAN in 1929, which revised the amount of reparations Germany was expected to pay.

With the onset of the GREAT DEPRESSION and the breakdown of coalition governments, Hindenburg pursued a policy using emergency decrees supporting his choice for chancellor, Heinrich BRÜNING, against the combined antirepublican majority of Nazis and Communists. He ran for president again in 1932 against HITLER, being considered the last bulwark against a Nazi dictatorship. After winning the election, he turned against Brüning because of land reforms that were disadvantageous to fellow landed aristocrats, and appointed the egotistic and ill-advised Franz von PAPEN and shortly thereafter, the political general Kurt von SCHLEICHER, both of whom were personal friends. Overcoming his distrust of Hitler, Hindenburg appointed him as chancellor on January 30, 1933, with Papen as vice chancellor, who along with other conservatives were supposed to restrain Hitler's dictatorial ambitions. Hindenburg lost control of the rapid radicalization pursued by the Nazis. In March 1933 Hindenburg presided over a purged REICHSTAG, and in 1934 tolerated the assassinations and purges connected with the infamous Roehm purge. Paul von Hindenburg died at Neudeck on August 2, 1934.

Hindenburg Program (1916)

The Hindenburg Program was a mobilization of industrial capacity and resources to further the war effort. As new leaders of the Supreme Command of the Armed Forces (OHL), Paul von HINDENBURG and Erich LUDENDORFF ordered a huge increase in weapons production. They insisted on production increases of 100 percent in small arms ammunition and 300 percent in artillery shells and machine guns. This required a total mobilization of the labor force and extensive control of production. This also required social changes by convincing many thousands of women to enter the labor force. This momentous shift in manufacturing priorities resulted in the closure of many small and medium peacetime industries. Attempting to give this total mobilization the appearance of a consensual and not dictatorial decision, the Patriotic Auxiliary Service Law was proposed and the War Office established, which had overall charge of economic mobilization.

Hitler, Adolf (1889–1945)
Nazi leader
Adolf Hitler, as leader of the National Socialist German Worker's Party (NSDAP) and chancellor of Germany from 1933 to 1945, was one of the world's most notorious dictators and responsible for WORLD WAR II and the HOLOCAUST.

On April 20, 1889, Adolf Hitler was born into the household of an Austrian customs official, Alois Hitler, and his third wife, Clara Pölzl, in Braunau-am-Inn. No substantial evidence exists that his grandfather was Jewish. A mediocre student in secondary school in Linz, he moved to Vienna in 1908 to pursue an artistic career. After his application to the Academy of Fine Arts was rejected, he drifted aimlessly, reading indiscriminately, discussing politics, and indulging a fascination for the operas of Richard WAGNER. Exhausting his resources, he chose to live in a homeless shelter and sell small paintings. He left Vienna in 1913 for MUNICH and enthusiastically volunteered for the army when WORLD WAR I began. Hitler served with distinction as a corporal, was wounded twice, and received the Iron Cross first and second class. Germany's defeat and surrender and the November Revolution (REVOLUTION of 1918–1919) were so shocking to him that the only believable explanation was the myth that it was caused by a Jewish-Marxist conspiracy.

After the war racial ANTI-SEMITISM provided Hitler with a rational structure for his prejudices explaining Germany's loss of the war, the revolution, and all the other evils and problems of modern society. Underlying all of Hitler's ideas was the social Darwinist principle of the struggle for survival and the racist view that all of human history was explicable in terms of blood. As a military spy he was sent to observe the GERMAN WORKERS' PARTY (DAP) in September 1919, which he joined, quickly becoming its most popular spokesman. In 1920 the party's name was changed to National Socialist German Workers' Party (NSDAP), the SA (Sturmabteilung) were organized to protect meetings, and a 25-point program declared the party's opposition to capitalism, democracy, and the Jews. A leadership (Führer) cult began, and after Mussolini's march on Rome, Hitler exhibited symptoms of megalomania. On November 9, 1923, Hitler headed an alliance of right-wing groups (*Kampfbund*), intending to take over the Bavarian government and then march on BERLIN.

This so-called BEER-HALL PUTSCH failed. Imprisoned in Landsberg, he dictated the first volume of MEIN KAMPF (*My Struggle*) to fellow Nazi Rudolf HESS. After his early release Hitler regained control of the party, changed its strategy to acquire power constitutionally, and promoted the Führer myth. Forming a temporary alliance with the GERMAN NATIONAL PEOPLE'S PARTY (DNVP) in a right-wing attack against the WEIMAR REPUBLIC, the Nazis won a new respectability. With the onset of the GREAT DEPRESSION the Nazis won an unprecedented 107 seats in the REICHSTAG elections of 1930.

Hitler's appointment as chancellor by President Paul von HINDENBURG on January 30, 1933, was the culmination of a long process, beginning with the creation in 1930 of an authoritarian presidential system by which emergency decrees gave the president the power to choose the chancellor regardless of majorities in the Reichstag. From 1930 through 1932 the Nazi electoral machine staged very dynamic campaigns, including demagogic oratory and street violence. The campaigns were astutely geared to appeal to different social groups, with emphasis on anticommunism, NATIONALISM, and Christian values, but downplayed anti-Semitism. Although Hitler lost his bid to defeat Hindenburg in the presidential election of 1932, the Nazi vote continued to rise. Backroom deals by Hindenburg's friends and advisers determined the rise and fall of chancellors Heinrich BRÜNING, Franz von PAPEN, and General Kurt von SCHLEICHER. Waiting for his opportunity, Hitler finally agreed to become chancellor in an alliance with the Nationalists, accepting Franz von Papen as vice chancellor.

A dictatorship was created by political manipulation and vigorous terrorism. Under emergency decrees, civil liberties were restricted on February 28, 1933, after the Reichstag fire. The ENABLING ACT (March 23, 1933) legalized the establishment of a dictatorship. Criticism by the Catholic Church was silenced through a CONCORDAT (treaty) with the Vatican (Reichskonkordat). The police came under Nazi control, and fear that the army would intervene was neutralized; the GERMAN COMMUNIST PARTY (KPD) was brutally suppressed, other political opponents were placed in CONCENTRATION CAMPS, and SA leaders were assassinated by the SS in June 1934. All state government and organizations were coordinated (GLEICHSHALTUNG). Hitler's popularity with so many ordinary Germans was probably based on his promises to restore Germany's national pride, overcome social divisions, and create a community inspired by German ideals.

Hitler claimed that his foreign policy was defensive and intended to include all Germans into one state, even though it aimed at war. Besides the defeat of France, his most important goal was the conquest of living space (LEBENSRAUM) in Russia. Hitler challenged the VERSAILLES TREATY by introducing conscription in 1935, rearmament, and in 1936 the occupation of the RHINELAND. Germany left the LEAGUE OF NATIONS. An alliance with Mussolini was signed in 1936. One step at a time, Hitler changed the balance of power, always saying that this was his last demand and he desired only peace. In 1938 he secured AUSTRIA. Also that year Hitler took over the borderlands of Czechoslovakia, which received international confirmation at the Munich Agreement (September 1938). With the occupation of the rest of Czechoslovakia Hitler moved beyond revising the Treaty of Versailles. He took an active part in military planning, even devising the successful strategy for the invasion of France in 1940, which especially fed his megalomania and conviction of infallibility. The tactics of lightning war (BLITZKRIEG) contributed to the success of German military campaigns. Preparing for the invasion of Poland, Hitler concluded a nonaggression pact with the Soviet Union (August 1939) in order to avoid a two-front war. Believing that England and France would continue their APPEASEMENT, the Nazis invaded Poland on September 1, 1939, starting World War II.

Hitler only gradually disclosed his true intentions concerning the invasion of Russia in 1941. At different times the conquest of Russia was presented as a way to defeat Great Britain, to acquire living space, and finally as a preemptive strike against an imminent Soviet invasion. At this time the plans for the FINAL SOLUTION to the Jewish question took form and orders were given at the WANNSEE CONFERENCE. Although no one has found the documentation to prove Hitler gave the order to annihilate the Jews, his approval was indispensable to authorizing Heinrich HIMMLER and the SS to execute the policy. In 1941 he assumed direct control of the military and meddled in tactical planning, which contributed to disastrous defeats in North Africa and at STALINGRAD. Shortly after the Normandy invasion (June 1944) by the Allies, an unsuccessful attempt was made to assassinate Hitler by the German RESISTANCE in the July 20, 1944, plot and take over the government. As the Soviets surrounded Berlin and Hitler hid in his bunker, he married Eva Braun, his mistress, and committed suicide with her on April 30, 1945.

Hitler Youth

The NAZI PARTY possessed its own youth organization, as did churches, political parties, and sporting associations. After HITLER became chancellor, the Hitler Youth absorbed all the other youth organizations and inculcated the ideology of the Nazi Party into German youths. It was a new type of youth organization that was totalitarian and fanatical in its support for Hitler the leader, the Aryan race, and the Fatherland.

The Hitler Youth emerged from the first Nazi Youth league established in 1922, which ended with the BEER-HALL PUTSCH. In 1926 the Hitler Youth was founded with Kurt Gruber as its leader. In 1931 Hitler replaced Gruber with the dynamic and aristocratic Baldur von SCHIRACH, who became Reich youth leader of the NSDAP and head of the Hitler Youth. At first the organization was under the control of Ernst RÖHM'S SA, but during summer 1932 it was given an independent status within the Nazi Party. When Hitler became chancellor, Schirach began to consolidate his control over all youth organizations, taking control of the Reich Committee of German Youth Associations. The only youth organizations that were exempt were Catholic because they were protected by the 1933 CONCORDAT (treaty with the Vatican), but that exemption ended in 1936. The Hitler Youth grew rapidly from less than 100,000 members at the end of 1932, and by the end of 1933 it had grown to 3.5 million members, then numbered 8 million boys and girls by 1939.

Hitler's ideals were inculcated into the youths, and the programs were organized to achieve those goals. The motto of the youths was "We are born to die for Germany." In their bodies and character Hitler conceived that National Socialist youths had to be "slim and slender, swift as the greyhound, tough as leather, and hard as Krupp steel." The organization's activities were intended to develop those traits whether it be sports, hiking, music, storytelling, or arts and crafts. The activities were competitive, and a great deal of emphasis was placed on community over individual interests. The competition glorified struggle, the fighter, and the heroic for the boys, while the Young Girls (Jungmädel) and the older girls in the League of German Girls (Bund Deutscher Mädel) were indoctrinated for service, discipline, and to be dutiful wives and mothers. The activities exhibited compulsiveness and dynamism. By 1938 for the boys the development of military arts took on a primary importance. Even the younger group, the Jungvolk, practiced small-arms drills, while those 14–18 years old used real rifles and performed army maneuvers. Specialized naval, glider, and motorized branches were established. All of this paramilitary training prepared the young men for six months service in the Labor Front and two years in the armed forces.

During the latter part of the war (1943–45) youths were called on to perform civil defense duties and even to man antiaircraft guns. They fought fires, patrolled the streets, and dug tank traps. They played an important role in the People's Army (Volksturm), the home defense force that included all males 16 to 60 not in the armed forces. In the BATTLE FOR BERLIN they were even committed to frontline combat.

Hoffmann, Ernst Theodor Amadeus (1776–1822)
writer, composer, painter, and critic
E. T. A. Hoffmann was the most multitalented of romantic storytellers. His novels and essays are

expressions of escape into the realm of the pure imagination where reality and hallucination are closely intertwined. Succeeding in blending weird romanticism with an almost scientific realism, Hoffmann's tales of horror and the grotesque are considered to have influenced the American writer Edgar Allan Poe.

Born in Königsberg, East Prussia, Hoffmann was trained as a lawyer and served as a Prussian state employee in Posen and Warsaw. He then turned to composing, working first in 1808 in Bamberg, then in 1813 as Kapellmeister (musical director) in DRESDEN and LEIPZIG, and in 1814 in BERLIN. There he enjoyed the association of romantic writers such as the poet Clemens BRENTANO. To be sure, though recognized as one of the most talented of the storytellers of the romantic period, it is thought that alcohol gave rise to Hoffman's inspirations. In 1816 he applied and was reinstated as a judge in the superior court. Most of his stories present a world of everyday events, but woven into them are specters, spooks, split personalities, and a motley array of gruesome creatures. He mixed these elements in his partly autobiographical novel *Murr, The Tom-Cat's Reflections on Life*. It is a story that mixes the life of a composer like himself with fragments of the autobiography of a cat.

One of Hoffmann's best-known works is *The Devil's Elixir*, published in 1815–16, which resembles a Dr. Jekyll and Mr. Hyde theme in which the desires, crimes, and insanity of a monk who deals with evil spirits are emphasized. Another novel, *The Entail*, has a plot concerning greed and murder in a storm-swept castle in which two brothers express a deadly hatred for each other. Hoffmann's *Fantastic Tales* (1814), otherwise known as the *Tales of Hoffmann*, are also a combination of reality and hallucination, which served to inspire Jacques Offenbach's opera of the same title. Hoffmann was most probably the most enthusiastically read author outside of Germany. On June 25, 1822, he died of a spinal infection in BERLIN.

Hohenzollern dynasty

The Hohenzollern family was the ruling dynasty of PRUSSIA from 1701 to 1918 as well as the dynasty that ruled IMPERIAL GERMANY from 1871 to 1918.

The Hohenzollerns of both the Swabian and the Frankish-Brandenburg-Prussian line derived their name from their ancestral castle on top of Mount Zollern in Swabia. As counts of NUREMBERG the members of the family increased their possessions by inheritance as well as by their repeated support of imperial policies and military campaigns. Frederick VI was given the Stadtholdership and later the hereditary possession of the Mark Brandenburg in 1415. Frederick WILLIAM, the Great Elector, the margrave of Brandenburg, turned this conglomeration of lands into a unified state and laid the basis for the rise of Brandenburg-Prussia as a great power. He freed East Prussia from Polish overlordship in the course of the THIRTY YEARS' WAR and acquired eastern Pomerania and some other territories in the TREATY OF WESTPHALIA. In 1614 through inheritance the three small duchies of Cleves, Mark, and Ravensberg on the lower RHINE became part of Brandenburg-Prussia.

The Hohenzollerns became kings of Prussia in 1701, when the elector Frederick III of Brandenburg became King FREDERICK I of Prussia. Under the reign of FREDERICK II (the Great) Prussia became a great European power during the WAR OF AUSTRIAN SUCCESSION and the SEVEN YEARS' WAR. The Hohenzollerns were responsible for the unification of Germany and became the emperors of Imperial Germany from 1871 to 1918. The last Hohenzollern emperor was WILLIAM II, who reigned from 1888 to 1918. A branch of the family (Hohenzollern-Sigmaringen) ruled in Romania from 1866 until after WORLD WAR II in 1947. The Hohenzollern Candidature of 1870 was an abortive proposal by a group of Spanish politicians that Prince Leopold of Hohenzollern-Sigmaringen should accept the crown of Spain. Although the candidature was forbidden by the king of Prussia, it caused a great deal of alarm in France and contributed to the causes of the Franco-Prussian War.

Holbein, Hans, the Younger
(1497–1543)

artist

A famous painter and graphic artist, Holbein was the first portrait painter to achieve international fame. He produced realistic portraits of humanist Desiderius ERASMUS, Thomas More, and King Henry VIII.

Born in AUGSBURG the son of the painter Hans Holbein the Elder, he received his initial training in the arts from his father. In 1515 Hans the Younger was sent to Basel, where he was apprenticed to the Swiss painter Hans Herbster. In 1519 he set up his workshop in Basel, where he became a citizen, married, had four children, and painted altarpieces, portraits, and murals, in addition to designing woodcuts and stained glass. One of his outstanding woodcut series was the *Dance of Death* (ca. 1521–25); he painted an exceedingly graphic *Dead Christ* (1521) in an altarpiece and a *Madonna and Child Enthroned with Two Saints* (1522). At this time he also made the acquaintance of Erasmus of Rotterdam, of whom he painted several portraits. Spending 18 months in England (1526–28), he painted the portraits of Thomas More and others. Returning to Basel between 1528 and 1532, Holbein continued his portrait painting, decorated the facade of the Kaiserstuhl and the city's council chamber, and designed woodcuts of the Old Testament (1531). During this period he also completed a portrait of his family, including his wife and two children, in the *Artist's Family*. During this period he painted the altarpiece, *Madonna of Mercy with the Family of Jakob Meyer*, in 1528. The religious turmoil of the REFORMATION and its iconoclastic attitudes forced him to flee Basel.

Holbein's career culminated during his second stay in England from 1532 to 1543. The subjects of his portraits were the king and his court and wealthy German merchants. He painted Henry VIII in full regal splendor and other members of his court, such as Jane Seymour, Anne of Cleves, and Edward VI as a child. Holbein perfected the technique of portrait miniatures. Also during this period he designed a triumphal arch for the merchants of the Steel Yard on the occasion of the coronation of Anne Boleyn.

Holbein's skills as a painter developed gradually. His superb technical skill included a realistic portrayal of detail, a grasp of three-dimensional form and space, and an outstanding sense of composition. A passion for objectivity is reflected in his portraits, although in the second English period he concentrated less on three-dimensional form and space and more on decoration in the style of mannerism.

Hölderin, Johann Christian Friedrich
(1770–1843)

philosophical poet

Friedrich Hölderin was a highly sensitive and spiritual poet who sought to express a religious vision in which man would be reconciled to everything through which God had revealed himself. Through his poetry he sought and "yearned to bring about a better, purer world condition." He had a vision that the Greek gods would be reawakened in German form, bringing about a new Golden Age, creating a new harmony between the conflicting forces of life.

Friedrich Hölderin was born in Lauffen am Neckar on March 20, 1770. His father died early in his life, but the mother remarried. His family relationships were said to have been harmonious and happy. In 1784 he left for boarding schools at Denkendorf and later at Maulbronn, where he began to write poetry. From 1788 to 1793 he studied for the ministry in the Lutheran seminary at Tübingen. He soon lost interest in the ministry and turned to philosophy and poetry, sharing his interests with other students of philosophy, such as G. W. F. HEGEL and F. W. J von SCHELLING. Some of his earliest poetry was on political IDEALISM fostered by the French Revolution. His personal experience, intellectual orientation, and artistic preoccupations place him with the romantics.

He was employed as a tutor in three different homes between 1793 and 1801. The one that had a deep impact on his life was the home of the FRANKFURT banker J. F. Gontard. His young wife, Suzette, and Hölderin became infatuated, but mainly as intimate friend and confidante. However, the husband was no fool, and he fired Friedrich as tutor. The poet called the woman Diotima, and she played the same role that Charlotte von Stein played in GOETHE's life. By 1799 Hölderin finished his great novel *Hyperion*. It is an apprenticeship novel like *Wilhelm Meister*, but in contrast it ends in disillusionment and death. It tells of a noble youth who tries to create a better world, and his efforts lead to terror and chaos. After the death of his noble friends, Diotima and Alabanda, with his ideals and faith shattered, he turns away from the world and becomes a hermit. The novel parallels some of Hölderin's own pathetic frustrations at his inability to find fulfillment as a man, a citizen, and artist, which nevertheless also provide the energy in his poetry.

Hyperion and *The Death of Empedocles*, which concerned a new messiah, demonstrate another attitude toward Greek antiquity other than Schiller's, whose Greece had been a past beautiful world that had been surpassed by Christianity. Hölderin, however, sees another Greece that is revealing itself in concrete shapes and appearances. For him the Greek gods were not dead and historical; they were merely in the process of transferring their home from Greece to Germany, to be reawakened in German form. He believed that his mission was to regenerate Germany during an age when all that Greece had stood for seemed lost.

His efforts at first focused on writing poetry in the style of Swabian poets and Friedrich Gottlieb KLOPSTOCK and was influenced by the ideals and strophic manner of Friedrich von SCHILLER. Poems written in classical metres were composed between 1796 and 1801 and are mainly odes and epigrams about Diotima. Toward the end of the period he wrote his three great elegies: *The Archipelago, Menon's Laments for Diotima*, and *Bread and Wine*. The latter two are more significant. In *Bread and Wine* the romantic propensity for dream moods is rejected, and the ideal attitude is described as "staying awake in the midst of the night." In this famous elegy he commemorates the religious happiness of the ancient Greeks and concludes with a decision for the poet to commit himself as a priest of Dionysius identified as Christ. In *Menon* the author employed the same resolution to the problems of love and compared himself to a stray deer wandering through the woods in the vain hope of relief. In his lyric poems that included "Sunset," "Bread and Wine," "The Rhine," and "Heidelberg," Hölderin reveals himself as a deeply tragic poet and one of Germany's great and dynamic lyricists. One of the greatest of these was "The Rhine," which turns from a meditation on the course of the RHINE to speculation on the reconciliation of mankind with all the gods ever worshiped.

Starting around 1801, Hölderin began experiencing some of the symptoms of schizophrenia; in 1806 he lost his librarian's post and then was confined to an asylum. His contact with reality became increasingly tenuous, and by 1808 he became hopelessly insane. From 1808 until his death in 1843 he lived a lonely life in a tower, under the care of a cabinetmaker.

Holocaust

The Holocaust, also known as the FINAL SOLUTION, is the name used to describe the annihilation of the Jews by the Nazis during WORLD WAR II. Although numbers are imprecise, about 6 million Jews were murdered, which amounted to about one-third of the Jews of the world. Most of the Jews came from Eastern Europe, and about 3 million were Polish Jews. That was a principal reason that the main killing centers were in Poland, including AUSCHWITZ-BIRKENAU, Chelmno, Treblinka, Sobibòr, Belzec, and Majdanek. In the Soviet Union another 2 million Jews were shot, starved, or died of disease.

The Holocaust was the logical outcome of the racist ideology of Adolf HITLER. German ANTI-SEMITISM had grown into racial anti-Semitism during the latter 19th century but was severely radicalized during WORLD WAR I. Radical nationalists liked to blame the German defeat in the war on Jews and socialists. During the WEIMAR REPUBLIC anti-Semitic activity grew step by step, especially among the right-wing parties and Nazis. Although anti-Semitism was a factor in the expansion of the Nazi vote, it actually was downplayed in the elections prior to Hitler's becoming chancellor. Once in power the persecution of the Jews by the Nazi regime went through three phases: (1) They were boycotted and excluded from professions, that is, from the law, medicine, teaching, press, and entertainment. (2) In 1935 Jews were again boycotted and terrorized, and were prohibited from associating in public places and in activities that were restricted for economic reasons. Emphasis was then placed on the NUREMBERG LAWS, which effectively separated Jews from Germans politically, legally, and socially. The laws defined who was a German and forbade marriages between Jews and Germans. (3) In 1938 Jewish persecution was again stepped up that spring and summer, culminating in the pogrom of Kristallnacht (*see* NIGHT OF BROKEN GLASS) on November 9–10. Synagogues all over Germany were torched, homes broken into, and many thousands of men sent off to CONCENTRATION CAMPS. In the aftermath of Kristallnacht the expulsion and emigration of Jews from Germany accelerated to a total of 317,000 Jews between 1938 and 1941. The SS were in favor of a vigorous expulsion program. An indication that the final decision to mass-murder Jews had not yet been taken was the formulation of the unrealistic Madagascar Plan, which aimed at the shipment of Jews to East Africa.

The war and the annihilation of the Jews became interrelated. Hitler's ambition was to obtain living space (LEBENSRAUM) in the Soviet Union, which he believed was ruled by Jewish Communists. So a war against Soviet Bolshevism and the annihilation of the Jews coincided, and the war provided the necessary cover-up to put his racial program into operation. When the four special strike forces (EINSATZGRUPPEN) followed the regular German army into the Soviet Union, Reinhard HEYDRICH ordered in summer 1941 the execution of all Jews in the service of the Communist Party. But the aim of the killing squads was even broader, that is, to eliminate Jewish life altogether in eastern Poland, Lithuania, Latvia, Estonia, and western Russia. The assistance of local police and paramilitary groups made the job easier. In cities such as Kiev with large Jewish populations, a total of 33,000 Jews were killed in three days, having been taken to a ravine called Babi Yar on the outskirts of the city. All those not killed were shipped to concentration camps in Poland. For instance in September 1941, 900 Soviet prisoners were gassed at Auschwitz in experimental trials of Zyklon-B gas. The Einsatzgruppen were extremely efficient in killing more than 1 million Jews in a two-year period.

More subtle and even more efficient methods were now thought to be necessary. Who was responsible for the decision for the Final Solution to execute the rest of the Jews of Europe? So-called intentionalist historians believe that Hitler had planned all along to kill the Jews and that his public speech and prophecy in the REICHSTAG on January 30, 1939, warned the world that a war would lead to the destruction of the Jewish race. The other school of historians, the functionalists, argue that the Nazis groped for a solution to the "Jewish problem" and resorted to the Final Solution during summer 1941. Nevertheless, Hitler was behind the decision, and he granted responsibility for the task to Heinrich HIMMLER. Himmler made it clear that the executioners bore no responsibility for the execution of the order; the responsibility was only Hitler's and Himmler's. The administrative responsibility for carrying out the Final Solution was given to Reinhard Heydrich as head of the RSHA. The plans for the genocide were discussed at the WANNSEE CONFERENCE in January 1942.

The technical problems in the creation of physical facilities to kill so many people were almost overwhelming. SS officers experimented with gas vans and also with the improvement of gas chambers and ovens for cremation. In summer 1941, orders were given to Rudolf HÖSS to enlarge Auschwitz because of its railway access, and five other death camps became operative by 1942 at Chelmno, Belzec, Sobibor, Majdanek, and Treblinka. At Auschwitz as many as 10,000 prisoners were sent to the gas chambers every day. In March 1942 another death camp was set up near Auschwitz outside the village of Birkenau. Jews brought here were used as forced labor in the hundreds of German factories located in this industrial region in east Upper Silesia. Those Jews who could not work were gassed and cremated immediately. Jews were brought to Auschwitz-Birkenau from as far away as Norway, the Atlantic coast of France, and Greece. Out of the 2.5 million deported to Birkenau, in some cases entire Jewish communities of various cities were annihilated: from the Greek city of Salonika—40,000; Polish city of Bialystok—10,000; Greek island of Corfu—1,800, and the Aegean island of Rhodes—1,700; from Theresianstadt—44,000.

Many other concentration camps existed in Germany, such as BERGEN-BELSEN and BUCHENWALD, and in Austria, France, and Yugoslavia where both Jews and non-Jews perished through forced labor, starvation, and murder. Little known were the executions of Yugoslav Jews in camps set up in Croatia, an ally of Germany; near Belgrade the Germans operated a camp at Zemun, where some 15,000 Serbian Jews were killed in gas vans. The killing campaign spread throughout Nazi-occupied Europe, continuing even though resources were being taken away from the war effort. During 1942 Jews were shipped from France, Belgium, Holland, and Norway. In 1943 Jews were deported from the cities of BERLIN, Vienna, and Prague and the countries of Greece, Luxembourg, southern France, Italy, and Denmark. The survivors of the Jewish revolt in the Warsaw ghetto were sent to their deaths at Treblinka. Almost a half million Hungarian Jews were among the very last to be sent to Auschwitz after the Germans occupied Hungary in 1944. Most of the Jewish citizens of Poland, Greece, Czechoslovakia, and the Netherlands died in the gas chambers, while half the Jews of Romania and Hungary survived. After the fall of Mussolini trains from Italy, Croatia, and Greece arrived at Auschwitz and Mauthausen. Most of the Jews of Denmark and Bulgaria survived where the local population actively aided them. Out of the 5 million to 6 million Jews who were killed, about 3 million died in the death camps.

Although the Holocaust was one of the worst cases of genocide in modern history, it arose out of the prejudices and hatred that inspired a terribly misguided fanatical ideology aimed at one group of human beings. Although there had been pogroms and violence against Jews throughout their history, the enormity of the Holocaust and its stain on German culture have been unforgettable. Nevertheless, in his final testament dictated in his bunker beneath Berlin, Hitler repeated his anti-Semitic misconceptions and exhorted Germans to continue to follow his racial laws.

Holy Roman Empire

The Holy Roman Empire was the name used to identify the first German Empire, which lasted from 962 to 1806. The largely Germanic and North Italian territory was organized by Otto the Great in 962. In response to several appeals of Pope John XII to enter Italy and restore law and order, Otto married Adelaide, the heiress of the crown of Lombardy, and pronounced himself king of Italy. The pope bestowed upon him the imperial crown, and the event marked the actual beginning of the Holy Roman Empire of the German Nation. This term was not applied to the Empire itself until the end of the 15th century. Continuity was reestablished with the traditions of ancient Rome, and the Carolingian Empire was reestablished. Primitive northern Europe once more came into a relation with the more advanced culture of the Mediterranean and Byzantine civilization. Under Otto III Rome became the capital of the Empire, while the emperor exercised almost complete control over the papacy.

The German monarchy under the Saxon and Salian emperors was still hereditary. Nominally, the ecclesiastical and secular electors (*Kurfürsten*) formed the electoral college, but in reality the more powerful ones among the German emperors exercised their authority to secure the succession of their eldest sons. Up to the year 1257 the ecclesiastical electors were the archbishops of Mainz, Cologne, and Trier; the secular electors were the Count Palatine, the duke of Saxony and the margrave of BRANDENBURG and the king of Bohemia. The number of electors was established in 1356 by the Golden Bull. In 1623 the electoral dignity was transferred from the Count Palatine to the ruler of BAVARIA, while in 1648 the Palatinate was once more added as the eighth, and in 1692 HANOVER as the ninth electoral district. After 1803 additional electoral provinces were created in Baden, Hesse-Kassel, Württemberg, and Salzburg.

At the Diet of Nuremberg in 1356 Emperor Charles IV promulgated the famous Golden Bull, whose significance has been compared by some with that of the British Magna Carta of 1215. It stipulated that the Empire was an elective institution and defined the powers of the electoral princes, dealt with the proceedings at elections and the order of succession to an electorate, and most of its provisions remained valid to the very end of the Holy Roman Empire in 1806. The Golden Bull gave legal sanction to the fragmentation and independence within the Empire, a kind of "legal anarchy." The electorates gained full sovereign power and were inheritable through the rule of primogeniture.

The seat of the emperor was dominated by the House of Habsburg between 1440 and 1806 with the exception of Emperor Charles VII, a Bavarian who ruled between 1742 and 1745. From 1512 to 1806 the Holy Roman Empire comprised 10 imperial districts encompassing 314 sovereign territorial states, as well as the lands of more than 1,400 independent imperial knights. In 1521 there also were 85 IMPERIAL CITIES, which had shrunk to fewer than 51 by the middle of the 18th century. HAMBURG was perhaps the largest with a population of 130,000, and the smallest was Buchau with fewer than 1,000. The size of the Empire stretched from the Duchy of Holland on the North Sea to the Bishopric of Trent on Lake Garda in the Austrian Tyrol; on the west from ALSACE-LORRAINE, which was to become French, to the Grand Duchy of Austria and the Kingdom of Bohemia in the east. This amounted to about 672,000 kilometers with an estimated population of 24 million. It was polycentric and possessed no common culture, economy, or even political center. The Empire was a patchwork structure as was evident in the location of its principal institutions: In REGENSBURG the REICHSTAG convened; in Mainz the imperial Chancellor resided; in Wetzlar the Imperial High Court of Justice met; and the coronation of the emperor took place in FRANKFURT. After the PEACE OF WESTPHALIA in 1648 the Empire was weakened further and had to be guaranteed by France and Sweden, to which was added Russia in 1779. When Napoleon sought to establish a French-dominated Empire, he insisted on the formal abolition of the Holy Roman Empire in 1806.

Honecker, Erich (1912–1994)
GDR leader

After the resignation of Walter ULBRICHT, Erich Honecker became the leader of the SOCIALIST UNITY PARTY (SED) and therefore of the GERMAN DEMOCRATIC REPUBLIC (GDR) from May 1971 until October 1989.

Born in 1912 in Neunkirchen in the industrial region of the Saar, Erich Honecker was the son of a Communist coal miner who grew up believing that communism was the solution to the problems of the working class. After Erich finished school in 1926, unable to attend the university, he joined the youth organization of the GERMAN COMMUNIST PARTY (KPD) and went on to apprentice in the roofing trade. He became head of the local youth group, and in 1930 the KPD offered him the opportunity to attend a party school in Moscow. After the Nazis took over in 1933, he participated in the underground and led the illegal Communist youth organization in BERLIN. Arrested by the GESTAPO, he was sentenced to life imprisonment until he was freed by the Russians in 1945.

Remaining in Eastern Germany, Honecker helped build a socialist state following the Soviet model. He rebuilt the Communist Youth Organization and the Free German Youth (FDJ), which he led until 1955. After studying security affairs in the Soviet Union, he returned and was placed in charge of security in the GDR and coordinated the construction of the BERLIN WALL in 1961. When Walter Ulbricht was forced to resign in 1971, Honecker was elected general secretary of the SED, which effectively made him head of state. From 1976 he was chairman of the Council of State.

Honecker was associated with the OSTPOLITIK of Willy BRANDT and signed the series of East-West treaties that provided international recognition for the GDR. Honecker signed three treaties with the FEDERAL REPUBLIC (FRG), including the "Transit Agreement" and "Traffic Treaty" of 1972, which facilitated trade and travel between the two countries. The two countries also agreed to respect their borders and sovereignty. Honecker achieved further recognition of the GDR's sovereign status by signing the Helsinki Accords. Trade with the West was facilitated and helped the economy. Significant were loans from the West, an interest-free credit line with West Germany, income from user fees, and millions of marks that were received annually from liberalized travel by Westerners. Internally, Honecker followed a policy of technological modernization, hoping that exports would propel the economy forward, but that proved illusory. The expansion of social programs such as a new minimum wage, raised retirement benefits, a shortened working day, and an ambitious program of housing construction to contain popular discontent also did not work. The policies were dependent on foreign loans and subsidies from the Federal Republic, which placed the GDR further in debt.

Changes were taking place in the 1980s. Tensions between the superpowers and the election of the conservative Helmut KOHL restricted any further changes with the West. By 1987 the signs of crisis were mounting as Honecker made a celebrated state visit to West Germany. An exodus of East Germans began in October 1989, which led to the end of the Berlin Wall and the Revolution of 1989. After the reunification of East and West Germany, Honecker was arrested on charges of treason and for ordering killings along the border. His trial began in November 1992, but he pleaded ill health and was allowed to immigrate to Chile, where he died in May 1994.

Höss, Rudolf Franz (1907–1947)
commandant of Auschwitz

Rudolf Höss had served at the Dachau CONCENTRATION CAMP between 1934 and 1938 and was appointed by Heinrich HIMMLER commandant at Auschwitz-Birkenau, which he administered to the end of the war.

In Baden-Baden on November 25, 1900, Rudolf Franz Ferdinand Höss was born the son of Franz Xaver, a shopkeeper who had earlier served in the German colonial army in East Africa. Until Rudolf was six years old, the family lived in an average home outside Baden-Baden near the Black Forest. Then they moved to MANNHEIM. Rudolf was raised in military fashion with a strong emphasis on obedience to orders. His family included two sisters and the mother, who were demonstratively affectionate. The family was pious, and the father fervently prayed that Rudolf had a vocation to the priesthood. When WORLD WAR I broke out, he secretly joined the army underage at 16, arriving in Turkey in 1917 on his way to the Iraqi front. Wounded several times, he was awarded the Iron Cross, both first and second class. Instead of being captured and placed in a camp, he and his unit found their way back to Germany. After the war he joined the FREE CORPS (Freikorps), volunteer units of soldiers who could not adjust to a peacetime existence. He served in the Baltic states, where he witnessed the Latvians commit horrors against civilians. He also served against the French in the Ruhr and the Poles in Silesia. In 1922 he joined the NAZI PARTY, and in 1923 was arrested for participation in a political murder. Released from prison in 1928 under a general amnesty, he turned to farming and became a member of the SS. Soon he and his wife joined Himmler's nationalist Artamanen Society. After Hitler came to power,

Höss was assigned to the Dachau camp in 1934, where he served under Theodor EICKE until 1938. In 1940 he was placed in charge of AUSCHWITZ and directed by Himmler to build it into a death camp for Jews.

Within two years Höss expanded Auschwitz-Birkenau into the largest killing center in the Third Reich. Höss was responsible for the execution of more than 2.5 million inmates, not counting a half million who starved to death. He felt that he carried out his orders to the best of his ability, had a difficult but necessary job to perform, and had do so without sympathy and pity. Late in 1943 he was temporarily assigned to BERLIN to assume responsibility for the Central Office for Camp Operation within the RSHA. He returned to Auschwitz in June 1944, when the Hungarian Jews arrived for annihilation.

Höss believed that what he was ordered to do relieved him of any responsibility. He was brought up with a compulsion to follow orders, and learned probably through Himmler that exterminating Jews was a form of pest control. He made it a mechanical system with the precision of modern industrial methods. He believed that his work was hygienic and clean.

After the war Höss at first avoided detection but was arrested early in 1946. He was extradited to Poland, where he stood trial for war crimes against the Polish people. On March 29, 1947, he was sentenced to death at Warsaw and was returned to Auschwitz, where he was hanged on April 16, 1947.

Hossbach Memorandum (1937)

The Hossbach Memorandum was the notes taken by HITLER's army adjutant, Colonel Friedrich Hossbach, of a meeting Hitler had convened on November 5, 1937, which documented Hitler's decision to unleash a war of aggression in the near future.

Hitler's decision was first presented and discussed at the Reich Chancellery in BERLIN on November 5, 1937. Among those invited to the meeting were Field Marshal Werner von BLOMBERG, Colonel General Werner von FRITSCH, commander in chief of the army, Admiral Erich Raeder, commander in chief of the navy, as well as Hermann GÖRING and Konstantin von Neurath, the foreign minister. The group was limited to the military command and the Foreign Ministry, though Göring represented the AIR FORCE and other offices. Hitler was in an elated and optimistic mood about the international situation, and for more than four hours presented his ideas and theories of race, population, economics, and the need for LEBENSRAUM (living space). He emphasized that "German policy was to make secure and preserve the racial community." Most of his arguments were almost verbatim reiterations of his expansionist-imperialist ideas, which he had developed in MEIN KAMPF. Germany's population could not be expected to experience healthy growth with its limited living space and could not maintain its living standards either through AUTARCHY or by participation in the world trading system. The logical conclusion was that Germany had to acquire more living space and resources to the East and that meant the use of force. He told them that the period of treaty revisionism had served its purpose and was over. Strategic planning now had to begin to realize this needed living space. This "road of force" was to begin with the "lightning" absorption of AUSTRIA and the destruction of Czechoslovakia. It was clear that his goal was not the resolution of the völkish issues of the Sudeten area, but the conquest of all of Czechoslovakia. In the event of a war with France Hitler recognized that Czechoslovakia would be too dangerous an enemy not to be destroyed first. The whole presentation clearly outlined the strategy and imperialistic nature of Hitler's policy goals.

Most of those present at the meeting were "silent and uneasy." The commander in chief of the army, Fritsch, protested that Germany had to avoid any situation in which Britain and France would go to war against Germany, a position that Blomberg supported. In the back of Fritsch's mind was the recent report submitted to him by the chief of staff, General Ludwig BECK, that Germany was not ready for war and that the German population saw no justification for it. The Hossbach Memorandum makes it clear that long before the crisis over the Sudeten, which Germans ignited, and the MUNICH CONFERENCE took place, Hitler had determined to crush Czechoslovakia.

Hubertusburg, Treaty of (February 1763)

After fighting the most powerful European coalition of powers to a standstill, FREDERICK II, the Great, could regard himself as victorious. He was able to retain all of his gains from the first two Silesian wars. Silesia was to remain in Prussian hands. What Frederick gave in return was his promise to vote for the election of Joseph as king of Rome. The Austro-Prussian negotiations took place in the dismal setting of the hunting lodge of August the Strong, which had been devastated by Prussian soldiers in 1761. In the negotiations Kaunitz had not given up hope that Austria might keep Glatz, but Frederick insisted that SAXONY not be awarded an indemnity, which along with Britain had paid the major share of PRUSSIA's war costs.

One significant result of the peace was that Prussia was constrained by the continental powers in its attempt to expand. For Germany as a whole it produced a 30-year period of peace. England and France ended their war through the Peace of Paris concluded in January 1763. In the negotiations with France the British failed to consult Prussia. The British disregarded the fact that the French still occupied Cleves, Mörs, and Geldern on the lower RHINE. France could turn them over to AUSTRIA and use them in negotiations with Prussia. While it drove Frederick into the arms of Russia, England deservedly earned the reputation of making peace at the expense of its allies.

Huch, Ricarda (1864–1947)
novelist and historian

Ricarda Huch was the greatest woman writer in modern German literature. Her work included well-researched works on history, historical novels, poetry, and literary criticism. She was involved in the German women's movement and was an outspoken critic of the Nazi regime.

She studied history at the University of Zurich because German universities still were not open to women. In 1892 she received her doctorate. Huch first became known for her poetry and novels, which reflected a passionate love for life and beauty. She had a great admiration for the political changes of 19th-century Italy rather than for the artistic Renaissance of the 15th century. Writing in a lyrical style she anticipated Thomas MANN's *Buddenbrooks* by describing the decay of a patrician family in HAMBURG. (Mann later described Huch as "Germany's first lady".) Perhaps her most lasting contributions are her works on Italian and German history in which she blends solid historical research with imaginative narration. The three works were: *Tales of Garibaldi* (1907); *Men and Destinies during the Risorgimento* (1908); and *The Thirty Years' War* (1914). In *The Thirty Years' War* she described it in dynamic scenes and images. Among her strictly scholarly works were *The Golden Age of Romanticism* (1899), *Gottfried Keller* (1904), and *Luther's Faith* (1916) as well as a three-volume *History of Germany* (*Geschichte Deutschlands*), which appeared in Switzerland during 1933. In the history she condemned the historical treatment of the Jews. She was an enthusiastic supporter of democracy, going back to her days in Switzerland. Although she remained in Germany during the Nazi regime, she was a critic of their brutality, ANTI-SEMITISM and violation of civil rights. Yet although she was slandered in the Nazi press, she was not imprisoned. She resigned from the Prussian Academy of Fine Arts in 1933 when it introduced "Aryanization."

At the end of the 19th century Ricarda Huch participated in the women's movement and tried to break down discrimination. Because she shared some of the values of conservative feminism, she opposed the NATIONALISM and militaristic policies of the FEDERATION OF GERMAN WOMEN'S ASSOCIATIONS.

Hugenberg, Alfred (1865–1961)
chairman of right-wing political party

Alfred Hugenberg was a wealthy founder of the Pan-German League and was a director of the Krupp enterprises in Essen. He was a staunch nationalist and advocate of expansionist war aims. In order to influence public opinion, he created a newspaper syndicate, and in 1927 his group bought control of Germany's largest film corporation, Ufa, and used its profits to support right-wing movements. Becoming a member of the German National People's Party (DNVP) in 1919, he soon took over the party. He favored a plebiscite against the Young Plan and provided Adolf Hitler with respectability. Hugenberg had hoped to include Nazis in a broad-based coalition, but the voters preferred Hitler. Even though Hugenberg was opposed to Hitler's socialism, he preferred him over democratic alternatives. In 1933 Hugenberg was appointed "economic dictator" in the Hitler cabinet. He resigned on June 26, 1933, after which the DNVP dissolved itself.

Huguenots
(French Calvinists)

Many immigrants came to Germany after the Thirty Years' War. The largest single group were the Huguenots, who arrived from France after the renunciation of the Edict of Nantes in 1685. Protestant states gained the most from foreign immigration. Frederick William, the Great Elector, through his Edict of Potsdam invited Frenchmen of the Reformed-Evangelical faith to come to Brandenburg. About 30,000 Huguenots sought refuge in Germany, and some 20,000 settled in Hohenzollern territories. More came later. Others immigrated to Ansbach-Bayreuth, Hesse-Kassel, the Palatinate, Brunswick-Lüneberg, Frankfurt, Emden, Bremen, Hamburg, and Lübeck. They were scattered through 240 different communities. Württemberg, which was strictly Lutheran, refused admission to the Huguenots. The port city of Hamburg also was open to Huguenots as well as Dutch, Portuguese, Jews, and others.

The Huguenots contributed greatly to the army of the Great Elector in Brandenburg. Of the Huguenots who came to Brandenburg, one-sixth were soldiers, and many of those were noblemen who easily received appointments in the army. Many of the Huguenots had a largely urban background, and they brought expertise not only in artisan production but also in wholesale commerce and luxury manufactures, finance, and industrial entrepreneurship. Many of these Huguenots kept aloof from the local German population, regarding themselves as a social elite. This was made easier for them by the special privileges granted the larger communities, including separate churches, law courts, army regimental organizations, and freedom from guild membership and regulations. They had their own remarkable social insurance system of poor relief, health care, and other charitable benevolences. In Prussia, as elsewhere, the prosperous Huguenots began to emerge from their self-imposed social and cultural isolation only after the Seven Years' War, but thereafter became well-accepted members of their communities at both noble and bourgeois levels.

humanism, German

Humanism is a philosophical and literary movement originating in Italy during the late 14th and early 15th centuries and diffusing to the rest of Europe. The Italian scholars who were called "humanists" devoted themselves to the study of classical writings of ancient Greece and Rome. They sought to exalt and ennoble man. The humanists wanted to create a new humanity modeled on the ideals of the old Roman culture, of which they considered themselves successors. Italian humanism was essentially an intellectual and philological movement. As a form of culture the Italian Renaissance focused on external forms and sensuous beauty and became for many a philosophy of life. The Italian humanists thought that their age was one of rebirth, believing it possible for the classical age to be reborn in the present. Hence, the French term, *Renaissance*.

When the Renaissance was diffused across the Alps to Germany, it was transformed into a strong moral and educational force. German thinkers had been much more concerned with the substance and not the appearances of things. While the Italian humanists were more interested in original pagan ideas and texts of Greece and Rome, German humanists focused more on the treasures of Christian antiquity, the writings of the Church Fathers, and the original texts of Scripture.

German humanism had its beginnings in the second half of the 14th century in Bohemia and adjacent regions where the Renaissance culture of the south was admired. As did the Italian princes, German princes were proud patrons and protectors of the movement. The history of humanism in Germany begins with Johann von Neumarkt at the court of Emperor Charles IV, who has been called "the father of German humanism." Neumarkt found followers, and in about 1400 Johann of Tepl's *The Plowman from Bohemia* was written, which was a humanistic disputation between the plowman and death. The Hussite rebellion ended this promising early start. Beginning again in the 15th century, the Italian humanists became the models for the Germans. German humanist literature originated in southern Germany. There the Swabian Heinrich Steinhöwel, the Swiss Nicholas von Wyle, and the Franconian Albrecht von Eyb distinguished themselves in translating many works of the Italian humanists such as Petrarch, Boccaccio, Aeneas Sillvious Piccolomini, and the Latin comedies of Platus and Terence. AUGSBURG and NÜRNBERG were centers of humanism, as were Basel, HEIDELBERG, Prague, Strasbourg, Vienna, and Erfurt, as well as cities along the RHINE, such as Mainz and Cologne. Princely courts patronized the poets and scholars. The emperor MAXIMILIAN, the "last of the knights," cultivated humanistic interests, and the courts of Württemberg, Saxony, Brandenburg and the Palatinate became centers of humanistic culture and education.

In Cologne the humanists encountered the first organized opposition from the old scholastics. A battle ensued between the humanists and scholastics, wherein the great Hebrew scholar and philologist Johannes REUCHLIN opposed the theological intolerance that demanded that all Hebrew books be burned. The scholastics were ridiculed as stupid charlatans, and the humanists won over many students to their cause. Humanistic ideas also were taken up in Swabia and BAVARIA, in the German east and north. In Nuremberg humanism was promoted by Wilibald Pirckheimer, and in Ingolstadt and Vienna by Conrad CELTIS. In the distant northeast Nicolaus Copernicus laid the foundations for modern astronomy.

German humanism did not play an important role as an ideal in political life nor as an ideal of a cultured personality as in Renaissance Italy. Humanists, however, played an important role in the reform of the universities. They complained that the university curriculum failed to adequately teach the arts, which had been neglected in favor of the professions. The humanists under the leadership of Jakob Wimpfeling introduced a new curriculum, which emphasized truly humanistic culture. ERASMUS of Rotterdam was the foremost humanist of the age, and although a Dutchman, can be considered a member of the society of the HOLY ROMAN EMPIRE. He edited the Greek text of the New Testament; Martin LUTHER's translation of the Gospels would have been impossible without his translation. What Erasmus did for the New Testament, Reuchlin did for the Old Testament by publishing his Hebrew grammar in 1506. Other humanists were model teachers rather than philosophers or philologists who proclaimed the new ideas by their personal example. Wilibald Pirkheimer belonged to this group of teachers, along with Conrad Peutinger and the Alsatian Jakob Wimpfeling. PARACELSUS, whose real name was Theophrastus Bombastus von Hohenheim, was a scientist who was one of the first to question the wisdom of medieval medicine in Latin books. It was Paracelsus who experimented and practiced personal observation through the dissection of bodies.

Humanitistic lyric poetry was of greater merit than that of contemporary German poetry. The humanistic poets wrote odes, eclogues, and all kinds of occasional poems. It even became customary to address friends and patrons in poetry, celebrating baptisms and weddings, funerals and eulogies. Even erotic sentiments were expressed by neo-Latin poets who spoke of love in sensuous terms. In Germany Conrad Celtis, the most elegant poet and propagandist of German humanism, wrote "Amorous Poems," which praised voluptuousness. Perhaps the greatest of the neo-Latin poets among the German humanists were Eobanus Hessus and Petrus Lotichius; these poets expressed themselves in stylistic perfection and metaphorical embellishments.

With few exceptions modern drama has been derived from the drama of the humanists. Terence and Plautus, Aristophanes, and Seneca were rediscovered by the humanists and were set up as technical and poetic models. The humanists no longer employed only themes from the Bible but wrote dramas with plots of all sorts. It did not take long before they wrote lively Latin dramas. Reuchlin and Celtis were the first to master this form.

Humboldt, Alexander von
(1769–1859)

traveler, geographer, mineralogist, and botanist

Alexander von Humboldt, the brother of Wilhelm von HUMBOLDT, was born in BERLIN on September 14, 1769, to a Prussian army officer and an aloof French HUGUENOT mother. He was early educated by a private tutor, later attended the universities of Frankfurt an der Oder and the modern university at GÖTTINGEN in 1787 and then went on to the School of Mines at Freiburg in SAXONY. In 1792 he joined the mining department of the Prussian government. In 1799 he started his five-year trip of exploration mainly to South America. From 1804 to 1827 Humboldt lived in Paris as a writer and scientist. In 1814 Humboldt accompanied the Prussian king FREDERICK WILLIAM III to London and in 1822 to Verona. Later, he lived in Berlin and in 1830 became an adviser to the king of Prussia. From 1830 to 1848 he performed several diplomatic missions to Paris. Starting in 1834 until 1862 he wrote the monumental *Kosmos*, the most com-

Alexander von Humboldt *(Library of Congress)*

prehensive presentation of the body of scientific knowledge of that era, published in Stuttgart in five volumes.

A splendid scientific observer, he observed the connection between deforestation and soil erosion. On his scientific expeditions throughout Europe, Siberian Russia, and Central and South America, Alexander von Humboldt pursued pioneering studies in the fields of geography, biology, and anthropology. During the five years he traveled in South America and Mexico, he discovered new material on volcanoes and in the structure of the Andes Mountains. He observed the relics of Aztec and Inca civilizations. Accompanied by the botanist Aimé Boupland, they collected extensive data on plant geography and climate. In 1800 he proceeded from the capital of Venezuela, Caracas, on his famous Orinoco expedition, during which he discovered the connection between the river systems of the Orinoco and the Amazon. The account of the whole expedition was published in French in 35 volumes between 1814 and 1819.

In December 1794 in JENA Alexander associated with GOETHE and SCHILLER and returned for several months in 1797. The classical influence of WEIMAR remained part of his thinking for the rest of his life. He never managed to marry, but found his happiness in friendships and the household of his brother Wilhelm. Benevolent but an acerbic personality, he died on May 6, 1859, in Berlin.

Humboldt, Wilhelm, Baron von
(Karl Wilhelm, Freiherr [Baron] von Humboldt) (1767–1835)
educator, statesman, and philologist

Baron Wilhelm von Humboldt was one of Germany's greatest educational reformers, a diplomat, philologist, and man of letters. He helped reform the Prussian school system, founded the Friedrich Wilhelm University (since 1945 Humboldt-University) of BERLIN, and contributed to the development of comparative philology.

Born in Potsdam on June 22, 1767, the older brother of Alexander von HUMBOLDT, Wilhelm was highly sensitive and analytical. He studied law at the universities of Berlin, and GÖTTINGEN and in 1794 began studies at JENA. In 1791 he married Caroline von Dacheroden. He had a sensitive character and during his youthful years became highly cultured and cosmopolitan through his association with GOETHE and SCHILLER and the humanistic circles of WEIMAR. In 1799 he published a critical essay on Johann Wolfgang von Goethe's *Hermann and Dorothea,* which gained him recognition on aesthetics. In 1802 he was appointed the Prussian minister to Rome, returning to PRUSSIA in 1809, when at the recommendation of Baron Karl vom und zum STEIN, he was made councillor of state and minister of public instruction. In 1810 Humboldt was appointed Prussian ambassador to Vienna and was instrumental in convincing AUSTRIA to unite with Prussia in defeating Napoleon. He participated in the CONGRESS OF VIENNA, where Prussia added parts of SAXONY, and acquired the Rhineland albeit against her will. He approved of the creation of the GERMAN CONFEDERATION as an association of German governments. As the Prussian representative to the diet of the confederation, he wrote to HARDENBURG that it could develop into a federal state. In 1817 he became ambassador to London, but in 1819 he resigned his government offices in protest over the repressive CARLSBAD DECREES.

When he accepted his position as education minister, he did not have a program of reform in mind, but derived his ideas from the German ENLIGHTENMENT, classical IDEALISM, and the new nationalist and liberal ideologies. Humboldt's reforms were influenced by Immanuel KANT, F. A. Wolf, J. G. FICHTE, F. W. Schelling, and F. SCHLEIERMACHER. In the process of making reforms he became the creator of the modern system of "humanistic" education in Germany. Humboldt aimed at the development of the humanistic ideal of a cultured personality and sought a radical division between the education of the individual based on a classical Greek model and vocational training. His humanistic secondary schools (*Gymnasien*) were the means to this end and the study of ancient and modern languages the basis of secondary education. For Humboldt, language in particular was a means for the creative development of intellectual forces and faculties. Humboldt looked to the educational ideas of the reformer Pestalozzi to bridge the gap between an educated intelligentsia and the common people. The unified school system that emerged from the reforms was tripartite, consisting of elementary schools (*Volksschulen*), "humanistic" secondary schools (*Gymnasien*), and universities for graduate study. Pestalozzi and the New Humanists argued that a well-balanced and liberally educated mind could master any scientific or professional problem. Humboldt's ideas on education were idealistic and did not allow much for the intellectual and moral limitations of human beings. In 1810 the University of Berlin was established, and for the first half of the 19th century it became the chief center of philological and philosophical studies in Europe.

Humboldt's contributions to political theory included *The Sphere and Duties of Government*

(1792; 1852), wherein he argued that a government is only one of the institutions that contributes to the development of the individual. Under the influence of ROMANTICISM he viewed individual nationality as part of divine life. In 1813 he wrote essays on a possible German constitution and in 1819 on the Prussian. He advocated a form of LIBERALISM and federalism that would respect the traditions of individual states, provinces, and regions. Not surprisingly, he rejected the liberalism of the French Revolution, which was based on the will of the individual.

Husserl, Edmund (1859–1938)
philosopher
Edmund Husserl was the father of phenomenology, the central goal of which was to establish a scientific basis for philosophy.

Edmund Husserl was born on April 8, 1859, in Prosnitz, Moravia. He attended schools in Vienna and Olmütz. Later he studied physics, astronomy, and mathematics at the University of LEIPZIG. He was especially talented in mathematics and went to study at the University of BERLIN with leading mathematicians, taking his doctoral degree in mathematics. In 1883 he returned to the University of Vienna, where he attended lectures of the philosopher Franz Brentano until 1886, becoming increasingly interested in philosophy. His then taught at Halle (1887–1901), GÖTTINGEN (1901–16), and finally at Freiburg (1916–29), where he spent the remainder of his life. It was during the last years at Freiburg that he was affected by the social and political pressures because of his Jewish ancestry. He died on April 27, 1938.

For Husserl philosophy was a "calling" to which he devoted his life, believing that it was primarily a science. Husserl's first systematic discussion of phenomenology appeared in his book *Logical Investigations* (1900–01). According to his thinking, human consciousness was the only source of objective data on which a universal philosophical system could be based.

His conception of philosophical science changed more than once. The truths that he called science did not concern a particular subject matter, but the unshakable foundations of all human knowledge. He pursued truth with almost a religious fervor, publishing eight books and writing thousands of manuscript pages. He spoke of himself as a "perpetual beginner" because he had to start over again abandoning his earlier views. His life was consumed by the pursuit of finding a radical foundation for rational thought. Consequently, Husserl never did produce a final Husserlian "system" of philosophical thought and did not arrive at an unambiguous phenomenological method. He did continue to insist that phenomenology was descriptive and distinct from psychology. Furthermore, phenomenology was distinguishable from philosophy, which is deductive, and describes what is believed to be true of the world based on prior assumptions. Consciousness had to be studied through the phenomenological method, which alone can discover what the world is really like.

As important as his ideas were and as difficult as they are to comprehend, he fascinated his students and influenced some other important 20th-century thinkers such as Martin HEIDEGGER in Germany and Jean-Paul Sartre (1905–80) in France.

Hutten, Ulrich von (1488–1523)
humanist, satirist, nationalist, and knight
Ulrich von Hutten was the political publicist of German HUMANISM. He transferred his warlike spirit as an imperial knight to the literary arena. He possessed a bitter hatred of the papacy and favored a universal German empire. Hutten supported LUTHER and the REFORMATION.

Hutten was born in a castle near Fulda in Hesse to impoverished Franconian nobility. At age 11 his parents sent him to a monastery school at Fulda. He left, however, at age 17, becoming an itinerant student at the various universities of Cologne, Erfurt, Greifswald, Wittenberg, and Vienna, enthused with the learning of the humanists. Later, he also attended Pavia and Bologna. It was between 1511 and 1513 that he went to Italy and because he was so poor decided to serve as a mercenary soldier in the imperial army in 1512. By 1513 he returned to Germany, served as a councillor to Albert, the new bishop of Magdeburg and Mainz, who also became his protector. In the meantime Hutten had won praise from ERASMUS, was protected by the Emperor MAXIMILIAN, and due to his increasing fame as a poet was designated poet laureate by the emperor in August 1517.

What made him famous was his sharp Latin diatribes against Duke Ulrich of Württemberg, who, coveting his cousin's wife, was responsible for the husband's death. Embittered at the duke, Hutten launched a series of devastating literary attacks. He wrote *Exposures of Ulrich* (1515) and a dialogue, *Phalarismus* (1516), which also developed into a denunciation of tyrants. In 1519 Hutten even participated in a war that evicted Duke Ulrich from his dominions. During the preparations for the campaign against the duke, Hutten became acquainted with Franz von Sickingen and promised to help Sickingen's friend Johannes REUCHLIN. Hutten was one of the two anonymous authors of the biting satire *Letters of Obscure Men*, which ridiculed Reuchlin's enemies and exposed the ignorance and bigotry of the clergy who supported the ANTI-SEMITISM of Johannes Pfefferkorn. It was the most devastating assault ever made upon Scholasticism and its Dominican commentators. Later, however, when Reuchlin condemned Luther's teachings, Hutten broke with him.

Hutten's aggressive resentments turned toward the papacy, which he attacked for immorality and greed. When he wrote the bitter dialogue *Vadiscus* (1520), directed against the papacy, he lost the patronage and protection of Archbishop Albert. His fierce hatred for the papacy also led him to support Martin Luther as a fellow fighter for German freedom in *The Arouser of the German Nation* (1520) and to support a national church and national culture. His lively NATIONALISM found expression in *Arminius* (1524), a dialogue in which the Roman Scipio, the Carthaginian Hannibal, and the German Arminius confronted one another over the issue as to who was the greater leader. It was Arminius who had unified the German tribes and was the defender of national soil. This work marks the beginning of the Arminius legend, which played an important role in German national aspirations into the 19th century.

Constantly involved in conflicts with powerful enemies, many of Hutten's hopes and dreams ended in disappointment. Some of them included the failure to enlist Erasmus as an ally in his projects and the failures to enlist Luther, Franz von Sickingen, and the emperors Maximilian and CHARLES V in his struggle for a stronger and independent empire. Hutten was an "imperialist" who believed that the emperor represented the German people and that the loss of the Empire's universal position was due to the Italian papacy.

Hutten is notable for his racy German style and was an outstanding satirist and developer of the dialogue literary style, which he borrowed from the Roman Lucian. Hutten had a fierce temperament and defended the weak against the strong. His body was weakened by his struggle with syphilis. In Switzerland the reformer Huldreich ZWINGLI protected him until his death in 1523.

idealism

The term *idealism* denotes a secularized version of a spiritual rather than a materialistic philosophy of human life and culture. It found its roots in ancient Gnosticism, through Neoplatonism, Renaissance nature philosophy, and the insights of PARACELSUS, Böhme, and LEIBNIZ into what became the idealistic movement. Idealism also was a true descendant of the Lutheran REFORMATION and its effort to create a life of the spirit outside the institutional church and state. Both the mystical communalism of PIETISM and the rationalism of the ENLIGHTENMENT nourished idealism and played a role in its development.

While philosophical materialism and empiricism did not take root in German thought as it did in France, an idealistic system of thought took shape with Immanuel KANT, Johann Gottlieb FICHTE, Friedrich Wilhelm Schelling, and Georg Wilhelm Friedrich HEGEL. For them true reality resided in the ideal form and not the material thing. Idealism in its philosophical sense emphasizes that the human mind and spiritual values are fundamental in the world. It is opposed to NATURALISM and the assumptions that ideas, the mind, and spiritual values are "reducible to material things and processes." First employed in the 18th century by Gottfried Wilhelm von Leibniz, the term *idealism* was used to describe antimaterialist philosophers like Plato and Leibniz's own "metaphysical idealism." Leibniz interpreted nature as not independently real. Immanuel Kant developed the next stage, termed *transcendental idealism*. The progress from Kant's idealism to what has been called "absolute or moral idealism" occurred in the thinking of Johann Gottlieb Fichte. Then Fichte's ideas were interpreted by Friedrich Wilhelm Schelling in his "aesthetic idealism," which concluded that the artist makes us aware of the Absolute. The giant and most comprehensive philosopher of idealism was Georg Wilhelm Friedrich Hegel. Other leading idealist thinkers were Johann Gottfried HERDER, Friedrich SCHILLER, and Johann Wolfgang von GOETHE. They were interested in the creative forces within man that shape religious faiths, artistic styles, and the forms of institutions and whole cultures.

Idealism also identified the orientation of German literature during the years from 1790 to 1805, which was a reaction to the dominance of French forms of rationalism and classicism. German writers emphasized the individual genius of the thinker. In this period Friedrich Schiller was influenced by Kant, and the great literary alliance between Schiller and Goethe occurred. Schiller understood that Kant split man's world into two halves, a physical part and an abstract and transcendental half. Schiller was a more abstract thinker who moved and thought in a world of ideal essences, which was more real than the world of sense experience. Schiller was a deductive poet whose reasoning descended from concept to facts. Goethe, on the other hand, was more of an inductive thinker who proceeded from daily experiences and facts to the ideas or generalizations behind them and the formation of ideal types and concepts

immigration

Since 1960 more than 30 million people have moved to Germany. By the late 20th century there were close to 8 million foreign residents, making up more than 7 percent of the population. In some densely populated urban areas they account for well over 20 percent. The largest ethnic groups are Turks with more than 1.7 million; Yugoslavs, around 700,000; some 500,000 Italians; 330,000 Greeks; and 270,000 Portuguese. Overall, the immigrant population increases by some 100,000 people annually.

As of the year 2000 the percentages of immigrants in the various German states were: BADEN-WÜRTTEMBERG (12.5 percent); BAVARIA (9.2 percent); BERLIN (12.8 percent); BRANDENBURG (2.4 percent); BREMEN (15.3 percent); HAMBURG (15.4 percent); HESSE (12.1 percent); Lower Saxony (6.7 percent); Mecklenburg-Western Pomerania (1.8 percent); NORTH RHINE-WESTPHALIA (11.4 percent); RHINELAND-PALATINATE (7.7 percent); SAARLAND (8.2 percent); SAXONY (2.4 percent); Saxony-Anhalt (1.7 percent); Schleswig-Holstein (5.5 percent); Thuringia (1.7 percent). The non-German population in the FEDERAL REPUBLIC is widely and unevenly distributed. Actually, four of the western states, Baden-Württemberg, Bavaria, Hesse, and North Rhine-Westphalia contain some 70 percent of all migrants. In the states composing the old East Germany the proportions of non-Germans in the population is small, as for example in Brandenburg with only 2 percent and Saxony with 2.4 percent.

Germany has experienced some foreign immigration throughout its history, except not as much as it has since the end of WORLD WAR II. In the late 19th century itinerant workers came from Poland and Italy, as well as Russian Jews who fled Russian persecution. The second stage in the process of migration was unleashed by the "guestworkers" who came based on the German-Italian Agreement of 1955, when there was an officially organized recruitment of non-German workers. After the building of the BERLIN WALL and the flow of East Germans was cut off in 1961, foreign recruitment was even more intense. This recruitment of guestworkers distinguished them from the "foreign workers" of the Nazi period. When the Arab oil crisis began in 1973, the recruitment was curtailed. Of the 14 million guestworkers who arrived, some 11 million returned home. The third immigration group since the end of the war has been the asylum seekers and other refugees who have been attracted by the words in the BASIC LAW that stated that "Anybody persecuted on political grounds has the right of asylum," which became the world's most liberal ASYLUM LAW. Many were legitimate seekers, but some also wished to take advantage of better economic opportunities in Germany. In 1993 limits were placed on the basic right itself.

After reunification antiforeign sentiment began to grow so that by 1992 it raged throughout Germany. Some of it occurred in the former GDR and was launched by the radicalism of Gerd Honsik's "stop foreigners movement." Part of it was fueled by the high rate of unemployment that occurred with the collapse of former state industries. The movement sought the expulsion of some 2 million Turkish workers. But the antiforeigner movement also was supported by nearly 2 million ethnic Germans who returned to Germany from Eastern Europe. Also resentful were the 1 million or so refugees who were protected by the liberal asylum laws. Unbelievably, there were a half million in 1992 alone. Most are forbidden to work and they live in camps, awaiting a court ruling on their status. In the meantime, popular resentment flourished against all aliens. And finally, the antiforeign sentiment provided support for racist neo-Nazi and skinhead movements.

Americans find it hard to understand the psychological underpinnings of the German debate on how to deal with immigration. The European nations have generally been more ethnically homogeneous, while the United States has been populated by a mix of racially and ethnically diverse European groups. The Polish miners who came to work in the RUHR coal mines in the 19th century integrated into German society and did not hold onto their traditions as do many of the Turks. Germany also had a short-lived colonial experience and consequently unlike the British, French, or Dutch has not had to deal with a legacy of colonialism and an influx of peoples from Africa or Asia. Finally, it is important for Americans to remember that Germans have felt overcrowded with approximately 80 million people living in an area the size of Montana.

Imperial Cities
(Reichsstädte)

Imperial Cities were towns and cities that received charters of freedom, which made them owe their allegiance directly to the Holy Roman Emperor, but were independent of any other sovereign prince. There were approximately 50 Imperial Cities, which included major cities, from NUREMBERG to tiny market towns. Examples of such cities are AUGSBURG, Nuremberg, Ulm, Dinkelsbühl, Memmingen and Wetzlar, FRANKFURT AM MAIN, and Strasbourg. The golden age of these cities was the 13th and 14th centuries, and some retained their importance through the REFORMATION. Few were significant after the THIRTY YEARS' WAR. Among those that declined were Biberach, Rottweil, Isny, Kaufbeuren, Ueberlingen, Hall, Gmünd, Windsheim, and Rothenburg. Cities that had been larger before the wars, such as Worms and Speyer, were also in decay. In northern Germany fewer free cities existed, and some of them also lost their freedom after the Thirty Years' War.

From about 1500 onward, the Imperial Cities encountered hostility from the territorial princes, who gradually expanded their territories at the expense of the cities. In 1489, however, the cities acquired the right to sit as the third college of the Imperial Diet (REICHSTAG). Many of the cities also played a major role in the REFORMATION by introducing Protestantism, and a few, including Nuremberg, Strasbourg, and Frankfurt am Main, would become important cities in modern Germany.

Imperial Constitution
(Reichsverfassung)

The empire that Otto von BISMARCK founded in 1871 was a centralized federal state, dominated by PRUSSIA, which was the largest, with two-thirds of the population of the new Germany. It comprised four kingdoms (PRUSSIA, BAVARIA, Württemberg, SAXONY), six grand duchies, five duchies, seven principalities, three free cities (HAMBURG, BREMEN, Lübeck) and the territory of ALSACE-LORRAINE, which was taken from France. Sovereignty was based in the Reich, but the states had control over education, courts, police, and fiscal affairs. The imperial government had administrative agencies only for naval affairs, foreign affairs, post and telegraph, and customs. The constitutional structure of the new Germany has been called "the Bismarckian compromise" and was based on three basic principles: first, the 1871 settlement froze the power relationships, not allowing for constitutional changes; second, Bismarck's power was maximized; third, it fused conservative political ideas with liberal economic ideas. The so-called compromise was of primary benefit to the conservatives and liberals who had been party to the original agreement and intended to exclude at first Catholics and later Socialists from sharing power.

The constitution was modeled on that of the NORTH GERMAN CONFEDERATION. There were some changes, and they had been approved by the German princes. Bismarck himself wrote the constitution. The office of emperor was to be held by a member of the Prussian royal family. There was a national bicameral legislature with an upper house, the Federal Council (Bundesrat), which was composed of representatives of the state governments. It was a kind of imperial senate, whose members held their offices by princely appointment and not by popular election. The lower house or Parliament was the Reichstag, which was elected by universal manhood suffrage of males over 25. Of the two the Federal Council was the more powerful and was dominated by Prussia. Not only did Prussia have 17 of the 55 votes (Bavaria had six, Saxony and Württemberg had four each), but the presiding officer always had to be a Prussian. Legislation was not legal until the Bundesrat approved it. Prussian dominance was even more extensive in that no changes could be made in military and customs, and no constitutional changes could be made without Prussian approval.

The legislative powers of the Reichstag were always limited by the prerogatives of the Kaiser, the chancellor, and the Federal Council. Until 1890 Bismarck continued to be the federal chancellor and was appointed by and was responsible only to the emperor. Since the chancellor was not responsible to the Reichstag, the constitution was not a parliamentary one, as was the case in England and France. Moreover, all federal legislation had to be approved by both the Reichstag and the BUNDESRAT, which gave Prussia a virtual veto over legislation. The Reichstag's right to initiate legislation also was limited, and for the most part it acted on matters submitted to it by the government. The chancellor was responsible to the emperor, and the cabinet ministers were responsible to the chancellor.

With the victories in the Austro-Prussian and Franco-Prussian Wars the popularity of the army was unprecedented. The Reichstag had no control over the command structure of the army, and only through the budget could it have any influence. During peacetime there was no federal army, only the forces of the states, which with the exception of Bavaria and Württemberg were part of the structure of the Prussian army. The power of the Reichstag over the army was strictly limited.

After unification a uniform criminal and civil law code and uniform commercial and industrial legislation was adopted. The administration of justice, and the judiciary, with the exception of the Supreme Court in Leipzig, was relegated to the authority of the individual states. With the reorganization of the ZOLLVEREIN in 1868, uniform weights and measures based on the metric system were introduced, as was a uniform currency, the German mark, based on the gold standard, which lasted from 1871 to 1924.

Imperial Germany (1871–1918)

The Second German Empire, which followed the HOLY ROMAN EMPIRE, was proclaimed at the end of the Franco-Prussian War at Versailles on January 18, 1871, by the king of Prussia, who became the emperor WILLIAM I of the new German state. In three wars of unification BISMARCK had achieved the creation of a "smaller German" state under PRUSSIA's leadership. Defeated France had to cede ALSACE-LORRAINE and pay huge reparations. In the patriotic enthusiasm of the war the southern German states joined with the NORTH GERMAN CONFEDERATION to defeat France and form the German Empire.

The long-sought German unity had finally come about not by popular decision, as had been hoped during the REVOLUTION of 1848, but by a treaty between princes, "from above." Prussia was the dominant state, having the largest number of seats (17) in the upper house of the BUNDESRAT, which constituted a veto over any reform legislation. The REICHSTAG was elected according to liberal principles by universal and equal suffrage. Although it had no say in the formation of the cabinet, it could influence government by its participation in lawmaking and its power over the budget. The Reich chancellor was accountable only to the Kaiser (emperor) and not to the Parliament, but he had to seek majorities for his policies in the Reichstag.

Each state had its own suffrage laws pertaining to state elections. In 11 of them it was still based on class suffrage, dependent on the taxes men paid. Women did not have the right to vote. In four states the old divisions of estates remained. The south German states, with their longer parliamentary tradition, reformed their electoral laws after the turn of the century. BADEN, BAVARIA and Württemberg modeled theirs after the Reich laws. Bismarck embraced liberal economic doctrines and throughout the rest of the century LIBERALISM influenced the reform of the legal code, as for instance in the CIVIL CODE of 1900. Although the MIDDLE CLASS grew and prospered, it was the ARISTOCRACY that still dominated the political system.

During the 19 years of Bismarck's rule peace prevailed, and through a system of complex alliances he tried to give Germany a secure position in the European balance of power. He was better in foreign policy than in domestic affairs, where he made a series of enemies. To him political opposition was "hostility towards the Reich."

He bitterly fought the left-wing liberals, suppressed Roman Catholicism in the KULTURKAMPF, and through the ANTI-SOCIALIST LAWS outlawed the Socialists for 12 years (1878–90). The working class grew rapidly along with the pace of industrialization. Despite Bismarck's attempt to induce their support of the government through progressive social legislation, the workers remained alienated from the state. After the young WILLIAM II came to the throne, he wanted to chart his own course and dismissed the aged Bismarck.

It was unfortunate for Germany that William II inherited the throne. He lacked knowledge and wisdom and bore the emotional scars of his crippled arm. He adopted a reactionary course after his early attempt to win the working class over to his idea of a "social emperorship" failed. His chancellors had to rely on changing coalitions of conservatives and National Liberals. Although the Social Democrats became the strongest party, they continued to be excluded from any participation in government. In foreign policy William pursued an imperialist policy and aimed to catch up with the greatest imperialist powers, especially England. This led to conflicts of interest with England and Russia. With England his construction of a world-class navy under Admiral Alfred von TIRPITZ did not force a change in England's policies and alienated her from an alliance with Germany.

Cultural changes also were taking place. Germany was modernizing and participating in the cultural changes affecting the rest of Europe. German society was becoming more materialistic, imperialistic, and militaristic. Chauvinism was on the rise, as was ANTI-SEMITISM. Cultural modernism fueled critiques of Christianity and stimulated a nostalgia for the past.

Imperial Germany was more responsible than the other great powers for precipitating WORLD WAR I. Germany's BLANK CHECK to AUSTRIA gave the green light for her ultimatum to Serbia. When the war broke out in August 1914, the system of alliances that was in place quickly made this a European-wide war, with the German violation of Belgian neutrality transforming it into a world war. The Germans committed a number of strategic mistakes, which contributed to the loss of the war. Some were the changes in the SCHLIEFFEN PLAN and the introduction of unlimited submarine warfare. Yet it was foolish for the Germans to believe that they could win against a world alliance that had more men and resources. The military dictatorship of Paul von HINDENBURG and Erich LUDENDORFF pushed the kaiser into the background. Even though there was a revolution in Russia in 1917, which removed Russia from the war, the entry of the United States in 1917 contributed to the inevitability of defeat. Ludendorff finally admitted so and sought an armistice. With military collapse came political collapse and the abdication of the Kaiser in November 1918, bringing Imperial Germany to an end.

Indemnity Bill (1866)

After the Prussian victory over AUSTRIA at the BATTLE OF KÖNIGGRÄTZ, BISMARCK came before the Prussian parliament (*Landtag*) and presented a bill of indemnity. It was a budget bill that was intended to retroactively legalize all the taxes that the government had illegally collected since 1862 in order to reform the army. Bismarck appealed to the parliament, which approved the measure by 210 out of 285. It marked the victory of authoritarian over representative government in PRUSSIA.

The constitutional conflict in 1862 centered on the control of taxation and of the army. According to the constitution parliament's consent was required for the additional taxes needed to pay for the reorganization and equipment of the army. Liberals in the Prussian parliament feared that the proposed reforms with their provisions to extend the period of compulsory military service would bolster the authority of the monarchy and strengthen the influence of the conservative-military clique, which might use the reformed army against its domestic enemies. New taxes were voted, but the Prussian parliament refused to vote for a permanent increase in military appropriations. Again in

March 1862 a new military budget was rejected. The dissolution of the Parliament and new elections failed to return a more agreeable parliament. Since King WILLIAM I refused to abrogate the constitution and did not abdicate the throne, he called on Otto von Bismarck to become prime minister, who then illegally collected the taxes.

The victory over Austria in 1866 led to an impassioned outburst of national feeling that affected even the liberal opposition. As news came in of the victories of the Prussian armies, the popular mood became ecstatic. Through conscription nearly every Prussian family had a member in the army, which now fueled patriotic feeling for the unaided Prussian victory over Austria and which combined with middle-class liberal opinion that favored German unification under Prussian leadership. Many liberals who were critical of the war at its inception, condemning it as a crime against "moral and legal principles," now changed their attitude to one of praise for Bismarck. The liberal deputies who had been returned to the parliament were also relieved that the triumphant Bismarck did not intend a coup against the constitution as they feared he might. Bismarck, as sly as ever, nourished the ground for the support of his Indemnity Bill. Soon after the parliament opened, he proposed a series of bills that appealed to every segment of the liberal opposition. The Indemnity Bill was proposed to appeal to those who favored the principle of legality. For Prussian chauvinists he had a bill of annexation, and for German nationalists a bill proposing a democratic suffrage for the new parliament (Reichstag) of the NORTH GERMAN CONFEDERATION. The liberals responded as expected, electing a moderate, Max von Forckenbeck, as their speaker, an action they believed would demonstrate to the Prussian people their unity behind the German policy of the government. The alliance of 1861 between the moderate right and the democratic left liberals dissolved. Most wanted to be relieved of the pressure of the constitutional conflict favoring national unity, even if under authoritarian auspices. While the democrats found it difficult to join the general rejoicing, the moderate liberals considered the constitutional conflict to be irretrievably lost and wanted to end it on the government's terms.

The great debate over the Indemnity Bill involved complex constitutional issues and electoral politics. Those who voted against the bill maintained that its passage would pardon four years of unconstitutional behavior on the part of Bismarck and the cabinet. The left liberals wanted to postpone the bill until after a legal budget was passed and another bill that established ministerial responsibility. The great victory over Austria, they argued, should not be confused with respect for constitutional law. On the other hand, the moderates feared the liberals would lose more voters than had already occurred, as voters had increased the number of conservative members from 28 to 142. Besides these incentives, Bismarck warned the chamber of the need for unity as the French were threatening to intervene and the Austrians to revive. Not surprisingly, the Indemnity Bill passed on September 3 by a vote of 230 to 75.

Independent Social Democratic Party of Germany
(USPD)

Antiwar members of the SOCIAL DEMOCRATIC PARTY who had broken away from the SPD formed a separate political party in April 1917, the Independent Social Democratic Party (USPD). The membership of the new party included a great deal of diversity, ranging from the reformist Eduard BERNSTEIN to such leftist radicals as Rosa LUXEMBURG and Karl LIEBKNECHT. All were, however, united by their opposition to the war. Having objected to the bureaucratization and centralization of the SPD, the Independents were loosely organized, leaving many caucuses with a great deal of independence. Two of the most important were the Revolutionary Shop Stewards and the Spartacus League. The USPD spread throughout Germany, but its organizational strength was greatest in BERLIN, HAMBURG, BREMEN, SAXONY, and the Rhine-Ruhr region. The party's strength grew throughout

1917–18, and it played a leading role in the strikes of 1918. Most members wanted to bring an end to the war and to have a nonviolent socialist revolution, but not to incite a violent revolution as did the Russian Bolsheviks.

During the REVOLUTION of 1918–19 the SPD and USPD shared power in the provisional government, and in the Council of People's Plenipotentiaries (CPP). The most important goal was to secure an armistice, but the USPD leaders also pressed for the nationalization of the economy, which was resisted by Friedrich EBERT and the SPD. Although Karl Liebknecht, who proclaimed the creation of a German Socialist Republic, wanted all power over the military and police in Berlin, the Berlin soldiers' and workers' council refused to make that decision. The USPD was opposed to the SPD's vision of the road to socialism and genuine democracy through a democratic suffrage and allowing capitalists to continue to control the economy. Therefore, the USPD favored retaining a role for the councils. By the end of 1918 the Independent members of the provisional government resigned. The radicals in the Spartacus League who favored a violent revolution split from the USPD to form the GERMAN COMMUNIST PARTY (KPD) in January 1919. That same month the Spartacus League staged its abortive second revolution. Although the vote for the USPD continued to rise in national elections, debates and conflicts within the party over its relation to the WEIMAR government weakened it. After the WEIMAR CONSTITUTION was adopted and a parliamentary system was established, the USPD refused to join with the SPD in a coalition cabinet with middle-class parties. In 1922 at the Gera Conference the party dissolved, and its members returned to the SPD or joined the new KPD.

indulgences and Martin Luther

According to Catholic theology, sins have both guilt and penalties attached to them. In Catholicism a sinner had to confess his or her sins in the sacrament of penance, repent, and be forgiven of the sin by the priest, after which there was still the matter of a penalty, a punishment that God justly imposed for sin. After absolution this eternal penalty was said to be transformed into a temporal penalty, a manageable "work of satisfaction" that the penitent could perform here and now, which included prayers, almsgiving, fasting, and pilgrimages. If, on the other hand, penitents did not complete their prescribed works of satisfaction, they could expect to suffer for them in Purgatory. This is where indulgences were pertinent. The so-called temporal punishment due to sin that priests imposed on the penitent as a "work of satisfaction" could be remitted through an indulgence, which the church could grant, but this never was a remission for the guilt of the sin itself.

Indulgences were introduced at the time of the Crusades for Crusaders who because of death did not complete their penances, but eventually indulgences became a comfort for the laity who feared future suffering in Purgatory. The doctrine of indulgences was expanded during the reign of Pope Clement VI (1342–52), who proclaimed the existence of a "treasury of merit," a reservoir of good works that the pope could dispense at his discretion. Based on this teaching, the church sold "letters of indulgence," which covered the works of satisfaction owed by penitents. This was further extended to Purgatory by Pope Sixtus IV (1471–84) in 1476. By LUTHER's time indulgences had become a major source of revenue not only for the Holy See but also for other purposes. They were regularly dispensed for small cash payments, which were regarded as good works of almsgiving. The laity were told that the indulgences remitted their own future punishments as well as those of their dead relatives presumably suffering in Purgatory.

In 1517 a Jubilee indulgence was proclaimed during the pontificate of Pope Julius II (1503–13) to raise funds for the rebuilding of Saint Peter's church in Rome. It was preached on the borders of SAXONY near Wittenberg in the territories of Archbishop Albrecht of Mainz, who was to receive one-half of the revenues in order to pay off his debts, which he had incurred in order to hold three ecclesiastical appointments simultaneously. Luther heard about the manner in which they were preached and handled. Apparently the Dominican monk and inquisitor John Tetzel was experienced in hawking the indulgences and must have made exaggerated claims for them. The audience was under the impression and told Luther that they were receiving complete remission of their sins and the assurance of going to heaven. Luther hesitated awhile, but soon addressed a letter on the subject to Archbishop Albrecht. He complained to him about the conduct of his indulgence commissioners, but diplomatically suggested that the archbishop was probably unaware of the shortcomings of his servants. Luther included with the letter his now famous Ninety-five Theses, which were more sharply critical, and his more moderate *Treatise on Indulgences*. The two have to be read together to understand Luther's point of view.

Luther did not completely reject indulgences. Rather he emphasized that indulgences could only release a sinner from punishments laid down by men, especially by the pope, thanks to the power of the "keys to the kingdom" conferred by Christ to Peter. Luther warned against the excessive expectations of plenary remission of punishments aroused by the indulgences; these would only give people a false sense of security about their salvation. Receiving forgiveness required contrition. Luther must have thought that he had to send the theses and the treatise to Albrecht to provide more details on indulgences than he had provided in his letter. While his theses were sharper criticisms meant to stir up debate, the treatise presented a more moderate and positive view of indulgences. He called the granting and gaining of indulgences a useful practice despite the corrupting commercial practices that surrounded their dispensation. He even praised the pope for coming to the aid of the departed. The treatise indicated that Luther believed in the existence of Purgatory and that indulgences could relieve souls of the torments they experienced there. Luther drew distinctions between the lifelong process of "justification" and the sacramental penance that was imposed or remitted. Luther was opposed to the concentration on particular sins and favored the deeper spiritual process of healing and prayer for grace.

inflation crisis of 1923

The crisis of inflation that culminated in 1923 had its beginnings with the manner in which IMPERIAL GERMANY financed its war on credit instead of through taxation. Besides entering the postwar years with a near empty treasury and the loss of overseas territories and markets, as well as the loss of its merchant fleet, the new republican government was faced by difficulties that induced it to follow an inflationary policy. It had to pay for demobilization and unemployment benefits and create jobs; confidence in the currency had been undermined by the VERSAILLES TREATY and the unspecified reparations burden. Between 1920 and 1921 the depreciated mark made it possible for Germans to recover some foreign markets. But deficit spending continued and did not scare away American investors who were speculating on the restoration of the German economy. The London Ultimatum on reparations was issued in May 1921. The instability of WEIMAR governments and the refusal of industrialists to support reparations led to a galloping inflation that depreciated the mark even further from about 84 marks to the dollar in May 1921 to 493 in July 1922. What precipitated the final stage of inflation leading to the the crisis of 1923 were a number of factors, including (1) failures in negotiations over reparations; (2) the assassination of Foreign Minister Walther Rathenau, who along with Chancellor Wirth had argued that Germany could not pay reparations according to the London protocol; (3) the need of a large foreign loan to stabilize its currency. The Allies objected to the practice of printing money in order to correct Germany's balance of payments and insisted that before Germany would qualify for a loan it would have to set its finances in order. In the meantime, the mark was devaluing at a rapid rate so that in the latter half of 1922 the mark depreciated from 1,134 to 7,589 to the dollar.

The governments of the Weimar coalition had relied on the policy of borrowing and printing new money to solve its political problems. Raising taxation to pay for the reparations demands of the Allies would have been politically undesirable because all classes would resent the taxation and a reduction of social services would alienate the workers. As the Allies refused to grant a reparations moratorium, the French decided to occupy the Ruhr in January 1923. The German government replied with passive resistance and continued to pay workers while they refused to work. The inflation went sky high as the government printed more money. At the end of 1923, 133 printing offices with 1,783 printing presses worked at breakneck speed. At that point the value of the mark to the dollar was 25 billion to one, and the paper money was practically worthless.

To answer the crisis, a new government was formed under Gustav STRESEMANN, who terminated the passive resistance, began an austerity program, and imposed new taxes. A new temporary currency was issued called the Rentenmark, which was secured by the landed and industrial wealth of Germany.

There were both winners and losers in this financial debacle. Some of the winners were the talented speculators, both German and American, who had profited from cheaper money. Export industries paid their debts in the depreciated mark and earned profits in stable foreign currencies. Some companies became debt free, while the concentration of industry occurred as competitors bought one another out. The losers were long-term investors, those living on savings or pensions, salaried employees, and the working classes who had to live on a reduced income and a lower standard of living. Many people lost all of their savings. The destruction of the currency produced a legacy of hostility against the republic, which promoted both left- and right-wing radicalism.

J

Jaspers, Karl (1883–1969)
existentialist philosopher

Karl Jaspers, a founder of existentialism, was a democrat, a liberal, a professor at Heidelberg, and a strong critic of National Socialism.

Born in Oldenburg on the North Sea coast on February 23, 1883, into the privileged family of a bank director, Karl Jaspers was able to attend a *Gymnasium* and then had the good fortune to study at the universities of Heidelberg, Munich, Berlin, and Göttingen. In 1913 he became an unsalaried lecturer at Heidelberg.

Jaspers began his career as a doctor after receiving his medical degree in 1909. For the following seven years he specialized in psychiatry at the university hospital attached to Heidelberg. During this time his interest in psychology flowered. He began to work out a classification system of basic personality types in conjunction with others, such as the social scientist Max Weber. As a result of these inquiries Jaspers produced his first major work, *General Psychopathology,* which included one of the essential themes of his philosophy, that man is so much more than he can know about himself through objective inquiry.

Existentialism for Jaspers meant transcendence and communication. He believed that "because man exists he can shape his own destiny by the exercise of his will in the face of a given set of potentialities. Man has freedom of choice and action through which he can influence other people; hence every individual is responsible to humanity as a whole." For Jaspers being an existentialist philosopher meant that human existence was the essence of "understanding value and knowledge." It was Jaspers's noble but unreachable goal to reconcile science, religion, and metaphysics. Like Immanuel Kant he had the idealistic ambition to develop history into a guide to human action. His first major work on philosophy was his three-volume *Philosophy* (1932), which many think was his greatest contribution. Nevertheless, *The Philosophy of Existence* (1938) was most often associated with him.

Jaspers was always opposed to the ideology and dictatorial practices of National Socialism, which made him the object of Nazi persecution. He not only opposed Nazi racial doctrines but also declared that they and the mass mysticism that the pseudo-religious practices of Nazism encouraged had no place in German culture. Consequently, starting in 1937 Jaspers was forbidden to teach in Germany. He remained loyal to his Jewish wife, and in 1945 both of them were to be deported to a death camp. The entry of the U.S. Army into Heidelberg saved them.

After the war he became rector of the University of Heidelberg, but in 1949 accepted a chair in philosophy at the University of Basel in Switzerland. He continued to publish on topics of international concern, such as German guilt (1945) and *The Atom Bomb and the Future of Mankind* (1957). In his reflections on freedom and democracy in the Federal Republic he published a number of volumes, especially one entitled *The Future of Germany* (1967), in which he questioned Germany's democratic progress. Altogether, he published 34 volumes. He died on February 26, 1969.

Jena

The city of Jena is located on the left bank of the Saale River not far from WEIMAR. The town was first mentioned as early as the ninth century. In 1230 it was chartered and from the mid–14th century belonged to the margraves of Meissen. After 1423 the House of Wettin held the margravate and the electorate of SAXONY. It was divided in 1485, and Jena came under the control of the dukes of the Ernestine branch.

The Friedrich-Schiller University was founded by John Frederick the Magnanimous, the elector of Saxony, in 1548 as an academy and was raised to university status in 1577. At first, Emperor CHARLES V refused to grant a charter to the university because it was religiously Lutheran. The charter was later granted by his successor, the emperor Ferdinand I. The university was noted for its school of medicine. Later, it became one of the principal centers for teaching the philosophy of Immanuel KANT. The dramatist Friedrich SCHILLER was a professor from 1789 until his death. In 1792 students threatened to migrate to the University of Erfurt, a move that was avoided due to the intervention of Johann Wolfgang von GOETHE. In the meantime, Johann Gottlieb FICHTE studied theology and philosophy at Jena and then was appointed a professor of philosophy from 1794 to 1799. During the last decade the early romantics, the brothers A. W. and F. SCHLEGEL, became the center of the Jena romantic group. Other philosophers on its teaching staff about this time were Georg HEGEL and Friedrich von Schelling. Goethe also wrote there *Hermann and Dorothea*. During the age of LIBERALISM the university was in the forefront of accepting new ideas. Even the evolutionist Ernst Haeckel was prominent there. And in 1841 Karl MARX received his doctorate in absentia.

During the 19th century Jena developed as an important industrial center. Most important, an optical instrument company was established by Karl Zeiss and continues to be important today. During WORLD WAR II the city suffered severe damage. Afterward, because of the division of Germany, Jena was located in the GERMAN DEMOCRATIC REPUBLIC under Russian dominance. Jena also has been known for its machinery, woodworking, printing, and publishing.

Jena, Battle of (1806)

The Battle of Jena was a decisive battle between the Prussian army and Napoleon's Grande Armée, which ended with the dismemberment of PRUSSIA. The battle was fought on the plateau northwest of the city on October 14, 1806. The Prussian army was under the command of General Hohenlohe and was outmaneuvered and outfought.

On the morning of October 14 the French columns fought their way across the Saale into Jena and then spread out into a line to the northwest. Hohenlohe only had some 38,000 troops and sent a message to WEIMAR, where another 15,000 men were waiting but came to his rescue too late. Marshall Ney tried to outflank Hohenlohe to the north and narrowly avoided disaster when his VI Corps was attacked by massed Prussian cavalry. Ney's men held, Napoleon sent reinforcements, and disaster was averted. But then Hohenlohe failed to follow up on this counterattack, and his infantry remained inactive and vulnerable to French fire. When the three French corps advanced, the tactics and lack of initiative of the old Prussian type army of FREDERICK THE GREAT proved disastrous. The Prussian line could not hold, and then the soldiers retreated to the northwest. Hohenlohe hoped to link up with the Prussian army at AUERSTADT under the duke of Brunswick, but the duke was killed, leaving the Prussian army leaderless.

The consequence of defeat at Jena and Auerstadt led to the collapse of Prussia and the occupation of BERLIN. The Peace of Tilsit followed, and Prussia was dismembered and lost all of her territories west of the ELBE RIVER and some lands in Poland.

Jesuits
(Society of Jesus)

The Society of Jesus was founded by Ignatius Loyola, who developed a program of *Spiritual*

Exercises and a society of companions to defend the church against PROTESTANTISM. Vowing absolute obedience to the pope, the Jesuits played a crucial role in the COUNTER-REFORMATION.

In June 1539 the Society of Jesus was formally instituted (and confirmed in 1550 by Pope Julius III) after Ignatius offered unconditionally the services of the society to the pope and added a special vow of absolute obedience (in addition to the other three monastic vows) to him. Ignatius was elected the general of the order and guided its growth for the next 15 years. So that the members of the society would not be identified with the bad reputation of some older religious orders, they were freed from wearing the monastic habit. The Jesuits now began to influence the Catholic reform movement. They exerted considerable influence on the proceedings of the COUNCIL OF TRENT. The order was favored by Pope Gregory XIII, who gave the Jesuits a new confirmation of their original constitution and supported them in their efforts to organize theological seminaries and institutions of higher learning.

The Jesuits had first come to Germany shortly after 1540 and attended the theological conferences of Worms and REGENSBURG in order to evaluate conditions. Permanent settlements followed in 1544 at Cologne, which became their most important center in Germany. Their influence in higher education expanded as they were allowed into the University of Vienna in 1551, and at Ingolstadt between 1549 and 1556. In 1577 they were placed in charge of the arts and theological faculties at Cologne. Their communities spread to Prague (1556), MUNICH (1559), Mainz and Trier (1560), Innsbruck (1561), Braunsberg and Dillingen (1564), Speyer and Würzburg (1567). The Jesuits gradually extended their influence to the leading Catholic universities of the Empire.

The most significant educational work accomplished in Germany was due to a great degree to the initiative of Peter CANISIUS (1521–97), the first German member of the society. Canisius was a Dutchman (Peter de Hondt) from Nijmegen, who was the most influential Jesuit of the first generation. German Catholics referred to him as the "Second Apostle of Germany" (St. Boniface being the first). He joined the Jesuits in 1543, then became a preacher, missionary, professor, and an adviser to Catholic princes in a number of southern areas. Not intellectually brilliant, he nonetheless was an effective missionary with the ability to communicate the Catholic faith to the people. In 1555 he was commissioned by Emperor Ferdinand I to author the new *Imperial Catechism*, which was printed in hundreds of editions and translated into 25 languages. Its simplicity of expression was comparable to Martin LUTHER'S. Also important for Canisius were his ambitions to improve the educational standards among Catholic youth and raise them to the level of Protestant schools, which had excelled under the reforms of Philip MELANCHTHON. Canisius's educational work was effective in Vienna, Ingolstadt, Augsburg, and Fribourg (Switzerland).

The mental discipline that developed from the *Spiritual Exercises* was carried over into the schools that the Jesuits established and where their greatest influence occurred between 1550 and 1650. The philosophy of Thomas Aquinas was made the basis of university education. Its Aristotelian rationalism, which had originally been fashioned to combat Muslim rationalism, was now useful in the combat against Protestant heresy. It provided intellectual discipline and assurance in debate. In the lower schools humanistic influence was apparent in the emphasis on ancient languages and literatures. Stress was placed on the grasp and retention of fundamentals by periodic drill and on the power and skill of persuasive argument. The Jesuit schools were excellent and gained an impressive reputation.

The great success of the Jesuits in the Counter-Reformation was largely due to their influence on educated Catholics who then became rulers. In the early 17th century the Jesuits became notorious in both Protestant and Catholic circles for their alleged political machinations. In general they refused to assume ecclesiastical offices but did serve as educators and father-confessors to the princes and kings of Catholic Europe. In some cases the Jesuits also influenced the use of force to defeat Protestantism, which was utterly destroyed in BAVARIA. Another instance occurred in Cologne when the archbishop became a Protestant. He was driven out of the city by Bavarian and Spanish troops and was replaced by a Bavarian prince. By the end of the 16th century all the bishoprics in western Germany were in the hands of Catholics.

Jews, status to 1869

Prior to the late 18th century, the idea of equality for Jews with all members of society would have had no meaning. It would have meant equality with another estate, either the nobility, MIDDLE CLASS (burghers), or peasants. Social position and rights were based on a grant of special privileges. It must be kept in mind that Jews wanted to practice their own religion, and in a society in which there was only one religion, Catholic orthodoxy, it is not surprising that the Jews were pariahs. Consequently, during centuries that witnessed the serious persecution of Christians who deviated from orthodoxy, such as Lutherans or Calvinists, it is not surprising that Jews were persecuted for their religious beliefs.

Some historians believe that had the Jews not performed an important function in society they might not have survived the Middle Ages. It is well known that Jews performed the tasks that society could not or would not perform. For instance, medieval society considered loaning money for interest as a violation of the teachings of the Bible, and sinful. Jews managed a substantial part of the long-distance trade, particularly in luxury goods and loan operations. The canonic prohibition had no parallel in Hebrew religious laws, and consequently Jewish social ethics presented no impediment to capitalistic attitudes. While the occupation and craft guilds were set up as Christian corporations, acquisition of land was also closed to them, as were schools, universities, and all public offices. Therefore, the Jews had to live outside society, but supplied the needs of kings and princes and also the church, and so received some protection for their services. When religious feelings ran high, or Jewish economic practices threatened the livelihood of gentiles, then Jews were persecuted. The violent persecutions of the Jews in the 15th and early 16th centuries forced many Jews in Germany to migrate to Poland.

Not all German cities had a Jewish population, whether large or small. NÜRNBERG and AUGSBURG were intolerant of any Jews within their walls. FRANKFURT was perhaps the largest German city with a Jewish population of 500 families. Its population gained considerable prosperity and cultural recognition. The REFORMATION did not change things for the Jews, even though LUTHER had hoped that they would convert to Christianity. When they did not, he condemned them to persecution. Their condition improved during the 17th and 18th centuries when they provided economic services that could provide contacts over larger areas. They also assisted in provisioning the new and larger armies. After 1648 Germany had to rely almost entirely on the importation of metals, and consequently Jewish connections were of great help. Coinage and currency operations became main activities of Jewish bankers. With the decline of the guilds and the growth of the "putting out" system of manufacture along with the factory system, Jewish capital was welcomed to facilitate these new capitalistic ventures.

In PRUSSIA there was an increase of Jewish families, especially in BERLIN, among them the Mendelssohns, Veits, and Friedländers, who became wealthy under FREDERICK II, largely the result of the silk factories that the king ordered developed. Jewish bankers also helped the king with his finances. That did not mean that all Jews were welcome. Frederick did not like Jews, and he did not want their numbers to increase very much. There had been laws restricting Jews in the kingdom, and in 1750 a revision of the restrictions was published. Only a Jew having the capital of 10,000 thalers could apply to live in Prussia, and his protected status could be inherited only by one of his children. Certain categories of Jews were not allowed to marry or own rural property. Dispensations were granted, but only if donations were made to the army recruitment fund. The career of Moses MENDELSSOHN illustrates the limits of Jewish assimilation. His participation with the cultural elite of Berlin seemed to indicate that the barriers to Jews in society were being reduced. Yet when he applied to the Prussian Academy, his nomination was rejected by the king.

In most of the German courts in the 18th century there were Jewish commercial agents to service the ruler's personal financial needs, which might include everything from luxury items to provisioning the army. The most famous of the 18th-century agents was Joseph Süss Oppenheimer (Jud Süss) who between 1732 and 1737 served Duke Carl Alexander of Württemberg and helped stabilize his finances. The estates feared that their rights were being undermined, and so executed Oppenheimer. Although some Jews had special privileges and made fortunes and some were merchants and participated in trade fairs, most Jews lived in small towns, ran a store, or were tradesmen. Overall, however, the conditions of Jews improved in the 18th century.

MARIA THERESA of Austria despised the Jews and expressed her prejudices in saying that the Jews "were the worst pest for the state." Her son, the great reformer, JOSEPH II, extended the toleration of the Jewish religion and broadened Jewish social rights, granting them a choice of occupation and place of residence. Although Joseph's religious reforms caused a great deal of controversy, most of them remained after his death. As far as results were concerned, Joseph II's famous edict of 1782 had limited consequences.

With the development of the ideas of the ENLIGHTENMENT as well as changes in Jewish social and economic positions, some Germans argued that their status as a minority needed to be revised. After the French Revolution, Napoleon's conquest of Germany, and the end of the HOLY ROMAN EMPIRE in 1806, the German states made changes. Reformers had every reason to add Jewish emancipation to their agenda, although German hostility toward the Jews was still too deeply rooted for equality to be achieved. Only in the RHINELAND areas annexed to France was emancipation achieved, as well as in satellite states such as Westphalia where a restricted emancipation was introduced. BADEN initiated the most progressive extension of rights but still not full civil equality. In 1812 Karl August von HARDENBERG and Wilhelm von HUMBOLDT, the Prussian reformers, issued an edict removing special restrictions and privileges governing the Jews and declared them citizens. In 1813 BAVARIA granted Jews state citizenship. During the reactionary restoration period, however, the emancipation movement slowed because of conservative pressures within governments and hostility within communities. The Jewish question had become a political issue and a matter of state policy. In 1848 at the National Assembly in FRANKFURT Jewish equality was made a fundamental constitutional right. Even though the revolution failed, a reversion to their former legal status did not happen to the Jews. During the process of German unification full emancipation was granted in 1869 in northern Germany and in all of Germany after 1871. Nevertheless, popular opposition continued and hatred toward the Jews was not unexpected.

The Jews of 1870, however, were a far cry from the ghettoized Jews who had been the cultural and political outcasts of the nation only a century earlier. In the period after 1780 many Jews had become culturally assimilated despite legal discrimination. The generation that had followed Moses Mendelssohn had an insatiable appetite for learning and education. They mastered the classic German literature and philosophy of the early 19th century. Many made the full conversion to mostly Protestant Christianity. Little survived of the old Jewish religion. German sermons and hymns dominated the worship of Jewish congregations, and by 1870 the old Jewish orthodox religion had vanished. The great majority of Jews belonged to the liberal or neo-Orthodox Jewish congregations.

Jews, status 1870–1933

Otto von BISMARCK's constitution of 1871 brought to legal fruition the process of Jewish emancipation that had begun during the Prussian reform period of the Napoleonic era. Jews expected that the new day that had dawned with the creation of the Second Empire was full of promise for the participation of Jews in German life. In fact, for decades Jews in Germany had considered themselves fortunate in their abilities and opportunities to assimilate. Germany had gone further than any other country in destroying the medieval ghetto. In 1880 the percentage of Jews to the total German population was in decline, so that by 1900 the 497,000 Jews in Germany was less than 1 percent of the population. The Jewish birthrate declined as middle-class families had fewer children, but IMMIGRATION from eastern Europe initially increased the total population to 615,000 by 1910. During the Weimar period the number declined again to 503,000 in 1933. Most Jews had migrated to the larger cities, and marriage to gentiles had become more common. The gates were open in business (not in government), and educational opportunities were afforded in the German universities. Even young Jews from eastern Europe created an "educational stampede" into universities, where they were not allowed in Russia. One of the foremost of these students was Chaim Weizmann, who later became one of the founders of Zionism and the first president of the state of Israel. By the turn of the 20th century in their attempt to become assimilated more Jews turned away from religious orthodoxy and adopted Reform Judaism.

German Jews took advantage of the opportunities in the new industrial economy. For the first time careers in business and the professions were open to them. Professorships were difficult to obtain, and few Jews were allowed into high school and grade school teaching. So university graduates flooded into the professions of journalism, law, and medicine. Jews in business and politics sought to build bridges between Jews and Germans. Names such as Gerson BLEICHRÖDER, who was Bismarck's banker, Max WARBURG, and Jakob Goldschmidt helped finance Germany's industrialization. Albert BALLIN built the largest shipping company in the world, the Hamburg-America-line (HAPAG), while Emil Rathenau built the General Electric Company, AEG. His son, Walther, administered the acquisition of raw materials during WORLD WAR I and contributed more than any other one to the war effort and was foreign minister during the WEIMAR REPUBLIC. Oskar Tietz introduced the department store in the 1880s, which enabled the German consumer to buy goods more cheaply. Contributions were made in many other fields: medicine, sciences, philosophy, literature, and the arts, all of which enriched German culture.

As Jews assumed a more visible profile and participated in the growth of the capitalistic economy, they also suffered the accusations of having caused the problems of capitalism. In the wake of the stock market crash of 1873, a new breed of Jew-hater was born with whom we associate the origins of ANTI-SEMITISM. The stock market boom in the early seventies had been stimulated by the large French indemnity, and hundreds of new business were established. Some of them were bound to fail, but unfortunately, the crash was precipitated by the overextension of the railroad empire of the Jewish entrepreneur Bethel Strousberg, in addition to the manipulations of less reputable Jewish traders and reckless small investors. On the other hand, the banker Gerson Bleichröder prevented the damage from the crash from being greater than it was. Nonetheless, the image of the Jewish businessman as a Shylock who took advantage or cheated others gained currency. This new anti-Semitism was racially and not religiously based and claimed that the Jews were an alien element in German society. Anti-Semitism became part of the program of the conservative parties. German Jews were unprepared for the expression of these strong prejudices. Politically, they relied on the PROGRESSIVE PARTY to counterattack. In the universities Jewish students founded their own fraternities. In 1893 the Central Union of German Citizens of the Jewish Faith was founded to oppose anti-Semitism, raise Jewish consciousness, and promote patriotism. The small number of Zionists established the Zionist Federation of Germany and supported the resettlement of Russian Jews in Palestine. When the war came, anti-Semitism became more pronounced, and after the war it was associated with the national defeat.

Jews made significant contributions to the Weimar Republic. Hugo Preuss, for instance, wrote the draft for the Weimar Constitution, and Walter Rathenau served as foreign minister in the early years of the republic. On the other hand, Jewish journalists predominated in the left-wing and liberal press. Jews were more creative in cultural life due to the religious emphasis on the life of the mind. They were very prominent in the theater, especially in avant-garde Expressionism. One example was Ernst Toller, who was a Communist among the expressionist dramatists in the New Objectivity movement. He was antimilitarist and antiwar and became a leader in the short-lived Bavarian Republic in 1919. The novelist Alfred Döblin wrote the psychological novel *Berlin Alexanderplatz*. Jews also were severe cultural critics and were not sensitive to German feelings. One Jewish historian interpreting the destructive criticism of some Jewish writers claimed that they had "split personalities" and were not sensitive toward German patriotism. But most Jews (60 percent) were employed in commerce, one-half of these being self-employed. Many were prominent in the wholesale business. In industry they were less prominent, except in Silesia, where more than half of the coal, iron, and steel businesses were owned or directed by Jews. Contrary to what the Nazis alleged, however, the Jews did not dominate the economy during Weimar.

Although some Jews agreed with the Zionist emphasis on making their future in Palestine, most supported the Central Association, affirming involvement in German politics and German patriotism. They supported the pro-republican political parties and made efforts to keep Hitler from gaining an electoral majority. It was not the anti-Semitism in Nazi political propaganda that attracted so many Germans to vote for Hitler and the Nazis. Rather, it was the crises of inflation and Depression and the collapse of the European financial structure in 1931 that affected the lower middle classes who were the major supporters of the Nazi Party.

Jodl, General Alfred (1890–1946)
Hitler's military adviser

Alfred Jodl was one of Adolf Hitler's principal military advisers and served as chief of the operations staff of the German High Command (OKW). He worked directly with Hitler and Field Marshal Wilhelm Keitel, chief of OKW.

Born in Würzburg, Bavaria, to a fourth-generation farming family, he served in World War I with Bavarian units as an artillery officer. Between the wars he served in staff and intelligence posts. In 1932 he was assigned to the Truppenamt, which was the clandestine replacement for the General Staff that had been forbidden by the Versailles Treaty. He was promoted to the National Defense Branch of the Armed Forces Office. In 1939 he was promoted to major general while serving as an artillery officer in Vienna. On the eve of the invasion of Poland in August 1939, he was assigned to the operations staff of OKW under his father-in-law, Field Marshal Wilhelm Keitel (1883–1946).

Jodl was an able and more independent officer than was Keitel, which made him the most important military planner next to Hitler himself. Hitler had taken a liking to Jodl when he met him on September 3, 1939; Jodl appeared and acted differently from the usual formal Prussian officer. Adolf Hitler had come to believe that he was always right. But Jodl demonstrated his abilities when in the swift occupation of Denmark and Norway he forestalled a British invasion of Norway and protected the iron ore supply from Sweden. After German victories in France and the Low Countries, Hitler's confidence knew no bounds. His plans to invade the Soviet Union were shared with Jodl, who viewed them skeptically. In general Jodl was a prudent and cautious man who preferred persuasion to confrontation. Jodl was spared some of Hitler's ruthlessness with the generals who were reluctant to follow Hitler's orders during the winter crisis of 1941. Hitler then had personally taken over command of the army. Hitler believed that the summer offensive of 1942 would be a great victory, especially with the capture of STALINGRAD. After Jodl returned from a negative assessment of the campaign, he and Hitler had an argument. Hitler had a vile temper and flew into rages when he did not get his way. Although Hitler threatened to discharge Jodl and Keitel, he kept them on the staff, even promoting Jodl to colonel-general on January 30, 1944. In the assassination plot of July 20, 1944, Jodl was injured but was not involved in the plot nor was he sympathetic with the RESISTANCE. His obedience and loyalty to Hitler led him into Germany's catastrophic defeat. On May 7, 1945, he signed the unconditional surrender of German forces, and on May 23, 1945, Jodl was arrested by the British. At the NUREMBERG TRIALS he was convicted of war crimes and crimes against humanity and hanged on October 16, 1946. A later German DENAZIFICATION court in 1953 did not agree with the sentence and exonerated him posthumously.

Joseph II (1741–1790)

Holy Roman Emperor

Joseph II was Europe's best example of an idealistic enlightened despot and revolutionary reformer. He was Holy Roman Emperor from 1765 to 1790, co-regent of AUSTRIA with his mother MARIA THERESA until 1780, and ruler of Austria to 1790.

Joseph was born on March 13, 1741, the eldest son of Maria Theresa, archduchess of Austria and Emperor Francis I (Francis Stephen of Lorraine, Grand Duke of Tuscany). Joseph's education had in mind the reform of the Austrian state machinery. He was intelligent, perceptive, and very energetic. His personality was solemn and earnest, but too dogmatic and single-minded for a successful ruler. Unfortunately, he thought he was infallible and ignored opposition to his ideas. In 1760 he married Isabella of Bourbon Parma, whom he adored, but she soon died, after providing him a daughter. An unhappy marriage of convenience followed with Josepha of Bavaria. After his daughter died in 1768, he remained desperately unhappy and preoccupied himself with the affairs of state. Considering himself the incarnation of reason and virtue, as well as an enemy of traditionalism, error and vice, he was an ardent reformer and pupil of the ENLIGHTENMENT. He distrusted his ministers who might have provided him with the wisdom of moderation.

Maria Theresa saw to it that Joseph was elected Holy Roman Emperor after his father died in 1765. Although Joseph desired greater responsibilities, after many arguments with his mother she restricted his activities as co-regent to army reform and foreign affairs, which he had to share with Count Kaunitz. Mother and son had their disagreements, one of them over the 1772 partition of Poland, which Prussia and Russia had initiated. Maria Theresa was opposed, but Joseph insisted that Austria take a share, receiving the southern Polish province of Galicia. After his mother's death he sought unsuccessfully to increase Austrian influence in

Joseph II *(Library of Congress)*

Germany, principally by trying to annex BAVARIA. He was opposed by FREDERICK II of PRUSSIA in the WAR OF THE BAVARIAN SUCCESSION (1778–79), and in 1785 again attempted to acquire Bavaria in exchange for the Austrian Netherlands. His disastrous foreign policy, which also undermined his domestic reforms, included an alliance with Russia against the Ottoman Empire (1778–91) in a war fought primarily by Austria, resulting in military defeat, great financial expense, and territorial losses. A rebellion arose in the Netherlands over the imposition of ecclesiastical reforms, and Hungary threatened to secede over Joseph's efforts at Germanization.

Joseph's attempts to rationally reorganize government and administration in which he disregarded regional traditions, the long-established relationships of serfdom, and the independence of the Catholic Church, have been described as "Josephinism." His program froze into a philosophy of rigid principles, which had at its center the system of an enlightened police state. At the core of Joseph's philosophy was the autocratic principle that only one man could govern and that all officials should receive their authority from him. Unlike his mother, Maria Theresa, Joseph enthusiastically admired the French philosophes and their proposals for a government and society based on reason. His program of reform, however, was too radical, and like those of other visionaries was soon overturned.

Joseph's reforms addressed the inequalities of the past. Called "the peasant emperor" in 1781, he abolished serfdom, allowing the serfs personal liberty to travel, marry, and enter the professions of their choice, while in 1783 he commuted the "robot" or work obligation of peasants into money payments to their nobles. Joseph also gave the peasants hereditary rights to their land. A more gradual reform would have been more enlightened, since Joseph angered his nobles more by taxing their lands equally with those of the peasants. More economic freedom was created with the abolition of the craft guilds. Most of the agrarian reforms were not retained after Joseph's death, and the social and economic emancipation of the peasants in Austria was not achieved until the REVOLUTION OF 1848.

His attempt to restrict the power of the Catholic Church and its monasteries was not anticlerical, but despite retaining Catholicism as the dominant religion, he sought to place the church under state control, all of which aroused alarm in Rome. Traditional ties with the archbishoprics of Salzburg and Passau were cut, as were the connections with the papacy. Joseph forbade the publication of papal documents without state permission. Monastic orders were placed under the control of local bishops, and those monasteries not operating educational institutions or providing nursing care were dissolved, a move that closed some 800 throughout the Empire. The education of priests was to be supervised by the state, and civil marriage was required and divorce made possible. Education was freed from church control.

The EDICT OF TOLERATION (1781) ended the identification of the state with the Roman Catholic Church, which had begun during the "Ferdinandean period" of the REFORMATION. Non-Catholics were given full rights as citizens and allowed the private exercise of religion. This may have been the beginning of religious toleration, but full religious equality did not occur until 1861. For the first time the legal position of the Jews was addressed. Their status was understandably complex. While the Jews had been expelled from Vienna in 1670, it was belatedly discovered that rich Jews were needed to administer state finances. Samuel Oppenheimer was one such important Jewish financier during the reign of Leopold I. In 1782 Joseph II decreed that the Jewish religion must be tolerated, broadening Jewish social rights as to their occupations and place of residence. Under the influence of the philosopher Cesare Beccaria, Joseph attempted to establish equality under the law, decreeing equal punishments for similar crimes, abolishing torture, and restricting the death penalty.

Joseph reorganized the Austrian Empire into new administrative districts of relative equal population. He followed this with a policy of Germanization, making German the official language of government and education. In his drive to create a single unified empire, he created a central office for Austrian internal administration, the United Court Chancellery, which was divided into 13 departments. Indicative of his fanatic reforming zeal were the 6,000 edicts he issued in 10 years. Because he feared that they would not be executed, Joseph even organized an extensive police system throughout the provinces responsible to the chiefs of provincial administration, who sent secret reports to the central government.

His reforms were resisted. In 1790 Joseph died on February 20, having written his own epitaph, "Here lies a prince whose intentions were pure, but who had the misfortune to see all his plans miscarry." Most of his reforms were abrogated by his brother, LEOPOLD II, who succeeded him.

Judenrat
(Jewish Council)

The Judenrat was a Jewish council that functioned as an executive committee, imposed by the Nazis on Jewish communities. These councils also were known as Councils of Elders or Ältestenräte. The Nazis had planned to set up Jewish Councils as early as 1933 in an attempt to govern Jews in an institutional framework separate from other Germans, but this original proposal was not implemented. Later, the councils were set up in Germany, where they were called the Reich Representative Council of German Jews. In German-occupied Europe they also were established and were simply called Jewish Councils (Judenrate).

On the eve of WORLD WAR II there were two models of Jewish organizations imposed by the Nazis. One was created under the auspices of Adolf EICHMANN in Vienna, which was a prototype of the later Jewish Councils and which was linked to the SS and the police. On the other hand, there also was a nationwide model that had a formal legal basis.

Shortly after the invasion of Poland the special killing squads, the EINSATZGRUPPEN, began to appoint Jews to local councils in various parts of Poland. Then, on September 21, 1939, Reinhard HEYDRICH sent a telegram to the leaders of the Einsatzgruppen instructing them to establish a council of elders in each Jewish community. According to the telegram a 24-man council was to be formed "from among the remaining rabbis and other persons of authority" with full responsibility to enforce obedience to directives. The terms *Judenrat* and *Ältestenrat* were used interchangeably. This was applied to the Polish situation and was modified to fit other countries. As a result of Heydrich's order, by November 1939 more than half of the Jews in Poland came to live under the Judenrat system.

Besides controlling the Jews and making sure they carried out orders, the councils also were multitasked, carrying out functions that the Jewish community usually had performed for its members. Some of the tasks carried out by departments under the councils were the registration of Jews, the survey of Jewish property, and internal administration such as police, housing, and health. Jewish leaders believed that temporary cooperation would lead to eventual liberation. In the hope of satisfying the Nazis and proving the productivity and necessity of Jewish labor, the Jewish Councils cooperated in the confiscation of property. The councils also tried to normalize ghetto life. They had responsibility for supplying and rationing food and for its payment. Even hospitals and clinics were established in order to prevent epidemics and high death rates.

Jugendstil (artistic style)

The "style of youth" or Jugendstil is the generic German name of the French art nouveau and the English and American modern style. Not so much a style but a mannerism, it was manifested chiefly in interior decoration, architectural ornament, typography, and the graphic arts. The name Jugendstil was derived from the art journal *Die Jugend,* founded in MUNICH in 1896, while the name was first used by critics in 1899. Its main centers became Munich, Darmstadt,

DRESDEN and Vienna. Starting in Britain and through the British art journal *The Studio,* the modernist manner soon was diffused throughout Europe. The Jugendstil artists were determined to change the arts and crafts. The movement paved the way for the modern style.

Jugendstil had its specifically national component and also different stylistic tendencies, a floral and a more abstract ornamental version as is also found in the Viennese Secession style. Sometimes it incorporated a poetical and irrational component. August Endell and Hermann Obrist created the facade and interior design of the Atelier Elvira in Munich (1897–98). The influence can be seen in architecture throughout the world, as for example in the work of Peter Behrens in Germany and Frank Lloyd Wright in the United States. Artists who reflected this influence of oriental art were van Gogh and Gauguin. In German EXPRESSIONISM there were exotic elements in Emil NOLDE and to a lesser extent in Paula Modersohn-Becker and Max PECHSTEIN. The first woodcuts of Ernst Ludwig KIRCHNER were influenced by Jugendstil, which also possessed a tendency to abstraction that later became widespread. The Secession artists in Munich, a group that included German impressionists at the turn of the century also came under the influence of Jugendstil. This included Kandinsky, who later aspired to create a totally new art.

Around 1900 many art journals and exhibitions promoted the new style. Decorative art and fine art were both exhibited, while in the last exhibition in 1902 in Darmstadt artists furnished houses as a total art work (Gesamtkunstwerk). Because of the lack of artistic sales, the Jugendstil artists left Munich and pursued other employment such as teaching.

June 17, 1953, Uprising (GDR)

After the establishment of the GDR its leaders strove to set up a Soviet-style republic. Besides purging pro-Westerners, Soviet-style collectives were introduced into factories and collectivization of agriculture intensified. The regime carried out ideologically inspired terror against whole social groups. All of this provoked a growing exodus of the middle-class and professional people, as well as farmers, to the West through a border that was still open. Even workers in the factories were becoming increasingly disgruntled after the first seven or eight years of socialism. The East German economy was continually burdened by heavy Soviet reparations and inefficiencies due to massive nationalization of industry. The party leaders coped with these problems by simply asking workers to work harder to achieve higher goals and accept heavier workloads. After Stalin's death the new Soviet leaders encouraged Walter ULBRICHT and East German leaders to reduce economic pressures and appease popular discontent. The measures introduced to do this, however, did not address a principal complaint of the workers, the increase in work norms. Refugees continued to increase from 110,000 in the second half of 1952 to 225,000 in the first half of 1953, which swelled by the end of the year to 330,000 or 2 percent of the East German population.

As the building workers in East Berlin could no longer tolerate the situation, a spontaneous revolt broke out on June 17, 1953. They stopped their work and called for a general strike. Their strike quickly spread to other branches of industry and some other big cities such as LEIPZIG and Magdeburg. At first the government responded cautiously. However, its attitude changed in response to the demands of the demonstrators for free elections, the restoration of their unions, parliamentary democracy, and reunification with West Germany. In many localities demonstrators set fire to SED offices and hauled down the red flags. By the next day the government had lost control of the situation. This was too much for Walter Ulbricht to bear, and he called on the Russians for help. Tanks of the Red Army garrisons were sent into action. The revolt was quickly suppressed, but not before 21 people had been killed.

This revolt was the first of its kind in postwar Communist Eastern Europe. The reaction of the East German leadership was harsh. Ulbricht and other Stalinists moved quickly against party reformers. Some were expelled from the party, others purged, and some even executed. Many party and county secretaries were dismissed, while a purge of the membership also took place. To quell the violence, the Russians were far from brutal, used firepower sparingly, and kept the death toll low. Some of the strike leaders were ex-army officers and former Nazi teachers from WORLD WAR II. The strike and its aftermath created considerable disillusionment among many who had hitherto been sympathetic to the new regime. One of those was the playwright Bertolt BRECHT, then living in East Berlin. In a poem never published in the GDR, he said that he regretted the official government view of the strike—that the people by striking had betrayed the government's trust; he sarcastically commented, "would it not have been simpler if the government had dissolved the people and elected another."

Nevertheless, in order to repair the damage the regime instituted a new era of liberalization, which lasted until the Hungarian revolution of November 1956.

Jünger, Ernst (1895–1998)
novelist and essayist

Ernst Jünger has been called one of 20th-century Germany's most original and influential authors. His book *Storm of Steel,* in which he elevates a soldier's life into a near mystical experience, claims that war makes a "new man." His book became very appealing to the nationalistic youth of the postwar period and to the Nazis.

He was born on March 29, 1895, in HEIDELBERG, the son of a druggist. At age 16 he ran away from home to join the Foreign Legion. After his return he joined the German army when war broke out. He excelled in shock-troop tactics and was wounded seven times with double wounds, achieving the distinction of receiving the highest military decoration of the Ordre pour le Mérite. After the war he remained in the army (Reichswehr) until 1923, and was active in the right-wing paramilitary group The Steel Helmets (Stahlhelm). During this period he published popular journals describing his war experiences, which combined vivid reporting of impressions with profound reflection on them: *The Storm of Steel* (1920), *Struggle as Inner Experience* (1922), and *Fire and Blood* (1925).

Through a prose that expresses vitality and violence, Jünger describes war as a great nihilistic experience. There was nothing romantic about the new form of technological warfare. It marked the end of bourgeois order based on security, leisure, and culture, which the war and the INFLATION CRISIS of the 1920s had destroyed. In war Jünger hoped to recover hard simplicity and Spartan discipline. There were no longer heroic deeds to perform, but a cold courage was necessary to become a functional unit in impersonal, technological warfare. Machines were a way of thinking and being.

In the latter part of WORLD WAR I he saw the outline of a new type of society emerging, which he sketched in the essays "Total Mobilization" (1931) and "The Worker" (1932). In these he asserts that war does not represent an exceptional situation, but is the most intense expression of the total mobilization that technological civilization seeks to realize. Its dynamic character is revealed in the frontline experience (*Fronterlebnis*) and mechanization, and the analogy of the gas engine, as "explosion and precision." No longer is there a distinction between the war front and rear or between soldier and civilian. There is a fusion in total mobilization, and individual freedom is obliterated. The worker operates like the soldier, and everybody becomes a worker. In fact work instead of being a means to an end now becomes the end in itself through which life achieves complete fulfillment. This has a totalitarian cast, and freedom is defined as total identification with the mass will.

Although Jünger was hailed by the Nazis as one of their foremost writers, he never joined the NAZI PARTY and moved out of Berlin. His ideas appeared more expressive of the thoughts of the National Bolsheviks, broken up in 1937 by the GESTAPO. Jünger's best-known work, *On the Marble Cliffs* (1939), demonstrates a change in his ideas, however, and is generally regarded as an allegorical critique of Hitlerism and the totalitarian state. It is a denunciation of a system that mobilizes frustration, fear, and greed to the end of destroying all noble cultural values. After a year the book was banned. During WORLD WAR II he served on the staff of the German commander in Paris. During that time he completed a manuscript of *The Peace,* which was written after his son was killed in the Italian campaign but not published until 1948. It revealed the author turning to a Christian position and speaking out for peace and a united Europe.

While most post–World War II novels emphasized the senseless horror of war, as the apostle of the "front experience" Ernst Jünger abandoned his belief that war forges a new man. His diary of World War II, *Rays (Strahlungen),* is a powerful statement of the author's recognition that his earlier ideals had become perverted and useless. The problems of force and resistance, of freedom of choice, appear again in the sharply analytical diaries he kept during World War II. In his usual masterly style Jünger wrote a utopian novel, *Heliopolis* (1949), a projection of an imaginary city of the future in which the dialectic tensions between power and love, individualism and collectivism, are enacted. On the one hand it appears to be an attack on Nazi ideals, but on the other it professes beliefs in a totalitarian ideology. Even more philosophical is Jünger's essay "At the Time Wall" (1959), which is a discussion of the changes and requirements of the human condition in the space age and under the impact of frequent revolutions. Having withdrawn from public life for some time, Jünger died in 1998 at the age of 102.

Junkers
(Prussian nobility)

Junkers were the Prussian country nobility, used by the Prussian kings to support the Crown, and came to dominate the army and offices of government. They were the core of the traditional ruling class in PRUSSIA.

The Junkers were a country nobility who owned large estates but lived an unassuming lifestyle that was little higher than that of the peasants. Living in timber and brick houses, their lives revolved around farming, producing the foods they consumed, hunting wild boar, horses, and shooting parties. During the REFORMATION and the THIRTY YEARS' WAR they were intent on developing a dominant position in society. The Great Elector reaffirmed their exclusive right to own land and possess seigneurial jurisdiction on their estates. No enforceable limitations were placed on their powers over their peasants, even to evict them and acquire their land. Economically, they also were permitted to export their products duty free and enjoyed freedom from taxation. They became a privileged caste because they provided the state with its military officers and high civilian officials. FREDERICK THE GREAT sought to protect the position of the Junkers.

In the 19th century the Junkers became pillars of an authoritarian monarchy. During the Restoration the policies of FREDERICK WILLIAM III enhanced the powers of the Junkers. After HARDENBURG's death in 1822 the king gave the owners of the largest estates the greatest representation on the provincial estates. After German unification the Junkers were represented by the GERMAN CONSERVATIVE PARTY in the Reichstag and the AGRARIAN LEAGUE. They supported WILLIAM II and Germany's role in WORLD WAR I. In the WEIMAR REPUBLIC their interests were represented in the antirepublican GERMAN NATIONAL PEOPLE'S PARTY (DNVP). They naturally supported one of their own, Field Marshal Paul von HINDENBURG for the Weimar presidency. Their power was undermined during the Nazi era and disappeared when the East German Communist regime, the GDR, took over eastern Prussia and other territories were lost to the new state of Poland.

Jutland, Battle of (1916)

The Battle of Jutland was the only significant naval battle between the British and German navies during WORLD WAR I. Although the Germans claimed victory, the battle proved indecisive, and the German fleet failed to break out of the blockade.

In February 1916 the new German naval commander, Vice Admiral Reinhard Scheer, began to make plans to engage the British fleet off the Danish coast. The engagement took place on May 31 and lasted through June 1. The British Admiralty had learned that German U-boats were moving to positions off the English coast. Warnings were sent to Admiral Sir John Jellicoe commanding the Grand Fleet at Scapa Flow and Vice Admiral Sir David Beatty commanding the battle cruisers at Rosyth. Both of these commanders put out to sea, ignorant that the German High Seas Fleet under Admiral Scheer was risking the open seas and steaming toward the Skagerrak, the waterway separating Norway from Denmark's Jutland peninsula.

The British had 28 battleships, nine battle cruisers, eight armored cruisers, 26 light cruisers, and 78 destroyers. The Germans had 22 battleships, five battle cruisers, 11 light cruisers, and 61 destroyers. The battle commenced when Admiral Beatty opened fire on the five German battle cruisers under Admiral Hipper. Before the hour was up, the British battle cruiser *Tiger* had been hit, Beatty's flagship, the *Lion*, had taken four shells from the German *Lutzow*, and the British *Indefatigable* was to sink within 30 minutes. As Beatty pulled away, steaming north toward the Grand Fleet, the Germans followed, and a running fight ensued. Now the Germans received the brunt of the battle with the *Von der Tann* knocked out of action, the *Seydlitz* set on fire, and the *Lutzow* and *Derfflinger* hard hit. About 6 P.M. the Germans saw the Grand Fleet coming. Rear Admiral Horace Hood signaled his squadron to form a single column. The ensuing battle was confusing. The *Black Prince* was sunk with no survivors. The *Defence* disappeared after she was hit by two salvos that blew its magazines. The *Warrior* was knocked out by shells that flooded her magazines. The *Invincible* was lost, and the *Warspite* was disabled. The Germans also suffered. The *Elbing* and *Frauenlob* sank as did the *Lutzow*. The *Pommern* blew up. Overall, the British had the worst of the battle.

The Battle of Jutland came to be known as the great naval battle of the war. It engaged 100,000 men in 250 ships for more than 72 hours. The German High Seas Fleet had sunk 117,025 tons of British warships, while the Grand Fleet had sunk about 61,180 tons of German naval power. The Royal Navy had lost 14 ships to the 11 of the Germans. On the other hand, of the German ships damaged only 10 were available for combat the next day, while the British could have put 24 capital ships to sea. Both sides claimed victory. For the British it was a calamity. In comparison, German armor had proved its superiority, and German gunnery had been more accurate. But that did not win the battle for the Germans because they still were trapped in their naval base. On July 4, 1916, Admiral Scheer confirmed this by renouncing any more fleet action. Jutland left the naval supremacy of the British intact.

Kaiser, Georg (1878–1945)
expressionist dramatist

Georg Kaiser was the dominant playwright of EXPRESSIONISM. A most gifted, skillful, inventive, and prolific dramatist, Kaiser did more than any other writer to transform German theater in the 20th century. A native of Madgeburg, he settled in the country near BERLIN. He became a businessman for a time; he spent three years in Buenos Aires, Argentina, and then had the dubious opportunity to spend time in prison for stealing furniture from a villa he rented. He justified this with the argument that an artist was a uniquely special individual and needed luxuries.

Kaiser's contributions to the expressionist movement were *From Morn to Midnight* and his trilogy, comprising *The Coral*, *Gas I* (1918), and *Gas II* (1920). These plays were attacks upon capitalism. In *From Morn to Midnight*, which was produced onstage by Max Reinhardt, the Bank Cashier is really not a character at all but a function. One morning at the bank the Cashier meets a women whom he mistakes for a possible flirtation, and he embezzles enough money to elope with her, but the fling ends with his suicide. The play is full of tricks, such as the audience watching the Cashier's adventures from the outside without becoming involved. A lot of the play is fantasy. At one point the Cashier discovers that a girl with whom he has taken up is a pasteboard figure with a wooden leg. Kaiser is saying that modern man is dominated by mechanism and artificiality. The hero's personality is developed in stages, which was typical of expressionism and rather common in the plays of Ernst TOLLER.

Kaiser tried to evolve the idea of a new type of man in his fight against the impersonal brutality of the time, but not a return to an old type of individualism. He approached his characters in an unsentimental way, and the usual outcome was the expression of a human catastrophe in search of religious meaning. *The Burghers of Calais* illustrates Kaiser's faith in the emergence of a new man who is a truly altruistic human being. *Coral* (1918) and *Gas II* (1920) are Kaiser's greatest achievements. In *Gas I* Kaiser shifts the emphasis to society and its regeneration. A billionaire is transformed by his attempt to change his identity with his secretary and double, whom he kills. Unfortunately, the billionaire's son is destroyed by the very workers whom he would save from enslavement to machines. *Gas II* is a futuristic play in which the world appears totally mechanized and man is victimized by machines and war.

Kant, Immanuel (1724–1804)
philosopher

One of the most influential philosophers in German history, Immanuel Kant elaborated a new systematic philosophy that joined the traditions of the 17th and 18th centuries into a creative synthesis. Kant sought to make reason secure against the skepticism of David Hume. He denied the metaphysical tradition that had come down from Aristotle to Descartes, Spinoza, and LEIBNIZ, and confined knowledge to experience while defending rationalism.

Immanuel Kant was born on April 22, 1724, into a poor family in the town of Königsberg. His

Immanuel Kant *(Library of Congress)*

father, Johann Georg, was an artisan and harness maker, and his mother, Anna Regina, was very religious. Both parents were sincere believers in Protestant PIETISM, which later had a profound impact on Kant's moral philosophy. Kant was educated first at the St. George's hospital school, and through the efforts of his mother and pastor he was admitted to the Collegium Fredericianum, where from 1732 to 1740 he diligently studied classical subjects, hoping to pursue a clerical career. Although he was registered in theology at the University of Königsberg, he principally studied philosophy, mathematics, and physical science, which made possible his mathematical conceptions and his understanding of Newtonian physics. For some years he had to work as a private tutor for wealthy students in East Prussia, then he resettled in Königsberg in 1755, offering private lectures because his application for a position at the university was rejected by FREDERICK II. In 1770 he finally received an appointment as professor in logic and metaphysics. In 1755 he also began to make a reputation for himself by advancing an original account of the origin of the universe in *General History of the Nature and Theory of the Heavens,* which has played an important role in modern science as the Kant-Laplace theory. Kant remained at the university for the rest of his life, never departing from the regular pattern of teaching, study, and writing. His iron regularity made it possible for housewives to set their clocks by his daily walks. The only break in this routine came on the day when he began to read Rousseau's *Social Contract,* which he could not put down. The only other incident that appears to have ruffled his calm life came when the king, FREDERICK WILLIAM II, through his obscurantist minister of education, Wöllner, threatened Kant with prosecution for publishing a book on the philosophy of religion, *Religion within the Bounds of Pure Reason* (1793), that was hostile to Christianity and the Scriptures.

Kant's masterpiece was *The Critique of Pure Reason* (1781). In it Kant investigated the legitimacy of the claims to objective reality made by pure reason. He assumed that the primary concepts have their origins in the mind itself and are created a priori. Kant argued that the human mind arranged the many impressions that humans experienced through universal patterns. The patterns included "intuition," by which he meant space and time, and "understanding," in which he included categories such as causality, reality, and unity into a coherent experience. His other works followed in rapid succession, including *The Critique of Judgment* (1788). Kant applied his critical philosophy to ethics, aesthetics, religion, theology, politics, and law. He also formulated categorical imperatives, basic ethical laws designed to instruct people in their moral duty.

Kant began his philosophical investigations with an explanation of the possible ways in which the human mind produces knowledge. He accepted the divisions of judgments formulated by Leibniz in which judgments are divided into analytic a priori and synthetic a posteriori types. Analytic judgments are necessarily true and universally valid. Synthetic judgments in contrast are the product of experience and are contingent upon context rather than necessarily true. But Kant created a third type of judgment, the "synthetic a priori judgment." This built on sense data just as synthetic judgments do, but they process this data according to a priori concepts in the mind that are activated by the sense data. These judgments occur in mathematics, physics, and ethics, transforming knowledge derived from sense data in accordance with notions contained in the structure of the mind.

In the first chapter of *The Critique of Pure Reason* Kant developed the general notion of the a priori concept into a system of categories of the mind. The categories were divided into four groups: causality, reality, relation, and modality. All sense data are given a special form or set of internal relations by these categories. The concepts precede actual experience and are a priori, which makes ordered experience possible. Reality is a universal order that originates with the experiencing subject through intuition and understanding. As a result nothing known about the world outside is known as it actually is. All sensory information has been molded and transformed by these categories, and minds are thus actively involved in creating knowledge.

Kant claimed that his new treatment of knowledge was a kind of "Copernican revolution" in epistemology, that he changed philosophy as Copernicus had changed astronomy. In exploring the basic epistemological questions, Kant offered a proof of the validity of Newton's belief in the uniformity of nature. He also developed the concept of transcendental ideas, ideas that lead into realms beyond the boundaries of human knowledge, such as ideas of God, freedom, and immortality.

In Kant's ethics he places freedom and dignity of the individual at the center. Kant argues that "we must believe that the will is free, even though we cannot know it, for otherwise morality is an illusion." His ethical system is explained in his *Foundations of the Metaphysics of Morals* (1785), which shows the influence of Rousseau, and in his *Critique of Practical Reason* (1788). He states that the moral law shows how obedience to it requires us to postulate the freedom of the will, the immortality of the soul, and the existence of God. The philosophy of freedom expressed in these works asserts that man is free because he is not morally molded by outside forces or experiences. His inner reasoning dictates his moral actions which are free actions. And it is this freedom that humans must accord to fellow humans regardless of social status, color, or creed. This was Kant's "categorical imperative," a universal command that is applicable to all human beings and that must always be obeyed. An example of a categorical imperative was never to use another human being as a means to an end.

Kant was extremely influential throughout the 19th century. Following his death the idealists, led by FICHTE, Schelling, and HEGEL transformed some of his concepts. Hegel and MARX developed complete systems based on Kant's categories. The nonprofessional philosopher Friedrich SCHILLER, who did more than any other to popularize Kant's ideas changed Kant's moralism into estheticism, while Friedrich SCHLEIERMACHER rejected Kant's ethics and philosophy of religion. The German reformers, such as HUMBOLDT, STEIN, CLAUSEWITZ and HARDENBURG also came under his influence. Schopenhauer and NIETZSCHE developed their concepts of the inner freedom of man. Henri Bergson developed the thesis of intuitions, and William James carried Kant's empiricism into the doctrine of pragmatism.

Kapp Putsch (1920)
This was the first serious threat to the republic from the political right. It was an attempt at overthrow (putsch) by a frustrated politician and agricultural expert Wolfgang Kapp (1868–1922) with military support from General von Lüttwitz (1859–1942). Irregular military forces called Freikorps provided them with capable military force, specifically the Erhard Brigade, one of the most political of the paramilitary units. Lüttwitz was the commander of the army's (Reichwehr) BERLIN district and believed that the simple solu-

tion to Germany's problems would be a military dictatorship. Kapp was a conspirator who dreamed up great plans. They were in alliance with other right-wing conservatives in the GERMAN NATIONAL PEOPLE'S PARTY and GERMAN PEOPLE'S PARTY. The Erhard Brigade commanded by a former marine commandant, Hermann Erhardt, favored extreme rightist and folkish ideas, and was stationed hardly 20 kilometers outside Berlin.

On March 13, 1920, Lüttwitz seized Berlin and proclaimed a new government with Kapp as chancellor. The extent of the territory under their rule was Berlin and some areas in East Elbia. The republican government escaped to the provinces and denounced the putsch as an attempt to restore the monarchy. The republicans then ordered a general strike, which quickly paralyzed the city, and without utilities travel was all but impossible. Although Erich LUDENDORFF supported the Kapp Putsch, the army remained uncommitted. Kapp failed to gain foreign recognition, and was hampered by the general strike and opposed by the Security Police, while the civil servants refused to carry out their orders. The putsch collapsed, and Kapp and Lüttwitz decided to flee on March 17. Although the putsch was a failure, it did have historical significance. It demonstrated that there was a group of militarists who were anxious to destroy the republic, which they considered to be Communist. The Erhard Brigade, which had recently returned from fighting in the Baltic region, returned with a new symbol on their helmets, the symbol of the swastika. Furthermore, the counterrevolutionaries of the Kapp Putsch were only a part of those who were opposed to the republic. To the south in BAVARIA a putsch did succeed when the commander of the army forced the democratically elected government to resign, replacing it with commissioner Gustav von Kahr.

Karl Theodor (1724–1799)
Imperial elector from the Bavarian Palatinate
Karl Theodor was the son of the Count Palatine Johann Christian Joseph and became the ruling count after his father's death in 1733. In 1742 he acquired the Electoral Palatinate by inheritance, and in 1777 he succeeded Maximilian III Joseph as elector of Bavaria. In 1778 he agreed to cede Lower Bavaria to the Habsburg Empire in return for the Austrian Netherlands. This exchange of territory was opposed, however, by the provincial diet and by PRUSSIA and SAXONY, which began the WAR OF THE BAVARIAN SUCCESSION (Bayrischer Erbfolgerkrieg). At the Peace of Teschen (1779) Karl Theodor abandoned the proposed exchange and ceded the area in Bavaria known as the Innviertel to Austria. Karl Theodor also encouraged the arts in MANNHEIM, creating a cultural renaissance. Just like his predecessor, Carl Philipp, he invited leading French and Italian architects to Mannheim, as well as sculptors, painters, and workers in porcelain. During his reign the Electoral Palace was constructed in the BAROQUE style. Between 1746 and 1752 the architect Pigage constructed the summer residence of the electors with its celebrated gardens and ROCOCO theater. An Academy of Sciences of the Palatinate also was founded in 1763. When Karl Theodor became elector of Bavaria in 1778 and moved his capital to MUNICH, this cultural flowering in Mannheim ended.

Kautsky, Karl Johann (1854–1938)
major theoretician of the Social Democratic Party
Karl Kautsky was a German-Austrian socialist who was one of the leaders in the SOCIAL DEMOCRATIC PARTY and the development of the international socialist movement. He was born to a Czech painter in Prague. Already a socialist by 1875, he became convinced that Marxism was the best socialist theory, and came to Germany in 1882 and introduced theoretical Marxism to the German SDP. Soon he became the editor of the leading Marxist theoretical journal, *Die neue Zeit*. Also contributing to MARX's popularity, he published *The Economic Doctrines of Karl Marx* in 1887. With the lapse of the Socialist Laws the party was allowed to reconstitute itself and had its first party congress in Erfurt during 1891. The Social Democratic ERFURT PROGRAM of 1891

became the official doctrine during the imperial period. It was largely the product of Kautsky's strongly Marxist thinking. Kautsky believed in the inevitable collapse of capitalism but not in change through revolution. Rather, he was part of the moderate centrist group that believed that change would come through political democracy. Yet he resisted the reformists on the right of the party led by Eduard BERNSTEIN, who wanted to revise the party ideology. Kautsky also disagreed with the new generation of radicals on the left led by Karl LIEBKNECHT and Rosa LUXEMBURG. While the radicals believed that imperialism was the last dialectical stage of capitalism, which would bring about world revolution, Kautsky thought that imperialism would end peacefully by the world powers coming to cartel-like divisions of colonial territories.

He found it impossible to agree with the majority of socialists who supported the German war effort by voting for war credits. Kautsky argued that Germany and AUSTRIA were the guilty ones in starting the war. In 1919 he helped edit a collection of documents that demonstrated the guilt of the Kaiser. Earlier in 1917 he joined the antiwar INDEPENDENT SOCIAL DEMOCRATIC PARTY (USPD), which came from the radical wing of the party and which led to his dismissal as editor of *Die neue Zeit*. His fellow Independents who favored the Bolshevik Revolution in Russia did not find him agreeable either, because of his outspoken criticism of the revolution in his *Dictatorship of the Proletariat* (1918). Although Kautsky briefly served in the early governments of the WEIMAR REPUBLIC, he failed to have much influence during the republican years and eventually moved to Vienna.

Keitel, Field Marshal Wilhelm
(1882–1946)
Hitler's chief military adviser
As chief of the High Command of the Armed Forces (OKW) from February 1938 to May 1945, Field Marshal Wilhelm Keitel was HITLER's closest military adviser as well as being one of his greatest admirers. He was an obedient officer, accepting Hitler's decisions without offering any resistance.

Wilhelm Keitel was born on September 22, 1883, on the family estate at Helmscherode in the Harz Mountains located in Brunswick. The family was anti-Prussian by tradition, having no desire to live in HANOVER after the last Hanoverian king, George V, had been deposed by BISMARCK. Although intelligent, Wilhelm barely succeeded in obtaining his *Abitur* from the *Gymnasium* in GÖTTINGEN. Because of the prestige of the army in the new Imperial Germany he was inspired to pursue a military career. He entered the artillery in 1901, and his superiors recognized Keitel's organizational abilities. During WORLD WAR I he began as a lieutenant in the artillery but soon was serving on the General Staff. During the latter part of the WEIMAR REPUBLIC he headed the Truppenamt, which was the clandestine replacement for the General Staff, which had been forbidden by the VERSAILLES TREATY. After Hitler became chancellor, Keitel between 1935 and 1938 served in the Armed Forces Office and was twice promoted, finally to lieutenant general. The Nazis then purged the command structure of the armed force initiated by Hermann GÖRING and Heinrich HIMMLER, who resented the leaders of the *Wermacht*. Generals Werner von BLOMBERG and Werner von FRITSCH were forced to resign. In addition to Hitler taking personal control of the armed forces, many pro-Nazi officers were now appointed to all branches. Hitler then abolished the Ministry of Defense in 1938 and replaced it with the High Command of the Armed Forces (OKW) and appointed Keitel as head and promoted him to general. Hitler now had become his own minister of defense, and Keitel had been placed in charge of the Wehrmacht and given the responsibilities of the Defense Ministry. In June 1940 Keitel conducted the armistice negotiations with the French and was promoted to field marshal.

Keitel was a colorless and nondescript officer and was despised as a "lackey" whose servility to and flattery of Hitler got worse as time went on. As Hitler's closest military adviser, he never questioned Hitler's decisions or encouraged discussion of an issue, bearing some responsibility for Hitler's belief in his own infallibility. Keitel realized, of course, that he would be dismissed if he disagreed with Hitler. Yet Keitel's subservience to Hitler went deeper than just military duty. In 1941 he had signed the commissar order that directed the execution of Communist leaders during the invasion of Russia. He also signed the order that began the reign of terror by the SS in Russian-occupied territory and he approved the Night and Fog Decree which permitted resistance fighters in the Reich to be secretly detained. If this was not enough to indict him for crimes against humanity by the Nuremberg court, he showed his unfailing devotion to Hitler when after the bomb blast on July 20 he rushed to embrace the Führer, then presided over the court that expelled from the army the officers implicated in the plot.

Keitel signed Germany's unconditional surrender in Berlin on May 9, 1945. He was arraigned before the International Military Tribunal (IMF) (*see* NUREMBERG TRIALS) and found guilty of planning a war of aggression and crimes against humanity. He was executed on October 16, 1946.

Kelly, Petra (1947–1992)

pacifist and environmentalist

Petra Kelly, a leading West German pacifist, was one of the most prominent founders of the GREEN PARTY. She was an ardent advocate of idealistic positions such as opposition to nuclear weapons, pacificism, feminism, environmentalism, and grassroots democracy.

Petra was born on November 29, 1947, in Gunzberg, Germany, and until age 13 attended a Catholic girls' boarding school. Her mother married an American officer, John E. Kelly, who returned the family to the United States in 1959, where Petra spent the next 10 years. During those years she participated in the civil rights movement, the anti-Vietnam and women's rights movements, and also studied political science at American University in Washington, D.C., in its School of International Service. She campaigned for presidential candidate Robert Kennedy and was distressed at his and Martin Luther King's assassinations.

The assassinations of Kennedy and King, the nuclear arms race, the Soviet invasion of Czechoslovakia, and the death of her sister from eye cancer moved her toward the advocacy of nonviolence, world peace, human rights, and against what she called the "the cancerisation of the world," which she believed was due to nuclear pollution. Disillusioned with U.S. policies, she returned to Germany, received a master's degree from the University of Amsterdam. In 1970 she founded a children's cancer research society. From 1972 to 1983 she went to work for the EUROPEAN COMMUNITY, concentrating on public health and environmental protection in addition to social and labor problems. During the 1970s she campaigned against the use of nuclear power and for disarmament.

Initially an admirer and supporter of Chancellor Willy BRANDT and a member of the SOCIAL DEMOCRATIC PARTY, she left the party in 1979, disillusioned over its defense policies. Earlier she had become active in environmental initiatives on the local and state levels and helped organize an "umbrella" organization (Bund Bürgerinitiativen Umweltschutz, BBU) for the citizen groups promoting these initiatives. This led to her participation in 1979–80 in the founding of the Green Party. This new party continued to emphasize the goals of the Citizen Initiative groups, such as environmental protection, nonviolence, and democracy. In 1979 she also protested against the NATO decision to deploy new U.S. missiles in West Germany and was nominated to the European Parliament in Strasbourg that same year.

Petra Kelly was one of the most outspoken founders of the Greens partly due to her quick wit, sharp tongue, and fluency in English. In March 1980 she was elected to the executive committee of the Green Party. After defeats in the national and state elections of 1980 and 1982, she finally was successful in the 1983 federal elections and was returned to the BUNDESTAG as member and speaker of the Green faction. She influenced the program of the newly formed Green Party and urged a broad program rather than just focusing on environmental issues. In one of her later writings Kelly justified the Greens' interest in focusing on a broad range of issues rather than just on environmental issues: "We can no longer rely on the established parties and we can no longer depend entirely on the extra-parliamentary road. The system is bankrupt, but a new force has got to be created both inside and outside parliament. In West Germany it is becoming increasingly important to vote for what we consider right and not just for the lesser evil."

For a while she belonged to the fundamentalist wing of the party and wanted the party to remain uncompromisingly idealistic. Perhaps unrealistically, she wanted the Green Party to continue to propose utopian goals and ask fundamental questions. She opposed the pragmatic politics of Joschka FISCHER and the compromises of the "Realo" wing of the party. From the mid-eighties her influence in the party declined, and her Bavarian district prohibited her from running for office more than twice, so she was not able to participate in the elections of 1990.

Kelly saw herself as part of a tradition of leaders who were reformers and revolutionary leaders, such as Martin Luther King, Gandhi, and Rosa LUXEMBURG. Her own ideas were collected in her book *Fighting for Hope: The Non-violent Way to a Green Future*. In 1992 she addressed the United Nations on Chinese human rights violations in Tibet. Although she could look forward to running as a Green candidate for the European Parliament in 1994, she mysteriously died in October 1992. It has been presumed that she and her companion, Gert Bastian, committed a murder-suicide, a not so honorable death for such a dedicated and influential idealist.

Kepler, Johannes (1571–1630)
astronomer and mathematician

Johannes Kepler was one of the leading founders of modern astronomy. He was an early supporter of the Copernican revolution and contributed his three basic laws underlying planetary motion, which postulated that planets revolve around the Sun in elliptical rather than circular orbits.

Johannes was born to Lutheran parents in the Swabian town of Weil on December 27, 1571. His father was a mercenary soldier who had fought in the Netherlands. A sickly child, he was brought up by his grandmother. When he turned 13, Kepler was accepted at the theological seminary at Adelberg. His poor health continued, and a proclivity to morbidness made itself evident during the following years. He went on to study at the University of Tübingen, where he graduated in 1591, after which he studied theology. While at Tübingen he learned of the Copernican heliocentric theory from professor Michael Mästlin. When the University of Graz requested a candidate for a professorial opening, Kepler was recommended as the "mathematician of the province," and began his duties as a professor in 1594. The next year he published a very successful almanac, which established his reputation. During July 1595 he conceived the basic ideas that became the main theme of his *Mysterium cosmographicum* (1596). In 1597 he began corresponding with Galileo Galilei, and in 1600 he had acquired a post as assistant to the famous Danish astronomer Tycho Brahe, who was the imperial mathematician and court astronomer for RUDOLF II, the Habsburg emperor of the HOLY ROMAN EMPIRE. In 1601 Kepler succeeded Brahe in both positions.

After Tycho Brahe died, Kepler fell heir to his extensive and immensely valuable astronomical tables. In preparing the collection for publication, Kepler made one of the most revolutionary assumptions in the history of astronomy. A mathematical discrepancy in the orbit of Mars led him to the conclusion that planets moved in elliptical rather than in a circular motion. A second law states that the line joining the planets to the Sun sweeps over equal areas in equal times. He also derived the mathematical equations that accurately describe the planetary paths, which have come to be known as Kepler's Laws and were published in the *New Astronomy* (1609). These formulations of the mathematical laws of motion of the planets describe their elliptical orbits about the Sun. His third law was published in Linz in the *Harmonies of the Worlds* (1618) long before Isaac Newton proved the law of gravity. Kepler also urged Galileo, with whom he had an unappreciative relationship, to stand fast with the Copernican view of the universe.

A devoted son, Kepler made several trips to Swabia in 1620–21 to defend his mother against accusations of witchcraft. His pay was often in arrears so he also worked on astrological tables for Albrecht von WALLENSTEIN. He moved to Ulm in 1626 and there in 1627 completed the *Rudolfine Tables,* which were published in 1628, a set of highly accurate astronomical tables that became standard for the next century. Kepler's last move occurred in 1628, when he moved to Sagan in Silesia. Kepler died on November 15, 1630.

Kiesinger, Kurt Georg (1904–1988)
chancellor

Kiesinger was a member of the CHRISTIAN DEMOCRATIC UNION (CDU) and served in the BUNDESTAG (Federal Lower House or parliament). He became nationally prominent in 1966 after the fall of Chancellor Ludwig ERHARD. Kiesinger won the chancellorship by advocating a grand coalition with the SOCIAL DEMOCRATIC PARTY (SPD), which ruled until 1969.

Born on April 6, 1904, in Ebingen, Württemberg, Kurt Georg Kiesinger was educated at BERLIN and Tübingen and completed his legal studies in 1934. After HITLER came to power, he joined the NAZI PARTY in 1933 but remained largely inactive. During the war he served as assistant chief of radio propaganda in the Foreign Ministry. After the war he was cleared by Allied and German DENAZIFICATION courts. In 1949 Kiesinger joined the CDU and was elected to the Bundestag, where he served as chairman of the Foreign Policy Committee. From 1958 to 1966 he served in state government as minister-president of BADEN-WÜRTTEMBERG and as president of the BUNDESRAT (Federal Upper House) between 1962 and 1963.

After Ludwig Erhard's position as chancellor had become untenable, the CDU executive committee selected Kiesinger as its candidate for chancellor out of a field of four. After negotiations Willy BRANDT of the SPD agreed to a coalition government with the CDU. On December 1, 1966, Kiesinger was elected the third chancellor of the FEDERAL REPUBLIC. A grand coalition between the CDU and the SPD was formed. Collective government by collaborating party leaders shaped the political style of the grand coalition from 1966 to 1969. It was an executive-centered coalition, but without a dominant chief of government. The coalition brought together the principal leaders of the two major parties in the name of stability at a time of economic crisis. For all practical purposes there was no longer an opposition party in the federal government, with the FREE DEMOCRATIC PARTY (FDP) constituting only 8 percent of the remaining seats. The CDU and SPD apportioned out authority and responsibility with the chancellorship going to Kiesinger (CDU), while the chairman of the SPD, Willy Brandt, became deputy chancellor and foreign minister. Governmental measures were decided by interministerial consultations. In these circumstances Chancellor Kiesinger was something like a board chairman and was restrained in using the powers that were his under the BASIC LAW. Kiesinger was thus a weaker leader of his government and party than Konrad ADENAUER had been, but on the other hand he was a more astute politician than was Erhard. As a chancellor he was a discreet mediator among his colleagues in the government. As chairman of his party he sought to use his personal charm and considerable political skills to mollify Christian Democratic critics of the grand coalition. Although he did both rather well, it was at the cost of muting his popularity with the voters. In the elections of 1969 the SPD did well enough at the polls so that it was able to form a coalition with the Free Democrats, who were eager to join in a Social-Liberal coalition. For the first time in the 20 years since the establishment of the Federal Republic the SPD became the principal government party, and the CDU/CSU became the opposition party.

It should be remembered that Kiesinger had considerable influence on the development of OSTPOLITIK, which was to reduce tensions with East Germany and improve relations with the Soviet bloc. It involved an informal abandonment of the HALLSTEIN DOCTRINE, which opposed the recognition of East Germany, although Kiesinger continued to oppose full recognition. Kiesinger died on March 9, 1988, in Tübingen.

Kirchner, Ernst Ludwig (1880–1938)
artist

Ernst Kirchner was a leading artist of EXPRESSIONISM, a founder of the famous group THE BRIDGE, and one of the greatest German painters of the 20th century. His paintings were noted for foreboding street scenes of prewar BERLIN and DRESDEN, horrifying scenes of the Great War, and women drawn in bright, wild, and garish colors.

Born on May 6, 1880, in Aschaffenburg, he attended secondary school in Chemnitz and began his professional training not as an artist but as an architect in Dresden and MUNICH. By 1905 he had decided to become an artist. His first experiments were in woodcuts influenced by the German version of French art nouveau called style of youth (JUGENDSTIL). In June 1905 he and his friends formed the artists' group known as The Bridge (Die Brücke), which stylistically paralleled the French fauvist school. His associates in The Bridge were Erich Heckel, Fritz Bleyl, and Karl Schmidt-Rottluff, who also were architects by training, but soon they attracted artists such as Emil NOLDE and Max PECHSTEIN. They began to host exhibitions during 1907 in Dresden and LEIPZIG. In 1911 they joined "The Blue Rider" group, which included Wassily Kandinsky, that organized an exhibition in Munich of graphic works and watercolor drawings. In 1913–14 Kirchner's own works were exhibited in Hagen, BERLIN, and JENA. As a soldier in the world war he became addicted to narcotics, which led to a nervous breakdown, several stays in sanatoriums, and release from the army in 1917. Moving to Switzerland to regain his mental and physical health, he continued to paint at a prodigious rate, and as earlier even designed his own furniture. Exhibitions of his works were held in Berlin in 1921 at the National Gallery, in FRANKFURT in 1925, and numerous locations in Switzerland. In 1931 he was admitted into the Prussian Academy of Fine Arts. When the Nazis came to power in 1933, his nervous condition worsened and intestinal cancer developed. The Nazis persecuted him, removing some 639 of his works from German museums and dismissing him from the Prussian Academy. Thirty-two of his works were included by the Nazis in their touring exhibition of DEGENERATE ART. When the Nazis took over AUSTRIA in 1938, he decided to marry his mistress, Erna Schilling, and together commit suicide, but she declined both requests, tragically leaving him to shoot himself.

Kirchner appreciated Rembrandt's focus on ordinary people and scenes of their lives and somewhat followed his example. In his youth he was a life-loving erotic bohemian and was fascinated by the beauty of the human body. Eroticism inspired his art as he painted nude models near Dresden and the Baltic Sea, and many of his mistresses posed for him in the nude. One of these portraits was of his mistress Doris "Dodo" Grosse, whom he depicted sitting nude with a hat (1909). Kirchner drew with fast strokes and used colors that were "bright, wild, and garish." But there was also a darker side to his art. Before the war he painted grimy scenes of jaded men and women in Dresden and Berlin in garish colors (*Five Women on the Street*), reflecting his sense of tragedy of the impending conflict. Kirchner like others in The Bridge group deformed the real object, the motif, of their paintings in order to express their inner feelings. For example, his experiences in the war evoked some horrifying paintings, as in *Artillerymen in the Shower* (1915), in which they are naked and vulnerable, and *Self-Portrait as a Soldier,* in which he depicts himself as a battle-weary soldier with his severed arm in his hand. Yet Kirchner has not been judged to be one of the humorless expressionist artists such as Max BECKMAN, George GROZ, or Otto DIX. His wide-ranging works are "at some times intimate and gently delightful, at others humorous, sensuous, psychologically probing or grandly romantic," having more in common with Picasso.

Klee, Paul (1879–1940)
artist

Although born in Switzerland, Paul Klee is associated with the school of modern art in Germany. Starting in 1898, he studied art in MUNICH and embraced EXPRESSIONISM and cubism, returned to Switzerland, and then went back to Germany in 1906, joining "The Blue Rider" group, a circle of artists associated with Wassily Kandinsky (1866–1944) and Franz Marc (1880–1916) who edited the "Blue Rider" almanac. After the war he was invited by Walter GROPIUS to join the faculty at the BAUHAUS in WEIMAR, which had to move to Dessau in 1925. He then taught at the academy in DÜSSELDORF.

Paul Klee found himself and his style of art in 1911. That year he made his most fruitful contacts with his contemporaries, not only Kandinsky and Jawlensky, but also Franz Marc Heinrich, Campendonk, and Gabriele Münter. He joined the Blue Rider group and took a modest part in their activities. In February 1911 he began to keep a catalogue of all he did, which amounted to 9,000 individual works, beginning with a preponderance of pen or pencil drawings, but gradually oil paintings. His art is elemental and has an almost childlike simplicity. He sought to reach the profound and complex reality of things— what he called the "prehistory of the visible." An essay he wrote in 1918 while still in the army summarized his "Creative Credo." Its main line of thought was that art does not render the visible but it makes visible. Klee believed that the artist's creativity was subjective, that it sprang from a discharge of energy and the resulting pictorial art was a fixed movement. In 1924 he published *Pedagogical Sketchbook,* which is mainly concerned with the analyses of elementary forms and movements. He always showed the greatest of respect for the science of the art of painting, and most of his pedagogical work is concerned with practical details. Some interpreters consider Klee's position in modern art as comparable to that of Newton in physics. His lectures at the Bauhaus and Weimar published in *Artistic Thought* (*Das bilnerische Denken*) are, it is said, "the most complete presentation of the principles of design ever made by a modern artist."

His works include: *Homage to Picasso,* 1914; *Red and White Domes,* 1914; *Villa R,* 1919; *The Boat Passes the Botanical Gardens,* 1921; *Battle Scene from the Fantastic Comic Opera, Sinbad the Sailor,* 1923; *Architecture,* 1923; *The Great Dome,* 1927; *High Roads and Byroads,* 1929; *Fruits on Blue,* 1938; and *Death and Fire,* 1940.

After the Nazis came to power, more than a hundred of his works were removed from art galleries and classified as degenerate. After returning to Switzerland, he was unable to work for the rest of his life because of illness.

Kleist, Field Marshal (Paul L.) Ewald von (1881–1954)
World War II panzer general

Ewald von Kleist was a member of one of the oldest landowning families in PRUSSIA. He served as a staff officer in WORLD WAR I. Remaining in the army during the WEIMAR REPUBLIC, he was an officer who did not always agree with HITLER, especially in the dismissal of General FRITSCH in 1938, was retired but reactivated at the beginning of WORLD WAR II. Kleist played a key role in the invasion of France, was given command of the first Panzer Group ever formed. He also commanded Army Group A in the invasion of Russia.

Kleist's career began in 1902, when he received a commission as a lieutenant in the Field Artillery Regiment 3. During World War I Kleist served as a field commander on the staff of Hussar Regiment 14. During the Weimar Republic he was an infantry commander in the Reichswehr, then became a commander of the

2nd Cavalry Division. He was forced into retirement over a clash with Hitler concerning General Fritsch. Reactivated, he was placed in command of the 22nd Corps, which fought in the Polish campaign. In February 1940 Kleist was given command of three panzer corps (including Guderian's 19th Corps), which played the crucial role in the invasion of France in 1940. With an army of tanks and motorized troops Kleist broke through the Allied lines and rolled across northern France. It should be pointed out that much of the credit is due to General Heinz Guderian, one of Kleist's corps commanders.

Why had Kleist been chosen over Guderian for the job of panzer commander? Hitler saw Guderian as a hothead who would be hard to manage and command. He saw Kleist as obedient, easy to command. But that did not always turn out to be the case with Kleist either. Hitler was not sure on a few occasions if he had made the right choice. The first was Kleist's disagreement over holding back the armor forces from destroying the British army at Dunkirk. The other would occur later in the Soviet campaign when Hitler finally dismissed Kleist.

Kleist was promoted to general in July 1940. His First Panzer Group invaded Yugoslavia. Then his group was part of the army group Centre during the invasion of the Soviet Union. His army group had a major role in the battle of Karkov in May 1942, and later spearheaded the German thrust toward the Caucasus, where he avoided encirclement. The survival of his army group at this time was due to his wisdom in relating to the local Russians and not alienating them. Many were anti-Stalinist and joined the Germans. About this time he clashed with Hitler over the retreat of his army behind the Bug River, which Kleist wanted and Hitler did not. Although Hitler allowed Kleist to do so, in the end Kleist was dismissed on March 30, not only for his insubordination, but also his lack of respect for the Nazis and his humane treatment of local populations.

The British army eventually captured Kleist in 1945 and subsequently tried him in Yugoslavia, where in 1948 he was sentenced to 15 years in prison. Then he was tried by the Russians for war crimes and died in a Soviet prison on November 5, 1954.

Klopstock, Friedrich Gottlieb
(1724–1803)
poet

Klopstock's poetry was passionate and unusual for his era. It demonstrated the poetic possibilities of the German language, which had not been appreciated. He played an important early role in the establishment of German as a literary language. In his ambivalence toward the French Enlightenment, he exemplified the complexities and tensions of the German Enlightenment.

Friedrich Gottlieb Klopstock was born at Quedlinburg in Lower Saxony on July 2, 1724. He obtained a sound classical education, attending the Protestant School of Schulpforta from 1739 to 1745. Then for a year he attended Jena University and for two years he studied theology at Halle. He was inspired by *Paradise Lost* of John Milton and decided to write his own great religious epic. In 1748 the first three cantos of his religious epic, *The Messiah,* were published. It is a landmark in modern German literature, for it destroyed the dictatorship that Johann Christoph Gottsched held over the arts and opened a new literary movement. *The Messiah* is written in hexameters and describes the last days of Jesus' life. In powerful visions the poet depicts the struggle between Heaven and Hell. He was influenced by the musical oratorios at the end of the 17th century, which through music spoke to the soul. (The style of these oratorios was brought to its zenith by Johann Sebastian Bach in his *St. Matthew's Passion*). The theme is not that of Milton's *Paradise Lost* but the salvation of mankind. The humanity of Jesus is continuously emphasized, his life, sufferings, and resurrection. Klopstock brought Pietism into the forefront in his poetry. *The Messiah* gave him a nationwide reputation as a poetic genius.

The odes he began to write in 1747 and continued to compose throughout his life constitute his most original achievement. The odes glorify religion, friendship, and nature; Klopstock never tired of expressing his awe of the infinite; in these odes his poetry is ecstatic in character. Nearly all of his odes and hymns were written without the use of rhyme, and he tried to emulate the varied meters of Horace, which was a better vehicle for the expression of his emotions. One of his earliest was the ode *The Zurich Sea,* which commemorates a boating picnic in mixed company, expressing in enthusiastic feeling a description of nature. The lyrical emotion foreshadows GOETHE's dynamic storm and stress language.

In 1751 Klopstock was invited to Copenhagen by King Frederick V at the instigation of Count Bernstorff and received a pension that continued throughout his life. In 1754 he married Meta Moller, but their happy marriage ended in 1758, when she died in childbirth. Although his plays are insignificant, he wrote his first, *The Death of Adam* (1757), followed some years later by *Salome* (1769) and *David* (1772). While in Copenhagen Klopstock's interest in German history bore fruit in his patriotic historical plays: *The Battle of Hermann* (1769), followed by *Hermann and the Princes* (1784) and *The Death of Hermann* (1787). In 1770 he settled in HAMBURG and published his odes in 1771, which renewed his influence on the younger generation, especially the circle around the young Goethe. Klopstock became an honorary French citizen during the French Revolution, but he was disillusioned by its outcome. In 1803 he died in HAMBURG on March 14.

Kluge, Field Marshal Günther (Hans) von (1882–1944)

World War II general
General Günther von Kluge served as a staff officer during WORLD WAR I, in which he was severely wounded at Verdun in 1918. He commanded the Fourth Army from 1939 to 1941 and became master of the BLITZKRIEG. He was commander in chief of Army Group Centre in the invasion of Russia from December 1941 until October 1943 and commander in chief in the West from July 1944 until he committed suicide.

Günther von Kluge was born on October 30, 1882, into an aristocratic Prussian military family in Posen. He served in various command and staff positions during WORLD WAR I. During the WEIMAR REPUBLIC he rose rapidly through the ranks. By 1936 he attained the rank of lieutenant general. When HITLER threatened to invade Czechoslovakia, Kluge was part of a plot to assassinate Hitler, which collapsed. In 1938, however, he was dismissed because of his disagreement with Hitler over the dismissal of General Werner von FRITSCH. In 1939, when the war broke out, he was recalled at age 57 and placed in command of Army Group VI. Kluge led the Fourth Army in the amazingly successful Polish campaign. He did, however, protest Hitler's plans to invade the West, but was placed in charge of the German offensive through the ARDENNES. His generalship in the French campaign established his reputation as one of the most brilliant German army commanders. After the fall of France he was promoted to field marshal in July 1940.

Kluge was one of the most successful commanders on the eastern front. He was appointed commander of Army Group Centre facing Moscow in December 1941. He remained on the eastern front until the battle of the Kursk Salient, which the Germans lost in July 1943. Significant for an understanding of his ambivalence was his veto of an attempt to assassinate Hitler on a visit to Smolensk in March 1943. That October Kluge was severely injured in a car accident and did not return to duty until June 30, 1944, when he replaced Runstedt (who was fighting the Allies in Normandy) on July 2 as commander in chief in the West.

One of the significant factors in Kluge's career was his vacillating support for conspiracies against Hitler. Two significant occasions were the Beck conspiracy of summer 1938 and the July 20, 1944, attempt to assassinate Hitler. Already in the 1930s Kluge and other generals feared that Hitler's militarism would lead Germany to disaster. Furthermore, he disliked the methods used by the Nazis to disgrace General von Fritsch, the persecution of the Jews, and the establishment of CONCENTRATION CAMPS. When General Ludwig BECK organized a plot to overthrow Hitler because of the planned invasion of Czechoslovakia, the plot was foiled due to the role of Chamberlain at the MUNICH CONFERENCE. Although Kluge and his friends General von Hammerstein and von Witzleben were ready to support the planned coup, since it failed, his attitude at another attempt proved ambivalent.

Although Kluge believed the government's fabricated propaganda of Polish atrocities against Germans in DANZIG, he quickly learned of and was appalled at the Nazi brutality against the Polish Jews and the indiscriminate slaughter of Polish civilians. Again Kluge and his fellow generals were disturbed at the news of Hitler's intention to attack France and the Low Countries, which they believed would lead to Germany's defeat. Kluge's plans to overthrow Hitler were abandoned, and he turned into an enthusiastic supporter of Hitler's plans.

More significant, however, was Kluge's fatal role in the July 20 plot. Kluge had agreed to cooperate if Hitler were killed. Kluge and Rommel had agreed that the war was lost and that they would support a Beck-Goerdeler government. After the failure of Claus von STAUFFENBERG's plot to kill Hitler and Rommel's severe injury, all conspiratorial hopes rested on Kluge, who had taken over command of Army Group B. When Kluge heard that Hitler was still alive, he backed out of the plan. After Kluge vanished for a whole day in August (he was trying to surrender to the Allied forces) Hitler did not believe his excuses and replaced him with Field Marshal Model. After trying to convince Hitler that the war was lost, Kluge committed suicide, knowing that his role in the July 20 plot had been revealed.

Koch, Robert (1843–1910)
physician

Robert Koch was a founder of the science of the relation between bacteria and medicine, known as bacteriology. He discovered the tuberculosis pathogen, the cholera bacillus, and the greatest discovery ever made with bacteria, the anthrax life cycle. He headed the Institute for Infectious Diseases in BERLIN and received the Nobel Prize in medicine in 1905.

Until the end of the 19th century wound infections were the mortal enemies of surgery patients and surgeons alike. No one could explain how they originated and spread. The first person to shed light on the subject was Robert Koch, who had been born on December 11, 1843, in the town of Clausthal-Zellerfeld, a mining region in the Upper Harz Mountains of HANOVER. Having studied medicine at the University of GÖTTINGEN, he became an army surgeon during the Franco-Prussian War. Later, he practiced as a district physician and pursued intensive medical research alongside his daily practice.

Koch discovered the cause of the deadly disease of anthrax in anthrax spores, a discovery that was sensational. He had cultivated anthrax spores on microscope slides, demonstrating that dormant spores could develop into bacteria that cause anthrax. For the first time a living microorganism was identified as the specific cause of an infectious disease and made visible to the human eye. Koch also had perfected the pure-culture technique whereby disease organisms could be cultured outside the human body. It was the beginning of a medical revolution. Later, in his laboratory in bacteriology at the German Health Office in BERLIN, he developed research techniques to isolate pathogenic bacteria. Although it was suspected that tuberculosis was caused by an infecting organism, Koch succeeded in discovering the tuberculosis pathogen. Later, in his research into the causes of cholera he identified the cholera bacillus and its means of transmission The discovery of the tubercle bacillus represented the turning point in the battle against tuberculosis, a disease that was widespread until well into the 20th century. During his career Koch also studied the diseases of leprosy, plague, malaria, and other livestock diseases. He became one of the creators of the science of bacteriology and influenced the work of Paul EHRLICH on immunology.

For his pioneering work Robert Koch received the Nobel Prize in 1905. He died on May 27, 1910.

Kohl, Helmut (1930–)
sixth chancellor of the Federal Republic

Helmut Kohl was born on April 3, 1930, in Ludwigshafen in the present state of the RHINELAND-PALATINATE. His family was Catholic and patriotic, but did not join the NAZI PARTY. Only 15 in 1945, he was too young to serve in the war. In 1947 he became one of the founders of the youth organization of the new conservative CHRISTIAN DEMOCRATIC UNION (CDU) in Ludwigshafen. After studying history, law, and politics, he received his doctorate in political science from HEIDELBERG University in 1958. His political career began when he was elected to the state legislature of the Rhineland-Palatinate in 1959 and then served as minister-president from 1969 to 1976. During these years Kohl's leadership expanded the CDU's share of the vote to 53.9 percent.

On the national level Kohl rose to prominence as one of the party's younger leaders. Defeated in the parliamentary elections in 1969, the CDU was out of the government for the first time in 20 years. In 1973 Kohl was selected to be the leader of the national party. He became the candidate for the office of chancellor in 1976 against the SPD's Helmut SCHMIDT, while in the election of 1980 Kohl had to defer to Franz-Josef STRAUSS of the CHRISTIAN SOCIAL UNION (CSU), who lost miserably to Schmidt. In 1982 the ruling coalition of the SPD and the liberal FDP fell apart, and the FDP decided to ally itself with the CDU/CSU to pass a "constructive vote of no confidence" as the BASIC LAW required. Kohl was elected chancellor in October 1982, which was confirmed in the parliamentary elections in 1983.

Kohl proclaimed that his government would try to solve three major problems facing the FEDERAL REPUBLIC. One was a crisis of economic growth and unemployment, second was the federal government's financial crisis, and third was an intellectual-political crisis. He planned to create new jobs through economic recovery, and provide tax relief as well as tax incentives for housing. His policies relied on the private sector just as Ronald Reagan's did in the United States and Margaret Thatcher's in England. A strong economic recovery stimulated economic growth, but unemployment remained high. Difficulties of agreement between the CDU and CSU over abortion and the punishment of public demonstrators made it difficult to carry out policies. Then three political scandals further rocked the administration. The most important one that hurt the CDU was the revelations concerning Rainer Barzel, which forced him to resign as parliamentary president. The scandal concerning illegal financial contributions also hurt the CDU and FDP. In foreign policy Kohl adhered to the treaties negotiated by the SPD, recognizing the national boundaries of Eastern European countries. Symbolic reconciliation with Germany's WORLD WAR II enemies, France and the United States, was also one of Kohl's important achievements. At Verdun he visited the graveyard of both French and German soldiers, and he convinced President Ronald Reagan to visit a military cemetery at Bitburg in 1985 during the 40th anniversary of the end of World War II. Kohl was determined to distinguish the younger from the older generation of Germans and refused to acknowledge any collective guilt for Nazi war crimes.

The Soviet premier, Mikhail Gorbachev, initiated the end of the cold war, which resulted in the fall of the BERLIN WALL on November 9, 1989, and the eventual collapse of the East German regime. Although a pragmatist and consensus-seeker, Kohl sensed the inevitablility of unification and took the initiative, proposing his Ten Point Plan for a confederation of the two Germanies. As the exodus of East Germans increased in early 1990, pressure for unification increased and Kohl promised quick unification with currency parity. Both the Soviet Union and the United States agreed to allow reunification. After concessions to the Soviet Union, renunciation of nuclear, biological, and chemical weapons, and payments for the removal of Soviet troops, unification happened rapidly. Kohl was elected the first chancellor of a united Germany. The challenges of reunification were more than expected, and the costs were compounded by a severe recession. Extreme unemployment in the five new eastern states caused resentment and neo-Nazi violence. Nevertheless, Kohl was reelected in 1994 as the economy recovered. Kohl, however, failed to solve some of Germany's other deep-seated problems, such as Germany's declining economic competitiveness and an overly expensive welfare state. He followed conservative policies, which, however, failed to solve the problems. He did succeed in integrating Germany into a unified Europe. In 1998 the CDU lost the parliamentary elections, and Gerhard SCHROEDER of the SPD replaced Kohl as chancellor.

Kokoschka, Oskar (1886–1980)
artist

Oskar Kokoschka painted the most compelling portraits in expressionist art in the first half of the 20th century. More persistently than any other modern artist he embodied in his painting a visionary and symbolic humanism.

Born in Pöchlarn, AUSTRIA, he studied art at the Vienna School of Decorative Arts while he was working at the Viennese Workshops, a renowned crafts workshop. His painting style, dominated by art nouveau influence, soon began to show features of EXPRESSIONISM, such as bizarre idiosyncrasies and distortions, as well as a tendency to psychological penetration. The following year at a Viennese art show he displayed drawings of young nude girls, which touched off a scandal that made him the talk of the Vienna scene. Between 1908 and 1912 there emerged a series of portraits in thin oils, applied almost like watercolor washes and agitated lines scratched with the brush handle into the wet paint, which established his early reputation. In these portraits Kokoschka stripped the mask of the centuries of convention from the human image. The facial features appear furrowed, the complexion flecked with various hues, and incised or scratched off with a brush handle or fine needle.

Kokoschka's expressionism bears covert traits of the BAROQUE. He was impressed by the expressionists of the 18th century. As in the baroque, so in Kokoschka there is something ecstatic and visionary, which is why his portraits are among the most compelling examples of expressionist art. The baroque artist Maulpertsch was especially admired for his super-cubist disposition of space and volume. Kokoschka deliberately rejected the "classicist Italian conventions of harmony," which implied the affirmation of transcendentalism and vision. What he meant was made clear in his work, which included dramas like *Sphinx und Strohmann* and *Hofnung der Frauen* as well as paintings, posters, and sculptures. In his portraits between 1908 and 1914 he was a merciless analyst of the human personality. In landscapes he recreated the romantic pantheism of Caspar David FRIEDRICH. In *The Tempest* he painted one of the great symbolic works, which epitomizes the age. It is a portrait of the artist himself and the woman he loves cast adrift in a boat driven by an irresistible force.

Kokoschka moved to BERLIN in 1910, then served in WORLD WAR I, was wounded, and moved to DRESDEN after the war. He fled from the Nazis to London in 1938, after which his works were condemned as degenerate, which he satirized in his *Self-Portrait of a Degenerate Artist* in 1937. After the war he finally settled in Switzerland in 1953.

Königgrätz, Battle of (1866)

This was the decisive battle that ended the Austro-Prussian War in 1866. It was fought on July 4, 1866, between the fort at Königgrätz and the town of Sadowa. The leading generals were Helmuth von MOLTKE on the Prussian side and Ludwig August Benedek on the Austrian. The Austrians had concentrated their forces in Bohemia along the rail lines north of Vienna and possessed a numerical advantage. Moltke's plan called for an offensive move into Bohemia by two separate armies that were supposed to unite once a battle commenced, then encircle and defeat the enemy. Yet communication between the Prussian armies was not very efficient, and orders were not always clear. On July 3 Prince Frederick Charles, the commander of the First Army, acted without orders and made a frontal attack against a large Austrian force that he had discovered. The battle lasted for 17 hours. The Second Army under the crown prince stabilized the Prussian front and also attacked on the Austrians' right flank. The planned encirclement of the Austrians was not complete, so Benedek was able to save a large contingent of some 180,000 of his troops to fight again. The Austrians suffered heavy casualties, especially as a result of the use of the Dreyse "needlegun," a breech-loading rifle that fired farther and faster than Austrian weapons. Austrian troops also had been trained in outmoded shock tactics against the superior firepower of the Prussians. Austrian leadership had its weaknesses inasmuch as Benedek was lacking in confidence and was saddled with officers who were imperial favorites. From the Prussian perspective and contrary to patriotic legend Königgrätz was not a model of military planning and leadership, for it did not occur in the location and manner that Moltke had expected.

Kreisau Circle
(German Resistance)

A small group of professional civilians and officers who opposed HITLER and made plans about the future of Germany, this group was formed on the initiative of Count Helmuth James von MOLTKE, who was the great grandnephew of the famous general of the Franco-Prussian War. The group met on weekends mostly in BERLIN, but a number of times at the estate Kreisau in Silesia owned by the Moltkes and from which the group received its name. Another leader was Count Peter Yorck von Wartenburg. By 1943 there were more than 20 members. Other members were Adam von Trott zu Solz (1909–44) and a Jesuit, Father Alfred Delp, S. J. (1907–45). The membership appeared to have been a motley group with different origins and temperaments. They were academicians, army officers, conservatives, liberals, socialists, Catholics, and Protestants. The so-called heart of the group was Yorck von Wartenburg, who was a descendant of the first American chief justice of the United States. Trott had been a Rhodes scholar, had many friends in England, and was employed in the Foreign Office. The group was basically Christian, but did try to attract undogmatic socialists. They formulated plans for the future of Germany and substituted a new philosophy in place of Nazism. Although there were many differences, most agreed that the age of the sovereign nation-state was over and some of its independence had to be given up in order to achieve peace in Europe. In a document drafted on August 9, 1943, they outlined their goals for a new Germany.

Some of its leading members were implicated in the July 20, 1944, plot to assassinate Hitler. Those tried and executed were Count Moltke, Trott zu Solz, Yorck von Wartenburg, Father Delp, and Count Fritz von der Schulenburg.

Krupp Industries
(House of Krupp)

The Krupp family were the creators of the largest industrial concern in modern Germany. It started the first major steelworks in 1811 and was part of the rapid industrialization of Germany. The firm also became Germany's leading supplier of armaments and mainstays of economic prosperity. As a weapons manufacturer, its links to the German military symbolized the power and influence of the military-industrial complex in modern states.

The history of the Krupps began in 1587 with Arndt Krupp, who was a prominent merchant in Essen. During the THIRTY YEARS' WAR the Krupps manufactured guns, but after the war returned to peaceful mercantile businesses. The beginning of interest in iron manufacturing is credited to a Krupp widow, Helene Amalie, who in 1800 acquired an iron foundry in Essen. Her grandson Friedrich (1787–1826) built on this foundation a steel-casting factory during Napoleon's continental system. In 1811 he founded the firm of Friedrich Krupp. His son, Alfred, became the real

The Krupp balloon gun *(Library of Congress)*

founder of the Krupp empire, becoming one of Germany's renowned industrial tycoons. In 1830 he began the manufacture of steel rails, which were used in the expanding market stimulated by the German Customs Union (1834) and the first railways. Friedrich developed new machinery and became famous at the London World Exhibition by exhibiting the world's first steel cannon and a four-ton steel ingot. Then he produced seamless steel railway wheels and became a major supplier of railway equipment. He introduced the Bessemer process on the Continent and in 1869 the open hearth method of steel casting. From a small ironworks employing 140 men in 1846, the Krupp works of Essen grew into one of the world's largest, employing 68,300 in 1912. Alfred Krupp had also pioneered the mixing of industries by adding mining, power, and transportation concerns.

Alfred Krupp secured a practical monopoly for the supply of the Prussian army. With the growth and modernization of the Prussian army and the success of Prussian artillery in the Franco-Prussian War, gun orders poured in from all over the world. Through Krupp agents who were army officers or noblemen the firm became notorious as "merchants of death."

Friedrich Alfred (1854–1902) succeeded Alfred as head of the firm. Even though he enjoyed the technical aspects of steelmaking, he expanded the firm into shipbuilding, steam shipping, and the manufacture of steel armor plate. By 1902 the firm had about 43,000 employees and expanded into scientific research. His oldest daughter, Bertha Krupp (1886–1957), inherited the firm and married Gustav Bohlen und Halbach (1870–1950), who with the permission of the Kaiser added the name of Krupp. He managed the firm from 1909 to 1943 and guided it through the boom of WORLD WAR I, the retrenchment of the WEIMAR REPUBLIC, the GREAT DEPRESSION, the Nazi accession of power, and the initial stages of WORLD WAR II. During World War I the famous field gun "Big Bertha" played a significant role in German advances and at Verdun. During the republic Krupp subsidiaries were engaged in the development of new weaponry. Although initially opposing Hitler's rise to power, Gustav Krupp von Bohlen adjusted his perspective, and his firm prospered through German rearmament and military expansion and the production needed during the war.

Alfred Krupp von Bohlen und Halbach (1907–67) succeeded Gustav in 1943 and directed the firm through the rest of the war. As Germany's largest arms supplier Krupp Industries supplied submarines (U-boats), the "Tiger Tanks," and the railway gun "Dora." The firm participated in the use of as many as 100,000 slave laborers.

At the end of the war the company was 70 percent destroyed and dismantled. Alfred was tried for war crimes and sentenced to 12 years, but released in 1951 by U.S. Commissioner J. J. McCloy. Probably because of the cold war, ownership but not control of the firm was returned to Alfred. With the Common Market and the economic recovery of West Germany the Krupp firm specialized in railroad and heavy machinery and nuclear plants. With the death of Alfred and financial crises, the firm was dissolved by his successor and eldest son, Arndt, and the company was converted to a corporation on January 31, 1968.

Krupp von Bohlen und Halbach, Gustav (1870–1950)

armaments patron of Hitler

Born in The Hague on August 7, 1870, to a well-known banking family, Gustav Krupp von Bohlen attended high school (*Gymnasium*) in Karlsruhe and earned a law degree in 1893 at HEIDELBERG. A diplomat and lawyer by training, his foreign service assignments were in Washington, Peking, and the Vatican. In 1906 he married Bertha Krupp (1886–1957) and headed the Krupp firm from 1909 to 1943, taking control of KRUPP INDUSTRIES in Essen, Kiel, Magdeburg, and elsewhere. Gustav Krupp von Bohlen was on socially friendly terms with Kaiser WILLIAM II, who even attended his wedding. Being Germany's most important armaments manufacturer, Krupp Industries profited from military expansion before the war, including the naval expansion, and played an important role and profited immensely in supplying weapons during WORLD WAR I. He was extremely proud of Imperial Germany. Although not democratically oriented and opposed to unions and collective bargaining, Gustav Krupp von Bohlen was politically flexible enough to seek out financial support from the Weimar government to restructure the firm for the production of nonmilitary products such as locomotives, farm implements, machinery, and cash registers. During the 1920s he was opposed to the politics of Alfred HUGENBERG of the ultraconservative GERMAN NATIONAL PEOPLE'S PARTY (DNVP). He also opposed the rabble-rousing NAZI PARTY, but another clue to his political flexibility was evident when within a month he quickly changed from being an opponent of HITLER's appointment as chancellor to a converted supporter. His expedient conversion took place on February 20, 1933, at a meeting of leading industrialists at which Hitler promised to oppose democratic elections and disarmament with Gustav Krupp von Bohlen publicly approving of the chancellor's remarks.

The alliance between Hitler and industrialists such as Gustav Krupp von Bohlen provided the foundation for German rearmament. Hitler made sure that the authority of the industrialists was maintained. In May 1933 he appointed Gustav Krupp von Bohlen chairman of the Adolf Hitler-Spende, a fund raised by the industrialists for the benefit of the Nazis. The Krupp firm adjusted to the anti-Semitic (*see* ANTI-SEMITISM) policies of the Third Reich and actually profited from the use of Jewish and other prison labor. In 1943 the eldest son, Alfred Krupp von Bohlen und Halbach (1907–67) took over control and became sole owner, directing the firm through most of the war due to the father's incapacity. In 1948 Gustav Krupp von Bohlen was to be tried by an American military tribunal, but was declared to be suffering from senility, while his son was convicted as a war criminal. Gustav Krupp von Bohlen did not stand trial and died at the family estate in Blühnbach, AUSTRIA, on January 16, 1950.

Kulturkampf (1871–1887)

The Kulturkampf was a "battle for culture" in the new Second German Empire between Otto von BISMARCK in alliance with the German liberals against the Catholic Church. As church and state were not separated in Germany, the government's anticlerical policies were intended to increase secular control over areas that the church had traditionally controlled or influenced. Bismarck feared that German, Polish, and French Catholics threatened the consolidation of the newly unified Germany. To some degree this dispute was generated by the Protestant majority in the new state along with liberals who desired to restrict the power of the Catholic Church. Roots of the dispute went back to the papal *Syllabus of Errors* (1864), a statement intended to guide Catholics in faith and morals, and which condemned the modern doctrines of LIBERALISM and materialism. It was coincidental that Pope Pius IX's declaration of papal infallibility was promulgated by the Vatican Council in 1870 about the same time as the founding of the Reich. Bismarck believed that there was a link between the declaration and German unification and feared a Catholic conspiracy against the new German state. Also at the root of this cultural war was the resentment in government circles against the newly formed Catholic CENTER PARTY and the suspicion that the Catholic clergy had an anti-German influence among the Polish minority living in eastern Prussia. Bismarck's fears were further provoked by the pope's refusal of his request to disband the Center Party in order to prevent it from organizing Catholic voters. A widespread anti-Catholic hysteria based on hostility toward Catholic loyalty to the pope, as well as traditional religious beliefs and values contributed to the government's policies. It would be a mistake, however, to assume that Bismarck advocated freedom of religion and separation of church and state. It also was not Bismarck's intent to destroy the Catholic Church, but to strengthen state authority over the churches.

Quickly escalating into a broad campaign, the Kulturkampf was waged on the state level (the federal states had jurisdiction over religion and education) through a variety of laws, regulations, and executive orders. It began with the abolition of the Catholic section in the Prussian ministry of ecclesiastical affairs and with criminalizing the use of the pulpit for political purposes. In 1872 restrictions were placed on ecclesiastical influence in administration, curriculum, and teaching in public schools. The hated JESUIT religious order was expelled from the country. During 1873 the May Laws were promulgated in PRUSSIA by the anticlerical minister of education, Adalbert Falk, instituting the supervision of seminaries and religious orders. The clergy were required to receive some of their education at state universities and pass exams in German culture. In 1874 compulsory civil marriage was required. When Pope Pius IX condemned these laws, the state responded by expelling bishops from their dioceses and priests from their parishes and allowed laymen to administer them.

Catholics rallied in support of the church and increased their support for the Center Party, whose representation in the REICHSTAG rose from 58 to 91 seats. Although Catholic bishops and priests were prosecuted, fined, jailed, and exiled, the state did not succeed in breaking the Catholic will to resist. Even the training and appointment of the clergy by the state was avoided. The measures taken against the clergy for violation of the May Laws proved to be largely ineffective. This was due primarily to the lack of bureaucracy and police, difficulties in enforcing the laws, and the legal protections in the traditional Prussian legal system. Indicative of the limits under which the state pursued its goals is the fact that the traditional state subsidies to the church were not ended until 1878 and income from church taxes never withheld.

Although negotiations to end the conflict had already begun in 1876, a major turning point occurred with the death of Pope Pius IX in 1878 and the election of Pope Leo XIII. Both parties were increasingly concerned with the rising treat of Marxism, while in Protestant churches there was concern that anticlericalism would affect them. Finally, in 1887 a compromise diplomatic agreement between Rome and BERLIN brought the Kulturkampf to an end. While Bismarck did not achieve his goals, the German state did retain influence over curricula in church schools and seminaries and in the appointment of clergy. Compulsory civil marriage also remained. While Catholics were no longer considered enemies of the state, they continued to experience the prejudices of a second-class minority.

L

Lagarde, Paul Anton de (1827–1891)
anti-Semitic writer

Paul de Lagarde was an orientalist professor, philologist, political thinker, and a forerunner of National Socialism. He was a real German revolutionary who yearned for a backward-looking utopia and wanted to find a religious basis for German nationalism. He demanded that contemporary Christianity be purged of Jewish influences. His writing was influential in the folkish movement and NAZI PARTY.

Born Paul Bötticher (later adopting the name Legarde from his maternal grandfather) in BERLIN on November 2, 1827, he decided on an academic career, became a teacher in Berlin, and in 1869 was elected a professor of oriental languages at the University of GÖTTINGEN. As an oriental philologist he became well known for his research into the Bible, and one of his greatest scholarly aspirations was to publish an edition of the Bible. Most of his later efforts, however, were dedicated to what Germans call the philosophy of culture (*Kulturphilosophie*). He was critical of the impact on German society of LIBERALISM, materialism, and secularism. He called for a moral cleansing of German life. Lagarde was strongly imbued with the 17th-century theosophist notion that a new world religion was needed and that Christianity had to be purged of its Roman and Jewish elements and that the German people had to adopt a national form of Christianity. He looked for the social roots for a new religious consciousness, which would not need ecclesiastical forms but would permeate the whole life of the community. This current of irrationalism would become manifest between the world wars.

His xenophobic ANTI-SEMITISM demanded an end to what he saw as the spiritual and economic power of the Jews who were foreign elements in German society and were "purveyors of decadence." He predated Nazism's depiction of the Jews as pests and parasites that needed to be destroyed, and he prefigured Hitler's policy of genocide. Lagarde was highly regarded by Alfred ROSENBERG, the leading ideologist of the Nazi Party. Lagarde died in Göttingen on December 22, 1891.

Lange, Helene (1848–1930)
feminist leader

Helene Lange was one of the founders of the German feminist (*see* FEMINISM) movement who advocated greater opportunities for women's educational and professional advancement. Because of her more moderate philosophy she became one of the most effective feminist leaders during the Empire.

Helene Lange was born in 1848 of middle-class origins in the city of Oldenburg in the state of Lower Saxony. She began her teaching career as a governess and received her teaching certificate in 1871. She headed a girls' school in BERLIN and worked with a group of women reformers whose patron was Crown Princess Viktoria. She perceived that women and girls were being discriminated against in education and in 1888 published her "Yellow Brochure," which petitioned the Prussian Education Ministry for reforms. In it she argued that female educational development could best be guided by women and not the then current male teachers. She founded continuing education courses for professional women in 1889 and in 1893 developed courses to prepare women for entrance to the university.

In 1890 she cooperated with others in founding the General Association of German Women Teachers and then became its president, calling for the reform of the educational system for girls. Upon also assuming the presidency of the General German Women's Association in 1902, she fought for self-determination, civil and political rights, and women's freedom of choice concerning their occupations. She did not advocate confrontation between the sexes, but rather equal opportunities for personal development. In 1893 she became editor of *Woman* (*Die Frau*) magazine. Some of her ideas included the claim to equal rights based on gender differences and the necessity for female qualities to improve the public welfare in male-dominated public spheres. However, she was opposed to radical tendencies in the feminist movement that favored sexual reform and reproductive rights. Although she opposed MILITARISM, she encouraged women to support the war effort in 1914. As for the goal of emancipation, she believed that there should "no longer be a leading sex but only leading individuals." From 1921 to 1930 she lived in Berlin as a writer.

Lasalle, Ferdinand (1825–1864)
founder of the General German Workers' Association (ADAV)

Ferdinand Lasalle was born on February 11, 1825, in BRESLAU, Silesia, the son of a prosperous Jewish textile merchant. He was educated at the universities of Breslau and BERLIN. He participated in the Berlin salons of Karl August Varnhagen von Ense, where he met other distinguished intellectuals such as Baron Alexander von HUMBOLDT. In Berlin Lasalle became known for his ideas in developing a socialist industrial system based on Hegelian principles.

Yet Lasalle was painfully aware of his Jewish heritage and resented the disabilities that the Jewish people suffered. He dreamed of becoming a heroic leader of the Jews, and it undoubtedly contributed to his desire to become a leader of the working classes to free them from their oppressive conditions. In the 1850s he gained great notoriety in his battle against the antiquated Prussian legal system in defense of a noble lady, the countess von Hatzfeldt, in her attempt to gain a divorce. He was active as a radical journalist, wrote some scholarly books, and became one of Germany's best-known political leaders through his many pamphlets and speeches. Workers from LEIPZIG requested his help in organizing a general workingmen's association. As a result he explained his ideas on the social question, which became the program and laid the foundations for the German Socialist Party. In Leipzig on May 23, 1863, along with 600 delegates, Lasalle formed the General German Workers' Association (ADAV), the first political organization of the German working classes, which became one of the parents of the later German SOCIAL DEMOCRATIC PARTY.

Lasalle was not a theoretician like Karl MARX but was principally a political leader. In fact he was a dictatorial leader by personality. In contrast to Karl Marx, Lasalle focused on the state and impressed on workers that they had to acquire political power in order to take over the state through universal manhood suffrage. He did not believe that social legislation would help them and neither would the cooperatives recommended by Hermann Schulze-Delitzsch. One of Lasalle's errors, for which Marx criticized him, was his acceptance of the Iron Law of Wages formulated by the Englishman David Ricardo. Workers could avoid being exploited, he urged, by forming producers' associations facilitated by the state whereby the workers could be owners. The defeat of the REVOLUTION OF 1848 convinced Lasalle that the liberal MIDDLE CLASS could not succeed by themselves against the power of the absolute monarchy and militaristic state. Through universal suffrage, Lasalle thought, the workers under his leadership could become a third force in bringing about social, political, and economic reforms. Unlike Marx, Lasalle did not accept the materialistic concept of the state, and in the German historical tradition of Otto von BISMARCK and Heinrich von TREITSCHKE, accepted the Hegelian theory of the state. Although his leadership was cut short in 1864 by his untimely death in a duel, Lasalle was "the greatest single figure in the history of the German Social Democratic party" and more than any other leader "made the social problem real and vivid to the broad German public."

Lasker, Eduard (1829–1884)
leader of National Liberals
Eduard Lasker was born a German Jew. The ideals of the French Revolution inspired him to enter politics and devote himself to German unification. In the REICHSTAG he was a good speaker and especially competent in fiscal affairs. He became the leader of the left wing of the NATIONAL LIBERAL PARTY, which was an outgrowth of the National Association (Nationalverein), which was officially constituted in 1867 when it split off from the Progressive Party. The party represented the MIDDLE CLASS and the professionals, people with education and property. When Otto von BISMARCK formulated the constitution for the NORTH GERMAN CONFEDERATION, it was Lasker along with the former leader of the Progressives, Max von Forckenbeck, who admitted that Bismarck had been the wiser concerning the reform of the army, and opted for supporting him now on the road to German unification. Belatedly, Lasker and the National Liberals decided to support the "further development of the Reich" and oppose the forces of particularism.

Lasker was intensely hated by Bismarck. Lasker's goals were to protect basic freedoms and to be an opposition party and restrict government spending. Lasker hoped to lay the foundations for an independent nationwide German press, which would be free from the restrictions that Bismarck had imposed on the Prussian press in 1863. Bismarck was thoroughly opposed to the kind of freedom that allowed editors the right to protect their sources and would not stand for allowing so-called irresponsible speculations that threatened the security of the state. Since Bismarck was opposed to the right of privileged editorial information, the Press Law of 1874 allowed for none of the protections that existed for journalists in the West.

The cause of German LIBERALISM was seriously damaged by the prosecution of the KULTURKAMPF, which both the liberals and Bismarck pursued. Eduard Lasker, however, was one of the few liberals who realized how much the liberals had violated their own principles. More true to the principles of liberalism was Lasker's exposé in the Reichstag of corruption in high places condoning legal irregularities on railway concessions during the economic boom that followed the Franco-Prussian War. These and other revelations weakened confidence in the stock market, which caused the economic boom to collapse. In 1881 Lasker left the National Liberals and united with the Progressive Party in the new German Free Thought Party (Deutsche Freisinnige Partei), which was widely known as the party of the liberal crown prince. Bismarck was afraid that this would transform the political system. When Lasker died during January 1884 while on a visit to the United States, Bismarck's hatred followed him to the grave. The chancellor failed to send a government representative to his funeral and also did not transmit an official message of condolences from the U.S. House of Representatives.

law, evolution of German
German law is rooted in continental European tradition and is derived from both Roman law and the laws of various Germanic tribes. Roman law came to Germany in the 15th and 16th centuries, but it by no means completely replaced German customary law.

German law began to reassert itself in the 18th century. Fundamental legislation in the form of the Prussian Law Code of 1794 and the Austrian General Civil Code of 1811 superseded Roman law in these fields and reintroduced a number of Germanic legal concepts, such as oral court proceedings. In PRUSSIA King FREDERICK WILLIAM I appointed as minister of justice Samuel von Cocceji (1679–1755), who combined a belief in natural law with a knowledge of state administration. The Prussian judiciary became salaried, and a new generation of jurists grew up under the enlightened thinkers Christian THOMASIUS and Christian von WOLFF, who singled out norms that gave expression to an enlightened state and the natural law. The Prussian Code enshrined the absolute powers of the monarchy and also made it legally permissible for Prussian rulers to levy taxes without popular consent. Criminal and procedural law, as well as public and administrative law, were influenced by the ideas of the French Revolution and embodied in the French codifications of the 19th century (e.g. the Code Napoleon), and by English legal concepts.

Uniformity was achieved after the founding of IMPERIAL GERMANY in 1871 through such major reforms as the Penal Code of 1871, the Judiciary Act, the codes of Criminal and Civil Procedure of 1877, the CIVIL CODE of 1896, and the Commercial Code of 1897. The Civil Code is a mixture of Roman and German law. Its significance also lies in its influence on the civil law of Japan and Greece, and the legal systems of AUSTRIA, Switzerland, Turkey, Brazil, Mexico, and Peru.

Law for the Equalization of Burdens
(refugee compensation)

In addition to other social welfare policies of the FEDERAL REPUBLIC, there were two major laws that were responsible for making the fruits of economic expansion available to all segments of society. One of these laws, the Law for the Equalization of Burdens (Lastenausgleichsgesetz), was approved by the BUNDESTAG during August 1952. It imposed a levy on fixed property and capital to help finance the integration of refugees. By the end of 1957 these measures enabled national and state authorities to relocate more than 890,000 displaced persons and to contribute more than 5 billion marks toward their housing. Under this law the government provided payments stretching over a number of years as partial compensation for war-related losses of either real property or liquid assets. By the end of 1986 more than 130 billion DM or $68.4 billion had been distributed to some 57 million applicants.

The Law for the Equalization of Burdens and Refugee Law (February 1953) neutralized some of the problems presented to the Federal Republic by the huge number of refugees that had been displaced to West Germany. The redistribution of income removed what might have become a source of political radicalism, and it undermined the strength of the refugee party, the BHE. The integration of the refugees into the Federal Republic was reflected in the 1957 Bundestag elections in which the BHE did not surpass the 5 percent hurdle for representation. The redistribution policy also neutralized the refugee opposition to Konrad ADENAUER's policy of Western European integration instead of making reunification its primary goal. The refugees were enabled to set up businesses, and they became an important source of innovation and growth in underdeveloped rural areas of BAVARIA, Lower Saxony, and Schleswig-Holstein. These measures were important contributing factors in creating a legitimacy for the Federal Republic, especially in the first decade after the war when prosperity had not reached most of the population and unemployment remained high.

Law for the Protection of the Republic
(Article 48)

The Law for the Protection of the Republic was contained in Article 48 of the WEIMAR CONSTITUTION. This article granted the president, who was popularly elected, extraordinary emergency powers to rule by decree. In case "public safety and order were seriously disturbed," the president could rule by decree, suspending certain fundamental rights that included the right of habeas corpus, secrecy of the mails, freedom of expression, inviolability of the home and of private property, and the right of coalition. In addition, he had the right to call upon the army to enforce his decrees. The virtually dictatorial power was theoretically subject to the approval of the REICHSTAG, but this check was of little protection from abuse because the president had the power to dissolve the Reichstag. For 60 days between the dissolution and reelection the president could rule without a parliament.

This article obviously was an offshoot of a period of insecurity and crisis, and in the beginning the first president, Friedrich EBERT, used his power to protect the republic. Although the Reichstag had the power to rescind the president's power, it failed to do so in the early 1930s, when Article 48 was used to support the authoritarian coalition governments of Heinrich BRÜNING, Franz von PAPEN, and General Kurt von SCHLEICHER. Hitler ruled under Article 48 until March 1933, when he was granted special powers under the ENABLING ACT.

League of Nations

The League of Nations was an international organization established in 1920 under the terms of the TREATY OF VERSAILLES to preserve peace and mediate international disputes through arbitration or conciliation. Its headquarters was in Geneva, Switzerland. Its initial membership consisted of 32 states, not including the United States, and 13 neutrals. Although the Central Powers were not initially included, following the LOCARNO TREATIES, Germany was admitted on September 8, 1926. Hitler withdrew Germany from the league in October 1933.

A league had been advocated during WORLD WAR I by a number of leaders in Britain and by President Woodrow Wilson of the United States. Wilson emphasized the importance of the league by including it in his Fourteen Points. The constitution or Covenant of the League was incorporated in each of the peace treaties following the war. When the U.S. Congress declined to ratify the Treaty of Versailles, the United States never became a member of the league. In contrast, Germany was a member of the league from September 1926 to October 1933. Even the Soviet Union was a member from 1934 to 1939. Turkey joined in 1932; Brazil, however, withdrew in 1926, then Japan in 1933 as it began its march of aggression in Manchuria. Italy quit the league in 1937 in protest of the league's condemnation of its war with Abyssinia. The league had no military forces to coerce states and relied on the "Sanction" policy, which was simply a boycott. The league succeeded in settling a number of international disputes, as for example in the Balkans and South America, and was able to assist refugees from Russia and Turkey in the 1920s.

As far as Germany was concerned, the League of Nations was responsible for the judicial administration of Upper Silesia and the maintenance of the Free City of DANZIG. Germany's entrance into the league aroused suspicion and ill-feeling among many Germans. They thought that the league was a club of the victors of the war, which existed for the defense of the status quo.

The League of Nations failed a number of times and ultimately did not prevent WORLD WAR II. It failed to prevent Japanese aggression in Manchuria and China, Italian aggression against Abyssinia, and the Russian attack on Finland in 1939, despite the fact that these were member states. During the war the league sought to continue its nonpolitical activities. It was formally dissolved in April 1946, handing over its remaining responsibilities to the United Nations.

League of the Three Emperors
(Dreikaiserbund, 1873 and 1881)

The Three Emperor's League was an agreement of cooperation between Germany, Austria-Hungary, and Russia intended by Otto von BISMARCK to preserve Germany's monarchical system and to protect Germany against diplomatic isolation and a French war of revenge.

In order to preserve Germany's authoritarian system of government, Bismarck decided to create alliances among what he considered the more stable nations of Europe, the monarchical and conservative regimes. While the Franco-Prussian War was still in progress, Bismarck sent a telegram in September 1870 to the Russian government in which he spoke of a "firm closing of the ranks of monarchical elements of Europe." Writing in a similar manner to the Austrian government, he urged a coordinated policy against the tide of revolution. One of Bismarck's primary concerns was to prevent France from securing an ally for a war of revenge against Germany. The first Three Emperor's League was based on agreements in May and June 1873 after a preliminary meeting of the emperors WILLIAM I of Germany, Francis Joseph of Austria-Hungary, and Alexander II of Russia, which occurred in BERLIN during September 1872 to discuss the possibility of a tripartite agreement. No agreement resulted at that time, but the next year a political formula was devised and signed on October 22, 1873. Except for some statements about the spread of revolutionary socialism, the agreement was basically a vague understanding of monarchical solidarity to preserve peace in Europe. It was nonetheless what Bismarck wanted because he did not like binding agreements and desired to maintain his diplomatic freedom of action.

The league did not survive very long, succumbing to the Eastern Crisis of 1875–78. In 1881 Bismarck negotiated the more formal and secret Alliance of the Three Emperors, which provided for prior consultation about changes in the status quo of Turkey. It also guaranteed benevolent neutrality should one of the participants be at war with a fourth power with the exception of Turkey. It was renewed in 1884, but was allowed to lapse in 1887 because of the tensions between the Austrians and Russians in the Balkans. In 1887 Bismarck established a separate alliance with the Russians through the Reinsurance Treaty.

lebensraum
(living space)

The concept of lebensraum did not originate with Adolf HITLER, but was popular in imperialist thinking prior to WORLD WAR I and afterward. As a slogan it was appropriated by Hitler to claim that Germany needed added living space in eastern Europe, especially in the agricultural Ukraine, for the expansion and health of the German population.

Before 1914 the concept of lebensraum was used to justify the acquisition of colonies. One of the philosophies from which lebensraum sprang was the theory of geopolitics, prevalent in Germany. Geopolitics was an offshoot of geography. As part of this political scientific study the theory influenced Nazi ideology and gave a sense of scientific legitimacy to the racial, militant, and nationalistic notions that surrounded lebensraum. In his geopolitical studies Karl HAUSHOFER merged politics and geography in his writings to produce a pseudoscientific formula for national expansion. According to geopoliticians a nation's strength lay in the amount of living space it possessed, which could provide a healthy agricultural base for its people. Geopolitics, however, was essentially based upon the principles of Social Darwinism, which proclaimed the "survival of the fittest." In the eyes of the Nazis the racially pure were the German people, who had the right to the living space that they needed.

The policy of lebensraum can be found in Hitler's *MEIN KAMPF* (1925) and Hitler's "Table Talk" (recorded between 1941 and 1944). In these writings it is clear that he had the Soviet Union in mind where the necessary living space was located. In Hitler's own words lebensraum was the only strategy that made sense in the Soviet Union. National Socialist policy was to "bring the soil into harmony with the population." In order to secure its place as a "great" nation, Germany had to carve a colony out of the East. Soviet territories would become for Germany what India was for Britain. As Hitler confided to Hermann Rauschning, the colonization of the Soviet lands was to be connected with the extermination of the racially inferior Slavs, while German colonizers would build a new elite order, based upon large agricultural estates, especially in Ukraine, which was thought to be a veritable land of milk and honey. The influence of Hitler's lebensraum policy was felt in the planning stages of OPERATION BARBAROSSA when Hitler issued the Commissar Decree by which Soviet political commisars would be executed.

Leibniz, Gottfried Wilhelm von (1646–1716)
mathematician and philosopher

Gottfried Wilhelm von Leibniz was Germany's greatest thinker of the 17th century. In Leibniz the mathematician, physicist, philosopher, theologian, diplomat, jurist, historian, and visionary of a Christian utopia were united. He was a man of universal knowledge who was the author of one of the three great systems of rationalism contributed by the 17th century to the ENLIGHTENMENT. He wrote to princes throughout Europe with his schemes of political reorganization, with plans for founding universities and scientific societies, the conversion of non-Christians, and the unification of the Christian churches.

Born in LEIPZIG on June 23, 1646, Leibniz was the son of a professor of moral philosophy at the University of Leipzig, and his mother was also the daughter of a professor. His early education was haphazard, but he immersed himself in his father's library, reading ancient classics, medieval scholastic philosophy, and the writings of the Christian church fathers. After receiving a traditional education in theology and the new natural philosophy of the Enlightenment at the University of Leipzig, he graduated with a bachelor's degree in 1663 at the University of JENA, where he studied mathematics under the direction of Erhard Weigel. Leibniz completed his formal education at the University of Altdorf, where he received his doctorate of laws in 1667. After that he visited Holland and NUREMBERG, where he studied alchemy and magic.

Although a Protestant, Leibniz began his political and intellectual career in the service of John Philip von Schönborn, the Catholic archbishop of Mainz, who was also an advocate for a Reich union against the menace from France posed by Louis XIV. The archbishop was actively interested in Leibniz's schemes for the union of the Christian churches. Leibniz worked on such legal problems as simplifying the laws of the HOLY ROMAN EMPIRE and began his extensive correspondence. He also began designing on a calculating machine, which he demonstrated before the French Royal Academy of Sciences and the Royal Society of London, a demonstration that led to his election to the Royal Society. Leibniz went to France during winter 1671–72 on a diplomatic mission trying to forestall French attacks on the Rhineland with the proposal that the French build an empire in Egypt. At the same time Leibniz immersed himself in the intellectual life of Paris, especially the mathematics of René Descartes, and initiated a friendship with the mathematician Christian Huygens. While trying to negotiate peace between England and the Netherlands, he became acquainted with such leading scientists in London as Robert Boyle. Later, while in Amsterdam he engaged in discussions with Anton Leewenhoek and discussed philosophy with the great Baruch Spinoza. From 1676 until his death in 1716 Leibniz held the position of librarian and other posts in the employ of the electors of HANOVER. At the Hanoverian court Leibniz had the sympathetic ear of the electress Sophia Charlotte, who was the daughter of the Hanoverian duke Ernst August, and also the wife of Elector Frederick III of BRANDENBURG. This remarkable woman not only gathered about her a circle of enlightened minds, but her influence extended to the courts of other states such as England and PRUSSIA. The connections of Hanover with England in the person of King George lifted this German state above the other small states in the Empire. In the course of the 18th century the university of GÖTTINGEN became an intellectual center of northern Germany along with Halle in Prussia.

Leibniz possessed a sharp and wide-ranging intellect that led him to investigate a great variety of subjects. He was a champion of rationalism and believed that the architectural model for the world was provided by the kind of reason used in mathematics. He wanted to create a comprehensive system of knowledge based on rigorous logical principles but also was anxious to avoid the atheistic and materialist implications that were contained in the mechanistic philosophies of Descartes and Spinoza. He tried to avoid the dualism of mind and body contained in Cartesian thought and offered a synthesis of concepts derived from medieval scholasticism and modern mechanistic philosophy. Leibniz described the principles of his view of the created world in his *Monadologie* (1714), which was written to Prince Eugene of Savoy.

Leibniz's most famous discovery was that of differential calculus, which he developed independently of Isaac Newton during his stay in Paris around 1676. He published it in 1684, some nine years before Newton announced his. Leibniz also invented the binary number system, a general method of integrating rational functions and the signs for similarity and congruence. In addition, he laid the foundation for the modern study of linguistics. Certain elements of his thinking also played an important role in the Enlightenment. One of his students, Christian Wolff, who had interpreted Leibniz's thought, influenced the German Enlightenment. Another great German philosopher, Immanuel Kant, who was trained in Leibnizian-Wolff philosophy, worked out a major restatement of epistemology.

Leibniz's concept of the body conceived as a collection of monads striving toward some goal entered the life sciences through the school of vitalism. His view provided an alternative for people dissatisfied with the Cartesian-inspired vision of the living being as a simple machine operating according to mechanical laws. From Leibniz's point of view, living beings have a purpose and are active in the world and are always striving toward some goal. The concept of a striving universe helped introduce the idea that the world and human beings change over time in an upward and progressive direction reaching toward perfection.

The hopes and dreams that Leibniz had for a restored Empire and Christian unity never materialized. He had envisaged an imperial academy of sciences and the arts in Vienna, which would serve as a central agency for world unity bringing together the best minds of Christendom in order to achieve Christian harmony. He was disappointed, as only the Academy of Sciences in Berlin was established. His death in 1716 went unnoticed.

Leipzig

Leipzig is located about 113 miles southwest of Berlin in east-central Germany in the western part of the state of Saxony. It is located near the junction of the Pleisse, Parthe, and Weisse Elster Rivers. It was first mentioned as a fortified town in 1015, and then chartered as a city around the year 1170. Its location where trade routes intersected stimulated the town's economic life, giving rise to important imperial fairs. It became a center of trade for the fur industry and later the printing industry. In 1519 Martin Luther held his great debate during the Reformation, which convinced many Germans to join the Protestant side. Besides its religious significance, Leipzig is also famous for writers such as Friedrich Schiller, one of Germany's greatest poet-dramatists, who was a student at the university. The city also drew many famous scholars, including Johann Wolfgang von Goethe, Johann Fichte, and Christian Gellert. The city also attracted such musical geniuses as Johann Sebastian Bach, Felix Mendelssohn, Robert Schumann, and Richard Wagner. In the history of literature and music Leipzig also was the home of the Kaffeebaum, a famous coffeehouse that opened in 1694 and became a meeting place of such figures as Goethe, Liszt, Wagner, and others.

Famous battles have also been fought in Leipzig. These included two battles at Breitenfeld in 1631, and one at Lützen in 1632 during the Thirty Years' War. These battles near Leipzig resulted in defeats for the Germans by Swedish forces. The more famous Battle of Leipzig (Battle of Nations) in October 1813 saw the defeat of Napoleon during the Wars of Liberation.

Leipzig's economic growth was also stimulated by the development of the printing industry and the furs, yarns, and textile industries. When the Holy Roman Emperor in the 18th century had imposed restrictions on publishing,

FRANKFURT AM MAIN declined as a center and Leipzig took its place. In 1839 the first German railroad opened between Leipzig and DRESDEN, which also stimulated the banking and metallurgical industries. Leipzig became the center of many railway lines. During the 19th century Leipzig witnessed the tremendous growth of industry and the industrial working class. Prior to WORLD WAR II the triangle that was formed by Leipzig, Dresden, and Chemnitz formed the industrial heartland of Germany and also was a stronghold of the SOCIAL DEMOCRATIC PARTY.

Leipzig is also a major intellectual and cultural center. The University of Leipzig, which was called Karl Marx University from 1953 to 1990, dates back to 1409. The city's libraries are also famous, especially the German Library (*Deutsche Bucherei*) and Europe's largest library specializing in education. It is a major center for publishing houses, is home to international book fairs, and has a college of graphic and book art.

Although a quarter of the city was destroyed during war, most of the historic landmarks were restored afterward. These include the Old Town Hall, the Old Commercial Exchange, the old residential and market squares, Auerbach's Cellar, and the 13th-century Church of St. Thomas.

Leipzig, Battle of (October 16–19, 1813)
(Battle of the Nations)

The Battle of Leipzig, also known as the Battle of Nations, was the largest battle of the NAPOLEONIC WARS (1803–15), a decisive defeat for Napoleon and a turning point ending his empire in Germany and Poland.

After the disastrous failure of the invasion of Russia, Napoleon succeeded in rebuilding his army and won some victories over coalition forces during spring and summer 1813. During that same period the Austrian minister, Klemens von METTERNICH, tried and failed to convince the French emperor that compromise was essential if he were to survive. An allied army was poised, which threatened to cut off the French lines of communication through LEIPZIG, leaving Napoleon with the choice of engaging in battle or falling back to the RHINE. Meanwhile, AUSTRIA declared war on August 12, 1813. Shortly thereafter, the allied armies moved their troops into position in the vicinity of Leipzig for the battle that was to decide Europe's future. AUSTRIA added 127,000 men to the allied armed strength, while PRUSSIA's new conscription law now provided 228,000 infantry, 31,000 cavalry, and 13,000 artillerymen with their 376 cannon. These were led by Prussia's toughest combat commander, General Gebhard BLÜCHER. To the north Swedish prince Jean Bernadotte commanded 110,000 troops, and Prince Schwarzenberg was positioned on the upper ELBE RIVER with his army. Napoleon's forces have been estimated from as low as 185,000 to as high as 442,000, though this latter number included many poorly trained recent conscripts.

Forced by political considerations, Napoleon found it necessary to leave a considerable number of troops in DRESDEN to protect his ally, FREDERICK, king of Saxony. After a victory near Dresden Napoleon then confronted the allied forces at Leipzig, where for three days fighting raged in the fields around the city. At first Napoleon successfully repulsed attacks by Schwarzenberg and Blücher, but the tide of battle turned when on the following day allied reinforcements arrived under Jean Bernadotte and General Bennigsen. On the 18th the assault against the French armies in Leipzig began, resulting in ferocious fighting with massive casualties on both sides. Napoleon ordered a retreat out of the city under cover of darkness but unintentionally left some 30,000 French soldiers behind because a bridge, their only avenue of escape, was accidentally blown up by a French corporal.

The battle cost a great number of casualties. The French armies lost some 38,000 killed and wounded and another 30,000 who were stranded in Leipzig. Napoleon left behind about 300 cannon and most of his transport and supplies. The allies lost some 54,000 soldiers killed or wounded, and another 5,000 defected to the French during the battle. Although Napoleon was able to conduct a successful retreat and cross the Rhine by early November, his empire disintegrated.

Leopold I (1640–1705)
Holy Roman Emperor

As emperor, Leopold was successful in raising the Turkish siege of Vienna (1683), challenging the threat from France, subjugating Hungary again, and incorporating Transylvania. Perhaps the greatest achievement was to end the Turkish threat to the Empire. In short, Leopold was able to expand and consolidate the power of the Habsburgs during his reign. These were tremendous accomplishments for an emperor known for his vacilation. When he became emperor in 1658, the HOLY ROMAN EMPIRE had been ravaged by war, its administration was chaotic, it was financially unstable, and most serious of all it was threatened by powerful empires of the French and the Turks on its flanks. The three French wars took up all 20 years of his reign, not even finishing the War of the Spanish Succession. He died soon after the great victory of the BATTLE OF BLENHEIM (1704). His wars with the Turks lasted from 1663 to 1683. Leopold's reign, therefore, can be assessed as one of the most successful in the early modern period.

Leopold should not have become emperor, but because his older brother Ferdinand died of smallpox, Leopold was first named king of Hungary in 1655, then king of Bohemia in 1656, and finally was elected Holy Roman Emperor in 1658. He was the second son of the Austrian Ferdinand III and the Spanish Habsburg infanta Maria Anna. He was said to have typical Habsburg physical attributes; he was reserved, short and thin, and of sickly constitution; his disposition was cold and reserved in public, but open with his close associates, and he generally was lacking in manners. His JESUIT education had a profound influence on him, and he was extremely knowledgeable in theology, metaphysics, jurisprudence, and the sciences, and was addicted to astrology and alchemy. He was proud of his knowledge of Latin style. He was a patron of musicians and encouraged the construction of buildings in the style of the BAROQUE. The emperor's indecisiveness could have been the result of policies and alliances with more powerful allies, such as the maritime powers of Great Britain and the United Provinces. He was tenacious in his convictions that the Habsburg claim to the Spanish Empire was inalienable; he also refused to give in to the Hungarians, who revolted in 1703. Leopold tried to extend royal ABSOLUTISM. The emperor was extremely pious and dedicated to the interests of the church, religiously intolerant and repressive of Protestants, especially in Hungary. He eliminated the traditional right of the Hungarian nobles to elect their ruler and resist the king. The Diet of Pressburg (1687) made the Hungarian crown hereditary in the house of Habsburg. During Leopold's reign the Holy Roman Empire became weaker, while AUSTRIA rose to the rank of a great European power.

There was a tradition among the Habsburgs going back at least as far as MAXIMILIAN I to glorify their lineage. The Habsburgs were skilled in the graphic and pictorial arts in presenting the mission of their dynasty. Under Leopold the arts of the theater and music were used to present the Habsburg motifs of dynasty and divine election. Leopold even staged some 400 theatrical productions in which he often had a leading role. The first major building of his reign was a large theater designed by Giovanni Burnacci, which seated up to 1,500 people. Austrian glory and victories over the Turks were depicted onstage. The tradition of presenting the whole Habsburg lineage was enlarged during the reign of Leopold as he was constantly depicted as the epitome of the triumphant Habsburgs. In one such allegory painted by Gerard von Horst in 1670 Leopold is shown as Hercules in full-bodied armor and wearing a court wig. Wielding a huge club, he is depicted standing on a monstrous three-headed hydra, which he has slain.

Leopold II (1747–1792)
Holy Roman Emperor

Leopold was the third son of MARIA THERESA (1717–80) and her husband, Francis I (1708–65). He became grand duke of Tuscany and carried out reforms that successfully improved the duchy's prosperity. In Florence he was influenced by the progressive views of the Italian ENLIGHTENMENT, and especially Cesare Beccaria, who promoted the abolition of torture and the death penalty. While his brother JOSEPH II was still alive, he refused to go to Vienna and be associated with the emperor's unpopular reforms and pathological insensitivity. When Joseph II died in 1790, he reluctantly left Italy to become the new Austrian ruler as Leopold II. Although not as fanatically absolutist as his brother, he was paranoid, subject to depression, and demanding. He differed from his brother's enlightened ABSOLUTISM and considered himself as the first servant of the state. Had he lived longer, he might have transformed the monarchy into a constitutional state.

After studying the situation in which Joseph had left the Empire, Leopold was determined to correct his brother's errors, following a policy of concessions and threats. Leopold was conciliatory toward the aristocratic and clerical elements in AUSTRIA, repealing Joseph's most controversial reforms. He revoked the hated tax reforms of 1789, but maintained the abolition of serfdom in Bohemia decreed in the Peasants' Patent of 1781. He agreed to be crowned king of Bohemia in Prague, but insisted that local rights be restricted to those existing in 1764. While reaffirming the position of the estates, he also encouraged the MIDDLE CLASS and peasantry. He also made it clear that education and the church were to remain under state authority.

In foreign affairs he also was an astute politician. Leopold was interested in consolidating his position at home and abroad. He tried to improve relations with PRUSSIA and in 1790 signed the Treaty of Reichenbach, which committed Vienna to ending the ongoing war with the Turks without annexations and respecting the territorial integrity of Poland. What Prussia promised was to go along with the restoration of Habsburg rule in Belgium. In 1791 he cooperated with the king of Prussia in the DECLARATION OF PILLNITZ, declaring the possibility of intervention in France even though it was well known that England opposed it. In 1792 he signed a defensive alliance with Prussia against revolutionary France. He attempted to avoid entanglement in the affairs of revolutionary France, even though he was concerned for the safety of his sister, Queen Marie Antoinette (1755–93) in the rapidly radicalizing situation. He quieted the Austrian Netherlands. He discouraged English aid to the Belgian insurgents. In Hungary he divided the nationalists. In 1790 he was crowned king of Hungary and became Holy Roman Emperor. Unfortunately, this ruler with so much promise, died suddenly and was succeeded by his less capable son, Francis, who became the last Holy Roman Emperor, FRANCIS II (1792–1806).

Lessing, Gotthold Ephraim (1729–1781)
dramatist, critic, and philosopher

Lessing was one of the most influential innovative thinkers of the ENLIGHTENMENT. Lessing was the first eminent German writer who made literature his profession. His plays, essays, and treatises presented the general educated public major philosophical issues in an attractive manner providing an appreciation for German literature and cultural life. He spread basic humanitarian values of the Enlightenment and the pantheism of Benedictus de Spinoza. He was a great modern literary critic.

Gotthold Ephraim Lessing was born the son of a Protestant minister in the town of Kamenz in SAXONY. After attending the University of LEIPZIG, he became involved in the world of journalism and theater. Settling in BERLIN in 1749, he wrote comedies, studied for a master's degree at Wittenberg, and became acquainted with such exponents of the Enlightenment as Moses MENDELSSOHN and Friedrich Nicolai. Lessing freed literature from superimposed rules. One of his important accomplishments during the early 1760s was the publication of a pioneering journal, *Letters Concerning the Newest Literature* (1759–65) in which he attacked the artificiality of French classicism and encouraged

German writers to use William Shakespeare as the source of their inspiration.

Although not an original thinker, Lessing embodied the rationalist ideals of the Enlightenment and dealt with basic questions facing Christians. He had abandoned the idea that the Bible was a direct revelation from God. Yet he could not simply abandon his religious beliefs in favor of a secular vision of the world. For a while he looked to Deism and the rationalism of FREEMASONRY, but without satisfaction. He came to believe that human reason should determine all actions, fear of the supernatural should be abandoned, and moral principles should be the foundation of one's life. Lessing fought against dogmatic orthodoxy and rationalistic theologians. He believed that God expressed the infinity of his essence in the universe. And conversely, individuals participated in the divine process by developing their potential. Lessing's philosophy depended on Gottfried Wilhelm von LEIBNIZ's emphasis on the individual, and also on the thought of Spinoza.

Lessing's most significant works are the plays *Miss Sara Sampson* (1755), *Minna von Barnhelm* (1767), *Emilia Galotti* (1772), and *Nathan the Wise* (1779). In *Miss Sara Sampson* Lessing introduced the domestic tragedy to the German theater and turned away from French tragedy. *Minna von Barnhelm* was his greatest work and the first German national drama in which Lessing attempted to counteract the hostility between PRUSSIA and Saxony following the SEVEN YEARS' WAR. In *Emilia Galotti*, whose theme is political power and arbitrary authority, Lessing criticized absolute government. *Nathan the Wise*, written in blank verse, manifests Lessing's progressive thinking and is a plea for religious tolerance. It is no comedy, but a drama of ideas. In it Lessing advances an Enlightenment theory that Christianity, Judaism, and Islam were all individuations of an original single religion.

Leuthen, Battle of (1757)

The Battle of Leuthen (named after the village) some 10 miles west of BRESLAU in Silesia was the location of FREDERICK THE GREAT's greatest victory during the SEVEN YEARS' WAR.

After having defeated a large force of 50,000 French and Germans at Rossbach with only 20,000 Prussian troops on November 5, 1767, he force-marched his Prussian blue coats to Silesia at the pace of 14 miles a day. There he found his army in a desperate situation. After having captured the chief fortress, Schweidnitz, which protected Lower Silesia, the Austrian prince Charles of Lorraine (1712–80), who was the brother of Emperor Francis I, had gone on to capture Breslau on November 25.

Frederick, however, restored the morale of his defeated army and with a total of 35,000 troops attacked an Austrian force on December 5, 1757, that was twice as strong (65,000) in the village of Leuthen. Frederick drove into the Saxon outposts at Borne and feinted toward the Austrian right wing, causing General Lucchese to pester Prince Charles with demands for reinforcements. Instead, Frederick's columns turned south to attack the Austrian left flank. Frederick employed his old stratagem of the oblique battle order, by which he held back one of his wings and threw his army with the greatest force upon a single wing of the enemy. The Prussian grenadiers routed the Bavarians and Württembergers who were allied to the Austrians, and then fell on the Austrian left flank at Sagschütz. As the Prussians fought their way through Leuthen, General Lucchese brought 70 squadrons to reinforce the Austrian line, charged by only 35 cuirassier squadrons of the Prussian left-wing cavalry, who defeated the Austrians. There resulted some 22,000 Austrian casualties, while Frederick suffered only 11,589. Frederick then continued his attack to the bridge at Lissa, forcing Prince Charles to retreat to the mountains. When Breslau surrendered to the Prussians, another 17,000 Austrians were lost. As a result Silesia had to be evacuated by the Austrians. It was a humiliating fifth defeat for Charles in two wars against Frederick, because of which he was relieved of his command.

This great victory by Frederick impressed Europe. Later Napoleon Bonaparte remarked that this battle alone would have sufficed to make Frederick immortal. Not only the troops of the Empire but also the elite regiments of the French had been defeated within a few hours by a smaller Prussian army. The sensational war news of Frederick's series of victories at Rossbach (1757) in Bohemia, Leuthen (1757), and Liegnitz and Torgau (1760) made him famous. His victories were aided by the advantages he had from his inner line of defense and the habitual jealousies of his coalition enemies and, of course, his military genius.

liberalism, German

Liberals had difficulty defining their own philosophy and presented themselves to society as a party of movement, of progressive change, and a better future. They were in a struggle during the Restoration against the reactionary conservative forces, which wanted to maintain order and preserve traditional society, culture, and monarchical power. Liberals could not deny the French revolutionary ideals of liberty, equality, and fraternity, but they were opposed to democratic agitation and revolutionary violence. Liberals were not necessarily against the state, but were ambivalent. They were not opposed to monarchy as such, but denounced despotism, arbitrary government, and unreasonable interference into private matters. On the other hand, liberals were not opposed to an enlightened state that had contributed to progress during the 18th century. Certainly they hoped to use the state to further their own agenda.

Liberals did not agree on a common set of political and economic beliefs. One division concerned how far freedom should be extended: its scope, its character, its consequences. They differed on who should get the right to vote, whether only the educated and propertied should vote or also the uneducated adult males. In the early 19th century most liberals were opposed to democratic suffrage, although some more democratically inclined would have included wage earners, apprentices, small farmers, and shopkeepers, but not women, children, and servants. On the subject of representation they differed as to whether it should be through an institution like a parliament as in England and France, or through an assembly of estates. Some believed in a strong bureaucracy and others in a weak one. Every liberal believed in some measure of political participation and in some sort of representative government.

The concept of the people, the *Volk*, was very important in liberal thinking. All liberals believed in constitutions that would in some instances limit the actions of the state, while in others direct its activities toward progressive ends. Although liberals believed that the *Volk* should be able to make its own laws, none believed that they should dictate what the government should do through the will of the majority. Liberals believed that governments should always act in a legally responsible manner. The liberal vision of the people, the *Volk*, was a distinct mixture of confidence and faith versus anxiety and fear. As time progressed, there was an increasing reluctance of the democratic wing of liberalism to work within the existing state framework, and with the people at the center of their thought a republic seemed more realistic and favored universal male suffrage. Democratic left-wing liberals did not think that the post-Napoleonic GERMAN CONFEDERATION could be transformed into the basis for German national unity and were prepared to create an entirely new political system.

German liberalism had its roots in German thought as well as foreign influences. Immanuel KANT and Wilhelm von HUMBOLDT provided the emphasis on personal freedoms and the development of individuality. Foreign influences came from England and the French Revolution. The Rhineland areas and southern Germany were more influenced by French ideas, while northern Germany was influenced by English traditions. From the University of GÖTTINGEN knowledge of English political institutions was disseminated. German liberals came to admire the role of English public opinion, trial by jury, and freedom of the press, and they found a kinship between German PROTESTANTISM and

English political liberalism. Influences of British economic liberalism came later in the 1850s. Before the REVOLUTION OF 1848 most of the leaders of German liberalism were professors who suffered for their liberal principles. German public opinion was aroused over the dismissal of the Göttingen Seven (professors who were dismissed because of their protests over the abrogation of the constitution of HANOVER by the new ruler, Ernst August). The revolution of 1830 in France stimulated liberalism in Germany as did the establishment of the Pressverein in 1832, which propagated liberal ideals. The high point of liberalism was the popular HAMBACH FESTIVAL, which was meant to inspire the new political spirit of the age. Liberal professors found allies in banking and merchant circles who made up the right wing of liberal leadership in the revolution of 1848. German liberalism was weak, however, because its middle-class base of support was much smaller than in England and France, and its ideals were considered an alien foreign doctrine that ran counter to the political spirit of Germany. Finally, the requirements of NATIONALISM and unity always took precedence over the liberal principles of liberty.

The liberal movement came to a climax during the Revolution of 1848 but then crashed. In spring 1848 as the wave of revolution swept over Germany, liberals gained the support of the masses and became the spokesmen of the nation. Liberals formed ministries in the various German states. Even in PRUSSIA a liberal ministry was formed and a constitutional monarchy established. Then delegates went to Preparliament (Vorparlament) in FRANKFURT, a congress of notables, where they decided to call a general election based on universal male suffrage. The majority in the Preparliament was composed of moderate constitutionalists. When the FRANKFURT PARLIAMENT was convened on May 18, 1848, all the aspirations of the liberals who wanted to create a parliamentary and constitutional state in Germany seemed to be on the verge of realization. Besides formulating a constitutional structure, the delegates wanted to secure the rights of the individual against the police-state. The Basic Rights guaranteed a citizen's constitutional state, and for the first time in German history a uniform bill of rights was established. Class privileges were abolished by a system of general equality before the law. Every citizen was to have freedom of thought and conscience, freedom of association, and rights over property. Individual actions were to be controlled by the rule of law. Social reform legislation was not approved and proved to be a stumbling block, creating a division between moderate liberals and the leftist democratic forces. Liberals considered the sanctity of property essential and would not consider a revolutionary land reform or the abolition of feudal obligations without compensation. So middle-class liberalism lost the support of the masses, which helped make the revolution possible. The liberals even used the police powers of the state to control public protests. Although the desire for national unity was the most important popular force in the revolution, the challenge of creating national unity was also a task that was too complicated to be solved while constitutional reforms were being decided. In the end, however, it was the military forces of the counterrevolution, first in AUSTRIA and then in Prussia, which led to the defeat of the Frankfurt Parliament.

Liberals did not lose all of the progress made during the revolution. As constitutions were modified by rulers, key demands of the liberal revolutionaries were left intact, such as civil rights, economic liberalism, and parliamentary control of the budget. Many German states kept their written constitutions and had popularly elected assemblies, though with restricted suffrage. The counterrevolution did not reverse the trend toward legal equality, which had been one of the goals of liberal revolutionaries. Conservatives did not reverse trial by jury and did not reverse laws emancipating the Jews.

The 1850s witnessed considerable economic expansion and industrial growth, creating a larger middle class receptive to liberalism. German economists agitated for free trade, a unified currency, and economic unity. In 1861 a chamber of commerce was organized, and among the many liberal organizations established was the National Association (Nationalverein), which became the first political organization in Germany transcending borders and including liberals and democrats in one party. The National Association stirred up the German middle classes to support Prussian leadership in the unification of Germany and to create a more liberal and constitutional Germany. It lasted until 1868 and was Otto von BISMARCK's strongest opponent on the army reform bill. The liberals were opposed to the elimination of the militia (Landwehr) and emphasized the parliament's control over the military budget. Bismarck proceeded to reform the army despite their opposition and proceeded to defeat Austria in 1866. The liberals proceeded with the INDEMNITY BILL (1866), which retroactively sanctioned the government's actions since 1862. Liberals sacrificed the principle of legislative control of the budget to the economic advances of the NORTH GERMAN CONFEDERATION.

The National Association was followed by the right-wing NATIONAL LIBERAL PARTY, which was officially constituted in 1867 when the left-wing PROGRESSIVE PARTY split with it over the issue of the Indemnity Bill. National Liberals became the right-wing liberals who supported Bismarck's constitution in the North German Confederation's REICHSTAG. Its leaders were Lasker, Forckenbeck, von Unruh, and Twesten, and its membership was largely men of education and property. After unification the National Liberals continued to support Bismarck in the KULTURKAMPF and were champions of government centralization. The Progressives continued to press for increased parliamentary rights. Yet, both parties until 1878 were dedicated to major liberal principles, which included free trade, anticlericalism, and civil liberties. Both parties appealed to the same middle-class electorate. The Progressives again split with the National Liberals over the support for protective tariffs on trade, which Bismarck enacted in the late 1870s. After that, liberal political power rapidly declined as is evident from their representation in the Reichstag: 155 deputies in 1874 to 47 in 1881. Liberals increasingly included bankers and industrialists who became strongly nationalistic and active supporters of colonial expansion.

The Progressive Party was the oldest of the Reichstag parties, founded in 1861, and was the strongest in the Prussian diet during the constitutional struggle with Bismarck. It was left-liberal and championed the principles of the Revolution of 1848. The party wanted Germany to become a full-fledged parliamentary state, promoted free-market economics, and in general was antimilitarist, antiprotectionist, and antisocialist. On the eve of WORLD WAR I (1910) another liberal party was formed, the PROGRESSIVE PEOPLE'S PARTY with the help of Friedrich NAUMANN.

This left-wing liberal group supported the political reforms initiated under Chancellor Max Von Baden and cooperated with the SOCIAL DEMOCRATIC PARTY and the CENTER PARTY in the founding of the WEIMAR REPUBLIC. Unfortunately, the liberal leaders on the left and the right could not merge their differences and consequently created two parties: the GERMAN DEMOCRATIC PARTY (DDP) and the GERMAN PEOPLE'S PARTY (DVP). The left-wing liberals in the DDP such as Hugo PRUESS contributed to the foundation of the republic, especially the writing of the WEIMAR CONSTITUTION. A key reason for the split was the unwillingness of the leaders of the DDP to include Gustav STRESEMANN because of his wartime annexationist positions. Consequently, he set up the DVP, which only accepted the republic in 1922. Throughout the 1920s the electoral base of liberalism was eroded partially because of the impoverishment of its constituency. The support declined from 23 percent in 1918 to 8.4 percent in 1930, which reflected the weakness of liberal ideas and the inability to defend the republic against the rise of National Socialism.

Liberation, Wars of (1813–1815)

The Wars of Liberation occurred after the defeat of Napoleon's Grand Army in Russia, a world-historic event and gigantic catastrophe, which emboldened PRUSSIA and AUSTRIA to form alliances whose goal was the collapse of Napoleon's European empire. In German history an important consequence was the stimulus for German national consciousness.

The wars originated with the revolutionary Convention of Tauroggen, a nonaggression pact signed by General Yorck von Wartenburg (1759–1830) on his own responsibility, which permitted Russian troops to cross the Niemen river and to enter East Prussia. Another event of revolutionary significance that led to the wars was the takeover of the administration of East Prussia by Baron Karl von STEIN, who proceeded to form the *Landwehr* and *Landsturm*. The rise of national sentiment resulted in the formation of numerous volunteer units in the Prussian army, and a volunteer reserve (*Landwehr*) was created to augment the regular army. The phrase *national liberation* was widely used while recruiting officers created a new military force. At the assembly of provincial estates early in 1813 both Stein as a representative of the czar and General Yorck von Wartenburg called for a crusade against the French. As a result the Prussian king moved to BRESLAU, and negotiations with Russia quickly led to an alliance. On March 16 the Russian czar and Prussian king declared war. The Prussian king addressed his people with the stirring "To My People," which explained the objectives of the struggle, and the young poet Theodor Körner (1791–1813) proclaimed that the Wars of Liberation were "a crusade, a holy war." Although the wars began as a struggle for national liberation and self-determination, they ended up being for the restoration of the European balance of power based on historical and legitimate dynastic and social relationships.

In spring 1813 Napoleon was on the strategic offensive, fighting both Russian and Prussian armies for control of Germany. With Britain, Spain, and Portugal presenting a united front in the Iberian peninsula and Prussia allied with Russia, Napoleon was put on the defensive. Organizing a counteroffensive, Napoleon raised an army of 120,000 men and planned to relieve DANZIG and then attack the scattered allied armies in Germany. Instead he had to divert to DRESDEN, where in late April Prince Eugène de Beauharnais's army was being threatened. Marching into SAXONY, the French confronted the Russian and Prussian armies near Lützen on May 1 and won the battle. Napoleon followed the retreating allies through Saxony and won the Battle of Bautzen on the banks of the Spree. The victories at Lützen and Bautzen restored Napoleon's strategic advantage, and he advanced to the ELBE RIVER, where he occupied Dresden to the south and HAMBURG to the north. The allies requested a six-week armistice to which Napoleon agreed on June 4, 1813.

During the armistice a diplomatic initiative occurred by which the coalition tried to involve new states. Britain was a key player by contributing war subsidies. British and Russian diplomats worked on the Swedes, whose troops occupied Pomerania. The Austrians were playing a diplomatic game under the direction of Prince Klemens Lothar von METTERNICH, waiting for the opportune time to become involved, which finally occurred in July when the Convention of Reichenbach was signed by which Austria agreed to join the Sixth Coalition against Napoleon.

When the campaign resumed in August, the allies decided to concentrate on defeating isolated French forces, which at first proved successful. While Blücher defeated the French at Katsbach to the west of Breslau, the Austrians threatened to attack the French in Dresden. At the battle before Dresden the outnumbered French were the victors. The retreating Austrians lost 38,000 killed and captured. After these defeats the allies were ready in September 1813 to concentrate against Napoleon's main army. Time was not on Napoleon's side as further defections occurred from his former allies. BAVARIA switched sides in early October, and it looked like members of the CONFEDERATION OF THE RHINE would soon desert. Napoleon needed a crushing victory to restore his credibility, which was not to happen. The first clash occurred on October 14, when the largest cavalry battle in history, although inconclusive, occurred between Prince Murat and Wittgenstein's army. Two days later, the "Battle of the Nations" occurred, otherwise known as the BATTLE OF LEIPZIG. As the allies attempted to encircle the French in LEIPZIG, the French withdrew. The battle ended in disaster for Napoleon, who lost more than 70,000 killed or captured and consequently lost military control of Germany as his army fled to the safety of the Rhine. The Confederation of the Rhine was dissolved.

The last battle of the German campaign was fought on October 30, 1813, on the north bank of the Main River as Napoleon pushed aside the Austrian and Bavarian blocking force. While the French remained in FRANKFURT for only a short while, they crossed the Rhine at Mainz in early December, and Napoleon prepared for the defense of France. The garrisons of French that remained surrendered with the exception of those in HAMBURG.

After disputes among the allies the campaign of 1814 proceeded. It was agreed that the Austrian and Prussian armies would advance separately on the premise that Napoleon could not attack both at the same time. On March 5 Blücher advanced along the shores of the Aisne with 85,000 men, while the main army followed the course of the River Seine. The allies suffered several setbacks that gave Napoleon hope, which encouraged him to attack allied supply lines followed by a retreat to Paris. The Austrian commander, Schwarzenberg, launched an attack immediately to prevent Napoleon from reinforcing the city. Most of the defenders were raw recruits, and on March 31, 1814, Paris surrendered and the war was over. By the Peace of Paris Napoleon agreed to abdicate to make way for the restoration of the Bourbon dynasty, and the French borders were to be reduced to those of 1792, which included Alsace. Napoleon was made sovereign over the island of Elba and provided a pension. When Napoleon returned from Elba, raised an army, and confronted the allies at Waterloo, he was decisively defeated and exiled to St. Helena, which was followed by the second Peace of Paris.

Liebknecht, Karl (1871–1919)
a founder of the German Communist Party (KPD)
Karl Liebknecht was born in LEIPZIG on August 13, 1871, the son of Wilhelm LIEBKNECHT. Karl was trained as a lawyer and defended others against charges of treason. In 1908 he won a seat in the Prussian parliament and in 1912 in the REICHSTAG. In 1912 he exposed the KRUPP armaments firm for bribery. Having joined the SOCIAL DEMOCRATIC PARTY (SPD) late in life, he became a very effective agitator.

Liebknecht was strongly opposed to German MILITARISM and even wrote about methods that could be used to subvert the army. He was opposed to WORLD WAR I and the SPD's policies that supported it. Early in the war he organized antiwar groups and public protests and was imprisoned because he was a member of the Spartacus League and for his antiwar agitation. In October 1918 he joined with Rosa LUXEMBURG and through the INDEPENDENT SOCIAL DEMOCRATIC PARTY (USPD) tried to foster social revolution. In January 1919 he helped found the GERMAN COMMUNIST PARTY (KPD) and supported the violent overthrow the government. The socialist government suppressed this attempt at revolution, and Liebknecht was arrested, then shot, allegedly while trying to escape.

Liebknecht, Wilhelm (1826–1900)
prominent founder of socialist organizations
A man of strong republican convictions, Wilhelm Liebknecht participated in the REVOLUTION OF 1848. Because of his revolutionary activity, like many others he had to flee into exile first to Switzerland and then to England, where he remained from 1850 to 1862. While in London he was closely associated with and learned from Karl MARX and Friedrich ENGELS their theories and experience. After returning to Germany in 1862, he joined the General German Worker's Association of Ferdinand LASALLE. His differences with the followers of Lasalle motivated him to join with August BEBEL in founding the Marxist-oriented SOCIAL DEMOCRATIC PARTY (SPD). From 1872 to 1874 he was imprisoned for his radical political activities and expelled several times from various German states. In 1875 he and August Bebel were responsible for merging the two socialist parties at the congress in Gotha (*see* GOTHA PROGRAM). He became editor

of two socialist newspapers, the most important being *Vorwärts*. In 1867 he became a Social Democratic deputy to the Diet of the NORTH GERMAN CONFEDERATION and continued to represent the SPD in the REICHSTAG until his death in 1900.

Liebknecht was a dedicated socialist whose optimism, dynamic personality, and ability to get people to work together was responsible for his success as a party leader. His speeches were printed and widely disseminated. He published a series of books on such subjects as the French Revolution, Robert Owen, and Robert Blum. His son was Karl LIEBKNECHT, whose socialist radicalism led to the founding of the GERMAN COMMUNIST PARTY (KPD) and contributed to the Spartacist Uprising in BERLIN during January 1919.

List, Friedrich (1789–1846)
advocate of a customs union (Zollverein) and a national economy

Friedrich List, a native of the former imperial free city of Reutlingen, became a professor of political science at the University of Tübingen. He was an economist who favored free competition within states but not between states. List proposed a doctrine of national economy that favored the subordination of the division of labor and competition to a closed national economy protected by import tariffs. He was essentially responsible for the creation of the ZOLLVEREIN. List explained his doctrine of an organized national economy in his *National System of Political Economy* (1840). He soon found himself at odds with the economic philosophy of Adam Smith, which was the dominant philosophy at the university. His outspokenness got him dismissed from the university and imprisoned by the reactionary government of Württemberg; he was offered amnesty only if he promised to emigrate to America. In the United States he became wealthy from his mining investments in Pennsylvania. Because of his prominence he was appointed an American consul, returning to Germany in 1830 and residing in LEIPZIG. He then became involved in the construction of a German rail line.

In the United States List's experiences had led him to conclusions different from the classical school of economics and its "cosmopolitanism, materialism, and individualism." He saw the United States prosper, not following a policy of free trade, but one of restrictive tariffs protecting its own growing industries. Whereas free trade, he thought, might be good for the advanced industrial economy of Great Britain, he thought that it was ruinous for Germany. He also came to the conclusion that the laws formulated by Adam Smith were not natural or eternal laws. He criticized German intellectuals and politicians for their lack of realism and practical experience, concluding that Germany had too many philosophers and writers who distracted people from economically useful occupations, resulting in a lack of technical and business skills. Both List and Adam Smith were materialistic and influenced by HUMANISM and the ENLIGHTENMENT, but they came to different conclusions as to how a nation's economy would promote prosperity and happiness. Whereas Smith believed that harmonization of conflicting interests would result from autonomous economic laws operating independently of society and culture without the state arbitrarily intervening, List concluded that the state and the nation were the guarantors of progress. For List the economy was linked to other aspects of culture and should have as its goal the development of the human personality, a just social order, and greater political freedom.

List never lost sight of his goal, which was the creation a unified German nation and a customs union as a preliminary step. He also thought that education would improve German national consciousness and Germany's industrial future. His vision also included a colonial empire that would furnish raw materials and unfinished products and provide a market for Germany's manufactured goods. He thought that the thinly populated eastern regions of Prussia offered opportunities for migration and agricultural development. All of his ideas were aimed at challenging the economic supremacy of Great Britain. Yet, his ideas were too advanced for the time. The ARISTOCRACY and their interest in land

and agriculture were opposed to industrialization; economists could not understand the interrelatedness of politics and economics; and businessmen opposed the interference of the state in the economy.

Liszt, Franz (1811–1886)
composer, conductor, and pianist

The Austro-Hungarian composer, conductor, and pianist Franz Liszt was one of Europe's preeminent artists who made important contributions to the German musical tradition.

Liszt was the son of an official at the Hungarian court of Prince Nikolaus Esterhazy. Demonstrating an impressive talent as a pianist, he held his first piano recital at the age of nine. By the 1820s he was a flamboyant virtuoso in Paris, where he met and was influenced by Paganini and especially by Chopin's romantic style. In 1834 he began an affair with Countess Marie d'Agoult, with whom he had three children, one of which was Cosima, who later married Richard WAGNER. Liszt separated from the countess in 1844 and later met Princess Carolyne Sayn-Wittgenstein, a new companion, in WEIMAR. His open affair with the not yet divorced princess and his support for avant-garde music led to his departure from Weimar in 1860. From there he went to Rome, where he received minor holy orders in 1860. Some of his later compositions include "The Legend of St. Elizabeth" (1857–62), the "Mephisto Waltzes" (1880–83) and "La lugubre gondola" (1882). Liszt died in BAYREUTH in 1886 while attending a music festival.

In 1848 Liszt became a director of extraordinary music at the ducal court in Weimar. His Weimar years from 1848 to 1859 represent the zenith of his career when he composed most of his major works. They include two pieces inspired by the Faust legend—*The Faust Symphony* (1857), which was based on GOETHE's work, and Episodes from Lenau's *Faust*—known as the *Dante Symphony* (1859). Other works of this Weimar period include more than a dozen symphonic poems, including *Tasso, Les preludes, Mazeppa, Hamlet,* and *The Battle of the Huns* (*Hunnenschlacht*). Other works include the E-flat

Franz Liszt *(Library of Congress)*

Piano Concerto, *The Dance of Death* for piano and orchestra, and works such as the *Transcendental Studies,* the B Minor Sonata, and his famous *Hungarian Rhapsodies.*

As director Liszt made Weimar the center of the New German School, devoting particular effort to the promotion of the music dramas of his son-in-law, Richard Wagner. Liszt also premiered the works of other new composers such as Robert SCHUMANN, Hector Berlioz, Giuseppe Verdi, Gaetano Donizetti, and others.

Locarno Treaties (1925)

The Locarno Treaties guaranteed the security of the Franco-German and Belgo-German frontiers and the demilitarized zone of the Rhineland.

In February 1925 Gustav STRESEMANN, the foreign secretary, whose motives were practical and not idealistic, desired to prevent another French incursion into the Ruhr as had happened in 1923, to remove the financial burdens of the VERSAILLES TREATY, and to gain long-range military parity with the other European powers. He offered a German commitment to respect the western frontier as defined by Versailles and suggested that the great powers should guarantee the inviolability of the French, Belgian, and German borderlands. Because of the recent failure to win approval for the Geneva Protocol, which had proposed that the LEAGUE OF NATIONS include in its covenant required arbitration to avoid war, Stresemann's proposal was finally negotiated at the multilateral conference that met at Locarno in October 1925.

Although France wanted Germany to renounce its revisionist claims not only in the West but also in eastern Europe for its allies, Stresemann rejected their demand because it would have weakened public support for his policy and alienated the army leadership. Therefore, Stresemann consented to no more than arbitration treaties with Poland and Czechoslovakia. As for Germany's admission into the League of Nations, Stresemann wanted a special condition that did not obligate Germany to participate in sanctions in order to protect its special relationship with the Soviet Union.

The treaty was signed by France, Germany, and Belgium and guaranteed by Britain and Italy. At the same time the Germans concluded arbitration conventions with France, Belgium, Poland, and Czechoslovakia; Franco-Polish and Franco-Czech Treaties of Mutual Guarantee were also signed. The treaty imposed limits on France's military freedom and made a repetition of her sanctions policy in the Ruhr impossible. The agreements were a triumph for Gustav Stresemann, Austen Chamberlain, and Aristide Briand. Because Stresemann and Chamberlain had refused to guarantee Germany's eastern borders, France concluded an alliance with Czechoslovakia in addition to her already existing alliance with Poland.

Lübke, Heinrich (1894–1972)
federal president

Heinrich Lübke served as president of the FEDERAL REPUBLIC for two terms from 1959 to 1969.

Heinrich Lübke was born in Enkhausen near Arnsberg in Westphalia. He completed his *Abitur* in 1913, studying building techniques and agriculture. During WORLD WAR I he served in the military, rising to the rank of lieutenant. After the war he continued his agricultural studies, but then also studied philosophy and administration at the Friedrich Wilhelm University in BERLIN. During the 1920s he was involved in the management of farming cooperatives, was a director of the German Farmer Association, and was elected as a representative of the CENTER PARTY in the Prussian legislature. He was imprisoned by the Nazis for a short time, but then was involved in various construction offices.

After the war he joined the CHRISTIAN DEMOCRATIC UNION of Westphalia. Under the British military administration he was appointed to the founding legislature of North Rhine Westphalia and from 1947 to 1952 served as minister of food and agriculture. Later, he joined Konrad ADENAUER's cabinet as minister of food, forestry, and agriculture. He believed that German agriculture needed to be reorganized and its productivity increased. During his tenure the number of inefficient farms declined by 340,000. Even though he was criticized by farmers, Adenauer reappointed him, and he became the main architect of the modernization of German agriculture and the agricultural policy followed by the EUROPEAN ECONOMIC COMMUNITY.

As the term of the first federal president, Theodor HEUSS, came to an end, Adenauer temporarily placed himself as a candidate for the office. This undermined the chancellor's authority, and he supported Heinrich Lübke for two terms as president, not because he particularly liked him. In the 1965 elections Adenauer also lured Lübke into a conspiracy to keep Ludwig ERHARD out of power, which did not work in the end. The president was a highly principled and no-nonsense official who sought to expand the importance of the office of president. Through a serious review of legislation and evaluation of appointments, he succeeded in strengthening his role. Lübke also tried to influence public policy in favor of friendly Franco-German relations, for the support of development aid, the support of West Berlin, and an alliance of parties in a Grand Coalition (CDU/SPD), which occurred. His stubborn personality and lack of diplomacy made it difficult for him to become very popular. In fact, he was frequently a target of media and press criticism for his partisanship. It also was alleged, though never substantiated, that he had participated as an architect in the building of CONCENTRATION CAMPS.

Ludendorff, Erich Friedrich Wilhelm (1865–1937)

general and military strategist of World War I
Erich Ludendorff was the most significant German leader of WORLD WAR I. Born on April 9, 1865, in Kruszewnia, Posen, Erich Ludendorff received his military education at a Prussian state military academy. He joined the army in 1882, was commissioned an infantry lieutenant in 1887, and due to his excellent performance was appointed to the General Staff in 1894. Gaining the confidence of the chief of staff, the younger Count MOLTKE, he became head of the important mobilization and deployment division of the General Staff. It was his responsibility to prepare the army's mobilization of the war plan designed by General Alfred von Schlieffen (*see* SCHLIEFFEN PLAN), which called for the invasion of neutral Belgium. Ludendorff's uncompromising personality brought him into conflict with the political opposition in the REICHSTAG, which resulted in his dismissal from the General Staff and assignment to command an infantry brigade on the French frontier. Shortly after the beginning of the war, as deputy chief of staff of the 2nd Army, he was responsible for the seizure of the Belgian fortress of Liege, which made him famous. He was then transferred to the eastern front as chief of staff for General Paul von HINDENBURG, where they won the BATTLE OF TANNENBERG and others.

Ludendorff was a joyless man of great energy whose life was dedicated to the military. His military competence was excellent, but he did not understand the connection between war and economics, politics, or diplomacy. Unfortunately, his ego convinced him that he was capable of leadership in these civilian areas as well. He liked to give but not take orders. He believed in the Darwinian survival of the fittest, and that Germany had to be ruthless to win the war. He was persuaded that the civilian government prevented him from exercising the brutal methods that were needed to win. He had contempt for pacifists and was opposed to any negotiated peace.

After the failure of General Erich von FALKENHAYN's Supreme Command in the murderous battle for the key French fortress of Verdun, the Kaiser in 1916 appointed Hindenburg as chief of the General Staff and Ludendorff became his quartermaster general. Ludendorff gained increasing control of the German war effort and in January 1917 ordered unrestricted submarine warfare, which Admiral Alfred von TIRPITZ predicted would bring England to her knees. In the process, Ludendorff forced the resignation of Chancellor Theobald von Bethmann Hollweg, who opposed submarines and favored a negotiated peace. Then Ludendorff began a program of total mobilization called the HINDENBURG PROGRAM and national emergency service. After the defeat of the Russians Ludendorff dictated the harsh TREATY OF BREST-LITOVSK in February 1918, whose punitive character indicated what awaited the Allies if they lost the war. After the spring 1918 offensive failed and Germany's position appeared hopeless, Ludendorff suddenly demanded armistice negotiations and reforms in the German government. President Woodrow Wilson's reply made Ludendorff again change his mind, demanding a last-ditch resistance. When he was overruled by the new chancellor, Prince Max von BADEN, he denied any responsibility for Germany's defeat and created the legend of the "stab in the back," which blamed the defeat on the Socialists and Democrats.

After the war Ludendorff gladly accepted the role of a betrayed and misunderstood leader. He participated in "folkish" ultranationalist movements and was involved in unsuccessful attempts to overthrow the republican government by Wolfgang Kapp (*see* KAPP PUTSCH) in 1920 and Adolf HITLER in 1923. He became an idol of the NAZI PARTY, entered the Reichstag as a Nazi in 1924, and ran for president on the Nazi ticket against his former commander in chief, Hindenburg, whom he had bitterly hated since the end of World War I. From 1924 to 1928 he was a Nazi member of the Reichstag. Ludendorff published his political and military views in his openly militarist *The Nation at War* (1936). Along with his wife he founded the mystico-religious Aryan-German Tannenberg League, which campaigned against Jews, Marxists, Freemasons (*see* FREEMASONRY), and JESUITS. After his resignation from the Reichstag, he wrote and lectured to declining audiences. He died in Tutzing, near MUNICH, on December 20, 1937, mourned by some but almost forgotten.

Ludwig I (1786–1868)
king of Bavaria

Ludwig was born in 1786 to Maximilian IV Joseph, elector of BAVARIA, who became Bavaria's first king. As crown prince during the NAPOLEONIC WARS Ludwig fought on the French side. Ludwig possessed great talents and had both romantic and classical interests. At first very liberal as a prince, shortly after becoming king in 1825 he turned politically very conservative. With the assistance of a group of nobles Ludwig overthrew the ministry of the great reformer Count Maximilian Joseph von MONTGELAS, whose administration was guided by the rationalism of the ENLIGHTENMENT and a spirit of toleration. Ludwig, however, did not intend to undo the modernizing reforms that Montgelas had made. While Max Joseph had issued a liberal constitution in 1808, which called for a representative parliament, by 1818 a new constitution was issued, which was the most conservative of the new South German constitutions. Crowned king in 1825, Ludwig at the age of 39 became a ruler in the manner of an 18th-century enlightened despot.

While still crown prince, Ludwig already had adopted his father's conviction that art and architecture should serve the purpose of the nation and the state and be a powerful educational instrument. Already on 1807 Ludwig began to plan a national shrine at the Walhalla near REGENSBURG, intending it to symbolize that all Germans shared a common fatherland. Eventually it was constructed between 1830 and 1842. MUNICH was more important, and Ludwig intended it to be a center of German culture so he adorned it with classical architecture. An urban plan was drawn up by the architect Leo von Klenze, which guided its development into the 20th century. Ludwig's talents were expressed in both romantic and classical directions. Promoting educational reform, he supported Friedrich Thiersch, who inculcated German neohumanism in schools and universities. Like so many others Ludwig was inspired by the revolution in Greece, which stirred strong Hellenic sentiments in him, while his brother, Otto, even became the new king in Greece.

Religious reform also was an important element in postrevolutionary Bavaria. While still crown prince, Ludwig patronized Johann Michael Sailer (1751–1832), who had the reputation of a rationalist, but whose piety and personal integrity were well known. After he became king, Ludwig's government was unwilling to give up controls over the church that had been acquired during the Napoleonic era, used religion to defend the established order, and encouraged religious revival and piety through missions, pilgrimages, and new liturgical forms. In 1827 at the initiative of Ludwig, Joseph GÖRRES (1776–1848) accepted a professorship in universal history at the newly established Ludwigs-University in Munich. There he established himself as a publicist and tried to influence Ludwig's government in a conservative, antiliberal, and church-oriented direction. At the university he joined the philosophers Franz von BAADER (1765–1841) and Friedrich Wilhelm Schelling (1775–1854), the jurist Georg Phillips (1804–72), the philologist Ernst Lasaulx (1805–61), and the church historian Ignaz von Döllinger (1799–1890). Becoming a professor at 27, Döllinger, the priest, quickly became the most influential Catholic historian of his day, being drawn into the growing debate over papal authority. Ludwig was also in the forefront of opposition to PRUSSIA over religious issues, developing a staunchly pro-Catholic policy, which soon alienated Bavaria's Protestant minority.

During the revolutionary disturbances in 1830, new elections returned a large number of liberal representatives to the parliament (*Landtag*), people who opposed Ludwig's conservative government. In response to student demonstrations at the University of Munich, the king tried to restrict freedom of the press. The progressive forces in the parliament fought with the government over the restrictive press law, first with some success, but then Ludwig responded repressively. He closed the parliament and tried to restore royal authority by appointing a conservative ministry. The center of liberal protest shifted from Munich to the RHINELAND PALATINATE, which had become part of Bavaria after the Napoleonic Wars. The liberal opposition had also been strong in Franconia, Würzburg, and Bamberg, where Ludwig followed the Austrian prince Clemens Lothar METTERNICH's lead in opposing the liberals who advocated reform. In June 1832 he appointed Prince Wrede extraordinary commissioner for the Palatinate, and with half of the Bavarian army established martial law in the troublesome Palatinate. Several of the speakers at the HAMBACH FESTIVAL were tried and imprisoned, and others deported or escaped to France. Similar repression of the liberal opposition occurred throughout the GERMAN CONFEDERATION. The reactionary shift in 1833 was greeted by protests in the Palatinate, where the government was condemned for violating the rights of the citizens. But the protests failed to stop Wrede's troops from dissolving political organizations and pacifying the Palatinate. Even though reaction triumphed in the early 1830s, political ferment continued across the German states. Ludwig's response was to attempt to undo decades of liberal political development and return Bavaria to monarchical ABSOLUTISM. He left the conduct of state affairs in the hands of his conservative minister, Karl von Abel, who promoted bureaucratic authority and the influence of the Catholic Church.

In 1846–47 the political climate in Munich was as threatening as it was in Vienna or Berlin. Discontent with the king increased with the arrival in Munich of the dancer Lola Montez, who became the object of his obsession, and eventually his mistress. His eccentricity and lavish spending earned him disrespect, ridicule, the opposition of Catholic leaders, and the resignation in 1847 of minister Abel and others. During the REVOLUTION OF 1848 Ludwig was the only king who was forced to abdicate in favor of his son.

Ludwig II (1845–1886)
king of Bavaria

Born in MUNICH on August 25, 1845, to the Bavarian crown prince Maximilian and his wife, Marie, a Prussian princess, Ludwig spent most of his early life sheltered at Hohenschwangau Castle in the company of his mother, servants, tutors, and farmers. He was tall, dark, handsome, and athletic. The paintings of German legends that decorated the castle and his love of the valleys and forests of the Bavarian Alps inspired a romantic outlook on life. His IDEALISM and ROMANTICISM were deepened by his love for the poems and dramas of Friedrich von SCHILLER (1759–1805). Ludwig's appreciation of the arts and pathological sensitivity made it possible for him to divorce himself from the real world into an imaginative paradise. Lacking a university education and having no practical exposure to politics and the conduct of government, he was unprepared to take on his future role as king.

At the age of 16, Ludwig experienced for the first time a performance of Richard WAGNER's (1813–83) opera *Lohengrin*. Both the music and the legendary theme inspired Ludwig to become a devoted collector of all of Wagner's compositions and publications. In 1864 after his father's death Ludwig invited Wagner to Munich. Ludwig supported the building of Wagner's opera house in BAYREUTH and had Wagner's operas staged for himself in Munich as the only spectator. Ludwig also planned the creation of a German

Music School in Munich to rival that of Vienna. He decided to build a big new opera house, which, however, was opposed by the government because of excessive costs, while the conservative citizens of Munich objected to his friendship with Wagner because of his participation in the REVOLUTION OF 1848 in DRESDEN. This antagonism of Wagner's enemies finally forced the king to ask Wagner to leave Bavaria in 1865 and alienated the king from Munich society, beginning a trend that was to make the king more comfortable in his rural residences.

Though ill-prepared to rule Bavaria, Ludwig at age 18 ascended the throne on March 10, 1864, after his father, King MAXIMILIAN II (1848–64). Contrary to expectations he took his responsibilities of government very seriously, attempting to realize his ideal of kingship, which emphasized art and culture instead of political power and conquest. Though he listened to his ministers, he often made decisions on his own. As crown prince in August 1863 Ludwig had the good fortune to meet with Otto von BISMARCK (1815–98), the new Prussian chancellor. Although Bismarck was a dynamic politician and Ludwig an artistic dreamer, the two maintained respect and a long correspondence. Shortly after becoming king, Ludwig was faced with the momentous decision to go to war. Ludwig would have liked to avoid involvement in the Austro-Prussian War of 1866, but was forced by the Bavarian parliament to support AUSTRIA. The surprising and disastrous defeat of Austria was costly for Bavaria, which had to pay PRUSSIA huge war reparations. However, diplomatic alliances changed during the following years with the Bavarians joining Prussia in a defensive alliance against France. When war between France and Prussia appeared inevitable, Ludwig again reluctantly signed the mobilization order demanded by the Bavarian government. After France was defeated, Bismarck persuaded Ludwig, though reluctantly, to agree to a declaration of a German Empire under the Prussian king. Ludwig was noticeably absent from the proclamation ceremony in the Hall of Mirrors at Versailles. Nevertheless, he secretly received a yearly stipend from Bismarck for his support.

Although controversial at the time, Ludwig built three extravagant palaces, which today have become among the greatest tourist attractions in Germany. Herrenchiemsee was modeled after Versailles of Louis XIV, Linderhof was constructed in neo-BAROQUE style, and his most famous in the Bavarian Alps was Neuschwanstein, a neo-Romanesque castle dedicated to Wagner. In the process of construction Ludwig accumulated huge debts, which the Bavarian government refused to assume and which created a great financial crisis for the WITTELSBACH family, threatening their family fortune. A conspiracy of government ministers under Minister-President Lutz tried to cover over their own financial irresponsibility by any means. Consequently, they manufactured a case against Ludwig, who was judged insane by a panel of physicians who had never even examined him. He was deposed as king on June 10, 1886, which required approval from BERLIN, though Bismarck did not personally support the action. Declared insane, he was banished to Castle Berg. As he and the escorting psychiatrist were walking along the Starnberger See, both strangely died in an apparent murder/suicide and were found floating in the water.

Lusitania, sinking of the (1915)

This state-of-the-art Cunard liner was the first express liner to be equipped with steam turbines and could outpace all of her transatlantic rivals. She became the pride of the British commercial fleet and restored British supremacy to the North Atlantic passenger service, which had been surpassed by the Germans. Popular with her passengers, she cast off on May 7, 1915, off the Old Head of Kinsale directly toward Liverpool, England. The German government had published a warning that such British ships might be sunk. Not only did the *Lusitania* carry 1,200 passengers in addition to her crew but also munitions for the military effort of the Allies. The German submarine *U-20* launched two torpedoes, and the huge ship sank within 18 minutes after the first one hit. Of those lost were 128 Americans, mostly women and children.

The sinking of the *Lusitania* became a symbol and rallying cry against the aggression of the Axis powers. American rage against Germany mounted, and public sentiment grew against neutrality. Neither German apologies, policy changes, nor compensation made any difference. The American president, Woodrow Wilson, sent a strong note to the Germans, but still resisted entering the war. The German chancellor, Bethmann Hollweg, considered abandoning submarine warfare, but was opposed by Admiral Alfred von Tirpitz, while the Kaiser vacillated. On September 1 the German sink-on-sight campaign was temporarily suspended. Nevertheless, the sinking eventually drew America into the war. Winston Churchill considered the sinking as one of the major causes of Germany's defeat in World War I.

Luther, Martin (1483–1546)
greatest religious reformer of the Reformation

Born in Eisleben, Saxony, on November 10, 1483, Martin Luther was the son of Hans and Margaret Luther. Hans Luther had been a peasant who managed to raise the family's status, first as a miner and then as an owner. Hans was ambitious for his family and also that his son be educated. The parents were very strict. "My father," Luther said many years later, "once whipped me so severely that I fled from him, and it was hard for him to win me back. . . . When I once stole a miserable nut, my mother beat me until the blood flowed. My parents meant well, but their strict discipline finally drove me into the monastery." The family cannot be said to have been a close one, because after Luther left home at age 13 he rarely saw and never wrote to them. Another aspect about his formation as a youth was the image he nurtured of God the Father and Jesus. They were represented to him as stern and cruel judges whose wrath had to be appeased through the intercession of the saints. Another of these early teachings that never left him was the belief in devils and witches.

In 1490 Luther first attended the local Latin school in Mansfield. In 1497 he was sent to the school of the Brothers of the Common Life at Magdeburg, where the brothers took their poverty seriously and regularly begged. At age 14 the impressionable Luther took this all very seriously, and he fasted and mortified his flesh so much that he turned himself into skin and bones. In 1498 Luther went to school in Eisenach, and in 1501 he matriculated at the University of Erfurt, where he studied Aristotle, who was still regarded as the authority even in natural sciences. In the study of philosophy the nominalism of William of Occam was the rage and the classics of the humanistic revival had reached Erfurt. Instead of the classics, Luther chose to concentrate on philosophical studies. Luther received his bachelor of arts in 1502 and master's in 1505. He began the study of law as his father wished, but that ended after only two months.

What prompted Luther to abruptly enter a monastery of the Augustinian Order, where he would take irrevocable vows of poverty, chastity,

Martin Luther, engraved by Theodor Knesing, from a picture by Lucas Cranach (Library of Congress)

and obedience, and in two years be ordained a priest? There has been much conjecture about his motives, but we can safely assume that his overpowering sense of sinfulness was the basic cause. His education in monastic schools would have encouraged such a possibility. As usually happens, however, external circumstances makes human beings manifest latent conflicts and desires. For one thing a plague had broken out in Erfurt in spring 1505, which is why Luther and other students left town. Later, on his return journey on July 2, Luther was caught in a thunderstorm that terrified him so much he believed the storm was an eruption of demonic forces in nature and the devil was present. Luther vowed to St. Anna that he would become a monk if he were spared. It changed the course of Luther's life, just as St. Paul's conversion had changed his, and both changed the course of Christian history. As Luther himself admitted, his vow was based on fear, a terror and agony of sudden death, but such a motivation was not valid. Luther was not aware of this and was determined to enter the monastic life. He expressed his monastic vows in 1506, was ordained a priest in 1507, and in 1508 was sent to the University of Wittenberg to lecture on Aristotle's Ethics and after his return to Erfurt on Peter Lombard's *Book of Sentences,* a theological textbook. After finishing his academic apprenticeship, he received a permanent position at Wittenberg in 1511.

Although Luther made many efforts to solve his spiritual struggles, his perceptions of God and himself did not change. He trembled at the thought of death and dreaded the day when he would stand before the judgment seat of God. He had an acute sense of his sinfulness and believed that man is incapable of extricating himself from his sinful state. It caused him anxiety and despair. He felt that he could never do enough to win God's favor and deserve God's pardon. After an intense period of crisis between 1508 and 1509, Luther discovered the answer for his troubled conscience in Paul's epistle to the Romans, 1:17, in the passage "the just shall live by faith." Luther privately came to the conclusion that the meaning of the Greek word *justice* was that God suspended sentence against sinners and saved their souls by giving them faith in his promise to save them through Christ the Mediator. Luther said that when he understood this he felt as if he had been reborn and entered paradise. Justification by faith became the cardinal doctrine of Luther's theology and of the REFORMATION. In simple language this meant that the church's doctrine of justification by works through man's active cooperation with grace was wrong. Luther now taught both a God of love, but also a pessimistic view of humans as wretched sinners who could no longer merit salvation through good works. Divine grace alone saved humans. Luther followed in the footsteps of William of Occam and narrowed the competence of human reason and denied freedom of the will. Luther ended with a conception of human nature that was neither of the Renaissance nor of medieval scholasticism.

At this stage of his life he still was friends with the humanists. In the famous heresy trial of Johannes REUCHLIN (1454–1522), Luther sided with the humanists against the inquisitors. It was also Luther's friendship with Spalatin, the private secretary to the elector, FREDERICK III, the WISE (1463–1525), that won Luther the friendship of this Renaissance prince and the protection that would save his life.

In 1517 the sale of INDULGENCES in nearby Saxony provoked Luther to go public with his criticism of the church. Luther reacted to the exaggerated claims that the promoters of the indulgence were making, by posting a notice of Ninety-five Theses that he would debate on indulgences. Originally written in Latin, the Theses were translated into German and publicized throughout Germany, becoming enormously popular. The papal legate, Cardinal Cajetan, called on Luther to renounce his theses, which he refused to do. In 1518 Luther debated with the theologian Johann Eck, which forced him into even more radical positions. Initially Luther's teachings on justification by faith had been in accord with those of St. Paul and the great theologian of the late Roman Empire, Augustine of Hippo. In 1518, however, Luther's justificatory concept advanced beyond Augustine's. Now justification was no longer a gradual cleansing of the believer by divine grace, but an instantaneous act whereby the believer appropriated the unmerited righteousness earned through Christ's death and resurrection. Luther was no fundamentalist giving equal value to all of Scripture. Calling the epistle to the Romans the most important in the New Testament, he did not literally accept the emphasis of St. James in his epistle on good works. Faith was also not an intellectual assent to a doctrinal creed but a childlike trust in the saving grace of the Christ the Redeemer.

Some of Luther's more radical ideas were expressed in three of his most famous tracts published in 1520: *To the Christian Nobility of the German Nation*, *On the Babylonian Captivity of the Church*, and *Of the Liberty of the Christian Man*, all three of which he published in 1520. Johann Eck secured a papal decree condemning Luther, and in 1521 Luther was summoned before the Imperial DIET OF WORMS, where he was asked to repudiate his writings. He refused to retract anything, saying that he was bound by his conscience and the word of God. Leaving the diet, he retired to the castle of WARTBURG under the protection of Frederick the Wise, where he began his translation of the Bible into German.

Luther returned to the University of Wittenberg, where he needed to moderate the reforming efforts of his colleague Karlstadt. Soon he published the LUTHERAN BIBLE, which revealed his mastery of German prose. His ideas also incited a great rebellion by the peasants who sought social and economic justice in the PEASANTS' REBELLION during 1524–25. Luther condemned their rebellion and supported the God-given authority of the princes. He also made the princes temporary emergency bishops. In 1525 Luther married a former nun, Katherine von Bora, creating a model Christian family with six children. His theological writings continued. Their antihumanist character brought him into conflict with the greatest humanist of the time, Desiderius ERASMUS (1465–1536). In 1524–25 Luther clarified his thinking on free will and directed his publication of *On the Will in Bondage* against Erasmus and humanist Christianity in general. Luther did not discourage good works, but did not believe that they were of any importance toward salvation. In 1528 he defended his theology on the Eucharist in *Confession concerning the Lord's Supper*. Luther's theology of the Eucharist was similar to Catholic teaching, and he opposed Ulrich ZWINGLI's emphasis on a symbolic presence of Christ in the Eucharist. In 1529 Philip MELANCTHON (1497–1560) arranged the MARBURG COLLOQUY, a debate intended to heal the differences between the Reformers. In 1530 Melancthon published the AUGSBURG CONFESSION, which although at variance with some of Luther's thinking, became one of the foundations of Protestant thought.

In the 1540s Luther struggled with diseases, and on February 18, 1546, he died after being called upon to arbitrate a dispute between two noblemen.

Lutheran Bible

Luther's translation of the Bible set the standard for the written German language. After Luther realized the inherent dangerous paths of subjectivity that the reform movement could take in the extremist sects, he increasingly emphasized the objective nature of divine revelation expressed in the Bible. The Bible thus became the exclusive foundation of Luther's reformed Christianity. But it had to be translated into the idiom of the common man, which task Luther undertook. His German translation was not the first of the whole or separate books of the Bible, but none of them had gone back to the Hebrew and Greek texts of the original. Luther, therefore, was the first translator to base his German version on the original text of the whole Bible and in a form of German that could be understood by people of every German region.

Luther began his translation at WARTBURG Castle in December 1521 and continued his work for more than 10 years. First published was the New Testament in 1522, while the books of the Old Testament were published individually until 1534, when the whole work was assembled and published as *The Bible or the Holy Writ* (*Die Bibel oder die Heilige Schrift*). Not satisfied with its accuracy, Luther continued to revise it in consultation with Philip MELANCHTHON and other scholars. It was published in its final form shortly before his death in 1546.

Even though Luther was not the first to write in a standard written German language, it was through his translation of the Bible that the German people received a unified language. Luther utilized a new dialect of the Saxon and Imperial chanceries and made it a vehicle for the expression of spiritual concerns. Luther's New High German was the first written standard language that could express the views and feelings of the common people as well as the thoughts and feelings of poets and philosophers. He enriched the German vocabulary by using words from the many dialects of the German people. He also rendered the spirit of the biblical passages in a such an excellent manner that his translation became a best seller and a part of German literature. The Lutheran Bible set the standard for German literature and for the great German poets and philosophers, including Johann Wolfgang von GOETHE and Friedrich NIETZSCHE.

Luther's pamphlets and hymns

Martin Luther wrote three important pamphlets in 1520, which were widely distributed. In them he presented his fundamental ideas of Christian liberty. They were entitled *An Address to the Christian Nobility of the German Nation*, *The Babylonian Captivity of the Church*, and *The Liberty of a Christian Man*.

In these pamphlets Luther attacked what he called the walls that constrained Christians. Fundamentally, they were found in the authority that the papacy claimed in calling councils and interpreting Scripture. In place of this broad claim, Luther presented his conception of the universal priesthood of believers. There was no intermediary, he wrote, between the believer and God; people were their own priests. What was necessary was faith that brings one directly into contact with God. Luther denied that the church was the authoritative interpreter of scripture since each believer, he asserted, must derive his own assurance of salvation from Scripture. The papacy's claim to infallibility therefore was a usurpation. But Luther went further, also claiming that not even a church council could stand between the believer and God. As far as the sacraments were concerned, he viewed them as symbols of inward change. Of themselves they had no inherent power to change people. These propositions were seen by Luther as a declaration of the freedom of the Christian person. It meant that there was no reform through any external agency of the church or the state. Only an inward transformation could bring about a real change in external behavior.

Luther's pamphlets inspired his contemporaries. The reformer was an excellent stylist and was able to write in more than one vein. He could use coarse language and also be gentle and delicate. None of his numerous disciples could write an equally forceful German, and the writings of his opponents were less appealing. Most of them wrote in a scholastic manner.

Luther wanted the congregation to take an active part in church services, so he composed his own hymns. Perhaps his greatest was the hymn "A mighty fortress is our God" (*"Ein feste Burg ist unser Gott"*). It bears the unmistakable stamp of Luther's religious genius and depth of feeling. Although inspired by the 46th psalm, the hymn became the battle hymn of the Protestant REFORMATION. Luther's personal feelings of penitence are evident in "From heartfelt need I cry to Thee!" (*"Aus tiefer Not schrei ich zu Dir!"*). Luther also translated into German some Latin hymns, such as *"Te Deum laudamus"* ("To Thee, O God, we sing our praise"). Popular texts were also used, especially in Christmas carols. The hymns appealed to the sense of hearing, beginning an emphasis in Protestant services on singing, which was in contrast to the traditional appeal of the visual in Catholic services and architecture.

Luxemburg, Rosa (1871–1919)
Polish-German Marxist theorist
Rosa Luxemburg was a brilliant Marxist theoretician and socialist party leader. She helped

found the Social Democratic Party of Poland and Lithuania. In BERLIN she became one of Europe's foremost commentators on the works of Karl MARX. She participated in the Russian Revolution of 1905, organized the Spartacus League in 1917, and was a founder of the GERMAN COMMUNIST PARTY (KPD).

Rosa Luxemburg was born in Zamosc, Poland, within the Russian Empire. Her father was a Jewish timber merchant and her mother the daughter of a rabbi. She was familiar with the writers of the ENLIGHTENMENT, especially GOETHE, and had a love of Russian literature. She attended the best girls' high school in Warsaw and while there became associated with the socialist movement, joining the Polish Socialist Party in 1886. The next year she fled to Switzerland after the czarist secret police became aware of her activities. In Zurich she attended the university, earning a doctorate of law in 1898. In order to get to Berlin, where she wanted to associate with the socialist movement, she made a marriage of convenience to obtain German citizenship. Luxemburg opposed the NATIONALISM of her day, as she believed patriotism distracted the proletariat from its economic identity. She opposed the reformist socialist ideas of Eduard BERNSTEIN, who had just published *Principles of Socialism*. Her arguments in *Reform or Revolution* (1899) were that participation in parliament and trade unions, which were created by the MIDDLE CLASS, distracted the proletariat from its goal of revolution. This position led her into an extended struggle with the leaders of the German SOCIAL DEMOCRATIC PARTY. She was also critical of Lenin's concept of party leadership, wherein a small group would direct and control the revolution. In 1905, when a revolution broke out in Russia during the Russo-Japanese War, Rosa went to Warsaw to participate. After imprisonment she returned to Berlin, and from 1907 to 1914 she taught Marxist philosophy in the school of the Social Democratic Party. She was criticized and opposed by other socialists and in less than flattering terms called a "doctrinaire goose," and repeatedly imprisoned by the government for insulting Kaiser WILLIAM II. In 1913 she published her most famous book, *The*

Rosa Luxemburg *(Library of Congress)*

Accumulation of Capital, arguing that capitalism could not sustain its own growth and had to spread into less developed countries. Later the economic doctrines of Keynesianism supported her thesis.

With the outbreak of WORLD WAR I she denounced socialist support of the war and participation in it. She was arrested and jailed for her revolutionary activities for the duration of the war. In letters from prison she communicated with her friend Karl LIEBKNECHT. Released for a short time in 1916, she helped found a group known as the Spartacus League, but was unable to win many followers. When she again emerged from prison in 1918, she was disappointed with the failure of socialist revolution in November and with Karl Liebknecht helped found the German Communist Party (KPD). She established and was the editor of the newspaper *Die Rote Fahne* and drafted its program. She and Liebknecht urged revolution against the WEIMAR government headed by Friedrich EBERT. In January 1919 the Spartacus revolt broke out in Berlin, even though Luxemburg and Liebknecht thought that the timing was not right. On January 15, 1919, both Liebknecht and Luxemburg were arrested and shot to death by soldiers. Her analysis of the Russian Revolution, which was posthumously published as *The Russian Revolution,* was a strong indictment of the revolutionary leaders who established a dictatorship over the proletariat.

M

Mann, Heinrich (1871–1950)
novelist and social critic

Writing in the realist and naturalist literary tradition, Heinrich Mann shared with the expressionists (*see* EXPRESSIONISM) the harsh, sarcastic criticism of the MIDDLE CLASS of the Wilhelmine Empire. He was especially critical of intellectuals and other leaders who left the issues of society and politics to those in authority. He hated the German lack of civic virtue. He opposed the Nazi regime and was a refugee from the regime, immigrating to the United States.

Like his younger brother, Thomas MANN, Heinrich was from Lübeck in northern Germany, his birth date March 27, 1871. Completing his education in Lübeck, he went to DRESDEN for a year and then entered a publishing firm in BERLIN. At first a disciple of the French realists, especially Émile Zola and Guy de Maupassant, he wrote impressions, sketches, novelettes, and some poetry. The early writings of Heinrich Mann indulged in the frenzied vitalism of Friedrich NIETZSCHE, in which orgiastic lust and sadism occurred in an Italian setting.

In Mann's first creative phase between 1900 and 1914 he wrote his realistic (*see* REALISM) and naturalistic (*see* NATURALISM) novel entitled *In the Land of Cockaigne* (*Im Schlaraffenland,* 1900). In it Mann vents his vitriolic hatred of the pillars of German middle-class society. He denounces with cruel humor the shallow and cheap intellectual ambitiousness of the newly rich. In a following novel, *Hunting for Love* (1904), he condemns as hypocritical the attitude of the "respectable" people on matters of love and sex. Mann's prewar fame was based on the novel *Professor Unrath oder das Ende eines Tyrannen* (*Blue Angel,* 1931), a study of the powerful sexual attraction of a cheap nightclub performer for adolescents and their professor, who falls into her snares and is professionally and socially ruined.

During the war years Mann started his powerful critique of German society, writing a trilogy entitled *The Kaiser's Empire—The Little Superman* (1911–13), *The Poor* (1917), and *The Chief* (1925)—which was to become his greatest success. Everyone had their turn as objects of derision from workers to officials and even the Kaiser himself along with other heads of government and the KRUPP armaments empire. The Kaiser is depicted as "power" uncontrolled riding horseback under the Brandenburg Gate. The lack of civic courage of the German citizenry is pilloried as one of Germany's leading vices. The books are devastating satires, which did not contribute to their popularity. In 1915 Heinrich Mann, a pacifist, expressed his opposition to the war when his brother, Thomas, publicly approved of it. It caused a rift from which the relationship never fully recovered.

Mann clearly saw the dangers that were facing Germany and was active with political speeches. His democratic views, however, inclined toward an idealistic communism, though not totalitarian. In 1931 he became president of the literary section of the Prussian Academy. In 1933 he was promptly dismissed from this office by the Nazis and deprived of his German citizenship. Mann took refuge in France, where he wrote about the victory of humaneness over tyranny in *The Young Henry of Navarre* (1935), which includes a description of the St. Bartholomew Massacre of

1572, and *Henry, King of France* (1938). In 1940 Mann escaped to the United States, where he settled close to his brother. After the war Mann hoped to return to Germany, mainly East Germany. In 1949 he accepted an appointment as president of the new founded Academy of Arts of the GERMAN DEMOCRATIC REPUBLIC, but died in preparation for the move.

Mann, Thomas (1875–1955)
novelist

Thomas Mann was one of the most gifted novelists of the 20th century. His works have been translated into most languages. He was awarded the Nobel Prize in literature in 1929. Rejecting National Socialism, he went into exile first to Switzerland and then to the United States. In view of the menace of Nazism, his novels *The Magic Mountain* and *Doktor Faustus* reveal that he was an astute critic and analyst of the German mentality of that period.

Thomas Mann was born in Lübeck, a Hanseatic seaport and commercial city near HAMBURG, on June 6, 1875. His family was prominent but had disintegrated by the time he became a young man. The famous old house where they had lived as leading citizens ended up becoming a local library. The father of Thomas and his brother, Heinrich MANN, was a grain merchant who died when Thomas was 15, after which the family fortune gradually evaporated. Their mother was partly German and partly Portuguese and West Indian Creole. She moved to MUNICH after her husband's death, joined by Thomas after he finished his education. Mann was bisexual, which he thought predestined him to be an artist. He nevertheless ended his bohemian lifestyle when he married Katia Pringsheim in 1905.

In his writing he was influenced by the German philosophers Arthur Schopenhauer (1788–1860) and Friedrich NIETZSCHE (1844–1900) and the composer Richard WAGNER (1813–83). Mann would stress the suffering artist (Schopenhauer's pessimistic worldview) that through suffering and determination works are produced that justify human existence. Mann found in Nietzsche's philosophy a confirmation of his own ironic attitude toward life. Wagner's influence was in Mann's adaptation of recurrent themes in his writings much the same way that Wagner used repetitive themes in his operas. In 1898 he became the editor of the journal *Simplicissimus*. His first published work was a collection of short stories, *Little Herr Friedemann* (1899), which enabled Mann to find a publisher for his first novel, *Buddenbrooks* (1901), which made him famous almost overnight. Mann here records in great detail how his family turned from respectable realism and a sense of social obligation to a touchy, anemic sentimentality and a withdrawal into romantic isolation. As the finer artistic sensibilities increase, the last Buddenbrook becomes a musician. Mann uses the theme of the healthy intellectual against the suffering artist and the dark Latin against the blue-eyed Nordic. Later in a number of short stories Mann reuses these themes of the contrast between the bourgeois and artistic modes of existence. Two outstanding examples are the novellas *Tristan* (1903), which is an ironic comedy set in a tuberculosis sanitarium, while *Tonio Kröger* (1903) is intensely autobiographical. About 1910 a change is evident in Mann's masterpiece *Death in Venice*, which shows the frustration and dissolution of the abnormal artist.

Thomas Mann *(Library of Congress)*

Mann's next novel, *Royal Highness* (1909), affirms social duty and bourgeois morality. During WORLD WAR I Mann published *Reflections of a Non-political Observer*, in which he tried to defend the traditional values of German culture. At first Mann had welcomed World War I, but later became a supporter of the WEIMAR REPUBLIC.

Just before the war Mann's wife had to enter a Swiss tuberculosis sanitarium for a few weeks' treatment, which later became the setting for *The Magic Mountain* (1924), which Mann wrote during and after World War I; in it he at last found a positive solution to the problem of German culture. His hero, Hans Castorp, visits a sanatorium for tuberculosis patients on a Swiss mountain peak, which becomes his "magic mountain" of detachment from healthy, normal life. Hans Castorp is flirting with death, but in the end death becomes a revelation for him. He listens to all the European debates between liberals and totalitarians, between skeptics and believers, between Eastern and Western ways of life. Mann's panorama of European prewar culture is astonishingly rich and exhaustive, but it is also somber and questioning. The disease of his patients is symbolic. In the end Hans Castorp is able to take a stand. It is a typically German stand, the creative mediation between conflicting forces. When the war breaks out in 1914, Hans Castorp chooses sides and shares the fate of his contemporaries as a voluntary soldier. Life is accepted both in its elevating and tragic aspects. The hero's devotion to the tasks of the day is seen as a reaffirmation. Time is seen with microscopic scrutiny. Many details are closely interwoven by leitmotifs and ironies. Mann has avoided all the easy simplifications and has emphasized the controversial aspects of the cultural situation. After the war Mann accepted German democracy and became a leading representative. In 1930 he published another short novel critical of FASCISM, *Mario and the Magician*, the story of a sensational event at an Italian seaside resort where a German family is on holiday. Cipolla, the arrogant magician and hypnotist (who is like Mussolini) makes the simple waiter, Mario, look ridiculous at a public demonstration, which is emblematic of fascism. This novel placed Mann as the first author of imaginative literature to show the evils of 20th-century totalitarianism. Between 1933 and 1943 he completed the tetralogy *Joseph and his Brothers*, which also ranks as one of his greatest works.

Mann never spoke or wrote in favor of Nazism. In Switzerland when HITLER came to power Mann did not return to Germany. In 1936 he attacked the Nazis as enemies of Christian and Western morality; in response the German government revoked his German citizenship and honorary degree from the University of BONN. Mann's letter to the dean at Bonn was a devastating indictment of Nazism. Moving to the United States in 1938, he taught at Princeton University and in California. There he wrote *Dr. Faustus* (1947), which ranks with *The Magic Mountain* as one of his greatest novels. In 1954 he returned to Zurich, where he died on August 12, 1955.

Mannheim

The city of Mannheim grew out of a fishing village founded in the early Middle Ages. The village was and the city is located on the right bank of the RHINE at the canalized Neckar River. A fortress was built on the site in 1606, and a municipal charter was obtained the following year. When the Germans were fighting the French during the War of the Palatinate Succession, the French devastated Mannheim. In 1720 the elector Karl Philip moved his princely residence from HEIDELBERG to Mannheim and built the present palace. Leading French and Italian architects, sculptors, and painters were brought to Mannheim by the following elector, Karl THEODOR (1743–78). An Academy of Sciences was established in 1763. Unfortunately, for the future of Mannheim, Karl Theodor became the elector of BAVARIA in 1778 and moved his capital to MUNICH. During the Revolutionary and NAPOLEONIC WARS with the defeat of AUSTRIA by the French, the Treaty of Luneville (1801) gave the left bank of the Palatinate to the French, and the right bank of the Rhine was ceded to Baden.

This changed again as a result of the CONGRESS OF VIENNA; the left bank of the Rhine was returned to Bavaria. The opening of the Rhine to shipping and the building of a port between 1834 and 1876 assured the economic future of Mannheim as a port on the Upper Rhine. The city of Mannheim suffered considerable destruction from bombing during WORLD WAR II but has been rebuilt.

An outstanding contribution to the history of music occurred during the 18th century under the elector Karl Theodor, who made Mannheim a musical center. He maintained a large orchestra and an opera and ballet company. He also employed a French and an Italian music director. The Mannheim orchestra had great soloists and composers. Johann Wenzel Anton Stamitz, a virtuoso violinist, was the founder of the Mannheim school, which established the norms for modern orchestras in its instrumentation and its characteristic sound. Musicians came from all over Europe, making their individual contributions to the development of the orchestra.

Famous examples of architecture in Mannheim are the beautiful BAROQUE Electoral Palace, which was one of the largest in Germany. The National Theater was originally built in 1779 but rebuilt in the 1950s because of its destruction during World War II. It was the site of the first performances of Friedrich SCHILLER's plays *Die Räuber, Fiesco,* and *Kabale and Liebe* in 1782 and 1784.

Two important technological innovations in transportation originated in Mannheim. Drais demonstrated his first foot-propelled bicycle in 1817. More important, Carl Friedrich BENZ (1884–1929) drove his first motor vehicle in Mannheim during 1885. To facilitate trade, Mannheim also built one of the largest inland harbors in Europe.

Manstein, Field Marshal Erich von
(1887–1973)
armored warfare strategist

Erich von Manstein was the master strategist behind the BLITZKRIEG invasion of France in 1940 and perhaps the best German strategist of the war.

Erich von Manstein was born in BERLIN on November 24, 1887, the son of Eduard von Lewinski, an artillery officer. After the death of his parents Erich was adopted by his uncle, General von Manstein, and took his surname. He entered the army in 1906 in the Third Regiment of the Foot Guards. He served in WORLD WAR I, mainly in staff positions on both the eastern and western fronts, but was wounded early on during November 1914. During the WEIMAR REPUBLIC he held various staff and regimental appointments in the Reichswehr. In 1935 he was appointed chief of the operations branch of the General Staff of the army. In 1936 he was made senior quartermaster and deputy to General Ludwig BECK, who then was chief of the General Staff. Manstein lost his staff position in the purge that accompanied the dismissal of General Werner von FRITSCH in February 1938 but was given command of the 18th infantry division, which participated in the occupation of the Sudetenland. After serving as chief of staff to General Gerd von Runstedt during the invasion of Poland, Manstein followed him to the western front.

Manstein questioned the plan for the invasion of France. He believed it replayed the old SCHLIEFFEN PLAN of World War I and would not work. What he recommended was a surprise attack through the supposedly impenetrable ARDENNES forest. HITLER adopted the plan over the objections of Generals Brauchitsch and Halder, and it became the key to the German victory over France. Manstein was promoted to general field marshal on July 19, 1940, after the fall of France. Transferred to the eastern front, he first led a Panzer Corps against Leningrad. Then his forces conquered the Crimea and Sevastopol, for which he was promoted to field marshal. In November 1942 he commanded Army Group Don and was involved in the Stalingrad campaign. He was unsuccessful, however, in rescuing the Sixth Army at Stalingrad. Manstein's Army Group South won a significant victory in the Kharkov area and later attempted to eliminate the Soviet Kursk Salient in July 1943. On March 30, 1944, Hitler's personal airplane landed at Manstein's headquarters in Lvov and took him and Field Marshal von KLEIST to Hitler's Obersalzberg, where both of them were dismissed from their commands.

In the meantime, as early as 1942 officers of the RESISTANCE had approached him to join in a plot against Hitler. After the successful siege of Sevastopol, he placed himself at the disposal of Col. Gen. Ludwig Beck. Manstein's feelings changed, however, after the performance of General PAULUS at Stalingrad. He reaffirmed his allegiance to Hitler and drew away from the plot.

At the end of the war Manstein was in British captivity and later transferred to Germany for trial. Tried before a military court in HAMBURG, he was sentenced to 18 years in prison. He was acquitted of the charge of authorizing the mass extermination of Jews. Subsequently, the sentence was reduced to 12 years, but he was released in 1953. He became a consultant to the West German government, advocating a citizen army and universal conscription. He died near Munich on June 12, 1973.

Marburg Colloquy (1529)

The Marburg Colloquy was a theological conference held between Lutheran and Zwinglian theologians in the Protestant university town of Marburg October 1–4, 1529. The main focus of the debate was over the real or symbolic presence of Christ in the Eucharist. The debate and the differences divided Protestants into Lutherans and Zwinglians.

In 1527 the Lutheran Philip of Hesse wrote to Martin LUTHER proposing a theological debate between the Lutheran reformers at Wittenberg and the Zwinglian reformers in Zurich. At first Luther rejected the proposal because Philip had a political alliance in mind in order to oppose the Catholics. Ulrich ZWINGLI believed that their differences were not insurmountable and enlisted the help of the scholar Martin Bucer, who believed that doctrinal compromise was possible. At the Diet of Speyer in 1529 Philip approached Philip MELANCHTHON to get his help in persuading Luther to meet with Zwingli. This prodding and that of his prince, John Frederick, persuaded Luther to attend a colloquy.

Although the debates were conducted in a friendly atmosphere, the participants were able to agree only on 14 out of 15 doctrines, with the exception of the most important, the Lord's Supper. Zwingli even agreed to most of Luther's points on the Eucharist, with the exception of the Real Presence. Nevertheless, both Zwingli and Luther signed the Marburg Articles in order to create political solidarity. The Zwinglians even signed all the articles but appended a statement concerning their disagreement on the Real Presence. The Marburg Colloquy signaled the final break between Luther and Zwingli and made a federation of Protestants in the Empire impossible, which had disastrous consequences in the religious wars of the next decades.

Maria Theresa (1717–1780)
empress of Austria

Maria Theresa was just 23 when she became the first female heir in the history of the Habsburg dynasty. She became archduchess of AUSTRIA, and queen of Hungary and Bohemia. She was the wife of Emperor Francis I, the grand duke of Tuscany but originally of Lorraine. She was the daughter of the last male Habsburg Emperor, CHARLES VI. Born in Vienna on May 13, 1717, Maria Theresa became one of the most beautiful women of her day, loved by her people and respected by her enemies. She developed a sense of duty toward her family and the Austrian state. She was happy to give birth to 16 children and believed that they should marry to further the family's interests and secure Austria's alliances. This resulted in the marriage of Marie Antoinette to the French dauphin, who later became Louis XVI of France.

Maria Theresa's father, Charles VI, did not marry her to a powerful prince who could protect Austria, rather allowing her to marry for love Duke Francis Stephen of Lorraine. To protect her succession to the throne, her father executed the

PRAGMATIC SANCTION. As soon as he died, some European states reneged on their promises, and PRUSSIA seized Silesia in the eight-year WAR OF AUSTRIAN SUCCESSION. Maria Theresa never reconciled herself to the loss of this rich province seized by FREDERICK II, that "evil man in Potsdam." In order to recover Silesia, Maria Theresa realized that reform was imperative and so enlisted the services of Count Frederick William von Haugwitz and Count Wenceslaus von Kaunitz to reform the government in the Habsburg hereditary lands of Austria and Bohemia. The central and local administration of government was strengthened, and the judicial and executive branches of government were separated. The chief offices of the state—defense, foreign affairs, justice, interior, and commerce—were made directly responsible to the monarchy. The right of the estates to collect taxes was abolished. She tried to improve the efficiency of government, levied taxes on the previously exempt Catholic Church, promoted industry to increase taxable wealth, and erected a tariff wall around Austria and Bohemia. In order to improve rural conditions she released the peasants on crown lands of their servile obligations. Although she was a devout Catholic, she tried to eliminate abuses in the church. In her efforts to establish a universal system of education, she eliminated the church's control of education.

Court life during the reign of Maria Theresa took on an atmosphere of gaiety and splendor. She had a veritable passion for dancing and organized elaborate masked balls. However, she would not tolerate aristocratic debauchery at her court, and for a number of years a notorious "chastity commission" operated moral inquisitions. Court architecture also changed during her reign from solemnity and symbolization of power to informal gracefulness and serenity. She also rebuilt Schönbrun and made it her summer palace, and the palace in Innsbruck was rebuilt in the 1750s and 1760s.

Maria Theresa reoriented Habsburg foreign policy and alliances. Following the advice of Prince Kaunitz, Maria Theresa abandoned her traditional alliance with Britain and allied Austria with France. This came to be known as the DIPLOMATIC REVOLUTION of 1756. During the SEVEN YEARS' WAR (1756–63) she failed in her attempts to get Silesia back from Frederick II. During the same period Maria Theresa habitually governed autocratically. In 1765 her husband, the emperor, Francis I, suddenly died of a stroke. Maria mourned his loss by continuously wearing black, and she never again was lighthearted and gay.

At the death of the emperor her son, who later was to become JOSEPH II, Holy Roman Emperor (1765–90), was appointed co-regent; he was determined to share in the governance of the state. Instead Maria placed him in charge of army reform and gave a share in the formulation of foreign policy with Prince Kaunitz. He lacked talent in either of these areas, and it was unfortunate that he was not able to influence internal affairs in which he could have made a difference. Mother and son struggled on for the 15 years of the co-regency. While Joseph was more religiously tolerant and resisted his mother's attempt to expel some Protestants from Bohemia, Maria was much more favorable toward the peasants. Some of the major reforms of the period were more due to the empress than Joseph. The new penal code of 1768 and the abolition of judicial torture in 1776 helped standardize judicial proceedings and punishments. Although she was a devout Catholic, Maria Theresa tried to reduce the power of the church and expanded the rights of the state. Neither papal bulls nor pastoral letters of bishops could be circulated without her permission. And in 1777 she banished the Society of Jesus (*see* JESUITS) just as other European rulers were doing.

During the first partition of Poland Maria Theresa became reluctantly involved but acquired Galicia so that Prussia and Russia would not expand at Austria's expense. She also reluctantly got involved in the WAR OF THE BAVARIAN SUCCESSION (1778–79) otherwise known as the Potato War, so known because soldiers spent more time digging potatoes than fighting. Joseph wanted to acquire Bavaria, which his mother resisted. When this led to war with Prussia in 1778, Maria was nonetheless able to acquire a small part of Bavaria, the Inn Quarter (Innviertel). The ratification of the peace treaty of Teschen was the last significant act of her reign. She died of a heart condition on November 29, 1780.

Marne, battles of (1914 and 1918)
The two battles of the Marne were decisive engagements in the valley of the River Marne in France. The first battle took place September 5–9, 1914, which stopped the German drive toward Paris. The second battle occurred in July 1918, ending the German spring offensive and led to the request for an armistice.

The SCHLIEFFEN PLAN had called for an invasion of France through Belgium. The Belgian resistance caused a delay in the German plans and the stubborn Allied retreat from the Sambre to Le Cateau slowed the German drive. At this time Field Marshal von MOLTKE, chief of the General Staff, transferred troops from the German right wing to Russia in response to a Russian invasion. At the same time another change occurred because of heavy casualties and fatigue in which the Germans, instead of encircling Paris from the west, decided to turn their forces to the east of Paris. This enabled the French commander in chief, Joffre, to engage his reserves from Paris against the German flank and rear. The French and British attacked the German flank from September 6 to 9, forcing the Germans on the defensive along the line of the River Marne. At this point Moltke departed again from the Schlieffen Plan by committing his left wing, which had been assigned a defensive function, to an offensive against Nancy. This wasted resources that could have been employed at the Marne. Moltke made a further mistake by sending a subordinate staff officer who had a confused understanding of the position of the armies and ordered a breakoff of the battle of the Marne and a general retreat to the River Aisne. The German advance had been stopped, and the Schlieffen Plan failed. Moltke had a nervous breakdown and resigned.

The second battle of the Marne was fought July 15–18, 1918. On July 15 the Germans opened an offensive east and west of Rheims with 51 divisions. Within three days the bulge they created was countered by an Allied attack with 600 tanks that tore through the German lines. The Germans were defeated at the Marne, which brought an end to Erich LUDENDORFF's spring offensives and was the greatest defeat of the war. It was followed by Allied counteroffensives that by November brought the war to an end.

Marshall Plan
The Marshall Plan was an American plan to aid Western European recovery after WORLD WAR II. The European Recovery Program provided a total of $13.3 billion to help finance European economic reconstruction.

The Marshall Plan was launched by Secretary of State George C. Marshall in a commencement speech at Harvard in June 1947, whose "purpose should be the revival of a working economy in the world so as to permit the emergence of political and social conditions in which free institutions can exist. . . ." It was a generous proposal to help the Europeans to reconstruct their economies and provide for social and political stability. The European countries had to take the first steps toward economic collaboration. The offer was made to all the countries affected by the war, including the Soviet Union and its satellites. Since the Russians declined U.S. help, the Marshall Plan became strongly identified with American anticommunist foreign policy intended to stop the spread of communism. The other pillars were the Truman Doctrine (1947) and NATO (1949).

Within weeks 16 countries got together in Paris to discuss their needs and promote economic recovery and to stabilize currencies. At the London Conference in 1948 the decision was made to extend the Marshall Plan to the occupation zones of Germany. The Organization for European Economic Cooperation (OEEC) assumed responsibility for distributing the Marshall Plan funds between 1948 and 1952. Germany was not an original member of OEEC, but the organization soon realized that European recovery required a prosperous Germany. The Marshall Plan aid (ERP) of approximately $3 billion accelerated the creation of the FEDERAL REPUBLIC, its admission to the OEEC, and its subsequent integration into the Western alliance.

The Marshall Plan was set up for four years (1948–52) and operated through a counterpart fund. About 70 percent of the funds were used to purchase commodities from U.S. suppliers. The recipient had to pay for the goods, and repayment was placed in a counterpart fund, which then could be used by ERP countries for further investment projects. Germany did not find out until 1953 whether it would have to repay its loans. Germany had already received U.S. aid amounting to $1.7 billion before the Marshall Plan was even started. Consequently, the amount of $1.4 billion was not that dramatic. Although Britain, France, and Italy received larger amounts of aid, Germany used its share better than any other country. Since Germany had not known if this would have to be paid back, it was particularly concerned that the money be given out only in a revolving loan system as loans at interest, which ensured that the funds would grow. The money Germany owed the United States was paid back by 1971. By 1995 the Special Fund had about 23 billion DM and had made loans that amounted to 140 billion DM.

Marx, Karl (1818–1883)
founder of scientific socialism

Karl Marx was a philosopher, economist, and political revolutionary. His basic ideas known as Marxism or "scientific" socialism provided the theoretical foundation for socialist and communist movements in the 19th and 20th centuries. He authored along with Friedrich ENGELS *The Communist Manifesto* in 1848; published the first volume of *Capital: A Critique of Political Economy* in 1867, followed by volumes two and three posthumously compiled by Engels from Marx's notes in 1885 and 1894.

Karl Marx was born on May 5, 1818, in Trier, Germany's oldest city, located in Rhenish Prussia, the son of a Jewish lawyer. Both of his parents were descendants of rabbis, but his father converted to Lutheranism. As a Jew Karl was barred from the practice of law. Although he attended a Lutheran elementary school, Karl later became an atheist and materialist. He studied a classical curriculum at the Gymnasium and matriculated at BONN University, having studied jurisprudence, philosophy, and literature. Marx transferred to the University of BERLIN, which was a hub of intellectual ferment, especially due to the teaching of the great philosopher G. W. F. HEGEL. While he studied at Berlin, he joined the Young Hegelians and was deeply influenced by their ideas. In 1841 he obtained a doctorate from the University of JENA and turned to journalism. After that he went to Paris to study economics and journalism.

Like other theoretical thinkers of his day, his thinking was colored by an intense involvement with Hegel's idealistic dialectic, which he sought to "turn upside down" from a materialist standpoint. He was furthermore influenced by the early French Socialists, the philosophy of materialism, and the theories of British political economists. His hopes of teaching philosophy at Bonn University were frustrated by the reactionary policies of the Prussian government, which also suppressed the liberal Cologne newspaper *Rheinische Zeitung,* which he edited. After moving to Paris, he came into contact with the working class and took up the study of economics. In Paris he also collaborated with the philosophic radicals Heinrich HEINE, Ludwig Börne (1786–1837), and Arnold Ruge (1802–80) in writing polemics against the left Hegelians. In Paris he also began his lifetime friendship and collaboration with Friedrich ENGELS.

In 1845 Marx was expelled from France and moved to Brussels, where he founded the GERMAN WORKERS' PARTY; he and Engels joined the Communist League, for which together they wrote the *Communist Manifesto.* They were expelled by the Belgian government, and he moved to Cologne, where he edited the *Neue Rheinische Zeitung,* which also was soon suppressed. Exiled again by both the Prussian and French governments, Marx landed in England, where he lived, researched, and wrote as a stateless person for the rest of his life.

The worldwide importance of Marx's thought is not to be found in his analysis of economic systems, which he derived from the classical economists Adam Smith and David Ricardo. Marx's book, *Capital,* is not primarily a work on economics, but one that uses economic materials to establish a moral-philosophical-sociological structure. What has made Marx so popular and influential is his theory of history and politics, which contains a moral approach to social-economic problems, provides insights into the relationships between institutions and values, and provides a modern materialistic conception of the salvation of humankind. Marx's fundamental thesis is the materialistic conception of history. This involves two basic notions: that the economic system at any given time determines the prevailing ideas; and that history is an ongoing process predetermined by economic institutions that have evolved in regular stages. Marx explained history as a dialectical progression from ancient precapitalism, through capitalism, and finally communism, which is the final and utopian stage of an earthly paradise.

Marx wrote hundreds of articles on political and economic subjects. Besides writing critiques of the Young Hegelians, Bruno Bauer, and the French socialist M. Proudhon, he wrote an analysis of the rise of Emperor Napoleon III, and from 1852 to 1862 wrote more than 300 articles for the *New York Daily Tribune.* He also involved himself in organizational development. He participated in the founding of the International Workers' Association (First International) in 1864. In general he was opposed to party organizations. Yet Marxism had a great influence in Germany, which may be because it still was a semi-feudal and military bureaucratic state where the church and industry were closely linked with the state. Because Germany lacked real parliamentary forms of government, the workers formed the Socialist Party, which expressed a militant opposition to the state.

His wife, Jenny von Westphalen, died in London during 1881, two years before Karl died in London on March 14, 1883, after being tormented for 20 years by various diseases. He had latent tuberculosis, was a heavy smoker, suffered from carbuncles, had hemorrhoids, pleurisy, headaches, and coughs, all of which kept him from accomplishing much intellectual work over the last decade of his life.

Maximilian I (1459–1519)
Holy Roman Emperor

Born in Wiener Neustadt, AUSTRIA, on March 22, 1459, Maximilian was the oldest son of Emperor Frederick III and Eleanor of Portugal. Maximilian received a thorough education in the liberal arts, was fluent in seven languages, was trained in music and painting, and learned practical subjects such as mining and carpentry. He was a congenial person with wit and intelligence and through his charm was at ease with all groups. In appearance he has been described

Karl Marx *(Library of Congress)*

as an ugly man with a Habsburg lip, a protruding jaw, and hooked nose. On the other hand, he demonstrated strength with his burly chest and strong neck.

Maximilian I's talents and career were said to be a product of successful dynastic marriages and the advantages of possessing the imperial title. He exemplified what became the motto of the house of Habsburg, "Let others make war, you, happy Austria, marry." His marriage in 1477 to Mary of Burgundy, who was one of the richest heiresses in Europe and the daughter of Charles the Bold, marked the beginning of the rise to European preeminence of the Habsburg dynasty. But it also plunged him into a long conflict with the king of France, Louis XI, over Burgundy, which included most of modern Belgium, the Netherlands, and Luxembourg and extended into France. Consequently, Charles was already in conflict with the king of France. When Charles the Bold was killed in the Battle of Nancy, Maximilian concluded his marriage to Mary by proxy and went to claim his wife in Ghent. Another example of Maximilian's prowess in the dynastic marriage market was the alliance that resulted from the marriage of his son and heir, Philip of Burgundy, to Juana, daughter of Ferdinand and Isabella of Spain, linking the Habsburgs to the Spanish house. In 1500 the offspring of Philip and Juana was Charles, who became CHARLES V, heir to Maximilian's Habsburg territories, but also claimant to the imperial title, Burgundy, and Spain. It established Spain's preeminence for the next century and gave the Habsburgs control of Spain and its colonial empire.

In 1486 Maximilian was elected king of the Romans and joined his father in the administration of the HOLY ROMAN EMPIRE. At the death of his father in 1493 he became sole ruler. As Holy Roman Emperor, Maximilian faced three major problems: the French in Italy; the Turks and the eastern frontiers; and the internal problems of the Empire and the need to reform its governing institutions. His political career was largely unsuccessful. He conducted numerous campaigns in the Netherlands, France, Italy, and Switzerland, most of which ended in failure. In 1494 Maximilian was forced to let his son, Philip, govern the Netherlands, but the problems of a regency in the Netherlands arose after the death of Philip in 1506. Maximilian's acquisition of Burgundy was a major reason for the great struggle between the Habsburgs and the French during the 16th century. Between 1500 and 1504 Maximilian was busy suppressing rebellions in Germany. The Empire was further weakened when the Swiss Confederation went to war in 1499 and their independence was recognized in the Treaty of Basel. The problem of the Turks and the frontiers in the east preoccupied him. He dreamed of expelling the Turks from eastern Europe, but was unsuccessful. After the death of King Matthias Corvinus of Hungary in 1490, Maximilian was, however, successful in expelling the Hungarians from Austria.

The problem of the Empire proved to be intractable. Maximilian hoped for the unity of Germany under a strong Habsburg monarchy with the right of taxation and a standing army to provide its defense, especially against the French and the Turks. Maximilian appealed repeatedly to the diets to support him in his view of the Empire's needs, but the princes refused to accept his position, mistrusting his policies, which they thought were intended to expand the Habsburg possessions. Consequently, the diets never provided him with the money and troops that he desired, and he had to resort to borrowing from bankers such as the Fuggers (See FUGGER, JACOB "THE RICH"). After 1508 there was no prospect of cooperation between Maximilian and the diets due to his war against Venice, which was opposed by German merchants.

A reform movement had emerged in 1495 that wanted to reorganize the Empire on a federal basis. The reformers accomplished some goals, outlawing personal feuds and establishing the Imperial Chamber Court (Reichskammergericht) in 1495 in which Roman law was to be used. An Imperial Council of Regency (Reichsregiment) also was established, which was intended to make Maximilian a figurehead monarch, but it failed to function. The impetus of reform came to a standstill in 1504.

Maximilian became famous as a patron of the arts and literature. He encouraged and surrounded himself with scholars and artists who were imbued with the current enthusiasm for HUMANISM and the culture of the Greeks and Romans. He did not neglect German culture inasmuch as he collected German folk poetry and songs and initiated the establishment of a German literary museum. He also wrote essays on his favorite arts. While in NUREMBERG in 1512 Maximilian enlisted Albrecht DÜRER on numerous projects. Hans Burgkmair also contributed illustrations for the emperor's literary works. He patronized humanists such as John Cuspinian and Conrad Peutinger. During his latter years Maximilian used humanists and artists such as Dürer to glorify his reign. Reflecting his own egotism, his most famous book was the quasi-autobiographical *Theurdank* (1517), which was a political allegory describing his journey to meet his new wife, Mary of Burgundy. Maximilian's autobiography was *White King* (*Weisskunig*). He died on January 12, 1519, of stomach and intestinal failures but had had a stroke in 1518 and had been afflicted by syphilis as early as 1497.

Maximilian I (1573–1651)

elector of Bavaria after 1623 and imperial statesman

Born in MUNICH, the son of William V and Renata of Lorraine, he was educated at the Jesuit (*see* JESUITS) University in Ingolstadt. He succeeded his father, Duke William, in 1598. He reformed the internal government and finances of BAVARIA so that it was economically stable at the beginning of the THIRTY YEARS' WAR. He reorganized Bavaria into a centralized absolutistic state and only assembled the estates in a *Landtag* once in 1612. Strongly influenced by his Jesuit advisers, Maximilian was an ardent supporter of the Catholic COUNTER-REFORMATION. Some said he had an exaggerated sense of responsibility for his subjects and followed a policy of moral reform, forbidding his peasants to dance, and even introduced the death penalty for adulterers.

Even before the Thirty Years' War Maximilian was active in the politics of the Empire. He sought to control the adjacent bishoprics of Salzburg, Freising, Passau, and REGENSBURG, and in 1607 he re-Catholicized the imperial city of Donauwörth. In 1609 he became the leader of the Catholic League (1609–35), which he organized against the Protestant Union organized by Frederick V of the Palatinate, who intervened in the Bohemian Revolt and started the Thirty Years' War. Maximilian ensured the election of his cousin, Ferdinand of Austria, as the Holy Roman Emperor, FERDINAND II, and pledged the support of the Catholic League for the new emperor. Bavarian forces composed the largest army in Germany and, led by Johann von Tilly (1559–1632), defeated Frederick at the battle of White Mountain (1620). For his services Ferdinand awarded Maximilian the honor of imperial elector (1623), and Bavaria also obtained the territory of the Palatinate to the right bank of the RHINE. Interpreting the victory of Catholic forces as a divine mandate to restore Catholicism in Germany, Maximilian supported the Edict of Restitution (1629). Maximilian feared that the emperor was using General Albrecht von WALLENSTEIN to transform the federal Empire into an absolute centralized state. Along with other League princes Maximilian forced the retirement of the powerful general in 1630. Although the elector had been ably served by General Tilly, during the Swedish phase of the war Bavaria suffered devastation. Wallenstein's return again prompted demands by the elector for his dismissal in 1633. When the war ended at the WESTPHALIA PEACE Congress, Bavaria sided with France, which enabled Maximilian to retain the electoral privilege and keep the Upper Palatinate although losing the Rhenish Palatinate.

Maximilian was the Empire's leading Catholic statesman and administrator, second only to the Habsburg emperor. He was superior morally to most of the other princes of his age. More than any other German prince he was responsible for stopping Ferdinand II in 1630 from turning the HOLY ROMAN EMPIRE into a centralized absolute monarchy.

Maximilian II (1527–1576)

Holy Roman Emperor

After the abdication of Emperor CHARLES V, Maximilian II, the son of Ferdinand I and Anna of Bohemia and Hungary, succeeded as Holy Roman Emperor. In 1548 Maximilian married his cousin Maria, daughter of Charles V. Although Charles V had to give the Imperial succession to Ferdinand I and his son Maximilian, he had tried to reserve the succession of Ferdinand for his own son, Philip II of Spain. Deep divisions between the two main branches of the Habsburg family occurred, but in the end the wishes of Charles V won out. Part of the problem was that the loyalty of Maximilian to Catholicism was questionable, and he was also on good terms with the German princes who had been the enemies of Charles V.

Maximilian was intelligent, cultivated, and tolerant. He was brought up as a Catholic but made a careful study of the LUTHERAN BIBLE. In Vienna he was influenced by the court chaplain who was neither Lutheran nor Catholic, but favored evangelical Christianity. Maximilian had many Protestant friends, was influenced by the Czech nobles, and distrusted the political maneuvering at the COUNCIL OF TRENT. He disliked the JESUITS, who were prominent in the COUNTER-REFORMATION. A turning point occurred when his father, Ferdinand, was reprimanded by Pope Paul IV for accepting the religious PEACE OF AUGSBURG in 1555 and who also labeled Maximilian a "wicked heretic son." Maximilian agreed to submit to the Catholic faith and sent his sons, Rudolf and Ernest, to Spain to be educated in a Catholic atmosphere. Although his cousin, Philip II, was named head of the house of Habsburg, Maximilian was elected Holy Roman Emperor in 1564. He believed that his role was to bring peace to his diverse people. He did not help the Protestant cause in the Empire, but in 1568 and 1571 he secured religious freedom for Lutherans in Lower Austria, while his brother, the Archduke Charles, extended similar toleration in Inner Austria, which included Styria, Carinthia, and Carniola. He favored limited reform of the church, which included the communion cup and priestly marriage. In his efforts to promote peaceful solutions through compromises he was unsuccessful. His relations with the Protestants were complicated by the dogmatic hostility between the various Protestant sects.

As a patron of the arts and sciences he was determined to make Vienna a cultural center. The emperor invited the distinguished botanist Karl Clusius and the physician John Crato von Krafftsheim, who were both Protestants. Musicians were also brought to Vienna from all over Europe, and he even tried to bring the famous Palestrina from Rome.

Maximilian was also unsuccessful as a warrior. The army that he led against the Turks in 1566 was ineffective, largely because of his own cautiousness. He tried to remain at peace with the sultan, continued to pay tribute to the Turks, abandoned efforts to reverse Turkish inroads and made a compromise treaty in 1568. In 1573 he was elected king of Poland, which, however, was opposed by the estates of the Empire. In 1574 he designated his Catholic son Rudolph II as his successor, securing the Catholic future of Habsburg lands. On October 10, 1576, he died, refusing to receive the last sacraments from the court chaplain.

Mein Kampf
(My Struggle)

Mein Kampf was the title of HITLER's book, which explained his political philosophy and program. It is not an autobiographical study but is a subjective political treatise explaining what he intended to do in the future. It presented Hitler's view of the world in which he grew up, of WORLD WAR I, why Germany lost the war, his anti-international and anti-Semitic prejudices, and his obsession with LEBENSRAUM. The second volume concerns the political struggle of the NAZI PARTY and the future Nazi state. It provides his insights into mass propaganda. The basic theme was that the German people should be a racially pure people to qualify them to be the leaders of humankind. Hitler's basic ideological plan was for racial supremacy and empire. The basic arguments were predominantly negative and appealed primarily to the dissatisfied people in Germany. Hitler's views were extremely nationalistic, socialistic, anti-Semitic, antidemocratic, antiliberal, antiparliamentary, anti-Catholic, anti-Marxist, and anti-French.

The first part of *Mein Kampf* was written in Landsberg prison after the BEER-HALL PUTSCH in November 1923. Hitler dictated it to Rudolf HESS and Emil Maurice. The second volume was written between 1925 and 1927 after the Nazi Party was reconstructed under Hitler's control. The style of the first edition was awkward and crudely written. The editors removed endless repetitions and crude expressions, and improved the style. The publisher was Max Amann, who after numerous revisions sold 5.2 million copies by 1939, making Hitler a millionaire. By his death almost 9 million copies were sold, and it was translated into English. Hitler dictated a second book to Amann, which was published posthumously as *Hitler's Second Book* in 1961.

Melanchthon, Philip (1497–1560)
humanist and theologian

Philip Melanchthon was a scholar and humanist who became the chief theologian of the REFORMATION and author of the AUGSBURG CONFESSION of 1530. Among his lasting achievements were those in education, which caused him to be known as the "teacher of Germany" (*Praeceptor Germaniae*).

Philip Schwartzerd (later to be known as Philip Melanchthon) was born to George and Barbara Schwartzerd at Bretten near Karlsruhe, where the father worked in the production of armor. After 1508 Philip's classical education was guided by his grandmother's brother, the famous humanist scholar Johann REUCHLIN, a Greek and Hebrew scholar. The name Melanchton, which is Greek for "Schwartzerd" ("black earth" in German), was given to Philip by Reuchlin because of his scholarly talents. The young student went on to study at Pforzheim and HEIDELBERG, receiving a bachelor of arts degree in 1511 and in 1514 a master's degree from Tübingen, which qualified him to lecture there in Latin and Greek literature. He participated in the editing of Reuchlin's satire of his ecclesiastical enemies, *The Letters of Obscure Men* (1514–15). In 1518 the prodigy was appointed professor of Greek at the University of Wittenberg and won the approval of Martin LUTHER through his inaugural address on the ideal program for the education of youth, which began their lifelong friendship.

Melanchthon lectured in the classics and became very popular. He also began to contribute intellectual services to Luther and the Reformation. In 1519 Melanchthon attended the LEIPZIG debates in which Luther and Johann Eck confronted each other. That same year he completed his bachelor of theology degree, arguing in his thesis a defense of Luther's principal positions. In 1521 he started his future role as the systematic theologian of Lutheranism, writing a basic text of theology, the *Main Topics of Theology* (*Loci Communes Rerum Theologicarum*), which Luther considered the most significant ever written. The *Loci Communes* based its doctrines on the writings of St. Paul. In subsequent revised and enlarged editions Melanchthon provided Lutheranism with a systematic theology, one of the foundations of Protestant thought.

Luther also looked to Melanchthon as a personal representative. Since the EDICT OF WORMS (1521) had made Luther an outlaw and politically handicapped, Melanchthon became the chief public representative for the theologians at Wittenberg in the councils of the Empire. Although not a religious figure like Luther nor a deep philosophical thinker, Melanchthon in 1530 answered Luther's Catholic critics at the DIET OF AUGSBURG. He also composed along with others the Augsburg Confession, in which he tried to provide Protestant Christians with common fundamental beliefs. His mild-mannered personality was the opposite of Luther's, who admitted that "Master Philip comes along softly and gently sowing and watering with joy." Melanchthon displayed the qualities of a dispassionate scholar and teacher who stood above the heated debates and slanderous name calling. Whether in discussion with

Zwinglians, as at the MARBURG COLLOQUY (1529), or in negotiations with traditional Catholic theologians, as at the Diet of Augsburg (1530), Melanchthon brought an air of emotional detachment. This resulted in his being able to successfully deal with complex issues and prepare statements of consensus of Christian doctrine. Luther's inflexibility and inability to compromise frustrated and disappointed the humanist teacher. Whereas Melanchthon desired to reconcile, Luther was adamant in his beliefs. In 1525 the differences came out into the open when in the controversy with Desiderius ERASMUS Luther emphasized with theological radicalness the sinfulness of man instead of his goodness. Melanchthon became frightened, as he did when the PEASANTS' WAR erupted in 1524–25. Immorality spread its wings as the old religious restraints evaporated, as did the appearance of the radical ANABAPTISTS and the divisions among the Protestants.

The Wittenberg professor exemplified reasonableness and responsible change, which appealed to the humanist community that Luther had alienated. Seen as the successor to Erasmus, Melanchthon provided respectability for the Lutheran leadership. But Melanchthon also wanted to bridge the gap Luther had placed between faith and reason. As a theologian Melanchthon's thinking was more rationalistic, and he wanted to bridge classical culture and Christianity. He wanted a more organized intellectual structure and identified faith with doctrine, eliminating some of the paradoxes that Luther thought were expressions of divine wisdom. So Melanchthon codified the Christian life into a system of doctrines. Later he introduced philosophical arguments and ancient church dogma. This was already evident in the 1535 edition of the *Loci,* in which he denied the "serfdom of the will and absolute predestination," giving the will a role in Christian conversion. He was also concerned with the moral laxity that emerged due to Luther's theory of justification and weak position on the role of good works in salvation. Other Lutheran leaders successfully opposed his desire to emphasize the necessity of good works in salvation. The situation in society helped resolve the problem as the new churches and the paternalistic state began to enforce moral standards. Melanchthon's desire for order in society also led him into taking an even stronger position than Luther against the rebellion of the peasants in 1524–25. The theologian also took Luther's social teachings and made them into a legal system, which supported the Christian authoritarian state with its police powers, though based on laws.

In other areas of his life Melanchthon provided diplomatic services for the Protestant princes and even for Catholic ones. The Protestant Philip of Hesse was one of his admirers, while Catholic princes such as King Francis I of France and Henry VIII of England sought his advice. It was in education perhaps that Melanchthon had a more lasting impact. In 1525 he established the Gymnasium in Nuremberg and later participated in establishing the University of Marburg. He reformed curricula, wrote textbooks on Latin and Greek as well as on many other subjects, and established a strong intellectual tradition at Wittenberg. Outliving Luther, Melanchthon died in April 1560 and was buried in Wittenberg.

Mendel, Johann Gregor (1822–1884)
father of genetics

Gregor Mendel has been called the father of genetics, laying the foundation for a scientific approach to human heredity. He experimented with plants, especially peas, in the Augustinian Abbey near Brünn in AUSTRIA. He issued the paper "Experiments in Plant Hybridization."

Gregor Mendel was born on July 22, 1822, at Heinzendorf in Austrian Silesia into a farming family. He attended schools in Leipnik, Troppau, and at age 18 enrolled at the Institute of Philosophy in Olmütz. In 1843 he joined the Catholic Augustinian order in Brünn. Education in the sciences was emphasized for members of the order, inspiring Mendel to study agriculture, pomiculture, and vine growing. In 1849 Mendel began to teach mathematics and Greek. From 1851 to 1853 he studied the natural sciences at the University of Vienna, where lectures by Professor F. Unger on plant anatomy and physiology influenced Mendel's ideas on the origin of plant variability, which led to his experiments with peas. In 1854 Mendel returned to Brünn as a teacher of physics and natural history, which duties he performed until 1868, when he was appointed abbot.

Mendel's energy was directed toward the problem of the origin of plant variability. He experimented with selected varieties of peas and then with artificial fertilization. His results were presented in a paper, "Experiments on Plant Hybrids," at a scientific meeting in Brünn in 1865, although unfortunately, his work or its significance was not appreciated. A reason was perhaps that his hypothesis of "particulate heredity" was contrary to the generally accepted theory of "blending heredity." After 1900 Mendel's segregation of the hereditary units later called genes was called Mendel's law of segregation. Mendel's law of independent assortment explained how the hereditary particles later recombined. Mendel also tried to prove the general validity of his theory in the plant kingdom. His experiments testing Lamarck's views concerning the influence of environment on plant variability disproved the French botanist's conclusions, finding that a hard line could not be drawn between species.

Mendel's attempts to carry out experiments on the hybridizing of bees were unsuccessful. His work as a meteorologist was well respected, and he initiated the first weather forecasts for farmers in 1878. Yet Mendel's paper of 1865 continued to be ignored until 1900, when scientists rediscovered it and formulated it as Mendel's law of heredity, but they still did not consider it generally valid. Mendel's theory was also mistakenly thought to be in conflict with the Darwinian theory of selection. Mendel was ahead of his time. Only in 1926 did S. S. Tchetverikoff demonstrate the synthesis of Darwinian and Mendelian theories. The reappraisal of Mendel's work has proved that his hypothesis of "hereditary particles" provided the explanation of heredity in all forms of life.

Mendelssohn, Felix (1809–1847)
one of the most popular composers of the romantic period

Felix Mendelssohn was born in HAMBURG into the family of a wealthy and cultured Jewish banker who had moved to BERLIN to avoid the terrors of Napoleon's invasion. Baptized a Christian as a child, Felix was accepted into privileged Berlin society, where he was exposed to writers, actors, artists, and musicians. Felix demonstrated musical talent quite early and by age 16 was composing brilliant octets and overtures. In 1837 he married Cécile Jeanrenaud, the daughter of a Huguenot pastor, and had five children. He eventually became an administrator and conductor in the Lower Rhine Music Festival in DÜSSELDORF and for the LEIPZIG Gewandhaus Orchestra. Founded in 1843 by Mendelssohn and under his direction, the Leipzig Conservatory of Music became famous throughout Europe. In response to the favor of the king of Prussia, Mendelssohn became the music director at the Berlin Academy of Arts. Besides these responsibilities he promoted the careers of Robert and Clara SCHUMANN, Hector Berlioz, and such violinists as Joseph Joachim, Ferdinand David, and Henri Vieuxtemps, as well as the pianist Anton Rubenstein.

Robert Schumann called Mendelssohn "the Mozart of the 19th century" who reconciled the musical contradictions of the period. In classical composition Mendelssohn was a successor to Ludwig van BEETHOVEN and Franz SCHUBERT. His romantic musical experiments such as the recycling of thematic material are to be found in his two piano concertos, the fascinatingly beautiful violin concerto, and the *Scottish* Symphony, which he completed in Leipzig after 1843. Other sources of inspiration for his compositions come from the works and friendship of the predominant literary personality of his time, Johann Wolfgang von GOETHE, but also from the plays of Shakespeare and the beautiful landscapes observed during his travels. A scherzo, for instance, was inspired by Goethe's *Witches Sabbath* (1825), and an overture was inspired by Shakespeare's *Midsummer Night's Dream* (1826).

Landscapes inspired the *Italian* Symphony (no. 4) as well as the *Hebrides* Overture. The latter was an inspirational response to his trip to Scotland in 1829, as was the *Scottish* Symphony (no. 3), which was dedicated to Queen Victoria of England. His two oratorios, *St. Paul* and *Elijah* were inspired by Georg Frideric HANDEL and were performed in London and Birmingham. Between 1829 and 1845 he also produced eight books of songs for the piano.

His health failed after 1844 and deteriorated quickly in 1847, when his beloved sister, Fanny, died, which devastated him. He died at the young age of 38 on November 4, 1847.

Mendelssohn, Moses (1720–1786)
German-Jewish philosopher of the Enlightenment

Moses Mendelssohn was born in Dessau on September 6, 1729. Small, homely, and crippled with curvature of spine, he nonetheless overcame his physical limitations and engaged in rigorous study at the Talmudic Academy of the renowned rabbi in BERLIN, David Fránkel. Mendelssohn pursued a course of studies that led him to create a dramatic turning point in Jewish history, by which Judaism began to cross over from the ghetto into the modern world. He wanted to make Jews acceptable to Christians, not through conversion to Christianity but as their fellow citizens through cultural enlightenment and civil emancipation. Mendelssohn became a key figure in the struggle to tear down the intellectual, social, and cultural barriers separating Jews from the outside world and to prepare the way for cultural and civic equality.

In Berlin he not only studied the Talmud but also explored other fields of knowledge, becoming familiar with contemporary philosophy, especially that of Gottfried LEIBNIZ and Christian WOLFF. Mendelssohn mastered German and learned French and English. Leaving Fránkel's academy, he became employed as a tutor for the children of a wealthy silk manufacturer, Isaac Bernhard, and later a partner in the firm. His friendship with Gotthold Ephraim LESSING, the writer and dramatist, led to his being the model of the enlightened Jew in Lessing's comedy *Nathan the Wise*. Lessing also published Mendelssohn's first essays and a translation of Jean-Jacques Rousseau's *Discourse on Unequality* (1756). Mendelssohn's mastery of the German language made him a leading figure on the German literary scene, even editing a popular literary magazine with Friedrich Nicolai. In the 1760s Mendelssohn married and soon had six children, of which two established banking houses, and his grandson, Felix MENDELSSOHN became a famous composer.

His most important works concerned the philosophy of religion and aesthetics. His book *Phädon* became the most popular work of German philosophy at the time. It was modeled on Plato's dialogue *Phaedo*, wherein Mendelssohn defended the immortality of the soul against the skeptics of his time. He also translated into German the *Pentateuch* (1778–83) of the Bible, which caused a cultural revolution among German Jews, introducing them to the German language and providing the key to world literature, science, and philosophy. It also influenced Jewish education, whereby Yiddish was replaced as the language of instruction and secular subjects were added to religious studies. Mendelssohn attempted to interpret Judaism as a religion of reason and not of faith, and he resisted attempts of Christian ministers to convert him, as the Swiss theologian J. K. Lavater attempted to do in 1769. Mendelssohn was ahead of his time by advocating religious tolerance and complete freedom and equality for Jews. In *Jerusalem* he opposed the traditional idea of the Christian state and pleaded for separation of church and state. In this regard his thinking was not compatible with traditional Christianity or Judaism. Mendelssohn's conception of Judaism distinguished revealed religion from Judaism as revealed law. As much as he tried to preserve the observance of the Jewish law, even among his children, all of them except Joseph converted to Christianity. Mendelssohn's attempt to bridge and harmonize Judaism with the rationalist culture of his time failed, but he raised the important questions that

Jews in the modern world had to face. He died in Berlin on January 4, 1786.

Mengele, Dr. Josef (1911–1979)
Auschwitz doctor

Josef Mengele was the notorious physician at AUSCHWITZ/BIRKENAU; he sent thousands of Jews to their deaths in the gas chambers and conducted terrible medical experiments.

Josef Mengele was born in Günzberg, BAVARIA, on March 16, 1911, to the owner of a farm machinery factory. While studying at the University of MUNICH, he met Alfred ROSENBERG, whose racial theories impressed him as scientific truths. After meeting HITLER, he became one of his most devoted followers. He received his doctorate in medicine in 1938 at the Frankfurt Institute for Hereditary Biology and Racial Hygiene, wrote his dissertation on hereditary deformities, and continued to do research on twins.

In 1940 he took part in the Nazi campaign of EUTHANASIA in which some 60,000 allegedly incurably insane Germans were killed. Then he served in the military with the 5th SS Panzer "Viking" Division, where he became a battalion surgeon. Repeatedly decorated, he was severely wounded on the Donets River during spring 1943. Declared unfit for duty, he was made an assistant to Dr. Hans Klein at Auschwitz that same year. After Klein was transferred to BERGEN-BELSEN, Mengele was promoted to chief medical officer by Heinrich HIMMLER. In association with other doctors Mengele had the task of choosing employable Jews to operate the industrial machines and sending others to the gas chambers. The process involved parading before Mengele, and he with the flick of his thumb or with his cane motioned either to the right, which meant the prisoner was saved, or left, meaning they went to the gas chambers.

Mengele became notorious for his medical experiments. On one occasion he supervised an operation by which two Gypsy children were sewn together to create Siamese twins, whose resected veins became infected. Other bogus experiments were conducted on the origins of dwarfs and cripples. He also researched methods in which multiple births would occur. His victims included Jews and Gypsies, adults and children. At one time he killed 750 women by gassing to rid the camp of lice, arguing that the danger of typhus had thereby been eliminated. An example of his horrible experiments were the eye injections he gave to children to change the color of the iris. Twins were the subject of much research to compare their dying process.

At the end of the war Mengele disappeared with his notes. Found, he was interned by the British in a hospital, but again disappeared underground. In 1947 he was arrested by the U.S. Army but released to the British for work as a spy. Then as the cold war developed, he lived in the U.S. zone and was not harassed because he was an old Nazi and anticommunist. He went to Rome in 1949 and then to Argentina. High on the list of wanted Nazi criminals, he became the object of a search by Interpol, Israeli agents, and the Nazi hunter Simon Wiesenthal. When he was found living in Paraguay, requests were made by the West German government to the Paraguayan military regime to extradite him for the murder of 2,000 people and for assisting in the killing of 200,000 more. In 1979 Mengele died at a beach resort in Brazil and was anonymously buried. In 1985 his body was dug up in Embu, Brazil, confirmed by forensic experts to be that of Mengele.

Merkel, Angela (1954–)
first woman chancellor

Angela Merkel is the first woman chancellor in German history and the first from the former East Germany. She was a "signal from the East" who was expected to be able to restore the CDU to power and bring to an end Gerhard Schroeder's (SPD) seven years in the chancellor's office. She also was expected to be an antidote to the strong showing of the center-leftist parties, which received 56 percent of the vote in the elections of 2002.

Angela Merkel was born on July 17, 1954, in Hamburg, but her parents soon moved her to Templin just north of Berlin in East Germany. Her father is a Protestant pastor who was a Christian Socialist who believed in the compatibility of Christianity and Marxism. Angela received her Abitur in 1973 in Templin and went on to study at the University of LEIPZIG, where in 1978 she earned a degree in physics. Between 1978 and 1990 she was a physical chemist at the Academy of Sciences in East Germany. She married a quantum chemist, Joachim Sauer, but did not have children. Merkel entered the CDU in 1990, became a representative in the Bundestag, and was a protégé of Helmut KOHL. Kohl actually did not discover Merkel but inherited her from Lothar de Maizière, who had become a Christian Democrat shortly before the Wall fell. Merkel worked in Maizière's press office in December 1989, and six months later she began to work for Kohl. Within a year she became Germany's minister for women and youth and in 1994 was named to the environmental ministry, where she became an environmentalist. By 2000 she had already become the chairwoman of the CDU. She took over the CDU parliamentary faction after Edmund Stoiber from the CSU, the sister party of the CDU, lost to Gerhard SCHROEDER in the elections of 2002. Nevertheless Merkel realized that the Schroeder era was nearing its end.

Because Gerhard Schroeder decided to call elections a year earlier some say that Angela Merkel was his "gift to Germany." By demanding to have a vote of confidence to receive a strong mandate, Gerhard Schroeder made an election inevitable. Had the election been a year later other CDU candidates would likely have replaced Angela Merkel. Schroeder was facing a rebellion in his own party over his economic reform program, Agenda 2010, and finally wanted a chance to bring about the reforms he had talked about in 1998. Yet Schroeder miscalculated in his expectations that he and the SPD could defeat Merkel and the CDU in the parliamentary elections that were held on September 18, 2005, and rightfully so as he was a more attractive campaigner.

On the other hand Angela Merkel has a shy personality, and her speeches are programmed. From the East German perspective, however, she is seen as quite normal, but uncommonly ambitious. In her secret police (Stazi) file from her East German days, even her police informant had little to comment about her. With many allies and few close friends Angela Merkel's rise is remarkable in the old boys' club of German politics where women's prospects for high office are meager. Part of the explanation of her success has been her capacity to deal with powerful men and to exercise power. One of her virtues is patience, the ability to wait for her competitors to eliminate themselves. Yet that did not make her an attractive candidate to many in the former East German states as the CDU's share of the vote dropped to 25.3 percent. Merkel's image was bad in the East, where she was accused of betraying the East German soul, but her image also fared badly in the West. She fared poorly in the East also because other CDU campaigners insulted easterners. Many easterners strongly opposed any talk of economic and social reform. After the elections and Schroeder's refusal to join a new government, a "grand" coalition was formed around Merkel in the so-called chancellor war. On November 22 Dr. Angela Merkel was elected Federal Chancellor. In the coalition with the SPD, the CDU will control the chancellery including six ministries and an additional cabinet post, while Merkel was forced to make concessions giving the SPD eight ministries.

Angela Merkel's policies for reform are expected to be harsher than the moderate economic and social reforms of Schroeder, which failed to reduce Germany's 11.6 percent unemployment. During the formation of the coalition with the SPD, Merkel designated the goals of cutting unemployment, stimulating the economy, and consolidating government finances as the central tasks of the Federal Government. Her goals of cutting unemployment and stimulating the economy will demand sacrifices of German citizens. A period of austerity will include an increase in the value added tax (VAT) in 2007, raising the retirement age to 67, and raising income tax levels. The economy will be given a boost during the next four years through a euro investment program, and a reform of corporate taxation is planned for 2008 to improve Germany's competitiveness. At this point changes in the social security and health-care systems have not been decided. In foreign policy Germany intends to remain a "responsible partner in Europe and the world." As far as Germany's policy toward the United States goes, experts expect that Merkel will create warmer ties to the United States but not bring about major policy changes. A major hurdle to improvement of ties is the restraint of German public opinion, which is fiercely opposed to the Bush administration and its foreign policy.

Messerschmitt, Wilhelm (1898–1978)
aircraft designer

Born on June 26, 1898, in FRANKFURT AM MAIN, "Willi," as he was called, received his basic technical education at the Munich Technical High School. Soon he became a designer for the Bavarian Aircraft Co. and later opened his own Messerschmitt Works in AUGSBURG. Within three years he produced his first all-metal plane. By 1933 he had military contracts to produce bombers for the German military. Then he designed the plane for which he has become famous, the Me 109, which had a square-tipped wing. It was first displayed at the Berlin Olympics in 1936 and tested during the Spanish civil war in 1937. It was so successful that throughout the war more Me 109s were produced than any other aircraft. HITLER praised Messerschmitt as a "genius." After the war he was convicted in 1948 as a Nazi supporter. He then resorted to building prefabricated housing, but it was not long that he was back at the drawing board, producing jet aircraft for the German air force due to the advent of the cold war. He died in MUNICH on September 15, 1978.

The Me 109 had its deficiencies as was discovered when the British Spitfire proved its superiority during the fight over Dunkirk. It was not long, however, before a new model, the Me 109F was produced, which outperformed the Spitfire at high altitudes. Messerschmitt made mistakes in the design of another plane, the two-engine fighter Me 210, which was replaced by the Me 410, a successful heavy fighter-interceptor powered by two inverted V-12 engines. Messerschmitt also designed the first turbojet fighter, but because its production was not given priority until 1945 it failed to be a significant weapon. A number of other Messerschmitt planes were produced, but the Me 163 was exceptional, the only interceptor fighter powered by a rocket motor, flying at 596 miles per hour but again not used until too late in the war.

Metternich, Klemens von (1773–1859)
Austrian statesman

Prince Klemens von Metternich was the most powerful and influential Austrian statesman since Count Wentzel Anton Kaunitz under MARIA THERESA. Metternich played a primary diplomatic role in the defeat of Napoleon, presided over the CONGRESS OF VIENNA, and as an opponent of LIBERALISM and NATIONALISM constructed a diplomatic system that preserved European peace until Italy and Germany were each unified.

Metternich's father was a count whose lands were situated in western Germany and who held the position of minister of the Austrian Netherlands. When he was a youth his family resided in the city of Koblenz, where he absorbed French culture and became fluent in its language. His first experience of the French Revolution was a popular demonstration at city hall while he attended the University of Strasbourg. Dismayed by the violence and goals of this mob, he continued his studies at the University of Mainz, where he came into personal contact with émigré French nobility. When the French armies occupied the lands of the Metternichs, they fled to the Austrian capital, Vienna.

With his marriage in 1795 to Eleonore von Kaunitz, the granddaughter of the former Austrian state chancellor, the ambitious Metternich gained entrance to AUSTRIA's elite social and political circles. Soon he received appointments as Austrian ambassador to BERLIN and DRESDEN, and then to France in 1806. While in France he seriously underestimated Napoleon, reporting him to be vulnerable and weak, encouraging Austria to go to war against Napoleon and lose. Metternich was able to negotiate favorable peace terms and was rewarded with an appointment as foreign minister in October 1809. That same year he arranged the marriage of Napoleon to Marie Louise, the daughter of the Austrian emperor Francis I, creating a temporary alliance. After Napoleon's disastrous retreat from Russia in 1812, Austria joined the allies and participated in Napoleon's defeat at the BATTLE OF LEIPZIG in 1813. With Napoleon's second defeat at the BATTLE OF WATERLOO, Metternich became the leader of the alliance against the conqueror.

At the Congress of Vienna during 1814–15 monarchs and princes were restored to their thrones and territories were divided. Metternich interpreted the successful congress as a personal triumph. His diplomacy earned him the title "coachman of Europe" and determined the future of Europe. In order to prevent the outbreak of future wars and secure the peace that had been gained with such difficulty, Metternich proposed the formation of the "Concert of Europe," by which the allies would act together to suppress revolutions. Metternich's goals were to keep Russian influence in Europe to a minimum and to frustrate PRUSSIA's expansionist ambitions in Germany. With the help of Great Britain he created an alliance system called the QUADRUPLE ALLIANCE. This was based on the concept of the balance of power, wherein four of the great powers would be able to suppress revolutions and prevent war. Metternich's goal was to suppress nationalism and liberalism, seen as serious threats to the survival of the multinational Austrian Empire, substituting confederations in place of German and Italian nation-states. Succeeding in Germany, the statesmen of the Congress of Vienna reduced the hundreds of German states to 35, including both Prussia and Austria. Actually, Metternich would have preferred to have the Austrian emperor as ruler over all of Germany, but FRANCIS II refused. Consequently, a weak GERMAN CONFEDERATION was established, which lasted until Germany was united under Prussian leadership in 1870.

Between 1815 and 1820 liberal political movements weakened the monarchs of western Germany. Metternich feared the subversive influence of the secret fraternities (BURSCHENSHAFTEN) as they staged patriotic demonstrations. After the assassination of Kotzebue, a politically conservative playwright, Prussia was convinced to join Austria in the declaration of the CARLSBAD DECREES (1819). These instituted censorship of the press, including books and pamphlets; the restriction of student societies and professors at universities; and the hunt for subversives. More than any other policy the decrees made Metternich a symbol of repression.

Above all else Metternich sought to preserve the Austrian multinational empire. He feared that under the influence of nationalism each nationality would eventually want to create its own state. Metternich, however, was far wiser than those Austrian ministers who followed the example of Emperor JOSEPH II and sought to unify the empire through the centralization of administration and standardization of the law. It was far wiser, Metternich thought, to allow each ethnic people to enjoy its own customs and laws, thereby eliminating one of the goals of revolutionaries and nationalists. The new emperor, Francis Joseph, however, would not listen and followed the advice of Count Kolowrat, the minister of state. As a consequence, Metternich's responsibilities were limited to foreign affairs, even though he was appointed Austrian state chancellor.

Metternich was a conservative statesman, but not a reactionary. His contemporaries accused him of developing a "Metternichian system" to suppress the forces of change. Instead, he tried to convince his contemporaries that he had discovered the immutable laws of "a world order" that reflected the rationalism of the ENLIGHTENMENT, especially the thought of Voltaire. He remained a classicist in an age of ROMANTICISM, abhorring the new concept of the sovereignty of the people, which he correctly believed undermined the continuity of the Austrian Empire to which he was so devoted. Being an émigré from the Rhineland and not an Austrian by birth, his perspective was more representative of a true European. Working for international peace and believing that each state was a sovereign entity, he encouraged princes to secure state boundaries by treaties. In order to preserve the balance of power in Europe, he thought it was necessary to establish a confederation of German states as a buffer between France and Russia. He was a flexible enough thinker to perceive that one form of government did not fit all peoples and tolerated Hungary's old constitution because of its ancient roots. Theoretically, he did not think that stability necessitated an absence of change, but in reality he was too rigid to conceive how an innovation in one part of society would not necessarily lead to the collapse of the whole.

When a liberal revolution established Louis Phillipe on the French throne in 1830, Metternich thought his efforts had failed. While Vienna had been spared during that revolution, that was not to be the case during the REVOLUTION OF 1848. After the first outbreak in Paris a revolution brought the angry mobs out into the streets in Vienna. They demanded Metternich's resignation. In the night he fled Vienna and went into exile in Britain. He returned to Vienna in 1858 and died a year later.

middle class, German
(*Besitzbürgertum; Bildungsbürgertum; Mittelstand*)

In German history a distinction has been made socially between the propertied upper middle class (*Besitzbürgertum*), the educated upper middle class (*Bildungsbürgertum*), and the lower middle class (*Mittelstand*). The term *Bürger* during the Middle Ages meant the inhabitant of a town, while *Bürgertum* in the 19th century generally meant upper middle class. In the late 19th century the new term, *Mittelstand*, came to be regarded as the lower middle class including master artisans, independent retailers, and small farmers.

During the 19th century the efforts of the propertied and educated middle class generally led to economic and social progress and had a liberalizing influence favoring constitutional government and NATIONALISM. After the nation was unified, industrialized, and technologically and scientifically advanced, the upper middle class became richer and the economy and society more complex and specialized. As a consequence, the upper middle class were represented in a variety of political and social orientations. Some became more conservative, antiliberal, antimodernist, and perhaps even anti-Semitic. Most were nationalistic, pro imperialist and probably supported WORLD WAR I. Many in the upper middle class were very critical of and opposed to the government of the WEIMAR REPUBLIC as too socialistic and liberal. Some even supported National Socialism and its emphasis on an authoritarian government.

As the Industrial Revolution and MODERNIZATION transformed German society, economic competition and special interests undermined the cohesion and collective identity of the middle class (*Bürgertum*). The middle class became increasingly fragmented into specific occupational groups. The upper middle class, of course, were the Ruhr industrialists, bankers, and owners of large businesses, while the lower middle class (*Mittelstand*) became increasingly fragmented. The *Mittelstand* were sandwiched between the wealthy *Bürgertum* and the organized working class. Retailers, master craftsmen, and large farmers were considered the traditional "old *Mittelstand*," while such salaried employees as schoolteachers, civil servants, and commercial employees were considered the "new *Mittelstand*." The *Mittelstand* were losing their businesses or jobs and were fearful of being reduced to industrial workers and a lower social status. This lower middle class also dreamed of an idealized and wonderful past of economic prosperity. Because of the stresses these social groups were experiencing, they were afflicted by atomization, alienation, depression, and suicide; some sociologists believe that they were the most revolutionary class in the country because they were resentful, lacked leadership, and were fluid in their political support.

The role of the *Mittelstand* is at the basis of the debate about whether the NAZI PARTY was a party of the lower middle class or whether it was a popular people's party, *Volkspartei*, appealing to people of many social levels and regions. It is generally true that the lower middle class gradually gravitated toward National Socialism after 1929. On the other hand, it is also true that in the analyses made of the electoral support for the Nazi Party, it came from every level of German society, including the upper middle class.

militarism

German history has provided one of the primary examples of the growth of militarism in modern Europe. A militaristic society is one in which the army plays a primary role in the state and society, and military attitudes and behaviors penetrate social, cultural, economic, and political spheres of a nation.

In German history the most prominent example of militarism can be found in the development of PRUSSIA. Early on in Prussian history there was a close connection between the feudal ARISTOCRACY and the army, by which that class maintained its unique position. At the end of the 15th century struggles between the peasantry and the nobility became increasingly violent and a number of instances of open revolt occurred. In the PEASANTS' WAR (1525) this antifeudal rebellion was crushed, and the powers of the landowning aristocracy were strengthened. Martin LUTHER provided the aristocracy with a powerful ideology against the demands of the peasants. Consequently, the suppression of the Peasant's War and the REFORMATION's emphasis on the state's connection with religion strengthened the power of the aristocratic JUNKERS. In fact, as church lands were secularized, the aristocracy strengthened its economic position, and they also seized common lands and forced the peasantry to work on their estates as landless serfs. Then the THIRTY YEARS' WAR further enhanced the power of the aristocracy, while that of the emperor was weakened. At this time the Great Elector, FREDERICK WILLIAM of BRANDENBURG consolidated state power and laid the foundation for a strong army and Brandenburg became a strong military power. The Great Elector coopted the aristocracy into his service and in return granted them control over their estates and peasantry with unrestricted police, legal, and economic power. From the Great Elector onward through FREDERICK the GREAT the army became an ever greater part of the state and an officer corps emerged in which the aristocracy predominated. A far-reaching militarization of society occurred whereby the aristocrats were controlled by the king and were given extensive privileges in the army and on their estates. The brutal discipline in the army influenced social relationships throughout the kingdom, while the economy of the country was geared to the maintenance of the army. The BAUERNSCHUTZ, which protected the peasantry, was added in the 18th century to the protection of the Junkers, and together the social structure was frozen into a feudalistic but growing capitalistic state. The soldierly and warlike spirit was stronger in Prussia than in any other German state.

The next phase of militarism took place as Prussia responded to the French Revolution, Napoleon, and the WARS OF LIBERATION. The old order of society was completely shattered. The reforms initiated by Napoleon and the leaders of the Prussian reform movement radically altered the character of social and political institutions. Political CONSERVATISM and ROMANTICISM became identified with German nationalism. A national hatred emerged against the rationalist ideas of the French Revolution and against foreign nations. Besides the growth of intense nationalism there arose anti-Semitic intolerance. The heroic and militaristic virtues of the ancient Germans were revived and glorified. The crushing defeats that Prussia experienced made the conservative reformers realize that changes were necessary in order to create an army that could match and perhaps defeat the mass armies of the French. Consequently the reformers were able to effect far-reaching changes such as liberating the serfs, purging the officer corps, establishing minimum educational standards, and relaxing discipline. Universal military service, or the idea of a "people's army" (Volksheer) was legally incorporated into the structure of the Prussian state.

After Napoleon had been defeated, the army, again separated from the rest of society, was purged of its liberal elements and used as an instrument of political repression. During the REVOLUTION OF 1848 the army was initially humiliated, but played a vital role in revolution and stabilized the power and authority of the JUNKERS in a changing society rapidly being transformed by capitalism and industrialization. After the revolution the main concern of the army was the internal enemies of the state, and plans for army reform were considered that would make the army an absolutely reliable tool of royal ABSOLUTISM. The militias, for instance, were to be brought under the regular army. A constitutional crisis ensued, and Otto von BISMARCK's use of the army to achieve foreign policy objectives and national unity diverted the attention of the liberals from constitutional questions. The military victories leading to the defeat of France in 1871 inflated the prestige of the army and the authority of the General Staff and proved the superiority of the Prussian army over those of BAVARIA and SAXONY.

Between 1871 and WORLD WAR I the army became the most important single factor in providing cohesion to the authoritarian and conservative state. It served to preserve the rights and privileges of the aristocracy. Criticism of the army as an illiberal institution was silenced, and control of the army by the REICHSTAG was diminished. The army was also a means of social integration, which occurred through the institution of the reserve officer corps, which reconciled many in the MIDDLE CLASS to the army, even to the extent of imitating the manners of the aristocracy. A military industrial complex emerged as industrialists profited from the expansion of the army, especially with the huge naval building program at the turn of the 20th century. The supremacy of the soldier, the peculiar attitude toward war and peace, and the view of the state as the center of power rather than for the general welfare were all reflective of militarism. Three factors were fundamental in the extension of military attitudes and behaviors after 1871. Germany's geopolitical location increased its fear of encirclement by a ring of implacable enemies. The growth of militarism in the new Reich was also due to the role the army played as a symbol of national unification. The glories of warfare were unfortunately used to stimulate a national patriotism. Both the army and the new navy played an important role in national integration as military training became a rite of passage of young men. Junker domination of the officer corps, however, declined, and its social composition broadened. New evidence now suggests that the German people were not so enthusiastic to go to war as has been previously reported. In 1914 and in 1939 the demonstrated enthusiasm was not a true indicator of the average German's interest in self-sacrifice and death. Nevertheless, it can be said that German militarism and the strategic planners during the July crisis of 1914 played an important role in precipitating the war. The extensive war aims of the pan-German expansionists were not secured by German militarism.

During the WEIMAR REPUBLIC militarism paid homage to trench comradeship. Weimar's militarism was essentially paramilitary and was effectively isolated from the general society. Yet, the army played an important role in dismembering the republic and bringing Hitler to power. Hitler and the ideology of National Socialism were primarily examples of the degree to which military virtues had been absorbed by a political party. And once in power the Nazis inculcated the army with its ideology. Warfare became the means to acquire the LEBENSRAUM that Germans supposedly needed. With defeat in the war German militarism as it had historically existed came to an end. That is not to say that the FEDERAL REPUBLIC and the GERMAN DEMOCRATIC REPUBLIC forswore the use of military power. The FRG created the Bundeswehr on a democratic base, removing, however, the role previously played as a rite of passage. Although the Communists needed the army to support their power in the GDR, its power was repudiated by its citizenry.

Mit brennender Sorge (papal encyclical, 1937)

The papal encyclical, *Mit brennender Sorge*, was a public statement concerning the ongoing persecution of the Catholic Church in Nazi Germany. It was the church's most forceful and dramatic condemnation of Nazi policy during the Third Reich.

In response to the pleas of German episcopal leaders, Cardinals Faulhaber, BERTRAM, and Schulte, and Bishops Galen and Preysing, that the papacy speak out forcefully and publicly against the Nazi persecution of the church, Pope Pius XI issued the encyclical *Mit brennender Sorge*. It was secretly distributed throughout the churches of Germany and read publicly from the pulpits on Sunday March 21, 1937. In keeping with Article 4 of the CONCORDAT OF 1933 pastoral letters and encyclicals could be read from pulpits as well as printed in diocesan newsletters, so only copies distributed outside of the churches were confiscated.

After introductory remarks the pope restated those articles of the Catholic faith that were contradicted by Nazi ideology. A true belief in God, the pope argued, was not consistent with the deification of a race, a people (as in German), or a state (such as Nazi). Belief in a national God or national religion was also erroneous. God could not be limited to a single people or race. The pope also spoke about the nature of divine revelation, a true belief in Christ, and the primacy of the Bishop of Rome (pope). He criticized the notion that what is advantageous for the people is "right." Furthermore, Catholics were not obligated in conscience to obey laws that were in violation of the natural law. The encyclical also forcefully protested the many violations of the Concordat of 1933, especially in the areas of education and the conflicts the Nazis had created between national education and religious duty.

With the publication of the encyclical HITLER concluded that the Catholic Church had declared war on Nazi ideology and that compromise was no longer possible. The government reacted angrily, condemning the open criticism and closing the publishing houses that remained open. Increasing pressures were placed on both the Catholic and Evangelical churches. Hitler may have considered abrogating the Concordat, but although Nazi intentions remained secret, it appeared that both Hitler and the Vatican preferred to retain the Concordat.

modernization crisis

Modernization is a process by which traditional societies that have existed in Europe and throughout the world have been transformed into so-called modern societies through an unprecedented and rapid process of change involving industrialization, urbanization, secularization, and rationalization. The modernization process has been racked by crisis all over the world, but in Germany it was concentrated in the experiences of the WEIMAR REPUBLIC. In general the Weimar political system forfeited its legitimacy and ceased to function when it was faced by deep-seated crises of economic, social, and cultural modernization. It was the strains within the process of modernization that gave opportunities for the rise of National Socialism.

The tensions of modernization existed in many areas of Weimar society. One area after another became an ideological or sectional battleground. Population increase led to conflicts between the generations and the sexes. Weimar's sick economy could not sustain a compromise between management and labor as had occurred at the beginning of the republic. Nor could it sustain the demands of a welfare state, especially during the GREAT DEPRESSION. Older social organizations gave way to a new mass society and to "totalitarian formations" dominated by the new mass media. The emerging mass culture and mass consumerism that created modern lifestyles were often labeled "Americanisms," which further generated bitter controversy. Freedom of maneuver for compromise solutions in the social and economic spheres continuously shrank. The traditional elites on the right were strong enough to bring the Weimar Republic to an end, but not to restore the prewar structure of IMPERIAL GERMANY.

It can be theorized that even without HITLER and the NAZI PARTY a major social and political transformation would have occurred. Imperial Germany had become an industrial but not a capitalist nor competitive society, economic ownership was highly concentrated, prices were high, and a small class of large landowners possessed great influence. Imperial Germany, furthermore, had a high birth rate until WORLD WAR I, which predicated that a large younger population would be looking for jobs after the war; there were also too many rural small farmers and an inflated urban lower MIDDLE CLASS. The conflicting demands were still manageable, following the pattern of the Bismarckian compromise, which balanced industry and agriculture, labor and capital, West versus East, centralism and particularism, Catholic versus Protestant, rich and poor. As long as there was general industrial and economic expansion and opportunities, these compromises worked. During the Weimar Republic, however, these conflicts attained crisis proportions. The compromises of the Imperial period failed to solve the problems of Weimar's industrial society. The economic consequences of the war, with the humiliating defeat, and the punitive VERSAILLES TREATY, changed the environment of cultural crisis. Other new conditions such as the lost generation of soldiers, a lack of career opportunities in the military, and the loss of markets and raw materials exacerbated the problem. The middle class lost its wealth through the liquidation of war loans, the INFLATION CRISIS OF 1923, and again as a result of the Great Depression. The failure or betrayal by leaders, beliefs, ideals, and values once held sacred and worth living by also created widespread disillusion. A crisis of legitimacy permeated the political order. A declining standard of living afflicted many in the population, as three-quarters were living on proletarian incomes. There also was a constriction in the avenues to the top of the social and economic ladder, and university graduates felt themselves exploited.

In the cultural sphere there was a "fear of modernity." People expressed a desperate need for roots and for community, sometimes repudiated reason, and looked for salvation from some charismatic leader. The cultural yearning for wholeness was filled with hatred and a range of enemies, whether it was communism, dehumanization through mechanization, capitalist materialism, godless rationalism, rootless society, cosmopolitan Jews, or the all-pervading city.

Modrow, Hans (1928–)
GDR leader

Hans Modrow was the last prime minister of the GERMAN DEMOCRATIC REPUBLIC. His goal was to democratize East Germany, but still keep it socialist. After unification he became honorary chairman of the PARTY OF DEMOCRATIC SOCIALISM (PDS), the successor of the SED.

Hans Modrow was born on January 27, 1928, into a baker's family in the village of Jasenitz in Pomerania near Stettin. Drafted into the militia (*Volksturm*) at the end of the war, he was captured by the Soviets, attended Soviet schooling, and made communism the credo of his life. Returning to East Germany in 1949, he joined the SED and became a party functionary in the East German Youth Movement (Freie Deutsche Jugend). In the 1960s he completed his doctorate in economics at Humboldt University in BERLIN. After joining the Central Committee of the SED in 1967, he held a series of political positions, but because of his stubbornness, which Erich HONECKER did not appreciate, he was sent to DRESDEN to become the regional district secretary in 1973. Before the political crisis of 1989 he had been an open advocate of economic reforms. Modrow was untainted by corruption, and when Erich Honecker could no longer maintain his position, Modrow was elected prime minister on November 13, 1989, as the only one who might be able to salvage the crumbling GDR.

As the GDR's political and economic crisis deepened, Modrow formed a new government on February 5, 1990, with 11 non-SED members. The opposition leaders now had access to state authority and infused new ideas and a new legitimacy into the cabinet. Yet, this cooperation between the government and the opposition did not solve the crisis. The new freedoms allowed liberal and conservative groups to emerge and form parties. While the German Social Union (DSU) even denounced Marxism, another 58,000 East Germans left for the West. Unification with West Germany seemed to be the only way out of the crisis. After a visit to Moscow and discussion with Gorbachev, Modrow agreed to work for a united Germany. Free elections were held on March 18, 1990, and Modrow had to resign in favor of Lothar de Maizière (1940–). Afterward Modrow served as honorary chairman of the PDS and in the elections of 1990 he was elected to the BUNDESTAG in BONN.

Moeller van den Bruck, Arthur
(1876–1925)
intellectual forerunner of National Socialism
Moeller was a leading intellectual and writer of the conservative revolution. Sympathetic to racial doctrine, he prefigured HITLER in his contempt for Western civilization and international law. His famous major work was *The Third Reich*, which called for a true revolution creating a mystical union of Germans in an authoritarian state.

Moeller van den Bruck was born in Solingen on April 23, 1876. As a young man he moved to Paris to escape the crass materialism of Wilhelmian Germany. He became a self-made historian, and cultural critic, and was greatly influenced by the philosophy of Friedrich NIETZSCHE and the Frenchman Maurice Barrès. Moeller collaborated with a prominent Russian writer in a German translation of Dostoyevski, whose nationalistic and messianic interpretation of Russian history asserted that Moscow was a Third Rome. This contributed to a cult of Dostoyevski in Germany after WORLD WAR I and an interest in Germany in an eastward orientation and the creation of a new cultural order.

While living in foreign countries, Moeller rediscovered the individuality and distinctive quality of his German nationality. Two books written after his return to Germany reflect this discovery. In *The Prussian Style* (1915) he stressed the virile and hard qualities of Prussianism, which were reflected in its army, bureaucracy, the kings and in Immanuel KANT. This Spartan PRUSSIA was contrasted with the neoromantic decadence of the Wilhelmian age. In his second work, *The Rights of Young Nations* (1919), which he directed toward the American president, Woodrow Wilson, Moeller contrasted the youthful and vital Germans with the decadence of Western peoples, especially the French. The young nations, among which he included the United States, he thought had not yet acquired a definite style, and so their *Kultur* was dynamic and creative. Moeller disagreed with Oswald Spengler's notion that all peoples would be caught up in mass society and technical civilization, reflecting a decline in creativity. Moeller saw the Western victory in World War I as due to the youthful Americans and Russians. The Russian Revolution was interpreted as an expression of national mission directed against liberal and socialist internationalism. He also held that the Germans were a young people who had the vitality and ability to create a new society, and that a German type of socialism could reconcile the antagonisms of Western individualism and the collectivistic society of the Soviet Union.

Moeller had nothing but contempt for what he imagined as the decadent West with its philosophy of right and reason, its LIBERALISM and dull and unheroic life. And when the Revolution of 1918 failed to produce the utopia he dreamed of, he became the enemy of the middle-class capitalist WEIMAR REPUBLIC. His compelling ideas made him the leader of young enthusiasts, among the conservative revolutionaries and a leading political guide. Even Adolf HITLER met with him in 1922 and suggested that the two work together, admitting Moeller's leadership in reconstructing Germany while Hitler humbly volunteered to be the drummer boy.

Combining all of his prewar prejudices and political aspirations, Moeller published his best-known political work, *The Third Reich*, in 1923. In it he sought to present the way of salvation that conservative Germans sought out of the divisions and impotence they saw in the Weimar Republic. He predicted that a revolution would occur, but that it would come from the right not the left as in the past, and provide a breakthrough to a new Third Age. The German people, he asserted, would effect a national revolution instead of the international revolutions that had occurred in the Western nations. Moeller's idea of a Third Reich was spiritualistic, having messianic significance embodying the sense of mission for the Germans in history. It was not the restoration of a Germanic past but a projection of new Third Age in which *Reich, Staat,* and *Volk* would be merged in a new dynamic vitality. The new national unity that Moeller imagined was to be based on the people. The revolution that he called for was a fundamental transformation of all the antitheses in German life from different churches, classes, regions, and political parties to creating a new synthesis of national consciousness directed toward the creation of a new Reich. The book accidentally provided the National Socialist movement with one of its slogans and the National Socialist state with its historic name.

Moltke, Helmuth, Count von (the Elder) (Helmuth Karl Bernhard, Graf [Count] von Moltke) (1800–1891)

strategist of wars of German unification

Helmuth, Count von Moltke was born in Parchim, Mecklenburg, to an impoverished noble family, his father an army officer. Educated in the Royal Cadet Corps of Copenhagen, he transferred to the Prussian army as an infantry lieutenant. He spent little time in regimental duty, attended the Berlin War Academy between 1823 to 1826, and worked in the General Staff's topographical office from 1828 to 1831. He also served as an adviser to the Turkish army, served on various staffs in Coblenz, BERLIN, and Magdeburg, and finally as adjutant to Crown Prince Frederick William. On October 29, 1857, he became chief of the General Staff. During the DANISH WAR over Schleswig in 1864, which was mismanaged by another general, Moltke was promoted to a field commander. The king, WILLIAM I, now admired Moltke so much that he made him chief of the General Staff, the ultimate authority under the king in Prussian military affairs. In the Austro-Prussian War of 1866 Moltke directed the deployment of Prussian forces by telegraph, bringing a narrow victory over the Austrian infantry. Although Moltke wanted to pursue the Austrians to Vienna and administer a punitive peace, Otto von BISMARCK objected for diplomatic reasons. In the Franco-Prussian War Moltke deployed the Prussian 2nd Army by railroad for a defense on the RHINE, which turned into an invasion of France. Moltke attended the proclamation of the German Reich (January 18, 1871) followed quickly by the armistice, the Treaty of Frankfurt, and his promotion to field marshal.

Starting with a firm foundation in Carl von CLAUSEWITZ's principles of war, Moltke revolutionized warfare during the years 1857–71 and through his innovations contributed significantly to Prussia's victories between 1864 and 1871. The wars were preplanned and were rehearsed in realistic war games. Moltke developed complex timetables and mobilization plans, and logistical requirements were worked out prior to battle. He learned from his mistakes and improved his plans until perfected. Moltke, "the general on wheels," introduced such new technologies as the use of railroads to transport troops quickly to the battle front and the telegraph for rapid transmission of orders. He also was responsible for giving general-mission type commands, which gave commanders more freedom in achieving their objective. Other innovations included future war planning, risk assessments, worst case scenarios, orchestration of weapons systems, clear short orders, and topographical maps. The Prussian army in the Franco-Prussian War that used these innovations was 1 million men strong. His creative military mind created the model for 20th-century armies.

Moltke was a remarkable man whose many talents included map maker, courtier, master of languages, artist, and devoted husband.

Moltke, Helmuth James, Count von (Helmuth James, Graf [Count] von Moltke) (1907–1945)

Resistance leader

Helmuth James, Count von Moltke was the founder of the KREISAU CIRCLE and a major leader of the German RESISTANCE. He was not directly involved in the July 20 plot, but was nonetheless tried and executed.

Born on March 11, 1907, at Kreisau in Silesia, the country estate of his parents, a German father and an English-African mother who both were Christian Scientists, his ancestors included the great field marshal Helmuth von MOLTKE, who helped found the Second German Empire in 1871. His mother was responsible for his appreciation of democratic institutions. As a youth he was active in the German Youth Movement, was interested in social reform, but finally decided to become an international lawyer, a profession he practiced in BERLIN.

His conception of human freedom, dignity, rights, and justice made him an adversary of National Socialism. As individuals began to flee the regime, he provided legal assistance. His most important contribution to the Resistance was the founding of the Kreisau Circle, which brought together Germans who discussed plans for a new government to replace the Third Reich. He envisioned a new Germany based on Christian principles with equal justice, a new Europe with a common parliament, and an executive that would direct Europe's economy. What separated him from the military Resistance was their desire to eliminate Hitler and the Nazi regime as soon as possible.

At the beginning of the war he held the position of a legal expert on international law in the High Command. In this position he was better informed than others in the Resistance about the atrocities committed by the German forces on the Eastern Front. He considered the war in

Count von Moltke during the trial for the attempt on Adolf Hitler's life, 1944 *(Library of Congress)*

Poland as disgraceful and the "bestialities of the SS" frightful. He worried about the guilt that Germans would carry far into the future over the corpses piled high due to executions, starvation, and typhus killing prisoners and Jews. He predicted that the nation was bound to lose the war and would have to pay a terrible price for its crimes.

Moltke, like General Ludwig BECK and Colonel Hans Oster of the Oster Conspiracy, tried to warn the West of Hitler's plans. Professional and family relations abroad, particularly in Britain, gave him the opportunity to warn British politicians of Hitler's plans before the war. His efforts proved unsuccessful, just as in 1943 when he tried to speak with representatives of the Allied nations concerning the possibility of capitulation on the Western front. In December 1943 Moltke wrote a memorandum to President Franklin D. Roosevelt stating that Germany's defeat and occupation were necessary for "moral and political reasons" and that the demand for unconditional surrender was "justified." Western statesmen were understandably distrustful but mistaken about the intentions of those Germans opposed to Hitler as merely an "aristocratic clique." In January 1944 Moltke was arrested for trying to warn an associate of his pending arrest. During the trials associated with the July 20 plot he was accused of not reporting the activities of the Resistance. The real reason for his trial was his Christian beliefs and unconditional rejection of Nazi doctrines. Dying for his beliefs, he was executed on January 23, 1945, at Plötzensee Prison.

Moltke, Helmuth Johann von (the Younger) (1848–1916)

chief of General Staff at start of World War I

The nephew of the elder Moltke, Helmuth was born the son of a Prussian official. He obtained combat experience in the Franco-Prussian War, graduated from the War Academy in 1879, and then was promoted to the General Staff. Serving as an adjutant to his uncle, the younger Moltke became friends with the crown prince William. Later, when the crown prince became Kaiser WILLIAM II, Moltke became his adjutant. Between 1891 and 1904 he remained in BERLIN close to Kaiser William II and, upon the retirement of Count Alfred von Schlieffen, became his successor as chief of the General Staff, a position for which he was ill-suited. His interests really lay elsewhere, in the arts, for which he maintained a studio where he painted and played the cello.

Moltke was in charge of the large General Staff of some 600 officers, which had been organized into an effective bureaucracy controlling a multimillion-man army. Moltke also was part of a small group that advised the Kaiser and was the driving force behind German political and foreign policy. Unfortunately, along with many others he believed that a war would cleanse the country of the ills brought about by industrialization, LIBERALISM, and socialism. In their thinking it was a "now or never" opportunity to defeat Germany's enemies, which would not be the case in two years. Moltke knew that it would not be a short war as many expected, and he disguised his doubts about the possibility of ultimate victory in his briefings with Chancellor von BETHMANN HOLLWEG. In the complicated international crisis brought about by the assassination of the Austrian archduke in 1914, the alliance systems, war plans, the arms race, and ultra NATIONALISM, Moltke advised the Kaiser to declare war in August 1914. It is difficult to believe that Moltke lost communication with his army commanders during the retreat from the Marne. All the planning of the great General Staff now had no effect. Faced by this crisis Moltke suffered an emotional breakdown and was replaced on September 14. He was officially replaced some months later, was given a desk job, and died two years later.

Montgelas, Maximilian Joseph von (Maximilian Joseph, Graf [Count] von Montgelas) (1759–1838)

bureaucratic reformer

Maximilian Joseph von Montgelas was perhaps the greatest statesman and reformer in the history of modern BAVARIA. He developed a centralized administration for the new Bavarian state.

Born in Savoy in 1759, his ancestors were French-speaking aristocratic landowners, and his father fought for both the Habsburgs and the WITTELSBACHS. He attended schools in Nancy and Strasbourg, learned German in the 1780s, and entered the Bavarian bureaucracy. His breeding imparted to him the tastes and manners of a courtier. He engendered the hostility of Karl THEODOR when he became a member of the Illuminati (see FREEMASONRY), which made him transfer to the service of his presumptive heir, the duke of Zweibrücken, Maximilian Joseph. In 1799 Montgelas became Bavaria's first minister, in 1803 finance minister, and in 1807 interior minister. On Napoleon's advice King Maximilian I Joseph (1799–1825) issued a constitution in 1808 that provided basic rights and freedoms, religious toleration, and a centralized government. Although the constitution mentioned representative institutions (Montgelas had little use for them), the king did not establish them. A new constitution was issued, however, in 1818, which Montgelas helped draft but which called for an Assembly of Estates instead of a legislative body.

Montgelas belonged to a generation of leaders who were old enough to have had some experience prior to the French Revolution but were young enough to grasp the opportunities for change that the new age offered. Montgelas believed that a state required a stable set of institutions and a cohesive polity, which would be bound together by loyalty and self-interest. This he believed could best be accomplished by an enlightened centralized administration. The first step for reform of the state was not going to be a parliament, an institution of public participation, but a reform of the administrative apparatus. The state building that he accomplished was a bureaucratic achievement of administrative reorganization. Soon after 1799 he replaced regionally rooted administrative bodies with five ministries, which divided up the responsibilities of the entire state. Then, in place of the previously poorly paid court favorites, he established a corps of professionally trained administrators. As far as the Bavarian constitution was concerned, Montgelas intended it to provide the Bavarian people with a closer association with administrative authority.

King Maximilian I Joseph married a Protestant princess, and so assured religious toleration and protection to the Protestant churches. With Napoleon's territorial reorganization important Protestant lands in Franconia were added to Bavaria. In 1803 all the South German states passed edicts that affirmed their right to both the authority and the property of the church. Officials assumed control over bishoprics, abbeys, and cloisters, and monastic lands were sold and monks and nuns expelled. The independence of imperial cities such as AUGSBURG was eliminated. Count Montgelas also tried to reform education, attempting to foster toleration although the Bavarian people were strongly opposed. His experiment in interdenominational elementary education failed. In the universities some Protestant influence was achieved as Montgelas brought Schelling to Würzburg and Friedrich Heinrich Jacobi and Friedrich Thiersch to MUNICH. The secondary schools were reformed by Thiersch in the neohumanistic spirit of WEIMAR. In 1806 he even made HEGEL the director of the Gymnasium in NUREMBERG.

Moravian Brethren

One of the founders of the Moravian Brethren was Balthasar Hübmaier (1480–1528), who had been a scholar and popular preacher before the REFORMATION. He had been vice rector of the university in Ingolstadt by 1515 but left the academic world to become a parish priest in REGENSBURG in BAVARIA and Waldshut on the RHINE. After intense study of the New Testament and contact with the reformer Ulrich ZWINGLI, he rejected the traditional belief in the validity of infant baptism. He wrote on the merits of adult baptism, was arrested and tortured in Zurich, but then went on to vigorously promote Anabaptism in Nikolsburg in southern Moravia near the Austrian border. He vigorously espoused religious toleration, but what set him apart from other Anabaptist leaders was that he believed that the state had the right to use force in a righteous cause as in the contemporary war against the Turks. Other leaders like Hans

Hut from Augsburg believed that the second coming was imminent and advocated communal ownership of property and goods and nonresistance to secular authority.

After Bohemia came under the jurisdiction of the Habsburgs in 1526, the Anabaptists were persecuted as heretics. Hübmaier was burned at the stake, but the community moved to Austerlitz, where it established a communal settlement (Brüderhof). The Moravian settlements were saved from their factionalism by the arrival of Jakob Hutter in 1533 from the Tyrol, where he had been the chief pastor of the Anabaptists. Hutter reorganized the Moravian Brethren into tight-knit congregations with common ownership of all property. They became an economically viable, socially cohesive, and religiously active community. Even though Hutter was executed in 1536, the community became the most successful survivor of 16th-century ANABAPTISM. These Hutterites spread into Hungary, Transylvania, and Ukraine.

Moroccan crises (1905 and 1911)

Both Moroccan crises were prompted by the French expansion of imperial interests in Morocco. In 1904 the British and French settled some of their outstanding international conflicts. While the French government recognized a British protectorate in Egypt, the British recognized Morocco as a French sphere of influence and that the French could provide order in that North African province. After waiting a year before it protested, the German government did so in a violent manner. The emperor himself, WILLIAM II, interrupted a Mediterranean cruise to make a theatrical landing in Tangier, where he visited the sultan and promised German support for his independence. The German government demanded that the Anglo-French agreement be set aside. Chancellor von BÜLOW considered the German Moroccan policy to be a bluff and for whatever Germany could gain, whereas military leaders thought it might destroy the Entente. In fact, the upper echelons of the army were thinking in terms of preventive war, and with Russia paralyzed with revolution, the time was advantageous. Interestingly, the Kaiser was nervous about the whole affair and never wanted to go to Tangier in the first place. The Kaiser had no desire to go to war over Morocco. German policy, however, had no coherence.

At the time of the original intervention the German government had insisted on an international conference to settle the Moroccan issue. Before the conference met in ALGECIRAS in 1906, the French attitude stiffened and the British had become determined to support them in the original agreement. The Germans blustered their way through the conference and found that they were virtually isolated. What started out as a German diplomatic victory now ended in defeat with the French keeping what the British had agreed to. The crisis actually strengthened the Anglo-French Entente by encouraging the beginning of talks between their military staffs and stimulated a fear of encirclement as a potent factor in German politics.

Tensions again broke out in 1911. On the pretext of protecting foreigners from native disorders, the French government dispatched troops to Fez. It technically was a violation of the Algeciras Treaty. The German intervention in 1911 was the brainchild of the foreign minister Alfred Kiderlen-Wächter. He aggressively reacted to the French action by dispatching the gunboat *Panther* to the Moroccan port of AGADIR, presumably thinking that a display of strength would gain compensation for Germany. When the French were not frightened, Kiderlen-Wächter absurdly demanded the compensation of the French Congo in return for their gains in Morocco. This was rejected by the French, who thought the affair was a pretext for war. The British, on the other hand, feared the Germans wanted to establish a naval base in Morocco. Fortunately, the crisis was peacefully resolved by worthless French concessions in the Congo in return for German recognition of French rights in Morocco.

The crisis had three important consequences. It increased tensions between Germany and the Entente; it accelerated the arms race; and it encouraged in the German leaders in the belief that war was inevitable. The ability of the chancellor, BETHMANN HOLLWEG, to deal with the complications of European affairs was considerably reduced. The humiliation Germany suffered in Morocco made Bethmann Hollweg appear as a weakling in the eyes of soldiers, conservatives, and patriotic societies.

Munich

Munich is the capital of the state (LAND) of BAVARIA and Germany's third-largest city after BERLIN and HAMBURG. It is located on the Isar River about 50 kilometers north of the Alps. Its population is approximately 1.3 million, and less than one-third of its population has been born there. The city is famous as a center of art and learning and possesses many institutions of higher learning, including the University of Munich, the Technical University, Academies of Television, Music, and Cinema and many scientific institutes, not to mention theaters and museums. Its attractive architecture includes examples of Gothic, Renaissance, BAROQUE and neoclassical architecture. The city is also the headquarters of the Roman Catholic archbishop and Evangelical bishop, radio and television corporations, and the yearly celebration of Oktoberfest. Munich's principal industries include the production of BMW motor vehicles, precision engineering, optical and electrical equipment, machines, publishing, and the brewing of beer.

The history of Munich began with Duke Henry the Lion, of Bavaria and Saxony, who in 1157–58 diverted the old salt road from Reichenall to Salzburg to cross the Isar River on a new bridge located near a monastery. That is why the city is called München (Munich), and its coat of arms includes a little monk, "the Münchner Kindl." In 1158 at a meeting of the diet in AUGSBURG Emperor Frederick I decided between the competing claims of Bishop Otto I of Freising and Henry the Lion in favor of the latter. In 1180 the city came under the authority of Otto von Wittelsbach, and later under Ludwig the Severe (1253–94) Munich became the permanent residence of the WITTELSBACHS. The size of the town increased fivefold under Emperor Ludwig the Bavarian, which in 1319 led to the building of a new town wall and four gateways. In the 15th century Jörg Ganghofer built Munich's Frauenkirche in late Gothic style, whose twin domed towers are a Munich landmark. In 1506 Munich became the capital of the united duchy of Bavaria. In the 18th century the ruling branch of the Bavarian Wittelsbachs died out and was replaced by Karl THEODOR, elector of Bavaria from 1777–99. His reign was followed by Maximilian IV Joseph who became Bavaria's first king as Maximilian I Joseph from 1806 to 1825. Because of extensive poverty there was a need to provide food and work for the impoverished. Benjamin Thompson from the American colonies immigrated to Bavaria and provided the solution, split pea soup, which came to be called Rumford Suppe, a much improved addition to their potato diet. He was given the title of Count Rumsford, joined the civil service in 1784, reorganized the army, and founded workhouses.

Among the artists and architects of the 17th and 18th centuries are the two famous Asam brothers, Cosmas and Egid, who extensively applied their craft as painters, stucco workers, and master-builders in Bavaria. Some of their most important works can be found in the frescoes of the Trinity Church, the parish church of St. Anna im Lehel, the little palace of Maria Einsiedel in Thalkirche, the St. Johann Neopomuk church, commonly referred to as the Asamkirche (1733–46), and in the decoration of the Freising Cathedral.

King Maximilian I Josef was followed by his son LUDWIG I in 1825. Ludwig built Munich into a beautiful city with art and architecture. Under the architectural direction of Klenze, the king built many fine buildings, including the Alte Pinakothek, opened in 1836 with a collection of paintings from the 14th to the 18th century, and the Glypotothek and the Feldherrnhalle, the latter honoring famous Bavarian generals. He also widened the Ludwigstrasse into a fine boulevard with the Feldhernhalle at one end and the Siegestor at the other. The scandalous relationship between Ludwig and the dancer Lola Montez lost him his throne in 1848. His son MAXIMILIAN II, who succeeded him, fostered learning and built the Maximilianeum, where since 1949 both houses of the Bavarian parliament have met. The Senate has been closed since 2000 due to a popular referendum. The Neue Pinakothek, displaying the art of the 19th century, was opened in 1853. In 2002 a third Pinakothek opened, displaying modern art. In 1864 LUDWIG II became king. Although he hated Munich, the city continued to flourish as a center of the arts and undergo economic and social changes. During this time the composer Richard WAGNER played a role in Munich's opera, but his declining popularity forced him to retreat to BAYREUTH. Following the death of Ludwig, Prince Luitpold governed as regent for 25 years. Between 1867 and 1908 the new city hall (Neuen Rathaus) was constructed in the neo-Gothic style, overlooking the Marienplatz. Luitpold was then followed by his son Ludwig III in 1912 as prince-regent, crowned in 1913. Germany's defeat in WORLD WAR I brought the end to the Wittelsbach dynasty, the king dying in Hungarian exile in 1921. The NAZI PARTY had its origin in Munich, which became known as the capital of the Nazi movement. In November 1923 HITLER's attempt to take over the government (Hitler putsch) was suppressed. Munich also was the site of the MUNICH CONFERENCE (1938) at which the Western powers gave in to Hitler's demands for the Sudetenland of Czechoslovakia. During WORLD WAR II Munich was severely damaged but afterward quickly rebuilt.

Munich Crisis/Conference (1938)

On September 29, 1938, a conference took place in Munich, which was to decide on the future of Czechoslovakia. HITLER, Mussolini, Neville Chamberlain, and Edouard Daladier agreed that the Germans could take over the Sudetenland of Czechoslovakia. Neither the Czechoslovakian nor Soviet governments were represented at the conference. Hitler had to abandon his plan for a war to destroy Czechoslovakia. It proved that neither Britain, nor France, nor the Soviet Union would come to the aid of Czechoslovakia.

After his success in annexing AUSTRIA, Hitler lost no time in turning his attention to the destruction of Czechoslovakia. Out of all the successor states of the Habsburg Empire Czechoslovakia was the only stable parliamentary democracy and had a well-balanced economy. The peace treaties had placed 3 million Germans and thousands of Poles and Hungarians within its boundaries. For a time there was harmony between the Germans and the Czechs until the DEPRESSION came, when relations turned sour due to government hiring practices that favored the Czechs. Konrad Henlein, a pro-NAZI PARTY leader, demanded increased political and cultural autonomy and also worked for the annexation of the areas of the Sudeten Germans into Germany. A diplomatic crisis emerged as Hitler used Henlein to provoke violence and escalating demands in spring and summer 1938. At first the Czechs resisted, secure in the knowledge that their defensive alliances with France and the Soviet Union would protect them if attacked by Germany. In September 1938 Hitler demanded that the Sudeten Germans be given the right of self-determination under the threat of war. The Czechs resisted, and war seemed inevitable.

APPEASEMENT, however, had sunk its roots deeply into British foreign policy. Lord Halifax had already promised Hitler that peaceful change in Eastern Europe would be tolerated by England. To Neville Chamberlain, the prime minister, the prospect of war was unthinkable. Fearing that the Sudeten crisis might escalate into a general European war, Chamberlain conferred with Hitler at his mountainous retreat in Berchtesdgaden on September 15, 1938. At that meeting they agreed on a peaceful cession of the Sudeten area to Germany. Later, Chamberlain worked out a deal with the French over ceding the Sudetenland to Germany and insisted the Czechoslovak government accept it. The Czechs still resisted, and Europe again appeared on the brink of war. Chamberlain met with Hitler a second time at Godesberg and again on September 22, but their meeting ended in an impasse, which in turn led to a summit conference at Munich on September 29–30, 1938.

The meeting in Munich involved Germany, Italy, France, and Great Britain and was held in the national headquarters of the Nazi Party. Without consulting either the Czechs or the Russians, the participants accepted a "compromise" proposal offered by Mussolini as a diplomatic solution to the Sudeten crisis. In reality Mussolini's proposal contained Hitler's latest demands. By the compromise Czechoslovakia was forced to yield the Sudeten areas to Germany without a plebiscite. Czechoslovakia was in a no-win situation, because her ally France would refuse to honor her treaty obligations. If Czechoslovakia accepted the so-called compromise, then the four participating states would guarantee the territorial integrity of what remained of Czechoslovakia. In effect, the Czechs were sold out in order to keep peace. Chamberlain returned to a worried England and announced that he had achieved "peace in our time."

Hitler got only part of what he wanted at the Munich Conference. He resented Chamberlain's success in maneuvering him into a peaceful solution, and he had to forgo the war he really had wanted with Czechoslovakia. He decided not to make the same mistakes over Poland and avoided the possibility of negotiation. Nonetheless, a second Czech crisis occurred in March 1939, when Hitler threatened a military invasion if the Czech leaders did not agree to be placed under German "protection." During the last days of his life in the Berlin bunker, Hitler reconsidered the causes of his failure and concluded that going to war in September 1938 would have led to a much more favorable outcome.

Münster Rebellion (February 1534–June 1535)

The rebellion occurred as a result of a group of radical Anabaptists who took control of the city of Münster and attempted to establish a New Jerusalem. The city became a haven for Anabaptists from northern Germany and the Netherlands. Their rule became radicalized under John of Leyden, who was appointed king, and under his rule a primitive communism and polygamy were practiced. As a result of the rebellion ANABAPTISM was no longer seen just as a heresy and religious problem but also as a menace to society.

The causes of the revolt were complex. For years before 1534 the city had been tottering on the brink of an upheaval. The city was torn apart by three groups who competed for power: the prince-bishop, Franz of Waldeck; the city council, which was predominantly Lutheran; and the guilds and lower classes that came under the influence of Anabaptism. Originally, the Lutherans, Zwinglians, and Anabaptists had cooperated in overthrowing the power of the bishop who had to leave the city in 1531. The situation changed radically when the Dutch Anabaptists under the leadership of John Matthys and John of Leyden (Jan Beukels), a onetime tailor, came to the city. In February 1534 the Anabaptists seized control of the city and elected one of them as mayor. Matthys, who was the true leader, insisted on universal baptism, ordering that only those people who adhered to Anabaptism could remain and Catholics and Lutherans had to leave under threat of death. A new heaven on earth was declared under the kingship of John of Leyden, who eliminated all human institutions, including family and property. Münster became the symbol of a New Jerusalem for persecuted Anabaptists throughout northern Germany.

After a year of unsuccessful fighting against the city, Bishop Waldeck was finally joined by the rulers of Cologne, Cleves, SAXONY, and HESSE, who had religious differences but joined in conquering the city. As the rebellion deteriorated, Matthys was killed before the walls of the city, after which power devolved to John of Leyden, who carried on excesses and was appointed king, the new David who would lead God's chosen people. He dissolved the city council, establishing a strict bureaucracy under 12 elders representing the tribes of Israel. Certain sins such as blasphemy, reviling parents, disobeying a master, adultery, spreading scandal, and even complaining were made punishable by death. Polygamy was introduced and defended as a necessity as there were four times as many women as men, and the purpose of marriage was to be fruitful. In reality John ruled as a secular ruler, himself taking 16 wives and engaging in pompous ceremonies; opposition to his rule was ruthlessly suppressed. Furthermore, a primitive communism was introduced. Finally on June 25, 1535, the gates of the city were opened to Bishop Waldeck's mercenaries, and King John and several of his leaders were brutally executed.

Napoleonic Wars (1803–1815)

The Napoleonic Wars were a continuation of the wars of the French Revolution, wars that lasted to the Peace of Amiens (1792–1802). The wars were a series of campaigns by Napoleon against four allied coalitions beginning in 1803 and ending with the Battle of Waterloo in 1815.

While Napoleon used the period of peace after 1802 to consolidate his power at home, Britain declared war and formed the Third Coalition in 1804, which included Austria, Russia, and Sweden. However, Napoleon tried to make Prussia an ally by offering Frederick William III Hanover, which he refused. Before the coalition could coordinate its forces, Napoleon defeated the Austrians at Ulm (1805) and an Austro-Russian army at the Battle of Austerlitz (1805). The main coalition victory was Lord Nelson's at the Battle of Trafalgar (1805). To defeat the Austrians at Ulm, Napoleon had marched through Prussian Ansbach, which moved Frederick William to join the coalition. The Prussian king demanded of Napoleon the independence of Germany as well as French concessions in Italy in favor of Austria. Because of his victory at Austerlitz, Napoleon imposed his own terms on Austria in the Treaty of Pressburg and on Prussia in the Treaty of Schönbrunn. In these treaties Napoleon began his reorganization of Central Europe. With Pressburg Austria was forced to cede Venice to Napoleon, the Tyrol and Vorarlberg as well as ecclesiastical principalities to the new state of Bavaria, and to hand over German territories to the kingdom of Württemberg and to Baden. At Schönbrunn Napoleon forced Prussia to accept Hanover and close its northern ports to British shipping, trying to force Prussia into war against Britain. Napoleon also created the Confederation of the Rhine in 1806 and forced it to support Napoleon's foreign policy and military command. The Holy Roman Empire was dissolved, and the emperor renounced his title and became Francis I of Austria.

War broke out again in 1806. Napoleon provoked Prussia into joining the Fourth Coalition allied with Russia and Saxony. Prussia was quickly defeated in October 1806 at the Battles of Jena and Auerstadt, which were followed by the surrender of a great number of fortresses. On October 25, 1806, Napoleon entered Berlin and decreed the Continental System, a blockade against Britain. It was economic warfare intended to coerce the rest of Europe into not trading with Britain. After the defeat of Friedland (1807) Russia withdrew from the war, and Czar Alexander met Napoleon on a raft in the Niemen River to decide on the Treaty of Tilsit and temporarily made Russia an ally against Britain. Prussia had to cede its territory west of the Elbe River to the new kingdom of Westphalia, in which Napoleon installed his brother Jérome as king. Prussian territories in Poland were turned into the Grand Duchy of Warsaw, which was given to the duke of Saxony. Prussia was reduced to half its size.

The year 1808 marked the high point of French rule in Europe. There were, however, signs of revolt, especially in Spain, where Napoleon's brother Joseph was deposed as king of Spain during the Peninsular War, which lasted until 1814 and cost 300,000 French lives. Revolts also occurred in the Tyrol, in Hesse, and in Stralsund, with an Austrian declaration of war in April 1809. Napoleon moved quickly to defeat Austria, which now had become a member of the Fifth Coalition. Napoleon suffered his first defeat at the battle of Aspern, but was ultimately victorious at the battle of Wagram (July 6, 1809). Severe terms were meted out to Austria at the Treaty of Vienna, comparable to those imposed on Prussia with the Treaty of Tilsit. Austria had to give Galicia to Russia, and the Grand Duchy and the Austrian possessions on the Adriatic were annexed by France, while the Tyrol and Salzburg went to Bavaria.

The turning point of the Napoleonic Wars came with the disastrous invasion of Russia and the crippling retreat of Napoleon's Grand Army in 1812. Napoleon went off to Moscow with 600,000 troops, of which about 200,000 were German. The final months of the Russian campaign were the turning point toward a Prussian recovery and the beginning of the WARS OF LIBERATION (1813–15). The initiative in the Wars of Liberation came from Baron Karl vom und zum STEIN and General Yorck with the Convention of Tauroggen (December 1812) when Yorck promised the czar the neutrality of Prussian troops. On March 17, 1813, Prussia declared war on France after Prussia had undergone extensive reforms under the leadership of Gerhard von Scharnhorst, Neithardt von GNEISENAU, Carl von CLAUSEWITZ, Karl von HARDENBERG, and Wilhelm von HUMBOLDT. For the time being not all Germans heard the call to rise up against Napoleon, as the Confederation of the Rhine remained loyal to him. Britain engineered the sixth and final coalition, which included Prussia, Russia, Sweden, and, after August 1813, Austria. Earlier in May, Napoleon had recaptured DRESDEN and won the battle at Bautzen. A second battle was fought at Dresden (August 1813), which was the last victory Napoleon would ever win in Germany. Now allied victories predominated, and the decisive battle of this last phase of the Napoleonic Wars was fought at LEIPZIG (October 1813), which came to be known as the Battle of Nations. After some negotiations France was invaded during the winter, and Paris surrendered on March 30, 1814. The First Treaty of Paris (May 30, 1814) terminated the war, and Louis XVIII was installed as king. While the coalition was negotiating at the CONGRESS OF VIENNA, Napoleon returned from exile in Elba, entered Paris, and prepared for a new campaign. War was renewed during Napoleon's "Hundred Days," but his army was decisively defeated at the Battle of Waterloo (June 16–18, 1815) by the armies of the duke of Wellington and the Prussian general Blücher. Napoleon abdicated a second time and was exiled to the island of St. Helena. In the Second Treaty of Paris (November 20, 1815) France was reduced to its territories of 1790. On the day the treaty was signed, the Great Powers formed the QUADRUPLE ALLIANCE, which tried to keep the peace after 1815.

National Assembly (1919)

The National Constituent Assembly was convened on February 6, 1919, in the city of WEIMAR, which was distant from the revolutionary events that had taken place in BERLIN. It accomplished three tasks: creating a legal government, making peace with the Allies, and writing a constitution.

The elimination of the revolutionary threats to the provisional government in Berlin made it possible to hold elections for a National Assembly. The decision on the date for the elections on January 19, 1919, was made by the First National Congress of Soldiers and Workers Councils, which met in Berlin in December. The Central Council of the Workers' and Soldiers' Councils resigned and handed over its authority to the assembly. The assembly was opened on February 11 in the city of Weimar, which was symbolically important as the residence of Germany's great poet, GOETHE. The delegates began to create a legal government by electing Friedrich EBERT the "President of the Reich" and authorized him to form a cabinet. The prime minister was Philip Scheidemann. The composition of the assembly showed that the nonsocialist forces in the country had recovered from the paralysis that had affected them in November and December. Of 423 deputies only 187 were Socialists (165 Majority, SPD); 22 Independents (USPD). The middle-class Catholic CENTER PARTY won 91 seats, and the new German Democratic Party (DDP), which was formed by the prewar Progressives, won 75 seats; 44 of the deputies were Nationalists (DNVP); and the new party formed by Gustav STRESEMANN, the GERMAN PEOPLE'S PARTY had 19 seats. It was clear that a coalition government had to be formed in which half of the ministers were Majority Socialists and the other half were from the Center and Democratic Parties. This constituted the Weimar Coalition, which proved to be the most loyal support of the WEIMAR REPUBLIC.

As early as November 15, 1918, the people's commissars (CPP) had appointed Hugo PREUSS secretary of the interior. Preuss was a distinguished scholar of constitutional law and a member of the DDP. Preuss had conducted conferences with officials and professors about the nature of a new constitution, and he wanted to build on the foundation of the principles of the 1848 FRANKFURT PARLIAMENT. The chief questions debated were the degree of centralization, the types of governments to be established on the local and state levels, the future of Prussia, and the powers of the presidency. At the insistence of the scholar Max WEBER, Preuss adopted the institution of a popularly elected president to balance the power of a parliamentary government. The draft constitution that emerged from all the various deliberations was debated by a constitutional committee of the National Assembly. Most of the deliberations were held in a cooperative spirit, and the constitution was certainly not the product of a single philosophy. Preuss's draft envisioned a parliamentary democracy modeled on Great Britain and France. Universal suffrage and a system of proportional representation guaranteed a representative system. What did change was Preuss's concept of a ceremonial president with a term of seven years. While Preuss limited the president's power to nominate the prime minister, the assembly gave the president emergency authority under Article 48. Preuss also had attempted far-reaching divisions of Germany's federal structure, dividing up Prussia into a number of states. The assembly disagreed, and Prussia remained intact. The new constitution was finally proclaimed to the German people on August 14, 1919.

Concluding peace was actually more difficult for the assembly. The Germans were informed of the treaty on May 7, 1919. Whether to accept or reject the terms of the dictated peace treaty was one of the biggest challenges facing the assembly. A passionate debate raged over the peace terms, which led to the resignation of the Scheidemann government. It was replaced by a new one under Gustav Bauer, and two of its members signed the treaty.

Another issue that aroused deep-seated emotions was that of the colors of a national flag. Perhaps one-fourth of the population were the political "outs" who favored retaining the imperial colors of white, red, and black. These were the conservatives, while the democratic-oriented "ins" favored the colors of the REVOLUTION OF 1848, black, red, and gold. The assembly eventually chose the latter.

National Democratic Party
(NPD)

The National Democratic Party was a political party of the far right in the FEDERAL REPUBLIC, a party that was founded in 1964. It was formed out a fusion of small rightist parties such as the neo-Nazi German Reich Party (DRP). The NPD cultivated a conservative image even though it had 12 former Nazis on its executive committee. Friedrich Thielen, leader of the rightist German Party, became the chairman. In 1965 the NPD had a membership of fewer than 14,000 members and received only 2 percent of the vote in the federal BUNDESTAG elections during that same year. Nevertheless, between 1966 and 1969 in 11 regional state elections the party won seats in seven legislatures. Due to the economic downturn in the late 1960s and the CDU/CSU formation of the grand coalition with the despised SPD, the votes for the NPD could be interpreted as a protest vote. In the federal elections of 1969 the party vote grew to 1.4 million votes, 4.3 percent of the total but short of the 5 percent minimum to be seated in the Bundestag.

The emergence of the NPD was not a reflection of a resurgent neo-Nazism as has been publicized in the United States. Adolf von Thadden, who became the party chairman in 1967, denied that he was neo-Nazi, but did protest that Germans were made to feel guilty for WORLD WAR II and that the gas chambers were built by American soldiers to place guilt on the Germans. The rise in the protest vote, however, was due primarily to an ailing economy, especially in the coal and steel industries, which were undergoing restructuring and created unemployment. In addition to the industrial workers there were the self-employed and farmers who blamed the governing parties for not solving the economic crisis. Also voting for the NPD were those conservatives and neo-Nazis who were outraged at the ongoing student revolt of the late 1960s. On the positive side these voters were also attracted to the ultranationalism of the party and its commitment to reunification. The support for the party, however, declined in the 1970s, when the economy recovered. The NPD's membership fell from 28,000 in 1969 to 6,000 in 1982, and its electoral support fell to less than 1 percent. After unification in the 1990s the party revived in the former East German states, where poverty and political disaffection became significant.

nationalism (German)

In the 18th century national loyalties were confined entirely to the cultural field. National pride centered on the special contribution that German philosophy and literature were making to the advancement of humanity as a whole. Germany, it was believed, was creating spiritual ideals, while France and Britain were engaged in political struggles. Initially, the French Revolution did not change this attitude. The early stages of the revolution found approval, but no one of importance demanded the same citizen rights for Germans. German thinkers viewed the Reign of Terror and the foreign wars as manifestations of the rationalism of the French ENLIGHTENMENT. Up until 1805 the educated classes remained cosmopolitan, but that changed with the defeat of AUSTRIA and PRUSSIA and the dissolution of the HOLY ROMAN EMPIRE.

In reaction to French nationalism and military occupation the national identity of the German people began to be emphasized. One of the new voices was Johann Gottlieb FICHTE, who in 1807–08 delivered his *Speeches to the German Nation* in BERLIN. Fichte preached a new conception of nationality in which the human mind could realize itself. He called upon his countrymen to resist French domination and to defend their nationhood. Yet, even here he still had a cosmopolitan vision of the role of Germans whose culture, he believed, could serve as a model for a future culture of humanity. In contrast to England and France, German national feeling did not develop in a political mold, but was concerned mainly with how the collective national will might be realized and safeguarded. German nationalism emphasized cultural individuality, which involved the peculiarities of language, literature, and religion, rather than political self-determination by the individuals of the state to which they belong.

German nationalism was a child of ROMANTICISM. Under the influence of romanticism, nationalism postulated that the collective past experience of an ethnic population was a guide to its future. That meant that each nation had a historic destiny that could be recognized through the study of history. German romantic nationalists became fascinated with the Middle Ages and the imagined glorious exploits of the German past. They saw the past Holy Roman Empire that had disappeared under Napoleon as a symbol of a great German future. They thought that a nationally unified Germany would once again occupy all or most of the territory of what had been the Holy Roman Empire. As dissatisfaction grew toward the repressive policies of the Restoration and with the recognition that economic expansion was fostered by political unity and the common market of a ZOLLVEREIN, support for a nation-state grew. The majority of German radicals in the period before the REVOLUTION OF 1848 used the concept of nationalism as a rallying cry for a movement to overthrow the despotic German rulers. The radicals emphasized that the people had common rights that could be realized only in a nation-state. The moderate liberals who were mostly in northern Germany, however, emphasized the role of history, which tied them closely to the traditional German states. As the agitation for national unity grew in the 1840s, they favored a federal state and were not as critical as the southerners of the monarchical and militaristic traditions of Prussia. By 1847 there was evidence that liberals throughout Germany were open to cooperation to advance national unity. These nationalistic sentiments were primarily a political ideology of the urban and educated MIDDLE CLASS. Nationalism at this time found little support from the rural peasantry or aristocratic elites. In fact, to most conservatives nationalism was a revolutionary and subversive force.

Nationalism became a popular force during the Revolution of 1848. It became a means of overcoming many of the centrifugal tendencies that stemmed from the regional and social divisions of the German people. The ideal of national unity brought about the political compromise between liberals and democrats, which created the majority in the FRANKFURT PARLIAMENT that voted for the constitution of March 28, 1849. The ideal of national unification even overshadowed the ideal of freedom.

Two important factors that stimulated the revival of national sentiment after 1848 was the succession of WILLIAM to the throne of Prussia in 1861 and the success of the unification movement in Italy. Germany and Italy were the two great European nations aspiring to unity at that time, and there was much in common between them. The nationalism of the period was mainly concerned with achieving national unification under Prussian leadership and was supported by liberals and progressives. German unification, however, was largely the work of Otto von BISMARCK and William I, neither of whom were nationalists and both wanted to make Prussia the dominant state in Germany. German unification was therefore the culmination of Prussian history and not the product of German nationalism.

Once IMPERIAL GERMANY had been established, the ideology of nationalism grew and was transformed by romantic and folkish (völkish) ideas, which stressed domestic and foreign threats to the nation. The search for un-German behaviors went hand in hand with radical nationalism and in one area merged with a biological ANTI-SEMITISM. A growing ethnocentrism and intolerance afflicted the nation, which was observable in regard to the treatment of its Polish minority. The PAN-GERMAN LEAGUE reflected this intolerance in its policy of uniting the German-speaking Germans of Eastern Europe. An imperialist ideology also developed disguised as a German cultural mission. The growth of MILITARISM, navalism, and imperialism in associations such as the Navy League, the German Army League, and the Colonial Society, which appealed to the nationalist-liberal middle class, also stimulated the growth of an aggressive nationalism. Nationalism had now become the new secular religion and was promoted through the educational system and public festivals.

Nationalism was one of the causes of WORLD WAR I, but also was extremely intensified by it. War propaganda emphasized nationalism, soldiers fought and were supposed to die for the nation, and imperialist ambitions sought to justify the costs and sacrifices of the war. The loss of the war was a nationalist humiliation, and the war-guilt clause of the TREATY OF VERSAILLES stimulated a nationalism of revenge. Returning soldiers fueled the resentments that focused on the liberal WEIMAR REPUBLIC as a foreign imposition.

The National Socialism of Adolf HITLER was an amalgam of various strands of German nationalism. Hitler promised an integrated utopian nationalist community, which satisfied the desire for national unity, and an end to the bitter divisions that plagued German society. Nazism was the manifestation of the most radical racist form of nationalism. Based on racist nationalism, Hitler launched WORLD WAR II in order to create an empire in which the German people could thrive with new LEBENSRAUM. The loss of the war brought a repudiation of the destructive nationalism and forced a reassessment of the role of nationalism in German history. There was a widespread acceptance of Germany's postwar division, while the loss of national identity was mainly the concern of a small group of intellectuals.

National Liberal Party

The National Liberal Party was the strongest party during the founding years (*Gründerzeit*) of IMPERIAL GERMANY, and supported the policies of Otto von BISMARCK up to 1878.

The National Liberal Party was an outgrowth of the National Association and was founded in 1867 as a result of a split within the PROGRESSIVE PARTY over the support of Bismarck's constitution for the NORTH GERMAN CONFEDERATION. Some of those who left the Progressive Party to form the National Liberal Party were Eduard Lasker, Max von Forckenbeck, Hans Viktor von Unruh, and others. The members of the party came from the MIDDLE CLASS, those with property and education who were Protestant and non-Prussian. The new National Liberals were the former members of the left and center of the Progressive Party who had come to the conclusion that Bismarck was achieving their goals of national unity and economic power. They still stood for freedom and unity, were willing to fight against particularism, and were champions of state centralization. This group demanded that the government support education and property, pursue a favorable fiscal policy, acquire overseas colonies as a means of expanding the German market, and impose high tariffs on the import of industrial goods to protect new German industries. The new party also agreed to support the demands of the aristocratic landed JUNKERS, who wanted high tariffs on the import of grain.

The National Liberal Party was split into two groups and lacked homogeneity. It had a conservative faction that harbored extreme nationalists such as Heinrich von TREITSCHKE, and a liberal faction that included the German Jew Eduard LASKER. Lasker was the leader of the left wing of the party, which advocated the basic rights of freedom and opposition to the government. Bismarck hated him. On the right wing was the leader Rudolf BENNIGSEN, who was the former president of the National Association, but who lacked the leadership ability to hold the party together. With these divisions the party could not be called a government party but rather a party of Bismarck since it did support him on the big issues. The party was strongly anticlerical and supported Bismarck's KULTURKAMPF against the Catholics. Nonetheless, it broke with Bismarck over his refusal to allow two more liberals into the cabinet along with Bennigsen and over the tariff policy of 1878.

In the elections of 1871 the National Liberal Party won the greatest number of seats (125) in the Parliament (REICHSTAG), to which it added another 30 in the elections of 1874. Its electoral strength declined to 128 in the elections of 1877 and to 99 in 1879. Its electoral support came from national, rather than from liberal groups. By 1912 the party received less than 14 percent of the vote. The party had split in 1880, with the rump of the party coming to terms with Bismarck. The reorganized party represented the interests of big business, which benefited from Bismarck's pro-tariff and anti-socialist policies. The left wing joined with other parties and continued its support for free trade.

naturalism

German writers after 1880 were aware that social conditions were changing. They began to pay attention to the problems of the working class and the degeneration of the MIDDLE CLASS, and to question traditional values. As these avant-garde writers searched for a new style, it had already been developed by foreign authors, among them: Leo Tolstoi and Fyodor Dostoyevsky, August Strindberg and Henrik Ibsen, Émile Zola with his novels that applied the scientific method to examining the horrible conditions in slums, as well as John Stuart Mill and Charles Darwin. The social plays of Ibsen had a powerful influence on the German avant-garde in the 1880s, especially *Ghosts* because of its discussion of the taboo subject of syphilis and heredity. As German writers took up the new style, they demanded that reality be rendered without embellishments and with scientific objectivity. Around 1885 theoretical tracts and periodicals begun to advocate naturalism. The movement crested in the early 1890s, then gradually declined, probably due to the monotony of its themes and limited style.

Naturalism was an extreme form of REALISM, which described slums, miserable lives, capitalism, and social problems. The writers took up the battle for emancipation where the earlier movements of storm and stress and YOUNG GERMANY had left off. The naturalists dwelt on the hypocrisy of the middle class and the struggle between social classes, and emphasized the influence of heredity and environment. No lyrical language was used; in fact, the authors often employed the vulgar language and dialects of the common people. Emotionally, the novels were depressing and militantly radical. Lengthy explanations stressed the importance of the environment in the stories. The characters were fixed, and their tragic situations appeared to be unsolvable.

The aims of the new literature were explained in two works of Arno Holz (1853–1929), one of which was *Art, Its Nature, and Laws* (1891). Along with Johannes Schlaf, Holz was an early stimulator of the movement. Together they published *Papa Hamlet* (1889), which recorded the minutest details of events—a method that came to be known as *Sekundenstil*. The most famous representative of the movement was Gerhart HAUPTMANN (1862–1946), especially as a playwright. Among his naturalist works were *Before Dawn* (1889) and *The Weavers* (1892). *Before Dawn* is a story of an alcohol-dominated family whose only decent member commits suicide; it made Hauptmann the leader of the school. *The Weavers* (1892) was acclaimed as the first socialist drama in German literature, recounting the sufferings of the Silesian weavers. Another naturalist was Hermann Sudermann (1857–1928), who was immensely popular and made good use of clever and sound dramatic technique. His celebrated drama *Magda* (1893) shows the bitter conflict between a Prussian father and an emancipated daughter. Richard Dehmel (1863–1920) was a lyric poet who wrestled with the conflict of sex and life. His best-known work is *Two Human Beings* (1903), about the relationship between man and woman. Clara Viebig (1860–1952) was one of the outstanding women writers of the early 20th century. She blended a naturalist description of the people with the regionalism of the Rhineland and the Polish borderlands.

Naumann, Friedrich (1860–1919)
pastor, journalist, and politician

Friedrich Naumann was a prophet of German LIBERALISM. As a critic of the liberalism of his day he preached the need for infusing social concerns into liberalism and creating a bridge to the working class. Early on he perceived the discrepancy between the agrarian nature of Imperial political institutions and the modern German industrial economy. He had a profound influence on the WEIMAR CONSTITUTION and political movements during the republic.

Naumann was a Protestant pastor's son and as a pastor himself developed a strong interest in the social question, which was influenced by the Christian social teachings of the court preacher Adolf STÖCKER, then by Marxism, and finally by such German economists as Max WEBER and Lujo Brentano. Gifted as a popular speaker and able to attract a wide audience, he urged better understanding between the social classes, with which the leadership of the Protestant churches did not sympathize and which intimidated many pastors into silence. As early as 1890 Naumann began to advocate the need to add social concerns into middle-class liberalism. In 1896 Naumann founded the National Social Association as an independent liberal party primarily concerned with social problems, but it failed at the polls. Then he joined the PROGRESSIVE PARTY (Progressive Association: Freisinnige Vereinigung) and after the death of Eugen Richter (1838–96) became the party's leader. In 1910 he cofounded the Progressive People's Party (Fortschrittliche Volkspartei, FVP). His hopes for the Kaiser's government were expressed in *Democracy and Empire* (1900), wherein a reformed and liberalized monarchy might be combined with genuine parliamentary democracy and social welfare. The new social conditions produced by industrialization required some modifications in the principles of classical liberalism. His motives, however, like those of Max Weber, were defective in their lack of concern for individual rights but were mainly intended to strengthen the German nation-state; one way to do that was to win over the workers. Kaiser WILLIAM II and the powerful ARISTOCRACY had ceased to be adequate defenders of Germany as a world power.

Naumann and the left-wing liberals in the Progressive Party joined the chorus of national support for naval armaments and imperialist expansion, believing that *nationalism* and *imperialism* would wean workers away from socialism. During WORLD WAR I, however, he opposed the radical annexationists who attacked Chancellor Theobald von BETHMANN HOLLWEG (1856–1921). During the last years of the war he spoke out in favor of the reform of the PRUSSIAN THREE CLASS VOTING SYSTEM, but argued that it would be a way to expand support for the monarchy and the war effort. In 1917 he founded a school for politics, later known as the Academy (Hochschule) for Politics in BERLIN.

Of greater consequence was his participation in the establishment in 1918 of the GERMAN DEMOCRATIC PARTY (DDP), which the leaders of the former Progressive Party founded. In 1919 the DDP became the third-largest party in the country with 75 seats in the NATIONAL ASSEMBLY, but it declined thereafter. Naumann led the party representatives in the National Assembly, was elected national party chairman in July 1919 but unfortunately died shortly thereafter.

Navy (Imperial to cold war)

With the founding of the Second Empire in 1871, Germany began to build a naval fleet. In 1872 the new chief of the Admiralty, Albrecht von Stosch, embarked on a 10-year building program that emphasized frigates, gunboats, torpedo boats, and coastal defense should there be a two-front war with France and Russia. In 1888 things changed when WILLIAM II ascended the Imperial throne. Soon he became an advocate of a battleship fleet, which was championed by the American admiral Alfred Thayer Mahan. Then in 1897 Admiral Alfred von TIRPITZ was appointed state secretary of the Navy Office. He was to lay the foundation for a fleet that would be one of the world's largest, with 60 battleships or battle cruisers. Tirpitz also believed in the "risk theory," by which he thought that Great Britain would be unlikely to risk its naval supremacy in a conflict with Germany.

Once WORLD WAR I broke out, it was clear that Britain was determined to maintain its naval supremacy. On the German side William II decided to withhold the battle fleet to use it as a bargaining chip in peace negotiations. In 1915, 1916, and 1917 the High Command decided to place its hopes on unrestricted submarine warfare. The failure of the submarine campaign in 1918 plus the entry of the United States led to a collapse of the Empire and the surrender of the High Seas Fleet to the Allies.

As the TREATY OF VERSAILLES placed restrictions on Germany's navy, it was to have a limited defensive role with six antiquated battleships, six light cruisers, and 12 destroyers. The REICHSTAG voted for six light cruisers and three pocket battleships, which was to give Germany an advantage in a conflict with Poland. Even before HITLER came to power, the Germans had built a revolutionary new warship, the "pocket battleship" (*Panzerschiff*), the first named the *Deutschland*. It was a long-range raider the size of a cruiser with the firepower of a battleship.

After Hitler came to power, he denounced the Versailles Treaty, signed the ANGLO-GERMAN NAVAL TREATY IN 1935, and began to rebuild the German navy. Erich Raeder, who was commander in chief of the navy, had convinced Hitler of the importance of naval expansion in combination with his plans to obtain continental LEBENSRAUM. Although a major expansion of the navy was included in the Z Plan, it was never fully completed. Nevertheless, at the beginning of the war Nazi Germany already had a powerful fleet, including two battle cruisers, *Scharnhorst* and *Gneisenau;* two battleships, *Bismarck* and *Tirpitz;* three heavy cruisers, *Admiral Hipper, Blücher,* and *Prinz Eugen;* three light cruisers, *Leipzig, Nürnberg,* and *Königsberg;* and numerous destroyers, torpedo boats, and U-boats. At the beginning of the war the raiders attacked commerce, disguising themselves and confusing the Royal Navy. Perhaps the most dramatic cruiser was the *Graf Spee,* which had sunk nine ships in the South Atlantic but was in turn sunk by three British warships in the Battle of the River Platte. By May 1941 the new battleship, *Bismarck,* went to sea and presented a formidable challenge to the Royal Navy. In the early part of the war the U-boats sank a great amount of tonnage, and after 1942 the German navy had come to rely mainly on the submarine fleet. On January 30, 1943, the submarine advocate Karl Dönitz (1891–1980) replaced Raeder as naval chief. With Allied dominance of the air and sea, the days of the German surface fleet were numbered. The *Scharnhorst,* which had been the mainstay of the fleet, was sunk late in 1943, and the *Tirpitz* sunk at the end of 1944, which restricted the navy to the Baltic. The last service that the navy provided was the evacuation of soldiers and refugees from the advancing Red Army.

During the cold war both West and East Germany wanted to protect the Baltic flank of their respective alliances, NATO and the WARSAW PACT. The navies of both sides were configured in frigates, missile boats, and minesweepers. But the FEDERAL REPUBLIC's navy had an extra mission to keep the North Atlantic sea lanes open, so they deployed submarines and destroyers. With reunification the East German navy was absorbed by West Germany and its personnel dismissed.

Navy League
(Flottenverein)

The Navy League was one of a number of radical right-wing pressure groups that flourished in Germany before WORLD WAR I. It was founded on April 30, 1898, by a group of leaders in heavy industry, the Free Conservative politicians in collaboration with allies in the Prussian government. It was an alliance between iron and rye. The group manifested a united front of imperialist opinion that helped pass the first Navy Law and was intended to prevent the extreme naval agitation of the PAN-GERMAN LEAGUE.

The Navy League started with just over 14,000 members but increased to 330,000 by 1914. Its grassroots membership was lower middle-class nationalist circles. There were conflicts between moderates and radicals as to its propaganda. The radicals thought that they were responsible for the tremendous growth of the league, which peaked at 325,000 members in 1907. During the ascendancy of the radical-nationalist faction (1903–08) propaganda innovation occurred with the use of film and other visual media. A new kind of right-wing populism emerged that attacked the monarchist establishment for its indifference to popular political mobilization.

Nazi Party
(National Socialist German Workers' Party, NSDAP)

The Nazi Party, officially called the National Socialist German Workers' Party (NSDAP), originated out of the small nationalist GERMAN WORKER'S PARTY (DAP) founded in January 1919 by Anton Drexler and Karl Harrer. It had precursors in right-wing folkish (*völkish*) nationalist groups in Germany and AUSTRIA. The most important in MUNICH was the Thule Society, which preached Aryan supremacy. At the time Adolf HITLER had been recruited as an instructor and spy for the military in BAVARIA. He was sent to observe the party's meetings, joined, became the organizing committee's seventh member and in 1920, due to his speaking ability, became head of its propaganda. On April 1, 1920, Hitler essentially took over the party and founded the NSDAP. Hitler was released from the army and began a speaking campaign between April and November 1920, during which he delivered at least 28 speeches in Munich alone. The party established locals outside of Munich, and by the beginning of 1921 its membership had reached 3,000. On January 22, 1921, the party's first annual congress was held. A party crisis occurred during 1921 when leaders wanted to merge with other folkish groups over Hitler's objections and threats to resign. The other leaders feared losing Hitler and agreed to his demand for dictatorial authority. From this time on Hitler emphasized the leadership principle as the central principle of the party.

Earlier, at the DAP's first mass meeting on February 24, 1920, Hitler took the opportunity to announce a 25-point party program formulated by himself and Drexler, which later became the program of the Nazi Party. It was clear that the movement was opposed to capitalism, communism, and democracy. The enemies of the German people were primarily the Jews, Marxists, the TREATY OF VERSAILLES, and the "November Criminals," the leaders of the WEIMAR REPUBLIC who had (according to popular myth) stabbed the army in the back. According to Hitler in MEIN KAMPF, propaganda and organization were the most important methods in the development of a mass political movement. In order to make members feel important and create a wider appeal by drawing attention to mass demonstrations, symbols were essential. Some of these physical trappings included the swastika, which was an ancient occult symbol invoking the power of the Sun. Party members were supposed to wear party badges carrying the symbol of the swastika. In 1920 the Heil salute was borrowed from Austrian folkish parties. Wearing uniforms and using flags and standards became common practice; ideas were to be simplified into propagandistic slogans, and newspapers such as the *People's Observer* (VÖLKISCHE BEOBACHTER) spread the party's ideas. The Nazi Party grew with the help of Ernst RÖHM and the Stormtroops (SA), which was a paramilitary association composed of young desperados. In 1923 Hitler and his SA were behind the attempt to push Gustav von Kahr into a march on Berlin on November 23, which has been called the

Members of the Sturmabteilung with Adolf Hitler on Nazi Party Day, Nuremburg, 1937 *(Library of Congress)*

BEER-HALL PUTSCH. The attempt failed but helped Hitler gain national notoriety at his trial when he appeared, together with General Erich LUDENDORFF. The 10 months of imprisonment that followed gave Hitler time to reflect and provided the opportunity to write about his political ideas, which were published in *Mein Kampf* (1925).

Major themes in Hitler's propaganda were the elimination of democracy and the destruction of communism. The party program came out against capitalism, and its appeal was to the workers and lower middle classes. Hitler thought that programs were a means to an end, and his anticapitalism referred to the nationalization of trusts and the communal ownership of department stores. National Socialism possessed a world view (weltanschauung) rather than a consistent ideology with programmatic content.

The party program was vague, which allowed various people to interpret the movement as they wanted. At first it may seem surprising that Hitler should have permitted contradictory ideas to coexist in the party, but doing so permitted the party to attract adherents from both the left and the right of the political spectrum and from all levels of the social structure.

After Hitler was released from Landsberg Prison in late 1924, he began to reconstitute the Nazi Party in February 1925. Hitler had come to the conclusion that his only hope of seizing power in Germany was by "legal" constitutional means and through elections. This meant a drive to expand the party's membership and successful participation in the electoral process. In both areas the party adopted an urban strategy, focusing its propagandistic efforts on labor, anticapitalist themes calculated to attract the support of the urban working class. Hitler's own position in the party's ideological debates remained characteristically vague while he concentrated on organizational issues such as creating a centrally directed party organization headquartered in Munich. The party, however, grew slowly until 1928, when in the REICHSTAG election it received only enough votes to return 12 delegates. With the onset of the GREAT DEPRESSION, however, electoral support for the Nazi Party grew in the September 1930 elections to return 107 delegates. The electoral returns grew from 800,000 votes in 1928 to more than 13.75 million in July 1932. As party membership grew from 27,000 in 1925 to 178,000 in 1929, the Nazis aggressively contested elections on all levels.

The propaganda effort was increasingly directed toward the middle classes and farmers. The electoral success that came in 1930 occurred mainly in small towns and in suburban districts. The party was stronger, too, in the Protestant north and east than in the Roman Catholic south and west. As the parties of the middle and far right splintered and their votes declined, the fortunes of the Nazi Party improved. However, electoral support for the Catholic CENTER PARTY remained stable, as did the vote for the Socialist and Communist parties. In the presidential election of 1932 Hitler ran against President Paul von HINDENBURG and was defeated, but his large vote demonstrated that he was a threat to the republic. The Nazi Party, however, could not gain an absolute majority of the vote because in a free election in July 1932 it managed to receive only 37.3 percent of the vote. In another election in November the vote for the Nazi Party dropped, so that it returned only 196 delegates. The tide had turned against the Nazis, but electoral success was not so important as the confidence of President Hindenburg, who was choosing chancellors, such as Franz von PAPEN and General Kurt von SCHLEICHER. Hitler was having a difficult time keeping the party together while he held out for the office of chancellor. In January 1933 Hindenburg was persuaded to appoint Hitler chancellor, surrounded by conservatives like Papen and Alfred HUGENBERG.

Party membership had grown from 3,000 in 1921 to 130,000 in 1930, then to 850,000 in 1933 and more than 8 million by 1945. The social composition of the party membership and its electoral support was complex and multiclass, not strictly lower and middle class. Between 1930 and 1932 in large cities the percent of middle-class support was consonant with the percent of the middle class in the population; there also was unusually heavy support from rural Protestant farmers, the small town middle class, and the urban upper class. Relatively weak voter support existed among women and the unemployed. Membership in the party, however, was disproportionately lower middle class but was increasingly proletarian in composition, including veterans, youth, and white collar. Half of the membership consisted of nonprofessional workers, and a minority were bureaucrats, intelligentsia, and the wealthy. Among the business leaders who joined the party only 12 percent had done so before January 1933, and most of those who joined did so only after 1936. Between 1932 and 1934 the SA became primarily (two-thirds) blue collar. In reference to the crisis of MODERNIZATION, it has been asserted that the Nazi Party represented a movement of losers, but this was generally not the case. The fact, however, that the party was composed of the younger generation does reflect a generational revolt of those who entered the job market and politics after World War I.

After 1933 the organization of party and the state gradually merged, with Hitler ruling by decree. The party kept its identity throughout the regime, with all those occupying key positions such as civil servants and teachers required to become party members. In summer 1933 Hitler declared Germany a one-party state. Hitler declared, "The party has become the state. All power rests with the Reich government." Except in a few cases like the Foreign Office the party did not take over the functions of the administrative offices of the state. In the early months Nazi leadership did everything possible to avoid conflicts between the party and state. There was rigid control of the party from above. In the bureaucracy the small number of democratic officials were purged, and the party relied on the functioning of government through a civil service that was favorable to an authoritarian government. So the primacy of the party was established only in specific instances.

With Germany's defeat in 1945 the Nazi Party was outlawed and disbanded.

Nazi-Soviet Nonaggression Pact

On August 23, 1939, it was announced that HITLER and Stalin had concluded a nonaggression pact. It was negotiated in 24 hours by Stalin and Molotov with German foreign minister Joachim von RIBBENTROP. Hitler had authorized Ribbentrop to sign a treaty and a secret protocol that specified separate spheres of influence in eastern Europe. The Soviets were to gain influence in Finland, the Baltic states of Estonia, Latvia and Lithuania, eastern Poland, and Bessarabia in Romania, while Germany would gain control of western Poland. The pact guaranteed the benevolent neutrality of the Soviet Union, providing that neither Germany nor the Soviet Union would attack each other nor assist another power at war with either of them. They promised not to join alliances against each other and to settle by peaceful means any differences between them. In addition to Soviet neutrality, Germany gained a steady supply of strategic minerals and foodstuffs in exchange for industrial equipment and machinery. The pact cleared the way for the German attack on Poland, thus marking the beginning of WORLD WAR II. In an elated mood Hitler told his generals: "Now Poland is in the position in which I wanted her. . . . I am only afraid that at the last moment some swine or other will yet submit to me a plan for mediation." Hitler obviously wanted war and not peace.

The pact guaranteed Germany that after a war with Poland a friendly border would exist between Germany and the Soviet Union. Germany then could concentrate all of its forces on Poland on the western front. In fact, it was the expectation of the Soviet Union that the German attack on Poland would be only a prelude to a German attack on the West. In fact, a war would weaken the imperialist powers. The pact further assured the leaders in Moscow that Japan would not dare to begin a new attack on East Asian territories. For Great Britain and France the pact meant that all of their hopes of a multifront war against Germany ended. Great Britain now stiffened its resolve. Prime Minister Neville Chamberlain stated that London would go to war with or without allies.

The conclusion of the pact shocked most Western statesmen, who had erroneously believed that the implacable conflict between communism and Nazism made the Soviet Union a partner with the democracies. In fact, the deep-seated distrust that the Soviets had of all imperialist powers, particularly France and Great Britain, was not displaced by the rise of Nazi Germany. The Soviet Union was hoping to strengthen its position and gain time for its future conflict with Germany. Stalin overestimated the power of England and France and underestimated the rapidity of German successes.

neo-Nazism

Neo-Nazism is a term used to describe the radical rightist or conservative political groups that sprang up in Germany and AUSTRIA after 1945 and resembled Nazism. These groups tried to reactivate the political and ideological ideas with which they had grown up. By 1950 there were about a dozen or so parties in which former Nazis remained politically active. Although the NAZI PARTY was prohibited, some former Nazis joined the GERMAN REICH PARTY (Deutsche Reichspartei) and soon got control. Electorally, it could not overcome the 5 percent hurdle, so its conservative members left to join the CHRISTIAN DEMOCRATIC UNION (CDU) and FREE DEMOCRATIC PARTY (FDP), while the ex-Nazis formed the Socialist Reichs Party (Sozialistische Reichspartei). This party had recognizable former Nazis in its leadership, and it professed fascist aims. Consequently, the FEDERAL CONSTITUTIONAL COURT outlawed the party before the 1953 election. These splinter parties were unable to gain a foothold in the political system.

In the 1960s the NATIONAL DEMOCRATIC PARTY (NPD) was formed out of a collection of rightwing splinter groups and again was temporarily successful. It was led by Adolf von Thadden, who preached a nationalist message, attacked the war crimes trials, and urged pensions for all those who had fought in the war. Eighteen of its executive board had been Nazi Party members. Although the party denied it was anti-Semitic, its speakers were often critical of Jews and Israel. It received the most votes in the later 1960s, receiving a high of a little more than 13 percent of the vote in NUREMBERG and BAYREUTH. By 1972 it was in steady decline. In its place the German People's Union (Deutsche Volksunion) was formed in 1971 as a movement of the radical right. Then, in 1983 The REPUBLICANS (Republikaner) formed a party that was temporarily successful.

After reunification Germany became engulfed in a wave of violence against foreigners. In 1991, according to police, there were more right-wing extremists than left-wing. Statistics showed that there were 1,483 instances of rightist violence in Germany, which was a 500 percent increase over the previous years. Although it is easy to identify them as neo-Nazi, many of these groups as well as the new rightist parties were actually without much political ideology. The surge in hostility to asylum seekers perhaps was motivated like the earlier situations, in increased support for radical-right parties. There is some question whether the protest movements and radical party formation are really a uniquely German expression of neo-Nazism. It is possible that voters support such radical parties as a protest against the lack of responsiveness of the major parties to social and economic change. It appears that when these stressful periods and economic recessions pass, support for these radical parties declines, which follows a pattern in other European countries and is not necessarily a function of neo-Nazism.

Neumann, Balthasar (1687–1753)
architect

Balthasar Neumann was the greatest architect of the early 18th century, following Fischer von Erlach of Vienna. Working for the Schönbrun family, he designed the Residenz in Würzburg and the Church of the Fourteen Saints (Vierzehnheiligen).

Balthasar Neumann was born in January 1687 at Eger in Bohemia. At first he worked in foundaries but soon was sent to Würzburg to study civil and military engineering. Joining the palace guards, he served with Imperial forces in 1717 as a military engineer. Returning to Würzburg, where he worked with the architect Johann Dientzenhofer, he spent the rest of his life building the residential palace of Prince-Bishop Philip Franz von Schönbrun.

The Residenz became the crowning achievement of Neumann's career and a testament to his architectural fantasy. His advice and designs were not the only ones involved, however. Other architects, principally Johann Lukas von HILDEBRANDT, made contributions, especially in the treatment of surfaces. The building that resulted was an extensive complex of courts surrounding a central block with a large octagonal dome over the main hall. Neumann designed his famous stairway with columns and arcades and decorated it with beautiful fresco painting by Giovanni Battista Tiepolo (1752–53). Tiepolo's fresco represents the four continents of the world. The stairway lacks a balustrade, but it does rise to a marble hall decorated with beautiful stucco ornament and frescoes by Tiepolo.

The challenge of building impressive, spacious, and floating stairways continued and was further perfected at Schloss Bruchsal and Brühl. Neumann employed oval landings, circling stairways, elaborately decorated main floors, lightened upper supporting walls with arches, and oval domes with windows. However, it was in church architecture that Neumann had his greatest success with the Church of the Fourteen Saints, built between 1743 and 1772. The altar of the church was to be built under the dome, but due to mistakes in construction, was placed in the center of the largest of a series of ovals, which gave the same impression. The design ended up being a compromise between a central plan and a longitudinal nave church. The perfection of this form of church can be seen at Neresheim, Neumann's last great church. Here the longitudinal oval combines with the ovals of the transept and the nave, creating a vast space over which the dome appears to float.

Neumann became swamped with commissions to design palaces, churches and convents, canonical residences, and the homes of the wealthy MIDDLE CLASS, as well as fortresses, barracks, streets, and bridges. Virtually no person of any status wished to build without his advice. He was also offered teaching positions. He did teach military and civil engineering at the University of Würzburg. At the same time he remained an officer in the bishop's military. Other accomplishments in civil engineering included a water supply for the city and a glass and mirror factory. Until his death on July 18, 1753, he continued his architectural planning for a complex stairway for the Hofburg in Vienna, and palaces in Stuttgart and Karlsruhe.

New Objectivity
(Neue Sachlichkeit)

A new cultural movement that appeared in the 1920s in response to the horrors of war, failed revolutions, political insecurity, economic disaster, and general MODERNIZATION, was called the New Objectivity, New Matter-of-Factness, or New Sobriety. The term was already in circulation before 1925, but in reference to art it was prominently used in 1925 as the title of an art exhibition in MANNHEIM at the gallery of Friedrich Hartlaub. In literature the movement proposed to replace the high-pitched emotionalism and IDEALISM of EXPRESSIONISM with a new perspective that claimed it was just looking at the facts and employing sober and sharply pointed language. The preaching of reform and the search for ideal humanity, which expressionism had emphasized, now turned to a more detached assessment of concrete circumstances. The movement was inaugurated by Joseph Roth, Hermann Kesten, and Erich Kästner (1899–1974) as embittered critics and satirists of society. It was their goal to expose the weakness, injustices, and hypocrisies of their time. Alfred Döblin described these critics as "disenchanted and disillusioned people." They felt that the moral fabric of society was beyond redemption. Döblin, himself, was extremely pessimistic about BERLIN as he describes it as "Sodom on the eve of destruction." Kästner's novel of the DEPRESSION years, *Fabian,* took a gloomy view of contemporary society. Even though they claimed to be objective analysts, they were one-sided opponents of capitalism, imperialism, MILITARISM, the JUNKER ARISTOCRACY, and the conservatism of the churches and the courts. In general, they were against the values and customs of the MIDDLE CLASS. But politically they were homeless, belonging to no political party because they would not submit to party discipline. Their journalism unfortunately was very critical of the WEIMAR REPUBLIC. They detested the political right, but played into its hands and inadvertently strengthened it. Kurt Tucholsky (1890–1935) was one of the most vocal critics of the failure of the REVOLUTION OF 1918–1919, who also detested the SOCIAL DEMOCRATIC PARTY and Friedrich EBERT, the president of the republic. Unfortunately, these left-wing critics did as much to undermine the republic as did the radical right.

One of the forerunners of the New Objectivity was Hans José Rehfish, who wrote on the problems of the returning soldier in 1918 and other contemporary themes. Other authors who participated in this movement were Ferdinand Bruckner, Hans Carossa, Marie Luise Fleiser, Gerhart HAUPTMANN, O. von Horváth, Max Mohr, Paul Kornfeld, Carl Zuckmayer, and Arnold Zweig.

In the art world a bitter and cynical social criticism was expressed in the work of George GROSZ, Otto DIX, and Max BECKMANN. The New Objectivity can be seen in the clear representation of a corrupt reality in the work of Dix and Grosz.

Nicolsburg, Peace of (1866)

The Austro-Prussian War was settled by the Peace of Nicolsburg. Otto von BISMARCK was able to reach an agreement with AUSTRIA to sign the peace at Nicolsburg on July 26. Austria was required to withdraw from Germany and pay a small war indemnity. She did not have to give up any territory. Bismarck also agreed with Austria that Saxony be preserved. King William objected to this mild peace settlement and wanted to impose territorial concessions on most of the states that had fought against PRUSSIA. Only gradually did he give in to Bismarck's arguments. Bismarck's reasoning involved making peace quickly before other European countries could intervene, and he wanted to keep the door open to future cooperation with Austria in European affairs. Bismarck also warned the king not to alienate the South German states with demands for their land. Instead, Bismarck looked to the future and the membership of the southern states in a German federal state. In North Germany Bismarck wanted to unite the western and eastern lands of Prussia by the annexation of HANOVER, Hesse-Kassel, Nassau, and FRANKFURT.

In order to make the peace possible, Bismarck had to find out where Napoleon stood. Napoleon agreed to give Bismarck a free hand in northern Germany and agreed to the replacement of the GERMAN CONFEDERATION by a NORTH GERMAN CONFEDERATION under Prussian leadership. The South German states were to be allowed to form their own federation. The provinces of Schleswig-Holstein were to become Prussian, except for North Schleswig, where a plebiscite decided which districts were to go to Denmark. Napoleon did, however, insist that the kingdom of Saxony survive.

Niemöller, Martin (1892–1984)

clergyman

The most famous and contradictory Evangelical minister in the Protestant resistance to the Nazi regime was Martin Niemöller. Having a distinguished career as a U-boat commander in WORLD WAR I, he was called to the ministry and ordained in 1924. Out of nationalist sentiment he welcomed the HITLER regime, expecting it to restore Christian faith and morality and Germany's international prestige. Opposing Nazi ecclesiastical policies for the Evangelical Church, he organized what became the CONFESSING CHURCH. From 1937 to 1945 he was incarcerated in CONCENTRATION CAMPS. After the war he was a leader in the German Evangelical Church and an outspoken pacifist opposed to nuclear war.

Born in Lippstadt, Wiesbaden, Martin became a naval officer on the battleship *Thuringia* at the beginning of World War I, then transferred to the submarine fleet where he became a U-boat commander. For his distinguished service as a captain he received the award Pour le mérite. His fervent devotion to IMPERIAL GERMANY was recounted in his autobiography, *From U-boat to Pulpit*. Like so many other Germans he was disillusioned at the end of the war. His NATIONALISM was still so strong that he refused to turn over two submarines to the British in accordance with the TREATY OF VERSAILLES and later thought the WEIMAR REPUBLIC lacked true leaders and great goals. The ideals of the republic and its materialism and rationalism, he thought, were contrary to the German spirit and imported from the West. So he sought other ways to give meaning to his life. Feeling called to the ministry, he studied theology at the University of Münster and was ordained into the Prussian Evangelical Church in 1924. By 1931 his reputation was sufficiently high to gain him an appointment to a prestigious church in the BERLIN suburb of Dahlem.

Niemöller, an avowed opponent of the Weimar Republic, approved of Hitler's dictatorship and his ambition to restore Germany's international prestige. He saw National Socialism and Christianity as complementary and the new regime as a return to Christian faith and morality. His opposition to the humiliating Versailles Treaty prompted him to approve of Hitler's withdrawal from the League of Nations in October 1933. Although his ANTI-SEMITISM did not have the undisguised animosity of Bishop Dibelius, he thought that the fate of the Jews were of no concern to German Protestants, and their persecution by the Nazis was divine retribution for the unpardonable crime of the crucifixion of Christ.

Niemöller soon found that the Nazis wanted to gain control of the Protestant Church by organizing the "German Christians," whose purpose was to control the church bureaucracy and dictate theological and policy changes. So in September 1933 he organized the Pastor's Emergency League, which in 1934 grew into the Confessing Church. Until 1937 he boldly criticized Nazi policies to restrict the autonomy of the church. His opposition to the Third Reich modified his attitude on the Jewish question; he believed that converted Jews deserved the full support of the church. Although he was arrested, tried in court, then acquitted, the Nazis rearrested him and placed him in the concentration camps of Sachsenhausen and DACHAU, from which he was liberated by the Allies.

Purged of his admiration for the Nazi regime, he led the effort in the German Evangelical Church to formulate the Stuttgart Declaration of guilt. Though it was an unpopular message, he emphasized the need for the church's repentance for its failure to resist the dictatorship. During his postwar career he continued to be a controversial leader because of his rejection of confessional Lutheranism, his strong pacifism, his insistence that the church provide leadership in the prevention of nuclear war, and for cooperation between democratic West and communist East Germany.

Nietzsche, Friedrich (1844–1900)
philosopher and critic

Friedrich Nietzsche was an important critic of German society, culture, and politics. He was opposed to the contemporary systematic philosophy of his time. A profoundly critical genius, he led a radical revolt against the values and traditions of Western civilization and Christianity. He believed that the vital forces of Western civilization had become so weakened in the 19th century that traditional values had lost their validity ("God is dead"), which left man to face a decadent and meaningless world ("nihilism"). Nietzsche sought to solve this problem and the dangers in himself by preaching a new gospel. Man must create his own values, using his will for self-conquest, which meant not so much a "superman," but an overcomer, as critic Walter Kaufmann prefers, an overman. For Nietzsche, the individual's faithfulness to himself and self-realization alone mattered, which was to be accomplished through overcoming and self-discipline.

Nietzsche was born on October 15, 1844, in the Saxon village of Röcken, where his father was a Lutheran pastor. His father's death when Friedrich was four had a severe impact and left him to grow up in a household of only women. In 1858, however, he was fortunate to win a scholarship to Pforta, one of Germany's best boarding schools, where he received a classical education. Sometime during this period he rejected his Christian upbringing and soon became a hardened atheist. At the University of BONN, where he enrolled in 1864, he studied under the classicist Friedrich Ritschl. Following his professor to LEIPZIG in 1866, he discovered the philosophy of the great pessimist Schopenhauer, who inspired and influenced him profoundly. There he met and and became an ardent admirer of the composer Richard WAGNER. Also while in Leipzig he contracted syphilis, which relentlessly undermined his health. In 1869 at age 24, without Nietzsche's having completed his doctorate, Ritschl recommended him for the chair of classical philophy at the University of Basel in Switzerland. His teaching was interrupted by his service as a medical orderly in the Franco-Prussian War and frequent long illnesses. Racked by headaches and eye trouble, he resigned in 1879 and until his collapse in 1888 produced 10 major contributions to German philosophy and literature.

During his tenure at Basel until 1879 he was preoccupied with the cultural values seen in his writings. Dedicated to Wagner, *The Birth of Tragedy* (1872) emphasized the Dionysian element in Greek culture and its expression in the Greek tragedies. He saw Wagner's music dramas as the revival of the same ecstatic and non-Socratic state of mind. In 1873 he expanded his critique of Greek culture, favoring earlier Greek thought over that of the honored place traditionally given to Socrates and Plato. That same year Nietzsche published the first of four long essays, this one depriving David Friedrich Strauss, author of *The Life of Jesus,* of any respect as a theologian or philosopher. The last two were devoted to praise of Schopenhauer and Wagner.

Nietzsche was severely critical of German society. He feared that Germans would become infatuated with their military victory over the French in 1871. As early as 1873, at the beginning of *Thoughts out of Season,* he pointed out the disastrous consequences that the victorious war had for Germany. He considered it an illusion that the German victory was due to the superiority of German culture, an idea he thought threatened the health of the German mind in favor of the German Empire. Nietzsche never equated, as did most German scholars and writers, cultural creativity and military power. Although he had praised Otto von BISMARCK for his victory over the Austrians for leadership in Germany, he severely criticized Bismarck for his policies in the 1870s. Nietzsche distrusted the state and rejected German NATIONALISM. He had contempt for the use of force and condemned the armaments race in which Germany was involved, which proved his independence from an age in which the cult of violence was rapidly spreading. He praised French civilization as superior to German culture and criticized the philistinism of the German MIDDLE CLASS. As for the idea that the materialistic worldview of modern science was the only acceptable one, Nietzsche countered that it was "stupid and naive."

In all of his works Nietzsche tried to provide a new meaning for existence in a world interpreted by Darwinian evolutionary theory, which he believed had destroyed the foundation for human dignity. Humankind could no longer be seen as created in the image of God but was a product of chance in nature, a creature without purpose or value. Nietzsche refused to bow to the pessimism of Schopenhauer on the tragic character of life and history. If life had no meaning in itself, then Nietzsche believed, humanity had to create meaning so as not to decline into nihilism and ultimately barbarity. He critiqued the traditional values of Western civilization found in Judaism and Christianity in *A Genealogy of Morals* (1887), and in *The Antichrist* (1888) he sought to help Europeans create a new set of values. These he found in the idea of "the will to power" through which humans can dominate and master themselves. He offered a concept of overcoming self by which the ideal person, a "superman," or perhaps better, an "overman," masters existence, orders passions, and forms character. The person of this ideal world would create a personal standard of value. Christianity's denial of self he considered to be prideful and constituted a "slave morality." To the contrary, Nietzsche proposed self-assertion and the elimination of the consciousness of guilt.

Nietzsche was alleged to be anti-Semitic, because of the publication after his death of *The Will to Power* (1906), a book in which his sister distorted his ideas. Among modern German writers Nietzsche was the most outspoken in his rejection of ANTI-SEMITISM and German nationalism. Neither did Nietzsche consider the Germans a master race. It is true that the Nazis quoted Nietzsche to support their own ideology, using brief excerpts out of context. Nietzsche was primarily interested in culture and did not consider it a product of race. To him racism was a distorted web of lies. Unfortunately, however unintended, many of Nietzsche's ideas had a perverted influence on some Germans in the early 20th century. In the preface to *The Will to Power* he warned against applying his ideas to anything other than the process of individual thinking. Yet it is easy to see how Nietzsche could be misinterpreted. Many young Germans in this manifestly materialistic period were attracted by Nietzsche's admonition to live dangerously, to wage wars, to overcome, to rule, and to own. In *The Gay Science* he welcomed the coming of a more manly and warlike age that honored courage. In his best-known work, *Thus Spoke Zarathustra,* he encourages his disciples to hasten the end of a decaying civilization. He gives his followers the commandment to become hard and impress "your will to power on thousands of years as if they were wax." Nietzsche's violent language in his latter writings extol a pitiless struggle. Yet, this insistence on brutality is one extreme in the dichotomy of his thinking, which is balanced by his gentleness and pure love of truth. This cultural critic who foresaw many of the developments of the 20th century was far from being accurately described by the two clichés, "the blond beast" and the "superman," often associated with him.

While in Turin, Italy, Nietzsche collapsed on January 3, 1889. Syphilis had finally overcome him. When he awakened, his sanity was gone. For another 10 years he was afflicted by increasing physical paralysis and detachment from reality, cared for by his mother and sister in Naumburg and WEIMAR until August 25, 1900.

Night of Broken Glass (November 9, 1938) (Crystal Night, Kristallnacht)

Terror attacks were made on Jewish synagogues and stores on November 9, 1938. Two days earlier, Ernst vom Rath, third secretary of the German Embassy in Paris, was assassinated by Herschel Grynszpan, a young Polish Jew whose family had been forcibly deported from Germany across the Polish border. Rath's death gave the signal to Joseph GOEBBELS to unleash a pogrom against the Jews. Reinhard HEYDRICH, chief of the SD, ordered the destruction of all Jewish places of worship in Germany and AUSTRIA.

The Nazi leadership had been preparing for the assault for a long time. The Nazis had been expelling Jews from the economic life of the country and trying to force hurried emigration. In October 1938 Hermann GÖRING indicated that Jews had to be removed from the economy and that in the coming weeks a general Jewish offensive was to take place. The Rath assassination provided the opportunity to begin the attack. But it was Joseph Goebbels who wanted to get back into HITLER's favor after having had an affair with a Czech actress. Goebbels proposed a coordinated attack against the Jews.

In 15 hours 191 synagogues were set on fire and 76 were demolished. Bands of Nazi hooligans systematically destroyed 800 Jewish-owned stores. The pillage and looting went on through the night. Streets were covered with broken glass, from which arose the name "Night of Broken Glass." In the end 91 Jews were killed and 20,000 arrested. The pogrom was not popular with the German people, who objected to the lawlessness and destruction of property. It was decided that the Jews would have to pay the cost of the damage to their property with 1 billion reichsmarks. Unfavorable worldwide publicity was gained for the Nazis, and they decided

Berlin Jewish shop owners survey the wreckage after the Night of Broken Glass, November 10, 1938. *(Library of Congress)*

that in the future a more rational course of persecution would exclude the public and be conducted by the SS.

Night of the Long Knives
(June 30, 1934)

At the end of June 1934 HITLER ordered the purge of leading Storm Troopers (SA). Eighty-five leading SA members, which included Ernst RÖHM and other provincial leaders, were executed by SS assassination squads. Ostensibly it was done to protect the regime against a second revolution and the growing power of the SA. It is now known that the SS and the leadership of the army, the Reichswehr, fabricated information that alleged Röhm was planning a putsch against the government and the NAZI PARTY leadership. Besides the SA leadership, others who had opposed Hitler were also killed. Those included Gregor STRASSER, General Kurt von SCHLEICHER and Gustav von Kahr. In BERLIN Hermann GÖRING and Heinrich HIMMLER supervised the arrests and executions. In MUNICH Hitler himself did so. The Nazis themselves gave the purge the name "Night of the Long Knives." Hitler announced that 77 persons had been executed, but it is more likely that some 200 persons had been executed and scores settled.

Hitler's conservative allies were silent about this dramatic breach of legality. Their reasons for silence was partly their beliefs that the most radical elements in the Nazi Party, the SA, were suppressed. Surprisingly, Hitler and the SS were seen as elements of moderation.

Nolde, Emil (1867–1956)
expressionist painter

Emil Nolde was a leading artist of the expressionist school who painted in highly brilliant and contrastingly glaring colors. He was strongly influenced by religion, a love of nature, German folklore, and the imagery of South Seas island culture. An exotic element entered EXPRESSIONISM through Nolde's art. Under Nazism he was placed on the list of so-called degenerate artists and forbidden to paint.

Born Emil Hansen on his family's farm near the village of Nolde in Schleswig-Holstein, he apprenticed as a wood-carver, and from 1892–1898 he demonstrated his talents as a drawing instructor at the Arts and Crafts Museum in St. Gall, Switzerland. From there he studied for a short time in the MUNICH area under the religious abstractionist Adolf Hoelzel. Nolde's artistic style was already forming as he demonstrated his interest in the landscape painting of German ROMANTICISM. Like many other artists of his generation he moved in 1899 to Paris, where he was so impressed by the impressionists that his art exploded with color. Yet he was disappointed with his formal training there and within a year moved to Copenhagen. In 1902 he married and changed his name to Nolde. During the most decisive years of his life he struggled with loneliness, inhibitions, and unfriendly provincial environments. Inspiration came from his subjective insights.

In the following years his artistic interests changed, and his circle of associates broadened. Originally his style had been dependent on his teachers in Munich and was symbolic in nature, which had included fantastic themes. By 1904 he had adopted something of an impressionist style, but under the influence of Vincent van Gogh and Eduard Munch he turned away from the impressionist style and adopted bright pigments, signaling his departure from impressionism. In 1905 his work was displayed in the Berlin Secession. Then he was invited to join the innovative circle of artists in DRESDEN called THE BRIDGE (1905–1913). He eventually rejected the emphasis on youth and ecstasy, which dominated *Wildly Dancing Children* (1909). In contrast to the calm refinement of classical art Nolde's expressionism distorted reality. From 1909 to 1912 a fantastic and mystical imagery emerged in his biblical scenes and lives of the saints with primitive figures with masklike faces reflecting non-Western cultures. In 1909 he painted his most famous masterpieces, *The Last Supper* and *Pentecost,* which demonstrated his emotional and symbolic use of rich colors. He also depicted Christ and his apostles as racial types instead of in the traditional manner. His celebrated triptych, *Life of St. Mary Aegyptiaca,* was produced in 1912. Alongside these productions were the symbolic scenes of life and nature. His paintings were rejected by the Berlin Secession in 1910, so he formed his own New Secession. In 1912 he contributed works to the Blue Rider exhibition in MUNICH. In 1913–14 he traveled to New Guinea to study the life of the aborigines, which explains the primitive motifs of his subsequent paintings, such as *The South Sea Islander* (1914).

Nolde's interest in "folk" and racial characteristics perhaps inspired him to join the Danish North Schleswig NAZI PARTY in 1920. In 1931 he was appointed to the Prussian Academy of Art. In 1932 he published the first volume of his autobiography. He failed to convince the Nazis that his work was true German art, and consequently in 1937 he was placed on the list of "degenerate" artists; his works were removed from museums and all his art confiscated. In 1941 he was forbidden to paint. This did not stop him from secretly producing more than 1,000 small watercolors known as "Unpainted Pictures." After WORLD WAR II his significance was attested in retrospective exhibitions. On April 13, 1956, he died in Seebüll.

North Atlantic Treaty Organization (NATO)

The FEDERAL REPUBLIC (West Germany) became a full member of NATO on May 5, 1955, some six years after its founding in 1949. In April 1949, 11 European countries joined with the United States in forming the North Atlantic Treaty Organization, a defense organization to resist Soviet aggression. The BERLIN CRISIS in 1948 provided a powerful stimulus for the integration of Western Europe into a military alliance dominated by the United States. Negotiations had begun in July 1948 after the U.S. Congress had changed its usual resistance to alliances with foreign states. The first secretary-general of the Atlantic alliance had described the original purpose of NATO in the following memorable way: to keep the Americans in, the Russians out, and Germany down.

After the quick disintegration of the wartime alliance that defeated Nazi Germany, the Atlantic alliance arose in May 1949 as a rampart against Moscow's claim to power, which had reached as far west as the ELBE RIVER. When Stalin died in March 1953, the international situation somewhat eased, but all hopes of a Soviet change of course with regard to Germany were shattered when the uprising of June 17, 1953, in East Berlin in the GDR was suppressed with the help of Soviet tanks. Unfortunately, on August 30, 1954, the treaty establishing the EUROPEAN DEFENSE COMMUNITY was rejected by the French National Assembly. Within a few weeks new treaties were negotiated and signed in Paris on October 23, 1954. Federal Chancellor ADENAUER pushed for the Federal Republic to become a member of NATO, which was part of his policy to integrate West Germany as much as possible into the West. As a result the Federal Republic was accepted as a member of NATO. The entry of the Federal Republic into NATO and the formal founding of the WARSAW PACT shortly thereafter was a consequence of the cold war. Germany's participation in NATO was an essential step in its desire for political sovereignty. NATO also deepened the division between West and East Germany.

After the Federal Republic's accession to NATO, the West German armed forces were rapidly built up. In November 1955 the first volunteers arrived at their barracks. In 1956 compulsory military service was introduced. The German contribution to NATO reached 270,000 in 1960 and 500,000 in the mid-1970s.

A number of crises dealing with the use of nuclear weapons arose. At first the FRG renounced the production of nuclear weapons but hoped to participate indirectly in nuclear defense through an Allied Nuclear Force, which failed to materialize. Then the FRG desired to have input into the use of nuclear weapons, but that conflicted with the American president's claim to sole responsibility. West Germany did, however, manage to have some influence in the

Seven Member Planning Committee's determination of nuclear policy, but without deciding on nuclear warfare itself. Germans also had fears of not having nuclear protection as the United States shifted its strategy from massive retaliation to a "flexible response." French withdrawal from NATO in 1966 weakened the alliance, but this was balanced by the growth of DÉTENTE between the Soviet Union and the United States through bilateral agreements on intercontinental missiles in the Salt I (1973) and Salt II (1979) treaties. This, however, was balanced off by the Soviet threat from medium-range missiles and the deployment by NATO of missiles on German soil. Chancellor Helmut SCHMIDT favored this counterarming with medium-range nuclear weapons, but linked it to a disarmament proposal that the Soviet Union ignored. The double-track strategy contributed later to the collapse of the Soviet Union and was a decisive step toward unification.

After unification and the elimination of the confrontation between East and West, the security situation improved. NATO was still considered as having an important role in Europe's stability and security. A new strategy was necessary, which was adopted in Rome in November 1991. It involved a sizable reduction in force strength and a reform of force structures. A German-American initiative in late 1991 led to the establishment of the North Atlantic Cooperation Council, which also embraced all the members of the former Warsaw Pact and the successor states of the Soviet Union, demonstrating a comprehensive security partnership for Europe. At the NATO summit in January 1994 the Alliance reaffirmed its offer to support peacekeeping and other operations under the authority of the United Nations Security Council.

In the early 1990s the cold-war role of the German army in a purely defensive role against an attack by the Warsaw Pact was reevaluated. The Bundeswehr had been organized as a citizen army and its defensive role was stressed in Article 87a of the Basic Law. After reunification the Federal Republic's military forces had already taken part in relief roles outside of NATO to Ethiopia, Cambodia, and Somalia. During the Gulf War of 1991 the air force had stationed units in Turkey as part of the NATO defense against an aggressive Iraq. In 1994 the Constitutional Court finally ruled favorably that the Bundeswehr could participate in all kinds of United Nations operations with parliamentary approval. When NATO became involved in the crisis in the former Yugoslavia in 1995 the Bundestag decided to approve the deployment of the air force in a combat role. In December 1996 the Bundestag decided that German troops could participate in "out of area" operations as long as they were sanctioned by NATO or the UN. Shortly thereafter 3,000 soldiers of the Bundeswehr became part of the multinational peace-keeping force in Bosnia-Hercegovina.

North German Confederation (1866–1871)

The North German Confederation was a federal association of German states north of the River Main, founded by Otto von BISMARCK in 1866 after the defeat of AUSTRIA in the Seven Weeks' War. It was designed by Bismarck as a transitional federation to a united Germany, so that it could be easily modified in the future. As a result of her victory, PRUSSIA annexed those north German states that had taken the Austrian side in the war (HANOVER, Electoral Hesse, Nassau, and the Free City of FRANKFURT), as well as the duchies of Schleswig and Holstein over which the war was fought.

A constitution designed by Bismarck was adopted that made the king of Prussia the hereditary head of state as the federal president. As president the Prussian king was the commander in chief, which secured for Prussia control of the army. Although the Prussian king had no legislative or veto power, he appointed the federal chancellor, Bismarck, placing executive power primarily in the chancellor's hands and giving him control of foreign affairs. In this constitutional monarchy a Reichstag (Federal Diet) was to be elected by direct and secret universal male suffrage. This was of little significance because the Reichstag had very limited powers and had no power over the formation of a government. Bismarck was responsible not to the Reichstag but to the king. The North German Confederation also was to have a Bundesrat (Federal Council) which represented the princes of the 43 member states, which exercised limited powers.

When the German Empire was proclaimed at Versailles on January 18, 1871, the North German Federal Constitution was modified to admit the three states south of the Main (BAVARIA, WÜRTTEMBERG, and BADEN). The institutions established in 1867 continued throughout the German Empire.

North Rhine-Westphalia

North Rhine-Westphalia is the fourth-largest of Germany's federal states and the most populous. Geographically, it lies to the north of the RHINELAND PALATINATE. The creation of the state of North Rhine-Westphalia occurred at the time of the British occupation after WORLD WAR II. In 1946 the greater part of the former Prussian Rhine province and the province of Westphalia were merged and later augmented by the inclusion of the former state of Lippe-Detmold. The political traditions were kept alive. Some of the most significant cities of Germany are located in the state, which include AACHEN, Bielefeld, Bochum, BONN, Cologne, Dortmund, Duisburg, Essen, Mönchengladbach, Münster, and Wuppertal.

The history of the state was determined by the administrative reforms of Napoleon Bonaparte, and the transfer of the territory to PRUSSIA. At the CONGRESS OF VIENNA (1815). Prussia profited from what became the industrial heartland of Germany, the Ruhr, with such important industrialists as KRUPP, STINNES, and THYSSEN. Its nickname, the "coal scuttle," was changed during the restructuring of the decades of the 1960s and 1970s. Forty-five of Germany's 100 largest firms are headquartered there. In the 19th century Germany's military-industrial complex was headquartered there, but after WORLD WAR II it played a peaceful role in promoting the SCHUMAN PLAN.

Noske, Gustav (1868–1946)
SPD minister of defense

Gustav Noske was Friedrich EBERT's choice as defense minister during the REVOLUTION OF 1918–1919. He organized the repression of the Spartacus rebellion in January 1919, then organized the right-wing volunteer forces (FREE CORPS), which repressed the Soldiers' and Workers' Councils and the Munich Soviet Republic. With the support of Ebert, Noske reestablished the authority of the military under General Wilhelm GROENER (1867–1939).

Noske was born in BRANDENBURG on July 9, 1868, earned a humble living in the trade of a basketmaker, and was a trade unionist and editor. He was among the second generation of leaders of the SOCIAL DEMOCRATIC PARTY (SPD) and became an outstanding speaker, agitator, and journalist. He developed expertise in military and colonial matters. Becoming an editor of an SPD journal in 1897, he was elected to the REICHSTAG from 1906 to 1920. Ebert chose Noske to pacify the marine uprisings in Kiel at the end of the war, which he successfully accomplished. At the end of December he was chosen by Ebert to a fill a cabinet seat vacated by the INDEPENDENT SOCIALISTS and was appointed minister of defense from 1919 to 1920. Noske had been known for his energy and determination and his hostility toward the radicals. Furthermore, he was not a doctrinaire antimilitarist. He accepted his new position, telling Ebert that he would not shirk his responsibility and would become a "bloodhound" for the republic. He became a member of the Council of People's Representatives in December 1918. Unfortunately, he had to turn to the career officers of the old army, such as General Freiherr Walther Lüttwitz and Majors von Stockhausen and Hammerstein for leaders of the volunteers, and he had to depend on the Free Corps because the so-called republican units were politically or militarily unreliable. In January 1919 he suppressed the Spartacus revolt in BERLIN, then moved to repress outlying centers of revolt between February and May 1919, especially the Munich Soviet Republic.

Although Noske had appealed for democratically oriented soldiers to join the Free Corps, he did not succeed. Most of the provisional Reichswehr came from the military units that were neither democratic nor republican. Little enthusiasm for the republic could be found in the army. Ebert and General Wilhelm Groener had reestablished the authority of the old military through the EBERT-GROENER PACT. When it came time for troop reductions required by the VERSAILLES TREATY, General Lüttwitz would not carry out his orders, refused to resign as Noske demanded, and was involved in the KAPP PUTSCH. After the revolt failed, largely due to a general strike in Berlin, Noske was the victim of severe criticism by Philip SCHEIDEMANN, who blamed the Reichswehr and Noske for the putsch; he was backed up by Carl Legien (1861–1920), the president of the Social Democratic unions in Berlin, who also demanded that Noske resign. The SPD organization excluded Noske from the cabinet and also prevented him from being elected to the Reichstag. Noske was not completely lost from public life when the new minister of the interior, Carl Severing (1875–1952), appointed him provincial governor (president) of the Province of Hanover, which post he held until 1933.

Nuremberg
(German: Nürnberg)

Nuremberg was an IMPERIAL CITY of great importance in the history of the HOLY ROMAN EMPIRE. It had its origins in the 11th century in connection with a fortress of Emperor Henry III. The emperors found it a good military and administrative center, with nearby forests a great place for hunting. Emperor Frederick I, Barbarossa (1152–90), made Conrad of HOHENZOLLERN (ancestors of the dynasty of PRUSSIA) the town's imperial overlord. In 1219 Frederick II held an important imperial diet at Nuremberg and granted the town its first charter, which declared the town free of authorities other than that of the emperor. The town flourished, and in the 13th century established itself as an important commercial center. A council of merchants became Nuremberg's ruling class and purchased its independence. A symbol of Nuremberg's importance in the larger history of the Empire was that it was granted in the Golden Bull (1356) the privilege of hosting the first diet of each newly elected emperor, and in 1424 the emperor Sigismund made Nuremberg the location where the imperial regalia was stored.

During the reign of MAXIMILIAN I (1493–1519) Nuremberg was prosperous commercially, and the emperor borrowed money from its rich inhabitants. Its population within the city was nearly 50,000, with a similar number living in the suburbs, which made it the largest city in the Empire. It was also the home of artists and intellectuals such as Albrecht DÜRER, Viet Stoss, Peter Vischer, Adam Krafft, Michael Wolgemut, Hans Sachs, Christoph Scheurl, Lazarus Spengler, Martin Behaim, and Regiomontanus. Humanists were especially well represented by Konrad CELTIS and Willibald PIRCKHEIMER. It also was a printing center. Anton Koberger dominated the printing trade as editor and publisher of a great many books. The guild of Meistersingers was later idealistically represented in Richard Wagner's opera *The Meistersinger from Nuremberg.*

Not all the inhabitants of the city were contented. The city expelled its Jews in 1499, and they were not allowed to return until 1850. The REFORMATION had a serious effect on the population of Nuremberg, even though the emperor favored Roman Catholicism. Martin LUTHER's preaching was eagerly received by the humanists as well as among the upper class and literate artisans. Even though Nuremberg professed loyalty to the emperor, the city council promoted Lutheranism by appointing Protestant clergy in its churches. The lower classes were dissatisfied, desiring more power, which under pressure of the PEASANTS' WAR in 1525 received concessions. Nuremberg's situation was complicated during this period. While it was the residence of the Catholics Charles and Archduke Ferdinand during the diets of 1522 and 1524, most of the city professed its loyalty to Lutheranism. In 1521 the DIET OF WORMS moved the Council of Regency and the Imperial Cameral Court to the friendlier environment of Esslingen. Nuremberg joined the Speyer protest in 1529 and signed the AUGSBURG CONFESSION in 1530, but did not join the Protestant SCHMALKALDIC LEAGUE. The city actually sent large amounts of money and some soldiers to help the emperor in his war against the Turks. The city's participation in the THIRTY YEARS' WAR shattered its economy and severely reduced its population. The population declined to 25,000 by 1806, and economic decline continued due to the wars of the 18th century. At the time of the dissolution of the HOLY ROMAN EMPIRE by Napoleon in 1806, Nuremberg became part of the kingdom of BAVARIA.

In 1835 the first German steam railway was opened between Nuremberg and Fürth, which was four miles away. Nuremberg became a favorite of the romantics, such as Wilhelm WACHENRODER and Ludwig TIECK, due to its maze of medieval streets. In the 20th century the National Socialists exploited the prestige of the city, holding its party celebrations (*Reichsparteitage*) there. During WORLD WAR II Nuremberg was heavily bombed and extensively destroyed. In early 1945 some 7,000 inhabitants were killed by Allied air raids. In the following decades the city was reconstructed. The war-crime trials by the International Military Tribunal were also held in there in 1945–46. Nuremberg has become a manufacturing center of mechanical and electrical products and a center of the toy industry, which sponsors a yearly fair.

Nuremberg Laws (1935)

After a spring and summer of acts of terror, boycotts, and bans against Jewish entry into cinemas, swimming pools, and resorts, and suspension of publication of Jewish newspapers, the so-called Nuremberg Laws were formulated to define the status of Jews in Germany and to restrict them in political and social life. The legislation derived its name from the city of Nuremberg, where HITLER announced the laws at the annual party rally on September 15, 1935. They were the formal legalization of Nazi biological-racist ANTI-SEMITISM and Hitler's personal obsession with the Jews. The laws also were a response to the urging of chief of the Reich Medical Chamber, Gerhard Wagner, who wanted more severe racial laws. The Nuremberg Laws effectively ended Jewish emancipation and civic equality.

A Reich Citizenship Law and the Law for the Protection of German Blood and Honor were announced. They went beyond earlier discriminatory legislation, which had excluded Jews from the civil service. The laws essentially withdrew German citizenship from all citizens who did not have so-called German blood. The first law, the Reich Citizenship Law, differentiated between a "citizen of Germany or kindred blood who was thought to be the bearer of citizen rights" and a "subject," who was anyone who enjoyed the protection of the German government. In a decree implementing this citizenship law, the basic definition of a Jew was provided, that is "anyone descended from at least three grandparents who are fully Jewish as regards race." The second law protecting German blood and honor forbade marriages and extramarital relations between Jews and "subjects of German or kindred blood." Jews were also forbidden to fly the German flag and employ German females of child-bearing age (to 45).

Additional regulations were appended to the Nuremberg Laws, which separated the Jews from Germans politically, legally, and socially. Jewish doctors were dismissed from hospitals, and other regulations affected pharmacists, restaurateurs, tutors, dietitians, legal consultants, and inspectors. The laws affecting the establishment of blood lines of Jews were arbitrarily applied, especially toward Jews of mixed ancestry (*Mischlinge*), that is, those descendant from two fully Jewish grandparents. No clear procedures were in place for determining the Jewishness of grandparents, but generally Jewishness of grandparents was based on their association with the Jewish religious community.

The Nuremberg Laws were an extension of Hitler's goal to establish a pure Aryan race, which he already had emphasized in the Nazi Party's Twenty-Five Point Program of 1920, which stated that only a member of the German race with German blood could be a citizen; this excluded Jews, who were alleged to be of different blood. In *Mein Kampf*, where he emphasized racial purity, he asserted that "The highest purpose of the folkish state is concern for the preservation of those original racial elements which bestow culture and create the beauty and dignity of a higher mankind. . . . A folkish state must therefore begin by raising marriage from the level of a continuous defilement of the race, and give it the consecration of an institution which is called upon to produce images of the Lord and not monstrosities halfway between man and ape." With the Nuremberg Laws Hitler took a major step toward realizing his long-cherished racial goal. As far as the Jews were concerned, it brought a pause to the wild uncontrolled street violence they had experienced, until the Night of Broken Glass (Kristallnacht) occurred in 1938.

Nuremberg Rallies
(Nazi Party Days)

The rallies of the Nazi Party were intended to publicize National Socialism, its message and its leaders and as well as the strength and prestige of the movement. Most of the rallies were held in Nuremberg, which possessed medieval architecture and trappings and its traditions of the troubadours. Nuremberg became known as the City of Party Congresses. The rallies included demonstrations, parades, flag ceremonies, and speeches by Nazi leaders in which all the enemies of Germany, such as the Jews and the Treaty of Versailles, were attacked.

The first and smallest of the rallies was held in January 1923 to celebrate the Nazi cause, yet it still managed to attract 20,000 participants. Besides various marchers and parades at the opening rally, what became the traditional ritual of the consecration of flags took place. The second rally took place in Nuremberg that same year in August, recommended by Julius Streicher as an ideal historic and central location. Besides the parades and speeches a new feature was the memorial service for the dead soldiers of World War I. Since the Beer-Hall Putsch occurred later that year and Hitler was later imprisoned, another rally was not held until 1926.

The third rally was held in the city of Weimar because Hitler had been forbidden to speak in most cities, even Nuremberg. The pageantry was more modest, but one of the future powerful leaders of the party, Joseph Goebbels, made an impressive speech praising Hitler. The fourth rally returned to Nuremberg in August 1927 and again was modest. The consecration of flags had now become a tradition, and the highlight of this rally was a torchlight procession through the narrow streets. At this rally Heinrich Himmler appeared in a top position in the party.

In August 1929 the first truly spectacular rally took place under the theme of "composure." The rally was a gigantic presentation, and all of the major buildings in Nuremberg were used. At the 1929 rally the theatrical scenes that later played such a prominent part were first used, elements such as the endless marches, human formation of swastikas, fireworks, and long speeches by the Führer.

After coming to power, the Nazis held their only annual rally until 1938 in Nuremberg. To celebrate Hitler's appointment as chancellor it was called the "Congress of Victory." Massive facilities were needed to accommodate the half million Nazis who came. The consecration of the flags ceremony occurred, as well as a roll call of the dead and long speeches. In 1934 Leni Riefenstahl filmed the five-day rally for her famous *Triumph of the Will*. Hitler dramatically arrived in his airplane, and the torchlight parades were impressive. At the rally in 1935 Hitler announced the Nuremberg Laws and displayed the new armaments the regime had been building. Two hundred and fifty thousand party members attended.

The ninth, final, and greatest of the rallies was given the theme of "Greater Germany," and was held September 5–12, 1938. More than 1 million people attended, and each day was dedicated to a separate topic. All the theater that had been developed, such as torchlight parades and fireworks, was employed. It was the final rally before the war.

Nuremberg Trials

The Nuremberg Trials were conducted by the International Military Tribunal at the end of WORLD WAR II to prosecute and punish Nazi war criminals, 22 principal German leaders, conducted from November 1945 to October 1946. The legal basis was established in London at a conference of jurists from the four Allied nations, convened on June 26, 1945. Agreement on a statute for the court was finally signed on August 8, 1945, by the Allied powers and subsequently endorsed by 19 member states of the United Nations. Special courts had been set up in the past, but there was no precedent and universal recognition for such a court. The responsibility to mete out justice was to last until 1948, when German courts were to take over this responsibility.

Legal and moral issues troubled many jurists; there had been no legal code functioning prior to the commission of the crimes, and applying the code retroactively was debatable. Many of the worst offenders, such as Adolf HITLER, Joseph GOEBBELS, and Heinrich HIMMLER were already dead. Robert Ley committed suicide in prison, and others, such as Adolf EICHMANN, had escaped or were in hiding (like Rudolf HÖSS); Gustav Krupp was too ill to stand trial. The trials were also criticized because they followed an Anglo-American form of procedure, but they

Hermann Göring stands in the prisoner's dock after hearing himself accused of war crimes. Seated beside him is Rudolf Hess, 1946. *(Library of Congress)*

surely were grounded in international law. The defendants were: Hermann GÖRING, Rudolf HESS, Joachim von RIBBENTROP, Alfred ROSENBERG, Wilhelm KEITEL, Ernst KALTENBRUNNER, Hans FRANK, Wilhelm Frick, Julius STREICHER, Hjalmar SCHACHT, Walter Funk, Karl DÖNITZ, Erich RAEDER, Baldur von SCHIRACH, Fritz SAUCKEL, Alfred JODL, Franz von PAPEN, Arthur Seyss-Inquart, Albert SPEER, Constantin von Neurath, Hans Fritzsche, and Martin BORMANN.

Only three of the defendants, the conservatives, Hjalmar Schacht, Franz von Papen, and Hans Fritzsche, were acquitted over the objections of the Soviet Union. Walter Funk, Rudolf Hess, and Erich Raeder were sentenced to life imprisonment, but Hess and Raeder were released in 1957 and 1955, respectively. Constantin von Neurath received a sentence of 15 years, while Karl Dönitz received 10. Both Baldur von Schirach and Albert Speer received 20 years. All the remainder of the defendants were sentenced to death.

Out of the many Nazi organizations that also were tried, such as the SS, SD, SA, NAZI PARTY and the OKW, only the SS, SD, and GESTAPO were found guilty and their members subject to trial.

October Edict (October 9, 1807)

The October Edict was based on plans that were long discussed by reformers who desired Prussia to become a free, progressive, and productive society. The Napoleonic Wars had put plans for these reforms on hold, but with the defeat of Prussia at the Battle of Jena changes in Prussian society had to be made. Plans for social emancipation and economic development had already had been circulating, which became the basis for the king's edict. It was entitled "On the Facilitation of Property Ownership, the Free Use of Land and the Personal Condition of Peasants," and issued on October 9, 1807. The main objectives of this first great Reform Edict was the abolition of serfdom, the free exchange and disposal of landed property, and the free choice of occupation. It should be remembered that up to this time two-thirds of Prussia's population was still in serfdom, which meant they were not able to leave their homes at will and were required to render services to the manorial lord. The nobility were also restricted by not being allowed to engage in trade or to own peasant lands, while it was also impossible for peasants or the middle class (burghers) to own mortgages on noble property. The edict eliminated these restrictions, allowing economic freedom, the entry of all citizens into any occupation, and social mobility.

Together with subsequent legislation the edict facilitated the development of civil equality, social mobility, and economic freedom. Although peasants were legally freed from historic servitude, they were, however, left exposed to market forces and the requirement to reimburse lords for their loss of manorial dues. The October Edict also introduced market forces in the sale of the estates of the nobility. Even though the power of the reactionary nobility had been weakened or redefined, they continued to wield considerable influence. Baron Karl vom und zum Stein and other reformers also sought to enable citizen participation in government, thinking that this would encourage citizens to fight for their country. One such reform was the restoration of self-government in 1808 to cities (*Städteordnung*) which, however, did not free the cities to make and administer laws independently of the state. But Stein did hope that this and other reforms of city government would free them from control of state bureaucracies. The reformers failed, however, to create effective representative institutions for Prussia. Following the example of the French Revolution, Stein abolished the inherited privileges of the merchant and craft guilds, replacing these protected rights with capitalism and private property. Jews and members of the armed forces, however, were denied citizenship and forbidden to own real estate, to engage in trade and industry, or to participate in city administration.

Oder-Neisse line

The Oder-Neisse line was the frontier established between Poland and Germany agreed upon at the Potsdam Conference in 1945 at the end of the World War II. The final recognition of the boundary came in 1990 during the process of German reunification.

The Oder-Neisse line between Poland and Germany had first been discussed at the Teheran and

Yalta Conferences and finalized at the Potsdam Conference (August 1945). Poland east of the "Curzon Line" was to be ceded to the Soviet Union, and Poland was to be compensated in the west with territory taken from Germany. The boundary line followed the Oder River and its tributary the Neisse from the Baltic to the border of Czechoslovakia. There was some ambiguity concerning the Neisse River, which possessed an eastern and a western channel. The Russians and Poles decided on the western Neisse at the Potsdam Conference. The Polish government in exile in London also demanded the Oder-Neisse boundary on historic grounds. The U.S. and British governments, however, were initially opposed to it because of the great number of Germans who would be expelled, and it also would make Poland too dependent on the Soviet Union. Yet the Red Army already occupied the area, and the United States and Britain desired to continue their wartime alliance into the postwar period. The line was finally accepted pending the conclusion of a peace treaty with Germany.

The Oder-Neisse line gradually was accepted. The GERMAN DEMOCRATIC REPUBLIC officially recognized the frontier in 1950. In 1971 it was accepted by the government of the FEDERAL REPUBLIC during the OSTPOLITIK of Willy BRANDT. German reunification in 1989–90 brought about the final peace settlement with Germany, which was signed in Moscow on September 12, 1990. In it Germany and the wartime allies agreed on the Oder-Neisse line as the permanent German-Polish border.

OKW
(Armed Forces High Command)

The High Command of the German armed forces (Wehrmacht) during WORLD WAR II was known as the OKW (Oberkommando der Wehrmacht). After the resignation of Field Marshal Werner von BLOMBERG in January 1938, HITLER abolished the War Ministry, which Blomberg headed and established the OKW. Overall direction of the German armed forces was retained by Hitler as leader and supreme commander (Führer and Oberster Befehlshaber). It was planned that the OKW was to function as Hitler's military staff. General KEITEL, a man of no character and an admirer of Hitler, was to function as chief of staff, and General JODL was to run the operations division. Keitel was to be Hitler's deputy and took over the functions of the war minister.

The organization of the OKW consisted of the Office of the Chief, General Keitel and his assistants; the Central Administrative Division, which administered OKW; and the main body, which was divided into four departments: (1) The Armed Forces Operations Office (Wehrmachtführungsamt, WFA), which consisted of three divisions—national defense, armed forces communications, and armed forces propaganda. These divisions were to handle military operations, provide information on the military situations, prepare Hitler's directives, and provide communications and propaganda. General Keitel was the officer in charge of WFA, who had the title of chief of the High Command of the armed forces. (2) The Armed Forces Intelligence Office was known as Amt Ausland ABWEHR, which interestingly was the largest of the offices in OKW. It was headed by Admiral Canaris and controlled the collection and dissemination of military intelligence. (3) The Armed Forces War Production Office (Wehrwirtschaftsamt) controlled procurement, allocation, and production for the war effort. (4) The Armed Forces Administrative Office (Allgemeines Wehrmachtamt) coordinated scientific research, prisoners of war, and casualties. A variety of smaller units composed the remainder of OKW: military justice, legal, and fiscal departments, and others.

The organization of OKW went through three phases: (1) 1938–39, (2) 1938–41, (3) 1941–45. The first period until the outbreak of WORLD WAR II (September 1939) involved the preparation of a national defense plan. It amended the plan presented by Hitler in June 1937 and prepared a new defense plan in April 1939 and planned for the occupation of AUSTRIA and Czechoslovakia. The OKW also functioned as Hitler's personal military staff and cooperated with the high commands of the ARMY, NAVY, and AIR FORCE. In the second period the OKW began to function as a supreme ground force headquarters, which started in spring 1940 at the time of the invasion of the Netherlands and Norway. Both of these armed forces commanders (Wehrmachtsbefehlshaber) received their orders under Hitler's directions from OKW. The third period began in early 1942 (May) when many headquarters of theaters of war were subordinated to OKW. These included the commanders of France and Belgium; Denmark; Netherlands, Norway, and the Balkans; Central Russia and Ukraine; northern Finland; and later in 1942, Italy and North Africa. The purpose of this command structure was to permit the Army High Command to concentrate on the Russian theater of the war. It is also related to Hitler's assumption of control of military strategy and tactical planning in December 1941 and imposing it on OKW, which became ground force headquarters. Because Hitler exercised command from various headquarters during the war, wherever he was there was OKW.

Olmütz, capitulation of (1850)

After the Revolutions of 1848 were suppressed, PRUSSIA under FREDERICK WILLIAM IV tried to establish a union of German states under Prussian and Austrian leadership. This originated in a plan set forth by Joseph Maria von Radowitz (1797–1853), a friend and adviser to the Prussian king. After all the revolutions in the Austrian territories had been repressed, the real director of Austrian policy, Prince Felix von Schwarzenberg (1800–52) decided to strongly oppose the Prussian plans for union. He wanted to reestablish Austria's dominant position in the German states and deal with the threat that the Prussian king, Frederick William IV, posed with his desire to form a German union under Prussian leadership. Neither was he ready to agree to Prussian demands that they share equal status in a restored GERMAN CONFEDERATION. After the middle of 1849 Schwarzenberg changed from using diplomatic means to forceful threats. In 1850 he made it clear to the Prussians that they would have to abandon their project or face war. This caused Prussian conservatives to give in, arguing that if war broke out Russia would side with Austria and revolution might even break out. In the name of Prussian honor, Radowitz and Prince William, the king's brother, advised the king to resist giving in to the Austrian demands. In the end Prussia decided to retreat from all of her former positions, which opened a road to a settlement.

One of the most important causes of Frederick William's collapse before Olmütz and his willingness to give up his cherished plan of Prussian union was a blunt warning from the Russian czar that he would consider changes in European treaties that were made without the approval of the cosignatories as acts of aggression. On November 29, 1850, the Prussian prime minister, Baron Otto von Manteufel (1805–82), and Schwarzenberg signed a convention at Olmütz. Prussia was required to agree to the restoration of the German Confederation, which had been superseded by the FRANKFURT PARLIAMENT. Prussia also had to promise not to interfere with the restoration of the elector of HESSE by the Federal Diet (BUNDESTAG). In order to avoid an armed conflict with Austria, Prussia was further humiliated by being forced to give up its plans for a German union. Prussia made some small concessions on the Hessian question. In Holstein the old order was restored with the appointment of Austrian and Prussian commissars who would be under the authority of the German Confederation. The conferences that were agreed upon to discuss the reform of the confederation proved to be inconsequential because of the unresolved conflicts between Austria and Prussia.

Among the consequences of "the humiliation of Olmütz," as it later was called by nationalists, was Prussia's loss of prestige in Germany, which she did not fully recover until its victory over Austria in 1866.

Olympic Games (1936 and 1972)

The Olympic Games of the Eleventh Olympiad were held in BERLIN in 1936. It was not HITLER's fame that brought the games to Germany, because they were awarded to Berlin in 1930 before he came to power. In 1933 the Nazi press had condemned the Olympic tradition as a "festival dominated by Jews." That changed, however, as Hitler decided that the prestigious sporting event could have great propaganda value, showcasing his regime and demonstrating to the world how much the Nazi regime was interested in world peace. The regime spent lavishly to build nine arenas, especially the Olympic stadium where the summer competitions would be held. The campaign against the Jews was also stopped for the three weeks of the competition. Some of the Olympic customs taken for granted today, originated in 1936, such as the lighting of the flame, the torch race, and the Olympic village.

In true nationalistic fashion the crowd and Hitler hailed the German athletes who won medals. Hitler honored the German athletes by personally greeting them, but refused to do so for the black American athletes, especially Jesse Owens, who won four gold medals and was the hero of the games. The outstanding performance of the black American athletes contradicted Hitler's racial theories, according to which he regarded blacks like Jews as inferior human beings. Because of their superior uncivilized strength, he said, they should not be allowed to participate in future games.

The Olympic Games of the Twentieth Olympiad held in 1972 in MUNICH also had a propagandistic purpose. The organizers wanted to present a new face of Germany to the world to erase the memory of its dreadful Nazi past. Most of the Games demonstrated that positive perspective, but on September 12 Arab terrorists struck at the Israelis living in the Olympic village. Nine were taken hostage, and all were murdered; five Arab terrorists were killed as was one policeman. The event became known as "Black September" and proved that the Olympic Games could not be shielded from the conflicts of the world.

OMGUS
(Office of Military Government for the U.S. Zone)

The American zone consisted mainly of BAVARIA, Hesse, and the northern parts of BADEN-Württemberg. It was administered by the Office of Military Government for the U.S. Zone (OMGUS) and was run by General Lucius D. Clay. The American occupation was at first hampered by an unclear chain of command as well as unclear policies. Initially, the chain of command was under General Joseph T. McNarney, who had been a subordinate of Eisenhower. Because he had little interest in his responsibility, his deputy, General Lucius Clay, replaced him in 1947. So for two years some confusion reigned while at the same time American administrators had unclear policy directives from Washington. One set of guidelines from the State Department, besides emphasizing the Four Ds (DENAZIFICATION, demilitarization, decentralization, and democratization), also made economic self-sufficiency a priority. At the same time the Joint Chiefs of Staff were influenced by the Morgenthau Plan and emphasized the negatives of dismantling factories and banning fraternization. Both sets of guidelines called for decentralization of both economic and political life.

Like the Russians, the Americans were determined to dismantle the factories that had provided German war-making potential. Again a conflict of goals emerged as the Americans wanted to make their zone economically self-sufficient. In the end relatively few plants were dismantled, and by 1949 the program had ended. Also, by January 1947 the British and American zones had been united in a "Bizone" in which a free market economy was established.

Denazification in the American zone was conscientiously attempted but inconsistent and only partially successful. To begin with, the International Military Tribunal was established which tried the major Nazi war criminals in what was called the NUREMBERG TRIALS. American military courts also tried groups of defendants representing SS officials, leading business and governmental officials, and those who had been involved in the HOLOCAUST. The Americans also followed two policies in order to punish former Nazis. The first policy was "guilt by office holding and membership," and by the end of 1945 had jailed 100,000 so-called dangerous Nazis. The second was the "questionnaire" phase where individual guilt was to be determined by the completion of 12 million questionnaires. This presented great difficulties. Those with minor offenses were tried first, while serious offenders had to be investigated. By 1948 and the heating up of the cold war some of these major offenders and war profiteers were needed as executives for the revival of German industry. If comparisons are revealing, the British were much more astute in evaluating the seriousness of Nazi associations. They recognized that there were many, especially in the political and educational fields, who held only nominal memberships.

Ostpolitik
(Eastern foreign policy)

Ostpolitik is a collective term for the Eastern foreign policy of the FEDERAL REPUBLIC, a policy initiated by the Social-Liberal coalition to improve relations with West Germany's Communist neighbors. The policy was declared by Chancellor Willy BRANDT in 1969 to normalize relations with the GERMAN DEMOCRATIC REPUBLIC, to renounce the use of force, and to respect its existing borders with East European states.

Upon taking office, Chancellor Willy Brandt declared that the new Federal Government was prepared to recognize the GDR and thus also to abandon the claim that the Federal Republic was the sole representative of Germany. The key to a solution of all further questions lay in an understanding with the Soviet Union, for which Brandt's closest foreign policy adviser, State Secretary Egon Bahr, had been preparing in Moscow since January 1970. The first step therefore was the conclusion of the Moscow Treaty in August 1970 between the Federal Republic and the Soviet Union. In the treaty both parties renounced the use of force and recognized existing borders. After the treaty was signed, the Federal Republic also declared that it would continue to seek the reunification of Germany.

In December 1970 the Warsaw Treaty was concluded with the Polish People's Republic. Up until then the normalization of relations had been blocked by the conflicting views of the two countries on the border issue. Poland regarded the ODER-NEISSE LINE as the definitive border and had as early as 1950 concluded a treaty with the GDR in which the latter had endorsed this view. The Federal Republic, on the other hand, had always invoked the Potsdam Agreement, which left the settlement of the frontier question open until a peace treaty was signed with a reunited Germany and said that expellees should not be deprived of their right to their homeland. It also emphasized that it had no intention of altering the border by force. The 1970 Warsaw Treaty stipulated that the Oder-Neisse line forms the western border of Poland. Both parties reaffirmed the inviolability of the existing borders and declared that they had no territorial claims on each other.

Negotiations also began with the GDR in 1970. Up until then the Federal Republic had refused to recognize the GDR as a state and insisted that it alone had the right to speak on behalf of all of Germany. This changed in the course of two meetings and a series of agreements. The first was the Four Power agreement on BERLIN, affecting transit traffic between the Federal Republic and West Berlin, and a treaty on traffic questions that facilitated travel in both directions. Finally, on December 21, 1972, the BASIC TREATY was concluded, by which the two states undertook to develop normal friendly relations, refrain from the use of force, and respect each other's independence. The treaty, however, did not establish formal international recognition of the GDR by the Federal Republic; instead the GDR was recognized as a sovereign state but not a foreign country. The treaty created the basis for the gradual development of cooperation in such areas as health, posts and telecommunications, and science and technology. Furthermore, each state set up a "permanent representation" in each other's capitals.

Ostpolitik was the cause of acrimonious domestic debates in the Federal Republic. The CDU/CSU was still strongly opposed to the recognition of the GDR. The disagreements culminated in an abortive attempt to oust Chancellor Willy Brandt by means of a constructive vote of no-confidence and subsided only after the next election in November 1972, when the Social-Liberal coalition emerged victorious.

P

Pan-German League

The Pan-German League was the preeminent and influential imperialist organization in IMPERIAL GERMANY. The league was founded in 1891 by Alfred HUGENBERG and Carl Peters and was originally called the General German League. In 1894 the name of the league was change to the Pan-German League. Surprisingly, academics were the largest single group in the league due to their conservatism and their belief that patriotism, NATIONALISM, and imperialism would swing the allegiance of the masses away from the Social Democrats to the monarchy. The membership had reached about 8,600 by 1896 and more than 20,000 at the turn of the century.

When the General German League was founded, its principal goal was to protest the Anglo-German treaty by which Germany gave up its interests in Zanzibar to England in exchange for Heligoland. The league was a radical nationalist pressure group that represented a strong desire for colonies and the promotion of patriotism and of national consciousness among German emigrants in North and South America. One of its founders was a young radical, a former official in the Prussian Ministry of Justice, Heinrich H. Class, who was critical of the weakness of German foreign policy between 1908 and 1914. Class became the league's leader in 1908 and in 1912 published a right-wing manifesto, *If I Were the Kaiser,* that was anti-Semitic and favored an authoritarian domestic policy and an annexationism in case of war. It was Class and others like him who established ANTI-SEMITISM as a new ideological base of the organization and acquired financing from among the Ruhr industrialists. The league also worked in secret to influence the Reich's political, military and industrial leaders.

When war did break out in 1914, the league was at the center of the war aims movement, which included the FATHERLAND PARTY and published its program of extensive political annexationist war aims in both western and eastern Europe. Class and Hugenberg, a director of KRUPP INDUSTRIES, formulated a 1915 memorandum on war aims. It is interesting how they considered balancing the acquisition of France's mineral resources with agricultural resources in the East. The memorandum, known as the Petition of the Intellectuals, was signed by the leading conservative organizations in the Reich and supported by many of Germany's intellectuals. They had blamed the coming of the war on the Entente powers, France, England and Russia, and believed that the enemy must be forced to pay for its aggression by being forced to cede its territory.

After the war the Pan-German League was superseded by the new radical right-wing parties, such as the NAZI PARTY, which succeeded in building up rightist support.

Papen, Franz von (1879–1969)

Center Party politician and chancellor

Franz von Papen's early career was in the military. He was promoted to the General Staff in 1911 and then became a military attaché in Washington, D.C., and chief of staff of a Turkish army in Palestine. After WORLD WAR I he became a CENTER PARTY deputy in the Prussian Diet from 1921 to 1932 and purchased control of the Catholic daily paper *Germania*. In June 1932 Paul von HINDENBURG appointed him to succeed Heinrich BRÜNING as chancellor. The Center Party opposed his appointment and cut its ties with him, leaving the conservative GERMAN NATIONAL PEOPLE'S PARTY as the only party to support him in the REICHSTAG. Papen was forced to resign and was replaced by General Kurt von SCHLEICHER on December 3, 1932. Conspiring against Schleicher, Papen then convinced the aging Hindenburg to appoint Hitler as chancellor on January 30, 1932. After the Röhm purge he was forced to resign the office of vice chancellor and continued to serve the Nazi regime, first as ambassador to AUSTRIA and later to Turkey. In Austria he helped pave the way for its annexation by Nazi Germany. Unfortunately, he was acquitted of war crimes at the NUREMBERG TRIALS.

Papen was a monarchist who had President Hindenburg's confidence. One of the most destructive actions that he took was to dissolve the government of Prussia headed by Otto BRAUN of the SOCIAL DEMOCRATIC PARTY, which had been a bulwark against a Nazi dictatorship. Another significant error in judgment was Papen's proposal of a Hitler chancellorship, in the belief that he could "tame" Hitler by surrounding him with non-Nazi conservative politicians and with Papen serving as vice chancellor.

Paracelsus, Theophrastus (1493–1541)
physician and theorist

What was his true name, this physician and medical experimenter, teacher, and scientist? It appears as variations on Philippus Aureolus Theophrastus Bombastus von Hohenheim. His professional name, Paracelsus, meant "greater than Celsus," who was an ancient Roman physician who wrote an encyclopedic work on medicine. Paracelsus became famous for his revolt against traditional medicine based on the classic writings of Galen and the Muslim Avicenna. In his teaching he emphasized observation and experimentation. He thought of the human body as a microcosm of nature and possessed of wonderful recuperative powers.

Born in Einsiedeln in Switzerland, his physician father from Württemberg introduced him to the practice of medicine at an early age. His father moved to Carinthia, a mining area, where Paracelsus learned about alchemy and mineralogy. Most of his education was informal and practical, although he studied medicine at Tübingen and certainly at Ferrara. He set up a medical practice in Salzburg in 1525 and began a lifelong pattern of entering into public controversy with the authorities. Leaving Salzburg, he became city physician and professor of medicine at the University of Basel in 1527. Paracelsus stimulated controversy with other professors, who resented his lack of respect for the ancients, that he lectured in German instead of Latin, and even threw copies of Galen and Avicenna into a bonfire in order to symbolize his rejection of traditional medical theory and practice.

Paracelsus learned from many sources, including nature and common folk where he gathered his knowledge of the properties of herbs, plants, and minerals and the peculiarities of human illness. His was one of those so-called sleepwalkers during the Scientific Revolution who wandered and stumbled on new truths, which were, however, mixed with many errors. Much of the basis of his knowledge was experiential, in which he was opposed to the humanists who relied on ancient authorities. His theories were firmly theistic and Neoplatonist, derived from Pico della Mirandola. Paracelsus believed that God could be recognized in nature and nature be known in God. He believed that nature was the greatest of all teachers and healers. Humans and physicians were mediators and interpreters of its laws. He rejected the magical interpretations of nature prevalent during the Middle Ages, dominated by demons and other spirits. He believed that chemistry could serve medicine and that remedies for diseases could be found in nature. He perceived the human body to be a "microcosm," which corresponded to the "macrocosm" of nature. Paracelsus assumed that nature contained an all-pervading vital force that was an expression of the immanent creative activity of God. As God's workshop, nature is a continuation of creation. He also praised the human mind, imagination, and will for their role in healing people.

The role of the physician in this process is as a priest, an intermediary between man, nature, and God. When human beings become sick, the harmony between them and the world has been disturbed. Each ailment has a distinct cure, and the physician must discover the appropriate time and remedy. Paracelsus thus fused spiritualized astrology and alchemy. It was a mystical nature philosophy that exerted an enormous influence on German thought up to the second half of the 19th century. Its basic notion of nature as a creative process is found in GOETHE and the romantics (*see* ROMANTICISM).

Party of Democratic Socialism (PDS)

The Party of Democratic Socialism (PDS) is the successor party of the SOCIALIST UNITY PARTY (SED), which had been the ruling party in the GERMAN DEMOCRATIC REPUBLIC. The party came into existence after the resignation of Egon Krenz on December 3, 1989. Shortly thereafter, delegates met in BERLIN in order to renew the party. Even though it rejected Leninism, the party was rapidly disintegrating because people had lost faith in its promises and could not believe in its ability to renew itself. Membership that had been 2.3 million had dropped to 130,000. The PDS deliberately remained the heir to the SED rather than re-forming itself as a completely new party, so that it could retain offices, staff, and financial resources. Nevertheless, many thought that the party would decline into political irrelevance.

In the 1990 election the party, with the help of its media star chairman, Gregor Gysi, managed to do fairly well and was successful in the BUNDESTAG election due to a special dispensation of the electoral system. The PDS received 1.1 million votes, most of them (except 109,000) in the former East Germany. That gave the party just 2.4 percent of the total German vote, but 11.1 percent of that of the former East. The Constitutional Court had ruled in September that the West and East each would have their separate voting areas with their respective 5 percent hurdles. So the PDS won entry to the Bundestag with 16 seats, which was twice as many seats as those who had opposed the Communist regime in the political group, Alliance 90/GREENS. It was quite a remarkable event because for the first time since 1949–53 a far-left party was represented in the BONN parliament when the Communists held 15 seats. Most observers thought that the PDS success would be short-lived, and that in the election of 1994 without separate East-West voting the PDS would fail to meet the 5 percent hurdle.

The party, however, managed to do even better. It had firm backing from the old Communist Party members who despised the process of unification. That included members of the intellectual elite of former East Germany as well as of ex-government ministries, the armed forces, and the Secret Police (the STASI). Most had lost their jobs, and virtually all had lost status. This discontent and economic insecurity of East German voters explains why the PDS did particularly well in the Bundestag elections of 1994, receiving more votes than in 1990 and overcoming the 5 percent hurdle, giving it 30 Bundestag seats. In the 1998 elections the PDS won 21.6 percent of the vote. It also won seats in all five of the East German state parliaments, as well as in the Berlin state legislature and in the European Parliament.

In 1997 the PDS had about 100,000 members with only a small number residing in West Germany. Its membership is the largest of any party in the East and is generally composed of older citizens who are already pensioners or unemployed; nevertheless, some members are under 50 years of age. Its program has focused on the problems in East Germany and is critical of the competitive capitalist economy. It is opposed to MILITARISM and participation in military alliances. Especially important to its voters is the demand that criminal proceedings against GDR politicians and others accused of "regime crimes" be terminated.

Paulus, Friedrich (1890–1957)
general

Friedrich Paulus was the general field marshal in command of the Sixth Army, which lost the BATTLE OF STALINGRAD.

Friedrich Paulus was born in Breitenau, a small town in HESSE, on September 23, 1890, into the family of a minor public servant. Healthy and of good physical bearing, he applied for cadetship in the IMPERIAL NAVY but was rejected due to his low social status. For a while he studied law at Marburg, but then became an officer cadet in the army when it began to accept cadets from his social background. Within two years he reached the rank of lieutenant. In WORLD WAR I he served in France, mainly as a staff officer, and later was assigned to the 2nd Prussian Jäger regiment, a part of the Alpenkorps, which served in Romania and Macedonia. He did not experience command of any size unit during the war. He remained in the small postwar army, but his weaknesses as a commander were already evident as it was reported he lacked "decisiveness." He probably approved of HITLER's expansion of the army, and in 1934 he was given command of one of the earliest motorized battalions, then the following year became chief of staff of the new Panzer headquarters.

In 1939 Paulus became a major general and was appointed chief of staff of the 10th Army, later redesignated the 6th, under General Walther von Reichenau. It served in Poland, then in Holland and Belgium, and he was present when King Leopold of Belgium signed the surrender of the Belgian army on May 28. Later, he received a new assignment as deputy chief of staff and chief of the Operations Section at OKW. He was immediately given the task of drafting plans for the invasion of Russia. His aristocratic Romanian wife, who had expressed her view that the invasion of Poland was immoral, now also judged the Russian invasion likewise. Like most other officers he told her that it was a political decision and that he had to obey orders. Once the invasion plans were complete, he was sent to North Africa to observe Erwin ROMMEL's campaign. His judgment of Rommel was that he was too headstrong and his supply requirements would hurt the future Russian campaign.

In December, after the initial victories in the invasion of Russia, OPERATION BARBAROSSA ground to a halt. While the Russians held out in Leningrad and Moscow, the German Army Group South had not reached the Caucasus. General Runstedt resigned, and Paulus's former commander, Reichenau, was then promoted to commander of Army Group South. A fateful mistake was made on December 30, 1941, when Reichenau asked Paulus, who had never commanded a unit in war, to become commander of the Sixth Army, made up of more than a quarter of a million men. Reichenau, however, soon died of a heart attack and was replaced by Field Marshal von Bock. Paulus's performance at Kharkov was only average, but the city was held against a Russian attack.

The old Barbarossa plan of 1941 was abandoned in summer 1942. The Germans had lost too many troops during the winter, and attention now was focused on the southern sector. The Sixth Army was ordered to push east to the Volga River at Stalingrad but not to capture the city. The Sixth Army moved forward on June 28, 1942, and had to cover 350 miles to Stalingrad. Along the way Paulus succeeded in taking 40,000 Russians prisoner. Hitler changed his plans again in regard to Stalingrad, wishing for a psychological victory over the city that bore Stalin's name. Paulus's Panzers were joined by a Panzer Army diverted from the Caucasus offensive that encircled the Russians. The decisive battle of WORLD WAR II, the Battle of Stalingrad was about to take place with General Paulus at center stage. The Germans began their attack on August 21, 1942, bombing the city into ruins, which was followed by an attack of nine infantry, five panzer, and four motorized divisions. Unbelievably, the Russian defenses held. In September Paulus and his Army Group commander, Weichs, flew to meet Hitler, explaining that they lacked supplies and troops and had lines of communication that were too long. Paulus and Weichs believed Hitler's promises of reinforcements and were obedient to his orders. When they returned to Stalingrad, the battle proceeded to be very costly, even though Paulus's forces were increased by two Romanian armies. On September 13 a major German offensive began, and during the urban warfare that ensued Paulus's army was decimated by 20,000 casualties a week. After weeks gathering their forces on his flanks, the Russians started a counteroffensive on November 19, which encircled the Sixth Army by November 23. Between 250,000 and 300,000 men were trapped in an area nearly 30 by 20 miles. Paulus's actions were timid and obedient, but disastrous. Prodded by subordinate generals into radioing Hitler for the freedom to break out, Paulus received the order to stand fast at all costs. Hitler's promises of supplies were never sufficient, and an Army Group under Field Marshal Erich von MANSTEIN failed to link up with Paulus by Christmas, making the situation hopeless. Paulus refused to surrender in keeping with Hitler's orders, but after three weeks of fighting the Russians gained Paulus's surrender on January 31. The prisoners numbered 107,800, including 24 generals. Only 6,000 of the prisoners ever returned home.

While held under house arrest in Moscow for 11 years, Paulus was urged to renounce Hitler, but he remained loyal until the July 1944 bomb plot, after which he supported the RESISTANCE. At the NUREMBERG TRIALS (IMT) he testified for the Soviet prosecution and later joined the National Committee for a Free Germany, a Soviet puppet organization. After his release by the Russians he settled in DRESDEN in East Germany in 1953 and died on February 1, 1957.

Peasants' War (1524–1525)

The Peasants' War was a rebellion against serious financial and political grievances of the peasantry against the princes. The REFORMATION did not cause the Peasants' War, but some peasant leaders saw in Martin LUTHER's teachings on freedom and justice relevance to their worldly problems and their desire to be released from serfdom. Luther turned against the peasants, and the princes suppressed their revolutionary efforts.

It had been common in Europe for almost a century before 1517 that the peasants were in sporadic revolt known as "*Bundschuh* rebellions." Agrarian revolts were common and had a number of causes. Clerical and noble landlords exploited their peasants and violated village rights and legal traditions. They encroached on the peasant's use of common fields, forests, and streams. In the courts the Roman law was increasingly practiced, which supported these usurpations while the peasants were left to appeal to customary law. Serious financial and political grievances also motivated the rebels of 1524. They complained about the problems of hoarding, speculation, new taxes, and unfair rents. This was the period of early capitalism, and this combined with the land pressures of a rising population often caused a struggle for the control of village affairs among lords, tenant farmers, and landless cottagers. What made things worse was a series of bad harvests. Finally, in 1524, there was a psychological expectation that a conflict between lord and peasant was inevitable.

The most common proposals of the peasants for reform was presented in the Twelve Articles. The demands were moderate, and obedience to rightful government was strongly emphasized. They called for the free use of fields, forests, and streams, which had been traditional in the Middle Ages; the influence of Lutheranism can be seen in their desire to elect their own pastors; and finally the easement of dues and labor services. When they spoke of equality, they did not mean the abolition of social ranks, but principally only the end of serfdom and bondage. The peasants did not initially intend to use violence, but to debate and compromise. Although there were exceptions, the nobility did not bargain in good faith, as the negotiations carried on by Archduke FERDINAND and the Swabian League were conducted to buy time to mobilize their military forces. The revolt therefore became violent and more widespread. Regional groups and armies were formed, but attempts to unite the regional forces failed. Gradually, radicals took over, especially in Franconia, where the peasants were joined by the town population. Unfortunately for the peasants most of their captains lacked military skills, which led to their ultimate defeat. Because of the chaotic nature of the Holy Roman Empire with its dispersion of political power, the peasants lacked a central target.

Martin Luther initially urged the landlords to treat their peasants more humanely, but when the peasants indulged in excesses, burning castles and murdering nobles, Luther's attitude toward them changed to anger, calling on the nobles to kill the "murderous and robbing peasants." Luther's violent reaction probably was due to thinking that the peasants had perverted the Word of God to justify their rebellion. The peasants also had raised their hands against divinely ordained authorities, which God used to restrain man's evil nature. Authority, according to Luther, existed primarily to maintain the ordered conditions of society, which would allow the preaching of God's Word.

In June 1524 the rebellion began in the southern Black Forest, and from there quickly spread throughout Hegau, Württemberg, Breisgau, and Klettgau. By February–March 1525 three major peasant armies developed in Upper Swabia. The army of Baltringen was the largest, growing to 7,000 and was led by Ulrich Schmid, a blacksmith. Schmid traveled to the imperial city of Memmingen, where he found an ally in Sebastian Lotzer, who drafted the Twelve Articles. On March 6–7 they held a parliament at Memmingen, and the three Upper Swabian peasant armies formed an alliance in a Christian Union. Meanwhile, the Swabian League now had troops available to suppress the rebels. After the defeat of the two peasant armies, the Lake Constance group decided to submit its demands to arbitration. From there the revolt spread to Franconia, where three major armies were organized in the area of Bildhausen. The second army formed in the Oden Forest and Neckar valley committed the most vicious act of the war at Weinsberg before the massacre that ended the rebellion. At this time the colorful knight Götz von Berlichingen was elected the commander of the army. The third Franconian force was composed of insurgents from the area between the Main River and the Thuringian Forest.

The three armies converged and unsuccessfully besieged the Marienberg fortress in Würzburg. The armies of the nobility were superior, at first defeating the rebels at the Battle of Böblingen under George Truchsess, who joined with the elector Louis of the Palatinate, the archbishop of Trier, and the bishop of Würzburg. The Swabian League routed the rebels at the Battle of Königshofen on June 2, and shortly thereafter at the Battle of Ingoldstadt the rebellion in Franconia was crushed. In Thuringia the free imperial city of Mühlhausen was the center of revolt, where Thomas Münzer through his millenarian preaching spread the rebellion during April–May 1525. At the Battle of Frankenhausen on May 15, 1525, the peasant army was defeated, which along with the arrest and execution of Thomas Münzer ended the Peasants' War in Thuringia. Pacification came last to Austria, where Michael Gaismair (1491–52), the leader of the Tyrolean Peasants' Revolt, was a visionary of political, economic, and social democracy in a Tyrolean republic. Gaismair became the leader of a revolt in Salzburg but was defeated by Archbishop Lang of Salzburg and the Swabian League.

Out of approximately 300,000 rebels, about 100,000 died. Luther's denunciation of the rebels diluted the appeal of Lutheranism to the peasantry, but together the peasant rebels struck a serious blow against the remains of feudalism and the Catholic Church. It was not until the 19th century that revolution again arose among Europe's peasantry and lower classes.

Pechstein, Hermann Max (1881–1951)
artist

One of the early expressionist (*see* Expressionism) painters and graphic artists, Max Pechstein was a member of The Bridge. His paintings were used to communicate a religious rather than a political or social message.

Born near Zwickau in Saxony, he studied at the School for Applied Arts in Dresden and after two years entered the Academy of Fine Arts, where he quickly became a "master-student." He early obtained commissions for wall paintings and stained glass windows through his professor, Otto Gussmann, and graduated in 1906. That same year he joined The Bridge group after meeting Erich Heckel and Ernst KIRCHNER. He then traveled to Italy, being impressed by Etruscan and early Renaissance art, and became acquainted with the fauvists on a trip to Paris, then finally settled in BERLIN in 1908. In numerous works he perfected his graphic techniques with woodcuts, lithographs, and sculptures. Probably the most popular of the expressionists at this time, he was also considered the leader of The Bridge group. When Pechstein's paintings were rejected by the Berlin Secession organization for an exhibition, he and others organized the New Secession movement and exhibited at the Galerie Macht. He participated in the Blue Rider exhibition in MUNICH during 1912. As his talents and abilities were recognized and his use of bright colors become more acceptable, Pechstein was able to exhibit with the older Secession, which, however, prompted his old friends in The Bridge to expel him from their group. He traveled to the Palau Islands, where he was exposed to the expressive powers of Oceanic and African art. After his return to Germany, during the war he was drafted. He returned to Berlin and with other expressionist artists tried to encourage the public acceptance of the WEIMAR REPUBLIC. He joined the two most active artist associations, the November Group and Workers' Council for the Arts, hoping along with others to be instrumental in the creation of a new society. Although this sounds naive today, there was a widespread expectation that a new world was possible. By this time he had become the leader of the expressionist movement and was honored by being elected a professor at the Prussian Academy of Art. After the Nazis came to power, he was prohibited to paint, lost his professorship at the academy, had 326 of his works removed from museums, and had his art included in the DEGENERATE ART exhibition. He was required to perform forced labor during the latter part of the war, was later interned by the Russians, and then returned to Berlin, where his studio and many works had been destroyed. He was appointed a professor at the Academy of Art, where he taught until his death.

Most of Pechstein's main motifs had been figures in nature, the human form in natural surroundings. This was well illustrated by the nudes dancing in *Under the Trees* (1911), which he had imagined even before he traveled to the Palau Islands. The attraction to primitive art was widespread among the young expressionists, but also was displayed in ethnographic museums. Pechstein never diverted from essentially humanistic ideals and used painting to communicate religious rather than political or social messages. Although his use of vibrant colors was part of his early development, after his return from the Palau Islands the colors he used softened and his compositions became more balanced.

People's Court
(Volksgericht)

The People's Court was established on April 24, 1934, to hear cases of treason and attacks on the president and other members of the German government. It was a court of first and last instance, meeting in the plenary chamber of the Berlin Law Courts, which was decorated with three large swastika banners and busts of HITLER and FREDERICK THE GREAT.

There were three five-member panels of judges, with only two being professional judges and the others selected from the NAZI PARTY or the military. For some time the court was inactive but was upgraded in 1936 and its functions clarified. Its purpose was declared to be not to render justice, but to destroy the opponents of the Nazi regime. With the beginning of the war its powers were upgraded to be competent to judge sabotage, draft dodging, subversion, and other criminal cases that were usually referred to special tribunals. The tribunal was supposed to suppress even the slightest opposition. It operated under Section 5 of the Decree of Martial Law that was to protect the military from having its morale undermined. Statements that were derogatory toward a Nazi leader or questioned Germany's ultimate victory were punishable by death.

Between 1934 and 1941 the court was active, pronouncing 210 death sentences. Between 1941 and 1945 the number of death sentences rose to 5,191, most probably due to the July 20, 1944, assassination attempt against Hitler. The conspirators were brought before Roland Freisler, who condemned them for treason. Hitler demanded that they be hanged within two hours on meat hooks at Plötzensee Prison. On March 3, 1945, the court was destroyed by a bomb dropped by the U.S. Air Force. It just so happened that a leading conspirator, Fabian von Schlabrendorff, who was being led into the court, escaped, but Roland Freisler was killed. Although Freisler was replaced, the court ended its proceedings at the end of April 1945.

Pieck, Wilhelm (1876–1960)
president of GDR

Wilhelm Pieck was the first and only president of the GERMAN DEMOCRATIC REPUBLIC (GDR). He participated in the founding of the KPD in 1919, and in 1935 was elected president of the Central Committee, while Ernst THÄLMANN was imprisoned by the Nazis. In 1949 he was elected president of the GDR and was given a second term in 1953.

Born into a working-class family in Guben, Niederlausitz, Wilhelm Pieck was apprenticed as a carpenter at age 14. He joined the SOCIAL DEMOCRATIC PARTY in 1895, and in 1905 got involved in party work. He opposed the political truce (Burgfrieden) of 1914 and the SPD support for war credits, served in the army but was put in prison in 1917 for distributing antiwar propaganda. In 1916 he joined the Spartacus League and in 1918 became a member of the Central Committee of the GERMAN COMMUNIST PARTY (KPD). He was arrested again in 1919, but released just prior to the execution of Karl LIEBKNECHT and Rosa LUXEMBERG during the Spartacus uprising.

During the WEIMAR REPUBLIC Pieck was elected to the Prussian state legislature between 1921 to 1928 and to the REICHSTAG in 1928. He held other high positions in the Communist International and in the Cominform. He also was chairman of the KPD during the Nazi imprisonment of its leader, Ernst Thälmann. He spent the Nazi years in exile in France and the Soviet Union. In 1943 he was cofounder of the National Committee for a Free Germany. Returning to Germany with the Red Army, he became one of the two presidents of the SED. At the founding congress of the SOCIALIST UNITY PARTY (SED) he and Otto Grotewohl clasped hands in a symbolic union of the German working classes. Pieck and Grotewohl represented the moderate forces in the SED, while Walter ULBRICHT was trying to organize the SED along Bolshevik lines. In 1949 Pieck was elected president of the German Democratic Republic (GDR) and in 1953 was confirmed for another term in 1953. He died in BERLIN in 1960.

Pietism

Pietism was a revival movement within 17th-century Lutheranism that stressed personal religious experience, penitence, conversion, and the values of a Christian's inner life. The predominance of rationalism in theology and rigid forms of orthodox dogmatism left individuals frustrated in their individual spiritual lives. Some Lutherans formed into small groups and sects, which converged in the pietistic revival movement.

In the Protestant German Christianity of the time there was a pessimistic spirit about the possibility of converting the world or resolving the differences between the Christian churches. So Pietism arose with an alternative focus on an individual spiritual awakening (the rebirth of the soul in Christ) and the expression of Christian belief in practical works of charity. Pietism began with the organization of special meetings for biblical study (*pietatis*) organized by Philip Spener (1635–1705), who formulated a reform program in his *Pia Desideria* (1675). Pietism aimed at bringing about the rebirth of the soul in Christ, which involved penitence and conversion. An elaborate scale of experiences was developed from a contemplation of sinfulness to penitence, humiliation, and conversion.

Following Spener's example, August Hermann Francke (1663–1727) opened a Bible College (Collegia Biblica) in LEIPZIG in 1686 and established orphanages and schools. The popularity of his Bible College alarmed the orthodox theologians, who had the civil authorities prohibit its meetings. Anti-orthodox resentments spread to HAMBURG and also grew into a popular movement. The revolt of the laity combined with political resentments developed into the first real challenge in Germany to the absolute supremacy of the state and church.

Pietism also became rooted in some institutions. One base was the city and university of Halle. Franke's schools and orphanages were popular and the university became a center of Pietist teaching. In fact, the faculties of philosophy, theology, and law for a time had pietist leanings under the influence of Francke and the philosopher Christian THOMASIUS. Although FREDERICK II reduced the prominence of Pietism at the university, the educational, printing, and charitable foundations survived.

Pietism was not antirationalistic since both Pietism and rationalism believed in the empirical understanding of God. Pietists believed that God could be experienced in feeling and imagination, while the rationalists thought that God could be known conceptually. It is not commonly understood that Pietism was also a stream of the ENLIGHTENMENT, which stresses individual, emotional, and subjective experience and has some parallels in psychology. Pietism and the Enlightenment also had in common their opposition to the orthodox churches and state-sponsored religion.

While most Pietists remained in their traditional churches, more radical expressions of the pietistic movement occurred in the foundation of the Union of MORAVIAN BRETHREN (Brüdergemeinde) at Herrnhut in Saxony, founded by Count Ludwig von Zinzendorf. Their numbers grew to more than 100,000 members, but with persecution they declined or migrated, some to PRUSSIA, some to Poland, and some to North America. The first German colony in Pennsylvania was founded by the pietist Mennonites who landed in 1683. Pietism also influenced Quakerism and reached John Wesley in England, contributing to his establishment of Methodism.

The deep religious feeling of the Pietists influenced Friedrich Gottlieb KLOPSTOCK to create new expressions of literary style and language. The passionate poet Gottfried Arnold under the influence of Spener developed a religious form of storm and stress. Pietism also contributed to the creation of the sentimental and autobiographical novel. The soul-searching and self-analysis in Pietism inspired the classical writers of the 18th and 19th centuries, who, like GOETHE, Jacobi, SCHLEIERMACHER, Novalis, Gerhart HAUPTMANN, and others, owed some of their formation to this pietistic heritage.

Pillnitz, Declaration of (1791)

This was an extension of the Austro-Prussian DÉTENTE entered into by the emperor LEOPOLD II of AUSTRIA and begun with the Treaty of Reichenbach. In August 1791 Leopold II and FREDERICK WILLIAM II met in Pillnitz in SAXONY. What had set the stage for the declaration was the agitation by the emigrant nobles for a counterrevolutionary intervention. The most prominent royalist was the youngest brother of Louis XVI, the Count of Artois. He insisted that there be a full restoration of the political and social rights of the crown and nobility, insisting that if the Germans would only make a show of force the revolution would quickly collapse. Although the Habsburg emperor and Prussian king rejected the count of Artois's demands, they did issue the Declaration of Pillnitz some weeks after the failed attempt of the royal family to flee from Paris. The declaration stated that the revolution in France affected all nations and that with the support of other states the emperor and king would intervene to restore the position of Louis XVI and that he would introduce a constitution.

In reality the German states did not want war. The declaration had made an eloquent statement of monarchical solidarity, but both Austria and Prussia were more interested in what was going on in the Reich, the Netherlands, and Poland. They were relieved when the French king accepted the new constitution in 1791, and Emperor Leopold thought that war was unlikely. Yet, the internal forces in France pushing for war proved irresistible. The declaration was twisted by both royalists and the Jacobins. In February 1792 Austria and Prussia concluded a defensive alliance, and on April 20, 1792, France declared war against the new Habsburg emperor, Francis II (1792–1835).

Pirckheimer, Willibald (1470–1530)
Nuremberg patrician and humanist
Willibald Pirckheimer served an important function in the city council and as a diplomat for the city of Nuremberg. He also was an accomplished humanist who translated numerous works. His single major original composition was a historical geography of Germany.

Pirckheimer's father was a legal adviser to the bishop of Eichstätt. Besides traveling widely with his father, Willibald studied law and Greek in Italy between 1488 and 1495. He was elected to the city council, where he remained until 1523. Besides participating in the governance of the city, he served in a diplomatic capacity for the city council of this very important independent imperial city. He defended Nuremberg's claim to territories it acquired in the War of the Bavarian Succession of 1504. He also defended the city's interests against the claims of the Franconian landed nobility. He was also for a while the city's representative at the Imperial Court in Innsbruck. His interests in the city's educational system was definitely related to his humanistic concerns.

One of the principal reasons that he was famous and well respected almost as much as Johannes Reuchlin and Desiderius Erasmus was for his abilities and association with German humanism. He was a patron and friend of Albrecht Dürer, and he entertained scholars, theologians, and princes. His literary work was not original and mostly included translations of classics into German. He was in agreement with Luther that good translation should render the sense of the original and not necessarily be a literal one. He favored the Greek Church fathers, especially Gregory of Nazianzus. Pirckheimer's one original work was a historical geography of Germany and a brief autobiography.

Before the Reformation began, Pirckheimer was calling for ecclesiastical and theological reform. When Luther became involved in controversies, at first Pirckheimer blamed the Catholic theologian John von Eck and the Dominicans for the religious turmoil. By 1525 Pirckheimer believed that Luther and his supporters were excessive. Eventually he rejected the Reformation. He was opposed to the dissolution of monasteries and defended monastic life.

Pius XII (1876–1958)
pope
Before being elected pope in 1939, Eugenio Pacelli was the papal nuncio to Germany until 1929, becoming secretary of state in 1930. He was the chief adviser to Pius XI on Nazism and the principal negotiator of the Concordat of 1933 with the Reich. He was the coauthor of the encyclical *Mit brennender Sorge (With Deep Anxiety)* (1937), which rejected the myths of race and blood but made no mention of Anti-Semitism. Elected pope in 1939, Eugenio Pacelli vainly tried to prevent World War II. During the war he followed a policy of neutrality as did Benedict XV during World War I. In following a policy of prudent diplomacy, Pius XII followed a less combative policy toward Nazi Germany than Pius XI would have. He did speak out against the death of innocents because of their nation or race but did not explicitly condemn the genocide of the Jews. After the war this position earned the pope condemnation for his "silence" in the face of Nazi mass murder. Pius XII was also opposed to the judgment of collective guilt, that all Germans were responsible for the crimes of Nazism. Pius believed that German

Pope Pius XII *(Library of Congress)*

Catholics had been "martyrs" and opponents of Nazism.

Eugenio Pacelli was born in Rome on March 2, 1876, to Fillipo and Virginia Pacelli. He studied at the Gregorian University, receiving degrees in law and theology. He was ordained a priest in 1899. From 1904 he was professor of ecclesiastical diplomacy at Rome. He entered the Vatican Secretariat of State, and in 1914 was named secretary of the Congregation for Extraordinary Affairs. Pacelli participated in Benedict's peace proposals to the Germans. In 1917 he became papal nuncio to BAVARIA, where he remained until 1925. In 1920 he became papal nuncio to Germany until 1929 and continuously made efforts to conclude a concordat with the WEIMAR REPUBLIC. He was successful, however, in negotiating concordats with Bavaria, PRUSSIA, and Baden. He was the chief adviser to Pius XI on Nazi Germany. In 1939 he was elected pope and was soon called the "pope of peace" as he tried to persuade governments against war. He failed in his attempt to keep Italy from entering the war, but was an uncompromising anticommunist. Establishing the Vatican Information Service, he instructed the church to give aid to the Jews. In fall 1943, when the Nazis began rounding up Jews, some 7,000 Jews and antifascists found refuge in the Vatican.

After the war Pius was criticized for his silence by Rolf Hochuth in his 1963 play *The Deputy*. The publication of documents from the war indicated that Pius had knowledge of the mass murder of Jews in Poland and deportations of thousands from various countries to death camps. In defense of Pius it has been argued that his protests would not have saved the Jews and would have caused additional danger to Catholics. Also, the pope did not want to undermine Germany's struggle against Soviet communism.

In postwar Italian politics Pius followed a conservative policy. He tried to encourage Catholic Action to intervene in parliamentary politics against the left. He reluctantly supported the creation of a separate Christian Democratic Party. He created resentment when he condemned the French "worker-priests." Politically, he endorsed Western European integration and denounced communism in Eastern Europe. In 1950 he proclaimed the dogma of the bodily Assumption of Mary to heaven. At age 82 he died on October 11, 1958, at Castel Gandolfo.

Planck, Max (1858–1947)
physicist

Max Planck was one of the major contributors to the advancement of modern science through his second law of thermodynamics. He discovered a law of radiation that states that radiant energy always amounts to the integral multiple of a finite quantum of action.

Born on April 23, 1858, in Kiel, he was the son of a famous jurist and law professor and was educated at the universities of BERLIN and MUNICH. The dissertation for his doctorate was on the second law of thermodynamics. In 1880 he completed his *Habilitation*, which qualified him for a lectureship at Munich. In 1885 he wrote a paper on "The Nature of Energy," becoming associate professor at Berlin in 1889, and full professor of physics in 1892. At Berlin his scientific research expanded. His contributions were included in his famous *Lectures on Thermodynamics* (1897). In 1900 he discovered Planck's Law, for which he was awarded the Nobel Prize in physics in 1918. Between 1912 and 1938 he was the permanent secretary of the mathematics-physics section of the Prussian Academy of Science and was president of the Kaiser Wilhelm Institute from 1920 to 1937.

Although Planck claimed that his discovery of the second law of thermodynamics was a "lucky intuition," further investigation proved that his understanding of the law had to undergo some change. He had to accept that the second law was an "irreducibly statistical law: the entropy is directly related to the probability that a given microscopic (atomic) state will occur." Then he had a second insight, which involved a break with all his earlier physical theory, known as "Planck's constant" or "Planck's quantum of action." Afterward he continued his research, looking into the statistical aspects of white light, statistical mechanics, and kinetic theory. In 1905 he supported Albert EINSTEIN's revolutionary insights in his special theory of relativity. In 1914 he succeeded in convincing Einstein to come to the University of Berlin.

During the Nazi regime he "hated Hitler's laws" but nevertheless believed they must be obeyed. He did not resign in protest over the Nazi persecution of his Jewish colleagues. He tried but failed to convince HITLER of the damage he was doing to science. Planck's son, Erwin, was involved in the July 20, 1944, plot and was executed. Shortly after the war on October 4, 1947, Planck died in GÖTTINGEN.

Poland, partitions of (1772, 1793, 1795, 1815)

This series of partitions resulted in the total extinction of the state of Poland in 1795. Poland had flourished from the 14th to the 16th centuries but in the 17th and 18th centuries progressively declined into weakness and anarchy. Its neighbors (AUSTRIA, PRUSSIA, and Russia) took advantage of its condition and divided Poland among themselves in what became known as the First, Second, and Third Partitions.

The First Partition in 1772 was instigated by FREDERICK THE GREAT of Prussia, who proposed the acquisition of some Polish lands by its three powerful neighbors. In the First Partition one-third of Poland's territory was divided between Prussia, Austria, and Russia. Prussia acquired the northwest frontier portion together with DANZIG. Austria annexed Galicia, including Lemberg, adding in 1775 the Bukovina. Russia took the eastern strip of White Russia.

During the Second Partition in 1793 a large tract of western Poland, including the towns of Posen and Kalisch, passed to Prussia (later the province of Posen). While Austria did not participate in this partition, the Russians acquired the rest of White Russia and the western Ukraine, including Minsk and Pinsk.

In 1794 a Polish rising under Kosciuszko led to the occupation of the rest of Poland, which was divided between the three monarchies in 1795. Prussia obtained the northern part of the remaining rump, which included Warsaw. Austria now took Galicia with Cracow and Lublin. Russia annexed an enormous area from the Baltic, including Courland in Lithuania, southward into Kovno, Wilna, Grodno, and Brest.

Napoleon resuscitated Poland as the Grand Duchy of Warsaw (1807–14), but there was a fourth partition through which the Russians extended their region westward, thereby including Warsaw. Prussia had lost all of its acquisitions of the Third Partition and part of the Second. Austria also lost to Russia most of the territory it had acquired in the Third Partition. Cracow was made a free republic in 1815.

Polish NATIONALISM remained the common enemy of the conservative monarchies but especially Russia, against the two great Polish revolts in 1830 and 1863. Poland was re-created in 1918 at the end of WORLD WAR I.

Polish Corridor

The TREATY OF VERSAILLES, by which territorial settlements were made after WORLD WAR I, took one-10th of Germany's prewar territory and population. Most of the German territorial losses were in the East, which re-created the state of Poland. Parts of the former Prussian provinces east of the Oder River were incorporated into the Polish Republic. Because the main seaport of Poland was the "free city" of DANZIG, which had previously been German, the landlocked Polish state was given a strip of territory along the Vistula River, which gave it access to the Baltic Sea. The corridor separated East Prussia from the rest of Germany. The population of the corridor was still predominantly Polish, and prior to the PARTITIONS OF POLAND in the 18th century had been a part of the Polish state. The population of the port of Danzig (Gdańsk) was, however, predominantly German.

This arrangement was bound to lead to conflict between Germany and Poland. The restoration of the corridor to Germany was a goal of revisionist German foreign policy. Nothing was changed during the WEIMAR REPUBLIC, but the corridor was given as a reason by HITLER for the invasion of Poland in 1939.

Porsche, Ferdinand (1875–1951)
automobile designer

Ferdinand Porsche was the designer of the Volkswagen and the Porsche sports car. As an inexpensive family sedan, the Volkswagen made him famous, while the sports car became a status symbol for the wealthy.

Born the son of a craftsman in Mallersdorf, Bohemia, Ferdinand Porsche was technically self-educated. He worked at the Lohner-Werke in Vienna from 1898 to 1905. In 1906 Porsche joined Austro-Daimler in Vienna as a technical director, building aircraft motors and sports cars. In 1923 he transferred to Stuttgart, where he remained until 1929, when he returned to Upper Austria, where he built two sports cars, the Steyr 30 and the Steyr 100. During the 1920s he gained an international reputation for compressor motors in his sports and luxury cars. In 1931 he established his own engineering firm and built a great reputation as a design engineer based on his development of combined gas and electric vehicles for civilian and military uses. One of his greatest ambitions was to design vehicles without economic constraints.

Porsche designed the inexpensive Volkswagen or "people's car" which was adopted by the Nazis and produced at the factory in Wolfsburg, which later became the largest automobile factory complex in Europe. His son, Ferdinand, was the actual designer of the VW. The VW had limited success before the war and did not reach its great popularity until after the war. During the war Porsche held leading positions in the economy and he and his son designed military vehi-

Hermann Göring, Robert Ley, Ferdinand Porsche, and Nazi officials looking at a Volkswagen convertible given to Göring, 1939 *(Library of Congress)*

cles. Besides being respected by HITLER, he was connected with Heinrich HIMMLER. Some of Porsche's success during the war was due to his employment of war prisoners, foreign workers, and CONCENTRATION CAMP labor. Not that he was the only one to do so, but he should have been punished more severely by the French, by whom he was imprisoned after the war.

Contributing to his postwar success was the launching of the Porsche sports car in 1950, which became a modern status symbol. Porsche did not live long to enjoy his success, dying in 1951.

Positive Christianity

The Nazi Party espoused a religious philosophy called "Positive Christianity," which it formulated in Article 24 of the party program adopted on February 20, 1920. Article 24 demanded "liberty for all religious denominations in the state, so far as they are not a danger to it and do not militate against the morality and the moral sense of the Germanic race. The Party, as such, stands for positive Christianity, but does not bind itself in the matter of creed to any particular confession." This vague religious platform in the Nazi program guaranteed religious freedom and avoided the pitfalls of the politics of religion and the alienation of potential supporters. When Alfred ROSENBERG published his *Myth of the Twentieth Century*, he provided specificity to the meaning of "Positive Christianity," explaining that its goal was to purify the German Nordic race, create a German church that harmonized belief in Christ with the forces of blood, race, and soil, do away with the Old Testament and purge the New Testament of "distorted and superstitious reports," restore the pagan Nordic values, and substitute the spirit of the hero for that of the Crucifixion. In fact, instead of the Christian cross, the symbol of Positive Christianity was the orb of the sun. Essentially, Positive Christianity meant the glorification of the Nordic race, contempt for divine revelation, and a demand for a German God and German Christianity. This interpretation was certainly contrary to traditional teachings of the Catholic Church and traditional Protestant churches, except those "German Christians" who in 1934 joined the German Faith Movement. Careful to avoid taking a public position defending the "German Christians" Hitler nevertheless approved of it.

Potsdam, Edict of (1685)

On November 8, 1685, FREDERICK WILLIAM, the Great Elector, issued an invitation to all Frenchmen of the Reformed-Evangelical faith to settle in BRANDENBURG. He offered them "a safe and free retreat" in his lands. As these so-called Huguenots were being persecuted in France by the revocation of the Edict of Nantes by King Louis XIV, some 20,000 Huguenots came and settled in HOHENZOLLERN territories. The Edict of Potsdam was a courageous act by the elector, who through the edict was inviting the Huguenots who were forbidden by Louis XIV to emigrate under severe penalties.

Potsdam Conference (July 17–August 2, 1945)

The Potsdam Conference, held in Potsdam, Germany, was the last of the Allied wartime conferences that discussed the future of Germany. Joseph Stalin continued to represent the Soviet Union, while the United States now had a new president, Harry Truman, and Britain a new prime minister, Clement Attlee.

The conference decided on the complete disarmament and demilitarization of Germany. It also agreed on the elimination or control of German industry that could be used for war production. In the administrative area the Allies created the Allied Control Council for coordinating their policies, but in reality each power could veto whatever was contrary to its interests. Little disagreement existed over the general policies of DENAZIFICATION, democratization, and demilitarization. Formal partitioning of Germany, which the Allies considered at the conferences of Teheran and Yalta, did not take place.

The conference approved the principle of reparations to the Soviet Union and other countries that had been victims of Nazi aggression. Rather than monetary, the Big Three agreed to permit reparations in kind. Each occupying power was permitted to remove German property from its own zone, but not so much as to jeopardize a tolerable German standard of living. In addition, the Soviet Union was to get 25 percent of the dismantled industrial equipment from the Western zones, since most Germany industry was located there, in exchange for food and raw materials from the Soviet zone. The conference participants also agreed to establish the Polish-German border along the Oder and western Neisse Rivers, which moved Poland 200 miles to the west, and agreed to permit the Soviet Union to retain the areas annexed in 1939. The conference also agreed that ethnic Germans from Czechoslovakia, Hungary, and Poland, who numbered more than 6 million, would be resettled.

Organizations that had served to support the German military tradition were to be abolished. This included all German land, naval, and air forces, the SS, SD, SA, and GESTAPO, the General Staff and officer's corps, reserves and military schools, war veterans organizations, clubs and associations that contributed to keeping the military tradition alive. The NAZI PARTY was destroyed. Education and the judicial system were to be reformed.

All of these arrangements were intended to be temporary and subject to a peace treaty with a united Germany.

Pragmatic Sanction (1713)

The Pragmatic Sanction was a new family law issued by Emperor CHARLES VI in order to secure the succession of his daughters to the Habsburg crown and the indivisibility of the Habsburg dominions. More to the point, it aimed to secure the succession of his eldest daughter, MARIA THERESA. In 1724 at the birth of their third daughter, Charles feared that he would not have a son as an heir. The problem of the Austrian succession had actually preoccupied Charles from the beginning of his reign. He had an elder brother, Joseph, whose children actually preceded his in the line of succession, which had been designated in a "mutual succession pact" by the emperor LEOPOLD when he left for Spain in 1703. It was supposed to settle the rights to the throne between the Austrian and Spanish Habsburg families. When Joseph, however, died in 1711, the pact lost its force, and Charles sought to change it, which he accomplished through the issuance of the Pragmatic Sanction in court in April 1713.

The Pragmatic Sanction was a revolutionary document. Previous documents that had allowed for a female succession had been hypothetical. For the first time the public declaration by Charles required a formal acceptance by the estates of the Habsburg lands. It was of particular importance relative to Hungary, which in the absence of a male heir could still elect its own king. Charles also desired foreign recognition to protect the succession of his daughter. Unrealistically, Charles placed too much faith in the document and its acceptance and should have followed the advice of Prince EUGENE of Savoy, who counseled that a full treasury and strong army would have been better insurance.

The imperial government announced the Pragmatic Sanction in 1718 and requested the consent of the estates in the Habsburg possessions. By 1732 the Pragmatic Sanction was recognized by the estates, and that same year the HOLY ROMAN EMPIRE gave its consent. The estates had consented with the provision that the Sanction did not lessen their existing rights, which was another way of saying that they were opposed to a strong central government. The estates gave their unanimous consent, indicating their loyalty to the Habsburg Empire. By 1738 all principal European powers had given their assent, which was of doubtful value as a guarantee, especially concerning FREDERICK II of PRUSSIA.

Preuss, Hugo (1860–1925)
constitutional lawyer

Hugo Preuss was most significant in his role in formulating the WEIMAR CONSTITUTION. He was also the cofounder of the left-liberal GERMAN DEMOCRATIC PARTY (DDP).

Born in 1860 into a middle-class Jewish family in BERLIN, he completed his doctorate at the University of Berlin. His *Habilitation,* which should have enabled him to teach at Berlin, did not succeed in getting him a professorial chair, not only because he was a Jew and a member of the new left-liberal Progressive People's Party (Fortschrittliche Volkspartei), but partly due to his sarcasm and Berliner wit. He was instead appointed to the new Commercial University of Berlin. Intellectually he was a disciple of Otto Gierke and developed a democratic version of his theory of Syndicalism. In practical politics he followed Theodor Barth, while his hero in history was Baron Karl vom und zum STEIN, whose reforms Preuss honored as the climax to his book *History of the Development of German Municipal Law* (1906). During the first year of the war Preuss published his political ideas in *The German People and Politics.*

Preuss was appointed secretary of the interior on November 15, 1918, and asked by the CPP (Council of People's Plenipotentiaries) to write a draft constitution to be presented to the constitutional convention, which was to meet in WEIMAR. Shortly after the revolution he published an article that advocated that liberals cooperate with the SOCIAL DEMOCRATS in establishing a republic. His constitutional draft envisioned a full-scale parliamentary democracy modeled upon those of France and Great Britain. Universal suffrage and proportional representation provided for a national parliament that was fully reflective of public opinion. The executive was to be subject to control by the popularly elected parliament (REICHSTAG). A cabinet was to serve only as long as it had the confidence of the national parliament. The National Assembly accepted this part of Preuss's draft. In place of the Imperial Federal Council where state officials were bound by the instructions of their governments, the delegates to the upper house or Reichsrat were to be free in their vote. Max WEBER urged that the president be popularly elected, which Preuss adopted. The president's seven-year term was to ensure that he would be above parties. Preuss also wanted the president to have limited powers, mainly nominating the Reich chancellor. This was not agreeable to the National Assembly, which gave the president considerable power in times of emergency and was expressed in Article 48. This gave the president the power to declare an emergency and govern without parliamentary approval. The assembly disagreed with Preuss's ideas on federalism and rejected the division of PRUSSIA into a number of states. When President Friedrich EBERT reviewed the draft, he wanted Preuss to give the constitution a popular ring by writing in the rights that the revolution had secured. They were included as freedom of press, assembly and association, freedom of person, freedom to select one's occupation, and freedom of academic teaching.

Preuss was the Reich interior minister in the period 1918–19 but resigned from the cabinet along with other DDP members in February 1919 in protest of the government's acceptance of the TREATY OF VERSAILLES.

Progressive Party
(Fortschrittspartei)

The Progressive Party was the oldest of the REICHSTAG parties. It was founded in 1861 in the Prussian *Landtag* by the left liberals who split from the main group of liberals. The leadership of the new party was composed of Max von Forckenbeck, Freiherr von Hovebeck, Hans Victor von Unruh, Hermann Schulze-Delitzsch, Theodor Mommsen, and Rudolf Virchow. They were landowners and members of the educated MIDDLE CLASS. It was the first modern national party in Germany and became the largest party in the Prussian parliament during the constitutional struggle of the 1860s. The Progressives led the fight in defense of parliamentary rights against the king over the army bill by which the government planned to strengthen the army.

The differences that the Progressives had with the old liberals were those of tactics and not goals. The Progressives were loyal to the king. They denied being opposed to the government but intended to champion the principles of the REVOLUTION OF 1848 and wished for Prussia to become a complete parliamentary state. They were liberal in their politics and economics. In general they were antimilitarist, antistatist, and against a protectionist tariff policy. Constitutionally, they wanted the protection of the administration of justice, freedom of the press, economic liberty, and separation of church and state. In reference to the reform of the army the Progressives demanded the continuation of the national guard, two years of active military service, and Prussian state takeover of the leadership in German unification. Moreover, they were bitter opponents of the SOCIAL DEMOCRATIC PARTY. The Progressives drew their electoral strength from the urban centers, from the commercial middle classes, from artisans, small merchants, lower officials, and intellectuals.

The king dissolved the parliament, concerning the conflict over the reform of the army. In the elections of December 1861 the German Progressive Party was victorious. While the conservatives retained only 15 of their 57 seats, the Progressives won 135 seats. The old moderate liberals lost considerable support, although 95 of them still entered the new parliament as did another 50 who represented moderate liberalism. The liberals enjoyed a parliamentary majority, which erupted into a parliamentary crisis over military reform. It was this crisis that led to Otto von BISMARCK's recall from Paris and appointment as prime minister.

The most important leader of the party was Eugen Richter (1838–1906). Together with Ludwig WINDHORST, Richter was an obstinate and sharp parliamentary debater. He was a conscientious and able parliamentarian, but habitually opposed Bismarck's policies. Richter was opposed to protective duties, imperialist expansion, armaments, and even a state system of welfare. He was said to be one of the best speakers of the Reichstag, a man of character, educated but abrasive and inflexible. He was, however, dull and lacked human appeal. Friedrich NAUMANN became the party leader following Richter's death. He was a more creative thinker. Naumann led progressive LIBERALISM away from laissez-faire economics and believed in the need to infuse social content into middle-class liberalism, creating a bridge to the working classes.

The Progressive Party lasted under this name until 1884, when it combined with a secessionist group from the NATIONAL LIBERAL PARTY and was renamed the Freisinnige Partei until 1893. A split again occurred, and the leftist groups became known as the Freisinnige Vereinigung. In 1910 the various left-liberal groups merged again to form the Fortschrittliche Volkspartei. During the WEIMER REPUBLIC it was again reconstituted as the Democratic Party (DDP).

Protestantism

The religious reform movement in the Roman Catholic Church that began with those reforms demanded by Martin LUTHER and that ended with divisions into distinct churches within the ranks of the reformers has been called Protestantism. The name Protestantism is derived from the name given to the princes and cities that at the imperial assembly of the Diet of Speyer in 1529 signed a "Protest" against the emperor, who had sought to enforce adherence to the pre-Lutheran beliefs of the Catholic Church. The term *Protestant* later came to be used to refer to non-Catholic forms of Christianity.

The Lutheran Church emphasized vernacular church services and communion for the laity both of the bread and wine, which Luther initiated in his German Mass. Luther as well as other reformers made the sermon the central part of the Sunday service and placed less stress on the Eucharist than Catholics had. One of Luther's most important associates was Philip MELANCHTHON, who developed the theological and administrative bases of the new churches. The theological principles of the Protestant churches, including the work of the Swiss reformers Ulrich ZWINGLI and John CALVIN, emanated from the simple notion of justification by faith alone and the return to the Scriptures.

The main Protestant Church in Germany was the Lutheran. The second was the Reformed Church, which was principally the work of Calvin and Zwingli. The division originated in 1529 at the Marburg COLLOQUY, where the reformers could not agree over the nature of the Eucharist, that is, whether the Lord's presence was real or symbolic. Luther's Biblicism was opposed to the philosophic rationalism of Zwingli, and unfortunately for the unity of the Protestant cause they would not compromise. Their writings on the sacraments had already sharply divided them. With some modifications the teachings of Zwingli were adopted beyond Switzerland in the cities of southern Swabia as well as along the RHINE from Strasbourg to as far as the Netherlands. The North German principalities and NUREMBERG, as well as the Franconian and north Swabian cities, followed Luther. There was always a political interconnection between religious reform and politics. In Germany religious decisions were left to the princes, while in Zurich religious reformation was always evaluated as to how it involved the republican politics of the city. From 1559 on, the Reformed Church was the officially recognized church of Switzerland and was recognized in Germany by the PEACE OF WESTPHALIA (1648). After the French Revolution the Lutheran and the Reformed Church were arbitrarily united in the Evangelical Union in 1817 by a decree of King Frederick William III.

Since the REFORMATION revision and revival of belief has been a prominent part of the Protestant experience. Protestantism has always been in a state of flux, and more intensely in Germany than in other countries. To begin with, the principal churches, both Lutheran and Calvinist, put a halt to the more radical reform of the ANABAPTISTS. In the 18th century Protestant theology came to be dominated by PIETISM and then the rationalism of the ENLIGHTENMENT. In reaction to the dry theology of the 17th century, Pietism was developed by Philipp Spener, who emphasized free associations outside of the authoritarian organizational church. It aimed at a deeper personal spiritual and moral life, a personalized religion through personal introspection, and prayer with extra emphasis on Bible study. This was carried out further by August Hermann Franke (1663–1727), who favored private discussions that were linked to the church services. Then Count Nikolaus von Zinzendorf, who founded the MORAVIAN BRETHREN, gave birth to an ecstatic kind of Pietism, which developed in the 18th century. Pietism was a very emotional form of Protestantism; it produced a number of great hymns.

The rationalism of the Enlightenment promoted an optimistic reappraisal of God's creation, which provoked skepticism, free thought, and criticism of hypocrisy. There also emerged those who stood for the belief in a personal relationship with God based on irrational and sensuous perceptions. With the moral philosophy of Immanuel KANT the paradoxical concept of a secularized religion arose. The philosophies of FICHTE, Schelling, and HEGEL did prepare the way for the naturalistic materialism of Ludwig A. FEUERBACH, who in his *Essence of Christianity* (1841) proclaimed that the Christian religion was the creation of man's wishful thinking. Materialism increasingly made inroads among the Protestant MIDDLE CLASS. The theology of Friedrich SCHLEIERMACHER stimulated a revival that was in tune with subjective idealism nurtured by the romantic age and from which a Christocentric subjective modern theology emerged. The influence of Kierkegaard was considerable, while Karl BARTH and Rudolf Bultmann became important theologians.

After German unification the Protestant churches had to respond to the growing industrialization and secularism that faced evangelical Christianity. They adopted a theology of conservative NATIONALISM and chose to oppose socialism and democracy while remaining defensive against Catholicism. This series of sentiments tied the upper and middle classes of society with the Protestant churches, but served to alienate them from urban workers. The basic unit, however, remained the territorial church (*Landeskirche*). Efforts at unity were frustrated by doctrinal and theological differences between the Lutheran and Reformed churches. The populations of both Lutherans and Calvinists have been the greatest in Prussia. Until 1918 the territorial ruler acted as "supreme bishop"of his church, which gave him final authority over ecclesiastical law, administration, appointments, and even doctrine. Even though in internal administration some autonomy had been gained from the state, the secular prince, especially the king, had the ultimate authority in the Protestant churches. German Protestantism remained the support of authoritarian monarchical government and resisted democratization, even though representative synods were introduced. During the Weimar years most Protestant leaders had difficulty reconciling themselves to the loss of the war, the abdication of the monarchy, and the introduction of parliamentary democracy. In general Protestant leaders welcomed the rise of National Socialism because HITLER promised a national revival, the destruction of communism and socialism, and an end to the hated advance of secularism. Some Protestants tried to make adjustments to the modern world as some followers of the theologian Karl BARTH did. After the Nazis came to power and the GERMAN CHRISTIANS challenged the institutional independence of the Protestant churches, the CONFESSING CHURCH under the leadership of Karl Barth protested with the BARMEN DECLARATION. That does not mean, however, that good Protestants opposed the policies of the Nazi regime.

After 1945 the position of Protestants was quite varied, both politically and socially. Protestants in the FEDERAL REPUBLIC lost their majority status, while in the GDR where Protestants were in the majority the churches lost their legal status. In the West Protestants politically supported both the CHRISTIAN DEMOCRATIC UNION (CDU) and the liberal FREE DEMOCRATIC PARTY as well as the SOCIAL DEMOCRATIC PARTY and the GREEN PARTY on the left. In the East church leaders found it necessary to break with their conservatism and accept the SOCIALIST UNITY PARTY (SED) and the East German state and in return were tolerated as a loyal opposition. A significant role was played by the churches when the East German dissidents were able to organize their protests of the regime in 1989 and bring about its collapse.

Protocols of the Elders of Zion, The

The *Protocols* is a forged anti-Semitic document of an alleged Jewish conspiracy to dominate the world. HITLER used it in his campaign against the Jews. The *Protocols* is supposedly an authentic report of the minutes of a secret Zionist congress that aimed to overthrow Christian civilization and to erect a Jewish world government in its place. The *Protocols* claims to be a verbatim transcript of a speech by an unnamed Jewish leader at 24 different meetings of the Elders of Zion. The *Protocols* emphasized two basic ideas: the belief that the Jews are the opponents of Christianity's divine plan for salvation and the vanguard of the Antichrist; and a conspiracy theory that saw the French Revolution as the work of transnational organizations such as the Freemasons, the Jacobins, and anarchists. The real enemies behind these organizations were revealed to be the Jews. Catholic circles were predominantly responsible for identifying FREEMASONRY with the Jews.

Previously unknown outside of Russia, it was Russian émigrés who after the Russian Revolution brought the *Protocols* to western Europe and North America to spread the word that Jewish Bolsheviks were responsible for the victory of the Antichrist in Russia. Although there were many versions of the *Protocols*, the version that was translated into German and was distributed in the West was written by Sergei Nilus (1862–1919), who had published two versions in Russia in 1905 and 1907. In Germany the *Protocols* appeared in winter 1918–19 among folkish nationalist groups in BERLIN and MUNICH. By the end of 1920 the *Protocols* had also been translated and published in Great Britain, France, Italy, Poland, and the United States. At the time there was the specter of the spread of communism, which helped fuel the spread of this conspiracy theory that fooled so many people, despite the *Protocols* having been judged a forgery. People had a need to find an easily understandable explanation for the disasters that had afflicted the world and Christian civilization, disasters such as WORLD WAR I, the Russian Bolshevik Revolution, the fall of European monarchies, and the GREAT DEPRESSION.

The *Protocols* contributed to Adolf Hitler's ANTI-SEMITISM. Hitler seldom referred to the Protocols in his speeches and in *MEIN KAMPF*, but he certainly believed and propagated the idea of a Jewish world conspiracy. His close relationship with Alfred ROSENBERG, who was the notorious proponent of the *Protocols* and the NAZI PARTY's theoretician and who published commentaries on the *Protocols*, undoubtedly influenced Hitler's thinking. The *Protocols* were consistently employed in the Nazi anti-Semitic campaign and were also recommended for use in the schools.

The *Protocols* are still being published and believed by a wide variety of groups that need to have conspiracy theories that explain the world. They have included Islamic fundamentalists, Christian millenarians, Russian chauvinists, white supremacists, black nationalists, and followers of NEO-NAZISM in postwar Germany.

Prussia

The state of Prussia had its origins in the 12th century, when the HOHENZOLLERN family from Swabia became rulers of the Mark BRANDENBURG. Its capital was BERLIN, which was founded in 1237. The significance of Prussia increased with the REFORMATION when the Hohenzollerns decided to adopt PROTESTANTISM. Unlike many of the other princes, however, the Hohenzollerns practiced religious toleration, which later led to the immigration of the French Calvinists under the Great Elector. During the THIRTY YEARS' WAR Prussia became a leader among the Protestant states of the HOLY ROMAN EMPIRE.

Prussia became a duchy in 1525 and a kingdom in 1701. Under the leadership of the Great Elector, FREDERICK WILLIAM (1620–88), the foundations of the state were laid. He succeeded as the elector of Brandenburg in 1640, and he made his territories into the provinces of a greater state. He was the founder of both ABSOLUTISM and centralization in the Hohenzollern domains. In 1701 the elector of Brandenburg, FREDERICK III, established the kingdom of Prussia as Frederick I of Prussia (1701–13). These two rulers raised Prussia into a major military power despite its meager resources. During the reign of FREDERICK II (the Great) in the 18th century Prussia challenged AUSTRIA's hegemony in the Holy Roman Empire. Prussia was strong enough to retain Silesia, which it won in the SEVEN YEARS' WAR and prevailed against a great alliance of European powers.

Besides its Protestantism, Prussia also early on developed a military tradition that later was impressed on the rest of Germany. This tradition included the special position of the army, the officers' corps, and the supremacy of the military over the civilian. Its origin went back to the Order of the Teutonic Knights, which was a military order that had controlled West and East Prussia. In 1525 it was secularized, and its territories became fiefs of the Hohenzollerns. Its code of behavior influenced the behavior of the Prussian officer corps. Closely connected to the code was the role played by the Prussian nobility, the JUNKERS. They came to dominate not only the officer corps of the army but also became leading officials in the bureaucracy and foreign office. Prussia with its first-rate army and modernized administration became through the efforts of its electors and kings a state dominated by soldiers and bureaucrats, with real political power exercised only by the king. No parliament was ready to challenge monarchical power, nor was a revolution brewing as in France.

The NAPOLEONIC WARS challenged the status quo in Prussia. After Napoleon defeated Prussia at the BATTLE OF JENA (1806), Prussia was reduced by the TREATY OF TILSIT (1807) to its size at the time of its founding as a kingdom. Due to its victorious position in the defeat of Napoleon, Prussian territory was restored, East Prussia was added, as was the Rhineland and Westphalia. This was to give Prussia an important position in the GERMAN CONFEDERATION with its establishment of the ZOLLVEREIN, and the process of industrialization centralized in the Ruhr. Besides the growth of LIBERALISM and NATIONALISM, it was these economic advantages that placed Prussia in the preferred role as the leader of German unification. Prussia did not intend to challenge Austria's leadership in the German Confederation and declined the honor that its king was given during the REVOLUTION OF 1848 to be the emperor of a united Germany. The career and ambition of Otto von BISMARCK tipped the scales in the Austro-Prussian struggle for dominance. Under Bismarck's leadership and after Prussia's victories in the Austro-Prussian War and the Franco-Prussian War, most of the German states were united in the Empire of 1871. Prussia also remained the dominant state within IMPERIAL GERMANY, with its king becoming emperor, its population and land mass equaling 60 percent, and the 24 remaining states plus ALSACE-LORRAINE totaling about 40 percent.

At this point in its development Germany's culture was, as Thomas MANN has pointed out, "spiritually forever the battlefield of Europe." The struggles between Germany and Western civilization mirror those between the Greco-Roman tradition and the Germanic, between the Renaissance and the Gothic, between LUTHER and Rome. Moreover, ROMANTICISM created the deepest divide in German culture, which affected both social and political life. It affected German nationalism, and along with the lateness of unification in the 19th century contributed to its aggressiveness and emphasis on superiority, both of which have been involved in the causation of the world wars.

Prussia dominated Germany both during the Empire and during the WEIMAR REPUBLIC. Under its domination Germany became a feudal-industrial state. Advances occurred in technology and industry, but the political system, even with universal male suffrage in the Reichstag, left much of the population in Prussia disenfranchised through the PRUSSIAN THREE CLASS VOTING SYSTEM (1849–1918). Most of the real political power remained with the Junker class and the monarchy. Critical decisions concerning the military and war were without civilian supervision. The Prussian ruling class was determined to hold onto power, even though the people demanded political reforms consistent with representative government. In some ways WORLD WAR I was a gamble to hold back reform and to maintain Prussian authoritarianism. Germany was unable to overcome the odds against its victory and was defeated. WILLIAM II was forced to abdicate, and the Empire ended.

It seems odd to say that during the republican years Prussia was a bastion of democracy in the new state. Yet social democracy was the strongest there. The WEIMAR CONSTITUTION did not divide Prussia into smaller units, but did reduce its influence. When the Nazis took over the republic, they established a dictatorship abolishing federalism and Prussia's influence. However, Nazi propaganda emphasized the historical connection between Hitler and Frederick the Great. The power of the Prussian ARISTOCRACY was broken by the involvement of so many in the July 20th plot against Hitler. After the war the loss of East and West Prussia, Silesia to Poland, and the confiscation of estates in the GERMAN DEMOCRATIC REPUBLIC effectively ended aristocratic Prussian power.

Prussia was dissolved in the Potsdam decrees of 1945. In the FEDERAL REPUBLIC the territory that had constituted Prussia became West Berlin, BREMEN, HAMBURG, HESSE, Lower Saxony, and NORTH RHINE-WESTPHALIA. In the German Democratic Republic Prussia became Pomerania, Silesia, and eastern Brandenburg.

Prussian Law Code (1794)

The greatest and most lasting political accomplishment of FREDERICK II was his reform of the Prussian legal system. His goal was to create a new community of justice, originating from and administered by the state. Karl Gottlieb Suarez (1746–98) was the chief author of *The Prussian Law Code* (*Preussisches Landrecht*). Suarez was a student of Christian WOLFF, and in the *Code* he wanted to carry out in a book of statutes the moral principles that the monarchy of Frederick II had developed. It was intended to give every citizen a clear conception of the state's purpose, and therefore the *Code* was confined not only to private civil and criminal law but also to constitutional questions. Frederick wanted a new code that was to be a "masterpiece of the human spirit." The codification process was immensely complex, not only because of the variety of statutes but also because of the diversity of interests that had to be pleased. Starting with the monarch, his sovereignty absolute, the *Code* defined as a right the Prussian ruler's imposition of taxes without popular consent. The king's rights were also defined as duties. His principal one was to act for the welfare of the people and respect those moral purposes that the human individual had a duty to realize in life. The general tenor of the *Code* pointed in the direction of contractual rights. The *Code* marked the beginning of a tendency of authoritarian government to limit its absolute powers by the rule of law. German terminology would express it in this manner: the *Obrigkeitsstaat* was supplemented by the *Rechtsstaat*.

The *Code* defined the rights of citizens according to the three social "estates"—peasants, MIDDLE CLASS (burghers), and noblemen. The scale of political and social rights was in accordance with the functions that the social class performed for the community. For instance, the nobility or "first estate" had its landholding protected and enjoyed preference to state positions provided the nobleman possessed the necessary skills for the job. Peasants had the right to remain on their land. General rights were recognized in the area of religion and less so in education. Complete freedom of religion and conscience was guaranteed. The state had authority over religion, but only in a practical way, such as loyalty to the state and the inculcation of good moral attitudes toward fellow citizens. Churches were prohibited from engaging in controversies with one another. PROTESTANTISM was the favored religion, although Catholics were tolerated, while papal interference was not. The state retained the power of censorship, and only members of the academy and universities were exempted. Private citizens had limited rights to criticize the government, the laws, and whatever endangered public order. The criminal law was liberal, torture was abolished, and its purpose was to prevent future crimes rather than exercise punishment.

The final code, the *Allgemeines Landrecht*, was published in 1794, eight years after Frederick's death. In the state's desire for legal reform it tried to overcome the centuries-old universalist customs of the HOLY ROMAN EMPIRE, as well as the local customs, privileges, and status of guilds, cities, corporate, and religious institutions. The new laws had as their goal the creation of a new human, called a *Staatsbürger*, who would be freed from community and caste restraints as long as the individual came under the authority of the state and paid taxes.

Prussian Three Class Voting System

The Three Class Voting System was introduced in 1849 in order to reform in a conservative direction the royal constitution promulgated in late fall 1848. The constitutions of both PRUSSIA and AUSTRIA were changed to limit the powers of parliament and to restrict the suffrage to the propertied minority.

The restricted suffrage was applied to state and local elections in Prussia. It remained in effect until 1918 and was the primary obstacle to democratic reforms. Prussian voters, only males over the age of 25, were divided into three groups, with membership dependent on the amount of property taxes each paid. The tax system did not include an income tax, and most taxes were based on indirect taxes that fell disproportionately on the poorer population. The taxes of each electoral district were divided into thirds, and the fewer wealthy contributed more per capita than did the lower class. The electoral system and consequently political power was skewed in favor of the rural and urban wealthy. Since there was no provision for a secret ballot until 1918, most of the voters in the poorer categories voted for the conservative candidates, who were favored by the wealthy landowners for fear of economic reprisals. The political imbalance in the system was demonstrated in 1908, when the breakdown of the groups was as follows: although 4 percent of the voters were in the first class, they elected as many representatives as the largest poorer group (82 percent) in the third class. Examining the elections of 1913, a similar outcome occurred. The conservative parties received 17 percent of the vote, which gave them 50 percent of the delegates in the parliament (*Landtag*). What created further imbalance was that the electoral boundaries for the Prussian state favored the lightly populated areas east of the ELBE RIVER. The whole system worked against the representation of the working class and the SOCIAL DEMOCRATIC PARTY.

Even when the Empire was established and a more progressive and democratic suffrage instituted for the elections for the imperial parliament (REICHSTAG), the Prussian electoral system remained the same. For the conservative leaders opposed to the modernization of the Reich, their fortress and defense was in the three-class system. The JUNKERS and their allies consequently controlled the politics in three-fifths of the Reich. After 1890 the political debate centered largely on the reform of the Prussian electoral system. There were promises of electoral reform during WORLD WAR I, but the system was not abolished until IMPERIAL GERMANY lost the war.

Pufendorf, Samuel, Baron von
(Samuel, Freiherr [Baron] von Pufendorf)
(1632–1694)
legal theorist and historian

Baron Samuel von Pufendorf was among the first German scholars to adopt the rationalistic principles of the French and English writers of his time. He was influenced by the English philosopher Thomas Hobbes and the Dutch jurist Hugo Grotius, who in his work *On the Law of War and Peace* had laid the foundations of modern international law. Pufendorf, who taught in the Universities of HEIDELBERG and Lund (Sweden), published his greatest work on natural and international law, *The Eight Books of the Law of Nature and Nations* in 1672. In the following year he summarized these ideas in *On the Duty of Man and Citizen*. He considered human nature to be the basis of all law and human reason as its supreme authority. He rejected Hobbes's notion that man in his natural state was continually at war, believing, however, that his natural state was one of peace. Pufendorf developed a concept of secularized natural law, holding that natural law was concerned with humanity in this life and was derived from human reason.

On January 8, 1632, near Chemnitz in SAXONY, Pufendorf was born the son of a Lutheran minister. It was natural that he would concentrate on theological studies when he began his education at the University of LEIPZIG. For whatever reason he developed a dislike for theology and turned to the study of the law at JENA. In 1658 on a trip to Copenhagen he became employed as a tutor to the children of the Swedish ambassador. He then went to Leiden and in 1660 published a book on legal theory, *The Two Books of the Elements of Universal Jurisprudence,* which was dedicated to the elector of the Palatinate, Charles Louis. As a reward, a new chair on political and natural law was established for him at the University of Heidelberg. While there, Pufendorf wrote a critical analysis on the constitutional law of the HOLY ROMAN EMPIRE (1664–65), which has been judged the greatest pamphlet on German national affairs after *To the German Nobility* by Martin LUTHER. It represented a new stage in German political thought based on the laws of politics. It proved to be quite controversial and was banned by the imperial censor, perhaps due to its criticism of the Habsburg emperors. Nevertheless Pufendorf argued that the Holy Roman Empire was not ruled by an ARISTOCRACY, but fell somewhere between a monarchy and a government by the estates. With its emphasis on Hobbes, Pufendorf's influence in academic thought prevailed.

After the publication in 1672 of his famous book on international law and another study of natural law and human freedom, wherein he argued that all people have the right to freedom and equality, Pufendorf turned his attention to historical studies. While professor of natural law at the University of Lund, he also served as the royal historian in Stockholm, writing a history of Sweden from King Gustavus II to Charles X Gustavus. Pufendorf also wrote *The Christian Religion and its Relationship to Civic Life* (1687), wherein he advocated religious tolerance and defended the absolute sovereignty of the state. This book impressed the Great Elector, FREDERICK WILLIAM of BRANDENBURG, who rewarded Pufendorf with the titles of Privy Councilor and Royal Prussian Historiographer. In his service Pufendorf completed a history of the elector's reign, using primary archival resources. In 1688 he became a baron, and in 1694 he died in BERLIN.

Q

Quadruple Alliance

The Quadruple Alliance was formed in 1813 by Austria, Britain, Prussia, and Russia against Napoleon in the final stages of the Napoleonic Wars. The alliance was concluded on March 1, 1814, at Chaumont, in which they pledged themselves not only to the common pursuit of the war and the avoidance of separate peace negotiations, but also to the common enforcement of the peace against French violations for a period of 20 years.

After the defeat of Napoleon, the four alliance members met at the Congress of Vienna (1814–15), where they established the Congress system, which was to protect against any further French aggression. They were surprised when the French people enthusiastically greeted Napoleon on his return from Elba and in the hundred days that ensued before he was defeated at Waterloo. This made a reaffirmation of the Quadruple Alliance appear essential. A declaration of solidarity on the same day as the second Treaty of Paris was designed as a guarantee of that treaty. By it each of the four powers pledged to supply 60,000 men in the event of a violation of the Treaty of Paris, particularly another attempt at a restoration of the Bonapartist dynasty. One of the articles of the Treaty of Paris called for periodic conferences for the discussion of their "common interests" and for those measures that would ensure the peace of Europe. Beneath the proposal for periodic conferences of the Great Powers lay an assumption concerning international relations, which differed from the view that had prevailed before 1789. It was that the Great Powers assumed responsibility for maintaining the welfare of Europe as a whole and that avoidance of war was a principal goal of the Concert of Europe. Four conferences were held in the years between 1818 and 1822. At the first conference in 1818 at Aix-la-Chapelle the alliance agreed to withdraw their army of occupation. The later conferences were at Troppau (1820), Laibach (1821), and Verona (1822).

The Quadruple Alliance was reaffirmed for the limited purpose of preventing violations of the Treaty of Paris, not to guarantee the broader settlement made at the Congress of Vienna or the general goals of the monarchs. After France had joined the alliance in 1818 at Aix-la-Chapelle, the Quintuple Alliance was established to suppress revolution wherever it threatened the interests of the member states.

Quidde, Ludwig (1858–1941)
historian and pacificist

Ludwig Quidde was born in Bremen. Educated in history, philosophy, and economics, he was well prepared for his life's work as a critic of Wilhelmian militarism and autocratic monarchism and as an advocate of pacifism. While still a student he published a pamphlet opposing the political Anti-Semitism of his time. As a pacificist journalist and historian he published a satire in 1894 critical of Emperor William II. Entitled *Caligula: A study on Roman caesarien megalomania,* he adroitly attacked William by carefully confining his indictment of Caligula to historical truths. He nevertheless paid a price by being banned from the exercise of his profession as a historian.

Quidde nevertheless possessed the historical perspective to realize that in IMPERIAL GERMANY there was a close association between historians and politics. In order to bring the historical truth to light, he founded the *German Journal for Historical Knowledge* in 1889. He had the credentials as secretary of the Prussian Historical Institute in Rome (1890–1902) to take a stand against the government.

Quidde then got involved in pacificist activities. In 1901 he began his leadership of the German delegation at the World Peace Congresses from 1914 to 1929. In 1914 Quidde became president of the German Peace Society and of the German Cartel for Peace from 1920 to 1929. During WORLD WAR I Quidde joined a small group of pacifists and professors who formed in 1915 the Association of a New Fatherland (Bund Neues Vaterland) to work for a compromise peace. Their voice of pacifism was drowned out by the exuberant patriotism of the majority of Germans at the beginning of the war. For these efforts he received the Nobel Peace Prize in 1927.

As far as his political affiliation was concerned, Quidde became a member of the South German Democratic People's Party and later during WEIMAR of the liberal DDP. In December 1918 during the November Revolution in BAVARIA, Quidde challenged Kurt EISNER, the revolutionary leader and prime minister of Bavaria, about his personal diplomacy. That January 1919 Quidde was elected to the NATIONAL ASSEMBLY that met in Weimar to write a constitution. When the assembly was informed about the punitive TREATY OF VERSAILLES, Quidde denounced the treaty and claimed for himself the special moral right to reject it. Once the republic had been stabilized, Quidde continued his efforts against German militarism. After the election of Paul von HINDENBURG as president of the republic in 1925, a White Book was published on secret rearmament plans of the German army to field 35 divisions. Professor Quidde struggled to make this information public, but along with others was decried as a traitor.

After the Nazis came to power, Quidde understandably immigrated to Switzerland.

Raabe, Wilhelm (1831–1910)
novelist

Wilhelm Raabe wrote in the age of REALISM and often has been called the German Charles Dickens. He was a North German novelist who observed the destruction of traditional values and the impact of industrialization with alarm. He acclaimed the movement toward national unification but was deeply critical of Prussian power politics and the ruthlessness of industrialization.

Wilhelm Raabe was born in Eschershausen near Hildesheim in 1831, the son of a civil servant who was assigned to Holzminden, where Raabe acquired his early education. After his father died, his mother settled in Wolfenbüttel. Raabe's education was undistinguished, but he supplemented it through extensive reading while he was an apprentice for four years (1849–53) to a bookseller. Afterward he went to BERLIN, where he attended classes at the university. Living on a street named Sperlingsgasse, he wrote his first novel about his life there, which was unexpectedly successful. Back home in Wolfenbüttel between 1856 and 1862 he tried with very little success to make a living by writing. He tried with historical novels to tell the tale of society after the NAPOLEONIC WARS and of the defense of the Lutheran city of Magdeburg.

Most distinguished among Raabe's works are three novels that form a trilogy and express his deep-seated pessimism about his times, lightened only by his humor: *The Hunger Parson* (1864), *Abu Telfan* (1867), and *The Plague Cart* (1870). *The Hunger Parson* describes the growing up of two friends in poverty, of a poor cobbler's son's rise into the ranks of the clergy, which is contrasted to Moses Freudenstein, who is an ambitious Jew. The parson, Hans, achieves satisfaction and serenity ministering to the material and spiritual hunger of a remote village on the Baltic coast; he is an epitome of the German soul in its fundamental goodness, dreamy impracticality, and high aspirations. The novel provides a black-and-white delineation, especially in the unrelieved evil of the Jew, Moses Freudenstein, and in the caricature of proud gentility of Frau Götz. In *Abu Telfan* a liberal survivor of the REVOLUTIONS OF 1848 has come home to a society that has little understanding and almost no place for him. *The Plague Cart* is a tale full of resignation and shows the destructive effect of the new industrial era on a girl raised by old standards of morality, a girl who is ruined through the lies and meanness of modern life. In *The Plague Cart* Raabe shed Schopenhauer's pessimism in favor of an active Christian HUMANISM, which in his later works showed up as a reverence for life deepened by an awareness of cruel realities. Later in life he wrote one of the masterpieces of German literature, *The Cake-Eater*, for which he received critical acclaim. It shows the slow progress toward a final affirmation of eternal moral values.

Yet Raabe wrote many other novels that never were successful. Some suggest that he wrote novels contrary to his times and in a complex narrative style. Perhaps what also contributed to his lack of success were his revelations of the unseemly side of change in German society. One of this type was *Pfister's Mill* (1884), which described the destruction of the environment caused by industrialization. Although

Raabe wrote from a fundamentally pessimistic point of view, he managed to inject positive qualities such as courage, kindliness, and humor into his stories, affirming that life can be rewarding.

racialism and Nazi ideology

Racialism was one of three principles at the core of the world view of Adolf HITLER. The idea of struggle is a fundamental concept that was derived from Social Darwinism and Marxism. Social Darwinism emphasized the role of struggle between peoples and nations, while Karl MARX posited a class struggle between economic groups, resulting in the victory of the proletariat. Adolf Hitler applied the idea of struggle to races, which for him was the dynamic of historical development. The second principle in his view was that the Aryan and the Jewish races were in a contest for supremacy and world domination. The third principle constituting the core of Hitler's ideology was the role of leadership. Out of the three, racialism, or his ANTI-SEMITISM, was the cement of the ideology.

The Nazis did not add any new elements to anti-Semitism, except the determination to carry it out. Racial doctrine emerged during the 19th century with the rise of NATIONALISM and capitalism. The emphasis on biological differences prompted the racialists of the time to erect a hierarchy within the white race. Out of this emerged the idea of Aryan superiority. They had confused the Indo-European group of languages with a so-called Indo-European race, which became the Germanic and then Aryan race. Racialists also believed that Aryan meant nobility of blood and that the Aryans were a superior race. All civilization supposedly resulted from a struggle between the Aryan race, which was creative, and noncreative other races. This racialism fused in Germany with ideas on German nationalism. It was believed that the Germans had their own distinctive culture and spirit, a *Volksgeist*. Among the promoters of this racialism were the Frenchman Arthur Comte de Gobineau and the English admirer of the Germans, Houston Stewart CHAMBERLAIN. The composer Richard WAGNER, who was also a racist, insisted the the Germans had a special heroic spirit. Racial differences were also confused with imagined blood differences. Among the Aryans it was thought that the Nordic race was the best.

Hitler made his racial doctrine the cultural core of his ideology. Already in 1921 he advocated the application of force against what he called the Jewish menace. In *MEIN KAMPF* Hitler expressed the belief that the soul of a person and the race was in the blood. He believed that God had created the Aryans as a perfect people, both physically and spiritually. The Aryans were supposed to be the rulers of the earth and the only race capable of creating higher civilization. What had caused the decline of the Aryans was the "original sin" of blood poisoning by the inferior Jewish race. To Hitler the Jews were not a particular religious creed but a specific race. They were not an original race created by God, but an inhuman and evil race and the personification of the devil. It was their goal to poison the Aryan race through miscegenation. The Jew was the cause of modern cultural decadence, but worse so in politics where through capitalism, liberalism, democracy, freedom of the press, and internationalism they hoped to dominate the world. But the worst and most powerful tool of the Jews was Marxism, which intended to create cultural chaos, making possible Jewish world domination. The Nazis, of course, saw no contradiction in the idea of the Jews controlling the capitalist West and at the same time Communist Russia; they explained it by demonizing the Jew. The Jews had hoodwinked the leaders of the modern world; they had created the twin foundations of the modern materialist world, international finance of capitalism and international socialism.

Hitler's anti-Semitism arose out of the pseudoscientific racialism of the 19th century and traditional Christian beliefs. *The PROTOCOLS OF THE ELDERS OF ZION*, which became available around WORLD WAR I, propagated the idea of a Jewish world conspiracy. The concept of the satanic Jew, however, was derived from Christianity, where some believed that only a people possessed by Satan could have killed Christ. The emphasis here should be on possession, because Nazi ideology identified the Jew as the devil himself. In popular Christian anti-Semitism it had been hoped to save the Jews through baptism. Nazism saw the Jew as a cosmic threat to human survival, which justified annihilation. In their worldview the Nazis actually were rationalizing what they desired to do themselves, control the world and destroy their enemies. The NAZI PARTY was thought to be a movement, a "spiritual movement," and its purpose was to promote the historic God-given destiny of the Aryan race.

Hitler realized that no pure racial group existed in the modern world. More racially pure Nordic Aryans were supposedly to be found among the Germans. The goal of the Nazi Party was to preserve the purity of the race and to save the culturally creative forces in the community. To save the Aryan racial community, the VOLKS-GEMEINSCHAFT, a new Aryan man had to be created who thought "with his blood" and worked for the good of the community. In building the racial community the Nazis also had to stop the "mongrelization" of the German people by the Jews and to prepare the Germans for a final contest, a racial Armageddon. The Volksgemeinschaft was the only true community, one organically unified and rooted in nature. It was the mission of the Nazi Party to be the vanguard, and the Nazi state the only instrument of this cultural regeneration.

Ranke, Leopold von (1795–1886)

historian

Ranke was the founder of the German school of objective historians, which focused on the investigation of sources in order to determine which facts explained the life and policies of states. This school also maintains that the course of history is affected by the will of humans, by human ideas, and by the initiative of great personalities.

Leopold von Ranke was born in 1795 in SAXONY into a family that had long provided lawyers and clergymen. His early education was in classical languages at the famous Schulpforta and philology and theology at the University of LEIPZIG. In 1818 he became a secondary school (Gymnasium) teacher in Frankfurt-an-der-Oder. It was there that he began researching and writing his first historical work, *The History of the Roman and Germanic Peoples*. Its publication in 1824 led to an appointment at the University of BERLIN. There he became a favorite of the rich and powerful attending their cultural salons, especially of the Jewess Rahel Varnhagen, and giving private lectures for his patron, the king of Prussia, FREDERICK WILLIAM IV. By the middle of the century he had become famous throughout Europe, and during the latter 19th century his students held most of the chairs of history in Germany. Even with extensive professional responsibilities he managed extensive research on the growth of the modern states, completing some 57 volumes. Some of his most important works were his studies of the popes and of Germany during the Reformation. In 1863 he was ennobled.

In Ranke's words his philosophy of history involved the explanation of how things happened (*wie es eigentlich gewesen*). This method started with archival research, then a criticism of the documents, and finally a rigorous evaluation of the evidence in order to get at the facts. The historian, he believed, had to be mindful of his personal biases, which might distort his narrative of the past; the facts had to speak for themselves. He had the advantage of access to archives which had not been opened to critical inspection. One set of documents that he made famous and which had a fundamental impact on his thinking were the reports of the Venetian ambassadors that were mined for *Princes and Peoples of Southern Europe in the Sixteenth and Seventeenth Centuries,* (1827) leading to his study of various conditions as the background for understanding the events.

The European community, Ranke thought, was based on a fusion of Latin and Germanic values and institutions and which comprised a family of states. The basis of public life was not the nation but the state. Each state was of divine origin, he thought, one of the "true ideas of God," that like the planets had cosmic significance. Each state was the rational framework in which each people pursued their divine destiny. It was the historian's purpose not to explain the present by studying the past but to understand each age and nation according to its own values. This historical relativism of Ranke wherein history revealed only the existence of many individual goals of states differed from Hegel's philosophy that assumed that an all-encompassing purpose ran through history. Furthermore, Ranke subordinated the internal politics of a state to its external efforts to protect its sovereignty and values. This approach influenced later German historians to emphasize the primacy of foreign over domestic affairs in the interpretation of a nation's development, an approach that contradicted that of the romantic and revolutionary doctrines that internal affairs such as the acquisition and protection of freedom were more important. Yet, Ranke was not without some roots in the romantic and idealist camps, which looked for a pattern of meaning behind events. Like the historians Barthold Niebuhr and Friedrich Savigny, Ranke believed in an order beyond events, which gave them meaning. Simply stated, he believed that the historian had a sacred calling to discover the ways of God and through history explain them to man. This fusion of the sacred and profane in the state's quest for self-preservation and power and his focus on PRUSSIA helped to glorify the study of the powerful state in the German historical profession.

Rapallo Treaty (1922)

This brief treaty between defeated Germany and revolutionary Russia was signed secretly on April 16, 1922, at the Soviet delegation's headquarters at Rapallo. Normal diplomatic relations were resumed, and both sides renounced claims for war costs and damages. Russia gave up its claims for reparations, and Germany gave up economic claims of losses German citizens incurred because of Bolshevik expropriations.

It was the first German independent act of foreign policy after 1918, and it sabotaged the Genoa Conference (1922), to which delegates had come from all over Europe to discuss solutions to Europe's postwar economic problems. This rapprochement between Germany and Russia aroused distrust in the West, especially in France, and became a special irritant in interwar diplomacy. This informal political cooperation between Germany and Russia lasted until HITLER's seizure of power and was renewed in 1939. It also represented the continuation of Germany's balancing act between East and West and the historic ties between the kingdom of PRUSSIA and czarist Russia.

Rathenau, Walter (1867–1922)

Jewish industrialist and statesman

Son of the founder of Germany's giant General Electric Company, AEG, Rathenau became one of Europe's great economic leaders. As a Jew he experienced second-class citizenship in IMPERIAL GERMANY, suffered the ANTI-SEMITISM of the time, but nonetheless sought to reconcile Judaism and German culture. His utopianism made him advocate state regulation and planning for the good of the community. During WORLD WAR I he was placed in charge of the War Materials Board, where he was given the authority to manage the use of scarce war materials, but until the institution of the HINDENBURG PROGRAM in 1916 Germany's wartime economy was only loosely coordinated. Rathenau opposed General Erich LUDENDORFF's armistice proposal and favored instead armed resistance in order to obtain better peace terms. He opposed the signing of the TREATY OF VERSAILLES.

During the WEIMAR REPUBLIC this outstanding patriot was appointed minister of reconstruction in 1921 and foreign minister in the early part of 1922, favoring a policy of reconciliation with the Allied powers and fulfillment of the terms of the treaty. An especially difficult issue was the reparations demanded by the Allies. Rathenau and the Reich chancellor of the time, the left-wing CENTER PARTY leader Joseph Wirth, favored the "fulfillment policy." Although this did not work, it attempted to use alternative forms of compensation instead of cash payments.

Walter Rathenau *(Library of Congress)*

At the economic Genoa Conference in April 1922 Rathenau pleaded Germany's case but undermined his efforts by concluding a separate TREATY OF RAPALLO with Communist Russia. Although Rathenau was warned of a plot to kill him, he refused added police protection, and on June 24, 1922, right-wing terrorists finally succeeded in assassinating him and defeating his efforts at reconciliation. The only positive thing that resulted was a spontaneous outcry and the passage by the REICHSTAG of the Law for the Protection of the Republic.

realism (literary)

The realistic movement in literature sought to describe the world of change in German society as it went through the process of modernization and industrialization. The failure of the REVOLUTION OF 1848 and the rising nationalistic spirit, the progress of natural science, and changing social mores all needed to be described in new terms. The literature of realism sought to describe people, actions, scenes, and speech in a manner that was lifelike and not distorted by the romantic imagination or social polemics and political propaganda. The writers were realists in that they desired to present an unadorned picture of contemporary life, and could also discriminate between the essential and the trivial. Some, such as Adalbert Stifter and the Swiss Gottfried Keller, concentrated on the great and lasting forces of life, the forces of nature and their impact on human beings shaped by history. The heroes of the realistic narrative were everyday people—clerks, cobblers, farmers, maids and ballerinas, widows and spinsters, and many others. These were common people and not particularly gifted or attractive. They were people who were respectable and had a healthy philosophy and succeeded in mastering life, more than the pretentious individualists whose egos were lacking in substance and who turned out to be losers.

German literature between 1848 and 1914 entertained a number of different schools and styles besides realism; there was NATURALISM, EXPRESSIONISM, symbolism, impressionism, neoromanticism, and neoclassicism. The realist movement was initiated by Berthold Auerbach (1812–82), whose *Village Tales from the Black Forest* (1843) harkened back to YOUNG GERMANY and LIBERALISM and expressed a poetic sympathy with the common folk. He thought that a cure for modern ills was a return to nature and the soil. He was one of the most popular realist authors besides the romanticist Ludwig Uhland (1787–1862) up to 1870. German realism reached its peak with the works of Friedrich Hebbel. His *Judith* marked a new era in German drama. Another author who incorporated national patriotism and race-consciousness was Gustav FREYTAG in his popular *Scenes out of the German Past*. Freytag, a historian in disguise, depicted the commercial MIDDLE CLASS in *Debt and Credit* (1855) as the foundation of the new German national state and the bearer of progress. He expressed the spirit of bourgeois realism the best, along with Theodor Storm,

Wilhelm RAABE, and Theodor FONTANE. Raabe became the favorite author of the academic classes, and his numerous novels were filled with the experiences of the educated. Nevertheless, Raabe's ideals were the embodiment of the "conscience of Germany" and birthed in pre-Bismarckian Germany. He and Theodor Storm idealized the regional towns and villages of their ancestors. One of the best of the novelists of social realism was Theodor Fontane in his later social novels. Friedrich Spielhagen (1829–1911) also should be placed in the realist school; he depicted much of German social and political developments up to the turn of the 20th century. Not to be ignored was the greatest poet of the group, Annette von DROSTE-HÜLSHOFF, whose nature and historical ballads and village novelette, *The Jew's Beach Tree*, where nature itself is the avenger of crime, is the first of the 19th-century realists.

Realpolitik

The term *Realpolitik* referred to practical politics instead of the execution of a political strategy based on IDEALISM and philosophical speculation. It meant the use of opportunism and power in politics, the belief that power ruled instead of principles. The term *Realpolitik* was coined by the political writer A. L. von Rochau (1810–73) in his book *The Foundations of Practical Politics* (2 vols., 1853–69). Von Rochau was interested in what it would take to unite Germany. Having been a radical before the REVOLUTION OF 1848, he moved to a moderate position. Like other moderate liberals, the "classical liberals" or "old liberals" were discouraged by the failure in 1848 to unite Germany. They were discouraged by the inability of revolution to achieve their goals, so their trust in the power of principle suffered a terrible blow. Now the moderates moved to a position they regarded as "realistic" and "practical," setting their hopes on the power of PRUSSIA to bring about German unity. They realized that neither law, principle, nor treaty would unite Germans, but a more powerful state like Prussia would be able to overwhelm and incorporate the rest.

Of all of Germany's statesmen, Otto von BISMARCK was the greatest practitioner of Realpolitik. In the popular Social Darwinism of his day he found a better explanation of the relation between science and society than believing that politics is a science based on natural law principles as emphasized in Manchesterism. Bismarck thought that politics was more of an art than a science and not a subject that could be taught. Politics was rather the capacity of a statesman to choose, between possible alternatives, that which is "least harmful or most opportune." Although Bismarck was well read in European history, he used its facts as a reservoir of argument to support his decisions. His political tactics were more based on his own experiences. The statesman also required patience and careful timing and an intuitive recognition of the best path and a well-informed understanding of his opponents. Bismarck also used a strategy of alternatives in the midst of shifting situations. He frequently entertained multiple solutions to problems and multiple possibilities of alliances with opposing political forces. This gave him the confidence that his opponents mostly lacked and the ability to maintain the initiative to achieve his goals.

Reformation (Protestant)

The reform of the Catholic Church initiated by Martin LUTHER was inspired by the Christian's quest for salvation. Even though the primary impulse was religious, Luther's attempt to solve his personal need to be assured of salvation gave rise to a backward-looking revolution that involved a humanist return to the sources that changed the course of history. Luther's protest against abuses in the church, his revival of Pauline and Augustinian theology on the role of faith in salvation, and his challenge to the authority of the popes and councils set Luther on a course that would irreversibly destroy the unity of the church and what was called Christendom. Luther challenged the institutional authority of the Catholic Church and emphasized personal interpretation of the Bible. The Protestant revolt divided Germany into two almost evenly divided denominations whose conflicts would scar her society, creating one of its many divisions.

Luther's reform movement was not the first in church history nor in the 16th century. A century earlier Jan Hus had preached the need for reform and been repressed. Ever since the Great Schism of the 14th century, church councils had failed to bring about needed reforms. Saints had prayed for reform. Humanists had sought to change the church and society at first by intellectually raising individuals to higher standards of moral behavior. Their reform program for the church and society was founded on education, a knowledge of the classics, new translations of the Bible, and the writings of the church fathers.

The problems in the church were enormous. Lax morality and corruption were rife. Ignorance and immorality, pluralism, simony, and a preoccupation with worldliness were widespread among the higher and lower clergy. Papal taxes drained money from Germany, and the church came to be seen as an oppressor of the poor, as was the ARISTOCRACY. Many Christians who sincerely wanted to feel assured of salvation became disillusioned with the clergy who would not live up to their expectations. Because of the fear of death that continued to be strong in Germany following the terrifying Black Plague of the 14th century, many Christians sought meaningful religious experience and a certainty of salvation. Besides the pious experiences associated with the Modern Devotion inspired by the mystical *Imitation of Christ* by Thomas à Kempis, there were other devotions associated with pilgrimages and veneration of relics. Perhaps the most controversial was the sale of INDULGENCES. Based on the church's spiritual treasury of merits gained by Christ and the saints, a Christian could gain the remission of the temporary penalties of sin one would have to suffer in purgatory. Conditions in Rome in the Papal Court under the Borgia and the Medici families were scandalously worldly and at times immoral. When Martin Luther visited Rome in 1511, these streams of criticism merged, linking the abuses in Germany with the authority of the church. When Martin Luther in 1517 indicted the corruption involved in the sale of indulgences by the Dominican monk Tetzel, he unintentionally sparked the Protestant Reformation.

What had prepared Luther for the formulation of his Ninety-five Theses in 1517 was a new understanding in 1512 of the relationship between grace, Scripture, and salvation. Catholic doctrine had long held that both faith and good works were necessary for salvation. Disagreeing with Desiderius ERASMUS and other humanists that humans could do good, Luther thought that human nature was so depraved that a Christian could never produce the good works that were required. Through long meditation on the Scripture, particularly St. Paul's letter to the Romans (1:17) stating that "the just shall live by faith," Luther came to the understanding that salvation came through faith in the promises of God earned by Christ's crucifixion. At first neither the Archbishop of Mainz, Albrecht von Brandenburg, nor Pope Leo X took Luther's theses seriously, believing that the controversy would soon dissipate. Yet, after they were printed and translated from Latin, they rapidly stirred up great discontent in Germany. In December 1517 Archbishop Albrecht condemned Luther as a heretic. In October 1518 Luther was called to defend himself at the DIET OF AUGSBURG where the heretical and revolutionary nature of his doctrines became more apparent. A pause in the prosecution for two years was due to political issues dealing with the election of a new emperor. LUTHER'S PAMPHLETS (three) published in 1520 openly challenged fundamental Catholic doctrines and challenged the authority of the pope. The *Address to the Nobility of the German Nation* was a plea to the princes to establish a reformed church in Germany. In *The Babylonian Captivity of the Church* he attacked the sacramental system administered by the clergy and demanded that clergy have the right to marry. Finally, *On the Freedom of the Christian Man* elaborated on Luther's doctrine of salvation through faith, though he did not deny the obligation of Christians to perform good works.

The seriousness of Luther's disbelief in traditional Catholic teachings finally brought a papal declaration of excommunication. In defiance, Luther burned it. Then he was summoned by the new emperor, CHARLES V, to defend himself at the imperial DIET OF WORMS. Not recanting, Luther said that he could not violate his conscience and change his position. The emperor Charles responded with the EDICT OF WORMS (1521), demanding that Luther be captured and Luther's teachings suppressed. Fortunately, Luther had the support of FREDERICK III, THE WISE, the elector of Saxony, and was protected in the fortress called WARTBURG. Luther's vigorous defense of his beliefs at Worms gained him the support of many Germans who also hoped for religious and social reform. A large number of princes established state-dominated churches in their territories. Luther also replaced the Catholic Mass with a new liturgy based on the reading of Scriptures, preaching, and the singing of hymns.

While Luther was at Wartburg he began his translation of the Bible; his teachings were now spread far and wide among the German people by his followers in the Augustinian religious order, lower clergy, and various humanists. A propaganda war ensued between Catholics and Protestants. Not only oral but especially printed propaganda became a potent weapon. The printing press was also a crucial medium that placed the dissemination of Lutheran ideas beyond the usual control of the church. The most influential accomplishment of Luther at Wartburg and of great literary significance was his translation of the New Testament (1522) from Greek into German; the rest of the Bible he published in 1534. It is undoubtedly true that the religious revolution associated with the Protestant Reformation is in large part due to the availability of these in thousands of copies.

Some of Luther's followers wanted to carry his teachings to more extreme conclusions. Some wanted to destroy all sacred images and statues. The ZWICKAU PROPHETS, who had adopted the teachings of the ANABAPTISTS, were opposed to infant baptism, which Luther still upheld. Luther turned out to be more conservative than some of his followers. Luther feared that religious and social anarchy would result if he did not establish a church that could restrict the freedom to dissent through authority. Instead of the authority of the pope, Luther chose to place the church under the civil government with "superintendents" who were appointed by the state to replace the Roman Catholic bishops. Although many doctrinal changes were made, a considerable portion of Catholic doctrine and practice was retained. The liturgy of the Mass was retained, but its sacrificial character was denied, and Latin texts were replaced by German. In the sacramental system there only remained Baptism and the Lord's Supper. Luther in contrast to Ulrich ZWINGLI and John CALVIN maintained the real presence of Christ in the Eucharist. He did, however, eliminate many pious practices such as pilgrimages, fasts, and the veneration of saints and their relics; monastic orders were dissolved and the clergy allowed to marry.

The consequences of the Reformation went far beyond the religious sphere. Social, economic, and political unrest coalesced with religious protest, sparking the first revolutionary movement in German history. The imperial knights were the first to organize. In August 1522 the imperial knight, Franz von Sickingen presided over a meeting of 600 knights at Landau on Lake Constance. They formed an association to defend their rights and the Lutheran faith, but their ultimate aim was the secularization of all ecclesiastical principalities. Most of the princes and cities failed to join the knights. On October 1, 1522 the Imperial Governing Council declared Sickingen an outlaw. The revolt of the knights ended when Sickingen was killed, many castles destroyed, and lands confiscated. The princes who were victorious in the struggle profited the most from the Reformation. In June 1524 a rebellion of peasants, The PEASANTS' WAR, occurred. They had taken Luther too seriously on the issue of social reform. Luther thought that the rebellion was inspired by Satan and condemned it in his pamphlet *Against the Thieving and Murderous Hordes of Peasants* and encouraged the princes to kill them. Finally, the princes brutally suppressed the rebellion, killing some 75,000, and the peasants slipped back into their despair. Lutheranism increasingly became dependent for its success and protection on the princes. In reality, the goals of the peasants for fundamental social reform were too utopian and could not have been realized. As a result of the rebellion the princes became reactionary, opposing any meaningful reforms.

The Reformation was more successful in the towns. The educated townsmen (*burgers*) were more influenced by Luther's writings. The town councils had not been able to control the independence of the Catholic Church, whereas a Protestant Church with its lay elders more easily controlled church finances and charitable services. Also, the married Protestant clergy were a more visible model for the Christian family. Some towns used PROTESTANTISM to revolt against their Catholic princes.

In the town of Münster the MÜNSTER REBELLION, one of the more radical millenarian phases of the Reformation, took place. By 1532 the town had become Protestant. Two years later, Johann Matthys, a baker by trade, came to Münster announcing the imminent second coming of the Lord. More than 1,500 townsmen were baptized and awaited Christ's coming in what Matthys called the New Jerusalem. The situation became more radical, and the town was besieged by the bishop's army. It all ended with the town being stormed and Anabaptist leaders being killed.

The attempts by the emperor Charles V to enforce the Edict of Worms were generally unsuccessful. His efforts provoked the Protest of 1529, signed by a large number of princes and towns. This was followed by the CONFESSION OF AUGSBURG, a vigorous exposition of the leading tenets of the reformers. Between 1521 and 1524 Charles was distracted by a series of wars with the powerful French king, Francis I (1515–47). As if this was not enough, Pope Clement VII (1523–34) had sided with the French king. Then the Ottoman Turks were threatening Habsburg domains from the East. Finally, the internal divisions in the HOLY ROMAN EMPIRE were unfavorable to Charles's goal of preserving religious unity. The independence of the hundreds of states ruled by princes and ecclesiastics, and the independent IMPERIAL CITIES had since the Middle Ages resisted imperial domination. Had the pope called a general council to reform the Catholic Church, Charles's efforts to stem the tide of Protestantism might have been more successful. In 1540 Charles sought to reach a settlement by agreement at the Conference of REGENSBURG. In spite of goodwill and moderation the conference broke down and the dividing line between the two doctrines became firm. As a result Charles resorted to warfare, challenging the SCHMALKALDIC LEAGUE formed by the Protestant princes in 1531. Charles was at first successful but then lost because the Leaguers had received support from France and the powerful Maurice of Savoy. By this time some four-fifths of Germany had become Protestant. Finally, Charles was compelled to agree to the PEACE OF AUGSBURG (1555). This was a turning point in the Reformation because it acknowledged the equality between Lutheranism and Catholicism, and the ideal of Christian unity was gone forever. The fundamental principle of the peace was that each prince was accorded the right to decide the religion of his own state. That did not mean religious toleration, which was a battle that had yet to be fought.

Regensburg

Regensburg is a city located in BAVARIA at the confluence of the Danube, the Regen, and Naab Rivers. The site of Regensburg was once occupied by the Celts, followed in A.D. 77 by a Roman camp for a cohort, and in A.D. 179 by a large legion, the location being named by emperor Marcus Aurelius as *Castra Regina*. The dukes of Bavaria resided here at the beginning of the sixth century, and St. Boniface instituted a bishopric in 739. In 788 Charlemagne made Regensburg the residence of the Carolingian rulers. The city became a free IMPERIAL CITY in 1245, developing into the most populous and wealthiest city in southern Germany. Testimonies to that era are found in the remarkable bridge of stone and as many as 20 of the remaining homes of wealthy merchants. At the end of the 14th century a slow decline set in with competition from the cities of AUGSBURG and NUREMBERG. In 1542 the city council decided to open the door to the REFORMATION. From 1663 to 1806 the "Permanent Imperial Diet" or parliament sat in Regensburg. In 1748 the princes of Thurn and Taxis, who had run the German postal service since 1595, took up residence as the principal commissioners of the diet. The role of the postal service declined as various states took over the postal functions themselves (Bavaria in 1812; Württemberg in 1852; PRUSSIA bought out the Turn and Taxis holdings in 1867). Having been secularized, Regensburg passed in 1803 to the former elector of Mainz, Karl von Dalberg. In 1809 the city was captured by the French and in 1810 was annexed to Bavaria.

The older areas of Regensburg survived WORLD WAR II with the exception of the cathedral church (*Obermünster*), which was rebuilt. The cathedral, the finest Gothic building in Bavaria, has two spires and was built starting in the 13th century and not finished until 1525 although restoration is ongoing. The city also has many medieval churches and buildings, including the ancient and important Benedictine Abbey of St. Emmeram, secularized in 1803. St. Emmeram is one of the oldest Benedictine abbeys in Germany, founded in the seventh century. St. Emmeram also has a magnificent BAROQUE interior crafted by the famous Asam brothers in 1731. In the latter 20th century the principal industries included electrical engineering, motor vehicles (BMW), chemical plants, clothing factories, sugar refining, carpetmaking, and brewing.

Reichstag (National Parliament) Building

The National Parliament building of the new German Empire was completed in 1894. Architecturally of the RENAISSANCE and BAROQUE-revival style, this building was intended to serve as the permanent home of the German Parliament. It was here during the Second Empire (1871–1918) that the Reichstag members were first elected by universal male suffrage and came to debate policy and make laws affecting the state.

The Reichstag has been affected by the events of modern German history. During WORLD WAR I, for instance, the Reichstag was altered in 1916 to reflect the country's move away from imperial rule when its facade was dedicated with bronze letters stating "to the German People" (*Dem deutschen Volke*). After Germany's defeat in the war, the formation of a republic in 1918 was announced from one of its windows. During the WEIMAR REPUBLIC the building continued to house the democratically elected members of the Reichstag.

On the night of February 27, 1933, about four weeks after the appointment of Adolf HITLER as chancellor, the Reichstag was destroyed by a fire that spread so quickly arson was suspected. The police arrested a Dutch Communist, Marinus van der Lubbe, who was found in the building. Van der Lubbe was tried in a show trial that September along with his alleged accomplice, the Bulgarian Communist Georgi Dimitrov. Van der Lubbe was convicted and beheaded. The Nazi government claimed that the fire was the first move in a Communist conspiracy to unleash a revolution in Germany. Dimitrov's trial had another outcome as he successfully defended himself, arguing that the fire was instigated by the Nazis to provide a pretext for taking emergency measures against left-wing parties. This interpretation was widely believed, although subsequent evidence suggested that van der Lubbe set fire to the Reichstag on his own initiative, but the Nazis exploited the incident. In any event, Hitler was able to rush through the Decree of the Reich President for the Protection of the People and the State, which emergency decree conferred totalitarian powers on the Nazi government.

Partially rebuilt, the structure was used in 1937 to host two Nazi propaganda exhibitions, the "Great Antibolshevist Exhibition" and "the Eternal Jew." During WORLD WAR II the Reich-

The Reichstag, Berlin, 1900 *(Library of Congress)*

stag was bombed and burned again, then bore the graffiti of invading Soviet troops. By 1961 it was rebuilt again, this time in the shadow of the BERLIN WALL. Its interior was covered by the high modernist, BAUHAUS-inspired design of Paul Baumgarten. On October 4, 1990, the edifice was the center of Unification Day celebrations. When the German government decided to move from BONN to BERLIN, rather than build anew the Federal Parliament decided to return to the Reichstag. After sponsoring an international competition, the German government selected the design of British architect Sir Norman Foster for the reconstruction. The structure is a remarkable project and a symbol of the new Germany's confrontation with its past. Foster kept much of the building's recognizable exterior form, rebuilding only the glass dome that had been destroyed during World War II. In the new Germany the dramatically visible dome has been interpreted as symbolizing the "transparency of democracy." On the inside, however, the building engages its historical past. Some of the physical marks that history left on its walls have been uncovered, the remnants of the ornate 19th-century decoration mingling with the traces of bullets, Russian slogans, and high-modernist style. Standing on the glass walkway, an observer can take in all of these historical fragments simultaneously.

Remarque, Erich Maria
(Erich Paul Remark) (1898–1970)
novelist

Erich Maria Remarque (pseudonym of Erich Paul Remark) was the author of the most popular pacifist novel, *All Quiet on the Western Front.* It was a worldwide best seller (later turned into a film) about a soldier's life in WORLD WAR I and vehemently condemned by the Nazis.

Born in Osnabrück on July 22, 1898, Erich Paul Remark attended a Teacher's Training College and the University of MÜNSTER. After serving in the army, he worked at various jobs such as press reader, clerk, even a racing driver. In a short period he wrote his famous novel *All Quiet on the Western Front* (*Im Westen nichts Neues*, 1929). Written in the first person, it is the story of a group of young German soldiers near the end of the war. The bloody experiences of the soldiers and the squalor of the trenches are portrayed with brutal REALISM, which are balanced by sentimentalized home-front sequences. Following the death of the hero's friend, it is pathetic that he himself is killed two weeks before the armistice on a day when all is reported quiet at the front. Considered a pacifist novel, it was bitterly criticized by the Nazis.

Remarque wrote a sequel, *The Road Back* (1931), which was less effective. In 1937 he published another war story of three young veterans during the postwar years. The three are emotional anarchists who believe in nothing, although when one of them is killed, the other two do not pursue the matter legally, but take matters into their own hands in the style of the new brownshirted Storm Troopers (SA), whose methods they believe they detest. Another novel Remarque published in 1941 is *Flotsam*, a story of a group of refugees fleeing from the GESTAPO. In *Arch of Triumph* (1946) Remarque abandons his pacifism and tells of a refugee surgeon in the Paris of 1939–40 who kills a Gestapo agent. In *Spark of Life* (1952) Remarque narrates how a small group of people survived the brutalities of a CONCENTRATION CAMP.

By 1929 Remarque had left Germany and from that time lived abroad. In 1938 he was deprived of his German citizenship. In 1939 he arrived in the United States and in 1947 became an American citizen. In 1948 he went to Switzerland and resided there until his death in Locarno on September 25, 1970.

Renaissance

Germany shared in the accomplishments of the Italian Renaissance primarily in the area of HUMANISM. Despite the interrelationship between Italy and Germany and the fact that one-third of Italy lay within the HOLY ROMAN EMPIRE, the spirit of the Renaissance with its appreciation of sensuous beauty in its art was not adopted by the Germans. The Italians were more concerned with form and a philosophy of beauty than were the serious and introspective Germans, who were more concerned with the substances of things. There was, nevertheless, a commonality between the South and the North in the concern for the humanities. In Germany, however, humanism had a strong moral and educational force. While the Italians had been more interested in the pagan literature of Rome, the Germans rediscovered the writings of the church fathers and the original texts of the Scriptures. German humanism also differed from that of other countries by stimulating religious discontent and hostility toward Rome, rather than pressuring the local church to reform itself. In the end the German humanists were swept away by Martin LUTHER's religious revolution. Their rationality contributed to the enlightenment of their German public and contributed to the reform of the universities, which until 1500 had been dominated by Scholasticism.

The earliest influences of Italian humanism were found at the University of Prague, and this phase died out with the persecution of the religious reformer Jan Hus. In the latter 15th century Rudolf AGRICOLA fathered German humanism, seeking to spread Renaissance learning. A disciple of Agricola was Conrad CELTIS, who became the foremost poet of German humanism. A champion of classical scholarship, he was also an advocate for religious renewal. Celtis, however, with other humanists, made his greatest contributions in the field of historical study about their German past. A member of the clergy and a humanist, Jakob Wimpheling hoped to reform the church from within. Another humanist was Willibald PIRKHEIMER, who was from NUREMBERG and a Greek and Latin scholar. Mutianus Rufus was an advocate of Christian humanism based on the moral teachings of St. Paul. Rufus was a leader of the humanists and influenced many students to practice a more devotional and ethical Christianity. Johannes REUCHLIN was the most respected and admired of the German humanists, an eloquent Latin stylist and the first competent Greek scholar in Germany. Most interesting was his mastery of Hebrew and the mysteries of the ancient Jewish Cabala. The goal of Reuchlin's Hebrew scholarship was to purify the church so that it could provide a more meaningful spiritual experience. Ulrich von HUTTEN was the chief nationalist among the German humanists and possessed a bitter hatred of the papacy. Hutten was only one of two humanists who supported Luther, Hutten for political reasons while the other, Philip MELANCHTHON, did so for religious reasons. Melanchthon was a humanist scholar and professor of Greek at the University of Wittenberg. Melanchthon became the chief systematic theologian of the REFORMATION. He also formulated the statement of Protestant doctrine that was presented to the emperor CHARLES V, a doctrine known as the AUGSBURG CONFESSION.

ERASMUS of Rotterdam was the leading spokesman of the Christian humanists and the greatest literary figure of his generation. He considered the church the greatest educational institution of humankind. He spoke of the "philosophy of Christ" as though it could be learned. Luther used his New Testament in his teachings on the epistle to the Romans. Too rationalistic for Luther, the theology of Erasmus, however, became a part of the thinking of Melanchthon and through him penetrated Lutheranism. Erasmian thought also influenced the Swiss reformation through Ulrich ZWINGLI.

Republicans, The
(Die Republikaner)

The Republicans have been a radical right-wing movement that emerged on the political stage in the 1980s. Before the fall of the BERLIN WALL the rise of the Republicans was another indicator of the continued life of NEO-NAZISM. The party was founded in 1982 by former members of the Bavarian CSU, Franz Schönhuber and others who were upset over the policies of Franz Josef STRAUSS. Schönhuber had been a Waffen SS sergeant during WORLD WAR II and after the war became an editor of a newspaper in MUNICH. He also had become a popular television political talk show host who was fired because he boasted of his SS background in his autobiography and became the chairman of the Republicans in 1985. The Republicans first built up their organization in conservative districts of BAVARIA and BADEN-WÜRTTEMBERG. Schönhuber idealized the Italy of the 1920s, which was led by the Fascist dictator Benito Mussolini, and the Republicans were opposed to a multicultural society and wanted a "Germany for the Germans." By 1989 there were some 20,000 members, mostly in their 20s, in all of the German states.

The program of the Republicans always carefully skirted accusations that it was a right-wing extremist party, and it affirmed its support for the federal government and democracy. Some observers had suspicions that the party really was undemocratic because of its anti-European, racist, and xenophobic ideas. It certainly could be said to be ultranationalist and superpatriotic, and it warned against immigrants and asylum-seekers whom it claimed would weaken the social safety net enjoyed by the German people. The party also was on the far right of women's rights, abortion, and homosexuality, asserting that women should stay home and raise their families. The party's platform in 1990, nevertheless, was more moderate than in 1987, but that was done to ensure that the party remained legal. Yet Schönhuber's speeches are loaded with hatred against minority groups such as Turks and German Jews. He accused the Jews of being responsible for the ANTI-SEMITISM in postwar Germany, that German history should not be reduced to AUSCHWITZ, and that Germany was being blackmailed by being blamed with sole responsibility for the war.

Voter support was unexpectedly strong. In 1989 the Republicans gained 7.5 percent of the vote in West Berlin's state election, and five months later they received 2 million votes (7.1 percent) in the vote for the European Parliament. By 1992 the party received 8–10 percent of the vote in the Berlin elections and received the greatest support in urban working-class districts from 18-to-24-year-old men who cast twice as many votes for the party as did women. Many had a minimum of education and were unemployed and sought community in right-wing groups that preached strong leadership, a German racial ideology, and hostility toward the Jews. Yet, the party also was supported by middle-class salaried employees and civil servants and police officers who favored the party's law-and-order goals. Some of these had shifted their votes from the CDU/CSU in protest against the government's IMMIGRATION policies, which they considered a threat to their jobs, housing, and social welfare. Small-town voters favored the party's opposition to foreign food imports and its patriarchal attitude toward women's rights. The party's NATIONALISM and emphasis on reunification was taken over by Chancellor KOHL in the 1990 campaign. The Republicans were also weakened by their continual strife, expulsions, defections, and litigation. It is easy to see that these problems accounted for the loss of one-half of its membership in the 1990s. Besides, a new rightist party, the German People's Union under the leadership of Gerhard Frey, a right-wing publisher from Munich, competed for the right-wing votes that were available.

Resistance/Opposition to Hitler, 1933–1945

Resistance against the Nazi regime was exhibited by individuals, political parties, churches, various organizations, the military, and by Germans in all social classes. After the war it had been widely believed that opposition to the Nazis existed only among army officers who tried and failed to kill Adolf HITLER on July 20, 1944. Opposition to the Nazi regime was actually much more extensive than in the military leadership. Even though most Germans accepted Hitler's dictatorship, thousands of others continued to resist Nazism in various ways after Hitler was appointed chancellor. In the last free elections as late as March 1933, under great duress, the majority of voters rejected Nazism. Once the dictatorship was in place, however, and became the legal government, most resisters mainly came from the bottom and upper ranks of society, although some middle-class groups also resisted. Most resistance activities spanned everything from quiet, inner self-assertion and conscious preservation of intellectual and religious beliefs to open disapproval such as distributing leaflets and criticizing Hitler and the government, and the ultimate opposition, attempting to assassinate Hitler and overthrow the government. Based on present research the term *resistance* and *resistance movement* were first used by the brave Hans and Sophie SCHOLL, encouraged by Professor Huber in the protest group called the White Rose. They were executed in 1943 after distributing their leaflets in MUNICH.

The resistance to the Nazi government was a direct response to its arbitrary persecution, criminal excesses, and dictatorial oppression; the brutality of the GESTAPO and the SS; the persecution of minority groups of non-Aryans (Jews and Gypsies); and the unleashing of another war. For others it was the persecution and genocide of the Jews that was the most important single factor pushing them into resistance, which was noted in the Gestapo interrogations of 700 of the arrested plotters as one of the principal ethical motivations for their participation in the July 20th conspiracy to overthrow Hitler.

In order to mount a resistance, there were interior obstacles that Germans had to overcome. First, there was the traditional obedience to authority and the oaths of loyalty that soldiers were required to take. Second, there were the multiplicity of fears for one's own safety, loss of one's job, punishment of one's family, or simply fear of torture and death. Opportunities for resistance were severely limited due to the terror apparatus and the effectiveness of political measures used to control society. In general, resistance efforts proved to be ineffective because the government had the unconditional loyalty of the security forces, the police, the Gestapo, the SD, the SS, and the army to counter subversion and provide security for the regime.

Active resistance by individual citizens was practically impossible under the totalitarian regime the Nazis established. Passive resistance in the form of a refusal to cooperate was more widely used. These could be for political, intellectual, ethical, religious, or humanitarian reasons. One such refusal was not to contribute to the numerous fund-raising campaigns that might be used for charitable purposes, but also to finance arms production. Some refused to join the NAZI PARTY, others resigned from their jobs, others emigrated. When the Nazis began their campaign of religious persecution, for many members of the German Catholic and Evangelical Churches the attendance at church services became an expression of opposition, which was so understood by the Nazi Party, which had observers at church services who regularly reported critical remarks in sermons. It took extraordinary courage not to greet others with the phrase "Heil Hitler!", not to sing the "Horst Wessel Song," not to salute the swastika flag, which had become the national symbol, or not to display this flag on official occasions. Courage was also shown by those who expressed criticism in literary or historical essays. Those who did not choose to emigrate might use their positions as civil servants or employees to implement the directives of the state and the Nazi Party as liberally as possible. Lawyers and judges might exploit whatever legal means might be available to protect the accused victims of political, religious, or racial persecution. There were examples of human heroism by clergymen and lawyers to protest against the system of terror, the violation of human rights, and the destruction of human life. Individual churchmen such as Clemens Cardinal von GALEN of MÜNSTER denounced the Nazi EUTHANASIA program of feeble-minded children. After calling upon his congregation to pray for the Jews, the Catholic priest, Father Bernhard Lichtenberg, dean of Berlin's St. Hedwig's cathedral, was sent to his death at DACHAU. The gifted Protestant theologian Dietrich BONHOEFFER joined the conservative anti-Nazi movement as early as 1935, and was later imprisoned and executed. Many Germans died for their religious beliefs. Paul Schneider, a Protestant pastor in the Rhineland, was imprisoned for ridiculing the Nazis and collecting money to help the Jews. Thousands of Catholic priests were arrested, and some sent to CONCENTRATION CAMPS.

Resistance went through phases. During the first months after January 1933 the old methods of political debate and criticism of the regime continued in newspapers and magazines until they were suppressed. By the end of 1933 the underground phase began. Here the trade unions and members of the SOCIAL DEMOCRAT PARTY (SPD) and the GERMAN COMMUNIST PARTY (KPD) were the most active. The Nazis first went after the Communists, who often suffered torture and death. Whereas the Communist resistance worked for the collapse of law and order in Germany, the Social Democrats concentrated from the beginning on forming a core of leaders and developing ideas for a new government after liberation. Communists and Social Democrats continued to see each other as opponents, but did make some efforts to bridge their differences and organize resistance groups, such as "New Beginnings," and "Red Raiding Party." Many members of the political left were placed in concentration camps, were executed, or went into exile, and by 1935 the Gestapo had crushed most of resistance groups.

The Roman Catholic and the Lutheran churches of Germany were the largest organizations that had a potential to oppose and undermine Nazi plans and ideology. The Nazis had considerable respect for and fear of the moral influence of the churches. The Catholic Church was anxious to avoid a repeat of the Bismarckian persecution of the church known as the KULTURKAMPF. The Catholic Church also wanted to protect itself against the encroachments of this new totalitarian government, and soon after Hitler came into power proceeded to negotiate a church-state treaty called a Concordat (Reichskonkordat) in July 1933. It was supposed to protect the church and clearly identify rights and obligations. Unfortunately, it also legitimized the Nazi regime internationally and gave the impression that the pope approved of the regime, which he did not. As it turned out, it also hampered the church's ability as an institution to protest and oppose the government because it had agreed not to involve itself in politics. Consequently, the church as a collective institution did not openly confront Nazi policy, while only a few bishops did. It was left to the lower clergy and laity to participate in resistance. After 1935 the Nazi leadership intensified the church-state struggle against Catholicism. Many priests were hauled before the courts for supposedly breaching the monetary exchange control regulations and for alleged moral misconduct. In 1937 Pope Pius XI responded to Nazi persecution with the papal encyclical *With Burning Concern* (Mit brennender Sorge). The church also opposed the regime's eugenic policies, the most outspoken bishop being Cardinal Graf Galen, who publicly criticized the murder of the mentally ill as did the Lutheran bishop of Württemberg, Theopil Wurm. There were other heroic individual acts of clergymen who knew that they would be inviting their own deaths, Catholic clerics such as Father Alfred Delp and Father Maximilian Kolbe and Bernard Lichtenberg, as well as Lutheran pastors such as Dean Ernst Gruber. Once the war began, Hitler ordered a moderation of the persecution of the churches for the sake of unity in the war.

In the Protestant churches there was more support for the government because of the traditional role of the state in church government. Early on, the group known as the German Christians wanted to establish a new church that integrated Lutheranism with the Nazi ideology under a new "Reich bishop," creating a centralized and nationalized Protestant church. Led by a Berlin minister, Martin Niemöller, many pastors and church members opposed this effort and protested by organizing the Confessing Church. It strengthened the spiritual independence of Lutheran Christians. It was led by the Reich Council of Brethren under the theologian Karl Barth. Many of its members were from the Pastors Emergency League. A national meeting (synod) was held at Barmen and produced the Barmen Declaration, which rejected the totalitarian claims of Nazism. Nonetheless, it was not a protest of a political nature, because its theologians remained loyal to Hitler, maintaining the traditional Lutheran respect for state authority.

The beginning of the war saw the creation of increasingly oppressive circumstances and increasing terrorism on the home front as military setbacks occurred on the eastern front. As the genocide of the Jews, Poles, and Russians was taking place, a wide assortment of individuals came to the decision that Hitler had to be eliminated and a new government established that respected basic ethical standards. By this time it had become clear that the chains that the Gestapo and the SS had placed on Germans could be broken only by the nation's armed forces. Yet, when we look at where the military leaders stood in the 1930s, there was little chance of that happening. Most high-ranking officers had become strong supporters of Hitler as Germany rearmed. However, some generals were not impressed and worried that Hitler was preparing for a new war. Chief of the General Staff, General Ludwig Beck, was a resister who refused to plan the invasion of Czechoslovakia. Beck, who no longer felt bound by his oath, called on the leadership of the army to resign all their offices in order to prevent a war, which they would not do. So Beck became the central figure in a resistance group that wanted to remove Hitler by force. Beck had been planning a coup as early as 1938 over Czechoslovakia, which failed to occur because of the Appeasement policies of the British prime minister, Neville Chamberlain in 1938–39. In winter of 1939–40 the chief of staff of the Abwehr, General Hans Oster, another leader in the resistance, carried out the Oster Conspiracy, in which he tried to inform both the Dutch and the Norwegians about Hitler's invasion plans for their countries, but without success. With Hitler's successful invasion of Poland and of France in 1940, the cohesion of the conspirators around Beck dwindled.

In 1939 Karl Friedrich Goerdeler, the former mayor of Leipzig, joined Beck's circle. At first Goerdeler was sympathetic to the goals of National Socialism and only gradually came to reject its excessive nationalism and fanatic racism and promoted the overthrow of the regime. After the war began, the group around Beck and Goerdeler repeatedly planned to assassinate Hitler, but these plans were hindered by the indecision of some conspirators, the lack of opportunity, as well as the transfer of officers involved. More decisive leadership came with the addition of Henning von Tresckow and Claus Schenk, Count von STAUFFENBERG. Tresckow had at first been enthusiastic about the Nazi goals, especially for the creation of a classless community. But the persecution of various groups and especially the Jews made him into an opponent of the regime. From 1938 Tresckow opposed Hitler's "cowboy policies" and was determined to kill the "tyrant" as a moral duty, but two assassination attempts in 1943 failed. Claus von Stauffenberg also had been fascinated with Nazism and liberated himself more slowly. Considered a military "genius" on the General Staff, Stauffenberg was involved in military operations and severely wounded, losing the use of one eye and one hand. In 1943 he became chief of staff at the General Army Office in BERLIN, where he became involved in the plans of Friedrich Olbricht to assassinate Hitler. In the meantime the KREISAU CIRCLE had been meeting under the leadership of Helmuth James, Count von MOLTKE, and Count Yorck von Wartenburg and had worked out a plan for a new government. The Kreisau Circle had brought together Conservatives, Socialists, Unionists, and Christians, but was not involved in the July 20th plot. It was perhaps unfortunate that Stauffenberg, who had gained access to Hitler's East Prussian headquarters known as the "Wolf's Lair," decided to act alone to attempt an assassination. Stauffenberg activated only one of his two bombs and had to leave the headquarters before it blew up. The attempt failed, and the leaders were arrested and executed. Even the members of the Kreisau Circle were executed. Overall, some 10,000 members of the resistance were executed by the Nazis.

Reuchlin, Johannes (1455–1522)
humanist Hebrew scholar

Johannes Reuchlin was born in Pforzheim in 1455. He studied law at the Universities of Freiburg, Paris, and Basel. He taught for a while and then entered the service of Duke Eberhard of Württemberg (1450–90) as a lawyer from 1484 to 1496. During this period he traveled to Italy and became acquainted with the leading Italian humanists, Pico della Mirandola and Marsilio Ficino. From 1502 to 1513 he was a judge for the Swabian League. His main interests, however, were philological, leading him to become a professor at Ingolstadt and Tübingen, where he taught Greek and Hebrew.

Reuchlin was an eloquent Latin stylist and the first fully competent Greek scholar in Germany. His scholarship involved the comparative study of scriptural texts. His philosophical interests led him from the study of Plato and Pythagoras to the Jewish occult lore in the Cabala. He also was the founder of Hebrew studies in Germany. He wrote *Rudiments of Hebrew* (1506), a Christian-Hebrew grammar. The goal of Reuchlin's Hebrew scholarship was to purify the church so that it could provide a more meaningful spiritual experience. In his philosophical-theological humanist writings *On the Wonder-Working Word* (1494) and *On the Cabalistic Art* (1517) he sought to integrate both ancient and modern philosophy in order to demonstrate divine truth. Reuchlin also wrote two Latin comedies, an important step in the development of German comedy.

His interest in Hebrew studies led to Reuchlin's involvement in one of the great controversies of the period. Dominican professors of Thomistic philosophy at the University of Cologne considered *The Eyeglasses* (1511), which defended the scholarly value of Hebrew studies, to be heretical. It was the Jew Johannes Pfefferkorn who converted to Christianity in 1505, became intolerant of existing Jews and Reuchlin's worst enemy. Pfefferkorn intended to eliminate Judaism in Germany, demanding that all Jewish literature be destroyed. Reuchlin responded by defending its existence as a source of religious and cultural truths. During this controversy the Dominican priests even opened inquisitorial proceedings against Reuchlin. He defended himself in *Letters of Famous Men,* a collection of letters from those who supported him.

Coming to his defense were the humanists Ulrich von HUTTEN and Crotus Rubeanus, who wrote an anonymous and satirical collection, *Letters of Obscure Men,* which lampooned Reuchlin's opponents. Reuchlin remained in the church and was opposed to the REFORMATION.

Revolution of 1848

In contrast to the negligible German response to the French Revolution of 1789, the response to the revolution in France of February 1848 was an epidemic of uprisings in March through all the German states. Economic problems and disease in the countryside, urban unemployment and misery caused by industrialization, and increased political repression by governments trying to stifle criticism combined to create an atmosphere ripe for revolution. Started in the countryside by farmers protesting taxes, protests and uprisings spread to towns and cities, first in the west and south and then north and east, including MUNICH, Vienna, and BERLIN. Some were armed clashes, while others consisted of peaceful demonstrations numbering some 30 separate revolts. During this first phase of the revolution the street fighting that took place in Berlin's Alexanderplatz killed some 230 people before FREDERICK WILLIAM IV ordered his troops to leave the city and granted liberal reforms. In Vienna the revolutionary turmoil forced the Austrian prince Klemens von METTERNICH to hurriedly flee to England and the emperor to retire to Innsbruck. The three major goals of the revolutionary leaders were the establishment of a nation-state; the liberal demands for basic civil rights and constitutional government with some measure of popular sovereignty; and social and economic reforms such as the complete elimination of serfdom, improved working conditions for urban workers, and economic freedom for business. An ultra-radical group preached socioeconomic egalitarianism, but it must be emphasized that the revolts were not caused by problems and class conflict emerging out of the Industrial Revolution.

The revolts proceeded through four stages. During the first phase moderate liberal goals were achieved, and political power was temporarily shared with the old ruler. In Berlin the king even toured the city clad in the new black, red, and gold flag. In May the German National Assembly met in St. Paul's church in FRANKFURT AM MAIN, known as the FRANKFURT PARLIAMENT. During the second phase, lasting from June 1848 to April 1849, the old rulers attempted to regain the power they had lost. The Austrian army attacked the revolutionaries in Prague and Italy, proving that the army could still be counted on as a bulwark of monarchical conservatism. Encouraged by these victories, reactionaries began to reassert themselves in the other German states, which ended in the defeat of most of the liberal agenda. This period ended when the Prussian king, Frederick William, in April 1848 refused to accept the crown of emperor of a united Germany offered to him by the Frankfurt Parliament. The third phase was a brief new wave of revolution that swept over most of the states from April to August 1849. Liberals and nationalists hoped to salvage at least a portion of their initial gains. In SAXONY, the Palatinate, and Baden the lower classes and democratic forces rebelled when they realized that all their sacrifices on the barricades had brought them no social or economic benefits. Repression of this second wave of revolution occurred during the fourth phase, and the Frankfurt Parliament was disbanded. Trials were held, thousands emigrated, and repression instituted the conservative reaction of the 1850s.

One of the greatest debates in the Frankfurt Parliament was between the "greater Germany" (*grossdeutsch*) versus the "smaller Germany" (*kleindeutsch*) solutions to the problem of which states and ethnic population would be included in a German nation-state. Austria insisted on bringing into the Reich all of its ethnic populations, encompassing more than a dozen different nationalities. The "smaller Germany" solution won the day. This was one example of the confusion and conflict among the three liberal revolutionary aims (national, liberal, and social). Middle-class liberals were forced to choose between unification and constitutionalism. The representatives at Frankfurt chose unification and doomed both. The MIDDLE CLASS also feared the egalitarian aims of the lower classes on whom they depended for their popular revolutionary support, which in the end made the middle class place its reliance on the conservative forces of order and stability. The entire revolution was doomed when Prussian troops dispersed the Frankfurt Parliament and repressed the popular uprisings.

It has often been said that Germany and Europe failed to make a decisive turn toward constitutional government during the Revolution of 1848. Yet, there were lasting accomplishments. Major German states kept written constitutions with some degree of popularly elected parliaments. The constitution of 1849 drafted in Frankfurt served as a model for subsequent German constitutions. Some of the language on basic rights was incorporated verbatim into the BASIC LAW adopted by the FEDERAL REPUBLIC in 1949. The freedom of peasants from manorial taxes and other burdens was not eliminated in Prussia, but artisans and journeymen in guilds were protected by the Prussian Commercial code of 1849. Neither was trial by jury eliminated nor the legal emancipation of Jews reversed. Economic LIBERALISM was not retarded as the states continued to encourage economic MODERNIZATION. And finally, legal equality for the middle class was not reversed, and its political and economic self-consciousness continued to grow.

Revolution of 1918–1919

Known as the November Revolution to contemporaries, the revolution broke out when the surprise of the Armistice spread throughout Germany. A reform of the government was already in the making that October as Prince Max of Baden had been appointed to head a reform government. But when the High Seas Fleet was ordered by mutinous admirals to strike a final blow against the British fleet, mutinies broke out among sailors in Kiel that spread to Wilhelmshaven on October 28, 1918. Then the rebellion spread to army units and to workers. By November 6, councils were established by sailors, soldiers, and workers in imitation of the councils (soviets) prevalent during the 1917 revolution in Russia. There was surprisingly very little resistance from officials of the Imperial government, and even in BAVARIA the WITTELSBACH dynasty was easily overthrown by Kurt EISNER on November 7 and a republic declared on November 8. That same day a republic was declared in Brunswick.

On November 9 the Kaiser abdicated; Prince Max handed over the chancellorship to Friedrich EBERT of the SOCIAL DEMOCRATIC PARTY; and Philip Scheidemann declared Germany a republic from a window of the REICHSTAG. WILLIAM II had resisted abdication, but in the end capitulated and sought refuge in Holland. The events were out of control, and if asked Ebert would have preferred a constitutional monarchy instead of a republic. Ebert, however, was also opposed by more radical elements in the establishment of a provisional ministry. The INDEPENDENT SOCIALISTS (USPD) insisted that sovereign power be given to the councils. Philip Scheidemann had taken his precipitous action to forestall the declaration of a socialist republic by the radical independent socialist, Karl LIEBKNECHT. But Ebert and Scheidemann took actions to restore order and call elections for a constitutional assembly. On November 10 secret negotiations for the EBERT-GROENER PACT took place between Ebert and the head of the army, General Wilhelm GROENER, for the army's help to contain the revolution against the radicals, provided the army was spared. Groener promised to bring the hundred of thousands of soldiers peacefully home from France and elsewhere.

In December the councils demanded more power, and clashes took place in BERLIN. The Spartacus League turned into the GERMAN COMMUNIST PARTY (KPD) and ignited a revolution in January, which was quickly suppressed. Gustav NOSKE, who was in charge of military affairs, used FREE CORPS troops to suppress revolutionary activity in BREMEN, Braunschweig, Bavaria, and the RUHR. The Spartacists leaders, Karl Liebknecht and Rosa LUXEMBURG, were killed by the military.

Elections and convening a constituent assembly were Ebert's goals. The elections were duly held on January 19, and the NATIONAL ASSEMBLY met in WEIMAR on February 6. When a new government was appointed by the assembly, the revolution officially came to an end, although in spring a Soviet style republic was still to be suppressed in Bavaria.

Rhine, River and Valley

The Rhine River is Germany's most important waterway, its most scenically beautiful and historically significant. It has a length of some 1,300 km. Beginning in Switzerland as the Alpine Rhine, it flows through Lake Constance (Bodensee), then westward, forming the Rhine Falls at Schaffhausen, and continues to Basel as the Higher Rhine. From Basel it flows northward through the upper Rhine plain. Between Mainz and Bingen it again flows westward, but shortly northwest through the Rhenish Uplands as the Middle Rhine. Around BONN it is called the Lower Rhine. As it enters the Netherlands it divides into a number of tributaries flowing into the North Sea.

Between Bingen and Bonn lies some of the most picturesque landscape in Germany if not the world. The legendary castles and picturesque walled towns and cobblestoned villages have been extolled by poets and memorialized by artists. Overlooking St. Goarshausen is Burg Katz—named for the Neukatzenelnbogen family—an impressive medieval castle dating back to 1371. Writers have often recalled the exploits of medieval knights and robber barons. One of Germany's famous legends is also associated with a great black rock outcropping near Oberwesel. The rock, rising some 400 feet above, is called the Lorelei after the nymph who sang to sailors below, luring them into crashing their ships on the channel rapids. The Rhine valley is also one of Germany's most beautiful wine-growing regions. Surrounding a castle at Rudesheim are vineyards that appear to flow toward the Bromserberg Wine Museum, which once had been a castle dating back to the ninth century. On the Rhine both passenger boats and barges travel, providing an artery connecting such cities as Ludwigshafen, Mainz, Koblenz, Kaiserslautern, Trier, Cologne, and Bonn. Magnificent cathedrals that recall its Catholic past are located in Speyer, Worms, and Mainz, as well as the abbey of Maria Laach in the Eifel, St. Catherine's Church in Oppenheim, and the Church of St. Paulinus in Trier.

During the NAPOLEONIC WARS patriots such as Ernst Moritz Arndt claimed the Rhine as "Germany's river, not Germany's boundary." The Rhine became a symbol of German NATIONALISM in the era of liberation from Napoleon and the age of ROMANTICISM. Even in Roman times both banks of the river had been settled by German tribes, and the past greatness of the HOLY ROMAN EMPIRE has been historically mirrored in its waters. The shores of the Rhine were where German patriots felt they needed to stand guard against the encroachments of the French, their "hereditary enemy." Arndt thought of the Rhenish people as the heart and soul of the German nation and imagined the river to be their lifeblood. Another staunch patriot, publicist, and prophet of national liberation, Joseph von GÖRRES (1776–1848) taught his readers the cultural and historical significance of the left bank territories of the Rhine.

Rhineland-Palatinate
(Federal state Rheinland-Pfalz)

The state of Rhineland-Palatinate was formed after WORLD WAR II on August 30, 1946, by the French military government. The federal state was merged out of part of the former Prussian Rhine province, the territory of HESSE on the left bank of the Rhine, Hesse-Nassau, and the Bavarian Palatinate. Mainz was designated as the capital of the new state. Since 1971 the political party that had dominated the elections was the CDU under Helmut KOHL, which won more than 50 percent of the vote until 1983. After German reunification in 1990 the SPD became the dominant party along with the FDP. Economically, the state is diversified, but its largest industrial employer is the chemical firm BASF.

The Rhineland is located in western Germany, bordering Belgium, Luxembourg, and France. The Rhineland was originally settled by the Celts, the Romans, the Burgundians, and the Franks. In the cities of Speyer, Worms, and Mainz some of Europe's greatest Gothic cathedrals were built, while in Worms the oldest synagogue in Germany dates back to 1034. Worms also was where the Imperial Diet of 1521 met, at which Martin Luther refused to renounce his theses.

The territory of the Rhineland had consisted of ecclesiastical states before the Napoleonic Wars and was ceded to Prussia in 1815 at the Congress of Vienna. In the Rhineland city of Mainz Johannes Gutenberg first printed books in movable type in Europe and the abbey church of Maria Laach was built; the famous liberal *Rheinischer Merkur* was published in the Rhineland; in 1832 the first democratic-republican festival took place at the castle in Hambach; the father of scientific socialism, Karl Marx, was born in the old Roman fortress city of Trier. Going back to the Middle Ages the emperor Frederick I Barbarossa built a castle in Kaiserslautern. Among the other cities are Ludwigshafen, Koblenz, Neustadt, Bingen, and Bad Kreuznach. The Rhineland-Palatinate is also one of the most beautiful valley landscapes dotted with castles, whose poets and musicians have sung about it. The Moselle River valley is a prime wine-growing area.

The mineral resources of the area were developed by the Prussians. In 1918 the French hoped to detach the then Rhineland area from Germany. The Treaty of Versailles stipulated that the Rhineland, although remaining German, was to be occupied by Allied troops for 15 years and that a 30-mile-wide demilitarized zone was to be created on the right bank of the river. The Locarno Treaties emphasized the permanence of the demilitarized zone. Gustav Stresemann secured agreements by which the British were to evacuate the Rhineland in November 1926 and the French by June 1930. After the advent of Hitler relations again became strained over the Rhineland question. During March 1936 Hitler ordered German troops to occupy the Rhineland, which violated the Versailles and Locarno treaties while the French and the British merely expressed feeble protests.

The Palatinate (Pfalz) lies to the west of the Rhine and consists of a flat (Rheingau) and a hilly and forested region (Pfälzer Bergland and Wald). Its urban centers are Kaiserslautern, Worms, Speyer, Mannheim, and Heidelberg. The name *Pfalz* presently refers to the central and southern part of the Rhineland-Palatinate, while the Upper Palatinate (Oberpfalz) is a district of Bavaria.

Palatine was a title given to civil servants of the Holy Roman Empire, and eventually it was the term applied to the territory of the plenipotentiary of the sovereign who ruled. These plenipotentiaries were called counts palatine, and they existed in Lorraine, the Rhineland, Swabia, Bavaria, and Saxony. Palatinate or pfalz originally referred to the buildings that the kings and their courts would occupy as their court seat. These later become an administrative center. The term *Palatinate* also came to identify the territory that the count palatine ruled. As time passed, all the Palatinates, such as Worms, Frankfurt, Aachen, and Lorraine were absorbed by local nobles with only the Palatinate of the Rhine remaining, which was acquired in 1214 by the Wittelsbach family of Bavaria. In 1329 the Rhine Palatinate along with the Upper Palatinate was separated from Bavaria and placed under a separate branch of the Wittelsbach family. The office of Imperial Elector remained hereditary until the dissolution of the Empire in 1806.

The Palatinate was ruled by one branch of the house of Wittelsbach, while the other branch provided the dukes, electors, and kings of Bavaria. The Palatinate became Protestant in 1542. The territory and electoral rights were given in 1623 to the elector of Bavaria, Duke Maximilian I when Frederick V, the "winter king," failed in 1619 to become king of Bohemia. After the Peace of Westphalia (1648) the Palatinate was split in two: the son of Frederick V, Karl Ludwig, recovered the Lower Palatinate, while the Upper Palatinate remained

Bavarian. The devastation of the Palatinate was perpetrated by the French in 1688–89, when they senselessly destroyed Worms, Speyer, Mannheim, and Heidelberg. This was the time when the Heidelberg castle with its treasures was destroyed. In 1816 after the Napoleonic Wars Bavaria and the Palatinate were unified, which continued until the end of WORLD WAR II.

Ribbentrop, Joachim von (1893–1946)
Nazi foreign minister

Joachim von Ribbentrop was a businessman who became the NAZI PARTY's foreign minister between 1938 and 1945. HITLER considered him a diplomatic genius and thought him "second to Bismarck." Ribbentrop's greatest diplomatic achievement was the NAZI-SOVIET NONAGGRESSION PACT in August 1939.

Ribbentrop was born on April 30, 1893, in Wesel on the RHINE RIVER of affluent middle-class parents. He experienced a good education at the Imperial Lyceum in Metz and also studied in France, Great Britain, and Switzerland. Serving in WORLD WAR I, he won the Iron Cross for bravery. His first diplomatic experience came when he assisted Franz von PAPEN on his military mission to the United States. In 1919 Ribbentrop was a member of the German delegation to the Versailles Peace Conference. Unable to obtain a government position in the WEIMAR REPUBLIC, he went into business as a wine merchant and was socially ambitious, marrying the daughter of the rich champagne magnate, Otto Henkell. Eventually he became co-owner of the Henkell-Trocken champagne firm and in 1925 added the aristocratic "von" to his name.

In 1928 he became interested in National Socialism and collaborated with Adolf Hitler with the hope of aiding his business prospects and even to put his Jewish competition out of business. He officially joined the Nazi Party in May 1932. Because of his wealth and connections he acted as a mediator between Hitler and the German government in the early 1930s, arranging the important meetings in January 1933 between Hitler and Franz von Papen and Hitler and Oskar von Hindenburg, son of the president. Out of these meetings came President Paul von HINDENBURG's decision to appoint Hitler chancellor on January 31, 1933. As a reward for promoting the Nazi ideology Hitler appointed Ribbentrop Reich commissioner for disarmament in 1934. The next year he was appointed ambassador-at-large and negotiated the Anglo-German Naval Treaty of June 1935. In October 1936 after the death of the German ambassador to Great Britain, Ribbentrop was named as his replacement. Holding this position for two years, Ribbentrop made great efforts as Gordon Craig writes "to cultivate a uniquely National Socialist style" which "had resulted in a tactlessness that was self-defeating," and "undertook to bully the British into an alliance." Mixing in polite English society, joining exclusive clubs, and making powerful friends, Ribbentrop tried to ingratiate himself, hoping the British would see things his way. He made the mistake of threatening the British with "dreadful consequences" if they did not enter into an alliance and give Germany a free hand in the East. He impressed many as being pompous and incompetent. What had been Anglophilia gradually turned to Anglophobia; he developed a deep anti-British feeling. Nevertheless, Ribbentrop was successful in signing the ANTI-COMINTERN PACT with Japan in November 1936. Hitler was overly impressed with Ribbentrop and considered him a diplomatic genius, second only to Otto von BISMARCK.

At this point the foreign minister, Konstantin von Neurath, was dismissed and Ribbentrop took over as foreign minister. From here he went on to negotiate the Munich Agreement of September 1938 and the March 1939 occupation of Czechoslovakia. In December 1938 he brought about a declaration of friendship with the French. But his greatest achievement was the Nazi-Soviet Nonaggression Pact signed in Moscow with Soviet Minister Molotov. One of Ribbentrop's great misjudgments concerned Great Britain's willingness to go to war if Germany invaded Poland. He did not think the British would and may have influenced Hitler's opinion. He may have prevented a peaceful settlement of the differences between Germany and England on the eve of the war.

Once the war had begun and after the Japanese Nonaggression Pact with the USSR in April 1941 and then Hitler's invasion of Russia that June, Ribbentrop's involvement in serious diplomacy declined. The Foreign Office was implicated in the July 1944 plot on Hitler's life, which further decreased his influence. He disappeared at the end of the war, but was captured by the British in HAMBURG in June 1945. He was found guilty of war crimes and crimes against humanity. The Foreign Office staff was found guilty of collaborating in the FINAL SOLUTION. He was hanged on October 16, 1946.

Riefenstahl, Leni (1902–2003)
film director

Leni Riefenstahl was a controversial film director who produced the Nazi propaganda films *The Triumph of the Will* (1935) of the 1934 NUREMBERG rally and *Olympia* (1938), a documentary of the Olympic Games of 1936. She was considered the "movie-queen of Nazi Germany." HITLER personally chose her to make propaganda films for the Third Reich.

Leni Riefenstahl was born on August 22, 1902, in BERLIN, the daughter of Alfred and Bertha Riefenstahl. She began her career as an actress and dancer and opened her film production company in 1931. Her career as a dancer was quite accomplished, dancing ballet for the Russian Ballet and modern dance with Mary Wigman. By 1920 she toured such cities as MUNICH, FRANKFURT, Prague, Dresden, and Zurich. Then she was employed by Max Reinhardt for dance performances between 1923 and 1926. She turned to acting in such films as *The Holy Mountain*. During the next seven years she made five more films, including *S.O.S. Eisberg*. Turning to film production, she wrote and produced the film *The Blue Light* in which she also played the leading role; the film was awarded in 1932 a gold medal at a Venetian festival. The film possessed the legacy of German EXPRESSIONISM, and Riefenstahl experimented extensively to create the desired special effects.

Hitler was so impressed with Riefenstahl's work in *The Blue Light* that he appointed her the director of films for the NAZI PARTY. After his power was consolidated, Hitler wanted Riefenstahl to film the 1934 party rally in Nuremberg. She produced "the propaganda film of all times," but later maintained that she had only made a documentary. What she did was carefully edit more than 60 hours of film without chronological accuracy but emphasizing certain themes like the solidarity and strength of the Nazi Party, the unity of the German people and the greatness of Hitler. The film had an emotional and irrational appeal and especially featured Albert SPEER's architectural decorations of swastikas, eagles, flags, flames, and music. It was awarded the German Film Prize for 1935. Less known is her next film on the German military; entitled *Day of Freedom: Our Armed Forces* (1935), which she shot to placate the army which was not pleased at the little attention it received in *Triumph of the Will.*

Riefenstahl received international acclaim for her two films on the Olympic Games of 1936. *Olympia* was divided into two parts: *Festival of Nations* and *Festival of Beauty.* Her meticulousness and inventiveness produced a great example of

Adolf Hitler (left) with Leni Riefenstahl during Nazi Party Day in Nuremberg, 1934 *(Library of Congress)*

sports photography, which included everything from nude dancers to the African-American athlete Jesse Owens.

After the fall of Nazi Germany Leni Riefenstahl had to defend herself from the accusation of Nazi collaborator. She rejected claims of her complicity and pleaded being duped by Hitler. She alleged that she did not understand Hitler's plans. In her 1993 film biography, *The Wonderful, Horrible Life of Leni Riefenstahl,* at 91 years of age she still claimed her innocence and said that she never realized the impact of her films promoting Nazism. She condemned the Nazis and expressed horror of the HOLOCAUST. She claimed that she deleted from *Triumph* almost every reference to racist policies. She probably was not an ideologue and was probably duped or "seduced by a monster" as were so many other Germans.

She was cleared of Nazi Party membership by the postwar courts, but was classed as a Nazi sympathizer, which resulted in her making only one more film, a marine life documentary. Earlier she had visited Africa twice and produced two books of still photography.

Rilke, Rainer Maria (1875–1926)
modernist poet

Transcending cultural boundaries, Rainer Maria Rilke is considered the greatest lyric poet of modern Germany. He recast German into a new literary language and wrote in a mystical sense of God and death.

Born in Prague, the capital of Bohemia in the Austro-Hungarian Empire, he was raised a Catholic in a lower middle-class culture. His father was frustrated in his life's ambition to become an army officer, which expectation was transferred to his son, something that tormented Rilke, who was effeminate and far from suited for the military. His parents separated, and he was sent to two military academies, after which he entered the German University of Prague to study literature. Then he went to study at the University of MUNICH, which began his wandering life during which he lived in France, Italy, North Africa, Scandinavia, Spain, and Switzerland. The beginning of WORLD WAR I found him living in Paris. At first he was caught up in the war enthusiasm but soon concluded that it revealed the desolation of modern culture. He was required to serve in the army and was assigned to the War Archives in Vienna, then released after the wife of his publisher, Frau Kippenberg, petitioned the army for his release from military service. From there he went to Munich, which also became intolerable during the REVOLUTION of 1918. So he moved to Switzerland, where his writing bloomed.

Rilke's early poems were indifferent love poems written in the tradition of Heinrich HEINE. Next came poems concerned with his native Prague. These and later prose works fail to indicate the achievements of his later genius. It was, however, in his second religious or mystic period (1899–1903) that he wrote *The Book of Hours,* wherein he opposes NATURALISM and he became a symbolist and religious prophet and humanitarian. His haunting verses express a longing for present-day transcendental confirmation. In his *New Poems* (1903–08) he achieved mastery over objective form with his ability to use the appropriate words expressed in effortless rhyme.

The year 1922 was described by him as his "great time," during which he was possessed by an energy and was able to write an amount of poetry unparalleled by any poet of the 20th century. The inspiration took place at the towered old Château de Muzot, which a friend placed at his disposal. Here he finished his greatest works, *Duino Elegies* (1922) and *Sonnets to Orpheus* (1923), the latter comprising 59 poems. The writing of the *Elegies* began in 1912, but was interrupted by World War I. The elegies attempted to conquer reality and to approach the transcendental. They begin with a moving lament for man's lonely insufficiency. The poet seeks to overcome his loneliness by communicating with his angels, who surprisingly are not the angels of Christianity but are closer to those of Islam in whom the transformation of the visible appears complete. Yet neither love, nor sacrifice, nor daily work are satisfying or explain life, and the poet becomes resigned to his existence. In the shorter poems of the *Sonnets to Orpheus* Rilke communicates a deep religious feeling of transformed reality. He concludes that life is continually changed by ever-present death. The transcendence here is not at all Christian. His attitude is almost agnostic, the god is not Christian but either Greek or Hindu. The sonnets are not chiseled, the images not self-contained, and the rhythms are multifarious.

A few years later in 1926 Rilke died. His attempt to reach beyond modern anxiety has been described as "neopagan aestheticism." Although raised a practicing Catholic, he already had rebelled against his Christian faith in his adolescence. His poetry is not imbued with Christian faith, and perhaps it is more meaningful to say that his work fused impressionism with romantic spirituality. In the *Sonnets* the everyday world of the West has been infused with Eastern mysticism. The mixture of Christian images presents some confusion and is not logical. He was a seeker of God, but did so through praise of the world in communication with his angel.

rococo culture

The rococo was the elegant concluding phase of the BAROQUE. The middle of the 18th century saw kings and ARISTOCRACY begin to prefer smaller residences where more intimate gatherings could comfortably take place. Although rococo art no longer reflected the baroque grandeur and flamboyance of ABSOLUTISM, it nonetheless was elegant and graceful. Two of the chief examples of rococo architecture actually were completed in the early part of the century, the Zwinger in DRESDEN (1711–22) already mentioned in reference to the baroque, and Frederick the Great's palace SANS-SOUCI (1745–47) in Potsdam. In Sans-Souci the décor is light and elegant in contrast to the grandeur and ostentatiousness of the baroque. Residences were generally not very high, and their design enclosed gardens in the non-geometric English style, in which trees and shrubs grew naturally. Rather than concentrate on the exterior of buildings, the rococo focused on interior design to accommodate social functions. For instance, chairs received backs, and bedrooms were separated from reception rooms. Windows bathed the interior with light, and the preferred colors were pastels. Music also reflected the new interests as did dress. The powdered wig became a symbol of the age, and the minuet the preferred form of dance. But it was in the Catholic South that Germany's great musical geniuses flowered. It was a golden age of German music that reflected a universality of meaning instead of a particular faith or region. The trinity of great composers were Joseph HAYDN (1732–1839), Wolfgang Amadeus Mozart (1756–91), and Ludwig van BEETHOVEN (1770–1827). Perhaps it was Mozart's chamber music that best expressed the elegance and grace of the rococo.

Röhm, Ernst (1887–1934)
SA leader

An early supporter of the Nazi Party and friend of Adolf HITLER, Ernst Röhm, became the leader of the Nazi Storm Troopers (Sturmabteilung), SA.

Born in MUNICH on November 28, 1887, into a family of Bavarian civil servants, Ernst Röhm decided on a military career. He earned his commission as an officer at the start of WORLD WAR I. He was wounded, enjoyed the comradeship of fellow soldiers, was a homosexual, and attained the rank of major. People were seen only as friends or enemies. Returning to Munich, he became a staff officer of General Franz Ritter von Epp's, who played a leading role in the overthrow the Soviet Republic. Röhm was one of the early members of the National Socialist GERMAN WORKERS' PARTY, provided it with considerable material support, and helped launch the career of Adolf Hitler. Until his resignation from the army in September 1923 he provided a liaison between the conservative Bavarian government and the many right-wing groups in BAVARIA. Röhm furnished important political connections for Hitler. He participated in Hitler's Munich BEER-HALL PUTSCH in November 1923, for which he was jailed but soon released. While Hitler learned from the failed putsch that a forceful overthrow of the government was impractical, Röhm did not learn the same lesson. Between 1925 and 1930, when Hitler called him back from Bolivia to lead the Storm Troopers (SA), Röhm earned a living as a factory worker and traveling salesman.

The Storm Troopers (SA) were Hitler's private army, through which he would win the battle of the streets with the Communists. In a few months Röhm had recruited 170,000 men under his command, but he had to pledge his allegiance to Hitler. By 1933 that number had grown to 2 million men in the SA. After Hitler came to power, he and Röhm again disagreed over the role of the SA in the new state and whether or not a second revolution was necessary. Röhm wanted the SA to be integrated into the army (Reichswehr), under his command making it a "people's army." The army was unalterably opposed, and Hitler needed the support of the generals, especially as he planned to take control of the army after the death of President Paul von HINDENBURG. On June 4, 1934, in a confrontation Hitler warned Röhm not to start a second revolution, after which Hitler decided to eliminate this socialist element from the party. Traveling to Bavaria, where Röhm and other SA leaders were vacationing, Hitler had him arrested and shot in his cell. Joseph GOEBBELS announced that the Führer had acted for the nation against these traitors. About 200 others were assassinated by the SS during the Blood Purge (NIGHT OF THE LONG KNIVES), including Gregor STRASSER and General Kurt von SCHLEICHER.

romanticism (1770–1830)

Romanticism was a cultural movement of protest against the rationalism of the ENLIGHTENMENT, of rejection of tradition and the emphasis on efficiency and relevance, as well as an optimistic belief that the future brings progress. It had its beginnings in the 1770s in the Storm and Stress movement when the poets of the time discovered an individual approach to life. It was, however, at the turn of the century that with the impact of the French Revolution the HOLY ROMAN EMPIRE came to an end, the Prussian state collapsed, and the German states were mainly a geographical expression. Old truths had been challenged, and no ideal or state or philosophy was predominant. As this old world disintegrated, an individual approach to life was promulgated by the German romanticists.

The romantics were convinced that life had dimensions that could not be comprehended by scientific analysis and that instinct and emotion were a better guide to the deeper truths than was reason. They sought to restore the intimate bond between man and nature, which the rationalism of the Enlightenment had broken with its conception of nature as a soulless mechanism for man's exploitation. They rejected the mathematical order of the philosophes and preferred the incoherence of life. They rejected the symbolical orderliness of the French garden and preferred the wild and mysterious world of the German forest. It was Schelling in particular, who, following PARACELSUS and Böhme, sought to overcome the alienation of nature from spirit.

While the Enlightenment had looked to the future, the romantics looked to the past, to the origin of things and the study of history, especially the Middle Ages. In place of the Enlightenment's belief in the recognition of the individual's rights within the framework of law, the romantics developed a cult of individuality. The romantics were preoccupied with the cult of genius, wherein superior individuals could realize their potential even at the expense of society's laws and conventions. One can imagine that this belief often became an excuse for eccentric behavior and mediocrity in thought and the arts. Rooted in this cult of individuality and originality was a strong emphasis on the *Volk*, the people, as a unique entity. This concept was given a new dignity by uniting the cultural community with the bonds of common ancestors, language, and native soil. Like Johann HERDER, the romantic school of historians looked to the past for authentic sources of the

Volk, researching sagas, myths, legends, customs, and language. Its popular influence is reflected in the famous collection of fairy tales published by the brothers GRIMM in 1812. Publication of the sources of German national culture significantly contributed to the growth of German NATIONALISM. Some romantics felt so strongly about the uniqueness of the German people that they were inspired to preach violence and war and claimed that the German nation was superior to all others.

Under the surface of life the romantics often found terror. Thomas MANN wrote that when he thought of romanticism, it was not happy wandering, joyful singing, or fantasies and dreamy longings that came to his mind, but rather the dark side of elemental forces that stirred behind the trees at night. There was something undeniably unhealthy with the preoccupation of the romantics with a world where good and evil spirits moved and above all with their fascination with death. The world of the romantic imagination was certainly colorful, rich in figures and association, nocturnal scenes, fairy tales and dreams, and incessantly changing. The variety of the Middle Ages fascinated them. When Herder uncovered the individuality of the historical periods and nations, he laid one of the important foundations for romanticism.

The romantics felt that there were states of mind in which a person was closer to understanding the mystery of existence. Novalis, for example, found that love and the death of a lover led to insights that could not be experienced in any other way. In the tales of Ernest HOFFMANN, madness, or what is mistaken for madness by most people, could break through the barriers of the rational and lead to deep and sometimes horrifying truths. Because of this orientation by the romantics they were interested in hypnotism, cataleptic states, the visions of stigmatized nuns, and somnambulism. Symbols were also common and thought to reflect the unknown or lead to the solution of mysteries. The Blue Flower was seen as a symbol of man's longing to transcend this world. Night had a variety of meanings and could be a symbol of the mother of all creation, the source of terror or even peace. The love of the beautiful Lorelei brought death. Messengers from another world brought to mind dangerous knowledge. The doppelgänger or spectral double shows man another side of his nature. And the solitude of the forest brought forth the divine and demonic.

During the romantic period there was a revival of religious consciousness, a reaction perhaps to the neglect and hostility that the Enlightenment had manifested toward religion. Great emphasis was placed on pure faith. Romanticism often felt itself akin to Christianity. The transcendental nature of religious experience was stressed as far superior to mere logic. The Protestant theologian Friedrich SCHLEIERMACHER in his *Reden über die Religion* (Lectures on religion) defined it as a feeling of absolute dependency. The romantics actually felt that they were standing on the brink of a new age of Christian unity in which all conflicting issues would be reconciled and a new spiritual unity would emerge. The Protestant Friedrich von HARDENBERG in his celebrated essay *Christianity or Europe* (1799) hoped that a new kind of Christian unity was possible that would be both hierarchical and evangelical, developing into a kind of Christian mystical solidarity. Schelling, on the other hand, preferred a synthesis in Roman Catholic solidarity. Rationalists such as Gotthold LESSING had asked whether religion really existed apart from philosophy and ethics. Rather than denying the existence of the supernatural as mere superstition, however, he accorded to religion a positive role in the continuous process of revelation and education of the community. Both the idealists and the romantics had a concept of God as an all-pervading creative spirit. The romantics even thought that cultures originated in the earliest forms of religion.

The romantics thought that it was the artist who as a type of magician could evoke and release the spirit in nature and the subject material from its material bonds. The goal of the artist was to bring about self-consciousness and freedom. The romantic artist whether in painting or poem or music sought to avoid a definite form, a finished product as had been the case in the classical period. Their creative subjectivity manifested itself characteristically in the romantic yearning for the limitless and the boundless. Feelings and the imagination were to be brought under the control of reason, as a guide, as a means for expressing the irrational. Artists must express themselves—instincts and passions—through work. A painting was to be the individual artist's vision of the cosmos. The greatest of the romantic landscapists was Caspar David FRIEDRICH, most noted for his landscapes and seascapes, reflecting the interest of the romantics with nature. His landscapes transformed nature, making it almost spiritually alive with imperceptible nuances of light and color. Individuals in his paintings are contemplating nature and convey a sense of the individual's longing for the infinite. His moods are gentle and softly melancholy, always truly romantic and never sentimental. Other painters wanted to tell stories and made their works illustrative of historical and literary themes while neglecting the requirements of artistic form. Ludwig Richter and Moritz von Schwind were chiefly illustrators of fairy tales, legends, and the intimate charms of German domestic life. Their works provided the perfect accompaniment to the family style of the early 19th century in its complacent middle-class comfort. Both of these artists, however, painted outstanding glorifications of the German landscape. Perhaps the most talented of the early romantic painters was Philipp Otto Runge, who saw in landscapes a human spirit, idea, or feeling. He dreamt of a synthetic fusion of all the arts. Another artistic genius of the movement was Karl Spitzweg, who best expressed himself in paintings of miniature size. In his treatment of light and color, Spitzweg, like Runge, anticipated some of the later impressionistic school of painting.

In music romanticism tended to be less revolutionary than in the visual arts. There was continuity between the classicism of the 18th century and the romanticism of the 19th. The classical forms that were developed by HAYDN, Mozart, and BEETHOVEN, such as the sonata, the string quartet, and the symphony, continued throughout the romantic period. Some reinterpretations and new meanings of the function of music were attempted by the early romantic composers such as Franz SCHUBERT, Robert SCHUMANN, and Felix MENDELSSOHN. They tried to work on the minds and senses of the listener, evoking a range of emotions and impressions. A fusion of poetry and music was attempted by Schubert and Schumann in the lied (song), which blended the words and melody in perfect harmony. Schubert's lieder give rise to a whole range of feelings, especially ones of sadness, nostalgia, or yearning.

Rommel, Erwin Johannes Eugen (1891–1944)

German general known as "Desert Fox"
Erwin Rommel was Germany's most popular war hero. A brilliant tactician, he helped defeat the French in 1940 and challenged and nearly drove the British out of North Africa. He tried but failed to defend against the Allied invasion on D-DAY and collaborated in a plot against HITLER.

Erwin Rommel was born into the family of a Protestant schoolmaster in Heidenheim near Ulm in Württemberg on November 15, 1891. His middle-class parents provided him with a traditional classical education, though he was an average student whose favorite subjects were science and mathematics. His father persuaded him to join the infantry as an officer cadet in 1910, and he was commissioned a second lieutenant in 1912. Serving in France during WORLD WAR I, he was awarded the Iron Cross in 1915; then he served in Romania, followed by the Italian front, and for exhibiting unusual bravery he received the Pour le Mérite. Remaining in the army after the war, in 1929 he held a series of positions in infantry instruction, first at a school in DRESDEN till 1933, then at the Potsdam War Academy, finally becoming commander of the war academy in Wiener Neustadt. He served as commander of the dictator's body guard when he entered Czechoslovakia and Poland.

Rommel's first field command in WORLD WAR II was of a tank division, which demonstrated lightninglike speed in reaching the Channel, even moving too quickly. In February 1941 Rommel was appointed commander of the AFRIKA KORPS, which was sent to Libya to support the Italian campaign. With orders only to fight a defensive action (his personal traits and tactical approaches lent themselves well to the fluidity of desert warfare) Rommel disobeyed orders and went on the offensive, initially meeting with brilliant success. His tactical skills were practical rather than theoretical. Bold and learning from his mistakes, he was a master of improvisation. Rommel's forces were not well supplied, and he constantly complained of shortages and inadequate efforts by rear echelons to meet even the minimum needs of the Afrika Korps. Yet, his risks and maneuvering paid off. On June 21, 1942, he reached Tobruk, which was the key to British defenses. By the end of June 1942 Rommel had driven the British all the way to EL ALAMEIN, which was 60 miles west of Alexandria. He was awarded the Knight's Cross and was promoted to field marshal. He did not, however, succeed in taking Alexandria. Rommel had to leave for Germany for medical treatment and did not return until the Battle of El Alamein was lost. Through a successful counterattack by Field Marshal Bernard Montgomery the Afrika Korps was driven back to Tunis. There Rommel encountered American forces under General Dwight Eisenhower and lost the final battle of Médenine on March 5, 1943.

After the African campaign Rommel acted as special adviser for Hitler and in the middle of 1943 became commander of Army Group B in Italy, where he was to prevent Mussolini's defection and to counter an Allied invasion of southern Europe. In December 1943 he was transferred to the so-called Atlantic Wall, and in January 1944 was made commander of the army in northern France. Rommel correctly thought that the best chances for defeating an Allied invasion were in its earliest stages on the beaches themselves where the invaders were the most vulnerable. This failed to happen. On July 17 he was seriously wounded in an air raid, forcing him to return home.

On two occasions, June 17 and 29, 1944, long after the German defeats at STALINGRAD and North Africa, Rommel and General von Rundstedt met with Hitler and attempted to convince him that the war was lost and he should end it. Hitler probably knew that the war was lost, but in a melancholic mood said that no one would make peace with him. It was also reported that Hitler became angry and enraged. By this time Rommel had become disillusioned with Hitler's unrealistic military leadership, which he believed would lead to Germany's destruction.

Up until late in the war Rommel was genuinely apolitical, and until the war's final stages he believed Hitler was ultimately susceptible to rational persuasion. Rommel became associated with the plot of July 20 but did not favor Hitler's assassination. Instead, he favored a trial that would reveal Hitler's crimes. Yet conspiracy was not part of Rommel's character, and his sworn oath of loyalty was difficult to break. After the German failure to defeat the D-Day invasion at Normandy, Rommel thought that to continue the war was senseless and would result in the destruction of Germany. He agreed to head a government that would seek an armistice with the Allies. Rommel's involvement was revealed by one of the conspirators. Hitler decided to offer Rommel the choice of suicide or standing trial for treason. There was also a threat against his wife and son, who would be spared if he committed suicide. On October 14 two generals came in a car; Rommel entered and took the poison. His body was cremated to eliminate incriminating evidence. A state funeral was held, and Hitler ordered national mourning.

Röntgen, Wilhelm Conrad
(1845–1923)
physicist

Wilhelm Röntgen was the physician who developed the X-ray technique. He discovered X-rays and their effects and applicability in 1895 and received the Nobel Prize in 1901. Germans formed a verb out of his name, to x-ray a patient is to "röntgen" a patient with Röntgen-Rays.

Wilhelm Conrad Röntgen was born in Lennep, Germany, on March 27, 1845. He was an only child, and his father was a well-to-do textile merchant. Wilhelm was not a serious student, quite a prankster and at one time was expelled from school. He did not have the credentials to enter a German university, but was finally accepted by the Swiss Federal Institute of Technology in Zurich. He blossomed at the institute, studying mathematics, technical drawing, mechanical technology, engineering metallurgy, hydrology, and thermodynamics. In 1868 he was awarded his diploma in mechanical engineering. Röntgen then took the advice of the German physicist August Kundt, who suggested he study physics for his doctorate, which he completed in 1869, then followed the professor as his assistant to the University of Würzburg. In 1874 the assistant finally was appointed a *privatdozent* at the University of Strasbourg and two years later became an associate professor of physics. Three years later, he became a full professor at the University of Giessen, where he remained until 1888, then returning to the University of Würzburg. In 1900 the Bavarian government requested that he come to Munich, where he stayed until he retired in 1920.

Röntgen published 48 papers on a variety of scientific subjects, but his most significant was on James Clerk Maxwell's theory of electromagnetism, which he confirmed while at the University of Giessen. The discovery for which Röntgen will always be the most famous, however, is that of X-rays. In 1895, while experimenting with cathode rays, the now professor of physics at the University of Würzburg made a far-reaching discovery. After repeating some of the earlier experiments on cathode rays, his research took an unexpected turn. In order to observe the luminescence caused by cathode rays, he darkened his laboratory and enclosed the vacuum tube in black paper. The cathode rays lit up a screen covered with barium platinocyanide crystals farther away than the centimeter the cathode rays could travel. His research continued for weeks and found that the radiation could pass through glass and wood and was even capable of exposing a photographic plate. Because the rays were so mysterious he called them X-rays. Just a few weeks later he published his findings on the rays, which opened up entirely new perspectives for diagnostic medicine and materials testing.

In 1901 he was awarded the first Nobel Prize in physics. Röntgen never applied for a patent because he felt that his discovery should belong to the whole of humanity. He gave the prize money to the University of Würzburg for scientific research. Other awards he received include the Rumford Medal of the Royal Society (1896), the Bavarian Royal Order of Merit (1896), the Baumgaertner Prize of the Vienna Academy (1896), the Elliott-Cresson Medal of the Franklin Institute (1897), the Barnard Medal of Columbia University (1900), and the Helmholtz Medal (1919).

The end of his life was neither happy nor prosperous. He experienced considerable grief over the death of his wife. Germany's defeat in the war also negatively affected him. The inflationary period afterward bankrupted him. His last years were spent in Weilheim near Munich, where he died of intestinal cancer on February 10, 1923.

Rosenberg, Alfred (1893–1946)
racial philosopher of Nazi Party

Alfred Rosenberg was a Baltic German born in the Russian Empire in the city of Riga/Tallinn on January 12, 1893. His middle-class family was of German-Latvian-Huguenot (Protestant) lineage. Having attended a German-Russian high school, he went on to study at the University of Riga, then in Moscow at the university in 1917. In 1918 he moved to Berlin and from there to Munich in 1919, where he met members of the Thule Society, which preached Aryan supremacy and believed in militant action. One of those members was Dietrich Eckart (1868–1923), whom Adolf Hitler accepted as a mentor; Eckart introduced Rosenberg to Hitler. Rosenberg joined the German Workers' Party (DAP), which later became the National Socialist German Workers' Party (NSDAP). At first Rosenberg contributed to the party newspaper, the *Völkischer Beobachter*, then became its editor, and finally the publisher between 1938 and 1945. After the Nazis came to power in 1933, Rosenberg was given the title Chief of the Foreign Political Office. He also held other ideologically oriented positions, the most important one being the Fuhrer's Deputy for the Supervision of the Entire Spiritual and Ideological Training of the Nazi Party. During the war he also became a general in the SS.

Rosenberg's initial platform for spreading his worldview (weltanschauung) was in the *Völkische Beobachter*. His ideas were pieced together from pseudo-scientific readings in works by Houston Stuart CHAMBERLAIN (1855–1927), Julius Langbehn (1851–1907), Paul de LAGARDE (1827–91), and Arthur Comte de Gobineau (1816–1882), ideas that were mixed with a German-Baltic brand of folkish (*völkish*) ANTI-SEMITISM, anti-Slavism, and radical anticommunism. In 1930 he published *The Myth of the Twentieth Century*, in which he attempted to provide a philosophy of history, and a "scientific" basis for the Nazi blood myth, which centered on a struggle between the Nordic spirit and the corrupting influences of inferior races. Among the many assertions of the book are that the highest value of the Nordic race is honor, which is a special attribute of the German people, and that the spirit of the Nordic race was personified by the god Wotan. Rosenberg warned that when Nordic blood was mixed with that of inferior races civilization was corrupted and declined. The ideas in the book were halfbaked and perhaps paranoid. His thinking completely ignored international cultural crosscurrents or they were repudiated. Physical heredity and geographical (environmental) factors called "blood and soil" (*Blut und Boden*) were sufficient explanations for determining the qualities of humans. In his analysis of German culture only the primitive Germanic elements were considered. All Germans were described as pure Nordics, blond and blue-eyed. Jewish citizens in Germany were branded parasites and were considered dangerous genetic influences whom the Nazis later herded into ghettoes or CONCENTRATION CAMPS. Rosenberg may have influenced Hitler's thinking, and we know Hitler reviewed the *Myth* in manuscript, but he claimed he never read the book. Yet, Rosenberg's book quickly became a best seller, second only to Hitler's MEIN KAMPF.

The *Myth* also had anti-Christian ideas that were strongly criticized by the Roman Catholic Church. Rosenberg denounced Christianity as a product of the Semitic-Latin spirit and a disintegrative Jewish concept. He urged the abandonment of the Old Testament of the Bible, replacing it with Nordic sagas. In place of the suffering crucified messiah he preferred the dream of honor and freedom in the Norse sagas. Instead of the false picture of Christ created by the Jewish and mongrel early fanatical theologians, he asserted that the real Christ was Nordic, courageous, aggressive, and a revolutionary. Rosenberg had the greatest contempt for the Roman Catholic Church, which he claimed enslaved civilization with its doctrines such as love, pity, and peace directly contradicting Nordic values. The pope was caricatured as a medicine man, and Rosenberg demanded that the "white race" be freed from this Asiatic Catholic influence. No wonder that the church engaged in a major battle over the *Myths*, and Catholics were forbidden to read it. In 1941 Rosenberg was appointed Reich minister for the Occupied Eastern Territories. His zealous application of his racial beliefs rapidly alienated the numerous Russians who had at first welcomed the German invaders. At the NUREMBERG TRIALS (IMT) Rosenberg was charged with originating race hatred, organizing the plunder of the occupied areas, helping to formulate the policies of forced Germanization, exploiting forced labor, and exterminating the Jews and members of other groups. He was executed on October 16, 1946.

RSHA: Reich Security Main Office

The Reich Security Main Office (Reichsicherheitshauptamt) was the main security office of the Nazi government. It was established in 1939 by Heinrich HIMMLER and combined the various security services. It was in Branch IV that the administration of the Final Solution took place.

In 1939 Heinrich Himmler reorganized the security forces of the Third Reich, combining them in the Reich Security Main Office (RSHA). The police forces that were consolidated were the SS, which included the SD, the intelligence branch of the SS under the leadership of Reinhard Heydrich, which was responsible for the security of Adolf Hitler, the Nazi Party, and actually for the whole Reich. The SD included SIPO, the Security Police, which included the Gestapo, the secret political police, and KRIPO, the criminal police. Reinhard Heydrich was in charge until he was killed by Czech partisans on June 4, 1942. As his successor Hitler appointed Ernst Kaltenbrunner, an enthusiastic Jew hater who hunted down Jews for the gas chambers. In the Nazi police state the RSHA was responsible for arresting all of its enemies and placing them in the concentration system under Oswald Pohl, its administrator. The RSHA was in effect the central office of the leadership of the SS, but also of the Ministry of the Interior. The Gestapo became Office IV of the larger organization. It was in Section B4 of Office IV that Adolf Eichmann was in charge of transporting Jews from all over Europe to their deaths.

Rudolf II (1552–1612)
Holy Roman Emperor

Born in Vienna, Rudolf was the eldest son of Maximilian II and Mary, the daughter of Emperor Charles V. Rudolf's early years were spent in Munich, and from 1563 to 1571 his uncle Philip II of Spain had Rudolf brought to live in Spain to strengthen his Catholicism. Rudolf was crowned king of Hungary in 1572 and king of Bohemia in 1576, also becoming Holy Roman Emperor on October 12 of that year. He was intelligent, aloof, and well educated. Throughout his life Rudolf remained a bachelor. Ill health troubled him in later years while he also became more stubborn and politically apathetic. His incapacity progressing after 1600 and lacking an heir, Rudolf was forced to transfer the government of Austria and Hungary to his brother, Matthias, who also succeeded Rudolf as emperor.

Rudolf II staunchly defended Catholicism and the reforms of the Counter-Reformation. Rudolf restricted or abolished religious freedoms. Protestant schools and churches were gradually closed throughout the Habsburg inheritance. Catholicism was restored in the bishopric of Strasbourg and the Protestant municipal government was thrown out of Aachen. In politics he was not very wise and found it difficult to carry out a sustained policy. His war against the Turks (1591–1606) lacked determination and adequate financing. He also failed to realize his dream of an international balance of power. He was, however, a very successful patron of the arts and sciences. The city of Prague became a great cultural center, where he promoted art, literature, music, and science. Albrecht Dürer and Peter Brueghel were his favorite artists, and he sent agents all over Europe to purchase works for his collection in Castle Hradschin. Artists were among his confidants. But Rudolf did more. He invited to Prague the astronomer Tycho Brahe, who recommended Johann Kepler for the position of court astronomer. Rudolf also supported many astrologers and alchemists.

Ruhr, industrial region of the

The region of the Ruhr has been Germany's largest industrial region, followed by Saxony and Berlin. The area is a little larger than 1,700 square miles north of the Ruhr River, which rises in the hill country of Westphalia and meanders westward for 144 miles, spilling into the Rhine at Duisburg. The Ruhr region is bordered by the Rhine to the east. The Ruhr is where the great industrial empires of the Industrial Revolution were located—the Krupps, Mannesmanns, Stinneses, and Thyssens. In the post–World War II era it was the source of more than 8 percent of the gross domestic product and was the location of the headquarters for 30 of Germany's 100 biggest companies. It also is Europe's most densely populated region with a dozen separate cities of more than 100,000 people. These cities include Bochum, Dortmund, Duisburg, Essen, Gelsenkirchen, and Oberhausen.

Traditional coal mining began in the Ruhr in the 15th century. The region's first ironworks, St. Anthony Hütte, was built in Oberhausen in 1758 and produced puddle steel and pig iron in the early 19th century. For nearly 150 years collieries, blast furnaces, iron foundries, steel mills, and factories covered the landscape. German industry was powered by the rich deposits of anthracite. Industrialists and their associations were influential in national developments, as for instance in the nationalization of the Prussian railways, canals, and higher tariffs, and infrastructure such as reservoirs for necessary water supply. After 1900 the Ruhr also became Europe's most important generator and distributor of electricity. After WORLD WAR I the republican government and the army prevented the radicals from nationalizing German industries. The rationalizing movement improved production, and cartels attempted to limit overcapacity. During World War II plants were destroyed, but mines were only slightly damaged. For a while production was restored and new investment made. Throughout the decades the Ruhr also became Germany's biggest environmental mess with slag heaps, poisoned rivers, and soot-blackened cities.

However, between 1960 and 1985 the prosperity due to coal and steel declined. The coal sector became hit first as Ruhr coal from its deep mines became too expensive in competition with cheap American coal and oil. The Ruhr's prosperity declined as coal pits were reduced from 172 to 39 and miners from more than 600,000 to 120,000. The steel industry's problems began 10 to 15 years later. Some of the causes were the import of less expensive foreign steel and new materials like aluminum and plastics. Since 1970 many plants have closed, and employment declined from 265,000 to about 100,000. The Ruhr became Germany's most depressed area with unemployment at twice the national average. By the 1990s a structural change had occurred with new companies producing environmental-protection technology, power generation, engineering construction, chemicals, plastics, retailing, and property development. In addition, higher education has expanded to five universities and nine polytechnical colleges, which has changed the Ruhr from rust belt to think tank. Today there are more universities and colleges than steel mills and more professors and students than coal miners and steel workers. To this has been added a Time-Warner Co. theme park, museums, business centers, and modern housing.

S

SA
(Nazi Storm Troopers; Sturmabteilung)

The SA was the paramilitary force associated with the Nazi Party (NSDAP). It had been first established as a Gymnastic and Sports division within the Nazi Party in August 1921. Initially, Hitler had organized squads of roughnecks, which were recruited primarily from the Free Corps. It was organized along military lines and was primarily intended to protect party meetings and to break up meetings of their opponents. There were a number of brawls that fall, and in October 1921 Hitler named the units Storm Troopers (Sturmabteilung) but regarded them as primarily a political rather than a military force. The SA was first led by a non-Nazi, Captain Pfeiffer von Salomon. By 1923 it had grown to 15,000 men, and even the University of Munich had a unit. After the Beer-Hall Putsch in November 1923 the organization was forbidden for two years in Bavaria. About 1925–26 the SA were dressed in brown uniforms, hence were known as Brownshirts. After Hitler was released from prison and the Nazi Party developed a new political strategy, the SA took on the extra role of political campaigning and agitation.

In January 1931 Captain Ernst Röhm became the leader and soon added thousands of veterans, enlarging the membership to 100,000; by 1932 its membership had grown to more than 400,000. During the Great Depression the SA also played a social role, providing through SA membership material support and purpose. The SA created considerable turmoil in the streets, confronting the Communist paramilitary, the Red Front, and the Reichsbanner of the Social Democratic Party. Hitler's goal was to have the SA harnessed to his political goals of gaining political power, while Ernst Röhm saw the SA as the nucleus of a revolutionary army to take over the republic. Because of the continued street violence, Chancellor Heinrich Brüning suspended the SA during the presidential elections in spring 1932, but the ban was lifted by Chancellor von Papen in July 1932.

After Hitler became chancellor, the SA and the SS were called upon to be auxiliary police. They broke into Communist Party headquarters and the offices of other organizations, creating a reign of terror. The SA leaders also demanded that they replace the regular army. This was resisted by Hitler, who ordered the assassination of Röhm and other SA leaders in the 1934 blood purge of the Night of the Long Knives. Afterward, the SA declined. It was reorganized in 1935. The younger members (18–35) were called into active service; those up to age 45 were placed in reserve and over that age in the local militia (*Landsturm*). Hitler said that its role was to provide internal security just as the army provided external defense.

Saarland
(state, Land)

The Saarland is the smallest federal state outside the city-states and is located in southwest Germany. The Saarland is an area rich in coal deposits, covering an area of more than 800 square miles along the basin of the Saar River. During the wars of the French Revolution and Napoleonic era, 1792–1815, it was occupied by the French. At the Congress of Vienna it was given to PRUSSIA as part of its Rhine province. Throughout the 19th century it became increasingly prosperous as the demand for coal increased. After WORLD WAR I under the TREATY OF VERSAILLES it was administered as a separate political unit by the LEAGUE OF NATIONS and the French took control of the coalfields as compensation for the damage German forces had inflicted on French coalfields during the war. A plebiscite was conducted by the league in January 1935 when 90 percent of the population voted for its restoration to Germany. On January 15 the Saar rejoined the Reich. The steelworks had to be repurchased. The area prospered with German rearmament. On the other hand, the Nazis persecuted all those opposed their rule.

At the end of WORLD WAR II the French desired to annex the Saar. The French tried to make the Saar a sovereign state under French administration until January 1957, when after another plebiscite was held it again became German territory. After the SCHUMAN PLAN was adopted, cooperation under the ECSC offered a solution. Although the French still desired to make the Saar an independent state, they finally agreed to return it to Germany on January 1, 1957. It became the 11th state of the FEDERAL REPUBLIC.

The Saarland takes its name from the Saar River, a tributary of the Moselle. The name Saar also appears in the names of the state's largest cities. For instance, the capital city is Saarbrücken, which has a population of about 200,000. Another is Saarlouis, which recalls the age of the French king, who had a fortress built to defend French conquests in the western part of Germany. The industries of the area include coal mining, engineering, chemicals, glass, and ceramics. Wine is also important to the economy. The ironworks like Völklingen, which was founded in 1873, was one of the principal producers during IMPERIAL GERMANY. Because of its inability to compete it was closed in 1986.

Sans-Souci
(Frederick the Great's summer palace)
Sans-Souci was the ROCOCO palace built for FREDERICK THE GREAT near Potsdam between 1745 and 1747. It was the king's favorite residence, built to Frederick's own plans by the royal architect and master builder Georg Wenzeslaus Knobelsdorff, who had been appointed in 1740 the director of royal palaces and gardens. The design was contrary to Knobelsdorff's ideas and the subject of argument. It was a long, single-story building crowning a terraced slope and set in a park of both French and English style.

This delightful summer palace at Frederick's country estate in Rheinsberg was surrounded by gorgeous gardens, which Knobelsdorff helped design. The land sloped down to the river in six glass-covered garden terraces that eventually provided grapes, cherries, figs, and pineapples. Frederick's additions to the palace included a Greek temple, an orangerie, a Chinese pavilion, and great art gallery. James Harris, the British envoy, wrote in 1772 "nothing can equal the splendor and magnificence of the new palace.... It is superior to Versailles [certainly an exaggeration], to the Escorial, to everything I ever saw or heard.... The costliness of the furniture exceeds all belief." As Harris indicated, Sans-Souci was furnished with expensive furniture and statues and was beautifully decorated. A magnificent gallery was completed in 1755 for Frederick's extensive art collection of about 100 paintings, while he soon expected to have some 50 more. He bought many of Watteau's works and some of Lancret, Correggio, Veronese, and Tintoretto, 12 of Rubens, and 11 of Van Dyck.

It was at Sans-Souci between 1745 and 1756 that Frederick entertained his famous guests in a small dining room. Voltaire was one of the prominent guests who spent some time there, while others included Francesco Algarotti, author of *Newton for Ladies,* La Mettrie, the author of *Man, the Machine,* and Jean Baptiste d'Argens, a severe critic of religion. After the SEVEN YEARS' WAR Frederick in 1763 had become increasingly a bitter misanthrope and his enjoyable soirées came to an end.

Throughout Frederick's reign Knobelsdorff directed the conversion and extension of the

CHARLOTTENBERG PALACE, the Opera House, and the Tiergarten in BERLIN.

During his final days Frederick the Great revived his spirits at Sans-Souci. Frederick had wished to be buried at Sans-Souci, but that was not to be. After a suitable royal funeral he was buried next to his father in the garrison church at Potsdam.

Saxony
(state, Sachsen)

Saxony is one of the new federal states reconstructed in 1990 from the Saxony of the early years of the East German state until 1552. The Silesian region to the west of the Oder River was added to the free state of Saxony, which was a kingdom until 1918.

The name of Saxony has historically been applied to a number of areas. The early medieval dukes ruled over a different area called Lower Saxony until the fall of Henry the Lion in 1180. From the 15th century onward Saxony became one of the more important German states. It played an important part in the REFORMATION under FREDERICK THE WISE, LUTHER's supporter. In the early 19th century its culture bloomed with LEIPZIG University enjoying a great reputation and with DRESDEN developing into a BAROQUE and ROCOCO city of great magnificence. The electors of Saxony, however, spent their wealth trying to succeed as kings of Poland against the pressures from AUSTRIA and PRUSSIA. They were continually losing territory by being on the losing side in the SEVEN YEARS' WAR (1756–63), the NAPOLEONIC WARS, and the Austro-Prussian War (1866–67). In between, Napoleon Bonaparte made Saxony a kingdom in 1806, but again some territory was lost at the CONGRESS OF VIENNA (1815). In the GERMAN CONFEDERATION Saxony remained a federal state, and it was a kingdom within the Second German Empire (IMPERIAL GERMANY) from 1871–1918.

During the 19th century Saxony was a leading industrial center, especially for textiles and machine construction, and it consequently became an important center of power for the SOCIAL DEMOCRATIC PARTY, which by 1912 polled more than 50 percent of the vote. It was in Leipzig that Ferdinand LASALLE founded the General German Workers' Association in 1863, and the SPD newspaper, *Vorwärts,* was founded in 1876. During the WEIMAR REPUBLIC the electorate favored the SPD and KPD, and toward the end of the republic the electorate shifted to middle-class parties, while the area of Chemnitz favored the Nazis. During WORLD WAR II beautiful Dresden, the "Florence on the Elbe" with its Semper Opera House, was bombed with incendiary bombs that incinerated large parts of the city.

Since World War II the Silesian area west of the Oder River was added to the Free State of Saxony which lasted until 1952, when it was divided into smaller governing districts. During the history of the GERMAN DEMOCRATIC REPUBLIC Saxony was the most heavily industrialized area and became well known for its automobile industry in Zwickau. Since reunification many of its unprofitable industries in textiles, mining, and steel have had to close. Repairing the environmental damage of the mining and industrial methods of the GDR has imposed a large financial burden on the state.

Schacht, Hjalmar Horace Greeley
(1877–1970)
economist and banker

Hjalmar Horace Greeley Schacht played an important role in the stabilization of the German currency after the runaway inflation of 1923. After he helped Adolf HITLER become chancellor, Hitler reappointed him to the Central Bank, presiding over Germany's economic recovery.

The parents of Hjalmar Schacht had recently returned from the United States, where they had been immigrants, and gave their son newly born on January 22, 1877, the middle name of Horace Greeley in honor of a great American. He went on to earn a doctorate in economics at the University of BERLIN in 1900 and entered the Dresdner Bank, one of the largest banks in Germany. During WORLD WAR I he helped set up a central bank in occupied Belgium. In 1916 he became a director of the National Bank for Germany. After the war was over, he helped found the politically liberal GERMAN DEMOCRATIC PARTY (DDP) in 1919.

Extremely ambitious, egotistical, and highly intelligent, Schacht gained a national reputation as a currency commissioner in 1923 and played a vital role in the stabilization of the currency after the runaway inflation of 1922–23 by the creation of a new "Rentenmark." This gained him the reputation as a financial wizard. His success also brought him an appointment to the presidency of the Central Bank (the Reichsbank), Germany's leading financial institution, which he held until 1930. In the meantime he became a strong nationalist and opposed what he thought was the unfair treatment of Germany by the Allies. In 1929 he participated in the negotiations for a new reparations plan, the YOUNG PLAN. When he returned home, however, he was faced with opposition from fellow nationalists. He then disowned the plan, deciding against the payment of reparations and opposing the growing national debt of the WEIMAR REPUBLIC. He blamed the republican government for the continuation of reparations in a pamphlet, *End of Reparations* (1931).

In 1930 Schacht became impressed with Hitler after reading *MEIN KAMPF* and after the huge Nazi electoral victory that stunned everybody in September 1930. Schacht helped Hitler to get much-needed financial support from leading industrialists. In October 1931 he participated in the organization of the nationalist HARZBURG FRONT, which was a coalition of industrialists, conservatives, and the Nazis. In November 1932 he recommended to President Paul von HINDENBURG that Hitler be appointed chancellor. In March 1933 Schacht was reappointed to the presidency of the Reichsbank. As Reich minister of economics Schacht presided over the vigorous rearmament program between 1934 and 1937. The mounting costs of rearmament threatened his conception of a balanced economy, which brought about serious disagreements with Hitler. He was retained as minister without portfolio between 1937 and 1943 and was renamed to the presidency of the Reichsbank. After it became clear that Hitler was bent on war, Schacht became involved with the RESISTANCE. After an attempted coup was unsuccessful in July 20, 1944, Schacht was arrested on suspicion of conspiracy. After the war was over, he was tried before the International Military Tribunal in Nüremberg and found not guilty. His contribution to rearmament was not considered a criminal act. Later he was tried before a German court and sentenced to eight years imprisonment. The decision was reversed on appeal. In retirement he helped several developing nations with their financial problems. He died on June 4, 1970.

Scheidemann, Philipp (1865–1939)
Social Democratic minister

Philipp Scheidemann was the SPD minister who without authorization from a democratically elected assembly declared Germany a republic.

A printer by trade, Scheidemann became a member of the SOCIAL DEMOCRATIC PARTY early in life. He became a newspaper editor, but also was distinctive as a speaker and able recruiter. Becoming a member of the REICHSTAG in 1903, he rose to membership in the SPD's executive committee by 1911. When war broke out, he led the party's Reichstag caucus in voting to support the war with war credits. During the war he decided to support a compromise negotiated peace and was opposed to the Hindenburg peace of the annexationists. The antiwar faction, known as the INDEPENDENT SOCIALISTS (USPD) left the SPD in 1917, while Scheidemann remained and became cochair of the SPD with Friedrich EBERT (1871–1925).

At the end of WORLD WAR I he was appointed secretary of state, one of the first two SPD members of the reformist cabinet of Prince Max of Baden. On the morning of November 9 with the Kaiser abdicating, Scheidemann, Friedrich Ebert, Otto BRAUN, and others presented themselves to Prince Max, and they agreed to form a new government on the basis of the constitution and not on the newly formed Workers' and Soldiers'

Councils. The new Reich chancellor Ebert proclaimed his intention to create a people's government based on peace and order. But what was happening in the streets of BERLIN and throughout Germany was pressing the revolutionary events forward. Kurt EISNER in BAVARIA, the Independent Socialists (USPD), and the Spartacists already had declared socialist republics so the Majority Socialists felt it necessary to quickly declare Germany a democratic republic. As the streets in Berlin swarmed with Berlin workers who formed in front of the Reichstag building, Scheidemann decided to counter the proclamation of a socialist republic by the Communist Karl LIEBKNECHT with his declaration that the "Hohenzollerns have abdicated. Long live the Great German Republic!"

It is difficult to understand why no military units or civilian groups resisted the revolution for the sake of the emperor. The military leadership under the authority of Generals Paul von HINDENBURG and Wilhelm GROENER kept the military and the monarchists under control. The main threat of violence against the new republic came from the left, from the councils, which Scheidemann clearly understood. In February 1919 Scheidemann became the first prime minister of a parliamentary cabinet, but as time progressed his inability as an administrator became evident. Then, when the VERSAILLES TREATY had to be accepted, he refused to sign it and resigned. During the 1920s he became a critic of his party. On December 16, 1926, he made a dramatic speech in the Reichstag, condemning the army, which sent the Nationalists and other conservative parties into an uproar accusing Scheidemann of treason, all of which resulted in a no-confidence vote. When Hitler came to power, Scheidemann fled to Denmark and lost his citizenship. He died in 1939.

Schiller, Friedrich (1759–1805)
dramatist, poet, and historian

Along with Johann GOETHE, Friedrich Schiller was one of Germany's greatest literary figures and founders of modern German literature.

The hero of Friedrich Schiller's drama *The Robbers* was Karl Moor, who came to epitomize the German classical ideal, a man who followed the voice of morality alone rather than the conventions of his birth and position in life. To Goethe, Schiller's friend, the prevailing impression was that the dramatist was in a continuous fight against nature, a heroic attempt to overcome the limitations of his self and of the whole contemporary culture by fighting for the ideal. Schiller fought within himself, and he fought against the outer world. He could not, however, overcome the opposition and the gap between ideal and reality. In his own life as a dramatist he lived a tragedy.

Even Schiller's personal life was a constant fight against hostile circumstances. Unlike the ruling patrician family of Goethe, Schiller's family was still fighting its way up the social ladder. He was born at Marbach, Württemberg, on November 10, 1759. His father started his military career as a Bavarian regimental surgeon and then served Duke Karl Eugen of Württemberg. His mother, Elizabeth, the daughter of an innkeeper in Marbach, was gentle and religious. Schiller's education was in subjects he did not like. Although at first he wanted to be a preacher, he had to study at the duke's military academy, then had to study law, and then medicine. He completed his dissertation even though he endured frequent illness and then was appointed medical officer in December 1780 to a regiment stationed in Stuttgart.

Schiller's play *The Robbers* was published in 1780 and first staged in MANNHEIM in 1782, which earned him public acclaim. The duke was not pleased, however, and when he absented himself from duty to see the second production of his play, the duke had him arrested, forbidding him to write on anything other than medicine. In the play Schiller was fighting against reality, challenging the world of the ENLIGHTENMENT with its princely despotism, and he expressed his personal feelings about it in the storm and stress tradition. The hero of the play ultimately realizes that revolutionary radicalism would not of itself solve the ills of the world.

Schiller looked to Rousseau's writings to confirm his judgments as to the unnaturalness of the age.

Schiller was immensely influenced by the philosophy of Immanuel KANT. Kant in contrast to Spinoza's pantheism did not believe in a godlike simplicity of man, so he formulated strong ethical laws, categorical imperatives that should guide man in the face of all temptation, which Schiller accepted. Schiller however softened Kant's sternness with a gentler sense of beauty, emphasizing that beauty should be pursued for its own sake rather than out of duty. Kant also taught that there is a world of pure thought beyond worldly sense experience, splitting man's world into a physical half and a transcendental half. As Schiller grew older, he realized that Kant's overly stern ethical teachings seemed to be directed not only against tyrants, but also against reckless rebels whose use of violent oratory endangered the cause of freedom. This indicated a moderation in Schiller's rebelliousness during his classical period.

The study of history has the effect of encouraging a person to be restrained in judgment, understand the complexity of past events, and generally to mature the mind. Something like this happened to Schiller. In 1789 he became professor of history at the University of JENA. One of his historical studies was written in 1788 before the appointment, *The Revolt of the Netherlands*. The other study represented the result of his extensive historical research, *The History of the Thirty Years' War,* 1802. Through history Schiller came to see that Divine Providence guided man on his slow march toward greater freedom. He therefore condemned tyrants but also those radicals who tried to accelerate God's work through shortcuts. One of the lessons learned from the French Revolution was that man should never strive merely for outer freedom as long as he does not possess inner freedom. People must first, Schiller thought, reform themselves before their governments.

His studies in aesthetics accompanied his historical research. Art became for Schiller the basis for education, through which people can rise above the crass materialism that drags them down and thus be ennobled. For Schiller reality was merely illusion, while truth was to be found in the higher, spiritual realm. In 1795 he wrote in his philosophical essay *On the Aesthetic Education of Man* that only through art can sensuous man be made rational. His important essay on aesthetics, *On naive and sentimental poetry,* written in 1795–96, forms the basis of modern poetry criticism. In his grandiose philosophical poem, *The Artist,* Schiller venerated art as a means to create a higher culture and teach man how to overcome his desires.

In 1799 Schiller moved to WEIMAR, where he assisted Goethe at the court theater. Schiller's later dramas are his best, starting with his great trilogy on Albrecht von WALLENSTEIN (1798–99), which he finished in Weimar, and ending with the popular *William Tell* (1804). The *Wallenstein* plays stress Schiller's view of man as a creative force portraying him as a great creative statesman who bows before the inevitability of fate. Wallenstein recognizes his guilt and acknowledges the justice of his end. *Maria Stuart* was written in 1800 and followed by *The Maid from Orleans* (1801). Schiller's technical mastery was outstanding in *William Tell* (1804), which presents the struggle of the Swiss against tyranny. In these latter tragedies Schiller is concerned with the profoundest experiences of humanity and maintains his claim of humanity's freedom of the will against the demands of the body and the world. Schiller died in Weimar on May 9, 1805.

Schinkel, Karl Friedrich (1781–1841)
architect and painter

Karl Friedrich Schinkel was the greatest master builder and one of the most influential architects of his time. Utility and harmonious clarity distinguish his structures as high points of the neoclassical style. He became famous with the New (Royal) Guardhouse (Neue Wache) and the Old Museum (Altes Museum).

Karl Friedrich Schinkel was born on March 13, 1781, to a pastor's family in the Prussian garrison town of Neuruppin. The family moved to

BERLIN, where he entered the *Gymnasium zum grauen Kloster* in 1792. In 1796 he had the good fortune to attend an exhibition of Friedrich Gilly's drawings of a projected monument of FREDERICK THE GREAT, which inspired him to become an architect. He began his studies as a student under Gilly's father, David, who was recognized in Berlin architectural circles. Chosen to be a member of the first class in the new Bauakademie gave him the opportunity to work with Henrich Gentz, who designed the Royal Mint, and Carl Gotthard Langhans, who designed the famous Brandenburg Gate. During 1803–04 he traveled to Italy and France in order to study classical sites and in the process painted romantic landscapes and panoramas. When he returned, the threat of war with France had brought public building to a halt, and architectural work was unavailable for the next decade.

After Napoleon's defeat a new era of public construction began in Berlin. In 1813 Schinkel already had designed the Iron Cross, which became Germany's highest military award. As the new Prussian state architect appointed by King WILLIAM III in 1815, he started work on his first commission in 1816, building the New (Royal) Guardhouse, a stone block construction with Doric portico, which established Schinkel as a master of neoclassicism. From then on he was occupied in major building projects. In 1818 he designed a monument to Napoleon's defeat, which is a cast-iron pinnacle. During the 1820s he reshaped the Lustgarten at the eastern end of Unter den Linden in front of the Royal Palace. Other projects were the Schauspielhaus with its ornamental grandeur in the Gendarmenmarkt (1821), which was meant to form a unit with the porticoed and domed French and German churches that flank it; a renovation of Humboldt's villa at Tegel (1824); the Neue Pavilion at Charlottenburg (1825); and the crown prince's palace of Charlottenhof (1827). Schinkel's masterpiece and a principal monument of European neoclassicism was the new museum that came to be called the Altes Museum (1822–30). Located opposite the palace, the museum had a central rotunda for sculpture flanked by courts and surrounded by galleries for paintings.

His later works include the Royal Customs Warehouse (1832) and the School of Architecture (Bauakademie, 1836) built on the Spree River near the Lustgarten. In Potsdam he created Charlottenhof Palace in Sans-Souci Park and the Church of St. Nicholas. Schinkel had been professor of architecture at the academy since 1820 and in 1830 was named the highest architectural official in the Prussian kingdom. On October 9, 1841, he died.

Schirach, Baldur von (1907–1974)
Hitler Youth leader

Baldur von Schirach became head of the HITLER YOUTH in 1931 and Reich Youth Leader in 1933. In 1940 he was appointed Gauleiter of Vienna and Reich defense commissioner, ending his leadership of the Hitler Youth.

Baldur von Schirach was born into a well-to-do aristocratic family. His father was Bailer-Norris von Schirach, who had been an officer in a guard regiment under WILLIAM II, while his mother, Emma Tillou, was an American with a lineage that went back to the American War of Independence. She claimed two signers of the Declaration of Independence among her ancestors. The father's career took an unlikely turn when he resigned in 1908 from the army and became a theater director in WEIMAR and then Vienna. Baldur grew up in an environment filled with the arts of music, theater, and literature, which perhaps encouraged his talent for poetry. He joined the Young German League, which promoted hiking and camping. At the university he had an unfortunate experience with a fraternity, which apparently turned him against Germany's aristocratic ruling class. He also was hostile to Christianity and became an anti-Semite after reading Henry Ford's racist *The International Jew* and *The Foundations of the Nineteenth Century* by the English admirer of Germany, Houston Stuart CHAMBERLAIN.

In 1924 while studying in MUNICH Schirach met National Socialists, and in 1925 joined the NAZI PARTY, becoming a member of the SA. With his poetry he flattered HITLER, who also was impressed by Schirach's contempt for the aristocracy and his rejection of Christianity. It also helped that he married the daughter of Hitler's photographer and associate, Heinrich Hoffmann. In 1929 Schirach was appointed head of the Nazi student movement, the National Socialist German Student's League, at the University of Munich. He proved that he had outstanding organizational talent when he was made Reich Youth Leader of the Nazi Party. On June 1, 1933, at the age of 26 Schirach became the official Youth Leader of the German Reich. Other youth groups were coordinated (Gleichschaltung), except the Catholic until 1936, into the Hitler Youth. In this position he sought to educate young Germans in the beliefs of Adolf Hitler. In 1936 Hitler banned all other youth organizations and required all German youths to belong to it and directed Schirach to project National Socialism through the youths. Schirach himself was praised as an embodiment of what was good in German youths. He succeeded in building up the youth organizations of the Reich, which by 1939 had 8 million members. Schirach became one of the most prominent Nazi leaders, and his enemies vilified him for his effeminate behavior. In July 1941 Hitler appointed him district leader (Gauleiter) of Vienna. When the Nazis deported the Viennese Jews, Schirach defended their deportation. After the war at the NUREMBERG TRIALS he was convicted of crimes against humanity for his participation in the deportation of the Jews to the death camps. Sentenced to 20 years, he was finally released in 1966 and died on August 8, 1974.

Schlegel, August Wilhelm (1767–1845), and Friedrich Schlegel (1772–1829)
theorists of romanticism

The Schlegel brothers were among the leaders of the romantic school. Their periodical *Das Athenaeum* (1798–1800) was not published regularly and lasted only for two years. Nonetheless, it was an important means of spreading their ideas about German ROMANTICISM. The brothers published model reviews, which were new at that time. They avoided measuring poems and artistic works by abstract yardsticks, evaluating them instead in a sympathetic spirit.

A. W. Schlegel was a gifted translator whose verse renderings of the plays of Shakespeare (17 volumes) became household books. He, like Johann Gottfried HERDER, the great philosophical leader of the storm and stress movement, achieved international fame among European romanticists through his excellent literary criticism. In BERLIN between 1801 and 1804 his lectures on literature and art were an attempt to break the hegemony of France. In 1808 Schlegel also presented lectures in Vienna on art and literature, which became his most important critical work. Becoming more of a scholar in his later years, he completed his translation of Shakespeare's plays with the help of TIECK's daughter and Count Baudissin. For a while he traveled throughout Europe with the famous Mme. de Staël. After her death in 1817 he became a professor of oriental languages at the university in BONN, devoting the rest of his life to Sanskrit and Indian studies as a translator and scholar. These laid the foundation for German Sanskrit philology. Unfortunately, his poems, which were his original works, were of little significance. He outlived his brother, dying in 1845.

Friedrich Schlegel, the younger brother, was the keenest critical thinker of the circle of romantics at the University of Jena. At Jena he was especially influenced by the philosophy of Johann Gottlieb FICHTE, whose teachings he later applied to literary theory. Friedrich's earliest publications were essays on classical antiquity (*History of the Poetry of the Greeks and Romans*) in which he theorized that the Greeks had established a perfect harmony between their civilization and their art. In *Das Athenaeum* he developed his literary theories, one of which was that romantic poetry was "progressively universal poetry," including all aspects of life. He tried to realize this theory in his experimental novel, *Lucinde* (1799), which was a glorification of free love and supreme emotionalism. In it he analyzed the details of his psychological relationship with Dorothea Veit, the daughter of the Jewish intellectual Moses MENDELSSOHN. In 1804 Friedrich and Dorothea married. He studied Oriental culture in Paris, then went to Cologne in 1808, where he converted to Roman Catholicism. In 1809 he settled in Catholic Vienna and became more and more closely associated with the political and religious reaction of the Restoration. He lectured on modern history (1810) and developed the idea of an alliance of European princes based on a common Christian foundation. This idea later became the basis of Metternich's Holy Alliance. Schlegel became an adviser to the Austrian delegation at the CONGRESS OF VIENNA. Near the end of his life he edited the conservative journal *Concordia*. He died in DRESDEN on January 12, 1829.

Schleicher, Kurt von (1882–1934)
general

Kurt von Schleicher became one of the most important politically connected generals during the WEIMAR period. Serving on the General Staff in WORLD WAR I, he worked under Generals GROENER and later von Seekt. In the Ministry of Defense he planned Germany's rearmament and helped create the Black Reichswehr, which was an illegal reserve army of 50,000 men.

Schleicher's close relationship with President Paul von HINDENBURG gave him increasing influence in the Weimar government between 1930 and 1933. He played a major role in the development of "presidential cabinets." Early on, Schleicher tried to bring the Nazis into the government, but failed. Then he convinced Hindenburg to replace Heinrich BRÜNING with Franz von PAPEN and later to appoint himself as chancellor. As chancellor Schleicher tried to bring the Nazis into his cabinet, but his efforts failed. Then Hindenburg dismissed him, but Schleicher advised the president to appoint HITLER as vice chancellor. After Hitler rejected this offer, Hindenburg dismissed Schleicher. At this point Papen persuaded Hindenburg to appoint Hitler chancellor, after which Schleicher lost his influence. Schleicher's efforts to bring Hitler into the government had given the NAZI PARTY respectability. Schleicher and his wife were assassinated with others during the RÖHM purge.

Schleiermacher, Friedrich Daniel (1768–1834)
Protestant theologian

Friedrich Daniel Schleiermacher was the greatest German Protestant theologian since the REFORMATION. He was one of the most influential religious writers of the 19th century. The central concept of his philosophy concerned how the needs and demands of the individual person could be reconciled with the state, society, the church, and God himself.

Friedrich Schleiermacher was born in BRESLAU in 1768, the son of an army chaplain. In his schooling he was influenced by the religious movement of PIETISM. He attended seminary and experienced what is commonly called a "crisis of faith." The questions and doubts were evidently resolved, his faith returned, and he was ordained and became a pastor at first in a small parish and then at a hospital in BERLIN. He came to know many of the leading romantic writers, especially Friedrich SCHLEGEL, whose scandalous book *Confidential Letters on Lucinde* he defended. He fell in love with a married woman who would not get a divorce, so he went to another pastorate in rural Pomerania. In 1804 he was teaching at Halle, and in 1810 he became a professor of theology at Berlin. During the Prussian reform era he was a collaborator of Baron Karl vom und zum STEIN and Wilhelm von HUMBOLDT, advocating stiffer resistance to Napoleonic expansionism and social reform.

Schleiermacher could balance the secular and the religious. He loved literature, but he did not identify the arts with religion or make the arts and science a substitute for God. Religion for him was not thinking or acting, "but intuition and feeling." The proper subject of theology, he thought, was the "pious sensibility of the believer." A person could learn about God's universe by getting to know oneself. Religion had its roots in the human personality, and he thought that the infinite could be perceived in the feeling of complete dependence. The proper study of religion therefore was not dogmatics but the religious life as it has been historically experienced. His concepts were neither in accord with the orthodoxy of revealed religion nor with the natural religion of the ENLIGHTENMENT. Rather, his understanding of religion was closely related to the New Humanists, who exalted the human personality, explaining it to be "the finite incarnation of the infinite spirit." He was more concerned with individual consciousness than with the revelation of supernatural truths. At the same time he originated the distinctive form of modern Protestant Christocentrism.

His interpretation of religious experience foreshadowed the development of psychology and the study of comparative religion. This intellectual character of Schleiermacher's thought denied it a popular appeal, but it did appeal to a theological faculty who tried to work out a synthesis between religion and philosophy. As far as church-state relations were concerned, Schleiermacher believed in a free church unregulated by the state, and was the chief opponent of Prussian church policy. Yet, he labored for the union of the Lutheran and Reformed Churches in Prussia.

Schlieffen Plan

The Schlieffen Plan was a strategic plan for a two-front war. It was conceived by Alfred, Graf von Schlieffen (1833–1913), who was chief of the German General Staff from 1891 to 1906. After 1871 General Helmuth von MOLTKE (the older) had adopted a plan to deal with the possibility of Germany having to fight a war both with France and Russia. He favored a quick defeat of Russia while conducting a holding operation against the French. General von Schlieffen reversed this strategy, deciding to attack France first. He concluded that a decisive victory over France could be achieved if the German army mounted a massive encirclement attack through Belgium and Luxembourg, going around the bulk of French forces in Metz and Strasbourg, crossing the Lower Seine River, and attacking the French rear. Schlieffen was confident that the French could be defeated in six weeks, and then the German armies could concentrate on defeating Russia.

Schlieffen's plan was technically brilliant and militarily advantageous. It used Germany's advantages in staff organization and speed of troop deployment to offset the numerical strength of the Russians and to outsmart the French dependence on defensive strategy. It was not, however, very wise and had serious political flaws. Germany's necessary invasion of neutral Belgium would violate international law and would label her as an aggressor. It is unfortunate that leading political figures did not object to this plan, which was a civilian capitulation to military plans.

The declaration of war in August 1914 triggered the immediate implementation of the Schlieffen Plan, which had been modified by the chief of staff, Helmuth von MOLTKE (the younger). As the German armies advanced through Belgium into northern France, they were stopped at the Battle of the Marne. Unexpectedly, the Russians had attacked more quickly than expected, and two army corps had to be transferred from the western front, thus weakening the German forces in France. Within two months Germany's strategy for winning a two-front war had failed. The defeat on the Marne also ended the career of the younger Moltke, who was succeeded as chief of staff by General Erich von Falkenhayn. After the war a controversy raged over Schlieffen's plan, some saying that it would have been successful had changes not been made, while others argued that it was fatally flawed.

Schliemann, Heinrich (1822–1890)
archaeologist

Heinrich Schliemann was the archaeologist who uncovered the ancient city of Troy in Asia Minor in 1868. He created the science of archaeology.

When Heinrich Schliemann discovered the legendary ancient city of Troy in 1868, a dream that had preoccupied him since his youth had finally come true. Schliemann was a linguistically gifted merchant who spoke 15 languages fluently. He began his career in Amsterdam and later amassed an immense fortune in St. Petersburg that enabled him to dedicate himself solely to his archaeological pursuits. After traveling extensively around the globe, he sought and—with the aid of the references in Homer's *Iliad*—ultimately found ancient Troy on the northwestern coast of Asia Minor. The ruins of Troy lie within the territory of present-day Turkey, south of the city of Hissarlik. Excavations in the 20th century have unearthed 46 stages in the city's history.

Several years after the discovery of Troy, he also discovered the Greek city of Mycenae. In that city the world-famous Lion Gate, the ruins of the citadel, and the enormous tombs of Mycenae are among the most impressive vestiges of ancient Greek civilization.

Schmalkaldic League (1531)

The League of Schmalkalden was a defensive alliance of Protestant estates to protect themselves against the threat of military force by the emperor CHARLES V and the Catholic estates.

The DIET OF AUGSBURG in 1531, where Philip MELANCHTHON had drawn up a list of Lutheran doctrines, the AUGSBURG CONFESSION, which were conciliatory and designed to prepare the way for mutual understanding between Protestants and Catholics, failed. With a strong Catholic refutation and the support of the emperor, Charles gave the Protestants six months to reconsider their position. Martin LUTHER supported those who now considered reconciliation impossible. Once the negative result of the diet had become clear, the Protestant princes decided to act and cast aside their scruples about resisting imperial authority. Luther supported their challenge to imperial authority and admitted that the princes had independent rights, especially in religious affairs. The imperial declaration of the Diet of Augsburg stipulated that Protestant innovations (Lutheran, Zwinglian, Anabaptist) had to be abandoned or that force would be used and the Imperial Cameral Court would prosecute them.

This paved the way for the coalition of Protestant estates, which formed the League of Schmalkalden, located in the town of Schmalkald in Thuringia, site of the palace of Wilhelmsburg, one of the most magnificent of late RENAISSANCE palaces. The charter was signed on February 27, 1531, by seven princes and 10 cities. The north German cities of Magdeburg and BREMEN signed at that time, and soon thereafter Brunswick, Einbeck, GÖTTINGEN, and Goslar joined. The leadership was alternately in the hands of the elector John of Saxony and Duke Philip of Hesse. In the next 15 years it brought together most of the Protestant estates of the Empire in an alliance for the defense of the Evangelical faith and doctrine. The league became the spearhead of all opposition against the imperial regime and was at times supported by the kings of France and England and even by the Catholic dukes of BAVARIA.

Although the Augsburg Confession was the league's doctrinal statement, other views were tolerated as other members such as south German cities partial to Zwinglianism joined, and Catholic Bavaria did also. The defensive nature of the alliance was stated in the charter, which emphasized that an attack on one member was an attack on all and was to be resisted by military force. Assessments were made, and a militia of 10,000 infantry and 2,000 cavalry were organized. In 1535 it was decided to double the force in case of emergency. Other political considerations worked to increase the membership of the league. For instance, Charles needed money and arms to fight the Turks and the French, while the Protestants threatened to withhold funds if the emperor moved against them. Others such as the Bavarians were opposed to making the imperial throne hereditary in the Habsburgs. Then Charles declared a so-called Nuremberg peace or "standstill" and even stopped the procedures at the Imperial Cameral Court and said that no action would be taken against the Protestants until a general church council was held. All of these things provided more time for the Schmalkaldic League to organize. By the mid-1540s much of the Empire had turned Protestant. Württemberg was lost to the emperor in 1534, and it joined the league in 1536. In 1539 there was bad news from SAXONY when it turned Lutheran. By 1545 all of northeastern and northwestern Germany had become Protestant, as well as large parts of southern Germany. Officially, only Bavaria, AUSTRIA, and the bishoprics along the Main River—Bamberg, Würzburg, Mainz, and the imperial abbey of Fulda—remained Catholic. Most of the electors had adopted PROTESTANTISM, and much of northern and southern Germany belonged to the league.

By 1545–46 Charles was finally in a position to use force against the Protestant league. He possessed inferior military forces and alienated many imperial estates, both Catholic and Protestant. Charles made many promises to sway some princes to his side. The largest positive factor was the support of the Protestant duke Maurice of Saxony (1541–53), to whom he promised the electoral title in addition to other concessions. Charles was able to assume control of southern Germany and the RHINELAND. The two major leaders of the Schmalkaldic League were captured by Charles, and his victory appeared complete. He proposed some reforms that were resisted by the estates, their entrenched interests wrecking his goals of reform.

In 1546–47 a number of battles took place between the imperial forces of Charles V and the Schmalkaldic League. Charles ostensibly won the war, but his victory was a hollow one. Nevertheless, the war probably marked the high point of Charles's personal reign.

Schmidt, Helmut (1918–)
chancellor

Helmut Schmidt rose to prominence through his expertise in foreign affairs and economics. In the administration of Chancellor Willy BRANDT, Schmidt became Brandt's crisis manager, the first Social Democratic defense minister since 1920, and later finance minister. Schmidt was the obvious replacement for Brandt in 1974 and remained chancellor until 1982.

Helmut Schmidt was born in HAMBURG in December 1918, the son of two teachers. Receiving a good education, he early on learned English and developed a passion for learning and an impatience with those who were lazy. In WORLD WAR II he served as an artillery officer on the Russian front, but at the end was captured by the English in April 1945. In the prisoner of war camp he became interested in politics and joined the SOCIAL DEMOCRATIC PARTY (SPD). His education continued at the University of Hamburg, where he studied economics. In 1953 he was elected to the BUNDESTAG (Parliament) as a Social Democrat and then soon became an expert on transportation and a good speaker. His knowledge of military defense led to the publication of *Defense or Retaliation* (1961), establishing him as an expert on military strategy. For a while he returned to participate in Hamburg politics and was skillful in coping with the devastating flood that killed 300 people in February 1962.

The year 1965 was a turning point as he got involved in the campaign that enabled the SPD to enter the "Great Coalition" with the CDU. Schmidt quickly obtained the important job of party floor leader. In the elections of 1969 Willy Brandt was elected the first SPD chancellor since 1930, and Schmidt was appointed defense minister in the Social-Liberal coalition, probably based on his new book indicating a policy of DÉTENTE, *Balance of Power* (1969). Schmidt became finance minister in 1972 and helped steer the SPD to victory again in the social-liberal, that is SPD/FDP, coalition. After Brandt's resignation in 1974 over a spy scandal, Schmidt became his logical successor. He continued Brandt's policy of reconciling West Germany with her eastern neighbors, and in his practical manner made Germany's presence in the Western Alliance more strongly felt, which was especially important as the United States was distracted by Vietnam and Nixon's Watergate scandal. Relations with France were consolidated. Schmidt's handling of the oil crisis of the 1970s earned him strong support and prestige abroad, and in 1977 he also dealt with the wave of terrorism afflicting the nation. In foreign policy he tried to steer a two-track policy for NATO, which involved the negotiation of arms control with the Russians while at the same time proposing the installation of medium-range nuclear weapons, principally in Germany. Schmidt became a statesman of international standing.

With the negative turn in international relations due to the Soviet invasion of Afghanistan and the Polish crisis, the political landscape changed. It is true that in the 1980 elections the voters rejected Schmidt's challenger, Franz Josef STRAUSS, yet the coalition of the SPD and FDP weakened. The Free Democrats defected to the CDU and formed a new government under Helmut KOHL. Even though Schmidt's chancellorship came to an end, he remained active in politics until 1987. In 1985 he published the critical *A Grand Strategy for the West*, which was critical of neutralists and at the same time of deficit spending of the American military buildup. He also continued his co-editorship of the liberal newspaper *Die Zeit*. In the later 1990s, after the Kohl government had built up mountains of debt, Schmidt levelled criticism at their mismanagement.

Scholl, Hans (1918–1943), and Sophie Scholl (1921–1943)
resistance leaders

Hans and Sophie Scholl were martyrs in an "idealistic" student-resistance group called the White Rose. They came to symbolize the resistance of the young to HITLER's dictatorship. They were arrested while distributing protest leaflets at the University of MUNICH. They were arrested, sentenced to death, and executed.

Hans and Sophie Scholl were born in Forchtenberg, Württemberg, in a liberal Protestant household to a father who had been a mayor of two towns and who moved with his family to Ulm to work as a business consultant. In opposition to their father's wishes, Hans and Sophie joined the HITLER YOUTH, optimistically believing in its program and promises. Hans had the advantage of appearing as the ideal Nordic type that the Nazis propagated. He had become a squad leader in the Hitler Youth, but became disillusioned by the militaristic narrow-mindedness that was required. After a fight with a ranking leader he left the organization and became opposed to the regime. Hans and Sophie joined one of the outlawed youth organizations even while he was in the army, for which he was imprisoned for some weeks. This was 1938, and the charges against Hans and Sophie were dropped due to an amnesty in connection with the union (ANSCHLUSS) with Austria. Hans was further alienated during his participation in the invasion of France, which strengthened his opposition to the Nazis.

Sophie was not so serious a person as Hans and appeared to others as happy and frivolous, although she took politics seriously. She was resigned to doing her duty, completing the labor service required of all youths and then another six months in war auxiliary service. Meanwhile, she had passed her examination as a kindergarten teacher and in May 1942 registered at the University of Munich for studies in biology, the place where Hans had been studying medicine since the autumn of 1940 as a member of an army student company.

The group of friends that made up the White Rose evolved very slowly. Besides the Scholls, it included Willi Graf and Alexander Schmorell. The main criterion of membership was not political opposition to the Nazis but the moral rejection of National Socialism and the affirmation of the religious, intellectual, and cultural values that it rejected. The students had a common interest in art and literature, singing in the Bach choir and attending cultural events. It was Hans Scholl in particular who succeeded in establishing contacts with Carl Muth, the former publisher of *Hochland*, an outlawed Catholic magazine. Through Muth contact with the Catholic writer Thedore Haecher was also established. The students met Professor Kurt Huber, whose lectures they began to attend, lectures where questions and thinkers were discussed that had been taboo. Initially, the interest was intellectual and not conspiratorial, but soon military and political issues opened up. They all agreed on the moral depravity of National Socialism. In fact Carl Muth and Thedore

Haecher felt that Hitler demonstrated demonic powers, which Christians had the obligation to resist, and by spring 1942 Hans Scholl had come to the conclusion that action had to be taken. So began the series of White Rose leaflets, the first four drafted in July 1942. The leaflets were mimeographed and sent to friends and addresses selected from the Munich phone book. The leaflets contained accusations against the Hitler regime, quotes from the classics, and passages from the Bible. Hitler was identified as the messenger of the anti-Christ. The students had made no concrete plans of resistance before the vacation of the winter semester of 1942–43. After the break the meetings were continued, and new contacts were made, including Falk, Harnack, Kucharski, and through Willi Graf, friends from the Catholic Youth Organization. In January 1943 a leaflet entitled "Appeal to all Germans!" was drafted, which rejected imperialism and militarism, called for cooperation among European nations, and demanded the restoration of guarantees for the rule of law. These were distributed not only in Munich but also in AUGSBURG, Salzburg, Linz, Vienna, BERLIN, Stuttgart, Saarbrücken, and Freiburg. On February 3 the arrival of the news that the German army had been defeated at the BATTLE OF STALINGRAD had a rattling effect, creating a feeling that a great turning point had been reached in the war. However, the members now mistakenly thought that the end of the war was near, and they were overly optimistic that a revolt might occur. Scholl, Schmorell, and Graf went about writing the words *Freedom* and *Down with Hitler* in white paint in the streets around the university and on the walls of the university three times in three weeks. The events led to the writing of a new leaflet, which declared that a "day of reckoning had come" and an appealed for a break with National Socialism. About 3,000 copies were printed, some mailed, while Hans and Sophie Scholl decided to distribute leaflets at the university, which is still a mystery. The Scholls were reported to the GESTAPO by a building superintendent. Both were arrested along with four others and brought before the PEOPLE'S COURT. No attempt was made to get away, and no attempt to cover things up. The Scholls were quickly tried and sentenced to death. On February 22, 1943, Sophie and Hans were both executed, as was Professor Huber on July 13.

Scholtz-Klink, Gertrud (1902–1999)
leader of Nazi Women's League

Gertrud Scholtz-Klink believed deeply in the Nazi worldview, especially women's roles as mothers, and was given the title of Nazi Germany's national Women's Leader (Reichsfrauenführerin). In 1934 she was appointed head of the German Women's Labor Service (Deutsche Frauenarbeitsdienst), established when all other women's organizations were disbanded. She held both the title and the position from 1934 to 1945.

She was born in Adelsheim on February 9, 1902. In appearance she was blond, blue-eyed, regular-featured, and slender. Earlier she had worked for the Red Cross, was active in labor organizations, and had been a district leader of women in Baden. She had been married three times and had four children by the time HITLER became chancellor. Her first husband was an SA member (brown-shirted Storm Trooper) who had died in 1930. Also a member of the NAZI PARTY, she deeply believed in its ideology. In 1933 she was appointed head of all women's organizations in the state of Baden, and in 1934 the chief of the Nazi Labor Service, Konstantin Hierl, appointed her head of the German Women's Labor Service.

In appearance she was the ideal Aryan to lead the women's organizations, and in demeanor she was obedient to Nazi male authority. She was to be seen but not heard; Hitler never consulted with her for advice on women's issues. The organizations that Scholtz-Klink headed were separate from the regular party organizations, and the women enjoyed considerable autonomy in their separate spheres.

The major policies affecting women did not come from Scholtz-Klink's office but from Nazi racial planners and eugenics experts who created social policy out of Hitler's prejudices and misinformation about both women and Jews. Nazi leaders also ordered the women's organizations to indoctrinate a new generation of girls, but the organizations did not receive either the budgets or the authority to accomplish their charge. By 1936 textbooks had not yet been Nazified and women were routinely insulted by male superiors. Changes in goals also were confusing. Beginning in 1933 women were encouraged to be good stay-at-home housewives, but soon, due to rearmament, were publicly urged to return to work. Other changes and challenges concerned the morality of eugenics programs, which were trying to improve the birthrate; also Hitler began attacking their favorite religious organizations. Conflicts of conscience arose because many women had thought that Nazi policies were not in conflict with Christian values. Now Hitler told them they had to choose between church and state.

By one estimate as many as 8 million women belonged to the organizations that she headed, even though most German women resisted joining those organizations. At the end of the war Scholtz-Klink was captured by the Russians, then escaped and lived in the French occupation zone for three years. She was captured again, tried as a war criminal, and received a short sentence. The FEDERAL REPUBLIC banned her from holding public office. In the 1970s she published a memoir and demonstrated that she was unrepentant and was still proud of her contributions.

Schroeder, Gerhard (1944–)
seventh chancellor of the Federal Republic

Gerhard Schroeder was born in Mossenberg in Detmold. His father was killed in WORLD WAR II, and his mother struggled to support five children as a cleaning lady. At an early age Gerhard Schroeder had to go to work to help support his poor family. Not able to attend the *Gymnasium,* he attended night school and earned his *Abitur,* a general certificate that qualified him for the university. He worked his way through law school between 1966 and 1971 as a construction worker, earning his law degree in 1976. In 1963 he had already joined the SOCIAL DEMOCRATIC PARTY (SPD), becoming chairman of the Young Socialists in Göttingen. In 1977 he became a member of the executive committee of Hanover and in 1978 national chairman of the youth wing, the Young Socialists, "Jusos." He was first elected to the BUNDESTAG in 1980, and from 1983 to 1993 he was chairman of the Social Democratic Executive Committee for Hanover. In 1986 he also was elected to lead the SPD opposition in the state assembly of Lower Saxony. Four years later Schroeder became minister-president of the state of Lower Saxony, forming a coalition with the GREEN PARTY. He held the post of president until October 1998. The people of Lower Saxony believed in his pragmatism and his desire for consensus politics. Voters returned him to office twice with an absolute majority because he was a man of action accomplishing such things as safeguarding jobs, slashing red tape in the ministries, and fighting crime. Early in his association with the Social Democrats he belonged to the far-left wing of the party, but as he grew older his political orientation shifted to the center. While he was a member of the supervisory board of Volkswagen AG, he became more sympathetic to business. This orientation placed him at odds with Oskar Lafontaine, who headed the party's left wing, favoring Keynesian policies.

In October 1998 he was elected seventh chancellor of the FEDERAL REPUBLIC of Germany with the votes of the SPD and Alliance 90/The Greens in October 1998. He was also elected national chairman of the SPD on April 12, 1999, a post he eventually resigned in February 2004. When Schroeder first became chancellor, the image he sought to portray was that of his Social Democratic predecessor, Helmut SCHMIDT, an image of a man of action and managerial type who could modernize the German bureaucracy. A media-savvy and consummate politician, he projected himself as a symbol of change. He promised to create a "New Middle" in German politics. There was, however, a cultural and political divide that separated Schroeder and Schmidt, the latter having been an officer during WORLD WAR II, and Schroeder having been born during the war. Nevertheless parallels were also there because Schmidt's policies favoring NATO's nuclear modernization were opposed by the SPD just as Schroeder's economic reform policies embodied in Agenda 2010 ran contrary to the opinion of most Social Democrats.

Schroeder won reelection in the 2002 general elections conducted on September 22 where he secured another four-year term, despite a reduction in the SPD majority from 21 to 9 seats. His successful reelection has been attributed largely to his firm opposition to the pending U.S.-led intervention in Iraq, which reflected the strong opposition to war among the German public. On the other hand his policies to reduce the welfare state were not well received by German voters who did not want a reduction in benefits. After the election of 2002 the SPD steadily lost support in opinion polls. Then in 2003 Schroeder announced Agenda 2010, which was his last attempt to make the tough reforms needed in Germany's social welfare system, to revitalize a stagnant economy, and to reduce high unemployment. Germany's high unemployment rate remained a lingering problem for the government through 2005.

While straining ties to Washington over the Bush administration's policies toward Iraq, Schroeder forged closer relations with Russia's Vladimir Putin and French president Jacques Chirac. While Schroeder bashed America, he paraded his friendship with the authoritarian Putin, describing him as a "flawless democrat," which obviously was not the case. This cultivation of closer ties to Moscow also had the purpose of facilitating a new natural gas pipeline built under the Baltic Sea to bypass Poland and supply Russian gas directly to Germany. That is not to say that Schroeder did not declare solidarity with the United States in the war on terrorism after the September 11 terrorist attacks. Under Schroeder German troops for the first time since WORLD WAR II were sent to Kosovo and to Afghanistan as part of NATO operations.

It was because of his plans to prematurely call new elections in 2005 that Schroeder's chancellorship came to an unexpected end. As a result of losing a regional election to the CDU in the SPD stronghold of NORTH RHINE–WESTPHALIA, Schroeder announced on May 22, 2005, a call for early federal elections. To force the holding of elections Schroeder even urged SPD members of the Bundestag (148) to abstain from a vote of confidence in his government. The election was held on September 18, 2005 and neither Schroeder and the SPD nor Dr. Angela MERKEL and the CDU obtained an absolute majority. With both claiming victory and because the election results were so close, a coalition government was negotiated which, however, did not include Schroeder. He announced that he would leave politics entirely as soon as Merkel became chancellor.

After leaving office as chancellor and resigning his Bundestag seat on November 23, 2005, Schroeder intended to resume his law practice and write a book. He accepted a position as a consultant with the Swiss publisher, Ringier AG, and also a position as head of a supervisory committee of the Russian-led consortium controlled by Gazprom which is building the Euro Baltic Sea gas pipeline. He and his fourth wife, the journalist Doris Koepf, whom he married in 1997, will continue to reside in Berlin and Hanover.

Schubert, Franz (1797–1828)
composer

Franz Schubert was born on January 31, 1797, in Vienna, the musical capital of the world. As a child he became skilled at the violin, viola, and keyboard and participated in a string quartet. Besides gaining experience in the Imperial Choir, he received an outstanding musical education. In the orchestra of the prestigious school in Vienna, he was honored with the position of the lead violinist, competent to play Mozart's G minor Symphony and BEETHOVEN's Second. By the age of 20 he completed his own Fourth and Fifth Symphonies. Schubert is considered the creator of the lieder form of music. He wrote more than 600 songs based on more than 90 poets, including GOETHE, KLOPSTOCK, and SCHILLER. Two famous song cycles composed by Schubert are *Die Schöne Müllerin* and *Die Winterreise*. Grasping the meaning of a poem, he had a remarkable instinct to apply the most suitable musical form to it, giving expression to the moods and thoughts in the text. He also composed impressive symphonies, the most famous perhaps are his *Unfinished* B Minor and the C Major (No. 9), and the music for several Catholic Masses, including the *Deutsche Messe*. Other forms he mastered were chamber music, sonatas, and operatic scores. He completed an enormous body of music due both to ability and incessant composition.

Unfortunately, he was not able to acquire a permanent musical position, and lived in poor circumstances with a circle of devoted bohemian friends. As his fame spread, he was invited to the homes of upper-class families and was admired by the dramatist Grillparzer and the opera singer Vogl. Social meetings known as "Schubertiads" were forums for literary readings and Schubert's compositions. His congenial personality, wit, and musical gifts gained him a devoted following. Schubert's style was essentially classical, but his inspiration looked to the future in his response to the great literary figures of his time, who composed such a great body of lyric poetry. Schubert gave expression to the ordinary human emotions of love, happiness, sorrow, and the beauty of nature.

Schumann, Robert Alexander (1810–1856), and Clara Schumann (1819–1896)
composer

Son of a bookseller in Zwickau, Germany, Robert Alexander Schumann developed an interest in literature at an early age. Yet, his musical interests also developed when he composed music as a boy. Although he went to LEIPZIG to study law, he soon began to study piano with the famous Friedrich Wieck and soon was inspired to follow a musical career. Unable to become a concert pianist due to an injury in his right hand, he concentrated on musical composition and criticism. By age 22 Schumann had published two major piano pieces, and two years later he founded the *New Leipzig Journal for Music*, through which he promoted new musical talent. Robert fell in love with Clara, the daughter of Wieck; she was a prodigy, debuting at the age of nine in the famous Gewandhaus in Leipzig. They married in 1840. Clara stimulated her husband's creative imagination and rightly deserves the reputation as one of the finest piano virtuosos of the age. She pursued her musical career despite her added family responsibilities, overcoming traditional prejudices against women in the arts. Her interpretations of classical and romantic piano literature set the standard for decades. Clara and Robert combined family life with separate careers.

A highly sensitive reader of poetry, Schumann set to music poems by GOETHE, SCHILLER, EICHENDORFF, HEINE, Chimisso, Kerner, Rückert, Mörike, and Lenau. His piano music, Opus 1 to Opus 23, written between 1830 and 1840, constitutes a landmark in musical history, paralleled by the early compositions of Chopin. This new music of the romantic world was graceful, lyrical, and songlike. His major works for the piano include *Carnaval* (1835), *Kinderszenen, Fantasie in C* and *Kreisleriana* (all in 1838). From 1840 onward Schumann entered his most creative period, composing his beautiful song cycles, one of which was a wedding present to Clara. In addition to chamber music, including a piano quartet and quintet, Clara encouraged his large-scale works, including the popular A Minor Concerto, his magnificent violin and cello concertos, four symphonies, and the *Manfred Overture*, inspired by Lord Byron. The recurring use of motto themes was one of his innovations. His large-scale vocal works include the secular oratorio, one opera, and choral music, including the cantata *Scenes from Goethe's Faust* (1853).

Schumann's creative energy, which enabled him to compose sometimes more than 20 hours a day was juxtaposed by periods of depression. It is thought that this quality was due to a bipolar disorder. Falling into depression in 1846, he could not compose at all. The psychiatric care of the time was of no avail, as his mental powers declined after 1853, forcing him to resign his position as municipal director of music in DRESDEN. He attempted suicide in 1854 and entered an institution for nervous diseases, where he died in 1856.

Schuman Plan (1950)

The Schuman Plan of 1950 proposed to combine French and German coal and steel production, which resulted in the EUROPEAN COAL AND STEEL COMMUNITY (ECSC) in 1952. It was proposed by Robert Schuman, the French foreign minister.

Robert Schuman (1886–1963), gained his fame as foreign minister when he was the foremost advocate of Jean Monnet's plan for combining French and German iron and steel industries in a common market. The coal and steel companies lay on either side of the Franco-German border in the SAARLAND, ALSACE-LORRAINE, the RHINELAND, and the RUHR valley. These areas had been fought over for a century by the French and the Germans. Attempts by the French and Belgians after WORLD WAR I had failed to control the area. Mighty trusts also dominated the area and prevented competition, which the Americans after WORLD WAR II were anxious to change, favoring decentralization in order to provide an equal start for the French and Germans in future competition.

Schuman's plan to place the French and German industries under a "higher authority" was opposed by the industrialists, who understandably preferred self-regulation. That sounded too much like the situation that prevailed in the 1920s and would not achieve the goals of integration. The plan was extended to include the industries of Belgium, Holland, Luxembourg, and Italy. Over the objections of the self-regulators, the Americans placed pressure on the governments, which successfully led to the establishment of the European Coal and Steel Community in 1952.

Jean Monnet became president of the High Authority and continued to face opposition of the industries involved. It was a first step, which led to the establishment of the future European Common Market.

SD
(Security Service: Sicherheitsdienst)

Under the leadership of Reinhard HEYDRICH, the SD was responsible for the security of HITLER and other Nazi leaders, the NAZI PARTY, and the Third Reich. Actually, it was the security service of the leader of the SS, Heinrich HIMMLER. In 1934, as there was a huge influx of new SS members, Himmler decided to organize this elite organization. In 1939 the SD along with the Criminal Police and the GESTAPO were all placed under Reinhard Heydrich as chief of the Reich Security Main Office (Reichssicherheithauptsamt). After Heydrich's assassination in Czechoslovakia, the organization was placed under the leadership of Ernst Kaltenbrunner.

Those who worked for the SD were largely professionals divided into five categories, ranging from confidants to agents, informants, and unreliables. The intelligence network had great power and was supposed to discover enemies of the state. This led them to report even on the private lives of ordinary citizens who were powerless against the SD. The SD had the power to arrest, to hold a person on preventative detention, and could send anyone to a CONCENTRATION CAMP. During the war it reported on the morale of citizens, was active against the partisans in occupied countries, and helped clear the ghettoes of Jews, sending them to concentration camps. Its victims included political and civil criminals, Communists, pacifists, Seventh Day Adventists, Jews, beggars, antisocials, homosexuals, prostitutes, and drunkards.

Seven Years' War (1756–1763)

In May 1756 a defensive alliance was concluded between France and AUSTRIA, an alliance known as the DIPLOMATIC REVOLUTION. One month later, war broke out between France and Britain in Europe. FREDERICK II of PRUSSIA was well informed concerning the alliances between the great powers and since neither France nor Russia presently could attack him, he decided to take his enemies by surprise. This preemptive invasion of SAXONY in August 1756 by Frederick started what came to be known as the Seven Years' War; Saxony was plotting with Austria and France the destruction of Prussia. What Frederick feared now took place. In spring 1757 a destructive alliance took place between France and Austria, who were joined by Russia, Sweden and smaller German states. HANOVER, Hesse, Brunswick, and Gotha continued their alliance with Prussia. Success in battle went back and forth as Frederick invaded Bohemia and then had to evacuate it. A noteworthy battle of the war was the Battle of Rossbach (November 5, 1757), which was a spectacular victory for Frederick. The French had hoped to liberate Saxony, but Frederick surprised and defeated them. Frederick's greatest victory over the Austrians occurred in Leuthen, a Silesian village 10 miles west of BRESLAU. After having force-marched his bluecoats to Leuthen, where Prince Charles had drawn up 65,000 of his men, the Prussians outmaneuvered the Austrians; they charged with their cavalry the white-coated Austrians, who broke and fled. The Prussian grenadiers then routed the soldiers from Württemberg and BAVARIA and rolled up the Austrian flank at Sagschütz. In the end the Austrians suffered twice as many casualties as the Prussians and lost a total of some 30,000 prisoners when Breslau fell. Certainly, Prussian military leadership proved to be superior. On the other hand, Charles of Lorraine, the brother of the emperor Francis I was relieved of his command after having been defeated by Frederick. Another great Prussian victory of the year was the Battle of Crefeld on June 23, in which Frederick defeated an invading Russian army.

In addition to Frederick's stubborn leadership, two factors saved Prussia from defeat. Britain provided considerable financial aid to the Prussians. Also, in 1762 the empress Elizabeth of Russia died. Her successor was Czar Peter III, who greatly admired Frederick and made peace, which allowed the Prussian king to hold off Austria and France. The war ended with the TREATY OF HUBERTUSBURG in 1763 with no significant changes in prewar borders. MARIA THERESA was extremely unhappy in not regaining control of Silesia. Because of Frederick's successes Prussia clearly stood among the ranks of the great powers, and the king came to be known as Frederick the Great.

Siemens, Werner von (1816–1892)
a founder of the German electrical industry

Werner von Siemens was one of Germany's best examples of the inventor who was also successful in business. Siemens, along with Emil Rathenau (1838–1915), who established the German Edison Company, was responsible for the creation of the German electrical industry and the rapid electrification of Germany. The Siemens and Halske Co. was the leading company in the field of heavy current and built Germany's extensive electrical trolley system.

Born in Lenthe near HANOVER on December 13, 1816, Werner was the eldest son of Christian and Eleonore. Receiving a general education near home, he later attended a neohumanistic *Gymnasium* in Lübeck. Dissatisfied with the lack of instruction in the natural sciences, he later attended the artillery and engineering school of the Prussian army in BERLIN. Between 1835 and 1849 he was an army officer where he was able to apply his engineering expertise. He obtained a General Staff position and was assigned to introducing the electric telegraph into the army and the construction of a military electric telegraph system.

In 1847 he founded an electrical telegraph factory in Berlin in association with the mechanic Johann Halske, whose main customer was the army, for which they installed and maintained electrical telegraphs. Siemens and Halske expanded their business into electrical telegraphs for railroads, and after 1852 entered the Russian market, building much of the telegraphic system there in the 1850s and 1860s.

Besides developing the first electric telegraph, Werner Siemens laid the first telegraph line in PRUSSIA between Berlin and FRANKFURT AM MAIN. In 1866 Siemens discovered and developed the dynamoelectric principle and invented the dynamo for generating high-voltage electricity for lighting. In 1879 he built the first electric locomotive and quickly developed the electric streetcar and built streetcar systems in Germany's larger cities. Siemens was also awarded the contract for laying a cable across the Atlantic from Europe to America via Ireland. It should not be forgotten that Werner Siemens had two brothers with whom he cooperated, Wilhelm and Carl. Wilhelm, for example, invented the Siemens-Martin furnace for melting steel.

Besides being an inventor and astute businessman, Werner Siemens had social concerns. As the Social Democratic movement expanded, the firm of Siemens and Halske responded with employee benefit packages that included profit-sharing, health insurance, and pension plans. Along with business activities Siemens also participated in the political arena. He was a political liberal and helped form the GERMAN PROGRESSIVE PARTY and from 1862 to 1866 he was a representative in the Prussian legislature. He supported the efforts of Otto von BISMARCK to unify Germany. Siemens recognized the importance of science in the modern world and that it was changing the social conditions of life. He was the first technologist named to the Prussian Academy of Science, and he worked to establish the Imperial Institute of Physics and Technology (1887).

Werner Siemens was ennobled in 1888 and died on December 6, 1892.

Social Democratic Party of Germany (SPD)

With the surge of economic activity in the 1850s there was increased organizational activity by workers. Some were cultural associations, and others were workers' cooperatives. At first they were taken under the wings of liberal groups, but political activity by the workers was prohibited. The National Association even refused to accept workers in its membership. It was in LEIPZIG, however, that the first steps were taken to organize workers into a Workers' Educational Association. After being turned down for membership by the liberal parties in BERLIN, leaders from Leipzig turned to Ferdinand LASALLE, who initiated the founding of the Social Democratic Party of Germany. It grew very slowly, and after 1869 its development was further impeded by the opposition of a new Social Democratic Labor party founded by two followers of Karl MARX, August BEBEL, and Wilhelm LIEBKNECHT. Not until 1875 at the Gotha congress did these two parties join forces to form the Socialist Workers' Party of Germany (SAPD). Later on, the party called itself the Social Democratic Party (SPD). In its GOTHA PROGRAM the new party combined the two socialist traditions: It was Marxist in its criticism of capitalist society and its proclamation of the international character of the socialist movement; it was Lasallean, on the other hand, in its emphasis upon political action to secure practical objectives. Those goals included universal male suffrage, the payment of parliamentary representatives, the abolition of inequalities of social class and property, the abolition of the standing army, the separation of church and state, free compulsory education, a progressive income tax, and state credit for producers' cooperatives. The party rejected the principle of revolutionary upheaval favored by Karl Marx and instead emphasized reform through political action.

Between the REICHSTAG elections of 1871 and 1877 the party grew rapidly and increased its Reichstag vote from 124,000 in 1871 to 452,000 in 1877. The chancellor, Otto von BISMARCK, considered the Socialists enemies of the state, was alarmed at their growing strength, and through the antisocialist laws of 1878 suppressed the party. Bismarck's persecution destroyed the party's institutions and gave the government extensive police powers. Suspected Socialists lost the customary protections of the law. Leaders were forced to leave the country, yet those few in the Reichstag did enjoy immunity but could not publicly speak or campaign. The party organization continued in exile and held congresses outside of Germany. In the Reichstag election workers were still able to vote for Socialist Party deputies, and after an initial decline an upward trend in elected deputies again occurred. After the dismissal of Bismarck by the new emperor, Wilhelm II, the Socialists were allowed to reconstitute themselves. In 1891 they held their first party congress in Erfurt and under the inspiration of its new theoretical leader, Karl KAUTSKY, adopted the ERFURT PROGRAM. It was Marxist in its social and political philosophy and was based on the theory of class struggle. An imposing party structure now developed, which made the German party the model Socialist Party of the entire Socialist International. By 1914 the party had more than 1 million members, and by 1912 the socialist vote in those Reichstag elections returned 110 deputies, which made it the largest party in Germany. The strength of the Socialist Party came primarily from the large industrial centers—BERLIN, Leipzig, HAMBURG, Cologne, and Schleswig-Holstein, SAXONY, Silesia, the RHINELAND, and northern BAVARIA. The bulk of its voting strength came from the industrial workers, with a small sprinkling of freelance intellectuals and professions.

One of the conflicts that arose within the Social Democratic Party was over the application of Marx's theories to the realities of economic and social conditions at the end of the century. Besides the revisionist opposition that emanated from southern Germany associated with Georg von Vollmar, the leader of the Bavarian Social Democrats, it was principally Eduard BERNSTEIN who provided the theories that radically interpreted Marx's ideas on class struggle and dialectical materialism. Bernstein argued that socialism had to develop in an evolutionary instead of a revolutionary manner. Although he still believed that socialism would replace capitalism, he advocated the pursuit of immediate improvements in wages and working conditions, and for greater political democracy. Although these ideas were popular with the reformists and union leaders, they were strongly opposed by such radicals as Rosa LUXEMBURG, who believed that imperialism signaled the coming of a revolution for which the workers needed to be prepared. Fearing a split in the party, most Social Democrats supported the position of the centrists, led by August Bebel and Karl Kautsky.

In order to understand the response of other Germans to the growth of socialism, some of the following perspectives might provide understanding. Before WORLD WAR I the Socialists had created a deep gulf between themselves and the rest of German society. They preached a gospel of revolution, which created fear and resentment. They often sneered at intellectuals, especially teachers and professors. They advanced very liberal ideas on marriage, the family, and the position of women in society. It is not surprising that churchmen considered the Socialists evil because of their attack upon religion. Above all, their internationalism and opposition to popular patriotism and chauvinism brought the Socialists into disrepute with the "respectable" elements of German society. The anti-Socialist persecution also left its mark. Socialists continued to be condemned as enemies of society by governmental leaders after the turn of the century as they were by Bismarck in 1878. However, Socialist leaders did not care to bridge this gap, proclaiming their hostility to the structure of capitalist society, the capitalist state, or capitalist culture. Socialist workers bound their sons to their party, and both looked down on all others. Academic people were generally not attracted to the socialist movement. In the Reichstag the Socialists displayed their lack of patriotism by consistently opposing increased armaments, naval appropriations, and colonial expansion, which were popular with other segments of society. This accounted for the anxious speculation as to what action the SPD would take when war broke out in 1914, whether they would oppose the war or join all the others in voting for war credits.

To everyone's surprise the Socialists reversed their opposition to war by voting in favor of financing the war. The party also supported the political truce known as the Burgfrieden. The war forced a split in the party between those who supported it and those who opposed it. In 1917 the antiwar group formed the INDEPENDENT SOCIAL DEMOCRATIC PARTY (USPD) under the leadership of Hugo Haase and Karl Kautsky. The radicals even went further and formed the Spartacus League, which advocated the use of violence. On the other hand, the main SPD supported the Peace Resolution of 1917 in cooperation with the CENTER PARTY. In October 1918 as the war was lost, the SPD joined the government. During the REVOLUTION of 1918–1919 the SPD managed to provide moderate leadership and avoided a Russian-style Communist revolution.

During the WEIMAR REPUBLIC the SPD participated in many coalition governments with the Center Party and the Democratic Party. The SPD leader, Friedrich Ebert, remained president until his death in 1924. Ebert like other leaders such as Philipp SCHEIDEMANN and Otto BRAUN were reformist Socialists. Throughout the republic the SPD's share of the electoral vote varied from a high of about 38 percent in 1919 to a low of 20.5 percent in 1924. During the DEPRESSION its voting strength further declined, while that of the Nazis and Communists rapidly increased. Membership in the SPD declined between 1919 and 1933, and the party attracted an insufficient number of younger members under 30. After HITLER became chancellor, the SPD was the only party that steadfastly voted against the ENABLING ACT in 1933, which gave Hitler dictatorial powers. The party was banned by the Nazis, and many of its politicians were imprisoned or went into exile.

During the Allied occupation after the war the SPD revived its organization. Kurt Schumacher emerged as the leader in the Western zones, while Otto Grotewohl was the leader in the Soviet zone. A merger between the SPD and the GERMAN COMMUNIST PARTY (KPD) was opposed in the Western zones, while the Soviets acted as patrons of a merger in 1946 between the SPD and Communist Party in the eastern zone, forming the SOCIALIST UNITY PARTY (SED). In the West Schumacher was elected leader at the first party congress, and Erich Ollenhauer was chosen his deputy. The Erfurt Program was reaffirmed, and the SPD strongly supported unification in opposition to the strong pro-Western position of the CDU'S Konrad ADENAUER. In some state elections during 1946–47 the SPD was successful and became the largest party in Hesse, BREMEN, HAMBURG, and Lower Saxony. In federal parliamentary (Bundestag) elections its vote increased steadily from 29 percent of the vote in 1953 to almost 46 percent in 1972, when it became the largest party. The SPD served as an opposition party to the dominant CHRISTIAN DEMOCRATS (CDU), having reservations about European integration and in 1954 opposing rearmament. In order to present a new face to the electorate, the SPD revised its program in the new Godesburg Program of 1959. It eliminated the Marxian principle of the class struggle and the requirement that property had to be socialized in order to accomplish social justice. On the federal level the party participated in the Grand Coalition from 1966 to 1969 and then provided the chancellor from 1969 to 1982, first Willy BRANDT and then Helmut SCHMIDT in coalition with the FREE DEMOCRATIC PARTY of Germany (FDP). Brandt represented a new type of leadership with a broad popular appeal. However, the first opportunity to participate in the federal government came when the CDU could not manage Germany's first postwar recession.

OSTPOLITIK was the new foreign policy initiative pursued by Willy Brandt. It meant normalizing relations with East Germany. The SPD also liberalized and modernized society, accepted the idea of a social-market economy, and generally became a people's party instead of a working-class party. After the SPD was forced into opposition in 1982, the popular vote fell to below 40 percent until the elections of 1998, when the SPD again became the largest party in the Bundestag. Since reunification the SPD lost some of its younger and more radical voters to the new GREEN PARTY in western Germany and the competition from the PARTY OF DEMOCRATIC SOCIALISM (PDS) in the states of the former East Germany. Its electoral support, however, remained in urban areas, particularly in the industrial areas of the

RUHR, the SAARLAND, Bremen, Hamburg, and Berlin.

Socialist Unity Party
(SED, Sozialistische Einheitspartei Deutschlands)

The Socialist Unity Party (SED) was a Marxist-Leninist party that became the ruling party of the new GERMAN DEMOCRATIC REPUBLIC (GDR) in October 1949 and kept its hold on power until German reunification in December 1989. It was founded on April 21, 1946, by the combination of the GERMAN COMMUNIST PARTY (KPD) and the SOCIAL DEMOCRATIC PARTY (SPD). Most of the leadership was SPD (Otto Grotewohl was the leader in the Soviet zone and cofounder of the SED) until 1949, when the SED became a Leninist party based on "democratic centralism," a fake kind of democracy in which the leaders make the decisions. The party's Central Committee, however, was not the decision-making body, but real power lay in the Politburo and party Secretariat. The Secretariat was divided into departments, which mirrored the administrative bureaus of the state, and often the same official was head of both. The Secretariat was the policy-executing body, whose general secretary was Walther ULBRICHT and in 1971 became Erich HONECKER.

The SED went through a number of phases in its development. The first was the Stalinist phase, which began about 1947 and lasted until 1962, led by Ulbricht. This Stalinist phase was intended to conform the economy and society of the GDR to the model of the Soviet Union. Even with Stalin's death Ulbricht persisted in this policy until 1962. Then the SED changed to an authoritarian-technocratic phase, which emphasized state planning and technocratic guidance. It was the first comprehensive economic reform in the Soviet bloc, and along with the construction of the BERLIN WALL enhanced Ulbricht's prestige with the Soviet leadership.

Ulbricht's prestige also rose within the GDR. In the 1950s the SED had still been dominated by old Communists of the Weimar and Nazi eras, but in 1963 the candidates for the Politburo were from a younger generation, and the majority of the Central Committee had become active after WORLD WAR II. This younger leadership was supported by a changing social composition of the party's membership. The SED was successful in attracting a large number of blue-collar workers, which in the decade after the Wall was built increased from about 34 percent to 57 percent. Perhaps, because there was now little chance of escaping the country, the SED became the accepted vehicle to success, even among the educated. Ulbricht had faith that the structural transformation of the economy to nationalization, collectivized farms and retail sales through state-owned stores was the key to success. The leaders also thought that they had solved the problem of economic planning, increasing the freedom of decision making without abandoning effective control

In 1971 Erich Honecker replaced Ulbricht, whose leadership of the SED lasted until October 1989. While Ulbricht had not followed the Soviet Union's emphasis on DÉTENTE, Honecker was willing to do so. In 1983 Honecker joined reform-minded Communists in Eastern Europe who sought to maintain détente as the Soviet Union and the United States renewed their confrontation. What had happened in Germany was that both West and East Germany had developed a vested interest in their cooperation, especially the financial advantages. The SED therefore wanted to retain the old policies, while Mikhail Gorbachev wanted to revitalize Soviet socialism through his reform policies. Perhaps not realizing that the East German system could not be maintained without the threat of Soviet military intervention, Honecker firmly opposed reform, while Gorbachev pulled out the rug of protection, withholding the promise of such support.

Demonstrations for reform of the regime began in autumn 1989, and by October 18 Honecker was replaced by Egon Krenz. The demonstrations went on to demand party democracy and new leadership, while Germans were fleeing to the West, and the rush of events led to the opening of the border to the West.

Some 600,000 SED members left the party as its monopoly on power ended on December 1. The party quickly transformed itself into the PARTY OF DEMOCRATIC SOCIALISM (PDS).

Speer, Albert (1905–1981)
Hitler's architect and minister of armaments
Albert Speer was HITLER's talented personal architect who designed for Hitler the future BERLIN as a capital of a vast empire. From 1942 to 1945 he was armaments minister who worked virtual miracles of armaments production during the latter part of the war.

Born in MANNHEIM on March 19, 1905, Albert Speer was the son of a prominent architect. He studied architecture in MUNICH and Berlin and became an assistant at the Berlin Technical College. It was not until 1930 that Speer heard Hitler speak and quickly became enthralled with his personality. In 1931 he joined the NAZI PARTY. It was as an architect that he caught Hitler's attention with the designs of the remodeled party district headquarters in Berlin, the Ministry of Propaganda, and the displays of the stadium in NUREMBERG, where party rallies were held. At age 28 Speer was made Hitler's designer-architect in chief. In 1937 he became inspector-general of the Reich, responsible for the rebuilding of German cities in the neoclassical style, which Hitler favored. All of the major edifices, squares, and monumental avenues were projected to exceed anything that other men had hitherto attempted. His designs for a triumphal arch would have towered above Napoleon's gigantic arch in Paris, his design for a congress hall was seven times the size of St. Peter's in Rome; a design for a palace for Hitler that dwarfed the great Chancellery completed in 1939 was 70 times as large as the building that Hitler had inherited. Speer designed a grandiose building program for after the war, which reflected Hitler's ambitions for conquest. Even timetables and sources of raw materials were analyzed, and foreign policy was tailored for these goals; the new Berlin was to be constructed by mid-century.

It was the accidental death in 1942 of Dr. Fritz Todt, minister of armaments, that provided the opportunity for Speer's appointment. As minister of armaments he achieved a tremendous increase in military production, almost doubling that of tanks between 1941 and 1944. He achieved these goals through relentless efforts and the unscrupulous use of slave labor, despite the massive Allied bombing raids. It is thought that he kept the German war machine in the field for two years longer than it could otherwise have been. In the final stages of the war he came to realize that the war was lost as well as the destructive nature of Hitler's megalomania. Speer urged Hitler to end the war. In the final weeks of the war he disobeyed Hitler's orders to destroy the German industrial complex before it fell into Allied hands.

In 1946 Speer was brought to trial before the International Military Tribunal (IMT) at Nuremberg. He was the only Nazi leader to admit personal responsibility for the crimes of the Third Reich, specifically the employment of slave labor. He did not use the defense, like all the others, that he was only following orders. His honesty and resistance to Hitler's last destructive orders saved him from the death sentence. Although the Russians wanted him to be executed, he was sentenced to 20 years

While in Spandau Prison he wrote *Inside the Third Reich* (1970), which was a self-critical memoir and one of the most reliable insights to the regime. Speer admitted his own guilt in the employment of slave labor; he showed how powerful Hitler's charisma was; he provided a close-up picture of Hitler's lieutenants and their competition for personal gain despite negative impacts on the war effort; and he reflected on the spiritual and cultural desert that was life around Hitler. Speer's futile pact with the devil was exposed too late. He died in London in 1981.

Spiegel Affair (1962)
In October 1962 *Der Spiegel* (*The Mirror*) published an article containing secret documents that demonstrated a lack of defense readiness of

some West German army units. The offices of the magazine were searched, and issues of the magazine were confiscated. Franz Joseph STRAUSS, the minister of defense, ordered the arrest of its editor, Rudolf Augstein, the defense correspondent, and some others on the charge of treason. The action by the government violated the freedom of the press and was a threat to liberal democracy. The citizenry throughout the FEDERAL REPUBLIC were outraged. Ulterior motives were suspected inasmuch as the magazine had for some time criticized Strauss. A government crisis resulted. The coalition partner, the FDP, threatened to leave the coalition in protest, and the FDP and many CDU/CSU politicians demanded a change in leadership. When Konrad ADENAUER, the chancellor, dismissed Strauss and promised to leave office in a year, the crisis ended.

SS
(Schutzstaffel)

The SS was first organized in 1923 as a personal bodyguard for Adolf HITLER and gradually developed into a police force and finally into a large and complex organization, including military units. In January 1929 Heinrich HIMMLER was appointed the leader, assuming the title of Reichsführer SS. Besides its function as a party police force, Hitler also designated it in 1931 to be an elite troop. After becoming chancellor in January 1933, Hitler used the SS in the so-called NIGHT OF THE LONG KNIVES to assassinate Ernst RÖHM, who planned to transform the SA (Sturmabteilung) Brown Shirts into a revolutionary army. On June 17, 1936, Himmler was appointed chief of the German police, and with the GESTAPO (Prussian Secret State Police) under his control was not subject to any legal authority.

Thereafter, the SS cast its shadow across the Third Reich, and by 1937 it consisted of five major divisions. Civilian security forces were in the General SS, while the Reserve SS assisted the regular police. Recruited from CONCENTRATION CAMP guards, the Death's Head Units were particularly brutal in upholding racial standards. Reinhard HEYDRICH was placed in charge of the Security Service (SD), which was charged with gathering ideological information for the NAZI PARTY and the state. Adolf EICHMANN, who played such a major role in the execution of the FINAL SOLUTION, headed one of the subunits of the SD. The Race and Settlement Main Office (RSHA) was given the mission to maintain racial purity and prepare for the future colonization in the East. Finally, the Waffen SS were heavily armed military units that would rival the regular army after the attempted assassination and coup on July 20, 1944.

The SS was the institutional embodiment of the ideology of National Socialism and symbolized the fusion of party and state. The SS ideal was racist, emphasizing the development of a Nordic German racial elite. SS members had to receive Himmler's permission to marry, prospective brides had to pass racial requirements, and eventually all recruits had to prove that they had no Jewish ancestry. The SS ideology was based on the idea of racial struggle for survival, was opposed to respect for modern human values, was antireligious, but emphasized honor, loyalty, and discipline. The SS developed into a secular order of knights with rites and symbols presumably from the German tribes. Himmler also developed an SS mystique, which included the black uniforms, symbols, and ceremonies.

In the Nazi police state the police functioned independently of the judicial system. People could be arrested without cause or on suspicion and would often end up in concentration camps. The SS was responsible for the establishment and conduct of the expanding concentration camp system. Beginning with the arrest and incarceration of many thousands of political opponents after the REICHSTAG fire on February 28, 1933, a system of concentration camps emerged first at DACHAU and then throughout Germany, at first housing mainly political opponents such as Communists, Socialists, clergy, and other dissenters. The police could arrest anyone under suspicion and intern them in the camps. Other groups, such as Gypsies, homosexuals, vagrants, habitual criminals, and especially Jews after 1938 were also placed in the camps.

With the occupation of Poland in 1940, the way was open for Hitler to pursue a "final" solution to the Jewish question. Himmler was given responsibility to resettle Poland along racial lines, which Reinhard Heydrich and special strike forces known as the EINSATZGRUPPEN were chosen to carry out policy. The units were sent into Poland to concentrate the Jews into ghettoes in the larger cities during 1939–40. With the invasion of Russia in June 1941, four more of these were organized as mobile units with the mission of killing Jews. During 1941–42 these strike forces and their auxiliaries killed some 1 million Jews. When the killing methods of the Einsatzgruppen proved to be inefficient and even Himmler was sickened, the decision was made to establish death camps with gas chambers. Himmler and the SS were given this responsibility with administrative responsibility delegated to Heydrich and Eichmann. Rudolf HÖSS was instructed to enlarge the AUSCHWITZ crematoriums, while other major annihilation camps were located at Chelmno, Belzec, Sobibor, Majdanek, and Treblinka.

Stalingrad, Battle of

The Battle of Stalingrad during winter 1942–43 was the most decisive battle on the Russian front. Its first phase was the German attack and occupation of Stalingrad, and the second was the Russian counteroffensive, and the defeat and surrender of the German army.

In the battle of Stalingrad Adolf HITLER hoped to deprive the Russians of their large tank factory and to gain a psychological victory by capturing the city that held Stalin's name. It also was the farthest point of penetration into Russia that the Germans made. The German Sixth Army under Field Marshal Friedrich PAULUS, which attacked the city, was the largest on the Eastern Front and comprised 14 divisions: 11 infantry, two panzer, and one motorized. On August 23, 1942, the Germans began their attack, attempting to encircle Stalingrad through a pincer movement that never succeeded. The Russians under General Vasili Chuikov were ordered to hold the city at all costs, which resulted in a war of attrition. In September the Germans shelled and bombed the city, destroying it but occupying it at great cost.

On November 19 the Soviet army began a counteroffensive under General Zhukov, which in five days succeeded in cutting off any retreat by the German army. Although they were surrounded, Hitler promised to break the encirclement. A relief army, Field Marshal Fritz Erich von MANSTEIN's Army Group Don tried to break through the encirclement from the south but was stopped 30 miles away. Now trapped inside Stalingrad, the German army was ordered to keep fighting and not to surrender. One German soldier who had dreamt of victory now recorded in his diary that he and his comrades were freezing and starving to death: "Soldiers look like corpses or lunatics. . . . haven't the strength to walk, run away and hide." By the end of December the Russians had destroyed the Sixth Army, and Paulus, along with 90,000 soldiers, was taken prisoner on February 2, 1943. Overall, the Germans lost some 200,000 men in the battle.

The Battle of Stalingrad was the most notable Soviet victory of the war and the German army's most disastrous defeat. It was the turning point of the war in Europe. The main reason for the disaster at Stalingrad was Hitler's decision to forbid the army to retreat and regroup, which was the most prominent example of his repeated prohibition of retreat in the face of overwhelming enemy strength and a special source of friction with his generals. It was precisely at this point in the war that Hitler had been freed to make decisions without the advice of the professional commanders who had the nerve to disagree with him, and had replaced them with compliant generals. Hitler now was in direct command of army operations and responsible for the defeat at Stalingrad.

Stauffenberg, Claus Schenk von
(Claus Schenk, Graf [Count] von Stauffenberg) (1907–1944)
conspirator in July 20, 1944, plot
Claus Schenk von Stauffenberg was a central figure in the plot to assassinate HITLER on July 20,

1944. Along with other German officers, conspirators in the Foreign Office, and the ABWEHR (Intelligence Office of the Armed Forces), Stauffenberg attempted to assassinate Hitler with a bomb at the Wolf's Lair at Rastenberg. The plot failed, and he and thousands of others were executed.

Stauffenberg was born on November 15, 1907, in Upper Franconia into a Catholic family whose father was privy chamberlain to the king of BAVARIA. Descended from ancient Swabian nobility, he had such ancestors as Count Neithardt von GNEISENAU, who established the Prussian General Staff, and Gerhard Johann von Scharnhorst of the Napoleonic war period. Stauffenberg was raised as a monarchist and Catholic, although his thought later turned in a more socialistic direction in his hopes for postwar Germany. He developed an interest in literature and the arts from his mother, absorbing ideas of the symbolist poet Stefan George, especially his IDEALISM, love of discussion, and patriotic dedication. Trained in the infantry, Stauffenberg was commissioned a second lieutenant in 1930 and by 1936 qualified to enter the General Staff College.

As an ambitious officer Stauffenberg served in the invasion of the Sudeten territory in Czechoslovakia, the war in Poland, and then France, where he participated in the General Staff. Assigned to North Africa in April 1943, he was severely wounded there by a low-flying plane, losing his left eye, right hand and forearm, two fingers on his left hand, and part of his leg. Expert care and his determination helped him recover, but it reveals something of his character that he resisted the use of pain killers. Lesser men would have lost the self-confidence to return to duty or even consider playing a role in assassinating Hitler.

Until the brutality of the anti-Semitic riots of November 1938, the NIGHT OF BROKEN GLASS (Kristallnacht), Stauffenberg like other officers supported the Nazi regime or at least were indifferent to it. For Stauffenberg his opposition had begun perhaps even earlier as was indicated by the testimony of a fellow officer, Friedrich Wilhelm von Loeper, that it was the oppression of the churches and persecution of the Jews that turned Stauffenberg against Nazism. It is thought that his active resistance certainly began after he observed the activities of the SS. He even likened Hitler to the Antichrist, which interpretation was perhaps inspired by a poem of Stefan George with the same title. With the military defeat before Moscow and the entry of the United States into the war, Stauffenberg joined the resistance in the latter half of 1942. In collaboration with Henning von Tresckow and members of the KREISAU CIRCLE they worked out a plan for a coup d'etat in conjunction with the army. Stauffenberg concluded that only the assassination of Hitler would permit peace with the Allies and save Germany from destruction. In 1943 the disastrous defeat of the German Sixth Army at the BATTLE OF STALINGRAD disillusioned Stauffenberg as well as many other officers.

After his recovery from his wounds in October 1943, he accepted a position in BERLIN at the General Army Office as chief of staff to General Friedrich Olbricht, who had been brought into the conspiracy by General Hans Oster, chief of staff of Army Counterintelligence (Abwehr), and a leading member of the military conspiracy against Hitler. When the leader of the Kreisau Circle, Count Helmuth James von MOLTKE, was arrested in January 1944, Stauffenberg carried on his work, becoming the leader responsible for the technical part of the assassination. After the Allies landed in Normandy on June 6, 1944 (D-DAY), and the Russians made a crucial breakthrough on the eastern front, the conspirators realized that the war was lost and Germany's position could not be improved by Hitler's assassination. Stauffenberg and Tresckow were nevertheless convinced that an assassination attempt was necessary to be a historical witness to the seriousness of purpose of the RESISTANCE. The conspirators decided that they also needed to kill Heinrich HIMMLER and Hermann GÖRING, which made the plot more complicated. As the only one who had ready access to Hitler, Stauffenberg assumed responsibility for the assassination, deciding to plant a bomb at the next scheduled meeting (after two aborted attempts (July 11 and 15) in Hitler's headquarters (Wolf's Lair) in the

Prussian woods. The plan was to kill Hitler, contact Berlin where the other conspirators were waiting to initiate a coup, arrest the Nazi hierarchy, and convince the military that they had been betrayed. Entering the compound, Stauffenberg avoided being searched, but he and his adjutant were interrupted in setting the fuses, which weakened the bomb's explosiveness. Setting the bomb (in a briefcase) under Hitler's map table, he excused himself; the bomb was moved, and consequently Hitler was not killed. Thinking that he had been successful, Stauffenberg left for Berlin to help direct the coup. That evening news came that the conspiracy had failed. Stauffenberg and Olbricht were arrested and executed immediately, others were strangled by wire hanging from meat hooks. Some 200 were tried and convicted. There were no further reported attempts on Hitler's life.

Stein, Karl, Baron vom und zum
(Heinrich Friedrich Karl, Freiherr [Baron] vom und zum Stein) (1757–1831)
statesman and reformer

Prussian statesman and reformer during the Napoleonic era, Baron Karl vom und zum Stein reformed the bureaucracy, abolished serfdom, and introduced land reform. His vision for a unified Germany was obstructed by the apathy of the German people and the self-interest and opposition of contemporary statesmen.

Karl vom und zum Stein was born into an old Westphalian family of Imperial Knights, who had preserved the medieval tradition of knightly independence and the idea of a unified German realm under imperial leadership. He opposed the selfish interests of the territorial princes and was loyal to only "one fatherland." Stein was a man of action and political realist who was inspired by a religiously based conviction that the state was a moral organism and should play a key role in social change and moral progress of the whole community. Though not a liberal, his thinking was influenced by British classical economics. His political strengths were his courage, moral character, and self-confidence, while his liabilities were his tactlessness, inflexibility, and willfulness.

Although he had served in the Prussian bureaucracy since 1780, it was not until 1804 that he received an appointment as minister of economic affairs. The reforms he introduced promoted freedom of trade by removing tariff restrictions within PRUSSIA, substituted private ownership for the state-run enterprises established under mercantilism, and eliminated the corporate restrictions that guilds had long placed on commerce. His uncompromising views on the need for reform challenged vested interests in Prussia, so he was dismissed by FREDERICK WILLIAM II in 1807 and accused of being an "obstinate, defiant, stubborn and disobedient state official."

Stein recognized the need for fundamental reform in Prussia if the state was to rise from the ashes. The catastrophic defeat by Napoleon at the BATTLE OF JENA (1806) resulted in its territorial dismemberment, its severe economic problems, and the breakdown in Prussian society. The paternalism and ABSOLUTISM of the government, he believed, had bred an attitude of irresponsibility and indifference among the population. Motivated by a vision of national regeneration, Stein thought that a transformation of the political and social order was necessary and envisioned that a reborn Prussia would become the future instrument of German unification. The reform program was embodied in the OCTOBER EDICT issued by the king on October 9, 1807. Together with subsequent legislation, the reforms facilitated the development of civil equality, social mobility, and economic freedom. Although peasants were legally freed from historic servitude, they were, however, left exposed to market forces and the requirement to reimburse lords for their loss of manorial dues. The October Edict also introduced market forces in the sale of the estates of the nobility. Even though the power of the reactionary nobility had been weakened or redefined, they still continued to wield considerable influence. Stein and other reformers also sought to enable citizen participation in government, thinking that this would encourage citizens to fight for their country. One such reform was the restoration of self-government in 1808 to cities

(Städteordnung), which, however, did not free the cities to make and administer laws independently of the state. But Stein did hope that this and other reforms of city government would free them from control of state bureaucracies. The reformers failed, however, to create effective representative institutions for Prussia. Following the example of the French Revolution, Stein abolished the inherited privileges of the merchant and craft guilds, replacing these protected rights with capitalism and private property. Jews and members of the armed forces, however, were denied citizenship and forbidden to own real estate, to engage in trade and industry, or to participate in city administration.

Under pressure from Napoleon, Stein was again dismissed in 1808, when it became known that he favored a revolt against Napoleon. Fleeing to AUSTRIA, he wrote his "political testament," in which he advocated reforms that were not realized until the REVOLUTION OF 1848. He became a special adviser to Czar Alexander I and worked to bring Prussia back into the war against Napoleon. At the CONGRESS OF VIENNA his ideals of a united Germany were not realized. He retired in 1816 and died at his castle on June 29, 1831.

Stinnes, Hugo (1870–1924)
industrial tycoon

Creator of the Stinnes combine, a giant vertical trust, Hugo Stinnes was one of the earliest financial backers of the NAZI PARTY, along with Fritz THYSSEN and Emil Kirdorf. He became the supreme example of the postwar business entrepreneur who expanded into businesses in many sectors of the economy.

Hugo was born in Mühlheim on February 12, 1870, into the wealthy merchant family of Mathias Stinnes, the owner of a coal shipping company. Educated as a mining engineer, he established his own company, which grew to include not only coal mines and depots, but also seagoing ships and iron and steel factories. He also was a principal investor in RWE, Rhenish-Westphalian Power Works, which supplied both gas and electricity to the area, and under his leadership became the largest in Europe. During WORLD WAR I he profited immensely from war-oriented production and even expanded into production of motor vehicles and airplanes at a time when horses were still the major motive power and the aeronautics industry was in its infancy.

With the end of the war he resented the loss of his overseas investments. As inflation increasingly affected the German economy, Stinnes built up one of the most spectacular postwar fortunes. He built up a vertical trust, branching out from the iron and steel industry into shipping, hotels, lumber, paper, newspapers, and politics.

With the establishment of the Weimar parliamentary system, he became more involved in politics. He became a spokesman for German industry and opposed the payment of reparations, which the Allies had increased to cover all war costs. As important for long-run relations between business and labor was his reversal on the issue of collective bargaining and his leadership in the conclusion of the Stinnes-Legien Agreement of November 15, 1918. This agreement helped stabilize the economic situation by establishing the eight-hour workday and the principle of collective bargaining. In 1922, however, he reversed his support for the eight-hour day, arguing that it was necessary for the country to pay its reparations debts. He did oppose the Allied demands for excessive reparations. An example of his diplomatic ineptness was his inflammatory theatrics at the Spa Conference in July 1920, ruining any hope of solving the problem of delivering coal supplies to the Allies. In 1923 Stinnes supported the passive resistance against the French in the RUHR. Politically, he was associated with the GERMAN PEOPLE'S PARTY of Gustav STRESEMANN and was elected a delegate to the REICHSTAG between 1920 and 1924. He did, however, oppose Stresemann's conciliatory foreign policy. Had Stinnes lived, he probably would have opposed Stresemann's great achievements in the LOCARNO TREATIES.

Two examples of his attempts to subvert democracy during the early 1920s were, first, his purchase of democratically oriented newspapers whose editorial perspectives he changed to suit his conservative views. Second was his early financial support for Hitler and the Nazi Party. Stinnes died prematurely in 1924 due to bungled surgery.

The Stinnes businesses declined and were liquidated. The economic interests lived on, however, in a new company formed in 1925. Under Hitler it became important in the armament and engineering industries and profited immensely from the war.

Stöcker, Adolf (1835–1909)
Christian-Social Movement leader

Adolf Stöcker was a founder of the Christian-Social Movement, which became part of the conservative effort to create a mass political following, just as Disraeli had in English politics. At one time a chaplain at the Imperial Court, he was a major critic of free-market (laissez-faire) capitalism and claimed that it was dominated by the Jews. German politics owes to him the responsibility of making anti-Semitism socially and politically acceptable.

Born into poverty and influenced by the new Pietism during the reign of Frederick William IV, he studied theology at the university of Halle, tutored the children of nobility, and due to his stirring sermons was appointed a preacher at the Berlin Cathedral in 1874. He saw firsthand the distress of the working class in his ministry at the Berlin city mission. Public immorality, crass materialism, which was the "spiritual cholera" gripping all classes, and the inabilities of the church to reach and convert workers in the new urban-industrial environment troubled him deeply. He wanted to combat the rising influence of godless socialism among the working class by social reform based on a "Christian foundation," and he alleged that the Jews were the major enemy of a Christian German culture. Leading the assault on economic liberalism from the conservative political right, he identified liberalism with Jewish domination. To Stöcker, then, liberals, Jews, the Social Democrats, and capitalists were all foreign and un-German, un-Christian, and basically evil. Since Stöcker considered Protestantism to be one of the most important foundations of the Prussian-German state, it is easy to understand why he was so hostile to the groups that were changing Germany.

Organizing the Christian Social Workers' Party in 1878, Stöcker soon changed its name to the Christian Social Party in 1881. Workers were not attracted to his ideas, so he appealed to the lower middle class, who had been economically hurt by the Depression of the 1870s. He blamed the Jews for their problems and compared their dramatic achievements since emancipation in 1869 with the declining status of the lower middle class. For a while he and the Christian Social Party were part of the Berlin Movement and were favored by Otto von Bismarck and the Imperial Court. Stöcker's political agitation combined economic reform with anti-Semitism, organizing mass meetings as one of the most volatile and controversial political demagogues of Imperial Germany. He became one of the most important forerunners of Adolf Hitler and the Nazi movement.

After he fell out of favor with Bismarck, Stöcker's greatest period of influence and prestige was during his alliance with the respectable German Conservative Party, which was closest to the throne. He helped anti-Semitism attain the greatest social respectability as part of the Conservative program in 1892, whereas previously it had been represented in small splinter parties. At mass meetings Stöcker viciously attacked the Jews and declared that a racial war existed because the Jews wanted to attack "our Christian religion, our Kultur, and our German spirit." Because of his radicalism, however, he was dumped by the Conservatives in the 1890s and was politically marginalized.

Stöcker's extreme anti-Semitism set the standard for Hitler's and inspired the Nazi movement. Hitler's dependence on Stöcker's concepts is evident in *Mein Kampf*, in which he literally uses Stöcker's words. What Stöcker theorized about the Jews was considered true fact by Hitler, whose fanatical seriousness led to the Final Solution.

Strasser, Gregor (1892–1934), and Otto Strasser (1897–1975)

Nazi Party leaders

Gregor and Otto Strasser advocated socialism and were early rivals for leadership in the NAZI PARTY.

The brothers were born in BAVARIA into a middle-class family, Gregor the older on May 31, 1892, in Geisenfeld and Otto on September 10, 1897, in Windsheim. Gregor, the more important of the two, served as a lieutenant during WORLD WAR I and was awarded the Iron Cross. Settling in Landshut, Bavaria, he became an apothecary. During the BEER-HALL PUTSCH he led some volunteers to MUNICH to help HITLER but arrived too late. Acting as cochairman of the NSDAP during Hitler's imprisonment he was a good organizer but not an effective speaker. He left Landshut and took over the party organization in northern Germany after Hitler's release from Landsberg Prison.

In BERLIN Gregor established the *Berlin Workers' Paper* under the editorship of his brother, Otto, and together with Joseph GOEBBELS the Strassers worked to build the Nazi movement in Berlin. Gregor considered himself more intelligent than Hitler and ambitiously wanted to replace Hitler as leader of the whole party. Becoming very popular among the lower classes, the brothers seriously believed in socialistic principles and were urban revolutionaries. Strongly disagreeing with Hitler over the extent of socialism in the party, a conflict arose that lasted from 1926 until Gregor's death. As Hitler began to form alliances with Germany's industrial magnates in return for financial support, it became clear to Otto that Hitler was using the party for his own agenda and that the Nazi Party would no longer stand for the workers and for socialism. Otto left the party in 1930 and founded the organization called the Black Front.

Gregor's popularity tempted him to challenge Hitler's leadership. It did little good, however, for Gregor to oppose Hitler's courtship of big business and his ANTI-SEMITISM. Yet in 1932 Hitler made Strasser the Reich organization leader of the party. After an argument between the two leaders, Hitler appointed Hermann GÖRING instead of Strasser the presiding officer of the REICHSTAG, which was made possible by the 230 seats the Nazis won in July 1932. Then with the intent of splitting the Nazi Party, Gregor was offered the positions of vice chancellor and premier of PRUSSIA by Chancellor Kurt von SCHLEICHER. Another argument ensued between Hitler and Gregor, each accusing the other of cheating and splitting the party. As a result Strasser resigned his leadership post and later was dismissed by Hitler as head of the political organization, being replaced by Rudolf HESS. During the Röhm purge, the NIGHT OF THE LONG KNIVES, on June 30, 1934, Gregor was arrested and killed. Otto, on the other hand, escaped the purge, left Germany, and settled in Canada. Returning to Germany in 1955 he failed in his attempt to reenter politics and died in 1975 in MUNICH.

Strauss, Franz Josef (1915–1988)

founder of the Christian Social Union (CSU)

This controversial political leader was born in MUNICH on September 6, 1915. Although a son of a butcher, he received a classical education in the Gymnasium as well as attending the *Maximilianeum*, a special school for gifted youth. At the University of Munich he studied history and political economy in addition to philology and German. His professional goal was to be an educator, which, however, was thwarted by the war, during which he became an artillery officer.

After the war he became involved in the political reconstruction of Germany and was active in the establishment of the CHRISTIAN SOCIAL UNION (CSU). He firmly believed that this new Bavarian party had to break from the traditional mold of the earlier BAVARIAN PEOPLE'S PARTY and its strong Catholic confessional program. The new party appealed to other Christians and a social cross section of the Bavarian electorate. Initially more liberal, the party gradually became more conservative, to which Strauss adapted, although he personally continued to have a more populist orientation.

Between 1946 and 1949 Strauss played a minor though growing role in Germany's rehabilitation. He served in the Bavarian Ministries of Culture and Interior, and in 1948 he was elected to the Economic Council of the newly combined Allied zones of occupation, where he actively supported the liberal economic reforms, known as the "social-market" system of Ludwig ERHARD (1897–1977). In 1949 he was elected to the West German parliament (BUNDESTAG) from his home district of Weilheim-Schongau. Quickly gaining attention with his critical speeches and his earthy personality, the energetic and controversial Strauss seemed to personify the conservatism of his home state of Bavaria. In 1961 he became the undisputed leader of the CSU, a position he held until his death, and served as minister-president of Bavaria after 1978.

In 1953 Strauss entered the cabinet of Chancellor Konrad ADENAUER and was soon called "the elbow minister" for his ability to push himself to the top. After a brief stint as minister of nuclear power he became minister of defense in 1956. The FEDERAL REPUBLIC had just instituted conscription, and when the NORTH ATLANTIC TREATY ORGANIZATION (NATO) authorized the use of tactical nuclear weapons, Strauss was successful in getting the parliament to support the policy. He also argued that West Germany must obtain nuclear weapons to remain on equal footing with her NATO allies, while the Kennedy administration insisted on American control. Strauss responded by seeking to cooperate with France to create a Europe willing to share nuclear weapons. Known as a "German Gaullist," Strauss was viewed with suspicion by the supporters of Adenauer's heir apparent, Ludwig Erhard, who favored a pro-American "Atlantic" posture. The liberal press also started writing in ominous tones that Strauss might become a hawkish foreign minister, or even Adenauer's eventual successor.

In 1962 the controversial SPIEGEL AFFAIR occurred, which forced Strauss to resign as minister of defense. The popular weekly journal *Der Spiegel* published an article criticizing the lack of preparedness of the German army and Strauss's management. Strauss, unwisely, had the police search the magazine's office, arresting the editor, the author, and some staff, claiming that they had revealed defense secrets to the public. Demonstrations protesting his role were so widespread that the partners of the ruling coalition, the liberal FREE DEMOCRATS, required him to resign. After leaving national office, he returned to private life for a short time and studied economics at the University of Innsbruck.

It was not long before he returned to active politics, being instrumental in bringing down the Erhard government of 1963–66 and afterward helping to establish the "Great Coalition" of 1966–69 led by the new CDU chancellor, Kurt Georg KIESINGER, and the Social Democrat vice chancellor and foreign minister, Willy BRANDT. Strauss became the minister of finance and cooperated in tackling the challenges of economic recession. The coalition ended when replaced with a Social Democrat-Liberal coalition after the elections of 1969. This placed Strauss in the opposition, and he tirelessly advocated German unity but opposed Willy Brandt's conciliatory foreign policy toward Eastern Europe. Besides taking the traditional German position of opposition to the 1945 settlements in the East, he also opposed Brandt's BASIC TREATY with the GERMAN DEMOCRATIC REPUBLIC. He did not succeed in stopping the acceptance of the treaties nor the reelection of the Brandt government in 1972. As Strauss tried to be a more dominant voice in the CDU/CSU, he weakened their opposition to the Social Democrats, and the CSU was increasingly becoming a national splinter party. In the 1976 election this resulted in a electoral victory for a Social Democratic/Free Democratic alliance led by Chancellor Helmut SCHMIDT.

The high point of Strauss's career was his candidacy for federal chancellor in the elections of 1980. The confrontation between Strauss and Schmidt was described as a "clash of giants." With no important issues dividing them, the campaign turned out to be a national campaign by the Social Democratic/Free Democratic alliance to "stop Strauss." His defeat did not, however, deter Strauss from active involvement in German politics as Bavarian minister-president (1978–88) and continuing as chairman of the CSU. When Helmut KOHL won the election against Helmut Schmidt in 1982, it ensured that Strauss would remain an important influence in the federal government. Between 1983 and 1984 Strauss served in the largely honorary post of president of the BUNDESRAT, the upper house of the federal parliament. He died in Regensburg, Bavaria, on October 3, 1988. After German reunification, evidence of Strauss's questionable dealings with East German leaders was made public.

Streicher, Julius (1885–1946)
Nazi anti-Semite

A virulent anti-Semite, Julius Streicher was a principal rabble-rouser of the NAZI PARTY, contributing to its success in Franconia. Because of his crudity and lack of organizational skills he was never promoted to higher office.

Born in Fleinhausen near AUGSBURG on February 12, 1885, he followed his father into the teaching profession. In 1909 he secured a position in NUREMBERG, in 1911 entered politics, and in 1913 married. During WORLD WAR I he served impressively, earning the Iron Cross both first and second class, and was promoted to lieutenant. After the war he returned to teaching in Nuremberg and got involved in right-wing politics, founding the anti-Semitic German Socialist Party. In October 1922 he joined Hitler's National Socialist GERMAN WORKERS' PARTY (NSDAP), merging his own party with it.

Streicher was an effective political speaker and his use of anti-Semitic rhetoric alleging that the Jews were responsible for Germany's problems won many converts in Franconia. In addition, he founded the anti-Semitic hate sheet *Der Stürmer* in 1922, which he edited himself until 1933. At first it circulated only in BAVARIA, then throughout the Reich until it was discontinued in 1943. The articles in the paper were rabble-rousing, anti-Semitic, hate-inducing, and Jew-denouncing. Hate articles, theories of a Jewish conspiracy, and even pornography filled its pages. Christ was declared not to be a Jew. Its most significant reader was Adolf HITLER, who read it from cover to cover. Streicher was a party gauleiter of Franconia from 1925 to 1940. In 1933 he was elected to the REICHSTAG, representing Thuringia, and was given the title of leader of a committee to counteract Jewish propaganda tales. Gaining a national reputation as an eccentric, he carried a riding whip and became rich selling properties expropriated from Jews. His personality was expressed with brutality, sadism, and an obsession with pornography, and his thinking was absolutely closed to compromise. Although Hitler had supported Streicher's campaign against the Jews, even he grew tired of the complaints about Streicher's behavior. After a commission organized by Hermann GÖRING had examined his activities, Streicher was stripped of party positions in 1940. He then lived in enforced retirement as a farmer.

Before the International Military Tribunal (IMT) (*see* NUREMBERG TRIALS) Streicher was indicted for incitement to murder and extermination of the Jews. Having taken no part in waging aggressive war and not having been a military or diplomatic adviser to Hitler, he nonetheless was convicted of crimes against humanity (count 4) and executed by hanging on October 16, 1946.

Stresemann, Gustav (1878–1929)
diplomat of the Weimar Republic

Gustav Stresemann was one of the leading political figures of the postwar WEIMAR REPUBLIC. He championed a policy of reconciliation and cooperation in Europe. He was born in BERLIN on May 10, 1878, the son of a beer distributor. Studying economics and political science at the University of Berlin, he earned a doctorate. Stresemann became the managing director of the Association of Saxon Industrialists and served as its director until 1918. In 1907 he was elected to the REICHSTAG as a deputy of the NATIONAL LIBERAL PARTY, which was economically liberal and strongly nationalist, favoring the expansion of Germany's economic and military power. His outstanding parliamentary skill earned him the chairmanship of the party in 1917. Stresemann was nationalist, but also expansionist, identifying with the PAN-GERMAN LEAGUE during WORLD WAR I. He also favored the goals of Admiral Alfred von TIRPITZ, the construction of a navy strong enough to rival that of Great Britain. Until the end of World War I Stresemann believed that Germany would be victorious, refusing to criticize General Erich von LUDENDORFF's policies. Germany's request for an armistice and then the revolution that followed shocked him. It was no surprise that he accepted the "stab-in-the-back theory," which blamed the civilian politicians for Germany's defeat.

After the war Stresemann founded the GERMAN PEOPLE'S PARTY (DVP) in December 1918. He hoped to reconcile Germany and its former enemies and regain international respect. At the height of the INFLATION CRISIS OF 1923 he became chancellor, and his government stabilized the currency and established an understanding with France over the reparations issue. Becoming foreign minister, he ended the occupation by French and Belgian troops of the RUHR in 1924. Then he began to initiate a revision of the VERSAILLES TREATY. Reparation payments were reduced, and payments revised in the DAWES PLAN of 1924. The LOCARNO PACT guaranteed Germany's western borders and provided the French with security. Germany then entered the LEAGUE OF NATIONS in 1926. Allied controls were removed in the following years. Both Stresemann and Aristide Briand of France received the Nobel Peace Prize for their policy of Franco-German rapprochement. Growing NATIONALISM in both countries put a stop to their attempt to resolve remaining problems. Yet, the YOUNG PLAN was Stresemann's last success, which further reduced reparations. Stresemann's death in Berlin on October 3, 1929, was a blow to the Weimar Republic and its future.

T

Tannenberg, Battle of (August 26–30, 1914)

In the middle of August the Russians sent two armies into East Prussia in response to an urgent plea from the French. The armies were commanded by Generals Rennenkampf and Samsonov. There was panic in the headquarters of the commander of the German Eighth Army, General von Prittwitz-Gaffron, who sent an urgent plea to the chief of the General Staff, Count Helmut von MOLTKE, the younger, for reinforcements. Prittwitz had temporarily thought of withdrawing his forces behind the Vistula River, and this cost him his command. On August 23, 1914, Colonel-General Paul von HINDENBURG was called from retirement to assume command and Colonel Erich LUDENDORFF was appointed his chief of staff. After initial German setbacks a plan for encircling the Russians was worked out by Colonel Max Hoffmann, who was informed of a deep personal feud between the Russian commanders. Hoffmann made the assumption that if Samsonov's army were surrounded at Tannenberg, Rennenkampf would not attempt to come to his aid. Hindenburg and Ludendorff decided to attack. They left only a small shielding force in front of Rennenkampf's Njemen Army and led 166,000 men against the 200,000 men of the southern Narew Army of General Samsonov. During August 26–31 they directed a masterly battle of encirclement at Tannenberg. Some three-fifths of the Russian army were killed, and some 92,000 were made prisoner, while the Germans sustained only moderate losses. Subsequently, the Germans turned against Rennenkampf's Njemen Army, which was cornered in the Battle of the Masurian Lakes, September 6–15, 1914, where the Germans captured a further 125,000 troops. By mid-September East Prussia was in full German control. The significance of the battle was that the Russians were never again able to launch an invasion into German territory during WORLD WAR I.

Thälmann, Ernst (1866–1944)

Communist Party leader

Ernst Thälmann became a Socialist early in life and joined the GERMAN COMMUNIST PARTY (KPD) at its founding in 1919. He led the party from 1925 to 1933, was extremely loyal to Moscow, and ran for the Reich presidency in 1925 and 1932.

Thälmann was born in HAMBURG on April 16, 1886, into a lower middle-class family of grocers and innkeepers. At age 17 he was already employed as a transport worker, was active in his trade union, and in 1903 joined the SOCIAL DEMOCRATIC PARTY (SPD). After service in the war he turned leftward and in 1918 joined the INDEPENDENT SOCIAL DEMOCRATIC PARTY (USPD). When the Communists split off and formed the GERMAN COMMUNIST PARTY (KPD), he joined them in 1919. He became leader of the party in Hamburg, was elected to the City Council, and in 1923 helped organize an uprising there. In 1921 he joined the Central Committee of the Communist Party and the Comintern in 1924. In the meantime he also had been elected to the REICHSTAG in 1924. In 1925 he became chairman of the Communist Party and was responsible for bringing the German Communists in conformity with Moscow's party line. In 1925 and 1932 he ran for the presidency of the republic, receiving only a small minority vote and losing to Paul von HINDENBURG.

The Communists waged political warfare against the Socialists, the SPD, who were considered traitors to their class, and weakened their support among the working class. Following orders from, Moscow Thälmann tried to outbid the Nazis on the national question and failed because of his unswerving loyalty to Moscow. Hated by HITLER, he was imprisoned in CONCENTRATION CAMPS until his death in BUCHENWALD on August 18, 1944.

Thirty Years' War (1618–1648)

Often called "the last of the religious wars" the sources of the conflict were certainly religious, between a militant Catholicism and a militant Calvinism. Secular dynastic interests were also involved, which included the desire of the German princes to resist the power of the emperor and the expansionist dynastic interests of other European monarchs. Since these were so powerful and involved the states of Denmark, Sweden, France, and Spain, perhaps the Thirty Years' War should be considered the first European civil war fought principally on German territory.

The PEACE OF AUGSBURG (1555) had been a compromise on the religious issue, but did not satisfy the participants and soon broke down. Under the weak emperor RUDOLF II (1576–1612), who had been brought up under Spanish and JESUIT influences, the COUNTER-REFORMATION began, which incited the renewed struggle between the religious confessions and the rulers who supported them. In 1608 the Protestant princes, under the leadership of the Elector Palatine, Frederick IV, concluded an alliance known as the Protestant Union (1608–1621), while the Catholic princes promptly responded with the Catholic League (1609–1635), which was led by the duke MAXIMILIAN I (1573–1651) of BAVARIA. While the main strength of PROTESTANTISM lay in the north and center of Germany, Bavaria became the center of the Counter-Reformation. Archduke Ferdinand of Styria, one of the bitterest enemies of the Protestants, who later became Emperor FERDINAND II (1619–37), reportedly stated that he would rather rule over a land that was a desert than over one populated by heretics. No sooner did this prince come to the ducal throne than he annulled the religious liberty of his Protestant subjects, expelled their clergy and teachers, and forced both the nobles and the people to return to Catholicism.

A decade of tensions and crises preceded the immediate cause of the Thirty Years' War. Ferdinand's accession as king of Bohemia in 1617 provided the event that mainly caused the Thirty Years' War. As the result of a collision between the two confessions in Prague, the Protestants, who formed the majority of the population both there and in the rural districts, set up a government of their own. When Ferdinand became emperor as Ferdinand II, succeeding the emperor Matthias, the Czechs rebelled. The Protestant princes met in a diet in spring 1618 and cast out of the window of Hradcin castle the two Habsburg governors, which has been memorialized as the "DEFENESTRATION OF PRAGUE." Then the Protestants chose the young Elector Palatine, Frederick V, the son-in-law of James I of England, as a rival king. Ferdinand responded to the challenge by sending a strong imperial army into Bohemia and crushed the rebellion at the Battle of White Mountain that November. With fierce vengeance the insurgents were punished. Twenty-seven prominent leaders were beheaded in the marketplace of Prague; thousands of families were exiled and dispossessed of their houses and chattels; and Protestant churches and schools were appropriated by Catholic priests and Jesuit teachers. In the end, Frederick, known as "the Winter King," lost both the Palatinate and the Bohemian throne.

The Protestant princes of Germany did not appear to be overly concerned for their coreligionists and stood by while the Bohemians were defeated and massacred. Then Spanish troops under General Johann Tserklaes, Count of Tilly, commander of the armies, ravaged the Palatinate.

Not until the emperor outlawed the ruler of that territory and proposed to install the Catholic Bavarian duke Maximilian in his place, did the Protestant princes become alarmed because it would have increased the number of the Catholic electors of the emperor at the expense of the Protestants. Of the two German princes who should have taken the lead in resisting the challenge to their faith and their independence but did not, were John George of electoral Saxony, who became an ally of the emperor, while George William, elector of BRANDENBURG, did not get involved. In the end the emperor made Maximilian an elector by presenting him with the Upper Palatinate.

While Catholics were determined to eliminate the Protestant heresy, Protestants wanted to expand their influence throughout Germany. Some princes were interested in attempting to expand their power and territories. Maximilian of Bavaria of the WITTELSBACH family even desired to rival the power of the Habsburgs. Other princes had designs on neighbors. The margrave of Baden desired Württemberg, while the city of Würzburg was desired by the landgrave of Hesse. Above all, the emperor wanted to consolidate Habsburg territories and extend his rule over Germany. Foreign rulers were no less altruistic, whether they were Gustavus Adolphus, Christian of Denmark, Maurice of Nassau, or Cardinal Richelieu, who ruled in France during the infancy of King Louis XIII. For instance, Richelieu financially supported the invasion by Denmark, and after 1631 French money financed the Swedish forces. What further complicated the dynamics of the war was that mercenaries were selling their services to the highest bidders and contributed to the brutality of the campaigns through wanton destruction and unnecessary killing.

In the long struggle that began in this fashion AUSTRIA and Spain, with Bavaria, supported the emperor and Catholicism, while Denmark, Sweden, Holland, France, and England supported the Protestant cause. The confessional questions over which contention first raged were soon overshadowed by those of purely political goals.

There were actually four wars, fought for the most part in different fields: the Bohemian phase and Palatinate war (1618–23); the Lower Saxon and Danish war (1624–29); the Swedish war (1630–35); and the Franco-Swedish war (1635–48). King Christian of Denmark, duke of Holstein, entered the struggle at an early stage, bent on acquiring BREMEN and other North German districts. France, which subsidized all the emperor's enemies in turn and attacked his armies in Spain, was primarily interested in weakening its southern neighbor. In 1630 Gustavus Adolphus, the warrior king of Sweden, invaded Pomerania with a well-equipped army of 15,000, said to be the only national army in the war. More than a year later, at the Battle of Breitenfeld north of LEIPZIG Gustavus brilliantly defeated the imperial army. This Swedish army moved westward toward the RHINE, then marched against the city of NUREMBERG, and then south into Bavaria. Although Gustavus was killed at the battle of Lützen two years later, Sweden continued to fight throughout the later phases. The involvement of England was mainly with money and naval assistance.

The war lasted until 1648 and was concluded by a series of agreements collectively known as the PEACE OF WESTPHALIA (October 27), which partitioned a large part of Germany. In addition, other agreements between the major European powers during the next two decades, as for instance Russia and Poland in 1667, marked a major turning point in European history. The states that benefited the most from this 17th-century world war were France, Sweden, and the Netherlands, which won what Austria lost. While France emerged as the dominant power in Europe, Sweden gained supremacy in the Baltic. France obtained Metz, Toul, and Verdun, reaching the Upper Rhine, which had been her ambition for a century. Spain, Denmark, and Poland were also on the losing side. Bavaria lost the Rhenish and kept the Upper Palatinate. The HOLY ROMAN EMPIRE was irreparably weakened through the recognition of the independence and the sovereignty of the states. Both the United Netherlands and Switzerland became independent states. The religious provisions of the Peace of Augsburg were reaffirmed, and all religious groups, rulers, subjects, and Calvinists were given equal status. Neither the Catholic nor the Protestant side achieved their goals, and Germany was still very much divided as before the conflict. The ruinous economic and social impact of the war has often been exaggerated, especially by German historians. The areas most affected by the destructiveness of the war were the militarily strategic ones along the Rhine, the Black Forest, the Leipzig plain, and the roads to the city of REGENSBURG and the Danube valley. Agriculture was hurt the most by the ravaging armies, but the disappearance of villages had begun already in the previous century due to the development of large estates. Economic breakdown in the commercial cities had already begun due to imperial bankruptcies, the inflation of the 1620s, and the changes in trade routes effected by the Atlantic trade. It has traditionally been thought that there was a disastrous population decline of from 5 million to 8 million people. Undoubtedly, the movements of often undisciplined armies and population migration contributed to the spread of typhus, one of the greatest killers of the 17th century, in addition to plague and even syphilis. It is now known that urban mortality in Germany was probably no greater than elsewhere, and perhaps there even was a modest increase in population. The economic consequences of the war that had supposedly turned back German development for 100 years have now been reinterpreted as a period in German history when income, productivity, and standards of living actually improved.

Thomasius, Christian (1655–1728)
philosopher and jurist
Christian Thomasius, along with Christian WOLFF, was one of the founders of the German ENLIGHTENMENT. In 1687 he was the first professor to give lectures in German since PARACELSUS, formally rejecting Latin as the vehicle of university instruction. He was a strong advocate of toleration and freedom of conscience and emphasized freeing the mind of dogma and superstition and appealing to "common sense" as the court of ethics.

Born in LEIPZIG on January 1, 1655, Christian Thomasius was the son of a teacher from whom he received his early education. He went on to study law at FRANKFURT and returned to teach at the University of Leipzig. While there he lectured on the natural law theories of Samuel von PUFENDORF. But then he stirred up opposition to himself by severely criticizing the prejudices and intolerance of the professors at Leipzig. In addition he began to publish a journal in German, which he used as a vehicle to further his attack on professorial stupidity. His views engendered such a strong rebuke that he was forbidden to lecture or publish.

In 1694 Thomasius accepted an invitation to teach at the newly founded university at Halle. There he sought to reconcile PIETISM and the Enlightenment, both of which had enemies in the BAROQUE scholarship of the day. Thomasius sought to develop a philosophy based on common sense and reason and not on divine revelation. He taught that theology should confine itself to purely religious problems and not become involved in philosophy. This distinction between religion and philosophy was a reflection of the Pietistic emphasis on an inward religion. Although his ideas lacked profundity, his philosophy idealized the honest man who lived according to the precepts of reason and aimed at the improvement of society.

According to Thomasius a chief obstacle to the illumination of reason was the superstition that pervaded the popular mind. People still believed in demonic possession and witchcraft. And if a person had a great deal of knowledge of physical phenomena, he or she was regarded by ordinary people of cooperating with the devil. Witchcraft was still a popular obsession. Although Thomasius still believed in the devil, he argued that witchcraft was difficult to prove. His Pietistic convictions concerning the soul led him to oppose the possibility of external control. In other religious matters he believed in freedom of thought and speech and condemned theologians who were always searching for heretics. In his personal life, however, he still believed that revealed religion was necessary for salvation.

In law and politics Thomasius attempted to free the study of jurisprudence from the control of theology. He thought that jurisprudence should be separated from theological ethics and derived from a rationalistic interpretation of natural law. He fought with great vigor against antiquated and inhuman concepts and procedures in the criminal law. Both Thomasius and Christian Wolff followed Thomas Hobbes in the construction of the authority of government. The German thinkers, however, disagreed with Hobbes's chaotic theory of the origins of society. Rather they considered humans to be a social animals. They thought there was a twofold social contract, the first expressing the general will in the community and the second concluded between this community and a ruler. The state was not of divine origin, and the inalienable rights of the individual could be maintained against the state. But most German political philosophers opposed the right of resistance to the government and refused to recognize institutions like parliaments, which limited the rights of the sovereign. Thomasius was zealous in advocating the reform of public administration, consequently exercising considerable influence on the future civil servants of the Prussian monarchy.

Thyssen, Fritz (1873–1951)

pro-Nazi industrialist

Fritz Thyssen was born on November 9, 1873, in the industrial city of Mühlheim in the RUHR, the son of August Thyssen, the founder of one of Germany's largest coal, iron, and steel empires. His company founded in Duisburg in 1871, August personified the classic German entrepreneurial virtues: independence, sole responsibility, risk taking, and absolute control of his own company. Son Fritz was trained to carry on the firm, educated in engineering, and possessing the talent to develop many international business contacts. As did many other nationalistic Germans, Fritz Thyssen found it difficult to accept the loss of WORLD WAR I and considered the punitive TREATY OF VERSAILLES a national humiliation. As a strong nationalist he was angered by the French occupation of the Ruhr and was arrested and tried by a French military court for helping organize the resistance. Politically, both he and his father had first been affiliated with the CENTER PARTY, but then turned to the political right. In 1928 Fritz Thyssen and his father established the United Steel Works, and Fritz became chairman of the International Steel Society.

Even before the BEER-HALL PUTSCH in November 1923, Thyssen had been impressed with the extreme NATIONALISM and demagoguery of Adolf HITLER, his contempt for the WEIMAR REPUBLIC and its politicians, and his promises to smash communism and even restore the HOHENZOLLERN dynasty. Thus began a long period of financial contributions to the NAZI PARTY, amounting to more than 1 million marks. He joined the Nazi Party in 1931 and soon thereafter invited Hitler to speak at a meeting on January 27, 1932, of 650 businessmen at the Industry Club in DÜSSELDORF. Hitler tried to persuade the audience that they did not have to fear the Nazi movement and interestingly made no mention of the Jews. While the Nazis claimed that they had won over big business, no large number of industrialists began to support the Nazi Party as once had been supposed. Thyssen, however, continued his support and subsidized the extravagant lifestyles of Hermann GÖRING and Gregor STRASSER. In the 1932 presidential elections Thyssen voted for Hitler instead of President Paul von HINDENBURG. After Hitler was appointed chancellor, Thyssen as an economic expert was chosen to direct a research institute on the corporate state, but nothing came of this. In reality there was a community of interest between industrialists and the Nazis and consequently industry enjoyed considerable freedom. It did not take very long, however, for Thyssen to become disenchanted with the Nazis because of their persecution of Christianity and the Jews.

His reservations began in 1935, and in 1938 he resigned from the Prussian Council of State in protest over the persecution of the Jews. He also denounced Dr. Robert Ley, head of the German Labor Front. Then in 1939 he publicly protested in the REICHSTAG the coming of war. Shortly thereafter he left the country for Switzerland.

On December 28, 1939, Thyssen sent a letter to Hitler chastising him for not keeping his oath to uphold the WEIMAR CONSTITUTION, and for persecuting Christianity and the Jews. In 1941 he published his autobiography, *I Paid Hitler*, wherein he explained his motives and patriotism and reveals his ill-fated cooperation with the Nazis. Unfortunately, the book is not trustworthy in regard to what it states about the finances of the party. The Nazis proceeded to revoke his German nationality and confiscated his property. Later, he and his wife were arrested in Vichy, France and placed in CONCENTRATION CAMPS. He was tried as a war criminal by the Allies and released in 1949. He died a bitter man in Buenos Aires, Argentina, on February 8, 1951.

Tieck, Ludwig (1773–1853)
romantic writer

One of the most versatile and productive writers of the romantic movement, Ludwig Tieck was born in BERLIN in humble circumstances, the son of a master rope maker. In his youth his intellectual and literary talents were already manifest. Initially he was a rationalist and a student of the ENLIGHTENMENT, but through his friendship with W. H. WACHENRODER he was converted to ROMANTICISM. Tieck pursued his university studies at GÖTTINGEN, Halle, and Erlangen. Initially, he studied theology but increasingly devoted himself to the study of literature. In 1794 Tieck returned to Berlin and wrote on rationalistic philosophy.

With his facile pen Tieck at a young age even before his collaboration with Wachenroder produced a horror novel (1795) and an amoral romantic story, *The Story of Mr. William Lovell* (1795–96), dealing with the corruption of a youth. He also edited German folktales and wrote fairy tales of his own, such as *The Blonde Eckbert* (1797), in which nature is described as a weird and mysterious reality until it is redeemed by poetry. Whereas the novel about Lovell is nihilistic and ignores the necessity of moral discipline, the Eckbert story concerns guilt, incest, and the supernatural.

Tieck also experimented with dramas, writing *Puss in Boots* (1797), a charming example of a witty romantic comedy in which the usual dramatic rules are ignored and the illusion of the play is destroyed. The basic plot of the children's story is used as a vehicle for satire. The story of Gottlieb and his astounding tomcat Hinze gave Tieck an opportunity to ridicule the dull rationalism of some of his contemporaries. Some critics regard it as a precursor of 20th-century experimental theater. Other dramas include *Knight Bluebeard* (1797) and *Prince Zerbino* (1797), which combined comedy, tragedy, satire, and the grotesque.

In 1797 Tieck met with Friedrich SCHLEGEL, and through Franz Sternbald's *Wanderungen*, Tieck became associated with Friedrich and August Wilhelm SCHLEGEL and their romantic literary circle in JENA. Others included Novalis.

In 1799 Tieck completed the novel begun with Wachenroder before his death. *The Wanderings of Franz Sternbald* turned out to be a glorification of the Middle Ages, a historical period that provided a dreamworld for the romantics. Under the influence of Wachenroder, Tieck replaced his playfulness with greater seriousness as in Sternbald's interview with Albrecht DÜRER. Later, however, Tieck succumbed to his fantasies and visions, which are difficult to endure. In international literature he was the first German critic to appreciate Shakespeare and also translated into German Cervantes's *Don Quixote* (1799–1801). Tieck and August Wilhelm Schlegel translated all of Shakespeare (1833), which became a standard work of German literature. He helped edit the literary remains of Wackenroder, Novalis, Kleist, and Jakob Lenz.

In 1804 he revised an old chapbook into a comedy, *Emperor Octavianus*, in which he intentionally mixed different verse forms to create an impression of change but which failed to attain its purpose. In 1819 he moved to DRESDEN, where he became a consultant for the city theater. In 1841 he was summoned to BERLIN by the king, FREDERICK WILLIAM IV of PRUSSIA, who invited him to be court author and reader in residence. He remained there until his death in Berlin on April 28, 1853.

Tilsit, Treaty of (1807)

After Napoleon had defeated the Russians at the battle of Friedland (June 14, 1807), he and Czar Alexander signed a peace treaty and negotiated an alliance at Tilsit on July 7, 1807. This peace settlement marked the height of Napoleon's power over Europe, and the alliance created a new European order.

After the defeat of the Russians at the battle of Friedland, Napoleon and Czar Alexander met to discuss peace terms. In a symbolic place of neutrality on the Nieman River at Tilsit an elaborate raft with a conference chamber was moored on which the two sovereigns discussed peace terms. After short daily discussions that lasted for two weeks, the two sovereigns signed a series of agreements, which collectively are called the Treaty of Tilsit, on July 7. A secondary treaty outlined the humiliating dismemberment of PRUSSIA. King FREDERICK WILLIAM III, who played no role in the negotiations, was summoned to the raft to hear the fate of his kingdom.

The Prussians had to sign the peace conditions within 48 hours. In a convention of July 12, the French were to evacuate Prussia east of the ELBE RIVER, which was to be dependent on the payment of a large indemnity. Napoleon only agreed to Prussia's continued existence as a favor to Alexander, and as a buffer between France and Russia. In return Alexander promised his assistance in ending the war between England and France, while Napoleon offered the same concerning the Russo-Turkish war. Napoleon refused to reconstitute the kingdom of Poland, but instead agreed to the creation of the Grand Duchy of Warsaw. The land for the duchy was to come from four of Prussia's provinces, the territories that Prussia had taken in the second and third partitions of Poland and the Netze district. Prussia not only lost all her possessions west of the Elbe but also had to cede Lower Lusatia to Saxony. Part of Prussia's land in Poland was to be given to Russia. The Oder River was brought under French control by the French occupation of the Prussian Oder fortresses. And finally, the kingdom of Westphalia was formed as a French bulwark in northern Europe.

The Grand Duchy of Warsaw was to form part of the pro-French Confederation of the Rhine. The ruler of SAXONY was to become the new ruler of Poland and also was to join the Confederation as the "King of Saxony." French power was extended to the Vistula River, where the city of DANZIG became a free city with a French garrison. Napoleon's intentions were to push Russia out of Europe and to expand in the Baltic, permitting the Russian conquest of Finland, then trying to steer the Baltic countries into a pro-French alliance. In the Mediterranean Russia had to give up to France some enclaves, and Napoleon in turn offered to support Russia in a struggle with Turkey.

As a result of the Treaty of Tilsit, Czar Alexander became a collaborator in the Continental System. The new Grand Duchy of Warsaw would supply for Napoleon a secure base for any future conflict against AUSTRIA, Prussia, or Russia.

Tirpitz, Alfred von (1849–1930)
founder of the Imperial German navy

He was born into a middle-class family in Küstrin and at age 16 entered the Prussian naval service. By 1877 he had become head of the torpedo division of the navy. In 1896 he was given command of a German flotilla stationed on the Chinese coast, where he became jealous of British predominance in China. Subsequently, he convinced the Kaiser that he should force the Chinese emperor to grant Germany a port in northern China, which occurred in 1896 at Kiaochow. In 1896 he was appointed state secretary of the Imperial Naval Office, which he occupied for 20 years. The egomaniacal Kaiser was also jealous of Queen Victoria's (his grandmother) navy and hoped that Tirpitz might provide the necessary leadership to build a strong German one. Autocratic and insistent on having his way, the admiral successfully lobbied for an increase in German naval strength and founded the Naval League to create public enthusiasm for the expensive shipbuilding program. The propaganda for the NAVY was rooted in the belief that a strong navy was required for national survival to provide the ability to play an important role in world affairs. Tirpitz's plan was completed in 1898 and was funded in the First Naval Law, which was followed by a Second Naval Law in 1900, which further expanded the navy. Tirpitz also developed a "risk theory," which theorized that Britain was jealous of IMPERIAL GERMANY's rising economic strength and sought to destroy it. So he argued that Germany had to maintain a naval ratio of two British to three German ships to seriously wound the Royal Navy. Tirpitz also theorized that neither France nor Russia would ever become Britain's allies. As international alliances changed prior to WORLD WAR I, Tirpitz found that France and Russia had become allies with Britain against Germany. Because naval superiority was too expensive to maintain, some politicians, such as Theobald von BETHMANN HOLLWEG, who was chancellor after 1909, favored a negotiated reduction of naval armaments, which Tirpitz opposed. He succeeded in undermining any of these attempts at compromise.

During World War I the British navy bottled up the Germany navy in its naval bases. It took until 1916 before the Kaiser allowed the German navy to engage the British in the BATTLE OF JUTLAND, which turned out to be a British victory, although both sides sank an equal number of ships. Then Tirpitz placed his hopes for Germany in submarines (U-boats) and argued for "unrestricted submarine warfare," which he predicted would bring England to its knees. The Kaiser decided to dismiss Tirpitz in 1916, disappointed with his failed naval schemes. Tirpitz fought back by influencing the dismissal of Chancellor Bethmann Hollweg. Then Tirpitz became a founder of the FATHERLAND PARTY which opposed a negotiated peace. When the war ended in an armistice, Tirpitz blamed Germany's defeat on parliamentarians and socialist traitors and the fickle Kaiser. During the WEIMAR REPUBLIC he favored the restoration of the HOHENZOLLERN monarchy and opposed the foreign policy of Gustav STRESEMANN, who sought to fulfill the VERSAILLES TREATY. Tirpitz died in 1930, most likely unaware that his naval policies had largely been responsible for making Britain an enemy in World War I and were a principal cause of Germany's defeat.

Toller, Ernst (1893–1939)
expressionist playwright

Ernst Toller was a young sensitive Jew who objected to the ANTI-SEMITISM around him. He preferred to study at Grenoble University. In 1914 he patriotically came home to Germany to enlist. The horrible experiences at the war front induced a breakdown, and he was released from the army in 1916. In the meantime he had become a pacifist and member of the left-wing INDEPENDENT SOCIAL DEMOCRATIC PARTY, which opposed the war. In January 1918 he became involved in antiwar protests in BAVARIA. In November 1918 the Bavarian revolution broke out under the leadership of Kurt EISNER (1867–1919), who along with other Jewish intellectuals (Gustav Landauer, Erich Mühsam, Eugen Levine), and Toller, who was the youngest, were involved in the revolutionary events of 1918–19. As the situation became more radical and a Bavarian Soviet Republic (Bayerische Räterepublik) was declared in spring 1919 (it lasted only six days), he was reluctantly elected its president. The Social Democratic government succeeded in repressing this Communist regime. Toller was again imprisoned, condemned to death, but the soldiers refused to fire on him. His sentence was changed to life imprisonment, but he was released in 1924. In the meantime his plays had been produced in BERLIN and other capitals of the world. Around 1925 he joined the circle of the NEW OBJECTIVITY movement, writing a play concerning the 1918 mutiny of German sailors in Kiel, *Fire from the Boilers* (1930), in which he attacks and expresses his resentment against the injustice of German courts. He also had a sensitive nature, which was revealed in his autobiography, *A Youth in Germany* (1933). After HITLER came to power, he fled Germany, first in Europe and then the United States. A few weeks after the German invasion of Czechoslovakia in 1939, he committed suicide by hanging in New York.

Toller was the leading Communist among the expressionist dramatists and belonged to the wing of EXPRESSIONISM that believed in pragmatic social reformation. Toller's first play, *The Transfiguration (Die Wandlung)* (1919), was written while he was in jail during 1918. The play was performed at the Tribüne theater in BERLIN in 1919. It was groundbreaking for the new style. As an expressionist production, the realistic representation of space found in naturalistic theater and the illusions and decorative sets were abandoned. Ideas were expressed by the symbolic use of space onstage and discontinuous episodic action. The plot of the play was autobiographical. Toller indicates the distance he had come from when the central figure, a young sculptor, becomes disillusioned with the war once he hears a nurse rejoice over a military victory that had cost 10,000 lives. The sculptor destroys the patriotic statue he has carved and decides to lead the masses in a revolution. The play employed the expressionist "speaking chorus" as well as the assistance of music and poetic speech. In his dramas heroes and heroines were submerged among the nameless masses, distinguished only by their professions. Many of his scenes were dreamlike projections on the borderline between reality and unreality.

Very successful was *Man and the Masses (Masse Mensch,* 1920), which explored the fundamentally important problems that are likely to arise between revolutionary leaders and their followers; it expresses Toller's doubts about the desirability of the dictatorship of the masses. The subject of *The Machine Wreckers (Die Maschinenstürmer,* 1922) is the English Luddite riots of 1812, when workers destroyed their machines. The hero of the play is an idealistic worker, Jim Cobbett, who is murdered by the mob when he tries to stop them from wrecking the machines. Here Toller repeats the expressionists' belief that machines destroy men's souls. The play presents an interesting contrast with an earlier play by Gerhart HAUPTMANN, *The Weavers* (1892), which approved of the destruction of machines by the workers.

Treitschke, Heinrich von (1834–1896)
historian

The historian and political publicist Heinrich von Treitschke was the most influential member of the Prussian school of history. He advocated a powerful state under Prussian leadership.

Born in DRESDEN on September 15, 1834, Heinrich von Treitschke was the son of a Saxon general who was ennobled in 1821. Showing academic promise, Heinrich was exposed to a traditional classical education—German literature, history and political economy, and philosophy—between 1851 to 1854 at the universities of BONN, LEIPZIG, Tübingen, and Freiburg.

He had always been a Prussophile. In the early stages of his career he was a strong Liberal, advocating a united Germany under a parliamentary and constitutional monarchy. At first he was opposed to BISMARCK's domestic policies, but after PRUSSIA defeated AUSTRIA in the Austro-Prussian War of 1866, Treitschke like so many other Liberals had a change of heart. His liberal principles became overwhelmed by his growing narrow-minded NATIONALISM. As a publicist he now became famous, and he was offered positions at Kiel and HEIDELBERG and finally at BERLIN, where he remained. His strong Prussian sentiments earned him the appointment as editor of the important historical journal *Prussian Annals,* and election to the German REICHSTAG in 1871. At first he had belonged to the NATIONAL LIBERAL PARTY, but resigned in 1879 to support Bismarck's protectionist commercial policy and held his seat until 1884 as an independent.

Treitschke's masterly multivolume *The History of Germany in the Nineteenth Century* made his reputation. He used only the Prussian archives, and it was beautifully written, but intensely nationalistic. He often oversimplified events, but he also was able to synthesize, which resulted in a unique general cultural history. His works have vivid and dramatic descriptions of historical events. In his writings and politics he became a leading propagandist for Prussian dominance in Germany. Other publications included *Historical and Political Essays* (1896) and his lectures on politics in *Politics* (1898).

Treitschke saw Germany as a vulnerable nation without the self-assurance or history of France or Great Britain. So like a youth Germany needed to be protected from harmful and immoral influences, which he described at different times as Catholicism, French culture, organized labor, the south German states, Austria, or the Jews. Since he had among his close friends a number of Jews, as did the contemporary composer Richard WAGNER, he was sympathetic toward them. A change took place in the 1870s, when Treitschke started to participate in the anti-Semitic movement. The famous historian now described the Jews as dangerous and as the embodiment of modern trends. He criticized their materialism, penchant for criticism, the liberal and democratic tendencies, and their cleverness. All of these characteristics supposedly stemmed from the rootlessness of modern Jews. Even if Jews were secularized but had a residual attachment to Judaism, they were not committed to the "German spirit." Although he had defended Jewish emancipation, he admonished Jews to become "fully German." His anti-Semitic essay published in the *Prussian Annals* was "A Word about Our Jews," (1879–80).

Treitschke died on April 28, 1896, in BERLIN.

Trott zu Solz, Adam von (1909–1944)
Foreign Office official in the Resistance

One of the more important figures in the RESISTANCE against HITLER, Adam von Trott zu Solz was the son of a former Prussian minister of education who also had an American grandmother. He was descended from the cosmopolitan and tolerant Hessian bureaucratic patriciate, received his education at two Gymnasiums, studied abroad as a Rhodes Scholar, developed friendships with foreigners and Jews, and had a positive attitude toward socialism, all of which motivated him to distrust Nazi doctrines. When Hitler became chancellor, Trott decided to resist the new regime. He refused to join the NAZI PARTY and did not enter government service until the outbreak of WORLD WAR II. He continued his contacts with Communists and Socialists. Yet, other evidence suggests that until war broke out he still felt duty-bound as a German to defend Nazism's attempt to rebuild Germany. He found its egalitarianism attractive and resented the criticism of foreigners, especially the English, whom he thought were hypocritical.

Trott was among those who tried to warn foreign governments of Hitler's intentions through clandestine contacts. Trott's efforts need to be seen in the context of attempts by other leaders of the Resistance, such as General BECK and Undersecretary of State Baron von WEIZSÄCKER, who were involved in several missions to London and Paris to get the western powers to resist Hitler's aggressiveness during the Sudeten crisis. Britain and France had given in so often to Hitler's revisionist foreign policy until the occupation of Prague on March 15, 1939, that members of the Resistance despaired of finding outside support. Yet Trott continued these efforts in June 1939, when he had interviews with the British foreign minister, Lord Halifax, and Prime Minister Neville Chamberlain with the goal of avoiding war and getting support for the military Resistance, but to no avail. After the invasion of Poland in October 1939, he traveled to the United States and participated in a conference at Virginia Beach with the goal of establishing contacts for the German Resistance. As expected, once the war began Resistance efforts became more complicated. The overthrow of Hitler might lead to Germany's defeat, making it difficult to get the German military to support a coup, without which one was impossible. Trott further believed that Germany's defeat and subjugation would make the realization of his ideas on a new international order impossible.

After the war began, the principal objective of the clandestine contacts with the Allies changed to securing favorable conditions of peace for a government of the Resistance after the overthrow of the Nazi regime. Trott made a number of trips abroad, one to the United States and neutral countries to obtain a clear idea of western war aims. His position in the Foreign Office from June 1940 onward provided cover for his efforts. In April 1942 Trott and other conspirators prepared a memorandum for Sir Stafford Cripps, Lord Privy Seal, and to Prime Minister Churchill, which sought acceptable peace terms and stated that it was in the interest of the Allies that an internal revolt take place instead of the victory of the Soviet Union. Trott did not know that Churchill had already decided to follow a policy of absolute silence so as not to disturb Britain's alliances with the Soviet Union (concluded in July 1941 after the German invasion) and the United States. Nonetheless, in 1943 and 1944 during trips to Switzerland and Sweden, Trott continued to plead for encouragement and support for the Resistance.

Between 1940 and 1943 Trott was a member of the KREISAU CIRCLE, which was discussing a number of proposals for the post-Hitler era. Trott was the foremost exponent of European internationalism, believing that NATIONALISM had become outmoded. These ideas influenced the Conservatives in the opposition to change their expectations of Germany's future, while on the other hand Trott zu Solz became more nationalistic and was concerned about Germany's future frontiers. Without any response from the Allies and Germany's defeat becoming inevitable, Trott believed that the Resistance had to act and attempt a coup in order to prove to the world that a resistance truly existed. When the July 20 plot failed, Trott was arrested, sentenced to death, and executed on August 26, 1944.

U

Ulbricht, Walter (1893–1973)
German communist politician

Walter Ulbricht, who ruled East Germany until 1971, was the most important German Marxist since Karl MARX. He succeeded in creating a fairly strong economy in East Germany and weathered many political storms.

On June 30, 1893, Walter Ulbricht was born into a poor, militantly socialist working-class family in LEIPZIG, joining the SOCIAL DEMOCRATIC PARTY (SPD) in 1912. During WORLD WAR I he was alienated from the moderate socialist party because of its support of the IMPERIAL GERMAN government. He believed that the capitalist system was based on inequality and economic exploitation, and that capitalism made the rivalries of the great powers and wars inevitable. Arrested for desertion twice, he regarded the recent revolution in Russia as the best model for radical change in Germany. The GERMAN COMMUNIST PARTY (KPD) had been founded in December 1918. Although Germany had no Communist revolution in 1918, Ulbricht joined the radical Spartacus group, which made a premature attempt to overthrow the SPD provisional government in January 1919. The rebels were brutally repressed, leading to the murder of Communist Party leaders Karl LIEBKNECHT and Rosa LUXEMBURG. Spartacus dissolved, and Ulbricht went to Leipzig as an organizer for the KPD, where he displayed remarkable talent and energy. During the 1920s he was invited to attend the Fourth Congress of the Communist International in 1922 in Moscow, where he subsequently received training.

By the late 1920s the KPD had become the tool of the ruthless successor to Lenin, Joseph Stalin. The party was organized into small cells, and Ulbricht was able to stop opposition to his efforts to obediently follow the directions of the Soviet Communist Party. Becoming a candidate in the REICHSTAG elections of 1928, he was returned to the Reichstag. Instead of cooperating with the Social Democrats (SPD), Ulbricht labelled them a "Social Fascist" organization. In the years before the Nazi takeover, the KPD believed that the middle-class democracy of the WEIMAR REPUBLIC would end in chaos and a Communist revolutionary takeover. To that end the Communists even cooperated with the Nazis in opposing the policies of the republic. When the Nazis won the struggle and Hitler was made chancellor in January 1933, the Nazi terror eliminated Ernst THÄLMANN, the party leader, imprisoned party members, and suppressed the party. Ulbricht escaped to Paris, where he continued to follow Stalinist policies. He even had another German Communist shot for refusing to denounce anti-Stalinist Communists in the underground party and cooperated with the Soviet Secret Police in ferreting out German and Austrian anti-Stalinists fighting in the Spanish civil war.

In 1938 Ulbricht moved to Moscow, where he was the tool of Stalinist policies. He supported the purges of the German Communist Party, especially between 1939 and 1941, when the Soviets handed over to the GESTAPO many German Communists who died in CONCENTRATION CAMPS. Chosen by Stalin to return to Germany in 1945, Ulbricht helped establish the Russian occupation. In April 1946 he along with Wilhelm

PIECK and other Communists helped merge the old SPD and KPD in the Soviet zone of occupation into the Soviet Unity Party (SED). The program of the SED espoused democracy for Germany, but under the influence of the occupying Soviets the Social Democrats lost any influence. The Soviets carried out land reform, confiscating thousands of Prussian aristocratic estates. DENAZIFICATION took place more rapidly than in the Western occupation zones, and educational reforms opened up opportunities to workers and farmers. Until 1949 it was not clear that two German states would be established. Soviet policy exploited its zone economically as reparations for the destruction of the war. Some weeks after the FEDERAL REPUBLIC of Germany (FRG) was created out of the Western occupation zones, a republic was established for East Germany called the GERMAN DEMOCRATIC REPUBLIC (GDR) on October 7, 1949.

In 1950 Ulbricht was elected general secretary of the Central Committee of the SED, which placed him in control of the political system. A harsh economic and political system resulted, modeled after the Stalinist regime. Economic conditions were terrible as much of East Germany's industrial plant lay in ruins or was exported to Russia, and raw materials and fuel were in short supply. The harshness of these conditions led to the worker's uprising of June 17, 1953, threatening the regime, which was saved only by the intervention of Soviet troops. From 1949 some 2,600,000 East Germans fled to the West. To stop this hemorrhage, Ulbricht decided in 1961 to build a wall around West Berlin to prevent East Germans from fleeing. Skilled workers now could no longer flee, and so contributed increasingly to building up the economy. By 1969 the GDR's industrial production had quadrupled, and it became second only to the Soviet Union. Ulbricht also promoted superb musical performances of world-renowned symphony orchestras of BERLIN, Leipzig, and DRESDEN. In theater the plays of Bertolt BRECHT were staged by the Berlin Ensemble. In sports, however, the GDR always excelled at the OLYMPIC GAMES. Ulbricht's hard-line orthodoxy did not produce blood purges as elsewhere, but dissidents were periodically "cleansed." The secret police (STAZI), which promoted extensive spying on fellow East Germans, also helped keep people fearful and in line.

When the economy of the GDR began to falter, Ulbricht was forced to resign in May 1971, succeeded by Erich HONECKER and a younger generation of leaders. More important, Ulbricht's Stalinist policies no longer were in favor with the Soviet leadership, which was now interested in opportunities of pursuing a policy of DÉTENTE in Central Europe, made possible by West German chancellor Willy BRANDT's new Eastern policy of OSTPOLITIK. After a stroke, Ulbricht died on August 1, 1973, in Berlin. He had thought of himself as a "little Lenin," a leader who showed no interest in luxuries, had little desire to contact relatives but was successful in creating a socialist society in at least part of Germany. Because of his longevity and political skill he has been described as the "last Bolshevik."

Versailles, Treaty of (1919)
The Treaty of Versailles was the major treaty that brought WORLD WAR I to an end, reorganized European boundaries according to the goals of the victorious Allies, and established the LEAGUE OF NATIONS. The treaty also included a clause by which Germany acknowledged responsibility for the war. Germany also had to accept the practical elimination of its military, as well as colonial, European, territorial, and population losses and economic reparations.

As the French premier, Georges Clemenceau, complained during the Paris Peace Conference in 1919 "it is much easier to make war than peace." That turned out to be the case as the victors of World War I, principally Britain, France, Italy, and the United States attempted to formulate the terms of the peace. The major decisions were made by the great powers, and some 20 other nations in attendance had little input. Germany was prohibited from participation in the discussions, which was a fundamental difference from the 1815 CONGRESS OF VIENNA, at which defeated France was allowed a prominent role in the peace settlement. That was not to be the case. Germany was forced to accept the peace treaty, and even moderate German opinion was so outraged that the treaty was considered a dictated one, the *Versailler Diktat*.

On May 7, 1919, the publication of the peace treaty shocked Germans like a thunderbolt. They had surrendered believing that the peace would be based on the Fourteen Points of the American president, Woodrow Wilson, only to receive a demand that rejected the spirit of Wilson's promises. The treaty required the loss of ALSACE-LORRAINE (taken from France by Germany after the Franco-Prussian War) to France, a few towns to Belgium, most of Posen and West Prussia, and all of the former colonial possessions. Furthermore, both the SAARLAND in the west and Upper Silesia (an important industrial center) to the east would be at least temporarily detached from Germany and their futures determined by plebiscites to be held under the supervision of the League of Nations. When the plebiscite did take place in Upper Silesia, resulting in a majority favoring Germany, the league violated the principle of self-determination and split the territory with Poland. The most northern German city, Memel, was awarded to the republic of Lithuania. The plebiscitory process did rightfully return the northwestern area of Schleswig to Denmark. The left bank of the RHINE was occupied by Allied troops and not evacuated for 15 years. While many of the territorial losses of Germany could be justified in nation-building (especially Poland and Czechoslovakia) in Eastern Europe, many Germans living in the lost areas lost their right to self-determination, which President Wilson had so loudly promised. The Germans were understandably angry over the creation of the Polish Corridor, which separated East Prussia from the rest of the Reich. The predominantly German city of DANZIG in East Prussia was declared a "free city." That is not to say a fairer way could have been found to establish the new states and realize the rights of other nationalities to have a nation-state. The peace makers had to consider factors other than ethnicity, factors that would make the new states economically viable. Nonetheless, as it turned out, the resentments aroused by these territorial arrangements would do much to make Europe unstable and eventually shatter the peace.

The treaty also called for the destruction of the German military. It was forbidden to possess large artillery and only a limited number of smaller ones. Tanks and military aircraft were prohibited. Fortifications in the occupied Rhineland zones had to be dismantled. In deference to the United States the Germans were forbidden to possess even one submarine, while in deference to the British only six warships and some smaller craft were allowed. The German army was to be reduced to a maximum strength of 100,000 men, including 4,000 officers. Germany also was forbidden to introduce conscription as the Prussians had done under Napoleon's rule because of the fear that a large army of trained men might be formed. This was an unwise decision because it resulted in a German army of elite professional soldiers who were loyal only to their commanders and their views of NATIONALISM. The hopes that German liberals had for a more democratically oriented army were thus disappointed, and the power of the officer corps remained intact.

In Article 231 of the treaty the victors required the Germans to accept full guilt for the outbreak of the war and consequently to be liable and pay compensation for all damage to civilians, mines, farms, and other infrastructure, as well as the cost of the armies of occupation. All German property in the Allied countries had to be sold for the benefit of the victors. The Allies forced the Germans to turn over all German merchant ships over 1,600 tons and half of those over 800, and one-fourth of the fishing fleet. The Germans were also to build for the Allies 200,000 tons of shipping annually. Large quantities of coal had to be delivered to France, Belgium, and Italy during the next 10 years. Germans had to internationalize their rivers and allow Allied warships to pass through the Kiel Canal. The sum of all goods the Germans had to deliver by March 1, 1921, amounted to 20 billion in gold marks. This was, however, only the beginning of war reparations and a total bill for 833 billion or 132 billion gold marks. This amount was scaled down throughout the 1920s by the DAWES PLAN (1924) and the YOUNG PLAN (1929) with Germany paying only about $4.5 billion, much of which was actually loaned to the Germans by American banks. The sum was actually less than the amount of indemnity the French had to pay to Germany after the Franco-Prussian War of 1870–71 and four times the amount of post–WORLD WAR II MARSHALL PLAN assistance given West Germany from 1948 to 1952. Nonetheless, the whole reparations issue caused much political turmoil in Germany after World War I and debate ever since by historians as to its impact.

Vienna (city)

Vienna is a city located on the Danube River near the northeastern corner of the modern state of Austria. It was a very important city during the HOLY ROMAN EMPIRE, the residence of the emperors of Austria since 1806 and the capital of the Federal State of Austria since 1918.

Vienna originated during the Roman Empire as the frontier fortress of Vindobona and the name of *Wenia* appeared for the first time in the Salzburg *Annals*. After centuries of slow growth the town was chartered in 1137. From 1156 until 1246 the dukes of Babenberg made Vienna their capital and in 1208 Leopold VI of the Babenberg family proclaimed himself the duke of Austria and Styria. After 1278 Vienna became the official seat of the Habsburgs and from 1438 to 1918 the capital of the Habsburg emperors. In 1279 the Habsburgs began to construct their Hofburg palace and the University of Vienna was founded in 1365 by Emperor Rudolf I of Habsburg who renewed the city's privileges as an imperial city and granted trading privileges to foreign merchants enhancing the city's commercial life. He also initiated the rebuilding of St. Stephen's Cathedral in the Gothic style.

Although other cities such as Prague and Graz were favored by some Habsburgs, during the Renaissance Emperor MAXIMILIAN I made Vienna the administrative capital of Lower Austria. Emperor MAXIMILIAN II lived in the city from 1564 to 1576 and Emperor FERDINAND II (1619–1637) moved the chancellery to Vienna from Prague. Threats to the city's existence took place during the two Turkish sieges, the first in 1529 and the second in 1683. Vienna was saved from any serious damage during the THIRTY YEARS' WAR, but like other cities was afflicted by a plague in 1679. Yet, the city lived on as one of the great cities of the Holy Roman Empire and the capital of the Habsburg's Danubian empire. Emperor Leopold (1685–1705) made extensive contributions to Vienna's cultural heritage. His deep interest in music made Vienna a leading center for composers in the city which included BEETHOVEN, HAYDN, and MOZART. The city's musical importance lasted to 1914 and further included Franz SCHUBERT, Johannes Brahms, Anton Bruchner, Gustav Mahler and Richard Strauss. Leopold also encouraged building projects which affirmed the imperial grandeur of his reign.

Vienna flourished during the 18th century and became a cosmopolitan center where architecture beautified the skyline. Vienna became an outstanding example of the late-BAROQUE style of architecture with architects Johann Bernard FISCHER VON ERLACH and Johann Lukas von HILDEBRANDT constructing magnificent palaces. These included the Schönbrunn palace for MARIA THERESA and the Belvedere for Prince EUGENE of Savoy. Other outstanding constructions during the baroque period included the beautiful Church of Saint Charles dedicated to Charles Borromeo, a principal religious leader of the Catholic Reformation. Famous palaces abounded including the Kinsky, Schwarzenberg, the Schönbrunn, the Bohemian and the Palace of the Sciences.

Besides being a center of government, Vienna also grew in economic importance. Coffee became an important commodity after the Turkish siege of 1683. Vienna became a busy port on the important Danube River. Its population grew to 100,000 in the 18th century. With the abolition of the Holy Roman Empire in 1806 Vienna became the capital of the Empire of Austria. In 1814–15 the CONGRESS OF VIENNA reflected its importance as a diplomatic center. During the Restoration Klemens von METTERNICH made Vienna the focal point of German and European politics and his reactionary policies were directed against liberals and nationalists. It also was the Biedermeier period, which was evident in Viennese middle class life. Its musical tradition continued and its literary traditions were enhanced by such novelists and dramatists as Franz Grillparzer (1791–1872), Arthur Schnitzler (1862–1931) and Hugo von Hofmannsthal (1874–1929). The early 19th century also witnessed economic development as the Danube Shipping Company was founded in 1831 and the first railway was constructed in 1837. Metternich's rule ended with the REVOLUTION OF 1848, which was ruthlessly repressed by the army. That same year the long reign of Emperor Francis Joseph (1848–1916) began. The expansion of the city occurred as outlying districts were incorporated, bringing about a population of 2,031,500 by 1910. Shortly before WORLD WAR I Vienna was the city where the young Adolf HITLER drifted and lived in a poorhouse while experiencing the rise of Austrian anti-Semitism in the contentious politics of Vienna.

After the war Austria lost its population of 50 million people from 12 different nationalities and Vienna became the capital of a small German-speaking republic. The city faced many adjustments during the republic and unemployment and distress during the DEPRESSION. A sizable number of its citizens did welcome the Nazi entry into the city in 1938 during the Anschluss. Vienna suffered from allied air raids during the war. Afterward the city was occupied and divided into four occupation zones by the Allied powers. The occupation ended with a treaty signed in 1955. The rebuilding of the destroyed areas of the city revived the beauty that it had earlier possessed. Presently, it is the headquarters of the Atomic Energy Authority (IAEA) and the Industrial Development Organization (UNIDO) of the United Nations. It also is the headquarters of the Organization of Petroleum Countries (OPEC) and the International Music Complex (UNESCO).

Völkischer Beobachter
(Racial Observer)

The *Völkischer Beobachter (VB)* was the official newspaper of the NAZI PARTY (NSDAP). Its origins go back to before WORLD WAR I to a scandal sheet called the *Münchner Beobachter (Munich Observer)*. After the war its name was changed to the *Völkischer Beobachter (Racial Observer)* to be more representative of its owner, the Thule Society, which was promoting racist ideas. By the end of 1920 the newspaper was deeply indebted, but its point of view attracted Dietrich Eckart and Ernst RÖHM, who were members of the same GERMAN WORKERS' PARTY (DAP) that HITLER had joined. Eckart, Röhm, and Major General Franz Xaver Ritter von Epp of the Reichswehr (army) raised 60,000 marks from wealthy friends and army funds. In 1921 Hitler took over the newspaper when he became leader of the new NSDAP. In 1923 with the help of a supporter, Putzi Hanfstaengel, the *VB* was made into a daily paper. The chief editor was Alfred ROSENBERG, who became the Nazi Party's philosopher. Max Amann, who was one of Hitler's earliest followers, became the party's business manager and after 1922 the director of the Eher publishing house, which published MEIN KAMPF.

The *Völkischer Beobachter* was nursed along by Eckart and Rosenberg, but as late as 1933 it only had a circulation of 127,000 which was small in comparison to the 17 million votes that the Nazis received in the March 5 election of that year. Until 1933 most of the circulation of the *VB* was confined to southern Germany, where it was published (Munich). There were other Nazi daily papers with a total circulation of 800,000, but that still accounted for one in 20 Nazi voters. Perhaps the small readership reflected the essential nature of the Nazi appeal, which was more emotional than conceptual; its emotions could be manipulated much more easily by a speaker and enthusiastic crowds than words read by a lonely reader of a newspaper. The pages of the *VB* were therefore more like the party's mass meetings and looked more like posters and front page headlines, such as calling the WEIMAR government "world champion belly crawlers."

Even so the *Völkischer Beobachter* led the growth of the Nazi press empire and Amann was to become Germany's greatest press magnate by 1942, controlling 82 percent of the country's press. It became the first national newspaper in German journalistic history, published after 1933 in both Munich and BERLIN simultaneously and in Vienna after 1938. It also was the first newspaper to top 1 million in circulation, partly due to a change in editorial policy that made it more informative and the provision of an improved news service. As unbelievable as it may seem, in a great European state, the paper lacked a single full-time correspondent in any foreign capital to match the expertise of the *London Times*. Perhaps that was reflective of the thinking of the half-educated Nazi leaders.

Volksgemeinschaft
(national community)

Hitler's ideal society was a Volksgemeinschaft, a racially homogeneous and harmonious national community. This concept of a society based on racial purity was joined by the Darwinian concept of struggle. All Germans in the Volksgemeinschaft were equal because of their Aryan blood. The Nazi ideal of community was to be based on the willingness of Germans to submerge their individual wills into a single-minded community of will that was well disciplined and obedient to the greater will of Adolf HITLER (leadership principle). The German people were expected to sacrifice their individual lives for the survival of the community.

The Nazis were not intent on creating a new social structure as were the Marxists. People were not to become socially and economically equal. Essentially, Hitler strove for a new national consciousness, which was to be inculcated through education and propaganda. In order to rid Germany of Marxism and overcome the divisions of society, Hitler aimed at simply overcoming the division between NATIONALISM and socialism with a vague concept of a "national community" based on race. In this manner nationalism and socialism would be fused into one, which would eliminate the conflict between the nationalist MIDDLE CLASS and the Marxist working class.

The appeal of Hitler's national community to the German people was rooted in a broad crisis that was afflicting the German people. The crisis was based on the shock and resentment created by the loss of WORLD WAR I, as well as the economic and social insecurity caused by the GREAT DEPRESSION. Bridging these experiences was what social scientists call the MODERNIZATION CRISIS and the shattering of traditional society and its values. The German social fabric was permeated by class conflict, alienation, rootlessness, and purposelessness. That is why Hitler often spoke of Nazism being a spiritual movement, like a new religion that could offer new meaning and purpose to life through a regeneration of the nation.

Volkssturm

The Volkssturm, People's Attack, was a militia or home guard created by HITLER near the end of the war in 1944–45. In execution of Hitler's order of September 25, 1944, all Germans from 16 to 60 were called to duty. The militia was composed of all able-bodied, mostly older, men up to the age of 60, and boys as young as 16, and maybe younger who were not already in the armed forces. It also contained men who were unfit for duty with the regular armed services. The basic unit was the battalion. In addition to these handicaps, the units were inadequately equipped. In short, it was a last-ditch effort, even though they were supposedly inspired by Nazi ideals. Units of the Volkssturm were supposed to be used in their own districts, but appeared on both the eastern and western fronts and were prominent in the final battle for BERLIN.

W

Wachenroder, Wilhelm (1773–1798)
romantic poet

Wachenroder was one of the group of early romantics who was too young to have found a position in the world before the French Revolution changed so much. This writer made his contribution to the romantic movement in the late 1790s and died prematurely at age 25. Like the other young romantics of his generation, personal relationships bound him to them, not a fixed set of ideas. For instance, Ludwig TIECK (1773–1853) and Wachenroder were the same age, were students together at the University of Erlangen, and were cooperating on a novel when the latter died.

The romantic movement (*see* ROMANTICISM) had its earliest production in the work of this sensitive young poet. *Effusions of an Art-Loving Friar* was published in 1797. The story tries to elevate reality into an artistic creation and saintly occupation. The artists of the Middle Ages who painted and built churches and artworks for the glory of God are described as divinely inspired. Wachenroder revealed his fine appreciation of art and music and contributed to the enthusiasm of others for medieval German art culture. A specific result of this book was the rediscovery of the beauty of the historic city of NUREMBERG with its wall, moats, towers, and churches. There was a personal story also involved, which linked the lives and experiences of Wachenroder and Tieck. In their student days while on a vacation trip from BERLIN, both of them visited Nuremberg, and Tieck's eyes and imagination were opened to the beauty of the artistic culture that had been produced in this imperial city.

Wagner, Richard (1813–1883)
opera composer

Richard Wagner was the most important opera composer, critic, and polemicist in the 19th century. He ruthlessly pursued his vision of creating a *Gesamtkunstwerk,* a total work of art, an organic union of music and drama. Wagner did not just link music and drama, as in BAROQUE opera, where music served mainly a decorative function with respect to the drama. He wanted to achieve an organic union in which each mode of expression retained its individuality, with no subordination of one to the other. In his great music dramas, especially in *The Ring of the Nibelungs,* both music and dramatic action carry the theme. The leitmotif is the special musical theme associated with an individual character or a dramatic idea throughout the opera. Nonetheless, music becomes the medium of the sensuous, while the drama carries the action. Wagner's musical dramas show an unmistakable romantic character; it was the dream of the romantics to combine all the arts for a common effect.

In some respects Wagner's life was like the plot of an opera. Shortly after his birth in LEIPZIG on May 22, 1813, his father died of typhus. Within the year his mother married a Ludwig Geyer, an itinerant Jewish actor and painter, and it is possible that he actually was Wagner's real father. His elder sisters were on the stage; he himself wrote poetry and horrific tragedies, as well as taking an interest in Shakespeare and ancient Greek literature. After impulsively marrying a singer-actress, Minna Planner, he fell in love with Cosima von Bulow. She was the daughter of Franz LISZT and wife of Hans von Bulow. In a drama worthy of any opera, Cosima gave birth to two of Wagner's children while still married to Hans. After Minna's death, Wagner married Cosima.

His musical training was a haphazard affair, but he was determined to become a composer to provide appropriate music for his dramatic work. He never desired to become competent on the keyboard, but nonetheless he did obtain some sound instruction for a year at the Thomaskirche in Leipzig. Wagner then began his career in 1833 with a series of appointments, beginning in Würzburg and ending up in Riga until 1839, when he decided to try his luck in Paris. There he hoped to launch *Rienzi,* hoping it would be a great success. Wagner, supreme egotist that he was, took the view that the world should be grateful and provide him with both the necessities and luxuries of life. Paris was a failure, and he left with a lifelong hatred for French musical culture. He participated in the REVOLUTION OF 1848 and had to flee from DRESDEN to Switzerland to escape arrest and was not allowed to reenter Germany and participate in its musical life until 1860. During this time, however, he composed much of the material for which he became famous. Later, he was befriended and patronized by the king of Bavaria, LUDWIG II, who rescued Wagner from debtor's prison and brought him to MUNICH. Ludwig encouraged him to begin *Parsifal,* and *Die Meistersinger* was first performed in Munich in 1867. Wagner was a supremely self-centered person, offensive to those around him and intolerant of any criticisms of his creations. So it is not surprising that after two years in Munich he was forced to leave. In 1876 his benefactor, Ludwig, made possible the performances of the *Ring* in BAYREUTH.

Wagner was a true revolutionary in the world of music; in fact, he became the founder of a cult. He attempted to teach a philosophy of life in the *Ring Cycle* (*Rheingold, Walküre, Siegfried,* and *Götterdammerung*), which was performed at the opera house (Festspielhaus) in Bayreuth. The ideas that Wagner wished to present were, or so he thought, new ideas of morality and human activity that would regenerate the human race, freeing humanity from slavery to the supernatural. Fear needed to be purged and in the *Ring Cycle* he presented standards for superior humans who would dominate lesser mortals. Only by submitting to sensuousness could individuals liberate themselves from rationalism. The perfect heroes are Siegfried and Brünnhilde, who are invincible, who become the superior ones to whom other average persons must submit. Wagner rejected the civility of the dominant Western moral values and turned to the strength and savagery of the Norse sagas. The myths of the *Ring Cycle* were really intended to express disillusionment with intellectual progress and contempt for the capitalistic and materialistic MIDDLE CLASS.

In Wagner German ROMANTICISM reached its climax. He became its arch-priest, in whom the genius of the theater reached its peak, and the artist had broken away from both social and moral conventions, freeing himself from bourgeois sentimentalism and from popular styles. Wagner's work was a tour de force of an artistic personality and a great showman. He wrote the words, composed the music, created the scenery, trained the singers, staged the whole production, and supervised the performances of his operas.

Wagner believed that the German people would be transformed by their racial myths, that it was a source of spiritual energy. He was influenced by the Frenchman Count Gobineau, who believed that race was continually subject to bastardization through the influx of alien racial (*see* RACIALISM) elements. Wagner wrote two essays criticizing the Jews, one in 1850 and the other in 1869. Because all art, for Wagner, was rooted in the VOLK, the Jews, who were foreigners, could not possibly be artistically creative. He thought that the Jews were undermining German culture and denied the validity of Jewish participation in German cultural life. Wagner was an inspiration for anti-Semites but did not support the anti-Semitic political parties that organized in the 1880s.

Wallenstein, Albrecht Eusebius Wenzel von (1583–1634)
Imperial general

A Bohemian general who led the Habsburg armies during the first half of the THIRTY YEARS'

WAR and one of the most controversial leaders in German history before Otto von BISMARCK, Wallenstein has been considered the first German nationalist by some, a great Czech nationalist by others, a mercenary captain, and even a traitor. Born on September 24, 1583, into the family of Wilhelm von Waldstein of the Bohemian Protestant gentry, he was orphaned in 1595. After attending Latin schools and university, the ambitious young man converted to Catholicism in 1602, married an aged widow, and as expected became a wealthy estate owner after her death. In 1615 Wallenstein was made the chamberlain of Archduke Ferdinand of Styria.

After gaining military experience in the Turkish wars and in Moravia, he militarily supported the Archduke Ferdinand and the Emperor Matthias against the Protestant Bohemian revolt, which broke out with the DEFENESTRATION OF PRAGUE (1618). In 1620 his troops played a significant role in the Battle of White Mountain (1620), which ended the Bohemian revolt. He became the commandant and subsequently commander of the Imperial armies. Shrewdly expanding and managing his holdings, he came to control nearly one-quarter of the territory of Bohemia. After the death of Emperor Matthias, Wallenstein lent considerable sums of money to the new emperor FERDINAND II. Wallenstein was rewarded with offices and titles, including governor of Bohemia, duke of Friedland in 1625, and in 1629 after victories in northern Germany, duke of Mecklenburg. The costs of Wallenstein's huge army, his opposition to the extremes of the Edict of Restitution (1629), and the threat he posed to their positions motivated the Imperial electors to demand of the emperor his dismissal in 1630. This restored the cooperative relationship between the emperor and his Catholic allies. With the invasion of Germany by a Swedish army under Gustavus Adolphus and the disastrous defeat of Imperial forces at the Battle of Breitenfeld (1631) north of LEIPZIG, Wallenstein was recalled in 1631. Out of his resentments and determination to gain the upper hand, he received from the emperor complete military authority and the right to negotiate with the enemy. The Swedes, however, were victorious over Catholic forces under General Johann Tilly, and at the Battle of Lutzen (1632) defeated Wallenstein's forces. At this juncture Wallenstein negotiated with the Protestant allies, bargaining at one time or other with Sweden, BRANDENBURG, and SAXONY, which led to the variety of interpretations of his motives. The huge costs of the generalissimo's army, his erratic performance and lack of decisive success, and accusations of treason led the emperor Ferdinand II to dismiss him in late 1633. When he refused to resign, an arrest warrant was issued, and officers murdered him on February 25, 1634.

Wannsee Conference (January 20, 1942)

At this momentous conference the decision to implement the FINAL SOLUTION to the Jewish question was officially made. The purpose of the conference was to ensure the smooth cooperation of the bureaucracy in the implementation of the plan.

Fifteen high-ranking officials of the NAZI PARTY, the GESTAPO, and the ministries of the German government were summoned to a villa in BERLIN by the notorious Reinhard HEYDRICH, head of the RSHA (Reich Security Main Office), who had been commissioned to make preparations for the execution of the Final Solution. Attached to the letters of invitation were copies of the letter by Herman GÖRING dated July 31, 1941, authorizing a more formal plan for the persecution and execution of the Jews that had begun years before. Heydrich outlined the general procedures for the Final Solution. He emphasized that the policy of trying to "solve the Jewish question," through other means, including emigration, had to be changed due to the war and the "possibilities in the east." After a statistical review of the Jews throughout Europe totaling 11 million, Heydrich expected that even the Jews of England and Ireland would eventually be transported to transit ghettos and then resettlement to the East.

The deliberations of the meeting were recorded in a protocol written by Adolf EICH-

MANN, with editorial modifications made by Heydrich. The protocol issued by the conference stated that "within the context of the final solution to the Jewish question, Jews will be put to work in the East in a suitable manner" which "would undoubtedly lead to great natural reduction in their numbers. Those who remain, who will be the most physically fit and represent the result of natural selection, must be given special treatment so that they will not be able to produce a new generation of Jews."

Those present did not always agree, and they varied in their culpability. For instance, Dr. Friedrich Kritzinger, state secretary of the Reich Chancellery, seemed appalled by the enormity of the proposed genocide, and he had to be threatened with death before he approved. Another participant, Dr. Wilhelm Stuckart, a high-ranking Reich official who authored the NUREMBERG LAWS was concerned the plan was illegal and argued instead for the sterilization of the Jews.

One of the issues that caused disagreement was Heydrich's attempt to modify the definition of a "Jew" in the Nuremberg Laws. He wanted to include in the Final Solution those previously exempted persons of a mixed racial background and those of mixed marriages. The practice of the SS already had not made distinctions in its efforts to rid eastern Europe of the Jews. After a long debate it was decided that the Nuremberg Laws would apply only within Germany, consequently making all persons outside Germany with any Jewish racial heritage subject to death, while those of mixed marriages had the choices of divorce, sterilization, or deportation.

Warburg, Max M. (1867–1946)
financier

Max Warburg was the director of the largest private bank in Germany from 1896 to 1938. He turned the family's bank, M. M. Warburg, into the leading private bank in HAMBURG. The bank was involved in the financing of industry, and Warburg and his partners were directors on the boards of 80 corporations in the 1920s. American capital flowed into Germany during the WEIMAR era through his bank.

Max Warburg was born into an upper-class Jewish family. One of his brothers, Felix (the other was Paul), married the daughter of Jakob H. Schiff, who was head of the banking firm Kuhn, Loeb & Co. of New York. Upon going to New York, Felix became wealthy, an elegant man of the world with his own racehorses. Soon he became a dedicated champion of the rights of the underprivileged and promoter of youth welfare and hospital care. He assisted Jewish immigrants to America and Palestine. In the meantime, Max Warburg was perhaps both honored and unfortunate to become a delegate to the Paris Peace Conference. Because the TREATY OF VERSAILLES was so punitive against Germany, and even though he rejected the treaty, anti-Semites blamed him for it. In the 1920s the Warburg bank played an essential role in transferring much-needed American capital into Germany. Max Warburg was honored with a seat on the board of directors of the Central Bank (Reichsbank). Because of the anti-Semitic atmosphere, he refused several offers of cabinet posts in the republican government but suffered as an object of anti-Semitic hatred.

The Hamburg bank declined during the GREAT DEPRESSION, losing some two-thirds of its clients, almost failed but was saved with the help of Warburg's brothers. After HITLER came to power, Max Warburg was protected until 1938 by Hjalmar SCHACHT. Two private Jewish-owned banks in Hamburg, the M. M. Warburg and Mendelssohn houses, were among the last Jewish enterprises to be taken over by the Nazis because they helped finance Hamburg's export trade and generated foreign exchange for the Reich. Also, the Warburg bank was part of a consortium of banks that floated loans for the government. In the meantime, Warburg helped finance Jewish emigration, although at the same time he encouraged Jews to stay and fight. After Schacht fell from favor with the Nazis in 1938, the Warburg bank lost its position in the government loan consortium. The Nazis demanded its liquidation, and the takeover of the bank was directed by Hermann GÖRING.

Max Warburg then immigrated to New York, where he died in 1946.

Warsaw Pact
The Warsaw Pact was the military alliance that united the Soviet Union and the other Communist states of Eastern Europe and subordinated their armed forces to Moscow. The Warsaw Pact was intended to counterbalance the western NORTH ATLANTIC TREATY ORGANIZATION (NATO). On May 14, 1955, East Germany was included as a charter member. In 1990 the GDR left the Warsaw Pact and the following year the remaining members dissolved it.

The Warsaw Pact precluded participation of its members in any other coalition or alliance and assured members of immediate assistance, including the use of armed force, in the event of armed aggression. For this purpose it created a joint command for the armed forces of the members, as well as a consultative committee to harmonize political action. The stationing of Russian troops in Eastern European countries, notably in Romania, Hungary, Poland, and East Germany, which until then had been justified by the need to maintain communications with the Russian occupation zones in Germany and AUSTRIA, was now guaranteed by bilateral treaties. The Warsaw Pact did not only have the purpose of strengthening military cooperation against the West, the Russians were also anxious to counteract the dangers of lessening of tension and the centrifugal consequences of greater economic autonomy in the satellite countries.

By a special announcement following the conclusion of the conference establishing the Warsaw Pact, the Russians declared that the supreme commander of the United Armed Forces should always be a Soviet officer, holding at the same time the office of the first deputy minister of defense of the USSR. The supreme commander was supported by a staff of the United Supreme Command, consisting of officers from all armies of the pact. The post of the chief of staff was always to be held by a Soviet officer.

At the time of the signing on May 14, 1955, the pact was apparently intended to regulate the relations of the Soviet Union to some of the satellites rather than to be used as the means of political and military integration of East Germany. The Soviets were required to withdraw from Austria after the signing of the Austrian State Treaty became valid, but also to withdraw from Hungary and Romania since their presence was only to maintain communications and supply lines to Soviet occupation troops in Austria. The Warsaw Pact enabled the Soviet Union to keep troops and commands in all satellite states, even in Czechoslovakia, where it had none, and in Poland, where it had only small units. After the revolutionary events in Poland and Hungary in autumn 1956, the Soviets used the Warsaw Pact not only as a political forum, but also as an institution to control the armed forces of its satellites.

Wartburg, The (castle)
The Wartburg was a 12th-century castle near Eisenach in Thuringia. It was the seat of the Landgrafen von Thüringen for three centuries and the scene of the childhood and married life of St. Elizabeth. The legendary contest of the Minnesänger is said to have taken place in the hall of the castle.

The poet Conrad Ferdinand Meyer wrote of Martin LUTHER's stay in the Wartburg from 1521 to 1522: "Concealed in a castle with greenery covered, the Bible and German thou hast discovered," concerning his translation of the New Testament into German. Not long thereafter Luther translated the whole Bible (1534), which decisively influenced the development of the German literary language.

Martin Luther's works, especially his Lutheran hymnbook, had a major impact on the development of German music as well. Johann Sebastian BACH was also strongly influenced by Luther. The Wartburg also played an important cultural role both before and after Luther. Around 1200 Landgrave Herman of Thuringia made it a gathering place for poets and singers. This fact formed the background for Richard WAGNER's opera *Tannhäuser*. The Hungarian-born landgravine Elizabeth, daughter-in-law of Landgrave Hermann, was canonized by the

Catholic Church. Inspired by a fresco cycle in the Wartburg, Wagner's Hungarian-born father-in-law, Franz LISZT, composed the *Legend of St. Elizabeth.*

In the year 1817 on the occasion of the 300th anniversary of the nailing of Luther's theses to the door of the church in Wittenberg, the Wartburg was the scene of a protest by students from JENA against militarism and the lack of freedom and for freedom and unity in Germany. The student movement of that time played a major role in the events leading up to the abortive German REVOLUTION OF 1848.

Waterloo, Battle of (June 18, 1815)

The Battle of Waterloo was one of the most famous in the history of warfare. The final defeat of the French ended the Napoleonic era. The battle occurred after Napoleon escaped in February 1815 from Elba and rallied the French people, organizing an army of some 280,000 men. In early June Napoleon moved his forces into the Low Countries, hoping to engage Lord Wellington and the Prussian general Gebhard BLÜCHER. Having superiority in troops and artillery, Napoleon first defeated Blücher's Prussian army at Ligny on June 16. Napoleon then turned against Wellington, their armies meeting on June 18, the French using fierce frontal attacks forcing their way through to Brussels, which was 11 miles to the north. The battle went on all day along a quarter-mile front between the village of La Belle Alliance and the ridge of Mont Saint Jean just south of Waterloo. The British infantry repulsed the French attacks and advanced on the French in the evening. The Prussians regrouped and rallied after the defeat at Ligny and during the afternoon came to the aid of the British. Blücher's cavalry routed the retreating French. The French army then disintegrated, and Napoleon abdicated four days afterward.

Weber, Max (1864–1920)

social scientist and economist

Max Weber was one of the founders of modern sociology. He became famous for his historical and comparative studies of great civilizations. In contrast to the economic theories of Karl MARX, he explained the rise of modern capitalism in the context of the Calvinist ethics of PROTESTANTISM.

Max Weber was born in Erfaut, Thuringia, on April 21, 1864, the son of a lawyer. Intellectually gifted, he read widely and attended the University of HEIDELBERG, studying history, economics, philosophy, and the law. Later, at the universities of BERLIN and GÖTTINGEN he studied jurisprudence, which led to a law degree in 1886. For his doctorate he wrote two studies, one a thesis and the other for the "habilitation" on legal, economic, and cultural history. In 1893 he married, then was appointed a professor of economics at Freiburg and in 1896 accepted a professorship at Heidelberg.

One of Weber's great contributions to the study of society was his development of an analytical method that was different from that of the popular philosopher Georg Wilhelm Friedrich HEGEL and the materialist Karl Marx. Weber went beyond their versions of historical development toward a deeper historical and comparative study of sociocultural processes in Western and Eastern civilizations. Some of his theories were explained in a classic of modern sociology, *Economy and Society,* which contains a wide range of comparative historical materials. Weber was concerned with processes of group formation, which included social classes, based on material interest. In *The Protestant Ethic and the Spirit of Capitalism* he linked the rise of modern capitalism with the religious ethics of Protestantism, especially Calvinism (*see* CALVIN, JOHN). Weber tried to show how irrational religious beliefs could influence rational social behavior. Christianity as interpreted by Calvinism developed a psychology within the rational framework of one's vocation, or "calling," which promoted an acquisitive activism along with rational calculation, both of which are characteristics of capitalism. The idea of a "calling" also constituted the chief rational framework through which people in Western civilization in modern times achieved success in the field of economics and science. In Calvinism the achievement of God's glory became transformed into a rational dynamic in a vocation, particularly when it was secular. Weber interpreted the relationship between irrational motives (beliefs) and economic rational ones differently from Karl Marx. Marxism insisted on the primacy of the material economic bases of society and asserted that religion was an ideological superstructure based on it. Weber did not think that a rational order was inherent in the universe and manifested itself in society or the state and gave expression to natural law and natural rights. Weber emphasized functional rationalism and "ideal types."

Weber analyzed power politics as constitutional issues. He was both a monarchist and at the turn of the 20th century one of Germany's most influential and representative liberals. Like Friedrich NAUMANN, he was very insightful of the shortcomings of the Empire, was critical of both the Kaiser and the German people, and understood the need to modernize Germany's political and social structure. The advancement of Germany as a power state (*Machtstaat*), however, was foundational to his political thought and even survived WORLD WAR I. Even though he quit the organization, Weber had been a member of the PAN-GERMAN LEAGUE, and believed that the Germans had the right to expand the German character of their Polish provinces. His nationalistic spirit was so strong and his passion for the German power state so instinctual that it was not open to rational criticism.

After the war he devoted his energies to anchoring parliamentary democracy in Germany. Along with Friedrich Naumann he joined the liberal GERMAN DEMOCRATIC PARTY (DDP), and sat on the committee that drafted the WEIMAR CONSTITUTION, and supported the popular election of the president, which was much more democratic than in the United States. Unfortunately, when it was combined with Article 48, which gave extraordinary powers to the president, it gave to President Paul von HINDENBURG, who was elected in 1925, the opportunity and power to undermine the constitution. Weber thought that the TREATY OF VERSAILLES was extremely unjust, and he strongly opposed its ratification. He contradicted himself on the principle of self-determination, believing in it for the Germans, but not for the Poles; he resented the loss of the eastern territories and the POLISH CORRIDOR to the "inferior" Polish population. Weber remained a strong Germanophile, and he yearned for strong personal leadership. Reflecting on the lost war, he blamed BISMARCK for the poor quality of leadership that he left behind. So Weber's liberal political thought was not always freedom-oriented, a judgment further strengthened by his continued admiration of the military dictator General Erich LUDENDORFF, and his strong desire to recreate the German General Staff as necessary for a strong German state.

Weimar (city)

Weimar is a city on the Ilm River in the principality of Saxe-Weimar-Eisenach about 65 miles southwest of LEIPZIG. It was founded most probably in the ninth century. After being under the control of a succession of counts and landgraves, it became a possession of the Ernestine branch of the house of Wettin. In 1547 the city was made the capital of Saxe-Weimar. During the RENAISSANCE the painter Lucas CRANACH the Elder painted an altarpiece. During most of the 18th century and the first decade of the 19th the city was the foremost cultural center of Germany. Outstanding literary figures came; for example, in November 1775 GOETHE at age 26 visited Weimar at the invitation of the young duke Karl August and his widowed mother, Anna Amalia, and decided to stay there for the next 60 years. Because of Karl August's young age, Anna Amalia headed the principality, trying to create a spirited artistic and intellectual climate. Christoph Martin WIELAND already was residing in Weimar, having been hired by Anna Amalia as a teacher for her son. It was Goethe's presence, however, that lured a number of other famous intellectuals to Weimar. Friedrich von SCHILLER also resided in Weimar, where he wrote his most famous dramas, *Wallenstein* and *William Tell*. Johann Sebastian BACH also lived in Weimar, where he composed 17 beautiful cantatas between 1708 to 1717. From 1842 to 1861

Franz LISZT resided in Weimar as the court orchestra director. A supporter of avant-garde music, he also supported the music of Hector Berlioz and Richard WAGNER. After Liszt left, Richard Strauss took up the musical leadership.

In the 20th century Weimar was the location where the NATIONAL ASSEMBLY met and wrote the constitution for the WEIMAR REPUBLIC. Later, it was the site of the development of the architecturally avant-garde BAUHAUS movement. In 1919 Walter GROPIUS was hired as director. The roster of the eminent artists who came to teach at the Bauhaus school is lengthy: Kandinsky, the American artist Lionel Feininger, Klee, Marcks, and Schlemmer. In 1937 the BUCHENWALD concentration camp was located outside Weimar. An estimated 65,000 people died there. American troops entered there in April 1945. During the postwar era Weimar became part of East Germany.

Weimar Constitution

Hugo PREUSS, a professor of constitutional law, had been commissioned to draft the constitution. He patterned it after the traditions of the United States, England, France, and Switzerland, and tried to combine the strong points of each. As in England and France at that time, the government (prime minister and cabinet) originated in the parliament (Reichstag) and was to be dependent on its confidence. For this reason, the system is called "parliamentary," and is different from the presidential system in the United States, where the president is elected by the majority of the people through the Electoral College. He is not dependent on the confidence of the Congress, he does not have to be from the party that has a congressional majority, and the Congress cannot vote him out of office. According to the traditional English and French constitutions, the will of the people is expressed through their representatives in parliament.

The NATIONAL ASSEMBLY convened in WEIMAR, and the committee that worked on Preuss's draft struck a compromise between the tendency to centralize power in the federal government or in the states, which wanted to locate more power there as had been the case under the Empire. The constitution provided for a democratic republic, and the states were to be known as lands (*Länder*); federal law was to override state law. Thus there was a limitation on states' rights, which was illustrated when the central government took over the German railway system and BAVARIA and Wurttemberg lost control of their postal and telegraph services, which they had controlled during the Empire.

There were to be two houses of the parliament. The upper house, called the Reichsrat, took the place of the former BUNDESRAT and represented the states. One of the principal changes was to put a limit on the power of the state of PRUSSIA and limit it to no more than two-fifths of the total, 66 seats. More important was its authority and power. While the old Bundesrat had derived its power from the Union of Princes, the Reichsrat derived its authority from the will of the people. Its power was limited by the power of the lower house, the Reichstag, which could overrule its decisions by a two-thirds majority or by a popular referendum. Although the Weimar Constitution was concerned with checks and balances, it set up a unicameral system with power anchored in the parliament (Reichstag).

The Weimar Constitution emphasized that supreme power emanated from the people. The new election system did away with the old smaller election districts and replaced them with large ones. The representatives of the people were to be elected by universal, equal, direct, and secret suffrage of all German citizens, men and women who were at least 20 years of age. The WEIMAR REPUBLIC committed itself to a system of proportional representation borrowed from France, which tended to make even the smallest minorities able to register their particular interests by electing representatives; unfortunately, this tended to weaken the parliamentary system. Votes were collected and entered into one central list, and any 60,000 of these votes elected a deputy, by which the minority attained the status of a political party and representation in the parliament. What this did was splinter the middle parties, and it strengthened the well-organized radical parties of the left and right. This enthusiasm for the most democratic method to ensure that minority opinions were represented by the use of the proportional system works best during times of social and political stability. That was not the case during the Weimar period. The electoral system tended to complicate the legislative process by increasing the number of parties, which made it difficult if not impossible for any one party to gain a majority. It made coalition government inevitable and also necessitated the inclusion in a cabinet of antirepublican splinter groups, which otherwise might have died out. The electoral system also had another weakness; party leaders were reelected to their seats in the parliament in each successive parliament and were able to hold onto the reins of power. This frustrated the voters, who saw that they could not alter the fundamental distribution of power without supporting extremists who promised radical reform.

The president (Reichspräsident) of the republic was elected for a term of seven years by direct ballot and could receive a second term. In some respects his powers exceeded those that the German emperor had before 1918. Some of the president's powers were: He was the commander in chief of the armed forces; he could appoint and dismiss the chancellor; he could dissolve the Reichstag; he could invoke a popular referendum against decisions of the Reichstag. Finally, he was given extraordinary emergency powers under Article 48 of the constitution, which gave him the power to rule by decree and suspend the constitution. These were virtual dictatorial powers. It should be noted that it was Article 48 that in the last stages of the republic undermined its foundations.

In the section of the constitution that defined and circumscribed a bill of rights, the Weimar Constitution showed the closest kinship with the ideals of the REVOLUTION OF 1848 and the FRANKFURT PARLIAMENT. The three parties of the Weimar Coalition, the Catholic CENTER PARTY, the GERMAN DEMOCRATIC PARTY (DDP), and the Majority Socialists, the SOCIAL DEMOCRATIC PARTY (SPD), were the champions of these rights and anchored them in the dignity of human beings. Besides the liberal democratic party, the Catholic and the socialist political parties defended the rights of the individual. Those rights regarded social justice, equality, and personal freedom. Special guarantees were also inserted to protect the rights of association and of national minorities.

Weimar Republic (1919–1933)

The Weimar Republic takes its name from the city of WEIMAR, where the National Constituent Assembly met in 1919 to formulate a constitution for the new republic. In the face of military defeat two extreme alternatives presented themselves. As during the Napoleonic conquest the Prussian leaders decided to reorganize the government in order to bring it in closer touch with the people. In the process the monarchy lost little of its prerogatives, and the state was strengthened to defeat the French enemies. In the course of WORLD WAR I, however, the monarchy had hidden behind a quasi-military dictatorship of generals. Paul von HINDENBURG and Erich LUDENDORFF had not achieved any great success and lost in popular appeal. The default of the military and the demand by the victorious Allies for the establishment of a democracy rendered a top-down reform impossible. On the other hand, a revolution from below in the 20th century after the example of the recently successful Russian Bolshevik Revolution was nondemocratic. A version of this type of revolution was attempted and aborted (Spartacus) in the early part of 1919 and was suppressed by Friedrich EBERT, leader of the SOCIAL DEMOCRATIC PARTY. He had taken over the leadership of the government at the end of 1918, and he and the Majority Socialists stood for the establishment of a democratic government. Not only did they oppose any ties to Russian communism, but they also resisted leftists from instituting the nationalization of the economy. Both the military defeat and fall of the monarchy in 1918 and the suppression of the leftist revolution in 1919 created new political problems for the future, that is the radicalization of the political right and the left. The right was made up of those who had been annexationists during the war and, resenting the German defeat, ascribed it to the "stab in the back" legend that socialist and democratic groups caused the defeat. The left was filled with resentment over the bloody suppression and the murder of their leaders, Karl LIEBKNECHT and Rosa LUXEMBURG, and the failure to establish a socialist republic. The history of the Weimar Republic became a conflict of the political moderates against these two extreme groups.

The Social Democrats had abandoned the revolutionary notions they had entertained in the 19th century. During the war a left-wing group had broken off and formed the INDEPENDENT SOCIAL DEMOCRATIC PARTY (USPD), whose most radical members later split off and formed the GERMAN COMMUNIST PARTY (KPD). The Social Democrats considered their main task to secure the orderly transition from the old to the new political order. Private ownership of industry and agriculture therefore remained untouched. Women, however, were given the right to vote. The PRUSSIAN THREE CLASS VOTING SYSTEM was abolished, and a very democratic proportional voting system was established. The eight-hour workday was established, and trade unions were given the right to negotiate wage contracts. Other steps in social progress were taken with the formation of the Works Councils Act (1920), under which workers were officially represented at their place of work. Unemployment insurance was introduced in 1927. Where they did make a mistake was to leave most of the antirepublican civil service and judiciary in office. The Imperial officer corps also retained command of the armed forces. Attempts by left-wing radicals to create socialism was stopped by force through the EBERT-GROENER PACT. In the beginning of the republic there were three unconditionally republican parties—Social Democrats, the liberal GERMAN DEMOCRATIC PARTY, and the denominationally oriented Catholic CENTER PARTY, which initially had a large majority and was known as the Weimar Coalition. By the Reichstag election of 1924 the Weimar Coalition was losing popularity, and those parties hostile to the republic grew in strength. Especially serious difficulties were presented by the postwar economic slump, the large reparations payments owed, and other oppressive terms of the VERSAILLES TREATY.

The city of Weimar on the Ilm River had a long tradition of LIBERALISM and was far enough away from the militarist and Communist dangers lurking around BERLIN. The WEIMAR CONSTITUTION, providing for a seven-year presidential office, a bicameral government, proportional representation, and a guarantee of federal rights, was adopted on July 31, 1919. The first president of the Republic, Friedrich Ebert, in office from February 1919 until his death in February 1925, was a moderate socialist and sought to organize the republic in the middle-class liberal spirit of the constitution. His successor, elected on the second ballot of the election in 1925, was a monarchist and a nationalist, Field Marshal Paul von Hindenburg, but who in practice upheld the constitution.

The republic suffered economic difficulties from the beginning, lasting into 1923. During 1923 France occupied the RUHR because Germany defaulted on its reparations payments. The government resisted this threat, but in the process the German currency shrank to an incredibly small part of its prewar value. Communist disturbances broke out in SAXONY and Thuringia, and in MUNICH Adolf HITLER attempted to take over the government in the BEER-HALL PUTSCH. The financial collapse in 1922–23 and political crisis was followed by a period of economic recovery and political stability, resulting partly from governmental economies, but even more from foreign loans and the DAWES PLAN. The foreign policy of Gustav STRESEMANN regained German political equality through the LOCARNO PACT and entry to the LEAGUE OF NATIONS. In this golden period of the 1920s, the arts and sciences flourished, and Berlin became one of the world's most interesting cultural centers. The election of Hindenburg as the candidate of the right as president moved the center of political gravity to the right of center, although he never developed a personal commitment to the republican state. The same applied to the army (Reichswehr), Germany's newly established regular army, which still formed a "state within the state." For the most part the army avoided parliamentary control.

The collapse of the Weimar Republic began with the world economic crisis of 1929. The American financial depression caused the withdrawal of funds from Germany, and within 18 months the major European central bank, the Austrian Credit Anstalt, worsened the crisis and increased unemployment. The economic disaster destroyed the political balance that had lasted from 1924 to 1929, the so-called Stresemann Era. Left- and right-wing groups exploited the unemployment and distress. It was no longer possible to find majorities in the Reichstag capable of forming a government. The president decided to appoint Heinrich BRÜNING chancellor, who was unable to obtain parliamentary majorities for his programs, so Hindenburg kept him in office through emergency powers from 1930 through spring 1932.

The National Socialist GERMAN WORKERS' PARTY (NSDAP) had been reorganized by Hitler after he was released from Landsberg Prison, and after 1928 it had chosen a new electoral strategy, focusing on farmers and the MIDDLE CLASS. In the parliamentary elections of September 1930 the NAZI PARTY shocked the country by increasing its seats in the Reichstag from 12 to 107. The party grew in strength and popularity, and Hitler even ran for president in spring 1932, though he lost to Hindenburg. By July 1932 the Nazis had become the largest single party with 230 seats. The Nazi program of anticommunism, anti-Versailles Treaty, and ANTI-SEMITISM increased its popular support and also secured for the party the backing of powerful capitalist interests. President Hindenburg attempted to change his chancellors from Brüning to Franz von PAPEN, then to General Kurt von SCHLEICHER in an attempt to keep Hitler out of the government. Nevertheless, in the end Hindenburg relented, and on January 30, 1933, through the influence of persons close to the Reich president Hitler was appointed chancellor in spite of the fact that his party was no longer enjoying as much political support. The conservatives around Hindenburg thought they could control Hitler and that his dictatorial rule could be prevented. On March 23 Hitler forced through the ENABLING ACT, which suspended the WEIMAR CONSTITUTION.

Weizsäcker, Ernst, Baron von
(Ernst Heinrich, Freiherr [Baron] von Weizsäcker (1882–1951)
diplomat in the Resistance

The permanent undersecretary of state in the Foreign Office, Baron Ernst von Weizsäcker participated in the RESISTANCE against Hitler, especially in warnings concerning Hitler's intentions in Czechoslovakia and the invasion of the Soviet Union. As ambassador to the Vatican from 1943 to 1945 he helped to protect Rome's Jews from deportation and advocated its status as an "open city."

Born in 1882, Weizsäcker was the son of the minister-president of Württemberg (1906–18), who lived in Stuttgart. Ernst entered the navy in 1900, where he enjoyed a career until 1920. He served in the BATTLE OF JUTLAND, but was opposed to unrestricted submarine warfare and the extreme war aims of the annexationists. Weizsäcker was fundamentally a monarchist, but decided to rationally accept the republic, voting for Gustav STRESEMANN'S GERMAN PEOPLE'S PARTY (DVP) and supporting his revisionist foreign policy. He did not approve of Hitler's appointment as chancellor and deplored the criminal excesses of the NAZI PARTY.

In 1920 he became a diplomat and was stationed in Basel, Copenhagen, Oslo, and Bern, and was finally selected in 1938 to be state secretary to the new foreign minister, Joachim von RIBBENTROP. During the Sudeten crisis of 1938 Undersecretary Weizsäcker along with General Ludwig BECK, was opposed to war with Czechoslovakia and the start of another European war, and was involved in several missions to London and Paris designed to arouse strong foreign opposition to Hitler. Because of the APPEASEMENT POLICY of Neville Chamberlain, this did not succeed. Through the historian Carl J. Burchhardt, the LEAGUE OF NATIONS high commissioner for DANZIG, Weizsäcker made another attempt to get a message to the British from Switzerland. Furthermore, Weizsäcker made it clear that the only way to prevent war was to eliminate Hitler. Later, when war with Poland loomed, Weizsäcker again informed the British through Erich Kordt, who was the leader of the Resistance circle in the Foreign Office, of Hitler's attempts to come to an agreement with the Soviet Union. Weizsäcker also opposed other policies of Hitler, which included the invasion of Denmark and Norway, Belgium and the Netherlands, and aid to Italy in North Africa, Yugoslavia, and Greece.

After his posting to the Holy See (Vatican) in 1943, the ambassador tried to help the Jews and protect Rome from destruction with the "open city" declaration. In 1946 he was arrested and tried by the International Military Tribunal (IMT) and sentenced to seven years' imprisonment (later reduced to five) for failing to protest Jewish deportations from France. He died a year after amnesty brought his release in 1950.

Weizsäcker, Richard von (1920–)
president of Federal Republic

Richard von Weizsäcker was born in Stuttgart in 1920, the son of the diplomat Ernst Heinrich von WEIZSÄCKER. Educated at Oxford University before the war, Richard served in the German army as an infantry officer from 1938 to 1945. Later, he served with the War Crimes Tribunal and learned about the crimes committed by the Nazis. Two times he served as lay president in the Protestant Church. In 1954 he joined the CHRISTIAN DEMOCRATIC UNION and was elected to the Federal Parliament (BUNDESTAG) in 1969. He also served as deputy leader of the CDU's parliamentary group. In 1981 he was elected mayor of West Berlin, which position he held until he became federal president in 1984, an office he occupied until 1994.

The role of the federal president has been largely symbolic, but at times could also be a means of shaping public opinion. A political moderate, Weizsäcker was unopposed by the SOCIAL DEMOCRATS as a candidate for president. In important areas he sought to influence public opinion. He made important speeches in three areas, seeking to raise the moral tone of German politics. The first occurred on the occasion of the 40th anniversary of the end of WORLD WAR II in 1985. He called May 8, 1945, a day of liberation, freeing Germans from the violent rule of Nazism, but also suggesting that more Germans knew of the HOLOCAUST than they had admitted. The second came on the occasion of the reunification of Germany, during which he warned against too hasty a process of unification, thinking that it might be synchronized with European integration. On October 3 he noted with pride that Germany had come to find its lasting place among the Western democracies. He warned, however, that material sharing had to take place and reconciliation needed to be tactful. Later, he argued in favor of moving the capital to BERLIN. After unification took place, extremists committed acts of terrorism. Although few other politicians attended the funerals of victims of right-wing extremism, President Weizsäcker chose to attend the funerals of victims to demonstrate his solidarity. A third occasion was his speech in 1992 in which he criticized the concentration of power in the FEDERAL REPUBLIC, which also suggested disagreement with Chancellor Helmut KOHL. In the early 1990s it had become fashionable to talk about a "disenchantment with politics," which prompted the president to criticize politicians for their skill in fighting political opponents.

Westphalia, Peace of (1648)

The Peace of Westphalia concluded the THIRTY YEARS' WAR (1618–48). Its main provisions were contained in two treaties negotiated in the Westphalian towns of Münster and Osnabrück between representatives of King Louis XIV of France, Queen Christina of Sweden, and Emperor

Ferdinand III and the German estates. The treaties were signed on October 24, 1648, and significantly affected both the Empire and its neighbors. They provided a framework for the European state system until the time of the French Revolution. The peace signified the end of the wars of religion. In fact, during the last phase of the wars Catholic and Protestant states acted in alliance, as the French were allied with the Swedes against the Catholic Habsburgs of Germany and Spain. The treaties inaugurated the modern phase of European history in which sovereign states are governed by international law.

The Peace of Westphalia checkmated the Catholic COUNTER-REFORMATION in Germany. Generally, the provisions of the PEACE OF AUGSBURG of 1555 were confirmed and broadened. All German states, including the Calvinist ones, were free to determine their own religion. Calvinism, which had not been officially recognized earlier, now was, and the princes retained their right to reform the church. A distinction was made, however, between the public practice of religion, which the princes could regulate, and the people's private practice of religion at home, where the rulers would not seek to impose their authority. Religion and politics were now separate worlds. The pope was completely ignored in all the decisions at Westphalia. Another step was taken in the treaties in making religion a question of personal conviction and individual choice.

Territorially, France gained parts of western Germany, part of ALSACE, and the three cities of Metz, Toul, and Verdun, giving the French control of the Franco-German border area and providing them with excellent bases for future military operations in Germany. Sweden and the German states of BRANDENBURG and BAVARIA gained some territory in Germany. As a result FREDERICK WILLIAM of Brandenburg now was the ruler of the largest territory in the Empire next to the Habsburgs. Although the Austrian Habsburgs did not really lose any territory, more important, the emperor, constitutionally, saw his authority diminished. The emperor's monarchical and centralistic ambitions were as effectively checked as was the Catholic Counter-Reformation. The territorial princes were the chief winners of the Peace of Westphalia as the more than 300 German states that made up the HOLY ROMAN EMPIRE became virtually independent. This weakened the Empire so much that it ensured German disunity for the next 200 years.

Wieland, Johann Christoph Martin (1733–1815)

poet of the rococo

Wieland was the poet of the German ROCOCO. He weaned educated Germans away from the fashionable literature of the French writers. In his novel *Agathon* Wieland treated the central problem of his life, the reconciliation of reason and sensuality. He was chiefly concerned with the problems of human happiness and the aesthetic education of humanity. Although not an original poet and having borrowed his themes from the literatures of other nations, he was nonetheless a great poet for the fluency, gracefulness, and refinement of his language. Wieland's place in German literature was to prepare the way for greater classical writers than he, GOETHE and SCHILLER.

Christoph Martin Wieland was a Swabian from Oberholzheim zu Biberach in Württemberg, born on September 5, 1733. His father was a believer in PIETISM and assuredly raised his son in this popular Protestant faith. Wieland spent his boyhood in Biberach and attended school in Kloster Bergen near Magdeburg, which was conducted according to pietistic principles. He attended the University of Tübingen to study law, but his literary talent led him to write an epic poem: *Herman; Twelve Moralistic Letters in Verse; and Anti-Ovid* (1752). This so impressed the famous J. J. Bodmar in Switzerland that he invited Wieland to live there while an inner change occurred. Most significant, his Pietism had been exchanged for a lighthearted philosophy of life before he returned in 1760, to Biberach where he was elected a senator and was appointed town clerk. He was betrothed several times but finally married in 1765 Dorothea von

Hillenbrand. In 1769 he was elected to a professorship at Erfurt University. His Socratic dialogues and a political novel drew the attention of the dowager duchess Anna Amalia of Saxony Weimar, who appointed Wieland the tutor of her sons, thus making him the first great German writer to come to WEIMAR, which under Goethe became the capital of German literature. In 1773 he launched the literary journal *The German Mercury*, which became the leading periodical in German intellectual life for many years.

Agathon was one of the great German novels of the 18th century and Wieland's chief work. It was a novel of apprenticeship in which the aesthetic rather than the religious or economic education of the young hero is emphasized. In this psychological novel Agathon is a Greek seeker of a philosophy of life whose head and heart are in conflict as the philosopher Hippias teaches him materialism and individualism and he is tempted by the wiles of a courtesan. The solution of a harmony between the senses and the spirit is unattainable for Agathon. An epic in which Wieland promoted the cheerful message of hedonism and epicurean sensuality is *The Philosophy of the Graces* (1768), in which a Greek youth seeks happiness in philosophy instead of a woman's arms. A social critical theme is developed in *The Abderites*, in which the inhabitants of an ancient Greek city modeled after Biberach, are ridiculed for their philistinism and narrow-mindedness. Wieland's best work, however, is the colorful medieval fairy tale *Oberon* (1774), which relates how the king of elves helped a Frenchman from Bordeaux perform wonders in the Orient.

William I (1797–1888)

king of Prussia from 1861 and German emperor from 1871

Keen expectations that the new king would be sympathetic to popular political trends greeted William in 1858, when he became regent, just as had been the case in 1840, when FREDERICK WILLIAM IV, his older brother, had become king. Unfortunately, the Prussian people would again be disappointed. Prince of Prussia in 1840, Regent in 1858 due to his brother's incapacitation from a stroke, William became king in 1861 and German emperor 10 years later. He was more like his father, FREDERICK WILLIAM III, than his elder brother had been. He was an old-fashioned conservative, confident of his military competence, but only of average intelligence and lacking the imagination and artistic interests of his brother. He was modest, but concerning the kingship of Prussia he certainly had an inflated pride in his office.

Not an uncritical observer of political affairs, he resented PRUSSIA's humiliation at OLMÜTZ and desired greater recognition for the contributions Prussia had made to the GERMAN CONFEDERATION. He objected to the power of state ministers interfering with the unofficial advisers in the court Kamarilla, and he was unalterably opposed to the use of religion for political purposes, especially the use of spies and the police to impose the government's religious views. Critical of the ultraconservatives, he favored the more moderate conservative party. Having served his country well as a member of the United Diet of 1847, he was elected to the Prussian National Assembly in 1848 and was placed in command of troops sent to suppress the revolution in BADEN. Afterward, he was the military governor in the RHINELAND and Westphalia until 1857, assumed the regency in 1858, and was crowned king (he placed the crown on his own head) in 1861.

The new king was determined to preserve royal authority, but did select ministers from various political groups to emphasize the independence of the royal government. People thought that a new liberal era was beginning as a cabinet of "liberal conservatives" was appointed and because the government ceased trying to influence the elections to the lower house of the Diet. In 1858 liberal political participation had increased the number of Liberals in the *Landtag* from 60 to 210. As a result of the war for Italian unification in 1859 and AUSTRIA's defeat by Italian and French forces, an increase of public involvement in political affairs took place. The future of the German question dominated German political life and aroused a deep desire for the early achievement of German unity. The failure of Prussia to come to the aid of Austria and the Peace of Villafranca between Italy and Austria, made William feel incompetent in conducting foreign affairs. Where William felt competent concerned reform in the army. The Italian war strengthened his determination to modernize the army, which he hoped would bring Prussia the respect she deserved in Germany. His choice for minister of war was General Albrecht von Roon (1803–79) whose entry into the cabinet marked the beginning of the end of the era of the new LIBERALISM. His desire to have a professional army set apart from the population contradicted the ideals of liberal reformers who wanted the army to be part of a national mobilization as was envisioned by Hermann von Boyen. The army reform bill consequently aroused immediate opposition in the Prussian Parliament, which refused to pass a bill that planned to double the size of the army, increasing the term of service to three years. Liberals feared that this would allow the army to "militarize" the conscripts and reduce the importance of the National Guard. The king considered abdication, but in the end appointed Otto von BISMARCK, a fiery conservative, as prime minister. After a failure to compromise with the parliamentary opposition, Bismarck decided to go ahead with the military reform without a budget being passed. Bismarck then led the king through the wars of unification. After the victory over France, William I became the German emperor in January 1871. The German states with the exception of Austria joined to form the new Second Empire. Bismarck wrote the constitution, which established a federal state, but in which Prussia held the preponderance of power.

William had a secondary role in government under Bismarck's leadership. Two assassination attempts were made in 1878, which resulted in the ANTI-SOCIALIST LAW. Although William made an accommodation to constitutionalism, he nonetheless continued to believe that the parliament should not limit his royal power. He was genuinely popular during his reign and was the incarnation of a heroic epoch of what has been called the "founders generation." He died at the advanced age of 91 on March 9, 1888, mourned by the German people and by Bismarck himself. William's son, the new emperor FREDERICK III, in whom the hopes of liberalism in Germany had centered, was unfortunately, a dying man at the time of his accession, suffering bravely for 99 days.

William II (1859–1941)
German emperor

William II was the German emperor from 1888 to 1918; he dismissed Otto von BISMARCK, altered his foreign policy, and very unwisely facilitated the formation of the formidable Triple Entente against Germany and her allies. An arrogant and enthusiastic nationalist and imperialist, he led Germany to the heights of military and industrial power, built the world's second-most powerful navy, and ruled over Imperial Germany until its defeat and his abdication during WORLD WAR I.

William, son of Crown Prince FREDERICK WILLIAM and grandson of Queen Victoria of Great Britain, was born into the HOHENZOLLERN family in 1859. Due to a deformed and paralyzed left arm, William was a disappointment to his parents, and his consequent resentments led to his disaffection from them. After two years at the University of BONN, he entered the army, which became his primary interest and surrogate family. He was able to overcome some of the limitations of his deformities, learning horsemanship and marksmanship. After Kaiser WILLIAM I died in March 1888, his son, FREDERICK WILLIAM, succeeded him, but after only 99 days died of throat cancer. The 29-year-old inexperienced crown prince William then ascended the throne as Kaiser William II. After serious disagreements with Bismarck, the old chancellor threatened to resign, and William surprisingly accepted. The young Kaiser was determined to rule by himself.

William possessed few attractive qualities, was not well educated, and had a personality ill-suited for an emperor. He was self-willed, arrogant, rude, impulsive, indiscreet, and insensitive to others and jealously guarded his prerogatives as emperor. He felt it was his duty to assert himself in both domestic and foreign policy. Quite unbearable to his ministers, he nevertheless was well liked by his companions, who were predominantly soldiers and bankers. His assertiveness masked his insecurities; he was unsure of his opinions and adopted the views of those around him. Excessively martial in his bearing, he sported a variety of uniforms. As Kaiser he wanted to be a "modern monarch," which he thought required him to be responsive to his subjects. Unlike his predecessors, he valued public opinion very highly in both domestic and foreign policy, which prompted him to pay more attention to the press to the neglect of official communications. It was unfortunate that he was advised by an oligarchy of some 20 mediocre men.

In the first years after Bismarck's departure from office, William hoped to check the rise of socialism by a broad program of legislation. He thought of himself as a king of the poor and talked as if he understood the "spirit of the people" and wondered if IMPERIAL GERMANY had been created to solve the "social question." Between 1891 and 1894 social legislation to improve the lives of the workers was introduced, but failed to win the hearts of workers away from the SOCIAL DEMOCRATIC PARTY. Disenchanted with this "treasonable horde" unworthy to be named Germans, the Kaiser turned his attention to issues of foreign and military policy, seeking to acquire an empire in order to enhance Germany's standing among the great nations of the world. To do this he increased Germany's armaments program and under the direction of Admiral von TIRPITZ built a world-class naval fleet, second only to that of Great Britain.

Although William desired good relations with and the respect of both Great Britain and Russia, he unfortunately failed to achieve these goals. It painfully annoyed him that Great Britain was not impressed with him. Dislike of his English mother and his often boorish behavior on visits did not ingratiate him with his English royal relatives. Attempting to gain their respect, he only succeeded in alienating Great Britain by building an imposing naval fleet. Because of the Kaiser's naval and imperial goals an arms race started, and because of his obstinacy efforts at arms reduction proved unsuccessful. His involvement in diplomacy only made matters worse. While the German ambassador in London tried to convince the British that Germany was interested in friendly relations, the German government began to act in a high-handed manner, believing that it could win imperial territory by demanding that Germany be compensated whenever the British tried to expand their colonial empire. The British, of course, were infuriated when the Kaiser during 1895 intervened in South African affairs, favoring the Boers during the Jameson Raid, and again during 1908 over the *Daily Telegraph* AFFAIR.

By 1912 the international situation had become perilous. Germany was allied with Austria-Hungary, which was internally weak and was threatened by the conflict among its nationalities and the two Balkan Wars. Within Germany the Socialists dangerously increased their seats in the 1912 REICHSTAG elections, which William felt threatened the monarchy. With war considered to be inevitable in the near future, the Kaiser ordered that plans be made. The crisis that started the World War I was the assassination of Archduke Franz Ferdinand on June 28, 1914, in Bosnia-Herzegovina. The Kaiser and the military secretly promised the Austrians their support with the BLANK CHECK, which encouraged the Austrians to issue an ultimatum to which the Serbians largely acquiesced. Considering the response unacceptable, the Austrians declared war. Now afraid of a European-wide war, William intervened at the last minute by appealing to Czar Nicholas II to halt the Russian mobilization already in progress. Not receiving a reply, the Kaiser declared war on Russia and then France. The strategic SCHLIEFFEN PLAN necessitated that France be invaded by violating Belgian neutrality, which had been guaranteed by Great Britain in 1831. The British responded by reluctantly declaring war, making a European war into a world war.

Although the Schlieffen Plan failed to provide Germany with a quick victory, there was still hope of victory during the early part of the war. William favored territorial annexations at the expense of Germany's enemies in order to create a greater German empire in Europe. He left the conduct of the war in the hands of the generals, especially Paul von HINDENBURG and Erich LUDENDORFF. Initially, the German people and even the Social Democratic Party supported the war effort, but with dismay at the deaths and sacrifices the German people soon blamed the Kaiser and his advisers and created disaffection and demands for constitutional reform. With the entry of the United States into the war in 1917 and the failure of Germany's spring offensive in 1918, the hopeless situation prompted the request for an armistice. By this time the Allies demanded the abdication of William II, who stubbornly remained at his headquarters at Spa in Belgium. The November Revolution broke out at the naval bases of Kiel and Wilhelmshaven, and on November 8 a republic was declared. William abdicated on November 9 and went into exile in Holland, where he lived for another 20 years, never returning to Germany and dying at age 82.

Windthorst, Ludwig (1812–1891)
leader of Center Party

Ludwig Windthorst was the foremost leader of the Catholic CENTER PARTY from 1874 to 1891. He became a great parliamentary leader of the Center's faction in the Prussian Diet and in the REICHSTAG. He was a principal opposition leader to the policies of Chancellor Otto von BISMARCK.

Ludwig Windthorst was born on January 17, 1812, in Kaldenhof near Osnabrück in HANOVER. After studying law at GÖTTINGEN and HEIDELBERG, he entered a law practice in Osnabrück. He was small in stature, had a big head, and could speak loudly. He was calm and deliberative, a hard worker and had a great memory for detail. His first political post was that of president of the Hanoverian chamber of deputies in 1851. Later he became the minister of justice (1851–52 and 1863–65), the only Catholic cabinet member in the predominantly Protestant state of Hanover. Even after Hanover was annexed by PRUSSIA in 1866 after the Austro-Prussian War, he continued to be a loyal supporter of the Guelph ruling house.

Windthorst's political views were those of his Catholic middle-class contemporaries. He advocated states' rights, constitutional government, judicial reforms, free enterprise, and monarchy. He also believed in the political leadership of AUSTRIA.

He was a fierce opponent of Bismarck, and Bismarck came to hate him. Windthorst was able to arouse passions and even hate, and certainly he could get Bismarck's goat, inciting the chancellor into tempestuous outbursts. The Center Party, a politico-religious party, was founded in 1852 and reorganized on a national basis in 1871. After the Center Party leader, Herman von Mallinchrodt, died in 1874, the leadership of the party passed to Windthorst. He became a master political strategist in the Reichstag and a bitter opponent of Bismarck. He was a fiery debater, and Bismarck was fearful of his political persuasiveness. His excellent memory compensated for his failing eyesight, and he was skillful in critiquing the weakest link in an opponent's argument.

Unlike the NATIONAL LIBERAL PARTY leaders who would announce their support or rejection of government bills on the first reading, Windthorst's strategy was to be noncommital until the final reading and vote on the bill to allow party members the freedom to vote for or against. Characterized as a "parliamentary wonder" Windthorst had more ability that the two liberal leaders, Rudolf von BENNIGSEN and Johannes Miquel, together. Accusations against him of political bargaining and a lack of sincerity in his religious convictions were inspired by the jealousy of his opponents.

Wittelsbach, House of

The House of Wittelsbach was the ruling dynasty of BAVARIA from 1180 to 1918, including the

German REVOLUTION OF 1918–1919. The Wittelsbach dynasty was founded by Otto von Wittelsbach, who was appointed duke of Bavaria in 1180. He was a loyal supporter of Frederick Barbarossa, who was Frederick I. The term *loyal supporter (Wittelsbacher Treu)* was proverbially applied to the family. During the HOLY ROMAN EMPIRE the Wittelsbachs were strong supporters of the Catholic COUNTER-REFORMATION. They also were electors of the emperor.

Under Napoleon's direction Bavaria became a kingdom and the Wittelsbachs its monarchs in 1806 when the elector received the title of King Maximilian Josef (1806–25). This was a consequence of Napoleon's policy of building up the middle states of central Germany as buffers against AUSTRIA and PRUSSIA. At the CONGRESS OF VIENNA Bavaria's existence as a kingdom was confirmed.

Wolff, Christian, Baron von (1679–1754)

Enlightenment philosopher

Christian von Wolff was a philosopher and mathematician and one of the founders of the ENLIGHTENMENT in Germany. He was especially important in transmitting the thought of Gottfried Wilhelm von LEIBNIZ.

Christian von Wolff was born in BRESLAU, Silesia, on January 24, 1679. It was his father's desire that he enter the Lutheran ministry, but after some exposure to theology he expressed a greater interest in mathematics, physics, and philosophy. Earning a master of arts degree he was able to teach at LEIPZIG and on the recommendation of Leibniz was appointed in 1706 professor of mathematics at Halle, where he remained until 1723, at which time he was expelled for his anti-Pietist and determinist teachings on human nature.

Wolff marks a transition to a phase of the German Enlightenment called that of "popular philosophy." That direction in his thought was indicated early in his career by his paper on universal practical philosophy. Wolff's philosophical thought was an eclectic mix of concepts that he did not draw from Christian theology. The orthodox clergy were understandably upset when he implied that the ethics of Confucius demonstrated that special revelation from God was not necessary to arrive at the highest moral code. Wolff's method of thinking obviously did not reflect PIETISM but the scholastic logic and encyclopedism that had infiltrated orthodox Lutheran theology. He used logic to transform the ideas of Descartes and particularly Leibniz into a comprehensive rational system that is determined by logical laws. He believed that all things existed for the good of humanity and were therefore intended for their use. Thus, the purpose of philosophy was practical, especially appealing to the MIDDLE CLASS, who were trying to give a meaning to life that was beyond what was prevalent in aristocratically dominated society in 18th-century PRUSSIA. The function of philosophy therefore was to reveal to people how the rational order of things was directed toward their happiness.

Contributing to the popularity of his philosophical thought was the fact that he wrote in German and had an explanation for everything. Wolff's ideas were spread throughout Germany in books, lecture halls, and even from the pulpit. Some of his publications include: *Rational thoughts on the powers of human understanding* (1713); *Rational thoughts on God, the world, and the human soul . . .* (1729); and *Rational thoughts on the purpose of natural things* (1724).

women and National Socialism

The Nazi attitude toward women was determined by the basic beliefs of the NAZI PARTY. The preservation of the Aryan race meant that women had a crucial role to play as mothers. The Nazis viewed the differences between men and women as natural, and women were designed to be mothers and wives. While men competed and struggled, women were reproductive, sacrificing for the sake of nurturing others. From the earliest beginnings of the Nazi Party HITLER promised to remove women from public life. Nazi social policy relegated women to becoming bearers of children and poorly paid workers in the lowliest jobs. Hitler was also opposed to women's role in politics, where opportunities had opened during the WEIMAR REPUBLIC. He was the strongest spokesman in German politics for the strong-man ideal. It is no surprise that the Nazis received so many votes from traditionalist sources such the conservative and Catholic political parties. Nazis had won support precisely because they opposed the progressive policies that the republic had instituted for women. National Socialism contributed nothing new to the discussion of woman's role in German society and only rehashed ultraconservative ideas, emphasizing that the inequality between the sexes was unchangeable. As far as voter support was concerned, far fewer women than men had voted for the Nazis before 1930, but as the GREAT DEPRESSION deepened and more women voted, nearly as many women as men voted Nazi between 1930 and 1932. It was not Hitler's charisma that motivated them as many observers thought, because so few voters actually saw or heard Hitler. It was the zeal and excitement of the local rallies that led many women to join the crusade to change Germany. They faced down hecklers, smuggled weapons, spoke on street corners, served as couriers, and marched behind Nazi banners while bearing insults like "brown goose" or "Hitler whore." However, the women kept folk traditions alive, gave charity to poor Nazi families, cared for SA men, and prepared food at rallies.

Although Hitler displayed little interest in the support of women and rejected the idea that females should have responsibilities in the movement, that did not alienate the women who supported Nazism. The elan and zeal of Nazism itself stimulated women to join Nazism's crusade. While endorsing the conventional roles for Nazi women, they played an active role and called themselves the "German Freedom Movement" and developed their own feminine political organizations. Some became so-called mother preachers, organizing new followers, emphasizing motherly roles. When women had seen how democracy had allowed the economic depression to destroy the material foundations of their homes, many turned against the materialistic Weimar system and to the promises of the Nazi Party. They believed that strong families would shelter them against poverty and chaos. They looked to a powerful state to defend their separate female spheres. They hoped for a harmonious public life and an adequate living space. The fascist vision of an ideal society actually incorporated a vision of a strong society founded on a separate but equal spheres. Nazi women even spoke of their living space (LEBENSRAUM), a harmonious living space outside of the material world of class and politics. The women saw themselves as different from men in their ability to make the nation healthy again through female solidarity, which would unite Aryans of all classes.

When the Nazis dissolved all women's organizations and coordinated them in the GERMAN WOMEN'S BUREAU (DFB) in 1933, Gertrud SCHOLTZ-KLINK (1902–99), who was the survivor of three marriages and mother of 11 children, was made head of this bureau. She fit the ideal Aryan image with blond hair and blue eyes, and she accepted the subservience of women to male leadership, and in 1934 was rewarded by Hitler with the title of Reich women's leader. With the help of thousands of volunteer workers, the German Women's Bureau provided instruction and welfare for mothers. The service set up classes in household management, child care, nutrition, housecleaning methods, and sewing. Families were urged to consume a "one-pot" main meal and to donate to Nazi charities what was saved. Charitable works were common, such as collecting money for the "winter relief" program, which helped poor families, almost 20 percent of the population.

During the last years of the Weimar Republic there were already complaints that women were keeping men out of work. Actually, the unemployment rate for women was much less than that of men. So the Nazi demand that the employment of males should take priority over females had great popular support. The Nazis wanted married women to care for their families, while single women could work in appropriate jobs such as social work, nursing, primary school teaching, and welfare services. Between 1933 and 1937 some 800,000 newly married women received government loans on condition of not seeking reemployment. The percentage of females in the labor force therefore declined to 31 percent in 1937. That same year, however, as the rearmament boom and the military draft for males created labor shortages, the government rescinded its requirement that women give up work, encouraging them to reenter the labor market. Once the war started, women were even pushed into men's jobs such as munitions production. This was supposed to be temporary, but it did mean that women had more opportunities for employment and education. However, many middle-class women preferred to stay at home and were happy with the regime's emphasis on domesticity. Women gained in health care and welfare as the regime showed concern for their well-being, even though it stemmed from Nazi racial policy and the desire to ensure that healthy children would be born. As the war progressed, women's presence in the labor force increased, accounting for three-fifths of wartime employment. By 1942 married women accounted for 40 percent of the female labor force, and by 1944 there were 14.5 million women workers, some who might be working up to 56 hours a week.

The Third Reich did manage to inculcate new notions about the sexual role of women in society. In German society and during the early Nazi period the double standard of morality had been predominant, characterized by the advantages men enjoyed in the sexual relations. The double standard of bourgeois society was replaced by immorality pure and simple. Under the strain of war and separation from their male partners, many women satisfied their erotic cravings in extramarital relationships. Even before the beginning of the war in 1939 young men had been herded in barracks or camps for long periods of time, which frustrated the opportunity for sexual relations. What became common then was that young women tended to have affairs with available older men. As prisoners of war and foreign workers came into Germany after 1939 and worked on farms and in industry, sexual contact, though forbidden, became a significant problem. During the final stages of the war the erosion of sexual taboos among women became pervasive.

World War I (1914–1918)

The immediate cause of the Great War was the spread of NATIONALISM in the Balkans and the terrorist assassination of the archduke Francis Ferdinand and his wife in Sarajevo. The Austrians had decided to destroy Serbian intervention in BOSNIA-HERZEGOVINA. It was difficult to localize the conflict that eventually became a world war. Among the reasons was the division of Europe into rival camps by a system of alliances, called the Triple Alliance and the Triple Entente. Originally they were defensive, but the two alliance groups became increasingly distrustful of each other through a series of crises that led up to the war—Morocco in 1905, Bosnia in 1908–09 and 1911, and AGADIR in 1911. Anglo-German relations had also worsened, and a naval rivalry grew because Germany was determined to build a naval fleet that could challenge the British.

Austria-Hungary declared war on Serbia on July 28, 1914; Russia mobilized along the German and Austrian frontiers on July 29; in response to the Russian threat Germany declared war on Russia on August 1 and on France on August 3; and Germany violated the neutrality of Belgium by its invasion on the same day. Britain declared war on Germany on August 4. The German-Austrian alliance broadened as Turkey joined them in November 1914 and Bulgaria in October 1915. Italy decided to change her alliances and in May 1915 joined the French and British Entente. The original Allies were supported by 17 other states, the most important being Japan (August 1914) and the United States in April 1917.

Before the war the German military had a strategic plan for a possible two-front war against the Russians and the French called the

SCHLIEFFEN PLAN. It was a military solution to compensate for a series of diplomatic blunders that had aligned Russia, France, and England against Germany and Austria-Hungary. It was a terrific gamble that required a knockout blow against France before the slower Russians could attack. The Russians surprised the Germans and quickly invaded East Prussian territories, causing a shifting of divisions from the western front, which caused the plan to fail in its objectives. As a result the general strategy of the war was lost sight of and the German military failed to develop an alternative plan.

The main area of fighting against Germany was along the western front, where, after the repulse of the initial German advance to the Marne, both sides constructed a line of trenches extending from Nieuport on the Belgian coast to Verdun. The fighting fronts were stabilized in fortified lines of trenches that were protected by barbed wire entanglements. The rapid firepower of machine guns and extensive use of artillery forced both sides into a defensive strategy. For three and a half years neither side advanced more than a few miles along this line, despite new weapons such as poison gas, which was first used by the Germans at the Battle of Ypres in April 1915, and tanks first used by the British on the Somme in September 1916.

By 1915 the Germans had to begin to conserve food and materials once the promise of a quick victory vanished. The essentials of a planned economy emerged in what was called "war socialism." The chief architect of the planned economy was Walther RATHENAU, the son of the founder of the great electric trust, AEG. The General Staff gradually came to realize that they faced a war for which there was no precedent, whether in strategy or policies, for conservation of raw materials and production of war materials. The war created "Fortress Germany." As the war entered its last phase in fall 1916, the preeminence of military over political considerations became apparent when the military dictatorship of Paul von HINDENBURG and Erich LUDENDORFF was established. Ludendorff, who was the real brains behind the military dictatorship, aimed at total mobilization as a means of fighting a mass war. All manpower up to 60 years of age was to be mobilized. Women were to work in the factories, and labor was to be recruited from subject peoples. All resources were to be mobilized by ruthlessly carrying out the policies of war socialism. In reality, most of these were carried out only halfheartedly because of public inertia and resistance.

On the Russian front after the initial Russian advances in the Carpathian Mountains and an offensive under General Brussilov against the Austrians in summer 1916, the Russians suffered defeat at TANNENBERG (1914) and then exhausted themselves in a defensive stalemate. Attempts were made by the Allies to assist them by opening the Dardanelles through a campaign at Gallipoli in 1915, but without success. Once the Bolshevik Revolution had occurred in 1917, the Communists secured an armistice in December 1917. The Serbs were defeated in 1915–16 by the Germans, Austrians, and Bulgarians. The Italian front was largely stabilized in the early part of the war, although the Italians were forced back from Caporetto in October 1917, but were victorious a year later at Vittorio Veneto. The Turks were decisively defeated in Palestine by the British and placed on the defensive in the Caucasus and in Mesopotamia. In Africa the South Africans fought for control of the German colonies, and in Asia the Japanese took over the German possessions.

Naval battles were few, the main one between the British and German fleets at JUTLAND (May 31–June 1 1916). Because the German surface fleet was ineffective, the navy decided to use the new U-boats to starve Britain, which, however, failed. Aircraft and dirigible airships were used to support military operations and brought total war to cities such as London.

The entry of the United States into the war brought about its decisive conclusion, which the Bolshevik Revolution and the peace of BREST-LITOVSK could not accomplish. Insisting that the Germans would achieve "peace through victory," Ludendorff planned one more offensive in spring 1918, which continued until September

1918. When it was clear the victory was impossible, he demanded an immediate armistice. Military collapse also meant political collapse. Kaiser WILLIAM II and the other German princes such as the WITTELSBACH king of BAVARIA yielded their thrones in November 1918 when the revolution broke out. The monarchy had lost credibility, and no one tried to defend it, as Germany was declared a republic.

World War II (1939–1945)

World War II was Adolf HITLER's war. Hitler's goal was war with the Soviet Union in order to obtain LEBENSRAUM for the survival of the German people. Already in MEIN KAMPF and later at a secret meeting recorded in the HOSSBACH MEMORANDUM, Hitler shared his ideas of the need for more living space to be acquired in the East. Hitler had already violated the TREATY OF VERSAILLES by remilitarizing the RHINELAND, annexing AUSTRIA, and absorbing most of Czechoslovakia. Encouraged by Hitler's success, the National Socialists promptly launched a new propaganda campaign aimed at the recovery of the POLISH CORRIDOR between East and West Prussia. Although the British and French had earlier given in to Hitler's demands over Czechoslovakia at the MUNICH CONFERENCE, Britain and France balked over Poland and negotiated a defensive alliance in April 1939.

What signaled the green light for war was the NAZI-SOVIET NONAGGRESSION PACT in 1939, which contained a protocol providing for the division of Poland between Germany and Russia. On September 1, 1939, German forces invaded Poland and overran the country in four weeks. Britain and France declared war on Germany on September 3 but did not attack Germany in the West. The Germans then occupied Denmark and Norway in April 1940. Then, against the advice of some of his generals, Hitler on May 10, 1940, invaded Belgium, Holland, and France in a "lightning war" (BLITZKRIEG), in which penetration by German tanks and the use of air power resulted in the defeat of the Netherlands in four days, Belgium within three weeks, and France within seven. The British evacuated much of their forces back to Britain from Dunkirk. Hitler thought that he had to defeat Britain before he invaded Russia and planned a crossing of the English Channel, but prepared the invasion with air bombardment in the BATTLE OF BRITAIN in 1940. This strategy failed for the Germans. Then to help his ally, Mussolini, Hitler diverted forces to Yugoslavia, Greece, and North Africa, where General Erwin ROMMEL and the AFRIKA KORPS almost succeeded in defeating the British.

On June 22, 1941, Hitler revealed the full extent of his imperialist ambitions when he launched a full-scale invasion of the Soviet Union along a 2,000-mile front with overwhelming force. Unfortunately for the Russians Stalin did not believe that Hitler would invade, while unfortunately for the Germans the campaign began too late and they nearly froze to death before the gates of Moscow, where the Russians counterattacked. The Soviets forged a military alliance with Britain and the United States; the Americans were bombed at Pearl Harbor by the Japanese on December 7, 1941, and besides the United States declaring war on the Japanese, Hitler and Mussolini declared war on the United States on December 10.

The British military efforts concentrated on the Italians, who in alliance with Germany (Pact of Steel) joined the attack on France on June 10, 1940. Soon, however, the Italians became a liability for Hitler. In Russia the Germans were gradually forced backward in November 1942. The Germans experienced a colossal defeat at STALINGRAD in January 1943, a major turning point in the war. In North Africa the second battle of EL ALAMEIN at the end of October 1942 stopped the German advance, and by May 1943 the Germans and Italians were defeated. The Allies invaded Sicily and Italy and forced the Italians to make a separate peace on September 3, 1943.

A second front was launched against Hitler on June 6, 1944 (see D-DAY) with the Anglo-American invasion of Normandy and the liberation of Paris on August 25, 1944. On the Russian front the German armies were in full retreat. In the meantime the naval war, which was primarily a submarine war, reached its climax in 1943. The air war over Germany in which the Allies gained superiority from July 1943 resulted in strategic bombing by thousands of Allied planes and the destruction of many cities. The worst occurred at the end of the war in the fire bombing of DRESDEN.

A German conspiracy by the RESISTANCE intending to assassinate Hitler and seize power occurred on July 20, 1944, but failed to kill the dictator. Almost 5,000 Germans were executed in retaliation. In August the British and American forces invaded southern France, and on October 11 the Russians crossed the German frontier. On March 23, 1945, the final offensive in the west crossed the Rhineland and on April 20, 1945, the Russian attack on BERLIN began. Hitler committed suicide on April 30 and Joseph GOEBBELS shortly afterward; on May 7 Germany surrendered unconditionally at Rheims. The war in the Pacific culminated with the dropping of atomic bombs at Hiroshima and Nagasaki, and the Japanese surrendered on August 14, 1945.

Worms, Diet and Edict of (1521)

The first meeting of the imperial estates with the recently elected emperor CHARLES V (1519–56) opened on January 27, and its decisions were signed on May 26. The religious problems arising from the REFORMATION were only some of the problems facing the estates, and its decisions would provide for the governance of the Empire for the next nine years while Charles was absent. The decisions of the Diet included a number of provisions concerning the organization of the imperial government, maintenance of public peace, and tax assessments. The Diet reestablished the Imperial Council of Regency (Reichsregiment) and reconstructed the Imperial Cameral Court (Reichskammergericht), which was to be installed in NUREMBERG (Nürnberg), and greater royal control over their operation was to be established. The earlier laws of the Empire were reaffirmed, especially the "Eternal Peace," which had been negotiated between MAXIMILIAN I and the estates to maintain law and order. Even feuds were outlawed. For his upcoming war with France, Charles was to be supported by the estates according to a tax register that was drawn up.

But Martin LUTHER's condemnation by the papal bull *Exsurge domine* of 1520 and his formal excommunication by *Decet pontificem romanum* of 1521 was the most important order of business at the meeting. At this stage of the proceedings against Luther he should have been handed over to the secular authorities for punishment, but FREDERICK III, THE WISE, who had convinced the emperor to agree that Luther should be given a hearing at the Diet of Worms, had prevented that. By then Luther had become an important international figure, and his journey to Worms in April 1521 was accompanied by an imperial herald. When the emperor and Luther confronted each other, Luther refused to renounce his views, basing his decision on the grounds that he had not been proven wrong either by Scripture or reason. Luther said that he could not act against his conscience in the following words:

> Unless I am convinced by the testimony of the Scriptures or by clear reason (for I do not trust either the pope or in councils alone, since it is well known that they have often erred and contradicted themselves) I am bound by the Scriptures I have quoted and my conscience is captive to the Word of God. I cannot and I will not retract any thing, since it is neither safe nor right to go against conscience. May God help me. Amen.

Although Charles wanted to impose the imperial ban immediately, the estates, however, wanted to make one last effort at a settlement, to which Charles agreed. Negotiations took place between an Imperial Commission and Luther, but to no avail. The ban on Luther was dated May 6, and the estates acted as a church council (the formal papal bull of excommunication had not yet been issued) declaring that Luther was a convicted heretic. Luther left Worms on

April 26 under an imperial safe conduct of three weeks. The Lutheran elector of Saxony decided to protect Luther, had him kidnapped on May 3, 1521, and hidden in disguise in the WARTBURG castle in Eisenach. Incidentally, Frederick the Wise, who did not want to anger the emperor, left Worms, disavowing an interest in Luther. The edict was approved on May 8, but was not passed by the Diet until May 25 after many of the princes had departed. The edict became law on May 26, 1521, which added the imperial to the papal ban on Luther. Luther was branded as a "devil in the habit of a monk," and characterized as a pagan because he denied free will. Even though civil unrest appeared to be in the making, for Luther what happened to Germany was only incidental to the church of God and any compromise with the Empire would have meant the betrayal of Christ. There was little hope that the provisions of the edict could be carried out, and many among the estates thought that the reformer had not been judged fairly and demanded that a real church council be called to decide on the religious issue.

Y

Yalta Conference (February 1945)
Between February 4 and 11, 1945, the most important conference of the Allied leaders took place at Yalta in the Crimea, located in the Soviet Union.

The Yalta Conference had been preceded by policy statements and a conference of the Allied leaders at Teheran. The civilian leaders had to make decisions concerning a postwar political settlement in Europe. Following a meeting with British prime minister Winston Churchill (1874–1965) in January 1943, U.S. president Franklin D. Roosevelt (1882–1945) announced that the Allies would seek Germany's unconditional surrender. When Roosevelt, Churchill, and Soviet premier Joseph Stalin (1879–1953) met for the first time, it was for a conference in Teheran in November 1943. The Allies agreed to the political and economic decentralization of Germany and the transfer of German territory east of the Oder River to the Soviet Union and Poland. Germany would also be divided into Allied occupation zones.

At the Yalta Conference the Big Three leaders confirmed the demand that Germany had to surrender unconditionally. The principal objectives of the Allied occupation would be demilitarization, DENAZIFICATION, political and economic decentralization, and partial territorial dismemberment. Supervising the implementation of these measures would be a four-power Allied Control Council, which would be composed of the supreme military commanders of the various occupation zones and would be located in BERLIN, the German capital, which was also divided into four sectors for occupation purposes. It also was agreed to include France as a fourth occupation power with its zone to be carved out of the American and British zones and to give France a seat on the Allied Control Council. Nazi leaders would be tried before an international court for their war crimes.

The Germans were to be provided with a minimum of resources for subsistence. Industry that could be used for rearmament had to be dismantled. Reparations were to be left to a separate commission. The future border of Poland was to be connected with the borders of Germany. Poland was to gain territory from Germany in the west, where the frontier would be moved to the ODER-NEISSE LINE. The eastern border was to be aligned with the Curzon Line of 1920, but no final agreement was reached.

Of particular interest to the United States was to enlist the Soviet Union's help against the Japanese. As a result Roosevelt made secret agreements that were favorable to the Soviets, hoping these would satisfy Stalin: The Soviets were to get control of South Sakhalin and the Kurile Islands, access to Darien and Port Arthur, and the Manchurian railways. Outer Mongolia was to be made independent of China. Although these were generous concessions, it was hoped that the Soviet Union's assistance would speed the defeat of Japan.

Further refinements of the future of postwar Germany were to be discussed in more detail at the POTSDAM CONFERENCE in summer 1945. There the Western powers acquiesced in the territorial arrangements the Russians made in the East, but got Soviet agreement that final boundaries had to be determined at a peace conference.

Young Germany

Young Germany was a short-lived literary movement of revolt that centered on and culminated in the two revolutions of 1830 and 1848. In their aggressive attempts to reform the political and social conditions of their time, these men are reminiscent of the poets of the earlier storm and stress movement. They appealed to youth and demanded not only social but also sexual emancipation; they spoke out for rationalism and democracy. They were not great writers with the exception of Heinrich HEINE, and they had no clear political plan. They had no cohesion as a literary school, nor were they bound by close personal relationships. They did, however, succeed in shocking the authorities and the reading public.

The repression of the age of restoration which was associated with policemen and censors provided the context for this movement. The state authorities gave the so-called young German writers their collective identity by a governmental decree in 1835. When Karl Gutzkow published his novel *Wally, the Doubter* in 1835, a series of laws culminated in an edict from the GERMAN CONFEDERATION, which banned the works of Gutzkow, Heine, Heinrich Laube, Ludolf Wienbarg, and Theodor Mundt, who it was asserted attacked the Christian religion, undermined the social order, and attempted to destroy discipline and morality.

Their leaders were the critic Ludolf Wienbarg and the novelist and playwright Karl Ferdinand Gutzkow. In 1834 Wienbarg dedicated his *Esthetic Campaigns* to Young Germany. He protested against monarchical legitimacy, ROMANTICISM, against Metternich and HEGEL, and for liberty. He was opposed to the orthodoxy of the church and the estheticism of the German classics. His slogan was "Life, this life," inspired by Heine's sensuality and not GOETHE's ideal of the perfect form. What he and the Young Germans demanded was the unrestricted expression of the senses. Heinrich Laube edited the works of the great eroticist Johann Jakob Wilhelm Heinse and wrote the novel *Young Europe*, published between 1833 and 1837. It was, however, the publication of *Wally, the Doubter* that stirred up the authorities with its attack on conventional matrimony and religion and became the most shocking novel of the 19th century.

The Young Germans shared a set of historical experiences in the 1830s, which gave their works a similar emotional tone but never the commonalty of a literary school. The following works express their common discomfort with traditional culture and the prevalent social values: Gutzkow's *Wally*, Wienbarg's *Esthetic Campaigns*, Mundt's *Life's Modern Confusions* and *Madonna*, Laube's *The New Century* and *Young Europe*. Heinrich Heine was the greatest of the group, especially with his criticism of German national vices in *Germany*. Ludwig Börne, like Heine a Jewish exile in France, wrote his important *Letters from Paris* (1831), which are models of German prose. His democratic convictions like those of Heine were expressed in their demand for radical reforms such as freedom of the press, civil emancipation, Jewish emancipation, male and female equality, sovereignty of the people, and the demand for a republic. He encouraged Germans to rise up and take their freedom from autocratic princes. Georg Herwegh, probably the most radical and Metternich-hating poet of his time, wrote *Poems of a Live Man* (1841). Finally, Ferdinand Freiligrath (1810–76), a lover of exotic romances, urged his countrymen to take revolutionary action.

Young Plan (1929)

The Young Plan was an American-inspired proposal for the definitive resolution to the war reparations problem that so plagued and embittered European relations in the 1920s. A committee was appointed and presided over by an American, Owen D. Young. It met in Paris in 1929 and worked out a plan by which German reparations payments that had been set by the DAWES PLAN in 1924 would be paid over a period of $58\frac{1}{2}$ years through a special Bank of International Settlement at Basel. At the same time, the cost of reparations was reduced to about a quarter of the figure originally asked in 1921.

The reduction of reparations and the removal of Allied troops from the RHINELAND was Gustav STRESEMANN's main objective after the conclusion of the LOCARNO TREATIES. The question of the withdrawal of troops and the Young Plan was agreed to at the Hague Conference of 1929. Stresemann succeeded in convincing the delegates that the downward adjustment of reparation payments would benefit the European economy. He also realized the political difficulty of getting popular support for any reparation payments, and thought that the simultaneous Allied evacuation of the Rhineland would increase German support. Because the GREAT DEPRESSION occurred, Germany was unable to make any payments in 1931–32. When in 1933 Hitler refused to pay any reparations, the Young Plan never was realized.

Z

Zabern Affair (1913)

Zabern was a village in ALSACE, which from 1871 to 1918 was part of the German Empire. As a consequence of the ill-feeling between the villagers and the German garrison, a trivial incident occurred in which a junior officer, Lieutenant von Forstner, struck a crippled civilian. A commotion resulted, and the military was called out. Police powers were assumed by the military authorities, and in defiance of normal process of law 28 people were arrested. The REICHSTAG protested against this action by the military, but a court-martial acquitted both Forstner and his commander. When the matter was raised in the Reichstag, the minister of war supported the military, as did the chancellor, Theobald von BETHMANN HOLLWEG. In this case an opportunity was missed to limit the power of the executive branch by transferring ministerial responsibility to the Reichstag. There was a vote of no confidence against the chancellor, but it did not lead to his resignation. Only the Socialists thought that Bethmann-Hollweg should resign. On the eve of WORLD WAR I Germany was still an absolute monarchy, even though it had a constitution.

Zeiss, Carl (1816–1888)
manufacturer of optical instruments

Carl Zeiss was a tool and dye maker of precision optical instruments who was responsible for Germany's international reputation in the field.

Carl Zeiss was born on September 11, 1816, in WEIMAR. In 1846 at age 30 he opened his own shop for the production of microscopes and optical instruments. Germany's reputation as a leading manufacturer of optical instruments began. He employed the physicist Ernst Abbe, who became his partner in 1866, forming the Zeiss Optical and Glass Co. in JENA, Thuringia. Then the chemist Otto Schott was also employed by the firm, and to his credit about 100 new types of glass were developed, which included heat-resistant types. Before WORLD WAR I the glass works was the world's dominant supplier of glass blanks for eyeglasses, microscopes, binoculars, cameras, and telescopes, which, however, had to be specially ground to customer specifications.

The war demonstrated that optical glass was a strategic material. Consequently, other manufacturers were supported by Western governments, including Bausch and Lomb in the United States. In 1945 at the end of WORLD WAR II the factory complex in Jena was destroyed. The American military government moved the management and 81 Zeiss scientists and technicians to Oberkochen, Württemberg, in West Germany, where another factory complex was erected. The East Germans had rebuilt the firm in Jena, and after unification in 1990 the two operations were merged into one firm. Leica cameras are one of the famous products produced by the company.

Zeppelin, Ferdinand, Count von (Ferdinand Adolf August Heinrich, Graf [Count] von Zeppelin) (1838–1917)
designer of dirigible airships

Count Ferdinand von Zeppelin invented the dirigible airship, which made him famous. They were employed by the German army over the western front and England.

Ferdinand Zeppelin was born on July 8, 1838, in Constance. As a young nobleman he entered upon a military career but was also allowed to study engineering and chemistry, which bore fruit in the development of his airships. During the American Civil War he was an observer and was able to experience balloon flight in Minnesota. He participated in the Austro-Prussian and Franco-Prussian wars, and observed the French use of balloons during the siege of Paris. Count Zeppelin continued in military service, was a military attaché in BERLIN, and then the ambassador and representative of Württemberg to the Federal Council. He ended his career as a major general.

In 1892 Zeppelin hired a design engineer to assist him in the construction of a dirigible. After many tests the government rejected his proposal of an airship in 1894. In 1898 he founded the Society for the Promotion of Motor Aviation and established an airship yard near Friedrichshafen. The first Zeppelin airship was constructed in 1900 and was launched at Friedrichshafen by Lake Constance. It was 416 feet long, had a speed of 17.3 miles per hour, and used hydrogen gas. It was not until 1908 that a 12-hour flight over Switzerland stirred up enthusiasm in Germany. In 1909 Zeppelin formed the first passenger air-travel company, the German Airship Company (DELAG), which flew 100,000 miles in five years. By the time WORLD WAR I broke out, the German army owned seven airships. The airships were used in the war by both the army and navy and played important reconnaissance roles in the BATTLE OF JUTLAND (1916). In February 1915 zeppelins crossed the North Sea and bombed Yarmouth in May 1915, extending their raids to London in the summer. Although they had a greater range and larger bomb load than aircraft, improved defenses made them vulnerable and ended their raids after a disastrous mass attack on London in November 1917.

Between the wars German zeppelins were commercially successful and from 1928 to 1937 maintained the first transatlantic airline service. After the burning of the *Hindenburg* in New York on May 6, 1937, flights were suspended.

Count Zeppelin had the foresight to recognize the superiority of airplanes over zeppelins and became co-owner of an aircraft factory at Friedrichshafen in 1912. Zeppelin died on March 8, 1917, in Berlin.

Zetkin, Clara (1857–1933)
Socialist leader and feminist

Clara Zetkin was a leading feminist (*see* FEMINISM) in the socialist movement. She joined the GERMAN COMMUNIST PARTY (KPD) at the end of the war and promoted international cooperation in the labor movement and more equality for women.

Born on July 5, 1857, the eldest daughter in a family of village schoolteachers, Clara Zetkin was educated in LEIPZIG, where she obtained a teaching certificate. While there she joined the ranks of German Social Democracy and met her future husband, Ossip Zetkin, whom she married in 1882. In Switzerland in the 1880s she served on the editorial board of the socialist newspaper, the *Social Democrat,* and contributed to the foundation of the socialist Second International in 1889.

A key to the success of the German socialist women's movement was the realization by the SPD that women needed a structure separate from men so that they could develop their own talents and ideas without fear of male disapproval. In 1891 Clara Zetkin became the editor of the women's newspaper of the party, *Equality* (*Die Gleichheit*), a position she held until 1917. These efforts motivated 30,000 women by 1908 to join the party, whose membership increased to more than 174,000 by 1914, twice the number in the French socialist party. It was the largest movement of women of any political orientation on the Continent. And it was Zetkin who expressed their radical orientation. She became prominent with her speech, "The Liberation of Women," given at the founding congress of the Second International in Paris in 1889. In it she argued that because of the weakness of middle-class democracy, it was left to the socialists to lead the struggle for women's rights. She was opposed to any limitation on gainful female employment, which she believed would provide proletarian women with independence and the basis of their social and political equality. When she returned to Germany, she moderated her position on the need to destroy capitalism, realizing that women joined the movement because their husbands were SPD members. Gaining suffrage, she argued, was only the first step in emancipation because it did not eliminate class differences and exploitation. Her ideas that women would be liberated and be politically equal only when socialism was created were incorporated into the party program of the GOTHA PROGRAM in 1896. Throughout the period before the war Zetkin cooperated with Luise ZIETZ (1865–1922) in developing the women's movement. She also was friends with Rosa LUXEMBURG and the left radicals in the party disputes prior to the war.

While most German women did not resist the euphoria and supported the war, Zetkin was totally opposed to the war and the Civil Truce (Burgfrieden). Luise Zietz, however, in the executive committee opposed only the approval of war credits, but then encouraged socialist women to provide community social services. Clara Zetkin and socialist women were generally more sympathetic to pacificism than the middle-class women's movement under Gertrud BAUMER. When the INDEPENDENT SOCIAL DEMOCRATIC PARTY (USPD) was formed, she was its representative in the REICHSTAG. Then she supported the Spartacus League and finally joined the newly organized Communist Party (KPD). She did not, however, support those Communists who wanted to forcefully take over the government; instead, she believed in the Marxian prediction that a revolution would soon occur. She lived in Moscow for a time and was friends with Lenin. After her return and election to the Reichstag, she had the honor of opening the 1932 session. After the Nazis came to power, she left for Russia, dying soon in Moscow on June 20, 1933.

Zietz, Luise Korner (1865–1922)
agitator for SPD women's movement

Luise Zietz became one of the early leaders of the SPD women's movement. Luise Zietz was the daughter of a cottage weaver. She was not able to attend school, so she largely educated herself. With those handicaps it is surprising that she even entered politics and was such an effective speaker. She was openly an agitator for the Social Democratic women's movement after the government legalized female participation in politics in 1908. She was notable for being the first female member of the Social Democratic executive committee. She used her leadership skills in integrating the socialist women's movement into the SPD. Yet some of the women leaders complained that Zietz allowed the male leadership to co-opt their autonomy.

When WORLD WAR I broke out, Luise Zietz opposed the approval of war credits. While she followed leadership directives and urged Social Democratic women to help in community social service, child welfare, and care for the sick and women in childbed, she carefully avoided any outbursts of hatred. She believed in and appealed to all socialist women to show international solidarity.

In 1917 Zietz was a principal agitator for the split in the party that led to the formation of the INDEPENDENT SOCIAL DEMOCRATIC PARTY (USPD). After the break she assumed a leadership role in the formation of the Independent's women's movement. She went on to play an active role in the REVOLUTION OF 1918–1919. In 1919 she was one of the first female members of the new REICHSTAG (1919–22) of the WEIMAR REPUBLIC. She opposed the republic's efforts to crush the radical left. She opposed those in the USPD who wanted to return to the SPD and also resisted a merger with the Moscow-dominated GERMAN COMMUNIST PARTY (KPD).

Zimmermann, Johann Baptist (1680–1758), and Domenikus Zimmermann (1685–1766)
rococo artist and architect

The creative artistic accomplishments of the stuccoworker and painter Johann Baptist Zimmermann and his architect brother, Domenikus, expressed the best of the Bavarian ROCOCO style. The beautiful and gloriously decorated rural church of Die Wies is their masterpiece.

The Zimmermann brothers were born at Gaispoint near Wessobrunn, Johann Baptist on

January 3, 1680, and Domenikus on June 30, 1685. Both brothers were trained at the abbey of Wessobrunn in the remarkable craft of coloring stucco to make it appear like marble. Domenikus went on to become a master mason, while Johann Baptist learned the specialty of fresco painting. For a time they concentrated on stucco work, although after 1724 Domenikus dedicated himself almost exclusively to architecture and Johann Baptist concentrated on fresco painting.

In his design of the pilgrimage churches at Steinhausen and Günzburg (1736–41) Domenikus solved the problem of combining a central plan church with a longitudinal one, resolving the difficulty with an oval nave surrounded by arcades, allowing devout pilgrims to move around unhindered. Large windows bathed the interior with light, which reflected on the pale pastel interior. The nave was beautifully frescoed by his brother.

One of the greatest achievements in the Bavarian rococo style was the construction of the pilgrimage church of Die Wies (1745–54, which stands in the middle of a forest clearing not far from Steingaden in Upper Bavaria. The white nave has touches of gold, and the richly colored sanctuary has fantastic ornamentation and a gaily colored ceiling fresco by Johann Baptist. The beauty of the church makes visitors believe they surely are in a heavenly place. It certainly is Domenikus's masterpiece, which he must have recognized because he lived there until his death on November 16, 1766.

The fresco artist, Johann Baptist, produced many works independently. He was appointed to the royal court in MUNICH in 1720, where he worked with the court architects, Joseph Effner and François Cuvilliés on the fresco decoration of the palace at Schleissheim, and in 1726 at Nymphenburg and in the Residenz in Munich. From 1734 on he produced some of his finest stucco ornamentation at Amalienburg. Frescoes and decoration for other churches were produced at Vilgertshofen (1734), Berg am Laim (1739–44), Dietramzell (1714), St. Peter's in Munich (1753–56), Andechs (1754), and Schäftlarn (1754–56). The ceilings of the Residenz theater (1752–53) in Munich and of the Great Hall at Nymphenburg Palace (1756–57) were his work. He died in Munich during February 1758.

Zimmermann Telegram (January 19, 1917)

The Zimmermann Telegram was a coded message dated January 19, 1917, from Arthur Zimmermann, the German foreign secretary (1916–17), to the German minister in Mexico routed via the German ambassador to the United States. The telegram urged that Germany and Mexico form an alliance if the United States entered WORLD WAR I against Germany in response to a German resumption of unrestricted submarine warfare against neutrals and belligerents on February 1. As a result of the alliance the Mexicans would attack the United States. In the peace settlement after a German victory the Mexicans would recover the territory they had lost in 1848 (Arizona, New Mexico, and Texas) as a result of the Mexican-American War. The telegram also indicated that Germany was encouraging Japan to join the Central Powers, thereby changing alliances and attacking the United States in the Pacific.

Possessing the German code, the British naval intelligence intercepted the message and forwarded it to Washington. It was released to the American press on March 1, which further enraged public opinion already angry over the submarine warfare. The telegram accordingly aroused a storm of protest. Additional resentment occurred because the telegram had been sent to the German ambassador in Washington, Count Bernstorff, over a private wire in the State Department, which the Germans had been given permission to use to facilitate the transmission of peace overtures. The telegram played a considerable part in inducing Congress to support war with Germany. Even so, President Woodrow Wilson tried to avoid war, requesting that Germany allow American shipping to flow unhindered to Britain. This was rejected, and the United States declared war on April 6, 1917.

Zollverein
(Customs Union)

An important step in the creation of German economic unity was begun by PRUSSIA in 1818 with the creation of a free-trade area within its boundaries. In 1834 the tariffs and trade barriers between 18 states were eliminated, and by the middle of the century all states except AUSTRIA had joined the Customs Union.

The establishment of a customs union that was to initiate the liberal economic era in the GERMAN CONFEDERATION was not begun as an economic measure, but rather one of enlightened bureaucratic rationalization. When the HOLY ROMAN EMPIRE was abolished in 1806, Germany was burdened by not only political particularism but also economic particularism. All bureaucratic proposals to establish a uniform currency and abolish trade barriers were foiled by the selfish interests of the territorial princes. At the end of the Napoleonic era Prussia acquired new territories at the CONGRESS OF VIENNA, including territories along the RHINE and in SAXONY to the southeast. Imports brought into Germany at ports along the Rhine had to traverse other states, which charged tariffs and generally made distribution to other parts of Prussia more difficult. As early as 1818 Prussian officials in the Ministry of Finance proposed the establishment of a customs union (Zollverein), attempting to lower costs and facilitate a more liberal trade policy by eliminating its 67 different tariff schedules. This single market favored the grain producers, mainly the noble landowners to the east (JUNKERS), but was disadvantageous for the infant German industries that needed protection from cheaper imported English goods. At the port of entry member states were to charge a tax that would be divided among the states according to population, but transit taxes were abolished. This applied to Prussia and its immediate neighbors, such as HANOVER and Hesse. The states to the south, BAVARIA, Württemberg, and Baden, traditionally distrusted Protestant Prussia and often allied themselves with Catholic Austria. Because of fears of losing their political independence, the proposals were not implemented for them until 1834. This political fear was balanced, however, by a greater fear of economic isolation, because the Austrian Empire had in the meantime established its own separate customs union, including its territories within the Confederation. Furthermore, the currency of the Prussian-led Customs Union of 1834 became the Thaler, the currency of Prussia. Consequently, these measures effectually left the economic leadership of the German Confederation to Prussia.

The actual economic unification of Germany under Prussian leadership was essentially the work of Friedrich von Motz (1775–1830) the Prussian minister of finance. He was a more progressive member of the Prussian cabinet who had grown up in the era of Prussian reforms. He was an advocate of the free-trade ideas of Adam Smith, appreciated the role of the MIDDLE CLASS in the Industrial Revolution, and had the support of the Prussian Junkers. He also predicted that the inclusion of the southern German states would eventually lead to their becoming part of a unified Germany under Prussian leadership.

Zwickau prophets

Among the radicals of Christian reform were the enthusiasts known as the "Zwickau prophets." They were itinerant preachers who inveighed against the corruptness of the clergy and the papal "Antichrist" in Rome. They called for a total purge of all the old sacramental forms of worship, which was contrary to LUTHER's view. The Zwickau prophets came from a small mining town of Zwickau on the Bohemian border where Hussite and Lutheran influences had mingled. The mining towns were turbulent places, but the weavers were the most active group. Luther's reforms had produced among the craftsmen a laicist radicalism. One of the leaders was a Nicolaus Storch, a poor clothier who taught a mystical approach to God based on a peculiar interpretation of the Bible. His approach to God started with the suppression of sensuality for a direct contact with God in which the ultimate sanctification and certainty of selection was achieved. A prophetic gift and mission sprang from this community. The secular order was seen as sinful and deserving of extermination if the inner voice commanded it. Another leader was Sebastian Frank (1499–1545), who eschewed a visible church and sacramentalism. He emphasized that Christ is in every person as an "inner light" illuminating the soul.

Among the radicals Thomas Müntzer was a champion of total destruction and the ablest opponent of Luther, being one of the most learned theological and humanist scholars of the time. He was influenced by Luther and gained a reputation as a preacher in Zwickau. In 1521 he was forced out of Zwickau and scattered his radical religious ideas throughout central Germany. That same year the Zwickau prophets came to Wittenberg, while Luther was at The Wartburg. Other leaders in Wittenberg appeared. At the university was Andreas Carlstadt, who made up in radicalism what he lacked in originality. He made new rules: He destroyed his books and writings and believed that Christian wisdom was given to simple people. What the Zwickau prophets advocated was a contempt for learning, the burning of religious art, the rejection of classical culture as pagan, and the adoption of such tactics as book burning, excommunication, and even death at the stake. All of this intolerance offended the humanists. The humanists were for church reform but had not counted on the radical ravings of the Protestants, which sounded like a return to medievalism

Müntzer's theology accepted the Joachimite idea of a third Age of the Spirit, which would manifest itself in a Thousand Year Empire. This was to be the actual fulfillment of the prophecy of Christ, that his spirit would eventually descend among humanity and reign over them. The gift of prophecy was also going to live again among the poor and uneducated, who have dreams and visions. In this way the "inner world" was to manifest itself against Luther's emphasis of the Scriptures as the Word of God. According to Müntzer Luther had created a new tyranny replacing the papacy. The third idea was that the elect, the real prophets, would eventually take over and destroy all the ungodly who were presently ruling in both the church and the state. It was not surprising that Müntzer was driven from place to place and in 1524 ended up in Mülhausen in Thuringia, where agitation prevailed. Finally, he became the ideological leader of the Peasants' War in 1525, during which upheaval he was killed.

Zwingli, Ulrich (Huldreich) (1484–1531)
religious reformer

Ulrich Zwingli became the leader of the Swiss Reformation. A key doctrinal difference with Luther concerned the Eucharist. Zwingli denied the real presence of Christ and insisted that the Eucharist was not a repetition of Christ's sacrifice but only a respectful remembrance.

Ulrich Zwingli was born on January 1, 1484, in the village of Wildhaus. He was one of 10 children. His education was humanistic. In 1494 he went to school in Basel and in 1498 to Bern, where he fell under the influence of a famous classicist, Heinrich Wölflin. Zwingli attended the University of Vienna, studying philosophy, was influenced by Conrad Celtis, and gained an appreciation of music. At 18 Zwingli returned to Basel, where he studied theology, receiving his baccalaureate in 1504 and a master's degree, and was ordained a priest in 1506. Some years later, he was an army chaplain at the battles of Novara (1513) and Marignano (1515). He pastored a church at Glarus, immersing himself in the Latin classics, the church fathers, and the Bible, improving his knowledge of Greek and learning Hebrew. In 1516 he became a hero-worshipper of Erasmus, whom he had met in Basel and with whom he carried on a correspondence. In 1516 Zwingli moved to Einsiedeln in the canton of Schwyz when he already was developing doctrinal opinions different from Rome. Zwingli was working his way toward a religion based on Scripture before he even heard of and applauded Luther. He not only attacked the sale of indulgences and the proliferation of false relics but also began to speak openly of a religion based only on the Bible. Independently of Luther, Zwingli concluded that the papacy was unfounded from Scriptures and that church tradition did not have equal validity with the Bible as a source of Christian truth. Late in 1518 he was appointed stipendiary or people's priest at the main church in Zurich. His appointment was not uncontested, and he had to defend himself against the accusation of fornication with a barber's daughter. Successfully defending himself, one of his first acts as a reformer was to petition for the right of the clergy to marry.

In the early years of Zwingli's ministry in Zurich, he preached frequently based on the Bible and from an Erasmian perspective on internal reform. He viewed Luther as a colleague in reform and not his leader. On his own, Zwingli turned his back in 1522 to the Erasmian idea of reform in the old church and moved to an evangelical theology. Very gradually in concert with the Zurich city council, Zwingli led the Zurich church to evangelical reform. Zwingli requested the abolition of the Mass in 1523, which was approved two years later by only a small majority. Zwingli's movement was centered much more than Lutheranism on a search for precise biblical authority. Images, pictures, and church music soon were denounced. In 1522 the Lenten fast was dramatically and solemnly broken. About the same time the bishop of Constance was petitioned to allow clerical marriage.

The year 1523 was a crucial turning point as the public debated Zwingli's 67 articles. The articles were formulated in response to the anger of the bishop over Zwingli's stand against celibacy. Zwingli successfully defended himself, and the city council severed the canton from the bishop's jurisdiction. Along with the abolition of the Mass on April 13, 1525, this completed the Reformation in Zurich. Yet, the radical ANABAPTISTS were already disputing the extent of the reform. Zurich became the center of the Swiss Reformation, and with the imposed discipline one of the first examples of puritanical PROTESTANTISM.

Zwingli's quarrel with Luther concerned the nature of the Eucharist: Was Christ's presence in the Eucharist a real physical presence as Luther maintained, or was the Eucharist a commemoration with emphasis on the spiritual presence of Christ? After some years of controversy, the landgrave Philip of Hesse (1504–67) was desirous to unite Swiss and German Protestants in a mutual defense pact against the emperor's determination to enforce the EDICT OF WORMS. Philip arranged a meeting at his castle in Marburg in early October 1529—the MARBURG COLLOQUY—to facilitate an agreement between Luther and Zwingli on the nature of Christ's presence in the Eucharist. No compromise resulted as Luther wanted no part of a spiritualized presence and Zwingli feared that Luther had not sufficiently broken with medieval sacramental theology. The Protestant movement split into two camps, which had important consequences for the Reformation in the Empire.

The quarrel was reflected in the competition for the allegiance of the IMPERIAL CITIES. Zwingli's doctrine was more popular in the republican cities where there was an emphasis on Christian community and republicanism. On the other hand, Luther's appeal was more to the aristocratic cities of the North and those in Franconia in the South. The concerns were not only theological but had two different basic approaches to ecclesiastical, political, and social issues. Even in its earliest stages Zwinglianism exercised an influence upon the towns of southwestern Germany, which were neighbors and trading associates with the Swiss. The south German towns had a greater social affinity and independence of outlook with the Swiss towns than they had with those of central and northern Germany. The most important of the Imperial Free Cities was Strasbourg, which sought to steer an independent course between Luther and Zwingli; it became a center of refuge for Protestant exiles and radicals. The hybrid religious scene in Strasbourg also illustrates that many of these towns were not exclusively Lutheran, Zwinglian, Anabaptist, Calvinist, or Catholic.

Zwingli expressed his theological view in the 67 articles of 1523 and in his tract of 1525, *De vera et falsa religione*. He consistently maintained that salvation depended on faith alone and was granted only to those souls whom God had chosen. In general his theology was absorbed in Calvinism. Besides not being able to unify with Luther, Zwingli also was disappointed that all of Switzerland did not join his Reformation. The conservative forest cantons remained faithful to Roman Catholicism and formed a league to fight Protestant movements. Civil war broke out in 1531, and Zwingli participated in the war as the chaplain of the citizens of Zurich. He was killed in the Battle of Kappel on October 11, 1531. His body was mutilated and burned.

CHRONOLOGY

962–1806
Holy Roman Empire

1414–18
Council of Constance and end of Great Schism in the church

1415
Jan Hus (1369–1415), a Czech nationalist opposed to the German control of the Czech church and advocate of the use of vernacular in the liturgy, is burned at the stake for heresy

1419–36
Hussite Civil Wars concern religious, national (anti-German), and socialistic issues erupting from Hus's execution

1438–39
Emperor Albrecht II; the crown of the Holy Roman Empire returns to the Habsburgs

1444–85
Rudolf Agricola, father of German humanism

1450
Printing invented by Johannes Gutenberg of Mainz

1452
Frederick III, the last German emperor to be crowned in Rome

1455–1522
Johannes Reuchlin, first competent Greek scholar in Germany and defender of Jewish literature

1459–1508
Conrad Celtis, foremost poet of the German renaissance

1466
The territory of the Teutonic Knights (West Prussia and Ermeland) ceded to Poland

1466–1536
Desiderius Erasmus, greatest literary figure of the northern renaissance

1471–1528
Albrecht Dürer, greatest German artist of the Renaissance

1477
Maximilian secures the Netherlands and Burgundy for the Habsburg family possessions

1480–1530
Matthias Grünewald, German religious artist of the Renaissance

1483–1546
Martin Luther, leader of the Protestant Reformation

1488–1523
Ulrich von Hutten, chief nationalist and poet laureate crowned by Maximilian I

1491–1556
Ignatius of Loyola, founder of the Jesuits

1491
Frederick III secures the hereditary succession in Hungary for the Habsburgs

1493–1519
Emperor Maximilian I, son of Frederick III

1493–1541
Paracelsus, physician and theorist whose knowledge was based on experience

1497–1543
Hans Holbein the Younger, Germany's greatest portrait painter of the Renaissance

1497–1560
Philip Melanchthon, humanist who became chief systematic theologian of the Reformation, and known as *praeceptor Germaniae* for his educational reforms

SIXTEENTH CENTURY

1500
Adages of Erasmus published

1502
University of Wittenberg founded

1503
Enchiridion of Erasmus published

1504
First postal route between Brussels and Vienna established by Francis of Taxis

1505–1507
Martin Luther enters monastery and is ordained a priest in Erfurt

1506
Latin-Hebrew grammar published by Johannes Reuchlin

1508
Maximilian I accepts the title "Chosen Roman Emperor"

1509
In Praise of Folly published by Erasmus

1510
Humanist controversy between Reuchlin and Pfefferkorn

1512
Luther completes doctorate at University of Wittenberg; Diet of Cologne divides the Empire into 10 major judicial districts

1516
New Testament published by Erasmus

1517
Martin Luther posts his Ninety-five Theses on the castle church in Wittenberg

1519
Charles V elected Holy Roman Emperor; Ulrich Zwingli's reformation in Zurich, Switzerland

1520
Luther's three major pamphlets defending his theology and attacking Rome: (1) *The Christian Nobility of the German Nation;* (2) *On the Babylonian Captivity of the Church;* (3) *On the Freedom of a Christian Man*

1521
Diet and Edict of Worms; Luther is banned by the church in the papal bull, *"Decet Romanum";* Ferdinand, the brother of Charles V, inherits the Austrian possessions of the Habsburgs

1521–26
War between Charles V and Francis I of France

1522
Publication of Luther's translation of the *New Testament*

1522–23
Revolt of the knights of the Empire

1524–26
Great Peasants' Revolt and War

1525
Luther marries Katherine of Bora; publication of Luther's pamphlet *Against the Murderous and Rapacious Hordes of Peasants*

1526
Peace of Madrid between Charles V and Francis I

1526–29
Second war between Charles V and Francis I

1527
University of Marburg founded

1529
The Second Diet of Speyer; debate over the interpretation of the Last Supper between Luther and Zwingli, called the Marburg Colloquy

1530
Diet of Augsburg and presentation of the Protestant statement of faith, the Confession of Augsburg, composed by Melanchthon; Schmalkaldic League formed

1531
Ferdinand I is crowned Roman-German king

1532
Religious peace of Nuremberg

1534–35
Anabaptist "Kingdom of Zion" in Münster succumbs to imperial armies

1536–38
Third war between Charles V and Francis II

1540
Society of Jesus founded by Ignatius of Loyola

1541
John Calvin's reformation in Geneva; Diet of Regensburg

1542–44
Fourth war between Charles V and Francis I of France

1544
Diet of Speyer; Peace of Crespy; alliance between Charles V and Protestants against threat from France and the Turks

1545–63
Council of Trent reforms Catholic Church

1546
Death of Martin Luther

1546–47
Schmalkaldic War between Protestants and Catholics

1548
Diet of Augsburg

1552
Betrayal of Charles V by Duke Maurice of Saxony; bishoprics of Metz, Toul, and Verdun occupied by Henry II of France

1555
Religious Peace of Augsburg was a compromise peace acknowledging the equality between Lutheranism and Catholicism, and that each prince could decide the religion of his state

1556
Abdication of Emperor Charles V

1556–64
Emperor Ferdinand I, brother of Charles V

1564–76
Emperor Maximilian II, son of Ferdinand I

1576–1612
Emperor Rudolf II, son of Maximilian II

1583–1634
Albrecht von Wallenstein, general during Thirty Years' War

SEVENTEENTH CENTURY

1600–50
Age of the baroque

1608
Protestant Union of Germany organized

1609
Catholic League organized, led by Duke Maximilian of Bavaria

1612–19
Emperor Matthias I, brother of Rudolf II

1618–23
Bohemian Revolt

1618
Defenestration of Prague, initiating Thirty Years' War

1619–37
Emperor Ferdinand II, grandson of Emperor Ferdinand I

1619
Election of Frederick V, Elector Palatine, as king of Bohemia

1620
Battle of White Mountain in which Bohemians are defeated by the emperor and the Catholic League under General Tilly

1623
Duke Maximilian of Bavaria (1598–1651) becomes an imperial elector and receives the Upper Palatinate

1625
Christian IV of Denmark invades Germany; Wallenstein placed in command of imperial army

1626
Wallenstein defeats Count Mansfeld at Dessau; Tilly defeats Danish forces at Lutter in Brunswick

1627
Johannes Kepler publishes *Rudolfine Tables*

1629
Edict of Restitution restores ecclesiastical estates to the emperor; Peace of Lübeck

1630
Wallenstein dismissed

1630–35
Gustavus Adolphus (1611–32) begins the Swedish phase of Thirty Years' War

1631
Tilly attacks the city of Magdeberg; Gustavus Adolphus defeats Tilly at the Battle of Breitenfeld; Prague occupied by Saxon army

1632
Wallenstein given supreme command of imperial forces; death of Tilly; Gustavus Adolphus killed at the Battle of Lützen

1633
Heilbronn Confederation formed

1634
Wallenstein assassinated in Bohemia

1635
Peace of Prague between emperor and electors of Brandenburg and Saxony whereby the electors ended their alliance with Sweden and relinquished German church lands acquired after 1627

1635–48
Swedish-French phase of Thirty Years' War

1637–57
Emperor Ferdinand III, son of Emperor Ferdinand II

1640–88
Frederick William, Great Elector of Brandenburg

1643–1715
Louis XIV, king of France

1646–1716
Gottfried Wilhelm von Leibniz, one of Germany's most original minds and contributor to the Scientific Revolution

1648
Peace of Westphalia ends Thirty Years' War

1652
Treaty of Passau secularizes ecclesiastical estates

1655–1728
Christian Thomasius popularizes the Enlightenment; first German professor to lecture in German

1658–1705
Emperor Leopold I, son of Emperor Ferdinand III

1663–1806
"Permanent Diet" located at Regensburg

1679
The "Great Elector" of Brandenburg required to return Pomeranian conquests to Sweden in Peace of St Germain

1679–1754
Christian Wolff, the heir of Leibniz and considered the greatest philosopher of the 18th century

1683–99
The Great Turkish War

1683
Turkish siege of Vienna repulsed with the help of John Sobieski, King John III of Poland

1684
"Holy League" alliance between Austria, the papacy, and Venice

1685
Potsdam Edict of Toleration invites French of the Reformed-Evangelical faith to settle in Prussia

1685–1750
Johann Sebastian Bach, baroque composer of organ music for church liturgies, including cantatas and *St. Matthew's Passion* (1772)

1685–1759
Georg Frideric Handel, composer of operas, oratorios, such as the *Messiah* (1742) and *Music for the Royal Fireworks* (1749)

1687
The Diet of Pressburg confers the male line of succession in Hungary on Austria; "Holy League" defeats Turks at Mohács in Hungary

1689–97
War of the League of Augsburg; French devastate the Palatinate, especially Heidelberg

1697
Prince Eugene of Savoy (1663–1736) defeats the Turks at Zenta, Hungary

1697
Peace of Ryswik requires Louis XIV to return conquests in the Palatinate

1699
Peace of Karlowitz requires Turks to surrender Hungary and Transylvania, marking the beginning of the Danubian empire of the Habsburgs

EIGHTEENTH CENTURY

1701
Frederick III, elector of Brandenburg, assumes title of "king in Prussia" as Frederick I

1704
Battle of Blenheim eliminates French forces from Germany in War of Spanish Succession

1705–11
Emperor Joseph I, son of Emperor Leopold I

1711–40
Emperor Charles VI, younger brother of Emperor Joseph I, the last in male line of Habsburg succession

1713
Pragmatic Sanction of Austrian emperor Charles VI provides for the succession of the emperor's daughter, Maria Theresa

1713–40
Frederick William I, king of Prussia, son of the elector of Brandenburg, Frederick III

1715–18
Second Turkish War

1716–17
Prince Eugene of Savoy victorious at battles of Peterwardein and Belgrade

1700–50
Expansion of religious Pietism

1718
Peace of Passarowitz ends the Turkish military threat to Hungary: The Turks surrender to Austria the remaining parts of Hungary, northern Serbia including Belgrade, and sections of Walachia and Bosnia

1722
Prussian General Directory organized, centralizing interior administration

1724–1804
Immanuel Kant, one of the founders of modern philosophy, a representative of the German Enlightenment and author of *Critique of Pure Reason* (1781), and *Critique of Practical Reason* (1788)

1732–1839
Joseph Haydn, one of four great Viennese composers of the classical period. Haydn practically invented the classical symphony

1733
Prussian cantonal system established

1740–80
Reign of Maria Theresa, empress of Austria (queen of Hungary)

1740–86
Reign of Frederick II, the Great, king of Prussia, son of King Frederick William I

1740–45
First and Second Silesian Wars

1744–1803
Johann Gottfried Herder, studied the cultural activities of humanity

1745
Treaty of Dresden, by which Austria ceded Silesia to Prussia

1745–47
Sans-Souci palace constructed in Potsdam for Frederick the Great

1746
Austrian Universal Directory of Commerce organized; in 1761 it becomes an independent central agency

1749
Austrian General Directory organized by Haugwitz; Prussian protection of the peasantry

1749–1832
Johann Wolfgang von Goethe, Germany's greatest intellectual and genius who ushered in the Storm and Stress literary period

1750–90
Cultural developments: Enlightenment and rococo

1756
Diplomatic Revolution involving change of alliances between Austria and France

1756–91
Wolfgang Amadeus Mozart, Viennese composer of the classical period, especially the opera *The Magic Flute*, symphonies, piano concertos, and church music

1756–63
Seven Years' War (Third Silesian War)

1763
Peace of Hubertusburg concludes the Seven Years' War, by which Frederick retained Silesia and all other gains of the first two Silesian wars

1763
Austrian military recruitment system established after model of Prussian "canton" system

1765
Prussian Transfer and Loan Bank founded

1769–1821
Napoleon Bonaparte, general of French revolutionary armies and emperor

1770–1827
Ludwig van Beethoven, great German composer of the French revolutionary period whose special musical genres were symphonies, piano concertos, string quartets, and piano sonatas

1770–1831
Georg Wilhelm Friedrich Hegel, idealist philosopher whose philosophy of history had a great impact; publication of *Encyclopedia of Philosophical Sciences* (1817, 1827, 1830)

1772
First Partition of Poland between Austria, Prussia, and Russia

1774
Sorrows of Young Werther by Wolfgang von Goethe published and has European-wide influence

1776
Sturm und Drang by Friedrich Maximilian Klinger published

1778–79
War of Bavarian Succession

1781
Emperor Joseph II issues Edict of Toleration for Protestants and Jews; peasants placed under imperial protection

1786–97
Reign of Frederick William II of Prussia

1789
French Revolution begins

1790–92
Emperor Leopold II, brother of Emperor Joseph II

1792
Declaration of Pilnitz threatens war against France, if the rights of German powers in Alsace not reinstated

1792–97
First Coalition War of Austro-Prussian alliance against revolutionary France

1792–1806
Emperor Francis II (Francis I as Emperor of Austria, 1804–35)

1793
The second partition of Poland between Prussia and Russia

1794
Prussian Civil Code includes private, criminal and constitutional law. It defines the rights of the absolute monarchy and the power to levy taxes without popular consent. Citizen rights are defined according to the three social estates—peasants, middle class (burghers), and nobility

1797–1840
Frederick William III, king of Prussia

1797–1828
Franz Schubert, Viennese composer of the classical period, who excelled in specialties of songs using Goethe's texts, but also composed symphonies and chamber music

1799–1802
Second Coalition War beween France and Austria, Russia, England, and others, in which the Austrians were defeated in the battles of Marengo and Hohenlinden (1800)

1799–1818
Maximilian von Monteglas (1759–1838) is chief minister of the Bavarian government, implementing ideas of the Enlightenment such as state control of education

1806–1825
Maximilian I Joseph, King of Bavaria

NINETEENTH CENTURY

1800
Battles of Marengo and Hohenlinden, where French defeat Austrians

1801
Peace of Lunéville ends war of Second Coalition

1803
Diet of Ratisbon; *Principal Decree of Imperial Deputation* of Regensburg remakes the map of Germany, secularizing clerical principalities

1804–14
Napoleon I, emperor of the French

1804–54
August Borsig, founded the first steam locomotive factory and limited English competition

1805
Third Coalition War between Austria and France; Napoleon defeats coalition at Austerlitz

1806
Holy Roman Empire dissolved by Napoleon; defeat of Prussian armies in battles of Jena and Auerstädt; Confederation of the Rhine established; Bavaria becomes a kingdom

1807
Prussian reform initiated by Baron Karl vom und zum Stein; edict of October 9 liberates peasants from personal duties, but nobles' patrimonial jurisdiction remains; by Peace of Tilsit Prussia forced to cede half her territory, including the Polish provinces; *Addresses to the German Nation* by J. G. Fichte; Napoleon makes triumphal entry into Berlin

1807–13
Prussian military reforms directed by Gerhard Scharnhorst including universal military service, a regular army, a reserve component, and a Home Guard of all men over 35

1808
New organization for urban communities by Baron Karl vom und zum Stein (1757–1831),

the self-administration of local communities was Stein's central achievement

1809
Peace of Schönbrunn deprives Austria of status as a great power and most of her valuable provinces; Prince Clemens von Metternich becomes chief minister in Austria

1810–12
Reforms in Prussia: Freedom of Trade and Occupation Acts; emancipation of Jews; University of Berlin and the War Academy founded

1810–22
Prince Hardenberg (1750–1822) becomes Prussian chancellor

1812
Defeat of Napoleon's "Grand Army" in Russia

1813
War of the "Great Coalition" against Napoleon; Battle of Nations at Leipzig frees Germany of the French and is decisive in the fall of Napoleon's empire

1813–83
Richard Wagner, revolutionary and prophet who created the "music drama" and composed the operas of the *Ring of the Nibelungs*

1814
Paris occupied by Allies; Congress of Vienna opens

1815
German Confederation founded; Napoleon returns and is defeated at Waterloo; Holy Alliance signed by Austria, Prussia, and Russia; founding of patriotic German Student Associations (Burschenshaft)

1815–98
Otto von Bismarck, Prussian prime minister and founder of the Second German Empire in 1871

1816
Federal Assembly opens in Frankfurt am Main

1816–92
Werner von Siemens, a co-inventor of the electrical dynamo applied to electric lights and streetcar systems; founder of Siemens and Halske corporation foremost in electrotechnology

1817
Wartburg festival of German Student Associations

1818
Prussia establishes a uniform tariff area making the state a single marketing unit; Bavarian concordat (treaty) with Rome, which severs the bond of Bavarian bishoprics with the bishop of Salzburg

1818–20
Modern constitutions for Baden, Bavaria, Hesse-Darmstadt, Weimar, and Württemberg

1819
Carlsbad Conference and Decrees suppress liberal and national movements

1819–98
Theodor Fontane, novelist and critic of the social scene of his time

1820
Federal Acts of 1815 extend into Acts of Vienna

1821–94
Hermann von Helmholtz (1821–94), one of the most important scientists of the 19th century, formulates the principle of the conservation of energy

1830
On War by General von Clausewitz; July revolutions in Paris spread unrest to Brunswick, Hannover, Kurhessen, and Saxony; constitutions enacted in the electorate of Hesse and the kingdom of Saxony

1832
Hambach Festival; repressive Six Articles

1833–97
Johannes Brahms, one of the greatest symphonic composers of the 19th century, was creative in all genres except opera

1834

German Customs Union Treaty (Zollverein) creates economic unification by removing tariff and trade barriers among 18 of the German states. By the middle of the century the rest of the states except Austria had joined the Customs Union; economic union of Germany under Prussian leadership was the work of Friedrich von Motz (1775–1830)

1834–1900

Gottlieb Wilhelm Daimler was a founder of the Daimler Benz Mercedes auto company

1835

First German railroad built in Bavaria from Nuremberg to Fürth

1835–48

Ferdinand I, emperor of Austria, son of Francis I

1837

Dismissal of seven Göttingen professors over protest against repeal of Hanover's constitution

1840s

Catholic social reform movement begins under leadership of Adolf Kolping (1813–65) and Bishop Wilhelm Emanuel von Ketteler (1811–77)

1840–61

Reign of Frederick William IV in Prussia

1841

Hoffmann von Fallersleben writes text of Germany's national anthem (*Deutschlandslied*)

1844

June uprising of Silesian weavers

1844–1900

Friedrich Nietzsche, philosopher of nihilism and critic of German materialism and nationalism

1845–1923

Wilhelm Konrad Roentgen, a physician who invents the X-ray technique and receives the Nobel Prize in 1901

1847

Convocation of the United Diet of Prussia in Berlin; Ludwig Jahn establishes Turnerbund; foundation of the Hamburg-America (shipping) Line

1848

Communist Manifesto published by Karl Marx and Friedrich Engels; revolutions throughout Germany in March; revolution in Vienna and flight of Metternich; National Assembly convenes at St. Paul's Church in Frankfurt am Main; National Assembly passes basic rights of the German people; repression of revolution throughout German states

1848–1916

Francis Joseph I, emperor of Austria

1849

Constitution for the German Reich; king of Prussia declines the German kaiser's crown; uprisings repressed in Saxony, Breslau, and Baden

1850

Prussian constitution implemented; treaty "humiliation" of Olmütz, by which Prussia relinquishes all plans for a German union under its leadership

1854

Establishment of Prussian House of Lords with a "Three-Class" suffrage

1857

Founding of North-German Lloyd (shipping)

1859

Franco-Piedmontese war against Austria for Italian unification

1860

German National Association established to support a small German nation state under Prussian leadership

1861

Promulgation of a new constitution for Austria; foundation of the Progressive Party in Prussia by Rudolf Virchow (1821–1902)

1861–88
Reign of William I, brother of Frederick William IV, king of Prussia and German emperor (1871–1888)

1862
Otto von Bismarck appointed Prussian prime minister; constitutional crisis over reform of the army

1863
General Association of German Workers founded in Leipzig under Ferdinand Lasalle (1825–64); Diet of German Princes in Frankfurt

1864
Austro-Prussian War with Denmark over Schleswig-Holstein

1865
Convention of Gastein, a compromise treaty between Austria and Prussia whereby Prussia would take over the administration of Schleswig and Austria that of Holstein

1866
Austro-Prussian War; Battle of Königgrätz/Sadowa; Treaty of Prague; dissolution of German Confederation; Indemnity Bill; founding of National Liberal Party

1867
Austro-Hungarian compromise settlement; foundation of North German Confederation; liberal "December Laws" begin new era

1869
Social Democratic Workers' founded in Eisenach by August Begel (1840–1913) and Wilhelm Liebknecht (1826–1900); Vatican Council convenes in Rome

1870
Bismarck's Ems Telegram; Franco-Prussian War; Battle of Sedan; siege of Paris; papal Declaration of Infallibility

1871
Proclamation of German Empire in Hall of Mirrors in Versailles (Jan. 18); Peace of Frankfurt am Main; cultural struggle (Kulturkampf) with the Catholic Church begins in Prussia; foundation of the German Center Party under leadership of Ludwig Windthorst (1812–91); first German Reichstag convenes; promulgation of the Imperial Constitution

1871–1950
Heinrich Mann, novelist and critic of false morals of the middle class in Imperial Germany

1871–88
Reign of Emperor William I

1873
Viennese stock market crash and beginning of Great Depression; Triple Alliance between German Empire, Austria-Hungary, and Russia; Falk's May Laws attempt to control Catholic Church in Prussia

1875–1955
Thomas Mann created the modern German epic novel

1875
Lasalleans and Marxists join in Gotha to form Socialist Workers Party; Reichsbank established; nationalization of railroads

1876
Central Association of German Industrialists founded

1878
Congress of Berlin; Anti-Socialist Laws; assassination attempt on Kaiser William

1879
Dual Alliance between Germany and Austria-Hungary; protectionist tariffs; publication of first volume of Heinrich von Treitschke's (1834–96) *German History of the 19th Century*

1883
Law on sickness benefits passed by Reichstag

1884
Accident insurance introduced; colonies acquired in South-West Africa, Cameroons, Togo

1885
Acquisition of colony in East Africa

1887
Reinsurance Treaty with Russia signed

1888
Death of Kaiser William I; terminally ill son, Friedrich III, succeeds him; accession to the throne by Friedrich's eldest son, William II

1890
Dismissal of Bismarck; General Leo von Caprivi becomes Reich chancellor; Reichstag rejects extension of Anti-Socialist Law; Reinsurance Treaty not renewed; colonial conflicts with England settled

1891
Pan German Association founded in Berlin

1893
Agrarian League of large landowners east of the Elbe founded

1894
Chlodwig, Prince Hohenlohe-Schillingfürst succeeds Caprivi as chancellor; secessionist Blue Rider art movement shocks establishment tastes; Federation of German Women's Associations (BDF) founded

1895
Kaiser William Canal opens connecting the North Sea and the Baltic

1898
Marxist ideology of the Social Democratic Party is revised by Eduard Bernstein (1850–1932); "New course" in naval and imperial policy

TWENTIETH CENTURY

1900
Bernhard von Bülow (1849–1929) succeeds Prince Chlodwig Hohenlohe (1819–1901) as Reich chancellor; Prussian Civil Code in force; Second Naval Bill passed

1901
New youth movement, Wandervögel, formed; publication of *Buddenbrooks* by Thomas Mann (1875–1955)

1901–76
Werner Karl Heisenberg, celebrated physicist and founder of quantum mechanics

1902
German Union of Women's Suffrage (DVF) organized by radical feminist Anita Augspurg

1905–06
First Moroccan Crisis between Germany and France; Schlieffen Plan for two-front war drafted

1908
Daily Telegraph Affair demonstrates Kaiser's irresponsibility

1909
Theobald von Bethmann Hollweg (1856–1921) replaces Bülow as chancellor

1911
Second Moroccan Crisis

1912–13
Reichstag debate on Army Bill

1913
Zabern Crisis provides opportunity for constitutional reform

1914
Assasination of Archduke Francis Ferdinand in Sarajevo; Germany gives Austrians a "blank check" of support; Austria-Hungary declares war on Serbia; German mobilization and declarations of war; German violation of Belgian neutrality; Battle of Tannenberg; Battle of the Marne; German war aims; Turkey joins Central powers

1915
Sinking of the *Lusitania;* secret Treaty of London promises Italy territory to join Triple Entente; Bulgaria joins Central powers

1916

Battles of Verdun and Jutland; Paul von Hindenburg (1847–1934) and Erich Ludendorff (1865–1937) assume supreme command of armed forces; death of Austrian emperor Francis Joseph; Romania enters war against Central powers in return for Allied promises of Bukovina and Transylvania

1917

German unrestricted submarine warfare; United States declares war on Germany; Independent Social Democratic Party (USPD) organized; peace initiative of Pope Benedict XV rejected; Peace Resolution; cease-fire with Russia; Chancellor Bethmann Hollweg dismissed; rightist and chauvinist Fatherland Party established

1918

Strikes in German cities; Peace of Brest-Litovsk deprives Russia of Baltic provinces, Finland, Poland, and Ukraine; Wilson's Fourteen Points; German army demands cease-fire; constitutional reform under Prince Max von Baden; naval revolt in Kiel; revolution spreads throughout Germany; workers' councils established; German republic declared by Philip Scheidemann (1865–1939); Kurt Eisner (1867–1919) leads revolution and establishes council government in Munich; Ebert-Groener Pact concerning military support for republic; armistice with Allies signed; William II abdicates

1919

Spartacus revolt in Berlin; National Assembly elected; Friedrich Ebert (1871–1925) elected first president; defeat of Soviet Republic in Munich; signing of Treaty of Versailles; Weimar Constitution adopted

1920

Kapp-Lüttwitz Putsch; Communist uprising in Ruhr and central Germany; Weimar coalition loses majority in Reichstag

1921

Matthias Erzberger (1875–1921) of Center Party assassinated; plebiscite in Upper Silesia

1922

Rapallo Treaty with Russia allows secret training of German army; assassination of foreign minister, Walter Rathenau (1867–1922) by radical right

1923

Passive resistance in the Ruhr occupied by French and Belgian troops; hyperinflation; Communist revolt in Saxony and Thuringia; conflict between Bavaria and the Reich; Hitler's Munich Putsch attempt (November 8–9); abandonment of Ruhr struggle by government of Gustav Stresemann (1878–1929)

1924

Dawes Plan on reparations accepted; period of stability begins; Hitler trial and imprisonment in Landsberg; Hitler writes *Mein Kampf*

1925

Death of President Friedrich Ebert; election of Field Marshal Paul von Hindenburg as Weimar president; Lacarno Treaties respect Germany's western frontiers as defined by Versailles Treaty

1926

Germany enters the League of Nations; Treaty of Friendship and neutrality with Soviet Union; Hitler begins rebuilding the Nazi Party

1928

Grand Coalition formed under Social Democratic chancellor Müller; problems with labor-management relations; Hitler appoints Joseph Goebbels (1897–1945) as Nazi propaganda minister

1929

Young Plan settles reparation problem; death of Gustav Stresemann (1878–1929), foreign minister and leader of the German People's Party (DVP); U.S. stock market crash begins world economic crisis

1930

Heinrich Brüning (1885–1970) of Center Party becomes chancellor; Emergency Decree; Reichstag elections produce a NSDAP landslide (107 seats)

1931

Harzburg Front alliance between NSDAP, DNVP and Stahlhelm; proposed Austro-German Customs Union rejected

1932

President Hindenburg reelected; Brüning resigns; Franz von Papen (1879–1969) forms right-wing cabinet; NSDAP becomes strongest party; Papen succeeded by General Kurt von Schleicher (1882–1934)

1933

Hitler appointed chancellor; Reichstag burns; Reichstag election gives majority to coalition between NSDAP and DNVP; Enabling Act passed, creating dictatorship; boycott of Jewish businesses; Concordat with Catholic Church; trade unions abolished

1934

SA leadership eliminated; death of Hindenburg; Hitler becomes the Führer; Army swears allegiance to Hitler; Labor Front established; Barmen Declaration of Confessing Church

1935

Saar joins Reich; military conscription; Air Force (Luftwaffe) created; Anglo-German naval agreement; Nuremberg Laws decree racial discrimination

1936

Olympic Games in Berlin; German troops occupy Rhineland; "Berlin-Rome Axis" formed; Anti-Comintern Pact signed with Japan; Four Year Plan; Heinrich Himmler (1900–45) appointed chief of police

1937

Hossbach Memorandum reveals Hitler's aggressive foreign policy; Pope Pius XI criticizes Nazi Germany in encyclical *Mit brennender Sorge*

1938

Hitler purges army and Foreign Office; Germany annexes Austria (Anschluss); appeasement at Munich Conference; Czech Sudetenland occupied; Reichskristallnacht riots against Jews

1939

Czechoslovakia invaded; Non-Aggression Pact signed with Russia; Poland invaded; Great Britain and France declare war; "euthanasia" order issued

1940

German invasion of Denmark, Norway, Belgium, the Netherlands, Luxembourg, and France; Franco-German cease-fire at Compiègne; Battle of Britain

1941

African campaign under General Erwin Rommel (1891–1944); Yugoslavia and Greece invaded; "Commissar" order issued; Soviet Union invaded (Operation Barbarossa); Final Solution ordered; declaration of war on United States

1942

"Wannsee Conference" announces Final Solution; Battles of El Alamein and Stalingrad; Battle of Atlantic

1943

Casablanca Conference demands "unconditional surrender"; German Sixth Army surrenders at Stalingrad; Total War declared; Rommel surrenders

1944

Strategic bombing of German cities accelerates; Normandy invasion; Russians defeat major army group; Claus Schenk von Stauffenberg (1907–44) attempts assassination of Hitler

1945

Yalta Conference; Hitler commits suicide; Germany surrenders; Potsdam Conference; West German Christian Democratic Party (CDU) and Christian Social Union (CSU) founded; military governments established in U.S. zone (OMGUS) and in Soviet zone (SMAD); Allied denazification programs begin

1946

Nuremberg International Military Tribunal (IMT); Socialist Unity Party (SED) established in Soviet zone

1947

Bizone formed by United States and Britain; trade unions reestablished in West; Marshall Plan;

Literary Group 47 organized; state of Prussia dissolved; Ruhr coal miners favor nationalization

1948
Berlin blockade and airlift; currency reform; Liberal Democratic Party (FDP) formed

1949
Basic Law considered provisional constitution; Bonn made the capital of the Federal Republic of Germany (FRG); Konrad Adenauer (1876–1967) elected first chancellor of FRG; Theodor Heuss (1884–1963) elected first president of FRG; East Berlin becomes the capital of the German Democratic Republic (GDR); Walter Ulbricht (1893–1973) becomes the leader of GDR; dismantling of GDR industries ends

1950
Coal and Steel Community between Germany and France; FRG joins Council of Europe; food rationing ends in FRG

1951
Equal worker-management status law passed in FRG; European Coal and Steel Community Treaty signed

1952
West German Equalization of Burdens Law; Germany Treaty signed; European Defense Community (EDC) Treaty signed; Reconciliation Treaty with Israel signed

1953
Uprising in East Berlin and East Germany; death of Stalin

1954
GDR reparations end; West Germany joins NATO and allowed to rearm

1955
West Germany gains sovereignty through Paris Treaty; diplomatic relations established with Soviet Union; Warsaw Pact founded

1956
East Germany creates People's Army

1957
Hallstein Doctrine; Saarland incorporated in Federal Republic; Treaty of Rome establishes European Economic Community; CDU/CSU absolute majority in Bundestag; Willy Brandt becomes mayor of Berlin (1957–66)

1958
"Berlin Ultimatum" issued by Soviet Union

1959
Social Democrats (SPD) reform party at Bad Godesburg; Heinrich Lübke (1894–1972) elected president of West Germany; Heinrich Böll (1917–85) and Günther Grass (1927–) publish novels

1960
Social Democrats accept rearmament and Western integration

1961
Berlin Wall built

1962
Spiegel Affair; Franz Josef Strauss (1915–88) resigns

1963
Franco-German Friendship Treaty; Chancellor Adenauer succeeded by Ludwig Erhard

1966
Grand Coalition formed between CDU/CSU and SPD

1967
West Germany establishes diplomatic relations with Romania; Stability Law passed by Bundestag

1968
"Easter Riots" in West Germany; assassination attempt on student leader Rudi Dutschke (1940–79); Bundestag declares emergency

1969
Gustav Heinemann (1899–1976) (SPD) elected West German president; coalition government formed between SPD and FDP; Willy Brandt

(1913–92) becomes chancellor and initiates Ostpolitik; West Germany rejects production of atomic weapons

1970
Ministers of West and East Germany hold meetings; German-Soviet Non-Aggression Pact signed; German-Polish Treaty

1971
Four Powers Agreement on Berlin; Erich Honecker (1912–94) becomes East German leader; Chancellor Brandt honored with Nobel Peace Prize

1972
Signing of Basic Treaty between West and East Germany; ratification of Moscow and Warsaw treaties; Olympic Games in Munich; Bundestag majority gained by SPD and FDP

1973
West and East Germany join United Nations; world oil crisis and embargo

1974
Chancellor Brandt resigns; Helmut Schmidt (1918–) (SPD) becomes chancellor; Walter Scheel (1919–) elected West German president; Red Army Faction begins terrorist campaign in West Germany

1975
Helsinki Council for Security and Cooperation

1976
East German writer, Wolf Biermann (1936–), exiled

1977
Murders, kidnappings, and hijacking by Red Army Faction

1978
Establishment of environmentalist Green Party

1979
Karl Carstens (1914–92) (CDU) elected federal president; European Parliamentary elections; NATO decides to deploy nuclear missiles in West Germany

1980
Chancellor Helmut Schmidt (1918–) visits Moscow

1981
Chancellor Schmidt visits East Germany; peace demonstration in Bonn

1982
Helmut Kohl (1930–) replaces Schmidt as chancellor

1983
Bundestag debate over NATO's force modernization; Green Party's first representation in Bundestag

1984
Chancellor Kohl visits Israel; strikes for 35-hour workweek; Richard von Weizsäcker (1920–) elected federal president

1985
President Reagan (U.S.) and Chancellor Kohl visit Bergen Belsen camp and Bitburg cemetery; EC summit on European Community reform; German identity debate

1986
The *Neue Heimat* scandal; Russian Chernobyl nuclear reactor accident impact

1987
CDU/CSU and FDP retain majority in Bundestag elections; Erich Honecker visits West Germany

1989
Fortieth anniversary of East Germany; East Germans demonstrate; Berlin Wall opened; Ten Point Plan for German unification proposed by Kohl

1990
Two-Plus-Four talks on Germany; German reunification effected on October 3; all-German elections won by Kohl-Genscher coalition

1991
Capital to be moved to Berlin; Maastricht agreements; 200,000 former East Germans migrated

to West; antiforeigner attacks increase dramatically; Emnid Institute reports that 32 percent of German respondents believes Jews partly responsible for own persecution; Holocaust museum opens at Wannsee; Erich Honecker protected by asylum in Chilean embassy in Moscow; first conviction in Berlin court of former East German guards

1992
East German (Stasi) files opened; Erich Honecker returns to stand trial; nationwide strike; Maastricht Treaty on European unity ratified; neo-Nazi violence against asylum seekers in Rostock

1993
Solidarity Pact on transfers to East German states; Basic Law on right of asylum amended; Erich Honecker exiled to Chile

1994
German military operations "out of area" approved; Kohl government reelected; Roman Herzog (1934–) elected seventh president of the Federal Republic

1995
Unprecedented jobless rate; budget deficit exceeds what allowed by Maastricht Treaty; the Trust Agency (Treuhandanstalt) completes privatization of 15,000 East German public enterprises; VE Day celebrated as liberation from Nazism; completion of modernization of 3 million East German dwellings

1996
Spy trader Wolfgang Vogel (1925–) acquitted on charges of blackmail and perjury; asylum seekers killed in Lübeck; right-wing violence; Bundesbank loan rates cut to stimulate economy; jobs alliance pact reached between IG Metal and employers; welfare reforms announced; neo-Nazi Gary Lauck convicted; Deutsche Telekom offers stock; Germany and Czech Republic reconcile

1997
1999 set for Berlin to become capital; joblessness hits postwar high; Krupp/Thyssen steel merger; Siemens buys Westinghouse; SPD slips in Hamburg elections; former East German leaders Egon Krenz and Guenther Schabowski sentenced; rightist politicians protest exhibitions of World War II atrocities by German soldiers; United States criticized at Bonn conference on global warming

1998
SPD candidate Gerhardt Schroeder and Red-Green coalition elected; CSU wins Bavarian election; rightists gain in Saxony-Anhalt election; Schaeuble replaces Kohl as CDU chair; Bertelsmann buys Random House; Daimler/Chrysler merged; influx of Kurdish refugees limited; Red Army faction disbanded; Holocaust reparations set; office of American Jewish Committee opened; bunkers used by Joseph Goebbels discovered

1999
SPD vote declined in state and local elections; Schroeder elected SPD chairman, replacing Lafontaine; election fund violations admitted by Helmut Kohl; last parliamentary session held in Bonn; jobless rate over 11 percent; Deutsche Bank/Bankers Trust merger completed; Siemens/Fujitsu merger; Holocaust memorial designed and reparations fund set; Germany participates in NATO bombing of Kosovo; Günther Grass wins Nobel Prize in literature

2000
CDU chair Schaeuble replaced by Angela Merkel; CDU loses election in Schleswig-Holstein; SPD wins in North Rhine-Westphalia; far-right parties banned; Kohl accused of destroying illegal fund documents; gay marriage legalized; Iranian president hosted by Chancellor Schroeder; Deutsche and Dresdner Banks merged; Holocaust Compensation Pact signed

2001
Chancellor Schroeder condemns 9/11 terrorist attack against United States; German troops deployed to Macedonia and Afghanistan; Greens back antiterrorist troop deployment; Schroeder reelected SPD chairman; court cancels fine on Kohl fund scandal; pension reform passes Bundestag; online music deal negotiated by Bertels-

mann; Deutsche Telekom buys Voicestream; Berlin Jewish Museum opens; anti-Semitic violence increases; World War II slave labor payment; Bavaria-Munich soccer team wins European championship

2002
Schroeder's SPD/Green coalition reelected; election campaign emphasizes anti-U.S. sentiment on Iraq war; election in Saxony Anhalt won by CDU; Schroeder and France's Chirac hostile to United Nations resolution threatening force; minister likens Bush tactics to Hitler's; Kohl's career ended; tax cut postponed; paintings of famous expressionist Ernst Kirchner and Emil Nolde sold; U.S. policy on global warming criticized; flood devastation affects 4 million Germans; Iraqi embassy in Berlin seized by opposition group

APPENDIXES

Appendix I
Rulers and Statesmen

Appendix II
Maps

APPENDIX I

HOLY ROMAN EMPERORS

A. Habsburg Rulers
1493–1519	Maximilian I
1519–56	Charles V (king of Castile and Aragon, 1516–56)
1556–64	Ferdinand I (king of Bohemia and Hungary, 1526–64)
1564–76	Maximilian II (king of Bohemia and Hungary)
1576–1612	Rudolf II (king of Bohemia, 1576–1611; king of Hungary, 1576–1608)
1612–19	Matthias (king of Bohemia, 1611–19; king of Hungary, 1608–19)
1619–37	Ferdinand II (king of Bohemia and Hungary)
1637–57	Ferdinand III (king of Bohemia and Hungary)
1658–1705	Leopold I (king of Bohemia and Hungary)
1705–11	Joseph I
1711–40	Charles VI

B. Habsburg-Lorraine Rulers
1740–80	Maria Theresa (empress consort 1745)
1745–65	Francis I (of Lorraine) (husband of Maria Theresa)
1745–65	Joseph II (Until 1780 merely co-regent in Habsburg lands)
1790–92	Leopold II
1792–1806	Francis II (Becomes first emperor of Austria, 1804–35)

HOHENZOLLERN DYNASTY (PRUSSIA AND GERMAN EMPIRE)

A. Kings of Prussia
1701–13	Frederick I (Frederick III of Brandenburg)
1713–40	Frederick William I
1740–86	Frederick II the Great
1786–97	Frederick William II
1797–1840	Frederick William III
1840–61	Frederick William IV
1861–71	William I

B. Emperors of Germany
1871–88	William I (of Prussia)
1888	Frederick III
1888–1918	William II

PRESIDENTS AND CHANCELLORS OF FEDERAL REPUBLIC 1949–97

Theodor Heuss (FDP) 1949–59	Konrad Adenauer (CDU)	1949–59
Heinrich Lübke (CDU) 1959–69	Konrad Adenauer (CDU)	1959–63
	Ludwig Erhard (CDU)	1963–66
	Kurt-Georg Kiesinger (CDU)	1966–69
Gustav Heinemann (SPD) 1969–74	Willy Brandt (SPD)	1969–74
Walter Scheel (FDP) 1974–79	Helmut Schmidt (SPD)	1974–79
Karl Carstens (CDU) 1979–84	Helmust Schmidt (SPD)	1979–82
	Helmut Kohl (CDU)	1982–84
Richard v. Weizäcker (CDU) 1984–94	Helmut Kohl (CDU)	1984–94
Roman Herzog (CDU) 1994–99	Helmut Kohl (CDU)	1994–98
Johannes Rau (SPD) 1999–2004	Gerhard Schroeder (SPD)	1998–2005
Horst Köhler (CDU) 2004–	Angela Merkel (CDU)	2005–

APPENDIX II

MAPS

Empire of Charles V, 1506–1519

The Reformation, 1517–1560

Europe in 1648 (Treaty of Westphalia)

Expansion of Prussia, 1683–1789

The Seven Years' War in Europe, 1756–1763

Europe after Congress of Vienna, 1815

Unification of Germany, 1866–1871

World War I in Europe and the Middle East, 1914–1918

Europe after World War I, 1919

Expansion of Nazi Germany, 1933–1939

Map of the Holocaust, 1939–1945

World War II in Europe and the Middle East, 1939–1945

Post–World War II Occupation Zones of Germany

Germany

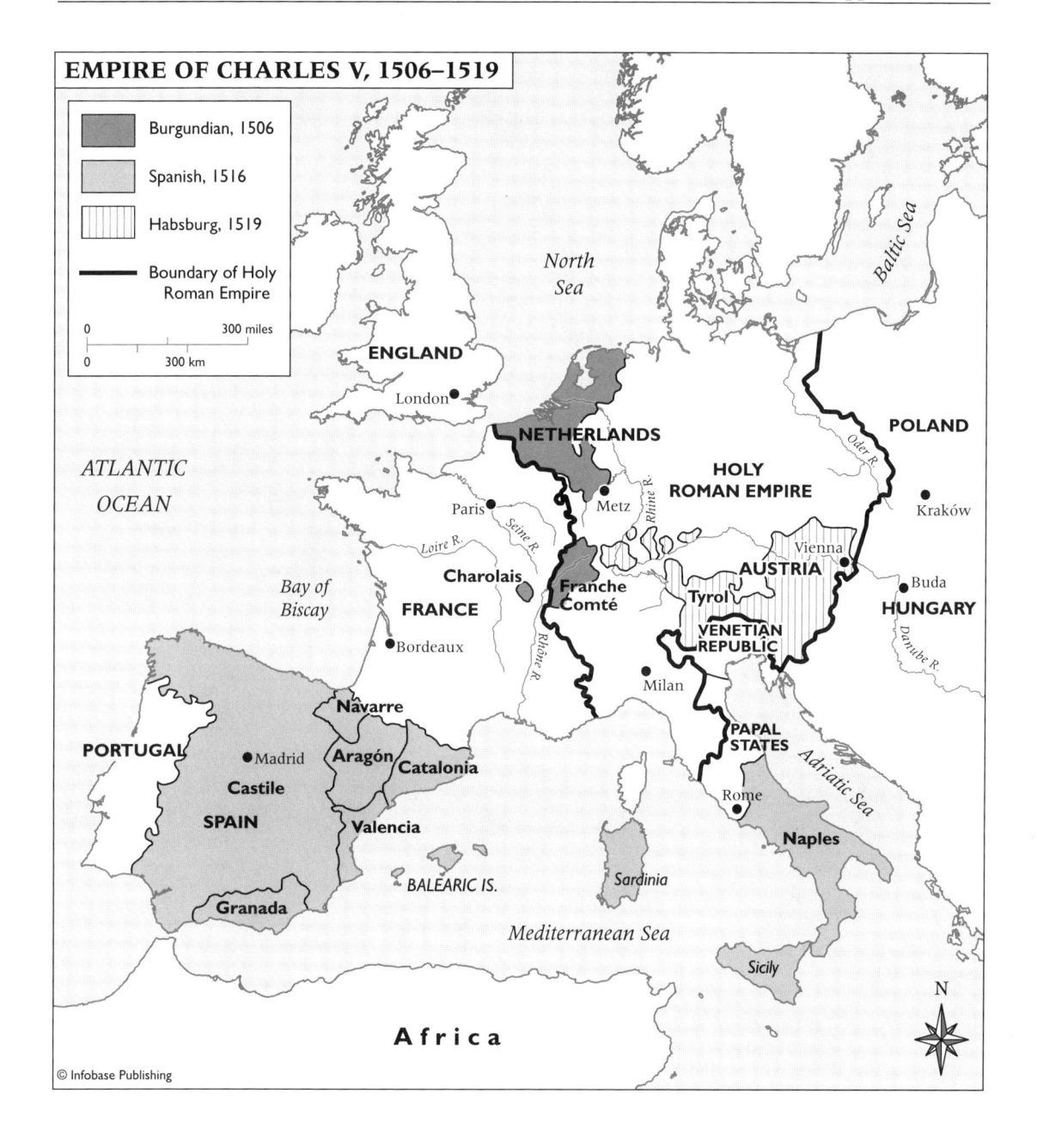

EMPIRE OF CHARLES V, 1506–1519

THE REFORMATION, 1517–1560

Religion in Europe by 1560
- Roman Catholic
- Roman Catholic with significant Protestant (Lutheran or Calvinist) minority
- Protestant (Lutheran)
- Protestant (Calvinist or Zwinglian)
- Anglican

- ← Spread of Protestantism, 1517–1560
- ▲ Concentration of Anabaptist and other radical reform groups
- ┈┈ Swiss Confederation, 1560
- ── Holy Roman Empire, 1560
- ✕ Battle of Frankenhausen, 1525

Reform Movements

Lutheran led by Martin Luther. Beginning 1517, Wittenberg, Saxony.

Zwinglian led by Ulrich Zwingli. Beginning 1519, Zürich, Switzerland.

Anabaptist led by Thomas Münzer. Beginning 1521, Wittenberg and Zurich.

Anglican led by Thomas Cranmer. Beginning 1534, London, England.

Calvinist led by John Calvin. Beginning 1536, Geneva, Switzerland.

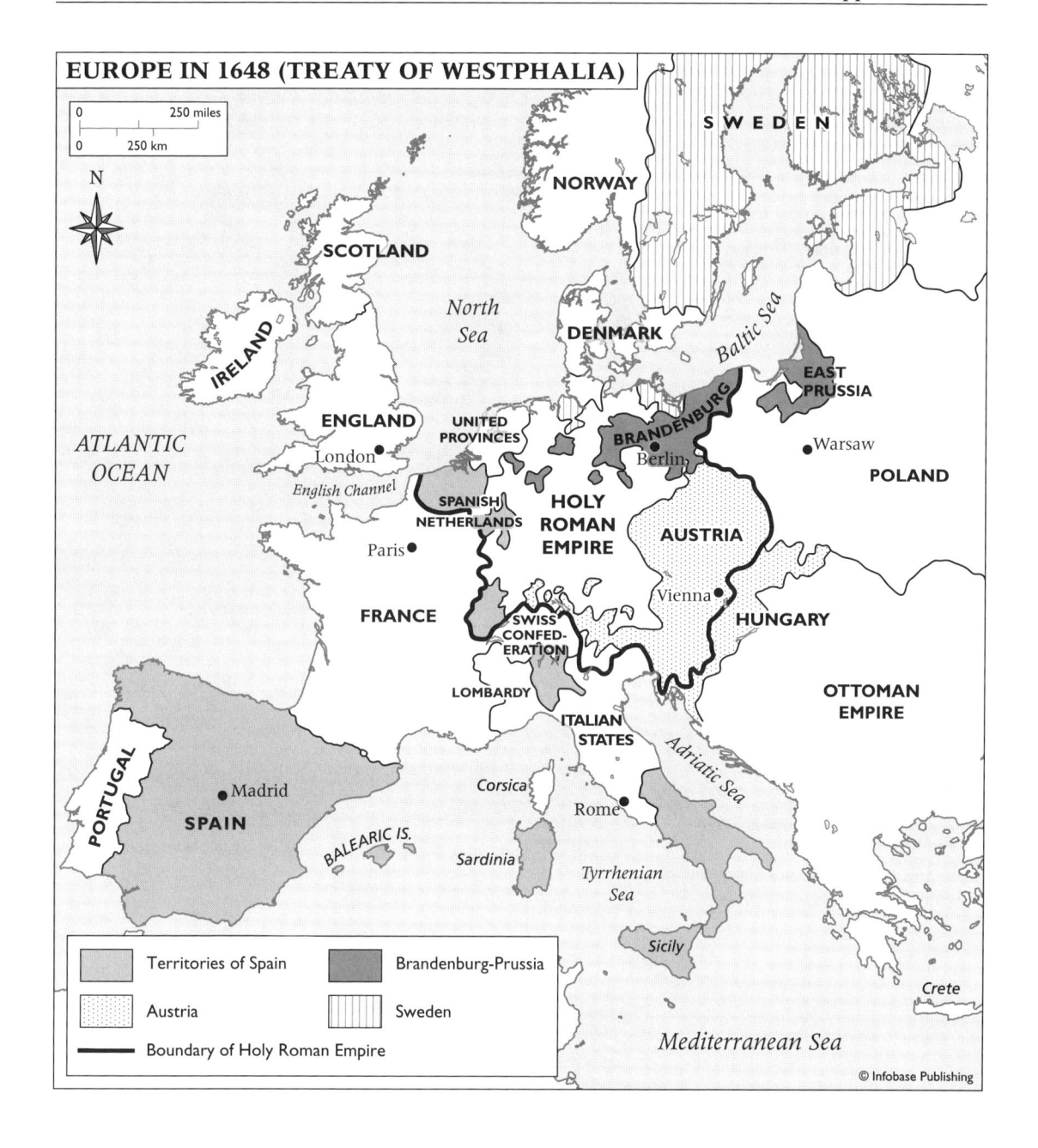

EUROPE IN 1648 (TREATY OF WESTPHALIA)

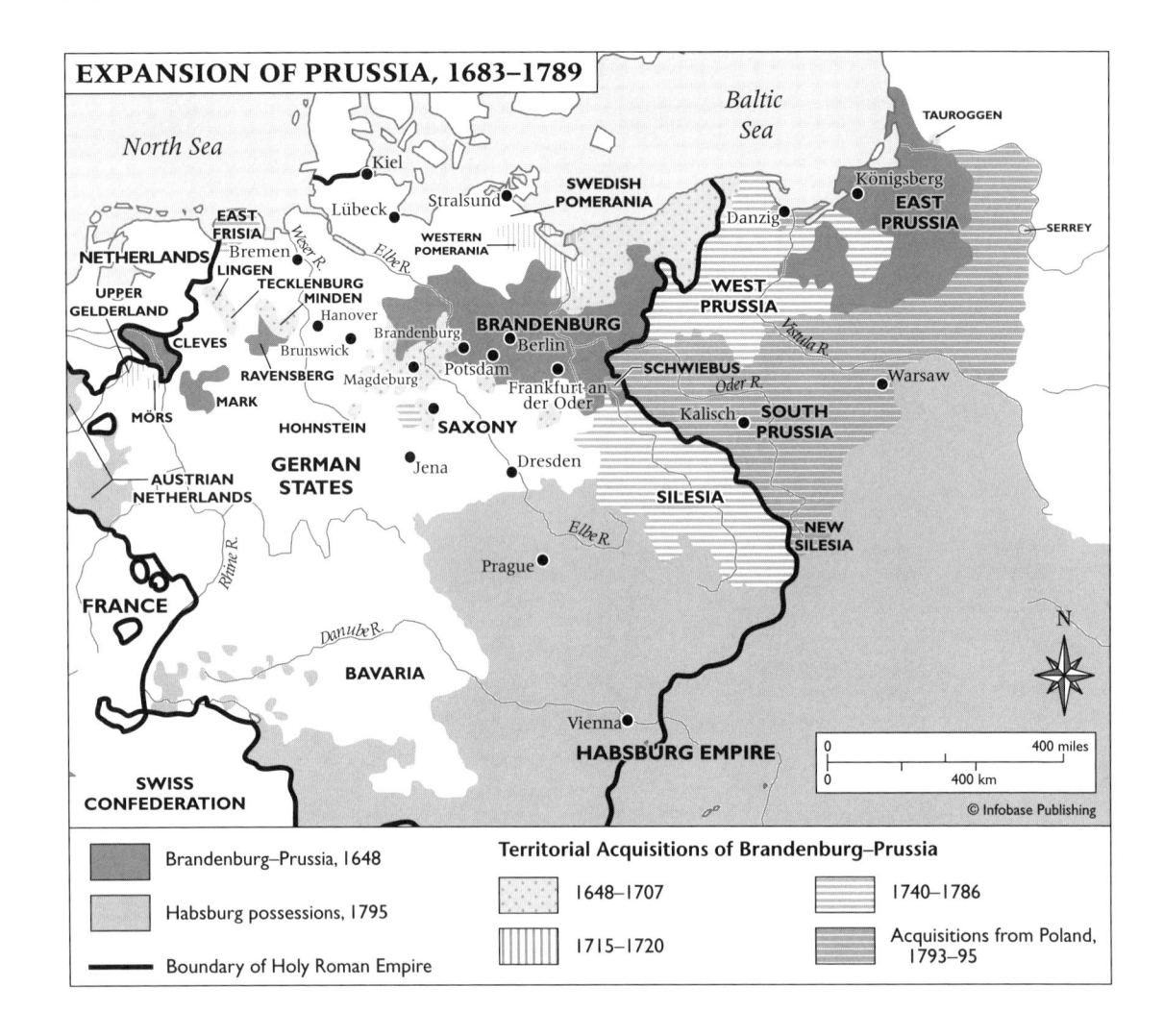

EXPANSION OF PRUSSIA, 1683–1789

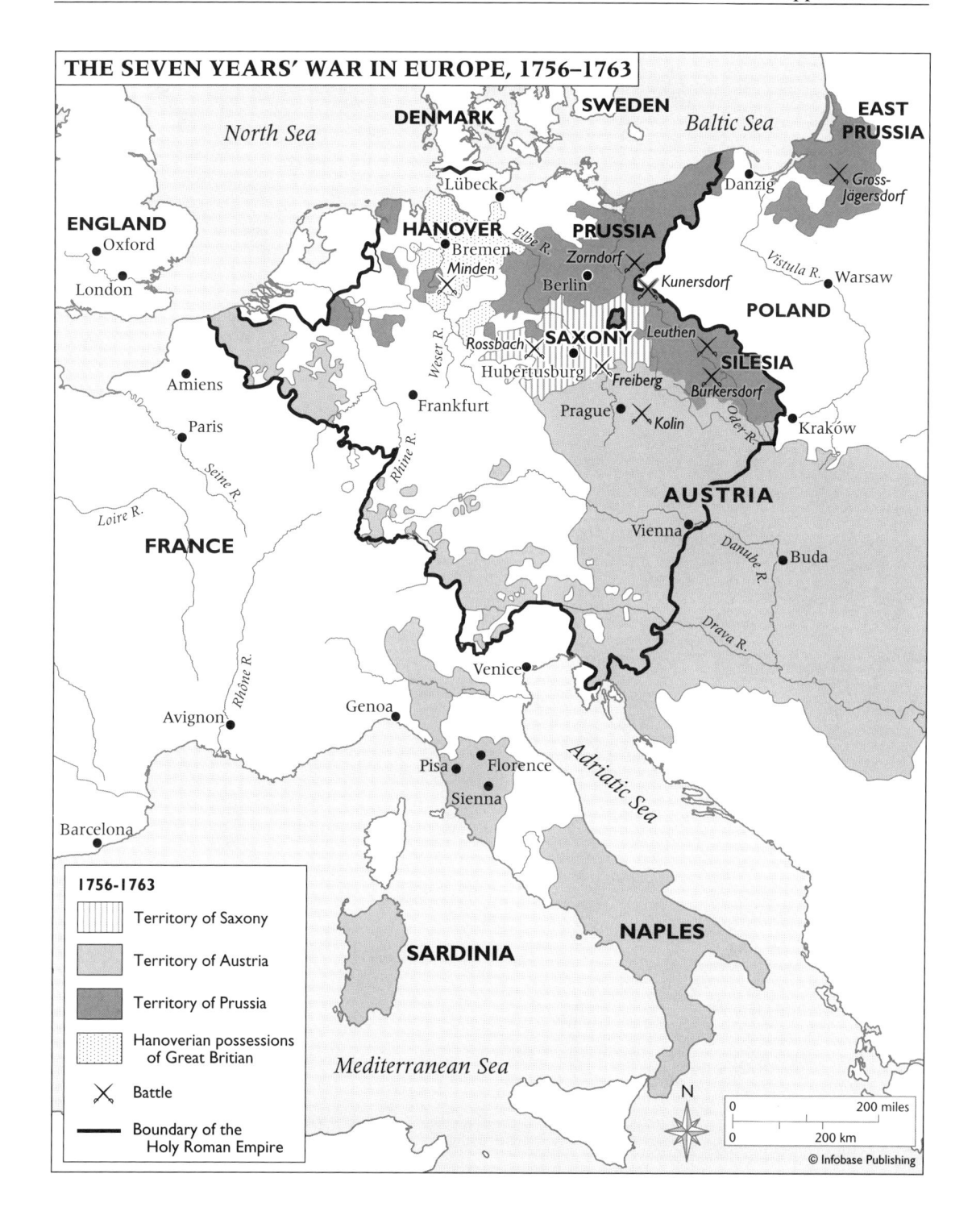

THE SEVEN YEARS' WAR IN EUROPE, 1756–1763

792 Germany

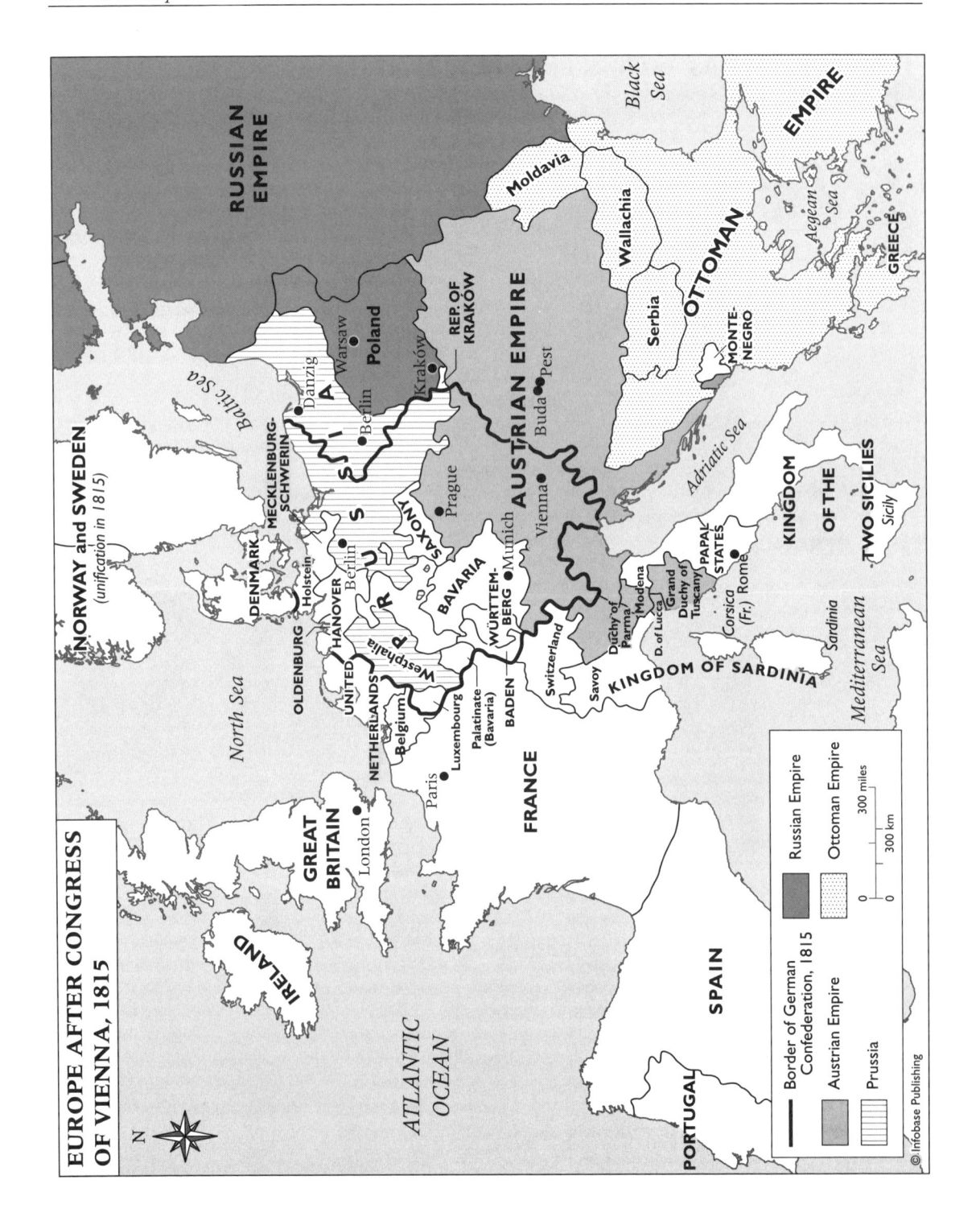

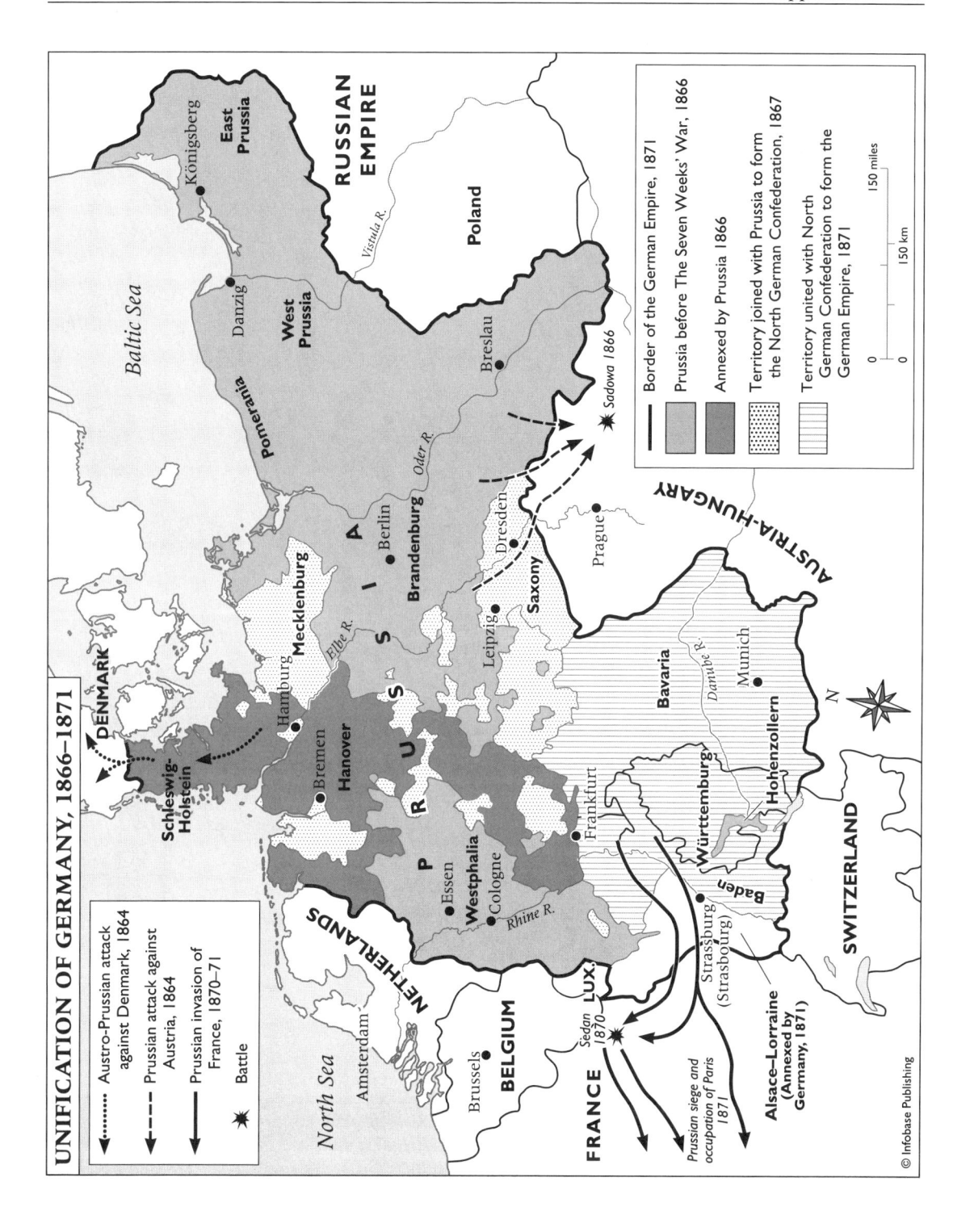

UNIFICATION OF GERMANY, 1866–1871

WORLD WAR I IN EUROPE AND THE MIDDLE EAST, 1914–1918

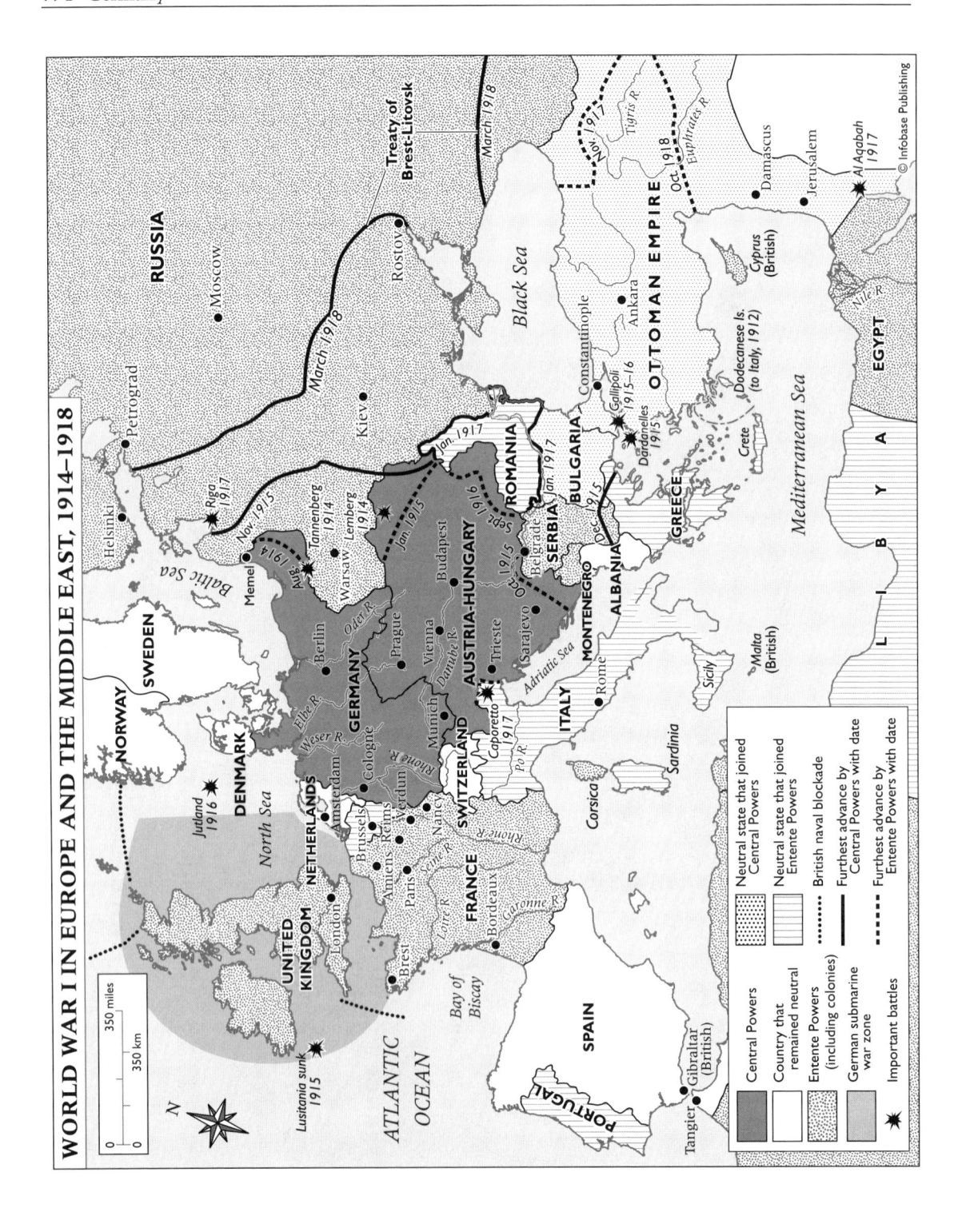

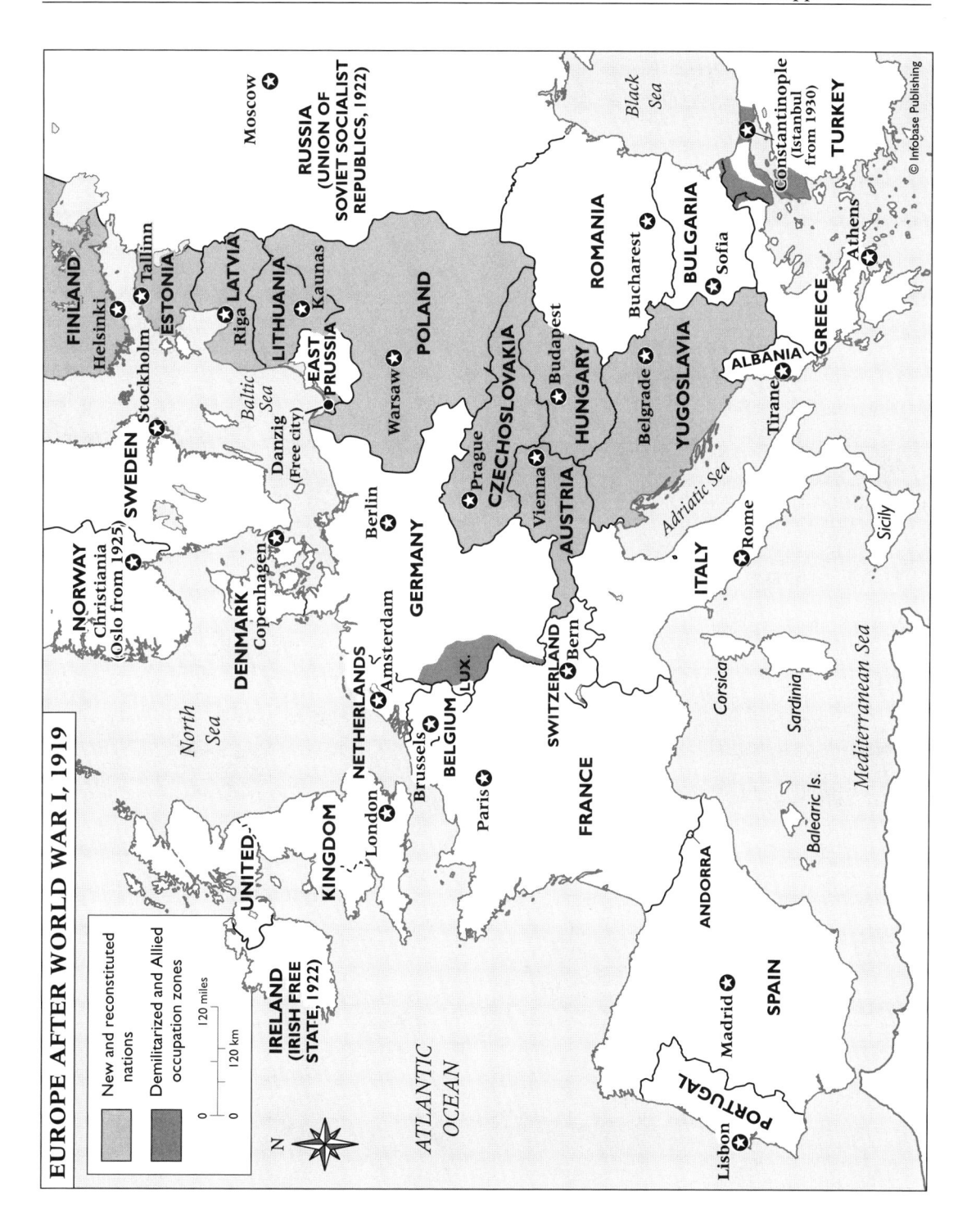

EUROPE AFTER WORLD WAR I, 1919

EXPANSION OF NAZI GERMANY, 1933–1939

Expansion of Nazi Germany, 1933–39
- Germany, 1933
- Saar region, 1935
- Rhineland, 1936

Territory annexed
- 1938
- 1939

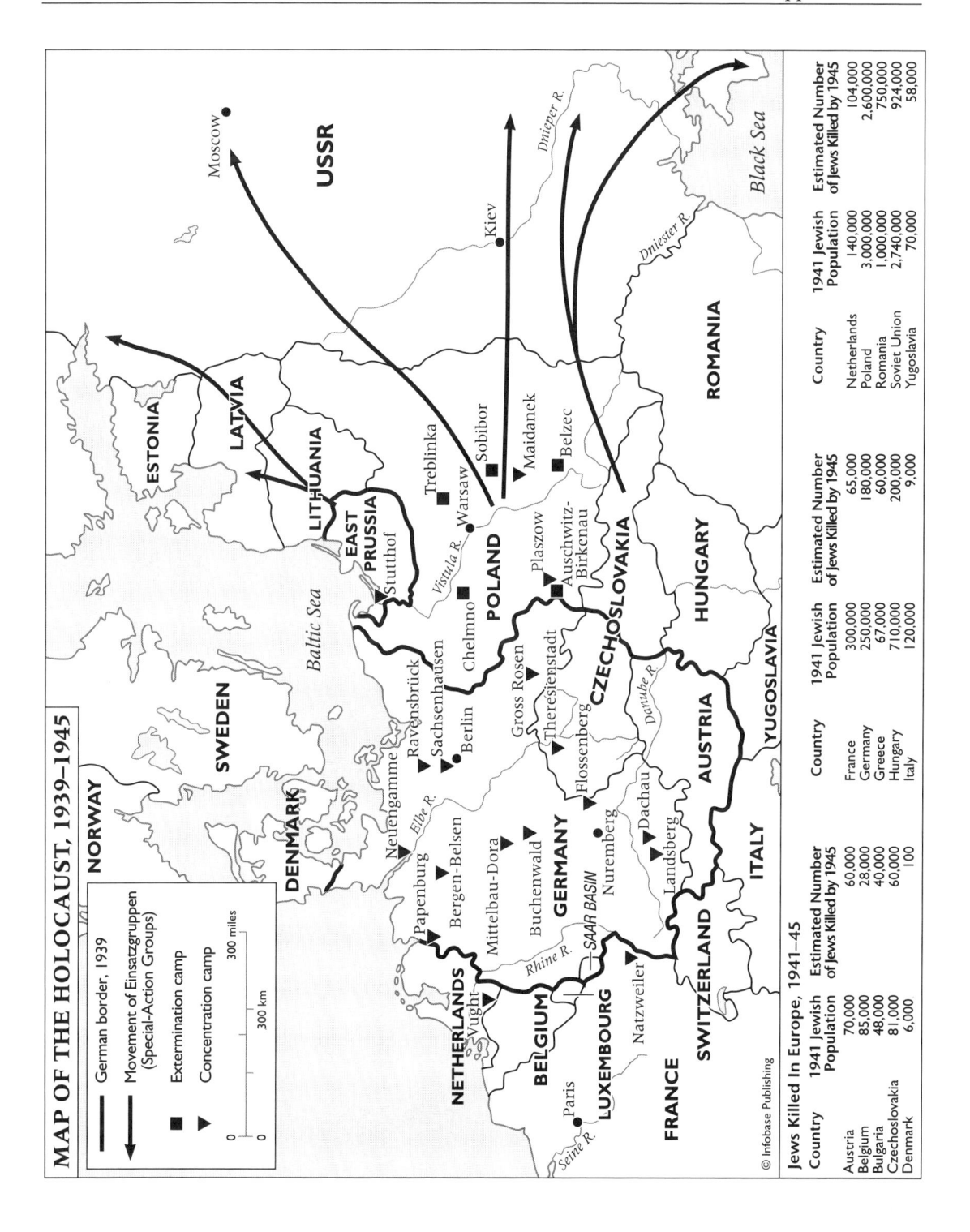

MAP OF THE HOLOCAUST, 1939–1945

Legend:
- — German border, 1939
- ↓ Movement of Einsatzgruppen (Special-Action Groups)
- ■ Extermination camp
- ▼ Concentration camp

0 — 300 miles
0 — 300 km

© Infobase Publishing

Locations shown on map:
- Norway, Sweden, Denmark, Netherlands, Belgium, Luxembourg, France, Switzerland, Italy, Germany, Austria, Czechoslovakia, Hungary, Yugoslavia, Romania, Poland, East Prussia, Lithuania, Latvia, Estonia, USSR
- Cities: Paris, Papenburg, Neuengamme, Bergen-Belsen, Mittelbau-Dora, Buchenwald, Nuremberg, Landsberg, Dachau, Natzweiler, Vught, Ravensbrück, Sachsenhausen, Berlin, Gross Rosen, Flossenberg, Theresienstadt, Chelmno, Stutthof, Warsaw, Treblinka, Sobibor, Maidanek, Belzec, Auschwitz-Birkenau, Plaszow, Kiev, Moscow
- Rivers/Seas: Seine R., Rhine R., Elbe R., Danube R., Vistula R., Dniester R., Dnieper R., Baltic Sea, Black Sea
- Saar Basin

Jews Killed In Europe, 1941–45

Country	1941 Jewish Population	Estimated Number of Jews Killed by 1945
Austria	70,000	60,000
Belgium	85,000	28,000
Bulgaria	48,000	40,000
Czechoslovakia	81,000	60,000
Denmark	6,000	100
France	300,000	65,000
Germany	250,000	180,000
Greece	67,000	60,000
Hungary	710,000	200,000
Italy	120,000	9,000
Netherlands	140,000	104,000
Poland	3,000,000	2,600,000
Romania	1,000,000	750,000
Soviet Union	2,740,000	924,000
Yugoslavia	70,000	58,000

WORLD WAR II IN EUROPE AND THE MIDDLE EAST, 1939–1945

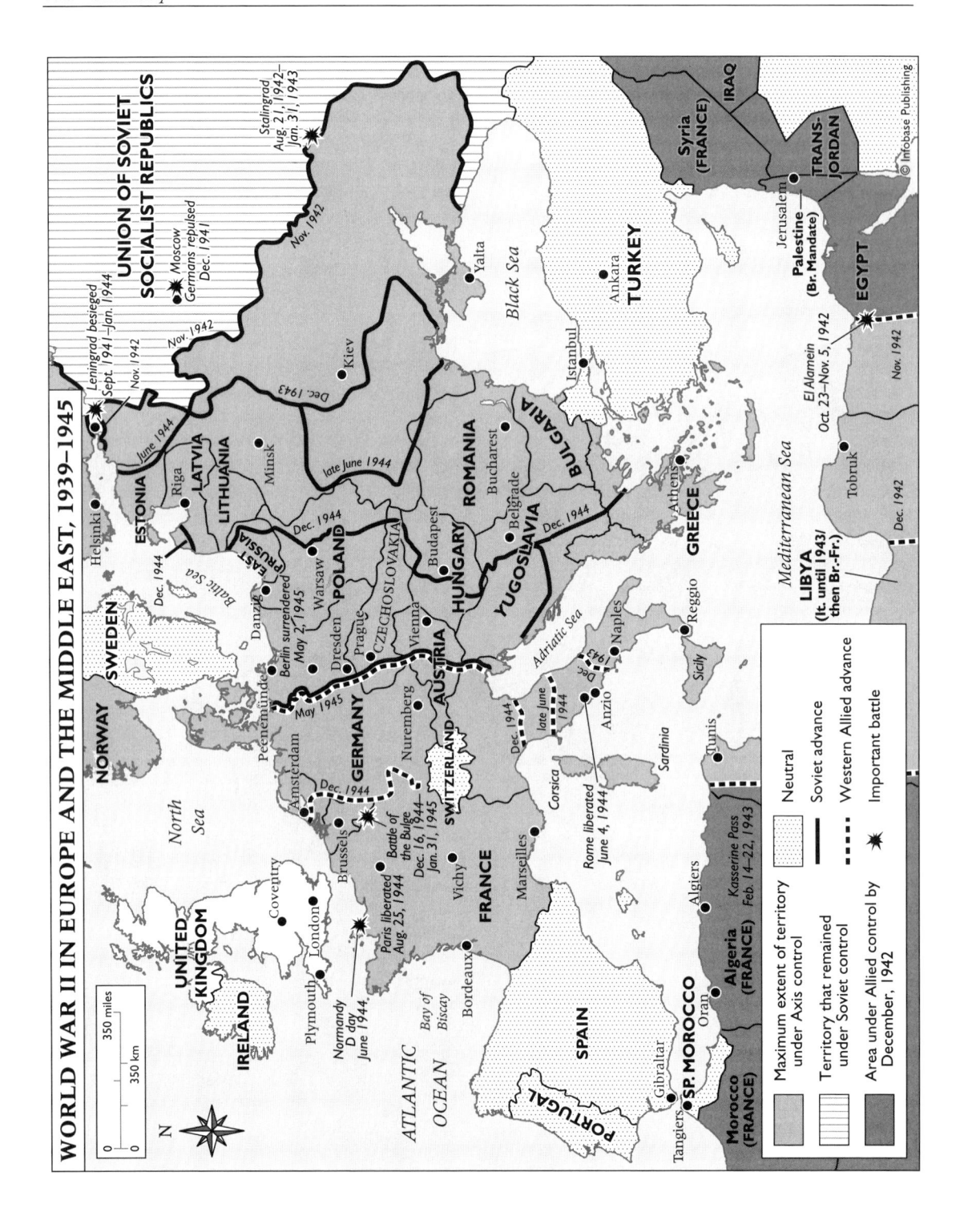

Appendix II 799

POST–WORLD WAR II OCCUPATION ZONES OF GERMANY

Legend:
- American Zone
- British Zone
- French Zone
- Russian Zone
- Taken over by Poland
- ○ Under Four Power control

Cities labeled: Hamburg, Bremen, Berlin, Bonn, Nuremburg, Munich, Vienna

Countries labeled: USSR, East Prussia, Poland, Denmark, Netherlands, Belgium, Lux., Czechoslovakia, Austria, Hungary, Yugoslavia, Italy, Switzerland

Water: Baltic Sea, North Sea

DIVISION OF BERLIN AFTER WORLD WAR II

- French Sector
- British Sector
- American Sector
- Soviet Sector
- West Berlin
- East Berlin
- East Germany
- Havel R.
- Spree R.

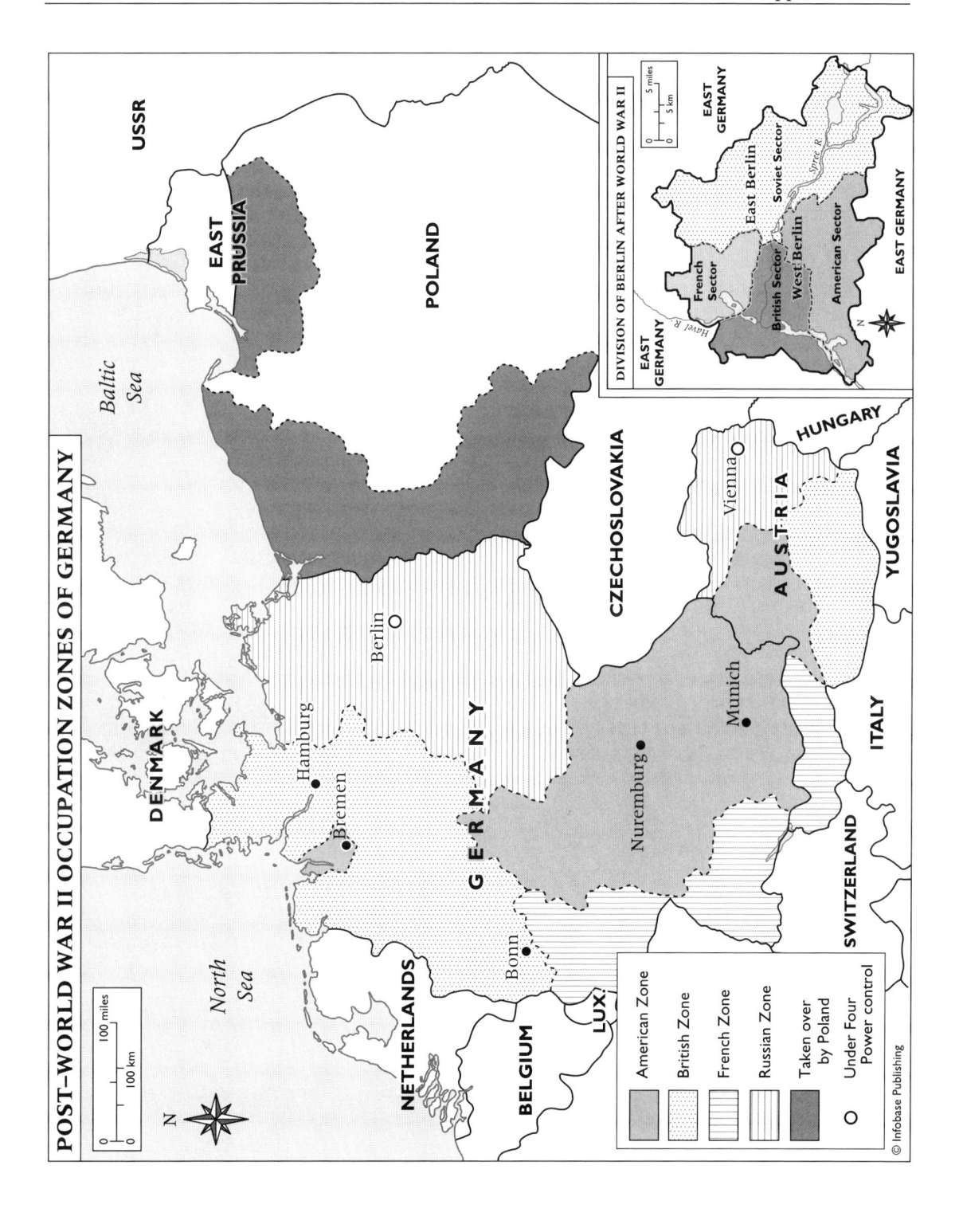

© Infobase Publishing

GERMANY
North Frisian Islands
DENMARK
Flensburg
Baltic Sea
Rügen
Fehmarn
North Sea
Kiel
Usedom
Rostock
Helgoland
East Frisian Islands
Cuxhaven
Lübeck
Wilhelmshaven
Hamburg
Schwerin
Emden
Bremerhaven
Oldenburg
Bremen
Weser R.
Elbe R.
Wittenberg
Oder R.
THE NETHERLANDS
POLAND
Meppen
Lingen
Brandenburg
Hannover
Wolfsburg
Berlin
Osnabrück
Potsdam
Hildesheim
Braunschweig
Bielefeld
Münster
Hameln
Magdeburg
Cottbus
Gelsenkirchen
Hamm
Oberhausen
Essen
Dortmund
Göttingen
Duisberg
Hagen
Ruhr R.
Bochum
Kassel
Weser R.
Halle
Leipzig
Krefeld
Düsseldorf
Wuppertal
Mönchen-gladbach
Solingen
Elbe R.
Dresden
Cologne
Erfurt
Weimar
Bonn
Siegen
Chemnitz
Aachen
Jena
Gera
Rhine R.
Zwickau
Lahn R.
BELGIUM
Koblenz
Frankfurt am Main
Bayreuth
Wiesbaden
Hanau
Main R.
LUX.
Trier
Mainz
Darmstadt
Bamberg
Moselle R.
CZECH REPUBLIC
Worms
Würzburg
Mannheim
Kaiserslautern
Heidelberg
Nürnberg
Saarbrücken
Heilbronn
Karlsruhe
Regensburg
Baden-Baden
Deggendorf
Stuttgart
Danube R.
Rhine R.
Tübingen
Passau
N
FRANCE
Ulm
Dachau
Augsburg
Munich
AUSTRIA
Freiburg
Lake Constance
Oberammergau
Friedrichshafen
Garmisch-Partenkirchen
0
100 miles
0
100 km
© Infobase Publishing
SWITZERLAND
LIECHTENSTEIN

BIBLIOGRAPHY

I. General

Barraclough, Geoffrey. *The Origins of Modern Germany.* New York: Capricorn Books, 1963.

Berghahn, Volker R., ed. *Militarism: The History of an International Debate 1861–1979.* New York: St. Martin's Press, 1980.

Berman, Russel. *The Rise of the Modern German Novel.* Cambridge: Cambridge University Press, 1986.

Bithell, Jethro. *Modern German Literature, 1880–1950.* 3rd rev. ed. London: Methuen, 1959.

Burns, Rob, ed. *German Cultural Studies.* Oxford: Oxford University Press, 1995.

Bossenbrook, William J. *The German Mind.* Detroit, Mich.: Wayne State University Press, 1961.

Carsten, Francis L. *A History of the Prussian Junkers.* Brookfield, Vt.: Scolar Press, 1989.

———. *The Origins of Prussia.* Oxford: Oxford University Press, 1954.

———. *Princes and Parliaments in Germany from the Fifteenth to the Eighteenth Century.* Oxford: Oxford University Press, 1959.

Clark, Jay A., ed. *Negotiating History: German Art and the Past: Prints and Drawings from Friedrich to Baselitz.* Museum Studies, vol. 28. no. 1. Chicago: The Art Institute of Chicago, 2002.

Craig, Gordon A. *From Bismarck to Adenauer.* Baltimore, Md.: Johns Hopkins University Press, 1965.

———. *The Germans.* New York: G. P. Putnam's Sons, 1982.

———. *Germany, 1866–1945.* New York: Oxford University Press, 1978.

———. *The Politics of the Prussian Army, 1640–1945.* New York: Oxford University Press, 1964.

Crankshaw, Edward. *The Habsburgs: Portrait of a Dynasty.* New York: Viking Press, 1971.

Daemmrich, Horst S., and Hiether H. Haenicke. *The Challenge of German Literature.* Detroit, Mich.: Wayne State University Press, 1971.

Dictionary of Literary Biography: German Writers from the Enlightenment to the Sturm und Drang, 1720–1764. Vol. 97. Edited by James Hardin and Christoph E. Schweitzer. New York: Gale Group, 1990.

Dictionary of Literary Biography: German Writers in the Age of Goethe: Sturm und Drang to Classicism. Vol. 94. Edited by James Hardin and Christoph E. Schweitzer. New York: Gale Group, 1990.

Dupuy, Trevor N. *A Genius for War: The German Army and General Staff, 1807–1945.* New York: Doubleday, 1997.

Emmel, Hildegard. *History of the German Novel.* Trans. Ellen Summerfield. Detroit, Mich.: Wayne State University Press, 1984.

Encyclopedia of World Art. 17 vols. New York: McGraw-Hill, 1959–1987.

Epstein, Klaus. *The Genesis of German Conservatism.* Princeton, N.J.: Princeton University Press, 1966.

European Authors 1000–1900: A Biographical Dicitionary of European Literature. Edited by Stanley Kunitz and V. Colby. New York: Wilson, 1967.

Evans, Richard J. W. *The German Bourgeoisie: Essays on the Social History of the German Middle Class from the Late Eighteenth to the Early Twentieth Century.* New York: Routledge, 1991.

———. *The German Peasantry: Conflict and Community in Rural Society from the Eighteenth to the Twentieth Centuries.* New York: St. Martin's Press, 1986.

———. *The Making of the Habsburg Monarchy, 1550–1700: An Interpretation.* Oxford: Oxford University Press, 1979.

Evans, Richard, and W. Robert Lee, eds. *The German Family: Essays on the Social History of the Family in Nineteenth- and Twentieth-Century Germany.* Totowa, N.J.: Barnes & Noble, 1981.

Eyck, Frank. *Religion and Politics in German History: From the Beginnings to the French Revolution.* New York: St. Martin's Press, 1998.

Fest, Wilfried. *Dictionary of German History, 1806–1945.* New York: St. Martin's Press, 1979.

Fichtner, Paula S. *The Habsburg Monarchy, 1490–1848: Attributes of Empire.* New York: Palgrave Macmillan, 2003.

Flinn, Michael Walter. *The European Demographic System, 1500–1820.* Baltimore, Md.: Johns Hopkins Press, 1981.

Fulbrook, Mary. *A Concise History of Germany.* Cambridge: Cambridge University Press, 1990.

———, ed. *German History Since 1800.* London: Arnold Press, 1997.

Garland, Henry B. *The Oxford Companion to German Literature.* New York: Oxford University Press, 1986.

Gillispie, Charles Coulston. *Dictionary of Scientific Biography.* New York: Scribner, 1970–90.

Goerlitz, Walter. *History of the German General Staff, 1657–1945.* New York: Praeger, 1958.

Hagen, William W. *Ordinary Prussians: Brandenburg Junkers and Villagers, 1500–1840.* New York: Cambridge University Press, 2002.

Hildebrand, Klaus. *German Foreign Policy from Bismarck to Adenauer: The Limits of Statecraft.* Boston: Unwin Hyman, 1989.

Hohenberg, Paul, and Lynn Lees. *The Making of Urban Europe, 1000–1950.* Cambridge, Mass.: Harvard University Press, 1985.

Holborn, Hajo. *A History of Modern Germany.* 3 vols. New York: Alfred A. Knopf, 1967.

Iggers, Georg G. *The German Conception of History: The National Tradition of Historical Thought from Herder to the Present.* Rev. ed. Middletown, Conn.: Wesleyan University Press, 1983.

Ingrao, Charles W. *The Habsburg Monarchy, 1618–1815.* 2nd ed. New York: Cambridge University Press, 2000.

Janssen, Johannes. *History of the German People at the Close of the Middle Ages.* 16 vols. New York: AMS Press, 1966.

Kahler, Erich. *The Germans.* Edited by Robert and Rita Kimber. Princeton, N.J.: Princeton University Press, 1974.

Kann, Robert A. *A History of the Habsburg Empire, 1526–1918.* Berkeley: University of California Press, 1974.

———. *A Study in Austrian Intellectual History: From Late Baroque to Romanticism.* New York: Frederick Praeger, 1960.

Kirk, Tim. *Cassell's Dictionary of Modern German History.* London: Cassell, 2002.

Kitchen, Martin. *The Cambridge Illustrated History of Germany.* London: Cambridge University Press, 1996.

———. *A Military History of Germany from the 18th Century to the Present Day.* Bloomington: Indiana University Press, 1975.

Koenigsberger, H. G. *The Habsburgs and Europe.* Ithaca, N.Y.: Cornell University Press, 1971.

Kohn, Hans. *The German Mind: The Education of a Nation.* New York: Harper and Row, 1960.

Krieger, Leonard. *The German Idea of Freedom. A History of a Political Tradition from the Reformation to 1871.* Chicago: University of Chicago Press, 1957.

Landes, David S. *The Unbound Prometheus: Technological Change and Industrial Development in Western Europe from 1750 to the Present.* Cambridge: Cambridge University Press, 1969.

Liptzin, Solomon. *Historical Survey of German Literature.* New York: Cooper Square Publishers, 1973.

Literary Culture in the Holy Roman Empire, 1555–1720. Chapel Hill: University of North Carolina Press, 1991.

Mann, Golo. *A History of Germany since 1789.* Trans. Marian Jackson. New York: Frederick Praeger, 1968.

McClelland, Charles. *State, Society, and University in Germany, 1700–1914.* New York: Cambridge University Press, 1980.

Modern Germany: An Encyclopedia of History, People and Culture, 1871–1990. 2 vols. Edited by Dieter K. Buse and Juergen C. Doerr. New York: Garland Publishing, 1998.

Moeller, Robert G., ed. *Peasants and Lords in Modern Germany: Recent Studies in Agricultural History.* Boston, Mass.: Allen & Unwin, 1985.

New Catholic Encyclopedia. 16 vols. New York: McGraw-Hill, 1967–70.

Okey, Robin. *The Habsburg Monarchy: From Enlightenment to Eclipse.* New York: St. Martin's Press, 2001.

Orlow, Dietrich. *A History of Modern Germany, 1871 to the Present.* 4th ed. Upper Saddle River, N.J.: Prentice Hall, 1999.

Pinson, Koppel S. *Modern Germany, Its History and Civilization.* New York: Macmillan, 1955.

Raynor, Henry. *A Social History of Music. From the Middle Ages to Beethoven.* New York: Shocken Books, 1972.

Reinhardt, Kurt F. *Germany 2000 Years.* Milwaukee, Wisc.: Bruce Publishing, 1950.

Robertson, J. G. *A History of German Literature.* 6th ed. Edinburgh: William Blackwood, 1970.

Rose, Ernst. *A History of German Literature.* New York: New York University Press, 1960.

Roseman, Mark. *Generations in Conflict: Youth Revolt and Generation Formation in Germany, 1770–1968.* New York: Cambridge University Press, 1995.

Sagarra, Eda. *A Social History of Germany, 1648–1914.* London: Methuen, 1977.

Sheehan, James J. *German History, 1770–1866.* New York: Oxford University Press, 1989.

Snyder, Louis L. *Documents of German History.* New Brunswick, N.J.: Rutgers University Press, 1958.

Vann, J. A. *The Old Reich: Essays on German Political Institutions, 1495–1806.* Brussels: Editions de la librairie encyclopédique, 1974.

Walker, Mack. *German Home Towns: Community, State, General Estate, 1648–1871.* Ithaca, N.Y.: Cornell University Press, 1971.

Zeydel, Edwin Hermann. *The Holy Roman Empire in German Literature.* New York: AMS Press, 1966.

Zophy, Jonathan, ed. *The Holy Roman Empire: A Dictionary Handbook.* Westport, Conn.: Greenwood Press, 1980.

II. SIXTEENTH CENTURY: RENAISSANCE AND HOLY ROMAN EMPIRE

Augustijn, Cornelis. *Erasmus: His Life, Works, and Influence.* Trans. J. C. Grayson. Toronto: University of Toronto Press, 1991.

Bainton, Roland. *Erasmus of Christendom.* New York: Scribner, 1969.

Benecke, G. *Maximilian I (1459–1519): An Analytical Biography.* Boston, Mass.: Routledge & Kegan Paul, 1982.

———. *Society and Politics in Germany, 1500–1750.* London: Routledge & Kegan Paul, 1974.

Bernstein, Eckhard. *German Humanism.* Boston, Mass.: Twayne Publishers, 1983.

Borchardt, F. L. *German Antiquity in Renaissance Myth.* Baltimore, Md.: Johns Hopkins University Press, 1971.

Busch, Harald. *Renaissance Europe.* New York: Macmillan, 1961.

Ellis, Frances H. *The Early Meisterlieder of Hans Sachs.* Bloomington: Indiana University Press, 1974.

Friedländer, Max J., and Jakob Rosenberg. *The Paintings of Lucas Cranach.* Ithaca, N.Y.: Cornell University Press, 1978.

Hitchcock, Henry-Russel. *German Renaissance Architecture.* Princeton, N.J.: Princeton University Press, 1981.

Hutchinson, Jane Campbell. *Albrecht Dürer: A Biography.* Princeton, N.J.: Princeton University Press, 1990.

Jensen, De Lamar. *Renaissance Europe: Age of Recovery and Reconciliation.* 2nd ed. Lexington, Mass.: D.C. Heath, 1992.

Osten, Gert von der. *Painting and Sculpture in Germany and the Netherlands, 1500–1600.* Baltimore, Md.: Penguin Books, 1969.

Ozment, Steven, ed. *Religion and Culture in the Renaissance and Reformation.* Kirkville, Mo.: Sixteenth Century Journal Publishers, 1989.

Mellinkoff, Ruth. *The Devil at Isenheim: Reflections of Popular Belief in Grünewald's Altarpiece.* Berkeley: University of California Press, 1988.

Panofsky, Erwin. *The Life and Art of Albrecht Dürer.* 4th ed. Princeton, N.J.: Princeton University Press, 1971.

Parente, James A., Jr. *Religious Drama and the Humanist Tradition: Christian Theater in Germany and the Netherlands, 1500–1680.* New York: E. J. Brill, 1987.

Pascal, Roy. *German Literature in the Sixteenth and Seventeenth Centuries: Renaissance, Reformation, Baroque.* New York: Barnes & Noble, 1968.

Rowan, Steven. *Ulrich Zasius: A Jurist in the German Renaissance, 1461–1535.* Frankfurt am Main: V. Klosterman, 1987.

Rowlands, John. *The Age of Dürer and Holbein: German Drawings 1400–1550.* New York: Cambridge University Press, 1988.

Smith, Jeffrey, ed. *German Sculpture of the Later Renaissance, 1520–1580: Art in an Age of Uncertainty.* Princeton, N.J.: Princeton University Press, 1994.

———. *New Perspectives on the Art of Renaissance Nuremberg.* Austin: University of Texas Press, 1985.

Snyder, James. *Northern Renaissance Art: Painting, Sculpture and the Graphic Arts from 1350–1575.* 2nd ed. Upper Saddle River, N.J.: Prentice Hall, 1975.

Spitz, Lewis W. *Conrad Celtis, The German Arch-Humanist.* Cambridge, Mass.: Harvard University Press, 1952.

———. *The Religious Renaissance of the German Humanists.* Cambridge, Mass.: Harvard University Press, 1963.

Stechow, Wolfgang, ed. *Northern Renaissance Art, 1400–1600: Sources and Documents.* Englewood Cliffs, N.J.: Prentice Hall, 1966.

Strauss, Gerald. *Nuremberg in the Sixteenth Century: City Politics and Life between Middle Ages and Modern Times.* Rev. ed. Bloomington: Indiana University Press, 1976.

Warnement, Julie, and Jody Shiffman. *From Schongauer to Holbein: Master Drawings from Basel and Berlin.* Washington, D.C.: National Gallery of Art, 1999.

Zeydel, Edwin H. *Sebastian Brant.* New York: Twayne Publishers, 1967.

III. Sixteenth Century: Reformation and Counter-Reformation

Arthur, Anthony. *The Tailor-King: The Rise and Fall of the Anabaptist Kingdom of Münster.* New York: St. Martin's Press, 1999.

Aveling, John Cedric H. *The Jesuits.* New York: Stein & Day, 1982.

Bainton, Roland Herbert. *The Age of the Reformation.* Malabar, Fla.: R. E. Krieger, 1984.

———. *Here I Stand: A Life of Martin Luther.* New York: Abingdon-Cokesbury Press, 1950.

———, and Eric W. Gritsch, eds. *Bibliography of the Continental Reformation: Materials available in English.* 2nd ed. Hamden, Conn.: Archon Books, 1972.

Baker, J. Wayne. *Heinrich Bullinger and the Covenant: The Other Reformed Tradition.* Athens: Ohio University Press, 1980.

Benecke, Gerhard. *The German Peasant's War of 1525: New Viewpoints.* Boston, Mass.: Allen & Unwin, 1979.

Bireley, Robert, S.J. *Refashioning of Catholicism, 1450–1700: A Reassessment of the Counter-Reformation.* Washington, D.C.: Catholic University Press, 1999.

Birnbaum, Norman. *Social Structure and the German Reformation.* New York: Arno Press, 1980.

Blickle, Peter. *The Revolution of 1525: The German Peasants' War from a New Perspective.* Trans. Thomas A. Brady, Jr., and H. C. Erik Midelfort. Baltimore, Md.: Johns Hopkins University Press, 1981.

Bouwsma, W. J. *John Calvin: A Sixteenth-Century Portrait.* New York: Oxford University Press, 1988.

Brecht, Martin. *Martin Luther: His Road to Reformation, 1483–1521.* Trans. James L. Schaaf. Philadelphia, Pa.: Fortress Press, 1985.

Cargill-Thompson, W. D. J. *The Political Thought of Martin Luther.* Totowa, N.J.: Barnes & Noble Books, 1984.

Christensen, Carl C. *Art and the Reformation in Germany.* Athens: Ohio University Press, 1979.

Classen, Claus-Peter. *Anabaptism: A Social History, 1525–1618: Switzerland, Moravia, South & Central Germany.* Ithaca, N.Y.: Cornell University Press, 1972.

Crossley, Robert N. *Luther and the Peasants' War: Luther's Actions and Reactions.* New York: Exposition Press, 1974.

Duggan, Lawrence G. *Bishops and Chapter: The Governance of the Bishopric of Speyer to 1552.* New Brunswick, N.J.: Rutgers University Press, 1978.

Dyck, Cornelius J., ed. *An Introduction to Mennonite History.* Scottdale, Pa.: Herald Press, 1981.

Edwards, Mark U., Jr. *Luther and the False Brethren.* Stanford, Calif.: Stanford University Press, 1975.

Estes, James M. *Christian Magistrate and State Church: Reforming Career of Johannes Brenz.* Buffalo, N.Y.: University of Toronto Press, 1982.

Forster, Marc R. *Catholic Revival in the Age of the Baroque: Religious Identity in Southwest Germany, 1550–1750.* New York: Cambridge University Press, 2001.

Gamble, Richard C., ed. *Calvinism in Switzerland, Germany and Hungary.* New York: Garland Publishing, 1992.

Goertz, Hans-Jürgen. *The Anabaptists.* Trans. Trevor Johnson. New York: Routledge, 1996.

———. *Thomas Müntzer: Apocalyptic Mystic and Revolutionary.* Trans. Jocelyn Jaquiery. Edinburgh: T & T Clark, 1993.

Greyerz, Kaspar von, ed. *Religion, Politics and Social Protest.* Boston, Mass.: Allen & Unwin, 1984.

Grimm, Harold J. *The Reformation Era, 1500–1650.* New York: Macmillan, 1965.

Harbison, E. Harris. *The Christian Scholar in the Age of Reformation.* New York: Scribner, 1956.

Harrington, Joel F. *Reordering Marriage and Society in Reformation Germany.* London: Cambridge University Press, 1995.

Hendrix, Scott. *Luther and the Papacy: Stages in a Reformation Conflict.* Philadelphia, Pa.: Fortress Press, 1981.

Hillerbrand, Hans, ed. *Oxford Encyclopedia of the Reformation* New York: Oxford University Press, 1995.

Hsai, R. Po-chia, ed. *The German People and the Reformation.* Ithaca, N.Y.: Cornell University Press, 1988.

———. *Society and Religion in Münster, 1535–1618.* New Haven, Conn.: Yale University Press, 1984.

Huizinga, Johan. *Erasmus and the Age of the Reformation.* New York: Dover Publishing, 2001.

Jedin, Hubert, and J. Dolan, eds. *History of the Church,* vol. 5. Trans. A. Biggs and P. W. Becker. New York: Seabury, 1980.

———. *History of the Council of Trent.* 2 vols. Trans. Ernest Graf. London: T. Nelson, 1957–61.

Jedin, Hubert, ed. *The Medieval and Reformation Church: an Abridgement of the Church.* Vols. 4–6. Trans. John Dolan. Abridgement by D. Larrimore Holland. New York: Crossroad, 1993.

Jensen, De Lamar. *Confrontation at Worms: Martin Luther and the Diet of Worms.* Provo, Utah: Brigham Young University Press, 1973.

———. *Reformation Europe: Age of Reform and Revolution.* Lexington, Mass.: D.C. Heath, 1992.

Lohse, Bernard. *Martin Luther: An Introduction to His Life and Work.* Trans. Robert C. Schulz. Philadelphia, Pa.: Fortress Press, 1986.

Lortz, Joseph. *The Reformation in Germany.* Trans. R. Walls. 2 vols. London: Darton, Longman & Todd, 1968.

Manschreck, Clyde. *Melanchthon: The Quiet Reformer.* New York: Abingdon Press, 1958.

Mathews, Thomas F. *Art and Religion: Faith, Form and Reform.* Columbia: University of Missouri-Columbia, 1986.

McNeill, J. T. *The History and Character of Calvinism.* New York: Oxford University Press, 1954.

Minnich, Nelson H. *Catholic Reformation: Council, Churchmen, Controversies.* Aldershot, Hants, U.K.: Ashgate Publishing, 1993.

Nischan, Bodo. *Lutherans and Calvinists in the Age of Confessionalism.* Brookfield, Vt.: Ashgate/Variorum, 1999.

Oberman, Heiko A. *The Dawn of the Reformation: Essays in Late Medieval and Early Reformation Thought.* Edinburgh: T & T Clark, 1986.

———. *Luther: Man between God and the Devil.* Trans. Eileen Walliser-Schwarzbart. New Haven, Conn.: Yale University Press, 1989.

O'Connell, Marvin R. *The Counter Reformation, 1559–1610.* New York: Harper & Row, 1974.

Ogilvie, Aheilagh, and Robert Scribner, eds. *Germany: A New Social and Economic History.* 2 vols. London: Edward Arnold, 1995.

Olin, John C. *Catholic Reform from Cardinal Ximenes to the Council of Trent, 1495–1563.* New York: Fordham University Press, 1990.

Ozment, Steven. *The Age of Reform, 1250–1550.* New Haven, Conn.: Yale University Press, 1980.

———. *Flesh and Spirit: Private Life in Early Modern Germany.* New York: Viking, 1999.

———. *The Reformation in the Cities.* New Haven, Conn.: Yale University Press, 1975.

Packull, Werner O. *Hutterite Beginnings: Communitarian Experiments during the Reformation.* Baltimore, Md.: Johns Hopkins University Press, 1995.

Pater, Calvin A. *Karlstadt as the Father of the Baptist Movement: The Emergence of Lay Protestantism.* Buffalo, N.Y.: University of Toronto Press, 1984.

Pelikan, Jaroslav. *The Christian Tradition: A History of the Development of Doctrine,* vol. 4, *Reformation of Church and Dogma, 1300–1700.* Chicago: University of Chicago Press, 1984.

Potter, G. R. *Zwingli.* New York: Cambridge University Press, 1976.

Reardon, Bernard M. G. *Religious Thought in the Reformation.* New York: Longmans, 1995.

Safley, Thomas M. *Let No Man Put Asunder: The Control of Marriage in the German Southwest, 1550–1600.* Kirksville, Mo.: Sixteenth Century Journal Publishers, 1984.

Scribner, Robert W. *Culture and Popular Movements in Reformation Germany.* New York: Oxford University Press, 1994.

Spitz, Lewis W. *Luther and German Humanism.* Brookfield, Vt.: Variorum/Ashgate, 1996.

Strauss, Gerald. *Law, Resistance, and the State: The Opposition to Roman Law in Reformation Germany.*

Princeton, N.J.: Princeton University Press, 1986.

———. *Luther's House of Learning: Indoctrination of the Young in the German Reformation.* Baltimore, Md.: Johns Hopkins University Press, 1978.

Strauss, Gerald. *Nuremberg in the Sixteenth Century: City Politics and Life between Middle Ages and Modern Times.* Rev. ed. Bloomington: Indiana University Press, 1976.

Tentler, T. N. *Sin and Confession on the Eve of the Reformation.* Princeton, N.J.: Princeton University Press, 1977.

Walton, Robert C. *Zwingli's Theocracy.* Toronto: University of Toronto Press, 1967.

Wright, William J. *Capitalism, the State and the Lutheran Reformation: Sixteenth Century Hesse.* Athens: Ohio University Press, 1988.

IV. Seventeenth Century

Aiton, E. J. *Leibniz: a Biography.* Boston, Mass.: A. Hilger, 1985.

Allison, Henry E. *Benedict de Spinoza: an Introduction.* Rev. ed. New Haven, Conn.: Yale University Press, 1987.

Benecke, G. *Society and Politics in Germany, 1500–1750.* London: Routledge & Kegan Paul, 1974.

Bourke, John. *Baroque Churches of Central Europe.* 2nd rev. ed. London: Faber & Faber, 1978.

Busch, Harald. *Baroque Sculpture.* London: B. T. Batsford, 1965.

Clasen, Claus Peter. *The Palatinate in European History, 1555–1618.* Rev. ed. Oxford: Oxford University Press, 1966.

Evans, Robert John Weston. *The Making of the Habsburg Monarchy, 1550–1700: An Interpretation.* Oxford: Oxford University Press, 1979.

———. *Rudolf II and His World: A Study in Intellectual History, 1576–1612.* Oxford: Clarendon Press, 1973.

Friedrichs, Christopher. *Urban Society in an Age of War: Nördlinger, 1580–1720.* Princeton, N.J.: Princeton University Press, 1979.

Gagliardo, John. *Germany under the Old Regime, 1600–1790.* New York: Longman, 1991.

Gutmann, Myron P. *Toward the Modern Economy: Early Industry in Europe, 1500–1800.* Philadelphia, Pa.: Temple University Press, 1988.

Hughes, Michael. *Early Modern Germany.* London: Macmillan, 1992.

Kayser, Rudolf. *The Saints of Qumrân: Spinoza and Jewish Literature.* Rutherford, N.J.: Fairleigh Dickinson University Press, 1977.

Koenigsberger, Helmut G. *The Habsburgs and Europe, 1516–1660.* Ithaca, N.Y.: Cornell University Press, 1971.

Krieger, Leonard. *The Politics of Discretion: Pufendorf and the Acceptance of Natural Law.* Chicago: University of Chicago Press, 1965.

Mann, Golo. *Wallenstein.* Trans. Charles Kessler. New York: Holt Rinehart and Winston, 1976.

McKay, Derek. *Prince Eugene of Savoy.* London: Thames & Hudson, 1977.

Meyer, Rudolf. *Leibniz and the 17th Century Revolution.* New York: Garland, 1975.

Pagès, Georges. *The Thirty Years War.* New York: Harper, 1971.

Parker, Geoffrey. *Europe in Crisis, 1598–1648.* Ithaca, N.Y.: Cornell University Press, 1980.

———. *The Thirty Years War.* New York: Routledge & Kegan Paul, 1987.

Pascal, Roy. *German Literature in the Sixteenth and Seventeenth Centuries: Renaissance, Reformation, Baroque.* New York: Barnes & Noble, 1968.

Powell, Nicholas. *From Baroque to Rococo: An Introduction to Austrian and German Architecture from 1580 to 1790.* London: Faber, 1959.

Rebel, Hermann. *Peasant Classes: The Bureaucratization of Property and Family Relations under Early Habsburg Absolutism, 1500–1636.* Princeton, N.J.: Princeton University Press, 1983.

Spielman, John P. *Leopold I of Austria.* New Brunswick, N.J.: Rutgers University Press, 1977.

Stein, K. James. *Philipp Jakob Spener: Pietist Patriarch.* Chicago: Covenant Press, 1986.

Steinberg, S. H. *The Thirty Years War and the Conflict for European Hegemony, 1600–1660.* New York: Norton, 1966.

Vann, J. A. *The Making of a State: Württemberg, 1593–1793.* Ithaca, N.Y.: Cornell University Press, 1984.

Wedgwood, C. V. *The Thirty Years War.* New York: Doubleday (Anchor Books), 1961.

V. Eighteenth Century

Allison, Henry E. *Lessing and the Enlightenment: His Philosophy of Religion and Its Relation to Eighteenth Century Thought.* Ann Arbor: University of Michigan Press, 1966.

Aris, R. *History of Political Thought in Germany from 1789 to 1815.* London: Frank Cass, 1936.

Asprey, Robert. *The Rise of Napoleon Bonaparte.* New York: Basic Books, 2000.

Barnard, Frederick M. *J. G. Herder on Social and Political Culture.* London: Cambridge University Press, 1969.

Beales, Derek Edward Dawson. *Joseph II.* Vol. 1, *In the Shadow of Maria Theresa, 1741–1780.* New York: Cambridge University Press, 1987.

Beiser, Frederick C. *Enlightenment, Revolution, and Romanticism. The Genesis of Modern German Political Thought.* Cambridge, Mass.: Harvard University Press, 1992.

Beck, Lewis White. *Early German Philosophy: Kant and His Predecessors.* Cambridge, Mass.: Harvard University Press, 1969.

———. *Immanuel Kant, On History.* Indianapolis: Bobbs-Merrill, 1963.

Bennet, Benjamin. *Modern Drama and German Classicism: Renaissance from Lessing to Brecht.* Ithaca, N.Y.: Cornell University Press, 1979.

Behrens, C. B. A. *Society, Government and the Enlightenment: the Experiences of Eighteenth-Century France and Prussia.* London: Thames and Hudson, 1985.

Berdahl, Robert M. *The Politics of the Prussian Nobility: The Development of a Conservative Ideology, 1770–1848.* Princeton, N.J.: Princeton University Press, 1988.

Bernard, Paul P. *Jesuits and Jacobins: Enlightenment and Enlightened Despotism in Austria.* Urbana: University of Illinois Press, 1971.

———. *Joseph II and Bavaria: Two Eighteenth-Century Attempts at German Unification.* New York: Twayne Publishers, 1968.

Blackall, Eric. *The Emergence of German as a Literary Language, 1700–1775.* Ithaca, N.Y.: Cornell University Press, 1978.

Blanning, T. C. W. *The French Revolutionary Wars, 1787–1802.* New York: St. Martin's Press, 1996.

———. *Joseph II, Holy Roman Emperor, 1741–1790.* New York: Longman, 1994.

———. *Reform and Revolution in Mainz, 1743–1803.* New York: Cambridge University Press, 1974.

Bruford, W. H. *Culture and Society in Classical Weimar, 1775–1806.* London: Cambridge University Press, 1962.

———. *Germany in the Eighteenth Century: The Social Background of the Literary Revival.* Cambridge: Cambridge University Press, 1965.

Brunschwig, Henri. *Enlightenment and Romanticism in Eighteenth-Century Prussia.* Trans. Frank Jellinek. Chicago: University of Chicago Press, 1974.

Butler, E. M. (Elizabeth Marian). *The Tyranny of Greece over Germany: A Study of the Influence Exercised by Greek Art and Poetry over the Great German Writers of the Eighteenth, Nineteenth Centuries.* Boston, Mass.: Beacon Press, 1958.

Copleston, Frederick. *A History of Philosophy.* Vol. 7, *Modern Philosophy.* Part 1. Fichte to Hegel. Garden City, N.Y.: Doubleday, 1965.

Chandler, David G. *The Art of Warfare in the Age of Marlborough.* New York: Sarpedon, 1997.

———. *Austerlitz 1805: Battle of Three Emperors.* London: Osprey, 1990.

———. *On the Napoleonic Wars: Collected essays.* Mechanicsburg, Pa.: Stackpole Books, 1994.

Clark, Robert. *Herder: His Life and Thought.* Berkeley and Los Angeles: University of California Press, 1955.

Dippel, Horst. *Germany and the American Revolution, 1770–1800.* Trans. Bernard Uhlendorf. Chapel Hill: University of North Carolina Press, 1977.

Dorwart, Reinhold. *The Administrative Reforms of Frederick William I of Prussia.* Westport, Conn.: Greenwood Press, 1971.

———. *The Prussian Welfare State before 1740.* Cambridge, Mass.: Harvard University Press, 1971.

Duffy, Christopher. *The Army of Frederick the Great.* Newton Abbot, England: David & Charles, 1974.

———. *Frederick the Great: A Military Life.* London: Routledge & Kegan Paul, 1985.

Ergang, Robert Reinhold. *Herder and the Foundations of German Nationalism.* New York: Octagon Books, 1966.

———. *The Potsdam Fuehrer: Frederick William I, Father of Prussian Militarism.* New York: Columbia University Press, 1941.

Fauchier-Magnan, Adrien. *The Small German Courts in the Eighteenth Century.* London: Methuen, 1958.

Fay, Sidney B. *The Rise of Brandenburg-Prussia to 1786.* Rev. ed. Edited by Klaus Epstein. New York: Holt Rinehart and Winston, 1964.

Fraser, David. *Frederick the Great: King of Prussia.* New York: Fromm International, 2001.

Fulbrook, Mary. *Piety and Politics: Religion and the Rise of Absolutism in England, Württemberg, and Prussia.* New York: Cambridge University Press, 1983.

Gagliardo, John G. *From Pariah to Patriot: The Changing Image of the German Peasant, 1770–1840.* Lexington: University of Kentucky Press, 1969.

———. *Reich and Nation: The Holy Roman Empire as Idea and Reality, 1763–1806.* Bloomington: Indiana University Press, 1980.

Gooch, G. P. *Germany and the French Revolution.* New York: Russell & Russell, 1966.

Henderson, W. O. *State and the Industrial Revolution in Prussia, 1740–1870.* Liverpool, England: Liverpool University Press, 1958.

Hertz, Frederick. *The Development of the German Public Mind: A Social History of German Political Sentiments, Aspirations and Ideas.* Vol. 2, *The Enlightenment.* New York: Macmillan, 1957.

Ingrao, C. *The Hessian Mercenary State. Ideas, Institutions and Reform under Frederick II, 1760–1785.* New York: Cambridge University Press, 1987.

Johnson, Hubert. *Frederick the Great and His Officials.* New Haven, Conn.: Yale University Press, 1975.

Kahn, Ludwig. *Social Ideals in German Literature, 1770–1830.* New York: AMS Press, 1938.

Kann, Robert A. *A Study in Austrian Intellectual History: From Late Baroque to Romanticism.* New York: Frederick Praeger, 1960.

Knudsen, Jonathan B. *Justus Möser and the German Enlightenment.* New York: Cambridge University Press, 1986.

Krieger, Leonard. *The Politics of Discretion: Pufendorf and the Acceptance of Natural Law.* Chicago: University of Chicago Press, 1965.

Lange, Victor. *The Classical Age of German Literature, 1740–1815.* New York: Holmes & Meier, 1982.

Lee, W. R. *Population Growth, Economic Development and Social Change in Bavaria, 1750–1850.* New York: Arno Press, 1977.

Link, Edith. *The Emancipation of the Austrian Peasant, 1740–1798.* New York: Octagon Books, 1974.

McCarthy, John A. *Christoph Martin Wieland.* Boston, Mass.: Twayne Publishers, 1979.

Melton, James Van Horn. *Absolutism and the Eighteenth-Century Origins of Compulsory Schooling in Prussia and Austria.* New York: Cambridge University Press, 1988.

Menhennet, Alan. *Order and Freedom: Literature and Society in Germany from 1720–1805.* London: Weidenfield & Nicolson, 1973.

Nicolson, Harold G. *The Age of Reason: the Eighteenth Century.* Garden City, N.Y.: Doubleday, 1960.

O'Brien, Charles H. *Ideas of Religious Toleration at the Time of Joseph II.* Philadelphia, Pa.: American Philosophical Society, 1969.

Padover, Saul K. *The Revolutionary Emperor: Joseph II, 1741–1790.* 2nd ed. London: Eyre & Spottiswoode, 1967.

Pascal, Roy. *The German Sturm und Drang.* New York: Philosophical Library, 1953.

Pick, Robert. *Empress Maria Theresa: the Earlier Years, 1717–1757.* New York: Harper & Row, 1966.

Raeff, Marc. *The Well-Ordered Police State: Social and Institutional Change through Law in the Germanies and Russia.* New Haven, Conn.: Yale University Press, 1983.

Reardon, Bernard, M. G. *Kant as Philosophical Theologian.* Totowa, N.J.: Barnes and Noble, 1987.

Reed, T. J. *The Classical Centre: Goethe and Weimar, 1775–1832.* New York and London, 1980.

Reill, Peter Hanns. *The German Enlightenment and the Rise of Historicism.* Berkeley: University of California Press, 1975.

Schroeder, Paul. *The Transformation of European Politics, 1763–1848.* New York: Oxford University Press, 1994.

Stoeffler, F. Ernest. *The Rise of Evangelical Protestantism. German Pietism during the Eighteenth Century.* Leiden: E. J. Brill, 1973.

Strich, Fritz. *Goethe and World Literature.* London: Routledge & Kegan Paul, 1949.

Sweet, Paul Robinson. *Wilhelm von Humboldt: A Biography.* Columbus: Ohio State University Press, 1978–1980.

Trebilcock, Clive. *The Industrialization of the Continental Powers, 1780–1914.* New York: Longmans, 1981.

Vierhaus, R. *Germany and the Age of Absolutism.* New York: Cambridge University Press, 1988.

Walker, Mack. *Johann Jakob Moser and the Holy Roman Empire of the German Nation.* Chapel Hill: University of North Carolina Press, 1981.

Ward, Albert. *Book Production, Fiction and the German Reading Public, 1740–1800.* Oxford: Clarendon Press, 1974.

Willoughby, Leonard Ashley. *The Classical Age of German Literature, 1748–1805.* New York: Russell and Russell, 1966.

Woloch, Isser. *Napoleon and His Collaborators: The Making of a Dictatorship.* New York: W. W. Norton, 2001.

VI. NINETEENTH CENTURY

Abrams, M. H. *Natural Supernaturalism: Tradition and Revolution in Romantic Literature.* New York: Norton, 1971.

Alsop, Susan Mary. *The Congress Dances: Vienna, 1814–1815.* New York: Harper & Row, 1983.

Anderson, Margaret Lavinia. *Windhorst: A Political Biography.* New York: Oxford University Press, 1981.

Andrews, Wayne. *Siegfried's Curse: The German Journey from Nietzsche to Hesse.* New York: Atheneum, 1972.

Aubert, Roger, et al., eds. *The Church between Revolution and Restauration.* New York: Crossroad, 1981.

Balfour, Michael. *The Kaiser and His Times.* London: Cresset Press, 1964.

Bendix, Reinhard. *Scholarship and Partisanship: Essays on Max Weber.* Berkeley: University of California Press, 1971.

Berlin, Isaiah. *Karl Marx.* 3rd ed. New York: Oxford University Press, 1963.

Bernd, Clifford A. *German Poetic Realism.* Boston, Mass.: Twayne Publishers, 1981.

Bernstein, Eduard. *Evolutionary Socialism: A Criticism and Affirmation.* New York: Shocken Books, 1961.

Bigler, Robert. *The Politics of German Protestantism: The Rise of the Protestant Church Elite in Prussia, 1815.* Berkeley and Los Angeles: University of California Press, 1972.

Blackbourn, David. *Class, Religion, and Local Politics in Wilhelmine Germany: The Centre Party in Württemberg before 1914.* New Haven, Conn.: Yale University Press, 1980.

———, and Geoffrey Eley. *The Peculiarities of German History: Bourgeois Society and Politics in Nineteenth Century Germany.* Oxford: Oxford University Press, 1984.

Bramsted, Ernest K. *Aristocracy and the Middle Classes in Germany: Social Types in German Literature, 1830–1900.* Rev. ed. Chicago: University of Chicago Press, 1964.

Bruford, W. H. *The German Tradition of Self-Cultivation: Bildung from Humboldt to Thomas Mann.* Cambridge: Cambridge University Press, 1975.

Bucholz, Arden. *Moltke, Schlieffen and Prussian War Planning.* Oxford: Berg Publisher; New York: St. Martin's Press, 1991.

Carr, William. *The Origins of the Wars of German Unification.* London and New York: Longman, 1991.

Chadwick, Owen. *The Secularization of the European Mind in the Nineteenth Century* Cambridge: Cambridge University Press, 1975.

Cecil, Lamar. *Albert Ballin: Business and Politics in Imperial Germany, 1888–1918.* Princeton, N.J.: Princeton University Press, 1967.

———. *William II.* Chapel Hill: University of North Carolina Press, 1989.

Cocks, Geoffrey, and Konrad H. Jarausch. *German Professions, 1800–1950.* New York: Oxford University Press, 1990.

Craig, Gordon A. *The Battle of Königgrätz: Prussia's Victory over Austria, 1866.* Princeton, N.J.: Princeton University Press, 1964.

———. *The Politics of the Unpolitical: German Writers and the Problem of Power, 1770–1871.* New York: Oxford University Press, 1995.

Dominick, Raymond H., III. *Wilhelm Liebknecht and the Founding of the German Social Democratic Party.* Chapel Hill: University of North Carolina Press, 1982.

Dorpalen, Andreas. *Heinrich von Treitschke.* New Haven, Conn.: Yale University Press, 1957.

Eley, Geoff. *Reshaping the German Right: Radical Nationalism and Political Change after Bismarck.* New Haven, Conn.: Yale University Press, 1980.

Evans, Ellen Lovell. *The German Center Party, 1890–1933.* Carbondale: Southern Illinois University, 1981.

Evans, Richard J. *Death in Hamburg: Society and Politics in the Cholera Years, 1830–1910.* New York: Oxford University Press, 1987.

———. *Proletarians and Politics: Socialism, Protest, and the Working Class in Germany before the First World War.* New York: St. Martin's Press, 1990.

———. *Society and Politics in Wilhelmine Germany.* New York: Barnes & Noble, 1978.

Eyck, Erich. *Bismarck and the German Empire.* New York: W. W. Norton, 1964.

Eyck, Frank. *The Frankfurt Parliament, 1848–1849.* New York: St. Martin's Press, 1968.

Fletcher, Roger, ed. *Bernstein to Brandt: A Short History Of German Social Democracy.* New York: Edward Arnold, 1987.

Fuerst, Norbert. *The Victorian Age of German Literature.* London: Dennis Dobson, 1966.

Gall, Lothar. *Bismarck, the White Revolutionary.* 2 vols. Trans. J. A. Underwood. London: Allen & Unwin, 1986.

Gay, Peter Jack. *The Dilemma of Democratic Socialism: Bernstein's Challenge to Marx.* New York: Columbia University Press, 1952.

Geary, Dick. *Karl Kautsky.* New York: St. Martin's Press, 1987.

Gillis, John R. *The Prussian Bureaucracy in Crisis, 1840–1860: Origins of an Administrative Ethos.* Palo Alto, Calif.: Stanford University Press, 1971.

Glaser, Hermann. *The German Mind of the Nineteenth Century.* New York: Continuum, 1981.

Geiss, Immanuel. *German Foreign Policy, 1871–1914.* London: Routledge & Kegan Paul, 1976.

Gregory, Frederick. *Scientific Materialism in Nineteenth Century Germany.* Boston, Mass.: D. Reidel Publishing, 1977.

Gutsmann, W. L. *The German Social Democratic Party, 1875–1933.* Boston, Mass.: Allen & Unwin, 1981.

Hamerow, Theodore S. *The Social Foundations of German Unification, 1858–1871.* 2 vols. Princeton, N.J.: Princeton University Press, 1969–72.

Harris, H. S. *Hegel's Development: Toward the Sunlight (1770–1801).* Oxford: Clarendon Press, 1972.

———. *Hegel's Development: Night Thoughts (Jena 1801–1806).* New York: Oxford University Press, 1983.

Heller, Erich. *The Disinherited Mind; Essays in Modern German Literature and Thought.* New York: Farrar, Straus and Cudahy, 1957.

Henderson, William O. *The German Colonial Empire, 1884–1919.* London: F. Cass, 1993.

———. *The Life of Friedrich Engels.* 2 vols. London: F. Cass, 1976.

———. *The Rise of German Industrial Power, 1834–1914.* Berkeley: University of California Press, 1975.

———. *The Zollverein.* Cambridge: Cambridge University Press, 1939.

Howard, Michael. *The Franco-Prussian War: The German Invasion of France.* 2nd ed. New York: Routledge, 2001.

Jarausch, Konrad H. *Students, Society and Politics in Imperial Germany: The Rise of Academic Illiberalism.* Princeton, N.J.: Princeton University Press, 1982.

Jensen, Jens Christian. *Caspar David Friedrich: Life and Work.* Woodbury, N.Y.: Barron's, 1981.

Johnson, Eric A. *Urbanization and Crime, Germany, 1871–1914.* New York: Cambridge University Press, 1995.

Kaufmann, Walter. *Nietzsche: Philosopher, Psychologist, Antichrist.* Princeton, N.J.: Princeton University Press, 1950.

Kelly, Alfred. *The Descent of Darwin: The Popularization of Darwinism in Germany, 1860–1914.* Chapel Hill: University of North Carolina Press, 1981.

———, ed. and tr. *The German Worker: Working-Class Autobiographies from the Age of Industrialization.* Berkeley: University of California Press, 1987.

Kennedy, Paul M. *The Rise of the Anglo-German Antagonism, 1860–1914.* London and Boston, Mass.: Allen & Unwin, 1980.

———. *The War Plans of the Great Powers, 1880–1914.* London and Boston, Mass.: Allen & Unwin, 1979.

Kent, George O. *Bismarck and His Times.* Carbondale: Southern Illinois University Press, 1978.

Kisle, John Van der. *Kaiser Wilhelm II: Germany's Last Emperor.* Gloucestershire, U.K.: Sutton Publishing, 1999.

Kitchen, Martin. *The German Officer Corps, 1890–1914.* London: Allen & Unwin, 1980.

Kraehe, Enno E. *Metternich's German Policy.* 2 vols. Princeton, N.J.: Princeton University Press, 1963–84.

Krieger, Leonard. *The German Idea of Freedom: History of a Political Tradition.* Boston: Beacon, 1957.

Lamberti, Marjorie. *State, Society, and the Elementary School in Imperial Germany.* New York and Oxford: Oxford University Press, 1989.

Laqueur, Walter. *Young Germany.* New York: Basic Books, 1962.

Lee, W. R. *German Industry and German Industrialization: Essays in German Economic and Business History in the Nineteenth and Twentieth Centuries.* New York: Routledge, 1991.

Lees, Andrew. *Revolution and Reflection: Intellectual Change in Germany during the 1850s.* The Hague: M. Nijoff, 1974.

Lichtheim, George. *Marxism: An Historical and Critical Study.* New York: Columbia University Press, 1982.

Lidtke, Vernon L. *The Alternative Culture: Socialist Labour in Imperial Germany.* New York: Oxford University Press, 1985.

McLellan, David. *Karl Marx: His Life and Thought.* New York: Harper & Row, 1973.

———. *Friedrich Engels*. New York: Penguin Books, 1978.

Meinecke, Friedrich. *The Age of German Liberation, 1795–1815*. Ed. and trans. Peter Paret. Berkeley: University of California Press, 1977.

Moses, John A. *Trade Unionism in Germany from Bismarck to Hitler, 1869–1933*. Totowa, N.J.: Barnes & Noble, 1982.

Mosse, George L. *The Nationalization of the Masses: Political Symbolism and Mass Movements in Germany from the Napoleonic Wars through the Third Reich*. New York: Meridian, 1975.

Muncy, Lysbeth. *The Junkers in the Prussian Administration under William II, 1888–1914*. Providence, R.I.: Brown University Press, 1944.

Nettl, John P. *Rosa Luxemburg*. 2 vols. London: Oxford University Press, 1966.

Nicholson, Harold. *The Congress of Vienna: A Study in Allied Unity, 1812–1822*. New York: Harcourt Brace, 1946.

Paret, Peter. *Art as History: Episodes in the Culture and Politics of Nineteenth-Century Germany*. Princeton, N.J.: Princeton University Press, 1988.

———. *The Berlin Secession: Modernism and its Enemies in Imperial Germany*. Cambridge, Mass.: Belknap Press of Harvard University Press, 1980.

Pascal, Roy. *From Naturalism to Expressionism: German Literature and Society, 1880–1918*. London: Wiedenfeld and Nicolson, 1973.

Pflanze, Otto. *Bismarck and the Development of Germany*. 3 vols. Princeton, N.J.: Princeton University Press, 1990.

Pinson, Koppel S. *Pietism as a Factor in the Rise of German Nationalism*. New York: Columbia University Press, 1934.

Prawer, S. S., ed. *The Romantic Period in Germany*. New York: Shocken Books, 1970.

Roth, Guenther. *The Social Democrats in Imperial Germany: A Study in Working-Class Isolation and National Integration*. Totowa, N.J.: Bedminster, 1963.

Reardon, Bernard M. G. *Hegel's Philosophy of Religion*. London: Macmillan, 1977.

———. *Religion in the Age of Romanticism: Studies in Early Nineteenth-Century Thought*. New York: Cambridge University Press, 1985.

Remak, Joachim. *The Gentle Critic: Theodor Fontane and German Politics, 1848–1898*. Syracuse, N.Y.: Syracuse University Press, 1964.

Richie, Alexandra. *Faust's Metropolis: A History of Berlin*. New York: Carroll and Graf, 1998.

Robertson, Priscilla. *Revolutions of 1848: A Social History*. Princeton, N.J.: Princeton University Press, 1952.

Röhl, John C. G. *The Kaiser and His Court: Wilhelm II and the Government of Germany*. Trans. Terence F. Cole. London: Cambridge University Press, 1995.

Ross, Ronald J. *Beleaguered Tower: The Dilemma of Political Catholicism in Wilhelmine Germany*. South Bend, Ind.: University of Notre Dame Press, 1976.

———. *The Failure of Bismarck's Kulturkampf: Catholicism and State Power in Imperial Germany, 1871–1887*. Washington, D.C.: The Catholic University Press, 1998.

Ruppel, Richard R. *Gottfried Keller: Poet, Pedagogue, and Humanist*. New York: P. Lang, 1988.

Sammons, Jeffrey. *Heinrich Heine: A Modern Biography*. Princeton, N.J.: Princeton University Press, 1979.

Schleunes, Karl. *Schooling and Society: the Politics of Education in Prussia and Bavaria, 1750–1900*. New York: Berg Publishers, 1989.

Schnädelbach, Herbert. *Philosophy in Germany, 1831–1933*. New York: Cambridge University Press, 1984.

Schulte, Regina. *The Village in Court: Arson, Infanticide, and Poaching in the Court Records of Upper Bavaria, 1848–1910*. London: Cambridge University Press, 1994.

Schulze, Hagen. *The Course of German Nationalism: From Frederick the Great to Bismarck, 1763–1867*. Trans. Sarah Hanbury-Tenison. London: Cambridge University Press, 1994.

Sheehan, James J. *German Liberalism in the Nineteenth Century*. Chicago: University of Chicago Press, 1978.

Showalter, Dennis E. *Railroads and Rifles: Soldiers, Technology, and the Unification of Germany*. Hamden, Conn.: Archon Books, 1975.

———. *Wars of German Unification*. New York: Oxford University Press, 2004.

Siemann, Wolfram. *The German Revolution of 1848–49*. New York: St. Martin's Press, 1998.

Simon, Walter M. *The Failure of the Prussian Reform Movement, 1807–1819*. New York: Howard Fertig, 1955.

Smith, Woodruff D. *The German Colonial Empire*. Chapel Hill: University of North Carolina Press, 1978.

———. *Politics and the Sciences of Culture in Germany, 1840–1920*. New York: Oxford University Press, 1991.

Snell, John L. *The Democratic Movement in Germany, 1789–1914*. Ed. and completed by Hans Schmitt. Chapel Hill: University of North Carolina Press, 1976.

Southard, Robert. *Droysen and the Prussian School of History*. Lexington: University of Kentucky Press, 1995.

Sperber, Jonathan. *Popular Catholicism in Nineteenth-Century Germany*. Princeton, N.J.: Princeton University Press, 1984.

Stargardt, Nicholas. *The German Idea of Militarism: Radical and Socialist Critics, 1866–1914*. London: Cambridge University Press, 1994.

Stern, Fritz. *Gold and Iron: Bismarck, Bleichröder, and the Building of the German Empire*. New York: Alfred A. Knopf, 1977.

———. *The Politics of Cultural Despair: A Study in the Rise of the German Ideology*. Berkeley: University of California Press, 1961.

Streidt, Gert, and Peter Feierabend, eds. *Prussia: Art and Architecture*. New York: Könemann, 2000.

Sweet, Paul. *Friedrich von Gentz, Defender of the Old Order*. Madison: University of Wisconsin Press, 1941.

———. *Wilhelm von Humboldt*. 2 vols. Columbus: Ohio State University Press, 1978.

Toews, John Edward. *Hegelianism: The Path toward Dialectical Humanism, 1805–1841*. New York: Cambridge University Press, 1980.

Vaughan, William. *German Romantic Painting*. New Haven, Conn.: Yale University Press, 1980.

———. *German Romanticism and English Art*. New Haven, Conn.: Yale University Press, 1979.

Von Laue, Theodore. *Leopold Ranke. The Formative Years*. Princeton, N.J.: Princeton University Press, 1950.

Wehler, Hans-Ulrich. *The German Empire, 1871–1914*. Trans. Kim Traynor. Dover, N.H.: Berg, 1985.

Willoughby, Leonard Ashley. *The Romantic Movement in Germany*. New York: Russell and Russell, 1966.

Windell, George G. *The Catholics and German Unity, 1866–1871*. Minneapolis: University of Minnesota Press, 1954.

Zeender, John. *The German Center Party, 1890–1906*. New Series. Vol. 66, Part I. Philadelphia, Pa.: Transactions of the American Philosophical Society, 1976.

Ziolkowski, Theodore. *German Romanticism and Its Institutions*. Princeton, N.J.: Princeton University Press, 1990.

VII. FEMINISM/WOMEN'S RIGHTS/ MOTHERHOOD IN MODERN GERMANY

Abrams, Lynn, and Elizabeth Harvey, eds. *Gender Relations in Germany History: Power, Agency and Experience from the Sixteenth to the Twentieth Century*. London: University College London Press, 1996.

Albisetti, James C. *Schooling German Girls and Women: Secondary and Higher Education in the Nineteenth Century*. Princeton, N.J.: Princeton University Press, 1988.

Allen, Ann Taylor. *Feminism and Motherhood in Germany, 1800–1914*. New Brunswick, N.J.: Rutgers University Press, 1991.

Bock, Gisela, and Pat Thane. *Maternity and Gender Policies: Women and the Rise of the European Welfare States, 1880s–1950s*. New York: Routledge, 1991.

Brauner, Sigrid. *Fearless Wives and Frightened Shrews: The Construction of the Witch in Early Modern Germany*. Amherst: University of Massachusetts Press, 1994.

Bridenthal, Renate, and Claudia Koonz, eds. *Becoming Visible: Women in European History*. 2nd ed. Boston, Mass.: Houghton-Mifflin, 1987.

———. *When Biology Became Destiny: Women in Weimar and Nazi Germany*. New York: Monthly Review Press, 1984.

Cole, Helena, ed. *The History of Women in Germany from Medieval Times to the Present:* Bibliography of English-Language Publications. Washington, D.C.: German Historical Institute, 1990.

Cosner, Shaaron, and Victoria Cosner. *Women under the Third Reich: A Biographical Dictionary*. Westport, Conn.: Greenwood Press, 1998.

Daniel, Ute. *The War from Within: German Women in the First World War*. Herndon, Va.: Berg Publishers, 1997

Douglas, Jane Dempsey. *Women, Freedom and Calvin*. Philadelphia, Pa.: Westminster, 1985.

Evans, Richard. *The Feminist Movement in Germany, 1894–1933*. Beverly Hills, Calif.: Sage, 1976.

Fout, John C., ed. *German Women in the Nineteenth Century: A Social History.* New York: Holmes & Meier, 1986.

Frevert, Ute. *Women in German History: From Bourgeois Emancipation to Sexual Liberation.* Trans. Stuart McKinnon-Evans with Terry Bond & Barbara Norden. New York: Berg, 1989.

Hafter Daryl, ed. *European Women and Preindustrial Craft.* Bloomington: Indiana University Press, 1995.

Harrington, Joel. *Reordering Marriage and Society in Reformation Germany.* Cambridge: Cambridge University Press, 1995.

Hull, Isabel V. *Sexuality, State and Civil Society in Germany, 1700–1815.* Ithaca, N.Y.: Cornell University Press, 1996.

Joeres, Ruth Ellen, and Mary Jo Maynes, eds. *German Women in Enlightenment and Nineteenth Centuries: A Social and Literary History.* Bloomington: Indiana University Press, 1986.

———. *German Women in the Nineteenth and Twentieth Centuries.* Bloomington: Indiana University Press, 1986.

Kolinsky, Eva. *Women in Contemporary Germany: Life, Work and Politics.* Oxford: Berg, 1989.

Koonz, Claudia. *Mothers in the Fatherland.* New York: St. Martin's Press, 1987.

Laska, Vera. *Women in the Resistance and the Holocaust: The Voices of Eyewitnesses.* Westport, Conn.: Greenwood Press, 1983.

Markwald, Rudolf K. and Marilyn Morris Markwald. *Katharina von Bora: A Reformation Life.* St. Louis, Mo.: Concordia Publishing House, 2002.

Marland, Hilary, ed. *The Art of Midwifery: Early Modern Midwives in Europe.* London: Routledge & Kegan Paul, 1993.

Meyer, Alfred G. *The Feminism and Socialism of Lily Braun.* Bloomington: Indiana University Press, 1985.

Moeller, Robert G. *Protecting Motherhood: Women and the Family in the Politics of Postwar West Germany.* Berkeley and Los Angeles: University of California Press, 1993.

Mor, Menachem, ed. *Jewish Assimilation, Acculturation and Accommodation: Past Traditions, Current Issues and Future Prospects.* Lanham, Md.: University Press of America, 1992.

Owings, Alison. *Frauen: German Women Recall the Third Reich.* New Brunswick, N.J.: Rutgers University Press, 1993.

Prelinger, Catherine N. *Charity, Challenge, and Change: Religious Dimensions of the Mid-Nineteenth-Century Women's Movement in Germany.* New York: Greenwood Press, 1987.

Quataert, Jean Helen. *Reluctant Feminists in German Social Democracy, 1885–1917.* Princeton, N.J.: Princeton University Press, 1979.

Roper, Lyndal. *The Holy Household: Women and Morals in Reformation Augsburg.* Oxford: Oxford University Press, 1989.

Rummel, Erika, ed. *Erasmus on Women.* Toronto: University of Toronto Press, 1996.

Snyder, C. Arnold, and Linda A. Huebert Hecht, eds. *Profiles of Anabaptist Women: Sixteenth-Century Reforming Pioneers.* Waterloo, Ont.: Wilfrid Laurier University Press, 1996.

Stephenson, Jill. *The Nazi Organization of Women.* New York: Barnes & Noble, 1981.

———. *Women in Nazi Society.* New York: Harper & Row, 1981.

Thönnessen, Werner. *The Emancipation of Women: The Rise and Decline of the Women's Movement in German Social Democracy, 1863–1933.* Trans. Joris de Bres. London: Pluto Press, 1973.

Wiesner, Merry E. *Gender, Church, and State in Early Modern Germany.* London and New York: Longmans, 1998.

———. *Working Women in Renaissance Germany.* New Brunswick, N.J.: Rutgers University Press, 1986.

Wilson, Katharina, M., ed. *Women Writers of the Renaissance and Reformation.* Athens: University of Georgia Press, 1987.

VIII. TWENTIETH CENTURY

A. General

Alen, Roy F. *Literary Life in German Expressionism and the Berlin Circles.* Ann Arbor: University of Michigan Press, 1983.

Alter, Robert. *Necessary Angels: Tradition and Modernity in Kafka, Benjamin, and Scholem.* Cambridge, Mass.: Harvard University Press; Cincinnati, Ohio: Hebrew Union College Press, 1991.

Belting, Hans, and Max Beckmann. *Tradition as a Problem in Modern Art.* Trans. Peter Wortsman. New York: Timken, 1989.

Dehio, Ludwig. *Germany and World Politics in the Twentieth Century.* New York: W. W. Norton, 1959.

Diest, Wilhelm, ed. *The German Military in the Age of Total War.* Dover, N.H.: Berg, 1985.

Gray, Ronald D. *Franz Kafka.* Cambridge: Cambridge University Press, 1973.

———. *The German Tradition in Literature, 1871–1945.* Cambridge: Cambridge University Press, 1965.

Hardach, Karl. *The Political Economy of Germany in the Twentieth Century.* Berkeley: University of California Press, 1980.

Hillgruber, Andreas. *Germany and the Two World Wars.* Trans. William C. Kirby. Cambridge, Mass.: Harvard University Press, 1981.

Joachimides, Christos M., Norman Rosenthal, and Wieland Schmied, eds. *German Art in the Twentieth Century: Painting and Sculpture, 1905–1985.* Munich: Prestel-Verlag, 1985.

Last, R. W. *German Dadaist Literature.* New York: Twayne Publishers, 1973.

Makela, Maria Martha. *Munich Secession: Art and Artists in Turn-of-the-Century Munich.* Princeton, N.J.: Princeton University Press, 1990.

Manchester, William. *The Arms of Krupp, 1587–1968.* Boston, Mass.: Little, Brown, 1968.

Moore, Harry T. *Twentieth-Century German Literature.* New York: Basic Books, 1967.

Sackett, Robert E. *Popular Entertainment, Class, and Politics in Munich, 1900–1923.* Cambridge, Mass.: Harvard University Press, 1982.

Samuel, Richard H. *Expressionism in German Life, Literature, and the Theatre, 1910–1924.* Philadelphia, Pa.: A. Saifer, 1971.

Schorske, Carl E. *German Social Democracy, 1905–1917: The Development of the Great Schism.* Cambridge, Mass.: Harvard University Press, 1955.

Schöllgen, Gregor. *Escape into War? The Foreign Policy of Imperial Germany.* Providence, R.I.: Berg, 1990.

Sokel, Walter Herbert. *The Writer in Extremis: Expressionism in Twentieth-Century German Literature.* Palo Alto, Calif.: Stanford University Press, 1959.

Spiegelberg, Herbert. *The Phenomenological Movement: A Historical Introduction.* 2 vols. 2nd ed. The Hague: Nijhoff, 1965.

Stachura, Peter D. *The German Youth Movement, 1900–1945.* New York: St. Martin's Press, 1981.

Stolper, Gustav, Kurt Haeuser, and Knut Borchart. *The German Economy, 1870 to the Present.* New York: Harcourt, Brace & World, 1967.

B. World War I, Revolution and the Versailles Treaty

Asprey, Robert. *The German High Command at War: Hindenburg and Ludendorff Conduct World War I.* New York: William Morrow, 1991.

Berghahn, Volker Rolf. *Germany and the Approach of War in 1914.* New York: St. Martin's Press, 1973.

———, and Martin Kitchen, eds. *Germany in the Age of Total War.* Totowa, N.J.: Barnes & Noble, 1981.

Birnbaum, Karl. *Peace Moves and U-Boat Warfare.* Hamden, Conn.: Archon Books, 1970.

Carsten, F. L. *Revolution in Central Europe, 1918–1919.* Berkeley and Los Angeles: University of California Press, 1972.

Chamberlain, Peter, and Chris Ellis. *Tanks of World War I: British and German.* New York: Arco Publishing, 1969.

Coper, Rudolf. *Failure of a Revolution.* Cambridge, Mass.: Harvard University Press, 1955.

Eksteins, Modris. *Rites of Spring: The Great War and the Birth of the Modern Age.* Boston, Mass.: Houghton Mifflin, 1989.

Farrar, Lancelot L. *The Short War Illusion: German Policy, Strategy, and Domestic Affairs, August–September 1914.* Santa Barbara, Calif.: ABC-CLIO, 1973.

Feldman, Gerald D. *Army, Industry, and Labor in Germany, 1914–1918.* Princeton, N.J.: Princeton University Press, 1966.

Hardach, Gerd. *The First World War.* Berkeley: University of California Press, 1977.

Herwig, Holger. *Biographical Dictionary of World War I.* Westport, Conn.: Greenwood Press, 1982.

———. *The First World War: Germany and Austria-Hungary, 1914–1918.* New York: St. Martin's Press, 1977.

———. *The German Naval Officer Corps: A Social and Political History, 1890–1918.* Oxford: Clarendon, 1973.

Horn, Daniel. *The German Naval Mutinies of World War I.* Rutgers, N.J.: Rutgers University Press, 1969.

Horne, Alistair. *The Price of Glory: Verdun 1916.* New York: Penguin, 1962.

Joll, James. *The Origins of the First World War.* New York: Longman, 1984.

Kennett, Lee. *The First Air War, 1914–1918.* New York: Free Press, 1991.

Kitchen, Martin. *The Silent Dictatorship: The Politics of the German High Command under Hindenburg and*

Ludendorff, 1916–1918. New York: Holmes & Meier, 1976.

Mayer, Arno. *Politics and Diplomacy of Peacemaking: Containment and Counterrevolution at Versailles, 1918–1919.* New York: Alfred Knopf, 1967.

Mitchell, Alan. *Revolution in Bavaria.* Princeton, N.J.: Princeton University Press, 1965.

Morgan, David. *German Left-Wing Socialism: A History of the German Independent Social Democratic Party.* Ithaca, N.Y.: Cornell University Press, 1975.

Morrow, John H. *German Air Power in World War I.* Lincoln: University of Nebraska Press, 1982.

Moyer, Laurence V. *Victory Must Be Ours: Germany in the Great War, 1914–1918.* New York: Hippocrene Books, 1995.

Ousby, Ian. *The Road to Verdun.* New York: Doubleday, 2002.

Pascall, Rod. *The Defeat of Imperial Germany, 1917–1918.* Chapel Hill, N.C.: Algonquin Books of Chapel Hill, 1989.

Ryder, A. J. *The German Revolution of 1918.* Cambridge, Mass.: Harvard University Press, 1968.

Schwabe, Klause. *Woodrow Wilson, Revolutionary Germany, and Peacemaking, 1918–1919: Missionary Diplomacy and the Realities of Power.* Chapel Hill: University of North Carolina Press, 1985.

Showalter, Dennis. *Tannenberg: Clash of Empires.* Hamden, Conn.: Archon Books, 1991.

Stone, Norman. *The Eastern Front, 1914–1917.* New York: Scribner, 1975.

Strachan, Hew. *The First World War.* New York: Viking Penguin Group, 2004.

Tarrant, V. E. *Jutland: The German Perspective: A New View of the Great Battle, 31 May, 1916.* Annapolis, Md.: Naval Institute Press, 1995.

Tuchman, Barbara. *The Guns of August.* New York: Macmillan, 1962.

Vincent, C. Paul. *The Politics of Hunger: The Allied Blockade of Germany, 1915–1919.* Athens: Ohio University Press, 1985.

Watt, Richard M. *The Kings Depart: The Tragedy of Germany, Versailles and the German Revolution.* New York: Simon & Schuster, 1968.

Whalen, Robert Weldon. *Bitter Wounds: German Victims of the Great War, 1914–1939.* Ithaca, N.Y.: Cornell University Press, 1984.

Wheeler-Bennet, John. *Brest-Litovsk: The Forgotten Peace.* New York: St. Martin's Press, 1966.

Winter, Jay, ed. *The Upheaval of War: Family, Work and Welfare in Europe, 1914–1918.* Cambridge: Cambridge University Press, 1988.

Wohl, Robert. *The Generation of 1914.* Cambridge, Mass.: Harvard University Press, 1979.

Zeman, Z. A. B. *A Diplomatic History of the First World War.* London: Weidenfeld & Nicolson, 1971.

C. Weimar Republic

Aldcroft, Derek H. *From Versailles to Wall Street: The International Economy in the 1920s.* Berkeley: University of California Press, 1977.

Angress, Werner T. *Stillborn Revolution.* Princeton, N.J.: Princeton University Press, 1963.

Bennet, Edward W. *Germany and the Diplomacy of the Financial Crisis, 1931.* Cambridge, Mass.: Harvard University Press, 1962.

Breitman, Richard. *German Socialism and Weimar Democracy.* Chapel Hill: University of North Carolina Press, 1981.

Carsten, Francis L. *Fascist Movements in Austria: From Schönerer to Hitler.* Beverly Hills, Calif.: Sage, 1977.

———. *The Reichswehr and Politics, 1918–1933.* Oxford: Oxford University Press, 1966.

Diehl, James M. *Paramilitary Politics in Weimar Germany.* Bloomington: Indiana University Press, 1977.

Dorpalen, Andreas. *Hindenburg and the Weimar Republic.* Princeton, N.J.: Princeton University Press, 1964.

Eberle, Matthias. *World War I and the Weimar Artists: Dix, Grosz, Beckman, Schlemmer.* Boston, Mass.: Houghton Mifflin, 1989.

Eisner, Lotte. *The Haunted Screen: Expressionism in the German Cinema and the Influence of Max Reinhardt.* Berkeley: University of California Press, 1969.

Epstein, Klaus. *Matthias Erzberger and the Dilemma of German Democracy.* Princeton, N.J.: Princeton University Press, 1959.

Evans, Richard J. *The Coming of the Third Reich.* New York: Penguin Press, 2004.

———, and Dick Geary, eds. *The German Unemployed, 1918–1936.* New York: St. Martin's Press, 1987.

Eyck, Erich. *History of the Weimar Republic.* 2 vols. New York: Antheneum, 1970.

Feldman, Gerald D., ed. *The German Inflation Reconsidered.* New York: De Gruyter, 1982.

Ferguson, Niall. *Paper and Iron: Hamburg Business and German Politics in the Era of Inflation, 1897–1927.* London: Cambridge University Press, 1995.

Fowkes, Ben. *Communism in Germany under the Weimar Republic.* New York: St. Martin's Press, 1984.

Frye, Bruce B. *Liberal Democrats in the Weimar Republic.* Carbondale: Southern Illinois University, 1985.

Gatzke, Hans. *Stresemann and the Rearmament of Germany.* Baltimore, Md.: Johns Hopkins University Press, 1954.

Gay, Peter. *Weimar Culture; The Outsider as Insider.* New York: Harper & Row, 1968.

Grathwol, Robert P. *Stresemann and the DNVP: Reconciliation or Revenge in German Foreign Policy, 1924–1928.* Lawrence: University of Kansas Press, 1980.

Hertzman, Lewis J. *DNVP.* Lincoln: University of Nebraska Press, 1963.

Hunt, Richard N. *German Social Democracy, 1918–1933.* New Haven, Conn.: Yale University Press, 1964.

Jacobson, Jon. *Locarno Diplomacy: Germany and the West, 1925–1929.* Princeton, N.J.: Princeton University Press, 1972.

Jones, Larry Eugene. *German Liberalism and the Dissolution of the Weimar Party System, 1918–1933.* Chapel Hill: University of North Carolina Press, 1988.

Kaufmann, Walter H. *Monarchism in the Weimar Republic.* New York: Octagon, 1973.

Kracauer, Siegfried. *From Caligari to Hitler: A Psychological Study of the German Film.* Princeton, N.J.: Princeton University Press, 1947.

Laqueur, Walter. *Weimar: A Cultural History.* New York: Putnam, 1974.

Lebovics, Hermann. *Social Conservatism and the Middle Classes in Germany, 1914–1933.* Princeton, N.J.: Princeton University Press, 1969.

Maier, Charles S. *Reconstructing Bourgeois Europe.* Princeton, N.J.: Princeton University Press, 1975.

Peukert, Detlev. *The Weimar Republic: The Crisis of Classical Modernity.* Trans. Richard Deveson. New York: Hill and Wang, 1992.

Plummer, Thomas G., et al., eds. *Film and Politics in the Weimar Republic.* New York: Holmes and Meier, 1982.

Schrader, Barbel, and Jürgen Schebera. *The "Golden" Twenties: Art and Literature in the Weimar Republic.* Trans. Katherine Vanovitch. New Haven, Conn.: Yale University Press, 1988.

Schuker, Stephen A. *The Financial Crisis of 1924 and the Adoption of the Dawes Plan.* Chapel Hill: University of North Carolina Press, 1976.

Stachura, Peter D., ed. *Unemployment and the Great Depression in Weimar Germany.* New York: St. Martin's Press, 1986.

Stehlin, Stewart A. *Weimar and the Vatican, 1919–1933. German Vatican Relations in the Interwar Years.* Princeton, N.J.: Princeton University Press, 1983.

Taylor, Ronald. *Literature and Society in Germany, 1918–1945.* Totowa, N.J.: Barnes & Noble, 1980

Tractenberg, Marc. *Reparations and World Politics.* New York: Columbia University Press, 1980.

Turner, Henry A., Jr. *Stresemann and the Politics of the Weimar Republic.* Princeton, N.J.: Princeton University Press, 1963.

Waite, Robert G. L. *Vanguard of Nazism: The Free Corps Movement in Post-war Germany, 1918–1923.* Cambridge, Mass.: Harvard University Press, 1952.

Waldemann, Eric. *The Spartacist Uprising of 1919.* Milwaukee, Wisc.: Marquette University Press, 1958.

Willet, John. *Theater of the Weimar Republic.* New York: Holmes and Meier, 1984.

D. National Socialism

Allen, William S. *The Nazi Seizure of Power: The Experience of a Single German Town, 1922–1945.* New York: Franklin Watts, 1984.

Barkai, Avraham. *Nazi Economics.* New Haven, Conn.: Yale University Press, 1990.

Barron, Stephanie. *Degenerate Art: The Fate of the Avant-Garde in Nazi Germany.* Los Angeles, Calif.: Los Angeles County Museum of Art, 1991.

Benz, Wolfgang, and Walter Pehle, eds. *Encyclopedia of Resistance to the Nazi Movement.* New York: Continuum Publishing, 1997.

Bergen, Doris L. *Twisted Cross: The German Christian Movement in the Third Reich.* Chapel Hill: University of North Carolina Press, 1996.

Bessel, Richard, ed. *Life in the Third Reich.* New York: Oxford University Press, 1987.

Beyerchen, Alan D. *Scientists under Hitler: Politics and the Physics Community in the Third Reich.* New Haven, Conn.: Yale University Press, 1977.

Biesinger, Joseph A. "The Reich Concordat of 1933," in *Controversial Concordats: The Vatican's Relations with Napoleon, Mussolini, and Hitler,* edited by Frank J. Coppa. Washington, D.C.: The Catholic University of America Press, 1999.

Binion, Rudolf. *Hitler among the Germans.* New York: Elsevier, 1976.

Bleuel, Hans-Peter. *Strength through Joy: Sex and Society in Nazi Germany.* Trans. J. Maxwell Brownjohn. London: Secker & Warburg, 1973.

Bracher, Karl Dietrich. *The German Dictatorship: The Origin, Structure and Effect of National Socialism.* Trans. Jean Steinberg. New York: Praeger, 1970.

Bramsted, Ernest K. *Goebbels and National Socialist Propaganda, 1925–1945.* East Lansing: Michigan State University Press, 1965.

Browder, George. *Hitler's Enforcers: The Gestapo and the SS Security Service in the Nazi Revolution.* New York: Oxford University Press, 1996.

Brozat, Martin. *The Hitler State: The Foundation and Development of the Internal Structure of the Third Reich.* London: Longman, 1981.

Burleigh, Michael and Wolfgang Wipppermann. *The Racial State: Germany 1933–1945.* Cambridge: Cambridge University Press, 1991.

Childers, Thomas. *The Nazi Voter: The Social Foundations of Fascism in Germany, 1919–1933.* Chapel Hill: University of North Carolina Press, 1983.

Conway, John S. *The Nazi Persecution of the Churches, 1933–1945.* New York: Basic Books, 1968.

Deist, Wilhelm. *The Wehrmacht and German Rearmament.* Toronto: University of Toronto Press, 1981.

Engelmann, Bernt. *In Hitler's Germany: Every-Day Life in the Third Reich.* Trans. Krishna Winston. New York: Pantheon Books, 1986.

Fest, Joachim C. *The Face of the Third Reich: Portraits of the Nazi Leadership.* New York: Pantheon Books, 1970.

Fischer, Conan. *Stormtroopers: A Social, Economic, and Ideological Analysis, 1929–1935.* London: Allen & Unwin, 1983.

Fritzsche, Peter. *Germans into Nazis.* Cambridge, Mass.: Harvard University Press, 1999.

Giles, Geoffrey J. *Students and National Socialism in Germany.* Princeton, N.J.: Princeton University Press, 1985.

Grosshans, Henry. *Hitler and the Artists.* New York: Holmes & Meier, 1983.

Grunberger, Richard. *The Twelve Year Reich: A Social History of Nazi Germany.* New York: Holt Rinehart and Winston, 1971

Haffner, Sebastian. *The Meaning of Hitler.* Trans. by Ewald Osers. Cambridge, Mass.: Harvard University Press, 1983.

Hake, Sabine. *Popular Cinema of the Third Reich.* Austin: University of Texas Press, 2002.

Hamerow, Theodore S. *On the Road to the Wolf's Lair: German Resistance to Hitler.* Cambridge, Mass.: Harvard University Press, 1997.

Hanser, Richard. *A Noble Treason: The Revolt of the Munich Students against Hitler.* New York: Putnam, 1979.

Hayes, Peter. *Industry and Ideology: I. G. Farben in the Nazi Era.* New York: Cambridge University Press, 1987.

Helmreich, Ernst Christian. *The German Churches under Hitler: Background, Struggle, and Epilogue.* Detroit, Mich.: Wayne State University Press, 1979.

Hildebrand, Klaus. *The Foreign Policy of the Third Reich.* Trans. Anthony Fothergill. Berkeley: University of California Press, 1973.

Hinz, Berthold. *Art in the Third Reich.* New York: Pantheon Books, 1979.

Hoffmann, Peter. *The History of the German Resistance, 1933–1945.* Cambridge, Mass.: MIT Press, 1977.

Höhne, Heinz. *The Order of the Death's Head.* New York: Coward McCann, 1969.

Homze, Edward L. *Arming the Luftwaffe: The Reich Air Ministry and the German Aircraft Industry, 1919–1939.* Lincoln: University of Nebraska Press, 1977.

———. *Foreign Labor in Nazi Germany.* Princeton, N.J.: Princeton University Press, 1967.

Hull, David S. *Film in the Third Reich: A Study of the German Cinema.* Berkeley: University of California Press, 1969.

Jäckel, Eberhard. *Hitler's World View: A Blueprint for Power.* Middletown, Conn.: Wesleyan University Press, 1972.

Kater, Michael H. *The Nazi Party: A Social Profile of Members and Leaders, 1919–1945.* Cambridge, Mass.: Harvard University Press, 1983.

Kele, Max. *Nazis and Workers.* Chapel Hill: University of North Carolina Press, 1972.

Kershaw, Ian. *The Nazi Dictatorship: Problems and Perspectives in Interpretation.* London: Edward Arnold, 1985.

———. *Popular Opinion and Political Dissent in the Third Reich: Bavaria, 1933–1945.* New York: Oxford University Press, 1985.

Koch, Hannsjoachim W. *The Hitler Youth.* London: Macdonald & Jane's, 1975.

Koehl, Robert L. *The Black Corps: The Structure and Power Struggles of the Nazi SS.* Madison: University of Wisconsin Press, 1983.

Krispyn, Egbert. *Anti-Nazi Writers in Exile.* Athens: University of Georgia Press, 1978.

Lebert, Stephan and Norbert. *My Father's Keeper: Children of Nazi Leaders: An Intimate History of Damage and Denial.* Trans. Julian Evans. Boston, Mass.: Little, Brown, 2002.

Lewy, Günther. *The Catholic Church and Nazi Germany.* New York: McGraw-Hill, 1964.

Manvell, Roger. *The Canaris Conspiracy: The Secret Resistance to Hitler in the German Army.* New York: McKay, 1969.

———. *The Conspirators: 20th July, 1944.* New York: Ballantine Books, 1971.

Mason, Timothy. *Nazism, Fascism and the Working Class.* New York: Cambridge University Press, 1995.

Mosse, George L. *Nazi Culture.* New York: Schocken, 1981.

Merkl, Peter H. *The Making of a Stormtrooper.* Princeton, N.J.: Princeton University Press, 1980.

Noakes, Jeremy, ed. *Documents on Nazism, 1919–1945.* Atlantic Highlands, N.J.: Humanities Press, 1974.

Orlow, Dietrich. *The History of the Nazi Party, 1919–1933.* Pittsburgh, Pa.: University of Pittsburgh Press, 1969.

———. *The History of the Nazi Party, 1933–1945.* Pittsburgh, Pa.: University of Pittsburgh Press, 1973.

Peukert, Detlev. *Inside Nazi Germany: Conformity, Opposition, and Racism in Everyday Life.* New Haven, Conn.: Yale University Press, 1987.

Pfanner, Helmut F. *Exile in New York: German and Austrian Writers after 1933.* Detroit, Mich.: Wayne State University Press, 1983.

Pridham, Geoffrey. *The Nazi Movement in Bavaria, 1923–1933.* New York: Harper & Row, 1973.

Rauschning, Hermann. *Hitler Speaks.* London: Butterworth, 1939.

Read, Anthony, and David Fisher. *The Deadly Embrace: Hitler, Stalin, and the Nazi-Soviet Pact, 1939–1941.* New York: Norton, 1988.

Rempel, Gerhard. *Hitler's Children: The Hitler Youth and the SS.* Chapel Hill: University of North Carolina Press, 1989.

Rhodes, James M. *The Hitler Movement: A Modern Millenarian Revolution.* Stanford, Calif.: Hoover Inst. Press, 1980.

Rhodes, Richard. *Masters of Death.* New York: Vintage Books, 2002.

Rinderle, Walter, and Bernard Norling. *The Nazi Impact on a German Village.* Lexington: University of Kentucky Press, 1993.

Ritchie, James M. *German Literature under National Socialism.* Totowa, N.J.: Barnes & Noble, 1983.

Scholl, Inge. *Students against Tyranny: The Resistance of the White Rose, Munich, 1942–1943.* Trans. Arthur R. Schultz. Middletown, Conn.: Wesleyan University Press, 1970.

Smith, Woodruff D. *The Ideological Origins of Nazi Imperialism.* New York: Oxford University Press, 1986.

Snyder, Louis L. *Encyclopedia of the Third Reich.* New York: Marlowe & Co., 1976.

Speer, Albert. *Inside the Third Reich.* New York: Macmillan, 1970.

Stachura, Peter D. *Nazi Youth in the Weimar Republic.* Santa Barbara, Calif.: ABC-CLIO, 1975.

Stein, George. *The Waffen SS: Hitler's Elite Guard at War 1939–1945.* Ithaca, N.Y.: Cornell University Press, 1966.

Steinberg, Michael S. *Sabres and Brown Shirts: The German Students' Path to National Socialism, 1918–1935.* Chicago: University of Chicago Press, 1977.

Stern, Fritz. *Dreams and Delusions: National Socialism and the Drama of the German Past.* New York: Vintage, 1989.

Sydnor, Charles W., Jr. *Soldiers of Destruction: The SS Death's Division 1933–1945.* Princeton, N.J.: Princeton University Press, 1977.

Turner, Henry A., Jr. *German Big Business and the Rise of Hitler.* New York: Oxford University Press, 1984.

Walker, Mark. *German National Socialism and the Quest for Nuclear Power, 1939–1949.* New York: Cambridge University Press, 1989.

———. *Nazi Science: Myth, Truth and the German Atomic Bomb.* New York: Plenum Press, 1995.

Wegner, Bernd. *The Waffen-SS: Ideology, Organization and Function.* Trans. Ronald Webster. Oxford: Basil Blackwell, 1989.

Weinberg, Gerhard L. *The Foreign Policy of Hitler's Germany: The Diplomatic Revolution in Europe, 1933–1936.* Chicago: University of Chicago Press, 1970.

———. *The Foreign Policy of Hitler's Germany, 1937–1939.* Chicago: University of Chicago Press, 1980.

Weindling, Paul. *Health, Race and German Politics between National Unification and Nazism, 1870–1945.* New York: Cambridge University Press, 1989.

Welch, David. *Propaganda and the German Cinema.* New York: Oxford University Press, 1985.

Zeman, Z. A. B. *Nazi Propaganda.* New York: Oxford University Press, 1964.

Zentner, Christian, and Friedman Bedürftig. *The Encyclopedia of the Third Reich.* 2 vols. Trans. Amy Hackett. New York: Macmillan, 1991.

E. World War II

Barnett, Corelli, ed. *Hitler's Generals.* New York: Grove Weidenfeld, 1989.

Barnouw, Dagmar. *Germany 1945: Views of War and Violence.* Bloomington: Indiana University Press, 1996.

Bartov, Omer. *Hitler's Army: Soldiers, Nazis, and War in the Third Reich.* New York: Oxford University Press, 1991.

Beck, Earl R. *Under the Bombs: The German Home Front, 1942–1945.* Lexington: University Press of Kentucky, 1986.

Beevor, Anthony. *The Fall of Berlin, 1945.* New York: Viking Penguin, 2002.

Bierman and Colin Smith. *The Battle of Alamein: Turning Point, World War II.* New York: Viking Penguin, 2002.

Breitman, Richard. *Official Secrets: What the Nazis Planned, What the British and Americans Knew.* New York: Hill & Wang, 1998.

Calvocoressi, Peter and Guy Wint. *Total War: Causes and Courses of the Second World War.* New York: Penguin, 1972.

Carell, Paul. *Hitler Moves East, 1941–1943.* Boston, Mass.: Little, Brown, 1964.

Dallin, Alexander. *German Rule in Russia, 1941–1945.* 2nd ed. London: Macmillan, 1981.

Fritz, Stephen G. *Frontsoldaten: The German Soldier in World War II.* Lexington: University Press of Kentucky, 1995.

Heiber, Helmut. *Hitler and His Generals: Military Conferences, 1942–1945: The first complete stenographic record of the military situation conferences, from Stalingrad to Berlin.* New York: Enigma Books, 2003.

Irving, David. *The Rise and Fall of the Luftwaffe: The Life of Field Marshal Erhard Milch.* Boston, Mass.: Little, Brown, 1973.

Jukes, Geoffrey. *Hitler's Stalingrad Decisions.* Berkeley: University of California Press, 1985.

Lewin, Ronald. *Ultra Goes to War.* New York: McGraw-Hill, 1978.

Macksey, Kenneth. *Invasion: The German Invasion of England, July, 1940.* London: Greenhill Books, 1990.

———. *Kesselring: The Making of the Luftwaffe.* London: Batsford, 1978.

———. *Military Errors of World War Two.* London: Arms and Armour, 1993.

Michel, Henri. *The Shadow War; European Resistance, 1939–1945.* New York: Harper & Row, 1972.

Milward, Alan. *The German Economy at War.* London: University of London Press, 1965.

Müller, Klaus-Jürgen. *The Army, Politics, and Society in Germany, 1933–1945: Studies in the Army's Relation to Nazism.* New York: St. Martin's Press, 1987.

Murray, Williamson, and Allan R. Millett. *A War to be Won: Fighting the Second World War.* Cambridge, Mass.: The Belknap Press, 2000.

Overy, Richard. *The Battle of Britain.* New York: W. W. Norton, 2001.

Rich, Norman. *Hitler's War Aims: Ideology, the Nazi State, and the Course of Expansion.* New York: W. W. Norton, 1992.

Ryan, Cornelius. *The Last Battle.* New York: Simon & Schuster, 1966.

Salisbury, Harrison E. *The 900 Days: The Siege of Leningrad.* New York: Harper & Row, 1969.

Schulte, Theo. *The German Army and Nazi Policies in Occupied Russia.* Oxford: Berg Publishers, 1989.

Steinert, Marlis G. *Hitler's War and the Germans.* Athens: University of Ohio Press, 1977.

Tarrant, V. E. *The U-Boat Offensive, 1914–1945.* Annapolis, Md.: Naval Institute Press, 1989.

Trevor-Roper, Hugh R. *The Last Days of Hitler.* 3rd ed. New York: Collier Books, 1962.

Watt, Donald Cameron. *How War Came: The Immediate Origins of the Second World War, 1938–1939.* New York: Pantheon Books, 1989.

Weinberg, Gerhard L. *Germany, Hitler, and World War II: Essays in Modern German and World History.* New York: Cambridge University Press, 1995.

———. *A World at Arms: A Global History of World War II.* Cambridge: Cambridge University Press, 1994.

Westphal, Siegfried. *The German Army in the West.* London: Cassel, 1951.

Whiting, Charles. *Bloody Aachen.* New York: Military Heritage Press, 1988.

———. *The Last Assault: The Battle of the Bulge Reassessed.* London: Leo Cooper, 1994.

Ziemke, Earl F. *Stalingrad to Berlin: The German Defeat in the East.* Washington, D.C.: Office of the Chief of Military History, 1968.

F. German-Jewish Relations and the Holocaust

Arendt, Hannah. *Rahel Varnhagen: The Life of a Jewish Woman.* New York: Harcourt Brace Jovanovich, 1974.

Bach, H. I. *The German Jew.* New York: Oxford University Press, 1985.

Barkai, Avraham. *German Jewish History in Modern Times: Renewal and Destruction, 1918–1945.* Ed. by Michael Berenner and Michael A. Meyer. New York: Columbia University Press, 1998.

Bauer, Yehuda. *A History of the Holocaust.* New York: Doubleday, 1982.

Breitman, Richard. *The Architect of Genocide: Himmler and the Final Solution.* New York: Knopf, distributed by Random House, 1991.

———. *Genocide and Rescue: The Holocaust in Hungary, 1944.* New York: Berg, 1997.

Browning, Christopher R. *Ordinary Men: Reserve Police Battalion 101 and the Final Solution in Poland.* HarperCollins, 1992.

———. *The Path to Genocide: Essays on Launching the Final Solution.* New York: Cambridge University Press, 1992.

Ciechanowski, Jan M. *The Warsaw Rising of 1944.* New York: Cambridge University Press, 1974.

Dwork, Deborah, and Robert Jan van Pelt. *Auschwitz 1270 to the Present.* New York: W. W. Norton, 1996.

Fleming, Gerald. *Hitler and the Final Solution.* Berkeley: University of California Press, 1984.

Friedländer, Saul. *Nazi Germany and the Jews: The Years of Persecution, 1933–1939.* Vol. I. New York: HarperCollins, 1997.

Gay, Peter. *Freud, Jews and Other Germans: Master and Victims in Modernist Culture.* New York: Oxford University Press, 1978.

Gay, Ruth. *The Jews of Germany.* New Haven, Conn.: Yale University Press, 1992.

Gellately, Robert. *The Gestapo and German Society: Enforcing Racial Policy 1933–1945.* Oxford: Clarendon Press, 1991.

Gidal, Nachum T. *Jews in Germany: From Roman Times to the Weimar Republic.* Trans. Helen Atkins, Patricia Crampton, Iain Macmillan, Tony Wells. Cologne: Könemann Verlag, 1998.

Gilbert, Martin. *The Holocaust: A History of the Jews of Europe during the Second World War.* New York: Holt, Rinehart and Winston, 1986.

Hacket, David A., ed. *The Buchenwald Report.* Trans. David A. Hackett. Boulder, Colo.: Westview Press, 1995.

Hagen, William H. *Germans, Poles and Jews: The Nationality Conflict in the Prussian East, 1722–1914.* Chicago: University of Chicago Press, 1980.

Hilberg, Raul. *The Destruction of the European Jews.* Rev. ed. New York: Holmes & Meier, 1985.

———. *Perpetrators, Victims, Bystanders: The Jewish Catastrophe, 1933–1945.* New York: HarperCollins, 1992.

Hirschfield, Gerhard, ed. *The Policies of Genocide: Jews and Soviet Prisoners of War in Nazi Germany.* London: Allen and Unwin, 1986.

Hsia, R. Po-chia. *The Myth of Ritual Murder: Jews and Magic in Reformation Germany.* New Haven, Conn.: Yale University Press, 1990.

———, and Hartmut Lehman, eds. *In and Out of the Ghetto: Jewish-Gentile Relations in Late Medieval and Early Modern Germany.* New York: Cambridge University Press, 1995.

Kaplan, Marion A. *Between Dignity and Despair: Jewish Life in Nazi Germany.* New York: Oxford University Press, 1998.

———. *The Campaign for Women's Suffrage in the Jewish Community in Germany.* New York: Yivo Press, 1976.

———. *The Jewish Feminist Movement in Germany: The Campaigns of the Jüdischer Frauenbund, 1934–1938.* Westport, Conn.: Greenwood Press, 1979.

Katz, Jacob. *From Prejudice to Destruction: Anti-Semitism, 1700–1933.* Cambridge, Mass.: Harvard University Press, 1980.

———. *Out of the Ghetto: The Social Background of Jewish Emancipation, 1770–1870.* New York: Shocken Books, 1978.

Lamberti, Marjorie. *Jewish Activism in Imperial Germany. The Struggle for Civil Equality.* New Haven, Conn.: Yale University Press, 1978.

Laqueur, Walter. *Generation Exodus: The Fate of Young Jewish Refugees from Nazi Germany.* Hanover, N.H.: Brandeis University Press, published by the University Press of New England, 2001.

———. *The Holocaust Encyclopedia.* New Haven, Conn.: Yale University Press, 1997.

Levy, Richard S., ed. *Antisemitism in the Modern World: An Anthology of Texts.* Lexington, Mass.: D.C. Heath and Co., 1991.

———. *The Downfall of the Anti-Semitic Political Parties in Imperial Germany.* New Haven, Conn.: Yale University Press, 1975.

Lifton, Robert Jay. *The Nazi Doctors: Medical Killing and the Psychology of Genocide.* New York: Harper & Row, 1986.

Lindemann, Albert S. *Esau's Tears: Modern Anti-Semitism and the Rise of the Jews.* New York: Cambridge University Press, 1997.

Lowenstein, Steven M. *German-Jewish History in Modern Times: Integration in Dispute, 1871–1918.* Vol 3. New York: Columbia University Press, 1998.

Mayer, Arno J. *Why Did the Heavens Not Darken? The "Final Solution" in History.* New York: Pantheon, 1989.

Meyer, Michael A., and Michael Brenner, eds. *German Jewish History in Modern Times: Tradition and Enlightenment, 1600–1780.* New York: Columbia University Press, 1996.

Mosse, Werner E., et al., eds. *The German-Jewish Economic Elite, 1820–1935.* New York: Oxford University Press, 1987.

———. *Revolution and Evolution. 1848 in German-Jewish History.* Tübingen, 1981.

Niewyk, Donald L. *The Jews of Weimar Germany.* Baton Rouge: Louisiana State University Press, 1980.

———. *Socialist, Anti-Semite, and Jew; German Social Democracy Confronts the Problem of Anti-Semitism, 1918–1933.* Baton Rouge: Louisiana State University Press, 1971.

Oberman, Heiko. *The Roots of Anti-Semitism in the Age of Renaissance and Reformation.* Trans. James I. Porter. Philadelphia, Pa.: Fortress Press, 1984.

Pulzer, Peter. *The Rise of Political Anti-Semitism in Germany and Austria.* New York: Basil Wiley, 1964.

Reinharz, Yehuda, ed. *The Jewish Response to German Culture.* Hanover, N.H.: University Press of New England, 1985.

Schleunes, Karl A. *The Twisted Road to Auschwitz: Nazi Policy toward German Jews, 1933–1939.* Urbana and Chicago: University of Illinois Press, 1990.

Steiner, Jean-François. *Treblinka.* New York: Simon & Schuster, l966.

Tal, Uriel. *Christians and Jews in Germany: Religion, Politics, and Ideology in the Second Reich, 1870–1914.* Ithaca, N.Y.: Cornell University Press, 1975.

Weiss, John. *Ideology of Death: Why the Holocaust Happened in Germany.* Chicago: Ivan R. Dee, 1996.

G. Postwar Germany

Backer, John H. *The Decision to Divide Germany.* Durham, N.C.: Duke University Press, 1978.

———. *Priming the German Economy; American Occupational Policies, 1945–1948.* Durham, N.C.: Duke University Press, 1971.

———. *Winds of History: The German Years of Lucius Dubignon Clay.* New York: Van Nostrand, 1983.

Balfour, Michael. *West Germany: A Contemporary History.* New York: St. Martin's Press, 1982.

Baring, Arnulf M. *Uprising in East Germany: June 17, 1953.* Ithaca, N.Y.: Cornell University Press, 1972.

Bark, Dennis L., and David R. Gress. *A History of West Germany.* 2 vols., 2nd ed. Oxford: Basil Blackwell, 1993.

Berghahn, Volker R. *The Americanization of West German Industry, 1945–1973.* New York: Cambridge University Press, 1986.

Braunthal, Gerard. *The German Social Democrats Since 1969: A Party in Power and Opposition.* Boulder, Colo.: Westview Press, 1994.

Browder, Dewey A. *Americans in Post–World War II Germany: Teachers, Tinkers, Neighbors, and Nuisances.* Lewiston, N.Y.: E. Mellen Press, 1998.

Bryson, Phillip J., and Manfred Melzer. *The End of the East German Economy: From Honecker to Reunification.* New York: St. Martin's Press, 1991.

Burkett, Tony. *Parties and Elections in West Germany: The Search for Stability.* New York: St. Martin's Press, 1975.

Buse, Dieter, and Juergen C. Doerr. *German Nationalisms: A Bibliographic Approach.* New York: Garland, 1985.

Cairncross, Alec. *The Price of War: British Policy on German Reparations, 1941–1949.* New York: Basil Blackwell, 1986.

Childs, David. *The GDR: Moscow's German Ally.* London: Alen & Imwom, 1983.

———. *The SPD from Schumacher to Brandt: The Story of German Socialism, 1945–1965.* New York: Pergamon, 1966.

———. *The Stasi: the East German Intelligence and Security Service.* New York: New York University Press, 1996.

Clemens, Diane Shaver. *Yalta.* New York: Oxford University Press, 1971.

Cooney, James A., ed. *The Federal Republic of Germany and the United States: Changing Political, Economic, and Social Relations.* Boulder, Colo.: Westview Press, 1984.

Dalton, Russell J. *The New Germany Votes: Reunification and the Creation of a New German Party System.* Providence, R.I.: Berg Publishers, 1993.

Davidson, Eugene. *The Death and Life of Germany: An Account of the American Occupation.* New York: Knopf, 1959.

———. *The Trial of the Germans.* New York: Macmillan, 1966.

Demetz, Peter. *Postwar German Literature.* New York: Pegasus, 1970.

Diner, Dan. *America in the Eyes of the Germans: An Essay on Anti-Americanism.* Princeton, N.J.: Princeton University Press, 1996.

Dönhoff, Marion Gräfin. *Foe into Friend: The Makers of the New Germany from Konrad Adenauer to Helmut Schmidt.* Trans. Gabriele Annan. New York: St. Martin's Press, 1982.

Ermarth, Michael, ed. *America and the Shaping of German Society, 1945–1955.* Providence, R.I.: Berg, 1993.

Evans, Richard J. *In Hitler's Shadow: West German Historians and the Attempt to Escape from the Nazi Past.* New York: Pantheon Books, 1989.

Feiss, Herbert. *Between War and Peace: The Potsdam Conference.* Princeton, N.J.: Princeton University Press, 1960.

Flores, John. *Poetry in East Germany: Adjustments, Visions, and Provocations, 1945–1970.* New Haven, Conn.: Yale University Press, 1971.

Frey, Erich G. *Division and Detente: The Germanies and Their Alliances.* New York: Praeger, 1987.

Fulbrook, Mary. *Anatomy of a Dictatorship: Inside the GDR, 1949–1989.* New York: Oxford University Press, 1995.

Gaddis, John. *The United States and the Origins of the Cold War.* New York: Columbia University Press, 1972.

Gedmin, Jeffrey. *The Hidden Hand: Gorbachev and the Collapse of East Germany.* Washington, D.C.: AEI Press, 1992.

Gerber, Margy. *Literature of the German Democratic Republic in English Translation: A Bibliography.* Lanham, Md.: University Press of America, 1984.

Gimbel, John. *The American Occupation of Germany: Politics and the Military, 1945–1949.* Palo Alto, Calif.: Stanford University Press, 1968.

Glaesner, Gert-Joachim. *The Unification Process in Germany: From Dictatorship to Democracy.* New York: St. Martin's Press, 1992.

Goschler, Constantin. "The Attitude toward Jews in Bavaria after the Second World War." In *Leo Baeck Institute Yearbook* 36 (1991): 443–458.

Griffith, William E. *The Ostpolitik of the Federal Republic of Germany.* Cambridge, Mass.: MIT Press, 1978.

Hallberg, Robert von. *Literary Intellectuals and the Dissolution of the State: Professionalism and Conformity in the GDR.* Trans. Kenneth J. Northcott. Chicago: University of Chicago Press, 1996.

Hanrieder, Wolfram, ed. *West German Foreign Policy, 1949–1979.* Boulder, Colo.: Westview Press, 1980.

Hearnden, Arthur, ed. *The British in Germany.* London: Hamilton, 1978.

———. *Education in the Two Germanies.* Oxford: Basil Blackwell, 1974.

Heineman, Elizabeth. *What Difference Does a Husband Make? Women and Marital Status in Nazi and Postwar Germany.* Berkeley: University of California Press, 1999.

Henderson, William O. *The Genesis of the Common Market.* Chicago: Quadrangle Books, 1963.

Höhn, Maria. *GIs and Fräuleins: The German-American Encounter in 1950s West Germany.* Chapel Hill: University of North Carolina Press, 2002.

Huebener, Theodore. *The Literature of East Germany.* New York: Ungar, 1970.

Jarausch, Konrad. *The Rush to German Unity.* New York: Oxford University Press, 1994.

Kerbo, Harold R. *Modern Germany*. (Comparative Societies Series). New York: McGraw-Hill, 2000.

Klineberg, Otto, et al. *Students, Values, and Protests: A Crosscultural Comparison*. New York: Free Press, 1979.

Kolinsky, Eva. *Parties, Opposition and Society in West Germany*. New York: St. Martin's Press, 1984.

Krisch, H. *German Politics under Soviet Occupation*. New York: Columbia University Press, 1975.

Large, David Clay. *Germans to the Front: West German Rearmament in the Adenauer Era*. Chapel Hill: University of North Carolina Press, 1996.

Markovits, Andrei S., ed. *The Political Economy of West Germany: Modell Deutschland*. New York: Praeger, 1982.

Mastny, Voitech. *Russia's Road to the Cold War: Diplomacy, Warfare, the Politics of Communism*. New York: Columbia University Press, 1979.

McAdams, A. James. *Germany Divided: From the Wall to Reunification*. Princeton, N.J.: Princeton University Press, 1993.

McCauley, Martin. *Marxism-Leninism in the German Democratic Republic*. London: Macmillan, 1979.

Merkl, Peter H. *German Foreign Policies: West and East*. Santa Barbara, Calif.: ABC-CLIO, 1974.

———. *German Reunification in European Context*. University Park: Pennsylvania State University Press, 1993.

Nagle, John D. *The National Democratic Party: Right-Radicalism in the Federal Republic of Germany*. Berkeley: University of California Press, 1970.

Opp, Karl Dieter, et al. *Origins of Spontaneous Revolution: East Germany 1989*. Ann Arbor: University of Michigan Press, 1995.

Papadakis, Elim. *The Green Movement in West Germany*. New York: St. Martin's Press, 1984.

Parkes, Stuart. *Understanding Contemporary Germany*. New York: Rutledge, 1997.

Peterson, Edward N. *The American Occupation of Germany: Retreat to Victory*. Detroit, Mich.: Wayne State University Press, 1978.

Pfanner, Helmut F. *Exile in New York: German and Austrian Writers after 1933*. Detroit, Mich.: Wayne State University Press, 1983.

Pond, Elizabeth. *Beyond the Wall: Germany's Road to Unification*. New York: Brookings Institution/Twentieth Century Fund, 1993.

Pridham, Geoffrey. *Christian Democracy in Western Germany: The CDU/CSU in Government and Opposition, 1945–1976*. New York: St. Martin's Press, 1977.

Pronay, Nicholas, and Keith Wilson, eds. *The Political Re-Education of Germany and Her Allies after World War II*. Totowa, N.J.: Barnes & Noble, 1985.

Roberts, Geoffrey. *German Politics Today*. Manchester, U.K.: University of Manchester Press, 1999.

Rückerl, Adalbert, ed. *The Investigation of Nazi Crimes, 1945–1978: A Documentation*. Trans. Derek Rutter. Heidelberg, FRG: C. F. Müller, 1979.

Sandford, John. *The Mass Media of the German-Speaking Countries*. London: Oswald Wolff; Des Moines: Iowa University Press, 1976.

Sanford, Gregory W. *From Hitler to Ulbricht: The Communist Reconstruction of East Germany, 1945–1946*. Princeton, N.J.: Princeton University Press, 1983.

Schick, Jack M. *The Berlin Crisis, 1958–1962*. Philadelphia: University of Pennsylvania Press, 1971.

Schissler, Hanna. *The Miracle Years: The Cultural History of West Germany, 1949–1968*. Princeton, N.J.: Princeton University Press, 2000.

Smith, Bradley F. *The Road to Nuremberg*. New York: Basic Books, 1981.

Spotts, Frederic. *The Churches and Politics in Germany*. Middletown, Conn.: Wesleyan University Press, 1973.

Thelen, Kathleen A. *A Union of Parts: Labor and Politics in Post-War Germany*. Ithaca, N.Y.: Cornell University Press, 1991.

Turner, Henry Asby, Jr. *Germany from Partitition to Reunification*. New Haven, Conn.: Yale University Press, 1992.

Wallace, I., ed. *The GDR under Honecker, 1971–1981*. Dundee, U.K.: GDR Monitor, 1981.

Willis, F. R. *The French in Germany, 1945–1949*. Palo Alto, Calif.: Stanford University Press, 1962.

Woods, Roger. *Opposition in the GDR under Honecker, 1971–1985: An Introduction and Documentation*. New York: St. Martin's Press, 1986.

Wyden, Peter. *Wall: The Inside Story of Divided Berlin*. New York: Simon & Schuster, 1989.

Yergin, Daniel. *The Shattered Peace: The Origins of the Cold War and the National Security State*. Boston, Mass.: Houghton, Mifflin, 1977.

H. Biographies

Balfour, Michael, and Julian Frisby. *Helmuth von Moltke: A Leader against Hitler*. New York: St. Martin's Press, 1972.

Bentley, James. *Martin Niemöller.* Oxford: Oxford University Press, 1984.

Black, Peter R. *Ernst Kaltenbrunner.* Princeton, N.J.: Princeton University Press, 1984.

Breitman, Richard. *The Architect of Genocide: Himmler and the Final Solution.* Hanover, N.H.: University Press of New England, 1992.

Brod, Max. *Franz Kafka: A Biography.* Trans. G. Humphrey Roberts and Richard Winston. 2nd ed. New York: Shocken Books, 1960.

Bullock, Alan. *Hitler: A Study in Tyranny.* London: Odhams Press, 1952.

Calkins, Kenneth R. *Hugo Haase: Democrat and Revolutionary.* Durham, N.C.: Duke University Press, 1979.

Deschner, Günther. *Reinhold Heydrich.* New York: Stein & Day, 1981.

Edinger, Lewis J. *Kurt Schumacher: A Study in Personality and Political Behavior.* Palo Alto, Calif.: Stanford University Press, 1965.

Ewen, Frederic. *Bertolt Brecht: His Life, His Art and His Times.* New York: The Citadel Press, 1967.

Fest, Joachim C. *Hitler.* Trans. Richard and Clara Winston. New York: Vintage Books, 1975.

Frank, Philipp. *Einstein: His Life and Times.* Trans. George Rosen. New York: Alfred A. Knopf, 1947.

Freedman, Ralph. *Hermann Hesse: Pilgrim of Crisis.* New York: Fromm International, 1997.

Graham, Cooper C. *Leni Riefenstahl and Olympia.* Metuchen, N.J.: Scarecrow Press, 1986.

Grohmann, Wil. *Paul Klee.* New York: H. N. Abrams, 1967.

———. *Wassily Kandinsky: Life and Work.* New York: H. N. Abrams, 1958.

Hamilton, Nigel. *The Brothers Mann: The Lives of Heinrich and Thomas Mann, 1871–1950, 1875–1955.* New Haven, Conn.: Yale University Press, 1978.

Hanrieder, Wolfram, ed. *Helmut Schmidt: Perspectives on Politics.* Boulder, Colo.: Westview Press, 1982.

Hess, Hans. *George Grosz.* New Haven, Conn.: Yale University Press, 1974.

Hinz, Renate. *Käthe Kollwitz: Graphics, Posters, Drawings.* New York: Pantheon Books, 1981.

Hoffmann, Peter. *Stauffenberg: A Family History, 1905–1944.* New York: Cambridge University Press, 1997.

Kaufmann, Walter. *Nietzsche: Philosopher, Psychologist, Anti-Christ.* 4th ed. Princeton, N.J.: Princeton University Press, 1974.

Kershaw, Ian. *Hitler: 1889–1936 Hubris.* New York: W. W. Norton, 1999.

———. *Hitler: 1936–1945 Nemesis.* New York: W. W. Norton, 2000.

Klein, Mina C., and H. Arthur Klein. *Käthe Kollwitz: Life in Art.* New York: Schocken, 1975.

Leopold, John A. *Alfred Hugenberg: The Radical Nationalist Campaign against the Weimar Republic.* New Haven, Conn.: Yale University Press, 1977.

Manvell, Roger, and Heinrich Fraenkel. *Dr. Goebbels: His Life and Death.* New York: Simon & Schuster, 1960.

———. *Goering.* New York: Simon & Schuster, 1962.

———. *Himmler.* New York: Simon & Schuster, 1965.

Marshall, Barbara. *Willy Brandt.* London: Cardinal, 1990.

McGreevy, Linda F. *The Life and Works of Otto Dix.* Ann Arbor, Mich.: UMI Research Press, 1981.

Mileck, Joseph. *Hermann Hesse: Life and Art.* Berkeley: University of California Press, 1978.

Nettl, John P. *Rosa Luxemburg.* 2 vols. London: Oxford University Press, 1966.

Overy, R. J. *Göring, the "Iron Man."* London; Boston: Routledge & Kegan Paul, 1984.

Planck, Max. *Scientific Autobiography and Other Papers.* Trans. Frank Gaynor. New York: Philosophical Library, 1949.

Politzer, Heinz. *Franz Kafka: Parable and Paradox.* Ithaca, N.Y.: Cornell University Press, 1962.

Powers, Thomas. *Heisenberg's War: The Secret History of the German Bomb.* New York: Alfred A. Knopf, 1993.

Prater, Donald. *A Ringing Glass: The Life of Rainer Maria Rilke.* Oxford: Clarendon Press, 1986.

Prittie, Terence. *Konrad Adenauer, 1876–1967.* London: Tom Stacey Ltd., 1972.

———. *Willy Brandt: Portrait of a Statesman.* New York: Schocken Books, 1974.

Russell, John. *Max Ernst: Life and Work.* New York: H. N. Abrams, 1967.

Schramm, Percy Ernst. *Hitler: The Man and the Military Leader.* Trans. Donald S. Detwiler. New York: Franklin Watts, 1971.

Schwarz, Hans-Peter. *Konrad Adenauer: From the German Empire to the Federal Republic, 1876–1952.* Providence, R.I.: Berghahn Books, 1995.

Skelton, Geoffrey. *Paul Hindemith: The Man behind the Music: a Biography.* New York: Crescendo, 1975.

Smelser, Ronald. *Robert Ley.* New York: Berg, 1988.

Smith, Bradley F. *Adolf Hitler: His Family, Childhood, and Youth.* Stanford, Calif.: Hoover Institution, 1967. Reprint, 1979.

Stachura, Peter D. *Gregor Strasser and the Rise of Nazism.* London: Allen & Unwin, 1983.

Speer, Albert. *Inside the Third Reich: Memoirs.* Trans. Richard and Clara Winston. New York: Macmillan, 1970.

Stern, Joseph Peter. *Ernst Jünger.* New Haven, Conn.: Yale University Press, 1953.

Volker, Klaus. *Brecht: A Biography.* Trans. John Newell. New York: Seabury Press, 1978.

Wagener, Otto. *Hitler—Memoirs of a Confidant.* New Haven, Conn.: Yale University Press, 1985.

Waite, Robert G. L. *The Psychopathic God: Adolf Hitler.* New York: Basic Books, 1977.

Wehr, Gerhard. *Jung: A Biography.* Trans. Shambhala Publications. Boston, Mass.: Shambhala Publications, 1987.

Weiss, Peg. *Kandinsky in Munich: The Formative Jugendstil Years.* Princeton, N.J.: Princeton University Press, 1979.

Wheeler-Bennet, John. *Hindenburg: The Wooden Titan.* New York: St. Martin's Press, 1967.

Witte, Bernd. *Walter Benjamin: An Intellectual Biography.* Ed. Liliane Weissberg, trans. James Rolleston. Detroit, Mich.: Wayne State University Press, 1991.

WEB SITES

www.auswaertiges-amt.de (Foreign office, embassies and consulates)
www.axishistory.com (Aspects of Germany during World War II)
www.bundesarchiv.de (Federal archives)
www.bundesregierung.de (Federal government)
www.bundestag.de (Bundestag homepage)
www.daad.de (German Academic Exchange) (DAAD: information on study and scholarships)
www.dwelle.de (Programming for Germany's international broadcasting)
www.finanzplatz.de (Stock market and business)
www.german-embassy.org.uk (German embassy in England)
www.German_History_Museum (Topics of German history)
www.germany.info (German politics and society)
www.goethe.de (Goethe Institute reports on cultural scene)
www.hdg.de (Historical events, pictures, museums)
www.magazine-deutschland.de (Articles about Germany in English)
www.perlentaucher.de (Arts, books, and newspapers)
www.policy.com (Current politics)
www.questia.com (On-line library and research on Germany)
www.reiseplanung.de (Travel information)
www.research-in-germany.de (Study and research in Germany)
www.spiegel.de (Articles from magazine *Der Spiegel*)
www.unwelt-deutschland.de (Environmental information)
www.wall-berlin.org (Information on Berlin wall)

INDEX

Boldface page numbers indicate primary discussions. *Italic* page numbers indicate illustrations. Maps are indicated by *m*.

A

Aachen **203**
Aachen, Peace Treaty of 40, 44, 241
Abernon, Edgar Vincent d' 126
ABM (antiballistic missile) Treaty 335
abortion 168, 181–182
Abraham a Santa Clara 249
absolutism **39–49, 203–204**
    abandonment of 65
    Austrian 41
    economics under 40
    Frederick William and 389
    French 39–41
    origins of 40
    pseudo-constitutional 95–96
    wars and 41–44
Abu Telfan (Raabe) 641
Academic Festival Overture (Brahms) 286
Acquainted with the Night (Böll) 281
Adages, The (Erasmus) 16, 357
Adam, Where Wert Thou? (Böll) 171, 281
Adam and Eve in Paradise (Cranach the Elder) 323
Addison, Joseph 60
Address to the Nobility of the German Nation (Luther) 21, 647
Adenauer, Konrad 160–163, *205*, **205–206**
    Basic Law and 250–251
    Christian Democratic Union and 309–310
    economic recovery and 345
    Erhard and 358
    European Defense Community and 361
    Strauss and 705

Adoration of the Trinity (Dürer) 342
Adorno, Theodor 434, 435
Adrianople, Battle of 4
Adultery (Fontane) 380
Adventurous Simplicissimus, The (Grimmelhausen) 35, 249
Affectionate Sisters, The (Gellert) 404
Afghanistan 199, 224, 335
Afrika Korps **206,** 352
Agadir Incident **206–207,** 272
Against the Thieving and Murderous Hordes of Peasants (Luther) 23, 648–649
Agenda 2010 197
Agrarian League **207**
Agricola, Rudolf 14, **207–208,** 652
agriculture 5, 50–51, 149, 181, 207, 334, 362
Agrippina (Handel) 437
Ahnen, Die (Freytag) 398–399
aircraft design 567
Air Force **208–209,** 314–315
airlifts, to Berlin *161,* **268–269**
El Alamein, Battles of 148, **352**
Alaric 4
Albers, Annie 252
Albers, Joseph 252
Albert I (Holy Roman Emperor) 9
Albert IV (duke of Bavaria) 210–211
Albert of Brandenburg **209–210**
Albert V (duke of Bavaria) **210–211**
Alemanni tribe 3, 4, 6
Alexander II (czar of Russia) 98
Algarotti, Francesco 675
Algeciras, Conference of **211,** 579
Allied Control Council **211–212,** 629

Allied Reparations Commission **329**
All Quiet on the Western Front (Remarque) 651–652
Alsace-Lorraine 80, 116, **212**
Altdorfer, Albrecht 18, **212**
American Zone, in postwar Germany 614–615
Amiens, Battle of **212–213**
Amiens, Peace of 397, 584
Amiet, Cuno 293
Anabaptism 24, 27, **213–214,** 333, 578, 648
Anatolian Railroad 268
Anglo-German Naval Treaty 143, **214**
Annenberg, Battle of 228
Annotations of the New Testament (Valla) 357
Annunciation (Günther) 33, 249
Anschluss 143, **214–215**
Antichrist, The (Nietzsche) 600
Anti-Comintern Pact **215**
anti-Semitism **215–218**
    Arendt on 221
    of cultural elites 324
    definition of 217
    economic depressions and 335
    of Eichmann 348–349
    of Federation of Farmers 100
    of Gobineau 89
    Holocaust and 463–464
    of Lagarde 519
    of Luther 215–216
    of Maria Theresa 489
    in Middle Ages 215–216
    under Nazis 140–141
    Nietzsche and 600–601
    19th-century 88–89

828 Germany

Nuremberg Laws and 607–608
origin of term 89, 217
origins of 140
Pan-German League and 616
Protocols of the Elders of Zion, The (unknown) and 634–635
racism and 217
Revolution of 1848 and 216–217
rise of 218
of Streicher 706
of Treitschke 88
of Wagner 90–91
Anti-Socialist Laws 97, 101, **218–219**, 258
Apocalypse (Dürer) 342
appeasement policy 145, 215, **219–220**, 459, 581
Aquinas, St. Thomas 320
archaeology 683–684
archetypes, in expressionism 364–365
Archipelago (Hölderin) 463
architecture
    baroque 32–33
    Bauhaus 252–253
    feudal 10
    of Fischer von Erlach 379
    in German Democratic Republic 183
    independence of sculpture from 17
    in Manheim 552
    under Maria Theresa 48–49
    in Munich 580
    of Neumann 596–597
    19th-century 92–93
    of Reichstag 650, 651
    rococo 38
    of Schinkel 680
    of Speer 697
    of Vienna 48–49
    of Zimmermann 756
Arch of Triumph (Remargue) 652
Ardennes, Battle of **220–221**, 336
Arendt, Hannah **221**, 349
Argentina 247, 348
aristocracy **221–223**
Armed Forces (Bundeswehr, Federal Republic) **224**
Armed Forces (Prussian to 1860) **224–227**

Armed Forces (Second Empire) **227–228**
Armed Forces (Volksturm, People's Attack) **725**
Armed Forces (Wehrmacht, 1939–1945) **223–224**
Armed Forces (Weimar Republic) **228–230**
Armed Forces High Command **612–613**
Arminius 4
Arminius (Hutten) 475
Arndt, Ernst Moritz 66, 70
Arnim, Achim von 62, 70, 292, 424
Arouser of the German Nation, The (Hutten) 16, 475
art
    absolutism and 204
    baroque 33–34, 248
    Bauhaus 252–253
    of Beckmann 259–260
    Bridge group and **293–294**
    of Cranach the Elder **322–323**
    degenerate **331–332**
    of Dix 338
    of Dürer 342
    of Ernst 358–359
    of Grosz 431
    of Kirchner 507–508
    of Klee 508
    of Kokoschka 513
    New Objectivity movement in 129–130
    19th-century 92–93
    of Nolde 602–603
    of Pechstein 622
    Renaissance 17–18
    in Weimar Republic 129–130
Article 48 118–119, 132, 344, **522–523**
Art Is in Danger (Grosz) 431
Artistic Thought (Klee) 508
Artists Group Bridge 92
Aryan race 138, 140–141, 305, 642–643
aspirin 257
assassination attempt on Hitler 150, 321–322, 700–701
Assault, The (newspaper) 419
Association of Women Teachers 371
astronomy 36

asylum laws 189, **230–231**
Ataulf 4
Atlantic, Battle of the **231–232**
Atlanticists 166, 169, 358
Atlantic Wall 330
Atlantis (Hauptmann) 442
Atomic Theory, The (Born) 283
Auerbach, Berthold 645
Auerstadt, Battle of **232–233**
Augsburg 10, 25–26, 28, 40, **233–234, 234, 234–235, 236,** 315, 360
Augsburg Confession 16, 21–22, 25, 28, 233, **236–237**
Augspurg, Anita 93, **237**
August, Nikolaus 326
August I (elector of Saxony, king of Poland) 203, 204
Augustus II the Strong (elector of Saxony, king of Poland) 340, 360
Augustus III (elector of Saxony, king of Poland) 42
Aüsburgerung 183–184
Auschwitz-Birkenau concentration camp 151–152, **237–238**
Austerlitz, Battle of 65, **238–239**
Austria **239–240**
    absolutism in 203–204
    Anschluss and **214–215**
    in Austro-Prussian War 77–78
    baroque architecture in 249
    Bethmann-Hollweg and 272–273
    Bismarck and 276
    in Danish War 76
    Ferdinandean period in 346
    in German Confederation 68, 385
    Metternich and 567–569
    in Napoleonic Wars 584–585
    nobility in 382
    Russia and, in Balkans 103–104
    Second Empire alliance with 98
    in Thirty Years' War 29, 30
    Vienna and 722–723
Austrian General Civil Code 521
Austrian Succession, Wars of **42–44,** 53, 203, **240–241,** 308
Austro-German Dual Alliance 98
Austro-Prussian War 77–78, 239, 276, 513–514, 575
autarchy **241,** 380–381

autobahns 139, **241,** *241*
automobiles 264, 326–327, *327,* *628,* **628–629**
Avicenna 17
Axis, The **242**

B

Baader, Andreas 243–244
Baader, Franz von **243,** 317
Baader-Meinhof Group **243–244**
Babylonian Captivity 12
Babylonian Captivity of the Church (Luther) 21
Babylonian Migration (Döblin) 338–339
Bach, Carl Philipp Emanuel 58
Bach, Johann Sebastian 35, 58, **244–245,** *245*
Bachmann, Ingeborg 170
Baden 68, 315
Baden, Max von 105, 344, 359
Baden-Württemberg **245–246**
Bad Gastein Convention 276
Bad Godesburg Convention 287, 309
Baghdad-Berlin Railway **268**
Bahr, Egon 169
Baldwin, Stanley 220
Balkans 146
Balkan Wars 103–104
Ballin, Albert 84, **246–247,** 490
banking 11, 85–86, 193, 278, **329–330,** 401
Barbarossa, Operation 146–147, *147,* **247,** 619
Barbie, Klaus **247**
Barlach, Ernst 364
Barmen Declaration **247–248,** 316
baroque **32–38,** 204, **248–250,** 403
Bartenstein, Johann Christoph 44
Barth, Karl 248, **250,** 281, 316
Basel, Peace of 398, 558
Basel, University of 250
Basic Law 156–157, 166, 224, **250–251**
Basic Treaty 169–170, **251–252**
Battle of Alexander, The (Altdorfer) 212
Bauer, Gustav 117
Bauernschutz 52, **252**

Bauhaus 127, *128,* **252–253,** 331, 430
Bäumer, Gertrud 94, 237, **253,** 373
Baumgarten, Paul 651
Bavaria **253–255**
 Albert V and 210–211
 in Confederation of the Rhine 315
 in Counter-Reformation 28
 Eisner and 351–352
 French Revolution and 254
 in German Confederation 68
 Napoleon and 254
 revolution in 109
 in Second Empire 95
Bavarian Party 156
Bavarian Patriots' Party 254
Bavarian People's Party 254, 255, **255–256,** *256*
Bavarian Succession, War of 46, **256–257,** 494, 554–555
Bayer, Friedrich 257
Bayer, Herbert 252
Bayer AG **257**
Bayreuth **257–258**
"Beautiful Childhood" (Benn) 262
Beaver Coat, The (Hauptmann) 442
Bebel, August 87, 101, **258,** 425
Bebel, Heinrich 14
Beccaria, Cesare 494
Beck, Ludwig August Theodor **258–259,** 319, 322, 656
Becker, Johannes 365
Beckman, Max **259–260,** 332
Beer Hall Putsch 124, **260–261,** 459, 561
Beethoven, Ludwig van 38, 58, 70, **261–262**
Before Dawn (Hauptmann) 90, 442, 590
Beggar's Opera (Brecht) 291
Behring, Emil von 346
Belgian Rexists 368
Belgium 145, 269, 362
Belvedere Palace 33, 48
Belzec concentration camp 313, 378
Benjamin, Walter **262**
Benn, Gottfried **262–263**
Bennigsen, Rudolf von **263**
Benz, Carl Friedrich **263–264**
Benz and Company 264

Benz Velo (automobile) 264
Berchtold, Count 272
Berg, Adolf von 343
Bergen-Belsen concentration camp **264**
Berghof retreat **264**
Berlin **264–266**
 airlifts to *161,* **268–269**
 blockade of 162, **268–269**
 bombing of *158*
 Brandenburg Gate in *286*
 Congress of 98, **267–268,** 341
 division of, after World War II 153, 169
 fall of **266–267**
 Olympics in 613–614
 origin of 264–265
Berlin, University of 66
Berlin Alexander Square (Döblin) 130, 338
Berlin-Baghdad Railway **268**
Berlin Conference **269–270**
Berlin Wall 180, 185–186, *186,* *270,* **270–271**
Bernstein, Eduard 101, 258, **271**
Bertram, Adolf **271–272,** 572
Bethmann-Hollweg, Theobald von 100, **272–273**
Beyer, Johann Wilhelm 49
Beyerlein, Fritz 206
Biberkopf, Franz 338
Bible 16, 17, 20, 21, 142, **545–546,** 564
Biedermeier 69, **273–274**
Biermann, Wolf 184, **274,** 411
Billiards at Half Past Nine (Böll) 171, 281
Birth of Christ (Altdorfer) 18, 212
Birth of Tragedy (Nietzsche) 600
Birth of the Virgin (Altdorfer) 212
Bismarck (ship) 231
Bismarck, Ferdinand 274
Bismarck, Otto von **74–81,** *75,* **274–277,** *275*
 Anti-Socialist Law and 218–219
 appointment of, as minister president of Prussia 227
 assassination attempts on 218
 Austria and 276
 in Austro-Prussian War 77
 Bavaria and 254
 Bennigsen and 263
 Bleichröder and 278–279

conservatism of 76, 318
constitution of 1871 and 95–96
in Danish War 76–77
Danish War and 328
dismissal of 98–99
Dual Alliance and 341–342
foreign policy of 97–98
in Franco-Prussian War 78–79
French Second Empire and 80
Lasker and 521
National Liberal Party and 589
Peace of Nicolsburg and 598
reactionary feudalism of 90
Realpolitik and 646
Social Democrats and 97
statecraft of 74–76
Stöcker and 703
Three Emperors League and 523–524
Treaty of Berlin and 267–268
on war 75–76
Windhorst and 304
Bitterfield Movement 183
Black Hand society 104
Blair, Tony 195, 199
blank check policy **277–278**
Bleichröder, Gerson von **278–279**, 490
Blenheim, Battle of 42, **279**, 360
Bleyl, Fritz 293
blitzkrieg 143, **279**, 552–553
blockade, of Berlin **268–269**
Blomberg, Werner von 135, 223, 230, **279–280**
Blomberg affair 400
Blood Purge 336
Blücher (cruiser) 144
Blücher, Gebhard Leberecht 65, **280**, 585
Blue Rider group 92, 365, 508
Blue Tiger, The (Döblin) 339
Bockelson, Johan 24
Böcklin, Arnold 92
Bodin, Jean 40
Bodmeer, Johann Jakob 427
Boer War 325
Bolivia 247
Böll, Heinrich 170, 171, 244, **280–281**
Bolshevik Revolution 105, 734
Bolshevism 440–441
bombings
of Berlin *158*

of Dresden 340
of England 209
of London 146
of Pearl Harbor 232
Bonhoeffer, Dietrich **281–282**, 316
Boniface, St. 10
Bonn 160, **282**
Book of Dialogues, The (Hutten) 15
Book of Hours (Rilke) 664
Borgia family 20, 647
Bormann, Martin 145, **282–283**, 332
Born, Max **283**
Borsig, August 83, **283–284**
Borsig Locomotive Works 83
Bosch, Robert **284**
Bosnia-Herzegovina 103, 224, **284–285**
Boxer Rebellion 366
Boxheim documents 133
Boyen, Hermann von 225, 226
Brahms, Johannes 91, **285–286**
Brandenberger, Erich 220
Brandenburg **286–287**
Brandenburg, Albrecht von 20, 647
Brandenburg Gate *286*
Brandenburg-Prussia **50–54**
Brandler, Heinrich 407
Brandt, Peter 244
Brandt, Willy 167, 168–169, **287–288**, 685
  Basic Treaty and 251
Brauchitsch, Walther von **288**
Braun, Eva 150, 264, **288–289**
Braun, Franziska 289
Braun, Karl Ferdinand **289**
Braun, Konrad 289
Braun, Otto **289–290**, 440
Braun, Volker 183
Braun, Wener Magnus Maximilian 290
Bread and Wine (Hölderin) 463
Bread of Early Years, The (Böll) 281
Brecht, Bertolt 130, 183, 233, **291**
  Benjamin and 262
Bremen/Bremerhaven **291–292**
Bremen (steamship) 84
Brentano, Clemens 62, 70, 292, 424
Brentano, Elizabeth "Bettina" 292

Brentano, Lujo 590
Brentano, Maximiliane 292
Breslau **293**
Brest-Litovsk, Peace of 105, 228, **293**
Brethren of Common Life 14, 16, 302
Breuer, Marcel 253
Briand, Aristide 538
Bridge, The **293–294**
Broad Field, A (Grass) 427
Bruchsal Palace 249
Bruck, Arthur Moeller van den 130
Bruckner, Anton 91
Brüning, Heinrich 132, 133–134, **295**, 319
bubonic plague 12, 20, 55–56
Bucer, Martin 16
Buchenwald concentration camp *152*, **295–297**, 312
Buddenbrooks (Mann) 89, 550
Bulgaria 242, 268
Bülow, Bernard von 100, 211, **297**, 326, 579
Bundesrat **297–298**
Bundestag 68, 162–163, 298, 352
Bürgersaal Church 33, 249
Burghers of Calais, The (Kaiser) 499
Burgundians 4, 6
Burke, Edmund 317, 405
Burns, Mary 354
Burnt Offering, The (Goes) 171
Burschenschaft **298–299**, 303
Bush, George W. 199
Byrnes, James F. 158

C

Cabala 15, 653
Cabinet of Dr. Caligari, The (film) 266
Cake-Eater, The (Raabe) 641
Calenberg family 438
Caligula: A study on Roman caeserien megalomania (Quidde) 639
Calvin, John 24–25, **300–302**, *301*
Calvinism 24–25, 27–28, 51, 234, **300–302, 447**, 731–732
Cameroons 269
Campo Formio, Treaty of 381, 398

Canaris, Wilhelm Franz 204, 322
Canisius, Peter **302**
canton system 225, **302–303**
capitalism 11, 56, 71, 87, 258, 333–334, 358
Caprivi, Leo von 99–100, 207
Capuchin order 321
Carl Eugene (duke of Württemberg) 245–246
Carl Friedrich of Baden-Durlach 245
Carlsbad Decrees 68, 226, **303,** 568
Carnot, Lazare 392
Caroline-Marianne-Palau islands 102
Carolingian Empire 6–7, 203, 233
Casimir IV (king of Poland) 328
Castlereagh, Robert 316
Cat and Mouse (Grass) 171, 427
Catherine II (czarina of Russia) 257
Catholic Center Party 120
Catholic Church. *See also* Reformation; religion
    Albert of Brandenburg and 210
    Albert V and 211
    anti-Semitism and 216
    baroque churches of 32, 249
    Bertram in 271–272
    Calvin and 301
    Center Party and 97
    Concordat of 1933 and 313–314
    Council of Trent and **319–320**
    Counter Reformation and **320–321**
    defenestration of Prague and 331
    Edict of Toleration and 346
    Erasmus on 356
    Erzberger and 359
    in Ferdinandean period 346
    Frederick II and 387
    Freemasons and 63
    French Revolution and 64
    Görres and 425
    Hitler and 142
    Joseph II and 47, 494
    Kulturkampf culture war and 517–518
    Maria Theresa and 45
    Middle Age crises in 12
    National Socialism and 571–572
    Peace of Augsburg and 25–26, 235
    printing press and 17
    resistance of, to Nazis 655–656
Catholic German Center Party 205
Caucasus Agreements 177
Cauer, Minna 237
Cavour, Count Camillo 74
Celtis, Conrad **14,** **303–304,** 472, 652
Center Party 96, 99, 114, **304–305**
    Bismarck and 277
    Christian Democratic Union and 309
    Erzberger in 359
    in National Assembly 586
    Windthorst and 742
centralization 389
Cézanne, Paul 332
Chamberlain, Austen 538
Chamberlain, Houston Stewart **305**
Chamberlain, Neville 126, 145, 219
Chamisso, Adelbert von 91
Charlemagne (emperor of the West) 6–7, 203
Charles IV (Holy Roman Emperor) 9, 12, 466
Charles of Lorraine 41
Charles V (Holy Roman Emperor) **305–307,** *306*
    Albert of Brandenburg and 210
    changing economic landscape and 11
    Diet of Augsburg and 234
    Diet of Worms and 748–749
    empire of 787*m*
    Erasmus and 357
    Frederick III and 388
    Luther and 21
    Melanchthon and 16
    Reformation and 25–26
Charles VI (Holy Roman Emperor) 33, 42, **307–308,** 630
Charles VII (Holy Roman Emperor) 39, 43, **308**
Charlottenburg Palace 33, **308–309**
Chelmno concentration camp 313, 378
chemical industry, in Industrial Revolution 84
chemotherapy 347
China 215, 714–715
Chirac, Jacques 199
Chirico, Giorgio de 332
cholera 511
Christ among the Doctors (Dürer) 342
Christian Democratic Union **309–310**
    Adenauer and 160, 162–163
    in Baden-Württemberg 246
    formation of 156
    in Grand Coalition 166
    Kiesinger and 506–507
    Kohl and 512
    Merkel and 566
    neo-Nazis and 596
    reunification and 187
Christian Democrat Party 178, 192, 200, 205
Christianity, Positive **629**
Christian of Denmark 29, 30
Christian-Social Movement 703
Christian Social Union 156, 166, 205, **310–311,** 704–705
chronology **763–779**
Churchill, John 279
Churchill, Winston 145, 211, 295
Church of St. Thomas 245
Church of the Fourteen Saints 33, 249
Ciano, Count Galeazzo 242
Cicero, John 209
Circus Caravan (Beckmann) 260
Cisneros, Ximenes de 321
cities, Imperial **478**
Civil Code of 1900 93, **311,** 372
Civil Constitution of the Clergy 64
Civil Service Rehabilitation 137
Class, Heinrich 368, 616
classes, economic
    culture and 323–324
    in 18th century 57
    Engels on 354
    middle **569–570**
    National Liberal Party and 589
    National Socialism and 594
    naturalism and 589
    in 19th century 89
    Prussian Law Code and 637
classicism 69, 422
Clausewitz, Carl von 226, **311–312**

Clay, Lucius 268
Clemenceau, Georges 114, 115–116, 721
Clement VII (pope) 25
clergy, in 18th-century social structure 57
Clinton, Bill 195, 199
Clovis (king of the Franks) 6
Clown, The (Böll) 171
coal fields 83
Cocceji, Samuel von 521–522
Cohn-Bendit, Daniel 378
Colet, John 16, 356
College of Cardinals 7
Colloquia (Erasmus) 356, 357
Combat League 260
COMECON 181
Commemoration Masque (Hauptmann) 443
Common Agricultural Policy 362
communism 112–113, 205–206, 353–354, 441, 556–557
Communist Party 155, 369, 466–467, 535
community, national **724–725**
compensation, principle of 67
concentration camps **312–313**, 797m
    Auschwitz 151–152, **237–238**
    Belzec 313, 378
    Bergen-Belsen **264**
    Buchenwald *152*, **295–297**, 312
    Chelmno 313, 378
    Dachau **325**
    Eicke and 349
    establishment of 140
    Final Solution and 312–313
    Flossenburg 264, 312, 349
    Heydrich and 455
    Himmler and 456
    Höss and 468
    Majdanek 378
    Mathhausen 312, 349
    Mengele and 565
    Natzweiler 264
    Ravensbrück 312, 349
    resistance in 297
    revolts at 238
    Sachsenhausen 312
    Sobibor 313, 378
    Treblinka 313
Concerning the Jews and Their Lies (Luther) 215

Conciliar Movement 12
Concordat of 1933 163, **313–314**
Condor Legion 143, **314–315**
Confederation of the Rhine **315**
Confessing Church 247–248, **315–316**
Congo 207, 269–270
Congress of Berlin 98, **267–268**, 341
Congress of Vienna 66–67, 68, **316–317**, 568, 639, 792m
Conrad I 7
conservatism 76, 205, **317–319**
Conservative Party 156, **408–409**
Constantinople, Turkish conquest of 13
constitution(s) **319**
    Daily Telegraph affair and 325–326
    of 1871 95–96
    in German Confederation 68–69, 385
    in German Democratic Republic 179
    revolutions of 1848 and 72
    of Second Empire 478–479
    Weimar Constitution 118–119, **733–734**
Contact Band Law of 1977 244
Coolidge, Calvin 125
coordination, policy of **418**
Copernican system 36
Corbusier, Le 253
Cordier, Mathurin 300
corporatism 367–368
corruption, Reformation and 20, 647
Cost of Discipleship, The (Bonhoeffer) 282
Council of People's Delegates 110
Council of People's Plenipotentiaries 344
Council of Trent 27, **319–320**
Counter-Reformation **27–28**, **320–321**
    Albert of Brandenburg in 210
    Albert V in 210–211
    anti-Semitism and 216
    baroque and 32, 249
    Canisius in 302
    Jesuits in 487–488
    Peace of Wesphalia and 738
coup of July 20, 1944 **321–322**

Court, Federal Constitutional **369**, 451
craft guilds 10–11
Cramer, Hans 206
Cranach, Lucas, the Elder 18, **322–323**, *323*, 337
Creation, The (Haydn) 58, 444
Crédit Mobilier 86, 330
Crimean War 275–276
Critique of All Revelation (Fichte) 376
Critique of Functionalist Reason (Habermas) 434–435
Critique of Pure Reason (Kant) 62, 500
Croissant-Rust, Anna 94
Crucifixion (Cranach the Elder) 322
Cruewell, Ludwig 206
Cuban missile crisis 166
cubism 331
culture
    absolutism and 204
    Benjamin as critic of 262
    Biedermeier and 273–274
    Chamberlain (Houston Stewart) on 305
    18th-century **55–63**, 58
    in Federal Republic 170–171, 172–173
    in German Democratic Republic 183–184
    of Germanic tribes 5–6
    Herder on 450
    Kulturkampf battle for 97, 263, **517–518**
    late Middle Age 11–12
    materialism and 92
    modernization and 573
    Reformation and 26
    Renaissance and 17–18
    rococo 665
    of romantic period 70
    in Second Empire 97
    of Weimar Republic 127–131
cultured elites **323–324**
Customs Union 71, **757**
Cyprus 198, 363
Czechoslovakia
    appeasement policy and 219
    Beck and 259
    in EU 363
    in German Confederation 68

Index 833

Munch Conference and 581–582
occupation of 142
Czech Republic, in NATO 198

D

Dachau concentration camp 312, **325**
Dada 129, 338, 358–359, 431
Daily Telegraph affair **325–326**
Daimler, Gottlieb 264, **326–327**
Daladier, Edward 581
Dalberg, Karl Theodor Anton Maria von 315
Dance of Death (Holbein the Younger) 18, 462
Danish War 76–77, **327–328**
Danube Landscape, The (Altdorfer) 212
Danube school of painting 18
Danzig **328–329**
Darwin, Charles 89, 442, 590
David (Klopstock) 510
Davout, Louis-Nicolas 232
Dawes, Charles 125
Dawes Plan 125, 126, **329**, 413
Days of the Commune, The (Brecht) 291
Day X (Heyn) 183
D-Banks **329–330**
D-Day 150–151, **330–331**
Dead Christ (Holbein the Younger) 462
Death and the Lover (Hesse) 454
Death in Venice (Mann) 550
Death of Adam (Klopstock) 510
Death of Empedocles (Hölderin) 463
Death of Hermann, The (Klopstock) 510
Death's Head 313, 325, 349
Debt and Credit (Freytag) 88, 399, 645
decentralization, 18th century 56
Declaration of Pillnitz 381
Declaration of the Rights of Man 64
De Clementia (Seneca) 300
Decline of the West (Spengler) 131
Decree for the Protection of the People 136–137
defenestration of Prague 331
Degenerate Art **331–332**

Dehmel, Richard 590
deism 59, 355, 397
Demian (Hesse) 453–454
Democracy and Empire (Naumann) 591
denazification 154–155, **332–333**, 614–615
Denck, Hans **333**
Denmark 29, 68, 144
Departure (Beckmann) 260
Depression, Great **333–334**
depressions (economic) **334–335**
Deputy, The (Hochhuth) 171, 626
Descartes, René 37, 59, 355
design, Bauhaus 252–253
détente 169, **335–336**
determinism 89
Deutschland (battleship) 144–145
"Deutschland, Deutschland über alles" **336**, 394
Development of Socialism from Utopia to Science, The (Engels) 354
Devil's Elixir, The (Hoffmann) 461
Devolution, War of 203
Diary of a Young Girl (Frank) 383
Dickens, Charles 380
dictatorship
  Nazi **135–143**
  road to 131–134
Die Freie Bühne 90
Diesel, Rudolf 233, **336**
diesel engine **336**
Die Technik des Dramas (Freytag) 399
Diet of Augsburg **234**
Diet of Nuremberg 466
Diet of Pressburg 41
Diet of Ratisbon 65
Diet of Speyer 213, 306
Diet of Worms 21, 648, **748–749**
Dietrich, Josef "Sepp" 220, **336–337**
Dietrich, Marlene 266
Dimitrov, Georgi 650
Ding (early tribal assembly) 5
diphtheria 346
Diplomatic Revolution 44, 46, **337**
Directory, General **404**
Discourse on Inequality (Rousseau) 564
Diskonto Gesellschaft 86, 330
Divided Heaven (Wolf) 183
divorce 58, 168, 182, 311
Dix, Otto 129, **337–338**

Djibouti 224
Döblin, Alfred 130, **338–339**
Dr. Faustus (Marlowe) 423
Dr. Huelsenbeack Near the End (Grosz) 431
Dr. Johannes Cuspinian and His Wife Anna (Cranach the Elder) 322
Doesburg, Theo van 253
Dog Years (Grass) 171
Doh, Hedwig 237
Dohm, Christian Wilhelm 216
Dollfuss, Engelbert 240
Don Carlos (Schiller) 62
Dongen, Kees van 293
Dönitz, Karl 339, **339–340**, 592
Donnersmarck, Guido Henckel 83
Dornier 208
Dostoyevsky, Fyodor 589
Dowding, Hugh 294
drama 60–62, 364–365, 441–443, 513, 529–530, 600, 716
Drayman Henschel (Hauptmann) 442
Dream of the Doctor (Dürer) 342
Dresden 53, 56, 240, **340–341**
Dresden china 340
Dresden State Opera House 340
Drexler, Anton 369, 592
Dreyse needle gun 77, 79
Droese, Felix 343
Droste-Hülshoff, Annette von 88, **341**, 646
Dual Alliance 100, **341–342**
Dufy, Raoul 332
Duineser Elegien (Rilke) 365, 664
Duisberg, Carl 257
Dumouriez, Charles 398
Dürer, Albrecht 17–18, 337, **342–343**
Durkheim, Emile 435
Düsseldorf **343**
Dutch War 40
Dutschke, Rudi 168

E

Eastern Treaties 335
East Franconian Kingdom 7
East German People's Council 178
East Germany. *See* German Democratic Republic
East German Youth Organization 184, 573

Ebert, Friedrich 110, 111–112, 115, **344**
Ebert-Groener Pact 111, **344–345**
Ecce Homo (Grosz) 431
Eck, Johann 234
Eckhart, Meister 12
Economic Council 158
economic miracle **345–346**
economics
    of absolutism 40
    under Adenauer 205
    of autarchy **241**
    banking in Middle Ages 11
    capitalism origins 11
    depressions in **334–335**
    dictatorship and 131
    of 18th century 56
    Engels on 354
    Erhard and 357–358
    of euro conversion 193
    of European Union 363
    feudal 10–11
    under Frederick William 50–51
    free-market 175, 358
    of German Democratic Republic 179, 180–181
    Great Depression and **333–334**
    of Industrial Revolution 85–86
    inflation and 483–484
    Lasalle and 520–521
    liberalism in 73, 82, 95
    List on 536
    under Marshall Plan 159
    Marx on 556–557
    nationalism in 82
    reconstruction after World War II 157–159
    Reformation and 23
    in Stresemann Era 124–126
    Thirty Years' War and 30–31
    of unification 191–193
    in Weimar Republic 122–124
Edict of Nantes 51
Edict of Potsdam 51, **629**
Edict of Restitution 375
Edict of Toleration 47, **346**
Edict of Worms 25, 234, **748–749**
education
    denazification and 155, 333
    French Revolution and 66
    in German Confederation 69
    in German Democratic Republic 181, 183

    Humboldt and 473
    in Industrial Revolution 86–87
    under Maria Theresa 45
    in 19th century 94
    Reformation and 19–20
    universities in Middle Ages 12
Effi Briest (Fontane) 89–90, 380
Egmont (Goethe) 422
Egypt 148, 206, 269
Ehrlich, Paul **346–347**
Eichendorf, Joseph von 62, 70, 91, **347**
Eichhorn, J. A. F. 394
Eichmann, Adolf 151, 221, **347–349**, *348*
Eichmann in Jerusalem (Arendt) 221, 349
Eicke, Theodor 312, 325, **349**
18th century **55–63**
    disease and 55–56
    economics and 56
    literature and 60–62
    music in 58
    nobility in 222
    philosophy in 62
    population expansion and 55
    secret societies in 63
    social structure in 57–58
Einsatzgruppen 151, **350**
Einstein, Albert 127, 283, **350–351**
Eisenhower, Dwight D. 148, 211, 330
Eisner, Kurt 109, 111, 121, **351–352**
El Alamein, Battles of 148, **352**
Elbe River **352**
Elective Affinities (Goethe) 421
Electoral Palace, Manheim 552
electrical industry 84–85
Elijah oratorio (Mendelssohn) 564
Emanuel, Max 279
Emanuel Quint (Hauptmann) 442
Emden (cruiser) 144–145
Emergency League of Pastors 142
emergency powers, in Weimar Constitution 118
Emergency Powers Acts 166, 168
Emperor Octavianus (Tieck) 713–714
Emperor's Bath (Altdorfer) 212
Empire, The (Mann) 89
Empire of Charles V 787*m*

empiricism 59–60, 89, 355–356
Ems Dispatch 79, **353**
Enabling Act 137, **353**
Enchiridon (Erasmus) 357
Engels, Friedrich 87, 271, **353–354**
engine, diesel 336
engine, gasoline 326–327
England 29, 71–72, 143, 145–146, 209, **294–295,** 396–397
English Royal Society 36
ENIGMA cipher **354–355**
Enlightenment **58–60, 355–356**
    conservatism and 317
    fascism and 368
    feminism and 372
    Frederick William II and 52–53
    Freemasonry and 397
    Hegel and 445–446
    Pietism and 624
    Prussian Academy of Sciences and 387
    romanticism and 69
Ensslin, Gudrun 243–244
Entail, The (Hoffmann) 461
Entente Cordiale 102, 579
environmentalism 174, 175, 427–428, 504–505
Enzenberger, Hans Magnus 171
epistemology 37
Epistle to the Romans (Barth) 250
Epp, Franz Ritter von 665
Equality (newspaper) 93–94
Erasmus, Desiderius **16–17,** 208, 234, *356*, **356–357,** 562, 653
Erfurt Program 258, **357**
Erhard, Ludwig 165, 205, 310, 345, **357–358**
Erhard Brigade 501
Erinnerungen aus mainem Leben (Freytag) 399
Erlach, Fischer von 33, 48
Ernst, Max **358–359**
Erzberger, Matthias 110, 121–122, 255, 305, **359**
Eschenbach, Wolfram von 35
Essay on Perpetual Peace (Kant) 62
Essence of Christianity, The (Feuerbach) 375, 633
Essence of Faith According to Luther (Feuerbach) 375
Essence of Religion, The (Feuerbach) 375

Esterházy, Paul Anton (Pál Antal) 48, 444
Estonia 198, 363
Ethiopia 219
Eugene of Savoy 41–42, 48, 279, **359–360,** 390, 526
Eugenics Laws 140
euro 193, 363
Europe, Ranke on 643–644
European Coal and Steel Authority 164
European Coal and Steel Community **360–361**
European Community 198
European Defense Community 205, 224, **361–362**
European Economic Community 206, **362–363**
European Economic Cooperation 555–556
European Recovery Program 159
European Union **363**
euthanasia **364**
Everyone His Own Football (Grosz) 431
Evolutionary Socialism (Bernstein) 271
existentialism, theological 250
exports, financing of, in Industrial Revolution 86
Exposures of Ulrich (Hutten) 474
expressionism **364–365**
    archetypes in 364–365
    Beckmann and 259
    as degenerate art 331
    of Döblin 338–339
    of Kaiser 499
    in 19th-century culture 88
    of Nolde 602–603
    of Pechstein 622
    in Weimar Republic 128, 129
Eyb, Albrecht von 471

F

Fables and Tales (Gellert) 403–404
Face of the Ruling Class, The (Grosz) 431
fairy tales 429
Falangists 143
Falk, Adalbert 97
Falkenhayn, Erich von **366**
Fallersleben, Hoffman von 394

Fall from Salvation, The (Cranach the Elder) 323
Fantastic Tales (Hoffmann) 461
Farewell Symphony, The (Haydn) 444
farming *See* agriculture
fascism **366–368,** 551
Fashoda conflict 102
Fatherland Party 105, **368–369,** 415
Faulhaber, Cardinal 572
Faust (Goethe) 61, 421, 422, 423
Fear and Misery of the Third Reich (Brecht) 291
Federal Constitutional Court **369,** 451
    formation of 369
Federal Republic of Germany **160–177, 369–371**
    Adenauer and 160–162, **205–206**
    armed forces of 224
    Basic Law in 156–157, 166, 224, **250–251**
    Bundesrat in **297–298**
    Bundestag in 298
    chancellors of **784**
    cold war and sovereignty of 163–164
    Constitutional Court in **369**
    culture in 170–171, 172–173
    economic boom (1950s) in 346
    electoral system **352–353**
    European Coal and Steel Community and 360–361
    foreign policy of 166
    foreign workers in 173
    as founding member of European Economic Community 362
    Frankfurt am Main in 384
    Free Democratic Party in 395–396
    German Democratic Republic and 184, 251–252
    Hallstein doctrine and 435–436
    Heinemann and 448–449
    Heuss and 454
    joins NATO 160, 224
    Kiesinger and 506–507
    labor management in 165
    literature in 170–171
    Lübke and 538–539

    population growth in 162, 172
    presidents of **784**
    Red Army Faction and 243–244
    social structure in 171–173
    Weizsäcker and 737
    women in 172
Federation of German Industry **371**
Federation of German Women's Associations 93, **371**
Fehn, Gustav 206
Fehrenbach, Konstantin 122
Feininger, Lyonel 252, 430
feminism **371–374**
    of Augspurg 237
    of Bäumer 253
    German Women's Bureau and 415–416
    Green Party and 427–428
    of Lange 519–520
    new 374
    of Zetkin 754–755
Ferdinandean period 346
Ferdinand I (Holy Roman Emperor) 27
Ferdinand II (Holy Roman Emperor) 28, 29, **374–375**
Fermi, Enrico 283
fertilizer 84
feudalism 9, 10–11, 90
Feuerbach, Ludwig 354, **375,** 633
Fichte, Johann Gottlieb 66, 70, **375–377,** 587
Fidelio (Beethoven) 262
Filbinger, Hans 246
Final Solution 151, 312–313, 348, **377–378,** 728–729
Finland, in Axis 242
First Coalition 65, 397
First Symphony (Brahms) 285–286
Fischer, Josef "Joschka" **378–379**
Fischer von Erlach, John Bernard **379**
fitness, physical 92
Five Women on the Street (Kirchner) 507
flag, National Assembly and 586
Fledermaus, Die (Strauss) 91
Fleming, Paul 34
Flesh (Benn) 263
Flight into Egypt (Cranach the Elder) 322

Flossenburg concentration camp 264, 312, 349
Flotsam (Remarque) 652
Flounder, The (Grass) 427
Focke Wulf 208
Follen, Karl 303
Fontane, Theodor 88, 89–90, **379–380,** 646
Fool in Christ, The (Hauptmann) 442
Forckenbeck, Max von 414, 481, 589, 631
Ford, Henry 680
foreign policy
　of Bush 199
　in Federal Republic 166
　of Hardenberg 440
　of Kohl 175
　of Maria Theresa 45–46, 554
　National Socialism and 142–143
　of Ostpolitik 169–170, 184, 335
　post-unification 197–199
　in Second Empire 97–98
foreign workers, in Federal Republic 173
Forster, Albert Maria 329
Forster, Georg 426
40-hour workweek 165
Foundations of the Nineteenth Century, The (Chamberlain) 305
Four Apostles (Dürer) 343
Fourteen Points 106, 114
Four Year Plan 241, **380–381**
France
　Aachen annexed by 203
　absolutism in 39–41
　Alsace-Lorraine and 212
　attack on, World War II 145
　Barbie and resistance efforts in 247
　declares war on Germany 143
　as founding member of European Economic Community 362
　in Franco-Prussian War 78–79
　Morocco and 211
　in Napoleonic Wars 584–585
　Second Empire collapse in 79–80
　in Thirty Years' War 29, 30, 711
　in Treaty of Versailles 115–116
　Treaty of Westphalia and 40
　victory over, 1871 98

Francis I (king of France) 25, 649
Francis II (Holy Roman Emperor) 48, 65, **381–382**
Francis Ferdinand (archduke of Austria) 104
Francis Joseph I (emperor of Austria) 98
Francis of Lorraine 43, 44, 240
Franco, Francisco 143, 146, 209
François Achille Bazaine 80
Franco-Prussian War 78–79, 276, 334, 575
Franco-Russian alliance 227–228
Frank, Anne 264, **382–383,** *383*
Frank, Hans 140, 325, **383–384**
Frank, Otto Heinrich 382
Franke, August Hermann 624, 633
Frankfurt, Treaty of 212
Frankfurt am Main **384**
Frankfurter Zeitung 351
Frankfurt Institute for Social Research 262
Frankfurt Parliament 72, **384–385**
Frankish kingdom 6
Franks 3, 4, 6
Frederick I (king of Prussia) *8,* 8–9, 225, **382–386**
Frederick II the Great (king of Prussia) 246, **386–388,** *387,* 636–637
Frederick III (king of Prussia) 11, 21, 51, 99, **388**
Frederick IV (king of Prussia) 28, 447
Frederick Augustus I (elector of Saxony) 340
Frederick William ("Great Elector" of Brandenburg) **50–51,** 224, 265, **389–390**
Frederick William I (king of Prussia) 51–52, 225, **390–391**
Frederick William II (king of Prussia) 9, 42–43, 52–53, **391–392,** 500
Frederick William III (king of Prussia) 225, **392–394**
Frederick William IV (king of Prussia) 72, 275, 319, **394–395,** 643
Free Corps 121, 229, **395,** 467
Free Democratic Party 156, 162, 167, 187, 194, 395–396

Free German Youth Movement 183
free-market economics 175, 358
Freemasons 63, **396–397**
Free Shooter, The (Weber) 91
Free Socialist Unions 100
Free Youth Movement 92–93
Freiburg School 357–358
Freie Bühne, Die 90
Freiherr, Karl von 83
French Revolution **64–73, 397–398**
　Bavaria and 254
　conservatism and 317
　Düsseldorf and 343
　feminism and 372
　Fichte and 377
　Frederick William II and 391–392
　German antipathy to 65
　German nationalism and 587
　German sympathy for 64
　Jewish people and 216
　Joseph II and 48
　militarism and 570
　nationalism and 64–65
　overview of 64
　secret societies and 63
　Stahl on 318
Freud, Sigmund 90, 127, 262
Frey, Agnes 342
Frey, Gerhard 654
Freytag, Gustav 88, 90, 335, **398–399,** 645
Frick, Wilhelm 135, 610
Friedrich, Caspar David 70, 274, **399–400**
Fritsch, Werner von 223, 280, **400**
Fritzsche, Hans 610
Froben, Johann 357
From Bacon to Spinoza (Feuerbach) 375
From India (Hesse) 453
From Morn to Midnight (Kaiser) 499
Fugger, Jacob 233, **400–401**
Fuggerei 233
Fuggers 210, 233, 400–401
Führerprinzip **401**
Funk, Walter 610
Future of Germany, The (Jaspers) 485

G

Gagern, Heinrich von 385, **402–403**
Galen, Clemens August von **403**
Galicia 554, 627
Galilei, Galileo 505
Gallén-Kallela, Axel 293
Gallicanism 19
Gambetta, Léon 79–80
Garbo, Greta 266
Gareis, Karl 121
Gauguin, Paul 332
Gaulle, Charles de 431
Gaullists 166, 169
Gay Science, The (Nietzsche) 601
Gefolgschaft 6
Geiler of Kaisersberg 12
Geiseric 5
Gelderland 386
Gellert, Christian Fürchtegott 403–404
Genealogy of Morals, A (Nietzsche) 600
General Directory **404**
General Electric Co. 330, 644
General German Workers' Association 87, 520–521
General History of the Nature and Theory of the Heavens (Kant) 500
General Psychopathology (Jaspers) 485
General Treaty 164
genetics, Mendel's work in 562–563
Genoa Conference 644
Genscher, Hans-Dietrich 170, 173, 175, 194, **404–405**
Gentz, Friedrich von 316, 317, **405–406**
George II of Hanover 44, 53–54
Gerhardt, Paul 34
Gerlach, Leopold von 76
German Center Party 156
German Christians (organization) **406**
German Communist Party 156, **406–407**, 535, 708–709
German Confederation **68–69**, 75, 319, 327–328, 384–385, 385, **407–408**
German Confessional Church 142
German Conservative Party **408–409**

German Democratic Party 253, **409–410**
German Democratic Republic **178–184, 410–411**
 agriculture in 181
 architecture in 183
 constitution of 179
 culture in 182–183
 détente and 335
 divorce in 182
 economy of 179, 180–181
 education in 183
 establishment of 162, 178
 Federal Republic and 184, 251–252
 Hallstein doctrine and 436
 literature in 183–184
 Modrow and 573–574
 morality in 182–183
 Pieck and 623
 Russian zone of 178
 uprising of June 17, 1953 179–180, 495–496
 women in 181–182
German Edison Company 85
German humanism 13–17
Germania (Tacitus) 14, 304
German Labor Front 137, 139, **411–412**
German language 5, 34, 47, 96
German National People's Party 207, 318, **412–413**
German People and Politics (Preuss) 631
German People's Party 115, 120, **413–414**
German Progressive Party 74, **414–415**
German Reich Party **415**
German Requiem (Brahms) 91, 285
German Social Union 187
German Theater, The (Gottsched) 426
German Union of Women's Suffrage 93
German Women's Bureau **415–416**
German Workers' Party **416,** 736
Germany, A Winter Tale (Biermann) 274
Germany, East. *See* German Democratic Republic

Germany, Imperial. *See* Second Empire (German)
Germany, map of 800*m*
Germany, West. *See* Federal Republic of Germany
Germany Illustrated (Celtis) 304
Germany Treaty 224, **416–417**
Gessler, Otto 121, 230
Gestapo 139, 140, 247, 322, *417,* 417–418
Gewerbe Insitut 284
ghettos, Jewish 141, 151, 455
Ghosts (Ibsen) 590
Gibraltar 146
Gilbert, Parker 125, 127
Gleichschaltung **418**
Globke, Hans 163
Glücks, Richard 349
Gneisenau, Neithardt von 65, 225, 226, 229, **418–419**
Gobineau, Joseph Arthur, comte de 88–89, 727
Goebbels, Joseph 137, 149, 150, 267, **419–420**
Goerdeler, Carl 258, 259, **420–421,** 656
Goes, Albrecht 170, 171
Goethe, Johann Wolfgang 60–62, *61, 421,* **421–423**
 Brentano and 292
 Fichte and 376
 Hauptmann and 443
 in Illuminati 63
 v. Leibniz 36
 romanticism and 69, 70
Goethe's Correspondance with a Child (Brentano) 292
Golden Age of Romanticism (Hoch) 469
Golden Bull 9, 466
Goldschmidt, Jakob 490
Good Person of Szechuan (Brecht) 291
Gorbachev, Mikhail 175, 185–186, 188, 512, 573
Göring, Hermann **423–424,** *628*
 air force and 208
 assassination attempt on 700
 Battle of Britain and 146, 294
 Beer Hall Putsch and 261
 Condor Legion and 315
 denazification and 332
 Final Solution and 151, 377

Four Year Plan and 381
 on law 140
 at Nuremberg Trials 154, 609
 Prussian police and 135
Görres, Johann Joseph von 70, **424–425,** 540
Gotha Congress 271
Gotha Program 357, **425**
Göthe, Esoander von 308
Goth tribe 3, 6
Göttingen, University of 250, 263, 283, **425–426**
Gottsched, Johann Christoph **426–427**
Götz von Berlichingen (Goethe) 60–61
Graf, Willi 686
Graf Waldemar (Freytag) 398
grain market collapse 207
Grand Alliance 42
Grand Coalition 166–168, 335
Grass, Günter 170, 171, **427–428**
Great Britain. *See* England
Great Depression **333–334**
Great Elector (Schlüter) 33
Greater Germany Art Exhibition 332
Great Philosophers, The (Arendt) 221
Great Schism 12, 19
Greece 146
Green Party 174, 196, 199, 292, **427–428,** 504–505
Gregory VII (pope) 7
Gregory XIII (pope) 487
Grien, Hans Baldung 338
Grillparzer, Franz 70, 273, 723
Grimm, Jakob 70, 292, **429**
Grimm, Wilhelm 70, 292, **429**
Grimmelhausen, Jacob Christtoffel von 35, 249
Groener, Wilhelm 111, 117, 133, 230, 344, **429–430**
Grolman, Karl von 226
Gropius, Walter 127, *128,* 252, *430,* **430**
Grosse, Doris 507
Grosse, Karl der. *See* Charlemagne
Grosz, George 332, 338, **431**
Grotewohl, Otto 410, 696
Grotius, Hugo 638
Group 47 170, 281

Group Portrait with Lady (Böll) 171, 281
Gruber, Kurt 460
Gruhn, Eva 280
Grünewald, Matthias 18, 338
Gryphius, Andreas 34–35, 249
Guardian Angel (Günther) 33, 249
Guderian, Heinz **431–432,** 509
Guernica 315
Guernica (Picasso) 315
Guggenheim, Peggy 359
Günther, Franz Ignaz 33, 249
Gustavus II Adolphus (king of Sweden) 29, 30, 375
Gutenberg, Johannes 17, **432–433**
Gutzkow, Karl Ferdinand 751
Gymnasium 323
Gysi, Gregor 187

H

Haase, Hugo 108
Habermas, Jürgen **434–435**
Habsburg dynasty 9–10, **39–49, 435, 783**
 Charles VI and 307
 establishment of 39
 foreign policy in 45–46
 Holy Roman Empire and 39
 Joseph II in 46–48
 Pragmatic Sanction and 630
 state reforms under 44–45
 Turkish Wars and 41
 Vienna and 48–49
 wars under 41–44
Haecher, Theodore 686
Haeften, Werner von 322
Hague Conference 127
Haller, Albrecht von 426
Haller, Carl Ludwig von 317
Hallstein, Walter 435
Hallstein Doctrine 169, 184, 335, **435–436**
Hamann, J. G. 450
Hambach Festival **436–437**
Hamburg 56, **437**
Hamburg-American shipping line (Hamburk-Amerika Linie) 84, 246–247
Handbook of the Christian Soldier (Erasmus) 16
Handel, George Frideric 35–36, 58, 250, **437–438**

Hanneles Himmelfahrt (Hauptmann) 442
Hanover 68, *438,* **438–439**
Hanseatic League 291
Hanseatic towns 10–11
Hansemann, David 86
Hardenburg, Friedrich von 62, 65, 70, **439**
Hardenburg, Karl August von 316, **439–440**
Harkort, Friedrich 82, 283
Harmonies of the World (Kepler) 36, 506
Harrer, Karl 592
Harvard University 425
Harzburg Front **440–441**
Hasenclever, W. 364
Hassel, Ulrich von **441**
Haugwitz, Count Friedrich Wilhelm 44–45
Hauptmann, Gerhart 89, 90, **441–443,** 590
Haushofer, Albrecht **443**
Haushofer, Karl **443**
Haussmann, Konrad 118
Haydn, Joseph 38, 48, 58, 261, **443–444,** *444*
Hebbel, Friedrich 645
Heckel, Erich 293
Hegel, Georg Wilhelm Friedrich 243, 353, 375, **445–446**
Heidegger, Martin **446–447**
Heidelberg **447**
Heidelberg, University of 25
Heidelberg Castle 33, 40, 447
Heidelberg Confession **447**
Heim, Georg 255
Heine, Heinrich 70, 91, 216, 343, **448,** 556
Heinemann, Gustav **448–449**
Heinrich, Otto 447
Heinrich von Ofterdingen (Novalis) 439
Heinse, Johann Jakob Wilhelm 751
Heisenberg, Werner 283, **449–450**
Held, Heinrich 256
Heller Altarpiece (Dürer) 342
Helsinki Agreements 335
Hendrick, Elisabeth 351
Henlein, Konrad 581
HE 111 bomber *208*
Herder, Johann Gottfried 59, 60, 63, 70, 355, 376, **450–451**

Hereditary Health Court 140–141
heredity, Mendel's work in
   562–563
Hermann and the Princess
   (Klopstock) 510
Hermann-Neise, Max 431
Hermann und Dorothea (Goethe)
   422
Herrenhausen Gardens 438
Herriot, Edouard 124
Herzog 5
Herzog, Roman **451–452**
Hess, Rudolf 145, 332, **452,** 610
Hesse **452–453**
Hesse, Hermann 130, **453–454**
Hesse-Darmstadt, in
   Confederation of the Rhine 315
Hetzer, Ludwig 333
Heuss, Theodor 396, **454**
Hewlett-Packard 246
Heydrich, Reinhard 138, 151, 204,
   377, **454–455**
Heym, Georg 365
Heym, Stefan 183, 184
Heymann, Lida Gustave 237, 373
High Authority 361
highways 139, 241, *241*
Hildebrand, Klaus 176
Hildebrandt, Johann Lukas von
   33, 48, 249, **455–456**
Hillgrubber, Andreas 176
Himmler, Heinrich **456**
   assassination attempt on 700
   Auschwitz and 238
   Bergen-Belsen and 264
   Dachau concentration camp and
      325
   Eichmann and 348
   Eicke and 349
   Einsatzgruppen and 350
   Final Solution and 151, 377
   Heydrich and 204
   Night of the Long Knives and 138
Hindemith, Paul 253, 291, 364,
   456–457
Hindenburg, Paul von *136,*
   457–458
   appointment of Hitler by 134
   armed forces of Weimar Republic and 230
   in Battle of Tannenburg 708
   Bavarian People's Party and 255
   Brüning and 295

conservatism and 318–319
death of 138
defeats Russians 228
depression and 133
Ebert-Groener pact and
   344–345
election of 125
Fatherland Party and 368
Free Corps and 395
Müller and 132
in World War I 105
Hindenburg Peace 368
Hindenburg Program **458**
Hirsh-Dunker labor association
   100
Historikerstreit 434
History of Germany (Hoch) 469
Hitler, Adolf 136, **458–460,** *593.*
   See also National Socialism
   Anschluss and 214–215
   appointment of, as chancellor
      134
   armed forces of Weimar Republic and 230
   art and 331–332
   assassination attempt on 150,
      321–322, 700–701
   in Battle for Berlin 267
   Beck and 258, 259
   Beer Hall Putsch and 124,
      260–261
   Berghof retreat of **264**
   on Bible 142
   Blomberg and 280
   Brauchitsch and 288
   Catholic Church and 142
   conservatism and 319
   Enabling Act and 353
   on feminism 415
   Final Solution and 377
   Four Year Plan of 241, 380–381
   Frank (Hans) and 384
   führerprinzip and **401**
   Goebbels and 419–420
   in Harzburg Front 440
   Hess and 452
   Holocaust and 463–465
   Hossbach Memorandum and
      468–469
   Jodl and 491–492
   Keitel and 503–504
   living space policy and 524–525
   Mein Kampf **560–561**

military and 223
military opposition to 321
mistakes made by 146–147
Moeller van den Bruck and 574
November Revolution and 111
Operation Barbarossa and 247
plans of 147–148
Reichstag dismissal by 135
religion and 141–142
resistance to **654–657**
   conservatism and 319
   Erhard in 357–358
   Goerdeler in 420–421
   Hassel in 441
   Manstein in 553
   military 321–322
   Scholls in 686–687
   Trott zu Solz in 717–718
   Weizsäcker in 736–737
   White Rose movement and
      150
suicide of 150, 267
Wagner and 258
women and 289
World War II, responsibility of
   144
Hitler-Ludenfordd Putsch 124,
   260–261
Hitler Youth 139, **460,** 680–681
Hobbes, Thomas 37, 249, 638, 712
Hochhuth, Rolf 171, 626
Hoffman, Ernst Theodor Amadeus
   70, **460**
Hoffman, Max 708
Hofmannsthal, Hugo von 723
Hohenberg, Ferdinand Hetzendorf
   von 49
Hohenlohe-Schillingfurst,
   Chlodwig zu 100, 101
Hohenstaufen dynasty 8–9
Hohenzollern dynasty 123, 353,
   461
Holbein, Hans, the Elder 233
Holbein, Hans, the Younger 18,
   462
Hölderin, Johann Christian
   Friedrich 62, 70, **462–463**
Holl, Elias 233
Holländer, Edith Frank 383
Holocaust **151–152,** 176, **463–465,**
   728–729, 797m. *See also* anti-
   Semitism; concentration camps
Holstein, Friedrich 211

Holstein, Fritz von 99
Hollweg, Bethmann 105
Holy Family at a Fountain, The (Altdorfer) 18, 212
Holy Night (Altdorfer) 212
Holy Roman Empire **465–466**
    absolutism in 203
    anti-Semitism in 215
    Charles V and 25
    constitution of 319
    courts in 558
    decentralization of 56
    demographics of 55
    dissolution of 48
    foundations laid by Charles IV 9
    v. Habsburg dynasty 39
    Habsburg family in 39, 435
    leaders of **783**
    Louis XIV attacks 40
    nationalist view of 70
    origin of term 9
    postal service in 172
    Pragmatic Sanction and 42
    Reformation and 19, 649
    Treaty of Westphalia and 40
Holz, Arno 89, 590
Holzmann, Philipp 330
home front, World War II and 149–150
homosexuals 138, 295, 400, 428
Honecker, Erich 411, **466–467**
    economic depression and 335
    Modrow and 573
    Schmidt and 174
    Socialist Unity Party and 696
    Ulbricht and 170, 184
    weakening of communism and 185
Horkheimer, Max 262
Höss, Rudolf 237–238, 312, 313, **467–468**
Hossbach, Friedrich 280
Hossbach Memorandum **468–469**
Hovebeck, Freiherr von 414, 631
Huber, Kurt von 686
Hubertsberg, Treaty of 46, 54, **469**
Hubmaier, Balthasar 333, 578
Huch, Ricarda 93, 311, **469**
Hugenberg, Alfred 127, 131, 319, 412, 440–441, **470**
Huguenots 40, 51, 265, 379, 390, **470**
Humanae Vitae (Böll) 281

Human Condition, The (Arendt) 221
humanism **470–472**
    Agricola in 208
    of Böll 281
    Celtis and 304
    Counter-Reformation and 321
    denazification and 155
    of Erasmus 356–357, 471, 653
    German 13–17
    of Hutten 474–475
    Italian 12, 13, 652
    in Middle Ages 12
    of Pirckheimer 625
    Reformation and 19–20
    in Renaissance 13
    of Reuchlin 657–658
human rights, Basic Treaty and 252
Humboldt, Alexander von 472, **472–473**
Humboldt, Wilhelm von 65, 316, 323, **473–474**
Hume, David 59, 355
Hungarian Revolution 180, 183
Hungary 242, 363
Hunger Parson, The (Raabe) 641
Hungerpastor (Raabe) 88, 335
Hus, Jan 13, 19
Husserl, Edmund 221, 262, **474**
Hutten, Ulrich von 15, **15–16, 474–475**, 653
Hutter, Jakob 579
Huygens, Christian 525
Huysman, Roelof. *See* Agricola, Rudolf
Hyperion (Hölderin) 463
Hypocrite, The (Gellert) 404

I

IBM computers 246
Ibsen, Henrik 89, 90, 589
idealism 88, 92, **476**
I. G. Farben 257
Ignatius Loyola, St. 321, **486–487**
Il Gesu 32
Illuminati 63, **396–397**
"Images of Decadence in Art" exhibit 332
Imitation of Christ (Kempis) 20, 647
immigration 189, 230–231, **476–478**
Imperial Chamber Court 558

Imperial Cities **478**
Imperial Constitution **478–479**
Imperial Council of Regency 558
Imperial Germany. *See* Second Empire (German)
impressionism 88, 331
Indemnity Bill **480–481**
Independent Social Democratic Party 105, 110, 114, 351, **481–482**, 755
India 102
Indipohdi (Hauptmann) 443
Indochina 269
indulgences, Luther and **482–483**, 544
Industrial Revolution 71–72, **82–87**, 569
industrial warfare 105
infectious diseases 511
inflation, in Weimar Republic 122–124, **483–484**
In the Land of Cockaigne (Mann) 89
Innocent XI (pope) 236
Innsbruck Palace 49
Inside the Third Reich (Speer) 697
Institute for Infectious Diseases 346
Institutes of the Christian Religion (Calvin) 25, 300
intelligence, Nazi military 204
International Military Tribunal 154–155, 332
    Frank (Hans) in 383–384
In the Land of Cockaigne (Mann) 549
Intoxicated Tide (Benn) 263
Investiture Controversy 7
I Paid Hitler (Thyssen) 713
Iphigenie auf Tauris (Goethe) 421, 422, 443
Iraq 199, 224
iron production 83–84
Isenheim Altarpiece (Grünewald) 18
Israel 161, 206
Italian humanism 652
Italian Symphony (Mendelssohn) 564
Italy
    baroque origins in 32, 248–249
    fascism in **366**
    as founding member of European Economic Community 362

in German Confederation 68
Goethe in 422
humanism in 12, 13, 471
Renaissance art in 18, 652
unification of 74
Itten, Johannes 252

J

Jacobi, Friedrich Heinrich 292
Jacobins 63
Japan, Anti-Comintern Pact and 215
Jarres, Karl 125
Jaspers, Karl 221, **485**
Jeanrenaud, Cécile 563
Jehovah's Witnesses 295
Jena **486**
Jena, Battle of 232, 393, **486,** 611
Jenny Treibel (Fontane) 90
Jerome, St. 18
Jerusalem (Mendelssohn) 564
Jesuits 45, 321, **486–488**
Jewish people. *See also* anti-Semitism
 under Civil Service Rehabilitation 137
 French Revolution and 216
 in Poland 151
 prior to 1869 **488–489**
 restitution to 161
 restricted to ghettos 141, 151
 stereotypes surrounding 642–643
 from 1870 to 1933 **489–491**
Jew's Beech Tree, The (Droste-Hülshoff) 88, 341, 646
Joanna the Mad (queen of Spain) 306
Jodl, Alfred **491–492**
Jogiches, Leo 121
Johann Albrecht of Mecklenburg 368
Johann of Tepl 471
John the Constant 322
John Frederick Magnanimous 322
John of the Cross, St. 321
John of Leyden 213–214, 582
Johnson, Uwe 171
John XII (pope) 465
Johst, H. 364
Jordan, Pascual 283
Joseph I (Holy Roman Emperor) 42

Joseph II (Holy Roman Emperor) 46–48, 204, 256, 346, *492,* **492–495**
Journalisten, Die (Freytag) 398
Journey to the Land without Death (Döblin) 339
Judaism and Music (Wagner) 91
Judgment of Paris (Cranach the Elder) 323
Judith (Hebbel) 645
June 17, 1953, Uprising **495–496**
Jünger, Ernst **496–497**
Junkers 50, 51, 52, 95, **497**. *See also* nobility
 Agrarian League and 207
 Bauernschutz and 252
 canton system and 303
 conservatism of 318
 Frederick William and 389
 Harzburg Front and 440
 Prussian army and 225
 Prussian dissolution and 161
 Reformation and 570
 revolution of 1848 and 571
Justinian Code 213
Jutland, Battle of **497–498**

K

Kaas, Ludwig 305
Kadinksy, Wassily 92
Kahlenberg, Battle of 41
Kahr, Gustav von 123, 124, 256, 260
Kaiser, Georg 364–365, **499**
Kaiser's Empire, The (Mann) 549
Kaltenbrunner, Ernst 151, 348
Kandinsky, Wassily 252, 430
Kant, Immanuel **499–501,** *500*
 empiricism of 59
 in Enlightenment 355
 Fichte and 376
 philosophy of 62
 romanticism and 69, 70
Kapital, Das (Marx) 87, 354, 556
Kapp, Wolfgang 121, 501–502
Kapp Putsch 121, 229, 255, **501–502**
Karl August of Saxony-Weimar 422
Karlowitz, Treaty of 41
Karlsruhe 246
Karl Theodor 56, 256, **502**

Kästner, Erich 129, 130, 597
Katte, Hans von 386
Kaunitz, Count Wenzel Anton 45, 337
Kautsky, Karl 101, 108, 258, **502–503**
Keitel, Wilhelm 145, 223, 332, **503–504**
Keller, Gotfried 645
Kellogg-Briand Pact 126
Kelly, Petra 378, **504–505**
Kempis, Thomas à 20, 647
Kennan, George 114
Kennedy, John F. 206
Kepler, Johannes 36, **505–506**
Kesselring, Albert 206, 208
Kessler, Emil 284
Kesten, Hermann 597
Kettler, Bishop Wilhelm von 87
Khrushchev, Nikita 166, 206, 270
Kiderlen-Waechter, Alfred von 207, 579
Kiel mutiny 108
Kiesinger, Kurt Georg 246, 310, **506–507**
Kiev 3
Kinkel, Klaus 405
Kipling, Rudyard 291
Kirchner, Ernst 129, 260, **507–508**
Kirchner, Ludwig 92
Kirkpatrick, Ivone 163
Klee, Paul 252, 430, **508**
Kleist, Ewald von **508–509**
Kleist, Heinrich von 62, 70
Klement, Ricardo. *See* Eichmann, Adolf
Klinger, Max 92
Klingsor's Last Summer (Hesse) 130, 454
Klopstock, Friedrich Gottlieb 60, 70, **509–510**
Kluge, Günther von **510–511**
Knight's Death and the Devil (Dürer) 342
Knight's Revolt 23–24
Knobelsdorff, Georg Wenzeslaus von 308, 675–676
Knowledge and Human Interests (Habermas) 434
Koch, H. Q. 354
Koch, Ignaz 44
Koch, Ilse 296
Koch, Karl Otto 295

842 Germany

Koch, Robert 346, **511–512**
Kohl, Helmut 174–177, *176*, 186–187, 194–195, 198, 363, **512–513**
Kokoschka, Oskar 332, **513**
Kollegienkirche 48
Kolping, Adolf 87
Konev, Ivan 267
König 5
Königgrätz, Battle of 276, **513–514**
Könignen II (Beckmann) 260
Korean War 164, 206, 224, 345
Körner, Theodor 66, 70, 91, 534
Kosovo 224
Kotzebue, August von 298, 303
Kramer, Josef 264
Kreisau Circle 321, 441, **514**, 576, 700, 718
Krenz, Egon 186, 187, 411, 696
Kreuzzeitung (newspaper) 409
Kristallnacht 141, 312, *601*, **601–602**
Kritzinger, Friedrich 729
Krupp, Alfred 83, 514–515
Krupp, Bertha 516
Krupp, Friedrich Alfred 336, 515–516
Krupp balloon gun *515*
Krupp Industries **514–515**
Krupp von Bohlen und Halbach, Gustav **516–517**
Kulturkampf 97, 263, **517–518**
Kursk, Battle of 148–149

L

Lady Jenny Treibel (Fontane) 380
Lafontaine, Oskar 195, 196
Lagarde, Paul Anton de **519**
Lamennais, Félicité Robert de 243
Lang, Franz Xaver 256
Lange, Helene 237, **519–520**
Langhans, Carl Gotthard 309
language, German 5, 34, 47, 96
Lasalle, Ferdinand 87, 258, **520–521**
Lasker, Eduard 334–335, **521**, 589
Lateran decree 7
Latin America, baroque in 249
Lattre de Tassigny, Jean de 211
law, evolution of German **521–522**

Law Code, Prussian **636–637**
Law for the Equalization of Burdens **522**
Law for the Protection of the Republic **522–523**
Law of Association 93
League of Augsburg 40
League of German Women 139
League of Nations 115, 126, 143, **523**
League of Three Emperors 98, 277, **523–524**
lebensraum (living space) **524–525**
Lectures on Thermodynamics (Planck) 627
Lefèvre, Jacques 300
legitimacy, principle of 66–67
Leibniz (Feuerbach) 375
Leibniz, Gottfried Wilhelm von **36–37**, 59, 249, 355, 356, 360, **525–526**
Leibstandarte unit 336–337
Leipzig **526–527**
Leipzig, Battle of 66, 226, **527–528**
Lenin, Vladimir 105, 228
Leo IX (pope) 7
Leo X (pope) 20, 210, 647
Leo XIII (pope) 304
Leopold I (Holy Roman Emperor) 41, 359, **528**
Leopold II (Holy Roman Emperor) 48, **528–529**
Leopold II (king of Belgium) 269
Lessing, Gotthold Ephraim 59, 60, 355, 376, **529–530**
Letters and Papers from Prison (Bonhoeffer) 282
Letters of Famous Men (Reuchlin) 15
Letters of Obscure Men (Reuchlin & Hutten) 15, 16, 475
Leuthen, Battle of 46, **530–531**
Ley, Robert 411, *628*, 713
Leyden 582
Liberal Democrat Party 192
liberalism **531–533**
  Bismarck and 274
  conservatism and 318
  Danish War and 76
  economic 73, 82, 95
  Hambach Festival and 436–437
  Industrial Revolution and 82
  Kant and 62

  in 19th century 88
  Progressive Party and 632
  romanticism and 70–71
  suffrage and 70
Liberal Party 156, 178
Liberation, Wars of **533–535**
Libya 206, 352
Lichtenberg, Bernhard 655
Lichtenberg, Georg C. 426
Liebknecht, Karl 110, 112–113, 121, 258, **535**
Liebknecht, Wilhelm **535–536**
Life of Galileo, The (Brecht) 291
Life of the Mind, The (Arendt) 221
Life of the Swedish Countess G . . . (Gellert) 404
Life Together (Bonhoeffer) 282
Ligurinus (Celtis) 304
Linde, Carl von 336
Lingen 386
List, Friedrich 82, **536–537**
Liszt, Franz 91, 285, *537*, **537**
literature
  Aüsburgerung and 183–184
  baroque 34–35
  of Böll 280–281
  of Brentano 292
  of Döblin 338–339
  18th-century 60–62
  in Federal Republic 170–171
  of Fontane 380
  of Freytag 398–399
  of Gellert 403–404
  in German Democratic Republic 183–184
  of Goethe 421–423
  of Hauptmann 442
  of Hoffmann 460–461
  of Huch 469
  of Jünger 496–497
  of Kaiser 499
  of Lessing 529–530
  of Mann (Heinrich) 549
  of Mann (Thomas) 550–551
  Maximilian I and 559
  of Raabe 641–642
  realism in 645–646
  of Remarque 651–652
  romantic school of 62
  of Schiller 678–679
  of Tieck 713–714
  of Toller 715–716
  Young Germany and 751

living space **524–525**
Lloyd George, David 115, 116, 207
Locarno Policy 121
Locarno Treaties 126, **537–538**
Locke, John 59, 60, 64, 355
Logical Investigations (Husserl) 474
Logic of the Social Sciences, The (Habermas) 434
Loibl, Martin 256
London 146, 276
London Conference 122
Lord's Supper 22–23, 648
Lorraine 84, 308
Lossow, Otto von 123–124, 260
Lost Honor of Katharina Blum, The (Böll) 281
Lottery Ticket, The (Gellert) 404
Louis Philippe (king of France) 80
Louis the German 7
Lubbe, Marinus van der 650
Lübeck, Peace of 375
Lübke, Heinrich **538–539**
Ludendorff, Erich Friedrich Wilhelm 105, 121, 123, 344, **539–540**
Lüderwitz, Adolf 269
Ludwig I (king of Bavaria) 254, **540–541**, 580–581
Ludwig II (king of Bavaria) 254, **541–542**, 581
Lueger, Karl 217
Lufthansa Airlines 192, 208, 330
Lunéville, Peace of 65, 551
Lusitania, sinking of 105, **542–543**
Luther, Hans 139
Luther, Martin 22, 543, **543–545**
  anti-Semitism of 215–216
  Augsburg Confession and 21–22, 236–237
  Bible translations of 21
  Cranach the Elder and 18, 322
  Diet of Augsburg and 234
  Diet of Worms and 748–749
  Dürer and 341
  Erasmus and 16–17, 357
  Frederick III and 388
  Hutten and 15
  hymns of **546**
  indulgences and **482–483**
  on Lord's Supper 22–23
  Melanchthon and 16, 21–22, 561

  music and 730
  pamphlets of **546**
  Peasants' War and 23, 621, 648–649
  Protestantism and 632–633
  Pufendorf and 638
  in Reformation 19, 20–23
  Reformation and 646–648
  on salvation 20
  von Brandenburg and 20–21
  Zwingli and 22–23
Lutheran Bible **545–546**
Lüttwitz, Walther 121, 501–502
Lützen, Battle of 30, 375
Luxembourg 68, 362
Luxembourg, Rosa 105, 112–113, 121, **546–547**, 547

M

Maastricht Treaty 198, 363
MacDonald, Ramsay 124
Machiavelli, Niccolò 40
machine tool industry 83
Mack, Heinz 343
Madam, The (Dix) 338
Madonna and Child (Cranach the Elder) 322
Maffei, Josef Anton 83, 284
Magda (Sudermann) 590
Magdeburg 10
Magic Flute, The (Mozart) 58
Magic Mountain, The (Mann) 130, 551
Magna Carta 466
Mahan, Alfred Thayer 591
Mahler, Gustav 91
Maidaneck concentration camp 313
Maier, Reinhold 245, 246
Main Topics of Theology (Melanchthon) 561
Mainz 56
Maizière, Lothar de 187, 188, 574
Majdanek concentration camp 378
Malta 363
Manchesterism 646
Manifesto of the Communist Party, The (Marx) 87, 354, 556
Mann, Heinrich 89, **549**
Mann, Thomas 89, 129, 130, *550*, **550–551**

Mannesmann Company 330
Mannheim 58, 246, **551–552**
Manstein, Erich von 145, **552–553**
Manteuffel, Edwin 227
Man with Fish (Beckmann) 260
maps **787m–800m**
Marburg Colloquy 23, **553**
Marburg Colloquy (Melanchthon) 16
Marc, Franz 508
Marcks, Gerhard 252–253, 430
Marconi, Guglielmo 289
Marcus Aurelius, statue of 249
Marcuse, Herbert 384
Margraves' Opera House 258
Maria Stuart (Schiller) 62
Maria Theresa (empress of Austria) **553–555**
  anti-Semitism of 489
  Diplomatic Revolution and 337
  Frederick II and 386
  Joseph II and 492
  marriage of 435
  reforms under 44–46
  Seven Years' War and 53
  Vienna and 48–49
  Wars of Austrian Succession and 42–44, 240
Mario and the Magician (Mann) 551
Marlowe, Christopher 423
Marne, Battle of 105, 441, **555**
Marr, Wilhelm 89
marriage 57–58, 140, 141, 311
Marshall Plan 159, 165, 345, **555–556**
Martel, Charles 6
Martyrdom of St. Catherine (Cranach the Elder) 322
Martyrdom of the Ten Thousand (Dürer) 342
Marx, Karl **556–557**, *557*
  Engels and 354
  Industrial Revolution and 87
Marx, Wilhelm 125, 256, 290
Mass in Time of War (Haydn) 444
materialism
  of Engels 353
  in Federal Republic 172
  of Feuerbach 375
  Lasalle and 520–521
  in 19th-century culture 88, 90, 92
Mathis the Painter (Hindemith) 457

Mathys, Jan 213–214
Matthys, Johann 24, 582, 649
Maurice of Nassau 29
Maurice of Savoy 25
Mauthausen concentration camp 312, 349
Maximilian I (Holy Roman Emperor) **557–558,** 722
Maximilian II (Holy Roman Emperor) 27, **560**
Maximilian I of Bavaria **559–600**
 absolutism and 203, 204
 Habsburg dynasty and 10
 Hutten and 15
 Thirty Years' War and 28, 29
Maximilian IV Joseph (king of Bavaria) 257
Maybach, Wilhelm 326–327
Maygar invasion 233
May, Karl 129
May Laws 97
Mazarin, Cardinal 359
Mecklenburg-Strelitz, Luise von 392
medical experimentation 313, 325
Medici family 20, 647
medicine 17, 346–347, 511–512, 562–563, 565
Meier, Heinrich Herman 84
Meineke, Friedrich 153
Meinhof, Ulrike 243–244
Mein Kampf (Hitler) 283, 305, 401, 452, 459, **560–561,** 593
Meissner, Otto 132
Meistersinger von Nürnberg, Die (Wagner) 91
Melancholia (Melencolia) (Dürer) 342, 343
Melanchthon, Philip **16,** 21–22, 234, 236, 322, 357, **561–562**
Melanchthon, Stephen 208
Melk, monastic church of 33, 48
Mencken, Wilhelmine 274
Mende, Erich 169, 396
Mendel, Johann Gregor **562–563**
Mendelssohn, Felix 91, 274, **563–564**
Mendelssohn, Moses 216, 489, **564–565**
Mengele, Joseph 238, 313, **565**
Men in Dark Times (Arendt) 221
Men Without Mercy (Döblin) 339
mercantilism 40

Mercedes-Benz *327*
mercy killing **364**
Mergel, Friedrich (fictional character) 341
Merkel, Angela 200, **565–567**
Messerschmitt, Wilhelm 208, 233, **567**
Messiah (Handel) 35–36, 58
Messiah, The (Klopstock) 509
Metropolis (film) 266
Metropolis 1917 (Grosz) 431
Metternich, Clemens von **567–569**
 appointment of 382
 Carlsbad decrees and 303
 Congress of Vienna and 316, 317
 Gentz and 405
 German Confederation and 68
 Hambach Festival and 436
 restoration of Holy Roman Empire and 66
 revolution of 1848 and 72
Mevissen, Gustav 86
Meyer, Conrad Ferdinand 730
Michaelis, Carolina 426
Michaelis, Johann D. 426
Michael Kramer (Hauptmann) 442
Michael Offensive 213
Middle Ages 7, **10–12,** 70, 215–216
middle class 11, **569–570,** 589
Midsummer Night's Dream (Shakespeare) 563
Milch, Eduard 208
militarism 82, 88, **570–571**
Military Reorganization Commission 225–226
Mill, John Stuart 590
Minna von Barnhelm (Lessing) 60
Mirabell Gardens of Salzburg 48
missiles, nuclear 335–336
Mit brennender Sorge (papal encyclical) **571–572**
Mitterrand, François 363
modernization crisis **572–573,** 594–595
Modrow, Hans 186, 411, **573–574**
Moeller van den Bruck, Arthur **574–575**
Mohács, Battle of 41
Moholy-Nagy, László 252, 253
Mollendorf, Richard Joachim Heinrich von 232

Moltke, Helmuth, Count von **575**
Moltke, Helmuth James, Count von **575–576,** *576*
 assassination attempt on Hitler and 319
 in Austro-Prussian War 513
 in Danish War 76
 Franco-Prussian War and 79
 in July 20, 1944, coup 321
 replacement of 100
Moltke, Helmuth Johann von **577**
Mommsen, Theodor 414, 631
Monadologie (Leibniz) 526
Mongolia, Outer 215
Monnet, Jean 361
Montez, Lola 580–581
Montgelas, Maximilian Joseph von **577–578**
Montgomery, Bernard 148, 211, 220, 352
Moravian Brethren **578–579**
Mörder, Hoffnung der Frauen (Hindemith) 364
More, Thomas 356
Moreau, Jeane 398
Morett, Joseph Hubert 18
Morgue (Benn) 262–263
Moroccan crises **579–580**
Morocco 102, 206–207, 211
Moscow, Treaty of 169
Moscow conference 153
Most Exalted Vision (Hindemith) 457
Mother Courage (Brecht) 291
movable type 432–433
movies 149, 266, 420, 663–664
Mozart, Wolfgang Amadeus 38, 58, 261
Mueller, Otto 293
Müller, Adam 317
Müller, Hermann 127, 132
Müller, Josef 317
Müller, Ludwig 315
Munch, Edvard 293
Müncher Post (newspaper) 351
Munggenast, Josef 33
Munich 56, 170, **580–581,** 614
Munich Agreement 173, 219
Munich Crisis/Conference **581–582**
Münster Rebellion **582–583**
Müntzer, Thomas 213, 758
Murr, the Tom-Cat's Reflection (Hoffmann) 461

music
  of Bach **244–245**
  baroque 35–36, 250
  of Beethoven 261–262
  Biedermeier and 273–274
  18th-century 58
  of Handel 437–438
  of Hindemith 456–457
  of Liszt 537
  Luther and 730
  of Mendelssohn 563–564
  19th-century 91
  rococo 38
  of Schubert 689–690
  of Schumann 690–691
  of Wagner 727
  in Weimar Republic 127–128
Music for the Royal Fireworks (Handel) 36, 438
Mussolini, Benito 143, 148, 242, 337
Muth, Carl 686
mutiny, naval 108
mysticism 11–12, 19, 243, 253, 262
Myth of the Twentieth Century (Rosenberg) 671

N

Nantes, Edict of 51
Naples 307
Napoleon Bonaparte **64–73,** 238–239, 254, 262, 315, 530–531
Napoleon III 75, 76, 78, 276
Napoleonic Code 216
Napoleonic Wars 50, 316–317, 527–528, **584–585,** 611, 635
NASA (National Aeronautics and Space Administration) 290–291
Nassau, in German Confederation 68
Nathan der Weise (Lessing) 60, 564
National Assembly **585–586**
National Democratic Party 166, **586–587**
nationalism **587–589**
  Bismarck and 75
  economic 82
  fascism and 367
  Fichte and 376
  French Revolution and 64–65
  Hegel and 446
  Holy Roman Empire in 70
  of Hutten 475
  inflation and 123
  religion and 141–142
  romanticism and 70–71
Nationality Acts 141
National Liberal Party 96, 100, 263, 277, 318, 521, **589**
National Socialism **592–595**. *See also* denazification; Hitler, Adolf
  Agrarian League and 207
  anti-Semitism and 140–141
  Aryan race and 138
  Barmen Declaration and 248
  Baumer and 253
  Bavarian People's Party and 256
  birth of 592
  Bormann and 282–283
  Catholic Church and 571–572
  Confessing Church and 315–316
  conservatism and 319
  economic policy under 241
  elections and 131–132
  in elections of 1928 127
  in elections of 1932 134
  expansion of Germany under 796m
  factors contributing to success of 131–134
  foreign policy under 142–143
  Frank (Hans) and 383–384
  Hassel and 441
  Heidegger and 446
  Hess and 452
  Jaspers and 485
  Locarno Pact and 126
  middle class and 569–570
  military and 223–224
  modernization and 572–573, 594–595
  Moeller van den Bruck and 574–575
  National Democratic Party and 586
  neo-Nazism and 595–596
  in Netherlands 368
  Nietzsche and 90
  Nuremberg Rallies and 608–609
  offices held by, after World War II 160
  parties as precursors to 120
  possible roadblocks to 133
  propaganda and 593–594
  Protestantism and 634
  racism and 642–643
  religion and 141–142
  resistance to **654–657**
    conservatism and 319
    Erhard in 357–358
    Goerdeler in 420–421
    Hassel in 441
    Manstein in 553
    military 321–322
    Scholls in 686–687
    Trott zu Solz in 717–718
    Weizsäcker in 736–737
    White Rose movement and 150
  Ribbentrop and 662–663
  status as sole legal party of 137
  Strasser brothers in 704
  "total" state under 139–140
  Wagner and 90
  women and 373, **743–745**
National Union 263
NATO (North Atlantic Treaty Organization) **603–604**
  Czech Republic in 198
  dual track decision of 335–336
  Erhard and 358
  Federal Republic in 164
  Federal Republic joins 160, 224
  Germany Treaty and **416**
  Poland in 198
naturalism 89, 364, **589–590**
Natural Philosophy of Cause and Chance (Born) 283
Natzweiler concentration camp 264
Naumann, Friedrich 94, **590–591,** 632
naval mutiny, after World War I 108
Naval Treaty, Anglo-German **214**
navy 229, **339–340, 591–592,** 714–715
Navy League **592**
Nazism. *See* Hitler, Adolf; National Socialism
Nazi-Soviet Nonaggression Pact **595**
Nazi Women's League **687–688**
Nehring, Walther 206
Nelson Mass (Haydn) 444
neoclassicism 49, 60
neo-idealism 92

neo-Nazis 163, 189, 194, **595–596,** 653
Neoplatonism 36, 342
neoromanticism 364
Neselrode 316
Netherlands 30, 145, 362, 368
Neuchâtel 386
Neumann, Balthasar 10, 33, 249, **596–597**
Neumarkt, Johann von 13
Neurath, Konstantin von 662
New Astronomy (Kepler) 36, 505–506
New Face of the Ruling Class (Grosz) 431
New Forum Party 186
New Jungle, The (Döblin) 339
New Objectivity 129–130, 259, 260, 338, 431, **597–598**
New Path of the German Woman, The (Baumer) 253
New State and the Intellectual, The (Benn) 263
Newton, Isaac 506
Nicholas Church (Leipzig) 186
Nicholas II (pope) 7
Nicolai, Friedrich 564
Nicolsburg, Peace of **598**
Nicolson, Sir Arthur 211
Niebuhr, Barthold 644
Niemöller, Martin 142, 163, 316, **598–599**
Nietzsche, Friedrich 89, 90, 262, 293, 351, 574, **599–601**
Nightingale of Wittenberg, The (Sachs) 14
Night of Broken Glass 141, 312, 601, **601–602**
Night of the Long Knives 138, 336–337, **602**
nihilism 90, 130
Nihilism (Benn) 263
Nijmegen, Treaty of 40, 389
19th century **88–94**
Ninety-five Theses (Luther) 20, 22, 210, 647
Ninth Symphony (Beethoven) 58, 262
Ninwegen, Peace of 40
Nobel Prize
  to Böll 171, 281
  to Brandt 168
  to Braun 289
  to Ehrlich 347
  to Einstein 350
  to Quidde 640
nobility 57, 64, **221–223,** 382. *See also* Junkers
Nolde, Emil 92, 293, 332, **602–603**
Nolte, Ernst 176
Norimberga (Celtis) 304
Normandy, invasion of 150, 330–331
North Africa 146
Northern Pacific Railroad 86
North German Confederation 258, 319, **604–605**
North German Lloyd Company 84, 100
North Rhine-Westphalia **605**
Norway, attack on 144–145
Noske, Gustav 112, 121, 230, **605–606**
Novalis 62, 65, 70, **439**
November Group 338
November Revolution **107–113,** 290, 318, 359, 640
nuclear power plants 196
nuclear warfare 335–336, 351
Nuremberg 315, **606–607**
Nuremberg, Diet of 466
Nuremberg Laws 141, **607–608**
Nuremberg Rallies **608–609**
Nuremberg Trials 154–155, 332, 383–384, **609–610,** 697, 706

O

Occupation Statute 164
occupation zones 799*m*
October Edict **611,** 701
October Reforms 105
Odeonsplatz 124
Oder-Neisse line **611–612**
Odessa (SS organization) 348
Ode to Joy (Schiller) 58, 62
Offenbach, Jacques 91
oil embargo 170
OKW (Armed Forces High Command) **612–613**
Olbricht, Friedrich 321
Old Beehead (Strittmatter) 183
Olmütz, capitulation of **613**
Olympia (film) 663–664
Olympic Games 170, **613–614**
Omaha Beach 331
OMGUS **614–615**
On Dialectical Invention (Agricola) 208
One Hour After Midnight (Hesse) 453
On German Poetry (Opitz) 34
On the Cabalistic Art (Reuchlin) 15
On the Concept of History (Benjamin) 262
On the Duty of Man and Citizen (Pufendorf) 638
On the Freedom of the Christian Man (Luther) 21, 647
On the Law of War and Peace (Pufendorf) 638
On the Wonder-Working Word (Reuchlin) 15
On War (Clausewitz) 311
Operation Barbarossa 146–147, 147, **247,** 619
Operation Sea Lion 145
Operation Valkyrie 321–322
Opitz, Martin 34, 249
Oppenheimer, Abraham 86, 330
Oppenheimer, Joseph 216
Oppenheimer, Robert 283
Oratorian order 321
oratorio 35–36
Origins of the Family, Private Property and the State, The (Engels) 354
Origins of Totalitarianism, The (Arendt) 221
Orlando, Vittorio 115
oscilloscope 289
Ostend Company 307
Oster, Hans 577, 700
Oster Conspiracy 577
Ostpolitik 169–170, 184, 251, 335, **615–616**
Ostrogoth tribe 3, 4
Oswolt Krell (Dürer) 342
Otto I 7, 580
Otto III 7
Otto, Louise 372
Ottokar II of Bohemia 239
Ottoman Empire 267, 387
Outer Mongolia 215
Oxford Symphony (Haydn) 444

P

Paasche, Hans 121
Pacassi, Nikolaus 49

pacifism 350, 640
Pact of Steel 143
paintings
   of Altendorfer 212
   of Cranach the Elder 322–323
   as degenerate art 332
   of Dürer 342–343
   expressionist 365
   of Holbein 462
   of Kirchner 507–508
   of Klee 508
   of Nolde 602–603
   Renaissance 17–18
   in romantic period 70
Pan-German League **616**
Papa Hamlet (Holz & Schlaf) 590
papal encyclical *Mit brennender Sorge* **571–572**
Papen, Franz von 132, 133, 134, 155, 610, **616–617**
Paracelsus, Theophrastus 17, **617–618**
Paris Commune 219
Paris Treaty 164
Parliamentary Council 156–157
Parma 307
Parsifal (Wagner) 91
Parsons, Talcott 435
particularism 96
Partnership and Cooperation Agreement 198
Party of Democratic Socialism 194, 196, **618**
Pas de Calais 330, 331
Passarowitz, Treaty of 360
Passau, Treaty of 307
passive resistance 654–655 *See also* resistance, to Nazis
Pastors Emergency League 316
Patrioteer, The (Mann) 89
patriotism, French Revolution and 66
Patterns of Childhood (Wolf) 183
Patton, George S. 220
Paul, Jean 62, 70
Pauli, Wolfgang 283
Paul III (pope) 27, 306, 320
Paul IV (pope) 27, 321
Paulus, Friedrich **619–620**
Pearl Harbor 232
peasantry 47, 57, **252**
Peasants' War 23–24, 210, 389, **620–621,** 648–649

Peasant War in Germany (Engels) 354
Pechstein, Hermann Max 92, 129, 293, **621–622**
Pelagianism 250
penal code of 1872 96
Penance of St. John Chrysotom (Cranach the Elder) 322
pension reform, under Schroeder 165, 192
People's Court 140, 418, **622–623**
Pétain, Henri 145
Peter Camenzind (Hesse) 453
Peters, Carl 269
Petersburg Agreement 164
petition politics 271
Petrarch, Francis 208
Peutinger, Conrad 233
Pfefferkorn, Johannes 15
Pfeifer, Anton 256
Pfister's Mill (Raabe) 641–642
Phalarismus (Hutten) 474
pharmaceutical industry 85, 257
Phenomenology of Spirit, The (Hegel) **445–446**
Philip of Hesse 307
Philipp, Karl 343
Philip V of Spain 42
Philip the Fair (duke of Burgundy) 306
Philistine Mirror, The (Grosz) 431
philosophy 221, 342
   of Hegel 445–446
   of Heidegger 446–447
   of Herder 450–451
   of history 643
   humanism in 470–472
   of Husserl 474
   of Jaspers 485
   of Kant 62, 500–501
   of Leibniz 525–526
   of Lessing 529–530
   of Marx 556–557
   of Mendelssohn 564–565
   naturalism in 589–590
   of Nietzsche 600–601
   of Ranke 643
   of Thomasius 711–712
   of Wolff 743
Philosophy (Jaspers) 485
Philosophy of the Future, The (Feuerbach) 375
physical fitness 92

Physical Principles of the Quantum Theory 449
physics 669–670, 283, 289, 350–351, 449–450, 626–627
Physics and Beyond (Heisenberg) 450
Piacenza 307
Pia Desideria (Spener) 37
Picasso, Pablo 315
Pieck, Wilhelm 410, **623**
Piene, Otto 343
Pierre Bayle (Feuerbach) 375
Pietà (Günther) 33, 249
Pietism 34, **37–38,** 249, 275, 356, **623–624**
Pillnitz, Battle of **624–625**
Pillnitz, Declaration of 381
Pimp and Whore (Dix) 338
Pirckheimer, Willibald 14, 342, **625**
Pister, Hermann 295
Pius IX (pope) 517
Pius XI (pope) 142, 313, 572, 656
Pius XII (pope) 171, **625–626,** *626*
plague, bubonic 12, 20, 55–56
Plague Cart, The (Raabe) 641
Planck, Max 350, **626–627**
plants, Mendel's work with 562–563
Plenary Council 408
Plowman from Bohemia (Johann of Tepl) 471
Plowman from Bohemia (von Saas) 13
Poe, Edgar Allan 461
poetry
   of Benn 262–263
   of Biermann 184, 274
   of Celtis 304
   of Droste-Hülshoff 341
   of Eichendorff 347
   emergence of 34
   of Gellert 403
   of Goethe 60–61
   Gottsched on 426–427
   of Heine 448
   Herder on 60
   humanism in 471–472
   of Klopstock 60, 509–510
   of Novalis 439
   of Rilke 664–665
   of Wieland 738–739
Poetry and Truth (Goethe) 421, 422

848 Germany

Pohl, Oswald 349
Poincaré, Raymond 124
Poland
   Death's Head in 349
   democratization of 185
   division of Germany after World War II and 153–154
   Einsatzgruppen in 350
   in EU 363
   Frank (Hans) and 383–384
   in German Confederation 68
   invasion of 143, 144, 223
   Jews in 151
   in NATO 198
   non-aggression pact with 142
   Oder-Neisse line and 611–612
   partitions of **627**
   Vilna seizure and 230
police 47, 135, 411. *See also* Gestapo; SS (Schutzstaffel)
Polish Corridor 116, 126, **628**
Polish Succession, War of 360
Polish War 308
political parties 96–97, 108, 114–115, 118, 125–126, 155–156, 223. *See also specific parties*
Political Testament (Frederick William II) 53
Pomerania 124
Pöppelmann, Mätthias 33, 249
population decline 12, 30
population expansion 55–56, 86, 172, 282
Porsche, Ferdinand 628, **628–629**
Portugal 269
Positive Christianity **629**
positivism 89, 274
postal service, in Holy Roman Empire 172
potash 84
potatoes 56
Potato War 46
Potsdam, Edict of 51, **629**
Potsdam Agreements 154, 161, 178, 611–612
Potsdam Conference **629–630**
Pragmatic Sanction 42, 53, 307, 308, **630**
pragmatism, of Hitler 147
Prague 12, 13, 77, **331**
Prague, Treaty of 276
Praise of Folly (Erasmus) 16, 356, 357

Prandtauer, Jacob 33, 48
Preparatory Theses on the Reform of Philosophy (Feuerbach) 375
Pressburg, Diet of 41, 65
Pressburg, Treaty of 239
Preuss, Hugo 586, **630–631**
Princes and Peoples of Southern Europe in the Sixteenth and Seventeenth Centuries (Ranke) 643
Princip, Gavrilo 104
printing, invention of 17
Prittwitz-Gaffron, General 708
Private Life of the Master Race (Brecht) 291
Problems of Atomic Dynamists (Born) 283
Prodigal Son (Dürer) 342
Professor Urath (Mann) 89
Progressive Party 96, **631–632**
Prometheus (Goethe) 60
propaganda 103, 149–150, 368, 419–420, 593–594
Protestantism/Protestant Church **632–633**. *See also* religion
   Barmen Declaration and 247–248
   Calvin and **300–302**
   Calvinism and 24–25
   Confessing Church and **315–316**
   Counter-Reformation and 27–28
   defenestration of Prague and 331
   Edict of Toleration and 346
   Erasmus and 17, 357
   Eucharist and 553
   Ferdinand II and 374–375
   in German Democratic Republic 184
   indulgences and **482–483**
   Marburg Colloquy and 553
   Melanchthon and 16, 561–562
   National Socialism and 634
   1989 revolution and 186
   Pietism and 37–38
   role of, in Nazi tyranny 163
   in towns 24
Protest of 1529 25
Protocols of the Elders of Zion, The (unknown) 217, **634–635**
Prussia **635–636**
   army of **224–227**

   in Austro-Prussian War 77–78
   Braun and 290
   canton system in 225, **302–303**
   in constitution of 1871 96
   cultural cultivation in 323
   Danish War and 76, 328
   defeat of, by Napoleon 65
   as economic power 74
   expansion of 790m
   in Franco-Prussian War 78–79
   under Frederick William II 52–53
   Hesse in 452–453
   militarism in 570–571
   nobility in 222
   peasants in 252
   police in 135
   population growth in 18th century 55
   suffrage in 96
Prussian Academy of Sciences 387
Prussian Icarus (Biermann) 274
Prussian Law Code 521, **636–637**
Prussian Three Class Voting System **637–638**
Pufendorf, Samuel von 59, 249, **638**
Puss in Boots (Tieck) 713

Q

Quadruple Alliance 568, **639**
quantum theory 283, 350
Quidde, Ludwig **639–640**
Quirnheim, Albrech Mertz von 322
Quisling, Vidkun 145

R

Raabe, Wilhelm 88, 335, **641–642**
Racial Observer (newspaper) **724**
racism 217, **642–643,** 670–671. *See also* anti-Semitism
Radek, Karl 112
Radowitz, J. von 395
Raeder, Erich 146, 591
Raidffeisen, Friedrich Wilhelm 87
railways 71, 83, 268, **268**, 283
Ranke, Leopold von **643–644**
Rapallo, Treaty of 123, 230, **644**
Rashid, Harun al- 203
Raspe, Jan-Carl 243–244
Rathenau, Emil 85

Rathenau, Walther 121, 122, 123, 218, 483, **644–645,** *645*
rationalism 59–60, 69, 355–356
Ratisbon, Diet of 65
Ravensbrück concentration camp 312, 349
Rawlinson, Henry 213
Reagan, Ronald 175, *176*
realism 88, 399, 645–646, 652
Realo faction 378–379
Realpolitik 75, **646**
reason, Enlightenment and 58–59
Recantation of Hans Denck, The (Denck) 333
reconstruction, economic, after World War II 157–159, 164–165
Red Army Faction 174, **243–244**
Reformation **19–26, 646–649,** 788*m*
   Augsburg and 233
   baroque and 32, 248
   Black Plague and 20
   Calvinism and 24–25
   Charles V and 25–26, 306
   consequences of 23–24
   Council of Trent and 27
   Counter-Reformation and 27, **320–321**
   Cranach the Elder and 323
   Diet of Augsburg and 234
   Dürer in 341
   v. Enlightenment 59, 355
   Erasmus and 356–357
   German character and 26
   Holy Roman Empire and 19
   humanism and 19–20
   issues leading to 20
   Junkers and 570
   Luther's role in 19, 20–23, 544–545
   Melanchthon in 16
   mysticism and 19
   need for 19–21
   Peace of Augsburg and 25–26
   printing press and 17, 21
   Protestantism and 633
   in Saxon dynasty 7
   in towns 24
   Zickau prophets an 757–758
   Zwingli in 758–760
Reformed Church 632–633
Reform or Revolution (Luxembourg) 547

refugee compensation 522
Refugee Law 522
Regensburg 10, **649–650**
Regent Luitpold (prince of Bavaria) 254
Rehfish, Hans José 597–598
Reich Security Main Office 204, **671–672**
Reichstag
   constitutions and 319
   Daily Telegraph affair and 326
   dismissal of, by Hitler 135
   Enabling Act and 353
   fire 136–137
   in Second Empire 96
Reichstag Building *650,* **650–651**
Reichstag Peace Resolution 359
Reign of Terror 64
Reinhardt, Max 291, 365
Reinhardt, Walther 112
Reinsurance Treaty 98, 102
relativity 350
religion. *See also* Catholic Church; Protestantism/Protestant Church; Reformation
   art and 17–18
   Barth on 250
   Bonhoeffer on 281–282
   Calvin on 300–301
   Denck on 333
   of early tribal peoples 5
   Enlightenment and 58–59, 355–356
   Feuerbach on 375
   Fichte on 376
   Hitler and 141–142
   Leibniz on 37
   Maria Theresa and 45
   Mendelssohn on 564–565
   Stahl on 318
Remarque, Erich Maria 129, **651–652**
Reményi, Eduard 285
Renaissance **13–18,** 32, 208, 470–471, **652–653**
Renner, Karl 239, 240
Rentenmark 124
reparations 116–117, 122–124, **329,** 630
Republikaner Party 194, **653–654**
Requiem Mass (Mozart) 58
Residenz 48

resistance, to Nazis **654–657**
   conservatism and 319
   Erhard in 357–358
   Goerdeler in 420–421
   Hassel in 441
   Manstein in 553
   military 321–322
   Scholls in 686–687
   Trott zu Solz in 717–718
   Weizsäcker in 736–737
   White Rose movement and 150
Restitution, Edict of 375
restitution, to Jews 161
Restless Universe, The (Born) 283
Restoration 226, 317–318, 382
Restoration, The (von Haller) 317
Reuchlin, Johannes **14–15,** 16, 652, **657–658**
Reuter, Gabriele 94
revisionism 271, 434
revolution, November **107–113,** 290, 359
Revolution of 1848 72–73, **658–659**
   anti-Semitism and 216–217
   Basic Law and 251
   Bismarck in 275
   conservatism and 318
   constitution and 319
   Frederick William IV and 395
   Junkers and 571
   nationalism and 588
   Prussian army in 226
   realism and 645
Revolution of 1918–1919 229, 344, 409, 482, **659–660**
Revolution of 1989 **185–190**
Rexists 368
Rhein-Main Air Force Base *161*
Rhein-Metal 230
Rhenish Confederation **315**
Rhenish League 40
Rhine, River and Valley **660**
Rhineland-Palatinate **660–662**
Rhine-Westphalia, North **605**
Ribbentrop, Joachim von 145, 215, 332, 610, **662–663**
Ricardo, David 354, 520, 557
Richter, Eugen 414, 590, 632
Richter, Ludwig 274
Richthofen, Baron Wolfram, von 315
Riefenstahl, Leni *663,* **663–664**

Riemenschneider, Tilman 23
Rilke, Rainer Maria 365, **664–665**
Ring Cycle, The (Wagner) 258, 727
Ritter von Thoma, Wilhelm 206
Road Back, The (Remargue) 652
Robbers, The (Schiller) 62, 678
Rochau, A. L. von 646
rockets 290–291
rococo 38, **665**
Rodrigo (Handel) 35
Rohe, Miles van der 253
Röhm, Ernst **665–666**
Rokossovsky, Konstantin 267
Roman Elegies (Goethe) 422
Roman Empire 3–5
Romania 242, 363
romanticism 62, **69–70,** 91, 347, 409, **666–668,** 727
Romantic Songs (Hesse) 453
Rome, Treaty of 175, 362, 363
Rome-Berlin Axis 143
Rommel, Erwin Johannes Eugen 146, 322, 330, 352, **668–669**
Röntgen, Wilhelm Conrad **660–670**
Roon, Albrecht 74, 227
Roosevelt, Franklin Delano 211, 351
Rose Bernd (Hauptmann) 442
Rosenberg, Alfred 140, **670–671**
Rossbach, Battle of 46
Roswitha of Gandersheim 14
Roth, Joseph 597
Round Table group 187
Rousseau, Jean-Jacques 64, 445, 501, 564
Royal Air Force 209
Rubble (Benn) 263
Rubeanus, Crotus 15
Rückert, Friedrich 66, 70, 91
Rückriem, Ulrich 343
Rudolf I (Holy Roman Emperor) 9
Rudolf II (Holy Roman Emperor) 27, 28, **672**
Rufus, Mutianus 14
Ruge, Arnold 556
Ruhr region 122–124, **672–673**
Rundstedt, Karl Rudolf Gerd von 220, 331
Runge, Otto 274
Ruppa, Wenzel von 331
Russia. *See also* Soviet Union
 Austria and, in Balkans 103–104
 blitzkrieg in 279

Einsatzgruppen killings in 350
Napoleon invades 66
Poland partitions and 627
post-unification relations with 198
revolution in 218
Second Empire alliance with 98
in War of Austrian Succession 386
Russian Revolution 228, 364
Russo-Japanese War 102
Russo-Turkish War 267, 341
Ryswick, Peace of 40–41, 236

S

SA (storm troopers) **674**
Saarland **674–675**
Saar valley 115–116
Saas, Johannes von 13
Sachsenhausen concentration camp 312
Sachs, Hans 14
Sailer, Johann Michael 540
Salian dynasty 7
Salian Frank tribe 4
Salome (Klopstock) 510
Salomon, Johann Peter 444
Salvarsan 346–347
salvation 20, 646
Salzburg 48, 56
Sans-Souci (palace) 38, **675–676**
San Stefano 267
Santa Clara, Abraham a 35
Sauer, Joachim 566
Savigny, Friedrich 644
Saxon dynasty 7
Saxon tribe 3
Saxony 315, **676**
Scandinavia, Germanic tribes in 3
Scenes from the German Past (Freytag) 399, 645
Scenes from the Life of Mary (Hindemith) 456
Schacht, Hjalmar Horace Greeley 124, 139, 155, 241, 440, 610, **676–677**
Schaeffer, Fritz 256
Scharnhost, Gerhardt von 65, 225, 226, 229, 585, 700
Scheel, Walter 169, 170
Scheer, Reinhard 498
Scheffler, Johannes 34

Scheidermann, Philip 110, **677–678**
Schelling, Friedrich Wilhelm Joseph von 70
Scherbius, Arthur 354
Schiller, Friedrich 58, 60, 62, 70, 422, **678–679**
Schiller, Karl 166
Schinkel, Karl Friedrich 87, **679–680**
Schirach, Baldur von **680–681**
Schlaf, Johannes 590
Schlegel, August 317, **681–682**
Schlegel, Friedrich 70, 317, **681–682**
Schleicher, Kurt von 132, 133, 134, 138, **682**
Schleiermacher, Friedrich Daniel 70, **682–683**
Schlemmer, Oskar 252, 430
Schleswig-Holstein question 76, 276, **327–328**
Schlieffen, Hans von 100, 227–228
Schlieffen Plan 104, 227–228, 555, **683,** 741–742
Schliemann, Heinrich **683–684**
Schloss Mirabell 48
Schlözer, August Ludwig von 426
Schlüter, Andreas 33
Schmalkaldic League 25, 210, 307, **684–685**
Schmidt, Auguste 93, 237, 371
Schmidt, Helmut 173–174, 174, 195, **685–686**
Schmidt-Rottluff, Karl 92, 293
Schmorelli, Alexander 686
Schneider, Paul 655
Schnitzler, Arthur 723
Schnurr, Wolfdietrich 170–171
Scholasticism 13, 652
Scholl, Hans 654, **686–687**
Scholl, Sophie 654, **686–687**
Scholtz-Klink, Gertrud 415–416, **687–688,** 744
Schönbrun Palace 48, 49, 379
Schönbruner, Franz 653
Schongauer, Martin 342
Schopenhauer, Arthur 70, 384, 599
Schrödinger, Erwin 283
Schroeder, Gerhard 192, 193, 195–197, 199, 358, 566, **688–689**

Index 851

Schubert, Franz Peter 70, 274, **689–690**
Schüle, Johann Heinrich von 233
Schulte, Cardinal 572
Schulze, Hagen 176
Schulze-Delitzsch, Franz Hermann 87, 414, 631
Schumacher, Kurt 156
Schumann, Clara 285, 286, **690–691**
Schumann, Robert 91, 285, 362, **690–691**
Schuman Plan 164, **691**
Schuschnigg, Kurt von 214, 240
Schwend, Karl 256
Schwind, Moritz van 70, 274
science, Benn on 263
Science of Knowledge (Fichte) 376
scientific revolution 36
Scottish Symphony (Mendelssohn) 564
SD (Nazi Security) **691**
Sea Lion, Operation 145
Seasons, The (Haydn) 444
Second Empire (German) **95–101, 479–480**
    army of **227–228**
    constitution of 1871 and 95–96, 319, 478–479
    foreign policy in 97–98
    Kulturkampf in 97
    nationalism in 588
    navy in **591**
    political parties in 96–97
    Reichstag and 650
    socialism in 97
    unification in 80–81
Second Empire of France, collapse of 79–80
Second Symphony (Brahms) 286
secret societies 63, **396–397**
Seeckt, Hans von 121, 124, 208, 229, 260, 279
Seghers, Anna 183
Seidel, Ina 129
Seisser, Hans von 260–261
Selbert, Elisabeth 374
Seldte, Franz 440
Self-Portrait as a Solider (Kirchner) 507
Self-Portrait for Charlie Chaplin (Grosz) 431
Semper, Gottfried 87

Seneca 300
Seven Weeks' War 254
Seven Years' War **53–54,** 60, 225, 340, 530–531, **691–692,** 791*m*
sexuality 89, 745
Seyss-Inquart, Arthur 214–215
Shaftesbury, Anthony Ashley Cooper, first earl of 59, 355
Shakespeare, William 60, 563, 713
shipbuilding 84, *84*
Sicily 9, 307
Sickingen, Franz von 23
Siddhartha (Hesse) 454
Siemens, Georg 86, 330
Siemens, Werner von 85, 330, **692–693**
Sigismund, Johann 51
silver trade 11
Simons, Menno 214
sin, Luther and **482–483**
slave labor 149
Slovenia 198, 363
smallpox 56
smelting 83–84
Smith, Adam 354, 557
Sobibor concentration camp 313, 378
Sobieski, John 41
Social Darwinism 94, 102
Social Democrat (newspaper) 271
Social Democratic Party 196, 197, **693–696**
    Anti-Socialist Law and 218–219
    Bebel and **258**
    Bernstein in 271
    Bismarck and 277
    Böll and 281
    Brandt in 287–288
    Braun in 290
    Bülow and 297
    Center Party and 305
    Ebert in 344
    economic system proposed by 158–159
    in elections of 1919 114
    in elections of 1949 162–163
    Fischer and 378–379
    Kautsky in 502–503
    Liebknecht and 535–536
    Luxembourg and 547
    November Revolution and 107
    reconstitution of (1945) 156
    in reunification 187

    in Socialist Unity Party 155
    on Stresemann 124
    in Weimar Republic 734–735
    World War I and 104
Social Democratic Workers' Party 87, 97, 101
socialism 97, 351, 353–354
Socialist Party 166, 357
Socialist Realism 183
Socialist Reich Party 163
Socialist Unity Party 155, 178, 185, **696–697**
Social-Liberal Coalition 168–169
social realism 90
social reforms, in Federal Republic 165–166
social structure
    18th-century 57–58
    in Federal Republic 171–173
    19th-century 93–94
social welfare 196, 522
society, in romanticism 69–70
Society of Sciences 37
sociology 434–435, 731–732
Soldiers' Council 345
Solidarity Pact 191
Soll und Haben (Freytag) 335
Solzhenitsyn, Alexander 281
Somalia 199
Sonnets to Orpheus (Rilke) 665
Sophie Charlotte (queen of Prussia) 37, 308
Sorrows of Young Werther, The (Goethe) 61, 421, 422
South Africa 102, 177
South America, Barbie's escape to 247
Soviet Union *See also* Russia
    Adenauer and 206
    in Battle for Berlin 266–267
    denazification campaign by 155
    détente and 335–336
    in division of Germany after World War II 153
    Four Year Plan and 381
    invasion of 146–147, *147*
    Kohl and 512–513
    Nazi pact with 143
    Operation Barbarossa and 247
    weakening of grip by, on Eastern Europe 185
Spain 29, 30, 78, 211, 242, 306

Spanish civil war 143, 209, 314–315
Spanish Succession, War of 39, **41–42,** 360
Spark of Life (Remargue) 652
spark plug 284
Sparticists 110, 112–113
Späth, Lothar 246
Spee, Friedrich von 34, 249
Speer, Albert 145, 149, 332, **697**
Spener, Philip 37, 356, 623
Spengler, Oswald 130–131
Sperrle, Hugo 314–315
Speyer, Diet of 213, 306
Sphere and Duties of Government, The (Humboldt) 473–474
Spiegel Affair 206, **697–698,** 705
Spielhagen, Friedrich 89, 90, 646
Spinoza, Baruch 59, 356
Spiritual Year, The (Droste-Hülshoff) 341
Spitfire (airplane) 567
Sponti movement 378
Sprickman, A. M. A. 341
Springer, Axel 168, 281
SS (Schutzstaffel) **698–699**
    Abwehr and 204
    Barbie and 247
    at Dachau 325
    Dietrich and 336
    Eichmann in 347–349
    Eicke in 349
    evolution of 140
    Final Solution and 377–378
    Himmler and 456
    mobile killing units (Einsatzgruppen) **350**
    resistance in 321
"stab in the back" legend 106, 161, 229, 256, 259
Stahl, Friedrich Julius von 318
Stalin, Josef 143, 146, 211, 267, 340
Stalingrad, Battle of 148, **699**
Stamitz, Johann Wenzel Anton 552
Stanley, Henry Morton 269
state formation, after World War II 156
states' rights 175
Static Poems (Benn) 263
Stationendrama 365
Stauffenberg, Claus Schenk von 150, 321–322, **699–701**

Steele, Richard 60
Steel Helmets 319
steel production 83–84
Stegerwald, Adam 310
Stein, Baron Karl vom und zum 225, 316, 393, 440, 611, **701–702**
Steinthal, Max 330
Steppenwolf (Hesse) 130, 453, 454
Stifter, Adalbert 645
Stinnes, Hugo 123, **702–703**
Stinnes-Legien Agreement 111, 702
Stöcker, Adolf 94, 217, **703**
Stöcker, Helene 237
Stoph, Willi 186
Storm, Theodore 88, 645–646
Storm and Stress movement 60
Storm of Steel (Jünger) 496
storm troopers **674**
Stramm, August 365
Strasser, Gregor 138, **704**
Strasser, Otto **704**
Strauss, Franz Josef 169, 274, 653, **704–706**
Strauss, Richard 91, 340
Strauss, Johann, the Elder 91
Strauss, Johann, the Younger 91
Stravinsky, Igor 253
Streicher, Julius 145, 261, 332, 610, **706**
Stresemann, Gustav 120, 124–126, 168, 413–414, 538, 702, **706–707**
Strindberg, August 89, 90, 364, 589
Strittmatter, Erwin 183
Stülpnagel, Carl-Heinrich von 322
Stumm-Halberg, Karl, Count 83
Stumpff, Hans-Jürgen 294
Stürmer, Michael 176
Stuttgart 246
submarines 231–232, *232*, 339–340
Subversion Law 101
Sudan 102, 269
Sudermann, Hermann 89, 90, 590
Sudetenland 143, 162, 219
Suevi tribe 3
Suez Canal 146
suffrage
    in Federal Republic **352–353**
    in German Confederation 69, 385

    liberalism and 70
    in Prussian Three Class Voting System **637–638**
    in Second Empire 96, 479
    of women 93, 237, 373
Sulieman the Magnificent (Ottoman sultan) 41
Supreme Command of the Armed Forces 344
surrealism 358–359
Swabian tribe 4
Sweden, in Thirty Years' War 29, 30
Switzerland, in Thirty Years' War 30
Syllabus of Errors 517
symbolism 89, 90

T

Tacitus 14, 304
Tales of Children and the Home (Grimm) 429
Tales of Hoffman (Offenbach) 91
Talleyrand-Périgord, Charles Maurice de 316
Tangier 579
Tannenberg, Battle of **708**
Tanning, Dorothea 359
Tauler, Johannes 12
taxes
    under Frederick William I 51
    Industrial Revolution and 71
    introduced by Hardenberg 440
    under Maria Theresa 45
    raised by Kohl 194
    Reformation and 20
    reforms under Schroeder 192
Technik des Dramas, Die (Freytag) 399
technology, Bauhaus and 253
Teheran conference 153, 178
telegraph 85
Telemann, Georg Philipp 437
telephone 85
television 172
Ten Point program 177, 187
terrorism 170, 174, 243–244
Tetralogy of the Atrids (Hauptmann) 443
Tetzel, John 20, 210, 647
Teutoburg Forest, Battle of the 4
Teutonic branch tribes 3

Teutonic Knights 328
Thälmann, Ernst 407, **708–709**
Thatcher, Margaret 188
Theatine order 321
Theodoric the Great 4
Theory and Practice (Habermas) 434
Theory of Communicative Action (Habermas) 434
Theory of Social Action (Habermas) 434–435
Theresa of Avila, St. 321
Theresian style of architecture 48–49
Thibaut, Anton 216
Thieneman, Marie 442
Thiers, Adolph 80
Third Coalition, War of 238
Third Reich, Moeller's conception of 574–575
Third Reich, The (Moeller) 130, 574
Third Symphony (Beethoven) 58, 262
Thirty Years' War **28–31,** 50, 239, 331, 514, 559, **709–711**
Thirty Years' War, The (Hoch) 469
This Book Belongs to the King (Brentano) 292
Thomas-Gilchrist open-hearth method 83–84
Thomasius, Christian 59, 624, **711–712**
Thomism 320
Thompson, Benjamin 580
Thor 5
Thoughts about Christa T. (Wolf) 183
Thoughts about Death and Immortality (Feuerbach) 375
Thoughts out of Season (Nietzsche) 600
Three Emperors, Battle of 65
Three Emperors League 98, 277, **523–524**
Three Leaps of Wang Lun, The (Döblin) 338
Threepenny Opera (Brecht) 130, 291
Thun, Johan Ernst 48
Thunderclap bombing campaign 340–341
Thuringians 6
Thurn, Matthias 331
Thus Spake Zarathustra (Nietzsche) 293, 601

Thyssen, August 83
Thyssen, Fritz **712–713**
Tiberius-4 3
Tieck, Ludwig 62, 70, 292, **713–714**
Tiepolo, Giovanni Battista 596–597
Tilly, Johann von 559
Tilsit, Treaty of 225, 440, **714**
Tin Drum, The (Grass) 171, 427
Tirpitz, Alfred von 84, 102, 228, 272, **714–715**
Tito, Marshall (Josip Broz) 179
Todt, Fritz 241
Togoland 269, 305
tolerance, Enlightenment and 59
Toller, Ernst 130, 715–716
Tolstoi, Leo 89, 589
Tonnies, Ferdinand 128
Torquato Tasso (Goethe) 421, 422
To the German Nobility (Pufendorf) 638
To the Moon (Goethe) 421
towns, Reformation in 24
trade unions, after World War II 155–156
Train Was on Time, The (Böll) 281
Trakl, Georg 365
Transplant, The (Dix) 338
treason, under Nazi law 140
Treblinka concentration camp 313, 378
Trecsckow, Henning von 700
Treitschke, Heinrich von 88, 217, **716–717**
Trent, Council of 27, **319–320**
Trials and Tribulations (Fontane) 380
tribes, early 3–6
Tridentine Decrees 27
Triple Alliance 274
Triple Entente 102
Tristan und Isolde (Wagner) 91
Triumph of the Will, The (film) 663–664
Trotsky, Leon 105
Trott zu Solz, Adam von **717–718**
Truman Doctrine 555
Tserklaes, Johann 29
Tsingau 102
Tucholsky, Kurt 130
Tunisia 148, 269
Turkey 104

Turkish conquest of Constantinople 13
Turkish immigrants 173, 194
Turkish Wars 41–42, 360
Twilight (Eichendorff) 347
Twilight of the Idols (Nietzsche) 90
Two Books of the Elements of Universal Jurisprudence (Pufendorf) 638
Two Children Are Threatened by a Nightingale (Ernst) 358–359
Two Gunners (Dix) 338
Two Human Beings (Dehmel) 590
Two-Plus-Four talks 177, 188
Two-Plus-Four Treaty 197
type, movable 432–433

U

U-boats 231–232, *232*
Uecker, Gunther 343
Uhland, Ludwig 70, 645
Ulbricht, Walter 170, 178, 180, 184, 410–411, 495—496, **719–720**
Ulm-Austerlitz campaign 315
Ulrich of Württemberg 15
ULTRA intelligence system 294
ULTRA security clearance 352, **354–355**
Under the Trees (Pechstein) 622
unemployment 189, 191–193, 334, 345–346, 744
Unfinished Story (Braun) 183
Unguarded House, The (Böll) 281
unification 370–371, 793*m*
  Bismarck and **74–81**
  consequences of 188–190
  economics of 191–193
  feminism and 374
  foreign policy post 197–199
  Kohl and 512–513
  in 1989 185–190
  politics post- 193–197
  in Second Empire 80–81
  unemployment after 191–193
Unification Treaty 177, 197
Union of Expellees and Dispossessed 163
Union of German Girls 139
Union Theological Seminary 281
United Court Chancellery 47
United Kingdom. *See* England
United States 105, 147, 153, 228, 232, 290, 334, 335–336

University of Basel 250
University of Berlin 66
University of Göttingen 250, 263, 283, **425–426**
University of Heidelberg 25
University of Prague 12, 13
University of Wittenberg 16
Unquiet Night, The (Goes) 171
Unruh, Hans Victor von 414, 631
urban guerrilla warfare 244
Ursuline order 321
Utah Beach 331
utilitarianism 274
Utrecht, Treaty of 307

V

Vadiscus (Hutten) 15
Valentine, Die (Freytag) 398
Valkyrie, Operation 321–322
Valla, Lorenzo 357
Valley of Thundering Hoofs, The (Böll) 281
Vandals 4, 5, 6
van Gogh, Vincent 332
Variations on a Theme of Paganini (Brahms) 285
Variations on a Theme of Schumann (Brahms) 285
Veit, Dorothea Mendelssohn 216
Velo (car model) 264
Venus (Cranach the Elder) 323
Verdun, Treaty of 7
Verdun offensive 105
Versailles, Treaty of **114–119, 721–722**
    Air Force and 208
    Alsace-Lorraine and 212
    armed forces limitations in 229
    Danzig in 328–329
    Dawes Plan and 329
    Erzberger and 359
    goals of 115–116
    military under 223
    reparations in 116–117, 122–124
    terms of 116
Vichy regime 145
Viebig, Clara 94, 590
Vienna **722–723**
    architecture of 48–49
    baroque and 32

Congress of 66–67, 68, **316–317**, 568, 639, 792*m*
1848 revolution in 72
Maximilian II and 560
as musical capital 58
Treaty of 316–317
Vietnam War 167–168, 378
Views of a Clown (Böll) 281
Village Tales from the Black Forest (Auerbach) 645
Violin Concerto (Brahms) 286
Virchow, Rudolf 414
Visigoth tribe 3, 4
Vögler, Albert 413
Volkgemeinschaft (national community) **724–725**
Völkischer Beobachter (newspaper) 260, **724**
Volkmann, Helmuth 315
Volkssturm (People's Attack) **725**
Volkswagen 628
Vollmar, Georg von 101
Voltaire 52
Von Hassel Diaries (Kreisau Circle) 441
voting. *See* suffrage
V-2 rocket 290

W

Wachenroder, Wilhelm **726**
Wacherle, Hilmar 325
Wadzek's Battle with the Steam Turbine (Döblin) 338
Wagner, Adolf 325, 340
Wagner, Richard 90–91, 258, 305, 550, 642, **726–727**
Waldburg, Otto Truchsess von 302
Waldersee, Alfred Graf von 100
Wallenstein, Albrecht Eusebius Wenzel von 559, **727–728**
Wallich, Hermann 330
Walser, Martin 171
waltzes 91
Wanderer's Night Song (Goethe) 421
Wanderings of Franz Sternbald, The (Tieck) 713
Wanderungen, Franz Sternbalds 713
Wandervögel 92
Wannsee Conference 377, **728–729**

Warburg, Max M. **729–730**
war crimes 154–155, 332, 348–349
War Cripples (Dix) 129
warfare, industrial 105
War Guilt Clause 117
War of the Second Coalition 393
wars 530–531. *See also* World War I; World War II
    Augsburg League, War of **236**
    of Austrian Succession **42–44,** 53, 203, **240–241,** 308
    Austro-Prussian 77–78, 239, 276, 513–514, 575
    Balkan Wars 103–104
    of Bavarian Succession 46, **256–257,** 493, 554–555
    Bismarck on 75–76
    Boer War 325
    Crimean War 275–276
    Danish War 76–77, **327–328**
    Dutch War 40
    Franco-Prussian War 78–79, 276, 334, 575
    Korean War 206, 345
    of the League of Augsburg 360
    of Liberation 66, 68, 69
    Napoleonic 50, 527–528, **584–585,** 611, 635
    Peasants' War 23–24, 210, 389, **620–621,** 648–649
    of Polish Succession 360
    Polish War 308
    Potato War 46
    Russo-Japanese War 102
    Russo-Turkish War 267, 341
    of Second Coalition 393
    Seven Weeks' War 254
    Seven Years' War **53–54,** 60, 225, 340, **691–692,** 791*m*
    Spanish civil war 143, 209, 314–315
    of Spanish Succession 39, **41–42,** 360
    Third Coalition, War of 238
    Thirty Years' War **28–31,** 50, 239, 331
    Turkish Wars 41–42, 360
    Vietnam War 167–168, 378
    War of Devolution 203
    Yom Kippur War 170
Warsaw, Treaty of 44

Warsaw Pact 187, 730
Wartburg Castle 21, **730–731**
Wartenburg, Peter Yorck von 321, 534
Waterloo, Battle of 66, **731**
Water Music (Handel) 35, 438
Weavers, The (Hauptmann) 90, 442, 590
Weber, Karl Maria von 70, 91, 340
Weber, Max 128, 435, 586, **731–832**
Wedekind, Frank 89, 90
Weidling, Helmuth 267
Weill, Kurt 291
Weimar 68, **732–733**
Weimar Constitution 118–119, 319, 353, **733–734**
    Bavarian People's Party and 255
    Center Party and 305
    correcting weaknesses of, after World War II 157
    female suffrage in 373
    Heuss and 630–631
Weimar Republic **120–134, 734–736**
    army of **228–230**
    autobahns in 241
    Berlin in 266
    cultural elites on 324
    culture of 127–131
    dictatorship and 131–134
    Dönitz in 339
    Ebert in 344
    economics in 122–123
    inflation in 122–124, **483–484**
    Jewish people in 491
    militarism in 571
    modernization and 572
    Moeller van den Bruck and 574
    National Assembly in 585–586
    nobility in 223
    November Revolution and 113
    Preuss and 631
    Prussia and 636
    Rathenau in 644–645
    Stresemann in 706–707
    Versailles Treaty and 114–119
    women in 129
Weishaupt, Adam 63, 397
Weizmann, Chaim 490
Weizsäcker, Ernst von 176, 441, **736–737**

Weizsäcker, Richard von **737**
Wels, Otto 353
Welsers 233
Werfel, Franz 365
Weser, Erich Koch 410
Weskott, Johann Friedrich 257
Westarp, Kuno von 412–413
West-Eastern Divan (Goethe) 421, 423
West Germany. *See* Federal Republic of Germany
Westphalia 315
Westphalia, Peace (Treaty) of 30, 39, 40, **737–738,** 789*m*
Wever, Walther 208
When Lilacs Last in the Dooryard Bloom'd (Hindemith) 457
White Mountain, Battle of 29, 331
White Rose movement 150
Widekind, Frank 364
Wieland, Christoph Martin 70, **738–739**
Wiesenthal, Simon 565
Wildly Dancing Children (Nolde) 602
Wilhelm, August 70
Wilhelm, Johann 343
Wilhelm Meister's Apprenticeship (Goethe) 422
Wilhelm Meister's Journeying Years (Goethe) 423
Wilhelm Meister's Travels (Goethe) 61–62, 70, 421
Wilhelm Tell (Schiller) 62
William I (emperor of Germany) 95, 99, 102, 275, **739–740**
William II (emperor of Germany) 99–101, 268, 277–278, 325–326, 442, 639, **740–741**
William IV of Bavaria 210
William of Orange 236
Will to Power (Nietzsche) 600
Wilson, Woodrow 106, 107, 114, 115
Wimpheling, Jacob 13, 14, 652
Windthorst, Ludwig 96, 304, 439, **742**
Wire Harp, The (Biermann) 274
wireless technology 289
Wirth, Joseph 122, 644
Witches Sabbath (Goethe) 563
Wittelsbach, Charles Albert 42, 240

Wittelsbach, House of 211, **742–743**
Wittenberg Concord (Melanchthon) 16
Wittenburg, University of 16
Witzleben, Erwin von 321
Wodan-Odin 5
Wolf, Christa 184
Wolff, Christian von 59, 356, 522, 712, **743**
Wölfflin, Heinrich 34
Wolgemut, Michael 342
Wolmar, Melchior 300
Woman, The (magazine) 253
women
    after World War II 373–374
    Augspurg's work for 237
    Baumer's work for 253
    in Civil Code of 1900 311, 372
    concentration camp for 349
    employment of, World War II 149
    in Federal Republic 172
    in German Democratic Republic 181–182
    German Women's Bureau and **415–416**
    Hitler and 289
    in Imperial Germany 372
    Nazis and 373, **743–745**
    in 19th-century Germany 93–94
    in Weimar Republic 129
Workers' Council 345
Workers' Party 87
World War I **102–106, 745–747**
    Aachen in 203
    alliances prior to 102–104
    Amiens, Battle of, and 212–213
    Beck in 258–259
    Beckmann in 260
    Bethmann Hollweg and 272–273
    Brest-Litovsk Treaty and 105, 228, **293**
    conduct of 104–105
    Dietrich in 336
    Dönitz in 339
    expressionism and 364
    factors leading to 102–104
    Falkenhayn in 366
    Fritsch in 400

German mistakes in 228
Great Depression and 333
Hassel in 441
Höss in 467
Jutland, Battle of, and **497–498**
Kluge in 510
Ludendorff in 539
Mann (Thomas) and 551
map of Europe after 795*m*
map of European and Middle Eastern theaters 794*m*
nationalism and 588
navy in 715
pacifism in 640
recruiting poster *103*
reparations for 116–117, 122–124
responsibility for 104
Second Empire and 81, 480
United States in 228
World War II 81, **144–152, 747–748**
   Aachen in 203
   Armed Forces High Command in 612–613
   Axis in 242
   Battle of Britain in **145–146,** 209
   Benn in 262
   Bonn and 282
   Brauchitsch in 288
   D-Day and 150–151, **330–331**
   Dietrich in 336–337
   economic recovery after **345–346**
   German expansion in 796*m*
   German home front and 149–150
   German surrender ending 153
   as Hitler's war 144
   Hossbach Memorandum and 468–469
   invasion of Soviet Union in 146–147, *147*
   Kleist in 508–509
   Kluge in 510–511
   League of Nations and 523
   Manstein in 552–553
   map of European and Middle Eastern theaters 798*m*
   Marshall Plan and 159, 165, 345, 555–556, **555–556**
   Nuremberg Trials and 609–610
   occupation zones after 799*m*
   Paulus in 619–620
   Potsdam Conference and 629–630
   Regensburg in 649–650
   Reichstag in 650–651
   start of 143
   turning of tide in 148–149
   Yalta Conference and **750**
Worms, Diet of 21, 648, **748–749**
Wortley, Stuart 325
Wrangel, Friedrich Graf von 328
Württemberg 10, 95, 315. *See also* Baden-Württemberg
Würzburg 10, 56
Würzburg Palace 10

X

X-rays 660–670

Y

Yalta Conference 153, 178, **750**
Yom Kippur War 170
Young, Owen D. 127, 751–752
Young Germany **751**
Young Plan 127, 707, **751–752**
Young Turk movement 285
youth movements 92–93, 167–168
Yugoslavia 179

Z

Zabern Affair 100, 228, **753**
Zeiss, Carl 486, **753**
Zeppelin, Ferdinand, Count von **753–754**
Zetkin, Clara 93–94, 372, **754–755**
Zhukov, Georgi 211, 266
Ziegler, Adolf 332
Ziegler, Heinz 206
Zietz, Louise 373, 755, **755**
Zimmermann, Arthur 756
Zimmermann, Domenicus **755–756**
Zimmermann, Johann Baptist **755–756**
Zimmermann Telegram **756**
Zinzendorf, Nicolaus von 34, 249
Zionism 338–339, 350, 490, 491, 634–635
Zola, Émile 89, 589
Zollverein (Customs Union) **757**
Zweig, Arnold 183
Zwickau Prophets 648, **757–758**
Zwinger Palace 33, 249, 340
Zwingli, Ulrich 16, 22–23, 213, 234, 357, 578, **758–760**
Zyklon-B 151, 238